The Handbook of Municipal Bonds

The Frank J. Fabozzi Series

The Handbook of Municipal Bonds

SYLVAN G. FELDSTEIN
FRANK J. FABOZZI

WILEY

John Wiley & Sons, Inc.

ISBN: 978-0-470-10875-8

Printed in the United States of America.

10 9 8 7 6 5 4 3 2 1

Contents

CHAPTER 57
How to Analyze Tobacco Bonds   **957**

Gerry Lian

CHAPTER 58
Toll Road Analysis   **981**

Robert H. Muller

CHAPTER 59
Water and Sewer Bond Analysis   **995**

Brian Winters

Foreword

Information is the lifeblood of markets. Indeed, economic theory tells us that the benefits of a free competitive market—an efficient and optimum allocation of resources—is only possible if all market participants have access to the same knowledge about a product and its price.

Without this information, buyers, sellers, dealers, and others have little way to determine whether to purchase or sell the product being traded. Market participants need to know what is being bought or sold and what value/price is being attached to the product. None of us would go into a food store to purchase food if everything were wrapped in brown paper with just the briefest description of the contents and prices only known when we reach the checkout counter. Everyone participating in a market needs to be informed so that rationale decisions can be made and resources allocated efficiently and optimally.

Over the years, I often heard people in the equity markets and in parts of fixed income markets talk about how "complex" they were. Market participants would talk about the large number of variables, alternatives, and such that they would have to consider. But, of all the financial markets, the municipal securities market has the greatest informational requirements.

One only needs to peruse the table of contents of this book to see the myriad types of municipal securities being offered in the market today. Multiply those different credit structures by the number of possible issuers (50,000+) and by the number of different possible maturities and one can understand easily why there are more than 1.5 million different securities outstanding in today's municipal bond market. At one point in my career, a database provider informed me that it took more than 120 possible data fields just to describe the range of municipal securities then outstanding. Today it undoubtedly would require even more.

Compare these statistics with the U.S. equity markets, where there are less than 10,000 outstanding equity issues. Moreover, it is not difficult to understand what it means to buy or sell a share of a company. Or consider the market for U.S. Treasury securities, where the number of different securities that can be traded is less than 1,000 and the credit quality is known! Participants in the municipal securities market, even those operating in a narrow segment of the market, are confronted with an almost overwhelming list of factors to be considered.

The Handbook of Municipal Bonds meets a critical need in filling the informational demands of this market. It provides a useful starting place for an issuer being presented with various financing alternatives, for an investor trying to choose among alternatives, and even for dealers and other professionals that wish to operate in segments of the market that are unfamiliar to them. It is the only comprehensive reference source for professionals in the municipal securities market—financial advisors, bond counsel, tax counsel, and trustees, to name a few. Reporters and other observers of the municipal securities market would be well advised to have *The Handbook* nearby.

Christopher "Kit" Taylor, Ph.D., CFA
Former Municipal Securities Rulemaking Board
Executive Director, 1978–2007

Preface

Since the mid-1980s, the municipal bond industry has undergone enormous growth and dramatic change. It is fair to describe the municipal debt market as continuing to evolve. As we go to press in early 2008, the municipal bond insurers, long a mainstay of the market with their triple A ratings and 50% market share, face significant financial and rating problems.

There are now more municipals outstanding than ever. According to the Securities Industry and Financial Markets Association (SIFMA), at the end of the third quarter of 2007, the par amount of municipals outstanding was $2,570.6 billion. Because of the lower interest rate environment in the years immediately after the terrorist attacks of 9/11, many older high coupon bonds were refunded at lower interest rates. This resulted in annual new issue volume also reaching new highs. In 2005, $408.3 billion was issued, an all time record. For calendar year 2006, the figure dropped slightly to $383.4 billion, tying it with 2003's total. By comparison, in the calendar year before 9/11, total new issue municipal volume was $200.88 billion. Trading in the secondary market has also become at times brisk, and "real time" trade transparency for investors and dealers has improved. Chapter 20 in this book describes this in more detail.

The industry also has many new buy-side participants. In addition to the traditional bank trust departments, mutual funds, property and casualty insurance companies, and high-net-worth individuals, buyers now include hedge funds, arbitrageurs, life insurance companies, cross-over buyers, and foreign banks, among other relative-value buyers. Even on the deal origination sell-side things are changing. While shrinkage among the dealer-brokers and investment bankers has occurred as Wall Street consolidated, the number of lawyers who represent themselves as "qualified experts" in the narrow legal specialty of municipal bond law has exploded as noted in Chapter 49 on analyzing revenue bonds. For all participants in this industry, greater scrutiny of qualifications and caution are in order. Because of the growth of the industry and the entry of so many new participants, in our opinion a handbook covering all aspects of the municipal bond market would be timely and useful.

In addition to the chapters on investment banking and trading that we cover in Parts One and Two, we have included chapters on municipal bond analytics and modern municipal bond portfolio management in Part Four and Part Five, respectively, in the book. These areas have substantially changed since the 1990s as the buy side participants have become more familiar with modern portfolio theory and fixed income analytics. In our previous writings on municipal bonds prior to the mid 1990s, we introduced and applied to the municipal market some of the techniques and concepts that are now widely used in the industry on both the buy and sell sides, including the proprietary trading desks of brokerage and investment banking firms. Book reviewers at that time thought that such concepts were not applicable for municipal bonds and criticized our book for that reason. Today, however, they have become important tools in the industry.

Compliance has also become of critical concern for both the buy and sell sides. For this reason, Part Three has several chapters addressing some of the more importance compliance issues in the industry.

Also, particularly since 2002, new synthetic instruments such as derivatives, structured notes, rate locks, and swaps have been introduced into the industry. As this book went to press in the fall of 2007, it was announced that four fund companies filed with the Securities and Exchange Commission to launch a total of 15 municipal bond *exchange-traded funds* (ETFs). Going forward, we expect these new instruments to increase in importance and have included some of the latest innovations in these areas within this book.

The trading and pricing of municipal bonds has also become more transparent while adopting analytical and quantitative concepts and principles from the taxable fixed income asset classes. There are now four different sets of municipal bond indexes available to investors in gauging portfolio performance and the market's performance. They include:

- *Lehman Brothers Municipal Bond Index*, a total return index that is widely used by mutual funds and other large portfolio managers. Their municipal bond indexes are based upon a universe of bonds across yield curves and credit sectors. In mid-2007, it had approximately 41,563 issues.
- Standard & Poor's, in conjunction with Investortools, publishes various municipal indexes. There are over 50,000 bonds, priced historically, in the *Standard & Poor's Investortools Municipal Bond Index*.
- Merrill Lynch fixed income research publishes a number of municipal bond indexes Their universe, as of mid-2007, included approximately 12,490 municipal bonds.
- *The Bond Buyer*, the trade daily newspaper, publishes weekly yield indexes.

As of 2007, there are two services that in the afternoon of each trading day make available generic scales for different maturities and different credit ratings. One is provided by Thomson Municipal Market Data, known in the industry as the MMD scale. The other is by Municipal Market Advisors (MMA).

The sale of bonds by issuers, both competitively and through negotiation, has also become more efficient and software based. Two companies offer this service for competitive bond sales. One is I-Deal/Ipreo, which also provides a software platform for negotiated bond sales and is discussed in Chapter 21. The other is Grant Street Group, which focuses on competitive sales in the municipal market.

The pricing of municipals, marked to market at the end of the trading day, is now done daily. The two most widely used services are FT Interactive Data and J. J. Kenny (Standard & Poor's Securities Evaluations). Chapter 27 describes the methodology and process used by FT Interactive Data.

Disclosure has become more immediate and accessible. The Securities and Exchange Commission as of mid-2007 has designated four information firms as Nationally Recognized Municipal Securities Information Repositories (NRMSIRs). Official Statements from issuers and "material event notices" are available at the NRMSIRs. While this is not the final solution to ongoing disclosure because the definition of what is "material" is still open to disagreement between bondholders and underwriters, it is a step in the right direction.

In the 1980s, the credit quality of municipal bonds was of major concern coming on the heels of New York City's general obligation note default in the mid-1970s and the Washington State Public Power System revenue bond default in the early 1980s. By 2007, though many on the buy-side and the credit enhancers maintained credit research resources, credit research on the sell-side was largely nonexistent. Many buy-side firms have become complacent. An exception is in the analysis of high-yield, project-type start-up financings. We have included several chapters and case studies in this book that cover the high-yield, high-risk credit sectors as well as the traditional credit sectors.

Perhaps the reason for the complacency in credit analysis is due to the high ratings that had been assigned to the new municipal issues. Approximately 50% of all new municipals up to 2008 were insured and given a triple-A rating by the commerical rating companies. Chapter 68 covers the analysis of these insurers that have become so important in the municipal bond market. Possibly another reason for the credit complacency is because municipals are becoming more commoditized with investors, traders, and speculators from all over the world participating in this market. Many view municipal bonds as being almost as safe as U.S. Treasuries. We disagree with this view despite the excellent track record of low municipal defaults and low yield spread volatility. In our view, the credit risk analysis component of the municipal industry is still important and in future economic down cycles will be very relevant. Accordingly, Parts Six and Seven of this book cover credit analyses written by recognized analysts in their sectors. The chapters in these two parts of the book cover most of the credit sectors.

We should also note that since the 1980s the "generally accepted accounting principles" of state and local governments have been set by the independent Government Accounting Standards Board (GASB). GASB has established uniform and more thorough reporting standards that municipal bond issuers and investors rely upon. GASB has helped improve the transparency of state and local government accounting. As this book goes to press, there is an assault on GASB by some issuers and politicians to weaken or eliminate its role. The result, if successful, in addition to introducing confusion to this area of the industry, would also allow issuers to obfuscate budget deficits and long-term liabilities. Years ago these practices resulted in budgetary disasters and bond defaults. We have included a chapter in this book by GASB to highlight its importance (Chapter 45) as well as one by the National Federation of Municipal Analysts, an organization of municipal bond credit analysts that has been in the forefront of fighting for more complete "material event" and financial disclosures (Chapter 43).

Finally, we note that many of our case studies provide the reader with detailed information on some of the more innovative financings and interesting problem bonds. The cases cover a wide range of topics arising from the 9/11 catastrophe, subprime loans, a major airline bankruptcy, and others. They are relevant for both buyers and issuers of municipals bonds.

ACKNOWLEDGMENTS

In addition to thanking the contributors in this book, many of whom also provided important advice on the structure of and topics in this book, there were others without whose assistance this book would not be as complete as it is. Many of these people helped us identify and recruit recognized authorities in their municipal bond specialties to write chapters and case studies. We thank Mark Adler (UBS), Alan Anders (New York City Office of Management and Budget), Dave Andersen (Merrill Lynch), Nancy Belz (Federated Investors), Gerald Benjamin (State University of New York, New Paltz), Kareem Drayton (Guardian Life Insurance Company of America), Frank Egan (Scott & Stringfellow), Gary Ellis (Wilmington Trust), Dall Forsythe (New York University), Bryan Gross (SIFMA), Brenda Horn (Ice Miller), John L. Kraft (Lomurro, Davison, Eastman & Munoz),

Richard Larkin (Royal Bank of Canada), Steve Letzler (DTCC), Donald R. Lipkin (Bank of America), Marvin Markus (Goldman Sachs), Robert J. Nelson (Thomson Financial/Municipal Market Data), Michael Belsky and Richard J. Raphael (Fitch Ratings), Samuel Ramirez, Sr. (Samuel Ramirez & Co), Samuel Ramirez, Jr. (Samuel Ramirez & Co), Gerald Roberts (Mission Capital), David Rowland (St. Paul Travelers Companies), Judy Wesalo Temel (Samson Capital Advisors), and John Zurlo (Siebert Brandford Shank).

Sylvan G. Feldstein
Frank J. Fabozzi

About the Editors

Sylvan G. Feldstein is Director of Municipal Bond Research in the investment department of the Guardian Life Insurance Company of America. Prior to joining Guardian in 1996, he was a research manager and analyst at major Wall Street broker-dealers and a rating agency. He earned a doctorate in Political Science from Columbia University in 1976 and has taught municipal finance at the School of Management at Yale University. He is a member of the National Federation of Municipal Analysts, where he was the recipient of the Analyst of the Year Award. From 1975 to 1999, he was editor of the New Jersey Municipal Bond News and has edited or authored four books about the municipal bond industry.

Frank J. Fabozzi is Professor in the Practice of Finance and Becton Fellow in the School of Management at Yale University. Prior to joining the Yale faculty, he was a Visiting Professor of Finance in the Sloan School at MIT. Professor Fabozzi is a Fellow of the International Center for Finance at Yale University and on the Advisory Council for the Department of Operations Research and Financial Engineering at Princeton University. He is the editor of the *Journal of Portfolio Management* and an associate editor of the *Journal of Fixed Income*. He earned a doctorate in economics from the City University of New York in 1972. In 2002, Professor Fabozzi was inducted into the Fixed Income Analysts Society's Hall of Fame and is the 2007 recipient of the C. Stewart Sheppard Award given by the CFA Institute. He earned the designation of Chartered Financial Analyst and Certified Public Accountant. He has authored and edited numerous books in finance.

Contributing Authors

Gregory Aikman	Mellon Private Wealth Management
David R. Bean	Governmental Accounting Standards Board
Bill Black	Morgan Stanley Investment Management
Paul R. Bockwoldt	JPMorgan Securities
Gerard Brennan	Interactive Data Pricing and Reference Data, Inc.
Richard Briffault	Columbia University School of Law
Harold B. Burger	AllianceBernstein
Lynn Cavallaro	Van Kampen Investments
Herman R. Charbonneau	Roosevelt & Cross, Inc.
Eric H. Chu	Bond Logistix LLC
Richard A. Ciccarone	McDonnell Investment Management LLC and Merritt Research Services LLC
Donald King Cirillo	Municipal Disclosure Advisors, Inc.
Gregory A. Clark	HVB Group
Daryl Clements	AllianceBernstein
Thomas H. Cochran	CivilCredit Advisors LLC
Thomas P. Dalpiaz	Fixed Income Securities, LP
Paul R. Daniels	Investortools, Inc.
William J. Darusmont	TBD Capital LLC
Roger L. Davis	Orrick, Herrington & Sutcliffe LLP
Michael P. Dorigan	PNC Capital Advisors
Cristy C. Edwards	Vinson & Elkins LLP
Frank Fabozzi	Yale University
Hilary E. Feldstein	Consultant
Sylvan G. Feldstein	Guardian Life Insurance Company of America

Jonathan A. Fiebach	Duration Capital
Philip Fischer	Merrill Lynch
Anthony H. Fisher	UBS Investment Bank
Thomas B. Fox	Bond Logistix LLC
Daniel J. Garrett	Investortools, Inc.
Wayne Godlin	Morgan Stanley Investment Management
Lisa Good	National Federation of Municipal Analysts
Terry J. Goode	Wells Capital Management
Laurie S. Goodman	UBS
Ankur Goyal	Morgan Stanley–Risk Department
Alexander Grant	Guardian Life Insurance Company of America and RS Tax-Exempt Fund
Cadmus Hicks	Nuveen Investments
Seth Horwitz	Morgan Stanley Investment Management
Bill Huck	Stone & Youngberg LLC
Perry E. Israel	Law Office of Perry Israel
Andrew Kalotay	Andrew Kalotay Associates
Stephen A. Keen	Reed Smith LLP
John L. Kraft	Lomurro, Davison, Eastman & Munoz, P.A.
Gary M. Krellenstein	JPMorgan Securities
Joseph Krist	Lord Abbett & Co. LLC
Kenneth A. Kriz	University of Nebraska at Omaha
Patrick Landers	Commonwealth of Massachusetts
Yingchen Li	JP Morgan Securities
Gerry Lian	Morgan Stanley Investment Management
Mychele Lindvall	Seattle Northwest Securities Corporation
David Litvack	Fitch Ratings
Douglas J. Lucas	UBS
Paul S. Maco	Vinson & Elkins LLP
Rebecca Manning	Harbor Asset Management
Diane R. Maurice	Morgan Stanley–Investment Management
Martin J. Mauro	Merrill Lynch

Sandra McDonald	McDonald Partners, Inc.
Jon A. McMahon	Bond Logistix LLC
James McSpiritt	Phipps Houses
Dean Michael Mead	Governmental Accounting Standards Board
Edward C. Merrigan	B.C. Zeigler & Company
Christopher J. Mier	Loop Capital Markets
Bradley D. Mincke	Van Kampen Investments
Ronald L. Mintz	The Vanguard Group
Jessalynn Moro	Fitch Ratings
Bart Mosley	UBS Securities LLC
Robert H. Muller	JPMorgan Securities
Tracy Neish	University of Arizona
Megan Neuburger	Fitch Ratings
Peter O'Brien	Guardian Life Insurance Company of America
William E. Oliver	AllianceBernstein
Michael Paladino	Fitch Ratings
A. Theodore Palatucci	J.P. McGowan & Company
Mark Paris	Morgan Stanley Investment Management
Anthony Pellegrini	Centennial Group
Jun Peng	University of Arizona
Jim Phillips	Morgan Stanley Investment Management
Marie S. Pisecki	BB&T Capital Markets
Edward A. Rabson	Landesbank Hessen—Thuringen (Helaba)
David Ratner	Industry Consultant
Kevin Reilly	Guardian Life Insurance Company of America
Leslie K. Ross	Reed Smith LLP
Michael J. Ross	Morgan Keegan & Company, Inc.
Evan C. Rourke	M.D. Sass Tax Advantaged Bond Strategies, LLC
Rich Saskal	The Bond Buyer
Mitchell Savader	The Savader Group LLC and Civitas Funding Group LLC
Maria C. Sazon	AllianceBernstein

Arthur E. Schloss	Morgan Stanley Investment Management
Ruben Selles	CIFG
Peter Shapiro	Swap Financial Group
Barnet Sherman	Morgan Stanley Investment Management
Albert Simons III	Orrick, Herrington & Sutcliffe LLP
Joseph A. Spiak	UBS Securities LLC
James E. Spiotto	Chapman and Cutler LLP
Stephen A. Spitz	Orrick, Herrington & Sutcliffe LLP
David Stevens	
Karen Szerszen	Allstate Investments, LLC
Jennifer Webster Taffe	Vinson & Elkins LLP
Richard Torkelson	JPMorgan Securities
Craig Underwood	Bond Logistix LLC
Kurt van Kuller	1861 Capital Management
Tom Weyl	Eaton Vance Management
David White	
Allen Williams	Ipreo
Mary G. Wilson	Sonnenschein Nath & Rosenthal LLP
Brian Winters	Van Kampen Investments
George G. Wolf	Orrick, Herrington & Sutcliffe LLP
William H. Wood	Frasca & Associates, LLC
Emily A. Youssouf	JP Morgan Public Finance
JonPaul Zaptin	JPMorgan Securities
Todd P. Zerega	Reed Smith LLP

The Sell Side:
The Originators of Deals

The Central Place of States and Local Governments in American Federalism

Richard Briffault
Joseph P. Chamberlain Professor of Legislation
Columbia University School of Law

Writing in Federalist Number 45, James Madison predicted that the states would dominate the new federal union created by the Constitution. The powers of the federal government were "few and defined," he pointed out, limited primarily to "external objects, as war, peace, negotiation, and foreign commerce." By contrast, the states, he explained, would have authority over "all the objects which, in the ordinary course of affairs, concern the lives, liberties and properties of the people, and the internal order, improvement, and prosperity of the State." As a result of their greater role in governance and their closer ties to the people, the states would also enjoy stronger popular support than the distant national government. Madison assumed the principal problem of federalism would be protecting a fragile federal government from the states, not protecting the states from the federal government.

For more than a century, American federalism developed largely as Madison forecast, with the federal government exercising a limited role in peacetime domestic life, and most government power wielded at the state and local levels. On the eve of the Great Depression, federal spending accounted for barely one-sixth of total domestic government—federal, state, and local—spending. The federal government provided few services directly to the people and only a modest amount of financial assistance to state and local governments.[1]

---

[1] J. Richard Aronson and John L. Hilley, *Financing State and Local Governments: Fourth Edition* (Washington, DC: Brookings Institute Press, 1986), p. 17.

Over the course of the twentieth century, this situation changed dramatically. The emergence of a national—and increasingly global—economy, two world wars, the rise of the United States to superpower status, and the ongoing cultural and technological transformations of our society have been accompanied by a tectonic shift in power to the federal government. The federal government now plays an enormous role in regulating the economy, promoting social welfare, enforcing political and civil rights, and protecting the environment.

Yet states and local governments remain central to American governance. As in Madison's day, "the ordinary course of affairs" is dominated by state and local governments. The rules that structure civil society—contract law, tort law, property and land use law, criminal law, family law, the incorporation of businesses, the regulation of the professions—are developed, implemented, and enforced primarily at the state and local levels. So, too, most public services that affect people in their homes and families—public schools, policing, incarceration of offenders, fire safety, clean water, removal of solid wastes and sewage, maintenance of roads and streets, public parks, public hospitals and emergency medical services—are provided by states and localities, not the federal government. The vast majority of the opportunities for participation in political life—such as running for office, campaigning for or against a ballot proposition, or appearing before such critical governing institutions as the school board, the planning and zoning commission or a town meeting—are at the state and local level, too.

The centrality of states and local governments to our federal system was dramatically underscored by three recent events: the 2000 Presidential election and the bitter postelection battle over Florida's 25 electoral votes; the terrorist attacks on the World Trade Center and the Pentagon on September 11, 2001; and Hurricane Katrina's devastation of New Orleans and the Gulf Coast in 2005.

The 2000 election reminded us that there is no national presidential election. Instead we undertake 50—actually, 51 including the District of Columbia—separate state elections. The winner is determined not by the national popular vote, but by the states' electoral votes, which are based in part on state population but also provide representation for the states as states. The collection, tabulation, and recounting of presidential votes is conducted by state officials, pursuant to state rules. Moreover, the states often delegate critical issues— selection of voting machinery, ballot design, whether to undertake a manual recount, whether to accept a technically flawed absentee ballot, whether dangling or dimpled chad is sufficient to mark the intent of a voter—to local officials. To be sure, as the Supreme Court's *Bush v. Gore*, 525 U.S. 98 (2000), decision indicates, the federal constitution constrains state and local decision making. And Congress reacted to the events of 2000 with new legislation increasing the federal role in the mechanics of voting. But the 2000 election remains a stunning reminder of how even with respect to our most important national office, states and local governments play a vital role.

September 11, 2001—9/11—demonstrated the crucial role of the states and especially local governments in dealing with issues of public safety and security. Although the terrorist attacks were an assault on our nation, most of the domestic response involved local governments. New York City police, firefighters, and emergency medical personnel responded to the attacks on the World Trade Center. Local public health and safety workers from the District of Columbia and various Virginia and Maryland counties battled the consequences of the terrorist attack on our most important federal military installation, the Pentagon. The vast bulk of the subsequent public effort to increase the security of public buildings, public spaces, and vulnerable infrastructure facilities has involved state and local security officers, not the federal government. More generally, in detecting and pursuing terrorists and preventing future terrorist attacks, the 600,000 local police officers are likely to play at least as great a role as the FBI and its 11,000 agents. This is not simply a matter of numbers—although the enormous difference in the magnitude of the local versus federal police forces is surely relevant. Local police forces are likely to have far greater knowledge of local conditions and dangers, including access to informants and awareness of unusual or suspicious incidents.[2]

The central role of states and local governments was underscored again in the aftermath of Hurricane Katrina. Once again, states and local governments were called upon to make critical decisions concerning evacuations, public safety, emergency health and medical assistance, and the provision of basic services. State and local actions directly affected the lives and property of hundreds of thousands, if not millions, of people. State and local governments are also continuing to play a key role in aiding victims of the disaster, rebuilding stricken areas, and planning future development in light of the needs of disaster prevention and preparedness.

The centrality of the states and local government is not simply a lingering aftermath of an earlier era. In recent years, the federalizing trend that marked the middle decades of the twentieth century has flattened, and the federal system has witnessed a modest tilt away from the federal government and back to the states and localities. This can be seen in the enhanced state and local share of public employment and public spending; in the greater discretion accorded to states and local governments in the manage-

---

[2] See generally Richard Briffault, "Facing the Urban Future After September 11, 2001," *The Urban Lawyer* 34 (Summer 2002), pp. 563–582.

ment of federally funded programs; and in the many policy initiatives that have sprung from the states and localities.

In 2002, the federal government civilian workforce was 2,690,000—down 13% from nearly 3.1 million federal employees 15 years earlier, and 170,000 workers smaller than the federal civilian workforce of 1966. By contrast, the combined state and local workforce in 2002 was 15,602,000—or nearly six times the federal. And while the federal workforce has been stagnating, the state and local workforce has been growing. The number of state and local employees in 2002 was 11% higher than in 1990—and roughly double the state and local workforce of 1966.

The state and local share of total government spending is also on the rise. In 1980, federal spending was 87% greater than state and local spending. In 2003, federal spending was just 48% greater than state and local spending. If federal spending on defense and foreign affairs, interest on the national debt, and the two major social insurance programs—Medicare and Social Security—are subtracted from the federal total, so that the focus is on domestic regulation and public services, then state and local spending actually dominates federal spending—by roughly 2:1. Moreover, although the federal government provides significant financial assistance to local governments, the federal aid share of state and local funds has been dropping. Federal aid amounted to 23% of state and local spending in 1980, and was slightly less than that in 2003. States and localities have not only expanded their programs but have also become more successful at cultivating their own resources.

Moreover, in recent years the federal government has given the states greater flexibility in spending federal dollars. The most famous instance of this is the 1996 welfare reform law, which gave the states broad new authority over federally funded welfare programs. Other federal aid programs in such areas as transportation and pollution control have been revised to reduce federal regulatory controls. This trend, however, is not unmixed, as the federal role has also increased in some areas, like primary and secondary education, that have traditionally been reserved to the states and localities.

States and localities have also been more aggressive in addressing a wide range of domestic policy issues. This is reflected in the unprecedented leadership role assumed by the state attorneys general in shaping national policy on tobacco; the initiatives underway in nearly a dozen states to tackle the sprawling pattern of urban growth; the states' exploration of new forms of school finance, HMO regulation, income assistance, and health insurance for the uninsured; the combination of voter-initiated and legislatively adopted measures to promote campaign finance reform; and the state and local legislative and judicial decisions reexamining family and marriage relationships. These developments demonstrate that states and localities are important, independent policymakers within the federal system.

THE STATES

The 50 states are the basic components of the United States. Although not all American land or residents are found within the states—the District of Columbia, the Commonwealth of Puerto Rico, and territories such as American Samoa, Guam, the Northern Marianas Islands, and the Virgin Islands are also parts of the United States—the federal government is structurally constituted out of the United States. As the Supreme Court has observed, "[t]he Constitution, in all its provisions, looks to an indestructible Union, composed of indestructible States." (*Texas v. White*, 74 U.S. 700, 725 (1869)).

The U.S. Constitution and the States

The Constitution includes multiple protections of the autonomy and equality of the states. The Constitution guarantees the territorial integrity of the states. No state may be created out of the territory of another state without its consent. So, too, no state may be deprived of its equal suffrage in the Senate. Under the Guarantee Clause, the United States is committed to protecting the states from invasion and domestic violence.

The states are in no sense arms of the federal government. They are not like federal administrative agencies or regional offices; the federal government does not appoint state officers. The states can legislate without having to demonstrate any authorization from the federal Constitution or by the federal government. Under the Tenth Amendment, the states have residual power over all aspects of government not granted to the federal government or not constrained by the Constitution or by the federal government acting pursuant to the Constitution. To be sure, the federal Constitution does impose significant restrictions on the scope of state law-making authority, and Congress acting pursuant to the Constitution's grant of power to the federal government can impose further limitations on the states. Nonetheless, the states continue to possess and exercise broad police power authority over their territory and their citizens.

Several recent Supreme Court decisions have underscored the protections that the Constitution provides for the autonomy of the states and their localities. Under *New York v. United States*, 505 U.S. 144 (1992) and *Printz v. United States*, 521 U.S. 898 (1997), Congress cannot "commandeer" states and localities to serve federal ends; that is, they cannot require the states to pass certain laws or enforce a federal regulatory program. Under the Court's recent Eleventh Amendment cases, Congress lacks the power to subject nonconsenting states to private damages actions in either federal, *Seminole Tribe of Florida v. Florida*, 517 U.S. 44 (1996), or state, *Alden v. Maine*, 527 U.S. 706 (1999), courts. Principles of federalism also limit the ability of Congress to enact legislation intended to remedy state and local violations of constitutional rights; such measures must be "congruent" with and "proportional" to the scope of state violations (see *City of Boerne v. Flores*, 521 U.S. 507 (1997), *Board of Trustees v. Garrett*, 531 U.S. 356 (2001)). Of course, Congress has broad powers under the Commerce Clause and other provisions of the Constitution to adopt economic and social legislation, preempt inconsistent state laws (see, e.g., *Lorillard Tobacco Co. v. Reilly*, 533 U.S. 525 (2001)), regulate state and local activity that affects commerce or constitutional rights (see e.g., *Garcia v. San Antonio Metropolitan Transit Auth.*, 469 U.S. 528 (1985), *Nevada Dep't of Human Resources v. Hibbs*, 538 U.S. 721 (2003)), and use conditions attached to federal grants to influence state and local actions (see *South Dakota v. Dole*, 483 U.S. 203 (1987)).

The inherent law-making power of the states includes fiscal affairs. Although the Constitution prohibits certain specific forms of state taxation and imposes other more general rules, such as nondiscrimination against interstate commerce, the states have enormous autonomy with respect to taxation, borrowing, spending, and lending money. They may innovate new forms of revenue-raising and new types of debt instruments, they may adopt new taxes and raise tax rates, and they may incur debt to raise the funds they need to pay for the programs they prefer. To be sure, state resources may be limited in practice, and interstate competition may constrain state activities. But the states' formal legal authority with respect to state fiscal matters is significant.

State Constitutions

Each state has its own constitution that establishes the basic structural framework for its state government. The federal constitution does not create the states or design their governments. Rather, a state's constitution provides for the basic component parts of state government, allocates powers among these components, and determines how these parts interact. So, too, like the federal constitution, most state constitutions impose limits on the scope of governmental authority. Many state constitutions contain limits similar to those in the federal constitution like the due process and equal protection clauses and the Bill of Rights. But state constitutions also differ from the federal in significant ways.

As a matter of theory, the federal constitution provides a *grant of enumerated powers* to the federal government. In other words, the federal government enjoys only those powers actually granted to it by the federal constitution. To be sure, expansive judicial interpretations of such open-ended constitutional provisions as the necessary and proper clause, the commerce clause, and the spending power have given the federal government broad authority; but still, in theory, all federal powers must be expressly or impliedly granted by the federal constitution. By contrast, state governments acting through their state legislatures are presumed to have broad, residual, plenary governmental powers. State constitutions are seen not as granting powers to state governments but, instead, as limiting the powers the states inherently possess.

A second major distinction between the federal and state constitutions is one of form. State constitutions tend to be longer and more detailed than the federal. This may be, in part, a reflection of the greater domestic responsibilities of state governments. Many state constitutions deal with the substantive responsibilities of state government, like public education. It may also reflect the relative frequency with which state constitutions have been revised or amended. The United States has operated under the same constitution since 1787. It has been amended 27 times. By contrast, the 50 states have had 147 constitutions, or nearly three per state. Nine states have had five or more constitutions. Only 19 states have operated under just one constitution. Moreover, not only do states frequently change their constitutions, but they even more frequently amend the ones they have. At the start of 2003, the states' current constitutions had been amended nearly 6,800 times, or approximately 136 amendments per state. As a result, many state constitutions include considerable statutory-like details.

To be sure, despite these differences most state constitutions produce state governments that look a lot like the federal government and the governments of their sister states. Thus, all 50 states have adopted the separation of powers, with three separate branches of government. All 50 states have an independently elected governor and an independently elected legislature; no state employs a parliamentary system in which the state legislature chooses the chief executive. In 49 states the legislature, like the federal Congress, is bicameral; and in most states the members of the upper house of the legislature serve for longer terms than members of the lower house. All 50 states also have an independent judiciary, and in all 50 states the courts engage in judicial review of state legislation. State bill of rights provisions frequently resemble those of the federal constitution, too.

Yet, in the areas of governmental structure and fundamental rights, many state constitutions include provisions that differ significantly from those in the federal constitution, or have no federal constitutional counterpart at all. Whereas federal judges are appointed by the executive, and, once confirmed by the Senate, enjoy life tenure, most state constitutions provide that most state judges are elected and serve for terms, rather than for life. Similarly, although the federal constitution places no limits on the number of terms federal legislators may serve, 18 states limit the number of terms state legislators can serve. Moreover, while the federal constitution creates only two executive branch officers—the president and the vice president—most states provide for numerous independently elected state officials who may exercise executive functions independently of the governor. In all but seven states, for example, the voters elect the attorney general, and in two of the other states, the attorney general is selected by an institution other than the governor.[3] The governor and attorney general may be of different parties and may clash over questions of legal policy. In addition to the independent attorney general, 38 states have an independently elected treasurer or comptroller, while in another four the official with these functions is elected by the legislature. Other officials who in some states are elected independently include the secretary of state, the commissioner of education, the commissioner of insurance, and the commissioner of agriculture.

Other structural innovations found in many state constitutions include the item veto and direct democracy. With respect to the former, the federal constitution enables the president to veto proposed legislation, but the president must veto an entire bill if he is to veto it at all. The constitutions of 43 states, however, allow the governor to veto "items" or "parts" of bills, although in every state but one that provides for this power the item veto is limited to appropriation bills.

The federal constitution makes no provision for direct democracy. The federal government is entirely representative: The people elect representatives to office who then do the governing. Apart from voting for candidates, citizens have no direct role in the ongoing processes of government. Most state constitutions, however, provide for some direct role for the people in governing. In every state but one, popular approval in a referendum is necessary to ratify changes to the constitution. Many state constitutions also condition the issuance of state or local debt on voter approval. Some state constitutions permit the voters to use referenda to block new legislation, while others authorize voter initiation of new legislation or amendments to the state constitution. In other words, in nearly half the states the voters can make or amend the constitution, without any action by the state legislature or the governor.

Direct democracy, particularly voter-initiated legislation and constitutional amendments, has had an enormous impact on the states that provide for it, particularly since California's adoption of Proposition 13 in the late 1970s. Today, in states like California, Colorado, Washington, and Oregon it is a central part of the political process. The voter initiative played a critical role in the adoption and spread of legislative term limits and in the imposition of limits on state and local taxation and spending.

---

[3] The attorney general is elected by the state legislature in Maine, and appointed by the judges of the state supreme court in Tennessee.

The State Fiscal Constitution

State constitutions pay considerable attention to state and local finances. The federal constitution says next to nothing about public finance, doing little more than authorizing federal taxation and borrowing,[4] and setting out the basic procedures for raising and spending money.[5] It places just a handful of substantive constraints on federal taxation,[6] and no restrictions on federal borrowing at all. By contrast, state constitutions accord extensive consideration to state and local spending, borrowing, and taxing.

State constitutions limit the purposes for which states and localities can spend or lend their funds and expressly address specific spending techniques.[7] These "public purpose" provisions narrow the range of government action and limit public sector support for private sector activities, although, in practice, judicial interpretations make these constraints far less binding that the constitutional texts might suggest.[8]

Nearly all state constitutions impose significant substantive or procedural restrictions on state and local borrowing. Some bar state debt outright or impose very low limits on the amount of debt a state may incur. Some cap state or local debt at a specified fraction of state or local taxable wealth or revenues. Many require a supermajority in the legislature, or of voters in a referendum, or of both before debt may be incurred.[9]

Many state constitutions also constrain state and local taxation. These provisions include prohibitions on certain types of taxes, such as the income

---

[4] See U.S. Const., art. I, § 8, cl. 1 (authorizing Congress to "lay and collect Taxes, Imposts and Excises"); id. at Amend. XVI (authorizing imposition of income tax); id. at § 8, cl. 2 (authorizing Congress "[t]o borrow Money on the credit of the United States").

[5] See U.S. Const., art. I, § 7, cl. (providing that "[a]ll bills for raising revenue shall originate in the House of Representatives"); id. at § 9, cl. 7 (providing that "[n]o Money shall be drawn from the Treasury, but in Consequence of Appropriations made by Law").

[6] See U.S. Const., art. I, § 8, cl. (providing that "[a]ll Duties, Imposts and Excises shall be uniform throughout the United States"); id. at § 9, cl. 4 (providing that "[n]o Capitation, or other direct, Tax shall be laid, unless in Proportion to the Census or Enumeration herein before directed to be taken); id. at § 9, cl. 5 ("No Tax or Duty shall be laid on Articles exported from any State").

[7] See, for example, Dale F. Rubin, "Constitutional Aid Limitation Provisions and the Public Purpose Doctrine," *St. Louis University Public Law Review* 12, No. (1993), pp. 143–148. Rubin finds that 46 out of 50 state constitutions contain some limits on spending.

[8] See, for example, Richard Briffault, "The Disfavored Constitution: State Fiscal Limits and State Constitutional Law," *Rutgers Law Review* 34 (Summer 2003), pp. 907, 910–915.

[9] Id., pp. 915–916.

tax; caps on the rates of certain taxes, such as the sales tax; and a variety of limits on the property tax, including the tax rate and annual increases in assessed valuation, as well as special procedural rules for new taxes or tax increases, including legislative supermajorities or voter approval requirements, some times with popular supermajorities.[10]

THE COMPLEX STRUCTURE OF AMERICAN LOCAL GOVERNMENT

Although American federalism can pose difficult questions concerning the allocation of governing authority between the federal government and the states, the position of the states in American government is reasonably familiar to most people. There are only 50 states, and many of us can name them all. The number of states is quite stable, as are state boundary lines. All but five states were admitted to the union before the start of the twentieth century, and the last two states, Alaska and Hawaii, were admitted in 1959, or nearly a half-century ago. The states are comparable to each other in powers, constitutional status, internal organization, and authority over their citizens even if they differ significantly in territorial size and population.

Local governments are quite a different story. There are nearly 90,000 of them and they differ dramatically in powers, status, organization, function, authority, and mode of creation across the country and, indeed, within a particular state. There is not even a consistent terminology for local governments; different states include such diverse local units as parishes, boroughs, townships, as well as the more common forms of local government such as county or city. Unlike the states, local governments may—and frequently do—overlap each other's territory. Unlike the states, local governments are frequently created, modified territorially, or abolished. Unlike the states, local governments lack inherent law-making authority. So, too, while the federal Constitution makes frequent reference to the states, the federal Constitution is entirely silent on the subject of local governments.

Local governments are crucial to American federalism. Approximately three-quarters of the aggregate total of state and local employees are actually employed by local governments. So, too, the overwhelming majority of state and local elected officials serve at the local level. The states may be formally responsible for the provision of most domestic public services, but local governments play the key role in actually delivering such basic services as education, policing, fire prevention, street and road maintenance, mass transit, and sewage and solid waste removal. Local governments are also the dominant actors in our intergovernmental system in regulating land use and in community development. A considerable portion of state spending is

---

[10] Id., pp. 927–929.

used not for the provision of state programs but consists, instead, of grants to local governments to help them finance local services and activities.

Part of the complexity of American local government derives from the fact that most localities are agents with two principals—their state government and their local constituents. On the one hand, local governments are creatures of their states, established by the states to discharge state functions locally. On the other hand, local governments are more than simply administrative arms of the state government. Local constituents play a critical role in directing local government activities and shaping their performance. This may involve local popular election of local government officials; appointment of some local officials by other, locally elected officials; or a requirement that the state appoint only local residents to the governance of the local unit. Local autonomy may also result from the powers and discretion accorded to the local government. Local governments, thus, have a bottom-up, that is, a local control aspect, as well as a top-down or state-control aspect.

Another part of the complexity of our local arrangements derives from the sheer variety of types of local governments. There are multiple forms of local government, and they often have overlapping territorial scopes and responsibilities. Most people in the United States live in at least two different local governments. Many are within the jurisdiction of multiple localities.

The County

One basic form of local government is the county. Descended from the old English shire, the county traditionally provided basic state services at the local level. Thus, the county was responsible for public prosecutions, recording deeds, keeping birth, death, and other public records, assessing property for tax purposes, registering voters, maintaining public roads, and providing poor relief and health care for the indigent. Most states are entirely divided up into counties. (Alaska uses the term *borough* for its counties; Louisiana uses the term *parish*.) There are exceptions: In Virginia, most of the cities are outside the jurisdiction of a county; in Connecticut and Rhode Island the county exists as a territorial unit but there are no county governments; and in a number of major cities—such as Boston, Denver, Honolulu, New York, Philadelphia, and San Francisco—city and county governments are combined. These and a few other exceptions aside, most of the land in most of the states lies within a county. A state's arrangement of counties is also usually quite stable, with counties only rarely created or destroyed, and county borders rarely changed. Indeed, in many states, the current county structure dates back to the state's entry into the Union. In 2002, there were 3,034 counties, or virtually the same as the 3,052 a half century earlier.[11]

Traditionally, the county was a regulatory and service-providing body, not a law- or policy-making one. Indeed, often there was neither a county executive nor a county legislature; instead the county government may have consisted of a group of independent officials, such as the Assessor, the Coroner or Medical Examiner, the Register of Deeds, the Board of Elections, the Sheriff, and the District Attorney. Although locally elected and thus to a considerable extent locally accountable, their function was to discharge state services locally. Counties were particularly important in providing basic services in rural and small town areas.

Beginning in the mid-twentieth century, however, counties, particularly those in urban areas, began to take on broader responsibilities and to assume a policy-making role. Frequently encompassing central cities, smaller outlying cities, and suburbs, counties are often well-situated to provide area-wide services in metropolitan regions. Many states have provided for stronger county governments, including elected executives and legislatures, and they have increased county functions to include such area-wide activities as housing, mass transit, airports, parks and recreation, water supply and sewage, planning, zoning, and regional governance.

Counties differ dramatically in population, ranging from under 100 people to nearly 10 million (Los Angeles County, California). At the start of the new millennium, the 671 counties that each had fewer than 10,000 inhabitants together had just 3.7 million people. But the 201 counties that each had more than 250,000 inhabitants together had 159 million people, or 56.5% of the total population in all the counties in the United States.[12] In 2001, county governments across the country raised and spent in the aggregate approximately $250 billion.[13]

The City

The city—or the municipality or the municipal corporation—is another basic unit of local governance. Here, too, terminology varies from state to state, so that municipalities may include the borough in some states (but not the Alaskan "borough," which is really a county), the town (but not the New England town), and the village. The city is closely associated with the idea of urbanness, that is, with greater population and greater population density, and the resulting need for more government regulation and public services. The city also relies on the concept of incorporation, that is, like a

---

[11] See U.S. Bureau of the Census, 1997 Census of Governments, p. 4.
[12] See U.S. Bureau of the Census, 2002 Census of Governments.
[13] Id.

private business corporation or a not-for-profit corporation, a municipality is incorporated when local people seek a new local entity to provide the services and undertake the functions they believe are necessary to deal with the consequences of population growth and density. Typically, the municipal government includes an elected legislative or policy-making body and an elected executive or appointed manager.

The number of municipal corporations is far more fluid than the number of counties. There were 19,431 municipal corporations in 2002—a 2,624 (or 16%) increase over the 16,807 municipal corporations in 1952. This increase reflects both population growth and dramatic population movements over the last half century. Some municipal corporations are also able to change their boundaries and increase their population through the annexation of unincorporated land. Although municipal corporations account for only a tiny portion of the United States' total land area, in 2002, nearly 174 million Americans, or almost 62% of the population, lived in cities. Like counties, cities vary widely in their population. Slightly less than one-half of all municipalities have fewer than 1,000 inhabitants each. The total population of these 9,361 small municipalities came to only 3.7 million people, or just 2.2% of the total municipal population. Conversely, there were just 241 cities with populations of 100,000 or more, but the total population of these larger cities was 76 million. Most cities—with the exception of many of the cities in Virginia—are located territorially within counties and are subject to county jurisdiction. So too, as previously noted, for a number of major cities, the city and county have been effectively fused.

The Township

A third form of local governance is what the United States Census Bureau calls *town* or *township governments*. These entities are located in just 20 states, concentrated in New England, the Middle Atlantic region, and the Midwest. (The New England states, New York, and Wisconsin use the term *town* while the other states use the term *township*.) Typically in these states, all or most of the counties or the parts of counties outside of incorporated municipalities are subdivided into towns or townships, much as the state is divided into counties. In New England and in the Middle Atlantic states, they are frequently found in densely populated urban areas and perform many municipal-type regulatory and service functions. By contrast, in the Midwest, many township governments perform only a very limited range of services for predominantly rural areas. There they resemble old-fashioned counties. There were 16,504 town or township governments in 2002, and, like the number of counties, the number of towns and townships is relatively stable, dropping only modestly from the total of 17,202 in 1952. With an aggregate population of 57 million, or around 20% of the total population of the United States, town and township governments play only a modest role in local governance in the United States as a whole. But they are significant in some states, including Connecticut, Illinois, Indiana, Kansas, Maine, Massachusetts, Michigan, New Hampshire, New Jersey, New York, Ohio, Pennsylvania, Rhode Island, Vermont, and Wisconsin.

Special Districts

Although no local government has the full range of powers of a state, counties, cities and townships are all considered to be general purpose governments in that they have relatively broad responsibilities over a significant number of areas—public safety, public health, land use, streets, highways, and transportation. However, a significant number of local governments are given very narrowly defined authority and are authorized to undertake only one or a very limited number of functions. These are known as special purpose local governments, and they are actually the most common form of local government in the United States today. The most common form of special purpose government is the school district. In 2002, there were 13,522 school districts in the United States. The Census Bureau lumps all other forms of special purpose government into the category of *special district governments*. There were 35,356 special districts in 2002, or nearly as many as the total number of municipal governments and towns and townships combined—and far more than the total number of municipal governments and counties. The special district has also been the most rapidly growing form of local government in the United States over the last half-century. The number of special districts in 2002 was nearly triple the 12,340 counted in 1952.

The vast majority—nearly 32,000—of the special district governments in 2002 were single-function districts, with responsibilities ranging from fire protection (5,725 districts), water supply (3,405), housing and community development (3,399), drainage and flood control (3,247), soil and water conservation (2,506), sewerage (2,004), cemeteries (1,666), libraries (1,580), health and hospitals (1,464), parks and recreation (1,287), highways (743), air transportation (510), and solid waste management (455). Other districts provide parking facilities, public utility services, industrial development, and financial assistance to other local governments. The remaining roughly 3,000 districts are multifunction districts that engage in two or more activities, particularly involving sewerage, water supply, and natural resources. Special districts other than school districts raised and spent approximately $90 billion in 1996–1997. That represented a 25% increase in special district expenditures over 1991–1992, which was itself a 35% increase over special district expenditures in 1986–1987.[14]

Special districts may be created for a variety of reasons. These include giving them independence from general purpose cities or counties; tailoring the territorial scope of the government to the proper dimensions of its function or activity; avoiding certain state constitutional restrictions that apply to cities or counties; obtaining some of the infrastructure and service benefits of local government without having to incur the full costs of general purpose local government.

Like general purpose governments, special districts combine top-down and bottom-up elements. They may be created by the state, by local constituents pursuant to state enabling legislation, or by other local governments. Those with locally elected or appointed governing bodies have a stronger bottom-up aspect. Unlike general purpose local governments, some special purpose districts, particularly those that are regional in scope, may be governed by state-appointed boards of directors, which reinforces their top-down element. Moreover, unlike general purpose governments, many bottom-up special districts are designed to be accountable to and controlled not by the local population generally but by discrete local groups, such as local landowners or users of the service provided by the special district. In these districts, representation in district governance may be tied to land values or assessment payments.

FROM DILLON'S RULE TO HOME RULE

The source and scope of local government powers has long been controversial. As a matter of federal constitutional law, local governments are creatures of the states. The states enjoy broad powers to create, alter, or abolish their local governments, change their boundaries, and modify or eliminate their powers, largely unconstrained by the United States Constitution. (See *Hunter v. City of Pittsburgh*, 207 U.S. 161 (1907).) Indeed, as a background legal principle in our system, a local government is a delegate or agent of its state, enjoying only the powers the state has delegated to it.[15] The scope of a locality's state-granted powers was traditionally further constrained by *Dillon's Rule*. Named after Judge John F. Dillon of the Iowa Supreme Court,

[14] See U.S. Census Bureau, 1997 Census of Government, Finances of Special District Governments 1 (September 2000). Because school districts are heavily funded by state aid and appropriations from general purpose local governments, school district expenditures may not be an appropriate measure of the importance of school districts in the state and local government system.

[15] See Richard Briffault, "Our Localism: Part I: The Structure of Local Government Law," *Columbia Law Review* 90, no. 1 (January 1990), pp. 7–8.

who first authored the rule in his Commentaries on the Law of Municipal Corporations shortly after the Civil War, Dillon's Rule provides that local governments may exercise only those powers granted in express words, or *necessarily or fairly implied* in the expressly granted powers, or essential to the accomplishment of the objects and purposes of the locality.

Protecting Local Governments

Dillon's Rule's crabbed approach to local power has long been criticized, and many states have taken steps to empower their localities. Two older limits on state power in order to strengthen their localities are state constitutional prohibitions on special state commissions that perform municipal functions and on special or local legislation. The special commission bans, many of which date back to the nineteenth century, were intended to protect the integrity of local governments by curbing the ability of the states to take important local functions and vest them in special bodies unaccountable to the local electorate.[16] The more widespread special legislation prohibitions were intended to limit the ability of state legislatures to target specific local governments.[17] Both types of provisions have had mixed success. In the middle and late twentieth centuries, a number of states added a new type of provision to their constitutions with the goal of protecting local governments from state legislative imposition—restrictions on unfunded mandates. Some of these measures are procedural, requiring the disclosure of the costs that state mandates impose on localities, but others are substantive, prohibiting certain categories of cost-imposing requirements unless the state provides the funds to offset the new costs.[18]

Home Rule

Restrictions on special commissions, special laws, and unfunded mandates may limit the ability of state governments to disrupt or impose upon local governments, but they do not empower local governments to act on their own. That has been the role of "home rule." The first home rule amendments to state constitutions date back to the late nineteenth century. The initial home rule measures often empowered just a single large city—St. Louis in Missouri, San Francisco in California—or a small number of very big cities. Today, most states accord home rule to most municipalities, and some states even make home rule available to counties, or at least some counties, too.

---

[16] See Richard Briffault and Laurie Reynolds, *Cases and Materials on State and Local Government Law: Sixth Edition* (St. Paul, MN: Thomson West, 2004), pp. 238–244.

[17] Id., pp. 244–259.

[18] Id., pp. 259–266.

Early versions of home rule sought to provide local governments with two powers—initiative and immunity.[19] The initiative power would enable local governments to undertake actions over a range of important issues without having to go to the state for specific authorization. In other words, home rule as initiative would undo Dillon's Rule and give local governments power to engage in policy-making concerning local matters. The immunity power would go further and protect local actions from displacement by state law. The combination of initiative and immunity powers would make a home rule city an "imperium in imperio," *St. Louis v. Western Union Tel. Co.*, 149 U.S. 465, 468 (1893), that is, a state within a state.

In practice, however, so-called "imperio" home rule often did not work out well for the cities. In many state courts, the Dillon's Rule philosophy lingered, leading to narrow interpretations of basic concepts such as "local" or "municipal." State courts were particularly reluctant to recognize claims that home rule immunized local actions from state regulation. Yet, with the same language used to establish both local initiative and local immunity, narrow judicial interpretations in immunity cases often led to equally narrow readings in initiative cases. In 1953, the American Municipal Association (later the National League of Cities), sought to remedy the deficiencies of the traditional imperio model by proposing a new approach under which all legislative powers that could be delegated to a locality were deemed to have been delegated to the locality, subject to the legislature's power to deny local authority by state statute. In other words, immunity was sacrificed to strengthen initiative. Later versions of the AMA/NLC model sought to provide a measure of immunity as well by requiring that state legislation limiting or denying local power do so expressly. This so-called "legislative" home rule approach influenced many home rule provisions in the second half of the twentieth century. In practice, however, many state home rule provisions blur these theoretically sharp distinctions and combine both imperio and "legislative" models. Moreover, the scope of home rule in any given state is inevitably influenced by both the constitutional or statutory text and the course of judicial interpretation. As a result, home rule powers and protections vary considerably from state to state, and from subject to subject.

FORMS OF LOCAL GOVERNMENT

There are three principal forms of local government in the United States: mayor-council, commission, and council-manager.

---

[19] See Gordon L. Clark, *Judges and the Cities: Interpreting Local Autonomy* (Chicago, IL: University of Chicago Press, 1985), p. 7.

Mayor-Council

Most of the largest cities in the United States use the mayor-council form, which tracks the traditional separation of powers between executive and legislative functions. Many cities have embraced the "strong mayor" form of mayor-council, with the mayor authorized to appoint and remove most city commissioners, propose the budget, and enter into contracts on behalf of the city. Other large cities, concerned about the power of the mayor and the potential for corruption and abuse in the strong mayor system, embraced a "weak mayor" model, with municipal functions splintered among multiple independent boards and commissions. In recent years, there has been something of a turn back to the strong mayor model, in the belief that government accountability can be promoted when the voters have one person whom they can hold accountable for government performance. Thus, in a number of large cities, such as New York, Chicago, and Boston, already strong mayors have been given greater responsibility for the public schools, which were traditionally the domain of independent boards of education.

Commission

The commission form of city government vests both legislative and executive powers in a single body—the commission—usually composed of five members. The commission model emerged in Galveston, Texas in 1901 in response to a tidal wave that devastated the city. The Galveston commission, initially composed of local business leaders, helped the city get back on its feet and by 1915 about 500 communities had adopted the commission form. One of the commission members may be designated the mayor, but he has no more formal powers than his colleagues. Individual commission members may also be given administrative responsibilities for different city services. Although the commission system was popular in the early decades of the twentieth century, there have been virtually no new adoptions since 1930, and only about 5% of cities use this form today.

Council-Manager

The council-manager system also arose in the early twentieth century as an alternative to the mayoral system. Here the innovator was Dayton, Ohio, which hired a city manager in 1914 to help recover from bankruptcy. After World War II, the council-manager system spread widely, particularly in medium-sized cities and suburbs, although a few large cities rely on managers as well.

The council-manager form draws on the model of the business corporation. The council as the elected representative body hires the manager as the chief administrative officer, who sits at the pleasure of the council. The manager has broad authority to hire and fire staff, administer the budget, and run day-to-day city operations. The council, which may be part time, sets overall policy. Although the manager works for the council, in many cities the city manager may actually take the initiative and emerge as the city's de facto leader.

Cutting across the issue of city form is the nature of city elections. Traditionally, most cities, including all but the largest, elected their councils or commissions in at-large elections, with all members of the body elected from the city as a whole. In the 1970s and 1980s, concerns grew that such electoral systems disadvantaged racial minorities, and especially following the 1982 amendments to the federal Voting Rights Act many at-large electoral systems in cities with large minority populations were challenged in court. In response to such suits as well as the greater political salience of minority representation, many local governments have shifted from at-large to district elections of their legislative bodies.

METROPOLITAN GOVERNANCE

Most Americans today live in large metropolitan areas, which may contain hundreds of thousands if not millions of people and sprawl across hundreds if not thousands of square miles, and include dozens if not hundreds of local governments. Some metropolitan areas cross state lines. Metropolitan area residents do not concentrate their activities within their home localities, but can live in one locality, work in a second, shop in a third, go to entertainment events in a fourth, and travel through multiple others in the course of these activities. So, too, metropolitan area businesses typically draw most of their workers or customers from outside their home localities. While the metropolitan area as an economic or social region has grown, only rarely is there a single local government with broad jurisdiction over such a region. Instead, most metropolitan areas are composed of large numbers of relatively small, some times overlapping, local governments.[20]

At one time, scholars and policy analysts sought the creation of large metropolitan area governments that would provide a legal and political structure congruent with the economic and social region. Much as many large cities had expanded territorially by annexation and consolidation with smaller outlying localities in order to follow population growth in the nineteenth and early twentieth centuries, they hoped that central city boundaries could be extended regionally. Widespread opposition from people in the

---

[20] See generally Richard Briffault, "The Local Government Boundary Problem in Metropolitan Areas," *Stanford Law Review* 48, no. 5 (May 1996), pp. 1115–1171.

outlying areas often precluded such expansion. Moreover, many scholars also came to oppose centralized regional governments, claiming that there are benefits from the competition of large numbers of relatively small localities as well as costs to very large local units.

The large number of metropolitan area governments creates numerous possibilities for interlocal conflicts and raises issues concerning efficient service delivery, interlocal inequalities, and the financing and maintenance of regional infrastructure. Many states and localities have sought to address some of these problems by developing new modes of interlocal cooperation and interlocal agreements. These can include contracts for services, whereby one government pays another to provide a service; joint services agreements, in which two or more governments provide a service jointly; or regional collaborative efforts to create new governmental entities that can provide government services.[21]

Many states also create, or authorize local creation, of regional special service districts. These are particularly important for building and operating infrastructure services, such as transit, airports, water supply, or wastewater treatment. Such arrangements enable people to maintain small local governments for services such as policing or land use regulation that people like to keep close to home, while taking advantages of the economies of scale for certain kinds of high-cost physical infrastructure. These districts or authorities are typically governed by appointees and financed by user charges, tolls, or special taxes. In a few areas—Seattle, Washington; Portland, Oregon; the Twin Cities region—there are multiple-purpose regional governments that handle a number of functions together.[22]

Only a handful of metropolitan areas have something that approaches a metropolitan area government. In smaller areas that fall entirely within a single county, the county may be given broader governing powers that make it effectively a regional government, or the central city and the county may be consolidated. Some prominent city-county consolidations, involving larger areas, in the late twentieth century include Miami and Dade County, Florida; Nashville and Davidson County, Tennessee; Indianapolis and Marion County, Indiana; and Jacksonville and Duval County, Florida. Typically in these so-called "two tier" consolidations, only the central city is consolidated with the county. Smaller cities within the county may remain. These consolidations strengthen the county government but also maintain possibilities of conflict between local and regional units.[23]

State governments have also been called upon to do more to address interlocal inequalities and the external consequences of local regulation.

---

[21] See Briffault and Reynolds, supra, pp. 449–472.

[22] See id., pp. 472–495.

[23] See id., pp. 496–507.

The school finance reform movement, which has led to often-protracted litigations in a majority of states, seeks to force the states to address the impact of interlocal tax base disparities on the funds available for the number one local expense, public education. In response, many states have determined to mitigate interlocal differences by supplementing locally generated revenues with more state aid, as well as by more actively overseeing locally provided education. A prime source of conflict over the external effects of local decisions is land use.

Zoning, subdivision controls, and other forms of land use regulation are important areas of local decision making. But with so many metropolitan area localities in close proximity to each other, local land use decisions will often affect neighboring communities. Local approvals of new development can create traffic, congestion, and pollution problems for nearby places. Conversely, local growth controls and zoning restrictions may either force unwanted development on other communities, or lead to the adoption of similar restrictions by adjacent localities, thereby contributing to the further movement of new development to outlying areas or the exclusion of certain land uses from a region. Some states have begun to take on a larger role in setting standards for and supervising local land use regulation to deal with these issues.

SUMMARY

State and local management of the problems of metropolitan development is an important example of the way American federalism works in practice. These issues of metropolitan organization, land use regulation, education finance, the cost and quality of local services, the construction and maintenance of basic infrastructure, and the like directly affect the economic well-being and quality of life of tens of millions of Americans, but they are addressed primarily by states and local governments. Different states and local governments come up with different approaches, with some taking these matters more seriously, or making greater progress, or engaging in more creative experiments, than others. The federal government almost certainly has the power to address many of these issues, and often provides some money or gets peripherally involved. But, much as Madison predicted in 1787, these and other key matters of domestic governance are the province of the states and local governments.

CHAPTER 2

An Overview of Investment Banking

Herman R. Charbonneau
Senior Vice President & Manager
Public Finance Department
Roosevelt & Cross, Inc.

This chapter provides an overview of investment banking from the perspective of the senior managing underwriter. The principles are basically the same for the large national broker-dealer as well as the smaller regional broker-dealer. This chapter also defines regional investment banking firms, and their share of the overall public finance market, and identifies the services that these firms offer to state-level and local government bond issuers. The competitive advantages and disadvantages of regional firms, vis-à-vis the national market leaders, are also discussed. The chapter concludes with a discussion of some of the challenges currently faced by regional public finance bankers as they seek to maintain and expand their market share.

OVERVIEW OF PUBLIC FINANCE BANKING

Public finance is the business of originating, structuring, and underwriting new municipal bond issues that are sold via a negotiated process. The business also encompasses financial advisory assignments, not entailing underwriting, for new issues. Public finance has grown rapidly over the past two decades as negotiated finance came to dominate the market.

Note: Quantitative date appearing in this chapter regarding municipal bond issuance volume, revenue bond issuance volume, and negotiated and competitive bond issuance volume were taken from *The Bond Buyer/Thomson Financial 2006 Yearbook* (New York, SourceMedia, Inc., 2006), and from prior annual editions of the *Yearbook* dating back to 1984. All data regarding the market shares and volumes for regional firms and national market firms were computed by the author from data appearing in the *Yearbook*, and the author takes sole responsibility for the computed data.

Role of Investment Banking In State and Local Capital Finance

Municipal bond issues may be sold either by competitive bidding, or by negotiation. In the former case, the issuer publishes a *notice of sale,* which establishes a time and place for submission of bids. Competing dealers submit bids at the appointed hour, and the bond issue is awarded to the bidder specifying the lowest cost to the issuer. In the latter case, the issuer engages a specific broker-dealer (or at times, a group of such firms) to act as investment banker for the transaction. The firm so engaged may be expected to perform a variety of services, including:

1. Assisting in the development of an appropriate credit structure for the bond issue.
2. Assisting in the development of the documentation embodying that structure.
3. Performing the quantitative analysis necessary to support and justify the structure.
4. Creating the maturity structure, preredemption or "call" features, and other technical aspects of the bonds.
5. Participating in presentations to the rating agencies.
6. Developing a comprehensive marketing plan for the bonds, and executing that plan.
7. Developing and justifying the final pricing for the issue.
8. Underwriting the issue, including any balances that remain unsold at the end of the marketing process.
9. Assisting in all of the technical aspects of closing the sale.

Not all of the services will be required on every transaction, but the marketing, pricing, underwriting and closing activities will be at the core of every investment banking engagement.

Dealer firms may also act as financial advisor to issuers of both negotiated and competitively sold securities. A dealer firm acting as financial advisor will supply independent advice to the issuer on many key aspects of the transaction, including the credit and security aspects of the issue, and the detailed technical features of the bonds. However, as financial advisor, the broker-dealer will not participate in the pricing, underwriting, and distribution of negotiated bond issues. Regulations of the Municipal Securities Rulemaking Board (MSRB) specifically prohibit a broker dealer from simultaneously acting as the financial advisor and underwriter for a negotiated sale. The advisor may, however, bid on a client's issue that is competitively sold providing it obtains the permission of the issuer.

Dealer firms that are active in the public sector may be able to act as either financial advisor or investment banker, but they clearly focus the preponderance of their efforts on the latter field. Broker-dealers acted as investment banker on over $330 billion of new municipal securities issues in 2005, but provided financial advisory services on only approximately $80 billion. Independent financial advisors, that are not affiliated with any underwriting firm compete actively with broker-dealers for advisory work, and have a very significant market share. Dealer concentration on investment banking assignments, as opposed to financial advisory work, rests on the relative profitability of the two segments. Underwriting negotiated transactions generally offers higher profits than fee-based advisory engagements.

Growth of Negotiated Public Sector Financing

The importance of public sector investment banking in the securities industry can be measured by the sharp rise over the past thirty years in the volume of negotiated municipal finance. Municipal issuers sold a total of $29.3 billion bonds in 1975, and only 40% of that total was negotiated. The total volume of municipal new issues rose to $408 billion in 2005, and slightly less than 81% of that amount was sold by negotiated, rather than competitive, means. Exhibit 2.1 shows the growth in negotiated finance over the past two decades.

Municipal industry professionals work today in a market that is essentially dominated be negotiated issuance, and the profitability of their munic-

EXHIBIT 2.1 Long-Term Volume by Type of Bid, 1988–2006

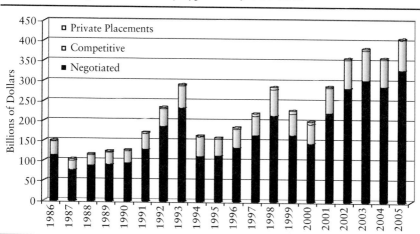

Source: Thomson Financial.

ipal operations pivots on their ability to obtain and sustain a viable share of that business. This is true for both national market and regional firms. The competitive method of bond issuance continues to be important in certain regional markets such as New England and the Middle Atlantic states, and it is also employed by a number of major State issuers of general obligation bonds. The real growth in volume and profitability has, however, been concentrated in the negotiated sector. Competition amongst broker-dealers for negotiated business is intense, particularly in periods when the overall growth rate for municipal securities issuance is constrained. Municipal issuers contemplating a negotiated sale frequently employ a formal *request for proposals* for investment banking services, and encourage the development of alternative ideas and approaches as part of that process.

Factors Driving Negotiated Volume

Negotiated volume has expanded rapidly for several reasons. First, municipal bond issuance has become more complex from a credit perspective, largely because of the increasing importance of revenue bond structures. Revenue bonds represented less than half of total issuance in 1975, but had grown to 65% of 2005's much larger total. Revenue bonds can be more difficult to structure and to market than general obligation securities, and negotiation permits the underwriter to devote more time and skill to the structuring, and eases the marketing process because the underwriter can search more thoroughly for appropriate buyers. These two factors may contribute to lowering borrowing costs. Second, periods of market volatility may also encourage negotiated sales of all kinds, since the underwriter and the issuer have more opportunity to optimize the timing of the sale, and so minimize borrowing costs. Third, the development of certain synthetic and derivative products has encouraged negotiation. Variable Rate Demand Bonds (VRDBs), Auction Rate Securities (ARS) and transactions based on interest rate swaps and other derivatives are frequently best done through negotiation because of their intrinsic complexity. Finally, many refunding transactions can be most efficiently accomplished via a negotiated sale, both because of their complexity and because of the need to carefully time these interest-rate sensitive transactions. Other factors have also contributed to the rising volume of negotiated sales, but the four outlined above account for much of the increase.

Role of National-Market Firms

Large national-market firms enjoy an exceptionally strong position in the market for public sector investment banking services. One method for defining national-market firms is to identify primary reporting government dealers that are also active in the primary market for municipal bonds. This definition currently encompasses nine firms. The best measure of their influence is to compute the volume of new negotiated issues on which these firms act as lead or *book-running* manager. These nine firms lead managed $218.2 billion of the $330.3 billion of negotiated issues sold in 2005. Their dominance is founded on a number of characteristics. First, the capital resources of each of these firms permit them to underwrite the largest municipal issues with no significant stress. Second, they have developed large and highly skilled staff capable of offering comprehensive services in all sectors of the market. Typically, these firms operate in almost all sectors, including among them health care, higher education, utility finance, and asset backed finance, and have developed a strong track record in all these areas. Third, these firms offer an array of services that goes well beyond traditional municipal finance. Within their organizations, they can call on resources in interest rate swaps and other derivatives and investment products that may prove to be very helpful to municipal issuers. Finally, they have developed marketing approaches that capitalize on all their varied resources and abilities.

REGIONAL BROKER-DEALER FIRMS

Regional firms active in municipal investment bank display wide range of characteristics. Their banking skills, staff, distribution capabilities, capital resources and sponsorship are quite varied. A significant number of participants in this market are owned by commercial banks. A number of these commercial bank owners have national stature or are international operations, but most are regional institutions. The majority of regional firms, however, are independent broker-dealers.

Regional dealers usually distribute the bonds they originate through their public finance operations to both institutional investors and retail sector buyers. Institutional coverage is national in scope for the larger regionals, but covers a more limited range for smaller firms. Retail distribution patterns are also varied. Some smaller firms and firms with a highly specialized public finance focus concentrate entirely on institutional buyers and forego retail distribution. The largest regionals have an extensive network of marketing branches, with a large numbers of sales representatives, and their coverage may be national in scope. Medium and smaller firms, however, tend to focus their retail sales efforts on a well defined regional area. Investmenbanking for state and local governments and authorities is regarded by most regional firms as an essential element of their business. Most regional firms, whether bank-owned or independent, use public finance as a means of originating financial products that can be profitably distributed through their retail and institutional marketing system. They act as well-integrated intermediaries between bond issuers, on the one hand, and final investors on the other. In this capacity, they originate municipal securities, structure and underwrite them, and then market the resulting products to final investors. There are some smaller firms that function primarily as originators; these entities rely on relationships with other regional dealers to distribute their products. However, firms employing this business model are a relatively small part of the industry.

Number of Regional Participants

National-market firms were defined above as institutions that function as primary reporting government dealers who are also active in the primary or new issue market for municipal securities. By exclusion, all other firms not falling into this category constitute the body of regional firms. The Bond Market Association (BMA), the trade group for dealers in all major categories of debt instruments, lists 75 members who are classed as regional dealers under this definition. Of these, some 47 are active in the municipal new-issue market. This number, however, somewhat understates the total, since it excludes firms that are not members of the BMA. Over 90 firms generate at least some new issue underwritings in the municipal market, but the top 41 handle most of the underwitings not controlled by national market firms. Regional dealers, as here defined, senior managed a total of $112 billion of new negotiated issues in 2005, but the top 41 firms captured slightly over 85% of the available amount.

Capitalization of Regional Firms

The capital resources of regional firms cover a very wide range. The largest firms in this category will have equity capital approaching $3 billion, while the smallest firms will have total resources that fall into $1 million to $5 million category. It is important to note that these gross measures of capital resources do not define the effective amount of capital allocated to a regional firm's public finance operation. A very large firm may have extraordinary amounts of capital on a firmwide basis. However, the amount allocated internally to the municipal securities business may be only a fraction of that total, and the amount allocated to a specific geographic area within the municipal market may be smaller still. A regional firm with $25 million in capital that is focused entirely on the municipal market in a limited geographic area of four to six states may well mobilize more "effective" capital to support its underwriting efforts than a much larger firm. The regional dealer may well have capital resources that are more relevant to the needs of its clients than does a much larger firm. Nonetheless, this relevance is only a tactical advantage in pursuing certain types of business. Regionals still tend to be capital-constrained in a strategic sense, in that they may lack the resources needed to develop a broad public finance capability spanning a large number of different product specialties.

Geographic Distribution

Regional dealer firms are headquartered in roughly half of the states. The largest concentrations are in the Middle Atlantic region, from Maryland north to New York, with over 25 firms. Other large concentrations are found in Texas, Missouri, Minnesota, Florida, and southern New England. A large proportion of regional firms have a public finance footprint that extends over many states and regions. It is not unusual for even smaller firms to have multiple origination offices in several states. A number of firms maintain a presence in disparate markets, such as the Midwest, the West Coast, and the Northeast. One large regional, for example, supports no less than fifteen regional offices located in all parts of the continental United States. Dealers that are positioned in this way treat each of these markets as a distinct region, and tend to target their services at a carefully defined population of issuers in each region.

Share of the Negotiated Market

Regional dealer firms have not been able to substantially increase their share of the negotiated bond market in recent years. Regional's share of the market stood at 37% in 2001, declined to a little less than 33% in 2002, and has fluctuated in a narrow band around 33% since then. The dollar volume of securities underwritten by regionals has risen over the last five years as the overall municipal market has grown. In 2001, regionals underwrote $81.7 billion. The total regional volume in 2005 was $112 billion, a sharp increase. However, this represented only 33.9% of the total market. The regional dealer community, absent an increase in market share, is vulnerable to the financial effects of a slow rate of growth in volume, or to an absolute decline.

STRATEGIC ADVANTAGES FOR THE REGIONAL FIRM

Regional underwriters have many advantages in building their business in their local niche. They know the local market for public finance investment banking products, and many can be very effective in marketing bonds to retail investors in their region. They also have access to governmental decision makers, a cost structure that is lower than that for national market firms, and the flexibility that goes with small size.

Knowledge of the Local Market

Regional firms frequently have more detailed knowledge about the local public finance markets in which they operate than do large national-market firms. They benefit from fairly intense interaction with local and state government officials and representatives of not-for-profit organization that sell tax-exempt bonds through conduit issuers. Regional firms monitor all local information sources carefully, and cultivate contacts with influential members of their communities. This interaction may provide early knowledge of developing projects that will require bond financing, and may also create opportunities to generate ideas that help shape and define the those projects. This is particularly true for small- to medium-sized projects that attract strong interest from the regionals, but less from the national-market firms. In any event, the better information flow received by regional public finance operations translates into a real competitive edge, and creates opportunities for business development.

Access to Local Decision Makers

Regional dealers may have frequent business, community service, and social interaction with the political and administrative decision makers for local governments and authorities. They are also usually a visible and significant force in the local economy, and have a well established identity. Local officials may well have a positive image of a regional firm with a significant presence, and they may develop real confidence in that firm and its representatives based on past service to community financing needs. That confidence, in conjunction with solid local contacts may translate into a moderate business advantage for the regional. The regional dealer will be able to exploit that advantage if it offers first-rate service at competitive fees; without the ability to deliver quality products, it will mean little.

Ability to Distribute Product Locally

The ability to market locally originated bonds to investors in the immediate area is a key competitive advantage for many regional dealers. Issuers generally respect a firm's ability to distribute their bonds to local accounts. The firm itself may also embrace local distribution as an effective means for maximizing profits.

Regional firms pursue varied approaches to marketing municipal securities. In general, there are four basic models:

1. Concentration on retail or household sector investors (including those buying through trust accounts and investment advisors) who are located in the geographic are of concentration for the firm.
2. Focus on institutional marketing, to national-level property and casualty insurance companies, managed mutual funds, major non-financial corporations, hedge funds, offshore banks, and similar institutions.
3. A balanced approach, combining a retail and institutional effort.
4. Foregoing an in-house marketing effort in favor of utilizing industry relationships with other firms to effect the sale of securities.

Firms using the approaches described in (1) and (3) have a clear advantage in local distribution. The emphasis on retail sales usually delivers financial benefits for the firm. The cost of maintaining a substantial retail sales force may be large, but in today's market the firm with this capability is able to obtain easier access to bonds, particularly those of an issuer employing a retail presale order period. Dealers capable of executing substantial retail business are frequently able to capture a larger portion of the profits on many underwritings.

The retail capabilities of regional firms may vary widely. The largest retail-oriented enterprises may have as many as 700 regional distribution offices, staffed by over 6,000 representatives. Smaller operations may make do with 10 to 25 retail sales representatives concentrated in one or two locations. However, a relatively substantial retail marketing strategy is a definite advantage to a public finance effort, no matter what the scale.

Cost Structure Supporting Profitable Small Transactions

Regional dealers may enjoy some cost advantages over national-market firms. The cost of local office space may be lower than in major financial centers, and lower living costs may facilitate marginally lower staff compensation. Regional public finance firms may also be able to size their staff in a more efficient way that national firms. The latter have to maintain large analytical and support establishments in order to accommodate wide fluctuations in their transactions volume. The regional firm may be able to operate with a leaner staff that is basically sized to handle average volume. Work surges can be handled with longer hours and a more intense work effort, and some of the technical work may be outsourced. Regional firms with a low cost structure can profitably handle a flow of smaller deals that might not be attractive to national-level operations.

DISADVANTAGES FACED BY THE REGIONAL FIRM

Disadvantages faced by regionals include a somewhat limited national distribution capability, especially to retail accounts, and constricted access to the staffing and capital needed to build a broadly based multiline public finance presence. These constraints impel regionals in the direction of smaller bond underwritings in certain well-defined product specialties. That, in turn, contributes to a stagnant share of the overall market for negotiated municipal issues.

Narrower Skill Base and Restricted Product Line

Regional firms have significantly smaller staff levels than national-market firms. They generally pursue public finance business in restricted range of product lines. Some firms have very narrowly defined business development efforts. For example, there are dealers that specialize entirely in areas such as health care finance, higher education, and housing. Other concentrate entirely on general and infrastructure finance for municipal and state governments.

The larger the firm, the more likely it is to pursue multiple product lines. However, even in the largest firms, four or five disciplines are likely to encompass the public finance effort. A larger firm, for example, might concentrate on general and infrastructure finance, and at the same time maintain specialties in higher education, housing, and education. Even the largest regionals will not approach the breadth of services offered by national-market firms; specialties such as resource-recovery financing, asset-backed securities, and specialized municipal derivative products departments are beyond the reach of most of these operations.

Decisions on product line concentration tend to be based on considerations of capital, staffing requirements, and the likely contribution of a given specialty to overall profitability. Capital considerations are always important. While a firm may have a sufficient concentration of capital to underwrite the larger issues in its geographic area of concentration, it must face the reality that the volume of business in certain specialty lines in that area is not enough to justify committing capital and personnel to those lines. Firms may also decide to opt out of certain lines of business because of difficulties in hiring the bankers and technicians needed to enter those specialties.

Regional investment banking is essentially a business of niches. Firms tend to focus on identifiable products that present significant product opportunities. The products might be selected because (1) volume in that specialty is high in the region the firm focuses on; (2) there is less competition in the specialty; and (3) available personnel have expertise in that area. Large firms may pursue several lines, though not as many as the national-market enterprises. Smaller players may have to make do with one.

Confined Scope for Distribution

Regional firms may have a significant advantage in distributing bonds to local retail investors. However, their overall distribution mechanism is weaker than that of the national-market firms. Some large regionals may have the branch structure and staffing required to market tax-exempt securities to retail accounts on a national basis, but the vast majority of firms in this classification confine their household sector sales to limited and well defined regions. This implies that they will turn in a relatively strong sales performance on small- and medium-sized financings ($5 million to $150 million), but will be only supporting players on large financings of up to $800 million.

National marketing to institutions can also be a problem for regional firms. The major national-market buyers receive intense coverage from the largest dealer firms, and get access to a major flow of new bonds through those same firms. Regionals, on the other hand, produce a more uneven supply of new issues for these buyers, and that supply tends to be concentrated in smaller bond sales. National-market firms also serve the needs of fund and insurance company buyers with a wide range of specialties, such as derivative products. Thus, regional firms may not be positioned to always extract the best possible terms from large institutional investors and indeed, may not be familiar with all of those buyers.

The net outcome of all these limitations is that regionals become biased towards smaller issues in their base areas, and in well defined product lines. They face many challenges in underwriting and distributing bond issues in the mid- to upper-end of the current size range.

IMPORTANCE OF A WELL-DEFINED PLAN

The success of a regional public finance effort rests on careful planning and disciplined execution. The business model chosen needs to achieve the most efficient matching of the firm's strengths to the characteristics of the local market in order to maximize profits and return on capital. Planning must be realistic, the goals must achievable, and the implementation process must move forward on a reasonable time scale. Overall, good management is the essential ingredient for success. A regional firm must have a well-thought-out vision of where it wants to position itself in the public finance industry, and it has to create and implement a practical, step-by-step process for reaching that goal. Management also has to recognize that public finance does not exist in a vacuum. A successful public finance effort needs solid support from the firm's underwriting, trading, and marketing arms. Meshing these other aspects of the firm with carefully constructed investment banking departments is the hallmark of outstanding regional firms.

Public Finance Product Line

Regional firms can opt to concentrate their public finance efforts on obtaining comanagerships, or they can focus on obtaining appointments as sole or senior manager on new issues. Comanagerships do not involve an extensive investment banking effort, since firms in this role are not expected to make many substantive contributions to the planning and structuring aspects of a transaction. However, profit margins are also low, since the firm's ability to directly market the securities to customers may be limited. Most regionals, as a practical matter, focus primarily on senior management appointments on new negotiated sales, but do devote some effort to obtaining comanagerships, particularly on larger transactions. The senior management role offers profit potential that is a significant multiple of the financial opportunities in comanagement appointments.

A firm focused primarily on the senior management role must decide where to concentrate its efforts. This requires:

1. A careful review of the pattern of bond issuance in the firm's geographic target area.
2. A review of the competitive situation in each major product line or type of issuance found in the area.
3. Estimating unit profit margins in each product sector.
4. A search for any unusual barriers to entry into specific market sectors.
5. The practicality and cost of acquiring the personnel and other assets needed to compete in each sector.

The analysis also has to take into account the existing business and assets of the firm. For example, a dealer with a very strong competitive bidding record in its home market, coupled with strong local retail distribution, has a real advantage in some specialties, such as general and infrastructure finance and utility bonds.

Regional dealers face varied challenges in their differing areas of geographic concentration. In New York, for example, where many local governments face credit quality problems and all have to deal with legal obstacles to revenue bond issuance, a dealer might elect to concentrate on refundings of all types. In order to mitigate the cyclical nature of the business, this same dealer might develop secondary lines such as financings for troubled credits, and conduit financings for independent schools, smaller colleges and universities, and other traditional and nontraditional not-for-profits. A New England dealer, on the other hand, might elect to place its main efforts squarely in the field of not-for-profit financing. Firms in rapidly growing areas of the South and Southwest might emphasize issues for infrastructure, utility, and education bonds. Some smaller firms have adopted themselves to highly specialized niches, such as tax increment financing, Qualified Zone Academy Bonds (QZABs), charter schools, and financing for Native American projects.

The product lines and specialties adopted will, in all cases, be the ones that offer the best return on capital to the firm over some reasonable period of time.

Target Audience

Once the firm has defined its preferred business lines, it needs to carefully research every potential user of its services, and identify those who make or influence the decisions on underwriter selection. Some elected officials and the staff of key governmental units will clearly be targets, as will board members and staff of any independent agencies or not-for-profits that have been targeted. Those who influence underwriter selection may include other professionals, such as accountants, law firms, and independent financial advisors The firm needs to strive to understand the decision-making process for each and every key issuer. It needs to know how those decisions are made, who makes them, and who influences them.

Marketing Plan

Public finance marketing plans are, in the best sense, a well-coordinated effort to establish the credibility of the firm as a provider of quality investment banking services. The regional banker has a specific message to deliver to the key decision makers for his chosen lines of business, the message that his or her firm can deliver effective financing concepts and bring them down to reality on a reasonable time frame. The regional firm needs to inspire trust in its professionalism, and confidence in its ability to bring in a bond issue at the lowest possible cost to the tax payers or fee payers. The popular press sometimes portrays public finance as a business dependent on political favoritism. No realist would deny that politics has been and will continue to be an influence on the public finance business. However, the most successful firms in the business cultivate real and substantive skills, and offer services of the highest quality. They also pursue the development of their business with careful attention to the ethical constraints that govern the interface between the public and private sectors.

Marketing plans can include an aggressive schedule of calls on all targeted potential clients. They can also call for indirect efforts, such as active support for and involvement with organizations such as the Government Finance Officers Association, the National League of Cities, and many others. Advertising rarely plays a significant role in public finance marketing, since it is not likely to be effective with the relatively small and sophisticated target audience. The heart of any successful plan is really the effort to develop new ideas that help the issuer accomplish its stated goals, and the ongoing campaign to articulate those ideas to the targeted decision makers.

Staffing Requirements

Staffing public finance departments is one of the most challenging tasks facing management of the regional firm. Skilled and dedicated professionals are the key to success, yet recruitment can be very difficult. Factors impeding hiring may include:

1. Reluctance of some individuals to working outside of major financial centers.
2. Concern about the volatility of future compensation, based on a perception that the narrower market faced by regional firms will lead to greater earnings variability.
3. A general perception that regional firms will have difficulty paying top compensation in good years.
4. A view on the part of some highly specialized bankers that regional firms will have difficulty generating a consistent and high level of activity in their sector.

Regionals have to work to hard to overcome these perceptions and to build around them. Firms with longstanding public finance operations normally recruit at least a portion of their staff locally and then train and develop these individuals until they can fill the senior banker role. Regional dealers may also offer creative—and generous—compensation packages that assure job security and high levels of average compensation over a number of years. Regional dealers have also been successful at hiring public sector and not-for-profit officials and guiding them through the potentially difficult transition to a successful investment banking career. .

Regional firms have a special need to emphasize and develop the technical skills of their staff. A national-market firm may be able to sustain its reputation despite occasional internal errors and problems. Regionals, with their lower transactions volume, are effectively held to a higher standard— one significant problem can seriously damage both the firm's reputation and its business development prospects. Successful regional firms have very high standards for the technical skills and performance of their professional staff, because their reputation and success depend on it.

Underwriting, Marketing and Sales Support

Many regional firms need to develop and enhance their skills in underwriting and sales and marketing to achieve real success in public finance. Credibility in public finance depends to a considerable extent on the firm's ability to price bonds at aggressive but realistic levels, and then market them effectively to final investors. The firm also needs to demonstrate an ability to underwrite unsold balances when that is appropriate. Unaggressive pricing, weak sales, and ineffective marketing will quickly undermine even the best-staffed public finance department. Regional firms achieve real success when they effectively integrate all their activities into their public finance effort, and seek to maintain uniformly high standards across all of their activities.

A successful underwriting effort in the market for competitively sold bond issues can also help to develop public finance business. A strong track record in buying competitively sold issues raises the firm's profile amongst government officials, demonstrates its willingness to take risk and underwrite bonds, and underscores the dealer's sales and distribution capabilities.

Administrative Support

Administrative support, particularly in the areas of compliance, accounting, and clearance, is an important element in the success of the regional firm. Compliance can be an especially critical factor. Failure to meet all of the mandates imposed by the regulations of the Securities and Exchange Commission, the National Association of Securities Dealers, the Municipal Securities Rulemaking Board, and the various state regulatory agencies can lead to substantial penalties, and those penalties will create reputational risk for the firm. Slipshod clearance and accounting can also create regulatory and public relations risks that can impact public finance. Strong administrative support is the mark of every successful regional firm.

RECENT CHALLENGES

The municipal securities market has undergone many changes over the past decade. Many new products, such as interest rate swaps, have assumed importance. Older products such as variable rate financing have assumed new forms, such as auction rate securities. The regulatory environment has also grown more intense and demanding. All these developments have represented significant new challenges for regional firms.

New Products

Interest rate swaps have become a very important product in the municipal market over the past decade. Swaps (and related options) have been used to create synthetic fixed rate and floating rate securities, to lock in favorable interest rates in a volatile market, and for synthetic-based refundings. Interest rate swaps have been utilized by the largest and most sophisticated issuers, and they have also been employed by a great many medium and small governmental units. They thus impinge directly on the business of regional public finance firms. The swap business, as it exists today, is dominated by large financial institutions. Large national and international commercial banks and the national market dealer firms offer swaps as a proprietary product and act as the counterparty on the vast majority of swap transactions involving municipal issuers. These swap dealers benefit from a large capital base, from their pool of highly skilled transactors and analysts, and from their investment-grade credit ratings. Most regional firms have few or none of these advantages, and have thus not been able to participate fully in this developing market. Regionals have typically participated in the swap market in more restricted ways. They have acted as swap advisors, charging a fee to the issuer for reviewing all documentation, arranging the terms of the swap, and locating a suitable counterparty. They have also played, at times, a more restricted role, blocking out the general terms of the transaction (for a fee or as part compensation for the overall engagement) and then bringing an independent swap advisor to arrange the detailed terms. Finally, regionals have formed ad hoc partnerships with national broker-dealers, with the latter acting as sole-source swap providers and the regional handling the issuer contact aspects of the transaction. These forms of involvement can be profitable, but to a much lesser extent than acting as a principal and counterparty. Regional firms will need to continue to probe for a more meaningful involvement in swap and similar derivative transactions. That involvement may be important both to insure that the public finance client gets the best possible terms and to convey reasonable compensation to the regional dealer.

Variable rate finance remains a very important product line for municipal dealers. Total sales of this type of bond were over $95 billion in 2005, including $62 billion of variable rate demand bonds and $33 billion of auction rate securities. Regional dealers have captured a significant share of the more traditional variable rate demand bond business, acting as senior manager on about one-third of the 2005 volume. However, they have only a very small share of the auction rate market, which is dominated by the large national-market firms.

Regional dealers need to devote considerable energy and thought to the problems created for them by the emergence of new products. In general, these new products demand scale and thus require large capital resources. They also demand relatively high and stable credit standing. These are resources that can be in short supply at many regional operations.

The Regulatory Environment

The regulatory environment has certainly become more complex and demanding over the past decade. In general, this complexity has emerged from a drive by regulators to achieve greater "transparency" in the market. *Transparency* means, on the marketing and sales side, a much better flow of information on trade volume and pricing. On the origination or public finance side it implies improved information flow from the issuer through the dealer regarding all material credit and other considerations impacting an issue. These requirements have laid additional burdens on public sector investment bankers, and those burdens can lay more heavily on smaller firms than on larger ones.

Restrictions on political contribution to officials of issuers, imposed both by Rule G-37 of the Municipal Securities Rulemaking Board and by certain states, have also had an impact. The regulatory environment today requires a regional firm to have both a technically proficient regulatory compliance program and a broad set of ethical guidelines and standards for its staff. The latter has to be woven into the culture of the dealer firm, and actively promoted and monitored by senior management.

THE OUTCOME OF REGIONAL BANKING EFFORTS

Regional dealer firms that are active in the public finance market provide a valuable service. They senior manage almost one-third of the total annual bond volume, and also provide advisory services to a wide array of local governments. Local governments, agencies and authorities, particularly smaller issuers, and not-for profit entities selling bonds though public-sector conduits benefit from these efforts. For many of these issuers the regional dealer community makes the difference between limited or no market access, on the one hand, and financings that move quickly and efficiently into the hands of investors. Regional dealers work in a difficult and demanding competitive environment in which success depends on good management and planning, and near flawless execution. Regional dealers have successfully surmounted these challenges in the past, and will undoubtedly continue to effectively serve their communities in the future.

CHAPTER 3

Role of the Financial Advisor

William H. Wood
Senior Technical Analyst
Frasca & Associates LLC

This chapter provides a description of the role of the financial advisor in both a competitive and negotiated transaction environment. It provides a comprehensive discussion of the tasks performed by a financial advisor for a municipal governmental entity and provides information designed to assist a typical governmental debt issuer in selecting the best possible financial advisor for its needs.

OVERVIEW OF FINANCIAL ADVISORS AND THEIR ROLES

Many issuers of municipal debt employ one or more financial advisors to assist them with their bond sales, the reinvestment of bond proceeds, and the structuring and pricing of related financial products such as interest rate swaps. A financial advisor may be a local or national firm and may have anywhere from one to several hundred employees. In all cases, however, the financial advisor is there to assist the governmental debt issuer in the successful structuring and/or sale of a bond issue or other financial product and to offer general financial advice and assistance, as requested, on budgeting, financial planning, and Treasury-related issues. Financial advisors principally help guide issuers through the complex process of debt issuance. In some cases, the financial advisor may be an investment bank that also underwrites municipal bond deals; more often the financial advisor is an independent firm that does not actually engage in the direct underwriting of debt or the sale of financial products such as swaps.

The actual role and involvement of the financial advisor is likely to vary significantly based upon whether the advisor is working on a negotiated transaction or managing a competitive bidding process. The scope of this assistance ranges from providing a valuable second opinion on elements of a negotiated securities dealer's pricing to actively working with bond counsel, the issuer and other parties to produce the documents and develop the structure necessary to offer a bond issue or other product to the market at competitive sale.

FINANCIAL ADVISORS IN NEGOTIATED TRANSACTIONS

During the past quarter century, the municipal market has become increasingly dominated by the negotiated sale method. In a negotiated transaction, the underwriter or interest rate swap provider is selected before the pricing of the bond or swap occurs. A negotiated underwriter or swap provider in many, but not all cases, has an ongoing relationship with the municipal issuer.

Financial advisors play several important roles in negotiated transactions. First, and perhaps foremost, the financial advisor will work closely with the issuer to select the team of bankers and/or swap providers who are deemed best qualified to provide the services necessary for the issuer to execute their transaction(s). Typically this is accomplished through a multistep process that begins with a *request for proposal* (RFP) being distributed to prospective underwriters and/or swap providers. The candidate firms will answer the RFP in writing. Next, in many but not all cases, those firms whose written responses are deemed most responsive are invited to make an oral presentation to the client. At the end of this process, the issuer and its financial advisor (sometimes with the assistance of other parties, like bond counsel) will determine which firm or firms will be selected. Most public debt issuers are anxious to insure that well-qualified parties are engaged and that the selection process itself is viewed as objective and unbiased. For this latter reason in particular, even experienced and regular debt issuers usually rely on a qualified financial advisor to assist them in this important selection process.

Once the investment banker or swap provider has been retained, the financial advisor in a negotiated transaction will monitor and review what the investment banker proposes regarding all aspects of the transaction: structure, marketing, pricing, and so on. Under this approach, the issuer gets the dedicated resources of an experienced investment banking firm to structure and market their financing, as well as comprehensive oversight from the financial advisor who insures not only that the pricing is fair, but that important ideas and concepts are not overlooked. This process is most effective when both the investment bank and financial advisor are well qualified and actively involved in the transaction. A less experienced advisor may be hesitant to mount a serious challenge to a banker or swap provider;

in these instances, the advisor's role may be reduced, in large part, to simply rubber stamping a recommendation.

FINANCIAL ADVISORS IN COMPETITIVE TRANSACTIONS

Even with steady growth in the use of the negotiated sale, certain issuers issue all or a substantial portion of their debt via competitive sale. Frequent and regular issuers with good quality ratings, such as certain state general obligation credits (e.g., Florida and California). On the other end of the spectrum, small school districts, borrowing small amounts of money (e.g., $1 million or less), typically choose the competitive sale approach. Some issuers, bound by long-standing policy or legal considerations, must competitively bid their offerings. Others prefer this approach because they believe it secures the lowest cost of debt. In this context, the investment bank or securities dealer will play no role prior to the pricing of the bonds. All of the documents and all structural considerations must be determined independently ahead of time. In these transactions, it is typical for the financial advisor, with assistance from bond counsel, to perform most of the functions otherwise performed by the investment banker in a negotiated bond transaction.

These functions include analyzing alternative financial structures, structuring the debt, determining whether and when to use bond insurance (including identifying available bond insurers), managing presentations to the rating agencies to secure bond ratings, assisting in the preparation of the offering and bidding documents, and assisting with the reinvestment of bond proceeds.

Proponents of competitive bond and swap transactions argue that the process of competitive bidding insures that the issuer gets the best possible price. Critics point out that absent the assurance of having the bonds to sell, no securities dealer will make an investment of time and resources comparable to the negotiated banker and, as such, the *best competitive bid* will not always be as good as the best negotiated price. Moreover, it is typically more difficult for a financial advisor on a competitive transaction to accelerate or delay the advertised time and date of a bond or swap bid to avoid adverse changes in the market that would warrant a last minute change (e.g., a heavy calendar of competing issues scheduled to sell on the same day).

SECURITIES DEALERS AS FINANCIAL ADVISORS

Broadly speaking, there are basically two kinds of financial advisors: those that are themselves securities dealers (or subsidiaries thereof) and those that are independent, unaffiliated companies. In the first type, it is common for the financial advisory personnel of a registered securities dealer to be the same as the investment banking personnel who pursue negotiated underwriting and swap business. Dealer-based financial advisors typically have immediate access to advanced market pricing information that independent financial advisors, who lack an underwriting or derivatives desk, will have to get from third parties or from an information service such as Bloomberg.

Proponents of using independent financial advisors will often assert that when a securities dealer serves as a financial advisor there is greater potential for conflicts of interest, even when the firm in question has agreed not to provide any fee-based services other than their advisory service.

INDEPENDENT FINANCIAL ADVISORS

The independent financial advisor does not typically offer any banking services (although in some cases they may provide fee-based services for items such as cash management, bond proceeds investing and arbitrage rebate calculation). Proponents of independent financial advisors argue that they typically are able to provide unbiased objective financial advice to issuers without any regard for possible future profit or gain. As noted above, proponents of securities dealers as financial advisors say that there is no substitute for having direct access to an active committing and trading desk in providing market intelligence. Advocates of independent financial advisors will counter that the independent advisor has access to pricing information from a large number of dealers or swap providers and is therefore better able to objectively evaluate pricing terms.

PRICING OF FINANCIAL ADVISORY SERVICES

While investment bankers almost always assess their fees on a contingency basis (i.e., no deal, no fee), financial advisors usually structure their fees according to one of two different rules. The first, which is similar to the standard investment banking fee, is transaction based. The second is simply to charge by the hour (and/or the day, month or year). In this second case, the actual advisory fee is based upon the scope of work performed without regard to how much debt is sold or how many swaps are executed. Proponents of this latter pricing approach will point out that a financial advisor may be more willing to give objective advice, especially if that advice is a recommendation against proceeding with a proposed transaction, if their compensation is not predicated on the issuance of debt.

Regardless of how the financial advisor is paid, unless specifically hired for one transaction, it is very common for the advisor to provide ongoing assistance throughout the year not only on transactional events (such as bond pricings), but also on more general debt and cash management issues.

DETAILS REGARDING THE FINANCIAL ADVISOR'S FUNCTIONS

Typical advisory services provided in connection with a bond issuance include:

- Evaluation of an issuer's outstanding debt and borrowing needs.
- Preparation of an RFP to solicit underwriter suggestions and ideas.
- Evaluation of proposals, whether unsolicited or prepared in response to an RFP.
- Advice on rating agency interactions, or assistance with the development and maintenance of issuer relationships with major rating agencies.
- Development and maintenance of issuer relationships with major bond insurers.
- Scheduling of investor meetings and information calls prior to bond pricing.
- Development of formal offering memorandum (official statement).
- Review and modifications to key legal documents (e.g., supplemental bond indenture).
- Independent mathematical analysis of financing alternatives under consideration.
- Development of bidding documents and procedures (competitive).
- Allocation of bonds.
- Review of all aspects of bond pricing (negotiated).

While bond counsel, the issuer, a negotiating underwriter, and certain other consultants are involved to varying degrees in many of the functions listed above, a financial advisor is likely to play an active and significant role in each of these functions.

In a negotiated transaction, the financial advisor's primary role is to cross-check and monitor the performance of the underwriting team. This includes working on the basic structure of the issue, and then negotiating the underwriting spread, or compensation, the interest rates, yields, and amortization schedule of the bonds. At the time of pricing, the financial advisor, independently monitoring the market and the disposition of other comparable issues in the marketplace, will advise the issuer when and if yields and/or coupons should be repriced. Finally, the advisor will also review the allocation of bonds among the underwriting syndicate to ensure that each firm is appropriately rewarded for its performance.

TYPICAL ADVISORY SERVICES PROVIDED IN CONNECTION WITH AN INTEREST RATE SWAP

Interest rate swaps and related derivative products, while often simple to understand in theory, can be difficult to properly evaluate, especially when they contain more complex features such as embedded options. As with bonds, the majority of swaps are priced through a negotiated rather than a competitive process. While a competitive market is available for the more standardized and more liquid derivative products (e.g., conventional LIBOR-based interest rate swaps), the majority of all derivative products bought by municipal issuers are purchased through negotiation.

In addition to securities dealers who make their own markets in derivative-based products, several independent financial advisors have developed the strong analytical expertise required to evaluate the increasingly broad range of derivative products available to issuers, including:

- Conventional fixed receiver swaps and fixed payer swaps using either BMA or a percentage of LIBOR.
- Forward delivery swaps using either BMA or a percentage of LIBOR.
- LIBOR to BMA (or vice versa) basis trades.
- Interest rate caps, floors and collars (either sold or purchased).
- Fixed payer issuer swaption for synthetic advance refunding.
- Fixed payer dealer swaption for enhanced swap yield.
- MMD rate locks.
- Investment contracts with flexible break provisions.

First, the financial advisor is responsible for evaluating whether the risks and/or benefits associated with a particular derivative product are appropriate for a given issuer based on a comprehensive analysis of the impact such product is likely to have under different market scenarios. This requires a thorough understanding not only of how the product works, but how including such a product will affect an issuer's overall debt profile and repayment obligations. Once a derivative product has been deemed appropriate, the advisor needs to be able to tell the issuer when market conditions are such that the issuer should move forward to lock in the pricing. The financial advisor then needs to determine whether to price the product through a competitive or negotiated process. In the case of a negotiated pricing, the financial advisor must be able to evaluate and ascertain the fairness of the price received for a derivative product, even when its structural details render it illiquid or unlike any other comparable transaction.

In certain cases, the structuring of certain interest rate swaps correspond with the issuance of bond issues (this is especially likely when fixed payer swaps or swaptions are used to create synthetic fixed rate debt when sold with a new variable rate issuance). If a swap advisor is separately engaged, it needs to work closely with the financial advisor in order to insure a seamless coordination of the debt issuance and derivative pricing.

HOW TO HIRE A FINANCIAL ADVISOR

Most of the nation's financial advisors are listed in the *Bond Buyer's Municipal Marketplace* or "Red Book." Every year, Thomson Financial ranks the nation's financial advisors (as they do underwriters and bond counsel firms) based on deal volume and on par amount. Volume is not always the best indicator of a firm's quality. An issuer needs to assess a variety of factors including, of course, experience, but also specialized knowledge, qualifications as well as the availability of senior professionals who understand the issuer's needs.

In evaluating a prospective financial advisor, a municipal issuer would typically ask for detailed information on the following subjects:

- Description of the firm, history and structure.
- Key employees to be assigned to your account.
- The firm's transaction/client experience over the past few years.
- Summary of the details of specific transactions completed (e.g., all swaps in past three years).
- If you are contemplating a particular transaction or want to elicit specific information regarding the firm's knowledge of your operations, a request for one or more specific proposals regarding your ongoing financial/debt management.
- Fee proposal (you may specify how you want the fee quoted; local laws may also apply).
- Disclosure of any possible conflict of interest.

In addition, you must be sure to ask those questions that are required under local or state law (for example, whether or not a prospective advisor is in compliance with relevant EEOC requirements).

Increasingly, issuers are using the Internet to post their RFPs for financial services, including RFPs for financial advisors. Additionally, the RFP is usually advertised in the *Bond Buyer*.

SUMMARY

Hiring a financial advisor is one of the first steps an issuer must take when confronted with the need to issue debt. Hiring the right advisor can provide many benefits to an issuer, not the least of which is having an experienced guide who can help them to successfully navigate the many complexities of the capital markets.

CHAPTER 4

Method of Sale in the Municipal Bond Market

Jun Peng, Ph.D.
Associate Professor
School of Public Administration and Policy
Eller College of Management
University of Arizona

Kenneth A. Kriz, Ph.D.
Associate Professor at School of Public Administration
University of Nebraska at Omaha

Tracy Neish
Doctoral Student
School of Public Administration and Policy
Eller College of Management
University of Arizona

Governments have to go through many steps to issue municipal bonds. The first step usually involves soliciting the advice of an independent financial advisor in structuring a potential issue. This involves setting the size of the issue and setting a general sketch of what the final bond issue will look like. Then the government must seek approval for the bond issue. Approval generally comes from one of two sources, the government's legislative body (city council, county board, state legislature) or the people as a whole through the referendum process. Once the government bond has been approved by voters or the legislative body, the government issuer will then start the issuance process. There are many key decisions that must be made during this phase of the issuance process. One of the most important is the method of selling the bond. The decision's importance stems from the fact that the method of sale will determine the responsibilities of most of the other key actors in the process.

In this chapter, we first discuss the chief differences between the two main methods of sale in the municipal bond market, competitive bidding and negotiated. We then discuss how these differences may affect issuer's decision over which method to choose.

METHOD OF SALE

There are three methods of selling municipal bonds: competitive bidding, negotiated sale and private placement. In a competitive bidding, the issuer solicits bids from underwriters. The underwriter (or the underwriting syndicate) that pays the highest price (providing the lowest interest rate) for the bond issue earns the right to sell the bonds to investors. A syndicate is a group of two or more underwriters who agree to bid or underwriter an issue. It is usually led by a senior underwriter. In a negotiated sale, an underwriter is hired by the issuer to sell the bonds to investors. In a private placement, the municipal bond is not sold to the public but is purchased directly by a preselected group of investors. Since private placement is used for relatively small-size bond issues and accounts for a very small percentage of the total sale volume (for example, less than half a percent of all issues in terms of volume were sold through private placement in 2005), the decision regarding method of sale is primarily between competitive bidding and negotiated sale.

Competitive Bidding

There are two main activities in the process of issuing a new bond, origination, and underwriting. Origination refers to all the work involved in preparing the bond to be sold and underwriting refers to selling the bond. In a competitive bidding, a financial advisor hired by the government issuer is responsible for origination and an underwriter who wins the bid is responsible for selling the bond. Governmental issuers are not always free to decide which method of sale to employ, however. A survey by Peng and Brucato[1] found that nine states have laws in place that specifically require *general obligation* (GO) bonds be sold by competitive bidding at the state level.[2] In six of

---

[1] Jun Peng and Peter Brucato Jr., "Do Competitive-Only Laws Have an Impact on the Borrowing Cost of Municipal Bonds?" *Municipal Finance Journal* 22 (2001), pp. 61–76.
[2] These nine states are: Delaware, Kentucky, Louisiana, Maryland, Minnesota, Missouri, Pennsylvania, South Carolina, and Tennessee.

those nine states, this competitive bidding only law also applies to GO debt issued at the local level.[3] No states have such a law for revenue bonds.

Once competitive bidding is chosen, whether through choice or by the law, a financial advisor is used to start the origination process. The major responsibilities of the financial advisor in the origination stage include:

1. Sizing and structuring the bond issue.
2. Preparing documents, such as the official statement and notice of sale, necessary for the bond sale, with help from the issuer's bond counsel.
3. Obtaining credit ratings from the various rating agencies.
4. Conducting cost benefit analysis on whether to purchase bond insurance.
5. Advising on the timing of the sale.
6. Soliciting and evaluating bids from underwriters.

In order to solicit bids from underwriters, the notice of sale is posted two to three weeks prior to the date of sale in nationally circulated newspapers and trade journals such as the *Bond Buyer*. Underwriters or underwriter syndicates who are interested in the bond issue will then do some preliminary analysis of the issue and engage in some presale effort to gauge investors' interest in the issue and the interest rate needed to sell the entire issue. Such effort will continue until the deadline for submitting the bid to the issuer. All bids submitted before the deadline are evaluated based on interest rate and the bid with the highest price (lowest interest rate) wins the bidding competition.

As the vast majority of municipal bonds are serial bonds, an overall interest rate needs to be calculated for the entire bond issue. Two methods have been used to measure the overall interest rate, *net interest cost* (NIC) and *true interest cost* (TIC). The formula for calculating TIC is

$$B = \sum_{n=s}^{m} \left\{ \sum_{j=1}^{2n} \frac{C_n P_n / 2}{\left(1 + \dfrac{TIC}{2}\right)^j} \right\} + \sum_{n=s}^{m} \frac{P_n}{\left(1 + \dfrac{TIC}{2}\right)^{2n}}$$

where

B = bond proceeds
C_n = coupon on bonds maturing in n periods
P_n = total par value of bonds maturing in n periods
N = number of years bond is outstanding
S = years to first maturity
M = years to final maturity
J = number of semi annual coupon periods

---

[3] They are Kentucky, Louisiana, Minnesota, Missouri, South Carolina and Tennessee.

The formula for calculating NIC is

$$NIC = \frac{\sum\limits_{n=s}^{m} nP_n C_n - \mathrm{Pr}}{\sum\limits_{n=s}^{m} nP_n}$$

where Pr is equal to the premium.[4]

The key difference between NIC and TIC is that TIC takes into account the time value of future debt service payment and thus accurately reflects the underlying interest rate born by the issuer.[5] TIC is the municipal bond's equivalent of *yield to maturity* (YTM) or *internal rate of return* (IRR). Despite the clear advantage of TIC over NIC and the prevalence of computing technology that makes TIC easy to calculate, NIC continues to be used by some issuers in evaluating bids.[6]

The compensation to the underwriter for the underwriting is in the form of *gross underwriter spread* (GUS). GUS is measured as the discount per bond (each bond has a value of $1,000). If a government issuer is to issue a $100 million bond and the GUS is $5 per bond, then the total compensation to the underwriter would be $500,000. It is a discount because this amount is deducted from the bond proceeds of $100 million, meaning the issuer will actually receive $99,500,000. In addition to GUS, the other major costs involved in the issuance process to the issuer are: the financial advisor fee, the bond counsel fee, credit-rating fees, document printing costs, and the bond insurance premium (if bond insurance is used). The GUS is by far the largest single issuance cost.

Negotiated Sale

In a negotiated sale, an underwriter is selected at the beginning of the issuance process to be responsible for both origination and underwriting. In this case, an underwriter is usually selected several months before the bond issue is expected to be sold. An underwriter can be selected in two ways. The first and easiest way is simply for the issuer to pick any underwriter it likes. The issuer may prefer a particular underwriter simply because it has pro-

---

[4] When the bond is priced above its face value, the difference is called the premium. This happens when the reoffering yield is below the state coupon rate.

[5] NIC, providing a quick and easy way of calculating the overall interest rate, was created in an era when the lack of computing technology makes calculating TIC very difficult and time consuming.

[6] Bill Simonsen, Mark Robbins, and Bernard Jump Jr., "State Rules about Using Net Interest Cost and True Interest Cost in Calculating Municipal Bond Interest Rates," *Municipal Finance Journal* 26 (2005), pp. 1–25.

vided similar service to the issuer before and thus is more familiar with the issuer's financial situation. In this case, the issuer does not have to justify to any outsider why a particular underwriter is chosen. The second way calls for the selection of an underwriter through a bidding process. This process starts with a *request for proposal* (RFP). The RFP discusses the project to be financed and specifies the information that the underwriter should include in its proposal to finance the project. Such information can include, among other things, the underwriter's previous experience with similar project financing, the experience of the major personnel involved, and the anticipated cost structure. Once the proposals are reviewed, a certain number of underwriters will be invited to make a presentation to the issuer and then one underwriter will be selected. The criteria for selecting an underwriter in a RFP process are more subjective that that in the competitive bidding process mentioned above. Since the interest rate is not known at the time of RFP, the selection of the underwriter will be based on a host of factors, such as experience, quality of proposal and financing cost. An RFP injects competition into the selection of underwriter in a negotiated sale to give the issuer some level of assurance regarding the quality and the cost of underwriter service. Over time, such competition in negotiated sale has significantly brought down the underwriter cost to the issuers. Exhibit 4.1 shows the negotiated

EXHIBIT 4.1   Underwriter Spread for Negotiated and Competitive Issues, 1988–2005

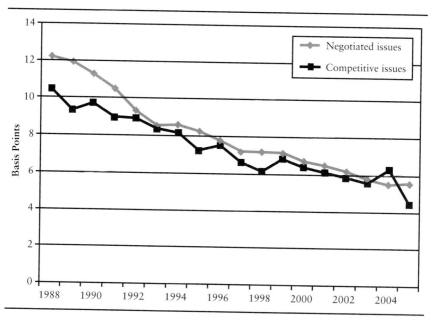

and competitive GUS over the last 20 years. It is easy to see that even if GUS has decreased for all issues over years, it has decreased by a much greater amount for negotiated issues, to the point that they are now comparable to that for competitive issues.[7]

Even in a negotiated sale, an issuer may still engage the service of a financial advisor. In this case, the financial advisor may help the issuer select an underwriter. If there is a RFP, the financial advisor may review the proposals and interview the underwriters. After the underwriter is selected, the financial advisor can also be retained by the issuer to monitor the underwriter's activities in terms of bond structuring and pricing. In this way, the financial advisor serves in a monitoring role for the issuer.

As the underwriter in the negotiated sale is responsible for origination, all origination activities done by the financial advisor in a competitive sale are now taken over by the underwriter. While conducting origination activities, the underwriter will also be involved in the presale marketing effort in terms of educating potential investors on the upcoming bond sale as well as gauging investor interest in the bond issue and the interest rate scale for the whole issue. These two efforts, origination and presale marketing, go hand in hand as the information on interest rate may have an impact on the size and structure of the bond issue. The presale marketing continues until the final date of sale. The underwriter has the opportunity to adjust the interest rate scale until the sale date depending on investor demand and interest rate environment with the goal of completing the sale of the entire bond issue.

Major Differences between Competitive Bidding and Negotiated Sale

Based on the description of competitive bidding and negotiated sale, two major differences need further discussion. The first notable difference is in the degree of flexibility in timing and structuring. A negotiated sale provides more flexibility to the issuer than a competitive bidding. In a competitive bidding, the final date of sale is set in the notice of sale used to solicit bids. This date cannot be changed by the winning underwriter. The principal amount and the structure of the bond issue are also set in the notice and cannot be changed in the future either by the issuer or by the underwriter. In a negotiated sale the final date of sale, the structure of the bond issue and the final borrowing amount are flexible to some extent depending on market conditions, primarily with regard to interest rate movement and investor demand for the debt issue. The total borrowing amount can be changed depending on investor demand. If there is high demand for the issue that can lead to a decrease in the yield, then the issuer has the option to increase the borrowing amount without an increase in debt service payment. The

---

[7] All data in this section are from *The Bond Buyer Yearbook* of various years.

structure of the issue can also be changed based on the specific demand profile of investors. The timing of the sale can also be changed depending on the prevailing interest rate environment and overall investor demand. The issuer can take advantage of a favorable movement in the interest rate to sell the bond issue earlier or delay the sale to avoid an unfavorable movement in the market interest rate. This is particularly important for refunding bond issues. Refunding bond issues are particularly sensitive to interest rate movements as their sole purpose is to reduce borrowing cost. Therefore, unfavorable movements in interest rate may cause the projected savings to disappear and the issuer may have to postpone the sale or cancel the sale altogether.

The second notable difference is that as the underwriter in a competitive sale is mainly responsible for underwriting, the underwriter in a negotiated sale is responsible for both origination and underwriting; and the length of time involved in the issuance process is vastly different for the competitive and negotiated underwriters. The competitive underwriter typically has only a week or so to get to know the issue between the posting of the notice of sale and the final sale date. The negotiated underwriter has much more time, usually several months, to become familiar with the issue. The major consequence of this difference in length of involvement is the level of "due diligence" expected of the competitive and negotiated underwriters. *Due diligence* refers to the effort spent examining and disclosing all information necessary for investors to purchase the bond issue. Because of their lengthy involvement with the issuer and the bond issue, the level of due diligence is expected to be higher for negotiated underwriters. This difference in level of due diligence in the municipal bond market is also recognized by the Securities and Exchange Commission (SEC). In its 1988 report on the bankruptcy of the Washington Public Power Supply System (WPPSS), the SEC stated that in the negotiated sale, the underwriter typically has a greater responsibility for disclosures and a greater role to play in the disclosure process since it is involved in the design of the issuance and the preparation of the official statement. In the case of competitive bidding, underwriters have a less intimate relationship and, therefore, there is a lower level of review responsibility.

DEBATE ON THE METHOD OF SALE

The method of sale decision is surely one of the most contentious topics when it comes to debt issuance. There are two aspects to the debate over which method to use, one political and the other economic.

Political Debate

The political debate is related to the political accountability in the government in awarding business deals to private companies. Competitive bidding, through which the underwriting business is awarded purely based on the cost, is not subject to any political influence. On the other hand, a negotiated sale, in which the underwriter is picked by government officials, is more susceptible to political influence. This susceptibility has been highlighted in several "pay-to-play" scandals. The pay-to-play problem results from the practice of awarding negotiated sale issues to underwriters who contribute to the political campaigns of elected officials or offer other financial incentives. There are two negative effects of pay-to-play. First, it can lead to political corruption. Second, the negotiated underwriter picked may not be the most competent, resulting in higher borrowing costs for the government issuer. From time to time, pay-to-play scandals surface that lead to public uproar and calls for limits on underwriting discretion.

To help address the pay-to-play problem, the Municipal Securities Rulemaking Board (MSRB), an agency created by Congress to regulate municipal securities dealers, issued Rule G-37 in 1994. This rule prohibits municipal securities dealers from doing municipal securities business for two years with issuers whose officials have received certain political contributions in excess of $250 from the dealer firm or its affiliated municipal finance professionals or political action committee. The rule also requires that dealers file quarterly reports with the MSRB disclosing any such political contributions. In 2005, MSRB further expanded on Rule G-37 with the issuance of Rule G-38. This rule prohibits any municipal securities dealer from paying anyone who is not affiliated with the dealer to solicit municipal securities business on behalf of the dealer. While Rules G-and G-38 may not have completely eliminated pay-to-play,[8] they have substantially reduced its possibility.

Economic Debate

The economic aspect of underwriting choice centers on the question of which method of sale leads to a lower borrowing cost. The effect of sale method on the issuer's borrowing cost is the most highly studied policy issue when it comes to state and local government debt management. Most of the studies

---

[8] In 2005, two securities dealers of Commerce Bank/Pennsylvania were convicted of conspiracy and other charges related to their relationship with former Philadelphia Treasurer Corey Kemp and Ron White, a friend of Philadelphia Mayor John F. Street in a pay-for-play scandal. The mayor's office paid out big fees to politically connected bond firms that gave money in exchange for contracts to arrange big debt issues . See John Shiffman, "Kemp Gets 10 Years for Corruption: The Sentence was Stiffer than Prosecutors Sought," *Philadelphia Inquirer*, July 20, 2005, p. A1.

can generally be divided into two groups, those that think competitive bidding is more cost effective in all instances and those that think negotiated sale may be a better method under certain circumstances.

As economic theory suggests, that increased competition should lead to lower costs, the first group of studies argues that competitive sale is more cost effective due to competition between underwriters. In this view, competition leads to a wider search for investors and lowers the borrowing costs for the issuer. Negotiated underwriters, given their unchallenged position in a sale, may not make their best effort to find the lowest cost for the issuer. Early studies on this question generally found interest cost savings from competition. To take just one example, Kessel[9] found that when the number of bids increased for a municipal bond issue, the interest rate decreased. Two later studies, Joehnk and Kidwell[10] and Sorensen,[11] found that competitive bidding led to lower borrowing costs compared to negotiated sale. More recently, Simonsen and Robbins[12] found that on average competitive sales result in lower interest costs when compared to negotiated sales and this difference increases as the number of bids received increases. Simonsen, Robbins, and Helgerson[13] studied municipal bond sales in Oregon that occurred during the mid-1990s and concluded that competitive issues result in significantly lower interest costs than negotiated issues.

In the second group of studies, the notion that competitive bidding will unconditionally lead to lower borrowing cost is disputed. It examines circumstances under which negotiated sale can be a more cost effective way of selling bonds. These circumstances can generally be categorized into two categories: timing uncertainty and demand uncertainty. These two circumstances reflect the major differences between the methods of sale discussed earlier.

Timing uncertainty has to do with the flexibility of sale date for each method of sale. Issuers using a negotiated offer have more flexibility in choosing the final sale date compared to competitive bidding. Such flexibility

---

[9] Reuben Kessel, "A Study of the Effects of Competition in the Tax-Exempt Bond Market," *Journal of Political Economy* 79, no. 4, pp. 706–738.

[10] Michael D. Joehnk,. and David S. Kidwell. "Comparative Costs of Competitive and Negotiated Underwritings in the State and Local Bond Market," *Journal of Finance* 34 (1979), pp. 725–731.

[11] Eric H. Sorensen, "Negotiated Municipal Bond Underwritings: Implications for Efficiency," *Journal of Money, Credit and Banking* (1979), pp. 366–370.

[12] William Simonsen and Mark D. Robbins, "Does It Make Any Difference Anymore? Competitive versus Negotiated Municipal Bond Issuance," *Public Administration Review* 56 (1996), pp. 57–64.

[13] William Simonsen, Mark D. Robbins, and Lee Helgerson, "The Influence of Jurisdiction Size and Sale Type on Municipal Bond Interest Rates: An Empirical Analysis," *Public Administration Review* 61 (2001), pp. 709–717.

can be an advantage during an unstable interest rate environment because the negotiated underwriter can better time the market. This is especially important for refunding bonds. One study, Joehnk and Kidwell,[14] found that negotiated sale resulted in lower spreads when the market was unstable and the issue received only one bid. Given the inherent difficulty of testing the timing hypothesis, most of the studies focus on the second hypothesis, demand uncertainty.

Demand uncertainty deals with the second difference between these two methods of sale, namely the length of time involved with the bond issue. The basic assumption that competitive bid underwriting is more cost effective is that it will lead to competition among underwriters. Such an assumption may not materialize under all circumstances. When underwriters do not have sufficient time to gauge investor demand for the bond issue, then they may not bid on the issue. As less issuers bid on the issue, the link between competition and lower interest cost through competitive bidding is broken. There are at least two important factors that can lead to such demand uncertainty, complexity of the issue and information asymmetry. Complexity refers to how complex the structure of the bond issue is. There are frequent innovations in bond structuring that will reduce the borrowing cost for issuers, such as variable rate issues and synthetic fixed rate issues. There are also various kinds of call features built into municipal bonds. The complexity of the issue takes more time to structure and also more time to educate and find investors. A negotiated sale allows the underwriter more time to market the issue and educate investors about the features of the bond. Leonard[15] believes that in some cases, such as when the bond being sold contains features that are unusual, negotiated sale will produce the lowest cost.

Information asymmetry refers to how familiar investors are with both the issuer and the purpose for which the borrowed proceeds are used. Information asymmetry problems arise whenever the parties involved in a transaction do not have the same information. Investors in bonds are concerned about the issuer's ability to pay back the debt and demand an interest rate commensurate with the underlying risk. When they are less familiar with the issuer or the financing of the future project, then they are either unwilling to purchase the bond or demand a higher interest rate to compensate for such uncertainty. There are several bond issue and bond issuer characteristics that can create a demand for more information and analysis:

---

[14] Michael D. Joehnk and David S. Kidwell, "The Impact of Market Uncertainty on Municipal Bond Underwriter Spread," *Financial Management* 13 (1984), pp. 37–44.

[15] Paul Leonard, "An Empirical Analysis of Competitive Bid and Negotiated Offerings of Municipal Bonds," *Municipal Finance Journal* 17 (1996), pp. 37–67.

- If the issuer borrows infrequently, then the investors may not be as familiar with the creditworthiness of the issuer and hence there will be more uncertainty regarding their creditworthiness.
- If the bond issue is revenue debt (where repayment is based on a project's revenue), there may be less certainty regarding the repayment prospects. On average, the information needed for assessing the repayment capability of a GO bond is less than that for a revenue bond. For a GO bond, investors need only to analyze the issuer's tax collection ability. For revenue debt, there may be less certainty about a specific project's ability to generate revenue.
- Even within revenue bonds, if the project is more "exotic," it may be more difficult to ascertain creditworthiness. Information requirements can be quite different depending on the projects the revenue bonds are used to fund. Some projects are easier to analyze than others. For example, the revenue projection of water projects is easier to analyze than that of a hospital project or development project.
- Bonds with lower credit ratings may face special challenges. For a bond with a high credit rating, the investors will feel more comfortable with its underlying risk without in-depth analysis. For a bond with a lower credit rating, investors will need to spend more time trying to understand the credit risk involved before they decide whether they want to buy into such credit risk or not.

When a bond exhibits one or several of these characteristics, competitive bidding may not generate sufficient bids to discover the best price. Negotiated sale gives the underwriter more time to educate investors and reduce information asymmetry and investor uncertainty about the risk, thus increasing the chance of discovering the best price for the bond.

Recent studies have highlighted differences in issue and issuer characteristics in the decision of which method of sale to use and the interest cost implications of that decision. Kriz[16] found that the decision to issue using negotiated underwriting is positively related to the decision to seek additional credit ratings. He concluded that the level of uncertainty surrounding the issue leads the issuers to choose a level of certification. Because of this uncertainty, the issuer may choose to issue using negotiated underwriting, which will give them time to deal with the uncertainty by conducting presale activities, such as seeking additional credit ratings. A later study by

---

[16] Kenneth A. Kriz, "Do Municipal Bond Underwriting Choices Have Implications for Other Financial Certification Decisions?" *Municipal Finance Journal* 21 (2000), pp. 1–23.

Kriz[17] found that negotiated offerings have the same or perhaps lower costs when compared to competitive offerings. After correcting for self-selection biases that lead issuers to choose one method over another, he found that there was no cost difference between the two methods of sale. A study by Peng and Brucato[18] yielded similar results. The authors found that issuers select a method of sale based on the perceived information asymmetry present. The more severe the information asymmetry, the more likely it is that an issuer will choose a negotiated sale.

HISTORICAL DATA ON USE OF SALE METHOD

Though there are many advantages to each type of sale depending on the issuer, negotiated issues have come to dominate the market. As shown in Exhibit 4.2, in 2005, slightly over 80% of all debt was issued using ne-

EXHIBIT 4.2 Negotiated Issues as Percent of Total Issuance, 1977–2005

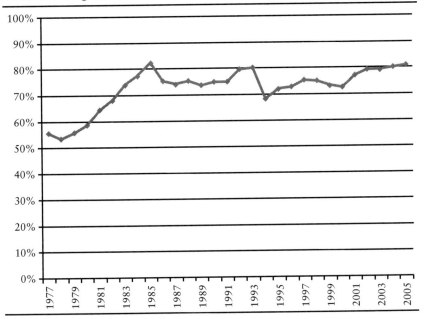

---

[17] Kenneth A. Kriz, "Comparative Costs of Negotiated Versus Competitive Bond Sales: New Evidence from State General Obligation Bonds," *Quarterly Review of Economics and Finance* 43 (2003), pp. 191–211.

[18] Jun Peng and Peter Brucato Jr. "Another Look at the Effect of Method of Sale on the Interest Cost in the Municipal Bond Market—A Certification Model," *Public Budgeting & Finance* 23 (2003), pp. 73–95.

gotiation. This is up from 55% in 1977. It would appear that negotiated issues have steadily become dominant. But the dynamics of the process are more complicated. In Exhibit 4.2, we show historical data on the method of sale. Negotiated issues did increase in dominance, but the period of greatest change was in the 1970s and early 1980s. From the 1977 starting point of 55%, in a mere eight years the percentage of negotiated issuance leaped to 82% of the market. From 1985 onward, the percentage has fluctuated more or less around a flat trendline. In this section of the chapter, we examine factors that can explain the change in the historical usage of negotiated sale. We pick three factors that have been discussed in the literature and for which historical data were available.

Revenue Bond Market Share

One possibility is that the nature of debt issuance changed. Bonds that are more risky need additional certification of their credit quality through the use of a negotiated issuer. One factor that could affect the market share of negotiated issues is a change in the share of revenue bond issuance. Revenue bonds tend to be more risky than general obligation bonds due to their largely limited, project specific repayment sources. Also, it may be harder to educate potential buyers regarding the feasibility of projects and hence the creditworthiness of the issuer. Therefore, one would predict that more revenue bonds would lead to more negotiated issues. In Exhibit 4.3 we include time-series information on the percentage of revenue issues in the debt market. It appears as though there is somewhat of a common trend between revenue bond issuance and negotiated sales market share. In the late 1970s into the early 1980s, revenue bond market share increased from 60% of total issuance to 73%. Then during the 1980s revenue debt market share declined, similar to the pattern observed in the negotiated issuance data. The only time period that is somewhat incongruous of a positive relationship between revenue issuance and negotiated issuance is during the early 2000s, when revenue bond issuance fell and negotiated sales increased.

Refunding Bond Market Share

Another factor which might account for increased negotiated issuance is the proportion of debt issued for refunding existing debt. Such debt should be less risky than other debt because the proceeds of the debt will go to pay off existing debt. Presumably the new debt service requirements will be less than before (since refunding only makes sense when interest rates fall). Even though refunding bond may be less risky on average, the timing of the issuance is more sensitive to interest rate change, as the projected refunding sav-

EXHIBIT 4.3   Negotiated Issues and Revenue Issues as Percent of Total Issuance, 1977–2005

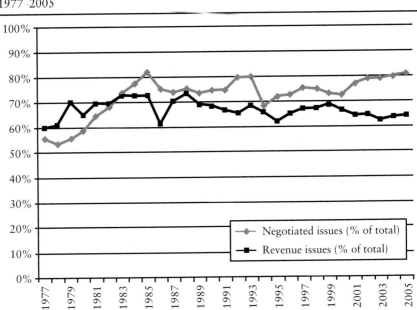

ings can disappear if the interest rate increases slightly. As explained in the first section of this chapter, refunding bonds may be more likely to be sold through negotiated sale due to its flexibility in timing. In Exhibit 4.4, we plot the relationship between refunding market share and negotiated market share. We see a more ambiguous pattern between these two variables.

Refunding issues rose dramatically in the mid-1980s, immediately following the high interest rates imposed by the Federal Reserve to combat the inflation of the late 1970s. This mirrors somewhat the rise in negotiated issuance, but it peaks after the peak of negotiation, and drops off dramatically in the late when negotiated issuance had turned flat to slightly downtrending. Then in the early 1990s refunding rose dramatically while negotiated issuance rose only slightly. After 1994, refunding activity has been highly volatile.

It was found earlier that the only time period that is somewhat incongruous of a positive relationship between revenue issuance and negotiated issuance is during the early 2000s, when revenue bond issuance fell and negotiated sales increased. This incongruity can be explained by the refunding bond share. Due to the interest rate drop in early 2000s, the refunding bond share almost doubled, from less than 20% in 2000 to about 40% in

EXHIBIT 4.4   Negotiated Issues and Refunding Issues as a Percentage of Total Issuance, 1977–2005

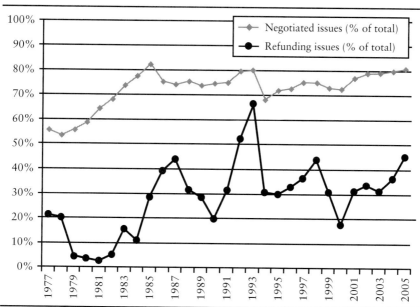

2005. This increase in refunding bond share helps explain why the negotiated sale share increased at a time when the revenue bond share decreased.

Interest Rate Volatility

Another factor that might lead to greater negotiated issuance is interest rate volatility. The uncertainty hypothesis suggests that issuers may switch to negotiated issues during times of greater volatility as a way to reduce uncertainty.[19] Exhibit 4.5 shows the relationship between negotiated issuance and interest rate volatility, as measured by the annual standard deviation of interest rates. Here there appears to be a relationship between the two variables in the earliest years of the data. Interest rate volatility jumped dramatically as rates rose in the late 1970s. The peak of interest rate volatility preceded the peak of negotiated issuance by three years. But after this point, the data on volatility bears little resemblance to negotiated issuance dynamics. Volatility declined throughout the next 20+ years while negotiated issuance remained relatively constant.

---

[19] Edward A. Dyl and Michael D. Joehnk, "Competitive Versus Negotiated Underwriting of Public Utility Debt," *Bell Journal of Economics* 7 (1976), pp. 680–690.

EXHIBIT 4.5 Negotiated Issues as a Percentage of Total Issuance and Interest Rate Volatility, 1977–2005

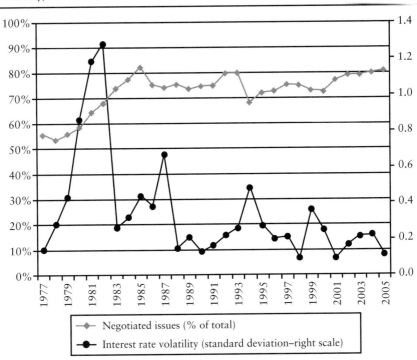

Negotiated issues (% of total)

Interest rate volatility (standard deviation–right scale)

SUMMARY

In terms of which method of sale (competitive versus negotiated) has a cost advantage, economic theory would suggest that when a bond does not require rigorous analysis from underwriters or investors to understand its credit risk, such as a simple GO bond with a high credit rating issued by an issuer with whom the market is familiar, then competitive bidding has the potential to discover the optimum price for the issuer by attracting multiple bids. On the other hand, negotiated sale may be preferred as a method to discover the best price if the bond needs more in-depth analysis by both underwriters and investors.

The economic theory is born out by historical data to some extent. We have found that negotiated issues have grown in market share over the last 30 years. Of the three factors we have examined, the market share of revenue bonds seems to have the most influence over the choice of sale method.

As predicted by theory, the relationship is positive with more revenue bond issuance leading to a larger market share for negotiated issues. Refunding bond share also can explain some of the changes in the share of negotiated issues, especially in years when there was a substantial increase in refunding bond share. There is less evidence in support of arguments that interest rate volatility affects the market share of negotiated issues. Over all, the historical evidence indicates that at least at the aggregate level, issuers' choice of sale method in the municipal bond market has been influenced by the characteristics of the bond to be sold.

Regardless of the economic effects, there exists concern regarding the political and ethical propriety of using the negotiated method of sale. Therefore, the ultimate decision of which method of sale to use may be reduced to a balancing of concerns for those issues who might benefit from using negotiated issuance. The only firm advice, as ever, is for issuers to carefully weigh the issues before settling on a method of sale.

CHAPTER 5

The Role of Bond Counsel in Public Agency Financing

John L. Kraft, Esq.
Partner
Lomurro, Davison, Eastman & Munoz, P.A.

Virtually all bonds issued by states and political subdivisions are accompanied by an approving legal opinion of a nationally recognized bond counsel. This is a law firm with an established reputation in the investment community for experience and reliability in municipal finance. The bond counsel's approving legal opinion is the investor's assurance as to the validity, security and tax-exempt status of the bonds. It states that the bonds are valid and binding obligations of the issuer enforceable in accordance with their terms and, when appropriate, that the interest income on the bonds is exempt from federal income taxes.

The assurances provided by the legal opinion stay with the bonds as long as they remain outstanding, passing from one owner to another. The owner of an outstanding municipal bond cannot expect to sell the bond unless he delivers with it a copy of the bond counsel's approving legal opinion.

This chapter will explain the role of bond counsel in public agency financing by exploring the history of bond counsel, the purpose of bond counsel in the twenty-first century, the legal issues addressed by bond counsel and evolving issues in public finance law that will be addressed by bond counsel.

HISTORY OF BOND COUNSEL

The role of bond counsel can best be understood from an historical perspective. In the 1800s a number of states and local governments issued bonds to fund capital improvements, often related to the development of railroad facilities. The ability of the issuer to pay the bonds depended upon the prosperity and the growing tax base that was expected to follow the development of the railroad industry. Unfortunately, prosperity was not universal, and a significant number of railroad bonds went into default. Bondholders brought suit in the local courts seeking to collect on the defaulted obligations. In order to avoid payment, the bond issuers asserted as defenses, technical defects in the procedures for the authorization and the issuance of the bonds. These technical defects were asserted to invalidate the bond issue and to relieve the issuer of the obligation to pay. The frequency of default through the use of these technical defenses in lawsuits caused investors to reject municipal bonds as investments.

In order to restore investor confidence, underwriters developed the practice of hiring an attorney of their choice, independent from the issuer, to review the legal procedures followed by the governmental unit in authorizing and issuing the bonds. The sale of the bonds to the underwriter was not final without the approving opinion of the independent attorney, who came to be known as the *bond counsel*. If the bond counsel found the slightest defect in the actions taken by the issuer, he (or she) would not render the opinion and the bond sale was aborted. Over time, the municipal issuers came to retain the bond counsel to guide them through the authorization process, so that the proper procedures would be followed and the issuer could be assured of obtaining the approving legal opinion at the time of the sale. Even though engaged by the issuer, the bond counsel retains its independence today, recognizing that investors will rely on its approving legal opinion when purchasing bonds.

The number of law firms providing these specialized services has grown over the years. The great majority of all bonds issued throughout the country still are approved by a small number of bond counsel firms. For many years *The Bond Buyer's Municipal Marketplace* (known as the "Red Book") has contained a section entitled "Municipal Bond Attorneys." The publisher disclaims any responsibility for the accuracy of the list, and a number of listed firms actually do little or no bond counsel work. However, all firms that do provide bond counsel services on a routine basis are listed in the Red Book.

REVIEW OF BOND COUNSEL OPINION

The present-day role of the bond counsel can be examined by focusing on a typical approving legal opinion. The comments in the following paragraphs will correspond to the numbers superimposed on the sample approving legal opinion set forth as Exhibit 5.1.

EXHIBIT 5.1 Sample of Legal Opinion

JOHN L. KRAFT, ESQ., L.L.C.   (1)

John L. Kraft, Esq.

Fellow of the
American College of
Bond Counsel

Township Committee of the
Township of Morris, in the   (2)
County of Morris, New Jersey

Dear Committee Members:

I have examined a record of proceedings relating to the issuance of $12,707,000 General Improvement Bonds of the Township of Morris, a municipal corporation of the State of New Jersey, situate in the County of Morris (the "Bonds"). The Bonds are dated November 15, 2006, (3) mature on November 15 in the principal amounts and bear interest at the rates per annum payable May 15, 2007 and semiannually thereafter on the fifteenth days of May and November in each year until maturity as described in the following schedule:

Year	Principal Amount	Interest Rate
2007	$ 515,000	3.50%
2008	520,000	3.50%
2009	520,000	3.50%
2010	520,000	3.50%
2011	770,000	3.50%
2012	900,000	3.75%
2013	925,000	3.75%
2014	950,000	3.75%
2015	955,000	3.75%
2016	1,000,000	3.75%
2017	1,025,000	4.00%
2018	1,030,000	4.00%
2019	1,030,000	4.00%
2020	1,030,000	4.00%
2021	1,017,000	4.00%

The Bonds are issued in the form of one Bond for each maturity, being fifteen in number, and are numbered GI-1 to GI-15, inclusive, in order of maturity. The are issued pursuant to the Local Bond Law of the State of New Jersey and a resolution of the Township Committee adopted October 18, 2006 and entitled, "Resolution Providing for the Combination of Certain Issues of (4) General Improvement Bonds of the Township of Morris, in the County of Morris, New Jersey (5) into a Single Issue of Bonds Aggregating $12,707,000 in Principal Amount" in all respects duly

70 South Orange Avenue, Livingston, NJ 07039

Phone: 973.992.4423   jkraft@kraftbonds.com   Fax: 973.992.5366

EXHIBIT 5.1   Continued

Township Committee of the
Township of Morris, in the
County of Morris, New Jersey
Page 2

approved and the various bond ordinances referred to therein, each in all respects duly approved
and published as required by law.

The Bonds are subject to redemption prior to their stated maturities. The Bonds will be
registered in the name of Cede & Co., as nominee of The Depository Trust Company, New York,
New York, which will act as Securities Depository.

In my opinion, except insofar as the enforcement thereof may be limited by any applicable
bankruptcy, moratorium or similar laws relating to the enforcement of creditors' rights, the
Bonds are valid and legally binding obligations of the Township of Morris and the Township has   **(6)**
the power and is obligated to levy ad valorem taxes upon all the taxable real property within the   **(7)**
Township for the payment of the Bonds and the interest thereon without limitation as to rate or
amount.

The Township has covenanted to comply with any continuing requirements that may be
necessary to preserve the tax exempt status of the Bonds under the Internal Revenue Code of
1986, as amended (the "Code"). In the event that the Township continuously complies with its   **(8)**
covenant, it is my opinion that interest on the Bonds is not includable in gross income for federal
income tax purposes under the current law.

In my opinion, the Bonds are not "private activity bonds" as defined in the Code and interest on
the Bonds is not an item of tax preference for purposes of computing the federal alternative
minimum tax imposed on individuals. Interest on the Bonds held by a corporate taxpayer is
included in the relevant income computation for calculation of the federal alternative minimum
tax as a result of the inclusion of interest on the Bonds in "adjusted current earnings." I express
no opinion regarding other federal tax consequences arising with respect to the Bonds.

Further, in my opinion, interest on the Bonds and any gain on the sale of the Bonds are not
includable as gross income under the New Jersey Gross Income Tax Act.

Very truly yours,

1. *Bond counsel firm.* The law firm rendering the opinion must be one
   recognized as a bond counsel firm. This reputation is established over
   years of involvement in the area of municipal finance.
2. *Heading.* Most approving legal opinions are addressed to the bond
   counsel's client, the issuer of the obligations. However, the bond counsel knows that investors will rely on its opinion throughout the life of
   the bonds. Investors have a right to expect that the bond counsel will
   be independent in rendering this opinion. The opinion will be rendered
   only after bond counsel has conducted a thorough review of all aspects
   of the bond authorization and issuance process and is certain that the
   opinion is correct. This is referred to as an unqualified opinion.
       If there are any factors present that might bring into question any
   aspect of the opinion, the bond counsel has the duty to put investors on
   notice by making reference to those factors and expressing the opinion
   either that such factors are without merit and do not affect the bond
   counsel's conclusion (a *no-merit opinion*) or that such factors do raise

some questions as to which the bond counsel cannot render an unqualified opinion (a *qualified opinion*). For example, if a lawsuit is started to enjoin the issuance of the bonds alleging some noncompliance with law, the bond counsel will analyze the situation. If the bond counsel is satisfied that there is no legal basis for the suit, it will issue a no-merit opinion. If there is any arguable basis to the claims, the bond counsel may issue a qualified opinion that expresses no opinion as to the outcome of the lawsuit. A qualified opinion usually will prevent the public sale of the bonds, since investors do not wish to gamble on a favorable resolution of legal uncertainties. A no-merit opinion can be the basis for a publicly offered issue if the original investors are willing to accept the bond counsel's conclusion that any questions raised will be resolved in favor of the issuer. Recognizing the great reliance placed upon the legal opinion, the bond counsel is very conservative in assessing whether a no-merit opinion should be issued.

3. *Description of bonds.* The bond counsel advises the issuer as to the form of the bonds. It should be noted that after July 1, 1983, all new-issue municipal bonds have to be in registered form in order to qualify the interest for federal tax exemption. The bond counsel also supervises the preparation, execution, and delivery of the bonds to the purchaser.

4. *Record of proceedings.* The basis for the bond counsel's opinion as to the validity and the security of the bonds is the record of the proceedings followed by the issuer to authorize the issuance of the bonds. As indicated above, the bond counsel's role originally was limited to an after-the-fact review of the proceedings. Sometimes, mistakes in law and procedure were uncovered that required the cancellation of the bond sale. The current practice is to have the bond counsel render advice and guidance to the issuer throughout the authorization process. The bond counsel then oversees the preparation of the record of proceedings to document that everything is in order. The record of proceedings usually includes proof of the proper establishment of the issuer as a political subdivision. There have been instances of bonds being "issued" by non-existent governmental agencies to defraud investors. This is virtually impossible today, when a well-known bond counsel approves the bonds to be sold. The record of proceedings also includes proof of the observance of all technical procedures for the authorization and the issuance of the obligations, such as the proper adoption of resolutions and ordinances in accordance with the requirements of law. The record of proceedings may also contain proof as to the validity and the enforceability of the security for the payment of the bonds, such as a mortgage or a security interest in personal property.

5. *Statement of authority.* Typically, reference is made in the opinion to the authority for the issuance of the bonds. In our example, the resolution referred to in the opinion was prepared by the bond counsel just prior to the bond sale. The ordinances referred to in the resolution were prepared by the bond counsel over a period of several years preceding the sale and constitute not only the authorization to sell the bonds but also the authorization to undertake the improvements financed by the bond issue.

6. *Validity.* The basic opinion of the bond counsel is that the bonds are valid and legally binding obligations of the issuer that must be paid when due. The obligation to pay, however, is subject to bankruptcy laws. The United States Constitution provides that the federal government has the supreme jurisdiction over bankruptcies, and the Bankruptcy Code has specific provisions governing municipal bankruptcies.

7. *Security.* The opinion discussed here applies to a general obligation bond issue. No specific stream of revenues is pledged to pay the bonds. The issuer promises to levy sufficient taxes "without limitation as to rate or amount" to pay the bonds in accordance with their terms. The bond counsel must be sure that the issuer has this general taxing power and that the issuer has invoked its use properly for the entire time the bonds will remain outstanding.

   The other major category of bonds is revenue bonds. These bonds are issued by public agencies that may or may not have the power to levy taxes. The source of payment of the bonds is the revenue derived from the project financed by the bonds or by some other specific source of revenue. When revenue bonds are backed up by a pledge to use the taxing power of the issuer if the pledged revenues are insufficient to pay the bonds, they are referred to as *double-barreled bonds.*

8. *Tax exemption.* In 1913, the United States Constitution was amended to authorize Congress to levy and collect income taxes. This created an additional responsibility for the bond counsel, namely to assure that interest on the bonds will be exempt from federal income taxation. The Internal Revenue Code always has provided that gross income of taxpayers does not include interest on the obligations of a state, a territory, or a possession of the United States or any political subdivision thereof or of the District of Columbia. Accordingly, the bond counsel renders the opinion that the holders of municipal bonds are entitled to this exemption, when appropriate. Because the interest on most municipal bonds is exempt from taxation, they can be sold at lower interest rates than securities bearing taxable interest, such as U.S. Treasury obligations.

FURTHER TAX DEVELOPMENTS

In 1968, Congress amended the Internal Revenue Code (the Code) to eliminate tax-exempt status for industrial development bonds (now called *private activity bonds*). The industrial development bond exception prohibits the use of tax-exempt bonds for projects which benefit private parties where the bonds are secured by the revenues of the project being financed. Subsequent amendments to the Code, numerous changes in the tax regulations, as well as pronouncements of the Internal Revenue Service in the form of revenue rulings and private letter rulings, make it increasingly complicated for the bond counsel to render an opinion that the interest on bond issues is exempt from federal income taxes. In 1969 the Internal Revenue Code again was amended to provide that arbitrage bonds would not bear tax-exempt interest. Arbitrage bonds are bonds that are issued for the purpose of reinvesting the bond proceeds in taxable investments for the purpose of making a profit. No one challenged these laws as being unconstitutional when they were adopted.

From 1913 to 1988, many believed that the basis for tax exemption was found in the U.S. Constitution. In 1988, the U.S. Supreme Court rejected this position and held that tax exemption is not a Constitutional right. Rather, it is a privilege granted by the federal government which can be withdrawn at any time. To date, the federal government has not eliminated tax exemption for municipal bonds, except as stated above.

Many states impose income taxes of their own. Currently, interest income on municipal bonds is subject to the state income taxes, except for bonds issued by the particular state and its political subdivisions. Bond counsel also expresses an opinion relating to tax exemption within the state where the bonds are issued, but this state tax exemption is under attack before the U.S. Supreme Court as described in the next section.

DISCLOSURE AND SECURITIES LAWS

In 1975, the City of New York defaulted on its general obligation notes because of its inability to pay the principal and interest on time. Criticisms were leveled against city officials, the underwriters of the obligations and other professionals advising the city, including the bond counsel. The Securities and Exchange Commission undertook a study to determine the causes of the default and the parties, if any, who might be responsible. In 1977, an SEC staff report criticized the role that the bond counsel played in the New York City fiscal crisis, charging that bond counsel did not critically analyze the financial information provided by the city. The SEC said that bond counsel should have conducted its own investigation when put on notice of circumstances that called into question matters basic to the issuance of its opinion. While the role of the bond counsel traditionally has been to do legal work and not to provide financial analysis, this report and the circumstances surrounding the default suggest that bond counsel has increased responsibilities in the area of financial disclosure, and bond counsel must evaluate carefully the legal standards to which it and its client, the municipal issuer, will be held.

In response to the New York fiscal crisis, the Securities Exchange Act of 1934 was amended in 1975 to regulate municipal securities professionals, that is, the brokers and the dealers involved in buying and selling municipal securities. Municipal issuers specifically were excluded from such regulation. However, municipal obligations are sold by the brokers and the dealers who are subject to this regulation. The bond counsel must be familiar with disclosure requirements and the rules of the Securities and Exchange Commission in order to advise the municipal issuer. Moreover, municipal governments have always been held liable under the antifraud provisions of the Securities Exchange Act of 1934. As this area of law develops through court decisions, changes in legislation and the practices of the trade, bond counsel must keep informed of these changes and must keep its client in conformity with acceptable practices.

RECENT DEVELOPMENTS

We conclude this chapter with a summary of the continuing development of the law of public finance from the nineteenth to the twenty-first centuries. The law continues to evolve even as this chapter is prepared for publication. Bond Counsel, individually and through the National Association of Bond Counsel, participate in this evolution. These developments include the following:

1. *Federal securities law.* The current Chairman of the SEC has proposed sweeping changes of the federal securities laws, including repeal of the "Tower Amendment." The Tower Amendment was part of the Securities Acts Amendments of 1975, which also created the Municipal Securities Rulemaking Board (MSRB) to regulate municipal securities dealers. The Tower Amendment prohibits direct or indirect regulation of municipal securities issuers. Repeal of the Tower Amendment could lead to presale registration requirements for municipal bonds and other onerous regulations that would greatly increase the issuance costs for municipal bond issuers.

2. *State tax exemptions for bonds issued by a state and its political sub-divisions.* As indicated above, the current practice of most states that impose state income taxes is to exempt from taxation interest on the bonds issued by the state and its political subdivisions. Interest on the bonds issued by other states and subdivisions is subject to the state income tax. New York and New Jersey are two examples of this practice. This tax preference is currently under challenge before the U.S. Supreme Court as being violative of the U.S. Constitution. A decision of the Court could come at any time.

3. *New accounting rules.* The Government Accounting Standards Board (GASB) has promulgated a new rule requiring governmental units to calculate and include in their financial statements, future liabilities called Other Post Employment Benefits ("OPEB"), principally retiree health benefits. The numbers are huge—New Jersey's potential liability is estimated by some to exceed $70 billion. This new GASB rule has created great controversy. The Government Finance Officer's Association has criticized GASB. Some have called for eliminating GASB altogether. Bond Counsel must engage in the controversy and then advise its clients on how to deal with this issue in the future.

The complexity and variety of public finance issues will continue to grow in the future. Bond counsel must address and solve them for the benefit of their clients and the investors in municipal bonds who rely on bond counsel to minimize legal risks from the municipal bond marketplace.

CHAPTER 6

The Role of Counsel to the Underwriters

Mary G. Wilson, Esq.
Partner
Sonnenschein Nath & Rosenthal LLP

In recent years the growth in securities laws and scrutiny of securities matters related to municipal financings have made the role of underwriter's counsel more complex and more important. Many counsel focus their practice on one or two areas such as general obligation government bonds, airport financings, housing financings, or financings for nonprofit educational institutions, health care providers or cultural institutions. While all public financings have certain basic elements in common, the specific rules, structures, risks and documentation varies from one type of financing to another. The underwriter plays a much more significant role in a negotiated financing in which it is hired at the beginning and involved in every element of the financing. In a competitive financing, the financing is structured and the disclosure prepared and, at the time of pricing, underwriters are asked to bid with the lowest bidder winning the role as underwriter. Underwriters often select counsel experienced in the particular type of financing involved. Each type of financing and each financing itself has differences, and the role of underwriter's counsel varies from financing to financing. In fact, in certain cases bond counsel may also serve as disclosure counsel with no counsel directly representing the underwriter. This chapter focuses on the primary responsibilities of an underwriter's counsel in a negotiated financing and does not address every possible financing structure or responsibility of an underwriter's counsel.

Underwriter's counsel has a variety of responsibilities in a municipal financing, including (1) assisting in structuring the financing and compliance with securities laws; (2) conducting due diligence; (3) drafting the offering document, the bond purchase agreement, any continuing disclosure agreement, any remarketing agreement and any agreement among underwriters; (4) reviewing and commenting on the bond documents prepared by other counsel; (5) preparing any blue sky survey; and (6) providing an opinion on the disclosure and certain other matters. The purpose of this chapter is describe each of these responsibilities.

STRUCTURING

The initial step in a public financing is generally for the underwriter and the issuer (or borrower in a conduit financing) to meet and discuss the financial needs and goals of the issuer and what financing structure can best meet those goals. After initial structuring discussions, the underwriter and the issuer often bring in bond counsel and underwriter's counsel to review the structure and determine whether the structure complies with all of the legal requirements. The analysis usually begins with the state law and federal tax analysis, which must be completed to allow bond counsel to give its opinion that the bonds have been validly issued and that interest thereon is excludable from gross income of the owners thereof for federal income tax purposes. Underwriter's counsel should be well versed in these issues and will often contribute to the analysis and changes suggested at this point. The next step is to review the structure for securities law and other legal concerns. Underwriter's counsel takes the lead on this step of the analysis.

SECURITIES LAWS

A key component of the underwriter's counsel role is ensuring that the structure and documentation of a financing comply with the securities laws. Initially, it may seem that public finance attorneys do not need to worry too much about securities laws. After all, most securities in public finance transactions are exempt from the registration requirements of the Securities Act of 1933, as amended (the 1933 Act). However, there are many other important applicable securities laws to consider in a public financing.

1933 Act Registration Requirement

The 1933 Act generally provides that it is unlawful for a person to use the mail or other forms of interstate commerce to sell or deliver a security unless a registration statement has been filed with the Securities and Exchange

Commission (SEC) and is in effect. It is important to remember that the definition of "security" in the 1933 Act is very broad[1] and a single financing may have multiple securities, including for example bonds, notes, letters of credit and insurance policies. Section 3(a) of the 1933 Act contains a list of exemptions from registration requirements which in most cases covers all identified securities in a municipal financing.[2] In each financing, underwriter's counsel is usually responsible for reviewing each security in the financing and making sure an exemption applies. If an exemption in Section 3(a) does not apply, counsel can turn to the list of exempt transactions in Section 4 of the 1933 Act to see if the financing can qualify as an exempt transaction. Unless the parties are willing to comply with the registration requirements of the 1933 Act, a financing must fit the securities or transaction exemptions.

Indenture Act Qualification Requirement

After completing the 1933 Act registration exemption analysis, underwriter's counsel may wish to confirm that the indentures in the proposed financing are exempt from the indenture qualification requirements of the Trust Indenture Act of 1939, as amended (the Indenture Act). The Indenture Act generally requires that any indenture[3] pursuant to which securities are issued be qualified by the SEC unless exempt from such requirements. Many of the exemptions tie to exemptions from the registration requirements of the 1933 Act, so that the Indenture Act analysis generally flows easily from the 1933 Act analysis.

The Antifraud Provisions

After concluding that the proposed financing is exempt from the registration requirements of the 1933 Act and the qualification requirements of the Indenture Act, underwriter's counsel gets to the securities laws from which public finance transactions are not exempt. Section 17 of the 1933 Act and Section 10(b) of the Securities Exchange Act of 1934, as amended (the 1934 Act), together with Rule 10b-5 promulgated thereunder are

---

[1] The term *security* includes, among other items, any note, stock, bond, debenture, evidence of indebtedness, certificate of interest or participation in any profit-sharing agreement, and guarantees of any of the foregoing. 1933 Act, Section 2(a)(1).

[2] See Rule 131 promulgated pursuant to the 1933 Act and related no action letters from the SEC for a more detailed discussion of separate securities, particularly with respect to conduit financing.

[3] Indenture is broadly defined to include indentures, mortgages, deeds of trust and similar instruments under which securities are issued. Indenture Act, Section 303.

known as the *antifraud provisions*. These provisions apply directly to municipal securities and are generally designed to ensure that securities are offered and sold to the public with complete and accurate material information, so that the purchaser can make an informed investment decision. Underwriter's counsel plays a primary role in preparing offering documents, and performing due diligence, to comply with the requirements of the antifraud provisions.

Rule 10b-5 covers purchases and sales of securities and prohibits a person from using interstate commerce or the mail to (1) employ a scheme to defraud; (2) make an untrue statement of a material fact or omit to state a fact necessary in order to make the statements made, in light of the circumstances under which they were made, not misleading; or (3) engage in any act which operates as a fraud on any person. A violation of Rule 10b-5 occurs when there is a misstatement or omission of a material fact made with an intent to deceive, manipulate or defraud upon which the plaintiff relied and which was the proximate cause of damages.[4] The intent requirement of Rule 10b-5 is known as the *scienter requirement.*

Section 17 of the 1933 Act applies to offers and sales and prohibits among other things the use of interstate commerce or the mail to obtain money or property by making any untrue statement of a material fact or any omission to state a material fact necessary in order to make the statements made, in light of the circumstances under which they were made, not misleading.

Rule 15c2-12

Rule 15c2-12, promulgated by the SEC under the 1934 Act, applies directly to municipal securities and has a number of requirements. Initially, underwriter's counsel must determine whether the proposed financing is exempt from some or all of the requirements of Rule 15c2-12 pursuant to the exemptions listed in Section (d). If not exempt, the underwriter must comply with the requirements of the rule including the requirement that the underwriter obtain and review a near final official statement prior to bidding on or purchasing municipal bonds.[5] Also, the underwriter may not purchase or sell any municipal securities in connection with an offering, unless the underwriter

---

[4] *Fundamentals of Municipal Bond Law 2004*, National Association of Bond Lawyers, Securities Laws, Chapter I, p. 6.

[5] Rule 15c2-12(b)(1) provides that unless an exemption applies, the underwriter must review an official statement deemed final by the issuer as of its date except for the omission of certain listed pricing information, which includes the offering prices, interest rates, selling compensation, principal amounts, ratings and other terms of the securities depending on such matters.

has reasonably determined that any obligated person[6] for whom financial or operating data is presented in the final official statement has undertaken in writing to provide designated repositories with certain annual financial and operating data and with timely notice of certain specified events, if material. Compliance with these requirements of the rule are usually achieved by adding a representation to the bond purchase agreement that the issuer (and/or borrower in a conduit financing) deems the preliminary offering memorandum (or other offering document then available) final and agrees to enter into a continuing disclosure agreement or undertaking pursuant to which the issuer (and/or borrower in a conduit financing) agrees to file the annual financial and operating data and material event notices as required by Rule 15c2-12.

In addition, the Municipal Securities Rulemaking Board (MSRB) has issued numerous rules which apply to municipal bonds. For more information on the MSRB and these rules, see Chapter 22.

Due Diligence

Underwriter's counsel takes the lead in a public financing in preparing and working with the financing team to produce an offering document (usually an official statement) which meets the standards of the antifraud provisions and Rule 15c2-12. The first step in preparing an offering document that complies with the security laws is often conducting due diligence.

Due diligence generally involves sending the issuer (or borrower in a conduit financing) a list of documents which counsel would like to review and a list of questions to answer in writing and conducting interviews with key operating, financial, legal and compliance management. The documents requested often include financial information, governance documents, agreements relating to the use of property to be financed with the proposed bonds, recent environmental reports, any documentation related to open investigations or regulatory matters, tax returns, and any operating, management, joint venture, or partnership agreements. The questionnaire and interviews are designed to highlight financial, tax, regulatory, litigation, labor, management, compliance, or operational issues that may be material and, therefore, should be disclosed. The reasonable scope and nature of the due diligence varies significantly based on the type of financing and the existing relationship between the underwriter, its counsel and the issuer. For example, healthcare

---

[6] Obligated person is defined in Rule 15c2-12 to mean any person, including an issuer of municipal securities, who is either generally or through an enterprise, fund, or account of such person committed by contract or other arrangement to support payment of all, or part of the obligations on the municipal securities to be sold in an offering (other than providers of municipal bond insurance, letters of credit, or other liquidity facilities).

institutions have extensive regulatory compliance requirements, so that in a tax-exempt health care financing all of those issues need to be reviewed. If an underwriter and its counsel work with an issuer on several financings a year, the due diligence only needs to be updated from the last financing.

Due diligence may also include obtaining an agreed upon procedures letter from the issuer's (or conduit borrower's) accountant outlining the review and procedures conducted by the auditor on the financial information in the offering document to confirm its accuracy and completeness. Underwriter's counsel usually takes the lead in negotiating this letter and arranging for its delivery. This letter is usually addressed to the underwriter and the issuer (or conduit borrower) and delivered prior to execution of the bond purchase agreement. If more than a week or so elapses between the execution of the bond purchase agreement and the issuance of the bonds or the original letter covered the preliminary official statement and a final official statement is issued, a bring-down letter may also be requested.

Why does underwriter's counsel conduct due diligence? There are a number of reasons that this occurs. The due diligence conducted by underwriter's counsel provides information for the offering document and provides the basis for underwriter's counsel's opinion. The opinion is discussed in more detail later in this chapter.

A second reason is to provide the underwriter with what is often called a *due diligence defense*. The applicable securities laws do not actually provide for a due diligence defense in municipal financings. The concept comes from section 11 of the 1933 Act which imposes liability on certain people for misstatements or omissions of a material fact in a registration statement. Pursuant to Section 11, a defendant, other that the issuer, may avoid liability by showing that the defendant had "after reasonable investigation, reasonable grounds to believe and did believe"[7] that the statements in question "were true and that there was no omission to state a material fact required to be stated therein or necessary to make the statements therein not misleading."[8] In addition, using similar language in a release related to Rule 15c2-12, the SEC has commented that by participating in an underwriting, the underwriter makes an implied recommendation and implies that the underwriter "has a reasonable basis for belief in the truthfulness and completeness of the key representations made in any disclosure document used in the offerings."[9]

The due diligence performed by underwriter's counsel does not eliminate the need for the underwriter to perform its own due diligence, but it assists the underwriter in preparing a due diligence defense analogous to that recognized in Section 11 of the 1933 Act and to meeting the duty

[7] 1933 Act, Section 11(b)(3).
[8] 1933 Act, Section 11(b)(3).
[9] SEC Release No. 34-26100 (September 22, 1988): Proposed Rule 15c2-12.

arguably arising under Rule 15c2-12. While Section 11 does not apply to municipal securities exempt from registration under the 1933 Act, a defense that the underwriter conducted reasonable due diligence and believed that the statements in the offering document were accurate and complete would make it difficult to prove the scienter element of a 10b-5 claim. This type of diligence and review of an official statement should also meet any requirements of Rule 15c2-12 related to review and belief in the accuracy and completeness of disclosure. This defense is stronger if the underwriter does some of its own diligence, if underwriter's counsel discusses any issues that arise during due diligence directly with the underwriter, and the underwriter participates in follow-up on identified issues.

On the practical side, it is also sometimes helpful for underwriter's counsel to play the tough guy in the due diligence process and ask the issuer or conduit borrower difficult questions or take the lead on an approach to disclosing sensitive information. This assists the underwriter in meeting its duty, but takes some of the pressure off the personal relationship between the underwriter and its client, the issuer or conduit borrower.

UNDERWRITING DOCUMENTS

Underwriter's counsel spends a significant amount of time drafting documents for the financing, including the offering document, bond purchase agreement, any continuing disclosure agreement, any remarketing agreement and any agreement among underwriters.

Official Statement

The role of due diligence in preparing the offering document and the Rule 10b-5 requirements that must be met have already been discussed in this chapter. The other key element to consider is that the offering document needs to effectively communicate the complete and accurate information it contains. Offering documents contain the key credit information on the issuer (or conduit borrower) (including financial performance, operational performance, key management personnel, risks and challenges) and also the features and mechanics of the securities being offered (including mode, conversion options, redemption features, tender provisions, and call provisions). Offering documents also generally identify the professionals (underwriters, attorneys, financial advisors) involved in the financing, describe the basics of the tax exemption on interest, attach a copy of the most recent audit of the issuer (or conduit borrower), summarize (or attach) the key bond documents, attach a form of bond counsel opinion, and contain financial information on any credit enhancers or liquidity providers (bond insurer or letter of credit/standby bond purchase agreement bank).

Many underwriters have particular styles and language that they like to use both for legal reasons and also so that potential purchasers recognize and are comfortable with the structure and style of offering documents. The underwriter and its counsel should discuss the style and content of the initial draft of the offering document, so that it effectively introduces the scope of disclosure that the underwriter and counsel determine is appropriate. Depending on the structure of the financing and marketing needs, there may be a preliminary official statement and a final official statement or just a final official statement. Underwriter's counsel generally also oversees printing and distribution of the offering document, so it is important to work with the underwriter to make sure timing expectations for delivery of the offering document are met.

Bond Purchase Agreement

The bond purchase agreement sets forth the financial and business terms of the underwriting agreement between the issuer and the underwriter and the conduit borrower, if any. The bond purchase agreement provides for the sale of the bonds to the underwriter and specifies the discount or fee the underwriter will receive, the pricing terms of the bonds, the representations and warranties of the issuer and any conduit borrower, the conditions precedent to underwriter's obligation to purchase bonds at closing, the events which enable the underwriter to terminate the bond purchase agreement without purchasing the bonds, the indemnification obligations of the parties, the documents to be delivered at closing, and who will pay what expenses/costs. Many underwriters have internal requirements for certain provisions of the bond purchase agreement such as indemnification, so underwriter's counsel should confirm these requirements before circulating the initial draft.

Continuing Disclosure Agreement

Underwriter's counsel also drafts any continuing disclosure agreement to meet the requirements of Rule 15c2-12. This agreement contains the undertakings of the issuer (and any obligated persons) to provide ongoing annual financial and operating data disclosure and timely event notices of certain events if material. The undertakings are made for the benefit of and are enforceable by the bondholders. The agreement may be between the obligated persons on the bonds and a dissemination agent (often a trustee) who agrees to disseminate information to the required repositories on behalf of the obligated persons or may be an undertaking of the obligated persons to disseminate the information with no dissemination agent involved.

Remarketing Agreement

In a variable rate financing, underwriter's counsel often drafts a remarketing agreement pursuant to which the remarketing agent (an investment bank and often the underwriter for the bonds) agrees to use its best efforts to remarket for a fee any bonds that are tendered. It should be clear from the agreement that there is no duty or obligation to successfully remarket, but just to use best efforts. The remarketing agreement must be coordinated with the bond indenture (or ordinance or resolution, as applicable), so that the timing and duties of the remarketing agent meet the requirements set forth in the bond indenture and disclosed in the offering document for re-marketing of the bonds. The remarketing agreement also protects the re-marketing agent by specifying the conditions under which the remarketing agent may suspend its duties, the indemnification provisions, and the duty of the issuer (or conduit borrower) to provide updated disclosure to the remarketing agent. Many underwriters have developed standard forms of remarketing agreements or at least termination provisions and indemnification, so underwriter's counsel should check with the underwriter before preparing the initial draft.

Agreement Among Underwriters

This agreement governs the relationship among the managing underwriter and the other designated underwriters setting forth the original participation amount of each, the financial agreement among the parties and the responsibilities of each of the parties. The agreement among underwriters is often drafted by counsel to the underwriter and is based on standard industry forms. Counsel must select the correct form for the type of underwriting. Depending on the financing, underwriter's counsel may also draft a *master selling group agreement* governing the selling group relationship and based on a standard industry form.[10]

REVIEW OF OTHER BOND DOCUMENTS

Underwriter's counsel also reviews all of the documents prepared by other counsels in the financing to make sure the interests of the underwriter are protected, that the financing documents work together and that the financing meets applicable legal requirements. These documents may include some or all of the following: a bond indenture; an ordinance or resolution; one or more loan agreements; a master indenture; a mortgage; escrow agreements;

---

[10] These forms are available on the Securities Industry and Financial Markets Association (SIFMA) web site.

reimbursement agreements; bond insurance policies; letters of credit; auction documents; and various closing documents.

BLUE SKY

Each state has its own laws for sale of securities. These laws are designed to prevent fraudulent practices and may impose requirements such as registration of entities selling or offering securities, registration of the securities or notice of sale. In a number of cases, municipal securities are exempt from state securities registration. The type of sales (institutional versus retail) will impact the application of the blue sky laws. The National Securities Markets Improvement Act of 1996 (NSMIA) amended the 1933 Act to preempt important areas of the blue sky laws affecting national markets. The effect of NSMIA is that municipal securities are included as "covered securities."

The states are prohibited from regulating covered securities, with certain exceptions. One significant exception is that a municipal security is not deemed to be a covered security in the state in which the issuer is located.

As a result, with the exception of the state in which the bonds are offered, the state securities laws may only require a filing of certain information and the payment of a fee. Underwriter's counsel usually takes the lead in reviewing the state laws and determining in which states, if any, action should be taken. Underwriter's counsel prepares a document called a blue sky survey which confirms which states will require action for sale of the bonds, which will not require action and in which states the underwriter has instructed counsel to proceed with the required action. The underwriter's counsel assists the underwriter with any required filings. Finally, counsel prepares a final blue sky survey which summarizes as of closing which states have been cleared for sale of the bonds. In addition, it is important to begin early enough that any filings required can be complete in time for the underwriter to undertake sales in those states.

OPINION

Underwriter's counsel is generally expected to deliver an opinion to the underwriter and in certain cases to the issuer either directly or through a reliance letter. The opinion usually covers three issues. First, it addresses the fact that neither the sale of the bonds to the underwriter nor the resale of the bonds by the underwriter to the public requires that the bonds be registered under the 1933 Act. Second, the opinion often has language to the effect that the bond indenture need not be qualified under the Indenture

Act. Third, it includes what is known as the 10b-5 opinion. A 10b-5 opinion generally outlines certain actions taken by underwriter's counsel in the financing and then has language to the effect that on the basis of the foregoing actions, but without independent verification of factual matters, nothing has come to the attention of such counsel that would lead them to believe that the official statement, as of its date and as of the date of issuance, contains any untrue statement of material fact or omits to state any material fact necessary to make the statements therein, in light of the circumstances under which they were made, not misleading. The 10b-5 opinion generally explicitly excludes financial and statistical data and lists certain sections of the official statement excluded from the opinion. In addition, underwriters may ask their counsel to opine that any continuing disclosure undertaking meets the requirements of Rule 15c2-12 for such an undertaking.

SUMMARY

Municipal financings are very complex and it is important that each counsel involved takes its role seriously. Underwriter's counsel not only contributes to the structure of a financing, but takes the lead for the legal team on securities law compliance and drafting disclosure on the important details of credit and structure of the financing. Underwriter's counsel needs to ask the difficult questions in a financing so that material issues are identified, explored, and disclosed in the offering document. All of the responsibilities of underwriter's counsel discussed in this chapter contribute to an effective and legally compliant financing.

CHAPTER 7

Summary of Federal Tax Requirements for Tax-Exempt Bonds

Perry E. Israel, J.D., LLM
Law Office of Perry Israel

This chapter provides a very broad outline of the federal income tax rules relating to tax-exempt municipal bonds. The topics covered include the rules relating to arbitrage, the private activity bond rules, and the remaining miscellaneous rules, including special rules for advance refunding bond issues.

The Internal Revenue Code (the Code) and the Income Tax Regulations (the Regulations) lay out a complex set of rules that govern whether the interest on municipal bonds will be excluded from gross income under Section 103[1] of the Code (i.e., whether the bonds will be what are generally called *tax-exempt bonds*). In typical convoluted fashion, the Code first provides that interest on obligations (bonds, notes, or other things treated as debt obligations for federal tax purposes, such as certain financing leases) issued by a state or local government will be excluded from gross income,[2] but then goes on to say that such interest will not be exempt if the bonds are private activity bonds, arbitrage bonds, or otherwise fail to meet other requirements.[3] Then the Code says that even private activity bonds may be tax exempt if they are "qualified private activity bonds," but the interest on such bonds will generally (but not always) be treated as a special preference item for purposes of the alternative minimum tax.[4]

---

[1] Even if interest on a municipal bond is excluded from federal gross income under Section 103, it may still be subject to special treatment under the alternative minimum tax or other specialized provisions of the Code, depending upon the tax status of the holder.

[2] Code Section 103(a).

[3] Code Section 103 generally.

[4] Code Section 57(a)(5).

All the provisions in the Code relating to the tax-exempt status of municipal bonds used to be contained in Section 103.[5] Originally, Section 103 was very short. However, beginning in 1968, Congress amended and added to Section 103, until by 1985, Section 103 was one of the longest sections in the Code. In the 1986 Tax Reform Act, Congress restructured the provisions relating to municipal bonds and spread them out through a number of sections of the Code.[6] As if the increasing complexity of the rules relating to tax-exempt bonds was not enough, since the mid-1990s the Internal Revenue Service has taken a much more active role in regulating tax-exempt municipal bonds. This has resulted in a substantial audit program, including fairly in-depth review of the investment and use of bond proceeds, and in some cases substantial settlement payments being made by issuers, bond counsel, underwriters, investment providers, and others to either preserve the tax-exempt status of a particular issue or to settle claims made under Code Section 6700.[7] In addition, the Securities and Exchange Commission and the Justice Department have also brought various actions or started investigations relating to alleged violations of the federal tax rules relating to bonds.[8]

As a result of the complex rules and fairly aggressive regulatory activities relating to tax-exempt bonds, it is important that qualified tax counsel be involved in any issuance of tax-exempt bonds (and potentially with respect to post-issuance matters) and also that participants in the municipal bond market have a general understanding of the federal tax rules relating to tax-exempt bonds. With such a general understanding, underwriters, investors, issuers, and others may have the chance to identify transactions that may raise potential tax questions and at least have the opportunity to question tax counsel and others to make sure that the transaction would have a good chance of surviving regulatory scrutiny. This chapter provides a very basic general background of the federal income tax rules relating to tax-exempt bonds. It should not be relied upon for ultimate determination of the tax status of bonds, but can at least be used for spotting issues.

As a general rule, the federal tax rules relating to municipal bonds can be roughly divided into three areas: arbitrage (or the rules relating to the

---

[5] Accordingly, lawyers specializing in the tax aspects of bonds are often called "103 lawyers."

[6] Generally, Sections 103 and 141–150, although there are special sections relating, for example, to Gulf Opportunity Zone bonds, New York Liberty Zone bonds, and Clean Renewable Energy Bonds, among others.

[7] Code Section 6700 relates to penalties imposed upon certain types of tax-shelter promoters. The IRS has taken the position that tax-exempt bonds are tax shelters within the meaning of Code Section 6700.

[8] See, for example, *Weiss v. SEC*, D.C. Court of Appeals, November 28, 2006.

investment and expenditure of bond proceeds), private activity (or the rules relating to the use of bond proceeds or facilities financed with bond proceeds), and other general rules (which include rules relating to who may issue tax-exempt bonds, refundings of tax-exempt bonds, and other miscellaneous matters). This chapter will follow that structure, even though it may not be clearly indicated in the Code or Regulations. Further information relating to the federal income tax rules are available from several other sources, including *Federal Taxation of Municipal Bonds* (Lexis/Nexis), prepared by an editorial committee of the National Association of Bond Lawyers.

ARBITRAGE[9]

Because municipalities are generally exempt from federal income tax, there is a natural "tax arbitrage" advantage created by the tax-exempt status of the interest on municipal bonds. Assume, for example, that an issuer of bonds invests its bond proceeds in United States Treasury obligations and pledges the earnings on the Treasuries to the repayment of the debt service on the bonds. Assuming an adequate pledge, the municipal bonds should enjoy the same AAA rating as the Treasuries. However, from the investor's point of view, the municipal obligations will typically be a much better investment than the Treasuries because the investor will not need to pay federal income tax on interest earned on the municipal obligations. Assuming a 35% marginal federal tax rate for the investor, if the investor would be willing to take, say, a 5% taxable return on an investment in Treasuries, the same investor should be willing to take a 3.25% return on the tax-exempt municipal obligations (i.e., 65% of 5%).[10] However, the municipality, which enjoys an exemption from federal income tax, would be happy to invest in the Treasuries at 5%, paying 65% of the return to the holders of the bonds and keeping the remaining 35% as a pure "arbitrage profit."

Congress and Treasury recognized in the late 1960s the opportunity for such tax arbitrage, and Congress ultimately adopted a law generally denying the luxury of tax exemption to bonds issued for the purpose of investing

[9] This chapter deals only with *tax arbitrage*—the arbitrage created by the difference between taxable and tax-exempt rates and the fact that issuers of municipal obligations are generally exempt from federal income taxation. Any reference to arbitrage should be taken solely as a reference to tax arbitrage and not, for example, to risk arbitrage or other market arbitrage opportunities.

[10] Of course, other factors may influence the investor's decision. For example, if the investor were afraid that Congress might amend the tax law in the future to eliminate the tax-exempt status of her investment or reduce taxes so that that investor's marginal tax rate would go down, the investor would take that tax risk into account in calculating the return she requires on her tax-exempt investment.

the proceeds at a yield that is higher than the yield on the bonds.[11] Munici-palities pointed out, however, that in most cases they were not issuing bonds in order to invest the proceeds, but to finance projects, and that acquiring yield-restricted investments would be difficult in many typical situations, including investments pending expenditures and investments in reserve funds.[12] Congress agreed, providing that there were a number of situations where a municipality could invest at an unrestricted yield.[13] At that point, municipalities, bankers, and lawyers started to become very creative to seize permitted arbitrage opportunities, and Treasury and IRS started to draw lines as to what was and was not permitted, typically about two or three years after a particular structure was developed. Finally, in the 1986 Tax Reform Act, Congress passed an additional arbitrage rule—the rebate rule, which generally provides that even if a municipality is permitted to invest at a yield above the yield on the bonds, it must generally pay its arbitrage earnings to the Treasury Department in the form of a 100% "rebate" tax on arbitrage profits.[14]

Yield Restriction Rules

The general yield restriction rule relating to tax-exempt bonds is that gross proceeds of a bond issue may not be used directly or indirectly to acquire investments with a yield materially higher than the yield on the bonds or to replace funds used to acquire investments with a yield materially higher than the bonds.[15] Thus, under the general rule, an issuer must identify what the "gross proceeds" of the bond issue are, determine the yield on the issue of bonds, and ensure that the gross proceeds are not used to acquire "invest-ments" with a yield "materially higher" than the yield on the bonds. How-ever, there are also significant exceptions to the yield restriction rule. These exceptions essentially take over the entire rule. Accordingly, as a practical matter, the best approach to determining compliance with the yield restric-tion rule is to identify the gross proceeds of the bond issue and generally identify what exception will apply to allow those proceeds to be invested at an unrestricted yield. Only if an issuer cannot find an applicable exception will it need to determine whether the proceeds are used to acquire invest-ments with a yield materially higher than the yield on the bonds.

---

[11] Today, those rules are contained in Section 148 of the Code.

[12] In addition, municipalities they felt that they should not be denied the opportu-nity to invest and make arbitrage profits pending the expenditure of the proceeds.

[13] See, e.g., Code Section 148(c), (d), and (e).

[14] See Code Section 148(f).

[15] Code Section 148(a).

Identifying Gross Proceeds

Many proceeds of a bond issue are relatively easy to identify. For example, the amounts received by the issuer from the sale of the bonds are easily identified as proceeds of the issue.[16] However, *gross proceeds* is a more encompassing term—it includes amounts that are not only "proceeds" of a bond issue, but also all amounts that might be "replacement proceeds" of the bond issue.

Proceeds consists of the sale proceeds (i.e., all amounts received from the sale of the bonds to the ultimate holders of the bonds in the initial offering[17]), *transferred proceeds*, and *investment proceeds*.[18] Transferred proceeds only arise when the proceeds of a bond issue are used to pay principal of another bond issue (the "prior issue") and consist of a pro rata amount of the unspent proceeds of the prior issue.[19] For example, if proceeds of a refunding issue are used on a particular date to pay one-third of the outstanding principal of the prior issue, one-third of all unspent proceeds of the prior issue become proceeds of the refunding issue. "Investment proceeds" consist of any amounts received from the investment of proceeds (including the reinvestment of investment proceeds).[20] Thus, "proceeds" generally means amounts that can be traced directly back to the sale of a bond issue or the investment of such amounts.

Replacement proceeds is a broader concept and consists of moneys that cannot be directly traced to the sale of bonds, but that nonetheless have some close relationship with the bonds so that the rules of the Internal Revenue Service will cause them to be treated as if they were proceeds.[21] For example, suppose that a college has raised funds to pay for a new geology building. Before the moneys are spent, however, the college is approached by an investment banker alumus who proposes that, rather than spending that money, the college issue tax-exempt bonds to pay for the geology building and invest the moneys that were raised through the fundraising in lucrative investments. The moneys raised through the capital campaign will be treated as "replacement proceeds" of the bonds because of the close *nexus*

---

[16] Regulation Section 1.148-1(b) defines these to be *sale proceeds*.

[17] And thus, sale proceeds technically includes amounts that may never be paid to the issuer of the bonds, such as amounts retained by the underwriter as *underwriters' discount* or compensation and amounts paid by the underwriter to a monoline bond insurer.

[18] Regulation Section 1.148-1(b).

[19] Regulation Section 1.148-9(b) describes the transfer mechanism is some detail.

[20] Regulation Section 1.148-1(b).

[21] See, generally, Regulation Section 1.148-1(c). Replacement proceeds can be created by an issuer, a conduit borrower, or another person who is related to the issuer or conduit borrower.

between the purpose for the bonds and the purpose for the capital campaign.[22] In addition to this *classic replacement* situation, there are four other situations where moneys other than proceeds will be treated as replacement proceeds of a bond issue:

- Moneys that are expected to be used to pay debt service on the bonds are treated as replacement proceeds, regardless of whether those moneys are pledged to the bondholders (so-called *sinking fund proceeds*).
- Moneys that are pledged to provide security for the bondholders (or persons providing credit support for the bonds) are treated as replacement proceeds if the moneys are pledged in a manner that provides reasonable assurance that the amount will be available to pay principal or interest on the bonds in the event of financial difficulties of the issuer or borrower. Thus, moneys set aside in a bond reserve fund, even if not funded with bond proceeds, will likely be treated as replacement proceeds of the bonds. A pledge of a general fund will not necessarily give rise to *pledge proceeds*. However, if the issuer or borrower retains the ability to spend moneys in the general fund for its general purposes and is not required to maintain any particular balance in the general fund.
- A requirement that an issuer or borrower maintain a cash balance in any particular amount with a covenant that it not pledge that balance to another other persons or grant superior rights to those of the bondholder or credit providers will give rise to pledge proceeds because of the *negative pledge* unless (1) the balance required to be maintained is reasonable for the issuer given the particular demands that might occur in its industry (for example, a hospital may generally need to maintain a 90 days' cash balance for rating and other purposes); (2) the issuer has the ability to spend the cash down below that level with no adverse effect other than the requirement that it be replenished by the next testing date; and (3) the balance is tested no more frequently than every six months.
- If the bonds remain outstanding longer than necessary to accomplish the governmental purpose of the bonds and the issuer or conduit borrower accumulates other funds during the time the bonds are outstanding that could be applied by issuer for any of its general purposes without the requirement that those amounts be replenished, the *available amounts* that accumulate will be treated as *other replacement proceeds*

---

[22] Whether the moneys raised in the capital campaign will be treated as "replacement proceeds" should be carefully examined by bond counsel. For example, if the capital campaign was to create an endowment fund to provide for programs in the new geology building, it is unlikely that they would be treated as replacement proceeds of bonds issued to finance the actual construction of the geology building.

(or ORPs). There is a safe harbor against the creation of ORPs that applies if the weighted average maturity of bonds that finance a capital project is no more than 120% of the of weighted average useful life of the capital project. ORPs most commonly arise in the context of long-term working capital financings, and any issuer or banker contemplating a long-term financing of noncapital assets should consult early and often with tax counsel.

In summary, gross proceeds consist of amounts received from the sale of the bonds and investments of such amounts, amounts expected to be used to pay debt service on the bonds, amounts pledged to secure the bonds, and various other funds (transferred proceeds and classic replacement amounts). Having identified those amounts, the question next is, may they be invested without regard to yield?

Exceptions to the Yield Restriction Rules

Congress recognized that complying with the yield restriction rules would be particularly onerous on issuers of bonds. Moreover, it was not anticipated that issuers would generally issue bonds solely for the purpose of investing and receiving an arbitrage profit. Accordingly, after fairly strenuous lobbying by municipalities, Congress provided fairly generous exceptions allowing gross proceeds to be invested at an unrestricted yield provided that the amounts were small enough or invested for a short enough period of time. This gave rise to three areas of exception to the yield restriction rule: temporary periods, reasonably required reserve and replacement funds, and the "minor portion."

Temporary Periods[23]   There are many different temporary periods during which and issuer may invest gross proceeds at an unrestricted yield. One of the most useful is the temporary period relating to the investment of bond proceeds pending their expenditure for acquisition or construction of capital projects—the so-called *three-year temporary period*.[24] To qualify for the three-year temporary period, an issuer must incur a binding obligation no later than six months after the date the bonds are issued that commits the issuer to spend at least 5% of the proceeds of the bonds of the net sale proceeds,[25] the issuer must reasonably expect to allocate at least 85% of the net sale proceeds to expenditures for the capital projects within

---

[23] See, generally, Code Section 148(c) and Regulation Section 1.148-2(e).
[24] Regulation Section 1.148-e)(2).
[25] Sale proceeds less costs of issuance, amounts deposited in a reasonably required reserve or replacement fund, and amounts invested pursuant to the minor portion.

the three[26] years following the date of issuance of the bonds, and the issuer must expect to proceed with the capital projects and the allocation of net sale proceeds to expenditures with due diligence.

Another useful temporary period applies to "bona fide debt service funds."[27] Remember that any moneys expected to be used to pay debt service on the bonds will be treated as replacement proceeds of the bonds. However, it is fairly common for an issuer to collect amounts to be used to pay current debt service in advance of payment, either in special bond funds or in the issuer's general fund. Notwithstanding the general yield restriction rule, these amounts may be invested without regard to yield to the extent that the amounts that are collected are used primarily to achieve a proper matching of revenues with principal and interest payments within each bond year and they are depleted at least once each bond year (except for a reasonable amount not to exceed the greater of the earnings on the fund for the immediately preceding bond year or 1/12th of the principal and interest payments on the issue for the immediately preceding bond year).

There are other special temporary periods for pooled financings,[28] replacement proceeds,[29] investment proceeds,[30] and other amounts not otherwise qualifying for temporary periods.[31] These are not widely used. The other temporary period used fairly frequently is the temporary period relating to "restricted working capital" borrowings[32]—in general, borrowings to finance temporary shortfalls in revenues, often referred to as *TRANs* or tax or revenue anticipation notes. The regulations provide in general for a 13-month temporary period for such working capital borrowings.[33]

Reasonably Required Reserve or Replacement Fund[34]   In addition to the generous temporary period rules, the Code and Regulations also provide for an exception to the yield restriction rule for investments in a "reasonably

---

[26] There is a special exception for long-term capital projects requiring more than three years to complete where both the issuer and a licensed architect or engineer certify that a longer period (no greater than five years) is required to complete the project), but this is rarely used.

[27] Regulation Section 1.148-2(e)(6).

[28] Regulation Section 1.148-e)(4).

[29] Regulation Section 1.148-e)(5).

[30] Generally, one year from the date of receipt. Regulation Section 1.148-2(e)(6).

[31] Generally, 30 days. Regulation Section 1.148-e)(7).

[32] Regulation Section 1.148-2(e)(3).

[33] It should be noted that a relatively minor amount of a capital project financing can be used for working capital costs relating to capital project, such as startup costs. These amounts qualify for the three-year temporary period if the capital project qualifies for the three-year temporary period.

[34] See, generally, Code Section 148(d) and Regulation Section 1.148-2(f).

required reserve or replacement fund" (also called a *4-R fund*). If a reserve fund is "reasonably required" (presumably for purposes other than generating arbitrage), amounts in it may be invested without regard to yield provided that the reserve is not greater than the least of (1) 10% of the stated principal amount[35] of the bond issue; (2) maximum annual debt service on the bond issue; and (3) 125% of the average annual debt service on the bond issue. A special rule prohibits using more than 10% of the sales proceeds to fund the 4-R fund and any other reserves.[36]

Minor Portion[37] Finally, the Code provides that a very small amount of bond proceeds (not in excess of the lesser of 5% of the sale proceeds of the issue or $100,000) may be invested without regard to yield even if no other exceptions apply. This rule can be useful to help with inadvertent investments that could otherwise cause the bonds to fail to qualify for tax-exempt status.

Refunding Bonds The temporary period and 4-R fund rules are modified when applied to bonds that are used to pay principal, interest, or call premium on other tax-exempt bonds (so-called *refunding bonds*).[38] In general, the temporary period for a current refunding issue (where the refunded bonds will be repaid within 90 days after the date the refunding bonds are issued) cannot exceed 90 days. Advance refunding bond issues may have a temporary period of no more than 30 days, although this is usually waived.[39] Transferred proceeds to a current refunding issue continue to get the remainder of the temporary period that would have applied to them without regard to the refunding. Transferred proceeds to an advance refunding issue lose any remaining temporary period when the advance refunding bonds are issued. If both the refunded issue and the refunding issue have a 4-R fund, the total amount that may be invested at an unrestricted yield cannot exceed the amount that could have been invested in a R fund for the refunding bonds.

Conclusion Between the temporary period rules, the 4-R fund rules, and the minor portion rules, most gross proceeds from most bond issues will be able to be invested at an unrestricted yield. Thus, the exceptions generally render the overall prohibition inapplicable. The only cases where yield

---

[35] If the issue has net original issue discount exceeding 2%, sale proceeds is used rather than stated principal amount.
[36] Code Section 148(d)(2).
[37] See, generally, Code Section 148(e) and Regulation Section 1.148-2(g).
[38] Regulation Section 1.148-9(d), (e), and (f).
[39] See Regulation Section 1.148-9(g).

restriction is likely to apply are (1) advance refundings; (2) bond issues involving substantial amounts of replacement funds; (3) bond issues financing very long-term projects; and (4) bond issues providing long-term financing for working capital purposes. In each of those cases it is important to determine the yield on the bonds and the yield on the investments purchased with gross proceeds of the bonds.

Determining Yield on Bonds and Investments[40]

If bonds have gross proceeds that do not qualify for investment at an unrestricted yield,[41] the issuer will need to calculate (or have someone else calculate) the yield on the bonds. In addition, if the gross proceeds are subject to yield restriction, yield will need to be calculated on the investments made with the gross proceeds to insure that the yield is not "materially higher" than the yield on the bonds.

The yield on an issue of fixed rate bonds is the discount rate that, when used to calculate the net present value of all future expected payments of principal and interest payments on the bonds gives a value equal to the issue price of the bonds. Present value is calculated using the normal formula ($PV = FV/((1 + i)^n)$), where i is the discount rate and n is the number of compounding periods). The regulations allow the issuer to use any compounding period it chooses, so long as the same compounding period is used for computing the yield on the bonds and the yield on the investments of gross proceeds. For a typical fixed rate bond paying interest semiannually, it is most common to use semiannual compounding. Bond yield is typically computed at the time of the issuance of the bonds and takes into account all future expected payments and expected payment dates as of the closing, including all mandatory prepayments and contingent prepayments that are reasonably expected to occur. Thus, for example, yield is computed taking into account sinking fund payments on term bonds.[42] The yield on a fixed yield bond issue is not recomputed to take into account actual facts that differ from expectations. However, if the issuer later sells or purchases any rights relating to the bonds (for example, sells a call waiver), a special rule

---

[40] The regulations relating to bond yield calculation are generally contained in Regulation Section 1.148-4. The regulations relating to calculation of yield on investments are generally contained in Regulation Section 1.148-5.

[41] Or if the bonds are not exempt from the rebate requirement, described below.

[42] Future expectations as to payments are subject to special rules if callable bonds are sold with a premium in excess of 25 basis points times the number of whole years to the first call date. Special rules also apply to bonds subject to option redemption within the five-year period following the issue date and callable bonds that bear a stated interest rate that increases in the future.

requires that the bonds be treated as if redeemed and reissued, with a new yield calculation.

The issue price of the bonds used in computing yield is generally defined to be the first price (for each group of substantially identical bonds, such as a particular maturity) at which at least 10% of those bonds is sold to the public. For this purpose, the public does not include investment bankers, bond traders, brokers, or similar organizations. Thus, tax counsel will generally ask the underwriter or winning bidder with respect to bonds to certify the prices at which the bonds were reoffered to the public and that at least 10% of each maturity was sold at those prices. However, it is often necessary to compute the yield on the bonds before any of the bonds have been resold to the public. For example, in an advance refunding, where all of the proceeds deposited into the refunding escrow must be invested at no more than the yield on the bonds, it is necessary to know the yield on the bonds in order to compute how much proceeds will have to be deposited into the escrow. For that purpose, Treasury provided a special rule that states that the issue price of bonds for which a bona fide public offering is made is determined as of the sale date of the bonds based on reasonable expectations regarding the initial public offering price.[43] Bankers should be prepared to explain to tax counsel why actual resale prices[44] differ from expectations as of the sale date, so it can be established that the expectations as of the sale date were reasonable.

The yield on a variable yield issue[45] is, by contrast, computed retrospectively, taking into account the actual payments of principal and interest on the bonds. In addition, the outstanding unpaid principal amount of the bonds on each computation date is treated as retired on that date for an amount equal to the value of the bonds[46] and also reissued on that date for purposes of the next yield computation. For a variable yield issue, yield must be computed no less frequently than once every five years. During the first five years, the issue may compute bond yield as frequently as once a year or may group two or more years together in calculating yield. However, after the fifth anniversary (or after the first date selected as a rebate payment date, see below), the issuer must compute yield every five years. If all of the bonds of a variable yield issue are converted to fixed or if all variable rate components are paid off and only fixed rate components remain, the issue is treated as paid off and reissued for its outstanding value, a final yield

---

[43] See the definition of "issue price" in Regulation Section 1.148-1(b).

[44] Shown, for example, at the Securities Industry and Financial Markets Association (SIFMA) web site, investinginbonds.com.

[45] Defined to be any bond issue that has any variable yield bonds as part of its components.

[46] Typically, either face value or accreted value, depending upon the amount of discount or premium at which the bonds were issued.

calculation is done with respect to the variable rate bonds, and yield on any remaining bonds is computed as of that date as if it were a newly issued fixed yield bond issue.[47]

In computing the yield on either fixed or variable rate bonds, amounts paid for *qualified guarantees* may be treated as if they were additional interest paid on the bonds.[48] Thus, the amount paid for a bond insurance policy, a reserve fund surety bonds, or a letter of credit providing credit or liquidity for the bonds may be taken into account when computing yield (increasing the yield on the bonds). There are a number of technical rules relating to having a qualified guarantee. The most important of these are that the cost of the guarantee must be expected to be less than the amount of interest saved on the bonds as a result of having the guarantee and the guarantor must not be a related party to the issuer (or the conduit borrower). For variable rate bonds, the cost of any nonperiodic guarantee fees (such as an up-front insurance premium) must be allocated to each year that the guaranteed bonds are outstanding.

Similar to qualified guarantees, so-called *qualified hedges*, such as interest rate swaps, may also be taken into account in computing the yield on the bonds.[49] For a swap or other hedge to be treated as a qualified hedge (taken into account in computing yield), a number of requirements must be met:

- The contract must be entered into primarily to modify the issuer's risk of interest rate changes with respect to one or more bonds.
- If the bond issue is a fixed rate issue (without regard to the hedge), the hedge must be entered into with certain time periods, generally no later than 15 days after the issue date.
- The hedge may not have a significant investment element. The regulations generally provide that a hedge will be treated as having a significant investment element if a significant portion of any payment by one party relates to an obligation to the other party (conditional or unconditional) to make a payment at another time. For example, a typical interest rate cap, where a single fixed payment is made by one party in exchange for the other party agreeing to make payments if interest rates exceed a threshold will be treated as having a significant investment element and will not be treated as a qualified hedge.
- The counterparty to the hedge agreement cannot be related to the issuer.

---

[47] There are special yield computation rules that apply to qualified mortgage bonds, qualified veterans' mortgage bonds, and student loan bonds. Regulation Section 1.148-4(g).

[48] Regulation Section 1.148-4(f),

[49] Regulation Section 1.148-4(h).

- The hedge must cover, in whole or in part, all of one or more groups of substantially identical bonds. Thus, for example, an issuer may hedge 30% of all identical bonds, but cannot hedge 100% of 30% of the bonds and leave the other 70% unhedged.
- The contract must be primarily interest based. The regulations state that a contract will not be primarily interest based unless, prior to hedging, the bonds meet certain definitions relating to fixed rate bonds or variable rate debt instruments and, after the hedging, the combination of the bonds and the hedge results in payments that would be made on fixed rate or certain variable rate debt instruments.
- The payments under the hedge must closely correspond in time to the interest payment dates that are being hedged.
- The payments made under the hedge by the issuer must be expected to come from the same source that the interest payments on the bonds will come from.
- The issuer must identify the hedge with the bonds no later than three days after the date on which the hedge is entered into (that is, no later than three days after the trade date, not the documentation date).

If all of these requirements are met, the net payments (whether to or from the issuer) under the hedge contract will be treated as additional payments on the bonds in computing the yield on the bonds.[50] In addition, if all of the variable rate bonds in the issue are hedged and, taking into account the hedge, it is expected that all payments made and received with respect to the bonds will be fixed and determinable, the hedge may be "superintegrated" and the bonds will be treated as a fixed yield issue from the date they are issued.[51]

Hedges entered into in anticipation of the issuance of bonds in the future may also be treated as qualified hedges if certain other requirements are met. Again, most importantly, the hedge must be identified by the issuer of the bonds in writing no later than three days after the hedge is entered into. Issuers or bankers considering the use of "anticipatory" hedges should consult early with tax counsel.

Computation of yield on investments generally follows the rules relating to computation of yield on bonds—yield on fixed yield investments is computed at the time the investments are acquired, based upon the acquisition price, and yield on variable yield investments is computed from time to

---

[50] There are special rules relating to termination payments.

[51] Because of some uncertainty about how the fixed and determinable rule is applied, typically only a BMA-based swap will result in variable rate bonds being superintegrated. Treasury has agreed to address concerns relating to superintegration of LIBOR-based swaps in the tax-exempt market, but has yet to do so.

time based upon actual payments made.[52] However, there are a number of important rules that should be kept in mind.

- If investments are not purchased at fair market value, the IRS may substitute what it believes fair market value to be when computing the yield on the investments. The regulations provide certain safe harbors for determining purchase price, in general involving bona fide bidding, in writing, with the lowest price (or highest yield) winning. It is important to be scrupulous in following the bidding requirements—the IRS, the SEC, and the Justice Department have all started investigations relating to bid-rigging allegations. In addition, investments purchased directly from the U.S. Treasury Department, such as Treasury Obligations—State and Local Government Series (or SLGS), will be deemed to have been purchased for fair market value.
- As a general rule, yield on all obligations of the same "class"[53] is determined on a composite basis. For example, all investments in a yield-restricted refunding escrow, whether or not held concurrently, are treated as a single investment with a single yield.
- No asset hedges are taken into account in computing yield on investments made with gross proceeds.
- For certain types of investments (generally not involving advance refundings), an issuer may make *yield reduction payments* to the Treasury Department to reduce the yield on the investments or the class to a permissible level.

As mentioned above, the yield restriction rule says that yield-restricted investment cannot have a yield that is materially higher than the yield on the bonds. In general, investments have a yield that is materially higher than the yield on the bonds if they have a yield that is more than 12.5 basis points higher than the yield on the bonds.[54] However, special rules apply to certain types of investments. Investment in refunding escrows or investments of replacement proceeds may not have a yield that exceeds the yield on the bonds by more than 1/1,000th of a percentage point. Investments in program investments may have a yield that is up to 150 basis points higher than the yield on the bonds. (A program investment is an obligation that must be acquired by the issuer to accomplish the governmental purpose of the issue, such as a loan made to a hospital for a qualified 501(c)(3) bond issue. Additional rules apply to qualify as a program investment.) The yield on student

---

[52] See, generally, Regulation Section 1.148-5.
[53] Each category of yield restricted purpose investments, yield-restricted nonpurpose investments, and all other nonpurpose investments are treated as separate classes.
[54] See Regulation Section 1.148-2(d) for definitions of *materially higher yield*.

loans acquired with tax-exempt student loan bonds may not exceed the yield on the bonds by more than 200 basis points. The yield on mortgage loans acquired with qualified mortgage bonds cannot exceed the yield on the bonds by more than 112.5 basis points. Finally, if an issuer uses bond proceeds to acquire other nonAMT tax-exempt obligations, no yield limitation applies. It should also be noted that, except for investments in nonAMT tax-exempt obligations, the permitted spread that is less than materially higher is still subject to the rebate requirement described below.

Proceeds that are allocated[55] to expenditures are no typically no longer treated as invested. However, there are certain types of expenditures that are treated as investments. These include expenditures for the purchase of annuity contracts or similar arrangements; the use of proceeds of a governmental bond to purchase residential rental property for family units which is not located within the jurisdiction of the issuer; and noncustomary prepayments. Special rules have been developed, however, for prepayments for natural gas and electricity prepayments.[56] These rules are complicated and any transaction involving such a prepayment such be carefully analyzed by tax counsel.

Rebate Requirement

In 1986, Congress decided that the yield restriction rules were not working properly and that issuers were undertaking too many transactions solely or in large part to take advantage of the permitted tax arbitrage. Accordingly, Congress imposed a new arbitrage rule: the rebate requirement.[57] In large part, this rule effectively imposes a tax on issuers of bonds equal to 100% of any tax arbitrage earned.

General Rule

The general rebate rule states that, even though an issuer may be permitted to earn arbitrage on the investment of nonpurpose investments[58] under the yield

---

[55] The regulations contain a special set of rules relating to the allocation of gross proceeds to investments and expenditures. In general, an issuer is provided with a great deal of flexibility in allocating proceeds to capital expenditures, including direct tracing or any other method of accounting for gross proceeds being spent for particular capital purposes. See Regulation Section 1.148-6.

[56] See Code Section 148(b)(4) and Regulation Section 1.148-1(e)(2)(iii).

[57] Today, this rule is contained in Code Section 148(f) and in Regulation Sections 1.148-3, 1.148-7, and 1.148-8.

[58] *Nonpurpose investments* are all investments other than those that must be made to accomplish the governmental purpose of the issue. *Purpose investments* are limited to those loans or investments required to accomplish the governmental purpose of the bonds, such as student loans, qualified mortgage loans, and loans to conduit borrowers.

restriction rule or because of the permitted materially higher spread, all those earnings must be paid to the Treasury Department to maintain the tax-exempt status of the bonds. There are limited exceptions to the rule, described below.

Similar to yield on bonds, rebate is calculated on an actuarial basis. Essentially, the issuer must make a list of all investments and all receipts from investments, do a net future value of those investments and receipts to the computation date at the yield on the bonds, and pay any positive amounts to the Treasury Department. Rebate payments in the amount of 90% of the accrued rebate liability must be made at least once every five years. These payments are also future valued at the yield on the bonds. Within 60 days after the date the last of the bonds in an issue is repaid, a final payment equal to 100% of the accrued rebate liability must be made. If an issuer makes a rebate installment payment and later, because of arbitrage losses, the amount of the liability is reduced, there is a procedure for the issue to recover the overpayments. Interest and penalties apply with respect to underpayments.

As an alternative to calculating rebate, an issuer of qualified construction bonds (described below under the exceptions to rebate) may elect to pay a penalty to the Treasury department equal to 1.5% of the amount of unspent proceeds every six months. Because this effectively results in an assumed arbitrage rate of 300 basis points, it is rare that the election to pay the penalty rather than rebate will be a wise choice.

Exceptions to the Rebate Requirement

Similar to the yield restriction rules, there are a few exceptions to the rebate requirement. These are much more limited than for yield restriction.

The regulations contain three expenditure exceptions to the rebate requirement that excuse the issuer from paying rebate if the proceeds of the bonds are spent fast enough. For each of these exceptions, the issuer can qualify for the exceptions even if the bonds have a reserve fund, but will still have to pay rebate on the reserve. The six-month exception will excuse the issuer from paying rebate if all gross proceeds of the issue are spent within six months after the date the bonds are issued. For this purpose, amounts in a bond fide debt service fund or a 4-R fund do not need to be spent, but will be subject to the normal rebate requirements. Similarly, amounts received by an issuer as payments on a conduit loan (which are also proceeds) do not need to be spent within the six-month period, but subsequent investments of those amounts will be subject to normal rebate requirements. The 18-month exception works just like the six-month exception, except that the issuer must spend at least 15% of the gross proceeds within the first six months after the issue date, a total of 60% of the gross proceeds within the first

12 months, and all[59] of the gross proceeds within the 18 months following closing date. The two-year exception applies only to governmental bonds, qualified 501(c)(3) bonds, and other qualified private activity bonds issued to finance property to be owned by a governmental unit or 501(c)(3) organization and only if at least 75% of the "available construction proceeds" (gross proceeds less amounts held in a reserve fund and or a bona fide debt service fund) are to be spent for construction purposes. Like the 18-month exception, the two-year exception has a spend down schedule: at least 10% within the first six months, 45% within the first 12 months, 75% within the first 18 months, and 100% within two years (and with a similar exception for a reasonable retainage).

All three expenditure exceptions are based upon actual facts, and, in the case of the 18-month and two-year exceptions, each expenditure milestone must actually be met or the entire issue will be subject to rebate. In addition, only the six-month exception is available for refundings. Any multipurpose issue (that is, any issue that both finances new assets and refunds a prior bond issue) will automatically be split into two (or more) issues for determining compliance with the expenditure exception. The issuer also may make a special election if it is financing a construction project where less than 75% of the proceeds will be used for construction purposes. In that case, the issuer may elect at the closing to treat the issue as two different issues for purposes of the expenditure exception: one issue that is at least 75% construction that contains all of the construction expenditures and one issue that may qualify for either the 6-month or 18-month exception. In any event, transferred proceeds of a refunding bond issue will only be eligible for an expenditure exception if that exception is met measured against the date the refunded bonds were issued.

In addition to the expenditure exceptions, a bona fide debt service fund may also be exempt from rebate. For governmental bonds, the bona fide debt service fund is exempt from rebate if the average maturity of the issue is at least five years and the bond issue is a fixed rate issue. For all bonds, the bona fide debt service fund is exempt from rebate in any year in which the gross earnings on the fund is less than $100,000. Treasury regulations state that a bond issue will automatically be treated as meeting the $100,000 test if the annual debt service on the bond issue is not in excess of $2.5 million.

Finally, there is an exception (the "small issuer exception") to the rebate requirement for bonds designated by a governmental unit that meet the following requirements:

---

[59] A special rule states that the 18-month rule will be met even if not all of the proceeds are spent within 18 months provided that the unspent amount is no more than a reasonable retainage not exceeding 5% of the gross proceeds and it is spent within the next 12 months.

- The issuer is a governmental unit with general taxing powers.
- The bonds are governmental bonds.
- At least 98% of the net proceeds of the bond issue (net of 4-R funds) are to be used for local governmental activities of the issuer.
- The aggregate face amount of all tax-exempt bonds (other than private activity bonds) issued by the issuer is not expected to exceed $5 million in the calendar year.

For purposes of the $5 million test, the issuer and all entities that issue on its behalf are treated as a single issuer and all bonds issued by a subordinate entity are treated as issued by the superior entity. Special rules apply to refunding bonds, excluding current refundings from the $5 million limit. Another special rule allows the issuer to issue up to $10 million more of bonds to finance the construction of public school facilities and designate those bonds as additional exempt from rebate.

Special Antiabuse Rules

Because Congress and the Treasury Department have a long history of seeing arbitrage abuses and fighting them retroactively, the current arbitrage regulations contain special antiabuse rules designed to eliminate abusive arbitrage devices and allow the Commissioner to depart from the arbitrage rules "as necessary to clearly reflect the economic substance of the transaction."[60] The abusive arbitrage device rules are designed to prevent issuers from overburdening the tax-exempt bond market and exploiting the difference between tax-exempt and taxable rates to obtain a material advantage. There are examples in the regulations of certain types of "window refundings,"[61] sales of conduit loans, and refundings of noncallable bonds that are treated as abusive arbitrage devices. The authority of the Commission to take other steps to reflect the economic substance of a transaction has not been clearly defined. As of now, this authority seems to be a tool in the IRS examiner's box that has not been widely used.

PRIVATE ACTIVITY BONDS

The other large set of federal tax rules relating to tax-exempt bonds are the private activity bond rules. In essence, the private activity bond rules are designed to insure that entities other than states and local governments

---

[60] Regulation Section 1.148-10.
[61] Refundings that carve out a "window" in debt service to allow investment activity during the period that debt service is reduced or eliminated.

will not benefit from the tax-exempt status of the bonds except for certain preferred types of financings. Thus, the Code provides that private activity bonds are taxable unless they are also "qualified private activity bonds."[62] For all bonds, then, one must determine whether the bonds meet the private activity bond tests. If they do met the private activity bond tests, then the bonds will be taxable unless they also meet the special rules relating to qualified private activity bonds.

Definition of Private Activity Bonds

Bonds meet the private activity bond test (and hence are private activity bonds) if any of three tests are met. These are the "private loan test," the "private business tests," and a special test relating to bonds that have an issue price in excess of $150 million.

Private Loan Test[63]

Bonds meet the private loan test (and are private activity bonds) if more than the lesser of 5% of the proceeds of the bonds or $5 million of the proceeds is loaned directly or indirectly to one or more persons who are not states or political subdivisions or instrumentalities of states or political subdivisions. Any arrangement that is characterized as a "loan" for federal tax purposes is treated as a loan for purposes of the private loan test. For example, if bond proceeds are used to finance a building that is "leased" under a capital lease to a nongovernmental persons and that person is treated as the owner of the building for federal tax purposes, the "lease" will be treated as a loan that was financed with bond proceeds. By the same token, a "forgivable loan" where it is expected that no repayments will ever be made may be treated not as a loan of bond proceeds but as a grant.

A special rule also treats certain prepayments for property or services as a loan if a principal purpose of prepaying is to provide a benefit of tax-exempt financing to the seller.[64] A prepayment is not treated as loan for these purposes if (1) the prepayment is on substantially the same terms as a substantial number of other prepayment arrangements where the persons making the prepayments are not the beneficiaries of tax-exempt financing[65]; (2) the prepayment is made within 90 days of the reasonably expected date of delivery of all of the property or services for which the prepayment is

---

[62] Code Section 103(b)(1).
[63] Generally contained in Code Section 141(c) and Regulation Section 1.141-5.
[64] Regulation Section 1.141-5(c)(ii) and (iii).
[65] This includes prepayments for maintenance, repair, or an extended warranty with respect to person property.

made; or (3) the prepayment meets the special prepayment arbitrage rules (mentioned above) concerning prepayments for natural gas or electricity.

In many states, local governments pay for capital improvements such as streets, curbs, sewers, lighting, schools, and parks by imposing "assessments" against affected landowners. The assessments go by different names in different states. However, for tax purposes, if the assessments are imposed on the basis of benefits conferred, the assessments are not treated as taxes imposed by the local government but are treated as "loans" to the local property owners.[66] The amount loaned is equal to the total amount of the assessment net of any interest charges imposed.[67] Because the assessment is treated as a loan for federal tax purposes, "assessment bonds" or any similar arrangement used to pay for the capital assets would meet the private loan test. However, there is a special exception for assessment bonds in the Code.[68] For this exception to apply, the following requirements must be met:

- The assessment imposed must be mandatory in nature and imposed for a specific purpose.
- The assessment must be used to finance one or more specific, essential governmental functions. Examples include sidewalks, streets and streetlights, electric, telephone, and cable television systems, sewage treatment and disposal systems, and municipal water facilities. The facilities must also be owned by a governmental person and available for use by the general public.
- Owners of both business and nonbusiness property benefiting from the financed improvements must be eligible, or required, to make deferred payments of the assessments on an equal basis. The terms for deferral must be the same for all assessed persons.

If these rules are met, the assessments will not be treated as loans for purposes of the private loan test.

Private Business Tests[69]

Bonds will also be treated as private activity bonds if they meet both of the private business tests. The private business tests consist of the "private busi-

---

[66] See IRS Publication 530.

[67] For example, it would not be uncommon to have an assessment for a new road imposed upon properties adjacent to the road. A typical assessment might be $10,000, with the property owner told she can pay $10,000 up front or $802 a year for 20 years (representing an implicit borrowing rate of approximately 5%).

[68] Code Section 141(c)(2) and Regulation Section 1.141-5(d).

[69] The rules relating to the private business tests are contained in Code Section 141(b) and Regulation Sections 1.141-3 and 1.141-4.

ness use test" and the "private payment or security test." In brief, bonds meet the private business use test if more than 10%[70] of the proceeds are used (directly or indirectly) in the private trade or business of one or more nongovernmental persons. Bonds meet the private payment or security test if either (1) the bonds are secured by any interest in property used or to be used for a private business use and such security is more than 10% of the amount of the bonds; or (2) payments are to be made (directly or indirectly) by one or more nongovernmental persons using bond-financed property and such payments have a present value that is more than 10% of the amount of the bonds.

The private business use test generally looks to any use either of the bond proceeds or of any facilities financed with the bond proceeds in any trade or business carried on by any person other than a governmental entity. This includes ownership of a bond-financed facility, leasing of a bond-financed facility, certain management and service contracts relating to financed facilities,[71] "output contracts" relating to bond-financed facilities (where the nongovernmental person has committed to purchase the output of electric or gas generation, transmission, distribution, or related facilities or water collection, storage, and distribution facilities under a take or take-or-pay contract), certain research contracts relating to research to be conducted in bond-financed facilities,[72] and any other arrangement that coveys special legal entitlements for beneficial use of bond proceeds or bond-financed facilities in a manner comparable to the other types of private business use.

There are, however, some exceptions to this broad rule that can be very helpful. Probably the broadest of these is a rule that says that use of bond-financed facilities as a *member of the general public* is not private business

---

[70] A special rule reduces the 10% amounts referred to in this paragraph to 5% if the private business use is *unrelated or disproportionate* to the governmental uses under the bond issue. Unfortunately, the statute and regulations are not entirely clear what "unrelated" means—based upon the legislative history, it appears that any private business use that is located in the same facility as the governmental use will be treated as "related" unless it is attorneys' office. The "disproportionate" rule is a very technical rule that only applies if more than one governmental facility is being financed and the private business use portion of one of those facilities exceeds the governmental use in that facility.

[71] Revenue Procedure 97-13 contains a set of guidelines defining certain safe-harbor management or service contract arrangements that will not be treated as private business use. In general, the safe-harbor guidelines require the issuer be at risk with respect to the operations of the facility, although for shorter contracts it does allow the manager or service provider to be compensated entirely on the basis of gross revenues.

[72] Revenue Procedure 97-14 contains a set of guidelines defining certain safe-harbor research contracts that will not be treated as giving rise to private business use.

use.[73] If trade or business use of bond-financed facilities occurs on the same basis as use by *natural persons*[74] not in a trade or business, there is generally no private business use for purposes of the test. Thus, if bond proceeds finance a freeway and more than 10% of the use of that freeway is by truckers conveying goods from one location to another in their trade or business, the freeway will not (absent some special arrangement with the truckers, such as giving them a priority right to use the freeway) be treated as giving rise to private business use. The use by the trucking companies is on the same basis as use by natural persons not in a trade or business.

If the issuer is going to rely upon the exception for "use on the same basis as the general public," it may not enter into an arrangement that gives priority rights to business users. However, the issuer may charge uniformly applied rates and charges applicable to different classes of users, such as volume purchasers, if the differences in rates are customary and reasonable. For example, bonds used to finance a municipal electric generator will not be treated as privately used as a result of large purchases of electricity on the same basis as any other member of the general public, even if volume users (such as a theme park) may get a substantially lower rate. However, if any arrangement is made to make volume purchasers the last persons cut off in the event of a power shortage, there probably would be private business use. In addition, an arrangement allowing for exclusive use or priority use "on the same basis as the general public" will not be permitted if it extends to more than 200 days of use. For example, suppose a city builds a parking garage using tax-exempt bonds. In general, the parking garage is available for parking by members of the general public. However, the city sets aside 20% of the garage for holders of long-term parking permits. It makes the parking permits available to the public on a general, first-come, first-served basis. If the term of the parking permit is longer than 200 days, holders of parking permits using the parking in their trades or businesses may give rise to private business use of the parking garage and, hence, the bonds.

Another set of useful exceptions are the so-called "short-term use" exceptions.[75] These include:

- Arrangements of no more than 100 days of total use based upon an established rates and charges table, even if the bond-financed facilities are not available on the same basis to natural persons not using the facilities in their trade or business. An example of this might be arrangements to rent a convention center in a city.

---

[73] Regulation Section 1.141-3(c).
[74] IRS terminology meaning *human beings*.
[75] Regulation Section 1.141-3(d)(3).

- Arrangements of no more than 50 days of total use where there is no rates and charges table, but the arrangement is negotiated at arm's length and the compensation under the arrangement is at fair market value. For this exception to apply, the facility cannot have been financed for a principal purpose of providing that property for use by that non-governmental person. Again, this might apply to a convention center.

Another useful exception is for so-called *incidental use* of a bond-financed facility that does not in total exceed 2.5% of the total proceeds of the issue used to finance that facility if the use if nonpossessory[76] and the use is unrelated to any other private business use by the same user in the same facility.[77] Examples of these types of arrangements include telephones, vending machines, advertising displays, and television cameras.

Private business use is measured over the life of the bonds.[78] Moreover, the amount of use is adjusted by the time there is private use. For example, suppose 30-year tax-exempt bonds are issued to finance a 10-story office building. Assuming that each of the floors has substantially the same allocated cost, the issuer could lease up to one full floor of the building to private business users for the entire term of the bonds so long as the other nine floors were used for governmental use. Alternatively, the government issuer might lease two full floors of the building to private business users for 15 years (using the remaining for governmental purposes) and use all ten floors of the building for governmental use the remaining 15 years. No concept of present value is used for this "space-time analysis."

The private security or private payment test is someone more difficult to apply than the private business use test. The easiest example of "failing" the private security or private payment test and avoiding private activity bond status is where proceeds of a general obligation bond are granted to one or more private business users. Even though 100% of the proceeds may met the private business use test, the bonds will still not be private activity bonds because they are not secured by any interests in property used in a private trade or business and no payments are expected from the recipients of the grants.

Apart from that simple case, it is important to get tax counsel involved early if it is expected that bond proceeds will be used in private trades or businesses but the intention is still to have governmental bonds by "failing" the private security or private payment test. In general, the private payment test is applied by comparing the present value of all expected payments to

---

[76] For example, a coffee cart in a lobby. The nonpossessory rule does not apply to vending machines, pay telephones, kiosks, and similar uses.

[77] Regulation 1.141-3(d)(5).

[78] Or over the life of the assets financed, if they have a shorter economic life.

the present value of all net debt service on the bonds. Because of the use of the present value test, it is possible that conclusions as to whether the private payment test is met may change during the process of pricing the bonds.

Bonds in Excess of $150 Million[79]

The 10% limit on private business use allows some marginal use of bond proceeds or bond-financed facilities for private business use so long as the bulk of the proceeds of an issue are used for government purposes. However, Congress was concerned that, where the size of the issue was quite large, states and political subdivisions might still be permitted too much private business use as an absolute number. Accordingly, the Code provides that if, even if the private business use portion of a bond issue meets the 10% limit, the bonds will nonetheless be treated as private activity bonds if the private business use and private security or payment for the bonds exceeds $15 million unless the issuer allocates a portion of it private activity bond volume cap to the bonds.[80] Thus, for any bond issue with an issue price of more than $150,000,000, the private business use limitation is effectively $15 million unless volume cap is obtained for the issue.

Special Rule for Certain Output Facilities[81]

Similar to the special limit for bonds with more than $15 million of private use, special limits apply to bonds where more than 5% of the proceeds are used to finance output facilities (such as electric generating facilities).[82] This rule states that, if the private use portion of the bonds exceeds $15 million less the aggregate amount of private use of other bond issues used to finance the same facilities, the bonds will be treated as private activity bonds. Unlike the general $15 million rule, the issuer cannot effectively overcome this limit by getting an allocation of the private activity bond volume cap.

Types of Qualified Private Activity Bonds

As stated above, private activity bonds generally do not bear interest that is exempt from federal tax income tax. However, Congress has approved the use of tax-exempt bonds to finance certain types of projects or to make certain loans that are considered to be worthy of federal tax exemption. Each of these types of "qualified bonds" has a multitude of special rules relating

---

[79] See Code Section 141(b)(5).
[80] See below, under "Volume Cap Limitation."
[81] See generally Code Section 141(b)(4) and Regulation Section 1.141-7.
[82] But specifically excluding water furnishing facilities.

to it. In all cases where qualified private activity bonds are being used, qualified tax counsel should be involved early in the transaction.

The types of "qualified bonds" are:

- *Exempt facility bonds.*[83] These are bonds where at least 95% of the proceeds of the issue (less any amounts deposited into a reasonably required reserve fund) are used to pay for depreciable capital assets that are airport facilities, dock and wharf facilities, mass commuting facilities, facilities for the furnishing of water, sewage facilities, solid waste disposal facilities, qualified residential rental projects (essentially, multi-family housing projects for low- or moderate-income persons), facilities for the local furnishing of electric energy or gas (so-called "two-county rule" facilities, since the user cannot be supplying electric energy or gas in more than two counties plus one adjacent city), local district heating or cooling facilities, qualified hazardous waste facilities,[84] high-speed intercity rail facilities, environmental enhancements of hydro-electric generating facilities, qualified public educational facilities, qualified green building and sustainable design projects, and qualified highway or surface freight transfer facilities. In addition to the specific qualifying rules that apply to each of these facilities, facilities for airports, docks and wharves, mass commuting, and environmental enhancements of hydroelectric generating facilities must be owned for tax purposes by a governmental unit and any office space located on the premises of the exempt facilities will not be treated as part of the qualified facilities unless they are almost entirely used for the day-to-day operations of the facilities. Finally, for airports, docks and wharves, mass-commuting facilities, and high-speed intercity rail facilities, there are special rules that treat lodging facilities, retail facilities located outside the exempt facilities, office buildings for persons who are not employees of the government unit or operating authority, and retail facilities located inside the exempt facilities that are designed to serve more than passengers and employees at the exempt facilities as impermissible costs.
- *Qualified mortgage bonds and qualified veterans' mortgage bonds.*[85] Qualified mortgage bonds are bonds that are issued to finance mortgage loans to so-called first-time homebuyers that meet certain income and purchase price cost limitations. Qualified veterans' mortgage bonds are bonds that are issued to finance mortgage loans to qualified veterans.

---

[83] Code Section 142 and Regulation Sections 1.103-8, 1.142-1, 1.142-4, and 1.142(a)(5)-1.

[84] But not radwaste.

[85] Code Section 143 and Regulation (and temporary regulations) sections 1.103A-2, 6a.103A-1, 6a.103A-6a.103A-3, and 1.143(g)-1.

- *Qualified small issue bonds.*[86] Qualified small issue bonds are bonds issued to finance manufacturing facilities and certain land acquisitions for first-time farmers. No more than $10 million of bonds may be issued for any project, and all capital expenditures of the borrower (and all related persons) in the jurisdiction of the issuer cannot exceed $20 million[87] (including the bonds) during the six-year period beginning three years prior to the date the bonds are issued. There is also a limit of $40 million on the total amount of small issue bonds that may be issued for the benefit of any taxpayer and related persons nationwide.

- *Qualified student loan bonds.*[88] Qualified student loan bonds are issued for the purpose of financing students loans made under programs (a) subject to the Higher Education Act of 1965 where the loans are directly or indirectly guaranteed by the federal government, the financing of the loans is not limited by federal law to the proceeds of tax-exempt bonds, and special allowance payments under section 438 of the Higher Education Act of 1965 are either authorized to be paid with respect to the loans or would be so authorized if the loans were not bond-financed or (b) subject to state law meeting special requirements.

- *Qualified redevelopment bonds.*[89] Qualified redevelopment bonds are permitted to finance specified redevelopment purposes in designated blighted areas. The usefulness of this program is highly limited.

- *Qualified 501(c)(3) bonds.*[90] Qualified 501(c)(3) bonds are probably the most widely used type of qualified private activity bonds. Qualified 501(c)(3) bonds are used to finance loans to organizations that are exempt from tax under Section 501(c)(3) of the Code, such as hospitals, schools, colleges, and museums. At least 95% of the proceeds of the bonds must be used either by 501(c)(3) organizations for their exempt purposes or by governmental entities. All property financed with the bonds must be owned by a 501(c)(3) organization or by a governmental entity. In addition, for bonds that finance capital assets prior to August 6, 1997, and for bonds issued after that date where more than 5% of the proceeds are used to finance working capital expenditures, there is a $150 million limit on the amount of bonds that can be outstanding for any beneficiary of the bonds at a particular time. The Code also restricts the use of such bonds to finance residential rental property for family units—if the proceeds do not finance property that is newly built using

---

[86] Code Section 144(a) and Regulation Sections 1.103-10, 1.144-0, 1.144-1, and 1.144-2.

[87] This number was newly raised from $10 million effective January 1, 2007.

[88] Code Section 144(b).

[89] Code Section 144(c).

[90] Code Section 145 and Regulation Section 1.145-0, 1.145-1, and 1.145-2.

the bond proceeds[91] or the property is not substantially rehabilitated within the two-year period ending one year after the date of acquisition of the property, the bonds will not be qualified 501(c)(3) bonds unless the special targeting requirements relating to low- and moderate-income multifamily housing bonds are met.

Volume Cap Limitation[92]

In general, qualified private activity bonds will only be tax-exempt if an allocation of state's private activity bond volume cap is made when the bonds are issued. Each state (including all of the political subdivisions of the state) is allowed to issue only a limited amount of private activity bonds in each calendar year. The volume cap is equal to the greater of $75 (in 2001 dollars, adjusted for inflation)[93] times the population of the state or $225,000,000 (in dollars, adjusted for inflation).[94] Each state has devised a scheme for allocating the volume cap among different issues and different issuers.

The private activity volume cap does not apply to qualified veterans' mortgage bonds, qualified 501(c)(3) bonds, or qualified exempt facility bonds issued to finance airport facilities, docks or wharves, environmental enhancements of hydroelectric generating facilities, qualified public educational facilities, qualified green building and sustainable design projects, or qualified highway or surface freight transfer facilities. It also does not apply to exempt facilities financing solid waste disposal facilities if those facilities are owned by a governmental unit. In addition, any exempt facility bonds issued to finance high-speed intercity rail facilities only need a volume cap equal to 25% of the bonds.

With the exception of high-speed intercity rail facilities, bonds that are subject to the volume cap need an allocation equal to the face amount of the bonds. It is not clear whether, for bonds that are sold at a substantial premium, there must be an allocation equal to the issue price of the bonds.

Refunding bonds do not need an allocation of the private activity volume cap unless the amount of the refunding bonds exceeds the amount of the refunded bonds, and then only to the extent of the excess. However, there are special rules for refunding student loan bonds and refunding qualified mortgage bonds that limits the permitted maturity of the refunding bonds unless volume cap is obtained.

---

[91] There is a special rule relating to interim taxable construction financings.
[92] Code Section 146 and temporary Regulation Section 1.103(n)-1T through -7T.
[93] $85 for calendar 2007.
[94] $256,235,000 for calendar 2007.

Finally, as described above, certain governmental bonds need an alloca-tion of the private activity volume cap if the private business use portion of the bond issue is less than 10% but still exceeds $15 million.

In the event that a state does not use its entire private activity volume cap in a calendar year, there are provisions allowing the state to carry for-ward the unused volume cap for up to three years for designated *carry for-ward purposes*. Once carried forward for a specific purpose, the state may not later change that purpose.

Other Private Activity Bond Limitations

There are a number of other special limitations on private activity bonds. These are:

- *Substantial use limitation.*[95] During any time period that a private activ-ity bond is held by a person who is a *substantial user* of the facility financed with that bond, the interest on the bond is not tax-exempt. This rule also applies to any person who is a *related person* to the sub-stantial user. Once the bond is transferred to another person who is not a substantial user or a related person, the interest will again be tax-exempt. This rule does not apply to qualified mortgage bonds, qualified veterans' mortgage bonds, qualified student loan bonds, or qualified 501(c)(3) bonds.
- *120% maturity limitation.*[96] The weighted average maturity of an issue of private activity bonds may not exceed 120% of the remaining (as of the issue date) weighted average life of the financed facilities. For this purpose, land is ignored unless more than 25% of the proceeds are used to acquire land. There is also a special rule relating to a pooled financing for making loans to 501(c)(3) organizations for the purpose of acquiring property. This rule does not apply to qualified mortgage bonds, qualified veterans' mortgage bonds, or qualified student loan bonds.
- *Land acquisition.*[97] No more than 25% of the proceeds of an issue of private activity bonds may be used to acquired land or interests in land. There is an exception for first-time farmer bonds. In addition, this rule does not apply to qualified mortgage bonds, qualified veterans' mort-gage bonds, qualified student loan bonds, qualified public educations facilities bonds, or qualified 501(c)(3) bonds.
- *Used property limitation.*[98] No proceeds of a private activity bond may be used to acquire used property. This rule does not apply to a build-

---

[95] Code Section 147(a).
[96] Code Section 147(b).
[97] Code Section 147(c).
[98] Code Section 147(d).

ing if the purchaser spends an amount at least equal to 15% of the amount of the bonds used to acquire the building to rehabilitate the building within the two years following the date of acquisition.[99] This rule doesn't not apply to qualified mortgage bonds, qualified veterans' mortgage bonds, student loan bonds, or qualified 501(c)(3) bonds.

- *Prohibited facilities.*[100] No portion of the proceeds of an issue of private activity bonds may be used to pay for any airplane, skybox,[101] health club facility,[102] facility primarily used for gambling, or liquor store.

- *TEFRA approval.*[103] All private activity bonds must be approved by an elected representative prior to issuance of the bonds. This approval is referred to as the TEFRA approval because the requirement first appeared in the Tax Equity and Fiscal Responsibility Act of 1982. TEFRA approval is required both from the issuer of the bonds and (if different) from the jurisdiction where the facility is located. Prior to the TEFRA approval, there must be a public hearing, at which all interested persons are given the right to participate. The hearing must be preceded by publication of a notice relating to the hearing (the TEFRA notice) describing the bonds to be issued, the project to be financed, and the initial owner or operator of the facilities as well as giving information about the hearing. The TEFRA notice must be published at least 14 days prior to the hearing. TEFRA notice and TEFRA approval are not required for current refunding bonds where the average maturity of the refunding bond issue will be no later than the average maturity of the bonds to be refunded. There are also special rules relating to airport bonds, high-speed intercity rail bonds, a subclass of student loan bonds called *scholarship funding bonds*, and bonds issued by certain volunteer fire departments.

- *Costs of issuance.*[104] No more than 2% of the proceeds of an issue of private activity bonds may be used to pay costs of issuing the bonds, including underwriters' discount. If the costs of issuance are excess of that amount, the issuer or conduit borrower must come up with sufficient equity to cover the extra costs. In addition, costs of issuance are treated as a "bad cost" for purposes of the 95% rules applying to the use of proceeds of qualified private activity bonds.[105]

---

[99] For structures other than buildings, the rehabilitation requirement is 100% of the amount of bond proceeds spent to purchase the structure. There is no exception for acquired equipment unless that equipment is purchased as part of the building.

[100] Code Section 147(e).

[101] Or similar luxury box at a sports facility.

[102] Except for qualified 501(c)(3) bonds.

[103] Code Section 147(f).

[104] Code Section 147(g).

[105] For small mortgage revenue bonds, with proceeds not in excess of $20 million, the costs of issuance limit is raised to 3.5%.

OTHER MISCELLANEOUS RULES, INCLUDING REFUNDINGS

The Code imposes a final set of rules that all tax-exempt bonds must comply with. In large part, these consist of rules relating to who can issue tax-exempt bonds, miscellaneous requirements either designed to help insure tax compliance or to stop perceived abuses, and rules relating to so-called "advance refunding bonds."

Issuers

The Code generally says that debt obligations of states and political subdivisions will qualify for tax-exempt status.[106] For this purpose, *state* includes not only the 50 states, but also the District of Columbia and any possession of the United States. A federally recognized Indian tribal government will also be treated as a state for this purpose if it is issuing the bonds for an *essential governmental purpose*, as provided in Code Section 7871. A political subdivision of a state is an entity that possesses a substantial amount of one of the three sovereign powers: the power to tax, the power of eminent domain, and the police power.[107] A state or a political subdivision may act directly or through an integral part of the state or political subdivision (such as actions taken by a department of the state).

In addition to states and political subdivisions, entities that act on behalf of the state or political subdivision may also issue tax-exempt bonds even if they do not independently possess sovereign powers.[108] Such an entity might be a *constituted authority* created pursuant to a specific state statute that specifically gives it the power to issue bonds on behalf of the state or a political subdivision (such as an industrial development board or a health facilities financing authority).[109] Alternatively, a nonprofit corporation may be treated as issuing bonds on behalf of a state or political subdivision if it meets various requirements.[110]

Finally, Congress has specifically authorized two other types of entities to issue tax-exempt bonds. Tax-exempt student loan bonds (otherwise meeting the tax requirements) may be issued by a nonprofit corporation

---

[106] Code Section 103(a) and 103(c)(1).

[107] See *Philadelphia National Bank v. United States*, 666 F.2d 834 (3rd Cir. 1981).

[108] See Regulation Section 1.103-1(b).

[109] See Revenue Ruling 57-187.

[110] Revenue Ruling 63-20 and Revenue Procedure 82-26. This type of issuance has largely fallen out of favor because of the restrictions imposed by Revenue Procedure 82-26 (such as the requirement that the governmental entity ultimately have title to the financed property) and because State laws have been amended to make constituted authority issuances easier.

established at the requires of a State or one or more political subdivisions of a State and operated exclusively for the purpose of acquiring student loan notes incurred under the Higher Education Act of 1965 provided that several other requirements are met.[111] In addition, certain volunteer fire departments will be treated as political subdivisions for purpose of the tax-exempt bonds rules.[112]

Miscellaneous Rules

Registration Requirement[113]

In general, bonds will not be tax exempt unless they are issued in a registered form, where ownership can only be transferred on books held by a trustee or paying agent. Because of the wide-spread use of the Depository Trust Company (DTC), this has largely resulted in bonds all being registered in the name of Cede & Co., with DTC and its participants maintaining further records. The registration requirement does not apply to bonds that have a maturity of not more than one year, bonds that not of a type offered to the public, and bonds that are of the type not intended to be sold to persons in the United States.[114] As a result of registration requirement, tax-exempt bearer bonds are largely a thing of the past.

Restriction on Federal Guarantees[115]

In the early and mid 1980s, Congress became concerned what it called *double dipping*: arrangements where a tax-exempt borrower not only got the benefit of the subsidy of the tax exemption, but also got the benefit of some other federal guarantee. Accordingly, for bonds issued since the 1984 Tax Act, tax-exempt status is generally denied if the bonds are also directly or indirectly guaranteed by the United States or any agency or instrumentality of the United States. This prohibition covers not only guarantees of the payment of principal or interest with respect to the bonds, but also the use of more than 5% of the proceeds to make loans which are guaranteed in whole or in part by the United States or its agencies or instrumentalities or to invest in federally insured deposits or accounts.[116]

---

[111] Code Section 150(d).
[112] Code Section 150(e).
[113] Code Section 149(a).
[114] The last of these would be unlikely with respect to tax-exempt bonds, since such a person would not get the benefit of the tax exemption.
[115] Code Section 140(b).
[116] Such as depositing bond proceeds into a federally insured bank account.

In addressing a perceived abuse, Congress wielded a very blunt tool and recognized the need to narrow it. Accordingly, there is a long list of exceptions to the federal guarantee prohibition. Bonds are not treated as federally guaranteed by reason of a guarantee from FHA, VA, FNMA, FHLMC, or GNMA, by reason of a guarantee of student loans by the Student Loan Marketing Association, or by reason of a guarantee by the Bonneville Power Authority pursuant to the Northwest Power Act as in effect on the date of enactment of the Tax Reform Act of 1984. In addition, bonds are not impermissibly federally guaranteed if the proceeds are invested for an initial temporary period until needed for the purpose for which they were issued, investments in a bona fide debt service fund, investments in a reasonably required reserve fund, investments in bonds issued by the United States Treasury, investments in a refunding escrow, or investments that are otherwise permitted by regulations. Moreover, the federal guarantee prohibition does not apply to private activity bonds issued for a qualified residential rental project, bonds subject to section 11(b) of the United States Housing Act of 1937, qualified mortgage bonds, or qualified veterans' mortgage bonds—unless the proceeds of such bonds are invested in federally insured deposits or accounts.

Information Reporting[117]

For bonds to bear tax-exempt interest, the issuer must file an appropriate information return with respect to the bonds no later than the 15th day of the second month of the calendar quarter following the date of issuance of the bonds. There are a number of forms, generically referred to as "Form 8038." A Form 8038-G must be filed for each governmental bond and a Form 8038 must be filed for each private activity bond. In the event that the information return is not properly filed, the IRS has established a procedure relating to late filings.[118]

Restrictions on Pooled Financings[119]

If more than $5,000,000 of the proceeds of a bond issue are expected to be used (directly or indirectly) to finance loans to two or more ultimate borrowers (so-called *pool bonds*), the bonds generally[120] will be taxable unless they meet certain requirements. For pool bonds to be tax-exempt, they must meet each of the following requirements:

---

[117] Code Section 149(e).

[118] Revenue Procedure 2002-48.

[119] Code Section 149(f).

[120] This rules does not apply to bonds that are subject to the private activity volume cap or to the special volume cap applicable to qualified mortgage veteran's bonds.

- At the time the bonds are issued, the issuer must reasonably expect that at least 30% of the net proceeds of the bonds[121] will be used to make loans within the first year following the issue date and that at least 95% of the net proceeds will be used to make loans within the first three years. For purposes of determining *reasonable expectations*, issuers may not take into account any expectations concerning changes in interest rates. In general, this rule requires that the issuer do some sort of bona fide demand study prior to issuing the bonds. Congress recently further tightened the expectations requirement as described below.
- The payment of legal and underwriting costs associated with the bonds must not be contingent upon the making of any loans and at least 95% of such costs must actually be paid not later than 180 days after the date of issuance of the bonds.
- Congress and Treasury were concerned that the "reasonable expectations" test described above was too loose. Accordingly, a new requirement was recently added that, prior to the issue date, the issuer must receive written loan commitments identifying potential borrowers of at least 30% of the proceeds of the issue. This rule does not apply to bonds issued by a State to make loans to subordinate governmental units of the State or to a State-created entity providing financing for water infrastructure projects through the federally sponsored State revolving fund program.
- To the extent that the expectations of 30% within one year and 95% within three years are not met, the shortfall in loans must be used to redeem bonds within 90 days after the end of the first or third year, respectively.

Requirements for Hedge Bonds[122]

Similar to pool bonds, there are special rules relating to so-called "hedge bonds." "Hedge bonds" are defined to be any bond issued unless (a) the issuer reasonably expects that at least 85% of the spendable proceeds of the bonds[123] will be spent within three[124] years after the date the bonds are issued for governmental purposes; and (b) the issuer does not invest more than 50% of the proceeds in some sort of investment that gives a substan-

---

[121] That is, net of reserve funds, costs of issuance, and capitalized interest.

[122] Code Section 149(g).

[123] Proceeds less costs of issuance and reserve funds.

[124] There are special rules allowing the three-year period to be extended to five years if the proceeds of the bonds are being used to pay for a construction project having a construction period in excess of five years and the issuer gets appropriate certifications from an independent architect or engineer.

tially guaranteed yield for four years or more.[125] If the bonds are *hedge bonds*, the issuer must reasonably expect at the time that the bonds are issued that at least 10% of the proceeds will be spent within the first year after the bonds are issued, at least 30% of the proceeds will be spent within the first two years after the bonds are issued, at least 60% of the proceeds will be spent within the first three years after the bonds are issued, and at least 85% of the proceeds will be spent by the fifth anniversary of the date of issue. In addition, the payment of legal and underwriting costs associated with the bonds must not be contingent upon the making of any loans and at least 95% of such costs must actually be paid not later than 180 days after the date of issuance of the bonds.

Hedge bond status can also be avoided by investing at least 95% of the proceeds of the bonds at all times in tax-exempt bonds that do not bear interest that is treated as an item of special tax preference for purposes of the alternative minimum tax.

Refunding Bonds

Just as with any other type of borrowing, issuers of tax-exempt bonds will often look at the interest rate on their outstanding debt and realize that they could borrow currently at a lower rate. If the bonds to be refinanced (the *refunded bonds*) can be currently repaid or paid within 90 days after the issuance date of the refunding bonds, all is well and good. However, it is not uncommon for tax-exempt bonds to be issued with "call protection," which creates a period during which the issuer does not have a right to prepay the bonds. An issuer may nonetheless want to "lock in" today's interest rate by issuing refunding bonds in today's market and setting aside the proceeds to be used to repay the refunded bonds when they can be called. If the refunding bonds are issued more than 90 days before the refunded bonds will be repaid, the refunding will be called an "advance refunding."

The IRS and Congress particularly dislike advance refunding bond issues, because there are two (or more) sets of bond issues outstanding at the same time bearing tax-exempt interest with only one project. The effect of this is to create a cost on the federal fisc without having new projects. Accordingly, advance refunding bonds are subject to a number of special rules.

■ Only governmental bonds or qualified 501(c)(3) bonds may be advance refunded.[126] Bonds issued to advance refund private activity bonds will be taxable.

---

[125] For refunding bonds, the test is applied by looking back to the original bonds being refunded.
[126] Code Section 149(d)(2).

- Only one set of advance refunding bonds may be issued with respect to any particular new money bond issue.[127] For example, bonds may be issued to advance refund governmental bonds that financed a project, but bonds may not be issued to advance refund the refunding bonds.[128] There are special rules where the new money bond issue was issued prior to 1986.

- As described above, the proceeds of the advance refunding bonds cannot be invested at a yield that is materially higher than the yield on the refunding bonds.[129] Accordingly, there is no economic savings from refunding noncallable bonds.

- When bonds are advance refunded, any remaining three-year temporary period with respect to the proceeds of the refunded bonds ends when the refunding bonds are issued.[130]

- If there are any present value debt service savings from doing the refunding, the refunded bonds must be called at the first call date (after the permitted 90-day *current refunding period*) giving rise to savings.[131] Again, there is a special rule for bonds issued before 1986.[132]

- When creating the refunding escrow, any amounts held in the debt service funds or construction funds for the refunded bonds put into the escrow must be invested in the earliest maturing investments in the escrow. Any amounts held in the reserve fund for the refunded bonds must be invested no more slowly than pro rata with proceeds of the refunding bonds.[133]

CONCLUSION

The federal tax laws relating to tax-exempt bonds are complex and (in some cases) not completely clear. It is important to make sure that qualified tax counsel is involved in all but the simplest transactions. In addition, even in the simplest transactions, bond counsel and investment bankers must be careful to ensure that special tax requirements will not apply and that the basic tax requirements are met. Failure to do so can result in taxability of the bonds and potential penalties being imposed upon bond counsel, bankers, and others.

---

[127] Code Section 149(d)(3)(A)(i).

[128] Even if the escrow is gone and even if there was a current refunding that took out the advance refunding bonds.

[129] Regulation Section 1.148-2(d)(2)(ii).

[130] Code Section 149(d)(3)(iv).

[131] Code Section 149(d)(3)(A)(iii).

[132] Code Section 149(d)(3)(A)(ii).

[133] Regulation Section 1.148-9(c)(2).

CHAPTER 8

The Role of the
Municipal Bond Trustee

James E. Spiotto
Partner
Chapman and Cutler LLP

The administration of a municipal bond issue presents unique challenges for the financial institution serving as bond trustee. Because of the pivotal role of the bond trustee in representing the municipal bondholders postissuance, an understanding of the bond trustee's duties and obligations generally and with respect to specified functions is instructive.

THE NATURE OF THE BOND TRUSTEE'S DUTIES AND RESPONSIBILITIES

Historical Overview

The role of the municipal bond trustee can be traced, in large part, to the development of the corporate indenture trustee. In the United States, the use of indenture trustees evolved from basic common law roots regarding paying agents and the ability to hold or act on behalf of others. The turning point in the use of indenture trustees came in the middle of the 1800s, when the United States Supreme Court was asked to review the issue of whether certain bondholders of a mortgage railroad bond issue could foreclose on the mortgage absent 100% of the holders.[1] The Supreme Court held that, without all the bondholders, the mortgage could not be foreclosed, since each bondholder should be present to defend his own claims and protect his

---

[1] *Nashville and Decatur R.R. Co. v. Orr*, 85 U.S. 471 (1873).

own interests.[2] This brought about the necessity of having an entity hold the mortgage for the benefit of the bondholders. At first, the railroads thought it wise to appoint one of their employees to act as the holder of the mortgage for the benefit of the bondholders. However, such appointment became a career threatening position when there was a default and the bondholders were screaming for action by the trustee to foreclose on the mortgage property held by the trustee's employer. The practical difficulties of this arrangement led to the common sense approach of obtaining the services of an independent, sophisticated institution that could act for the benefit of others. The use of a bond trustee developed to take action on behalf of the holders, to hold the collateral if any was granted and, generally upon default, to protect the rights and interests of the holders as a prudent person would do with regard to his own property.

The next stage in the development of the bond trustee came during the early part of the 1900s. During the 1920s and 1930s, given the financial turmoil of those times, there were numerous instances where bond trustees did not give priority to the interests of the bondholders. One case in particular is representative of the problem.[3] The bank serving as the bond trustee was also a lender. The bank as lender liquidated the obligor, thereby paying off the obligor's loans from the bank. After the bank had been paid off, the bank as bond trustee gave notice to the bondholders of existing defaults. In fact, there was no need for further action by the bond trustee, since there were no assets available to pay the holders of the securities. The court's conclusion was not surprising, nor was the court's impatience with the bond trustee. The horror cases that arose out of the 1920s and 1930s brought about the enactment of the Trust Indenture Act of 1939,[4] applicable to corporate issues. The requirements embodied in the federal legislation, an independent, qualified, compensated institution to protect the rights of bondholders, became the standard in municipal transactions as well.

The Concept of the Bond Trustee: Contracting Party or Fiduciary?

It is against this historical backdrop that the current municipal bond trustee has its role, duties and responsibilities defined. There are many different ways of describing what a bond trustee is. The basic definition of its duties and responsibilities will flow from the fact that its origins arose out of the necessity of having someone, in the time of default, capable of either holding collateral and realizing thereon, or taking actions on behalf of a disparate group of public debt holders in an effort to maximize the recovery and return.

---

[2] Id. at 474-75.

[3] *Drueding v. Tradesmen's Nat'l Bank and Trust Co.,* 319 Pa. 144, 179 A. 229 (1935).

[4] 15 USC §§ 77aaa et seq.

As previously noted, the law regarding bond trustees is primarily derived from cases regarding corporate trust indentures. A trust indenture is a unique sort of document, and the trustee acting thereunder has unique duties and obligations. Over the years, various courts have characterized the role of the indenture trustee in different ways. An *indenture trustee* has, from time to time, been characterized as a fiduciary,[5] agent,[6] contracting party,[7] or a combination of the above.[8] Municipal finance has borrowed the concept of a trustee acting for bondholders in the administration of bond ordinances or resolutions.

At times, various courts have combined the above approaches to rationalize how a bond trustee should act. As a practical matter, the bond trustee by and large has been viewed as the party who has contracted for specified duties and responsibilities prior to default; and, upon default, the bond trustee is the party who will take such action as is reasonable and prudent under the circumstances to protect the rights and interests of the holders.

It is frequently said that the nature of the trustee's responsibilities differ before and after default. The trustee's duties are passive until some default by the obligor occurs.[9] After default, the duties become active, proactive and responsible, akin to those of the ordinary fiduciary (this is the very origin of the prudent person rule). This standard finds its source in the Vermont case of *Sturges v. Knapp*.[10] However, the court defined the role of the bond trustee after default as follows:

> [A]fter the forfeiture occurs, either by nonpayment of interest or principal, or both, as in the present case, the duties of the trustees become not only active and responsible, but critical and delicate. It not only is not a dead, dry trust, but it is one of the most active and momentous responsibility.[11]

Then, the court described the powers and the duties of the trustee after default. According to the court, they are not limited by the language of the agreement, but are "to be estimated by surrounding circumstances, and

---

[5] *York v. Guaranty Trust Co.*, 143 F.2d 503 (2nd Cir. 1944), rev'd, 326 U.S. 99 (1945).

[6] *First Trust Co. v. Carlsen*, 129 Neb. 118, 261 N.W. 333 (1935).

[7] *Hazzard v. Chase Nat'l Bank*, 159 Misc. 57, 287 N.Y.S. 541 (N.Y. Sup. Ct. 1936).

[8] *Dunn v. Reading Trust Co.*, 121 F.2d 854 (3rd Cir. 1941).

[9] Quindry, Bonds and Bondholders, §§ 205, 211 (2d ed. 1934); Jones, Bonds and Bond Securities, § 1030 (4th ed. 1935); *Northampton Trust Co. v. Northam on Traction Co.*, 270 Pa. 199, 112 A. 871 (1921); *Colorado and Southern Ry. v. Blair*, 108 N.E. 840, 842 (N.Y. 1915).

[10] *Sturges v. Kanpp*, 31 Vt. 1 (1858).

[11] Id. at 55.

determined on the basis of what a prudent owner would deem reasonable under the circumstances."[12] This legal analysis parallels the development of a *prudent person* rule for personal trustees and general fiduciaries.[13]

Later Developments

In the succeeding years since the decision in *Sturges v. Knapp* was handed down, the leading authorities have made is clear that, predefault, unlike those of an ordinary trustee, the duties of a bond trustee are generally defined by and limited to the terms of the agreement.[14] An exception to this rule is that, at all times, a bond trustee must avoid conflicts of interest.[15] After an event of default occurs, it has been widely held that the standard of care rises to that of a fiduciary and the bond trustee is required to perform the duties set forth in the indenture in the same manner as a prudent person would do so under the same circumstances. However, this change does not render the document creating the basic obligation, namely the trust indenture, bond ordinance, or resolution (*the Agreement*) irrelevant. While the trustee must in the postdefault context act prudently, this standard is applied only in the exercise of those rights and powers granted in the Agreement. The scope of the trustee's obligation then is still circumscribed by the Agreement, albeit less narrowly. The trustee is not required to act beyond his contractually conferred rights and powers, but must, as prudence dictates, exercise those obligations in order to secure the basic purpose of any Agreement, the repayment of the underlying obligation.[16]

Implied Powers of the Bond Trustee

An evolving area of the law is that grey, predefault period with which trustees are all too familiar. It has been said with regard to predefault duties, to regard the bond trustee as a mere stakeholder is to understate its responsibility; to treat the trustee as though it were an ordinary trustee is to overstate the extent of its duties and to subject it to a standard of conduct

---

[12] Id. at 58.

[13] *Harvard College v. Amory*, 9 Pick 446, 461 (Mass. 1831).

[14] *LNC Inc. v. First Fidelity Bank*, 935 F. Supp 1333, 1346 (S.D.N.Y. 1996); *Meckel v. Continental Resources Co.*, 758 F.2d 811, 816 (2nd Cir. 1985); *Lorenz v. CXS Corp.*, 736 F. Supp 650 (W.D.Pa. 1990), aff'd, 1 F.3d 1406 (3rd Cir 1993).

[15] *Elliott Assocs. v. Schroder Bank & Trust Co.*, 838 F.2d 66 (2nd Cir 1988). See also *Dabney v. Chase Natl. Bank*, 196 F.2d 668 (2nd Cir 1952), as supplemented 201 F.2d 635 (2nd Cir.), cert. dismissed per stipulation 346 U.S. 683 (1953); *AMBAC v. Bankers Trust Co.*, 151 Misc. 2d 334, 573 N.Y.S.2d 204 (N.Y.S.Ct. 1991).

[16] *Beck v. Manufacturers Hanover Trust Company*, 218 A.D.2d 1, 632 N.Y.S.2d 520 (N.Y.App.Div.).

not required by the nature of the trust.[17] The duties and powers of a bond trustee prior to default are circumscribed by the contract, but not to the extent that trustees are stymied in their efforts to protect holders. The courts have long held that the law does not imply any duties on a trustee that are inconsistent with those provided for in the trust Agreement.[18] All implied covenants are derived directly from the language of the Agreement.[19] Bond trustees have duties that are expressly declared in the instrument itself, as well as those incidental duties which the law imposes upon the trustee as a necessity in bringing to fruition those obligations which the Agreement expressly defines.[20] One court has expressed this concept by drawing a distinction between the limitations that an Agreement may place on a trustee's duty and the trustee's duty to discharge whatever obligations it does assume with absolute single-mindedness of purpose.[21]

Implications of the Prudent Person Rule

It is clear that courts in applying the prudent person rule were concerned about protection of the rights of the bondholder. A bond trustee who fails to record a mortgage promptly and protect the security of the holders would be liable, even though the Agreement had exculpatory language.[22] The delay in notice to the holders of a default while the obligor liquidates to pay the bond trustee bank debt is actionable.[23]

Generally, bond trustees, while viewed as being more than stakeholders, whose duties are exclusively defined by the terms of the Agreement, have been protected when they reasonably rely on the terms and conditions of the Agreement. For example, in a case involving whether or not the bond trus-

---

[17] Louis Posner, "Liability of a Trustee Under the Corporate Indenture," *Harvard Law Review*, Vol. 42 (December 1928), pp. 198–242.

[18] See, for example, *Hazzard v. Chase Nat'l Bank*, 159 Misc. 57, 287 N.Y.S. 541 (N.Y. Sup. Ct. 1936).

[19] *Gardner and Florence Call Cowles Foundation v. Empire, Inc.*, 589 F. Supp. 669 (S.D.N.Y. 1984), vacated on other grounds, 754 F.2d 478 (2d Cir. 1985).

[20] Renzo Bowers, *The Law of Bonds and Bond Security: 4th ed.* (Indianapolis: Bobbs-Merrill, 1935). Cf. *Marine Midland Trust Co. v. Continental Bank and Trust Co.*, 28 F. Supp. 680 (S.D.N.Y. 1939) (obligation to maintain stated minimum ratio of collateral imposed on obligor when Agreement was construed as a whole and read in light of certain correspondence).

[21] *Dabney v. Chase National Bank*, 196 F.2d 668, 671 (2d Cir. 1952), *cert. dismissed*, 346 U.S. 863 (1953).

[22] *Benton v. Safe Deposit Bank of Pottsville*, 134 Misc. 727, 236 N.Y.S. 36 (N.Y. Sup. Ct. 1926).

[23] *Drueding v. Tradesmen's Nat'l Bank and Trust Co.*, 319 Pa. 144, 179 A. 22-9 (1935).

tee could be held liable by the bondholders for redemption of the bonds consistent with the terms of the Agreement prior to default, the court held that the contractual provisions regarding redemption applied regardless of arguments by the bondholders concerning the necessity of other provisions.[24]

THE MUNICIPAL BOND TRUSTEE PRECLOSING

Acceptance Considerations

It should always be kept in mind that, while the bond trustee may, in its sole discretion, review the documentation to make sure that the trust can be effectively administered and that the rights and interests of the bondholders are properly protected, including the bondholders' receipt of the benefit of the bargain, it is generally not perceived to be the duty, responsibility, or liability of the municipal bond trustee to perform a preclosing review in order to accomplish these results. The structure of the financing and the compliance with the disclosure contained in the official statement should be the duty of others involved in the transaction. The review typically is taken for the purpose of helping the bond trustee to determine if it wishes to accept the trusteeship.

Function of the Bond Trustee Preclosing

As set forth above, the duties of the bond trustee, prior to default, are those circumscribed by the terms of the bond resolution or other relevant Agreements. However, from a practical standpoint, prior to closing, it is not unreasonable to expect that the trustee should interject itself into closing issues to the degree necessary to insure that (1) the trust created by the documents can be effectively administered; and (2) based on the face of the document, the bondholders are receiving the benefit of the bargain as set forth in the offering documents. In other words, while it is not the responsibility of the trustee to see to it that the transaction is a "good deal," it certainly makes practical sense for a bond trustee to review the documents prior to closing to satisfy itself that the transaction, at least from the trustee's standpoint, is clear and workable. In particular, the bond trustee should want to make sure that any provisions requiring administration on its part are unambiguous and capable of compliance. Typically, bond counsel is opinionating with respect to the tax-exempt status of the bonds. Underwriter's counsel may be concerned about compliance with the applicable securities law, but not

---

[24] *Meckel v. Continental Resource Co.*, 758 F.2d 811, 816 (2nd Cir. 1985); *Elliott Assoc. v. J. Henry Schroder Bank and Trust Co.*, 838 F.2d 66 (2nd Cir. 1988).

necessarily with protecting the bondholder to the fullest. There may very well be no one at the table who has put the bondholders' interests first. It therefore makes practical sense for the bond trustee to be certain prior to assuming a trusteeship that, if the trusteeship is accepted, the bond trustee will be able to function under the terms of the documents and to protect the rights of the bondholders.

Examine the Indenture and Related Documents

All too often, the bond trustee is provided with the closing documents microseconds before the scheduled closing. It is sound practice for the bond indenture trustee to notify the participants to the proposed transaction early on that it will require final drafts of the documents within a reasonable period of time prior to closing so that such documents can be examined by the appropriate parties. The bond trustee will want to make sure that the documents are in such a form that will permit it to exercise its duties. In complex transactions, the bond trustee should obtain a checklist or flow chart from bond counsel.

Review of Security, If Any

In a secured issue, there is a granting clause in the recitals or other provisions at the beginning of the bond resolution or security agreement. Sometimes, when municipal bonds are secured by a pledge of revenues (subject to the issuer's needs for operation and maintenance), the pledge is created by statute with a resulting statutory lien. The trustee should check to make sure that the legal description in the granting clause in the document is the same property covered by the statutes, title insurance policy, if any, and represented to be conveyed or assigned in the official statement. The definition of *trust estate* should be provided for in the bond document. Counsel's opinion should reflect any security interest conveyed to the trustee. If there are mortgages or UCC statements which need to be filed, although the recording is typically not the duty of the indenture trustee, the trustee should insist upon evidence of perfection. If a statute is being enacted, the trustee should insist upon evidence of its effectiveness.

Review Remedial Provisions

Every bond ordinance or resolution should provide for effective remedies upon the failure of the obligor to comply with the terms and conditions of the agreement. Prior to closing, the bond trustee should assure itself that the remedy section is adequate to permit the trustee to protect the rights of the holders if such action is ever needed. In general, the bond resolution should provide for events of default, for acceleration of the maturity, including acceleration upon the direction of a certain percentage of the holders, for rescission or waiver of acceleration or default upon the direction of a certain percentage of the holders, and provisions regarding collection of the indebtedness by the trustee as the trustee of an express trust. In secured conduit issues, there should be a provision with regard to foreclosure on the collateral.

Examine Necessary Opinions and Certificates

The trustee should assure itself that it has received and can rely upon all necessary opinions and certificates. These include the opinion of bond counsel as to the tax-exempt status of the bonds. Opinions should be directed to the trustee and should indicate that the trustee may rely on such opinions. Frequently, incumbency certificates and certificates of compliance are given. A resolution of the obligor authorizing the issuance of the bonds certainly must be obtained.

Receipt of Original Documents

As set forth above, it is important for the trustee to leave the closing room in receipt of all closing documents. It is important to receive *original* documents, if such is possible. Should litigation arise or the authenticity of documents be called into question, it is always helpful to have a paper trail to the original documents.

The Holmes Harbor Case: An Aberration?

Upon default, a bond trustee is judged by hindsight. The procedures used in acceptance of an account and the general administration of that account, prior to and after default, may be subject to careful scrutiny.[25] For example, in the case filed in the Superior Court of the State of Washington in and for the County of Island, *Robert Trimble v. Holmes Harbor Sewer District et al.*,[26] bondholders sued all the parties to the transaction when it was determined that the defaulted bonds had been illegally issued. The complaint asserted that the bonds were illegally issued and invalid since the bonds were not in fact revenue bonds and therefore the trustee was not qualified to serve. In the State of Washington, a water and sewer district must use

---

[25] See, for example, *Broad v. Rockwell International Corp.*, 614 F.2d 418 (5th Cir. 1980).

[26] Case No. 01-2-00751-8.

the county treasurer or its designee as trustee for all municipal bonds issued with the exception of revenue bonds. In the case of revenue bonds, an institutional trustee may be appointed. The issuer, Holmes Harbor, and bond counsel both represented to the trustee that the bonds being issued were revenue bonds.

There was extensive motion practice in the case. In a hearing before the trial court, the court ruled that the bonds in fact were not revenue bonds, therefore making the Agreement between Holmes Harbor and the bank as trustee invalid and unenforceable. Most troubling for trustees, the court also held that the trustee should have discovered the illegality of the issuance prior to entering into the Agreement. It is unclear whether the court's ruling was influenced by testimony that two other banks had rejected the trusteeship and that the legal opinion as to the capacity of the trustee to serve was not unqualified. Among the allegations against the trustee was that the trustee relied on bond counsel's opinion inappropriately and that the trustee should have performed its own due diligence on Washington State law.

The members of the Corporate Trust Committee of the American Bankers Association submitted a declaration in the case explaining the longstanding principle in the industry that, prior to default, an institutional trustee has duties limited to those spelled out in the Agreement and that, prior to the execution and delivery of the Agreement, the proposed trustee has no obligation to bondholders or any other party. They explained the long-held principle that a trustee is not expected to conduct its own independent investigation into whether an issuer has authority under applicable law to issue the proposed bonds. The court denied the trustee's motion for reconsideration. The court stated it relied on the testimony of Robert Landau, coauthor of *Corporate Trust Administration and Management,* 4th edition (New York: Columbia University Press, 1992) that trustees are supposed to insure that they have "believable authority and capability to discharge their required duties" before signing a trust agreement. The case was eventually settled by the bond trustee and others.

ADMINISTRATION OF THE TRANSACTION BY THE BOND TRUSTEE

Postclosing, the administration of the transaction by the indenture trustee, governed by the terms of the basic Agreement, normally a bond resolution, indenture or ordinance, falls into three areas of responsibility:

- *The control of the principal amount of the securities authorized and outstanding.* The registrar function is basic to the financing and accurate records must be kept at all times as to the securities outstanding and securities canceled. With the advent of the Depository Trust Company, to be described below, what used to be a time consuming function for the trustee has in large part become the responsibility of others.

■ *The monitoring of performance and compliance with the indenture or bond resolution.* All resolutions contain covenants by issuers and/or borrowers that they will completely maintain projects, collect pledged revenues, abide by specific restraints and prohibitions in their financial affairs, and maintain and protect the trustee's title to any property or equipment collateralized under the issue. They also covenant to report on these matters on a specific schedule so that the trustee can study it and make determinations as to compliance with the resolution or ordinance. In making these determinations, the trustee may rely on the representations made in the reports as long as they are in the form required and signed by the officers authorized to do so.

■ *The holding of the security.* Not all bond resolutions or indentures require collateral, but for those that do, the trustee has the responsibility to preserve its title to property for the benefit of the bondholders. If revenues are pledged by statute or resolution, the trustee must determine that the appropriate accounts to receive the pledged revenues are established and complied with to achieve the desired result. The bond trustee may be called upon to direct the use of pledged revenues to pay operation and maintenance of the municipal operation or to fund bond reserve or special accounts, such as for replacement of obsolete equipment. The trustee must see that adequate provision is made for title, fire, liability and flood insurance on real property pledged and must prohibit the borrower from taking any action that would jeopardize the trustee's title to the property, and the borrower must not release any collateral unless other collateral of equal value is substituted or an amount of bonds proportionate to the value of the collateral is redeemed.

As previously discussed, predefault, the municipal bond trustee is protected by complying with the language of the Agreement. Although this rule would appear on its face to be easy to follow, in application, results have varied. Thus, based on an examination of the language of the Agreement, courts have held that a bond trustee has no duty to evaluate the precarious financial condition of the issuer[27] and meets notice requirements by utilizing the mails as provided for in the Agreement.[28] A similar analysis resulted in a conclusion that a bond trustee had no duty to perfect the security interest.[29]

---

[27] *Baker v. Summit Bank*, 46 Fed. Appx. 689 (3rd Cir. 2002).

[28] *Meckel v. Continental Resources Co.*, 758 F.2d 811 (2nd Cir. 1985).

[29] *Harriett & Henderson Yarns, Inc.*, 75 F. Supp. 2d 818 (W.D. Tenn. 1999).

Conversely, the contractual responsibility to disburse funds based upon requisition certificates has resulted in some decisions holding that the requisition certificate must provide sufficient detail to justify the expenditure[30] and that a bond trustee who failed to reject a certificate that did not use the required language breached its duty to noteholders.[31] As will be discussed below, recent changes in the municipal finance industry itself have resulted in new roles for the municipal trustee, all of which must be examined in the light of the previously discussed standards of behavior.

SELECTED CHALLENGES AND ISSUES FOR MUNICIPAL TRUSTEES POSTISSUANCE

Postissuance Tax Compliance

While few issues are more important to the municipal bondholder than compliance by the issuer with the restriction of the federal tax code, the role, if any, of the municipal trustee in policing such compliance differs from transaction to transaction based upon the language of the documents. The basic statutory rule is that interest on a bond is not tax-exempt if it is an *arbitrage bond* under Section 103(b)(2) of the Internal Revenue Code. As a general rule, the arbitrage restrictions limit the amount of investment return that can be made or retained with respect to the proceeds of a tax-exempt bond issue. The rebate requirement, which originally applied to private activity bonds and now extends to virtually all tax-exempt bonds, requires that investment return over the yield on the issue, if earned, is paid over or rebated to the United States Treasury. Typically, the bond trustee's arbitrage rebate duties are ministerial and, frequently, by contract, the trustee takes no responsibility under the documents for making arbitrage calculations. In fact, often the documents provide the trustee may conclusively rely upon the opinion of counsel or a CPA firm as to the compliance with the arbitrage rules and the structure of the transaction should appropriately provide that there will be funds available to pay for such advice.

It is routinely noted that tax-exempt bonds are based upon basic expectations as to use of the proceeds, the ability of the issuer to repay the bonds and the timing of when principal, agreed upon interest and other basic terms will be repaid. When any of these key expectations is modified postissuance, the tax-exempt status may be jeopardized. The determination of taxability, unless it is met with a mandatory redemption of the bonds, is normally an event of default under the bond resolution, raising the level of the trustee's

---

[30] *Shawmut Bank, N.A. v. Kress Associates*, 33 F.3d 1477 (9th Cir. 1994).
[31] *In re Bankers Trust Co.*, 450 F.3d 121 (2nd Cir. 2006).

duties and responsibilities and requiring the exercise of remedies. While the specifics of the application of the Internal Revenue Code are not the subject of this chapter, it is obvious that the trustee could be a key player in resolving postclosing tax situations which could lead to a determination of taxability and ultimately an event of default under the bond documents. The Internal Revenue Code has established a voluntary closing agreement program (IRS Notice 2001-60, 2001-40, I.R.B. 304) intended to encourage issuers and conduit borrowers to exercise due diligence and compliance with the Internal Revenue Code and applicable regulations by providing a vehicle to correct violations. While IRS negotiations are necessarily with the issuer, the municipal bond trustee may wish to, at the very least, monitor the proceedings to determine that the interests of the bondholders are being appropriately considered. This procedure is voluntary on the part of the issuer. In the event the issuer receives an audit letter with respect to the transaction, the trustee will need to be even more aggressive in monitoring the proceedings, to the degree possible, to prevent an adverse impact on the bondholders.

Bondholder Relations in a DTC Era

In earlier times, paper certificates evidenced the debt for which the trustee was acting, and the trustee could determine its holders by reviewing the bondholder list the trustee itself maintained. Notices required under the indenture could be given by the trustee via publication in a newspaper of general circulation in the "area" or in the mail to the parties on the trustee's bondholder list or both. The Depository Trust Company (DTC) was established in 1973 to reduce costs and provide clearing and settlement efficiencies by immobilizing securities and making "book-entry" changes to ownership of the securities. Now, certificates evidencing ownership of bonds are generally registered with the trustee in the name of the nominee for DTC, Cede & Co. The beneficial owners do not receive physical delivery of the certificates. Large securities firms who are DTC participants record their ownership position in the bonds at DTC. Customers of the DTC participants in turn have their ownership of the bond issue reflected on the books of the DTC participant. Firms who are not DTC participants may contract to have their ownership position handled by a DTC participant firm. These non-DTC participants may act as broker, nominee or agent for the ultimate beneficial holder, an institutional or individual investor. Further, a number of the DTC participants are themselves broker dealers or banks that hold for other persons. The result is that actual beneficial ownership of the securities is frequently removed from the registered owner of the bonds by many levels. All transfers of beneficial ownership interest in the bonds are made in accordance with the rules of DTC. The trustee has no responsibility or liability for transfers of beneficial ownership interest in the bonds.

How does a trustee with notice responsibilities under the documents provide for or meet the requirements of the documents when the trustee does not know the identity of the actual beneficial owners of the bonds? In the past, many indentures, bond ordinances and resolutions have continued provisions for the publication of notice in newspapers of general circulation in a specific area. With the use of DTC, reliance on such publication provisions has lessened or has been combined with the notice to DTC, the registered holder. The trustee forwards a notice electronically to DTC. However, unless a DTC participant has requested hard copies of the notices sent by the Trustee, DTC will simply notify the DTC participants of the availability of notices with a listing, by issue, of the notices that have been received. The notice is described in short-hand fashion, with just the first few words of the notice included. For an important notice, trustees may wish to obtain a position list from DTC for the bond issue and mail the notice to the DTC participants on the position list. Further, it may be possible for the trustee to obtain from the DTC participants the names of nonobjecting beneficial owners who do not oppose the disclosure of their name and address as bondholders. It is by no means clear, however, that even diligent efforts by the trustee will produce contacts with beneficial holders of a majority of the outstanding securities. While certain services purport to provide expertise in identifying beneficial holders, the greatest assistance to the trustee is the existence of large holders who actively seek out the trustee and make their identity known to the trustee. There is a school of thought that, in voluntarily taking action in addition to the limited notice requirements of the indenture, the trustee is exposed to possible liability and that the trustee's best protection is to religiously follow the exact terms of the documents. This should be kept in mind by beneficial holders who should not assume any extraordinary efforts will be made to notify them of important developments. It may behoove beneficial holders to be proactive and provide the trustee with a written request to notify the beneficial holder individually at the time the trustee is providing notice to DTC. Further, DTC has an electronic bulletin board for notices and mailings by the issuer or trustee which DTC participants, nominees, brokers and institutional holders, as well as individual holders through their nominee or broker, can access by CUSIP number.

Rather than being identified by the name of the transaction, issues are identified at DTC through CUSIP numbers. *CUSIP* is an acronym for the Committee on Uniform Security Identification Procedures of the American Bankers Association. The procedures regarding the assignment of CUSIP numbers were adopted in 1967. A standard numbering system is used by all segments of the securities industry. The CUSIP number consists of nine numerals; the first six are the issuer number, the next two are the issue number and the last are a check digit. The numbers that appear on the face of each stock and bond certificate are assigned by the CUSIP service bureau of Standard and Poor's Corporation. CUSIP numbers should be indicated on all notices provided by the trustee. The issuer and the trustee execute and deliver a letter of representations. All payments of principal, redemption premium, if any, and interest on the bonds and all notices with respect thereto, including notices of full or partial redemption, are made and given at the times and in the manner set out in the letter of representations. The trustee must be sure to include the CUSIP number in any communication with bondholders.

A working group composed of representatives of the National Association of Bond Lawyers, the Bond Market Association, the American Bankers Association, the Government Finance Officers Association, the National Association of State Auditors, Comptrollers and Treasurers, and the National Federation of Municipal Analysts made joint recommendations for better communication with the beneficial owners of defaulted municipal securities. In the year 2000, the National Association of Bond Lawyers issued its form indenture and commentary (which was updated in 2002) with respect to indentures governing municipal securities. The form indenture suggests recommended language to provide a method for beneficial owners to receive notices directly and to take certain steps to help notices get to the depository system after an event of default. Also, postissuance material events and notices should be available in varying degrees through nationally recognized municipal securities information repositories and state information depositaries and Disclosure USA as described in the next section.

The Municipal Trustee's Role in Continuing Disclosure

On November 10, 1994, the Securities and Exchange Commission (SEC) published amendments to Rule 15c2-12 that require commitments to continuing secondary market disclosure as a condition to accessing the municipal securities market. The amendments make it unlawful for a broker-dealer or municipal securities dealer to purchase or sell municipal securities in connection with a primary offering of an issue of municipal securities with an aggregate principal amount of at least $1 million unless it has reasonably determined that the issuer or an "obligated person" has undertaken in a written agreement or contract for the benefit of the holders of such municipal securities to provide certain information to specified information repositories annually and also upon occurrence of certain material events. The nationally recognized municipal securities information repositories are known as NRMSIRs and state information depositaries are known as SIDs.

Where a municipal transaction involves an active trustee, depending upon the structure, the undertaking to provide continuing disclosure may contain a recitation of the issuer or obligated person's undertaking to provide ongoing disclosure so that such undertaking can be enforced by the trustee on behalf of the bondholders. The issuer may covenant to provide to the trustee annual financial information, audited financial statements, if any, and material event notices. Material events include principal and interest payment delinquencies, nonpayment related defaults, unscheduled draws on debt service reserves reflecting financial difficulties, unscheduled draws on credit enhancements reflecting financial difficulties, substitution of credit or liquidity providers or their failure to perform, adverse tax opinions or events affecting the tax-exempt status of the security, modification to rights of security holders, bond calls, defeasances, release, substitution or sale of property securing repayment of securities and rating changes. Sometimes, the issuer undertakes to provide to the trustee the information required by the Rule and the trustee in turn agrees to provide such information received from the issuer to the repositories. Each material event notice provided by the trustee to the NRMSIRs and SIDs is also to be provided to the Municipal Securities Rule Making Board and is to be captioned and to prominently state the date, title and CUSIP number of the bonds. Further, the trustee may agree to promptly advise the issuer whenever, in the course of performing its duties as trustee, the trustee identifies an occurrence which, if material, would require the issuer to provide a material event notice provided that the failure of the trustee to so advise the issuer does not constitute a breach by the trustee of any of its duties and responsibilities. Despite the requirements of Rule 15c-2-12, continuing disclosure compliance by issuers is often poor, leaving trustees and bondholders in the dark.

It has been the experience of certain market participants that direct filing with the NRMSIRs can be cumbersome and attempts to retrieve the data can yield inconsistent results. A coalition of municipal securities market trade associations known as the Muni Council came together to address problems with the then-existing system of NRMSIRs. The Muni Council created a new disclosure entity, Disclosure USA, to enable parties who have the responsibility to file disclosure documents to deal with a single entity free of charge rather than with each of the NRMSIRs. To the degree contracts impose an obligation on the trustee to make filings with the NRMSIRs, the new central post office has agreed to transmit information to the NRMSIRs and SIDs as appropriate. In a letter dated September 7, 2004, the Office of Municipal Securities of the SEC articulated its position that transmitting required filings either directly or indirectly through a trustee or designated agent to Disclosure USA for submission to the NRMSIRs and any applicable SID without also separately submitting such filings to the NRMSIRs and SIDs by some other means is consistent with the intent of Rule 15c2-12. Accordingly, while the trustee itself does not assume disclosure obligations, it can, by contract, play a key role in the dissemination of required information to the secondary market.

The Bond Trustee and Bond Insurance: The Advantages and the Complications

Since the early 1970s, municipal bond insurance has emerged as the credit enhancement of choice for municipal bond issues. The attractiveness of municipal bond insurance to cautious investors has increased with the massive default of the Washington Public Power Supply System, the bankruptcy of the Allegheny Health, Education and Research Foundation and the Chapter 9 filing by Orange County, California.

Bond insurers typically conduct extensive due diligence before agreeing to insure a municipal bond issue and the credit rating of the major municipal bond insurers is AAA. Accordingly, even if the underlying issuer would not qualify for such a rating, bonds that are insured by the premier insurers normally have that top rating, which reduces the borrowing cost for the issuer. In effect, the insurance pays for itself.

Bond insurers assume responsibility for the timely payment of principal and interest as it becomes due if the issuer is unable to meet those obligations. Municipal bond insurance also covers sinking fund payments. However, the bond insurer normally does not have an obligation to make full payment of the accelerated principal balance of the bonds upon default. The policy guarantees the timely payment as scheduled over the life of the bonds.

Given the obligations assumed by the bond insurers, it is not surprising that the bond insurer often demands the time and attention of the trustee with respect to monitoring the underlying bond issue. That is particularly because the issuer is the first source of payment of principal and interest on the bonds. Documentation for insured municipal bond issue outlines the relationship between the trustee and the insurer. The trustee will require the consent of the insurer to any amendment of the documents that affects the insurer's rights, the execution of any supplemental indenture or bond ordinance or any significant action by the trustee. In the event of an insolvency, the insurer will have the right to vote on behalf of all the holders of insured bonds, absent a default by the bond insurer under the policy. Further, upon the occurrence and continuance of the event of default, the insurer will be entitled to control and direct the enforcement of all rights and remedies granted to the bondholders and the right to approve all waivers of events of defaults. Normally, the bond insurer will have its own counsel and thus, while the presence of bond insurance guarantees a payout of the bonds, the trustee will necessarily have to be sensitive to the views of the insurer.

This special consideration can prove especially challenging when bonds are issued in various series, only some of which are insured. Although normally the insured bonds will be entitled to a priority of payment vis-à-vis the other series, the interplay between the bond insurer and the majority holders of other series can test the abilities of the most experienced trustee.

The Trustee as Administrator of Variable Rate Securities

Bonds with special investment features present the trustee with particular demands. Floating rate and variable rate bonds are particularly attractive to investors in a rising interest rate environment. Interest on such security is recalculated periodically based upon certain criteria such as the prevailing rate for treasury bills or other interest rates. Other references for the variable rate may include LIBOR, or the price of a specific commodity, or the price of a specific financial instrument that normally changes over time in response to market pressure. The prevailing interest rate is the current interest rate based upon the specified standard for the issue for the period until the next reset.

While the earliest variable rate issues were private placements that paid an interest rate based upon a percentage of an agreed upon index, later versions have included an ability of bondholders to tender their bonds back to the issuer at par through a put. Obviously, a remarketing agent is responsible for setting the new interest rate and remarketing any tendered bonds. The liquidity facility to permit payment of the tendered bonds is often a letter of credit. The letter of credit backstops any failure to remarket the bonds by the remarketing agent. Unlike bond insurance, which pays the scheduled principal and interest when due, the letter of credit covers the accelerated principal and interest amount due on the securities. Even more complicated is the type of variable rate demand bond in which rates are reset monthly, weekly or even daily by the remarketing agent. The transaction documents should spell out with specificity the duties of the trustee for the bonds with respect to the calculation of interest and the interaction between the trustee, the remarketing agent and the tender agent, if any. Such securities are a far cry from the plain vanilla general obligation bonds that municipal indenture trustees first administered. Moreover, it goes without saying that the more complicated the transaction, the more challenging will be any contractual obligation of the trustee to monitor the required payments and compliance by other parties with the deal documents.

Swaps

The role of the municipal indenture trustee has become even more difficult with the advent of municipal derivative products. The use of interest rate derivative products by the municipal issuers has grown in number and innovation in recent years. A derivative product refers to a contract such as an interest rate swap agreement which derives it value from the value or changes in value of another financial instrument or index. An interest rate swap contract is a legal agreement between two parties to exchange cash flows. In its simplest form, an interest rate swap arrangement is one in which one party agrees to make fixed payments and the other party agrees to make payments based upon a floating rate of interest. Payments can be structured to coincide with fixed bond interest payments and the amount of the swap amortizes as the bonds mature or are redeemed. The International Swap and Derivatives Association, Inc. has developed standard forms to document the typical interest rate contract, although, the terms can be heavily negotiated. Inherent in interest rate swaps is the counterparty risk, the risk that the counterparty will be unable to perform under the terms of the swap. In addition, depending on the relationship between the rate on the bonds and the floating rate on the swap, the issuer could suffer a shortfall. There are numerous variations on these products ranging from the straightforward to the supremely complex. Today's municipal bond trustee must not only understand the structure of the transaction the trustee has been engaged to monitor but also be sensitive to the practical and legal issues inherent in these structures.

SUMMARY

The breath of the municipal financial products for which institutions act as trustee have evolved in intricacy and yet the basic principles established in case law regarding the scope of the responsibility of the bond trustee should remain constant. Because the trustee is a creature of the contract creating the transaction prior to default, municipal practitioners must take care to describe in detail the functions expected of the trustee in today's transactions. Further, current technology is a mixed blessing to the bond trustee, greatly simplifying certain tasks, but complicating others, including the providing of notice to the bondholders. With the consolidation of the corporate trust industry, there is increased pressure on institutions acting as trustee to assume the challenges of new products without abandoning the basic limited nature of their role.

Chapter 9: The Last Resort for Financially Distressed Municipalities

James E. Spiotto
Partner
Chapman and Cutler LLP

In instances of extreme financial distress, a municipality may consider instituting a proceeding for municipal debt adjustment under Chapter 9 of the Bankruptcy Code or face acrimonious lawsuits which are both injurious to the municipality and unproductive in providing an economic solution to the problem. However, as graphically illustrated in Exhibits 9.1 through 9.5, municipalities have sought the protection of the bankruptcy courts over the years. The appendix to this chapter provides a list of the municipal bankruptcy cases filed through February 8, 2007. The purpose of this chapter is to explain the structure and significance of a Chapter 9 filing.

Our system of federalism grants local governmental bodies the independence and the freedom to be able (with the consent of their citizens) to finance various necessary improvements through the issuance of municipal bonds. Under virtually every other form of government, the local governmental body, regardless of the merits of such proposals, must first request approval and financing from the central government before the local government is able to proceed with such commonplace municipal improvements as bridges, sewers, roads, and public buildings. Our Founding Fathers ordained that certain independence and power should be given to the states and their local governmental bodies.[1] Thereafter, during the late 1700s and early 1800s, a method of finance evolved whereby municipalities would issue their own debt obligations either based on their full faith and credit

---

[1] See *The Federalist* No. 31 (A. Hamilton).

Note: A more detailed discussion by the author appears in M. David Gelfand (ed.), *State and Local Goverment Debt Financing*, Cumulative Supplement issued June 2007 (St. Paul, MN: Thomson West).

EXHIBIT 9.1   Frequency of Municipal Bankruptcies, 1937–2007 (as of 02/08/07)

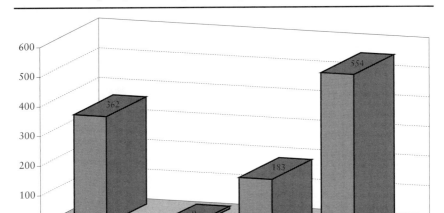

ª Since passage of the Bankruptcy Code.

EXHIBIT 9.2   Chapter 9 Filings by Year, 1980–2007 (as of 02/08/07)

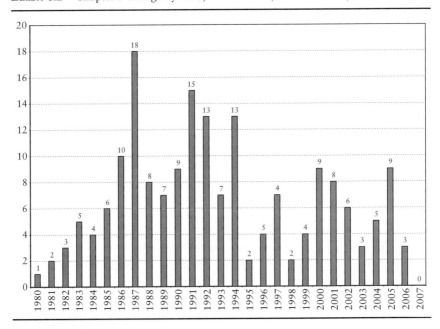

EXHIBIT 9.3   Chapter 9 Filings by State, 1980–2007 (as of 02/08/07)

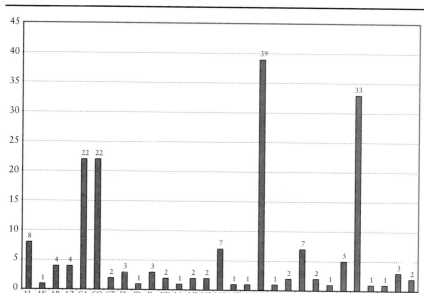

EXHIBIT 9.4   Chapter 9 Filings by Type, 1980–2007 (as of 02/08/07)

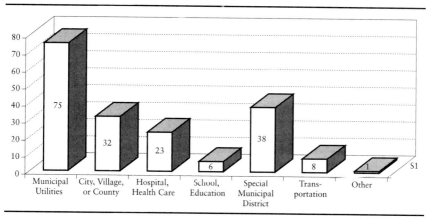

(general obligation bonds) or based upon the revenues to be collected by the municipal body in connection with the financed improvement (revenue bonds). This system of municipal finance has allowed citizens to determine on a local basis what improvements they desire and to finance such improvements without the need for federal financing or approval.

EXHIBIT 9.5   Chapter 9 Filings by Region, 1980–2007 (as of 03/14/06)

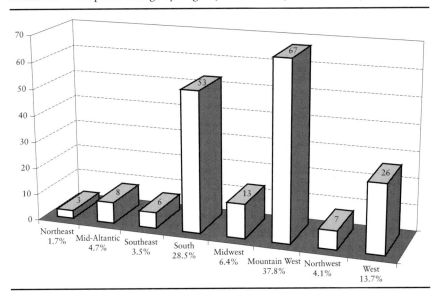

As our municipalities have grown and prospered, so has their need for continued financing. The confidence of the municipal bond market is essential, and municipalities traditionally have made every effort to honor their public debt obligations. States have enacted statutory provisions waiving sovereign rights in connection with financings to assure the bondholders that if they purchase the revenue bonds of municipalities within these states, the pledge of revenue to the bondholders cannot be diverted or terminated.[2] These statutory provisions were not only for the bondholders but also for the citizens of the state so that by providing assurance to bond investors of adequate remedies, all municipalities could make use of municipal bond financing when necessary. Currently, municipalities both large and small are facing severe economic hardship. Ironically, during times of financial crises, a municipality needs the support of the municipal bond market.

Chapter 9 of the Bankruptcy Code can be an alternative to municipalities from which the market does not shrink provided that the principles and practical realities of municipal financing are not disturbed. This material will analyze the viability of Chapter 9 as a remedy for municipalities. Particular attention will be directed to the amendments to Chapter 9 which became

---

[2] Most states have statutory provisions authorizing the pledge of revenues for the payment of certain bond indebtedness. Some state statutes specifically provide that the revenues so pledged cannot be diverted or used for purposes other than first making the required payment on the bond indebtedness. See Cal. Educ. Code § 1525.

law on November 3, 1988[3] (Municipal Bankruptcy Amendments). The Municipal Bankruptcy Amendments have made Chapter 9 a real option for municipalities since they have cured many of the ambiguities and uncertainties which existed under prior law. A modification to Chapter 9 made in the Bankruptcy Reform Act of 1994[4] clarified the eligibility of municipalities to institute Chapter 9 proceedings.

HISTORICALLY, BANKRUPTCY HAS BEEN A MECHANISM OF DEBT ADJUSTMENT IN OTHER COUNTRIES

The notion of bankruptcy as a mechanism of debt adjustment was present in some of the earliest forms of law, including Greek and Roman law, which regarded the discharge of debt and the prompt and equitable liquidation of assets as a necessary ingredient of civilized society. During the fourth and fifth centuries BCE, 10 out of 13 Greek municipalities belonging to the Attic Maritime Association had defaulted on their loans from the Delos Temple, and the notion of municipal receivership was recognized[5] when a Greek banker took over the administration and collection of taxes of Atarneus to pay off a defaulted loan. While under early Roman practices a debtor who could not pay his creditors over time met with a certain radical penalty—death—later procedures included the purportedly more humane remedy of the sale of the debtor's assets and distribution to creditors.[6] English common law, which was, for the most part, the source from which our legal system arose, recognized bankruptcy as a necessary ingredient of its legal system from the late seventeenth and eighteenth century, although imprisoning debtors for nonpayment of debts was common. Basic American Bankruptcy law is less harsh and presents a debtor with a method for putting its financial affairs in order.[7]

In enacting the Constitution of the United States, the Founding Fathers determined that the legislative branch of the federal government should be vested with establishing laws regarding bankruptcy in order to ensure

---

[3] Municipal Bankruptcy Amendments, Pub L No 100597, 102 Stat 3028 (1988).
[4] Bankruptcy Reform Act of 1994, Pub L 103394, 108 Stat 4106 (1994) (the "1994 Bill").
[5] Hillhouse, *Municipal Bonds: A Century of Experience* (New York: Prentice-Hall, Inc., 1936).
[6] See generally Wenger, Institutes of the Roman Law of Civil Procedure (1940); *Continental Illinois Nat. Bank & Trust Co. v. Chicago, Rock Island & Pacific Ry. Co.*, 294 US 648, 70 L Ed 1110, 55 S Ct 595 (1934).
[7] See generally Holdsworth, *History of English Law* VIII (London: Sweet & Maxwell, 1936).

uniform and consistent resolution of insolvency matters. Accordingly, the Constitution provides that "Congress shall have the power . . . to establish . . . uniform laws on the subject of bankruptcies throughout the United States . . . ."[8] However, while provisions have evolved which govern bankruptcy of municipalities, the Tenth[9] and Eleventh[10] Amendments to the Constitution preclude the power of the federal government to supervise the bankruptcy of a state.

BRIEF HISTORY OF MUNICIPAL BANKRUPTCY LEGISLATION IN THE UNITED STATES

Prior to 1934, federal bankruptcy legislation did not provide a mechanism for municipal bankruptcy, insolvency, or debt adjustment.[11] During the period 1929 through 1937, there were 4,700 defaults by governmental bodies in the payment of their obligations.[12] In 1934, the House and Senate Judiciary Committees estimated that there were over 1,000 municipalities in default on their bonds.[13]

Units of local government were dependent upon property tax. During the Depression, there was widespread nonpayment of such taxes. Bondholders brought cases for accountings, secured judgments and obtained writs of

---

[8] US Const art I, § 8, cl 4.

[9] "The powers not delegated to the United States by the Constitution, nor prohibited to the States, are reserved to the States respectively, or to the people."

[10] "The Judicial power of the United States shall not be construed to extend to any suit in law or equity, commenced or prosecuted against one of the United States by Citizens of another State, or by Citizens or subjects or any Foreign State."

[11] The Bankruptcy Act of 1800, 2 Stat 19 (1800); The Bankruptcy Act of 1841, 5 Stat 440 (1841); The Bankruptcy Act of 1867, 14 Stat 517 (1867); The Bankruptcy Act of 1898, 30 Stat 544 (1898). That is not to say that there were no defaults in government obligations in the 19th century. Indeed, the 1842 default by the State of Pennsylvania on its bonded debt inspired William Wordsworth to pen the sonnet "To the Pennsylvanians" in which he spoke of "won confidence, now ruthlessly betrayed." It was the defaults of local utility districts and municipalities in the 1800's that tarnished the integrity of the "new frontier's" obligations. George Peabody, an eminent financier, sought to be admitted to polite English Society only to be rebuffed, not due to his lack of social grace, but because his countrymen did not pay their debts. It was the defaults by governmental bodies in the latter half of the 1800s and early 1900s which brought about the procedures that are now taken for granted, including debt limitations on municipal issues, bond counsel, and clearly defined bondholders' rights.

[12] See A Commission Report, City Financial Emergencies: The Intergovernmental Dimension (Advisory Commission on Intergovernmental Relations, Washington, D.C., July 1973).

[13] S Rep No 407, 73rd Cong, 2d Sess 2 (1934).

mandamus for levies of further taxes. The first municipal debt provisions of the Bankruptcy Act of 1898 as amended from time to time (the Bankruptcy Act) were enacted as emergency legislation for the relief of such municipalities, and became effective on May 24, 1934.[14] These provisions were to be operative for a two year period from that date, but this period was later extended to January 1, 1940.[15]

The municipal debt adjustment provisions of the Bankruptcy Act enacted in 1934 reflected an attempt to protect municipalities and corporation from debilitating disputes with creditors.[16] The 1934 legislation provided a procedure whereby a local governmental unit, if it could obtain acceptances from two thirds of its creditors, could have a plan of readjustment enforced by the federal courts. Under the 1934 legislation, the court, and to some extent, the creditors, through the court, had certain control over the municipality's revenues and governmental affairs. In 1936, the Supreme Court of the United States held, in the case of *Ashton v. Cameron County Water Improvement Dist., No. 1*,[17] that the 1934 municipal bankruptcy legislation was unconstitutional in that it infringed on the sovereign powers of the states.

The invalidation of the 1934 legislation left many municipalities hopelessly insolvent and without any real practical remedy. In fact, at the time of the decision in Ashton, there were approximately 89 petitions pending for relief.[18] In 1937, new legislation was passed which attempted to cure the

---

[14] 48 Stat 798 (1934).

[15] 49 Stat 1198 (1936).

[16] HR Rep No 207, 73rd Cong, 1st Sess 103 (1933); HR Rep No 517, 75th Cong, 1st Sess 34 (1937); HR Rep No 686, 94th Cong, 1st Sess 541, 542 (1975); HR Rep No 595, 95th Cong, 1st Sess 397398 (1977); S Rep No 95989, 95th Cong, 2nd Sess 110 (1978).

[17] *Ashton v. Cameron County Water Improvement District, No. 1*, 298 US 513, 80 L Ed 1309, 56 S Ct 892, rehg denied, 299 US 619, 81 L Ed 457, 57 S Ct 5 (1936), with Mr. Justice Cardozo among the four dissenters. Justice Cardozo noted the widespread existence of municipal defaults and the nominal as opposed to real remedies of bondholders.

"Students of government have estimated that on January 1, 1933 out of securities to the extent of $14,000,000,000 issued by units smaller than states, a billion were in default. The plight of the debtors was bad enough; that of the creditors was even worse. It is possible that in some instances the bonds did not charge the municipalities or other units with personal liability. Even when they did, however, execution could not issue against the property of the debtor held for public uses, and few of the debtors were the owners of anything else. In such circumstances, the only remedy was a mandamus whereby the debtor was commanded to tax and tax again." 298 US at 534.

[18] See George H. Hempel, "An Evaluation of Municipal Bankruptcy Laws and Procedures," *Journal of Finance* 28, no. 3 (1973), pp. 1339–1351. Hempel discusses a number of examples illustrating how Chapter IX worked in practice. In the case of Fort Lee, New Jersey, municipal bankruptcy court jurisdiction was exercised con

defects outlined by the court in Ashton and to protect municipalities from the injurious protracted litigation some were enduring.

The 1937 municipal bankruptcy legislation[19] enacted in response to the Ashton decision required: (1) no interference with the fiscal or governmental affairs of political subdivisions; (2) a limitation of the protection of bankruptcy to the taxing agency itself; (3) no involuntary proceedings; (4) no judicial control or jurisdiction over property and those revenues of the petitioning agency necessary for essential governmental purposes; and (5) no impairment of contractual obligations by states. This legislation was upheld by the *Supreme Court in United States v. Bekins*,[20] which noted that the statute was carefully drawn not to impinge upon the sovereignty of the states. Like the 1934 legislation, the 1937 provisions were deemed emergency in character, but expiration dates were repeatedly extended.

In 1946, the termination clause was repealed,[21] thereby making the municipal bankruptcy legislation a permanent part of the Bankruptcy Act, Chapter IX. In addition, the 1946 amendments also: (1) extended the benefits of Chapter IX of the Bankruptcy Act to incorporated counties, authorities, commissions, or other similar public agencies organized for the purpose of constructing, maintaining or operating revenue producing enterprises; (b) provided for reference of special issues of fact to a referee in bank-

---

tinuously over several decades from 1928 through the 1970s. Fort Lee lost more than 40% of the assessed real estate valuation because of the construction of the George Washington Bridge. In 1938, a plan of composition was filed whereby bondholders received refunding bonds maturing in 1979 equal to the face value of their claims plus any interest in arrears. Saluda, North Carolina was prevented from filing a successful Plan of Debt Adjustment by one bondholder who held more than half of the outstanding bonds. While the default occurred in the 1930s, the case was not filed until 1971 with the bondholders getting over 40 cents per dollar of debt. Ranger, Texas filed at various times (1940, 1946, 1971) three refunding plans. In Medley, Florida, a plan of compensation extending the nonbonded debt was approved. The bonded debt of Medley was left untouched. (Hempel, "An Evaluation of Municipal Bankruptcy Laws and Procedures," pp. 1344–1345.) The case of San Jose School District is an example for any municipality that desires to live successfully after a Chapter 9 proceeding has been filed. From the outset of the Chapter 9 proceeding, San Jose maintained that its bonds would continue to be paid; they were, and San Jose is existing outside a Chapter 9. The cases of Ft. Lee, Saluda, Ranger, and San Jose all demonstrate the need for a practical resolution of temporary as well as permanent cash flow problems. The resolutions differ and if the municipality is not realistic in the beginning (overly optimistic as to revenue, payoff) a harsher and more drastic resolution will be obtained in subsequent proceedings.

[19] 50 Stat 654 (1937).
[20] *United States v. Bekins*, 304 US 27, 82 L Ed 1137, 58 S Ct 811, rehg denied, 304 US 589, 82 L Ed 1549, 58 S Ct 1043 (1938).
[21] 60 Stat 409 (1946).

ruptcy or Special Master; (c) provided for a preliminary stay of proceedings against a municipality upon the filing of a proceeding under Chapter IX; and strengthened the effectiveness and workability of Chapter IX by means of certain procedural changes.[22]

Chapter IX then, while part of the Bankruptcy Act, provided a forum whereby a municipality could voluntarily seek an adjustment of indebtedness. A Chapter IX was not a proceeding to adjudge the city a bankrupt. The court's jurisdiction did not extend to declaring the city bankrupt or to administering its affairs as a bankrupt. The court was limited to disapproving or carrying out a proposed plan of reorganization of a municipality's debt.[23]

This humble birth of municipal debt adjustment must be remembered. The principles enumerated in Ashton and the 1937 legislation are important in understanding the role of a Bankruptcy Court in a Chapter 9 proceeding today.[24] The Court cannot constitutionally interfere with the revenue, politics or day-to-day operations of the municipality. The Bankruptcy Court cannot replace by its rulings or appointments the City Council or any other elected or appointed official. The limited but vital role of the Bankruptcy Court is to supervise the effective and appropriate adjustment of municipal debt. This is significant when assessing the role of the Bankruptcy Court in municipal debt adjustment. Historically, Chapter IX and its successor Chapter 9 were intended to facilitate rather than mandate voluntary municipal debt adjustment and not municipal debt elimination.

EXISTING MUNICIPAL BANKRUPTCY PROVISIONS

Despite the economic difficulties facing New York in 1975, Chapter IX was not perceived to present a viable solution to the problems. In particular, New York would have been required to show that, prepetition, 51% of its creditors (including the holders of bearer bonds), accepted the plan of composition. Further, the law in effect had no mechanism for raising funds to pay the municipality's postpetition expenses. Having observed the deficiencies of the old Chapter IX in practice, Congress set about creating a mechanism to manage the financial troubles of a municipality. On April 8, 1976, the

---

[22] See HR Rep No 6682, 79th Cong, 2d Sess 112 (1946).

[23] *Leco Properties Inc. v. R.E. Crummer & Co.*, 128 F2d 110 (CA5, 1942). Further, the court had no jurisdiction to determine the existence of the city or boundary disputes in the nature of quo warranto. *Green v. City of Stuart*, 135 F2d 33 (CA5, 1943).

[24] Upon the adoption of the Bankruptcy Reform Act of 1978 (hereinafter referred to as the "Bankruptcy Code"), the roman numerals which had previously been used to identify chapters of the Bankruptcy Act were abandoned in favor of arabic numbers. Hence, since the effective date of the Bankruptcy Code, "Chapter IX" has become Chapter 9.

bill amending Chapter IX of the Bankruptcy Act was signed into law, Public Law 94260 (the 1976 Legislation).[25] Among the major changes was the elimination of the requirement that the municipality obtain the prepetition consent of 51%[26] of its creditors. The 1976 Legislation allowed the city to file for bankruptcy without the approval of its creditors and permitted the city to continue borrowing for essential government services. The provisions regarding municipal bankruptcy were further modified in the Bankruptcy Reform Act of 1978 (the Bankruptcy Code)[27] whereby Chapter IX was redesignated Chapter 9. Chapter 9 was amended slightly by the enactment of the Bankruptcy Amendments and Federal Judgeship Act of 1984 (the 1984 Act).[28]

On November 3, 1988, President Reagan signed into law substantive amendments to Chapter 9 which corrected some of the inconsistencies between existing bankruptcy law and municipal law, the Municipal Bankruptcy Amendments. The Municipal Bankruptcy Amendments became effective as of that date. The Municipal Bankruptcy Amendments are designed to harmonize bankruptcy law with existing municipal law and financing practices. Their focus includes assurance that liens on "special revenue" not be extinguished, that prepetition payments on bonds and notes be free from the taint of possible preference attack, and that revenue bonds not be

[25] 90 Stat 315 (1976). For a general discussion of the 1976 Legislation see *Norton Bankr L & Prac* § 47.01 et seq; Robert Bond, "Municipal Bankruptcy under the 1976 Amendments to Chapter IX of the Bankruptcy Act," *Fordham Urban Law Journal* 5 (1976), pp. 1–12; Kenneth Ellison, "The Recent Revision of the Federal Municipal Bankruptcy Statute: A Potential Reprieve for Insolvent Cities?" *Harvard Journal on Legislation* 13 (1976), pp. 549–592; Lawrence King, "Municipal Insolvency: Chapter IX, Old and New; Chapter IX Rules," *American Banker Law Journal* (1976), pp. 55–56; Joseph Patchan and Susan Collins, "The 1976 Municipal Bankruptcy Law," *University of Miami Law Review* 31 (1977), pp. 287–306.

[26] The prior consent requirement was workable during the depression when most refundings were accomplished through the vehicle of the Reconstruction Finance Corporation which bought a large portion of the outstanding bonds.

[27] 11 USC § 101 et seq.

[28] On July 10, 1984, President Reagan signed the Bankruptcy Amendments and Federal Judgeship Act of 1984 ("1984 Act"), Pub L No. 98353. This legislation consists of three main parts: creation of a new Bankruptcy Court to replace the Bankruptcy Reform Act provisions found unconstitutional in Northern Pipeline in the Supreme Court's decision of June 28, 1982, (Title I of the 1984 Act); creation of additional district and circuit court judgeships (Title II of the 1984 Act); and Amendment of the Bankruptcy Code making changes in areas where either certain abuses or concerns were raised regarding the Bankruptcy Reform Act of 1978. Such areas included rejection of labor contracts, grain storage facility bankruptcies, repurchase agreements, timesharing agreements, shopping center bankruptcies, discharge of debts incurred by drunk drivers and consumer credit (Title III of the 1984 Act).

transformed into general obligation bonds. Further, the Amendments make a general failure to pay debts the criterion for municipal insolvency and eligibility for filing.[29] The 1994 Bill clarifies the split which had developed in case decisions and provides that municipalities must be specifically authorized by the State in order to be eligible to file for bankruptcy.[30]

Chapter 9 is not a vehicle for elimination of debt but rather for debt adjustment. A Chapter 9 proceeding is a mechanism for a debtor municipality, through a court supervised proceeding, to attempt to settle disputes with its creditors. Since a municipal unit cannot liquidate its assets to satisfy creditors and continue to function as a municipality, the primary purpose of Chapter 9 of the Bankruptcy Code is to allow the municipal unit to continue operating while it adjusts or refinances creditor claims. Indeed, one of the stated purposes of the Bankruptcy Code was to provide a "workable procedure so that a municipality of any size that has encountered financial difficulties may work with its creditors to adjust its debts."[31] Under this legislation, a city cannot be forced to take any specific action without the state's consent.

The causes of these municipal bankruptcies include large judgments which the local governments are unable to pay,[32] other court action,[33] burdensome labor contracts,[34] related real estate developments which went into private bankruptcy,[35] changes in government structure,[36] poor financial planning,[37] or declining land values and real estate deflation which have plagued special districts.[38] One of the causes of the Orange County crisis was the imposition

---

[29] Municipal Bankruptcy Amendments, Pub L No 100597 (1988).

[30] 1994 Bill at Section 402.

[31] HR Rep No 137, 93rd Cong, 1st Sess 237248, reprinted in [1978] US Code Cong and Ad News 6221.

[32] Bay St. Louis, Miss., South Tucson, Ariz., and Wapanucka, Okla.

[33] North and South Shenango Joint Municipal Authority.

[34] San Jose School Dist.

[35] Grimes County Municipal Utility Dist. No. 1; Sanitary & Improvement Dist. No. 5 of Cass County, Neb.; Sanitary & Improvement Dist. No. 4 of Lancaster County, Neb.; Sanitary & Improvement Dist. No. 42 of Sarpy County, Neb.; Sanitary & Improvement Dist. No. 7 of Lancaster County, Neb.

[36] The Management Institute of San Leandro; San Jose School District; Jersey City Medical Center; Monterey County Special Health Care Authority.

[37] Pleasant View Utility Dist. of Cheatham County; Pulaski Memorial Hospital.

[38] For example, Colorado Centre Metropolitan District; Villages at Castle Rock Metropolitan District No. 4; Hamilton Creek Metropolitan District; Summit County, Colorado; WillOWisp; Wolf Creek Valley Metropolitan District No. II, Mineral County, Colorado; Wolf Creek Valley Metropolitan District No. IV, Mineral County, Colorado; Dawson Ridge Metropolitan District No. 1.

of a constitutionally imposed lower tax cap (Proposition 13).[39] Interestingly, as of the date of this writing, not a single municipality in Louisiana, Mississippi or Alabama filed for Chapter 9 in the wake of Hurricane Katrina. This result was credited to a combination of federal assistance and financial support provided by states and the prevalence of bond issuance.[40]

INITIATION OF CHAPTER 9 PROCEEDING AND EFFECT ON BONDHOLDER RIGHTS AND REMEDIES

Only a municipality may be a debtor under Chapter 9 of the Bankruptcy Code.[41] Only a municipality can initiate a Chapter 9 proceeding. There can be no involuntary Chapter 9 proceeding. Not only are involuntary proceedings constitutionally prohibited, as set forth in *Ashton v. Cameron County Water Improvement Dist. No. 1,*[42] but also there is no statutory basis for such an involuntary action. Only § 301 of the Bankruptcy Code, providing for voluntary cases, is incorporated into Chapter 9. A municipality is a political subdivision, or public agency, or instrumentality of a state.[43] A municipality is not eligible to be a debtor pursuant to any other Chapter of the Bankruptcy Code.[44]

Moreover, under the 1994 Bill, in order to proceed under Chapter 9, state law must have specifically authorized the entity to be a debtor under Chapter 9.[45] Some states have specifically authorized a municipality to so

---

[39] Article XIIIA of the California Constitution.

[40] *The Bond Buyer*, September 1, 2001.

[41] 11 USC § 109(c). Claims by holders of industrial revenue bonds are not governed by Chapter 9, and amounts owed by private companies to the holders of industrial development bonds are not to be included among the assets of the municipality. S Rep No 95989, 95th Cong, 2d Sess 109 (1978). The determination of whether or not an entity is a "municipality" can be difficult. Although originally Chapter 11 relief was sought and denied because of the debtor's status as a municipality, the Court in *In re Jersey City Medical Center*, 817 F2d 1055 (CA3, 1987), ruled that a public municipal hospital was a proper debtor under Chapter 9. Conversely, the cases *American Milling Research and Development, Inc.*, No. 7400129 and *Fort Cobb Irrigation District*, No. 7600679, were initially filed under Chapter 9 but were converted to Chapter 11 bankruptcies.

[42] *Ashton v. Cameron Water Improvement District No. 1*, 298 US 513, 80 L Ed 1309, 56 S Ct 892, rehg denied, 299 US 619, 81 L Ed 457, 57 S Ct 5 (1936).

[43] 11 USC § 101(29).

[44] Only a "person" is eligible for relief under Chapters 7 and 11 of the Code. "Governmental unit" is excluded from the definition of "person." 11 USC § 101(33).

[45] 11 USC § 109(c)(2).

proceed.[46] Some states have specifically prohibited municipalities from filing under the Bankruptcy Code.[47]

Prior to 1994, a number of states had been silent on the issue of whether local governmental bodies were authorized to file under Chapter 9. The power of a municipality "to do all acts necessary, proper or convenient" including the right to sue and be sued had been held sufficient to authorize a municipality to file.[48] Given the judicial and legislative history surround-

---

[46] *States that specifically authorize municipal bankruptcies:*

Ala. Code 1975 § 11-81-3	Minn. Stat. Ann. § 471.831
Ariz. Rev. Stat. Ann. § 35-603	Mo. Ann. Stat. § 427.100
Ark. Code Ann. § 14-74-103	Mont. Code Ann. § 7-7-132
Cal. Gov't Code § 53760	Neb. Rev. St. § 13-402
Colo. Rev. Stat. Ann. § 32-1-1402	N.Y. Local Finance Law § 85.80
[Note limitations discussed below]	Okla. Stat. Ann. tit. 62 §§ 281, 283
Fla. Stat. Ann. § 218.01	S.C. Code Ann. § 6-1-10
Idaho Code Ann. § 67-3903	Tex. Loc. Gov't Code § 140.001
Ky. Rev. Stat Ann. § 66.400	Wash. Rev. Code § 39.64.040

States that conditionally authorize municipal bankruptcies:

Conn. Gen. Stat. Ann. § 7-566	N.C. Gen. Stat. Ann. § 23-48
La. Rev. Stat. Ann. § 39-619	Ohio Rev. Code Ann. § 133.36
Mich. Comp. Laws § 141.1222	53 Pa. Cons. Stat. Ann. § 11701.261
N.J. Stat. Ann. § 52:27-40	

Colorado has enacted legislation specifically authorizing its beleaguered special taxing districts to file a petition under Chapter 9. Section 32-1-1402 of the Colorado revised statutes states that "any insolvent taxing district is hereby authorized to file a petition authorized by federal bankruptcy law and to take any and all action necessary or proper to carry out the plan filed with said petition . . . ."

[47] See, for example, Ga Code Ann § 36-80-5.

[48] *In re Pleasant View Utility Dist. of Cheatham County, Tenn.*, 24 BR 632 (BR MD Tenn, 1982). The court concluded that the term "generally authorized" as used in § 109(c) mans only that the state should give some indication that the municipality has the necessary power to seek relief under the federal bankruptcy law. The court so held despite legislative history of the section which indicated that the Senate rejected the House's proposal that a municipality would be eligible to file a Chapter 9 petition unless such filing was prohibited by state law. See HR Rep No 595, 95th Cong, 1st Sess 263264, 318319, reprinted in [1978] US Code Cong & Admin News 5963, 62206222. The Senate's position was a departure from the earlier notion that a municipality's authority to file a municipal bankruptcy was an inherent element of existence. See *In re South Beardstown Drainage & Levee Dist.*, 125 F2d 13 (CA7, 1941). See also *In re City of Wellston*, 43 BR 348 (BR ED Mo, 9184), in which the court held that a grant of powers to act for the preservation of peace and good order and for the benefit of trade and commerce was sufficient to authorize the filing of a Chapter 9 petition.

ing municipal debt adjustments and state authorization to file a Chapter 9, it was important to note there could have been an overlooked problem in this regard. Commentators cited the reported decisions in North and South Shenango Joint Municipal Authority as a statement of law.[49] This case as reported could stand for the proposition that home rule power granted to a municipality is sufficient authority for it to be eligible to institute a Chapter 9 proceeding even though there is no expressed statutory power to file. However, such was not the final result in North and South Shenango, in which the Bankruptcy Court was reversed by the District Court in an unreported decision.

In a decision arising out of the filing by a Colorado special purpose district before the 1994 legislation, the court revisited the same issue. The special purpose district had, under applicable statute, the ability to be a party to suits, actions and proceedings, to borrow money, incur indebtedness and issue bonds, to refund any bond indebtedness, to manage, control and supervise all of the business and affairs of the district and to exercise all rights and powers necessary or incidental to or implied from the special powers granted by the statute. The statute further provided that the specific powers granted should not be considered as limitations upon any power necessary or appropriate to carry out the purposes and intent of the statute. The court found that the express and specific authorization to file a Chapter 9 is not required by 11 USC § 109(c)(2) and the aforementioned general powers were sufficient to constitute a general authorization for a Chapter 9 filing. The court held that the ability to file a Chapter 9 was necessary or incidental to the power to refund bond indebtedness and the

---

But see *In re North & South Shenango Joint Municipal Authority*, No. 8100408 in the United States Bankruptcy Court for the Western District of Pennsylvania. There, the Bankruptcy Court found that a joint municipal authority which had been created under Pennsylvania law to construct and operate sewer systems, had been "generally authorized" to file a petition under Chapter 9. The court relied on the distinction in Pennsylvania law between municipal authorities like the debtor authorized to do all acts "necessary or convenient for the promotion of their business," and political subdivisions, which were required to obtain the approval of the state Department of Community Affairs before they could file a petition for relief under the federal bankruptcy law. The court found that the decision to restrict political subdivisions' resort to bankruptcy evidenced a contrary intent regarding municipal authorities. 14 BR 414 (BR WD Pa, 1981). The Third Circuit declined to exercise jurisdiction over the appeal. *Pennbank v. Washbaugh*, 673 F2d 1301 (CA3, 1981). However, the District Court, to which an appeal was also taken, reversed the Bankruptcy Court and held that there was no sufficient showing of state authorization. 80 BR 57 (BR WD Pa, 1982). The case was then handled in a state court proceeding. (Letter of Kirkpatrick, Lockhart, Johnson & Hutchinson, Pittsburgh, Pennsylvania to author dated August 8, 1984).
[49] See for example, 4 Collier on Bankruptcy, §900.03 n 12.

District's ability to manage, control or supervise its business and affairs.[50] However, a Philadelphia bankruptcy court decision,[51] citing the North and South Shenango case, held that the right to sue and be sued did not constitute the requisite affirmative action required by the Bankruptcy Code. In the Bankruptcy of the City of Bridgeport, to be discussed later, the court also concluded that specific authorization to file a Chapter 9 petition was not required.[52] The legislative history behind the 1994 Act specifically noted the controversy and the purpose of the amendment to clarify the matter. The state law must specifically authorize the filing.[53] The court in the Orange County bankruptcy ruled that the Orange County Investment Pool was not specifically authorized to file a Chapter 9 petition by a statute which referenced a laundry list of public entities that are authorized to file but which did not refer to an investment fund.[54]

Further, the municipality must be insolvent or unable to meet its debts as they mature, and desire to effect a plan to adjust its debts.[55] The determination of insolvency is not as easy as it seems. The Municipal Bankruptcy Amendments have clarified the definition of insolvency and resulted in a more workable definition from a municipal law standpoint.[56] In addition, it must be demonstrated that one of the following has occurred:

1. The municipality has obtained the agreement of creditors holding at least a majority in the amount of claims of each class that such entity intends to impair under a plan in a case under Chapter 9.
2. The municipality has negotiated in good faith with creditors and has failed to obtain the agreement of creditors holding at least a majority

---

[50] Villages at Castle Rock Metropolitan District No. 4, No. 89 B 16240 (D Colo, May 11, 1990).

[51] *In re Carroll Township Authority*, 119 BR 61 (BR WD Pa, 1990).

[52] *In re City of Bridgeport*, 128 BR 688 (D Conn 1991).

[53] See Bankruptcy Reform Act of 1994 Section by Section Description appearing at 140 Cong Rec H 10771 (daily ed 10/4/94).

[54] *In re County of Orange*, 183 BR 594 (BC CD Cal. 1995). See also *In re Alleghany Highlands Economic Development Authority*, 720 BR. 647 (BC WD Va. 2001).

[55] 11 USC §§ 109(c)(3) and (4).

[56] In the case of *In re Sullivan County Regional Refuse Disposal District*, 165 BR 60 (BR D NH 1994), the court held that the failure of the debtors to impose a special assessment, as they had a right to do, did not raise a question with respect to their insolvency. Rather, it was held that such failure to do so was relevant with regard to good faith. See also *In re City of Desert Hot Springs*, 2003 WL 22682471 (9th Cir. 2003).

in the amount of claims of each class that such entity intends to impair under a plan in a case under Chapter 9.[57]

3. The municipality is unable to negotiate with creditors because such negotiations are impractical.

4. The municipality reasonably believes that a creditor may attempt to obtain a transfer that is avoidable under § 547 of the Bankruptcy Code.[58]

With regard to an unincorporated tax or special assessment district which does not have its own officials, an action is commenced under Chapter 9 by filing a petition by such district's governing authority or board or body which has the authority to levy taxes or assessments to meet the obligations of each district.[59]

The fact that a municipality has filed a petition does not necessarily ensure that its debts will be adjusted in that proceeding. Section 921(c) provides that, after objection to the petition, the court, after notice and a hearing, may dismiss the petition, if it can be shown to the Bankruptcy Court that a petition was not filed in good faith or not in accord with the require-

---

[57] The issue of good faith negotiations often is subject to dispute. In the case of *In re Chilhowee RIV School District*, 145 BR 981 (BR WD Mo 1992), the school district had transferred funds from the incidental fund into the salary fund and into the equipment fund so that those funds would have more money than originally budgeted. The incidental fund (which would be subject to attack by former teachers) would not have substantial funds subject to disbursal. The court held that the mere fact that the debtor attempted to place itself in as good a position as it could for entering a bankruptcy situation was only one factor to be considered. The mere fact that prebankruptcy planning had occurred was not indicative of bad faith as such. The court held that it was only when prebankruptcy planning left the stage of preparation and became fraud on creditors that there was a serious problem. However, in the case of *In re Ellicott School Building Authority*, 150 BR 261 (BR D Colo 1992), where the Authority held a meeting with bondholders regarding its proposed plan describing the proposal as a take it or leave it situation and expressed unwillingness to compromise, the court found that no true good faith negotiations had taken place. Similarly, in the case of *In re Sullivan County Regional Refuse Disposal District*, 165 BR 60 (BR D NH 1994), where the districts did not seriously attempt until four or five weeks prepetition to develop a feasible prepayment plan, the districts never exercised their assessment powers, and the districts never set out for creditors comprehensive workout plans dealing with all their liabilities and assets in terms comparable to a Chapter 9 plan, the debtors failed to establish prepetition good faith negotiations.

[58] 11 USC §§ 109(c)(5) (A)(B).

[59] 11 USC § 921(a).

ments of Chapter 9.[60] Further, if a creditor can show that any of the following has occurred, the court may dismiss the petition:

a. There has been a want of prosecution of the municipal debt adjustment proceeding.
b. There has been an unreasonable delay that is prejudicial to creditors.
c. There has been a failure to propose a plan within the time fixed by the court to propose such a plan, or such plan has not been accepted by the appropriate percentages of creditors.
d. The court has denied confirmation of the plan as being in the best interests of creditors and feasible.
e. If a court has maintained continuing jurisdiction after confirmation, there has been a material default by the municipality with respect to such a plan or a condition specified in the plan for termination of the plan has occurred.[61]

UNIQUE FEATURES OF CHAPTER 9

Chapter 9 specifically incorporates by reference a number of provisions of the Bankruptcy Code.[62] This procedure has created a number of open issues. Of key interest to bankruptcy practitioners is the fact that Section 901 of the Bankruptcy Code does not incorporate Sections 327 through 331, which are the professional retention and compensation provisions.[63] Those sections permit the employment of professional persons for the debtor, including counsel and financial advisors, and payment of compensation to such professional persons retained pursuant to court order. Assumedly, it was be-

---

[60] 11 USC § 921(c) See *In re Jersey City Medical Center,* 817 F2d 1055 (CA3, 1987). Section 901(a) of the Bankruptcy Code incorporates Section 301 of the Bankruptcy Code which states that "the commencement of a voluntary case under a chapter of this title constitutes an order for relief under such chapter." Section 921(d) provides that if the petition is not dismissed under subsection (c) of this section the court shall order relief under this chapter. Colliers has indicated that this provision is superfluous. Collier on Bankruptcy, § 921.04 (15th ed). However, one court has rejected Colliers' conclusion, and has found that, given the complexities of the qualifications for Chapter 9 filing, Congress clearly intended that a distinct "order for relief" would be entered by the court in Chapter 9 cases. *In re Colorado Centre Metropolitan District,* 113 BR 25 (BR D Colo, 1990).

[61] 11 USC § 927. The effect of dismissal is governed by § 349 of the Bankruptcy Code. Dismissal generally does not bar discharge in another proceeding or institution of another proceeding except as provided in § 109(f) (180 day rule as to institution of cases dismissed).

[62] 11 USC § 901.

[63] 11 USC §§ 327–31.

lieved that legislating in that area would infringe on the municipality's rights contrary to the strictures of § 904. There is no provision in the Bankruptcy Code for the payment of the attorneys' fees of counsel or other advisors to the debtor. Unless the debtor consents, there does not appear to be an ability for counsel for the debtor to obtain payment from the court.

While Section 503(b)(4) of the Bankruptcy Code, which provides for payment of counsel or accountants to a creditor, indenture trustee, equity security holder or committee which has made a substantial contribution to a case under Chapter 9, is incorporated by reference, Section 503(b)(4) makes no mention of counsel for the debtor. The provisions for retention and compensation of counsel for the debtor in a corporate bankruptcy do not require the substantial contribution test.[64] Particularly in many of the special purpose district bankruptcies, where funds are scarce, the source of payment of fees to counsel for the debtor is a difficult issue which must be reckoned with if the debtor is to receive adequate representation. Further, if the debtor does determine to pay its counsel out of funds which other creditors deem inappropriate, it appears that the court will not interject itself.[65]

Section 901 also does not incorporate by reference the sections which provide for initial creditors' meetings or examinations of the debtor.[66] Although, in fact, in many cases, the U.S. Trustee's Office proceeds to insist on such a creditors' meeting, there does not appear to be specific statutory authority for such.

Section 541, "Property of the Estate," is not incorporated into Chapter 9. This section typically creates the estate of the debtor. In a Chapter 9 proceeding, there is no debtor-in-possession concept and the debtor retains title to, possession of, and control over all of its property other than "special revenues" pledged to certain obligations as defined in § 928. Any other approach would run afoul of the concerns discussed in the Ashton case. The priority of expenses and claims is embodied in Section 507 of the Bankruptcy Code.[67] This section, which governs the seniority of certain types of unsecured claims, includes special treatment for wage claims, contribution to employee benefit plans, etc. Chapter 9 only incorporates by reference the provision giving priority to administrative expenses allowed under 503(B).[68] Thus, it would appear that there are no priority unsecured claims under Chapter 9, except for such administrative expenses. As more Chapter 9s

---

[64] 11 USC § 503(b)(4).

[65] See *In re Sanitary and Improvement District No. 7 of Lancaster County, Nebraska*, 96 BR 966 (BR Neb, 1989).

[66] See 11 USC §§ 341 and 343.

[67] 11 USC § 507.

[68] 11 USC § 507(a).

are filed, problems which may exist on account of the format of Chapter 9, incorporation of provisions from other chapters, may become apparent.

THE REQUIRED MAINTENANCE OF MUNICIPAL SERVICE DURING A MUNICIPAL BANKRUPTCY

While in a Chapter 9 proceeding, the municipality will still have to function as a municipality. Depending upon the statutory mission of the municipality, there are certain necessary and basic municipal services which must be provided, such as police, fire, and under certain instances, sewer, water and electrical services. Defining what these necessary municipal services are is a question of state law and may by itself be a complex issue. A bankruptcy court and creditors will not be able to successfully interfere with such service. Section 904 of the Bankruptcy Code recognizes this reality. Accordingly, certain revenues and activities of the municipal body which may be the cause of the "insolvency" may not be able to be restrained, curtailed, or modified without a compelling reason. Even municipal debt secured by *special revenues*, which pledge is preserved by reason of Section 928 of the Bankruptcy Code, is subject to the payment of necessary operating expenses.

Given the fluctuation and delay in cash flow (tax collection), it is evident that a municipality which traditionally has had to rely on the municipal bond market for financing its operation must consider how such financing will be accomplished in a Chapter 9. Section 364 of the Bankruptcy Code, which provides for voluntary credit extension on a priority basis is applicable to a Chapter 9, but the paucity, if not absolute lack, of large municipal Chapter 9 filings leaves doubt in the minds of many investors as to whether any Chapter 9 financing is prudent. States as well as regions should consider establishing emergency funds for financing of municipal operations during times of financial crisis when traditional sources are unavailable.[69] At least some states—Pennsylvania under the Financially Distressed Municipalities Act,[70] and Illinois in an action to assist the City of East St. Louis—have done so to a limited extent.

---

[69] See for example, Ohio Rev Code Ann § 118:17 et seq; NY Pub Auth Law § 3001 et seq.

[70] Pa Stat Ann Tit 53, § 11701.102 et seq.

LABOR CONTRACTS ARE AN IMPORTANT ELEMENT OF THE MUNICIPAL BUDGET WHOSE STATUS IN A CHAPTER 9 HAS BEEN SUBJECT OF DISCUSSION

On February 22, 1984, in the matter of *National Labor Relations Board v. Bildisco & Bildisco*,[71] the Supreme Court held that § 365(a) of the Bankruptcy Code[72] provides that, with certain limitations, the trustee may unilaterally assume or reject "any executory contract" of the debtor, including a collective bargaining agreement.

Bildisco & Bildisco (Bildisco), a New Jersey general partnership in the business of distributing building supplies, filed a voluntary petition in bankruptcy for reorganization under Chapter 11 of the Bankruptcy Code. Prior to filing, Bildisco had negotiated a three-year collective bargaining agreement with the International Brotherhood of Teamsters, Chauffeurs, Warehousemen and Helpers of America (Union) which provided that the agreement was binding on the parties and their successors regardless of bankruptcy. After filing, Bildisco requested permission from the bankruptcy court pursuant to § 365(a) to reject the collective bargaining agreement. At the hearing on the matter of rejection, Bildisco presented a sole witness, a general partner who testified that rejection would save his company $100,000 in 1981. The bankruptcy court granted permission to reject the collective bargaining agreement on January 15, 1981.

A collective bargaining agreement is an executory contract which is subject to rejection under § 365(a). According to the Supreme Court, the fact that Congress did not exclude collective bargaining agreements from the scope of § 365 indicates that § 365 does apply to such agreements. However, because of the "special nature" of labor agreements, the Court found that a standard for rejection more stringent than the normal "business judgment" rule should apply.[73] According to the Court, a Bankruptcy Court should permit rejection of a collective bargaining agreement subject to § 365(a) but only if the debtor can show both that the agreement burdens the estate and that the equities balance in favor of rejection. This would include a consideration of the likelihood and consequences of:

1. Liquidation for the debtor absent rejection.

---

[71] *National Labor Relations Board v. Bildisco & Bildisco*, 465 US 513, 79 L Ed 2d 482, 104 S Ct 1188 (1984).
[72] 11 USC § 365(a).
[73] See *Group of Institutional Investors v. Chicago, M., St. P. & P.R. Co.*, 318 US 523, 87 L Ed 959, 63 S Ct 727 (1943); *In re Minges*, 602 F2d 38 (CA2, 1979); *In re Tilco, Inc.*, 558 F2d 1369 (CA10, 1977).

2. Reduced value of the creditors' claims that would follow from affirmance and the hardship that would be imposed on them.
3. Impact of rejection on the employees.

In striking the balance, the Bankruptcy Court must consider not only the degree of hardship faced by each party, but also any qualitative difference between the types of hardship each may face. Nevertheless, the Supreme Court rejected the test espoused by the Union that Bildisco should not be permitted to reject the collective bargaining agreement unless it could demonstrate that its reorganization would fail unless rejection was permitted.

Given the fact that labor obligations are among the most burdensome problems faced by municipalities, as evidenced by the San Jose School District bankruptcy,[74] the Bildisco result obviously could be attractive to some local governments. However, municipal workers generally perform a governmental function. Absent a resolution by the debtor municipality's legislative body approving or disapproving rejection, the provisions of § 904 of the Code require that the Bankruptcy Court cannot interfere with the political or governmental powers of the debtor. Accordingly, the jurisdiction of the Bankruptcy Court is limited, and the termination of a labor contract contrary to the wishes of the municipality's elected officials may be subject to attack as beyond the court's power. Further, if Bildisco is to be applicable to a Chapter 9, a clearer standard for review by the Bankruptcy Court should be promulgated to ensure no violation of § 904 or the Tenth Amendment.

STATUTE GOVERNING THE REJECTION OF COLLECTIVE BARGAINING AGREEMENT IN CORPORATE CONTEXT

Congress, in the Bankruptcy Amendments and Federal Judgeship Act of 1984, responded to the Supreme Court's decision in Bildisco[75] which permitted unilateral rejections of a collective bargaining agreement by a debtor. The Supreme Court in Bildisco rejected the standard whereby a collective bargaining agreement could be rejected only if it was demonstrated to be onerous and burdensome and would thwart the efforts to save the debtor from collapse.[76] In response, Congress added § 1113 to the Bankruptcy

---

[74] *In re San Jose Unified School Dist.*, No. 58302387A9 (BR ND Cal, 1983).

[75] *National Labor Relations Board v. Bildisco & Bildisco*, 465 US 513, 79 L Ed 2d 482, 104 S Ct 1188 (1984).

[76] See *Brotherhood of Railway & Airline Clerks v. REA*, 523 F2d 164 (CA2, 1975) cert denied 423 US 1017. For a discussion of the conflict between labor and bankruptcy law in this case and under the Bankruptcy Code, see Note, Labor Law

Code. This provision had the effect of modifying the Supreme Court's ruling so as to prohibit unilateral rejection without a court hearing and ruling upon an application for such rejection.

There is no reference or amendment contained in the 1984 Act or § 901 of the Bankruptcy Code that would indicate that § 1113 would be applicable to a Chapter 9 proceeding. As a result, Bildisco may be applicable and still valid as to a Chapter 9 to the extent it is not inconsistent with § 904 of the Bankruptcy Code or the Tenth Amendment.

"SPECIAL REVENUES" PLEDGED TO BONDHOLDERS

Many municipal bonds are revenue bonds secured by a pledge of revenues derived from the project or a special tax levy. Prior to the enactment of the Municipal Bankruptcy Amendments, there was real concern as to the continuation of such a pledge after the filing of a Chapter 9 petition. Section 552(a) of the Bankruptcy Code, which is applicable to a Chapter 9, provides that any prepetition pledge terminates upon bankruptcy as to property acquired after the filing of a petition, except for "proceeds, product, . . . etc." of property already subject to the lien.[77] This section invalidates the reach of after acquired property clauses to property acquired by the debtor after the filing of the petition. The only exception is for *proceeds*, a term that is largely undefined by the Bankruptcy Code or cases. Thus, prior to the enactment of the Municipal Bankruptcy Amendments, Section 552 could have been interpreted to defease the lien on revenues assigned by the debtor to secure bonds unless the revenues collected after the filing of the petition could be traced as proceeds of some other property of the debtor which was subject to a lien prior to the filing.[78] The fear was that if a municipality filed a Chapter 9 petition, Section 552 would permit general creditors of the municipality to seek payment from the pledged revenues. Not only would such a result eliminate the difference between general obligation and revenue bonds, but it would have a serious effect on the municipal bond market.

These concerns are addressed by Section 928 of the Bankruptcy Code, one of the Municipal Bankruptcy Amendments.[79] Subsection (a) renders Section 552(a) inapplicable to revenue bonds secured by special revenues. Thus, in the case of special revenues, the security interest in special revenues remains valid and enforceable even though such revenues are received after

Bankruptcy Collective Bargaining Agreements and Chapter 11 Reorganizations Under Subtitle J of the Bankruptcy Amendments and Federal Judgeship Act of 1984, 59 *Tul L Rev* 1694 (1985).

[77] 11 USC § 552(a).

[78] See S Rep No 506, 100th Cong, 2d Sess 5 (1988).

[79] 11 USC § 928.

a Chapter 9 filing. Subsection (b) of Section 928 provides that in the case of project or system financing, the bondholders' lien on special revenues is subject to necessary operating expenses of the project or system. Section 928 is intended to negate Section 552(a) in the municipal context. The legislative history makes clear that this section is not intended to create new rights that otherwise would not exist under state law and constitutional provisions. Section 928 removes the limitation on preexisting rights created by Section 552(a) where special revenues are concerned.[80]

Particular attention should be directed to the definition of special revenues, the pledge of which survives bankruptcy. Special revenues are defined as:

"(A) receipts derived from the ownership, operation, or disposition of projects or systems of the debtor that are primarily used or intended to be used primarily to provide transportation, utility, or other services, including the proceeds of borrowings to finance the projects or systems;

(B) special excise taxes imposed on particular activities or transactions;

(C) incremental tax receipts from the benefited area in the case of tax increment financing;

(D) other revenues or receipts derived from particular functions of the debtor, whether or not the debtor has other functions; or

(E) taxes specifically levied to finance one or more projects or systems, excluding receipts from general property, sale, or income taxes (other than tax increment financing) levied to finance the general purpose of the debtor."[81]

Examples of the special revenues mentioned in clause (A) include receipts derived from or received in connection with the ownership, financing, operation or disposition of a municipal water, electric or transportation system. An excise tax on hotel and motel rooms or the sale of alcoholic beverages would be a special excise tax under clause (B). "Special excise taxes" are taxes specifically identified and pledged in the bond financing documents and are not generally available to all creditors under state law. A general state sales tax would not be a special excise tax. In a typical tax increment financing referred to in (C), public improvements are financed by bonds payable solely from and secured by a lien on incremental tax receipts resulting from increased valuations in the benefited area. Although these receipts may be part of the general tax levy, they are considered to be attrib-

---

[80] See S Rep No 506, 100th Cong, 2d Sess 12 (1988).

[81] 11 USC § 902(2).

utable to the improvements so financed and are not part of the preexisting tax base of the community. Examples of revenues from particular functions under clause (D) would include regulatory fees and stamp taxes imposed for the recording of deeds or any identified function and related revenues identified in the municipality's financing documents, such as tolls or fees related to a particular service or benefit. Under clause (E), an incremental sales or property tax specifically levied to pay indebtedness incurred for a capital improvement and not for the operating expenses or general purposes of the debtor would be considered special revenues. Likewise, any special tax or portion of a general tax specifically levied to pay for a municipal financing should be treated as special revenues.[82] By its terms, Section 552(a) only applies to liens resulting from security agreements, not other types of liens such as statutory liens.[83] In the Orange County case, the District Court held that the lien securing the payment of certain notes was a statutory lien that secured the filing of the County's Chapter 9. For this purpose, although a project or system may or may not be revenue producing, the incremental tax must be specifically identified with such project or system.

PAYMENTS TO BONDHOLDERS ARE NOT PREFERENCES

Section 547 of the Bankruptcy Code,[84] which is applicable to a Chapter 9 proceeding,[85] would give the municipality the ability to avoid any transfer to or for the benefit of a creditor made on account of an antecedent debt while the debtor was insolvent within 90 days of the date of the filing of a petition. The concerns raised by the applicability of this section to municipal revenue bond financing were several.[86] An argument could be made that interest payments made during the 90-day period, either from revenues obtained before or during the 90-day period, were preferential and had to be returned to the debtor municipality.[87] Further, there was fear that deposits made pursuant to the defeasance provisions of indentures, if made within 90 days before the filing of a Chapter 9, could be deemed to be preferential.

The Municipal Bankruptcy Amendments not only address the problem of revenue bondholders, but actually provide assurance to holders of all municipal bond or note obligations.[88] Section 926(b) of the Bankruptcy Code now

---

[82] See *Heffernan Memorial Hospital District*, 202 BR. 147 (BR S.D. Cal. 1996).

[83] *In re County of Orange*, 189 BR. 499 (CD Cal. 1995).

[84] 11 USC § 547.

[85] 11 USC § 901.

[86] See S Rep No 506, 100th Cong, 2d Sess 7 (1988).

[87] But see the decision of the *United States Supreme Court in the Matter of Union Bank v. Wolas*, 112 S Ct 527 (1991).

[88] 11 USC § 926.

provides that a transfer of property of the debtor to or for the benefit of any holder of a bond or note on account of such bond or note may not be avoided under Section 547. While this section refers to "bonds or notes," there is nothing in the legislative history to support the view that this provision is limited only to instruments bearing such titles. The intent appears to be that Section 926(b) should be applicable to all forms of municipal debt.

USE OF LETTERS OF CREDIT AS BACKING FOR MUNICIPAL AND CONDUIT OBLIGATIONS

Letters of credit are not guarantees, and are not considered to be *ultra vires* for national banks. A letter of credit is considered to be the full faith and credit of a financial institution in the amount set forth therein, and, as a general rule, when the conditions of the letter of credit are met, payment cannot be enjoined.[89] In drafting any letter of credit transaction, it is important that all documents clearly indicate that the letter of credit is not a guarantee. Upon presentment of specified documents and fulfillment of certain conditions, a letter of credit is an unqualified obligation to pay.[90]

A letter of credit is an independent contract between the issuing bank and the beneficiary.[91] As such, if the stated conditions are satisfied, it survives the bankruptcy of the debtor for whom it was issued.[92] Neither the letter of credit nor its proceeds are property of the estate. In issuing the letter of credit, the bank agrees to pay out of its own assets.[93] In the case of conduit financing, the debtor for this purpose would be the corporation for whose benefit the municipality issued the bonds.

---

[89] Circumstances that will justify an injunction against payment of a letter of credit are limited to situations of fraud in which the wrongdoing of the beneficiary has so violated the entire transaction that the legitimate purposes of the independence of the issuer's obligations would no longer be served. *Intraworld Industries Inc. v. Gerard Trust Bank*, 461 Pa 343, 336 A2d 316 (1975); *Edgewater Const. Co. v. Percy Wilson Mortgage & Finance Corp.*, 44 Ill App 3d 220, 357 NE2d 307 (1976); *Crocker Nat. Bank v. Superior Court of State of California*, 434 US 984 (1977), 68 Cal App 3d 863, 136 Cal Rptr 481 (1977).

[90] See *Wichita Eagle & Beacon Publishing Co. v. Pacific Nat. Bank of San Francisco*, 493 F2d 1285 (CA9, 1974). See also *In re Eastern Freight Ways, Inc. v. Seaboard Surety Co.*, 9 BR 653 (SD NY, 1981).

[91] UCC § 5114, Official Comment, § 2.

[92] *In re Page*, 18 BR 713, 715 (DCD, 1982); *In re Marine Distributors, Inc.*, 522 F2d 791, 795796 (CA9, 1975); *Courtaulds North America, Inc. v. North Carolina Nat. Bank*, 387 F Supp 92 (MD NC, 1975) revd on other grounds 528 F2d 802 (CA4, 1975).

[93] *In re Page*, 18 BR 713, 715 (DCD, 1982).

A number of years ago, the municipal finance community was jarred by a bankruptcy court decision holding that a letter of credit obtained for a conduit financing could not be drawn on by the indenture trustee on account of the bankruptcy of the company despite the fact that such was an event of default under the documents.[94] The court, assuming that the trust indenture was an executory contract, held that such ipso facto clauses were not enforceable. The court would not permit the draw because the effect of such a draw would be to increase the liabilities of the debtor because of the increased monetary obligations of the debtor under the reimbursement agreement with the letter of credit bank. This decision is contrary to other cases,[95] and was reversed by the District Court. However, a recent case has not extended that reasoning to include situations where the letter of credit secures performance under a lease instead of a bond indenture.[96]

PLAN OF ADJUSTMENT FOR MUNICIPALITY TIME, CONTENT, IMPAIRMENT OF CLAIMS AND ACCEPTANCE

Section 941 of the Bankruptcy Code provides that the debtor shall file a plan for the adjustment of its debts.[97] If such plan is not filed with the petition, the debtor shall file such plan at such later time as the court fixes.[98] The cumbersome requirement of obtaining prepetition consents by creditors is abolished. The municipality may modify the plan at any time prior to confirmation provided such modification is consistent with the requirements of Chapter 9.[99]

Sections 1122 and 1123(a)(14) of the Bankruptcy Code,[100] which are applicable to Chapter 9 and Chapter 11 proceedings,[101] govern the required contents of a reorganization plan. The United States Supreme Court, in con-

---

[94] *In re Prime Motor Inns*, 123 BR 104 (BR SD Fla, 1990), rev'd 130 BR 610 (SD Fla 1991).

[95] *In re Zenith Laboratories, Inc.*, 104 BR 667 (BR NJ, 1989).

[96] *In re Metrobility Optical Systems, Inc.*, 268 BR 326 (BR NH 2001).

[97] 11 USC § 941. This section gives the debtor the exclusive right to propose a plan. HR Rep No 595, 95th Cong, 1st Sess 399 (1977). The exclusivity is consistent with § 904 of the Code which precludes any interference in the affairs of the Chapter 9 debtor. For the elements of a plan pursuant to Chapter 11, see generally Norton Bankr L & Prac § 59.01 et seq.

[98] Bankruptcy Rule 3016(a) provides that a Chapter 9 debtor may file a plan at any time.

[99] 11 USC § 942.

[100] 11 USC §§ 1122 and 1123(a)(14). The general provisions concerning the contents of a Chapter 11 plan are made applicable here, with two exceptions relating to the rights of stockholders, which are not applicable in Chapter 9 cases.

[101] 11 USC § 901.

sidering a plan of adjustment under the old Chapter IX, held that before a plan could be confirmed, it must appear to the court that, based on past and prospective tax revenues and operating expenses, the municipality will be able to make payments under the plan.[102] Such a test does not take into consideration federal and state aid and grants to municipalities. The plan must be based upon an analysis of the debtor's cash flow including taxes and other revenues and a determination of the validity and amount of claims pursuant to § 502 of the Code. Once a feasible plan has been developed, consideration must be given as to any voter or regulatory approval necessary based upon the structure of the plan. Discussions with key creditors and creditors' committees as to their views regarding any proposed plan is central to developing a plan that can be confirmed without lengthy litigation.

A fundamental aspect of a municipal bond is the exemption from Federal income taxation which is enjoyed by interest paid on the bonds. Determination of whether or not interest paid on the bonds is so exempt is normally made by bond counsel who are hired by the municipal issuer when the bonds are issued to give such an opinion to the purchasers and owners of the bonds. There are complex Federal tax requirements which are preconditions for the tax exemption and accordingly part of any municipal debt adjustment plan must deal with a determination of whether or not the interest paid on the new obligations will be tax exempt. Indeed, this can be of critical importance for holders of mutual funds or unit investment trusts which are generally restricted by their organizational documents to only owning tax exempt securities.

The plan may provide for, among other things, sale of property of the estate, either subject to or free of any lien; cancellation or modification of any indenture or similar instrument; extension of a maturity date or a change in an interest rate or other term of outstanding securities; or issuance of securities of the debtor for existing securities; and may impair any class of claims secured or unsecured.[103]

The plan shall include the following:

---

[102] *Kelly v. Everglades Drainage District*, 319 US 415, 87 L Ed 1485, 63 S Ct 1141 (1943).

[103] 11 USC §§ 1123(a) and (b). For example, the Plan of Reorganization in *In re San Jose United School District*, No. 58302387A (BR ND Cal, Sept. 1, 1983), treated the following topics: (1) Definitions; (2) Administrative Expenses; (3) Classification of Claims; (4) Treatment of Claims (including bondholders whose claims were not impaired by the Plan: "The Plan shall not alter any legal, equitable or contractual rights to which each claim entitles the holder thereof)"; (5) Amendments and Waiver; (6) Retention of Jurisdiction; and (7) Executory Contracts (including the rejection of the labor contract).

1. Designation of the classes of claims that exist specifying any class of claim or interest that is not impaired under the plan.

2. Statement of the treatment of any class of claims or interests that is impaired under the plan.

3. Statement providing for the same treatment for each claim or interest in a particular class unless the holder of a particular claim or interest agrees to a less favorable treatment of such claim or interest.

4. Statement of a means for the execution of the plan such as the sale of property, transfer of property; the satisfaction or modification of any lien, the cancellation or modification of any indenture or similar instrument, the curing or waiving of default, extension of a maturity date, the change of interest rate or other terms of outstanding securities, or the issuance of new securities.

5. Statement, if appropriate, of the settlement or determination of any disputes belonging to the debtor.

6. Assumption or rejection of any executory contracts or unexpired leases.[104]

The plan can include any other appropriate provision not inconsistent with the applicable provisions of the Bankruptcy Code. Section 1122 which governs the classification of claims is applicable to a Chapter 9 proceeding. Under § 1122, the plan may place a claim or interest in a particular class only if such claim or interest is substantially similar to other claims or interests of such class, except that the plan may designate a separate class of claims consisting of every unsecured claim that is less than or reduced to an amount that the court approves as reasonable and necessary for administrative convenience. Classification of claims becomes important because under § 1129, it is necessary to obtain the acceptance of at least one class of impaired creditors before the debtor may move the court to cram down the plan. Courts have held that there must be some limit on the debtor's power to classify creditors in such a manner to assure that at least one class of impaired creditors will vote with the plan and make it eligible for cram

---

[104] Id. It has been held that it is not unfair to treat bondholders of the same issue alike in a Chapter IX regardless of what they paid for the bonds. *Equitable Reserve Assoc. v. Dardanelle Special School District, No. 15 Yell County, Ark.,* 138 F2d 236 (CA8, 1943); *West Coast Life Ins. Co. v. Merced Irrigation District,* 114 F2d 654 (CA9, 1940). Similarly, it has been held that there is nothing unfair in Chapter IX in refusing special treatment to bondholders who had obtained judgments or writs of mandamus prior to the bankruptcy. *Evergreen Farms Co. v. Willacy County Water Control & Improvement District No. 1,* 124 F2d 1 (CA5, 1942); *Vallette v. Vero Beach, Fla.,* 104 F2d 59 (CA5, 1939). See also *In re Illinois California Exp., Inc.,* 50 BR 232 (BR Colo, 1985).

down consideration by the court. Using such a standard, a court in the bankruptcy of a municipal medical center approved the separate grouping of the claims of medical malpractice victims, employee benefit plan participants and trade creditors.[105] Further, where bonds and warrants are treated differently under state law, their separate classification in a plan of reorganization under Chapter 9 has been held to be appropriate.[106] While separate classification has been denied for nonsubstantive reasons, differences in security or other reasonable distinctions will likely be supported.[107]

The impairment of claims provisions of § 1124 of the Bankruptcy Code[108] are applicable to a Chapter 9 proceeding.[109] The confirmation standards adopted in Chapter 9 are the same as those of Chapter 11. This is a change from the prior Chapter IX, which required compliance with the fair and equitable rule.[110] A claim or interest is impaired under the plan unless:

1. It remains unaltered as to its legal, equitable, and contractual rights.
2. Any default which caused the acceleration of the indebtedness is cured; and in addition:
   a. The original maturity of such claim or interest is reinstated as such maturity date existed before the default.
   b. Any damages suffered by the holder of such claim or interest as a result of reasonable reliance by such holder on such contractual provisions or such applicable law is appropriately compensated.
   c. After curing the default, the equitable, legal and contractual rights of the holder of the claim or interest are not altered or modified.
3. The holder of such claim or interest receives on account of such claim or interest cash equal to the amount of such claim or the greater of:
   a. Any fixed liquidation preference to which the terms of any security representing such interest entitles the holder of the interest.
   b. Any fixed price at which the debtor under the term of such security may redeem such security from such holder.[111]

The plan of adjustment must be tailored to the specific needs and revenue projections of the municipality. Subject to state law restrictions, debt

---

[105] *In re Jersey City Medical Center*, 817 F2d 1055 (CA3, 1987).

[106] *Sanitary and Improvement District No. 65 of Sarpy County, Neb. v. First Nat. Bank of Aurora*, 79 BR 877 (D Neb, 1987).

[107] See, e.g., *Taylor v. Provident Irrigation District*, 123 F2d 965 (CA9, 1941) (different maturity dates not basis for separate classification).

[108] 11 USC § 1124.

[109] 11 USC § 901.

[110] HR Rep No 595, 95th Cong, 1st Sess 394397 (1977).

[111] 11 USC § 1124.

service on the bonds may be extended, reduced or otherwise modified in a plan of adjustment. Creditors including bondholders and indenture trustees should consider the feasibility of any proposed plan and its compliance with the terms of both state law and the Bankruptcy Code. The plan must not only be feasible and in compliance with the terms of the Bankruptcy Code and state law, but also be acceptable to the requisite creditors.

Section 524(a) governs the effect of discharge that voids judgment, remedies or collection efforts on preconfirmation obligations other than as provided for in the plan. The order of confirmation discharging certain prepetition indebtedness is in effect an injunction against any further actions to collect that debt other than provided for in the plan.[112]

POSTPETITION DISCLOSURE AND SOLICITATION

The disclosure standards of § 1125 of the Bankruptcy Code[113] are applicable to a Chapter 9 proceeding.[114] An acceptance or rejection of a plan may not be solicited from the holder of a claim or interest unless at the time of or before such solicitation there is transmitted to such holder the plan or a summary of the plan and a written disclosure statement approved by the court after a notice and hearing as adequate.[115] Adequate information is defined in the Bankruptcy Code as "information of a kind, and in sufficient detail, as far as is reasonably practicable in light of the nature and history of the debtor and condition of the debtor's books and records, that would enable a hypothetical reasonable investor typical of holders of claims or interest of the relevant class to make an informed judgment about the plan."[116] In essence, adequate information is similar to the type of facts that the municipality must disclose in its official statement to those who purchased its bonds. In the disclosure statement the municipality must disclose all facts which would be material and relevant to a creditor's evaluation of the plan including the feasibility of the plan based upon claims and available reve-

---

[112] 11 USC § 524(a)(2).

[113] 11 USC § 1125. See Norton Bankr L & Prac § 62.13 et seq for a discussion of its application in a Chapter 11.

[114] 11 USC § 901. Under the Bankruptcy Act, the Supreme Court held that a municipality ought to have disclosed that the fiscal agent soliciting acceptances was also a bondholder. *American United Mut. Life Ins. Co. v. Avon Park, Florida*, 311 US 138, 85 L Ed 91, 61 S Ct 157 (1940). Query whether, in the light of 11 USC § 903, the language of § 1125 relieving the court from the necessity of following state law regarding disclosure should be applicable to a Chapter 9.

[115] 11 USC § 1125(b).

[116] 11 USC § 1125(a)(1).

nues.[117] The benefits and detriments of the plan to creditors and the effect of delayed confirmation must be spelled out. In its disclosure materials, the San Jose School District stressed its nonimpairment of bonded debt.[118] A municipality may tender different disclosure statements (differing in amount, detail or kind of information) to different classes of creditors.[119]

ACCEPTANCE OF THE PLAN

In order to be accepted, a plan must have the assent of at least two thirds in allowed amount of each class and more than one half of the number of creditors of each class voting.[120] Accordingly, a municipality, in devising its plan of adjustment in classifying debt, must consider the type and amount of debt which must accept the plan. If too many diverse creditors are put into one class, it could adversely affect the ability of the municipality to gain acceptance of the plan. If a plan is carefully crafted, it will define separate classes for varying interests, keeping the amount of indebtedness and creditors per class to a manageable level. However, some plans classify unsecured bonded indebtedness with trade debt and employee claims with the view toward avoiding nonacceptance by the class. As referred to previously, Section 1122(a) of the Code provides that claims can be classified together only if such claim or interest is "substantially similar" to the other claims or interests of such class. Improper classification of claims would be a basis for objecting to confirmation pursuant to § 1128.

Acceptance by a class is not required if the class is not impaired.[121] Assuming one impaired class has accepted the plan, acceptance of other classes is not required if the plan does not discriminate unfairly, and is fair and equitable with respect to each class that is impaired and has not

---

[117] See Robert Fippinger, "Securities Law Disclosure Requirements for the Political Subdivision Threatened With Bankruptcy," *Fordham Urban Law Journal* 10 (1982), pp. 541–594.

[118] *In re San Jose Unified School Dist.*, No. 58302387A (BC ND Cal, 1983).

[119] 11 USC § 1125(c).

[120] 11 USC §§ 1126(c) and 1129(a)(8)(A) are made applicable to Chapter 9 pursuant to 11 USC § 901. See generally Norton Bankr L & Prac § 61.12.

[121] 11 USC § 1129(a)(8)(B). There is a split of authority as to whether the requirements of § 1129(a)(10), requiring acceptance by at least one class of claimants for confirmation, is satisfied by an unimpaired class which is deemed to have accepted the plan. § 1126(f). See *In re W.E. Parks Lumber Co.*, 19 BR 285 (BR WD La, 1982); *In re Landau Boat Co.*, 13 BR 788 (BR WD Mo, 1981); Contra *In re Pine Cove Village Apartment Co.*, 19 BR 819, (BR SD NY, 1982); *In re Barrington Oaks General Partnership*, 15 BR 952 (BR D Utah, 1982).

accepted the plan.[122] If a class is to receive nothing under a plan, that class is deemed to have rejected the plan.[123] Under § 946 of the Bankruptcy Code an exchange of a new security as part of a workout before the case is filed can constitute an acceptance of the plan of reorganization if the exchange was under a proposal that later became the plan. However the plan must be in accordance with the prepetition exchange agreement. Furthermore the disclosure requirements of § 1126(b) require adequate prepetitioned disclosure. Although in the corporate sphere prepackaged Chapter 11s have found popularity as a means of binding nonconsenting creditors, at least one case has held that a municipality may not file under Chapter 9 immediately following the exchange if the purpose of filing is to force dissenting creditors into submission.[124]

CONFIRMATION OF PLAN

The confirmation requirements of § 1128 of the Bankruptcy Code are applicable to a Chapter 9,[125] and there are additional Chapter 9 requirements.[126] After notice to all interested parties, the court shall hold a hearing on the confirmation of a plan. A party in interest and a special taxpayer may object to the confirmation of a plan.[127]

The court shall confirm a plan only if it meets the specific requirements of Chapter 9, including being proposed in good faith and not by any means forbidden by law. This means that there are no hidden agreements between the parties not specifically set forth in the plan nor any acceptances of the plan obtained through such hidden agreements.

In addition, at least one class of claims which is impaired under the plan and which is not an insider claim must have accepted the plan, or the court must have determined that the plan does not discriminate unfairly and

---

[122] 11 USC § 1129(b)(1), commonly known as the *cramdown provision*. See generally Norton Bankr L & Prac § 62.06.

[123] 11 USC § 1126(g).

[124] *Wright v. City of Coral Gables*, 137 F2d 192 (CA5, 1943).

[125] 11 USC § 901. See generally Norton Bank L & Prac § 63.01 et seq for confirmation under Chapter 11.

[126] 11 USC §§ 1128 and 1129.

[127] 11 USC §§ 1128(a) and (b); 934(a). A special taxpayer means record owner or holder of legal or equitable title to real property against which a special assessment or special tax has been levied, the proceeds of which are the sole source of payment of an obligation issued by the debtor to defray the cost of an improvement relating to such real property. 11 USC § 912(2). A general change in all assessments or in the tax rate would not qualify any property holder in the district as a special taxpayer affected by the plan.

is fair and equitable with respect to each class of claims or interests that is impaired under, and has not accepted, the plan.[128] In other words, even if such claimants constituted impaired classes, the acceptance of the plan by affiliates, elected officials or relatives of elected officials would not support confirmation since such claimants are insiders.[129]

In addition to the requirements set forth above, the court shall confirm the plan if:

1. The plan complies with the provisions of Chapter 9.[130]
2. The plan complies with the provisions of other Chapters of the Bankruptcy Code made applicable to Chapter 9.
3. All amounts to be paid by the municipality to any person for services or expenses in the case or incident to the plan have been fully disclosed and are reasonable.[131]
4. The municipality is not prohibited by law from taking any action necessary to be taken to carry out the plan.[132]
5. The plan provides that each holder of a claim of the kind specified in § 507(a)(1) of the Bankruptcy Code (administrative expenses during the course of the proceeding) will receive, on account of such claim, property of a value, as of the effective date of the plan, equal to the amount of such claim, except to the extent that the holder of a particular claim of such kind has waived such payment on such claim.
6. The plan is in the best interest of the creditors and feasible.[133]

---

[128] 11 USC § 1129(a)(2), (3), (8), (10), and (b).

[129] An affiliate may include the municipality which leases substantially all of the property of a municipal lease authority. 11 USC § 101(2)(D).

[130] 11 USC § 1129(a)(1).

[131] 11 USC § 1129(a)(4).

[132] 11 USC § 1129(a)(3).

[133] 11 USC §§ 943, 1129. The "best interest of creditors" test does not mean liquidation value. It is expected that the court will be guided by standards set forth in *Kelly v. Everglades Drainage District*, 319 US 415, 87 L Ed 1485, 63 S Ct 1141 (1943) and *Fano v. Newport Heights Irrigation District*, 114 F2d 563 (CA9, 1940). In Kelly, the court found that, in approving a plan, the bankruptcy court must make adequate findings bearing on the probable future tax revenues of the district, such as the revenues received in the past from each source of taxation, the present assessed value of property subject to each tax, the tax rates currently prescribed, the probable effect on future revenues of a revision made in the tax structure, the extent of past tax delinquencies, and any general economic condition of the district which may reasonably be expected to affect the percentage of future delinquencies. Similarly, in Fano, which involved a Chapter IX filed by an irrigation district which had a $15,000 deficit on accrued interest on its bonds, a plan to pay 62.50 cents on the dollar was not confirmed as "equitable" or in the "best interest of creditors" where

The debtor may modify a plan at any time prior to confirmation so long as the modified plan meets the requirements of Chapter 9.[134] The court will dismiss a case under Chapter 9 if confirmation of a plan under Chapter 9 is refused.[135] If a plan is confirmed, the Court may retain jurisdiction over the case for such period of time as is necessary for the successful implementation of the plan.[136]

A party in interest (creditor, special taxpayer or debtor) may request the court within 180 days after the date of confirmation to revoke such order if and only if the order was procured by fraud.[137] Such an order revoking an order of confirmation should contain necessary provisions to protect any equity acquiring rights in good faith reliance on such an order and should also revoke the discharge of the debtor.

A decision reflects the interplay between the various requirements for plan confirmation imposed by Chapter 9 and state law considerations.[138] Like so many of the Chapter 9 filings, the case involves a special district. The debtor had issued unsecured bonds and warrants prepetition. Under state law, bonds had priority over warrants. That is, the law required that bonds be fully paid according to their terms prior to utilizing revenues for payments of warrants. The plan of adjustment did not pay the bondhold-

---

the district was debt free, except for interest, with assets in good condition and in value greatly exceeding the indebtedness of the district, and there was no sufficient showing as to why the district's tax rate could not have been increased sufficiently to meet the district's obligations.

It may by helpful in evaluating whether the requirements of Chapter 9 are met to review other cases applying the more stringent "fair and equitable" test. Where a court was presented with a dismal history and bleak financial future of a drainage district, it approved a play for payment of 20 cents for each dollar of principal amount of the bonds. *Delno v. Market St Ry Co.*, 124 F2d 965 (CA9, 1942). See also *Mason v. Paradise Irrigation District*, 326 US 536, 90 L Ed 287, 66 S Ct 290 (1946) (52.521 cents on each dollar of principal). Also interesting is the decision in *Getz v. Edinburg Consol. Independent School District*, 101 F2d 734 (CA5, 1939) which approved a plan pursuant to which refunding bonds which included accrued overdue interest were issued and 51% of moneys held in the sinking fund were permitted to be used to fund the maintenance of schools.

Of course, a plan cannot benefit some unfairly. Where some bondholders who purchased the bonds at bargain prices acquired an appreciable quantity of taxable property in the city, a plan which would result in the lowering of tax levies would not be approved. *Town of Belleair, Fla v. Groves*, 132 F2d 542 (CA5, 1942) cert den 318 US 769, 87 L Ed 1140, 63 S Ct 762 (1943).

[134] 134 11 USC § 942.
[135] 11 USC § 927(b).
[136] 11 USC § 945(a).
[137] 11 USC § 1144.
[138] *In re Sanitary & Improvement District No. 7*, 98 BR 970 (BR Neb, 1989).

ers the full amount of their claim with interest but paid some recovery to warrantholders. Despite the state law constraints, the court held that under the Bankruptcy Code, the debt of the municipality could be adjusted, and therefore, the plan was not objectionable in this respect.

However, the new bonds and warrants to be issued to the holders under the plan received different scrutiny. The zero bonds had a call provision that permitted payment at less than par and permitted payments on the new warrants even if the bonds were taken out at less than par. In other words, the bondholders, as contemplated under the plan, could receive securities under the plan which would not be paid in full. Because of the state law requiring priority of the bondholders, the court held that such treatment was in violation of state law and the plan could not be confirmed. The case stands for the proposition that the plan can modify the existing prepetition debt, regardless of state law prohibitions, but the plan cannot contemplate the violation of the law going forward.

Chapter 9 is one mechanism for resolution of disputes regarding the allocation of resources of a troubled municipality. It is difficult to achieve a consensual plan after a contested confirmation hearing. As a result, a debtor should consider negotiation with trade and public debt and employee groups to work out the terms of the plan. To be confirmed, a plan must be fair. If creditors are unreasonably "crammed down" so that the distribution to public debtholders is less than justified, the municipality may find it difficult to have any plan confirmed. Further, the market will recall such unfair treatment the next time the municipality attempts to enter the market.

APPENDIX: CHAPTER 9 CASES FILED AS OF FEBRUARY 8, 2007

No.	Year	Code	Debtor	Court District	Docket Number	Plan of Adjustment	Confirmation of Plan
1	2004	(B)	Town of Millport	N. Alabama	04-73885		
2	2002	(A)	Etowah Solid Waste Disposal Authority	N. Alabama	02-42175-JSS-9		Case closed 10/23/02
3	2002	(E)	The West Jefferson Amusement and Public Park Authority	N. Alabama	02-04303-BGC-9	11/04/02 11/15/02 amendment	Confirmation 12/20/02
4	1998	(A)	West Walker Water Authority	N. Alabama	98-71559	04/26/99 06/16/99 amendment	Confirmation 09/27/99
5	1994	(E)	Alabama State Fair Authority	N. Alabama	94-03695-BGC-9	12/16/96 02/03/03 amendment	Confirmation 04/04/03
6	1992	(B)	Town of North Courtland	N. Alabama	92-82747	09/29/03 09/30/94 amendment	Confirmation 02/23/95
7	1991	(B)	City of Lipscomb	N. Alabama	91-3033	10/24/91	Confirmation 01/6/92
8	1999	(B)	City of Prichard	S. Alabama	99-13465-9-MAM	10/31/01 12/5/01 amendment	Case closed 1/2/02
9	1986	(D)	Cooper River School District	Alaska	3-86-00830	02/17/88	Confirmation 04/11/88
10	1997	(E)	Superstition Mountains Community Facility District 1	Arizona	97-00210	04/02/97	Case Closed 04/22/98
11	1994	(E)	New Magma Irrigation & Drainage District	Arizona	94-00211-TUC-JMM	06/21/95	Confirmation 6/21/95 Case closed 01/08/04
12	1994	(E)	Central Arizona Irrigation and Drainage District	Arizona	94-02043-TUC-JMM		Confirmation 4/1/96
13	1983	(B)	South Tuscon, Arizona	Arizona	83-00866	12/23/83 02/21/84 amendment 04/05/84 amendment	Confirmation 04/09/84; Case closed 03/23/88
14	2006	(E)	East Hot Springs Multi-Purpose Municipal Owners	W. Arkansas	06-70041		
15	2005	(E)	Ridges Mater Property Owner's Improvement District	W. Arkansas	05-74966		Dismissed 12/28/2005
16	2003	(E)	Madison County Property Owners Improvement Dist 1 - Cedar Bluff Sub. Proj.	W. Arkansas	03-73321	08/26/03	Confirmation 11/05/03 Case Closed 10/06/04

No.	Year	Code	Debtor	Court District	Docket Number	Plan of Adjustment	Confirmation of Plan
17	2002	(E)	Bentonville Municipal Property	W. Arkansas	02-74392	07/15/02 11/20/02 amendment	Confirmation 12/17/02 Case Closed 06/17/03
18	2005		Sierra Nevada Public	C. California	05-27696	Filed 08/03/2005	Case opened in San Fernando Valley and Transferred to L.A.
19	2001	(B)	City of Desert Hot Springs	C. California	RS01-30756 DN	09/09/02 12/20/02 amendment 05/03/04 amendment	Confirmation 07/26/04
20	1997	(E)	Ventura Port District	C. California	97-55269		Confirmation 12/10/98 Case closed 12/29/98
21	1994	(B)	County of Orange	C. California	SA 94-22272-JR		Confirmation 5/16/96
22	1994	(B)	Orange County Investment Pools	C. California	SA 94-22273-JR		Case dismissed 05/24/95
23	2003	(C)	Coalinga Regional Medical	E. California	03-14147	01/07/04 02/24/04 amendment	Confirmation 05/13/04
24	2002	(A)	Alpaugh Irrigation District	E. California	02-16206	01/27/03	Confirmation 05/23/03
25	2001	(C)	Alta Healthcare District	E. California	01-17857		
26	2000	(C)	Chowchilla Memorial Hospital District	E. California	00-13597	03/30/01 05/25/01 amendment	Confirmation 09/14/01 Case Closed 05/05/04
27	2000	(C)	Sierra Valley District Hospital	E. California	00-30288	06/28/02	Confirmation 07/03/02 Case Closed 11/21/02
28	1997	(C)	Kingsburg Hospital District	E. California	97-15254	04/14/99 08/26/99 amendment 11/18/99 amendment	Confirmation 04/05/00
29	1996	(C)	Corcoran Hospital District	E. California	96-15051-A-9F	08/29/97 06/15/98 amendment 08/10/98 amendment	Confirmation 04/29/99 Case closed 07/07/04
30	1990	(C)	Corning Hospital District	E. California	89-28568		Discharge 3/29/95
31	1986	(D)	Lassen Community College District	E. California	2-86-01379	01/12/89 05/30/89 amendment 01/24/91	Confirmation 07/24/91

No.	Year	Code	Debtor	Court District	Docket Number	Plan of Adjustment	Confirmation of Plan
32	2006	(C)	West Contra Costa Healthcare District	N. California	06-41774		
33	2005	(E)	Reclamation District Number 768	N. California	05-14658	Filed 11/17/2005	
34	2001	(A)	Aromas County Water District	N. California	01-52689		Case Closed 11/05/03
35	1999	(C)	Southern Humboldt Community Health Care District	N. California	99-10200	01/20/00 04/19/00 amendment	Confirmation 10/26/00 Case closed 12/29/03
36	1991	(D)	Richmond Unified School District	N. California	91-42434	No plan filed	Case closed 12/18/91
37	1985	(C)	Monterey County Special Health Care Authority	N. California	85-00649	01/08/86	03/27/86
38	1983	(D)	San Jose School District	N. California	83-02387	02/07/84	Case dismissed 05/08/84
39	1981	(E)	The Management Institute of San Leandro	N. California	81-02265	No plan filed	Case closed 08/21/85
40	1997	(E)	Mount Carbon Metropolitan District	Colorado	97-20215-HRT	01/21/03	Confirmation 6/19/03 Case closed 01/20/05
41	1997	(E)	Hamilton Creek Metropolitan District	Colorado	97-1099		Case dismissed 3/30/99
42	1996	(E)	Hamilton Creek Metropolitan District	Colorado	96-18180 RJB		Case dismissed 08/04/98
43	1994	(E)	City of Colorado Springs Spring Creek General Improvement District	Colorado	94-15333-MSK	09/08/94	Confirmation 09/20/95; Case closed 09/09/97
44	1994	(E)	Aurora CentreTech Metropolitan District	Colorado	94-11247-PAC		Case closed 08/05/94
45	1993	(E)	Castle Pines North Metropolitan District	Colorado	93-21925-RJB		Case closed 08/02/94
46	1992	(D)	Ellicott School Building Authority	Colorado	92-20479		Case dismissed 03/10/93
47	1992	(E)	Powderhorn Metropolitan District No. II	Colorado	92-11439-SBB		Case dismissed 03/07/95
48	1991	(A)	Cottonwood Water and Sanitation District	Colorado	91-25763		Case closed 06/24/94
49	1991	(E)	Northern Metropolitan District, Adams County, Colorado	Colorado	91-26399-RJB		Case closed 06/15/93
50	1991	(E)	Castle Pines North Metropolitan District	Colorado	90-17548-RJB		Case dismissed 11/13/92
51	1991	(E)	Colorado Springs Cottonwood General Improvement District	Colorado	91-10684		Case closed 01/03/96
52	1991	(E)	Paint Brush Hills Metropolitan District	Colorado	90-18984-CEM		Case dismissed 01/22/93

No.	Year	Code	Debtor	Court District	Docket Number	Plan of Adjustment	Confirmation of Plan
53	1990	(E)	Wolf Creek Valley Metropolitan District No. II, Mineral County, Colorado	Colorado	90-11905		Case closed 08/17/95
54	1990	(E)	Wolf Creek Valley Metropolitan District No. IV, Mineral County, Colorado	Colorado	90-11906		Case closed 06/12/95
55	1990	(E)	Dawson Ridge Metropolitan District No. 1	Colorado	90-15400		Case closed 08/28/96
56	1990	(E)	Villages at Castle Rock Metropolitan District No. 7	Colorado	90-18922		
57	1990	(E)	Will-O-Wisp	Colorado	89-17447		
58	1989	(E)	Colorado Centre Metropolitan District	Colorado	89-16410		
59	1989	(E)	Villages at Castle Rock Metropolitan District No. 4	Colorado	89-16240	09/12/91	Confirmation 12/17/91
60	1989	(E)	Hamilton Creek Metropolitan District, Summit County, Colorado	Colorado	89-07269	11/07/89	
61	1987	(E)	Eagles Nest Metropolitan District	Colorado	87-15212		
62	1992	(F)	Westport Transit District	Connecticut	2-92-20404 92-50044		Petition dismissed 4/29/94
63	1991	(B)	City of Bridgeport	Connecticut	91-51519		Case dismissed 08/01/91
64	1989	(F)	Lake Grady Road and Bridge District, Extension #1, Hillsborough County, Florida	M. Florida	89-4507-8P9	06/27/89	Confirmation 1/19/90
65	1987	(F)	Lake Grady Road and Bridge District, Hillsborough County, Florida	M. Florida	87-1590	08/31/87	Confirmation 01/15/88
66	1987	(A)	Water & Sewer District "A" Pasco County, Florida	M. Florida	87-3218	03/04/87	Confirmation 07/20/87
67	1998	(C)	East Shoshone Hospital District	Idaho	98-20934-9	02/05/99	Confirmation 6/29/99 Case closed 05/22/00
68	2005	(A)	Slocum Lake Drainage District of Lake County	N. Illinois	05-63193		Filed 10/25/2005 Dismissed 01/19/2006
69	2005	(B)	Village of Alorton	S. Illinois	05-30055		
70	2004	(B)	Village of Washington Park	S. Illinois	04-31911		
71	1985	(A)	Bell County Garbage and Refuse Disposal District	E. Kentucky	85-143	05/08/88	Case dismissed 06/30/88

No.	Year	Code	Debtor	Court District	Docket Number	Plan of Adjustment	Confirmation of Plan
72	1984	(A)	Whitley County Water District	E. Kentucky	84-00089	no plan filed	Case dismissed 04/17/85
73	1999	(C)	Lower Cameron Parish Hospital Service District	W. Louisiana	99-21290	04/19/00	Confirmation 9/29/00 Case closed 07/26/01
74	1992	(C)	Addison Hospital	E. Michigan	92-02336	06/25/93	
75	1987	(B)	Village of Merrill, Michigan	E. Michigan	87-09455	06/19/87	Case dismissed 12/09/87
76	1997	(B)	Town of Winstonville	N. Mississippi	97-91794		Case Closed 02/10/98
77	1987	(B)	City of Mound Bayou, Mississippi	N. Mississippi	87-00295-BKC-DN1	Settled prior to filing plan	
78	2001	(B)	Village of Hillsdale	E. Missouri	01-52989		Case Closed 12/12/02
79	1994	(B)	City of Kinloch, Missouri	E. Missouri	94-43315-399		Confirmation 07/18/96; Case closed 03/18/98
80	1984	(B)	Wellston City, Missouri	E. Missouri	84-01492	02/19/84 01/03/86 amendment	Plan not Confirmed; Case closed 10/01/86
81	2002	(B)	City of Reeds Spring	W. Missouri	02-31360	03/03/03 9/22/03 amendment	Confirmation 11/14/03 Case closed 10/07/04
82	2000	(B)	City of Macks Creek	W. Missouri	00-21435	06/06/01 10/10/01 amendment	Confirmation 12/27/01
83	1992	(D)	Chilhowee R-IV School District	W. Missouri	92-42256-9-FWK	4/7/93 5/24/93 amendment	Confirmation 6/16/93 Case closed 06/28/95
84	1984	(C)	Pulaski Memorial Hospital	W. Missouri	84-00082	08/14/85	Confirmation 10/10/85; Case closed 01/08/88
85	1991	(E)	City of Columbia Falls, Montana Special Improvement Districts Nos. 25, 26, and 28	Montana	90-31775-9 91-31360-9 91-31355-9		Confirmation 1/23/95, Case closed 06f11/98; Confirmation 1/23/95, Case closed 06/11/98; Confirmation 1/23/95, Case closed 06/11/98;
86	2005	(A)	Sanitary and Improvement District No. 425	Nebraska	05-85871		Filed 10/26/2005
87	1992	(A)	Sanitary and Improvement District No. 113	Nebraska	92-81195	12/21/92	Confirmation 03/18/93; Case closed 09/30/93

No.	Year	Code	Debtor	Court District	Docket Number	Plan of Adjustment	Confirmation of Plan
88	1992	(A)	Sanitary and Improvement District No. 284	Nebraska	92-80761	01/12/93	Confirmation 03/26/93; Case closed 05/09/94
89	1991	(A)	Sanitary and Improvement District No. 289	Nebraska	91-80274		Confirmation 12/18/92 Case closed 04/21/93
90	1991	(A)	Sanitary and Improvement District No. 89	Nebraska	91-80674		Confirmation 1/16/92 Case closed 03/30/94
91	1991	(A)	Sanitary and Improvement District No. 151	Nebraska	91-80989		Confirmation 8/19/91 Case closed 04/06/94
92	1990	(A)	Sanitary and Improvement District No. 235	Nebraska	90-80387		Confirmation 1/15/91 Case closed 04/10/96
93	1990	(A)	Sanitary and Improvement District No. 330	Nebraska	90-81351		Confirmation 10/22/90 Case closed 04/21/93
94	1989	(A)	Sanitary and Improvement District No. 257	Nebraska	89-81086		Case closed 04/06/94
95	1989	(A)	Sanitary and Improvement District No. 264	Nebraska	89-81343		Confirmation 7/30/90 Case closed 04/21/93
96	1988	(A)	Sanitary and Improvement District No. 252 of Douglas County, Nebraska	Nebraska	88-1427	02/21/89 05/12/89 amendment	
97	1988	(A)	Sanitary and Improvement District No. 52 of Sarpy County, Nebraska	Nebraska	88-81614		Case closed 10/23/92
98	1987	(A)	Sanitary and Improvement District No. 117 of Sarpy County, Nebraska	Nebraska	87-01724	05/28/87	Confirmation 05/26/88
99	1987	(A)	Sanitary and Improvement District No. 93 of Sarpy County, Nebraska	Nebraska	87-00062	01/09/87	Confirmation 12/14/87
100	1987	(A)	Sanitary and Improvement District No. 122 of Sarpy County, Nebraska	Nebraska	87-00178	01/22/87	Confirmation 05/29/87
101	1987	(A)	Sanitary and Improvement District No. 103 of Sarpy County, Nebraska	Nebraska	87-00826	03/18/87	Confirmation 11/07/88
102	1987	(A)	Sanitary and Improvement District No. 92 of Sarpy County, Nebraska	Nebraska	87-82507	08/14/87	Case closed 01/13/93

No.	Year	Code	Debtor	Court District	Docket Number	Plan of Adjustment	Confirmation of Plan
103	1987	(A)	Sanitary and Improvement District No. 75 of Sarpy County, Nebraska	Nebraska	87-01089	04/31/87	
104	1988	(A)	Sanitary and Improvement District No. 69 of Sarpy County, Nebraska	Nebraska	88-81752	04/01/88	Case closed 02/04/93
105	1987	(A)	Sanitary and Improvement District No. 267 of Douglas County, Nebraska	Nebraska	87-00487	02/20/87	Confirmation 08/17/88
106	1987	(A)	Sanitary and Improvement District No. 253 of Douglas County, Nebraska	Nebraska	87-01878	06/12/87	Confirmation 04/11/88
107	1987	(A)	Sanitary and Improvement District No. 301 of Douglas County, Nebraska	Nebraska	87-02662	08/28/87	
108	1987	(A)	Sanitary and Improvement District No. 251 of Douglas County, Nebraska	Nebraska	87-02134	07/10/89	
109	1987	(A)	Sanitary and Improvement District No. 3 of Saunders City, Nebraska	Nebraska	87-80051	01/08/87	Confirmation 06/30/87 Case closed 03/26/93
110	1987	(A)	Sanitary and Improvement District No. 6 of Platte County, Nebraska	Nebraska	87-80780	03/13/87	Confirmation 12/18/87 Case closed 03/30/93
111	1986	(A)	Sanitary and Improvement District No. 67 of Sarpy County, Nebraska	Nebraska	86-02941 86-82941	10/10/86	Confirmation 5/26/92 Case closed 03/21/94
112	1986	(A)	Sanitary and Improvement District No. 187 of Douglas County, Nebraska	Nebraska	86-1798	06/20/86	Confirmation 11/17/86
113	1986	(A)	Sanitary and Improvement District No. 97 of Sarpy County, Nebraska	Nebraska	86-00601	03/05/86	
114	1986	(A)	Sanitary and Improvement District No. 229 of Douglas County, Nebraska	Nebraska	86-1885	06/27/86 10/30/86 amendment	Confirmation 11/07/86
115	1986	(A)	Sanitary and Improvement District No. 87 of Douglas County, Nebraska	Nebraska	86-01738	06/20/86	Confirmation 11/17/86
116	1986	(A)	Sanitary and Improvement District No. 250 of Douglas County, Nebraska	Nebraska	86-01266	05/01/86	Confirmation 04/18/88

No.	Year	Code	Debtor	Court District	Docket Number	Plan of Adjustment	Confirmation of Plan
117	1986	(A)	Sanitary and Improvement District No. 4 of Saunders City, Nebraska	Nebraska	86-82126	07/25/86	Confirmation 11/17/86 Case closed 04/21/93
118	1985	(A)	Sanitary & Improvement District No. 265 of Douglas County, Nebraska	Nebraska	85-2384	12/27/85 01/24/86 amendment 07/10/86 amendment	Confirmation 10/07/86
119	1985	(A)	Sanitary & Improvement District No. 7 of Lancaster County, Nebraska	Nebraska	85-0039	01/15/86 11/18/86 amendment 05/02/88 amendment 08/30/88 amendment 11/23/88 amendment 02/15/89 amendment 05/03/89 amendment 06/02/89 amendment	Confirmation 06/22/89
120	1985	(A)	Sanitary and Improvement District No. 65 of Sarpy County, Nebraska	Nebraska	85-756	05/01/86 09/02/86 amendment	Confirmation 10/30/86
121	1984	(A)	Sanitary & Improvement District No. 63 of Sarpy County, Nebraska	Nebraska	84-01263	06/29/84	Confirmation 03/11/85
122	1983	(A)	Sanitary & Improvement District No. 4 of Lancaster County, Nebraska	Nebraska	83-01456	10/06/83 04/17/84 amendment 06/18/84 amendment	Confirmation 08/02/84
123	1983	(A)	Sanitary & Improvement District No. 42 of Sarpy County, Nebraska	Nebraska	83-00956	06/02/83 07/27/84 amendment	Confirmation 09/26/84
124	1982	(A)	Sanitary & Improvement District No. 5 of Cass County, Nebraska	Nebraska	82-01671	11/01/83 10/24/86 amendment 11/12/86 amendment 01/22/87 amendment	Confirmation 02/26/87
125	1993	(E)	Sullivan County Regional Refuse Disposal District	New Hampshire	93-12640-JEY 93-12639		Case closed 11/29/96
126	1999	(B)	Camden, New Jersey	New Jersey	99-16569		Case dismissed 07/29/99
127	1983	(C)	Jersey City Medical Center	New Jersey	83-00829	03/29/85	Confirmation 08/06/87
128	2004	(A)	South Brunswick Water and Sewer Authority	E. North Carolina	04-09053-8-JRL		
129	2005	(B)	Town of Muldrow	E. Oklahoma	05-7621		Filed 04/21/2005

187

No.	Year	Code	Debtor	Court District	Docket Number	Plan of Adjustment	Confirmation of Plan
130	2005	(A)	Muldrow public Works Authority	E. Oklahoma	05-71622		Filed 04/21/2005
131	1997	(E)	Eufaula Industrial Authority	E. Oklahoma	97-71225	03/26/98 Third amendment	Plan not confirmed
132	1989	(A)	Valliant Public Works Authority	E. Oklahoma	89-70108	12/08/89 03/15/90 amendment 07/10/90 amendment	Case closed 10/23/90
133	1982	(B)	Wapanucka, Oklahoma	E. Oklahoma	82-00231	No plan filed	Case dismissed
134	2004	(C)	Watonga Hospital Trust Authority	W. Oklahoma	04-10415		
135	2000	(B)	City of Tyrone	W. Oklahoma			
136	1988	(B)	Borough of Shenandoah	E. Pennsylvania	88-20603	No plan filed	Case dismissed
137	1981	(E)	North & South Shenango Joint Municipal Authority	W. Pennsylvania	81-00408		Case dismissed 05/26/82
138	1988	(F)	Low Country Regional Transportation Authority	South Carolina	88-01944		
139	1994	(A)	East Sevier County Utility District	E. Tennessee	94-30103		Case closed 09/06/95
140	1991	(A)	Sale Creek Utility District	E. Tennessee	91-11216	04/24/91	Confirmation 05/11/95; Case closed 11/07/00
141	1988	(B)	City of Copperhill	E. Tennessee	88-00710		
142	1986	(F)	Chattanooga Area Regional Transportation Authority	E. Tennessee	1-86-00564	03/13/86	
143	1982	(A)	Pleasant View Utility District of Cheatham County, Tenn.	M. Tennessee	82-01139	04/12/82 12/22/82 (refiled)	Case dismissed 05/19/83
144	2006	(B)	Town of Marshall Creek	E. Texas	06-40072		Filed 01/23/2006
145	2004	(B)	City of Westminster	E. Texas	04-41856		Dismissed 07/28/04 Case Closed 08/11/04
146	2000	(B)	City of Westminster	E. Texas	00-41266		Case dismissed 2/6/01
147	1993	(F)	Denton County Reclamation and Road District	E. Texas	93-40306	03/08/93	Case closed 09/12/94
148	2001	(C)	Hall County Hospital District	N. Texas	01-21283	08/28/02	Confirmation 10/28/02
149	1992	(A)	Northwest Dallas County Flood Control District	N. Texas	92-31469-RCM	5/12/92	Case closed 11/20/92
150	1988	(C)	South Eastland County Hospital District d/b/a Black-well Hospital	N. Texas	88-10005	07/07/88 11/17/88 amendment	Confirmation 12/16/88

No.	Year	Code	Debtor	Court District	Docket Number	Plan of Adjustment	Confirmation of Plan
151	2003	(A)	Roman Forest Public Utility District No 3	S. Texas	03-36168		Confirmation 02/02/05
152	2002	(B)	City of Rio Bravo	S. Texas	02-50287	01/13/05	Confirmation 05/09/02
153	2001	(B)	City of Kendleton, Texas	S. Texas	01-37013	09/24/01 10/15/01 amendment 05/06/02 amendment	Confirmation 05/09/02 Case Closed 04/01/04
154	2000	(C)	Chambers County Hospital	S. Texas	00-80240	07/01/03	Confirmation 10/20/03
155	2000	(C)	Bayside Community Hospital	S. Texas	00-80240	7/1/03	Confirmation 10/20/03
156	2000	(A)	Roman Forest Public Utility District No. 4	S. Texas	00-30662-H4-9	12/12/01	Confirmation 4/22/02 Case closed 04/01/04
157	1996	(A)	Northwood Municipal Utility District No. 1	S. Texas	96-48226-H3-9		Confirmation 5/15/98
158	1995	(A)	Harris County Municipal District No. 250	S. Texas	95-49649-H5-9		Confirmation 11/4/96
159	1995	(A)	Montgomery County Municipal Utility District No. 42	S. Texas	95-41259		Confirmation 9/20/96 Order Amended 10/30/96
160	1994	(A)	Greens Parkway Municipal Utility District	S. Texas	94-47421-H5-9		Confirmation 12/26/96
161	1994	(A)	Harris County Municipal Utility Districts No. 202	S. Texas	94-42132-HA-9		Confirmation 8/22/95
162	1994	(A)	Harris County Municipal Utility District No. 216	S. Texas	94-45424-H5-9		Confirmation 12/9/96
163	1994	(A)	Rankin Road West Municipal Utility District	S. Texas	94-40920-H5-9		Confirmation 6/1/95
164	1993	(A)	Montgomery County Municipal District No. 56	S. Texas	93-49490	06/01/95 09/15/95 amendment	Confirmation 12/5/95 Case closed 09/20/96
165	1993	(A)	Cypress Hill M.U.D. No. 1	S. Texas	93-48643-H4-9	02/14/94	Confirmation 4/14/94 Case closed 03/21/95
166	1993	(A)	Big Oaks Municipal Utility District	S. Texas	93-42397	03/18/94 05/18/94 amendment 08/01/94 amendment 01/12/95 amendment	Confirmation 1/14/95 Case closed 09/20/96
167	1993	(A)	Harris County Municipal Utility District No. 165	S. Texas	93-43120	04/21/93	08/23/93 amendment Case closed 02/13/95
168	1992	(A)	West Harris County Municipal Utility District No. 7	S. Texas	92-45173-H4-9		

No.	Year	Code	Debtor	Court District	Docket Number	Plan of Adjustment	Confirmation of Plan
169	1987	(A)	Northwest Harris County Municipal Utility District No. 19	S. Texas	87-02498	03/10/87	Confirmation 04/20/81
170	1980	(A)	Grimes County Municipal Utility District No. 1	S. Texas	80-010948	08/19/80	Filed 08/05/2005
171	2005	(B)	City of Camp Wood	W. Texas	05-54480		Case Closed 04/30/04
172	2001	(C)	Whitney Hospital Authority	W. Texas	01-60808	09/01/03	Case Closed 04/30/04
173	2000	(C)	Rockdale Hospital District	W. Texas	00-61862	02/04/02 04/17/02 amendment	Confirmation 05/17/02 Case Closed 06/17/03
174	1996	(E)	Retama Development Corporation	W. Texas	96-51115	02/13/97	Confirmation 3/12/97
175	1992	(F)	Southeast Williamson County Road	W. Texas	92-12887	11/10/92	Confirmation 02/17/93
176	1992	(F)	Southwest Williamson County Road District No. 1	W. Texas	92-12274	04/16/92	Confirmation 06/29/93
177	1990	(C)	Timpangos Community Mental Health	Utah	90-612		
178	2001	(E)	Alleghany Highlands Economic Development Authority	W. Virginia	01-01576		Case dismissed 11/08/01
179	1985	(A)	Badger Mountain Irrigation District	E. Washington	85-03136-299	11/23/87	Confirmation 11/26/97 Case closed 08/17/04
180	1991	(A)	Whatcom County Water District	W. Washington	91-00941	07/31/98	Confirmation 09/04/98 Case closed 04/23/02
181	1991	(B)	City of North Bonneville	W. Washington	91-34125		Case dismissed 02/16/94
182	1992	(A)	Jefferson County Solid Waste Authority	N. West Virginia	92-30352	02/01/93 05/28/93 amendment	Confirmation 08/11/93; Case closed 12/01/97
183	1988	(A)	Arbuckle, WV Public Service District	S. West Virginia	88-50151	06/09/88	Case closed 01/08/93

Subnational Infrastructure Finance in the Emerging Markets: A Financial Guaranty Perspective

Thomas H. Cochran
CivilCredit Advisors LLC

Anthony Pellegrini
Centennial Group

David Stevens

Richard Torkelson
JPMorgan Securities

David White

The closely related fields of public project finance and subnational infrastructure finance are developing rapidly in the world's emerging market economies for a variety of reasons beyond the rapidly increasing demand for infrastructure driven by high population and GDP growth rates. Two other key drivers of this phenomenon are:

1. The rapid growth and improving quality of local credit and capital markets in the developing world as local contractual savings pools are formed and grow at often explosive rates, and as economic and financial institution reforms stabilize local economies.
2. The "devolution revolution" which is pushing responsibility for infrastructure finance down from central governments to lower levels of

The authors also wish to gratefully acknowledge the contributions of Roger McDaniel.

government in many countries of Latin America, Central and Eastern Europe, Africa, and Asia. Even in countries such as Chile which have chosen to stay quite centralized governmentally, responsibility for infrastructure finance has been shifted outward to private sector partners through various public-private partnership arrangements such as concessions.

The purpose of this chapter is to convey the basic approach being taken by monoline financial guaranty insurers and other guarantors which are beginning to apply time-tested public finance credit and structuring principles in some of the better-developed emerging market countries, which have become the new frontiers of essential public infrastructure finance.

THE DEVELOPMENT AND GROWTH OF LOCALLY DENOMINATED CONTRACTUAL SAVINGS POOLS AND CREDIT MARKETS

In virtually all but the most deeply impoverished emerging market countries, private savings are being accumulated and managed contractually by institutions acting in a fiduciary capacity for growing groups of individual and corporate savers. In many countries, such as Chile and Mexico, the often rapid development of private pension funds has been an important corollary of this growth of private savings pools. In other countries such as South Africa and Vietnam, the banking and insurance sectors appear to be more dominant institutional players controlling the investment of rapidly increasing amounts of private savings. Any of these institutions will find themselves challenged to invest the money in a diverse set of relatively safe, locally denominated equity and/or debt securities. While sovereign government treasury and agency bonds will always be one key mainstay of the fixed income portions of such investment portfolios, all portfolio managers seek greater diversity. They tend to welcome the appearance of well-structured securities issued by prudently managed nonsovereign public and private entities providing essential public services because these instruments provide both a positive yield spread above similar maturity sovereign securities and enough safety to meet stringent fiduciary guidelines and other relevant regulatory requirements.

In most cases, the growth of this incipient "buy side" for high-quality locally denominated equity and debt securities has been initiated or accelerated by fundamental policy decisions about retirement savings and the basic issue of how much control individual savers should have over the investment of savings. In many cases, these fundamental decisions have been based on recommendations by the International Monetary Fund (IMF) and such multilateral and bilateral international development finance institutions (IFIs) as the World Bank and USAID, respectively. Equally important, IFIs have devoted increased resources to assisting the development of national legal and regulatory frameworks, and the creation and strengthening of the public and private agencies and institutions which regulate and intermediate the private contractual savings pools developing within the countries.

These decisions about the treatment of long-term savings were typically just one key part of the adoption of some free (or freer) market policies. Few countries have achieved all of their goals in this regard. Moreover, in some cases (e.g., Venezuela, Argentina, Bolivia, and Ecuador) a political backlash is threatening to roll back some of these changes as this is being written. However, in most of the middle- and upper-income emerging market economies—and a surprising number of low-income emerging market economies—increasing central bank independence has encouraged more stable financial policy making emphasizing control of inflation and lower nominal and real interest rates. In addition, financing tenors in some local debt markets are lengthening, in some cases with startling rapidity, as the burgeoning "buy sides" grow comfortable with the relative safety provided by new classes of securities (e.g., subnational general obligation bonds in Vietnam and public enterprise revenue bonds in South Africa).

The growth in contractual savings began in many developing countries well before the Asian currency crisis of the late 1990s. However, that crisis and its aftermath in such nations as Indonesia, Thailand, and Korea vividly demonstrated the dangers inherent in the incurrence of large amounts of debt denominated in the "hard" currency of the most highly developed economies when the revenues expected to service the debt are paid by indigenous consumers in local currency, and it was impossible or prohibitively expensive to obtain reliable currency hedging with the tenors necessary for efficient financing of essential infrastructure. Consequently, local currency financing in the emerging markets appears to have embarked on a period of long-term secular growth. According to various sources, the compounded annual growth rate of local currency financing from 2000 to 2004 in Mexico was 18%; in Chile, 35%; and in South Africa, 54%. We believe there is a substantial number of developing countries where locally denominated financing is becoming an increasingly attractive option, displacing foreign currency financing, and creating an environment where local investors are seeking well-structured private sector fixed income securities as an alternative to central government treasury bills.

Our own direct observations working in countries as different as Indonesia, Vietnam, South Africa, Chile, Brazil, Poland, and Ukraine strongly bear out the accuracy and importance of this observation. While by no means do all developing countries yet possess sufficiently developed local capital markets, reasonable legal and regulatory frameworks, and a sufficiently promising macroenvironment to permit local currency investments, most of those countries with sovereign ratings in the BB to A range either have achieved that status or are making strides toward that objective.[1] A number of lower-rated countries are also moving in the same direction.

Decision makers in many countries and within the IFIs, as well as some private sector lenders and other capital market participants such as credit rating agencies, are recognizing that local currency financing of essential public services and other basic human needs such as shelter is also healthier for the borrowers and for the countries where they are located. Financings in local currency not only are likely to better match each particular borrower's financial inflows and outflows, they are also likely to reduce the country's vulnerability to future currency crises and diminish the severity of those which do occur.

One of the hallmarks of the well-developed local capital markets is the involvement of credit rating agencies and the establishment of rational credit spreads for investments with different credit ratings. When credit spreads are based on objective risk criteria rather than simply the historic relationships between specific borrowers and lenders which characterize less well-developed credit markets, opportunities for a far broader range of investors to participate tend to emerge rapidly. A typical public policy objective in many emerging market countries has been to encourage investments that are sufficiently safe that they will be attractive to long-term investors such as pension funds and insurance companies and, at the same time, produce the longer tenors and principal amortization schedules required for many public infrastructure projects to be affordable to taxpayers and ratepayers.

Three rating scales are now in simultaneous use by the major credit rating agencies and most independent rating agencies active in developing countries:

1. The international currency rating scale, which provides guidance on the statistical probability of default for bonds denominated in one of the world's hard currencies.
2. The international local currency rating scale, which provides guidance on the statistical probability of default for bonds denominated in local currencies.

---

[1] For a thorough review of the status of subnational financial market development through 2003, see Mila Freire and John Petersen (eds.), *Subnational Capital Markets in Developing Countries from Theory to Practice* (New York: Oxford University Press/World Bank, 2004).

3. The recently introduced country-specific national rating scales, which provide guidance on the relative credit quality of locally denominated bonds without explicit statistical support. The benchmark comparison for relative credit quality is to locally denominated central government (sovereign) treasury bonds, viewed by local capital market investors as providing the "risk-free" interest rates in that market, and consequently rated triple AAA on the national scales.

While the international currency and international local currency rating scales give investors guidance on the statistical probability of default and a means of comparing credit quality across all borders, the national rating scales do not provide this guidance. However, this has proven to be of little or no consequence to local capital market traders and other participants in establishing rational credit spreads off local risk-free interest rate benchmarks.

Rational credit spreads also allow the introduction of a variety of third-party credit enhancements including partial risk and partial credit guarantees by IFIs and bond insurance by monoline financial guaranty insurance companies that can further improve the safety and attractiveness of securities. In order to price guaranty products, interest rate savings and other benefits to the issuer for using them need to be estimated and this can be done only in markets which exhibit rational credit spreads.

We see local capital markets with this important characteristic in most but not all middle- and upper-income emerging market countries in Latin America, Central Europe, Africa, and Asia. Mexico, Malaysia, India, Chile, and South Africa are examples of countries where we often see reasonably wide spreads. Central European and some Asian countries, such as South Korea and Taiwan, are examples of countries where a relatively long history of fierce bank competition for a relatively small number of high-quality transactions has combined with low interest rates to compress credit spreads into the range usually seen in the OECD countries.

THE DEVOLUTION REVOLUTION: DECENTRALIZATION AND/OR PRIVATIZATION IS CONTINUING IN VIRTUALLY ALL EMERGING MARKETS

Fiscal and administrative decentralization and/or involvement of the private sector in the operations of essential public facilities and services is continuing in most nations of the developing world. Over the past 15 to 20 years, transitional post-Communist and developing countries have been redefining the roles and financing systems of their various levels of government. Dramatic shifts in the roles of various levels of government have emerged in response to changing economic and political conditions, including the failure of centralized planning, global macroeconomic and financial instability, and increasing pressures for popular participation and democratization. Latin America and Central and Eastern Europe, in particular are witnessing an era of unprecedented political and fiscal decentralization in which the reform agenda has focused on increasing private sector participation, streamlining central government operations, and devolving substantial powers and responsibilities to lower levels of government in a profoundly important "devolution revolution."

As we noted above, there has been a political backlash against aspects of this trend in a few countries, particularly in the water and sanitation sectors.[2] For example, the successful presidential campaign of Evo Morales in Bolivia appears to have been at least partially catalyzed by popular discontent with water and sanitation privatizations that may not have sufficiently accounted for the greater proportion of deeply impoverished consumers in that country. More broadly, water and sanitation finance experts around the world are now taking a far more sober view of privatization than that espoused by the World Bank and other IFIs in the 1990s due to the many shortcomings of privatization transactions completed in that period. However, few critics of water and sanitation infrastructure privatization are espousing a return to sole reliance on central government agency construction, ownership and operation of essential public facilities. The far more common stance is to advocate renewed efforts to strengthen subnational governments and the regional and local public utility enterprises that are so prevalent in many developing countries. As the *New York Times* reported in its coverage of a global conference held in 2006: "At the fourth World Water Forum, a six-day conference . . . of industry, governments and nongovernmental organizations, there is little talk of privatization. Instead, many people here want to return to relying on the local public utilities that still supply 90 percent of the water to those households that have it."[3]

Subnational entities and/or the private partners engaged by national or subnational governments to take on essential public service infrastructure development responsibilities through concession and similar *public-private partnership* (PPP) arrangements will all have to mobilize a massive amount of capital from a variety of sources. One aspect of this transformation is that intermediate and local governments are being given increased responsibilities for the delivery of public services in many countries. Consequently, they

---

[2] The role of the private sector in providing such other essential public services as power, air and surface transport appears to be much less politically sensitive than in water and sanitation.

[3] Elizabeth Malkin, "At World Forum, Support Erodes for Private Management of Water," *New York Times*, March 20, 2006.

are becoming more involved in the development, operation, and financing of the public infrastructure that is required to deliver those services. They face a daunting task: It is estimated that the Latin American and Caribbean region alone will require approximately US$70 billion per year to finance the region's infrastructure investment needs.[4] Though increased transfers from central governments will be able to fund some portion of these investments, private sector funding will have to be brought to bear either through broadened commercial bank lending and/or the development of subnational bond markets. In addition, multilateral development banks and bilateral official development institutions represent an important source of funding that needs to be tailored to the changing environment of decentralization. Finally, a variety of intermediate and local governance reforms that increase revenues or lower expenditures can have the effect of increasing the amount of available local resources. Regardless of the source, securing financing for infrastructure development represents a very challenging objective for subnational governments in emerging market countries throughout the world.

The challenge is great because without the explicit or implicit sovereign guarantees which they were often able to rely upon in the past, many subnational governments in emerging market countries now lack perceived creditworthiness due to financial deficiencies and institutional limitations. A history of reliance on central government transfers coupled with the paucity of predictable local revenue sources creates an environment in which intermediate and local governments experience difficulty convincing domestic lenders to invest in the infrastructure required to deliver basic services. The lack of technical management skills in functional areas such as budgeting, accounting, and financial management only serves to exacerbate reluctance on the part of investors and limit financing opportunities. As a result, only some of the largest jurisdictions in the emerging markets, a handful of unusually well-managed midsized governmental entities, and a small number of subnational public service enterprises have tapped their domestic capital markets and managed their debt without serious problems of the kind seen in such countries as Brazil and Argentina during their economic crises. In many cases, the explicit or implicit sovereign guarantees covering lending done prior to the enactment of major decentralization reforms was masking a multitude of operational and financial weaknesses in the state-owned enterprises and subnational governmental and utility entities which were the ultimate recipients of foreign and local capital for infrastructure.

As a result, projects are now being sponsored not by central governments but increasingly by subnational governments, utilities, and other pri-

---

[4] Antonio Vives and Jorge Rivas, *Private Infrastructure and the Inter-American Development Bank Group*, Inter-American Development Bank Publication, January 1998, p. 2

vate players, all without explicit or implicit central government guaranties. However, these local and private sector players are often not viewed as sufficiently creditworthy to enjoy access to long term, reasonably priced funding for required development projects.

Large, well-capitalized international players in PPPs are increasingly reluctant to enter the emerging markets due to a series of negative experiences in the power, transportation, and water sectors which highlighted flaws in many countries' first attempts to set up concession and similar privatization schemes, and in the hard currency debt financing strategies. Some indigenous capacity exists to step into equity and/or managerial roles from which multinational sponsors are withdrawing (e.g., in Chile where experienced indigenous and regional companies are replacing multinational water and sanitation companies in both ownership and operational roles). However, in most low- and middle-income developing countries in Asia, Africa, Central and Eastern Europe, and Latin America, sufficient local public or private capacity to meet rapidly growing infrastructure needs is absent or at least has not been given the institutional and policy framework to succeed. The raw talent often exists in most countries but the bureaucratic environment maintained by many public systems prevents people from managing properly. Recognizing this, IFIs have been responding not only with increased capacity-building technical assistance resources, but also with financial products such as *partial risk guarantees* addressing various forms of regulatory risk, equity for indigenous PPP partners, and *output-based aid* (OBA), designed to facilitate the entry and retention of multinational expertise in the operation and management of infrastructure facilities in such key sectors as water and sanitation, and energy distribution. The involvement of the IFIs is often key to obtaining the policy and institutional changes required for more efficient management of local systems.

DEVELOPING FINANCIALLY SUSTAINABLE SUBNATIONAL INFRASTRUCTURE CREDITS IN THE EMERGING MARKETS

The credit criteria being used by rating agencies and credit enhancers such as monoline financial guarantors and IFIs providing partial guarantees in evaluating public project and subnational infrastructure risk in emerging market countries closely parallel those used for decades in the United States and other OECD markets. The traditional tripod of sound public finance—ability to pay, willingness to pay and essentiality—continues to be the foundation for credit analysis and structural design, as in the developed world. However, the ways in which these generally familiar criteria are applied and the financing structures used in emerging markets are both being adjusted to accommodate such distinctive general emerging market circumstances as:

- Increased volatility of macroeconomic performance and the resulting increased volatility in tariff revenues, as demand for even essential services gyrates in a more pronounced fashion than in fully developed countries.
- Increased price elasticity of demand for some essential services, resulting from the inescapable fact that public service tariffs in emerging market countries will constitute markedly higher percentages of personal income than they do in OECD countries.
- Relatively short periods over which reliable financial information and performance data which are needed for comparative analytic purposes will have been collected and reported.
- Relatively less-well developed legal and regulatory systems governing the delivery of essential services by regulated utilities and subnational governments.

For all categories of infrastructure finance except general obligation debt issued by subnational general-purpose governmental entities, the accurate projection of revenue generated by demand for the public service being provided by the borrower is, of course, fundamental to the credit analysis. Whether the sponsor is a concession company, a public-private partnership, or a public agency, infrastructure demand forecasting in emerging market countries is more challenging than it is in OECD countries for a variety of reasons including difficulty obtaining reliable historical and current demand data, lack of knowledge about price elasticity of demand for public services, and the unfamiliarity of demand forecasters with country-specific circumstances for specific sectors (e.g., willingness to pay for trip-time savings in a given country's personal and commercial transport sector).

Some statistical techniques—including probabilistic techniques more traditionally used with asset-backed securitization transactions—can be employed in single-risk analysis, to provide a better understanding of the range of uncertainty inherent in particular demand forecasts. However, these will be of limited use if the underlying data are poor or if historically unprecedented demand risks emerge, as they did for commercial aviation after the 9/11 attacks. Also, because sponsor bias has been strongly suggested by the rating agencies as a major contributing factor in the demand forecasting errors which have undermined the creditworthiness of infrastructure transactions in several sectors, third-party demand analysts with no connection to project sponsors are increasingly being used by financial guarantors in their due diligence.

Some countries have recognized how real or perceived demand risk can increase the cost of an essential infrastructure financing—or prevent it altogether—and are finding ways to relieve project sponsors and their lenders of some or all of this risk. Chile and other countries have included minimum revenue guarantees in transportation concession agreements, and several countries have experimented with concession terms which vary with demand (the lower the actual demand, the longer the concession term). Chile has turned the variable concession term concept into a formulaic demand risk management tool for highway and aviation infrastructure with the adoption of its Mechanism for the Distribution of Income (MDI) program. This concession agreement modification is provided to the private sector partners at a price set by a probabilistically driven formula to make sure that it is ultimately "revenue neutral" to the government, and is thus likely to be politically defensible for the long term.

Monoline financial guaranty insurers and other credit enhancers will apply the general principles already in widespread use in the United States and other OECD countries with robust subnational infrastructure finance sectors rather than the exact criteria applying to each subsector (e.g., as published by Standard & Poor's in its publication Public Finance Criteria) when underwriting subnational credits.

First, both the overall legal provisions for creditors and the political environment of a given emerging market country will be carefully evaluated to make sure that they provide adequate protection for bondholders and other lenders in the event of fiscal stress and or default. In a number of emerging market countries, borrowing by subnational entities is either forbidden or severely restricted. In addition, great care must be taken to ensure that the legal charters of the borrowing entities allow them to undertake the specific kind of transaction under consideration. Even lenders in developed countries such as the United Kingdom have been burned by entering into ultra vires transactions (e.g., the derivatives transactions with certain UK municipalities in the 1990s).

This country level analysis will include but will not necessarily be limited to such systemic factors as:

1. The national legal system's treatment of public sector and corporate contracts and property rights, as well as the system's longevity, stability, and responsiveness.
2. The intergovernmental oversight environment within which subnational entities operate.
3. The intergovernmental fiscal system, including the dependence of regional and local governments on superior levels of government for revenue, the reliability of revenue flows from superior levels of government, and the freedom of subnationals to levy taxes, fees, and the like in order to generate "own-source" revenue.
4. The degree of development of banking and securities law and regulation, particularly as they apply to subnational borrowing, cash investment, and use of trust services.

5. The lien position of subnational debt holders and the ability of debt holders to perfect and enforce if necessary their security interests in:
   a. Cash flows of public or quasi-public subnational entities.
   b. Hard assets such as rolling stock, land, commercial and industrial properties, and the like.
   c. Stock shares and other financial instruments held by subnational entities.
6. The treatment of subnational entities under bankruptcy statutes.
7. The ability of debt holders to enforce in a timely fashion security interests in assets of subnational entities.
8. The extent to which subnational entities enjoy an explicit or implicit sovereign guaranty.
9. The degree to which sometimes long existing tension and animosity between the central government and its provinces or states may embroil the transaction in domestic political fights between different levels of government. (Brazil, India, and China are examples of where this may be a consideration.)

Second, in order to obtain investment-grade ratings and to be eligible for credit enhancement, subnational borrowers will have to pass the baseline ability and willingness to pay, and essentiality tests. In emerging market settings the willingness to pay question needs to be especially thoroughly considered, as central governments differ markedly in their oversight of intermediate levels of general and special purpose governments, and of municipalities. Best practices in central government oversight of emerging market subnational public finance can be found in countries such as South Africa operating under its Municipal Finance Management Act (Number 56, 2003), Mexico with its strictly enforced regulatory requirements that any subnational wishing to borrow in any form must first obtain two independent ratings, and Poland with its revamped system of intergovernmental finance. These and other countries' systems tend to be effective because they clearly define subnational governmental roles and responsibilities, set expectations for financial performance, have active oversight systems, and have the power for senior levels of government to intervene and take remedial action well in advance of a financial crisis likely to result in a default on debt.

Just as in the OECD countries, it is useful to distinguish between tax-backed and enterprise credits in the analysis of subnational infrastructure credits.

Tax-Backed Credits

Tax-backed bonds in the emerging markets are likely to develop in many varieties; credit analysts must be vigilant about distinguishing among seemingly similar instruments. As discussed earlier, security may range from very strong to highly speculative. Three key tax-backed bond types will be considered by rating analysts and financial guaranty insurance underwriters:

General Obligation, Unlimited Tax Bonds

General obligation, unlimited tax bonds will be secured by the unconditional, full faith and credit of the issuer, to the fullest extent permitted by the legal systems in which the issuer operates. Depending on the laws of the nation in which the debt is issued, the issuer pledges to raise sufficient property and/or other broad-based taxes, without limit, to pay debt service on the bonds. The use of third-party trustees, and the ability of such bondholder representatives to invoke *mandamus* or similar procedures to force the issuer to raise tax rates to pay debt service will be considered credit-strengthening features for this bond type. At the individual taxpayer level, the willingness and ability of tax authorities to impose and enforce meaningful penalties (e.g., foreclosure against property, etc.) against delinquents will be another key credit factor. Clear legal authority of the issuer to incur debt in general and to incur the specific debt being scrutinized will have to be demonstrated in the fundamental legal analysis; voter approval of the specific issuance will be regarded as a significant additional credit strength for this bond type. This type of structure will usually have a higher shadow rating and a lower capital charge to financial guarantors than the following two structures.

Limited Tax, General Obligation Debt

Limited tax, general obligation debt is secured by broad-based taxes which have a ceiling on the tax rate. In some cases, limited tax debt will be found to be functionally similar to unlimited tax debt because the issuer is well below the tax rate limit, although the political willingness to raise taxes should be examined very carefully. In other cases, the tax rate may be close to or equal to the tax rate limit, which limits flexibility and reduces credit quality of the debt. However, in contrast to an unlimited tax bond, debt service supported by a limited tax pledge must compete with other functions which are also funded by the broad-based tax source. An issuer may have both unlimited and limited tax debt, although the approval process is typically easier for the limited tax bonds.

Lease Obligations and Other Forms of Debt Carrying Appropriation Risk

Lease obligations, often taking the form of certificates of participation, and other securities carrying at least a theoretical risk of nonappropriation of sufficient money to cover debt service by the governing body are a common and growing type of tax-backed debt in the United States. Financing of this kind gained favor in the United States because no voter approval is needed and leases typically do not count against debt limitations. However, lease payments are made from the General Fund and must compete with other operating budget priorities.

The use of leases grew dramatically as property tax limitations and voter rebellions have made it difficult to issue general obligation debt. In emerging market settings, financial guaranty insurers will generally not guarantee this form of debt, unless systemic issues make it impossible for subnational entities to incur both general obligation unlimited tax debt and limited tax general obligation debt. We can envision situations where a lease structure may be under consideration in emerging market public finance settings because, for example, a vendor has offered a municipality attractive long-term financing for telecommunications equipment. In situations where leasing is simply a financing alternative, most of the questions which traditional monoline bond insurers have used to assess municipal leasing in the United States and other OECD nations will apply in emerging markets, including:

- What historical and prospective indicators speak to the municipality's ability to pay?
- How essential is the project? Is the project somewhat discretionary, making lease default more likely? Conversely, is the project so essential that a creditor would lose the recourse of repossession in the event of default?
- Is the lease subject to annual or periodic appropriation and, if so, what process is followed? Is the lease obligation binding on the governing body in the future?
- Is the lease subject to abatement?
- How would a payment default on the lease affect the municipality's general reputation, its access to debt markets, its relationships with other creditors, its relationships with other governments (particularly provincial or central governments), and its relationship with debt rating agencies (if any)?
- What "outs" are available to the municipality under the lease?
- What structural protections may be afforded to creditors under the lease documents (e.g., reserve funds, pace of principal amortization, timing of payments, use of trustees)?
- What is the creditor's ability to repossess leased assets?

However, the evaluation of lease and other structures which entail appropriation risk in emerging markets will also have to account for structural weaknesses more often seen to a more pronounced degree in the subnational sectors of emerging market countries than in developed countries. As discussed more fully below, these shortcomings can include problems with (1) governance, management and administration; (2) the regional and/or local economy; (3) basic financial performance; and (4) tax and other revenue collection systems. Weaknesses such as these will be regarded by credit analysts as more dangerous in debt structures with annual appropriation risk than in those which do not entail appropriation risk.

Structuring Strong Tax-Backed Credits in Emerging Markets

Interest in the various "flavors" of subnational tax-backed debt discussed above is growing rapidly in emerging markets around the world. As noted above, the analytic approach to tax-backed subnational debt issues in emerging market countries is likely to generally resemble that used in the United States. The increasing number of municipalities achieving reasonably good credit ratings from major rating agencies illustrates this point. However, there are a great many municipalities which will not be able to so readily and successfully establish high credit quality. This will be true either because of weaknesses in factors intrinsic to the municipality or regional government like or because of systemic weaknesses affecting all debt, such as problems establishing, perfecting, and/or registering liens on specified tax or tariff revenue flows.

In emerging market settings, with the processes of governmental decentralization and capital market development continuing to occur more or less simultaneously, establishing that all necessary legal authority exists and will continue unimpaired in the future can be particularly challenging. Understanding and obtaining all necessary regulatory and other approvals for the specific transaction can also be difficult. Thus, all tax-backed issuers will have to demonstrate their established legal authority and provide a realistic schedule for obtaining all necessary approvals at the outset of the underwriting process.

One means to improve the credit quality of a tax-backed issue is to establish the creditor in a lien position above other tax revenue claimants (public employees, suppliers, etc.) to the extent that this is legally possible in the country. Use of assets other than taxes to further enhance the tax-backed credit (e.g., real property, financial assets such as stock shares, and "interception" of reliable aid flows from higher levels of government) are also used with success in some subnational tax-backed transactions around the world. Structural transaction enhancements such as debt service reserve funds, requirements to set aside weekly or monthly debt service payment amounts in lock-boxed *accumulation accounts,* and the like may also be somewhat helpful in some instances. However, in the long run, the best ways to increase the creditworthiness of tax-backed debt issuers include national efforts to reduce or eliminate weaknesses in the systemic factors; and local and regional initiatives to further develop tax bases, and improve financial and operational capabilities.

The subnational tax-backed sector is likely to include a range of bond types and risk profiles in the emerging market countries qualified for financial guaranty operations. This sector is likely to offer some of the most highly secured debt in some emerging markets countries—debt of municipal governments with diversified tax bases, supported by an unlimited tax on property, or municipal governments which are part of strongly unitary state governance structures such as Vietnam in which the debt may be morally, if not legally, a sovereign debt. Credit quality may be so strong that some offerings can be awarded the highest triple-A rating on the relatively new national scale rating systems without the benefit of third-party credit enhancement. However, the tax-backed sector is also likely to include some of the riskiest types of subnational debt, such as debt secured by special assessments or other narrowly based taxes, or by broader taxes (e.g., those with unlimited tax general obligation tax pledges) imposed on smaller tax bases (e.g., special districts).

Tax-backed credit analysis will focus on at least four principal credit factors which bear on the credit principles of willingness to pay, ability to pay, and project essentiality:

1. Management/administration
2. Regional and local economy
3. Financial performance
4. Tax and other revenue collections
5. Debt profile

These five key analytical areas may be supplemented by examination of special credit enhancements which may be offered by a higher level of government such as intergovernmental transfer intercepts. Structural credit enhancements such as debt service reserve funds, debt service accumulation lockbox accounts, double-barreled structures, and additional bonds tests can also be used to strengthen subnational debt structures in emerging markets as they are routinely used in more developed markets. In fact, such structural enhancements may need to be larger or stronger in emerging markets than in developed markets because each can help a credit structure survive the more pronounced fiscal stresses likely to be encountered in emerging markets for reasons such as increased macroeconomic volatility.

For example, debt service reserve funds are amounts set aside in highly liquid form to help meet debt service requirements in case of unforeseen stress on the pledged tax or other revenues. Additional bonds tests are designed to prevent the development of unsafe debt burdens on the same pledged tax or other revenue stream. Larger debt service reserve funds and more stringent additional bonds tests can each provide the greater liquidity subnational issuers may need to ride out the higher levels of mid- to long-run economic volatility typical of emerging markets. Similarly, debt service accumulation lockbox accounts ensure that amounts of pledged revenue are regularly being set aside between debt service payment dates (e.g. 1/6 of the next debt service payment in semiannual payment structures) to mitigate the risks posed by unanticipated delays in the collection of pledged tax or other revenues, caused by systemic weaknesses or other problems likely to be more severe in emerging markets than in developed markets. Double-barreled structures provide a backup pledged tax or other revenue stream in case the primary source should prove inadequate to cover debt service and can help mitigate both mid- to long-term and short-term risks to pledged revenues.

Risk mitigation products offered by such high-quality providers of credit enhancement as multilateral and bilateral development banks (e.g., partial risk and partial credit guarantees of the World Bank, the International Finance Corporation, European Bank for Reconstruction and Development, and the U.S. Overseas Private Investment Corporation), and philanthropic institutions (e.g., the Aga Khan Foundation) can also be used to improve the credit quality of tax-backed transactions.

Management/Administration

The strength of management represents potentially the most challenging factor of subnational credit analysis, since this is the least quantifiable of all factors. Analysts will favor managements that are proactive, knowledgeable about debt practices and the capital markets, and conservative in financial policies and practices. Management and governance structure will also be assessed to determine, for example, whether decision making is vested in one official or a broader legislative board; whether the governing body is relatively unified in outlook, or highly factionalized; and whether there has been a history of continuity in key positions. The political environment in which the management works and the extent to which political allegiance rather than technical competence determines the careers of public employees must also be examined carefully.

The extent to which policies and practices are formalized will also be an important credit factor. Well-managed entities will project and monitor cash flows, develop financial projections, establish 5- or 10-year capital plans, and implement risk management programs. They also may develop debt capacity guidelines to evaluate the impact of debt financing and set reasonable limitations. Other indicators of strong management are formal policies to maintain operating and major maintenance reserves at specific levels, as well as procedures to limit withdrawals from reserves to specific, critical purposes. While this area of analysis tends to be more qualitative, if not subjective, management behavior is indicative of willingness to pay and can mean the difference between debt payment and default.

Credit analysts will have to recognize that the quality of management can be highly transitory, often changing with political election cycles. This is a particularly pronounced problem in governmental systems characterized by weak civil service recruitment, training, advancement, and retention policies and practices, and/or by relatively low degrees of civil service independence from political interference. Credit analysts examining subnational credits in emerging markets will be especially vigilant about whether management standards have been developed and maintained through changes in elected political leadership, mitigating the risk that poor political leadership will undermine management quality.

Regional and Local Economy

The area economy is a key element in assessing the credit quality of the issuer, since the health of the economy will be an important driver of revenues and of expenditure demands. The diversity of local taxpayers and employers, historical unemployment rates, wealth levels, and cyclicality of the economy are good indicators of its resiliency and stability. Information on tax base growth, age, growth rate and education levels of the population, trends in building permits, and bankruptcies can also provide insight. A rapidly growing, young population will drive demand for schools and other infrastructure, whereas an older, retired population, while requiring fewer services, may resist tax rate increases that would impinge on its fixed incomes. An over reliance on one employer or sector is a vulnerability; diversity and continued, steady growth are positive factors providing stability and predictability to an issuer's performance.

Financial Performance

An issuer's historical financial performance will be closely scrutinized to evaluate whether sufficient resources will be available to meet debt service. The ability of management to control expenditures and meet budget targets is a good indication of their degree of control over financial operations, including the payment of debt service. This is an important indicator not only when payment of debt service must compete with other budget priorities, such as the case of a limited tax, but even when debt service is paid from a dedicated tax not originally intended to be used for any other purpose.

Because a subnational government generally does not face competition for its services, the many financial ratios and measures used to evaluate a corporate credit or a municipal enterprise system, such as a water enterprise or power generator, will often not be as useful in tax-backed credit analysis. For example, in evaluating *general obligation* (GO) debt, the typical meaning of debt service coverage is irrelevant, if the issuer has pledged to levy whatever amounts are necessary to pay debt service and has the clear legal authority and demonstrated willingness to do so and if the tax payers who are expected to pay the increased taxes have—and are expected in the future to have—the ability and willingness to assume the burden of the required higher taxes.

Equally or more important is the affordability and political viability of the general obligation pledge. Useful indicators of this factor will include:

- The ratio of debt to the tax base.
- The level of an entity's tax rates in comparison to neighboring jurisdictions.
- Current and projected future debt service as a percentage of the budget.
- Voter support for government funding needs.

Similarly, a subnational government does not measure its financial performance in terms of operating profit or net income, but in terms of whether it generates a surplus or deficit. Surpluses generated add to an entity's "fund balance"; deficits reduce its fund balance. The fund balance is usually a measure of cash and near-cash receivables and may be viewed as the subnational near-equivalent of net working capital in a corporation. As for longer-term assets, a GO issuer's property, plant, and equipment assets are shown on a different schedule of accounts than the general fund, if recorded. While these and other general principles of subnational accounting are likely to hold true in most middle- and upper-income emerging market countries, there is substantial variation among countries with respect to the details of municipal accounting standards, the degree to which each country's standards are adhered to, and the extent and quality of independent, third-party auditing. The subnational credit analyst in emerging market settings will need to understand these differences and their implications for the predictability and volatility of revenue streams pledged to debt service in a given transaction.

Review of three to five years of audited financial statements will be the primary means of analyzing an issuer's historical financial performance, and separate reports to supervening levels of government will provide a second source of financial performance information. So-called structural balance, whereby ongoing revenues equal ongoing expenditures, will normally be viewed as an indication of good financial control and an indicator of mid- to long-term fiscal stability.

The diversity and volatility of revenues will also be scrutinized. Different subnational governments will have different mixes of revenues depending on the composition of the local economy as well as different statutory authorization for specific revenue sources. Only issuers which can demonstrate stable, predictable, and growing revenue sources are likely to be considered for financial guaranty insurance. Population and economic growth are generally viewed as positive factors but can be a mixed blessing because while population increases tend to raise property values, they also create demand for public services.

Sales and income taxes will be considered more volatile than property-based taxes due to their sensitivity to economic conditions, but will capture an economic upturn more quickly. On the other hand, a sales tax-based budget will quickly suffer from reduced collections during an economic downturn, at the same time that counter-cyclical government spending may begin to rise. A diverse mix of revenue types is considered to be a positive credit factor, particularly if the issuer has the ability to increase the tax rates.

On the expense side of a subnational budget, spending pressures can come from supervening governmental mandates, rapid population expansion, the need to serve a preponderantly elderly and/or less affluent population, or aging infrastructure. The ability to accumulate reserves in anticipation of unexpected events is another important credit factor. Specific reserves may be established in anticipation of uncollectible taxes or other receivables. They may also be established as "rainy day" funds and to provide for future operating contingencies. The latter are generally funded through specific appropriations, or by earmarking a portion of an operating surplus (i.e., the excess of revenues over expenditures). The general fund balance may also serve as an informal, nonspecific reserve. The degree of liquidity of reserves will also be evaluated to determine how useful such funds would be in a crisis.

The tax assessment systems employed by issuers and the collection rates and trends in tax collection rates will also require careful scrutiny. Delinquencies and the systems used to track and recover on delinquent accounts will receive particular attention.

Tax and Other Public Revenue Collection

Tax-backed credits in developing countries face challenges not encountered to anything like the same extent in more advanced economies. First, the rate of collection in richer countries is a much higher percentage of GDP. For example, in richer OECD countries, the tax collection rate is about 38% of GDP whereas it is less than 20% in developing countries. This means that a tax pledge in a developing country encumbers a scarcer resource. Second, tax collection is less evenly distributed in developing countries because many businesses are informal or unregistered, and because there may be large informal slum communities where property is not registered and therefore not taxed. Raising tax rates may be more difficult in such circumstances because the base is smaller than it otherwise should be. Third, fiscal and administrative decentralization may be part of an unfinished institutional process. For example, there may be decentralization of responsibility for service delivery without full decentralization of corresponding authority for tax rate setting or collection. When a local authority in such circumstances pledges tax revenues its ability to act in case of difficulties may be constrained by the decisions of higher governmental authorities.

Tax rate collection is generally lower in developing than developed countries. Much of the difference is due to administrative reasons. One study found that the cost of compliance with tax collection was ten times higher as a proportion of revenue collected in India than in the United States. This difference is attributable to a variety of factors such as costs of training, public education, accounting standards and systems, and the costs of real and/or personal property registration. Tax avoidance in developing countries is more common because registration systems are incomplete and costly to maintain. There may also be political motives for limiting the ability of local authorities to reform or improve elements of the current system such as registration systems and delinquency enforcement actions.

Theft of service and unaccounted for service is much more common in some (but not all) developing countries. While there is a widespread perception that the poor are unwilling or unable to pay for services, many studies have shown that the poor actually pay much more for services such as water when they buy it from informal vendors than they would if it were available from a utility. Good management, good incentive systems and strong surveillance may be the key factors affecting collection rates. In fact, evidence for the presence or absence of good management can often be found in the data on collection rates, leakage, unaccounted-for services, and theft of services. Often performance on these indicators is consistent among subnational entities within a country, and may be evidence of strong central or provincial government oversight of local bodies. For example, in countries like Vietnam and China where management of services is considered a technical function rather than a political function, collection rates are very high. In countries where local management of services is affected by political considerations such as, India, collection rates are much lower and the rates themselves cover a lower percent of system operating costs.

Debt Profile

Each tax-backed debt issuance is analyzed for its specific characteristics, such as rate of amortization, peak debt service payment, and legal covenants. The rate of debt amortization should reflect the useful life of the project being financed. Debt used for durable fixed assets such as buildings is typically amortized over 20 to 25 years, while debt for equipment or vehicles may be financed over 5 to 10 years and computer equipment should be financed over only 3 to 5 years, given the rapid obsolescence of the equipment and technology. Debt service should be relatively level; attempts to defer dramatically higher levels of debt service until later years may signal fiscal stress. Any refinancing of existing debt should match, if not improve on, the existing amortization rate. The amount of parity and other debt relative to the issuer's ability to pay will also be carefully scrutinized to the extent that measures of ability to pay such as full value of a property tax base, per-capita income for a personal income tax base, or total sales for a sales tax base, can be found.

The establishment of a lockbox or escrow system, which reliably insulates tax revenues dedicated to debt service from being used for operating expenses, can materially improve an issuer's credit quality. The debt profile analysis should also take operational and capital reserving policies and practices into account.

Structured Financing of Multiple Subnational Credits

Financial guaranty insurers and other credit enhancers will also consider underwriting well-structured pools of subnational tax-backed and/or enterprise credits in "bond bank," "revolving loan fund," and similar formats in circumstances where a creditworthy supervening governmental entity is guaranteeing the debt or is providing sufficient credit enhancement to both "homogenize" the credits included in the pool and to raise the credit rating of the pool. Normally, such pooled transactions would include subnational credits from the same country. In general, the ownership of the underlying loans and/or bonds in the pool is retained by the originating and servicing entity, which is usually a special purpose governmental agency. However, there may be circumstances in which the ownership of underlying debt instruments is transferred to a *special purpose vehicle* (SPV), for example, when individual loans for the pool are obtained from one or more commercial banks seeking capital relief. The pool sponsor itself will be analyzed as an enterprise, with careful attention to origination and portfolio management skills. If an SPV structure is employed, servicer evaluation guidelines similar to those used for ABS servicers will be used.

Enterprise Credits

Subnational enterprise credits may be classified as "pure enterprise" systems which are totally reliant on fees collected by the enterprise, and hybrid or double-barreled systems, which supplement the fee-reliant revenue stream with taxes, assessments, or other broader support. Major characteristics of both systems include:

- *A pure enterprise system* must rely only on its system revenues to pay operating, maintenance and debt service costs, so user charges must be set high enough to cover all these costs, with a cushion for unanticipated contingencies. User charge revenues will fluctuate directly with use of the enterprise.

- *A hybrid or double barreled system* may impose assessments or other charges not tied to usage, in order to reduce user charges, thus making it more competitive as well as providing creditors a more stable revenue stream. Such fees are usually established on a per-user basis, and while they may fluctuate with population or housing trends, they are not sensitive to demand fluctuations and therefore add stability to the revenue stream.

- *In its strongest form, a double-barreled security will include system revenues as well as a covenant by the supervening subnational government to make up shortfalls* from its general fund, or a pledge of its full faith and credit. This additional backup pledge will strengthen security significantly, often resulting in a rating equal to that of the direct debt of the subnational governmental entity.

Subnational public enterprise financings are being structured with many country-to-country variations under both purely public and mixed public-private systems such as *public finance initiatives* (PFI), *public-private partnerships* (PPP), and concessions where the public participant is either a sovereign or subnational government. All such mixed public-private financings will generally be treated as public project credits because of the heavy involvement of one or more purely corporate entities in such transactions.

Credit analysis of both management and financial performance of all subnational enterprise credits will always include a particular focus on four major problems which tend to challenge such entities far more in emerging markets than in developed markets:

- *Extension of service to underserved or unserved populations, usually the poor and near-poor.* Although most public attention has been paid to the issue of extension of clean water and sewage treatment services to the poor and near-poor due in part to this issue's inclusion in the Millennium Development Goals, most essential public service enterprises are under increasing political pressure to extend or substantially improve existing service to underserved or unserved populations and to do so on a financially sustainable basis. Our observations in many different countries strongly suggest that continued governmental and popular support for subnational public enterprises will depend, in part, on their demonstrated ability to plan and execute service extensions and improvements to these populations. Therefore, plans to extend financially sustainable service to underserved populations will receive particularly close attention in the review of all management and financial performance elements of subnational enterprise credits. This has been a particularly sensitive and politically loaded issue in many countries as different as Mexico and Peru in Latin America, Poland, and Ukraine in Central and Eastern Europe, and South Africa and Indonesia in the Asia/Africa region. The difficulty of finding ways to extend service to underserved populations in a financially sustainable, yet politically acceptable fashion has contributed substantially to the marked decrease in the attractiveness of privatized water transactions from both the investors' and the consuming public's point of view.

- *Recruitment and retention of high-quality technical and financial personnel.* For reasons ranging from low public sector wage scales to gaps in secondary and post-secondary education systems, to poor incentive systems for good performance, it continues to be difficult for subnational public enterprises to recruit and retain high-quality managers and technicians. This is often one of the root causes of poor maintenance, and deteriorating service quality, the consequences of both ranging from physical leakage of water, electricity, or gas, and growing maintenance costs to increased theft of services and payment delinquencies. For this reason, professional recruitment and retention plans and performance will receive close scrutiny in the management element of every subnational enterprise credit review.

- *Billing and collection of user fees.* Even with highly qualified personnel on the job, billing and collection problems challenge emerging market service enterprises due to a variety of problems ranging from "cultures of nonpayment" in specific communities, to technical gaps in the software and hardware systems needed to conduct these critical functions, to poorly functioning banking systems which may imply heavy reliance on cash or even barter payments with all the risks that implies. Consequently, particularly close attention will be paid to this element of the financial performance and management function of each subnational enterprise credit analyzed.

■ *Legal authority, supervening governmental approval and ongoing regulation.* In emerging market settings, where the ongoing processes of governmental decentralization and capital market development are continuing to occur more or less simultaneously, establishing that all necessary legal authority exists and will continue unimpaired in the future can be particularly challenging, as can the assessment of the regulatory process in the future. Understanding and obtaining all necessary regulatory and other approvals for the specific transaction can also be difficult. Thus, all subnational enterprise issuers will have to demonstrate their established legal authority and provide a realistic schedule for obtaining all necessary approvals.

Illustration: Water and Sanitation

During the 1990s and well into the new millennium, there has been much stronger interest in various forms of privatization for water and wastewater entities in emerging markets than had been typical in the United States, where subnational public enterprises have long been the dominant means of delivering water and sanitation services. In many cases, the World Bank and other IFIs ardently promoted the privatization of water and sanitation services, where arrangements involving the private sector range from:

■ *Operating contracts or leases* of facilities, or contracting out of various maintenance functions let by public entities.
■ *Concession agreements* for the operation of existing systems, the construction of new facilities for existing systems, and green-field projects.
■ *The full purchase of systems* by private utilities.

We also see many systems continuing as public enterprises, departments of municipal or regional governments, or as quasi-independent authorities in forms analogous to patterns found in the United States. The high failure rate in emerging market water and sanitation privatization agreements which were originally concluded in the 1990s and early 2000s has led to the withdrawal of many global water companies from the emerging markets and a renewed interest in the role of subnational public enterprises in meeting the Millennium Development Goals for water and sanitation.

In any case, significant elements of standard municipal risk remain in water-related privatizations and public-private partnerships. While specific forms of water-related credit risk discussed may be shifted away from the public sector under the more complete forms of privatization, they nonetheless must be carefully analyzed from the perspective of whatever party is taking these risks.

Some form of rate regulation for private water and waste-water entities appears to be virtually universal. Public entity rate regulation can come from a central government ministry or a specialized regulatory body, preferably one with a degree of independence. Alternatively, in places as far apart as such Central European states as Latvia and Lithuania and Asian states like China, water, sewer (and other utility) rate regulation can be a local or regional governmental function. Whether it is imposed from the center or from the local level, the rate regulation system poses a form of risk that must be carefully analyzed.

The key analytical areas associated with water and sanitation financings in emerging market settings will include:

1. The service area and customer profile.
2. The water system and projected capital improvements.
3. The legal covenants.
4. Rate setting authority and other regulatory trends.
5. Historical and projected financial operations.
6. Environmental considerations—both in the developing country and international or development bank requirements if relevant.

Service Area and Customer Profile

Analysis of the service area and customer profile focuses on the enterprise's economic base, with a particular focus on the relative economic strength of enterprise customers and their ability and willingness to pay currently authorized and anticipated rates. When assessing the service area and customer profile, rating and credit analysts will consider key factors including but not necessarily limited to:

- *Population history for a minimum of the last 5 to 10 years* to identify historical customer growth or decline and projected growth or decline in the future and estimates of any future capital needs for capacity improvements. Credit analysts can then assess whether the proper financial planning processes and operational mechanisms are in place to avoid unanticipated capital expenditures.
- *Major employers, by sector,* to understand the general status of the employment sector and expected outlook and to help project the future economic strength of the service area. In addition, analysts will look closely at historic, current and projected employment rates, income trends, and other wealth measures, particularly in comparison to state and national averages (with analyses similar to those we use for tax-backed credits).

- *User concentration,* if any commercial, industrial or residential customer contributes more than 5% to the operating revenue of the enterprise, credit analysts will "drill down" further into the credit risk that accompanies moderate to high degrees of user concentration.

Water System Assessment: Projected Capital Needs

The adequacy of the system's facilities and present or future capital needs that may affect service costs will be carefully evaluated with particular care in emerging market settings. Ultimately, the enterprise must provide efficient service in order to generate sufficient net revenues to retire the debt. The need for future capital expenditures which may hinder the water system's ability to both pay for operating costs and provide coverage of debt service, or which may require additional debt, will also be examined. Analyses which must be undertaken in this area include, but will not necessarily be limited to:

- *Projection of sales.* Given the water usage over a fiscal period, a unit rate can be determined such that sufficient revenues are collected to cover all operating costs and debt service during that period.
- *The assessment of system demand.* Demand projections will take into account the socioeconomic information developed in the service area analysis. Historic and projected results of demand-side management (e.g., such conservation measures as providing flow control devices to customers) are taken into account. Where necessary, use of multivariate analysis, Monte Carlo techniques and other advanced statistical analysis will be used to further analyze demand risk. These techniques will typically yield far more helpful credit guidance than single-variant stress testing, which typically fails to take into account such key information as the probability of single stress factors occurring, the degree of correlation among single stress factors, or the probability of several uncorrelated stress factors occurring at the same time.
- *The analysis of system capacity.* The capacity analysis will evaluate the system's ability to meet peak flow demands given current capacity, including a review of historic and projected efficiency improvements that are achievable through leak detection, repairs, and other measures. If analysis of demand and capacity reveal substantial future capital requirements, the capital improvement plan is carefully scrutinized to ensure that such needs are projected to be met in a timely manner. Analysts will also consider whether these needs will be met through internally generated funds, governmental grants, additional debt, or some combination thereof.

Demand and capacity analysis must also take into account an often shifting national and/or intermediate level regulatory environment. In the advanced economies, the last three decades have seen dramatic tightening of wastewater treatment standards. Similar change in potable water standards, requiring substantial future investments, is projected for the near future. The possibility of similar shifts in the emerging markets must also be considered. The analysis will also assess the impact of both current and likely future changes in standards on the water entity's capital improvement program.

- *The evaluation of management.* This part of the analysis will typically cover (1) the training and experience of the senior personnel; (2) plans and performance for the recruitment and retention of qualified technical and financial management personnel; (3) the quality of the capital improvement program; (4) the process for developing the operating budget and financing plans; (5) the history of adherence to financial planning documents; (6) the ratio of labor to total operating costs relative to entities; (7) the collection policies of the entity and the enforcement penalties for late payers and nonpayers; and (8) the use of professional engineers to perform an independent assessment of the systems performance and capital needs on a regular basis.

Legal Covenants

Among the most essential legal pledges for a well-structured subnational water and sanitation enterprise financing are:

- *Pledge of gross revenues or net revenues (i.e., payment of debt service after operation and maintenance expenses).* Whether a gross or net pledge is used is less important than more fundamental supply, demand and operating factors. One of the primary concerns is whether both operating expenses and debt service will be paid. If bankruptcy is declared by a water enterprise, having a pledge of gross revenue will be beneficial. The pledge of gross revenues will generally require payment of the debt service first and then all other expenses thereafter, which may assist in efforts to cut costs. However, care must be taken to identify possible super-senior claims for taxes due, labor claims, and the like in the legal system of the host country. Note that this view differs from that of some rating agencies, which typically analyze water and wastewater enterprises as always offering a pledge of net revenues, regardless of the actual legal pledge, because they assume that revenues will always be used to continue to operate the system before debt can be paid.

- *Senior versus subordinate lien on revenue.* Financial guaranty insurers will be likely to wrap only senior lien debt transactions in this as in every other form of financing for emerging market public infrastructure. Exceptions may be made if the senior lien for previously issued debt has been irrevocably closed, so that no more debt may be issued on a parity with the senior lien or if a "double-barreled" structure is being used whereby a supervening level of government of equal or greater credit quality is providing a strong back-up guarantee. Other kinds of guarantors such as IFIs and philanthropies may be willing to enhance subordinate lien credits.

- *Additional pledged revenues.* Additional revenues may include excise or other special taxes, special assessments, contractual payments from other parties, or pledged revenues. The latter are generally insignificant in municipal utility finances, but possibly important in certain project financings.

- *Minimum debt service coverage ratio.* This feature provides important bondholder security and is common in the water and wastewater sectors. Net revenues to annual debt service ratios of 1.2× to 1.25× are considered average in the developed world and will generally be regarded as minimally acceptable by rating analysts and financial guaranty insurers for pure enterprise financings in emerging markets. This ratio is a key factor which creditors will be monitoring in their ongoing surveillance. Surveillance experience suggests that establishing very high coverage ratios as a credit cushion when underwriting systems where management may have exhibited reluctance to raise rates does not necessarily protect the creditor. Managements in these cases may choose to create technical defaults by not meeting, say, a 1.35× test while avoiding payment defaults by covering debt, for example, 1.2×. This places the creditor in the difficult position of seeking legal enforcement of rights in local courts, which may hold that a significant injury to the creditor's position has not occurred.

- *Additional bonds test.* Before additional debt can be issued, the enterprise must meet an earnings test. The intent of this test is to assure that rates are sufficient to support any additional debt. The *additional bonds test* (ABT) affirms that payment of the debt service on the current issue will continue to be paid even in the event that additional senior or parity debt is issued in the future. A typical ABT will require that no debt may be issued unless historical net revenues for the prior 12 or 18 months are sufficient to provide 1.25× coverage (or some other specified level) of existing and new debt service. Tests which rely on projected revenues as well as historical revenues are even stronger, but tests that use only projected revenues are considered weaker.

■ *Debt service reserve fund.* Rating analysts and financial guaranty insurers will typically require a reserve fund equal to either (1) maximum annual debt service; (2) 10% of the bond proceeds; or (3) 1.25× average annual debt service, with the ultimate decision depending upon the results of stress analysis and, where appropriate, probabilistic risk analysis. This *debt service reserve fund* (DSRF) covenant typically affords at least one year of additional financial security, giving creditors additional time to begin remediation. Usually the trustee must be notified if there is a draw on the DSRF, providing an early warning system of fiscal stress. The trustee is usually required by the trust agreement to contact a guarantor, to enforce covenants, and to pursue remedies as the guarantor may direct, but our experience has been that trustees often fail to do so. Any draw on the reserve fund will be an event of default which must be remedied immediately. Ideally, the enterprise will also have other funds available to meet debt service in addition to the DSRF, although these funds may not be pledged to bondholders. Of course, this can only work if the legal documentation requires that the issuer furnish adequate operational and financial information to the guarantor on a frequent basis.

Rate Setting Authority and Other Regulatory Trends

The ability of the water enterprise to raise revenues by passing costs through to customers is fundamental to bondholder security. In the United States, municipal water and wastewater systems are typically not subject to rate regulation by a superior governmental body such as a state board of public utilities. This is less likely to be the case in emerging market settings. Whether or not there is rate regulation from a supervening level of government, the enterprise may be a subunit of a city, in which case rates would typically be approved by the city's governing body. If the enterprise is established as a quasi-independent agency, the governing board probably would be separately elected or appointed. However, even with this degree of autonomy, financial guaranty insurers and other credit analysts will favor the maximum possible autonomy for decision makers within the enterprise. For example, it will be preferable that independent, appointed officials serve on the governing board of water agencies. Water enterprise boards composed of elected officials are traditionally less willing to raise rates because of the potentially negative political consequences.

It is generally desirable for the financing documents to include a "rate covenant," under which the enterprise promises to maintain rates at a level sufficient to provide a specified minimum debt service coverage ratio. Rate covenants can be very valuable, but they are not foolproof; rate trends are just as important as rate authorization issues. Historic compliance with debt service coverage covenants does not always provide an accurate picture of the future financial strength of a water system. For example, a utility might keep rates low by postponing capital improvements only to find itself in danger of violating environmental regulations. Guarantors in the United States have encountered situations in which a city is suddenly faced with a mandated and unexpectedly large capital improvement project requiring significant rate increases. An interim effect on the community might include restricted usage of water, an outflow of untreated effluent into nearby waterways, or a moratorium on new construction that would increase demand on the system. Any or all of these effects can be accompanied by large rate increases.

Citizens often view the cost of water and sewer services provided by governmental enterprises as a form of taxation and will not react favorably to significant increases despite the evident essentiality of the service. As a result, capital projects may be delayed or postponed indefinitely, leading to an ever-increasing backlog of projects, deterioration of system operations, and possibly violations of environmental regulations. Generally, financial guaranty insurers will prefer frequent, lower rate increases, rather than drastic rate increases or "rate shocks." One method of avoiding rate shock is to establish a *rate stabilization fund* (RSF). RSFs are funded from annual excess revenues and are used to phase in future rate increases. They may also be used to pay for future capital projects and so eliminate associated rate increases.

Historical and Projected Financial Performance

The audited annual financial statements serve as the fundamental means of disclosure of the enterprise's ability to support debt, as well as providing a variety of other indicators of financial and operational strength. This review will cover at least three to five years of audited financial statements, and any accompanying "management letters" provided by the auditors. Financial performance projections for at least the term of the debt to be guaranteed will also be required. Three aspects of financial statement analysis will be emphasized in both initial credit approval and surveillance:

- *Detailed analysis of the balance sheet and income statement.* The balance sheet and income statement provide evidence of the ability of the enterprise to meet operating expenses, pay debt service, support the obligations of the system, and comply with the legal covenants. They also help the credit analyst identify the accumulation of cash reserves and any working capital problems.
- *Scrutiny of accounts.* A review of at least three years of all key accounts yields valuable information on the strength and stability of financial

performance. Particularly close attention will be paid to the debt service reserve fund(s); cash and investments to determine liquidity; and capital levels.

- *Detailed analysis of the enterprise's flow of funds.* Gaining a thorough understanding of the priority in which the enterprise must meet its obligations, as outlined in existing and contemplated bank loan and/or bond documents, is fundamental to identifying financial risks. It is important to identify whether the financial flow of funds works under an "open-" or "closed-loop" system. Under a closed-loop financial system, all the revenues derived from the utility stay within the enterprise. This allows the enterprise to accrue cash reserves for major maintenance, equipment replacement, and other system development and financing programs. This approach is preferred since all net revenues generated by the system remain available for the benefit of the system, including debt service, which benefits bondholders. An open-loop financial system, in contrast, allows transfers to be made to the subnational government of which the enterprise is a subunit.

  This can be problematic, particularly in cases where the financial standing of the enterprise is strong, but the subnational government's general fund is weak. For example, if a city comes to rely on cash transfers from the enterprise in order to improve its general fund, the enterprise will be limited in its ability to accumulate reserves or working capital, possibly hindering its ability to pay the debt service and meet any cushion ratios. Furthermore, enterprises that experience low cash levels generally have to issue additional debt to finance capital improvements, which in turn can result in high debt to capital ratios. When water enterprises operate under an open loop system, effective creditor surveillance practices may help ensure that transfers do not grow excessively. It is important to understand where the transfers fit within the flow of funds; if they may be made prior to payment of debt service, it is important that they also be defined as an expense of the system. This will ensure that any rate covenants and debt service coverage requirements will make provision for the transfers. It is also helpful if the amount of transfers are made more predictable, either as a fixed amount or through formal policy linking the amount of transfers to some indicator, such as a fixed percentage of gross revenues.

Environmental Considerations

As with any type of infrastructure, water and sanitation facilities must conform to increasingly rigorous environmental standards as each country adopts and enforces these regulatory regimes. Thus credit analysts will need to pay particularly close attention to such issues as:

- *The current status of the host country's environmental regulatory system* and foreseeable changes in standards, such as in potable water quality or effluent characteristics.
- *Environmental requirements of multilateral institutions* if such institutions are ever likely to be needed for co-financing, and the like.
- *Risk of sanctions and negative political and social repercussions* if there are environmental accidents or serious pollution affecting the public and the local economy.

CONCLUSIONS

Several global phenomena are driving the expansion of locally denominated capital market solutions for essential public infrastructure finance in middle- and upper-income developing countries. The most powerful forces driving local capital market development include an enormous and rapidly growing backlog of unmet demand for essential public infrastructure, the global movements to decentralize key public functions requiring large capital investments and/or to fully or partially privatize essential public services, the sustained emphasis on financial and legal reform by official donors, the rapid accumulation of private savings, and the development of rational credit spreads using national rating scales. The development and growth of local bond markets is requiring the adaptation of long-established public project finance techniques and shaping the subnational finance credit principles used in these novel settings.

As the example of water and sanitation illustrates, mobilizing local financial resources in emerging market countries will continue to be the most challenging frontier of public infrastructure finance because each country's local capital market is developing in unique political, economic and cultural circumstances. Additional challenges are posed in virtually all developing nations in such critical areas as financial and operational management expertise, stable and predictable inter-governmental fiscal relations, and constructive oversight by supervening levels of government.

CHAPTER 11

The Role of the Rating Agencies

Edward A. Rabson
Muncipal Credit Analyst
Landesbank Hessen–Thuringen (Helaba)

When investing in municipal bonds, the investor's primary concern is the issuer's ability to meet its financial obligations, the full payment of its debt service on a timely basis. Over time, as shown in various municipal default studies, most municipal bond issuers have an outstanding record of meeting principal and interest payments in a timely manner. Issuers disclose information on their financial condition through various documents that are publicly available for an investor to review. However, not all investors have the time, ability, and training to access and review such data and reach an accurate determination of the issuer's ability to meet its financial obligations.

Another avenue open to an investor to evaluate an issuer is to examine its credit rating. Credit ratings are important benchmarks as they reflect a professional assessment of the issuer's ability to meet its financial obligations. Many municipal bonds are rated by one or more of the three recognized credit rating agencies: Moody's Investors Service, Standard & Poor's, and Fitch Ratings. While a number of the banks, brokerage firms and mutual funds have their own research departments which also analyze municipal bonds, credit ratings provided by the municipal rating agencies receive general market acceptance.

Rating agency credit evaluations are intended to measure the probability of the timely repayment of principal and interest. Municipal securities' ratings are typically issued upon initial bond issuance and are periodically reviewed. The ratings may be revised by changes impacting the issue or the issuer's credit position, its creditworthiness. Municipal credit ratings may also be affected by a credit enhancement feature such as bond insurance, a guaranty of the timely repayment of principal and interest and a letter of credit or standby bond purchase agreement. Bonds with credit enhancements often carry dual ratings; both the credit enhanced rating and the underlying or unenhanced rating. Variable rate demand obligations often carry both long-term and short-term ratings. Credit rating agencies will continue to play an important role in the functioning of the municipal market.

MOODY'S INVESTORS SERVICE

Long-Term Ratings Defined

According to Moody's, its "long-term ratings are intended to be measures of expected loss, and therefore incorporate elements of both probability of default and severity of loss in the event of default . . . Moody's long-term ratings are opinions of the credit quality of individual obligations or of an issuer's general creditworthiness, without regard to individual debt obligations or other specific securities . . . ."[1]

Global Scale Ratings

"The default and loss content for Moody's municipal long-term rating scale differs from Moody's general long-term rating scale . . ." (global rating scale).[2] This difference in rating scales, wherein municipal issuer ratings are typically lower than ratings for similar corporate issuer obligations, goes against data obtained in municipal and corporate default studies. The studies have confirmed that default levels for investment-grade municipal obligations are lower than for investment-grade corporate debt. In response, and given intense interest in the municipal market and the growing number of crossover buyers of municipal debt, Moody's is now expanding its Global Scale Ratings (GSRs) to include the mapping of more U.S. municipal ratings to its global scale. It is likely that, over time, many municipal obligations, in the near term only those issued into taxable bond markets, will receive GSRs; GSRs that, primarily based upon the results of the default studies, are higher than their current municipal ratings. Moody's is reviewing for future determination whether it will eventually also make GSRs available for tax-exempt debt.

Specifically, in March 2007, Moody's announced that it was implementing a new approach for mapping U.S. long-term taxable municipal ratings to the global scale it uses to rate all bonds in other markets. Further, Moody's also announced that the GSRs would apply to taxable municipal bonds sold

---

[1] *Moody's Rating Symbols and Definitions*, Preface (August 2004), p. 1.
[2] *Moody's Rating Symbols and Definitions*, U.S. Municipal and Tax-Exempt Ratings (August 2004), p. 9.

within the United States in addition to only those sold outside the United States, as was previously the case. Additionally, Moody's is expanding GSR municipal debt sectors covered from only tax-backed and water and sewer debt to other municipal sectors including "healthcare, transportation, electric power, higher education and certain subsectors of municipal housing."[3] Moody's intends to implement a "U.S. municipal scale flag" that it will attach to all ratings on its municipal scale, while municipal GSRs will not have the flag attachment, including certain long-term municipal debt already carrying GSR ratings and short-term municipal ratings, which are already based upon the global scale.

Long-Term Ratings

Moody's long-term municipal bonds rating scale incorporates "the analysis of four primary factors relating to municipal finance: economy, debt, finances and administration/management strategies . . . ." The scale is comprised of nine symbols, ranging from Aaa, the highest investment grade rating, to C, the lowest speculative grade rating. Investment grade ratings incorporate the four highest rating grade categories; Aaa, Aa, A and Baa. Speculative or noninvestment grade ratings incorporate the five lower rating grade categories; Ba, B, Caa, Ca and C. Moody's adds the numerical modifiers 1, 2 and 3 to bonds rated within the Aa through Caa categories; with 1 indicating that the issuer or obligation lies within the higher end of its rating category; 2 indicating a midrange ranking and 3 indicating a lower-end ranking.

Moody's bond rating scale also uses Conditional Ratings, using the prefix (Con.), where the security for bond issues is dependent upon (1) earnings of a project under construction; (2) earnings of a project with limited operating experience; (3) rentals required to begin upon project completion; or (4) payments dependent upon some other limiting condition.

Exhibit 11.1 provides a summary of the Moody's ratings and corresponding municipal long-term rating definitions.

Short-Term Ratings

Moody's short-term debt rating scale incorporates three investment grade categories within Moody's Investment Grade (MIG); MIG 1, MIG 2, and MIG 3, and one speculative grade category; SG. Exhibit 11.2 provides a summary of the Moody's ratings and corresponding municipal short-term debt rating definitions.

---

[3] Moody's Public Finance Credit Committee, "The U.S. Municipal Bond Rating Scale: Mapping to the Global Rating Scale and Assigning Global Scale Ratings to Municipal Obligations," *Rating Methodology* (March 2007), p. 1.

EXHIBIT 11.1 Moody's Ratings and Municipal Long-Term Rating Definitions

Rating	Municipal Long-Term Rating Definitions
Aaa	Issuers or issues rated Aaa demonstrate the strongest creditworthiness relative to other U.S. municipal or tax-exempt issuers or issues.
Aa	Issuers or issues rated Aa demonstrate very strong creditworthiness relative to other U.S. municipal or tax-exempt issuers or issues.
A	Issuers or issues rated A demonstrate above-average creditworthiness relative to other U.S. municipal or tax-exempt issuers or issues.
Baa	Issuers or issues rated Baa demonstrate average creditworthiness relative to other U.S. municipal or tax-exempt issuers or issues.
Ba	Issuers or issues rated Ba demonstrate below-average creditworthiness relative to other U.S. municipal or tax-exempt issuers or issues.
B	Issuers or issues rated B demonstrate weak creditworthiness relative to other U.S. municipal or tax-exempt issuers or issues.
Caa	Issuers or issues rated Caa demonstrate very weak creditworthiness relative to other U.S. municipal or tax-exempt issuers or issues.
Ca	Issuers or issues rated Ca demonstrate extremely weak creditworthiness relative to other U.S. municipal or tax-exempt issuers or issues.
C	Issuers or issues rated C demonstrate the weakest creditworthiness relative to other U.S. municipal or tax-exempt issuers or issues.

EXHIBIT 11.2 Moody's Ratings and Municipal Short-Term Rating Definitions

Rating	Municipal Short-Term Debt Rating Definitions
MIG 1	This designation denotes superior credit quality. Excellent protection is afforded by established cash flows, highly reliable liquidity support, or demonstrated broad-based access to the market for refinancing.
MIG 2	This designation denotes strong credit quality. Margins of protection are ample, although not as large as in the preceding group.
MIG 3	This designation denotes acceptable credit quality. Liquidity and cash-flow protection may be narrow, and market access for refinancing is likely to be less well-established.
SG	This designation denotes speculative-grade credit quality. Debt instruments in this category may lack sufficient margins of protection.

Commercial Paper Programs

Moody's short-term debt rating scale incorporates three investment-grade categories within Moody's Prime ratings (Prime); Prime-1, Priime-and Prime-3, and one speculative grade category, Not Prime (NP). Exhibit 11.3

EXHIBIT 11.3 Moody's Ratings and Municipal Short-Term Commercial Paper Rating Definitions

Rating	Municipal Short-Term Debt Commercial Paper Rating Definitions
P-1	Issuers (or supporting institutions) rated Prime have a superior ability to repay short-term debt obligations.
P-2	Issuers (or supporting institutions) rated Prime have a strong ability to repay short-term debt obligations.
P-3	Issuers (or supporting institutions) rated Prime have an acceptable ability to repay short-term debt obligations.
NP	Issuers (or supporting institutions) rated Not Prime do not fall within any of the Prime rating categories.

provides a summary of the Moody's ratings and corresponding municipal short-term commercial paper rating definitions.

Variable Rate Demand Obligation Ratings

Moody's *variable rate demand obligation* (VRDO) rating scale incorporates a two-component rating; a long- or short-term debt rating and a demand obligation rating. The long- or short-term rating represents the evaluation of the risk associated with making timely payments of scheduled principal and interest. The demand obligation rating represents the evaluation of the likelihood to receive the purchase price upon demand (demand feature). The rating categories are a variation of the three MIG investment grade categories; Moody's Variable Municipal Investment Grade (VMIG); VMIG 1, VMIG 2, and VMIG 3, and one speculative grade category; SG. When either of the two-components is nonrated, it is rated NR (e.g., Aaa/NR or NR/VMIG 1).

Exhibit 11.4 provides a summary of the Moody's ratings and corresponding municipal demand obligation rating definitions.

STANDARD & POOR'S

Long-Term Ratings

Standard & Poor's (S&P) long-term municipal credit ratings are provided for an issuer and for an issue, as appropriate. S&P uses a similar rating scale for both municipal issuers and issues. The issue scale is comprised of ten symbols, ranging from AAA, the highest investment grade rating, to D, an obligation in payment default. Investment grade ratings incorporate the

EXHIBIT 11.4 Moody's Ratings and Municipal Demand Obligation Rating
Definitions

Rating	Municipal Demand Obligation Rating Definitions
VMIG 1	This designation denotes superior credit quality. Excellent protection is afforded by the superior short-term credit strength of the liquidity provider and structural and legal protections that ensure the timely payment of purchase price upon demand.
VMIG 2	This designation denotes strong credit quality. Good protection is afforded by the strong short-term credit strength of the liquidity provider and structural and legal protections that ensure the timely payment of purchase price upon demand.
VMIG 3	This designation denotes acceptable credit quality. Adequate protection is afforded by the satisfactory short-term credit strength of the liquidity provider and structural and legal protections that ensure the timely payment of purchase price upon demand.
SG	This designation denotes speculative-grade credit quality. Demand features rated in this category may be supported by a liquidity provider that does not have an investment grade short-term rating or may lack the structural and legal protections necessary to ensure the timely payment of purchase price upon demand.

four highest rating grade categories; AAA, AA, A and BBB. Speculative or noninvestment grade ratings incorporate the six lower rating grade categories: BB, B, CCC, CC, C and D. S&P adds the modifiers Plus (+) or Minus (–) to bonds rated within the AA through CCC categories to show relative standing with those rating categories. The issuer rating scale is similar except that the C category is excluded and an SD (selective default) symbol is added to the D category.

According to S&P, an "issuer credit rating is a current opinion of an obligor's overall capacity (its creditworthiness) and willingness to pay its financial commitments" and "it does not apply to any specific financial obligation, as it does not take into account the specific provisions of the obligation, its standing in bankruptcy or liquidation . . . or any forms of credit enhancement . . . ." An "issue credit rating is a current opinion of the creditworthiness with respect to a specific financial obligation, a specific class of financial obligations or a specific financial program. It takes into consideration the creditworthiness of guarantors, insurers or other forms of credit enhancement . . . ."[4] Issuer and issue credit ratings can be either long-term or short-term.

Exhibit 11.5 provides a summary of the S&P ratings and corresponding municipal issuer/issue long-term rating definitions.

---

[4] "Issuer Credit Rating Definitions," *Standard & Poor's Ratings Definitions* (September 2006), p. 5.

EXHIBIT 11.5   S&P Ratings and Municipal Issuer/Issue Long-term Rating
Definitions

Rating	Municipal Issuer/Issue Long-Term Rating Definitions
AAA	An obligor/obligation rated AAA has extremely strong capacity to meet its financial commitments.
AA	An obligor/obligation rated AA has very strong capacity to meet its financial commitments, differing from AAA rated issuers/issues only to a small degree.
A	An obligor/obligation rated A is somewhat more susceptible to the adverse effects or changes in circumstances and economic conditions than higher rated categories, but has strong capacity to meet its financial commitments.
BBB	An obligor/obligation rated BBB has adequate capacity to meet its financial commitments, but is somewhat more susceptible to the adverse effects or changes in circumstances and economic conditions than higher rated categories.
BB	An obligor/obligation rated BB is less vulnerable in the near term than other lower rated issuers/issues; however, it faces major ongoing uncertainties and exposure to adverse business and economic conditions which could lead to inadequate capacity to meet its financial commitments.
B	An obligor/obligation rated B is more vulnerable to nonpayment than issuers/issues rated higher, but has the capacity to meet its financial commitments. Adverse conditions will likely impair the ability to meet the financial commitments.
CCC	An obligor/obligation rated CCC is currently vulnerable to nonpayment and is dependent on favorable business, financial and economic conditions to meet its financial commitments.
CC	An obligor/obligation rated CC is currently highly vulnerable to nonpayment.
C	An obligation rated C to cover a situation where a bankruptcy petition has been filed, or similar action has been taken, but payments on this obligation are being continued.
D SD	An obligor/obligation rated D is in payment default on one or more obligations, rated or unrated, when it came due. An SD rating is assigned when the obligor has selectively defaulted on a specific issue but will continue it meet its payment obligations on other issues in a timely manner.

EXHIBIT 11.6   S&P Ratings and Municipal Short-term Note Rating Definitions

Rating	Municipal Short-term Note Rating Definitions
SP-1	Strong capacity to pay principal and interest. An issue determined to possess the strongest capacity to pay debt service is given a plus (+) designation.
SP-2	Satisfactory capacity to pay principal and interest, with some vulnerability to adverse and economic changes over the term of the notes.
SP-3	Speculative capacity to pay principal and interest.

Short-Term Note Ratings

S&P's short-term debt rating scale incorporates the liquidity factors and risks unique to notes and applies to notes due in three years or less. Notes maturing after three years will likely receive a bond rating. S&P's notes rating scale has two investment grade symbols, SP-1 and SP-2, and one speculative grade symbol, SP-3. Exhibit 11.6 provides a summary of the S&P ratings and corresponding municipal short-term note rating definitions.

Short-Term Commercial Paper Ratings

S&P's short-term issuer ratings have a similar rating scale to S&P's rating scale for commercial paper. The rating scale has three investment grade symbols, A-1, A-2, and A-3, two speculative grade symbols, B and C, debt under regulatory supervision, rated R, and debt in payment default, rated D or SD (selective default).

S&P's commercial paper ratings reflect an assessment of the likely timely payment of debt having an original maturity of up to 365 days. The rating scale has three investment grade symbols, A-1, A-2, and A-3, two speculative grade symbols, B and C, and debt in payment default, rated D. Exhibit 11.7 provides a summary of the S&P ratings and corresponding municipal short-term commercial paper rating definitions.

Dual Ratings

S&P's assigns dual ratings to all debt issues that have a put option feature as part of their structure. The first rating is an evaluation of the likelihood of repayment of principal and interest and the second rating covers the demand feature. For example, for long-term debt, AAA/A-1+; and for short-term debt, SP-1+/A-1+.

EXHIBIT 11.7   S&P Ratings and Municipal Commercial Paper Rating Definitions

Rating	Municipal Short-term Commercial Paper Rating Definitions
A-1	Capacity for timely payment is strong. Issues with extremely strong safety characteristics are given a plus (+) designation.
A-2	Capacity for timely payment is satisfactory. However, the relative degree of safety is not as high as for A rated issues.
A-3	Capacity for timely payment is adequate. However, the relative degree of safety is not as high as for higher rated issues.
B	Issuers rated B are regarded as having only speculative capacity for timely payment.
C	This rating is assigned to short-term debt with a doubtful capacity for timely payment.
D	Debt rated D is in payment default.

FITCH RATINGS

Long-Term Ratings

According to Fitch, in general, its international long-term ratings are "used as a benchmark measure of probability of default . . . . The major exception is within public finance (municipal) . . . where market convention has always focused on timeliness and does not draw analytical distinctions between issuers and their underlying obligations . . . ."[5] Exhibit 11.8 provides a summary of the ratings by Fitch Ratings and the corresponding municipal long-term rating credit rating definitions.

Short-Term Ratings

Fitch assigns short-term ratings for obligations that are due in up to three years. The ratings "reflect unique risk characteristics of bond, tax and revenue anticipation notes . . . and place greater emphasis on the liquidity necessary to meet financial commitments in a timely manner . . . ."[6] The rating scale has three investment grade symbols, F1, F2 and F3, two speculative grade symbols, B and C, and debt in payment default, rated D.

Exhibit 11.9 provides a summary of the ratings by Fitch Ratings and the corresponding municipal short-term credit rating definitions.

---

[5] "International Long-Term Credit Ratings," *Fitch Ratings Definitions* (November 2006), p. 1.
[6] "International Short-Term Credit Ratings," *Fitch Ratings Definitions* (November 2006), p. 1.

EXHIBIT 11.8   Fitch Ratings and Municipal Long-term Credit Rating Definitions

Rating	Municipal Long-term Credit Rating Definitions
AAA	Highest credit quality. AAA ratings denote the lowest expectation of credit risk, assigned only in case of exceptionally strong capacity for payment of financial commitments. This capacity is highly unlikely to be adversely affected by foreseeable events.
AA	Very high credit quality. AA ratings denote expectations of very low credit risk and indicate very strong capacity for payment of financial commitments. This capacity is not significantly vulnerable to foreseeable events.
A	High credit quality. A ratings denote expectations of low credit risk and indicate strong capacity for payment of financial commitments. This capacity may, nevertheless, be more vulnerable to changes in circumstances or in economic conditions than is the case for higher ratings.
BBB	Good credit quality. BBB ratings indicate that there are currently expectations of low credit risk. The capacity for payment of financial commitments is considered adequate, but adverse changes in circumstances and economic conditions are more likely to impair this capacity.
BB	Speculative. BB ratings indicate that there is a possibility credit risk developing, particularly as the result of adverse economic change over time; however, business or financial alternatives may be available to allow financial commitments to be met.
B	Highly Speculative. For issuers and performing obligations, B ratings indicate that significant credit risk is present, but a limited margin of safety remains. For individual obligations, B ratings may indicate distressed or defaulted obligations with potential for extremely high recoveries. These obligations would possess a Recovery Rating of RR1 (Outstanding).
CCC	For issuers and performing obligations, CCC ratings indicate that default is a real possibility. For individual obligations, CCC ratings may indicate distressed or defaulted obligations with potential for average to superior levels of recoveries. These obligations would typically possess a Recovery Rating of RR2 (Superior), RR3 (Good) or RR4 (Average).
CC	For issuers and performing obligations, CC ratings indicate default of some kind appears probable. For individual obligations, CC ratings may indicate distressed or defaulted obligations with a Recovery Rating of RR4 (Average) or RR5 (Below Average).
C	For issuers and performing obligations, C ratings indicate default is imminent. For individual obligations, C ratings may indicate distressed or defaulted obligations with potential for below-average to poor recoveries. Such obligations would possess a Recovery Rating of RR6 (poor).
RD	RD indicates an entity that has failed to make due payments (within the applicable grace period) on some but not all material financial obligations, but continues to honor other classes of obligations.
D	D Indicates an entity that has defaulted on all of its financial obligations.

EXHIBIT 11.9   Fitch Ratings and Municipal Short-term Credit Rating Definitions

Rating	Municipal Short-term Credit Rating Definitions
F1	Highest credit quality. Indicates the strongest capacity for timely payment of financial commitments. Issues with extremely strong safety characteristics are given a plus (+) designation.
F2	Good credit quality. A satisfactory capacity for timely payment of financial commitments, but the margin of safety is not as great as for F1 rated issues.
F3	Fair credit quality. An adequate capacity for timely payment of financial commitments; however, near term adverse changes could result in a reduction to noninvestment grade.
B	Speculative. Minimal capacity for timely payment of financial commitments, plus vulnerability to near term adverse changes in financial and economic conditions.
C	High default risk. Capacity for meeting financial commitments is solely reliant upon a sustained, favorable business and economic environment.
D	Indicates an entity that has defaulted on all of its financial obligations.

SUMMARY

For municipal bond investors, rating agency credit evaluations will continue to provide an important and independent view of creditworthiness. Of course, bond issuers, investment banks, broker-dealers, and government regulators will also all continue to use credit ratings for their own purposes. Although periodic criticisms of rating agencies can be expected, the future role of rating agencies in the municipal marketplace is assured.

CHAPTER 12

Municipal Bond Refundings

William H. Wood
Senior Technical Analyst
Frasca & Associates, LLC

This chapter describes the various types of municipal bond refundings that are sold, the typical reasons that a governmental issuer will sell refunding bonds, and the different ways in which refunding bond issues can be structured. Broad recommendations are also provided regarding how to determine the best time to refund outstanding bond issues as well as whether the use of derivative instruments should be included as part of the refunding structure.

REFUNDING OVERVIEW

An outstanding municipal bond is said to be refunded when a new bond is sold and the proceeds of that new bond are used to pay all of the remaining principal and interest (and, in some cases, early redemption premium) on such outstanding bond. In a refunding, all or some of the maturities from one or more prior issues are discharged with the proceeds of a refunding issue.

Mechanically, an issuer will sell a new issue of bonds and use the proceeds to buy investment securities (described as *nonpurpose obligations* by the tax code) which will fund the payments due on the refunded bonds. These investment securities are typically held by an independent trustee and the portfolio that holds them is called an escrow. The tax law requires that this portfolio of escrow securities not earn a yield in excess of the yield on the refunding issue which purchased them.

The most common form of investment securities used in refunding escrows are Treasury securities. The Treasury allows issuers to subscribe for special custom tailored securities called SLGS (for State and Local Government Series), which are specifically designed to provide maximum cash flow efficiency in a typical refunding escrow. The SLGS program is also designed to allow issuers to purchase a portfolio of escrow securities at yields below market Treasury yields such that the escrow yield can be set equal to the refunding bond yield. In certain cases, as we will see, the issuer will be better off purchasing Treasuries (or other investment securities) in the open market.

REASONS TO SELL REFUNDING BONDS

There are, generally speaking, three nonmutually exclusive reasons for an issuer to undertake a municipal bond refunding:

- To redeem bonds on an early redemption date prior to their maturity in order to realize interest rate savings from refinancing those bonds at a lower cost.
- To restructure debt service (i.e., the annual schedule of outstanding principal and interest), typically to extend the payments of principal and interest in order to achieve budgetary relief.
- To defease or amend an issuer's bond documents.

We discuss each reason below.

Debt Service Savings

By far the most common types of refundings are those sold to lower bond interest cost and/or to stretch out debt service payments. The first type uses the optional redemption provision embedded in an outstanding bond to redeem that bond before its maturity date. Calling the bond early allows the issuer to take advantage of lower interest rates to refinance the bonds being called. The second type may also may involve calling some of the refunded bonds, but its primary goal is to create a refunding debt service structure which is longer and, in the earlier years, lower than the previously outstanding debt service.

Debt service savings is typically measured in two ways: present value savings and total savings. (Both should be adjusted for items like changes in reserve balances and their earnings rates.) Showing a particular level of positive present value savings is typically an important requirement for approving a refunding for savings, even when the primary purpose of that refunding may be a restructuring of debt service. Depending upon local law and practice, there may be a legal or policy requirement that a certain level of present value savings be realized in order to move forward with a refunding issue.

The federal tax code provides some tricky rules regarding when you have to call bonds before their maturity dates. While an issuer should always rely on its bond counsel for a definitive determination regarding when a refunded bond must be called (if at all), the rule basically goes like this: When all or a portion of a prior issue is being refunded, those bonds which are subject to optional redemption must be called on the first call date that produces present value savings with respect to that issue. As a practical matter, in the vast majority of cases an issuer who is refunding bonds for present value savings will call its outstanding callable bonds on their first call date.

Document Changes

Some refundings are issued to defease or amend an issuer's master legal document. The majority of revenue bonds are sold pursuant to a master legal document which controls the terms and method for issuing debt under the same security agreement (*parity debt*). Depending on the nature of the issuer, this legal document may be an indenture, a resolution or an ordinance. But in each case the effect is pretty much the same. The master document sets items like which revenues are pledged as security, what can be financed, the basis for issuing additional bonds, limitations regarding the term and form of the debt, and the like.

It often happens that as municipal issuers evolve and revenue sources change, they need to modify this master legal document to make it conform with current needs and requirements. One of the ways to accomplish this to refund and defease all or a portion of the outstanding bonds sold under the current master document.

In order to modify a master bond document, an issuer must fund a special kind of escrow called a *defeasance escrow*. What makes a defeasance escrow different from a regular escrow is that it can only contain investment securities approved by the master document as being eligible to effect a defeasance. Historically, this was most commonly Treasury securities. Over the past two decades the standards for permissible investments have evolved and it is now quite common to find certain Agency securities, certain receipt securities, certain AAA municipal securities and others included in the list of permissible defeasance investments. (Most refundings for savings also rely on the use of eligible defeasance securities since the use of any other escrow security would mean that the refunded bonds would still be deemed legally outstanding and this would, in turn, impair an issuer's ability to issue new debt.)

In some instances, based upon bond counsel's interpretation of the documents, certain changes can be made to a master bond document with the approval of, say, 50% of the outstanding bondholders. In this case, it may be possible to amend a master document by issuing new and refunding bonds.

Assuming the new and refunding bonds represent 50% of all outstanding bonds (after giving effect to any prior bonds defeased with proceeds of the refunding portion), the underwriter of the bonds may effect the consent required to amend the master document before distributing the new bonds to investors. This approach can require a substantially smaller refunding issue than a conventional full defeasance.

It is common to combine a refunding issue to make changes to a master document with a refunding issue to lower bond interest cost and/or to stretch out debt service payments.

ISSUES RELATING TO STRUCTURING A REFUNDING BOND ISSUE

Advance Refunding versus Current Refunding

Municipal bonds sold in the United States are frequently refunded well before they reach either maturity or their first call date. Broadly speaking, there are two types of refundings: current refundings and advance refundings.

The specific difference between these two types of refundings is defined by the tax code. Under current tax regulations, all or a portion of a prior bond issue is said to be *current refunded* when all of the refunded principal and interest from that issue is paid within 90 days of the closing date of the refunding issue. If 91 or more days elapse between the closing of the refunding issue and the final payment of any bond principal and interest on the refunded issue, those bonds are said to be *advance refunded*.

Negative Arbitrage

Federal tax regulations and normal market conditions typically give an issuer of municipal bonds a unique advantage in the refinancing its debt compared with any other fixed income issuer. This advantage derives from three basic facts:

1. The tax law typically allows a municipal bond issuer to invest the proceeds of a refunding issue at a yield that does not exceed the yield on the refunding issue.
2. The issuer is able to use the refunding bond proceeds to buy Treasury (and other high grade) securities to pay the refunded principal and interest.
3. Because of the tax exemption of municipal bonds, the yields on municipal bonds are usually substantially lower than the yields on comparable

taxable bonds, even U.S. Treasury securities which are viewed as having no credit risk.

The result of these three factors is that a municipal issuer, in most market environments, can invest the proceeds of its refunding bond issue at a yield equal to the refunding bond yield. This leads to a very important consequence: it becomes economically efficient to refinance debt long before it matures or becomes subject to optional redemption.

Consider the following simplified example. Assume that an issuer has approximately $125 million of noncallable bonds outstanding at an average interest rate of 5%. The annual debt service on these bonds is roughly $10 million per year over the next 20 years. Now, lets say the issuer needs to refinance this debt in order to achieve a legal defeasance, but current market rates are 8%, not 5%. Ignoring costs of issuance, the issuer will need approximately $98 million to fund an advance refunding escrow which, assuming 8% treasuries are available (a near certainty in this case), will be sufficient to fund the 20 years of annual debt service remaining of $10 million a year. What will the debt service on that $98 million refunding issue be? It will be $10 million a year, basically identical to the debt service on the 5% bonds being advance refunded.

When an issuer is able to invest the proceeds of an issue of refunding bonds at that issue's bond yield, the escrow is said to have no *negative arbitrage*.

Now, there are actually a fair number of cases where negative arbitrage does come into play and where it makes a refunding issue more expensive than it would otherwise be. An issuer only avoids negative arbitrage when its escrow, which is typically invested in Treasuries, is able to earn its refunding bond yield. While tax-exempt rates are generally lower than taxable rates, the yield of an escrow invested in Treasuries may be lower than the corresponding tax-exempt refunding bond yield. Following are the three most common causes for negative arbitrage.

First, negative arbitrage often occurs when the average life of the escrow portfolio is much shorter than the average life of the refunding bonds. Treasury yields are usually higher than corresponding AAA tax-exempt yields for the same maturity. But yield curve is also generally upward sloping, which means that the 10-year yield is greater than the five-year yield, and the five-year yield is greater than the two-year yield. This means that negative arbitrage is far more likely when you are selling bonds with a 20-year average life if the refunding escrow has an average life of two years versus, say, 10 years.

A second factor is the refunding issuer's credit rating. While AAA yields are likely to be substantially below Treasuries for any given maturity, this is much less likely to be the case for a BBB issuer. In other words, a lower rated issuer is, all other things being equal, much more likely to experience negative arbitrage than a higher rated issuer.

A final determinant of negative arbitrage is overall market conditions. In certain circumstances, tax-exempt bond rates approach Treasury rates and the favorable spread between the two disappears. This can be caused by different factors such as oversupply of municipal product (versus Treasuries) or by an overall fall in interest rates. In the latter case, when rates, especially short-term rates, get very low, compression is likely to occur such that taxable and tax exempt rates are much closer than they would otherwise be.

SLGS versus Open-Market Securities

Unless an issuer is faced with the prospect of negative arbitrage, it will usually purchase SLGS to construct an efficient yield restricted escrow portfolio. If the issuer chooses to use open-market securities instead, the tax law now requires that it acquire those securities through an open and competitive bidding process.

In the past, issuers were able to negotiate with securities dealers to purchase open market Treasury securities for refunding escrows. This gave rise to a practice known as *yield burning,* which reached its peak in the early 1990s. Under this practice, a securities dealer would artificially inflate the price of an open market portfolio until the yield was reduced to the exact level of the refunding bond yield. While this cost the issuer nothing, it was judged to constitute an inappropriate profit for the dealer and subsequent Internal Revenue Service (IRS) regulations required that open market escrow securities be acquired through a bidding process involving at least three disinterested parties providing *bona fide* bids.

There are, however, instances where SLGS are not the best answer. First, SLGS rates are set daily at levels which are slightly below Treasury yields. This means, if negative arbitrage is present, an issuer may be able to increase its refunding savings by bidding a Treasury portfolio instead of subscribing for SLGS. Second, in certain instances where negative arbitrage is present, an issuer will want to be able to use Agency securities instead of Treasuries in its refunding escrow. Agency securities can earn 50 basis points or more above the yields on comparable Treasury securities. That kind of yield difference can soak up a lot of negative arbitrage.

Typically, an issuer will only consider using Agency securities if they are explicitly permitted as defeasance securities or if, in the case of most general obligation debt, there is no explicit contractual provision for defeasance.

What Can Be Current Refunded?

Under current tax law, most callable tax exempt bond issues can be current refunded once their first call date is within 90 days. This means that just about any tax-exempt issuer can issue current refunding bonds to refinance existing indebtedness at a lower interest rate. Given the right interest rate environment, it should always be possible to structure the refunding debt service to realize savings in every year. It will also be possible, in many circumstances, to simultaneously extend the refunded debt's final maturity as part of a refunding program.

In order to determine whether an issuer can extend the final refunding maturity, bond counsel needs to make a careful analysis of the original use of proceeds of the bonds being refunded. In general the tax law limits the final maturity of the refunding issue to 120% of the useful life remaining of the assets which were originally financed by the bonds being refunded. In addition, if there is a master document governing these bonds, that document must not prohibit refundings which extend the final maturity.

What Can Be Advance Refunded?

For many years, there has been an active public policy debate regarding what constitutes appropriate limitations on advance refunding bonds. The IRS has long disliked advance refunding bonds because they perceive these issues to overburden the tax-exempt bond market. From the perspective of the IRS, there is an implicit tax subsidy associated with each dollar of tax-exempt bond principal for each year it remains outstanding. When an issuer sells an advance refunding bond issue, until the prior issue is fully paid down—which is often 5 to 10 years down the road—there will be two issues of tax-exempt debt outstanding in the marketplace instead of one. The IRS views this as a doubling the federal subsidy and they don't like it.

This has resulted in changes in the tax law that, most notably as part of the Tax Reform Act of 1986, have restricted the ability of issuers to advance refund certain bond issues. In addition, certain types of issuers and certain types of debt can only be current refunded. Broadly speaking there are two categories of restrictions here:

1. An issue sold after the effective date of the 1986 tax act is only entitled to one advance refunding.
2. Generally speaking, issuers of industrial development bonds (typically now categorized as private activity bonds) are prevented from ever issuing any kind of tax-exempt advance refunding bond.

Over the last decade, highly rated callable bonds which can be advance refunded almost always have been refunded before they reached their first call date. When this happens, the investor loses term but gains credit. Since bonds will always trade to the lower price of call or maturity, the substitution of AAA Treasury securities in an escrow means the investor actually gets a price boost when a callable bond is advance refunded since the term used to set the price is unchanged but the credit is improved. Curiously, there is no measurable difference in the pricing of bonds in the primary market based upon whether or not they are eligible for an advance refunding. All other things being equal, an astute investor buying new issue municipals should favor those securities which are able to be advance refunded (typically new money issues) versus those that can't be (typically advance refunding issues and private activity bonds).

WHEN SHOULD AN ISSUER REFUND PRIOR BONDS?

Advance Refundings

When an issuer should refund prior bonds is a very important question, especially as applied to advance refundings. It is also one in which all investment bankers and many financial advisors are, unfortunately, naturally biased. The source of their bias comes from their compensation being dependent on the completion of the bond sale which they are proposing. An issuer should always be wary of a recommendation to refund outstanding bonds when it comes from someone whose only source of compensation results from a deal happening. Moreover, how much the investment banker or the financial advisor earns is not likely to have any meaningful correlation to how much an issuer saves from doing a refunding. This is not to say that an issuer should not carefully evaluate an investment banker's unsolicited advance refunding proposal. Many advance refundings make good business sense, particularly for risk averse issuers.

Historically, the most common test for determining whether a particular bond maturity should be advance refunded for savings was to measure the marginal present value savings produced from refunding that maturity as a percentage of the par amount refunded. Typically issuers or their financial advisors set minimum per bond savings targets at levels such as 3% and 5%. While this is somewhat crude, it is also simple and reasonably reliable. The ever increasing sophistication of computer technology now allows bankers to compute complex call option valuations in order to show more complicated rationales for selecting which bonds to refund. These models may well be valid, but it is much harder to understand what goes into them and they are open to manipulation.

For example, it is common to use what is known as a *forward yield curve* in valuing the call option on a bond that is a candidate for an advance refunding. What this means is that future interest rates are said to be implied by the shape of the yield curve today. This logic says the one-year rate one year from now can be predicted by looking at today's one- and two-year rates. Today's one-year rate and the one-year rate one year from now must equate to the two-year rate today. While this is a totally valid approach for determining forward pricing, it is also very suspect when used for pricing bond call options. The reason is that because the municipal yield curve has always been upward sloping, the forward yield curve is always higher than the spot yield curve. In other words, investment bankers who use this model always assume that on average future interest rates will be higher than today's rates rather than, say, the same. In reality, of course, rates are just as likely to go up as down over time. But the mathematics serves the bankers' purpose because it always makes doing the deal today look better.

In practice, there are three important facts to keep in mind when considering a normal advance refunding of callable bonds for savings:

1. The present value savings virtually all comes from the reduction in interest rates after the call date.
2. An issuer can only sell one advance refunding during the first 10 years preceding the typical first call date on a new money issue.
3. Assuming the refunding bonds are structured to match the maturity of the refunded bonds, every year an issuer waits it "moves down the yield curve." This means that it gets the benefit of the lower rates, assuming market rates remain unchanged, because each year it waits, the refunding issue is one year shorter.

These three factors taken together all make a strong case for having solid present value savings prior to doing an advance refunding, especially if there are no broader objectives for restructuring debt service or changing documents.

There is one significant counter-factor in favor of an issuer locking in savings by selling advance refunding bonds today. To use an old metaphor, a bird in the hand is worth two in the bush. In some contexts it will be better for a risk-averse issuer to take modest present value savings today when the alternative is an uncertain future outcome which includes some probable outcomes in which there are no savings whatsoever.

Current Refundings

Once an outstanding bond becomes callable, the call option becomes a *wasting asset*. In general, the test for refunding bonds which are currently callable should be far looser than the test required for bonds that can only be advance refunded. In addition, it is legally possible to advance refund a current refunding of a new money bond issue (assuming, of course, that the original bond issue met the tax law test to be advance refundable).

REFUNDINGS AND DERIVATIVES

The last decade has seen an explosion in the use of synthetic fixed rate debt to advance refund outstanding issues. Synthetic fixed rate debt typically involves an issuer selling floating rate tax-exempt bonds while simultaneously entering into an interest rate exchange agreement (i.e., interest rate swap) in which the issuer pays fixed and receives floating. The floating receipt cancels out the variable interest rate cost and the issuer is left with fixed rate debt.

Synthetic fixed rate debt is likely to be proposed for outstanding bond issues, which are not legally able to be advance refunded and which can't be current refunded because their first call date is more than 90 days in the future. An issuer can lock in a fixed rate for a future refunding one or more years in the future by entering into a forward starting swap. For example, let's assume a high coupon bond issue first becomes callable in three years and that it is not legally able to be advance refunded. An issuer can use a forward starting swap that begins three years from now to lock in refunding rates today. In the simplest scenario, the issuer will enter into the forward swap today and three years from now it will issue variable rate debt (which, together with the forward swap, create synthetic fixed rate debt). The proceeds of this borrowing are then used to retire the outstanding high coupon debt on its first call date. This approach provides a very attractive alternative for locking in refunding savings when IRS rules prohibit an issuer from selling advance refunding bonds. The forward interest rate swap can also function as a hedge: in this case, rather than selling variable rate debt which is hedged by the forward starting swap three years from now, the issuer would unwind the swap for a profit (if rates have risen) or a loss (if rates have fallen) and issue conventional bonds at prevailing market rates to current refund the outstanding high coupon debt (with the refunding issue size adjusted, either down or up, depending upon whether the hedge produced a profit or loss respectively).

Historically, most synthetic fixed rate debt—whether initially structured in the current or forward market—has been structured as noncallable. This creates what can be a misleading bias in favor of synthetic fixed rate debt since it is most often compared with conventional callable coupon bonds. For example, refunding savings will always be greater if an issuer decides to replace existing high coupon debt with new debt which is noncallable rather than callable. Unfortunately, it is not uncommon for an issuer to see a refunding proposal which appears to produce significant present value savings but where the savings don't come from falling market interest rates but rather from replacing higher yielding callable debt with lower yielding noncallable debt. An issuer should always require its investment banker to analyze a hypothetical refunding issue using conventional coupon bonds with a 10-year call before committing to any refunding structure which is itself noncallable. If that hypothetical refunding issue doesn't meet an issuer's savings targets, the issuer should be very wary of undertaking a refunding for savings using a noncallable structure since it will be probable that the savings the issuer is realizing aren't coming from the call at all. This is particularly true in the LIBOR market, where synthetic fixed rates are often substantially lower than the comparable rates found in the BMA or conventional bond market. If an issuer likes the attractive rates associated with noncallable synthetic fixed rate debt and if it also wants to limit the total amount of synthetic fixed rate debt on its balance sheet, it will often be better off using synthetic fixed rate debt for new money borrowings rather than for refundings.

Recently some of the major participants in the municipal swap market have begun to provide issuers with the option of entering into callable swaps. These callable swaps create synthetic fixed rate debt which has the economic equivalent of a 10-year par call. While callable synthetic rates will always be higher than comparable noncallable rates, an issuer should carefully evaluate the benefits and costs associated with issuing callable and noncallable synthetic fixed rate debt.

An issuer also needs to carefully evaluate the variable rate components. No swap payment, unless the swap is a so-called "cost of funds" swap, will ever exactly match an issuer's own interest cost. While the Bond Market Association (BMA) index will correlate closely with a typical issuer's tax-exempt variable rate interest cost, it is not perfect. When an issuer chooses to use a LIBOR swap instead of a BMA swap, this difference in floating rate amounts (technically called *basis risk*) becomes far greater.

When an investment bank pitches a LIBOR swap, it is important to identify what assumptions they are making about the relationship between LIBOR and BMA. This is not to say that it's bad to use a LIBOR swap to create synthetic fixed rate debt. Under most market conditions the expected benefits are substantially greater than those available from a comparable BMA swap. But there is also greater risk. It is important that the issuer understand that risk.

Another important fact relates to the way yield is computed on a bond issue. Without getting too technical, if your bond counsel determines that your swap qualifies for something called "super-integration"—this is much more likely to occur with a BMA swap than with a LIBOR swap—you are able to compute your refunding bond yield using the synthetic fixed rate over the life of the bonds. If, however, bond counsel only determines that you qualify for "integration," you will have to recompute your yield every five years. Depending on the structure of your bond issue, this recurring five-year computation period may require you to restrict your escrow to a substantially lower yield than that which you could have earned under super-integration.

COMPETITIVE VERSUS NEGOTIATED SALE

The vast majority of advance refundings are sold via negotiated sale. In most cases, this is likely to present a smoother path for most issuers. It is, however, possible to sell most advance refundings on a competitive basis if a highly experienced financial advisor is retained.

CONCLUSIONS

Refundings represent a very important debt management tool for municipal issuers. The relationship between taxable and tax-exempt interest rates creates a unique opportunity for these issuers to efficiently refund their bonds well in advance of the first redemption date. Meanwhile, tax law restrictions can complicate an issuer's ability to refinance much of its debt more than 90 days before that first call date. Interest rate swaps can provide an effective work-around for locking in rates when an issue can't be legally advance refunded. Whenever an issuer is refunding prior bonds for savings, that issuer should be cautious, especially when bonds to be refunded aren't yet callable. On average, issuers who have waited to refund a bond issue which was not yet subject to optional redemption have realized greater present value savings than those who have refinanced their outstanding debt at the first hint of profit.

CHAPTER 13

Public-Private Partnerships

Robert H. Muller
Managing Director
JPMorgan Securities

A substantial public policy debate has emerged in recent years regarding which services can be best provided by governmental entities and those that the private sector can better supply. Governments have begun to realize the potential and substantial financial benefits from the leasing or sale of various assets. As a result, a whole range of proposals have been offered about the best ways that governments can divest or shift service delivery or the operation of important infrastructure assets from themselves to private companies. Implementation of these goals has been tried under various labels including contracting, public-private partnerships, privatization and concessions. Distinguishing these terms is not an easy task.

The Government Accounting Office in July 1997 released a special publication discussing the process and procedures related to privatization. The GAO stated:

> Under a public-private partnership, sometimes referred to as a joint venture, a contractual arrangement is formed between public-and private-sector partners that can include a variety of activities that involve the private sector in the development, financing, ownership and operation of a public facility or service.[1]

The GAO went on to define privatization "as any process aimed at shifting functions and responsibilities, in whole or in part, from the govern-

---

[1] General Accounting Office, *Terms Related to Privatization Activities and Processes*, GGD-97-121,www.gao.gov/special.pubs/gg97121.htm, p4.

I would like to thank Elizabeth Hillenbrand and Benjamin Djiounas, Associates, JPMorgan Securities, for their review of this chapter.

ment to the private sector."[2] Many governmental activities both today and in the past fall under these definitions.

This chapter will provide a review of the history of public-private partnerships within the United States and their reemergence in the past 10 years as a new funding alternative for state and local government capital improvements. Toll road privatizations have garnered the most visibility but the sale or lease of other assets such as airports, lotteries, port facilities, and parking garages have also been accomplished or are under active discussion. This chapter focuses on the key terms and provisions of concession agreements that affect both the possible price for the asset and the future relationship between the private operator and the governmental owner. An overview of the investors in these transactions and the methodologies for determining purchase price is also provided. The chapter concludes by highlighting the potentials benefits and risks for governments undertaking asset privatization.

HISTORY

From the 1790s to 1913

Public-private partnerships and privatization have a long history within the United States, dating back as far as the creation of the New York City municipal water system. Alexander Hamilton had proposed a public-private partnership to build the water system creating a private company of which "the city would be entitled to a third of the shares" and "the project would be overseen by appointed commissioners."[3] In the end, Aaron Burr subverted the plan under the guise of creating a mostly private water company, while actually funding a bank. As cities grew and mass transit became more important, many cities granted concessions, first to horse drawn street cars and ferries and later to trolley cars, elevated railways and eventually subways.

The creation and expansion of the New York City subway system around the turn of the twentieth century was perhaps the greatest public-private partnership in American history. The debate surrounding its inception still provides the best single record of the benefits and drawbacks of public versus private ownership of infrastructure assets. The agreement that the city and state finally signed in 1913, known as the *dual subway contracts*, provided for a massive expansion of the original single-line system to serve four boroughs, including areas without substantial development. The concession finally granted to the private operators (known as the IRT and

---

[2] *Terms Related to Privatization Activities and Processes.*
[3] Gerard T. Koeppel, *Water for Gotham: A History* (Princeton, NJ: Princeton University Press, 2000), p 77.

BMT) unwittingly contributed to the demise of private transit. Private companies agreed to freeze the subway fare in exchange for the right to build additional subway lines.[4] Subsequent inflation, the spread of the private automobile and the Great Depression all ultimately contributed to the City takeover of the private lines. Subway fares were finally increased in 1948.

1913–1980

After that period of debate, governments dominated the construction, ownership, and operation of transportation assets. Concessions and public-private partnerships mostly faded away in the transportation sector. In contrast, regulated private companies and governments generally split ownership and operation of utility services for electricity, gas, and water. Governments primarily owned water and sewer systems and the private sector owned electric and gas operations. Very few shifts in ownership between the public and private sectors took place despite periodic efforts to privatize utility assets. Occasionally, a government acquired the assets of a private operator. By and large, the balance of financing transportation and utility assets went unchanged for many decades.

Many governments entered into contracts with private companies to provide various services, such as building maintenance or school food services. These contracts were generally short term in nature and did not involve the operation or leasing of infrastructure or other hard assets. Such operating contracts rarely gave private companies the ability to collect any fees or user charges from the general public for the provision of the specific service.

1980–2003

During the Reagan years though, attitudes towards public-private partnerships began to change as the federal government started encouraging governments to enter into more extensive contracts with the private sector. Public recognition was growing of the fact that many government assets were being inadequately maintained, inefficiently operated, under invested, over staffed, and providing poor service. Morcover, foreign governments in areas such as Europe and Australia began to privatize governmental assets. Prime Minister Margaret Thatcher of the United Kingdom led these efforts in the 1980s by privatizing the national water system and the British Airports Authority that operated the principal airports including Heathrow.

---

[4] Brian J Cudahy, *Cash, Tokens, and Transfers: A History of Urban Mass Transit in North America* (New York: Fordham University Press, 1990), pp. 122–123. Also see Peter Derrick, *Tunneling to the Future: The Story of the Great Subway Expansion that Saved New York* (New York: New York University Press, 2001).

In the United States, efforts to implement change took root more slowly for a number of reasons. The governmental structure in the United States is more fragmented, with ownership and oversight of infrastructure assets often divided among assorted local, state and federal governments. State and local governments can finance capital improvements through the issuance of tax exempt bonds. The existence of the municipal bond market permits infrastructure to be financed at low rates using long-term bonds. All sizes of local governments can access debt but if a government chooses to enter into a long-term operating contract with a private entity, it may lose the advantageous tax-exempt status. Furthermore, the federal government may require grants to be repaid if a local or state government privatizes or sells off assets financed by the federal government. All of these factors delayed the pursuit of the types of privatization underway in the United Kingdom and other countries.

Nevertheless, governments were encouraged to enter into more extensive operating lease and management contracts for their water and sewer systems. In 1997, the IRS allowed "operating contracts of up to 20 years without sacrificing the tax free status of these facilities . . .".[5] As a result, by 2002 Public Works Financing reported that "cities contracting out water system operations now include Indianapolis, Phoenix, Seattle and Tampa Bay."[6]

Public-private partnerships also began to gain popularity in transportation. States started to permit different bidding and construction rules for highway construction, known as *design build*. This approach shifted risk to the private contractor and freed up the private contractor from needing to comply with expensive employment and bidding rules that added to the cost of new construction. Of more importance, a few states began to experiment with the notion of allowing private companies to not only design or build new roads, but also to operate and manage toll roads. As a result, private toll roads opened in Southern California and Northern Virginia. The Federal Aviation Administration (FAA) promulgated rules in the late 1990s that allowed for the privatization of up to five U.S. airports of different sizes. The FAA waived the repayment of the FAA grants but stipulated that 65% of the airlines, by number and volume, serving the market must consent to a privatization. Despite this opportunity, only one airport, Stewart International Airport in Newburgh, New York was fully privatized. Stewart was sold back to a governmental entity in 2007. The remaining applications stalled.

[5] *Privatization of Water Services in the United States: An Assessment of Issues and Experience* (Washington, D.C.: National Academy of Sciences, 2002), pp. 44–45.
[6] Elizabeth Brubaker, "Revisiting Water and Wastewater Utility Privatization," prepared for the Government of Ontario Panel on the Role of the Government. Presented at "Public Goals, Private Means" Research Colloquium, University of Toronto, October 3, 2003, p. 9.

Then in 2003, privatization and public-private partnerships appeared to suffer a serious setback when Atlanta backed out of a long term contract to operate its water system. In 1998, Atlanta granted a 20-year contract to United Water Service Atlanta to operate its water system. The Atlanta system had been poorly operated and maintained for many years and suffered from serious underinvestment. Operating performance, however, did not materially improve during the initial years of the contract and in 2003, a new mayor determined that the private company was not performing sufficiently and terminated the contract. Reaction was widespread. Critics of privatization exploited the cancellation, calling it a "debacle . . . and a huge setback for privatization."[7] Despite the setback in Atlanta, several states including Texas and Washington continued to enact and implement legislation to permit the creation of public-private partnerships, principally directed at building new toll road assets.

2004–2007

The seminal event that sparked privatization efforts, however, was Chicago Mayor Richard Daley, Jr.'s announcement in 2004 that he was exploring leasing the city's long neglected Chicago Skyway to a private company under terms of a concession lasting 99 years. The toll road runs only 7.8 miles through the southeastern part of the city to the Indiana border and had been in default on its debt for many years following its completion. The city initially anticipated that the concessionaire might offer as much as one billion for the right to collect tolls and operate the project. Yet when the three bids were opened, a venture consisting of Macquarie Infrastructure Group of Australia and Cintra Concesiones de Infraestructuras de Transporte, S.A. of Spain, global operators of toll roads, stunned the government finance world by offering to pay $1.83 billion for the long-term lease. This sum exceeded gross revenues by more than 40 times. A 144A taxable debt offering for more than $1.4 billion was sold in 2005. FSA insured the entire bond deal and the rating agencies assigned an underlying investment grade rating. After providing for outstanding debt, net proceeds were set aside in various investment accounts of the city.

As a result of this substantial bid and successful financing, governmental officials throughout the United States began to examine the untapped value not only of their toll road assets but also of other municipal assets. Less than a year later in 2005, newly elected Governor Mitch Daniels of Indiana announced that he would pursue a similar privatization to that of the neighboring Chicago Skyway for the state's own toll road. After a process lasting less than four months, four separate private consortiums offered

---

[7] Brubaker, "Revisiting Water and Wastewater Utility Privatization," p. 12.

bids. The team of Macquarie and Cintra submitted the winning bid of $3.85 billion, exceeding initial expectations by a substantial margin. The concession extended for a 75-year term. The governor earmarked the net proceeds for future state transportation needs.

After receiving bids, substantial opposition developed within the state against the private lease and the legislature approved the transaction by very small margins. Various parties contended the state had not been offered enough money, while others opposed toll increases or opposed foreign ownership. Shortly thereafter, the Virginia Department of Transportation agreed to a concession with Transurban of Australia to operate the Pocahontas Parkway, a nine-mile highway and bridge in the eastern part of the Richmond area. This road initially opened in 2003 and was generating far less traffic and revenues than had been forecast. The winning bid was $611 million.

Since the Indiana lease was completed in June 2006, numerous states and localities have explored privatization and concessions including New Jersey, Pennsylvania, Illinois, and Harris County, Texas among others. Additionally, the City of Chicago has privatized parking garages and has announced its intention to lease Midway Airport under terms of the FAA program. The FAA has granted approval to Chicago, which could allow for the privatization of the first large hub airport in the United States. However, concerns about national security still need to be addressed. Finally in late 2006 and early 2007, several states led by Illinois, California, and Texas announced they are considering the privatization of their state lotteries.

THE PROCESS OF PRIVATIZATION

Background

This section discusses privatization of infrastructure assets in greater detail. In contrast to private operators who simply manage governmental assets, a true privatization entails a private company leasing or even acquiring a governmental asset in exchange for a substantial upfront payment. This process entails a complex transaction. Although the government retains title to the asset in the case of a lease or concession, a private owner is ceded the right to operate the asset, collect fees and other charges to generate profit and invest capital in the asset. The private owner pays the government for the opportunity to lease the assets, expecting a future return on his equity investment. To set forth these arrangements, governments and private owners enter into a concession or regulatory agreement detailing various terms of their relationship. Financing structures often differ from those seen in traditional public finance and may resemble corporate mergers and acquisitions.

A winning bid usually is awarded through a public, competitive and transparent process. In addition, the investor base is substantially different from the traditional purchasers of tax exempt municipal debt. Finally, this section will conclude with some of the advantages and disadvantages governments face in deciding between full public ownership, contracting, leasing, or selling an asset to a private company. Since private owners enter into a transaction to maximize their profit, a private company's motivation may differ markedly from the mindset when operated by the government.

American state and local governments own and operate a significant number of assets that generate substantial revenues from the provision of a specific service and produce net income after providing for routine operation and maintenance expenses, debt service, and depreciation. Assets such as these include toll roads, airports, parking garages, power projects, port facilities, water and sewer systems, convention centers, and assets without bricks and mortar, such as lotteries and even liquor stores. All of these assets can be leased or sold to a private company that will make large payments for the right to lease or purchase such assets. Agreements involving past sales or leases often contained provisions with regard to the continued provision of services. However, because the government surrenders all control over the asset in those instances, future regulatory control usually passes to a state rate setting body that usually already regulates the private company.

Terms of a Concession Agreement

A government granting a concession to a private company to lease an asset for a specific number of years may become the prevailing privatization format. To implement the concession, a detailed legal agreement is usually created between the government and private operator to govern their relationship during the term of the lease. These agreements are often of a quasi-regulatory nature and define the terms under which the private company may operate the asset. Since virtually all of the agreements so far entered within the United States involve the leasing of new or existing toll roads, most of the relevant provisions in this discussion are drawn from that background. Concession agreements pertaining to airports are common in foreign countries but not yet in this country. Provisions for airports when developed, while potentially similar to a toll road, will be shaped by the continuing presence of the federal government and the airlines as important parties to any agreement.

For a toll road, important provisions dictate the length of the concession, the tolling and pricing regime, maintenance and operating requirements, limitations on competition, level of service provided to the user, capital expenditures and governmental rights in the event of nonperformance.

These terms may be set forth as given conditions before potential bids are open or evolve as part of the negotiation process between the government and a potential winning bidder. These terms will differ depending upon the asset up for privatization. For example, in the case of a lottery, the government may proscribe the terms under which the private company can promote the activity due to a desire to limit the promotion of gambling. In essence, the government needs to determine the right balance of control it wants versus permitting the relatively unfettered operations desired by the private operator to maximize returns. Since these agreements may be in place for a very long time, care must be given in their drafting since a government unwittingly may give away revenue-setting or operating authority which in the future could conflict with the public benefit expected from such an asset. Conversely, the terms may prove so inflexible that the private owner cannot generate a reasonable profit in the future. For example, insufficient rate setting flexibility could become a problem during a period of high inflation.

To date, concessions granted for toll roads in the United States have been for long terms, running from 35 years for the South Bay Expressway in San Diego County to 75 years for the Indiana Toll Road, and 99 years in the case of the Chicago Skyway. In general, these terms are longer than those granted in many foreign countries. Shorter concessions are viewed as an opportunity for the government to regain control of an asset, to reexamine the basis for the original concession and allow for changes in public policy to be implemented. Longer concessions have usually been granted on the assumption that they maximize upfront payments or that the asset is not viewed as having future important policy considerations (a noncore asset). At the end of the concession term, the asset reverts fully to the government once again.

Toll Pricing Regime

The tolling or pricing regime is a second key provision. For a toll road or parking garage, for example, initial tolls or parking rates are typically set at the commencement of the lease. Thereafter, the agreement usually stipulates a formula by which tolls may be increased. The formula may be based upon a number of different options. For most toll road concessions signed so far in the United States, tolls have been permitted to be increased annually or at some set interval. The pricing regime has usually been tied to annual increases in the consumer price index, nominal gross domestic product per capita or gross state product per capita sometimes with a floor set at a predetermined percentage annually. For the CPI based regime, toll increases generally lag increases in personal income. However, increases tied to CPI usually do not produce the maximum revenue for the private operator and thus constrain their bid amounts. A nominal GDP formula will result in higher toll rates for the users, particularly with compounding over time, and tolls may actually increase faster than incomes if the regional economy is growing less robustly than that of the nation. In contrast, such regimes will more closely approximate revenue maximization and result in higher concession payments. They also will produce more traffic diversions off the toll road to nearby non tolled assets, thereby causing higher congestion and costs to the government. A gross state product methodology has many of the same attributes as one tied to nominal GDP, except that toll increases are likely to more closely match income growth in the state.

Other formats exist. Virginia requires rate increases on the Dulles Greenway to be approved by the state regulatory commission. For the South Bay Expressway, no restriction on tolls exists but the return on invested capital is limited, resulting in an unknown but de facto limit on toll increases in the future. In at least one recent case, the 407 ETR in suburban Toronto, Canada, no limits were placed on tolls and significant toll increases have created friction between the provincial government that granted the concession and the private operator. The absence of any rate setting formula may represent a surrender of regulatory authority by the government involved and is unlikely to be a favored choice in the future.

Water, sewer and airports have different types of limitations. In the case of potential airport concessions, any pricing regime for airport charges is more complicated than for a toll road. Revenues are derived from numerous sources including landing fees, passenger facility charges, space rental, parking charges and retail revenues, which make indices harder to implement. Any charge affecting the airlines will require approval from the airlines utilizing the airport under current regulations. Individual retail leases would be negotiated in a fashion not dissimilar to current practice. The federal government is likely to influence or even limit the level of passenger facility charges that can be levied. In various privatized foreign airports, government concessions have usually attempted to limit the overall rate of return that the private operator can generate, making the concession pricing terms more akin to a regulated public utility. Permitted returns may exceed those allowed by state regulators in the case of investor owned utilities, but exactly how concession agreements for U.S. airports will evolve awaits the completion of the first privatized airport transactions. Since few precedents exist, pricing regimes for water and sewer concessions are open to question.

Asset Maintenance

The need to maintain the asset throughout the period of the concession is another important part of the agreement. At a minimum, governments usually stipulate that the asset must be returned in at least the same condition as when it was leased. For a toll road, this can be defined by requirements for a specific level of service or the condition of the pavement and bridges. Toll collection operations also fall under this rubric. State highway departments and the Federal Highway Administration have defined and published standards for road quality. If such standards are not met, the document specifies that the private operator may need to invest capital to restore the road to the condition provided for in the agreement. For example, when the level of congestion rises to a D, the owner may need to widen the road to comply with this provision. Despite the supposed clarity of these standards, they may become subject to interpretation over time, as what is deemed adequate today may be obsolete and inadequate to serve the public in 40 years and subject to dispute. Standards of operating and service quality are also reasonably well defined for water and sewer systems as well. The government should be able to enforce such requirements. For airports, defining service quality will be much harder to monitor and enforce.

Noncompete

Limits on competition are often an important component of the legal protections sought by private owners. The question of competition again only pertains to certain types of asset privatizations. For example, since water and sewer systems are inherently natural monopolies, limitations on competition are unnecessary. For toll roads, parking garages, even airports where competition exists, limitations are sought by the private company involved in a lease.

Most toll roads are embedded in a complex transportation network often containing other toll roads, limited access highways and important arterial roads. To the extent that government could choose to add traffic capacity on these alternative routes, it could reduce or even divert traffic from the toll road. As such, private operators want either to put prohibitions on such expansions or seek monetary compensation for their financial losses. The agreement for the Indiana Toll Road included selective limits on competition.

These restrictions produce some of the stickiest public policy issues in drafting a concession agreement. A basic conflict exists between the governmental need to promote mobility and the private operators desire not only to limit competition but also to be compensated for proper execution of public policy. Therefore, noncompete agreements are important to maximizing upfront proceeds paid to the government. This inherent conflict was an important factor in the decision by the Orange County Transportation Authority to purchase the SR91 HOT lanes from the private owner because constant disputes and demands for payments resulted from every effort by government to relieve traffic on the highly congested SR 91 freeway. Noncompete issues also became important in the disputes between the Province of Ontario and the operators of the 407 ETR.

Attempts to limit competition for airports are at the same time less important and more problematical to implement. Since no substantial airport in the United States has been privatized to date, no reference points exist on this topic. In many foreign countries, because airports are owned and controlled by the national government, the ability to limit operation or construction of new airports is controlled by the government granting the concession. Even so, in the United Kingdom, a substantial public policy debate is ongoing related to restoring competition to the British airport system. Nevertheless, for many airports within the United States, it may be impossible to limit competition since it already exists in places such as San Francisco, Boston, Los Angeles, and South Florida, among others. Moreover, it will be hard to place limitations on air carriers, particularly low cost carriers who have already sought out secondary, lower cost airports in major metropolitan areas and might be viewed as a restraint on trade. Yet at a practical level, adding significant airport capacity is very expensive and maybe more difficult than expanding a highway network

Numerous other clauses exist within concession agreements, each tailored to the specific asset undergoing privatization relating to indemnification, enforcement services, force majeure, use of nontoll revenues, property tax exemptions and remedies and procedures in the event that either party fails to perform. From the government perspective, if the private operator fails to perform, at the extreme, the government retains the right to cancel the concession and resume the operation of the asset. Since the private operator acquisition of the asset has usually been financed using substantial amounts of debt, these agreements typically contain protections and remedies against mismanagement or even a financial default triggering a cancellation of the lease. Conversely, governments retain the right to repurchase the concession from the private operator.

Financing and Investors

The financing of privatized assets differs materially from the traditional sources of capital that support the public tax-exempt debt markets. To encourage investment, investors in state and local government bonds historically benefit from tax exemption on the interest of such securities. This has provided low cost financing for public projects. As a result, individuals or their mutual fund proxies have been the dominant class of investors. Certain classes of corporate investors, such as property and casualty insurance companies, have been granted limited exemption as well from federal taxes when investing in municipal bonds. By and large, such investors are risk adverse and seek a proven stream of income. The nature of this investor base and the concerns of government regarding taking on too much risk or leverage largely have shaped the financing of infrastructure within the United States for decades.

The foreign privatization of the 1980s and 1990s created a new type of global investor. These companies were interested in investing equity and saw the use of debt as a tool to maximize equity returns. In effect, they borrowed a page from the corporate financing technique known as leverage buyouts. They also viewed infrastructure assets as capable of providing proven revenue streams over long periods of time and thus, could be matched well against long-term liabilities, such as pension obligations. They even afforded some protection as an inflation hedge because of the relatively inelastic nature of usage patterns of infrastructure assets. Forced savings provisions in Australia and Canada created large pools of equity capital that were first applied to projects in those countries. However, as most public infrastructure assets became privatized, particularly in Australia, these investors began to search elsewhere for infrastructure assets in which to invest.

Events in the United States discussed earlier coincided with the foreign investors need to invest equity capital. As a result a whole new investor class in public infrastructure emerged with the bid for the Chicago Skyway. In place of steady tax exempt interest income, these equity investors seek a return on their invested equity generally determined off a calculation of the presumed *internal rate of return* (IRR). This return is generally being matched against the risk. New projects viewed as riskier than established assets require higher IRRs. Unlike tax-exempt debt, however, these returns can vary over time. Equity returns are maximized through a capital structure that provides for the issuance of as much debt as possible. Because cash flows on toll road assets are believed to be highly predictable, bond investors accepted lower debt service coverage and very low or even below investment grade ratings. In the initial concession agreements financed in the United States, leverage was very high ranging from 65% to more than 80%.

The combination of high leverage, the ability to deduct interest from taxable income and to accelerate depreciation has produced overall financing costs that, although somewhat higher than tax exempt debt, are not a constraint on project feasibility. Thus, a new class of investors has emerged to compete with traditional municipal bond financing. This new class of investor is willing to make substantial up front payments to governmental owners for the right to operate an infrastructure asset under the terms of a concession. With many governments strapped for capital, the combination of a private operator that may bring efficiencies to the operation of infrastructure assets and big cash payments seem likely to accelerate privatization within the United States.

Determination of Valuation

The determination of the purchase price by a private operator is based upon techniques borrowed from corporate rather than municipal finance. The essential building blocks include a detailed understanding of historical financial performance, competitive and operating factors, the implications of the requirements set forth in the concession agreement and the bidding documents created by the government and its financial advisors.

Forecasts for future cash flows over the life of a concession are critical inputs into determining potential valuations. For toll roads, such forecasts are often generated by sophisticated traffic and revenue models but such projections can be generated in numerous ways depending upon the type of asset involved. These cash flows can then be used as the basis for building financial models. A potential bidder can choose from a variety of well-established corporate financing methodologies to achieve desired internal rates of return. Discounted cash flow techniques and even data from valuations on other transactions are used to substantiate their bid price. Desired internal rates of return are then achieved through the practice of financial engineering to optimize the mix of equity and debt. Interest rates on the debt, access to alternative funding sources, such as bank loans, bond insurance and mixes of investment grade and noninvestment grade are all essential ingredients in the equation of price. In general, the longer the term of the concession, the higher the bid price, but in very long concessions, the discount on future cash flows is substantial and governments may not realize the full benefits of surrendering an asset to a private operator for such a long period. Needless to say, valuations tend to be the highest when markets are most amenable to the use of leverage which is generally during periods of tight credit spreads and low interest rates.

Benefits and Risks for Governments

The risks inherent in financing infrastructure assets in this fashion are largely unknown. Although infrastructure assets are believed to produce predictable returns, significant leverage amid a goal of revenue maximization may create performance characteristics that differ from those displayed in more traditionally funded projects. Some insight into this risk is evident in the performance of start up toll road projects in the United States during the the period 1993–2006 where a combination of financial engineering, high leverage and steep and escalating tolls have resulted in distressed outcomes for such roads as Connector 2000, Dulles Greenway, and the Garcon Point Bridge in Florida. Moreover, the ability to maximize prices paid to governments for their assets is highly dependent on market conditions. The middle of the first decade of the twenty-first century was characterized by low interest rates, very tight quality spreads and an overall willingness on the part of investors to tolerate or discount risk. A different credit and rate environment may make privatization more difficult and nudge governments back toward contracting for operating and management services.

Privatization has clearly arrived as a new source of funding for state and local governments. Many governments are rich in assets that have historically not been viewed as sources of capital. In this new environment though these assets may present opportunities to raise significant amounts of needed capital. Yet governments need to be very careful in viewing such assets in only a monetary way. The allocation of the proceeds of any privatization should be applied to programs producing the best future returns. However, the risk that moneys will be allocated to balancing budgets and tax cuts is substantial particularly during periods of fiscal stress.

Governments may pursue alternatives to privatization. Having realized that substantial untapped monetary value is locked up in its assets, governments could extract value utilizing more historical governmental financing techniques. For example, governments could issue more debt against the revenues of toll roads and direct proceeds towards purposes other than those associated with the toll road. Also, they could transfer excess net revenues from the enterprise to the general fund of the government. This is a common practice already for many municipally owned water and power systems. In the case of airports, federal constraints on the use of airport funds act as a limitation on any such effort. For other assets such as toll roads, most existing financing structures limit the use of moneys for any purpose not related to the revenue generating enterprise. The debt and legal documents would need to be restructured to realize this value. A change in government ownership and a willingness to incorporate some aspects of privatization such as legally binding toll setting regimes might be required as well. Both rating agencies and bond insurance companies, however, remain concerned about the potential for future political interference.

Infrastructure assets, by their very nature, provide valuable, even essential services to large parts of the public. The public purpose goal of serving the citizens in the best way to promote the public good may not coincide over time with the desire of a private entity to maximize its profits. Large amounts of cash can be generated quickly through privatization but future returns and well-being could be affected if the current officials do not approach such efforts using a well thought out strategy. Privatizations both in the United States and elsewhere have already been met by stiff opposition from various interests, even the general public, and this is unlikely to change going forward. The battle between whether private owners or the government best represent societal interests in the provision of infrastructure goes back to the beginning of the republic and will undoubtedly emerge in new forms in the years ahead.

SUMMARY

Since the earliest days of the nation's founding, governments have entered into agreements with private companies to build, own, and operate public assets and infrastructure. After many years, where most infrastructure improvements were financed by governments, capital shortfalls have led a range of state and local governments to focus again on building partnerships with private companies and accessing new sources of financing to meet a major backlog of capital needs. Although a great deal of attention has been paid to a few visible toll road transactions in Chicago, Indiana, and Virginia, major legal and governmental impediments such as federal restrictions on the sale of airport assets as well as political reticence on the part of governmental officials continue to constrain the actual number of privatization deals which have been completed. Tax-exempt bonds continue to offer a very attractive financial alternative to the financing approaches required to fund a privatization. Governments are also learning to adopt and apply some practices such as more defined toll setting regimes in lieu of actual privatization. Nevertheless, with vast pools of private capital assembled to support privatizations and many governments financially strapped and unable to fund needed improvements, the creation of public-private partnerships is likely to expand in the years ahead. Risks exist for governments that do not explore all of the alternatives and some clashes are inevitable between private sector companies motivated to maximize earnings and public sector entities committed to meeting the needs of a larger community. Financial troubles may also ensue but properly done, these partnerships may prove to be beneficial to all parties involved.

The Sell Side: Distribution and Market-Making Roles

CHAPTER 14

The Role of the Underwriter

Christopher J. Mier, CFA
Managing Director
Loop Capital Markets

This chapter discusses the complex role of the underwriter in a new issue municipal financing. The underwriter artfully stands in between the issuer and investor and seeks to price new issues such that an efficient and fair market is created for both buyer and seller. The discussion in this chapter touches on the many functions an underwriter must perform in meeting the challenges of bringing new issues to market in ever-changing market environments.

THE UNDERWRITER'S ROLE IN CONTEXT

A municipal bond originates as an idea. Initially, a unit of government—a city, a county, or a school district, for example—has a project that needs financing. It could be a new courthouse, jail, or water treatment facility. Or perhaps it is a new generating plant for an electric utility, or an expansion of a hospital. The list of possible uses of tax-exempt financing available through the municipal market is enormous. In any case, what starts out as a project in the gleam of a finance director's eye gets transformed into a municipal bond issue through a process that starts within the unit of government and winds its way through various professional organizations it has hired to assist in the creation and distribution of a municipal bond issue. The end result of this process is a bond issue that has been sold to the investing public—both retail and institutional. In return, the governmental issuer receives the financing that it needs to construct the project.

The various parties that are involved with a newly germinated municipal bond issue include the issuer's finance director (and staff) and in-house legal counsel. The issuer will frequently select a financial consultant, a bond counsel, and a senior managing underwriting firm (and other comanaging underwriters, as well) to underwrite the new issue. The senior managing underwriter may have their own counsel to represent them. The firm that is the senior managing underwriter will have numerous investment bankers working with the issuer to help construct the financing plan for the project. In addition, that firm will have someone called an *underwriter* whose principal responsibility is to commit the firm's capital towards the pricing and distribution of the new securities in the primary marketplace. While the involvement of all of the various participants is essential in the financing process, the role that the underwriter plays is a particularly pivotal one. The underwriter will, in essence, take the issue from the investment banking staff and shepherd it the rest of the way until it reaches the hands of the investor—the ultimate destination for the bonds along the new issue pathway.

The process of initiating a municipal bond issue and guiding it to its ultimate destination—the hands of the investor—is a lengthy process that never follows the exact same course twice. When the marketplace functions effectively, the issuer is able to sell bonds to finance its projects at a cost that is satisfactory, and the investor is able to buy bonds at a price that he also deems acceptable. The underwriter, in effect, stands at the crossroads of the supply and demand for capital and ensures that a market clearing transaction takes place for each bond issue that his firm underwrites. During this process he has to satisfy the diverse constituencies of issuer and investor, all while putting the firm's capital at risk.

WHEN DOES THE UNDERWRITER BECOME INVOLVED IN THE PROCESS?

As previously mentioned the underwriter bridges the gap between issuer and investor and is principally responsible for the successfully pricing and selling of a new issue municipal bond. An underwriter is at the center of the creation and distribution process of a new municipal bond issue. The underwriter contributes to the investment banking process—the creation stage—by providing valuable market feedback on current conditions in the bond market and how they might impact the transaction. As the day of the issue will be priced approaches, the underwriter helps the sales manager kick start the selling process by providing a detailed explanation of the salient aspects of the financing to the sales manager, who coordinates the sales effort. On pricing day the underwriter proposes a pricing to the issuer which, if accepted, will be used by the underwriting team to start the sales and distribution process.

In a typical financing, an underwriter first enters the process shortly after the senior managing underwriting firm has been chosen, along with an underwriting group, to underwrite the issue. The underwriter of the lead firm will participate in conference calls between the issuer, its financial consultant, and the firm's investment bankers, bond counsel, and others. At this stage of the process, the underwriter will mostly be providing useful commentary about market conditions currently prevailing, and any preliminary feedback that might be appropriate relative to the structure of the bond issue that the issuer and its financing team (the issuer, and their financial consultant and investment bankers) have considered. For example, if the financing contemplates the use of zero-coupon bonds as part of a refunding strategy, the underwriter may have a valuable contribution to make in terms of the current receptivity in the marketplace for zero-coupon bonds, and the price they are likely to command as part of the new issue. If there has been a lack of zero-coupon bonds in the market, and the few that are available are commanding huge prices, the underwriter will highlight this to the financing team. If the market is reeling from stronger than expected economic reports that are giving off worrisome inflation signals, and interest rates have been rising, the underwriter will be sure to mention this as well. If the pricing date that is tentatively scheduled turns out to be a heavy one for the municipal market, the underwriter will point this out. In the early goings, the underwriter is the financing team's eyes and ears of the market. He (or she) points out all salient market conditions that may influence the reception that a bond issue might expect to receive in the prevailing market environment, whether they are positive or negative.

As the pricing date of the issue approaches, the frequency with which the underwriter will communicate with the issuing client and the rest of the financing team will increase dramatically. Simultaneously, the underwriter will continue to gather additional market information to prepare for the pricing and sale of the issue. This reconnaissance is a vital function of the underwriter and is critical to providing the information that will enable the success of the issue upon pricing. The underwriter will be monitoring other issues in the market place that have similar characteristics to the issue that he will be pricing. He will use all of his available sources of information—street contacts, other underwriters, his own sales force, and the like—to better understand the level of demand and the prices being paid for various types of bond characteristics in the marketplace. These characteristics include the general category of the bond, general obligation or revenue bond, the term or maturity structure of the financing, the coupon structure, the state of origin, the call feature, the rating and many others. The underwriter will monitor all relevant new issue financings in both the competitive and negotiated markets. Additionally, he will watch the secondary market for indications of how various types of bonds are trading. If his firm is going to bring to market a local California school district general obligation bond with a 30-year serial structure and MBIA insurance, for example, the underwriter will carefully monitor market conditions with respect to all of these features, and any others he thinks may yield valuable information that will help him price and sell the transaction for the issuer.

The underwriter has a significant arsenal at his disposal with which he can gather information, but the underwriter must select his sources of information carefully. For example, let's say the issuer has indicated an interest in nine-year par calls instead of the standard 10-year call feature. In surveying the landscape, the underwriter notes that there hasn't been an issue in the market with a nine-year call in over a month. The underwriter must discreetly ascertain what reception the contemplated structure would likely receive without divulging information to the marketplace prematurely. The underwriter must have a sixth sense as to where and how to gather as much accurate information as possible so that on "game day"—the day the issue is initially priced—he can price an issue that satisfies the pricing requirements of both issuer and investor.

THE LEAD-UP TO PRICING

The day before pricing there will typically be a conference call between the issuer, its financial advisor, and the senior manager of the underwriting team. The underwriter for the senior managing firm will play a key role in this call. He will lead the group in discussing and analyzing market conditions that relate specifically to the bond issue that is to be priced. The financing team will finalize the proposed structure of the issue, and the underwriter will supply a likely scale for the transaction. The group will determine a game plan for the day of pricing. They will select a time for an early conference call to make any last minute revisions to the pricing scale and for the underwriter to receive formal approval from the issuer to release the scale. They will plan for a call when the group will reconvene to discuss the orders that have been received and any plans for repricing, if necessary.

During the course of the sales process hundreds of clients will be contacted by the firm's sales force to determine their interest in the issue. The sales force will relay critical feedback from investing clients back to the underwriting desk. The feedback will include the specific orders that some clients will have at the existing pricing, as well as what changes a client might require before being willing to present an order. An example might be an indication of interest subject to a change in structure or price ("I would take $5 million in 2025, if you can do a 5.00% coupon instead of a 4.75%

coupon."). The order period is like a huge electronic bazaar with sales people interacting vigorously with their clients and relating vital information back to the underwriting desk.

If the issue has required repricing—raising or lowering prices—the underwriter has to wait to see if the orders will stay or if investors will choose to drop. A reprice is, in effect, a free option for the investors. Now that the price of the issue has been changed, the investor can watch the market and wait for more market information to decide if he is going to stay or drop. The sales person covering the account provides a vital function during this time by supplying the underwriter with valuable feedback as to the customer's state of mind and probability of staying or dropping. The underwriter is putting both the firm's capital at risk as well as the quality of the firm's relationship with the issuer. A deal that does not go well can result in significant underwriting losses. Gauging investor sentiment is critical to the process of underwriting new issue securities.

To be a good underwriter an individual needs to have strong negotiation and presentation skills. Being able to justify a price change to an issuer of municipal bonds who is convinced that their bonds are worth gold is not an easy task under time-constrained circumstances! The timing and presentation of the deal to the investor community is important as well. Such things as whether to go out with pricing before a competing issue or after, whether to offer a short or a long order period, creating a pricing structure that maximizes the interest of the investing community while minimizing the cost the issuer has to pay are all key factors in a successful underwriting.

What kinds of things can go wrong with a new issue underwriting? Rapidly changing market conditions can make new issue underwriting difficult and may result in the underwriter incorrectly gauging investor interest relative to a given proposed pricing structure. As an additional example the issuer may decide that they are being short-changed on the proposed pricing of their bond issue. "Let's go out with a 4.23% yield on the 30-year-term bonds instead of a 4.25%." The underwriter, bound by the necessity to get the best possible price for the client's issue, may feel compelled to swallow hard and release a pricing that he may feel is too high in price (and too low in yield) for the market to embrace. While, on the surface, this may not seem like a problem since any bonds that fail to generate sufficient interest from buyers during an order period can be repriced, unsold bonds in a new issue syndicate can taint the issue and create negative momentum in the execution of the transaction that may ultimately cost the issuer more than if they had gone out with the original recommended price. Ultimately, it is unpredictable movements in the market that wreak havoc on new issues. When the bond market falls 30 minutes after the initial price release of a new issue and investors turn cautious, the underwriter must rely on experience and sound judgment to guide the issue towards a satisfactory completion.

What's the mark of good transaction? A good transaction is one that satisfies all parties that a fair transaction has been effected in a fair process that has provided adequate transparency to all parties involved. While there are no set standards, an example of a "classic" underwriting might be one where the bonds are priced into a receptive market, receiving a subscription of about 1.5 to 2 times across all maturities, enabling the bonds to get "bumped" in price slightly, while losing only a nominal amount of business. A "Goldilocks" level of subscription (not too hot, not too cold) of around 1.5 to 2 times provides assurance to the issuer that their bonds have been priced correctly, and simultaneously reassures buyers that they have bought a reasonably "tight" deal where they will get allocated adequate amounts of bonds that are well placed. An issuer will generally regard a small re-price as a signal that the bonds were not priced too cheap for starters (a large price increase can be upsetting to issuers) while buyers want access to reasonable allocations on deals that they feel have been fairly priced by the underwriter.

A difficult task that the underwriter must perform after the pricing phase has been concluded is the allocation of bonds. When the final pricing has been transmitted, and all investors have had the opportunity to stay or drop, the underwriter will take the order pad (a computer printout) and head for an undisclosed location to decide how to allocate the bonds. The underwriter must decide how the bonds are to be allocated among the investors. If the 2020 maturity has $5 million in par value, but has received orders of $5 million, $3.5 million, and $1.5 million, a two times oversubscription, then a decision has to be made as to how to distribute the bonds between the investors submitting orders. In allocating bonds, the underwriter must be bound by his duty to the issuer, and a responsibility to be fair to his investor clients. Within those broad parameters there is room for the underwriter to use his own judgment. From a buyer's perspective, ideally, the bonds will be allocated to investors who sincerely want them for long-term investment purposes and who will not sell them in the secondary market at the first possible opportunity for short-term profit, thereby reducing the perceived value of the bonds of the customers who continue to hold the issue.

In conclusion, the underwriter fulfills a key function in the process of creating and bringing a bond issue to market. The underwriter must stand squarely in the middle of supply and demand and settle on a market clearing price that can make two diverse and inherently conflictual parties satisfied. Then, after the price is finalized, he must allocate the bonds to investors in a manner that is fair and that helps create a reasonable secondary market. An underwriter should be highly market savvy, a good negotiator and reconciler, and able to artfully price a bond issue under changing market circumstances.

SUMMARY

The underwriter acts as a key intermediary in the process of ushering new issue municipal bond issues from the issuers to investors. The underwriter performs many key activities such as gathering and disseminating vital market information, determining the best bond structures with which to generate interest from investors, and, of course, establishing a market clearing price for the new issue and subsequently allocating bonds to investors. The underwriter must seek to satisfy the needs of two important constituencies: issuers, who seek financing, and investors, who provide it.

CHAPTER 15

The Roles of Traders and Brokers

JonPaul Zaptin
Vice President
JPMorgan Securities

In the middle of a municipal bond department on a bustling trading floor, the roles and responsibilities of a trader are very clear and well understood by those around him—or her—usually. Place that trader at a dinner table or at a party with friends and family and listen to a conversation about what he does for a living and the confusion can often be comical. One trader here at JPMorgan has a mother who tells her friends that he's a stockbroker for Morgan Stanley. What is a trader? A dealer? A salesperson? A market maker? This chapter will define many of the characteristics and responsibilities of municipal traders and brokers and how their jobs intertwine.

TRADERS

Under normal circumstances, a fair amount of work goes into getting a trade done. Often to get the wheels in motion, a trader will quote a two-sided market or a salesperson will ask the trader for a bid on a customer's behalf. These steps are usually just the beginning of a series of phone calls or Bloomberg messages that comprise a negotiation process that may or may not result in a trade. After all the marketing efforts cease and price negotiations are finalized, it is a trader who sits at the center of a transaction and ultimately decides to write the trade ticket or not. Weighing many factors, and acting on behalf of his firm and with his own risk position and profitability in mind and at stake, it is the trader who decrees "I buy!" or "Sold to you!" While it sounds simple enough, trade execution is the most important responsibility a trader carries through his day, though it is by far not his only duty. Additional responsibilities include but are not limited to:

- Efficient and profitable capital commitment
- Evaluating bonds and identifying relative value opportunities
- Trade idea generation
- Bidding competitive loans
- Negotiated loans and trading the break
- Inventory management

At most larger municipal bond shops, the trading desk is part of a larger department including syndicate/underwriting, sales, proprietary trading, short-term/money market trading and derivative trading and marketing. Secondary traders often go by other names such as dealers, market makers and flow traders and in many cases wear multiple hats as they assist with pricing bids on competitive new issues and interact directly with investor clients. Most fundamentally, a trader looks to write trade tickets that are profitable or that make sense in some other way. He continuously tries to generate customer flow and add value with two-sided market quotes, swap ideas, and relative value observations.

Capital Commitment

A trading desk is given a line of capital by upper management, and that line is further subdivided by trader on a desk. The overall capital committed may be indicative of the size and condition of the firm's balance sheet, its risk appetite, or relative value view of municipals at a point in time. For example, a prudent trading desk is able to pare back its market exposure heading into a heavy issuance cycle, or willing and able to "load the boat" when it determines that municipals look cheap or visible supply looks lighter than expected. Or perhaps, a trading firm identifies a potential revenue or league table opportunity on the competitive new issue calendar (i.e., $1 billion California State GOs or $500 million Washington State GOs), and decides to lighten up on its secondary inventory in order to free up some capital with which it can aggressively bid the new issue.

At the individual trader level, an aggressive market maker generally seeks to own as many bonds as his position limits allow while turning his book over as often as possible. A flow trader generally doesn't take long-term views of bonds though sometimes a patient approach is necessary. To paraphrase what a well-respected customer once told me, every bond has its day. A given credit or structure may be in vogue one week and not so the next. One key to successful trading is being present in the market with a bid to buy the bonds and warehouse them when they are cheap and to feed the inquiry when they are in demand. The other side of this trade usually requires having the discipline to let another bond go, perhaps slightly cheaper than they were worth, to keep the flow going and the position in compliance with its limits. A trader will often base his bid-side price on where he can or cannot sell bonds that he owns. For example, "If I can't sell Salt River 5s at a 4.20%, what should my bid be for uninsured Illinois GOs?" Based on market conditions and known customer inquiries, a trader may prefer a specific part of the yield curve, or sector, or bond structure (coupon, call feature, etc.), and his inventory will often include bonds that he finds attractive and/or thinks his sales force can sell.

Part of committing capital but sometimes separate from relative value trading is a trader's role as a liquidity provider. Buyers of bonds expect that when they need to sell bonds, they can turn to dealers for a bid. The quality of a bid shown may depend on the tone of the market or the day of the week, but customers take notice of what firms provide a bid side when they are looking to sell bonds and the onus falls on the trader. Oftentimes, a trader is asked to bid a block of bonds as he wonders how he might muster a bid out of someone for any block of bonds that he owns, but still, showing the bid and providing liquidity is part of the job.

Identifying Relative Value and Evaluating Bonds

At any given moment, a trader must have the ability to determine and communicate what he thinks a bond is worth in the context of fundamental and technical factors in both the municipal and taxable markets. There is not one correct trading model or formula to accomplish this. In fact, providing evaluations and/or bids is where the art and science of trading municipal bonds come together and where experience is paramount. In the context of how the market "feels," the trader must instantly know and consider where a bond or similar bonds have traded recently, what customer inquiries exist for like bonds, what comparable bonds may be on the new issue horizon, what similar bonds may be in the hands of the competition ("in the street") or of customers who may also be ready sellers. Is it a liquid trading issue? And most importantly, can the sales force sell it? Two sayings come to mind here. "A trader's best hedge is a good salesperson." And, "a bond is not bought, it is sold." A trading and sales operation works most effectively when the traders and sales force are in continuous and direct dialogue and contact, and a trader can turn to his sales force and ask two questions, and reasonably rely on the answers. Can you sell this bond, and at what price? The first question is critical, as the sales force should have a pretty intimate understanding of what bonds their customers will buy. More times than not, the price is going to be driven more by the trader's input because a buyer has little incentive to put her best foot forward when discussing what she might pay for a bond. Though it seems very obvious, both traders and customers look to buy bonds as cheaply possible, but showing too cheap of a bid can ultimately insult the seller and discourage future business. An effective trader must be able to reflect a bid where he is comfortable owning bonds, ideally with a decent chance of making money, with the goal to have his bid-side hit, or to get a counteroffer nearby so that he can shop the market to his customer base.

Generating Trade Ideas, Creating Customer Flow, and Managing Inventory

One of the most vital skills a successful trader brings to a "room" is his ability to market his position and his logic to his sales force, so they may in turn help their customers see the value in his inventory. Perhaps Louisiana Gas 4.75s look cheap to where 5.00s are trading. Or maybe a duration sensitive account can pick-up call protection for little to no cost versus a short call bond that another customer views as a probable refunding candidate. Maybe a block of Puerto Rico noncalls look cheap to the manager of a state specific fund in need of duration. Or maybe low absolute rates will make it difficult for underwriters to print long-dated bonds with 5% coupons, creating a bit of a scarcity premium on outstanding bonds. An effective trader is constantly thinking about bonds through the eyes of his customers so he may hone in on what trades there are to do. Isolating and capturing the cross-current of customer buy/sell objectives is what makes trades happen and the trader must constantly frame those cross-currents long enough to get a trade done. Absent considerable new supply and/or significant price action, the municipal cash market can often become lethargic and unmotivated to trade, and frankly terribly boring for a flow trader. A proactive committer may try to instigate that flow by proposing swap or switch ideas where one bond is traded for another at an agreed upon spread. The greatest benefit of a swap, especially in a slow market, is that it establishes "printed" trading levels, and gives buyers confidence in what other bonds may be worth relative to the printed prices. Swaps are also an effective way for a trader to turnover his merchandise and give his sales force new inventory to work with.

Competitive Loans

At many trading firms, underwriters, and traders work hand in hand at structuring and pricing bids competitive new issue loan. The key element to such capital commitments is a firm's ability to gauge and balance customer demand for paper with where its traders see value and may wish to own bonds, and with any management "axe" to gain market share and/or improve league table standings. The flow traders are in the trenches day in and day out and are in the best position to offer up to the final minute market color and price guidance and to help determine whether customer orders are used in the bidding process.

Negotiated Loans and Trading the Break

On most trading desks, a secondary flow trader is responsible for making markets and supporting a new issue when it "breaks," or becomes free to trade in the secondary market. He is in position to know how well received a deal was, which customers participated and whether those customers will be better buyers, sellers, or holders once a deal has been allotted. A trader uses all available information to make markets in the new issue, establish a position in the name, and attempt to redistribute the bonds between buyers and sellers.

TYPES OF TRADERS

Trading firms employ risk-taking teams of many different structures and varying emphasis, but most institutional trading desks are composed of some mix of dollar bond traders, serial bond traders, note traders, retail traders, and special situation traders.

Long-revenue bond traders and *dollar bond traders* generally focus on bonds with maturities greater than 20 years. Historically these bonds traded in dollars (as opposed to yield), though as bid/offer spreads have been compressed and pricing has become much more exact, even most long-dated bonds are now traded in yield terms. Many new issues that come to market with long-weighted debt will include at least one term bond or a longer-dated security, often with at least a 25- to 30-year maturity and a large issue size, allowing in theory for increased liquidity and trading volume.

Intermediate/serial bond traders generally trade the maturity curve from 2 to 20 years, although some firms clearly delineate the short-intermediate (2- to 10-year) range from the 10- to -20 year part of the curve. Traders in this range may focus on AAA rated high-grade state GOs such as Maryland, Virginia, and North Carolina or comparably lower rated credits such as New York City GOs or a gas prepay deal such as TEACs or Main Street Gas, or anything in between. While many serial structures come with smaller issues sizes than dollar bonds, larger issuers (LA USD, New York State Thruway) can print substantial maturities in the serial range.

Note traders typically trade securities with durations of one year or less. Many municipalities use the note market to finance short-term projects or to raise cash in advance of tax receipts, or proceeds from a scheduled longer term bond issuance. The municipal note market is by definition very sensitive to the taxable money market sector (U.S. Treasury bills, commercial paper) as well as cash flows driven by seasonal factors such as tax dates and financial reporting dates (quarter-end and year-end).

A *special situation* trader focuses on a distinct and unique sector of the market. This is an area where no two firms are organized identically. Some firms have traders who focus on bonds issued in certain states, such as New York and California, or on certain regions, such as the southeast or the Midwest. A trader may also focus only on housing bonds, or zero-coupon bonds, or taxable municipal securities. Or maybe a trader is tasked with trading all structures and maturities, but is limited to positions under a certain size threshold (e.g., $5 million). Another important niche to recognize is the high-yield market. High-yeld traders may traffic in uninsured sectors such as airlines, hospitals, and tobacco bonds to name a few, and usually have dedicated salespeople and credit analysts to support their businesses.

A *retail trader* is one whose primary responsibility is to provide an inventory of municipal bonds for his sales force of registered representatives to distribute to individual investors. The retail trader must also be willing and able to provide liquidity (i.e., a bid) to customers needing to sell bonds.

WATCHING THE TAXABLE MARKETS

Today more than ever, the municipal bond market is linked to the taxable markets as the universe of tax-exempt participants includes more hedged and "RV (relative value)" players such as dealer proprietary desks (arbs), hedge funds, asset managers, and corporations. Even traditional real money accounts like bond funds and insurance companies have developed methods to insert leverage with hedges into their investment portfolios. What this means is that flow traders and customers alike keep an eye on one or more "hedge proxy" such as U.S. Treasury bonds, bond futures, interest rate swap rates (LIBOR), swap spreads, and BMA, a derivative of the LIBOR market developed by the tax-exempt community. Each of these markets can experience moderate to massive flows and price-action in their own right, which have a direct, though not fully predictable impact on the performance of municipal bonds. The unpredictability of how municipals bonds perform relative to the hedge instruments discussed is the arbitrage that our market's RV players seek to exploit: This is, as they say, what creates markets.

TRADING DISCIPLINE AND MENTAL ATTITUDES

Every trader follows some semblance of a daily routine. Most traders get an early start, checking the status of the overnight market as they wake up either on their Blackberry, the Internet, television, or radio, or some combination of all of the above. Geopolitical events and significant market moves in global fixed income and equity markets can impact a municipal trader's risk position before he even gets out of bed so it is best to arrive at the office as fully informed as possible.

Once logged into a Bloomberg terminal and armed with a cup of coffee, a trader begins to set the day's game plan in motion. He will scan newswires (Dow Jones, Reuters, and Bloomberg) for any headlines or information that may affect the markets. He may check in with a broker's broker to refresh any late day markets from the previous day, or to get some early markets going. Taking note of what economic releases are on tap and what deals are set to be priced on the new issue front, a trader may opt to aggressively quote two-sided markets for his sales force and customers, or to take a less aggressive approach and wait to see if any data or customer flows give the markets a strong direction to the upside or downside.

A seasoned trader will sense whether the market feels firm or heavy at different points in the day and adjust his markets accordingly. Alertness and attentiveness are paramount as a trader must have six ears and four eyes for often there are 8 or 10 situations he must be involved in at once. He sometimes needs three hands just to field incoming phone calls. Like a bloodhound, he must be able to detect the "hidden fox" and he must be able follow his gut instincts. Like a good scout, a trader must find the trail where some leaves have been rustled and be able to identify and ignore the false alarms. How a trader responds to a situation one moment may be totally wrong the next, so the ability to remain focused on the task at hand in the context of the most current events will often determine whether a trader makes a good decision, or one he regrets. It is true that some of the best trades are the ones that aren't executed.

The requisite constant awareness produces a very tense intellectual and emotional environment on a trading floor, often best accompanied by a bottle of Advil or a container of Tums. Sometimes tempers fly and frustrations abound over a missed trade or situation. A good desk will channel that energy into capturing the next trade and the one after that.

WHO BECOMES A TRADER?

An entrepreneurial individual who likes the smell of battle, who enjoys using his wits to the utmost, and who likes to make money is a candidate to become a trader. A good trader is extremely competitive and refuses to be beaten in any situation, and aspires to the highest ethical business standards.

One interesting aspect of trading bonds is the respect that traders have for each other. Because of the rapid pace at which trades can occur, traders must have the complete confidence of all the counterparties they talk to.

Traders buy and sell millions of dollars worth of securities solely on their word. If a trader buys $10 million (par value) worth of bonds from another trader over the phone, there can be no question as to the trader's validity. If a trader reneges on a trade and develops a reputation, his effectiveness in the trading community is finished. A trader's word is his bond (no pun intended).

Another interesting trait of trading is the dual role of competitor and colleague that traders play. Because traders work for different firms, their allegiance is obvious. They compete for the same business each day and try to beat the next guy. But at the same time, traders need each other to make a market and create competition and at times provide liquidity.

BROKERS

A municipal bond broker is an agent who works between two traders for a commission. He does not take any risk and must execute simultaneous transactions. Because brokers do not take positions, their skills must be subtle as they establish working relationships with traders and find situations in which people will pay their commission.

A broker provides anonymity and allows a trader to operate in a sector of the market without his identity being given up, and can be useful in providing swift execution for a trader when necessary. A broker can also be the eyes and ears in the market for a trader in terms of identifying pockets of supply and demand, and ascertaining support and resistance levels. A broker might say the market is 4.10–4.07, but size comes at 4.05, or there is a great deal of interest at 4.13. This information can be very helpful if a trader is looking to build a position in a particular security, or assessing the downside risk in a sell situation.

The broker's commission is always paid by the initiator of the business. For example, if the broker's market is 4.10–4.07, and dealer A instructs the broker to "hit" the bid (sell the bonds), the broker will sell the bonds to the 4.10 bidder and buy the bonds from dealer A at 4.10 less his commission. A locked market occurs when the broker has a bid and an offering at the same price, and the broker's commission stands in the way of the trade. If the offering is lifted (i.e., bonds are bought), the lock is said to be broken to the upside, and conversely, the break is to the downside if the bid is hit.

Finally, when a trader has a block of bonds that he wishes to sell, he may give them to a broker "for the bid." The broker will call other traders at other dealers and obtain the best bid for the bonds. The price including the broker's commission is conveyed to the potential seller who then decides whether or not to trade the bonds. Many municipal brokers also accept for the bid lists of bonds in retail sizes that many institutional desks cannot effectively focus on.

A WORD ON E-COMMERCE

Though still many years behind the efficiency of electronic trading platforms found in markets such as equities and U.S. Treasuries, the municipal bond market continues to move toward broader based e-trading. Improved price transparency has granted retail investors and their registered representatives new found confidence in the secondary municipal market. One way for institutional bondholders to advertise their inventories to retail inquiries is to post them on external e-trading platforms like the Municenter, Bond Desk, and Valubond, in addition to internal retail offering systems. On these platforms, investors can compare bond offerings with specific characteristics and search for the best value. From an institutional perspective, the transition to e-trading is still in its infancy as the majority of buyers have resisted moving away from the traditional offer/bid/counteroffer protocol practiced over the telephone for so many decades. While it remains to be seen how widely accepted the concept becomes going forward, it is certain that sellers of bonds will look to utilize every available channel of distribution so these platforms are likely here to stay.

SUMMARY

As noted in the opening paragraph, the goals in this chapter were to describe the roles, challenges, characteristics, and responsibilities of traders and brokers. Their activities are complex and busy. Hopefully this chapter has provided insights into this world.

CHAPTER 16

Municipal Arbitrage and Tender Option Bonds

Bart Mosley
Managing Director, Cohead of Municipal Proprietary Trading
UBS Securities LLC

One of the most striking changes in the municipal bond market over the past two decades has been the growth of "arbitrage" programs utilizing leveraged municipal bond portfolios made possible by *tender option bond* (TOB) structures and hedged trading strategies to profit from relative value opportunities in the municipal market. The list of participants engaging in this activity includes the proprietary trading desks of municipal bond dealers, the investment arms of banks, hedge funds, and other alternative investment providers. Whether directly involved or not, all participants in the market are affected by municipal arbitrage activity. Municipal arbitrageurs are often the most active trading accounts in the market, providing a source of liquidity and price discovery. Also, through the use of TOBs, they provide short-term investors such as tax-exempt money market funds much needed product in which to invest.

Municipal arbitrage strategies fall into two general categories that look to profit from the well-documented[1] tendency of longer maturity municipal bonds to trade at cheaper levels than would be expected by comparison to taxable fixed income investments of equivalent tenor and credit risk. One category consists of tender option bond programs that look to extract a yield premium over time as a yield spread earned over and above hedging costs—also called *municipal carry trades*. The second category consists of

---

[1] See, for example, Richard C. Green, "A Simple Model of the Taxable and Tax-Exempt Yield Curves," *Review of Financial Studies* 6, 2 (1993), pp 233–264; or Merle Erickson, Austan Goolsbee, and Edward L. Maydew, "How Prevalent is Tax Arbitrage? Evidence from the Market for Municipal Bonds," NBER Working Paper W9105 (August 2002), available at SSRN: http://ssrn.com/abstract=324047.

trading-oriented strategies that look to capture trading profits made possible by volatility in the relative value of municipals—sometimes called *municipal basis trades*. This chapter looks at the relative value of municipals and why the arbitrage opportunity exists and persists. We also examine the financing techniques and hedging strategies municipal arbitrageurs use.

Describing something as "arbitrage" often conjures the idea of a free lunch, or a risk-free profit opportunity. This is not the way that the term applies here. On the contrary, as countless members of the municipal arbitrage community can attest, there is no small amount of risk in this activity. Like other fixed income "relative value" arbitrage strategies, municipal arbitrage attempts to profit from a *perceived pricing inefficiency* via a *market neutral* strategy, meaning there is an attempt to hedge market exposures so that profitability is not dependent on the direction of interest rates. The other salient feature of fixed income arbitrage is the ability to use *leverage* to minimize the amount of invested capital required to control large positions. Mortgage security arbitrage, for example, looks to earn an excess yield spread by exploiting variations in the pricing of prepayment risk in mortgage securities—such a position can be advantageously financed via dollar rolls (a form of repurchase agreement) and, assuming that prepayment risk is accurately modeled, interest rate risk can be hedged. Correctly modeling prepayment risk can be dauntingly complex, which helps to give rise to the arbitrage opportunity. By contrast, the analysis needed to understand the relative pricing of municipal bonds is quite straightforward and the arbitrage opportunity comes from structural factors in the supply and demand for municipals.

RELATIVE VALUE—WHAT "SHOULD" A MUNICIPAL BOND BE WORTH?

The distinguishing characteristic of municipal bonds is the tax exemption from U.S. federal taxes for interest paid by state and local governments. Given the high credit quality of high-grade municipals, we would expect that, after adjusting for the tax exemption, municipal bond yields should compare closely with high-quality taxable fixed income instruments, such as U.S. Treasuries and agencies, or the LIBOR swap curve. We use LIBOR swap rates as the benchmark for taxable yields when performing relative value comparisons for municipal bonds because it avoids complications stemming from liquidity concerns for individual bonds as occurs with on-the-run U.S. Treasuries, for example.

Given two bonds equivalent in all respects except that the income from one is taxable and the other tax-exempt, the main driver of relative value between the two should be the expected tax rate an investor would pay on the interest of the taxable bond over its life. If we label this expected tax rate τ, we can relate the yield on a tax-exempt bond and a taxable bond as

$$\text{Yield}_{\text{tax-exempt}} = \text{Yield}_{\text{taxable}} \times (1 - \tau)$$

When we compare the value of tax-exempt and taxable bonds, we usually look at the ratio of the two bond's yields, expressing as the tax-exempt bond's yield as a percentage of the taxable yield, as opposed to as a yield spread (i.e., the difference between the two yields). By rearranging the above equation, we can relate the yield ratio to the implied tax rate between a taxable and tax-exempt bond:

$$\text{Yield}_{\text{tax-exempt}}/\text{Yield}_{\text{taxable}} = (1 - \tau) = \text{Municipal yield ratio}$$

Exhibit 16.1 compares the yield curves for Aaa rated municipal bonds and LIBOR swap rates as they appeared in August 2006. The exhibit analyzes the municipal yield into the rate that would equate the LIBOR swap rate adjusted for taxes, assuming a tax rate of 35%, and a yield premium over that "tax-equivalent" level. Clearly, there is a yield premium that increases for longer maturities.

If we know, or think we know, the appropriate tax rate that should apply for the marginal buyer, call it τ', then we can separate the yield ratio

EXHIBIT 16.1 Municipal Yield Curve versus USD LIBOR Curve

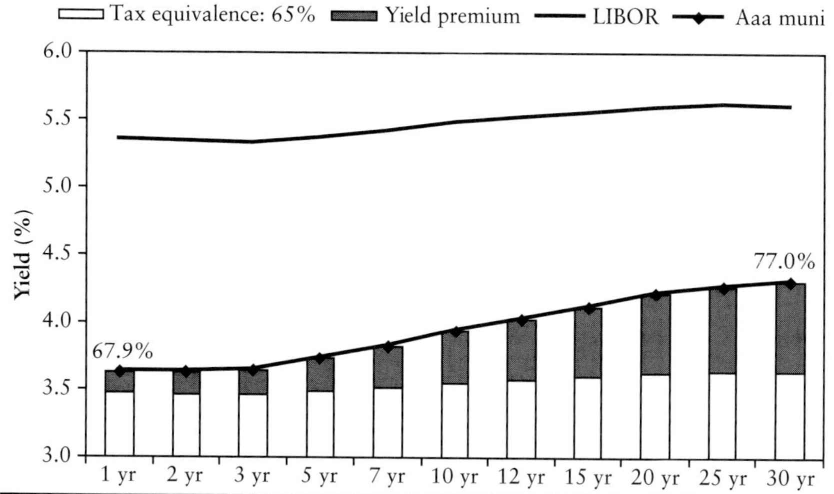

Source: Municipal Market Data, UBS Securities LLC.

we observe in the market into two components: the contribution required by tax adjusting for equivalence with taxable yields, and the yield premium.

$$\text{Municipal yield ratio} = (1 - \tau') + \text{Yield premium}$$

Exhibit 16.2 shows the historical yield premium for 30-year Aaa municipals, assuming the marginal tax rate is the corporate income tax rate, which was 34% to 35% during the timeframe shown. Two facts that are immediately discernable from the chart provide the motivation for municipal arbitrage activity: (1) the yield premium has consistently been positive, indicating the potential for an arbitrageur to earn an excess spread by isolating the premium, and (2) the yield premium varies considerably over time—indicating a volatile relative value relationship which creates trading opportunities.

HOW MUNICIPAL ARBITRAGE WORKS

We will use the information in Exhibit 16.3 for a typical municipal arbitrage trade involving a 20-year municipal bond, hedged with a LIBOR interest rate swap to examine the hedging and financing aspects of municipal arbitrage.

The interest rate swap used to hedge interest rate risk in the position entails a semiannual fixed payment, a market rate set at the time the swap is entered into, in exchange for receiving a variable payment of three-month

EXHIBIT 16.2   Historical Yield Premium

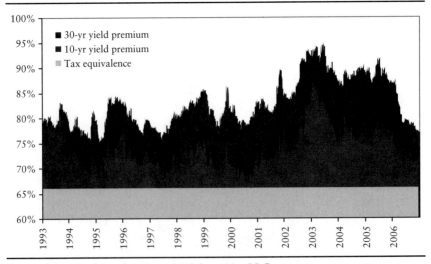

Source: Municipal Market Data, UBS Securities LLC.

EXHIBIT 16.3 Hypothetical Municipal Arbitrage Position

Bond Position		Hedge Position	
$50 million face value, 20-year maturity yield = 4.25%		$34.1 million face value LIBOR swap: Pay fixed rate and receive floating three-month LIBOR	
Dollar duration	$53,651.46	Dollar duration	$40,717.63
Hedge beta	75.9%		
Municipal bond income	$2,125,000	Pay fixed@5.60%	$(1,909,650)
Less		Less	
TOB interest	$(1,633,500)	Receive three-month LIBOR	$1,824,398
Program costs	$(90,000)		
Equals net tax-exempt income	$401,500	Equals hedge Cost	$(85,252)
Pretax equivalent income	$608,333		
		Net portfolio income	
		Net hedged carry	
		(Income less hedge cost)	$316,248
		Pretax equivalent carry	$523,081
		Net spread (basis points on bond face value)	105 bp
		Return on invested capital	10.46%

LIBOR set quarterly. The value of this interest rate swap will vary as interest rates go up or down in a similar manner to a short position in a bond. *Dollar duration*, also called *price value of a basis point* or *PV01*, is the change in value of a position for a one basis point parallel change in interest rates across the yield curve. We have chosen to use a hedge position with a lower dollar duration than the bond position to account for the fact that we expect changes in municipal bond yields to be more muted than changes in taxable bond yields. We have chosen to scale the hedge ratio, the ratio of the dollar durations of the swap and bond positions, by the municipal/LIBOR yield ratio. This factor in the hedge ratio is termed the *hedge beta* and is an important consideration, as we will discuss below.

The *net spread* is the income we expect to earn on the position, after accounting for financing and hedging costs. This represents a benefit earned by locking in the municipal yield premium. The objective of municipal carry trades is to capture this net spread. The other source of profit and loss in this position is changes in the municipal versus LIBOR yield ratio. Exhibit 16.4 summarizes the net profit and loss in different scenarios.

Valuation and Hedging: The Basis

The difference in value between a hedge and the security being hedged is referred to as *the basis* of the hedged position. Basis risk—the risk that changes in the value of a hedge position will differ from changes in value for the hedged position—reflects the degree that the hedged position and the hedge instrument are dissimilar. An arbitrageur chooses a specific hedge in order to offset a specific risk factor, isolating the basis risk that differentiates the security that is thought to be mispriced. In our example, the interest rate swap is hedging interest rate risk and we choose a hedge of the same tenor as our bond position in order to control for yield curve risk. The basis risk in the transaction encompasses tax risk (changes in the tax code or the value

EXHIBIT 16.4   Summary of Profit and Loss in Different Scenarios

	Bond Position	Swap Position	Net
Rates Unchanged			
Yield	4.25%	5.60%	
Price	100.000		
Ratio	75.9%		
Value	$50,000,000	0	
Swap Rates Decline 50 basis points			
Rate	3.95%	5.100%	
Price	102.459		
Ratio	77.5%		
Value	$51,229,321	–$2,122,159	
Change	$1,229,321	–$2,122,159	–$892,838
Swap Rates Increase 50 basis points			
Rate	4.45000%	6.100%	
Price	97.369		
Ratio	73.0%		
Value	$48,684,679	$1,954,755	
Change	–$1,315,321	$1,954,755	$639,434

of tax-exempt income), specific credit risk (the risk of the issuer defaulting) and liquidity (the supply and demand dynamics affecting the general market or a specific instrument).

The municipal/LIBOR yield ratio is a measure of the basis for the hedged position, representing the aggregate pricing of the tax, credit and liquidity risk factors for the municipal bond position.

Hedge Ratios: An Art, Not a Science

Once a hedging instrument is chosen, the next question is, "What is the correct hedge ratio to use?" That is, how many Treasuries to short, or what notional amount of interest rate swaps to enter into to insure that the hedge value changes the appropriate amount given a change in the market? The usual hedge ratio for a bond is one that balances the dollar value of a basis point (DV01) of the bond and the hedge, creating a zero DV01 position:

$$\text{Hedge ratio} = \text{DV01}_{bond}/\text{DV01}_{hedge}$$

However, what if we do not expect the yield on the bond and the yield on the hedge to change in lockstep? This is certainly the case in hedging municipal bonds. On one hand, we have discussed the fact that municipal yields are generally expressed as a yield ratio when comparing tax-exempt and taxable yields—the relative changes in yields should reflect this ratio. Also, empirical evidence suggests that the tax-exempt/taxable yield ratio is itself sensitive to interest rate moves—how do we incorporate this into our hedging strategy? If we assume we know how municipal yields will change given a change in taxable yields, we can restate our hedge ratio as

$$\text{Hedge ratio} = \beta \times (\text{DV01}_{bond}/\text{DV01}_{hedge})$$

where β, which we'll term the *hedge beta*, is the expected change in municipal yields given a change in taxable yields, or

$$\beta = \Delta\text{Yield}_{muni}/\Delta\text{Yield}_{taxable}$$

There are a number of different valid approaches available to estimate β. The choice of hedge beta is one of the primary differentiating factors between arbitrageurs. We can identify three generic approaches:

1. *Ratio-based hedging.* If the basic arbitrage is looked at as a mean-reverting process on the yield ratio, it would seem to be appropriate to use the yield ratio as an approximation for the hedge beta. Obviously, the yield

ratio itself changes, so some practitioners may use long-term averages or dynamically adjusted ratios to reflect the changes in the market.

2. *Regression based hedges.* One argument with the above approach is that the resulting mark-to-market will show a definite correlation to the direction in interest rates. As mentioned earlier, yield ratios tend to move in inverse relationship with the level of rates. If the objective is to obtain a hedge that makes results more or less independent of rates, a so-called regression-based hedge may be used:

$$\text{Yield}_{muni} = \beta \text{Yield}_{taxable} + \alpha$$

3. Alternatively, the arbitrageur may look at the interest rate relationship to be hedged as the funding component of the position, rather than the duration component. For a LIBOR swap hedge, then, the important relationship is the relationship between three-month LIBOR received on the swap versus weekly BMA paid on TOB position.

A complicating factor in all this is the fact that most municipal bonds that are longer than 10 years to maturity when issued are callable. Market convention is for the quoted yield on callable municipals to be based on *yield-to-worst*, meaning the yield is calculated assuming the bond will be called with certainty on the first call date if the call is currently in the money for the issuer (generally, if the bond's price is a premium), and as though the bond will remain outstanding to maturity otherwise. Some market participants attempt to hedge using DV01 calculations based on this yield-to-worst methodology. For bonds trading close to a price of par, however, this can result in unstable hedge ratios as the bond trades from a discount to premium. Many arbitrageurs therefore use option-adjusted DV01 calculations to control for this callability.

Financing: TOBs and Leverage

Most municipal arbitrage programs utilize tender option bond programs, or TOBs to create leveraged positions in municipal bonds. TOBs are securitization vehicles of municipal bonds that allow a bond or portfolio of bonds to be effectively financed at tax-exempt rates.

In the taxable fixed income markets, arbitrageurs will usually fund the purchase of securities through the repurchase—or repo—market. In a repo transaction, the owner of a security will simultaneously sell the security to a counterparty and agree to repurchase the security at a higher price on a later date. The price differential reflects the interest rate at which the original owner of the security has in essence borrowed money to cover the purchase price of the security. If we try to apply this to the financing of a tax-exempt municipal bond a problem immediately presents itself. The lender to whom we are turning to finance the municipal bond will receive taxable interest from us and will therefore charge fully taxable rates. The tax code disallows the deductibility of this interest cost for the borrower since the proceeds are used to purchase a tax-exempt security. So, in the end, we would receive a relatively low yield on the bond, reflecting its tax-exempt status, while having to finance it at a higher, taxable rate.

To achieve an efficient financing of a municipal bond, we want to in effect split the bond into two parts: one part that is priced tax efficiently and one that carries the tax, liquidity, and other risks that create the municipal yield curve premium. This is what TOBs do—a tender option bond trust creates a short-term, variable rate instrument that is collateralized by an underlying long-term municipal bond. As we have seen, short maturities tend to be priced more tax efficiently than longer maturity municipal bonds. The trust then creates a second instrument that passes all the "residual" risk and return of the underlying collateral to an investor who wishes to obtain leveraged exposure to a municipal bond. The details of how TOBs work are covered in the appendix to this chapter.

The tax code does allow some firms to finance municipal bonds in a tax efficient manner without resorting to the TOB structure. These include broker-dealers in municipal bonds and firms with an appropriate balance sheet structure.[2] Section 265 of the Code generally disallows the deduction of interest costs "incurred or continued to purchase or carry obligations the interest on which is wholly exempt from [federal taxes]." The primary exception is if the tax-exempt obligations represent a *de minimus* portion (defined as less than 2%) of the taxpayer's assets. Broker-dealers can limit the amount of interest costs that are disallowed by calculating the portion of their inventories of municipal bonds that are attributable to equity funding rather than debt. This is not actually an exception to the general Section 265 disallowance, but a limitation that recognizes that broker-dealers utilize a mix of funding sources.

The next section will look at various arguments that attempt to explain the existence of the municipal yield curve premium and the relative value arbitrage opportunities it brings, which will provide a context in which to understand the fundamental risks of municipal arbitrage.

---

[2] Prior to the Tax Reform Act of 1986, commercial banks had the ability to deduct the interest costs associated with holding portfolios of municipal bonds. The 1986 Act retained a limited sphere of bank-qualified bonds for which banks still receive this beneficial treatment, but that segment of the market is limited and specialized enough to be excluded from the present discussion.

WHERE DOES THE MUNICIPAL YIELD CURVE'S STEEPNESS COME FROM?

If credit risk—the risk that a municipality will default on its obligations and leave the bondholder with nothing to show for his investment—is minimal, there must be some other factor at work that would explain the municipal yield curve premium. The explanations put forward to explain the persistence of the yield premium fall into three broad categories: (1) tax risk, (2) liquidity and market segmentation, and (3) supply/demand. In reality, of course, each of these effects plays some role and the volatile relationship of municipals to taxable bonds is in part the result of shifts in the relative importance of these factors.

The Tax Risk Argument

Perhaps the most often cited reason for a the municipal yield curve premium is the risk that the value of the tax exemption for municipal bond income could either be eroded or eliminated completely by Congressional action. The certainty about what the tax treatment of municipals will be is obviously less as the investment horizon expands for longer maturities. This risk was brought home most acutely during the 1996 Presidential election when Steve Forbes ran on a platform centered on shifting the country to a flat tax system that would have eliminated taxation of investment income and thereby would have eliminated the benefit of holding municipal bonds. During the summer of 1995, when the chances of Forbes' proposal being more widely taken up looked the brightest, the municipal market did see significant decline in value (increase in yield ratios), with the ratio of 30-year municipal yields to 30-year Treasury bond yields increasing from 78% campaign started in February of 1995 to 87% by September 1995. Prior to that, in March 1986, Oregon Senator Bob Packwood's proposal to tax all municipal bond income under the newly proposed *alternative minimum tax* (AMT) caused such turmoil the municipal market essentially closed down for several days until he rescinded his proposal.

While these episodes illustrate that the municipal bond tax exemption is not written in stone, they also highlight the difficulties that face the enactment of any other tax regime. Based on the yield ratios on long maturity municipal bonds, which have ranged between 74% to 96% of 30-year LIBOR swap rates since 1994, it would appear that the market is pricing in a much more uncertain future for the value of the tax exemption than is warranted.

What about changes in tax rates? Perhaps the risk that Congress could lower tax rates and erode the value of tax exemption warrants a significant yield premium. Consider that the top marginal tax rate for individuals since

1994 has ranged from 39.6% to 33% and that the corporate tax rate has remained at 35%; these tax rates imply yield ratios of between 67% (for a 33% tax rate) and 60.4% (for a 39.6% tax rate). These implied ratios are much lower than those that have been seen in the market. Even the lowest ratio we have seen for long municipals, 74%, over the past decade would imply a tax rate of only 26%, while the average municipal yield ratio of approximately 82% implies a tax rate of 18%. Since World War II, the top marginal income tax rate has ranged from greater than 90% to a low of 28% in the late 1980s (even then, many taxpayers were subject to a 33% rate). This would seem to imply that the odds of a tax rate as low as 26% over the life of a 30-year bond are quite low. So, while tax risk is certainly real, the municipal yield premium would appear to overstate its potential impact.

The Liquidity Argument

We can also look at the diverse nature of the municipal market for an explanation. There are over 80,000 issuers who raise money via the municipal bond market, many in relatively small amounts. The market comprises well over 1 million individual bonds most of which trade infrequently, if ever, after issuance. So it is reasonable to suppose that there should be some liquidity premium associated with the need to keep track of the large number of credits in the market. That is, investors who develop the expertise to understand the diverse sectors that make up the municipal market should expect to earn some premium. This does not, however, explain why such a premium should be greater for longer maturities. Also, large, liquid issuers such as the City of New York or the State of California do not show any significant decrease in the yield curve premium seen in all municipal bonds.

The Supply/Demand Argument

Lastly, we can look at supply and demand patterns in the municipal bond market. On the demand side, the market for municipal bonds is somewhat limited. Pension funds, life insurance companies, and European and Asian banks are all significant buyers of fixed income assets who do not benefit from the tax exemption on municipal bonds. Indeed, direct retail investors, or proxies for retail investment such as mutual funds hold roughly half of all municipal bonds. Financial institutions and property and casualty insurance companies account for the largest share of the remainder. One thing that all these investors have in common is that they tend to be relatively risk averse. The very high credit quality of most municipal bonds conforms to the risk profile of most of these investors. Another implication of this risk profile is that these investors are most comfortable with shorter maturity bonds. On balance, then, we would expect to see demand for municipals most constant for shorter maturities.

On the other hand, the issuers of municipal bonds—state and local governments—tend to prefer long-term fixed rate borrowings. This is an outgrowth of the fact that municipalities rely on future tax receipts to repay their borrowings, and so want to minimize the variability that comes from having to frequently rollover their debt. This combination of demand for shorter maturity tax-exempt bonds and a bias in supply towards longer maturities contributes to the steep yield curve bias seen in the municipal bond market. As would be expected given this supply/demand mismatch the yield premium for long maturity municipals is quite sensitive to the level of supply in the municipal bond market as Exhibit 16.5 illustrates. The exhibit shows the yield premium, given by the difference between the Aaa municipal/LIBOR yield ratio for 30-year maturities and 1-year maturities, compared with new issue volume for municipal bonds.

CONCLUSION

A classic textbook definition of arbitrage is "the simultaneous purchase and sale of the same, or essentially similar, security in two markets for advan-

EXHIBIT 16.5 Municipal Yield Ratio versus 30-day Supply

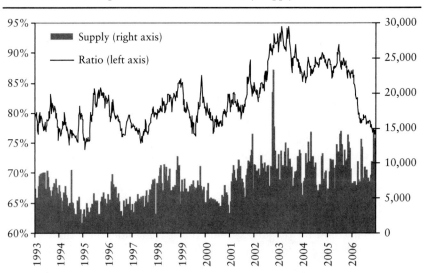

Source: Bond Buyer, Municipal Market Data, UBS Securities LLC.

tageously different prices."[3] Nassim Taleb provides a real-world trader's definition of arbitrage as an activity where "the expected value of a self-financing portfolio (that can be negative) is positive."[4] Taleb's characterization emphasizes the fact that most real world arbitrage opportunities are not sure things and rely on some key assumptions:

1. The securities involved really are the same or essentially similar—that is, that the observed pricing differential does not actually account for an overlooked risk factor differentiating the securities.
2. The portfolio can be financed without the cost of financing erasing the perceived pricing differential.
3. The market will behave in such a way as to allow the arbitrageur to profit from the pricing differential—that is, the pricing differential won't move against the arbitrageur, either wiping out the capital allocated to the trade or causing one's risk managers, investors or management to withdraw support for the trade. An old trader's aphorism puts it succinctly: "Markets can remain irrational longer than you can remain solvent."

We've looked at the how the first two questions impact the two key components of municipal arbitrage trades: (1) valuation and hedging and (2) financing. The last assumption relates to the question "what can go wrong?"

We started by commenting on the fact that municipal arbitrage, like most real world fixed income arbitrage strategies, is not without risk. We have covered a number of risk factors that are both endogenous (correctly assessing basis risk and municipal valuation) and exogenous (changes in the tax treatment of municipals, liquidity, supply and demand pressures). It is important to always keep in mind that any of these factors, as well as other unforeseen factors, can turn any "arbitrage" into a losing proposition.

Still, the field of municipal arbitrage continues to grow and evolve. Tender option bond programs develop new wrinkles, such as the broader use of "pooled" trusts that facilitate the financing of large portfolios. New markets for hedging risks, such as credit default swaps, are beginning to find their way into municipal arbitrageur's portfolios. Finally, the derivatives markets are allowing non-traditional and non-U.S. taxpayers to participate in the market through BMA Municipal Ratio swaps. Municipal arbitrage activity will continue play an important role in how municipal bonds get priced and

---

[3] William Sharpe and Gordon Alexander, *Investments*, 4th ed. (Englewood Cliffs, NJ: Prentice Hall, 1990).
[4] Nassim Taleb, *Dynamic Hedging* (New York: John Wiley & Sons, Inc., 1997).

distributed. Further the techniques of municipal arbitrage will continue to find application in more portfolios manager's toolkit.

APPENDIX: TENDER OPTION BONDS IN A NUTSHELL

Most major municipal bond dealers sponsor tender option bond programs, branded under various names: UBS Muni CRVs (UBS), ROCs & ROLs (Citigroup), RITES & P-FLOATs (Merrill Lynch), PUTR & DRIVERS (J.P. Morgan), to name a few. They use these programs both for their own proprietary trading capabilities and to allow their customers to benefit from the ability to create leveraged municipal bond positions. Despite the different names, they all perform the same function: issuing short-term, money-market securities which are backed by long-term municipal bonds and residual securities which represent a leveraged position in the underlying bonds. The UBS Muni CRVs program dubs the short-term and residual securities CRV floaters and CRV residuals, respectively, and we will use this terminology in this appendix.

Exhibit 16.6 depicts the mechanics of how a TOB trust works. The investor deposits a bond with the TOB trust, which is overseen by a trustee bank. The trust issues two securities which receive different shares of the principal and interest payments on the deposited bonds: (1) variable rate demand obligations representing 90% or more of the principal amount of the underlying bonds (the CRV floaters), which are generally purchased by tax-exempt money market funds; and (2) residual interest securities (the

EXHIBIT 16.6   Tender Option Bond Trust Structure

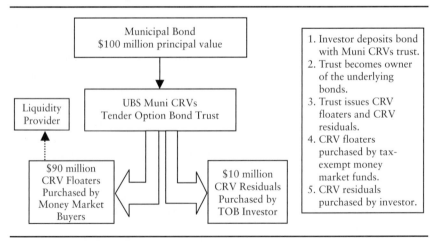

CRV residuals), which are purchased by the original investor and which represent the remaining principal. The CRV floaters are structured to trade at a price of par, so that the CRV residuals carry most of the remaining market risks of the underlying bond.

The residual securities reflect a leveraged position in the underlying bonds. Much of the control over the disposition of the underlying bonds rests with the CRV residual holders. The trust provides the CRV residual holder with the right to require the CRV floater holders to tender their securities on seven-day's notice, allowing the residual holder to terminate the trust and liquidate the underlying bonds. In exchange, the CRV floaters receive first priority on payments from the trust. So if short-term rates rise, there is the possibility that all of the coupon income on the underlying bonds will be paid to the CRV floaters, leaving nothing for the CRV residuals.

The name *tender option bond* actually derives from the short-term security created by the trust. The mechanism that allows the CRV Floaters to be treated as short-term securities is a liquidity facility that allows holders of the CRV floaters to tender them for redemption on short notice, usually seven days. This *tender option* allows a purchaser to classify the CRV floaters as short-term instruments under Rule 2a-7 of the Investment Company Act of 1940—enabling tax-exempt money market funds to buy the CRV floaters. Either the dealer sponsor of the TOB program or the residual investor often provides the liquidity facility, but it is not uncommon for the sponsor to contract a third party to provide liquidity. The liquidity facility is a 364-day conditional facility that must be renewed each year. Because the liquidity facility terminates in the event of a default on the underlying bond, it is not considered a credit enhancement.

As for traditional *variable rate demand obligations* (VRDOs), the rate on the CRV floaters is set by the remarketing agent at a level that allows the bond to be remarketed at a price of par. While the CRV Floaters can be remarketed in various modes, ranging in terms from daily to yearly, the most common mode is weekly corresponding to the reset frequency of the BMA Municipal Swap Index of short-term, tax-exempt rates.

Upon deposit of the underlying bonds, the trust (not the trustee) becomes the legal owner of the bond. The trustee's role is to administer the trust on behalf of the beneficial owners of the trust, represented by the two classes of securities issued from the trust: the floating rate securities and the residual interest securities. The holders of each of these new securities holds a participation in the underlying bonds held by the trust, meaning that they are entitled to specific cash flows of principal and interest from the bonds. The TOB trust is setup to be a partnership for tax purposes, so that the tax-exempt character of the interest on the underlying bonds is preserved.

In order for the trust to be able to pass through tax-exempt income, the Code requires that each class of participant (i.e., the CRV floater and CRV residual holders) share in both the benefits and burdens of ownership of the underlying bonds—in investment terms, the risks and rewards must be to some extent shared. Two key provisions of the TOB structure in this regard are *gain sharing* and *tender option termination events* (TOTEs).

Gain sharing is designed to cover the benefits side of the equation. Since the CRV floaters generally receive the smallest share of the interest income on the bonds, their portion of the return on the bond needs to be boosted somehow. This is accomplished by providing that a portion of any gain on the bond at the time the trust terminates be shared with the CRV floater holder. There are various mechanism for this, but the most common is for 5% of any gain, but not a loss, be added to the redemption price for the CRV floaters if they are redeemed for a reason other than the exercise of the floater holders tender option—for example, the CRV residual holder exercising his right to redeem the CRV floaters and terminate the trust.

On the burdens side, TOTEs convey credit risk on the underlying bonds under some circumstances to the CRV floater holders. TOTEs are generally "really bad" events that result in the liquidity provider automatically terminating the right of the CRV floater holder to tender the securities for redemption. These typically include a payment default on the underlying bonds, the bonds being declared taxable or subject registration under the Securities Act of 1934. In this case, the CRV floater holders will continue to hold a beneficial interest in the bonds.

A last thing to note is that TOB securities, both CRV floaters and CRV residuals are private placement securities that are eligible to be purchased only by sophisticated investors. Also, the gain sharing provision in particular and the tax partnership nature of TOBs in general do not lend themselves to active trading of the underlying bonds.

CHAPTER 17

Interest Rate Swaps and Their Application to Tax-Exempt Financing

Eric H. Chu
Managing Director
Bond Logistix LLC

Craig Underwood
President
Bond Logistix LLC

Thomas B. Fox
Managing Director
Bond Logistix LLC

Jon A. McMahon
Financial Consultant
Bond Logistix LLC

Roger L. Davis
Chair, Public Finance Department
Orrick, Herrington & Sutcliffe LLP

Stephen A. Spitz
Partner, Public Finance Department
Orrick, Herrington & Sutcliffe LLP

Albert Simons III
Partner, Public Finance Department
Orrick, Herrington & Sutcliffe LLP

George G. Wolf
Chair, Tax Department.
Orrick, Herrington & Sutcliffe LLP

This chapter is reprinted in its entirety courtesy of its authors and publishers Bond Logistix LLC, a registered investment advisor and derivative advisor (www. bondlogistix.com) and Orrick, Herrington & Sutcliffe LLP a global law firm with a finance emphasis (www.orrick.com).

The global interest rate swap market is remarkably vast, both in terms of size and scope of products, and it continues to grow rapidly. Within the U.S. public finance sector, the use of interest rate swaps and their close relatives is becoming more common as increasing numbers of governmental entities utilize them to reduce their borrowing costs, better manage or limit their interest rate risk, and effect better matching of assets and liabilities. Written for the benefit of issuers of tax-exempt debt (referred to in this chapter as *agencies*) and other entities that have access to the municipal capital markets, this chapter serves to help agencies enhance their understanding of interest rate swaps and related financial tools.

Included is an overview of common types of swaps and discussions of how they work. Additional topics addressed are transaction mechanics and documentation, potential benefits and risks, legal and tax issues, and post-trade management. Special emphasis is placed on the most common type of transaction, the so-called *fixed rate swap*, in which an agency receives a floating rate and pays a fixed rate. When combined with an issue of floating rate bonds, this swap is intended to create a structure which, on a net basis, results in synthetic fixed rate debt for the agency.

Like other areas of finance, the swap industry has developed its own terminology to describe the financial and legal terms of a transaction in a practical and concise manner. Several of the most commonly used terms are listed in the Glossary of Key Terms in the appendix to this chapter.

WHAT ARE SWAPS AND HOW DO THEY WORK?

An interest rate swap is a contractual agreement between two parties who agree to exchange (or *swap*) certain cash flows for a defined period of time. Generally, the cash flows to be swapped relate to interest to be paid or received with respect to some asset or liability. Accordingly, the swap is designed to generate a net change in the interest rate cash flow related to that asset or liability (typically investment securities or bond indebtedness, respectively), but neither impacts the principal of that asset or liability nor results in the creation of any new principal. As a result, the size of a swap, for purposes of describing the computational base on which the swapped payments are calculated, is referred to as the *notional amount*. As part of any swap, both parties agree to:

- The notional amount.
- The rate or rate formula each party will use to compute the amounts to be paid to the other on that notional amount.
- The dates on which cash flows will be exchanged.

■ The term of the swap.

Interest rate swaps do not typically generate new funding like a loan or bond sale; rather, they effectively convert one interest rate basis to a different basis (e.g., from floating to fixed). There are also swap variations, which are structured to have an up-front payment made from one party to the other. Such swaps, or *off-market* swaps, can be a useful tool when an agency's financing objective includes the need for additional, up-front cash. However, an agency should consider the fact that such a swap can be characterized as having an embedded loan. Later in this chapter, we discuss these off-market swaps in greater detail and also address later on the additional legal issues that they present.

Whether entering into a plain vanilla fixed rate swap, or one tailored to a set of special circumstances, agencies should note that issuing variable rate bonds and then entering into a fixed rate swap is not the same as issuing fixed rate bonds, even though the agency's future debt service obligations should be similar under both. Exhibit 17.1 compares a conventional fixed rate bond issue arrangement to a swap transaction creating a synthetic fixed rate that, in fact, involves two separate transactions.

Structure of an Interest Rate Swap

Each swap transaction has its own terms and features; but the typical interest rate swap used in the municipal marketplace provides that one party's

EXHIBIT 17.1   Conventional versus Synthetic Fixed Rate Debt

Fixed Rate Bonds

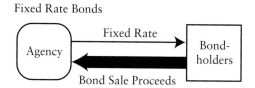

Variable Rate Bonds and Floating to Fixed Rate Swap

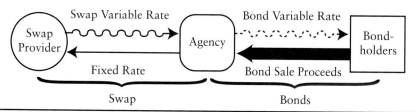

payments are calculated using a fixed rate (the *fixed leg*), while the other party's payments are calculated using a variable rate (the *floating leg*). The swap documentation identifies:

- The set fixed rate.
- The specific variable rate index.
- The notional amount (including any scheduled increases or more likely, decreases or amortization).
- The dates of cash flow exchange.
- The conditions of optional and mandatory termination.
- The scheduled termination date, which defines the term (sometimes referred to as the *tenor*).

The fixed rate is generally set for the term of the swap. The variable rate can be based on any index (e.g., BMA Index or LIBOR), or even a specific security (e.g., an agency's variable bond rate). The underlying index, or other instrument, from which the floating leg payments are calculated is known as the "underlying."

If scheduled to occur on the same dates, the fixed payment by one party is netted against the floating payment by the other, such that only a net settlement is made by one of the parties on a given payment date. These exchanges take place on the preestablished payment dates and reflect the differences between the two rates during the applicable period.

The Counterparties' Perspectives

In the municipal marketplace, the two parties to a swap are the agency (or, in the case of a conduit bond deal, the conduit borrower) and a financial institution (the *provider*), typically a commercial bank, an investment bank, or an insurance company (or a subsidiary of one of these entities). While the agency accomplishes some financial goal (e.g., hedging variable rate exposure, improving asset/liability matches, reducing borrowing costs, etc.) by entering into the swap, the provider will be compensated for establishing its own hedges and the ongoing costs of carrying the swap on its books.

What is a Hedge?

In finance, *hedge* generally refers to a tactic (or a financial product) used to offset losses or potential losses associated with an existing financial position. For example, a put option is a hedge that can be used to reduce or eliminate the risk of adverse price movements in a security. However, the cost of the hedge limits the amount of any future gain on the security as well. If a hedge completely eliminates any possible future gain or loss (put another way, if it eliminates the uncertainty of the security's return), it is called a perfect hedge.

Specifically, in the case of a fixed rate swap, an agency's variable rate debt is said to be hedged by the swap since, on a net basis, the agency is paying a fixed rate of interest and the swap has eliminated the possibility of having to make higher (or lower) interest payments to its bondholders should short term interest rates rise (or fall). In this way, the agency has eliminated any potential loss (higher rates) or gain (lower rates) on the variable rate bonds. As discussed in the next section, there are varying degrees of hedge effectiveness among commonly used interest rate swap structures.

The Provider's Perspective

Providers typically enter into particular interest rate swaps as part of a large, hedged portfolio. To illustrate, a provider might enter into swap transactions with two different agencies of similar credit, with matching variable interest rates, notional amounts, and terms. The provider would be the receiver of the variable interest rate in one transaction and the payer in the other. However, for the transactions to be economically feasible for the provider, there needs to be a difference in the fixed rate components of the swaps. For example, if in the first transaction the provider is obligated to make payments computed using a fixed rate of 5.00%, the provider would look to structure the second transaction to receive 5.00% plus a spread. This way, the provider will earn that fixed spread, or bid/ask spread, between the two agreements.

Even with the use of very sophisticated financial engineering programs, in practice, providers are unlikely to be able to achieve a hedge that is completely without credit and related risks and perfectly matched in terms of both the timing and amounts of the cash flows. There are some risks to a swap (e.g., counterparty credit risk or change in tax law risk) that cannot be hedged to any significant degree; that is, cannot be quantified in dollars with any precision. Additionally, there are other risks inherent in the swap agreement provisions themselves (e.g., one-way termination upon downgrade, default by a counterparty to the agreement or the invalidity or unenforceability of the agreement) that a provider is also unable to completely hedge, especially if those provisions differ from completely balanced, two-way industry norms.

Thus, for the same reasons that a lower credit rating may require an agency to issue debt at higher interest rates, an agency's swap rate can also be higher than that of other agencies with higher credit ratings or if it contains nontraditional swap terms that are difficult to hedge. Therefore, in a fixed rate swap, the interest rate the agency is charged by the provider will include a component used to offset the incremental costs for hedging greater risks. The greater the risk perceived by the provider, the higher the interest rate that will be charged to the agency.

Subject to the caveat that there is a limit to the amount of the unhedgeable risk a provider can and will take on, swap agreements are very flexible. As mentioned, features that are difficult for the provider to hedge (or cannot effectively be hedged) come at a cost; and there may be features, if analyzed separately, that cost the provider more than they can benefit the agency and therefore may not be to the agency's advantage. Thus, in evaluating and negotiating a proposed swap transaction, it is important that the agency be able to delineate the cost components of the swap and understand not only its own needs and objectives, but also the needs and objectives of the provider.

The Agency's Perspective

Unlike a provider making its business from earning the bid/ask spread on a transaction, an agency generally enters into a swap in order to achieve some specific financial objective, such as achieving a lower borrowing cost or hedging interest rate exposure. For example, the most commonly used swap structure—the synthetic fixed rate transaction—is attractive when the net synthetic fixed rate (the fixed swap rate plus the ongoing costs associated with variable rate debt, taking into account reasonable assumptions for basis spread and other risks) is lower than the fixed rate on a traditional fixed rate bond structure. In this scenario, the agency achieves an important financial objective—lowering its borrowing cost—while maintaining the predictability of a fixed interest rate. However, as with any financing structure, the agency must first evaluate the risks associated with a swap and conclude that they can be adequately managed and that the swap is otherwise suitable for the agency.

Conversely, a synthetic variable rate transaction may be attractive if an agency wishes to increase the proportion of variable rate exposure in its debt and/or asset structures in an effort to reduce a mismatch between its assets and liabilities. An appropriately structured swap can convert fixed rate debt to a variable rate, and may be the most efficient, and perhaps the only viable, method of reducing such a mismatch, given the costs and tax limitations associated with restructuring debt and limitations on investment maturity terms. As with the synthetic fixed rate structure referenced above, an agency must compare the costs and associated risks of the available swap structures with other, perhaps more traditional, financing techniques, in order to make a prudent, informed decision.

Regardless of structure, an agency should go beyond the financial analysis required to determine if a swap will achieve its economic objective and review a proposed swap transaction with the same level of diligence it would apply to the consideration of any bond issue. Issues such as rate exposure, basis risk, transaction costs, covenant obligations, security, redemption or refunding flexibility, termination risk, counterparty creditworthiness and other similar issues should all be carefully considered prior to entering into a swap.

TYPES OF SWAPS AND OTHER HEDGES

Interest rate swaps can be used to achieve goals beyond creating synthetic fixed or variable rate debt. Agencies seeking to achieve a variety of financing objectives have a choice between several interest rate swap structures in use today, each having its own set of features and variations. Swaps can be structured as floating-to-floating rates swaps, in which one variable rate index is swapped for another (also known as a *basis swap*). Additionally, instead of debt, they can be associated with investment assets in order to effectively convert the interest earned on such investments from fixed to floating or vice versa. Swap agreements may also incorporate a variety of features, such as an off-market swap component, which is economically equivalent to a loan, generally made from a provider to an agency. Other features might include a tax reform trigger event, which is used to hedge against changes in tax law, or an embedded option such as a call option. These different types of swaps as well as other forms more generally described as hedges, are described in this section.

Interest Rate Swaps

As previously mentioned, an interest rate swap is an agreement between two parties to exchange future cash flows. The term of the swap and its notional amount will typically mirror the dates and amounts of the hedged debt or asset. The most common variations found in tax-exempt financing are:

- The floating-to-fixed rate swap (fixed rate swap)
- The fixed-to-floating rate swap (floating rate swap)
- The floating-to-floating rate swap (basis swap)

Floating-to-Fixed Rate Swap (Fixed Rate Swap)

As an alternative to issuing fixed rate bonds, an agency can instead sell floating rate bonds and simultaneously enter into a receive-floating, pay-fixed interest rate swap, or fixed rate swap. The goal is to create, on a net basis, a fixed rate obligation. A key consideration for the agency will be the formula and floating rate index to be used in computing its receipts on the floating leg of the swap (e.g., percent of LIBOR, percent of LIBOR plus a fixed spread, BMA Index, or cost of funds). The goal is to select a formula and index that will best match, or hedge, the agency's bond interest payments. To the extent the floating leg receipts do not match the variable rate bond interest payments, the agency's net debt service will vary over time and, accordingly, will result in somewhat higher or lower net debt service payments from period to period.

How Fixed Is Synthetically Fixed?   A properly structured swap will provide an effective hedge, but more often than not, a less than perfect one. A perfect hedge would be defined by floating leg receipts that match the interest payments due on the hedged bonds exactly, which is known as a *cost-of-funds swap*. This structure results in a true fixed rate obligation for the agency, but may not result in the lowest overall cost of funds. This is because market rates charged for the fixed leg on a cost-of-funds swap will be considerably higher than the fixed leg of a swap, where the underlying is more liquid and traded in greater volume, such as the BMA Index or LIBOR.

Simply put, a provider can more effectively hedge a BMA or LIBOR-based swap, which is reflected in the rate charged on the fixed leg. For this reason, cost-of-funds swaps have been rare. Furthermore, cost-of-funds swaps generally include provisions converting the swap to an index under certain circumstances (such as a decline in the credit quality of the agency) and may give the provider significant control over factors that may influence the agency's cost of funds (e.g., interest rate mode, remarketing agent, or similar ongoing costs).

An agency's net future debt service obligations under a synthetically fixed rate structure may not be determined with the absolute level of precision of a fixed rate bond issue. However, from a budgeting perspective, absolute precision is not likely to be essential so long as the agency under-

EXHIBIT 17.2   Floating Rate Option Scorecard (agency's perspective)

	Floating Rate Option		
	LIBOR	BMA	Cost-of-Funds
Fixed rate coupon	Lowest	Higher	Highest
Liquidity	High	Medium	Low
Hedge effectiveness	Good	Better	Best (perfect[a])

[a] True synthetic fixed rate.

stands the underlying mechanics and factors that will affect its net debt service requirements and the degree to which those requirements may vary.

The fixed rate achieved through this structure can be lower than the fixed rate that can be attained through a traditional fixed rate bond offering. This is especially true if an agency structures its swap using a LIBOR-based floating payment in exchange for a fixed payment. The rate advantage of a LIBOR-based swap is the result of a combination of factors, including the greater liquidity and efficiency of the taxable swap markets and the agency's assumption of basis risk, including change in tax law risk. Also, because the agency can generally terminate a swap only at market value and not at par value, the synthetic fixed rate arrangement should be evaluated against the cost of noncallable fixed rate bonds as opposed to typical fixed rate bonds with optional redemption provisions.

Basis Risk, Including Change in Tax Law Risk The term *basis risk* refers to the potential or actual mismatch between an agency's floating receipt from a swap and its floating payment obligation on the underlying debt. This mismatch exists when each cash flow references different underlying securities or ones of differing maturity terms. For example, every month an agency might receive a preset percentage of the one-month LIBOR rate from the provider, and pay interest on its tax-exempt variable rate bonds once every 35 days. Both the timing difference and the fact that interest will accrue at different rates, even if neither is significant, technically results in basis spread. Moreover, the magnitude of the basis spread will vary over time. It is the cumulative basis spread over the term of the swap, or more practically over each fiscal year, that will be important for the agency in terms of cash flow budgeting.

Change in *tax law risk*, or *tax reform risk*, is the risk that there will be an unanticipated structural change to the current tax law (e.g., a reduction in marginal income tax rates), which would then impact the relationship (i.e., the spread) between tax-exempt and taxable rates. This is the risk agencies undertake whenever they issue floating rate bonds. It can also arise in the context of a swap. To illustrate, suppose an agency currently has outstanding tax-exempt variable rate bonds at 3.5% as well as taxable variable rate bonds at 5.0%. If the marginal tax rate was, for example, reduced from 30% to 10%, the yield on the tax-exempt bonds might increase to 4.5%. In the case of a fixed rate swap wherein the provider is paying the BMA Index (and receiving a fixed rate) and the rate on the agency's bonds is substantially the same as the BMA Index, the provider is exposed to tax risk because if there is a reduction in the marginal tax rates and the BMA Index suddenly rises, the provider's payment obligations under the swap will increase.

While the agency's payment obligations under the bonds will also increase, that increase will be offset by the increased swap receipts. On the other hand, if the agency had entered the same swap, but instead of receiving payments based on the BMA Index, it received payments based on LIBOR (70% of one-month LIBOR for example), the agency would be exposed to tax reform risk. In this example, assuming that if since inception the swap receipts had closely approximated the bond interest payments, then a sudden reduction in the marginal tax rate could adversely impact the agency.

Fixed-to-Floating Rate Swap (Floating Rate Swap)

As an alternative to issuing variable rate bonds, the agency can instead sell fixed rate bonds and simultaneously enter into a receive-fixed, pay-floating interest rate swap. The goal is to create, on a net basis, a floating rate obligation.

Floating-to-Floating Rate Swap (Basis Swap)

In a basis swap, the agency enters into a receive-floating, pay-floating interest rate swap where, for example, the underlying for the first floating leg is the BMA Index and for the second floating leg is based on the one-month LIBOR rate (see Exhibit 17.3). A basis swap may be used to reduce risk associated with potential changes in tax law, decrease basis risk, or to move from one index to another.

EXHIBIT 17.3   Synthetic Fixed Rate Debt with a Basis Swap

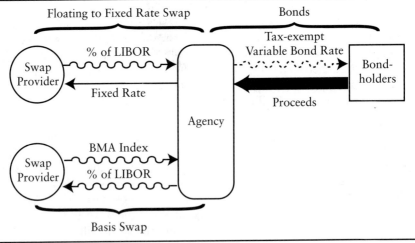

EXHIBIT 17.4 Off-Market Swap versus On-Market Swap

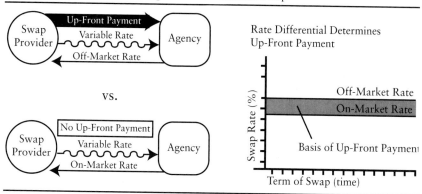

Off-Market Swap

An *off-market swap* is a variation of an interest rate swap in which one or both of the referenced rates is priced off the market, resulting in an up-front cash payment, usually paid by the provider to the agency. For example, in the case of a floating-to-fixed rate swap, if the coupon rate for the fixed leg is set above the market rate, the agency would receive an up-front payment from the provider (which is somewhat similar to a loan to the agency which it, in effect, pays back as that portion of the fixed rate that is above the market rate.) See Exhibit 17.4.

Forward Swap

Forward swaps are interest rate swaps in which the accrual and exchange of cash flows commences at a later date (the effective date) rather than the current date (on or around the trade date), thereby affording the opportunity to lock in rates today while accruals begin in the future. While forward swaps allow rates to be locked in, the rates will be determined via the forward rate curve, which is not the same as the current yield curve. These types of transactions are often used to approximate the benefits of an advance refunding when one is not otherwise permitted under tax law. The forward swap locks in a fixed rate, and then variable rate bonds are issued in the future as current refunding bonds upon the effective date of the swap. Although mechanically different from a swap, agencies can achieve similar results by utilizing what is known as a rate lock agreement, which entails entering into an agreement with an underwriter to issue fixed rate bonds in the future.

Agencies who have entered into a forward swap often determine to optionally terminate the swap prior to its scheduled effective date, and

EXHIBIT 17.5   Forward Starting Swap (synthetic advance refunding)

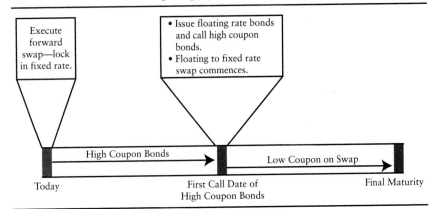

essentially utilize the forward swap as a cash settlement hedge. If, for example, interest rates have risen since the trade date, the swap is "in the money" for the agency; that is, if the swap were terminated the provider would be required to pay the agency a termination amount. Depending on market conditions, including the relationship between the tax-exempt and taxable yield curves, the agency might be able to achieve a better financing result by terminating the swap (and collecting its settlement amount) and either leaving the bonds that were to be refunded outstanding, or issuing conventional fixed rate bonds as a current refunding. See Exhibit 17.5.

Swaption

A swap option, or a swaption, is similar to a forward swap in that the swaption outlines the terms of a swap to be entered into in the future. However, in a swaption, one party, usually the provider, has the right, but not the obligation, to enter into (or modify or cancel) that swap with the other party, the agency, at a specified fixed rate and floating rate formula, on a specified date or during a specified period in the future. In exchange for that right, the provider will pay an option premium to the agency on the trade date, which can be months or years prior to the swap's potential effective date.

   This structure is sometimes used in connection with the refinancing of debt that cannot be advance refunded because of tax law restrictions. In such a case, the fixed rate on the swap that underlies the option is the *strike rate* (which might be structured to equal the average coupon on the outstanding bonds) and the provider may only have a limited time frame (on or just before the first call date of the bonds) to exercise its option. If the provider exercises its option, the agency will issue variable rate bonds at that time, call the outstanding bonds, and on a net basis have a synthetic fixed rate as a result. The payments associated with that fixed rate will be approximately the same as prior to the swap. The option premium received by the agency then would be reflective of the agency's refunding savings. If the provider does not exercise its swaption, the agency will have received its premium while retaining the ability to call the old debt at a later date and, therefore, may have yet another opportunity to refund those bonds.

Option or Obligation?

An *option* is a contract that provides the right, but not the obligation, to enter into or effect a transaction for prespecified terms within a predetermined time period, or *exercise period*. The entity that sells the option (and usually receives an up-front payment in exchange), has an obligation to fulfill the terms of the transaction if the option is exercised. The exercise period can vary from a single date in the future (a European option), to a series of single, periodic dates (a Bermudean option), to any date within a specified date range (an American option). Agencies that utilize these tools should be aware of the associated obligations that may arise in the future and plan accordingly.

Interest Rate Caps, Floors, and Collars

An *interest rate cap* is a hedging tool that protects the purchaser of the cap from rises in short-term interest rates through receiving a payment from the provider when the interest rate on the underlying exceeds a specified strike rate (the *cap rate*). By contrast, in the case of an *interest rate floor*, the agency would receive a premium and would be obligated to make payments to the provider to the extent the strike rate (the *floor rate*) exceeded the rate on the underlying. An *interest rate collar* is a combination of both an interest rate cap and interest rate floor which can be structured such that the cap premium and floor premium offset each other and, therefore, on a net basis, no premium(s) are paid by the agency. Similar to an interest rate swap, basis risk will exist to the extent the rate on the *underlying* does not equal the agency's bond interest rate in any given period. Exhibit 17.6 shows an example of an interest rate cap (with a strike rate of 4.75%) and an interest rate floor (with a strike rate of 2.25%) and, when combined, the two represent an interest rate collar.

USES AND BENEFITS

Although a swap does not itself represent debt, it is usually tied to one or more debt issuances. As such, swaps are used to change the economics of ex-

EXHIBIT 17.6   Interest Rate Cap, Floor, and Collar

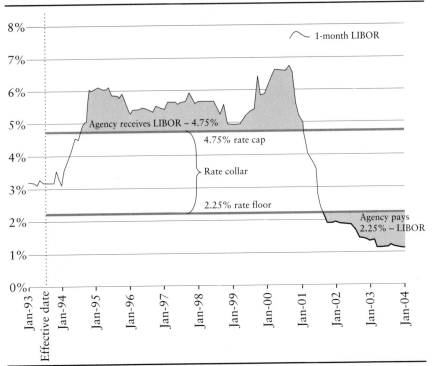

isting or future debt without changing the size or structure of the debt itself. When used as part of a coherent strategy, swaps provide access to different markets and more flexible structures than have been historically available to agencies when straight fixed rate or variable rate debt were the only options. Swaps can also be entered into for any term, and can therefore be useful for addressing near-term cash flow and other liability management needs, for example, during the construction period of a debt-financed project in which an agency does not wish to change the underlying structure of outstanding long-term debt.

Swap structures are most commonly explored because of the potential reduced borrowing costs, but entering into a swap agreement can benefit an agency in other ways. Beyond any cost savings, the uses and benefits of debt-related swaps by agencies can generally be described as falling into four broad categories:

- Swaps afford increased flexibility in the design of an agency's asset/liability matching strategy.

- Swaps serve as a way to hedge certain interest rate and market risks.
- Swaps can enable an agency to access interest rate markets otherwise either unavailable or unattractive with traditional debt structures.
- Swaps can be used to generate cash payments to the agency in exchange for certain adjusted terms or options sold to the provider.

Asset/Liability Matching

Agencies are becoming increasingly attentive to comprehensive asset/liability management strategies. Historically, debt and investment decisions were often made independently of each other, and governmental agencies typically borrowed at long-term fixed rates and invested at short-term rates. Particularly in an interest rate environment where the yield curve is steep, agencies with significant funds invested short-term have felt the adverse impact of a debt strategy which does not account for such an environment. With their relative ease of structuring, implementation, and termination, swaps can be a useful tool in restructuring the debt side of an agency's balance sheet to better reflect certain asset positions. Such a unified and coordinated strategy can allow an agency to use either side of the balance sheet to more readily anticipate uncertain cash flow needs that might be presented by the other side.

Hedging of Interest Rate and Market Risks

The most common type of debt-related swaps is the floating-to-fixed and fixed-to-floating rate swap. In the first scenario, a swap is used to create a synthetic fixed rate obligation where the underlying debt is variable. This presents an alternative to issuing true fixed rate debt by allowing the agency to utilize the short-term capital markets while not exposing it to interest rate risk. Under certain market conditions, influenced by factors such as the steepness of the yield curve, credit spreads, and current or expected income tax rates, true fixed rate debt will carry a higher interest cost, and so a floating-to-fixed rate swap can serve to lower the borrowing costs of the debt. Such swaps are also useful when an agency wishes to convert existing variable rate debt to a fixed rate obligation without the time and costs of a bond refunding. This is particularly common when an agency anticipates a future period of rising interest rates, and wishes to limit its variable rate exposure in connection with given debt for a certain period of time.

In the fixed-to-floating rate swap scenario, synthetic variable rate debt is created where the underlying debt is fixed. In this context, an agency is able to create variable rate debt exposure without the traditional costs of true variable rate debt (e.g., liquidity, letter of credit, or remarketing fees, etc.)

and without exposure to the risk the bonds will be tendered by their holders and not remarketed. In this way, an agency can also achieve a better matching of a given bond issue's short-term assets with the debt, thereby mitigating the risk of significant negative arbitrage on large cash balances. Additionally, this structure is useful for certain borrowers that are unable to easily acquire the necessary insurance or liquidity support for true variable rate debt.

When structured on a forward basis, a floating-to-fixed swap can be used to hedge against rising interest rates. This can be particularly valuable in the context of large or long-term debt restructurings. For example, a forward funding swap can enable an agency to achieve a synthetic advance refunding of fixed rate debt when it is otherwise precluded from doing so by the tax rules limiting advance refundings. By entering into a forward swap today, an agency can lock in today's fixed rates, while the swap payments do not actually begin until after the call date of the old bonds. At that point, variable rate current refunding bonds are issued, and the agency has thereby replaced the old true fixed rate debt with synthetic fixed rate debt at today's rates (but determined via the forward yield curve). This provides an effective hedge against interest rate risk if an agency considers today's environment to be favorable, and is concerned that such an environment might no longer exist once the call date of the old debt is reached.

An important element of swaps is the ease with which they can be terminated or renegotiated. Early terminations can be motivated by the desire to regain the exposure of the underlying debt structure, or the opportunity to monetize a market gain on the swap. Some agencies have a swap management strategy to terminate the swap (in whole, or in part) when a significant termination fee would be owed to the agency and then subsequently replace the swap when interest rates cycle in the opposite direction.

Achieving Access to Different Interest-Rate Markets

Swaps are frequently used to lower an agency's borrowing costs by providing access to interest rate markets otherwise unavailable or unattractive with traditional debt structures. For example, while the traditional tax-exempt fixed income market generally provides governmental issuers access to cheaper capital than its taxable counterpart, the greater liquidity and flexibility of the swap market can often present even more borrowing cost savings opportunities. Also, in certain interest rate environments (e.g., historically low rates), the difference, or "compression," between taxable and tax-exempt rates can increase the pricing advantage of synthetic fixed rate bonds over traditional fixed rate bonds. As will be discussed in the next section, when considering these relative advantages, agencies must carefully analyze the possible impact of basis cost and the potential that it might reduce and/or eliminate the projected cost advantage. Further, swaps can allow an agency to diversify its exposure to different markets, which is often a goal in and of itself.

The creation of synthetic fixed rate or variable rate debt can also enable an agency to maintain some characteristics of one type of debt while accessing some characteristics of another. This allows the agency to optimize its debt positions while also simplifying its overall asset/liability position.

Generating Cash Payments

While most swaps contain defined commencement and maturity dates, it can be advantageous for an agency to sell one or more options to the provider relating to a swap or potential swap. Two examples of these are options to extend and options to cancel (or suspend) the swap. In either case, the option gives the provider increased flexibility in the future management and maintenance of the swap, which may be valuable in certain changing interest rate environments. The benefit to the agency may come in the form of an increased rate on its receipt under the swap (or decreased rate on its obligation under the swap). Alternatively, these options can be monetized in whole or in part in the form of a cash payment to the agency upon execution of the swap.

A swap can also be structured such that the agency's obligation under the swap is greater (or its receipt is lower) than would otherwise be the case (i.e., its payment obligations are above the current market). This is an off-market swap, and is characterized by the agency receiving an up-front payment from the provider in exchange for higher future net swap payments from the agency.

Another way to generate cash is through the use of a basis swap with an up-front payment. This can be a standalone structure or it can be layered on top of a floating-to-fixed rate swap. This is most appropriate when the agency either (1) is comfortable that the up-front payment outweighs the basis risk being assumed; or (2) already has a basis position to be neutralized by the basis swap. An additional way to generate a cash payment today is to enter into a swaption, under which the provider is sold the option to enter into a swap over a given term.

BUSINESS RISKS

When entering into a swap, the agency anticipates that the provider will honor its obligations for the full term of the swap (unless the agency exercises its early termination option). Further, when entering into a synthetic fixed rate swap, to convert variable rate debt to a fixed rate obligation, the agency expects that the variable rate payments it receives under the swap will closely approximate the interest rate on the related debt. There are risks, however, that such expectations will not be fulfilled. These risks include:

- Provider credit risk
- Termination risk
- Collateralization risk
- Basis risk and tax risk

We discuss each risk in this section.

Provider Credit Risk

The value of a swap to the agency depends on the ability of the provider to meet its payment obligations under the swap. This risk is addressed, though not eliminated, by requiring some level of provider credit (e.g., AA/Aa2 or A/A2) as a condition to entering into a swap. Provider credit can often be enhanced through an unconditional guarantee by an affiliate of the provider. Credit risk can also be addressed with collateralization requirements and/or provisions that, in the case of provider downgrade, allow for termination of the swap, or require a transfer or assignment of the swap to a creditworthy provider. (See the discussion later in this chapter regarding credit annex).

Termination Risk

Swap agreements allow for termination of the swap in the case of certain *termination events*. Such events may include, in addition to payment defaults on the swap, adverse credit indicators such as a downgrade or a cross default on other obligations, *force majeure*, a challenge to a party's legal obligation to perform its obligations under the swap beyond the parties' control, or other factors. If there is an early termination, one party will owe the other a termination payment reflecting the valuation of the swap under then-current market conditions. If market rates have changed to a party's disadvantage (e.g., if the party is a fixed rate payer and interest rates decline), or even if rates have not changed but the party received an up-front payment on an off-market swap, that party will be "out of the money" on the swap and will owe the other party a termination payment. A termination of a swap, therefore, could result in a substantial unanticipated payment obligation on the part of the agency. This risk can be addressed to a degree through credit enhancement of the agency's obligation and swap agreement provisions basing termination events on the credit of the credit enhancer as opposed to the agency. Because swap agreements generally provide for "two-way" termination payments at market value, an agency may be obligated to make a substantial payment even if termination is the result of provider default or deterioration of the provider's credit.

Collateralization Risk

Swap agreements often require a party that is out of the money on a swap above a negotiated threshold to post collateral even if that party is performing and no termination event has occurred. This may be burdensome for an agency and may raise significant legal issues. Since collateralization thresholds are tied to credit ratings, collateralization risk can also be addressed in part through credit enhancement.

Basis Risk and Tax Risk

When an agency enters into a swap in connection with variable rate debt, for any payment period the variable rate received by the agency under the swap (calculated in accordance with the terms of the swap agreement) may be either greater than or less than the interest rate paid by the agency on the underlying debt. As explained earlier in this chapter, the potential for a disadvantageous mismatch is known as basis risk.

If the variable rate payable to the agency under the swap is calculated based on a taxable index (e.g., 67% of one-month LIBOR) and the related debt is tax-exempt, then the agency is also exposed to tax risk, the risk that the spread between taxable and tax-exempt rates will be less than anticipated (perhaps because of a reduction in marginal tax rates). See Exhibit 17.7 for a historical comparison between LIBOR and the BMA Index, which is often used as a proxy for an agency's floating rate tax-exempt debt.

Basis risk and tax risk can be addressed by structuring the swap as a cost of funds swap. Cost of funds swaps are uncommon, however, since (1) pricing is not as efficient as with an index-based swap; (2) the agency must generally cede some control over the administration of its debt (e.g., interest rate mode changes, monitoring of remarketing agent performance) to the provider; and (3) cost of funds swaps generally convert to an index-based swap under certain adverse circumstances (e.g., agency credit event, challenge to tax-exemption of the debt).

HOW TO ACQUIRE A SWAP

The emergence of swaps has introduced an additional complexity to the issuance of public debt, which is already complicated by a myriad of federal and state rules and regulations. Along with the real world benefits of the

EXHIBIT 17.7   BMA Index versus 67% of One-month LIBOR: Historical Comparison

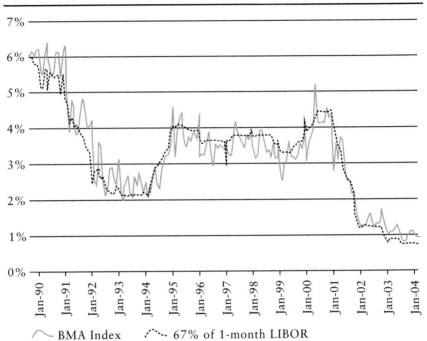

prudent use of swaps comes the responsibility of understanding the mechanics, benefits, and perhaps most important, the risks. Thus, because of the added intricacies that a swap can bring to tax-exempt financing, there are additional issues that an agency must consider when entering into a swap agreement beyond those of a traditional issue of tax-exempt debt.

When an agency undertakes to issue new tax-exempt debt, one of its first and most important tasks is to assemble the appropriate financing team. In the case of a traditional offering, a financing team usually consists of the agency, underwriter(s), bond counsel, financial advisor, disclosure counsel, and trustee. However, given the unique and specialized nature of swaps, if a swap is utilized in a debt offering, the agency may wish to add a swap advisor and/or swap legal counsel to the financing team. It is not unusual for some bond counsel and financial advisory firms to lack the required expertise to advise issuers on the specifics of swap structures, documentation, and pricing. In these instances, the agency will often supplement the financing team's capabilities with firms possessing substantial swap expertise. A swap advisor can offer an agency a diverse line of services tailored to help the agency analyze, develop, and implement a comprehensive swap strategy. Such services include: development of internal swap utilization policies; independent evaluation of proposed interest rate swap structures; risk assessment and stress-testing evaluation; swap structuring and pricing services; competitive bidding services; swap documentation review and consulting; fair market pricing certification; termination valuation and negotiating services; and swap position monitoring and reporting services. With specialized expertise in the swap industry, a swap advisor often proves to be an invaluable tool employed by agencies seeking to maximize the benefits of utilizing swaps as part of a diversified asset and liability portfolio.

The roles of the swap advisor include:

- Transaction structuring
- Pricing negotiations
- Document review
- Competitive bidding
- Pricing certification
- Ongoing monitoring

We discuss each role in this section.

The Bidding Process

An agency has two basic approaches to acquiring, or entering into, an interest rate swap:

- Conduct a competitive bid process.
- Negotiate the terms with a preselected provider.

As with the sale of bonds or other governmental debt, the advantages and disadvantages of the competitive versus negotiated transaction are debatable and difficult to quantify given the complexities of today's financial markets. With appropriate prudence and safeguards, an agency can acquire a fairly priced swap with either approach.

Competitive Bid

Once an agency has concluded that entering into a swap agreement is a prudent option to achieve its financial objectives (e.g., hedging interest rate exposure, improving asset/liability matches, achieving a lower borrowing cost, and so on), its first step is to work with its swap advisor to draft a comprehensive bid package for eventual dissemination to qualified bidders. Qualified bidders would typically consist of appropriately experienced and creditworthy institutions, which also qualify under the agency's general policy standards.

The bid package would typically include:

- A description of the agency's financing plan.
- A term sheet with the desired terms of the swap (which can be very detailed in order to avoid protracted negotiation over the swap documentation and should address all of the terms likely to be included in the swap documents that are material to the agency).
- Relevant information on the agency's credit.

Exhibit 17.8 identifies what a term sheet might include.

EXHIBIT 17.8   Term Sheet

General	
Counterparty party A (provider)	[to be awarded]
Counterparty party B (agency)	City of Anytown
Notional amount	See Exhibit A [typically the bond amortization]
Currency	U.S. dollars
Trade date	January 15, 200__
Effective date	February 1, 200__
Termination date	February 1, 203__
Fixed Amounts	
Fixed rate payer	Agency
Fixed rate option	[to be awarded]
Fixed rate payment dates	August 1 and February 1 beginning August 1, 200__
Fixed rate day count fraction	30/360
Floating Amounts	
Floating rate payer	Provider
Floating rate payer payment dates	1st day of each month beginning March 1, 200__
Floating rate option	67% of the USD-LIBOR-BBA (one-month maturity)
Floating rate day count fraction	Actual/Actual

Once a draft bid package has been circulated and commented on by the agency's financing team, including legal counsel, the agency and/or its swap advisor would then distribute the draft bid package to qualified providers. Circulating a draft bid package allows the agency to solicit feedback and address any concerns that the provider community may have regarding the agency's credit and/or financing plan.

Often the feedback received during this premarketing effort can provide the agency with important structuring considerations for its overall financing plan. For example, less creditworthy agencies may benefit from swap dealer feedback to determine the additional cost of their "credit penalty" and the advisability of credit-enhancing the swap through either third-party insurance or some type of collateral arrangement (referred to as a *credit support annex*), much like evaluating bond insurance.

After receiving feedback from an adequate number of interested swap dealers and reasonable assurances of sufficient interest, the agency would schedule a formal bid and circulate the final terms it desires. On the bid date, swap dealers submit bids and the swap is entered into with the winning bidder.

If an agency is offering to pay a fixed rate and receive a floating rate, the winning bidder will be that conforming bidder which is willing to accept the lowest fixed payment in exchange for the desired floating payment. If an agency is offering to pay a floating rate and receive a fixed rate, the winning bidder will be that conforming bidder that is willing to pay the highest fixed rate in exchange for receiving the floating payment. Often, dealers will submit conditions with their bids. In these instances, the agency and its financing team must evaluate the conditions of each bid to determine if it still conforms to the terms of the bid process.

Once a winning provider has been selected, the provider offers draft documents detailing the terms and conditions of the swap. (An overview of swap documentation is provided later in this chapter.) The agency and its financing team then review the draft documents and negotiate any specific terms that they might find objectionable or absent from the documents. Once these negotiations are complete, the agency and the provider will execute the swap documents and the exchange of payments will commence as prescribed.

Negotiated Bid

As with a negotiated sale of bonds, where an agency negotiates the debt structure and cost with an underwriter, an agency can select a single swap dealer (or limited group of dealers) with which it can negotiate the terms of an interest rate swap. The selection of a provider in a negotiated swap transaction is usually based on a number of factors including past relationships, special expertise, experience, size and overall capabilities, creditworthiness, innovative ideas, fees, and the like. An agency should consider all of these factors prior to selecting the provider in a negotiated swap transaction.

Typically, an agency will utilize an interest rate swap in connection with a debt financing. In such cases, the agency often selects its senior bond underwriter as the designated provider. The senior underwriter structures the swap as an integrated part of the overall financing plan, and collects a fee for its usual underwriting and structuring services, while also being compensated for its principal position as the provider.

Once financing and swap structures have been settled upon, the agency and its underwriter will set a pricing date on which the bonds and the swap will be priced. The underwriter, acting as the swap dealer, will offer the agency the swap at a price that it deems to be fair market.

Once the agency has accepted an offer for the swap pricing, the underwriter provides draft documents setting forth the terms and conditions of the swap. After reviewing these documents and negotiating the final terms, the agency and underwriter execute the final documents and the swap commences.

Pricing and the Swap Advisor

As mentioned previously, a recently emerging role in the public finance industry has been that of the swap advisor. Given the complexities and nuances of the swap market, many agencies have elected to utilize the specialized skills and capabilities of a swap advisor whose responsibilities can include a wide range of services, such as policy development, transaction structuring, pricing negotiations, document review, competitive bidding, pricing certification, and ongoing monitoring.

Of all the elements to a swap transaction that these services address, perhaps the most important is pricing. While transparency in the pricing of vanilla swap transactions has improved significantly, the pricing on transactions that include more exotic elements can differ significantly from one swap dealer to another. In order for an agency to be secure that it is entering into a swap at a fair market price, it is important that some criteria or process for establishing the fair market price for its swap be in place. In addition to using publicly available or subscription-based pricing data (e.g., Bloomberg), a Swap Advisor will monitor the prospective providers' pre-trade date pricing indications and then advise the agency on final pricing.

Also, posttrade, agencies will generally need ongoing pricing updates ("marked-to-market") on existing swap transactions for accounting purposes. (See the discussion on accounting issues later in this chapter.)

Swap Policies

It is increasingly considered prudent financial management for governmental entities considering the use of an interest rate swap to put into place a written swap policy. Such a policy should be approved by the entity's governing body and clearly address the following:

1. The entity's rationale for utilizing interest rate swaps
2. Permitted instruments
3. Approved transaction types
4. Risk and benefit analysis procedures
5. Procurement and execution procedures
6. Counterparty eligibility requirements
7. Collateral requirements
8. Documentation requirements

A swap advisor and legal counsel expert in swap transactions can assist in the development and implementation of swap policies.

LEGAL ISSUES

Public agencies, unlike other entities, are characterized by limited powers and compartmentalized revenues and obligations. State constitutions and statutes can raise challenging issues and care must be exercised in the integration of swaps with an agency's other obligations, in particular the agency's debt.

The legal issues to be discussed in this section include:

- Authority to enter into swaps
- Sources of payment and security
- Integration with bond documents

Legal Authority

In states, or for particular entities, that do not have legislation granting express authority to enter into swap agreements, an agency's authority to enter into a swap must be derived from that agency's general power to enter into contracts in furtherance of its governmental purposes. Often the particular statute authorizing the related bonds may also authorize other actions necessary or appropriate in connection with issuing the bonds.

A number of states, however, do have statutes expressly authorizing public agencies (or certain types of public agencies) to enter into swaps and similar transactions. Such statutes often impose procedural requirements. Public agencies may, for example, only enter into swaps following a determination by the agency's governing body that the proposed swap is designed to achieve one of the purposes specified in the authorizing statute (e.g., reducing interest rate risk, lowering the cost of borrowing, enhancing the relationship between risk and return on investments). Some states require providers to satisfy various credit criteria.

Constitutional Issues

In addition to concerns about legal authority to enter into swaps, constitutional issues may arise as well. For example, in the case of public agencies subject to constitutional debt limits, when the agency's obligations under a swap are payable from the agency's general fund, as distinguished from enterprise revenues, such obligations might qualify for the broadly recognized special fund exception to the debt limit. Interest rate swaps are unique. They are unlike debts, investments, insurance, or anything else, and there is very little case law analyzing how swaps or certain swap features, such as an obligation to pay a termination payment, are to be treated for such legal purposes. Counsel asked to opine that a particular swap is not a prohibited indebtedness must evaluate carefully both the particulars and the overall economic substance of the transaction and in some cases may require structural changes to certain swap provisions (e.g., eliminating or qualifying the agency's obligation to make a termination payment to a defaulting provider or subjecting the agency's payment obligation to an appropriation contingency). In most cases, however, state constitutional debt limitation issues have a greater effect on the swap opinion than on the swap itself.

Sources of Payment and Security

It is common and generally appropriate for an agency's obligations under a swap agreement to be payable from the same source as the debt or asset to which the swap relates. If a swap is entered into in connection with an agency's general fund debt or with respect to the investment of general fund assets, for example, the agency's obligations on the swap are usually payable out of the agency's general fund. If the swap is entered into in connection with debt issued under an agency's master trust indenture, it is appropriate for the agency's obligations on the swap to be secured by such master indenture; and if a swap is entered into in connection with the debt or investments of an agency's enterprise fund, the agency's obligations on the swap would normally be payable solely out of the revenues of such enterprise. Swap documents should limit the agency's obligations accordingly. Similarly, cross-default and credit events (usually included in termination events) should be limited to the same source of funds.

Further, with respect to swap obligations payable from enterprise revenues, the priority of payment versus other obligations payable from such revenues must be specified. Often revenues have been pledged to secure bonds and the swap either cannot qualify as a parity obligation or it is not desirable to treat it under the additional indebtedness or rate covenant tests. Accordingly, many swaps are secured by and payable from revenues on a subordinate basis to the bonds. Many modern indentures specifically contemplate parity swaps. However, even in those cases, because a termination payment on a swap could be a significant lump sum and could distort debt service coverage ratios, and even the ability to pay debt service on the bonds, it is common for termination payments on a swap to be payable on a basis subordinate to the payment of regular swap payments and enterprise revenue debt.

Integration with Bond Documents

Provisions relative to payments and receipts on swaps entered into in connection with bonds or other debt obligations should be integrated into the bond documents. This is of particular importance if the intention is to produce synthetic fixed rate debt by combining a swap with variable rate debt. An indenture executed and delivered in anticipation of a swap should provide for regular swap payments on a parity with debt and should treat amounts received on swaps as a reduction in debt service (as opposed to an addition to revenues). Otherwise, debt service coverage calculations will not reflect the integration accurately.

Bankruptcy

Should the provider go into bankruptcy, or become the subject of some other type of insolvency proceeding, the agency may face a number of different risks. The provider may be able to repudiate the swap and refuse to perform further. The provider may have a period of time in which to decide whether or not it wants to continue to perform, and it may be able to suspend its performance while it makes that decision. The provider may be able to transfer the swap to another provider without the consent of the agency, even if the transfer is in violation of the terms of the swap. In addition, the agency may be required to continue performing under the swap even though the provider is not required to do so. The netting provisions of the swap may not be enforceable. The agency may be required to return all payments that it has received under the swap for a specified period of time prior to the bankruptcy or insolvency; such period may be as long as one year. The agency may be required to return the collateral that secures the swap. The agency may be unable to foreclose on any collateral securing the swap without court permission, and the court is not required to give its permission. Similarly, the agency may be unable to take any other action to enforce the provisions of the swap without court permission. The agency may not be able to terminate the swap, even if the swap provides that it can be terminated upon the bankruptcy or insolvency of the provider. There are a number of other possible risks associated with the bankruptcy or insolvency of a provider and the bankruptcy and insolvency risks that are present in any swap will depend on the specific facts of the transaction. As a result, an agency that has concerns about bankruptcy and insolvency issues should consult with counsel experienced in this area.

TAX ISSUES

A swap entered into in connection with an issue of tax-exempt bonds may impact certain tax matters relating to those bonds. Specifically, the nature of the swap structure will determine if the agency may or must take into account the payments under the swap in its determination of arbitrage rebate liability in connection with the bonds.

Section 103 of the Internal Revenue Code of 1986 (the Code) provides generally that income on a state or local government bond is exempt from gross income for federal tax purposes so long as, among other things, the bond in question is not an *arbitrage bond* within the meaning of Section 148 of the Code. An arbitrage bond is generally defined by the Code as "any bond issued as part of an issue any portion of the proceeds of which are reasonably expected (at the time of issuance of the bond) to be used directly or indirectly to acquire higher yielding investments . . . ." Therefore, the relevant benchmark in determining whether a bond is an arbitrage bond is the yield on the bond.

The Treasury Regulations under Section 148 of the Code (the Treasury Regulations) provide detailed rules for determining the yield on an issue of bonds, whether fixed or variable rate. In determining that yield, the agency is permitted to take into account certain payments associated with a *qualified hedge*. A hedge is a contract entered into primarily to modify the agency's risk of interest rate changes, such as an interest rate swap contract.

Amounts paid or received by an agency pursuant to a swap contract which meets the definition of a qualified hedge have the effect of increasing or decreasing, respectively, the yield on the bonds, and accordingly will impact the agency's potential arbitrage rebate liability and yield restriction limitations. Amounts paid by an agency pursuant to such a swap contract will permit the agency to invest the proceeds of the bonds at a higher return. Conversely, amounts received by an agency will lower the rate of return an issuer may earn on investments made with bond proceeds.

Qualified Hedges: Regular Integration

For an issuer of bonds to take into account or *integrate* payments made or received on a swap in the determination of bond yield, the swap must meet the definition of a qualified hedge set forth in the Treasury Regulations. In order to meet the definition of a qualified hedge, the following eight criteria factors must be satisfied:

- Interest rate hedge
- No significant investment element
- Unrelated parties
- Contract covers substantially identical bonds
- Interest-based contract
- Payments closely correspond
- Same source of payments
- Hedge must be identified

We discuss each factor next.

If a swap satisfies all eight of the criteria, the swap is treated as a qualified hedge, and accordingly payments made or received by the agency under the swap are included in the determination of yield on the bonds. A swap satisfying the definition of a qualified hedge in the Treasury Regulations is terminated upon the sale or disposition of the swap by the agency, when the agency acquires an offsetting swap, when the bonds subject to the swap contract are redeemed, or when the swap ceases to be a qualified hedge as discussed above. Upon the termination of a swap that is a qualified hedge, the agency must treat any payments received or paid in connection with the termination as payments made or received on the hedged bonds for purposes of determining bond yield. If such payments are made by the agency, bond yield will be increased; and if such payments are received by the agency, bond yield will be decreased.

Interest Rate Hedge

The swap contract must be entered into primarily to modify the agency's risk of interest rate changes with respect to a bond.

No Significant Investment Element

The swap contract must not contain a significant investment element. Generally, a swap contract contains a significant investment element if a significant portion of any payment by one party relates to a conditional or unconditional obligation by the other party to make a payment on a different date. For example, a swap contract requiring any payments other than periodic payments (such as a payment for an off-market swap), or an interest rate cap which calls for the agency to pay an up-front premium, might be determined to have a significant investment element. If a single payment for an off-market swap is made by the provider to the agency; however, the agency may still treat the swap as a qualified hedge if: (1) the provider's payment to the agency and the agency's payments under the swap in excess of those that the agency would make if the swap bore an on-market rate are separately identified in a certification of the provider; and (2) the payments described in (1) are not treated as payments on the swap.

Unrelated Parties

The agency and the provider must be unrelated parties.

Contract Covers Substantially Identical Bonds

The swap contract must cover, in whole or in part, all of one or more groups of substantially identical bonds of the issue. For example, the contract may cover all of the fixed rate bonds having the same interest rate, maturity, and terms. The contract may also cover a pro rata portion of each interest payment on a variable rate bond issue. This somewhat formalistic requirement necessitates special drafting when an agency wishes to hedge only part of its interest rate risk on particular maturities.

In addition, the issue of bonds resulting after all payments pursuant to the swap contract are taken into account must also have terms substantially similar to a bond described in the Treasury Regulations. In the context of variable rate debt instruments, agencies are generally comfortable that the terms of the resulting bonds satisfy this requirement if the variable interest rate on the swap is within, or would be within, 25 basis points (0.25%) of the hedged bonds if otherwise issued as variable rate bonds.

Interest-Based Contract

The contract must be primarily interest based. That is, the hedged bonds must, without regard to the swap contract, be either fixed rate bonds or one of several variable rate debt instruments described in the Treasury Regulations. In addition, after all payments pursuant to the swap contract are taken into account as additional payments on the hedged bonds, the terms of the resulting bonds must be substantially similar to a bond described in the preceding sentence. Generally, issuers are comfortable that the terms of the resulting bonds are similar to a variable rate debt instrument if the variable interest rate on the swap and the interest rate on the hedged bonds are or would be within 25 basis points (0.25%) of each other on the date the swap contract is entered into.

Payments Closely Correspond

The payments received by the agency from the provider must correspond closely in time to either the specific payments being hedged on the hedged bonds, or specific payments required to be made pursuant to the bond documents, irrespective of the hedge. These payments might include payments to a sinking fund, debt service fund or similar fund maintained for the issue of which the hedged bond is a part.

Same Source of Payments

Payments by the agency to the provider must be reasonably expected to be made from the same source of funds that, absent the swap, would be reasonably expected to be used to pay principal of and interest on the hedged bonds.

Hedge Must be Identified

While a qualified hedge may be entered into by either the actual issuer of the bonds or a conduit borrower, the actual issuer must identify the hedge on its books and records maintained for the hedged bonds not later than three days after the date on which the hedge contract is entered into. The identification must contain sufficient detail to establish that the requirements of a qualified hedge have been satisfied and must specify the provider, the terms of the swap, and the hedged bonds. In addition, the hedge transaction must be noted on the first form relating to the issue of which the hedged bonds are a part that is filed with the Internal Revenue Service (i.e., the form 8038 or 8038–G submitted in connection with the issuance of the bonds).

Qualified Hedges: Superintegration

Certain qualified hedges relating to floating-to-fixed rate swaps have been accorded unique tax treatment—although variable rate bonds, the yield on the variable rate bonds will be treated as a fixed rate yield. While regular integration calls for the inclusion of payments made or received on a swap in the determination of bond yield, in these certain cases the bond yield is simply the stated fixed rate of the swap.

These swaps are often referred to as *superintegrated swaps*. Superintegrated swaps, and the accompanying ability to treat a variable rate bond issue as a synthetic fixed rate issue, offer several advantages over the normal qualified hedge rules set forth above.

Because the yield on a fixed rate issue does not change, an agency may more effectively plan its investment of bond proceeds, making certain that the yield on its investments does not violate applicable arbitrage restrictions. An issuer of bonds seeking to advance refund (i.e., use the proceeds of a refunding bond issue to refund bonds more than 90 days from the date of issue of the refunding bonds) an older issue of bonds, where the proceeds of the refunding bonds are invested in an escrow for a long period of time until the prior bonds can be refunded, will desire certainty that the yield on the investments in the refunding escrow does not exceed applicable arbitrage yield restrictions on the refunding bonds. This certainty results from being able to disregard any differences (so-called *basis differences*) between the variable rate on the bonds and the variable rate on the swap.

Finally, because the yield on a fixed yield bond issue is calculated only once, on the issue date, where true fixed rate bonds and synthetic fixed rate bonds are combined in a single bond issue, the yield on a synthetic fixed rate issue will usually be higher during initial computation periods than the yield on a similar variable rate issue. This is because the higher yielding, longer term bonds will have a greater effect in the fixed yield calculation, as compared to the more limited effect those longer term, higher yielding bonds would have in initial computation periods in a variable yield calculation.

In order to qualify as a superintegrated hedge, the swap contract must meet the rules set forth above, as well as the following:

- Maturity
- Payments closely correspond in time
- Aggregate payments fixed

We discuss these additional hedge features to achieve superintegration next.

Maturity

The term of the swap contract must be equal to the entire period during which the hedged bonds bear a variable rate of interest, and the agency must reasonably expect that the swap contract will not be terminated before the end of that period.

Payments Closely Correspond in Time

Payments to be received by the agency or the provider under the swap contract must correspond closely in time to the hedged portion of payments on the hedged bonds. According to the Treasury Regulations, payments received within 15 days of the related payments on the hedged bonds generally correspond closely.

Aggregate Payments Fixed

After taking into account all payments made and received under the swap contract, the agency's aggregate payments must be "fixed and determinable" as of no later than 15 days after the issue date of the bonds. Payments on the bonds are treated as fixed if: (1) payments on the bonds are based on one interest rate; (2) payments received on the swap are based on a second interest rate that is substantially the same as, but not identical to, the first interest rate; and (3) payments on the bonds would be fixed if the two rates were identical.

For example, the BMA Index is likely to be substantially the same as an agency's individual seven-day interest rate, and a swap whereby the provider is required to make payments to the agency based on the BMA Index (possibly increased or decreased by an appropriate spread) should be eligible for superintegration. A more thorough analysis would need to be undertaken, however, to determine whether a swap under which the provider is required to make payments to the agency based on an index which is not a tax-exempt variable rate index (such as a percentage of LIBOR chosen to approximate the BMA rate) may be eligible for superintegration.

For accounting purposes, the interest payments an agency makes on the hedged bonds are treated as equal to the payments received by the agency under the superintegrated swap when calculating the yield on the hedged bonds. Accordingly, the only payments taken into account in calculating the yield on the hedged bonds are the payments the agency makes under the superintegrated swap.

If an agency terminates a superintegrated swap within five years of the date of issue of the bonds, the agency must recompute the yield on the bonds as if the bonds were originally issued as a variable rate issue. If the swap is terminated after five years of the date of issue of the bonds, the issue of which the hedged bonds are a part is treated as if it were reissued as of the termination date of the swap for purposes of calculating the arbitrage yield on the bonds.

The deemed reissuance or recomputation of arbitrage yield due to the termination of a superintegrated swap is only applicable for purposes of the arbitrage rebate rules and does not apply to the rules with respect to yield restrictions set forth in Section 148 of the Code. This distinction is most relevant in the context of an advance refunding escrow; if the termination of a swap results in a recomputed arbitrage yield which is lower than the escrow yield, this presents only a potentially positive arbitrage rebate liability and not a yield restriction violation.

Anticipatory Swaps

Often, an agency will want to enter into a swap prior to the issue date of its bonds in an effort to, among other things, hedge against interest rate fluctuations prior to the bond issuance. This is called an "anticipatory hedge." The Treasury Regulations divide anticipatory swaps into two categories:

1. Swaps expected to be terminated upon the issuance of the bonds.
2. Swaps not expected to be terminated upon the issuance of the bonds.

For swaps expected to be terminated substantially contemporaneously with the issuance of the bonds, the amount paid or received, or deemed to be paid or received, by the agency to terminate the contract is treated as an adjustment to the issue price and proceeds, respectively, of the bonds. Special rules apply if the swap is not actually terminated substantially contemporaneously with the issue date of the hedged bonds.

For swaps not expected to terminate upon the issuance of the bonds, the agency does not take into account payments made or received before the issuance of the bonds, but will take into account the payments made after the issue date. Special rules apply if the swap is, in fact, terminated in connection with the issuance of the hedged bond.

Anticipatory hedges must, within three days of the date the hedge contract is entered into, meet the identification requirement set forth above and must specify the reasonably expected governmental purpose, issue price, maturity and issue date of the hedged bond, the manner in which interest is reasonably expected to be computed on the hedged bond, and whether the swap is expected to terminate upon issuance of the hedged bonds.

DOCUMENTATION AND NEGOTIATION

Documentation

Swap agreements are generally based on the ISDA (International Swaps and Derivatives Association, Inc.) master agreement, which was developed with the hope of creating uniformity within the market. The *master agreement* itself is a preprinted form, and is accompanied by the schedule and, if applicable, the credit support annex. The *schedule* designates the parties' elections among options presented in the master agreement, amends master agreement provisions as negotiated by the parties, and addresses additional deal terms not covered by the master agreement. The *credit support annex*, when present, details collateralization requirements, terms and mechanics. A confirmation, detailing the terms of that particular transaction, is entered into in connection with each trade. An overview of each of these documents required in a swap agreement is outlined below.

- *ISDA master agreement.* The standardized master legal agreement for all derivative transactions between the agency and a provider that states standardized definitions, terms and representations governing the swap transaction(s).
- *Schedule to the master agreement.* A schedule amending or supplementing the ISDA master agreement in order to set out the specific business terms and conditions governing the transaction(s) executed under the agreement.
- *Credit support annex.* A document governed by the ISDA master agreement which states the provisions regarding the mutual posting of collateral, if required, under the ISDA schedule to the master agreement. The need to post collateral is triggered by designated events (e.g., if the credit rating of one party drops below an agreed upon rating level, or if the market value of the swap exceeds a threshold for a given rating level of either the agency or the provider).
- *Confirmation.* A document governed by the ISDA master agreement that is executed for an individual transaction, itemizing the specific terms and conditions for that particular transaction. Each confirmation contains the pricing terms of the particular swap transaction (e.g., fixed or variable rate, notional amount and amortization, termination options) and is executed by the parties at the time of the trade.

The master agreement, schedule, and credit support annex are designed to apply to all of a series of swaps entered into between the parties.

Swap documentation can be difficult to read and understand because the basic documentation forms do not address precisely the legal and business issues particular to public agencies and tend to be oriented toward the provider. Additionally, swap documentation can cover termination event/payment and other real financial risks to the agency, which can be narrowed or eliminated through careful negotiation. It is, therefore, essential that an agency considering a swap take it as seriously as the issuance of bonds and be assisted by legal and financial advisors experienced with municipal swaps.

Major Points of Negotiation

As with any negotiated contract, understanding the needs and perspectives of the other party, as well as one's own, is essential to reaching a mutually satisfying outcome. The process of such negotiations will reflect the relative values assigned by each party to various structures, with the optimal result that the needs of both parties are addressed. Because the early termination of a swap can have a significant adverse impact and because various dispute resolution approaches are unsuitable for governmental agencies, termination, credit, and dispute resolution issues, for example, are usually diligently negotiated. The following is a brief list of some of the points that are often subject to negotiation.

Termination and Credit Related Points

Termination and credit related points include:

- *Downgrade termination.* Swap agreements generally allow one party to terminate the swap at its market value if the other party's long-term, unsecured debt rating falls below a given level. This provision allows the nondowngraded party an opportunity to exit the swap and eliminate its credit exposure to the downgraded party. The threshold level can vary (below A–/A3 and below BBB/Baa3 are common).
- *Cross-default termination.* Swap agreements generally allow one party to terminate the swap at its market value if the other party defaults on other obligations of particular types (*specified indebtedness*) above a specified size (the *threshold amount*). Specified indebtedness should be limited to obligations germane to the sources from which the agency is obligated to make payments on the swap. The specified indebtedness and threshold amount should reflect an order of magnitude indicating significant financial difficulty in the case of default. It is therefore not uncommon for the threshold amount for the provider (generally a

large financial institution) to be significantly greater than the threshold amount for the agency.

■ *Incorporation of bond documents.* Swap agreements generally incorporate provisions of the indenture or other documents pursuant to which the related bonds are issued or secured. This is appropriate to the extent that the incorporated provisions are important in securing the agency's obligations under the swaps. However, since any default of an incorporated provision is typically a termination event under the swap, many provisions of the indenture or other documents (like accounting, notices filings, maintenance, covenants) are not appropriate for incorporation.

■ *Incipient illegality.* Swap agreements may contain provisions allowing the provider to terminate the swap upon the occurrence of an "incipient illegality" (e.g., introduction or enactment of legislation, a public declaration by the agency, etc. challenging the validity of swaps similar to the agency's swap). The rationale is that if an event occurs that would make the swap agreement invalid, or would assert that the swap agreement is not a valid obligation of an agency, the provider should be empowered to take action before such illegality is in fact formalized. The agency must be certain that the definition of incipient illegality is not so broad as to result in an unwarranted termination of the swap. Thus, events such as a public official expressing his or her views about swaps in negative terms, the introduction of resolutions or legislation that are never implemented and would probably not affect existing swaps in any event, or even judicial cases finding a swap to be invalid in an unrelated setting, should not be allowed to cause termination due to an overinclusive definition of incipient illegality.

■ *One-way termination/two-way termination.* *Two-way termination* is a (nondefaulting party required to pay defaulting party on termination if nondefaulting party is out of the money). It is the norm for swap transactions. But since, for a public agency, the prospect of an obligation to make a potentially very large unexpected payment to a defaulting provider can be politically unpalatable, an agency may wish to consider *one-way termination*, when only a defaulting party is obligated to pay a termination payment).

■ *Collateralization.* Swap agreements may require a party that is out of the money above a certain threshold to post collateral or provide for collateralization as an alternative to termination for credit downgrade. Points of negotiation include the thresholds at which collateralization will be required (which generally depend upon the long-term, unsecured debt rating of the party at the time), the types of collateral permitted, the level of collateralization, and the frequency of valuation. An obligation to post collateral may present significant financial, and in some cases legal, difficulties for a governmental agency.

- *Setoff.* A *setoff provision* enables a party that is entitled to a payment under the agreement (e.g., a termination payment) to satisfy that obligation by reducing the amount it owes the other party in another transaction. Accordingly, setoff is a way to manage credit exposure. Setoff would allow a provider to debit any deposit accounts the agency has with the provider or an affiliate of the provider to satisfy amounts payable to the provider. For public agencies, for whom moneys are not necessarily interchangeable, a setoff provision can complicate the agency's other business dealings with the provider.
- *Term out.* A *term-out provision* allows the agency to make payments over time for any amount it may be required to pay upon termination of a swap.
- *Optional termination.* An agency should have the right to optionally terminate a swap at market at any time. The particular mechanics, though, can be the subject of further negotiation. Typically, providers can unilaterally terminate the swap agreement only upon the occurrence of agency downgrade or default.
- *Transfer or assignment.* The parties' ability to assign their rights and obligations under a swap (e.g., to an affiliate, to another bond indenture) are often heavily negotiated since an assignment can have major credit implications.
- *Swap insurance.* Swap insurance provides that the agency's payment obligations under the swap are insured. The terms of such insurance are fairly standardized, however, the presence of swap insurance can have a significant impact on negotiations relating to other credit related points described above.

Dispute Resolution Points

Dispute resolution points include:

- *Settlement amount calculations.* When a swap terminates at market, the market value (i.e., the settlement amount) must be determined. The methodology for such determination (e.g., *market quotation* vs. *firm bid*) and identification of the party entitled to manage the process should be described in the swap agreement.
- *Choice of governing law.* Providers uniformly ask that swap agreements be governed by New York law. Providers wish to reduce uncertainty by having their agreements governed by a single jurisdiction's law to the extent possible, and New York has the most developed body of law

relating to sophisticated financial transactions. The agency may request that issues relating to its power and authority to enter into the swap be governed by the laws of its home jurisdiction.

- *Jurisdiction and venue.* Each party would prefer that any dispute arising under a swap agreement be resolved in its local courts. Silence on this matter or mutual, nonexclusive jurisdiction are often acceptable compromises.
- *Jury trial waiver.* Waiver of jury trial is a common provision in sophisticated financial transactions. Some agencies, however, have a firm policy against such waiver, and in some jurisdictions a jury trial waiver may not be enforceable.
- *Waiver of sovereign immunity.* Agreements often purport to have the agency waive sovereign immunity. As a general matter, the exercise of remedies against public agencies is governed by state statute, such that procedural and substantive requirements cannot be waived by contract. A representation that remedies are available should be sufficient.

AFTER THE CLOSE: POSTTRADE MANAGEMENT

From hedging interest rate risks to lowering borrowing costs to introducing flexibility into an agency's overall debt management strategy, the economic motivations for developing and implementing a comprehensive swap strategy are clear. Part of such a strategy should be well conceived plans for:

- Monitoring the performance and effectiveness of the swap.
- Accounting for a changing valuation position of the swap.
- Periodically disclosing consistently the associated terms and risks.

Financial Management

When initially structured, a given swap will contain a stated termination date. This is the date through which the swap will remain in effect in the absence of any voluntary or involuntary termination under the swap documents. However, an agency should not simply assume that all will go as planned, or that the scheduled termination date will or should be reached. Rather, procedures should be in place to monitor the potential advantages of a negotiated (voluntary) termination, and to monitor the risks and consequences of any other kind of early termination.

It is important that an agency that makes use of swap structures have a strategy in place for monitoring changes in the interest rate environment. Changing market conditions will impact the effectiveness and value of a swap, and may even create opportunities for terminations or restructurings with substantial payments to the agency from the provider or with terms more favorable to the agency. As with other financing structures, swaps are very sensitive to changing market conditions and a successful swap strategy should allow for quick action to take advantage of favorable market conditions while those conditions still exist.

Two other examples of options which may present themselves given interest rate environments different from those at the time a swap commenced, are (1) reversing or layering an offsetting swap on top of an existing swap and (2) changing the underlying basis or index of an existing swap. In both examples, the agency that is prudently monitoring existing swap positions may be able to either realize substantial monetary gains or improve the economics of their original swap.

Risk Monitoring

In addition to monitoring for financial strategy and planning reasons, an agency should also monitor changing business risks, such as those outlined earlier in this chapter. While each of those risks is considered at the time a swap is structured, changes in market conditions, counterparty creditworthiness, and even the tax and regulatory environments might effect a change in how the agency values and accounts for the swap. In the case of counterparty solvency, it is important that the agency develops a plan of action in the case of downgrade or other rating triggers or, in the extreme, an event calling for an early termination of the swap. Similarly, the agency may have its own obligations if its ratings are downgraded or it suffers other changes to its financial condition. Markets and circumstances can change rapidly, and it can be costly for an agency to be caught reacting to changes after they occur (even if they effect directly only the provider) without monitoring procedures and plans in place.

Accounting and Disclosure

Before the introduction of FASB 133 ("Accounting for Derivative Instruments and Hedging Activities") and GASB Technical Bulletin No. 2003–1 ("Disclosure Requirements for Derivatives Not Reported at Fair Value on the Statement of Net Assets"), swaps were off-balance-sheet transactions and there was very little consistency regarding how swaps were accounted for or reflected in financial statements, if recognized at all. With the introduction of FASB 133 and GASB Technical Bulletin No. 2003–1, an agency using swaps in connection with the issuance of tax exempt debt should be aware of the additional accounting and disclosure requirements for swaps and the potential impact on its balance sheet. Unlike in the case of accounting for traditional outstanding bonds, an agency using swaps must generally account for and reflect the performance of its swap portfolio in its financial statements.

Under FASB 133, agencies reporting financial results under FASB guidelines must report payments made and received under a swap with interest expense on the balance sheet. Furthermore, all swaps must be recorded as assets or liabilities (depending on whether the swap is in a gain or loss position) at fair market value. Unrealized gains or losses for a given period must be reflected in the earnings for that period. In volatile environments, this can result in large differences from one period to the next. There may be an opportunity, however, if a given swap qualifies as a cash flow hedge, for the agency to make use of hedge accounting, thus reducing some of the impact of changes in unrealized gains and losses on earnings statements. An agency desiring to make use of such hedge accounting should be certain to consult with the proper experts before entering into a swap agreement so as to be sure the swap meets the necessary requirements.

For agencies reporting under the guidance of GASB, GASB Technical Bulletin No. 2003–1 outlines a number of items, which should be disclosed in the financial statement notes for swaps not reported at fair market value on the balance sheet on a given reporting date:

- *Objective.* The agency should disclose its objectives in entering into the swap, and its strategies in achieving those objectives. Also to be disclosed is the broader context leading to the development of those objectives.
- *Significant Terms.* The agency should disclose significant terms of the swap, such as notional amount, interest rates, other financial terms and options, the effective date, and scheduled termination date.
- *Fair Value.* The agency should disclose the fair market value of the swap, as well as the methodology for determining that value.
- *Risks* (e.g., basis, termination). The agency should disclose its updated exposure to various risks through use of the swap, including those outlined earlier in this chapter, as well as changing interest rate risks and market access risk.
- *Associated debt.* In the case that the swap is associated with an underlying debt obligation, the net cash flow of the swap should be disclosed along with the requirements of the underlying debt.

Swaps may have a significant impact on an agency's overall financial position and may present risks material to the holder or purchasers of an agency's bonds. An agency must take care, therefore, to insure that its swaps and attendant risks are adequately disclosed in official statements and continuing disclosure reports. In order to comply with their financial reporting obligations, agencies need to have in place a mechanism to periodically value (mark-to-market) swaps for annual and internal account purposes, in addition to the other purposes set out earlier in this chapter.

APPENDIX: GLOSSARY OF KEY TERMS

Agencies. For the purposes of this chapter, issuers of tax-exempt debt and other entities that have access to the municipal capital markets.

Arbitrage. For federal tax law purposes, the resulting dollar amount, positive or negative, generated by an agency investing tax-exempt bond proceeds at interest rates above (positive arbitrage) or below (negative arbitrage) the rate an agency is paying on an issue of tax-exempt debt obligations (see arbitrage yield).

Arbitrage yield. For federal tax law purposes, the yield on an issue of tax-exempt debt obligations used to calculate the amount of arbitrage earned, positive or negative, by an agency.

Assignment. The transfer of a party's rights and obligations under a swap to another party.

Basis risk. The risk of a mismatch between an agency's floating rate receipt (or payment) on a swap and its floating rate payment (or receipt) on the underlying debt (or asset) as a result of different indexes or terms being used to determine payments and receipts.

Basis spread. The difference in interest rates between an agency's floating rate received (or paid) on a swap and its floating rate paid (or received) on the underlying debt (or asset), which results from different indexes or terms being used to determine payments and receipts.

Basis swap. A floating-to-floating rate swap in which one variable rate index is swapped for another; commonly used to modify basis risk.

Bid date. In a competitive bid transaction, the date on which swap providers submit bids and the swap entered into with the winning provider is priced.

Bid package. Documentation package distributed by or on behalf of an agency to qualified providers, detailing the terms and structure of the swap desired by the agency, which the providers will use to formulate their bid on the scheduled bid date.

BMA index. The BMA Municipal Swap Index (formerly the PSA Municipal Swap Index) is the principal benchmark for the floating rate interest payments for tax-exempt issuers. The BMA Index is a national rate based on a market basket of seven-day non-AMT tax-exempt variable rate demand obligation issues of $10 million or more (typically 650 issues). In 2007, the BMA Index became known as the SIFMA Municipal Swap Index when the The Securities Industry Association and the Bond Market Association merged to become the Securities Industry and Financial Markets Association

Cap. A financial contract under which the provider, in exchange for charging a set premium, will make payments to the agency whenever and to the extent the interest rate on the underlying exceeds a specified strike rate, also known as the cap rate.

Change in tax law risk. The risk that there will be an unanticipated structural change to current tax laws, which would impact the spread between tax-exempt and taxable rates.

Collar. A combination of an interest rate cap and an interest rate floor.

Collateralization risk. Risk that the circumstances under which an agency would have to post collateral pursuant to certain swap agreement provisions will arise in the future.

Competitive bid. Process of entering into a swap agreement where interested swap providers submit bids to the agency on a specified date, and the swap is entered into with the winning provider; usually the provider offering the interest rate terms most favorable to the agency.

Confirmation. Document governed by the ISDA master agreement that is executed for an individual transaction, itemizing the specific terms and conditions for that particular transaction.

Cost of funds. Refers to an agency's actual interest rate cost on its debt obligations, which may or may not include carrying costs such as remarketing fees, liquidity fees, letter of credit fees, and the like, that is sometimes used as the underlying in a swap transaction.

Cost of funds swap. A swap under which the floating leg receipts match the interest payments due on the underlying debt exactly.

Counterparty. A party in a swap transaction. From an agency's perspective, this is synonymous with provider.

Counterparty credit risk. The risk that a party to a swap will not be able to meet all of its financial obligations under the swap.

Credit penalty. The additional requirements (e.g., a higher interest rate, additional insurance, etc.) of a party to a swap imposed due to that party's lower credit rating.

Credit support. Collateral that can be in the form of cash and/or marketable securities posted by one party to a swap agreement to reduce the credit exposure of its counterparty. See also *Swap insurance*.

Credit support annex. Document governed by the ISDA master agreement that states the provisions and circumstances under which posting of collateral is required.

Cross-default termination. The ability of one party to terminate the swap at its market value if the other party defaults on other obligations of particular types.

Downgrade termination. Provision in some swap agreements allowing one party to terminate the swap at its market value if the other party's long-term, unsecured debt rating falls below a given level.

Effective date. The first date on which payment obligations begin to accrue, including the date any up-front payment is exchanged. In the case of a forward swap, payment accruals may not begin for months or even years into the future. When a swap is entered into in connection with an issue of bonds, the effective date is often set to coincide with the issue date of the bonds.

Exercise period. In an option contract, the period of time in which a party has the right to exercise its option and effect a prenegotiated transaction.

Fixed leg. In a swap transaction, the payments made by one party to another based on a predetermined fixed interest rate.

Fixed rate swap. A swap, under which an agency pays a provider a fixed rate in exchange for receiving a floating rate; most commonly used to convert variable rate bonds into synthetic fixed rate obligations.

Fixed-to-floating rate swap. See *Floating rate swap.*

Floating leg. In a swap transaction, the payments made by one party to another based upon a predetermined floating (variable) rate index.

Floating rate swap. A swap, under which an agency pays a provider a variable rate and receives a fixed interest rate; usually associated with an issue of fixed rate bonds that an agency wishes to convert to a synthetic floating rate.

Floating-to-fixed rate swap. See *Fixed rate swap.*

Floor. A financial contract under which an agency will make a payment to the provider when the underlying falls below the predetermined strike rate, or floor rate.

Forward rate curve. The yield curve, as of a future (or forward) date, constructed using currently prevailing rates on instruments settling in the future; commonly used to price many interest rate derivative instruments.

Forward swap. An interest rate swap under which the accrual and exchange of cash flows commences at a later date, rather than the current date.

Hedge. A tactic (or a financial product) used to limit potential losses or gains associated with an existing financial position, asset or liability. Also see *Perfect hedge.*

In the money. Refers to a party's financial position if it would be owed a payment by the other party if a swap were terminated at the prevailing market price.

Integration. For tax law purposes, the ability of an issuer of bonds to take into account (or "integrate") payments made or received on a swap in the determination of bond yield.

Interest rate risk. The risks associated with changes in interest rates (i.e., the risk that changes in interest rates will adversely effect an agency's position with respect to borrowing costs, reinvestment opportunities, at-market investment termination, etc.)

Interest rate swap. A contractual agreement between two parties who agree to exchange certain cash flows, calculated at different interest rates, for a defined period of time.

ISDA master agreement. The standardized master legal agreement for all derivative transactions between an agency and a provider that states standardized definitions, terms, and representations governing the swap transactions.

LIBOR. London Inter-Bank Offered Rate is the interest rate banks charge each other for short-term money, up to a 12-month term. LIBOR is commonly used as the underlying for the floating leg of a swap. The British Bankers' Association (BBA) sets the rates daily.

Mark-to-market. Calculation of the value of a financial instrument (e.g., an interest rate swap) based on the current market rates or prices of the underlying.

Negotiated bid. Method of entering into a swap agreement where the terms, including the rates, are negotiated between an agency and the provider.

Notional amount. Similar to bond principal amount; used as the basis to determine the amount of swap interest payments. The notional amount will often amortize over time to match the amortization of the bonds to which the swap is related.

Off-market swap. A variation of an interest rate swap in which one or both of the referenced rates are priced above or below the market, usually resulting in an up-front payment from one party to the other.

Option premium. The amount paid by a party in exchange for an option.

Optional termination. The right of a party to terminate a swap at any time at the prevailing market price. In most swap agreements only the agency has this right.

Out of the money. Refers to a party's financial position if it would owe a payment to the other party if a swap were terminated at the prevailing market price.

Perfect hedge. A hedge that completely eliminates any possible future gain or loss on the hedged asset or liability.

Provider. For the purposes of this chapter, the financial institution that enters into a swap agreement with an agency, usually a commercial bank, investment bank, or insurance company.

Rate lock agreement. An arrangement under which an agency enters into an agreement with an underwriter to issue fixed rate bonds in the future, at a predetermined net interest cost.

Schedule to the master agreement. Schedule amending or supplementing the ISDA master agreement which sets out the specific business terms and conditions governing the transactions executed under the agreement.

Setoff. Swap provision that enables a party that is entitled to a payment under the agreement (e.g., a termination payment) to satisfy that obligation by reducing the amount it owes the other party in another transaction.

Strike rate. In an interest rate cap or interest rate floor, the predetermined interest rate that, when reached in the market, automatically triggers a payment under the contract.

Swap curve. The name given to the swap's equivalent of a yield curve. The swap curve identifies the relationship between swap rates at varying maturities.

Swap insurance. Insurance policy purchased to guarantee obligations on a swap, which can be underwritten to insure only the regularly scheduled payments under the swap, or also any termination payment that may be required under the swap.

Swaption. A type of swap in which the terms of the swap are agreed to in advance and where one party has the right, but not the obligation, to enter into that swap on a future date or during a specific period.

Synthetic fixed rate. The resulting rate an agency will pay on an issue of variable rate obligations after entering into a floating-to-fixed interest rate swap.

Synthetic floating rate. The resulting rate an agency will pay on an issue of fixed rate obligations after entering into a fixed-to-floating interest rate swap.

Tax risk. The risk that the spread between taxable and tax-exempt rates will change as a result of changes in income tax laws or other conditions.

Term out. Provision of a swap agreement that allows the agency to make payments over time for any amount it may be required to pay upon termination of a swap.

Termination eate. The scheduled maturity date of the swap, when the final payment obligation is made (barring an early termination of the swap). When a swap is entered into in connection with an issue of bonds, the termination date is often set to coincide with the maturity date of the bonds.

Termination events. Events that allow for the termination of a swap, such as a credit downgrade.

Termination payment. Payment made from one counterparty to the other if the swap is terminated prior to its scheduled termination date.

Trade date. The date on which swap terms are set and the agreement is priced; formal documents are sometimes exchanged some time later. Also called the *Sale date.*

Underlying. The variable interest rate, security price, commodity price, or index of prices or rates on which the derivative's payments are based. A derivative's payment is based on the interaction of the underlying and the notional amount.

CHAPTER 18

The Regional Firm: Its Customers, Traders, and Institutional Salespeople

Mychele Lindvall
Vice President
Manager of Institutional Sales and Trading
Seattle Northwest Securities Corporation

In this chapter, I describe the mission and nuances of the "regional" municipal trader, institutional salesperson, and his or her customers.

UNDERSTANDING "REGIONAL"

There are several factors to consider as we look to understand the expertise of the regional trader and salesperson. These factors focus on:

- States with a personal income tax
- Demographics
- Regional economy
- Weather/nature
- Politics

States with a Personal Income Tax

Most states with a personal income tax treat interest, or in the case of mutual funds dividends, paid by municipal issuers outside their state as taxable. There are some exceptions to this. Utah, for example has a personal income tax, but does not tax income on bonds issued in states that do not tax Utah bonds. State of Washington residents do not have a personal income tax, so by this very virtue, issuers in this state enjoy reciprocity with Utah. This is the case in several states. The local personal income tax can factor into the relative value of a bond issued in a particular state.

Demographics

The demographics of the state often play an important role in how a state and local municipal bond trade. For example, Montana has a relatively high personal income tax. A trader or salesperson might conclude accordingly that bonds issued in Montana should carry a premium to the general market. A look at the demographics in this state would shed another perspective. There are not a whole lot of people in Montana and, therefore, not a whole lot of people buying double tax-exempt Montana bonds! Whereas California's demographic picture is obviously much different and robust. As a result, from time to time, California municipal bonds can demand a hefty premium.

Regional Economy

The various regions in the United States form their own economic landscapes, for example, agricultural versus industrial, tourism versus high tech, and so on. This is a consideration for many institutional and high net worth retail investors as many strive for diversity in their municipal bond portfolios.

Weather/Nature

Mother Nature, I'm not kidding (i.e., hurricanes, earthquakes, and floods) have a major economic impact on several regions. Local bonds, after these events occur, can undergo dramatic credit and pricing deteriorations and result in unstable trading situations for many months. Examples include the Northridge earthquake in southern California, the flooding of the Mississippi River, and Hurricane Katrina. All of these events impacted the values and trading of local bonds in their respective regions.

Politics

Politics . . . enough said! But seriously, even what appears on the surface to be the smallest local political issue can and will continue to affect the security of a bond. Politics can determine the issuance of bonds, as voter approval is required for many projects. Also, grassroots taxpayer revolts, ballot initiatives, budget impasses and political fights are constant worries that can change overnight the value of local bonds. Many investors look to their regional contacts for information on local politics and public policy.

TRADING

The consolidation of trading desks among the *bulge bracket firms* (i.e., the bigger Wall Street firms), coupled with the purchase of independent fixed income companies by the national and/or super regional firms, has resulted in fewer traders involved in the business of traditional municipal bond trading. What has emerged are many other types of trading instruments including derivative programs and arbitrage trading desks. Some of these are capital intensive and, therefore, usually prohibitive for the smaller regional.

Many firms house public finance, trading, and sales under one umbrella with one common goal: profitable distribution of product through high quality customer service. The municipal trader plays an important role here. By being involved in the market, the trader can advise bankers in a timely fashion of market conditions, interest rates, and differentiate the trading dynamics from one part of the yield curve to another. In addition, the trader can aid bankers in understanding how various coupons or callable versus noncallable structures are trading at any particular time in the marketplace. A regional trader should always understand the spread relationships between the states in the trader's region and the various credits within those states.

This last point has been somewhat lost over the past few years as we have had record-breaking new bond issuance in virtually every state in the country. This has helped to commoditize the municipal market and has reduced the specialty state aspect. In 2006, we saw a dramatic decline in issuance and a return to the need to effectively evaluate the worth of a bond not only on its structure but by accessing the local specialty state supply and demand factors.

There are several factors to consider when organizing a trading desk and determining how many traders are required. A desk with a $50 million trading line versus one with a $500 million trading line has to be particularly focused in its use of capital as it cannot be all things to all people. A regional trader's first priority is to provide the best market for bonds issued in the local region. As many institutional customers' daily routine includes the sale of bonds via competitive bid wanted, it is the responsibility of a regional firm to focus its attention and use of capital first on bonds sold by its firm and/or those in its regional footprint. Additionally, a good regional firm should keep a robust inventory of the region's bonds always available so that customers across the country will think of its firm when looking to buy and sell local bonds. Bearing all this in mind, the remaining capital on the trading desk can be used to buy and sell securities issued throughout the country (i.e., national trading names when trading opportunities present themselves).

Often trading responsibilities and personnel assignments on the trading desk are broken down by maturity, geography, credit quality, tax status, bonds subject to the *alternative minimum tax* (AMT), structure, and type or some combination of these. A trader assigned to trade single-A rated student loan bonds subject to AMT probably is not the same person who should trade general market triple-A rated insured, local school district paper. The knowledge requirements and wide range of credit and pricing differences between these two bonds could be too confusing for the trader who works in a fast response, minute-to-minute environment bidding, and selling a wide range of names. An example of the usual assignment, one trader might be assigned to trade all California single-A or better-rated bonds out to 30 years on the yield curve. The trader sitting to the right may be assigned general municipal bonds across the nation from 10 to 30 years. And yet the trader sitting to the left may be responsible for all states including California out to 10 years, rated triple B to nonrated. Most lower-rated credits in the sectors of hospital bonds, continuing care retirement community bonds, student loan-backed bonds, and local or regional airport bonds among others take a fair amount of credit analysis to determine the value of the security. This requires the attention of a dedicated trader. On the flipside, the trader who trades general market insured triple A paper can quickly determine the value of a bond by the coupon, maturity, call features, and tax advantages of the state where it is issued.

Additionally, bank-qualified paper and zero-coupon bonds generally trade differently than general market coupon-bearing bonds and require special trading attention. In regard to bank-qualified bonds, the issues are under $10 million each and because of the special financial attractiveness of the bonds for bank portfolios, they generally trade at a premium to general market bonds.

In regard to zero-coupon bonds, when interest rates are relatively high and investors think interest rates will go lower, these bonds trade at a narrower spread to general market coupon-bearing bonds. Also, institutional investors sometimes find these bonds attractive as a way to add duration to their portfolios. In a lower interest rate environment when zeros trade at a wider spread to general market coupon bonds, investors will buy them for the incremental yield.

With access to Bloomberg and the Internet on almost every trader's and salesperson's desk, the ability to technically analyze a bond is made a snap while making various assumptions on volatility, yield curve progression, and so on. Instead of dragging out the atlas from under one's desk, the resources available from various Internet search engines can give the whereabouts, the populations, and employment bases of such diverse and remote places as Puyallup, Washington, or Truth Or Consequences, New Mexico including just about everything you ever wanted to know about these places and more! Also available, via various web sites are bond ratings, rating reports, official statements, escrow documents, and so on. This is information that in the past could take up to a week or more to obtain by begging someone, usually a local government worker, to whom you have never talked to in your life, to please, please, please locate the document, copy it, and then mail or maybe even fax it to you!

Traders gain access to the municipal marketplace in various ways. Customer *bid wanteds* are on Bloomberg, which has become the central meeting place for most portfolio managers, traders, and salespeople. Early each morning traders and salespeople go through all the bids wanted and decide where to risk their firm's capital. With so many customers putting bonds out for bid on a daily basis, most traders will prioritize in some fashion. "Good" customers of the firm always get first look, then consideration depends upon the type of bond, how many, and, in the case of a regional trader, special consideration is given to bonds issued in the same region. The bidding process is like that of a silent auction. Traders from a dozen firms or more submit bids until a previously specified time, say noon, when the highest bid is selected. If the customer decides to sell the bonds, then you own them.

Another silent auction process is by bidding bonds on what's called the broker's "wire." This is an old-fashioned term because a "wire" is not used anymore. The nation's major brokers have electronic trading platforms that allow traders to input bids. The process is then the same as previously described with one major difference. When you bid the broker wire, you bid to buy only at a price that is of opportunistic value to you. However, when you bid a customer's bond, there is an obligation to provide a competitive bid.

This process can be tricky because buying (bidding on) bonds at an aggressive price usually results in an aggressive offering. I remember one trader some years ago getting all wound up when I questioned his bid for one of my customers. In my capacity as a salesperson acting on behalf of an important institutional client, I said "I really need to make sure we are on the market and competitive." His sharp reply, which is almost commonplace in the industry when traders talk to salespeople, was to say: "You salespeople always want the highest bid for your customers and the cheapest offerings!" It does not work that way. A trader either has good bids or good offerings. But I do understand the frustration of traders and the tight, competitive markets in which they work.

Another way to add bonds to the inventory of a regional firm, or to fill customer requests, is to buy bonds offered by other accounts or to buy bonds from other dealers. I remember buying my first block of bonds. I bought it in a competitive bid situation from a customer. I was thrilled and reported to the head of our department that I outbid something like 30 other bidders. He responded by yelling at me that I was dumb to pay that much more than 30 other professional traders for those bonds. "And now you expect a customer will pay even more?" he added.

Buying bonds is one thing. Selling them is another. How does the trader effectively access and manage the risk of a multimillion dollar inventory? There are many tools to use. The first one is common sense. As a trader tries to buy a block of bonds he needs to ask the question: "What customer would be looking for these bonds?" In other words, the trader needs to not only know the value of a security but utilize relationships with the sales force to make sure he knows the firm's customers and how to appropriately "stock the shelves." I have worked with traders who just could not resist buying a block of bonds from another dealer because the bonds were so cheap. Question number one, if the bonds are so cheap, why couldn't the dealer sell them to its own customers? Question number two, if the bonds are cheap, are they cheap for a reason? Maybe there is no demand for the structural features of the particular bond (i.e., put/calls, maturity, or state income tax exemption)

I have come to the conclusion that regional firms primarily service either retail or institutional investors. Very few do a good job of servicing both. Some may have a few high-net-worth account components with a primary institutional customer base. This market focus does limit distribution of the traders' inventory at such a firm. Since trading desks are not investors, the name of the game is turnover. However, other traders, at more retail-oriented firms, can be helpful in marketing these positions to their retail customers. Also, over the past 10 years or so, the use of Bloomberg and other electronic platforms to offer bonds directly to many retail brokers has provided a great deal of liquidity, which, of course, is a big hedge against market risk for the trader.

Risk management has evolved in the computer age from the traditional practices to "buy low, sell high," and own bonds in an up-market but not in a down-market. Risk on the trading desk should be monitored and managed on an hourly and a daily basis. There should be computer programs at work that show how many bonds are long, the average maturity, and the dollar value per 01 for the total bond inventory. There should also be programs that show how long the bonds have been in the inventory and when it is time for the trader to push the eject button (i.e., sell them).

Almost all trading desks hedge their inventory. There are computer programs available to help select the right product to use as the hedge, be it U.S. Treasury futures, Bond Market Association (BMA), or Municipal Market Daily (MMD) rate locks. These hedges can help to protect an inventory from interest rate swings, but unfortunately not from spread risk. And if you happen to hedge your municipal position with 10-year Treasury futures and they outperform municipals, a trader could find himself sideways really fast. I have heard more than once from traders employed at regional and national desks say that "The best hedge is a good sales force!"

Finally, tools needed to actually trade bonds now are almost all electronic. The brokers have web sites that list dealer offerings and bid wanteds. There are also several electronic trading platforms that allow traders to offer their inventory and customer offerings directly to a large number of retail brokers. This allows traders to access the largest holders of municipal bonds (i.e., the individual investors). These platforms are very helpful to a regional trading desk that has something shy of the thousands of sales people employed by the large national brokerage firms.

THE REGIONAL INSTITUTIONAL SALESPERSON AND THEIR CUSTOMERS

Institutional salespeople representing a regional firm for the most part cover all of the major institutional accounts across the country. In addition, they are focused on covering the smaller banks, asset managers, trust companies, and other money managers in their particular region. The goal is to create and sustain customer relationships by providing value in the primary and secondary markets for primarily the local bonds.

This also creates a consistent and strong customer base for a regional public finance group to competitively distribute its bond issues. The ability to be creative in structure and offer attractive investment opportunities to institutional buyers is enhanced by having a strong local presence in trading and banking.

Sometimes on the sales side you can have a chicken-and-egg discussion that goes something like this: "Did the salesperson get the customer because of our new issue product, or did the salesperson get the order because of their relationship in the secondary market?" I believe there is truth to both as customers that primarily do secondary business in large size may never give the time of day to a small regional trading operation, except for our proprietary product.

Institutional customers are partially distinguished and separated by the size and type of bonds they are interested in. One breakout would include the following:

Arbs, TOBS and hedge fund participants in the regional markets, sometimes referred to as *flow accounts*, will trade anything from

$500,000 to $500,000,000 plus, zero coupons to big premiums, and 2- to 40-year maturities. Their trading decision is usually very technical in nature and they, as "crossover buyers," view municipals as a commodity. The salesperson may want to know what type of hedge is being employed and is the bond going into a derivative program? Sometimes it serves the salesperson best to just show the bond offering or the bid and wait for the account to put the numbers into the black box and see what comes out! A successful salesperson covering this type of account should nonetheless become well acquainted with their approach and learn a little about their methodology.

Banks have been a long time customer in the municipal market. The traditional structure and security of municipal bonds are attractive to the conservative bank trust customer. Trust departments today have evolved from traditional "buy and hold" purchasers of securities with strict dollar price parameters, to a more sophisticated asset management model of actively managed portfolios. Many banks have *common funds* or *specialty state funds*. A portfolio manager assigned to these funds is usually charged with providing income with total return performance.

Besides trust departments of banks, their own portfolios are managed by the bank's Treasury department. This is the investment department that manages the banks own assets. Managers of bank portfolios often find that the investment in bank qualified municipal bonds is a sound addition to their overall investment scheme. In accordance with the Tax Equity and Fiscal Responsibility Act act of 1982, securities are granted this qualification if issued by a municipality that has borrowed $10 million or less in the year of issuance. Many bonds deemed bank qualified are issued by small local municipalities and are usually issued through a regional underwriter and traded on regional trading desks.

Corporations are also buyers of municipal bonds. Many large corporations require outside asset management and have strict investment guidelines for investments. Cash management is invested with short-term paper usually out to two years. Some corporations will invest out to 10 years.

Foreign banks have emerged in the past few years as the biggest buyer of taxable municipal bonds. Issuance of pension obligation bonds dominated this market in 2003–2005.

Insurance companies including property and casualty, bond insurers, and life companies are consistent customers for the regional dealer. Property and casualty companies in particular will invest in regional credits across the country. As some are *buy-and-hold* accounts, they are not as concerned with how a bond is going to behave in the marketplace. Instead, their concerns include income and matching assets with their companies' anticipated liabilities. They also look at the specific structure and *book yield*. Other insurance companies are performance oriented and have more of a *total return approach*. Some do both buy and hold and total return. One example of total return is a bond offering in a specialty state that can potentially outperform the general market due to varying supply and demand characteristics. Some accounts that are total return will buy such a bond hoping to sell it prior to maturity at a greater spread to its benchmark then when it was bought.

Mutual funds were the dominant investment group in the 1980s through 1994. Now, they are important, but not as much as they were. In 1994, interest rates screamed up and many retail investors did not understand the decline in the *net asset value* (NAV) of their mutual fund shares as opposed to their owning a particular bond, clipping the coupon and waiting for it to mature at par. Many mutual funds saw severe outflows in 1994 and 1995. Eventually, the assets stabilized. The fund managers are charged with outperforming against their peer groups with the goal of attracting new investors. A good mutual fund can produce much better results than individual bonds to the individual investor while providing diversity. Many mutual funds were created specifically for investors residing in high tax states. For example, there are many California and New York funds. The bonds purchased for these funds can only be issued in that state and, therefore, the dividend paid is federal and state tax exempt. The managers of these funds find it beneficial to have strong relationships with the regional dealer that will underwrite issues and actively trade bonds in the states they manage.

Money managers, also called *asset management people*, describe a group that would potentially invest assets for any of the above listed participants in the municipal market including high-net-worth individuals. This has been one of the fastest areas of growth in the financial services industry and in particular the municipal market over the past five years through midyear 2007. Many of the large retail firms are moving to private wealth management, changing the role of the retail broker from selling particular products to acquiring assets to be managed by portfolio managers of the firm. Asset managers also manage investments for insurance companies, corporations and banks, and municipalities.

THE SKILLS OF THE SALESPERSON

Electronic tools available to the institutional salesperson are also generally the same as to the trader. Sales peoples' tools include broker wires, retail platforms, and portfolio management software. And like the traders, salespeople should have a commitment to their customers and be well versed in the credits in the geographic region that they are selling. Knowledge of these credits and how they will trade provides great value to the investor.

Each individual salesperson has, of course, his or her personal skill set and style that has been influenced by education, market experience, and employment in the business. Regional salespeople are generally a colorful bunch, coming from many walks of life. One is just as likely to meet a regional salesperson with a degree in underwater photography and an MBA from UCLA as a Harvard graduate with a degree in finance that just wants to live in the Northwest. While there are many stereotypes of salespeople, let me suggest a few:

- The technician
- The emotionally invested
- The sports fan
- The intellectual
- The artist
- The schmoozer
- The specialist in relative value

Admittedly, the "sports fan" and the "schmoozer" are less successful than in previous years as both buyers and sellers have become more sophisticated. Having said this, I believe that most successful salespeople possess some of all of these qualities, except perhaps the "sports fan." It might be the "artist" that finally gets through to the customer who always insists you not call but send a message. This is sometimes thought of as going into the big black hole of the Bloomberg message system. If the account finally agrees to talk with you about his or her buying and selling objectives, it calls on the "technician" and the "intellectual" to understand just what he/she is saying. Finally, it takes the "emotionally invested" to go after trading opportunities that will surely enhance the customer's portfolio performance.

Lastly, let me conclude by summing up with a true life story of what I believe should be the attitude of a successful regional sales and trading person. Several years ago I was talking with a rookie salesperson about his career. He told me that he had, in fact, decided against a career selling municipal bonds. I was surprised as I thought he was coming right along. It seemed to him that working at a small regional firm without all the glamour of a major trading operation was not all that appealing. He added that he realized this even more when he reflected on a conversation that he had overheard between myself and one of our firm's customers. He told me that not only could he never feel what I was describing, he would certainly never truthfully say the words that he heard me say: "I love these bonds!!"

CHAPTER 19

Changing Roles of Buyers and Sellers of Municipal Bonds: One Participant's View

William J. Darusmont
Managing Partner
TBD Capital LLC

There have been more changes since the early 1970s in municipal bonds than in any other securities class except derivatives. The closest would probably be the conversion to negotiated commissions by the New York Stock Exchange.

I was hired as a junior investment officer in the largest multistate bank holding company, which, at $18 billion, was one of the top 20 financial institutions in the United States (how things have changed). My boss and mentor in a four-person department had over 20-years experience selling municipal bonds for some of the top firms in the company and this gave me the advantage of learning both the buy and sell side of the business. It also afforded me the opportunity to meet some of the top names in the business. Our banks portfolios were about 60% U.S. government securities and 40% municipal bonds.

It was a very close-knit community and your word was your bond. Over the phone, bonds were purchased and sold with confirmations arriving three or more days later and settlements a week or more away. This was distressing to our chief financial officer who thought everything should be in writing. Yet over my ten years with the organization, I never saw one of those verbal contracts broken.

As a major buyer, and with three dealer banks in our system, we were treated very well. Even on new issues with major interest, we usually received all of the bonds that we put in for.

The largest buyers of municipals were commercial banks, followed by casualty insurance companies, and then trust departments and individuals. Several changes to tax laws have altered that mix significantly with mutual funds now the largest buyers followed by individuals, casualty insurers then banks and personal trusts.

Most of the major firms and dealer banks were headquartered in New York City with other major cities being Chicago, San Francisco, and Los Angeles. There were also large regional operations in other major cities.

Large cities had bond clubs and municipal bond clubs that served more of a social than an informational purpose but that function cannot be understated as municipal bonds, more than any other investment class, were a relationship business. The business was largely self-regulated and knowing the participants personally was very important. In 1975, Congress created the Municipal Securities Rulemaking Board (MSRB) to regulate the business with oversight from the Securities and Exchange Commission.

Business lunches were important ways to communicate but sometimes became much more social than informative, except in getting to know what a person is really like over a two-martini lunch. Just about anything that happened was soon known by just about anyone on the street who was interested. It was possible for a large buyer to be invited to lunch every day of the week.

It was a wonderful business and one I was proud to have chosen for a career. Not a day would go by without at least one newspaper article pertaining to municipal bonds either directly or through some other aspect such as tax laws.

In response to the oil crisis of the early 1970s, President Nixon imposed wage controls. These had the unforeseen result of people leaving their firms in the financial services industry for other companies for significantly more money. This became a game of musical chairs and bid up the price of new employees at the expense of those who remained. As I was on a fast track at this point, it didn't impact me. I believe this was significant as it broke the bond between the employer and the employee. Later, defined benefit pension plans were abandoned for 401(k) plans along with significant downsizing due to mergers so that eventually civil servants had both higher salaries and higher retirement benefits.

The job of Bank Investment Officer was about the most secure in banking. I often quipped that if a bank went out of business, the investment officer sold off the securities, swept up the floor, and turned the keys over to the landlord—the last one to leave. I never thought I would do anything else than become the department head as I was being groomed for that position. But, as in everything, the business changed and I went over to the other side of the street as an institutional bond salesman.

The first thing I learned, upon changing sides of the street, which my boss had warned me of so it really came as no shock, was that the salesmen who had been my friends became just passing acquaintances, with the exception of two of them. Once again my mentor's advice had proved correct and true.

In this chapter, I provide a perspective on the changing role of the municipal bond market since the early 1970s based on my experience in the market.

COMMUNICATIONS AND TECHNOLOGY

The telephone was the primary instrument of communication. That was followed by the *Bond Buyer*, a daily publication with news on coming bond issues and statistics; the Blue List, a daily listing of positions in bonds by all dealers; and Munifacts, a sort of teletype that provided market news, who had purchased an issue, and the reoffering yields as well as members of the selling group. Compucorp and Wang had just invented desk-sized computers that could compute bond prices and yields and calculate bids for bond issues. Prior to that, prices were calculated using a basis book that provided prices for various coupons and maturities and interpolation was used to calculate the exact price. The computers were expensive and slow by today's standards, but Compucorp then invented a smaller and easier to operate machine the size of a desk calculator that had present value formulas built into it to determine the exact price as well as principal and interest. Several people developed programs to analyze bond swaps, the most famous of whom was Michael Bloomberg who created the state of the art system for Salomon Brothers that was the best until he left there and started his own firm developing Bloomberg Analytics along with Merrill Lynch as a limited partner, which remains the top system in the business. He even managed to create a database of every municipal security in existence, a daunting task since the large number of serial maturities. There are well over 50,000 issues in existence. This dramatically improved communication and analysis, but, as with the Internet, it came at a price.

THE LEGAL OPINION AND INDENTURE OF A MUNICIPAL BOND

The legal opinion and the indenture are the two most important components of a municipal bond and both are included in the offering statement for a bond issue. The indenture is a contract that specifies coverage requirements, sources of revenue, and remedies. The legal opinion was written by one of a few competent law firms in municipal bonds. Without a clean opinion as to the tax exemption and terms of the bond, it was worthless. In the late 1980s, the importance of who wrote the opinion diminished, perhaps because banks were no longer the major buyers (or because bond attorney's migrated to new firms), and opinions by lesser known firms emerged. One such instance ended in a major bankruptcy due to the attorney going to a new firm and operating too closely with the financial advisor. As with Michael Milken and other West Coast offices of New York firms operating without close supervision, the chances of a problem intensifies.

THE ROLE OF CREDIT AGENCIES

In the early 1970s, there was just Moody's and Standard and Poor's. Their ratings were based on historical payment histories, much as credit agencies do today for individuals. Other than key ratios and evaluating the indenture (the terms of the agreement), the rating was little more than an indication of the ability to pay, not of forecasting trouble ahead. For this reason, New York City and other issuers defaulted without being first lowered to sub-investment grade. Most recently Orange County, California filed for bankruptcy protection less than six months after the rating agencies had affirmed the bond rating.

Subsequently, rating agencies increased the quality of their analysis due to government pressure as well as competitive pressure from another rating agency, Fitch.

Perhaps due to familiarity, we, being on the West Coast, observed that similar quality issuers on the East Coast had higher ratings than those west of the Mississippi. Municipal bond insurance (which pays the principal and interest as it comes due in the event of an issuer default), has become quite cheap and is provided on most new issues and has reduced credit risk substantially.

CHANGES IN TAX-EXEMPT STATUS

While the tax-exemption of municipal bonds was established by the Internal Revenue Service Tax Code, there is no Constitutional guarantee of reciprocity. The Supreme Court has upheld the tax exemption on numerous occasions that the interest is exempt from federal income taxes. Still, whenever a case comes up, it roils the municipal bond market.

These changes brought about the issuance of taxable municipal bonds. The market for these was fragmented in the early years and they suffered from a lack of liquidity. Today the market has grown in size with buyers being taxable bond funds, life insurance companies, and mutual funds. The advent of hedge funds has also increased marketability of taxable municipal issues.

There have been changes however, regarding municipal arbitrage primarily due to refunding a prior issue at a lower rate of interest and then investing the proceeds in U.S. government bonds at a higher interest rate. Regional dealers primarily in the West made frequent use of arbitrage by refunding some issues within months of their issuance. For us, this was a distinct advantage as the issues in our region, primarily single-A rated, would then be escrowed with U.S. government bonds and be upgraded to a triple-A rating. As a result our portfolios had extremely high credit quality.

PRICING TRANSPARENCY

There was no pricing transparency except on new issues until the MSRB mandated that dealers report prices on all trades to them. Secondary offerings could be marked up and sold at whatever the market would bear. This was especially true of odd-lot trades to individuals but even institutional buyers didn't know how much profit there was until the MSRB required the markup to be disclosed on "agency" trades (when the seller didn't own the security). The next step was for the MSRB to require sellers to report all trades within minutes of the trade thus providing some measure of transparency although there are still big price differences depending on the size of the trade and whether it was a buy or a sell.

THE BUYERS OF MUNICIPALS

For several reasons, banks were the major force in the municipal bond market. In order to serve their communities they became major underwriters of bonds but it also enhanced their chances of having the banking relationships for the municipalities and with no money market funds they could be quite lucrative. In addition, they bought large amounts of bonds for their portfolios due to the tax-exempt interest but also since they could deduct the interest cost on the deposits while earning the bond interest tax free. A lesser-known reason was that the federal tax laws allowed them to carry forward losses to the next year. Consequently, banks would have one year of all gains and one of all losses, effectively eliminating any tax consequences. The Tax Reform Act of 1969 eliminated the gain/loss advantage and the Tax Equity Fiscal Responsibility Act of 1982 (TEFRA) eliminated the deductibility of interest used to purchase municipal bonds with few exceptions. Starting in 1987 due to grandfathering existing holdings, banks gradually became less of a factor in the municipal bond market and shrank rapidly in importance being replaced by tax-exempt bond mutual funds as the largest buyer. Banks were primarily buyers of 15 years and shorter maturities.

Casualty insurers were the next largest participants and they remain large today, but the rapid increase of wealth of individuals in the 1990s moved them down to third place. Insurance companies prefer the long end of the market for yield purposes as those are normally the highest and some come at deep discounts.

As for portfolio managers, some are content to "buy and hold" and don't provide much information to the salesmen, while others are active traders looking for swap opportunities. The former tend to be less forthcoming about their portfolio holdings while the latter provide them to get swap ideas. I have always been in the middle: communicating what I am trying to do, but withholding my total portfolio because I don't want to be bothered by a constant stream of swap ideas.

SELLERS OF MUNICIPAL BONDS

In addition to dealer banks, large brokerage firms have municipal bond departments and there is an even larger network of "boutique" dealers throughout the country. Whereas the relationships developed by salesmen (even today most are men) were highly valued, it was common for them to start a career with a bank on a salary and subjective bonus (on the West Coast, Bank of America and United California Bank were spawning grounds—at one time or other it seems that most people had once worked either there or at Merrill), and then migrate to a firm that offered the "carrot" of partnership, still for a salary and bonus, or to a smaller firm that paid high commissions. All of these can exist in the same market since municipal bonds are sold on a yield basis and the markup is included in the offering price. Municipal bonds are unique in that whereas government securities and corporate bonds are only sold by large dealers, there is plenty of room in municipals for boutique specialty houses.

Some salesmen were always disgruntled with their compensation and kept trading down to smaller and smaller firms for higher commission payouts, eventually winding up in an obscure firm too small to be used by large institutional buyers. Over the early 1990s, some firms have sprung up that hire experienced salesmen for their "client book." They are paid on commission only with very high payouts, but receive health benefits, which are costly to individuals.

Salesmen use many techniques to win business:

- *The Entertainer.* He may be very knowledgeable of the securities (in the old days they had to be), but feels that his best opportunity to sell bonds is to entertain his clients frequently and sometimes lavishly. Even the ones who aren't as knowledgeable attempt to provide a steady stream of information so you don't forget who they are.
- *The Informer.* These are people who research new issues thoroughly and are very well versed on them. Again, in the old days, most salesmen knew the bonds thoroughly and could recite much of the data such as interest coverage ratios.
- *The Gofer.* This is a person who pays close attention to what your normal buying parameters are and watches for offerings within and outside of his firm. He will then call the client without telling him who owns the bonds that meet his requirements, hoping to make the sale. He will buy less a commission and sell the bonds to a you at the quoted price although if you deal direct with the firm they may cheapen the offering.
- *The Wheeler-Dealer.* This type of salesman is one who is in the business to make money quickly and then retire or do something else. I have seen them misrepresent offerings or "front-run" orders in syndicate that should have been for the benefit of the selling group, so they can make the sale to the client. Whenever someone did this to me I would reject the bonds, but some other buyers allowed this practice.
- *The Jock.* Some firms hire professional athletes, not as salesmen per se, but to do client relations. One was a baseball player who gave us tickets whenever he was in town. Another was a former NFL fullback who was an announcer. Who would turn down an opportunity to have dinner with someone like that?
- *Mr. "I haven't a clue."* The downside of improved communications and offering bonds over the Internet has allowed individuals with little knowledge of the business or the bonds to put offerings out to buyers and hope to snag a trade—most of them do not last long.
- *The Perma-Bear.* I once knew a salesman who was one of the most successful salesmen to individuals in his firm; he was always bearish on bonds and convinced his clients to keep maturities within one year. He had a huge desktop calendar with every square filled with when his clients bonds were going to mature. It was like having an annuity. While the yields may have been lower his clients never complained about losses!

THE FUTURE AS PROLOGUE

Whereas bond salesmen once held the upper hand within the firm, the size of the largest accounts have become so huge that they no longer rely on a salesman but will work with whoever the dealer assigns to them. Also, the diminished use of phone calls relative to e-mails of inventory positions has also reduced the salesman's exposure to the client. Additionally, for a number of reasons, including ethics and a changing breed of buyer, firms are doing far less client entertaining and gift-giving and instead focusing more on having group luncheon meetings with economists and analysts. The relationship business of the old days is fading away in favor of more quantitative analysis. Casual dress codes have also decreased the amount of entertaining.

Historically, this closely knit group of buyers and sellers found reasons to enforce ethical behavior. Unfortunately, that has fallen apart over concerns that chastising someone for bad behavior might impair the buyers ability to get the bonds they need. I was subpoenaed before two grand juries to testify against a major firm. The first time, several other buyers who were holders of the affected bonds also appeared. I was called a second time and told that I was the only one willing to testify as the others were concerned about retribution in the form of not being able to get their bonds from the dealer in the future. I felt this was preposterous and in any event a bad reason to not confront a wrong deed.

I believe a major reason for short-term versus long-term thinking is that other than the dealer banks, most bond firms were partnerships. As more and more converted to publicly held corporations, a change occurred in the way business is done. In a partnership, the partners were entrepreneurs and the only way they could get a good return on their investment, and in general be able to take their capital out, was to insure that new employees were carefully screened and then instilled with the firm's philosophy. The saying was, "Think of the customer first, the firm second, and yourself last." That was a good philosophy, as if the customer is taken advantage of in the short run, they won't be around in the long run. I went to work for a boutique municipal bond firm that, as a partnership, was proud of the way it controlled expenses . . . spend it as if it is your own, because it is. Shortly after that they went public and things changed. Top executives had limousines, and the sales manager told me, "Think of the firm first, the customer second, and yourself last." I also had an intern sit by me for three hours and the first question he asked was, "How much did you make on that trade?" His second was, "Why not split the profit with the (institutional) buyer so he will do more business with you?" This anecdote sums up how the business has changed. When there is no hope of partnership, and management is focusing on short-term goals, quality and integrity suffer, at the expense of long-term gain. A corporation exists to make profits but that should be measured within the context of long-term profitability, not a quick profit at the expense of one's reputation.

While there will be significant changes for the sellers of municipal bonds, there will also be big changes for issuers as more pension obligation bonds are issued to fund employee retirement plans which until 2007 were grossly underfunded. State and local governments now must also fund for retiree healthcare expenses. As a result, this will cause increased sales of municipal assets such as toll roads, bridges, airports and water, and sewer systems in an effort to reduce the number of employees and improve cash flow. For holders of outstanding bonds this may prove beneficial in terms of improved credit quality but there could be fewer conventional issues as these assets are sold off and are replaced with new and more exotic forms of financing.

A top salesman once told me, "Bonds are sold not bought." That may well have been true, but increasingly they are bought as needed rather than on the encouragement of a salesman and close friend. The bond market of the future may one day consist of the buyer doing all trading via computer screens with no faces behind them. Indeed, both functions could eventually be outsourced to places such as India, where some of the brightest analysts and mathematicians reside. It will be a challenging era for all as technological change always is. There will always be a municipal bond market; but it may not resemble anything we know today. It will be the challenge of today's youth and young people in the business to meet that challenge, and human nature will ensure that it is met.

CHAPTER 20

The Depository Trust Company and Real-Time Price Transparency

Sylvan G. Feldstein, Ph.D.
Director, Investment Department
Guardian Life Insurance Company of America

David Ratner
Industry Consultant

This chapter explains the structure of the Depository Trust Company (DTC) and its sister organization, the National Securities Clearing Corporation (NSCC), as well as the important roles they play in the municipal bond market. These roles include securities trade settlement operations, trust services, and reporting. Investors, issuers, and bankers are most familiar with DTC and not NSCC, possibly because only DTC is briefly mentioned, usually near the end of the document, in most new issue municipal bond official statements.

THE DEPOSITORY TRUST & CLEARING CORPORATION

DTC is actually a subsidiary of the Depository Trust & Clearing Corporation (DTCC). DTCC is primarily a depository, or limited purpose trust com-

The sources for this chapter include *The U.S. Model for Clearing and Settlement* (New York: The Depository Trust & Clearing Corporation, October 2006); "Response to the Disclosure Framework for Securities Settlement Systems," The Depository Trust Company (June 2002); "National Securities Clearing Corporation," National Securities Clearing Corporation (undated); "Bond Market Goes Real-Time: DTCC to Automate New-Issue Information," *@dtcc Newsletter* (January 2006); "FICC's RTTM Service Ushers in Real-Time Price Transparency for Municipal Bonds," *@dtcc Newsletter* (March 2005); and, informant interviews with DTCC personnel in March 2007.

pany, that holds the securities. Another affiliated subsidiary of DTCC is NSCC. Other subsidiaries of DTCC, which cover other asset classes, include the Fixed Income Clearing Corporation (FICC), which has a U.S. government securities division and a mortgage-backed securities division. This chapter focuses mostly on DTC and NSCC, as they are the most relevant to the municipal bond industry.

DTCC is industry-owned by its financial community customers such as banks, broker-dealers, mutual funds, and other financial institutions. DTCC has approximately 450 participant shareholders and a 21-member board. Seventeen board members are from participant firms, one each is from the NYSE and the National Association of Securities Dealers (NASD), and two are from DTCC senior management. DTCC operates on an at-cost basis, returning excess revenue to its member firms. In 2005, it had revenue of $1.3 billion and gave back $528 million. DTCC's DTC, NSCC, and FICC subsidiaries are all rated AAA/A-1+ by Standard & Poor's.

DTC and NSCC were integrated into DTCC in 1999. These two companies grew out of Wall Street's paperwork crisis in the late 1960s and early 1970s. They were primarily created to provide securities clearing for the stock exchanges, initially for the New York Stock Exchange (NYSE), American Stock Exchange (Amex), and over-the-counter market (now the Nasdaq). As volumes and processing costs grew across the country, business pressures grew to centralize the process.

Although DTCC has always maintained multiple facilities, DTC and NSCC are headquartered a few blocks from the NYSE building in downtown Manhattan. After 9/11, DTCC established other physical facilities over a thousand miles away.

While DTC and NSCC were born out of the back-office and paper processing crises in securities processing, in the 1970s it was also a time of security firm changes. During this earlier period, employment on Wall Street, particularly among back office securities processing employees, also underwent consolidations and massive layoffs. The NYSE and DTCC, having unionized workers, were seen as desirable places to work in terms of job security and compensation.

After the 1999 consolidation of DTC and NSCC into DTCC, three more clearing corporations were brought into DTCC. Two of those clearing corporations, the Government Securities Clearing Corporation and the Mortgage Backed Securities Clearing Corporation, were combined to form the FICC.

The Function of DTC

DTC started as the Central Certificate Service in 1966 as a part of the NYSE and became a separate, limited purpose trust company called DTC in 1973.

DTC is now the world's largest securities depository. Securities deposited with DTC are usually registered in the name of Cede & Co., DTC's nominee name. At the end of 2006, DTC had overall, including municipals, $36 trillion dollars worth of securities in custody and had handled annual book-entry deliveries overall of securities valued at $179 trillion. In 2006, it had also made payments, including municipals, of about $3.3 trillion in cash dividend, interest and reorganization payments. At the end of 2005, it held more than 99% of all outstanding municipal bonds.

DTC is a banking organization, as it is a limited-purpose trust company, organized under the New York State banking law; a securities clearing corporation within the meaning of the New York Uniform Commercial Code; a securities clearing agency, as it is registered under Securities and Exchange Commission (SEC) provisions in Section 17A; and a member of the U.S. Federal Reserve System. DTC holds and provides servicing for over 2.7 million issues of U.S. and non-U.S. securities, including municipal bonds. DTC facilitates settlement of sales and other securities transactions in deposited securities through electronic computerized book-entry transfers. The direct participants in DTC include securities brokers and dealers, banks, trust companies, clearing corporations, and other financial organizations.

At year end 2005, DTC maintained a committed line of credit of $1.5 billion with 21 major participant banks to support settlement and participated in a $50 million shared credit line with DTCC and NSCC to support short-term operating cash requirements.

The Function of the National Securities Clearing Corporation

The National Securities Clearing Corporation (NSCC) was founded in 1976 and its original owners were the NYSE, the Amex, and NASD. Its roots go back to 1892 when the Stock Clearing Corporation was established. NSCC is where the clearing and matching of securities trades takes place in the secondary market for the more than 6,000 financial intermediaries such as brokers, dealers, banks, mutual funds, and others. In 2006, it processed, including municipal bonds, more than 8.5 billion transactions valued at more than $174.9 trillion and had an average daily number of transactions of 34 million.

By the 1980s, NSCC began the automated clearance and settlement of municipal bonds as well as corporate bonds. This was once a colorful but cumbersome process of armies of messengers from various securities firms scurrying through Wall Street clutching bags of checks and bond certificates. Now, the process is automated, and most municipal bonds don't exist in paper certificate form.

NSCC's work begins after a trade or purchase of a municipal bond. It now clears and settles virtually all broker-to-broker equity, corporate or municipal bond transactions in the United States and is also the leading processor of mutual fund orders. NSCC in accordance with regulatory and industry standards, generally completes the clearance and settlement process in three business days after the trade. (Other settlement cycles are supported by NSCC as well, and other fixed income instruments, such as U.S. government securities or mortgage-backed securities, settle on totally different settlement cycles. The communication is by computer. This settlement process is known by municipal bond traders as *T plus 3*.)

Most equity trades are locked in, that is, the marketplace or electronic trading platform has already matched all the trade terms. Most corporate and municipal bonds are not locked in, however. Instead, both the buying and selling broker report trade details to FICC. FICC performs a comparison function to match the trades and then passes them to NSCC for clearance and settlement. After midnight on the day the trade is reported, NSCC reports back to the participants the trade as compared. It now assumes responsibility for settling the transaction in the event of an insolvency of one of the parties. From this point on the parties are dealing with NSCC. In the case of municipal bonds (and all other securities handled by NSCC), the seller has to deliver the security to NSCC and the buyer has to pay NSCC for the security delivered to it by NSCC.

Paper certificates do not actually change hands. DTC's role in the process is to keep custody of a single bond for the entire issue, and DTC tracks the transfer of ownership between brokers and banks using an automated book-entry system. NSCC first nets all trades to a single movement to or from NSCC for each security, and then nets all the financial obligations for all trades to a single dollar amount owed to or from NSCC by the participant firm. This reduction, or *netting* process, into one daily payment brings greater efficiency and standardization. During the settlement period, NSCC electronically instructs DTC to move the securities from the account of the seller to the NSCC account at DTC and then to that of the buyer, and to collect the money owed and due. Funds to pay from the buying firm are electronically wired from its designated settling bank using the Fedwire system. Since all the money payments for all trades are netted, only a single end of day wire transfer is needed to settle all NSCC transactions through their settlement bank.

NSCC provides three benefits to the municipal bond industry. First, it has an infrastructure in place to handle not only average daily trading volumes, but spikes in volume as well. Second, it guarantees the trade will be completed on the original terms even if, in a worse case scenario, an insolvency were to occur to one of the firms involved. Third, NSCC, through a continuous net settlement system, consolidates all debits and credits for each trading firm to a single money balance, and nets the securities movements as well. This reduces the total number of financial obligations requiring settlement and reduces the securities movements required. On an average day in 2006, NSCC netting eliminated about 98% of the financial obligations requiring settlement. While municipal bonds were a part of that 98% figure, the exact figure for netting of municipal bond trades is not available, but is undoubtedly less than 98% for equities, corporate and municipal bonds combined.

Besides this role, NSCC also provides related ancillary services, including an automatic system of transferring customers' brokerage accounts from one financial company to another, known as the *automated customer account transfer service*, and a standardized methodology to reprice *aged fails*, that is, municipal bond (or other equity or bond) trades that were not completed between traders.

Overall, across all equity and fixed income classes it handles, NSCC averaged by 2007 almost $700 billion in daily volume. At year-end 2005, NSCC maintained a committed line of credit of $2.6 billion to provide for potential liquidity needs.

It should also be noted that another subsidiary of DTCC, DTCC Deriv/SERV LLC, provides global matching and confirmation for over-the-counter derivatives such as credit default swaps and interest rate derivatives, which are also used sometimes in conjunction with municipal bonds.

The Function of the Fixed Income Clearing Corporation

The FICC was created in 2003 from two other DTCC clearing corporations. Among other activities, it is the unit of DTCC that established the *real-time matching system* (RTTM) for all fixed income instruments, including municipal bonds. It is discussed below in conjunction with the real-time reporting of municipal bond trades to the Municipal Securities Rulemaking Board (MSRB).

DTCC's Relationship to "CUSIPs"

The acronym CUSIP came into being in 1964 when the American Bankers Association established the Committee on Uniform Security Identification Procedures to establish an identification system for securities. In 1967, CUSIP numbers consisting of nine alphanumeric digits came into existence. Standard & Poor's operates the CUSIP Service Bureau, which assigns the numbers. DTCC along with all other segments of the financial community endorses this identification system and has a representative on the CUSIP Agency Board of Trustees.

DTC and NSCC's Relationship to Real-Time Price Reporting and the MSRB

On January 31, 2005 after several months of system testing, DTCC's FICC through its *real-time trade matching* (RTTM) service improved the MSRB's ability to bring price transparency to the municipal bond market. RTTM was first applied to U.S. government securities in 2000 and then to mortgage-backed securities in 2002. Prior to 2005, price reporting for municipal bond trades was done in batch mode at the end of the day and publicly available on a day-after basis.

Working with the NSCC, the arm of DTCC that operates the clearing and settlement services for municipals, FICC provides the support to the MSRB's mandatory 15-minute price reporting requirement for all municipal bond trades. By 2005, there were some 30,000 interdealer and customer municipal bond trades a day reported.

Approximately 250 broker-dealers and others submit municipal trade data to the real-time matching service. This is done in one single, interactive message that serves two business purposes. FICC does the comparison and matching of municipal bond trades for NSCC, and forwards the matched data to NSCC for processing, netting, and settlement as discussed above. The data are simultaneously forwarded to the MSRB for the 15-minute price reporting requirement. The price data are forwarded within seconds to the MSRB that performs automated error checking and then electronically disseminates prices. This is the first time investors have near real-time price data for municipal securities. It is available at the Securities Industry and Financial Markets Association, the municipal industry trade group, web site, www.bondmarkets.com

The DTCC, through its DTC subsidiary, is also planning to automate and streamline the information distribution process by municipal bond underwriters on municipal new issues. New-issue security information will be sent electronically to DTC. After review, DTC will send the data to market participants in a real-time electronic format until settlement day. Currently, the system is decentralized and involves a variety of manual processes including phone calls, faxes, e-mails, and even messengers.

SUMMARY

It can be said that over the years technological advancements and regulatory requirements have created significant challenges for the municipal bond industry. On the operations side, DTCC and its two subsidiaries DTC and NSCC have become critical to a well-functioning municipal bond marketplace.

i-Deal/Ipreo:
The Transaction Platform

Allen Williams
Executive Vice President & Managing Director
Global Capital Markets
Ipreo

Tailored software platforms have become critical and integral to the timely pricing and distribution of new issue municipal bonds and notes. Communication among underwriters during these phases for competitive and negotiated sales now depends upon sophisticated software platforms. The platforms are dramatically changing to improve the efficiencies. This chapter, written from the perspective of a software developer and vendor who specializes, traces this history and explains the specific processes in use as of mid-2007.

THE EVOLUTION OF NEW-ISSUE TECHNOLOGY

For over 25 years, i-Deal (now Ipreo, following its merger with UK-based Hemscott in December 2006) has been servicing the municipal broker-dealer new issue market. Throughout the development of Ipreo's software offerings and numerous name changes (from Dalcomp to Thomson to i-Deal to Ipreo), its role as the primary provider to broker-dealers of new issue software has remained constant. The i-Deal/Ipreo municipal software system manages all aspects of the new-issue workflow for municipal securities—from bidding and origination through allocations and settlement, and all the stages in between. Since 2000, these software platforms have facilitated the raising of over $1 trillion in new issue capital in the global municipal markets.

The i-Deal/Ipreo municipal new issue platform traces back to the system that was originally created in 1981. It was called the Dalcomp Bookrunning System. Dalcomp later enhanced its mission statement to create an electronic community in the municipal market. All of the functionality built in the early years was intended to allow the municipal market to operate in a seamless, electronic way. These earlier software platforms have created the foundations for the new issue pricing and distribution in the municipal bond market as we know it today.

Initially, back in the 1980s, the goal of software development was to establish a proprietary network where municipal new issue information could be delivered among broker-dealers unencumbered or interrupted by anything else. This allowed municipal underwriters to receive deal information that focused only on its participation in a deal. Previously, it was received as part of a news information platform. Dalcomp installed dedicated printers on the underwriting desks of the broker-dealers that received only new issue deal information.

The first and perhaps most significant enhancement made by Dalcomp was the provision of allotments via a "syndicate wire." In the early 1980s, it was the prevailing wisdom that allotments could only be delivered verbally over the phone. The bookrunning platform with the syndicate wire gave the lead manager the ability to customize a myriad of wires that served to expand their ability to communicate electronically with other syndicate members. At the same time, there was also a need to provide extensive profit and loss bookkeeping reporting so as to integrate the back office into the workflow process. Heretofore, the accounting process was looked at separately and not seamlessly integrated.

While these innovations were state-of-the-art at the time, deal members still had to manually manipulate the information they received electronically on the wire (i.e., enter it in a document or spreadsheet and distribute it, mostly via fax to their internal sales force). This led to the concept of *shared data*. The underwriters went to the market with a proposition: If you are willing to share information electronically when you are the lead manager, you could receive information directly into your system when you are the deal member. This eliminated the need for each deal group member to rekey security description and order and allotment information. The result was that municipal transactions could be done at a much quicker pace, with a significantly fewer errors than in the past. This was truly the beginning of an electronic community.

ORDER ENTRY

From that time on, a great deal of time and effort was spent examining clients' business processes and creating software solutions to enhance the efficiency of those processes. An example of this is the process of order entry in the municipal new issue market. Historically, firms took orders over the phone, wrote them down on a paper order pad, and then entered them into the book of the deal manager. In the late 1990s, i-Deal introduced *electronic order entry* (EOE), which allowed a syndicate member to enter an order and have it sent electronically to the lead manager of a deal. No more lost orders, busy signals, or little pieces of paper to keep track of.

These software processes were further enhanced by adding an issue monitor feature. This gave the bond issuer a view offsite into the real-time bookbuilding process. This made it possible for the issuer to be able to be in its own office and not in the lead manager's office or on the trading floor of the underwriter as was the prevailing method for an issuer who wanted to track the sales of the deal minute by minute.

THE ISSUER AND PROSPECTUS DELIVERY

Once the issuer was established as a receiver of electronic information, the next step was to automate the delivery of official statements and preliminary official statements. This was traditionally accomplished via hard copy mail delivery service. This was not only costly but required extensive storage, wasted paper, and long lead times. Electronic delivery allowed an issuer and underwriter of a deal to deliver documents electronically, providing an immediate financial benefit as well as streamlining a process that had been the same for many years. The end result was that these offering documents could be delivered in hours instead of days and at a fraction of the cost. This allowed issuers to bring their deals to market when the timing was right, not when the documents were done.

Exhibit 21.1 shows the nine steps involved in marketing, selling, and executing a competitive municipal bond issue today. The electronic software systems and platforms covered in this chapter are included in parentheses with the applicable steps. Exhibit 21.2 shows the 20 steps involved in a comparable negotiated bond sale.

THE FUTURE

So where is new-issue technology going now? Most recently, i-Deal has focused on addressing the distribution of primary new issues to the dealer's internal sales force. This is a process that is still saddled with a great deal of unnecessary manual intervention. Like the bookrunning process in the last quarter of the last century, sales distribution is the next area ripe for auto-

EXHIBIT 21.1   Competitive Process

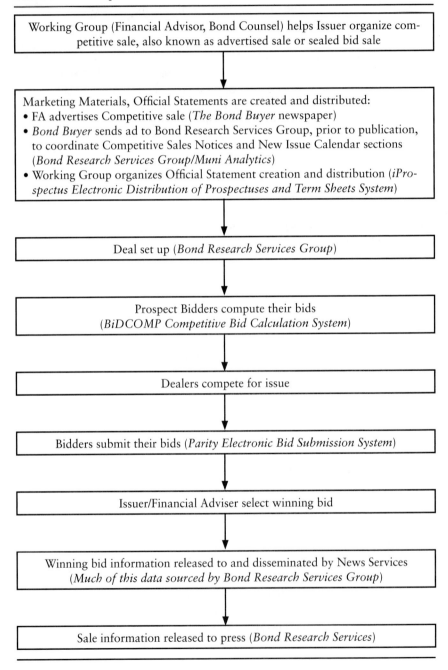

Working Group (Financial Advisor, Bond Counsel) helps Issuer organize competitive sale, also known as advertised sale or sealed bid sale

Marketing Materials, Official Statements are created and distributed:
- FA advertises Competitive sale (*The Bond Buyer* newspaper)
- *Bond Buyer* sends ad to Bond Research Services Group, prior to publication, to coordinate Competitive Sales Notices and New Issue Calendar sections (*Bond Research Services Group/Muni Analytics*)
- Working Group organizes Official Statement creation and distribution (*iProspectus Electronic Distribution of Prospectuses and Term Sheets System*)

Deal set up (*Bond Research Services Group*)

Prospect Bidders compute their bids
(*BiDCOMP Competitive Bid Calculation System*)

Dealers compete for issue

Bidders submit their bids (*Parity Electronic Bid Submission System*)

Issuer/Financial Adviser select winning bid

Winning bid information released to and disseminated by News Services
(*Much of this data sourced by Bond Research Services Group*)

Sale information released to press (*Bond Research Services*)

EXHIBIT 21.2 Negotiated Process

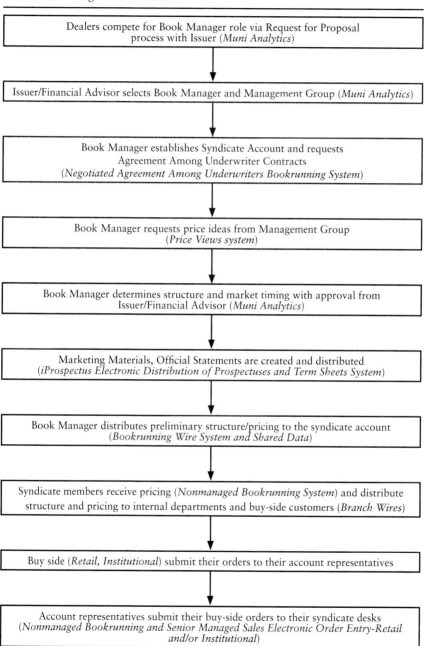

Dealers compete for Book Manager role via Request for Proposal process with Issuer (*Muni Analytics*)

Issuer/Financial Advisor selects Book Manager and Management Group (*Muni Analytics*)

Book Manager establishes Syndicate Account and requests Agreement Among Underwriter Contracts (*Negotiated Agreement Among Underwriters Bookrunning System*)

Book Manager requests price ideas from Management Group (*Price Views system*)

Book Manager determines structure and market timing with approval from Issuer/Financial Advisor (*Muni Analytics*)

Marketing Materials, Official Statements are created and distributed (*iProspectus Electronic Distribution of Prospectuses and Term Sheets System*)

Book Manager distributes preliminary structure/pricing to the syndicate account (*Bookrunning Wire System and Shared Data*)

Syndicate members receive pricing (*Nonmanaged Bookrunning System*) and distribute structure and pricing to internal departments and buy-side customers (*Branch Wires*)

Buy side (*Retail, Institutional*) submit their orders to their account representatives

Account representatives submit their buy-side orders to their syndicate desks (*Nonmanaged Bookrunning and Senior Managed Sales Electronic Order Entry-Retail and/or Institutional*)

EXHIBIT 21.2 (Continued)

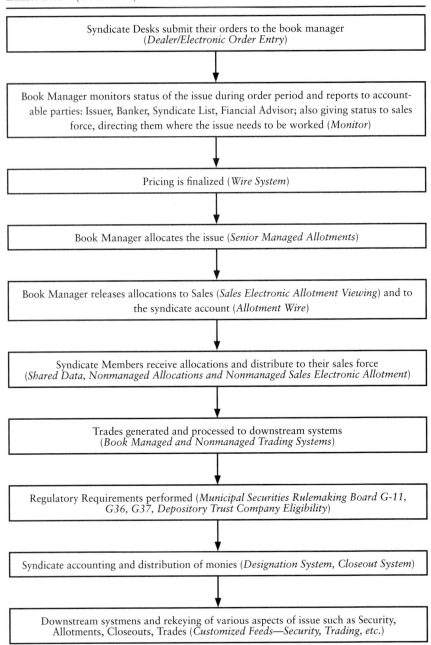

Syndicate Desks submit their orders to the book manager
(*Dealer/Electronic Order Entry*)

Book Manager monitors status of the issue during order period and reports to accountable parties: Issuer, Banker, Syndicate List, Fiancial Advisor; also giving status to sales force, directing them where the issue needs to be worked (*Monitor*)

Pricing is finalized (*Wire System*)

Book Manager allocates the issue (*Senior Managed Allotments*)

Book Manager releases allocations to Sales (*Sales Electronic Allotment Viewing*) and to the syndicate account (*Allotment Wire*)

Syndicate Members receive allocations and distribute to their sales force
(*Shared Data, Nonmanaged Allocations and Nonmanaged Sales Electronic Allotment*)

Trades generated and processed to downstream systems
(*Book Managed and Nonmanaged Trading Systems*)

Regulatory Requirements performed (*Municipal Securities Rulemaking Board G-11, G36, G37, Depository Trust Company Eligibility*)

Syndicate accounting and distribution of monies (*Designation System, Closeout System*)

Downstream systmens and rekeying of various aspects of issue such as Security, Allotments, Closeouts, Trades (*Customized Feeds—Security, Trading, etc.*)

mation and software development. This will allow a seamless interface with the new issue workflow. The tracking and distribution of either municipal fixed or variable rate inventory is another area of continued technological advancement. Firms use dedicated software platforms to both show and distribute municipal inventory to the secondary market. This process has resulted in speeding up the trading process and allowing inventory tracking to be more efficient.

SUMMARY

Software platforms are now used to facilitate new-issue execution to the municipal broker-dealer community. The next stage will involve software platforms that will be capable of distributing data in a timely manner to the regulatory agencies. As of mid-2007, Ipreo is working closely with the DTCC on its NIIDS (New Issue Information Dissemination) initiative to make descriptive information more readily available.

Compliance Issues

The Municipal Securities Rulemaking Board

Paul S. Maco
Partner
Vinson & Elkins LLP

Jennifer Webster Taffe
Associate
Vinson & Elkins LLP

The Municipal Securities Rulemaking Board (MSRB) was established in 1975 pursuant to a Congressional directive contained in the Securities Act Amendments of 1975 (the 1975 Amendments).[1] Prior to that time, the municipal securities market was substantially unregulated. The Securities Act of 1933 (the Securities Act) and the Securities Exchange Act of 1934 (the Exchange Act) governed the regulation of the corporate securities markets but generally contained exemptions for municipal securities for reasons that included the local nature of markets, a perceived absence of abusive practices, the predominance of institutional investors, and federal-state comity. Both securities acts, however, contain general prohibitions against fraud.[2] These antifraud provisions prohibit fraudulent or deceptive practices

---

[1] Municipal Securities, Pub. L. No. 94-29, 89 Stat. 131 (1975).
[2] Securities Act of 1933, 15 U.S.C. § 77q(a); Securities Exchange Act of 1934, 15 U.S.C. § 78j(b).

Note: This chapter is intended for educational and informational purposes only and does not constitute legal advice or services. If legal advice is required, the services of a competent professional should be sought. These materials represent the views of and summaries by the author. They do not necessarily reflect the opinions or views of Vinson & Elkins LLP or of any of its other attorneys or clients. They are not guaranteed to be correct, complete, or current, and they are not intended to imply or establish standards of care applicable to any attorney in any particular circumstance.

in the offer and sale of all securities, including municipal securities, regardless of whether the securities are required to be registered with the Securities and Exchange Commission (SEC) under the Securities Act. Antifraud provisions served as the basis for regulation of the municipal market until market abuses prompted the addition of statutory provisions regulating municipal securities dealers in 1975.

In the early 1970s, municipal securities dealers known as *bond daddies* were selling investors often worthless municipal bonds out of offices in various cities in the American South.[3] Little regulation and lax enforcement enabled municipal securities dealers to prey on naïve investors and made it difficult for legitimate firms to do business. Some of the most common scams included selling vastly overvalued bonds, switching (substituting less valuable or risky securities for those actually paid for by an investor), bucketing (pocketing the purchase price for securities without delivering the securities), and making false representations about the security securing the payment of debt service and the level of risk associated with particular securities. In one of the most egregious cases, a municipal securities firm in Fort Lauderdale, Florida, solicited the business of Prisoners of War (POWs) returning from Vietnam in order to defraud the POWs of substantial amounts of back pay they had amassed while imprisoned.[4]

The SEC responded to fraudulent activities in the municipal market through a series of highly publicized enforcement actions under the antifraud provisions of the securities laws.[5] Such enforcements actions provided remedies after the fact, but had little preventive effect on bad conduct. In order to address the need for deterrence of fraudulent activities, Congress amended the securities laws and creating a limited federal regulatory framework for the municipal market as part of the 1975 Amendments.

In enacting the 1975 Amendments, Congress's approach to regulating the municipal market was through regulation of municipal securities dealers rather than direct regulation of the issuance and delivery of new issues of municipal securities by municipal issuers. The new regulatory framework established under the 1975 Amendments mandated that municipal securities dealers register with the SEC, created the Municipal Securities Rulemaking Board to provide for self-regulation of municipal securities dealers, and gave the SEC broad rulemaking and enforcement authority over all municipal securities dealers. The 1975 Amendments created the tripod of regulation for the U.S. municipal securities market that exists today: SEC broker-dealer regulation, MSRB regulation, and the antifraud provisions. SEC and MSRB

---

[3] See generally "Bond Daddies: The Birth of the Memphis Blues," *Institutional Investor* (June 1997), pp. 155, 156.

[4] See *SEC v. R.J. Allen & Assoc., Inc.*, 386 F. Supp. 866 (S.D. Fla. 1974).

[5] 1993 Staff Report on the Municipal Securities CCH at 6 (1993).

efforts to improve price transparency, provide a framework for continuing disclosure, curb conflicts of interest and corruption, and improve disclosure to investors in the municipal market all rest upon this tripod of authority. This chapter focuses on the role of the MSRB.

ORGANIZATION OF THE MSRB AND THE SCOPE OF RULEMAKING AUTHORITY

Congress instructed the SEC to establish the MSRB as a self-regulatory organization, similar in concept to the self-regulating National Association of Securities Dealers (NASD) and registered stock exchanges. Under the Exchange Act, Congress granted the MSRB primary rulemaking authority for municipal securities dealers, subject to approval of the MSRB's rules by the SEC. As a self-regulatory organization, the MSRB is financed through fees and assessments paid by municipal securities dealers rather than through public funds, and new board members are elected by the existing MSRB rather than appointed by Congress.

The MSRB is composed of 15 members consisting of five representatives of securities firms, five representatives of bank dealers, and five representatives of the general public at least one of which must represent issuers and one investors. Public representatives are subject to SEC approval to assure that no one of them is associated with any broker, dealer, or municipal securities dealer. Members serve three-year staggered terms with five new members elected each year. A nominating committee of nine persons including six MSRB members and three nonmembers nominate new members for election by the MSRB. Boardmembers may not succeed themselves in office, and a securities firm representative or bank dealer representative may not be succeeded by someone associated with such member's firm.

MSRB rules govern municipal securities dealers. Municipal securities dealers include municipal securities brokers, municipal securities dealers, and banks that have identifiable departments effecting transaction in municipal securities. The Exchange Act requires that municipal securities dealers register with the SEC thereby enabling identification of organizations engaged in the municipal securities business for examination and enforcement purposes and imposing qualifications for acting as a municipal securities dealer. Brokers and dealers are required to be members of NASD even if they are engaged solely in the municipal securities business, however, transactions in municipal securities are governed by MSRB rules and are not subject to NASD rules. Bank dealers are not required to be members of NASD.

The MSRB is responsible for adopting rules to prevent fraudulent and manipulative acts and practices, promote just and equitable principles of trade, and protect investors and the public interest. Under the Exchange Act, a violation of the MSRB rules is expressly made a violation of federal law, however, the MSRB has no enforcement or inspection authority. The MSRB makes rules and has substantial power to interpret its rules both generally and with regard to specific circumstances, through interpretive letters and notices promulgated by the MSRB, but its rules are enforced for securities firms by the NASD, for bank dealers by the Office of the Comptroller of the Currency, the Federal Reserve Board and the Federal Deposit Insurance Corporation, and for all municipal securities dealers by the SEC.

Since the MSRB is not a voluntary association of industry members but instead was created by an Act of Congress, it was necessary for the MSRB to establish rulemaking procedures that provide for industry participation. The MSRB generally issues rulemaking proposals in exposure draft form and provides for a public comment period. Draft rules are frequently modified in response to public comment. Proposed final rules are filed with the SEC and provided to the bank regulatory agencies charged with enforcement of MSRB rules. The SEC typically publishes the rules in the Federal Register and provides for an additional public comment period.

MSRB rules address a broad range of topics including matters pertaining to election and administration of the MSRB, standards of professional qualification of municipal securities dealers, supervision and compliance requirements pertaining to MSRB rules, recordkeeping requirements, uniform practices, market transparency, fair dealing, fair pricing and suitability requirements, conflict of interest disclosure and prohibitions relating to political contributions that could potentially influence the award of municipal securities business. The MSRB categorizes its rules into three categories: administrative rules, definitional rules and general rules. Administrative rules relate to internal operation of the MSRB. Definitional rules provide definitions for certain terms used throughout MSRB rules. Substantive regulation is primarily contained in the general rules. The remainder of this chapter focuses on the general rules.

PROFESSIONAL QUALIFICATIONS, SUPERVISION, RECORDKEEPING AND COMPLIANCE

The MSRB is responsible for providing rules setting forth professional qualifications for municipal securities dealers. Professional qualifications and related requirements are primarily contained in MSRB Rules G-2 through G-7. Under such rules, municipal securities professionals are classified into five categories (municipal securities principals, municipal securities sales principals, financial and operations principals, municipal securities representatives and municipal fund securities limited principals). Specific qualification requirements regarding testing, training and continuing education apply to each category of professionals. All municipal securities dealers are required to meet the applicable professional qualification requirements.

Municipal professionals categorized as principals are charged with supervisory responsibilities. Firms are required to employ a certain number of persons qualified as municipal securities principals in order to ensure compliance with MSRB rules. Each municipal securities firm or department is required to designate one or more qualified municipal securities principals and finance and operations principals and may designate one or more sales principals to perform certain supervisory functions. In addition, each firm or department is required to adopt, maintain, and enforce written supervisory procedures including procedures pertaining to the review of written and electronic correspondence with the public. Supervisory procedures are subject to review by the appropriate regulatory agency.

Municipal securities dealers are required to comply with restrictions imposed pursuant to disciplinary actions by the organizations responsible for enforcement of MSRB rules. Generally, a municipal securities dealers will be disqualified under MSRB rules if they have been expelled or suspended from membership or participation in any national securities exchange or the NASD. Municipal securities dealers are required to obtain certain types of information about the municipal professionals they employ, including employment history and professional background, any disciplinary sanctions, and the bases claimed, if any, for exemption from the MSRB's examination requirements. Brokers and dealers registered with a securities association must meet such securities association's requirements with regard to obtaining fidelity bonds to insure against losses caused by bonded employees.

In order to facilitate internal monitoring of compliance with MSRB rules as well as periodic compliance examinations by the appropriate enforcement organizations, MSRB Rules G-8 and G-9 contain recordkeeping requirements. Municipal securities dealers are required to make and keep current certain specified records concerning their municipal securities business, including information required to be obtained under other MSRB rules such as information about political contributions and information pertaining to recommendations of particular transactions to customers. Specific periods of time for preserving different types of records relating to a firm's or bank dealer's municipal securities business are prescribed under the rules.

Periodic compliance examinations of municipal securities dealers to ascertain compliance with applicable rules and regulations of the MSRB, the SEC and the Exchange Act are conducted in accordance with the requirements of Rule G-16.

UNIFORM PRACTICE RULES

The MSRB adopted a series of rules intended to standardize the business practices of municipal securities dealers in order to promote a more free and open municipal securities marketplace. These rules address uniform procedures for underwriting syndicates, clearing, transferring and settling municipal securities transactions, price quotations, and identification of securities through the CUSIP numbering system.

Underwriting Syndicates

Many municipal securities issues are sold by an issuer to a group of underwriters, referred to as a syndicate, rather than to a single underwriter. A syndicate is a group of underwriters that enter into a contractual agreement to jointly purchase and distribute securities. The purpose of Rule G-11 is to standardize many aspects of syndicate practice in order to facilitate the orderly marketing of securities among a variety of investors over a wide geographic area to enhance an issuer's access to capital and an investor's access to investment opportunities.[6]

Rule G-11 requires the lead manager in a syndicate to establish priorities for different categories of syndicate orders to apply during the initial public offering period and requires certain disclosures to syndicate members which are intended to assure that allocations are made in accordance with those priorities. In addition, in order to assure the accountability of managers for syndicate funds, the rule requires that the manager provide certain accounting information to syndicate members including an itemized statement setting forth the nature and amounts of all actual expenses incurred on behalf of the syndicate. In order to further standardize syndicate practice, the Municipal Bond Association has developed uniform agreements, consistent with Rule G-11, known as Master Agreements Among Underwriters for use in competitive and negotiated sales.

Uniform Settlement Procedures

Prior to the development in the 1970s of uniform procedures for clearance and settlement of transactions through clearing agencies and immobilization of securities through securities depositories, the trading and transfer of securities was highly disorganized and inefficient.[7] For municipal securities in bearer form, it was necessary to physically deliver securities and receive

---

[6] Robert A. Fippinger, *The Securities Law of Public Finance*, § 9:5.1 (New York City: Practising Law Institute, 2d ed. 2006).

[7] Fippinger, *The Securities Law of Public Finance*, §§ 9:1.2, 9:1.3 and 9:5.2.

a check in exchange, and repeated counting of securities was required.[8] Technological advances facilitated the development of automated systems for comparison, transfer and settlement of securities transactions, greatly enhancing the ability of municipal securities dealers to efficiently conduct securities transactions.[9]

Under Rule G-12, all interdealer transactions in municipal securities that are eligible for automated comparison must be compared in an automated comparison system operated by a registered clearing agency and must be registered in book-entry form.[10] Today, the Depository Trust Company (DTC) together with the National Securities Clearing Corporation (NSCC), both of whom are subsidiaries of the Depository Trust & Clearing Corporation (DTCC), provide this service for municipal securities. NSCC uses automated systems to compare submissions made by trading counterparties to make certain there is agreement as to the terms of the trade. NSCC's accounting system provides for continuous net settlement that summarizes and nets trades and payments among its participants at the end of each day, thereby reducing the volume of securities and payments that need to be exchanged. DTC acts as a central depository for holding securities in bulk form and maintaining ownership records of securities on its books, thereby enabling book-entry rather than physical transfer of securities from one owner to another.

Rule G-12 sets forth uniform practices for clearance and settlement of inter-dealer securities transactions including uniform practices relating to the following matters: (1) establishment of uniform settlement dates for transactions in municipal securities; (2) exchange and comparison of dealer confirmations and standard information required to be contained in such confirmations; (3) procedures for resolving discrepancies in confirmations which result in unrecognized transactions; (4) establishment of uniform requirements for good delivery of municipal securities; (5) procedures for rejection and reclamation of municipal securities; (6) close-out procedures for transactions in municipal securities; and (7) the time periods within which good faith deposits must be returned, syndicate accounts settled, and credits from designated orders distributed. The rule requires municipal securities dealers to include CUSIP numbers, if assigned, on interdealer confirmations and delivery tickets, as a means of uniform identification of the securities involved.

Bona Fide Price Quotations

Under Rule G-13, it is unlawful for a municipal securities dealer to distribute or publish a bid for or offer of a security unless the dealer is ready to buy

---

[8] Id.

[9] Id.

[10] Id.

or sell a security for its own account at the quoted price. The purpose of the rule is to promote efficient markets by preventing market manipulation.

CUSIP Numbers

CUSIP numbers are used to identify all registered municipal securities and are assigned by the CUSIP Services Bureau operated by Standard and Poors (S&P). CUSIP numbers consist of nine characters that identify the issuer, particular issue of securities, interest rate, and maturity. Rule G-34 requires that underwriters take certain steps to ensure that the issues they underwrite can be processed through the mandated systems for clearance, settlement and transaction reporting. Underwriters of new issues are required to apply to S&P for assignment of CUSIP numbers prior to the date securities are sold to such underwriters. In competitive sales, financial advisors subject to MSRB jurisdiction are required to obtain CUSIP numbers prior to the time of sale of the securities to an underwriter, thereby relieving the underwriter of such obligation. Rule G-34 also requires that underwriters of new issues apply to DTC to make such issues depository eligible.

MUNICIPAL MARKET TRANSPARENCY AND THE MSRB

In the United States, municipal securities are traded over-the-counter in a "negotiated" market. There are no organized exchanges operating auction-based markets for municipal securities as there are for corporate securities.[11] Municipal securities dealers publish a list indicating the municipal securities they are willing to sell, without quoting a firm price, and negotiate the price with dealers willing to buy the security. Until the MSRB mandated transaction reporting, current market transaction prices for municipal securities were difficult to access. A transparent market provides equal and immediate access to all quotations and reports of price and volume of all trades effected in the market to all market participants.[12] Without access to firm bid and ask quotations and last sale reports, market participants are disadvantaged in assessing the value in the secondary market of securities they own or might purchase. Access to prices paid by other market participants also enables investors to determine whether they have paid a fair price.

The MSRB initiated transaction reporting in 1995 and fully implemented a real-time transaction reporting system (RTRS) in 2005. Subject to certain exceptions, municipal securities dealers are required to report trades to the MSRB within 15 minutes of the time of execution of a trade through

---

[11] Public Securities Association, *Fundamentals of Municipal Bonds* 29 (1990).
[12] *1993 Staff Report on the Municipal Securities* CCH (1993).

electronic portals. Information on CUSIP numbers and description of issues traded, par values, prices, yields and dates and times of trades are available through the RTRS. The MSRB publishes price information on municipal securities transactions using data reported by municipal securities dealers. *The Daily Report of Frequently Traded Securities (Daily Report)* is free and is made available to subscribers each morning by 7:00 A.M. Currently, it includes details of transactions in municipal securities issues that were traded two or more times the previous business day. The *Daily Report* is one of the primary public sources of municipal securities price information and is used by a variety of industry participants to evaluate municipal securities.

The MSRB also publishes a *Daily Comprehensive Report*, providing details of all municipal securities transactions that were effected during the trading day one week earlier. The *Daily Comprehensive Report* is available by subscription. Along with trades in issues that are not "frequently traded," this report includes transactions reported to the MSRB late, interdealer trades compared after trade date, and transaction data corrected by municipal securities dealers after trade date. The MSRB Transaction Reporting Program provides market participants and the public with information about the municipal securities pricing for transparency purposes, and at the same time provides agencies charged with enforcing MSRB rules with a surveillance database to assist regulators in inspection for compliance with, and enforcement of, MSRB rules and securities laws.

FAIR DEALING AND SUITABILITY

MSRB fair practice rules address fair dealing, suitability and fair pricing and are designed to assure that municipal securities dealers observe high professional standards in dealing with customers.[13] Such rules address the disclosure responsibilities of municipal securities dealers, fair compensation requirements and the affirmative obligation of municipal securities dealers to make suitable recommendations and offer and purchase securities at market value.

Rule G-15 requires that customers in secondary market transactions receive a written confirmation pertaining to each transaction and also prescribes the form and content of such confirmation. The confirmation must contain information concerning the identity of the parties to a particular transaction, a description of the securities, the trade date, the settlement date, yield to maturity or dollar price, the capacity in which the municipal securities dealer is acting, and other specified information. The rule imposes

---

[13] MSRB Rules G-17 (fair dealing), G-19 (suitability) and G-30 (fair pricing); MSRB Manual CCH §§ 3581, 3591, and 3646. See, generally, *1993 Staff Report on the Municipal Securities* CCH (1993).

affirmative obligations on municipal securities dealers to disclose important details about securities including items such as call features, credit enhancement and the source of payment pledged to the securities. Additionally, municipal securities dealers are required to forward notices regarding securities to the beneficial owners of such securities.

Rule G-17 requires that municipal securities dealers deal fairly with all persons and prohibits municipal securities dealers from engaging in any deceptive, dishonest or unfair practice. The rule is interpreted by the MSRB to have both an affirmative disclosure component and an antifraud component. As part of a municipal securities dealer's obligation to deal fairly, the MSRB has stated that a municipal securities dealer has an affirmative obligation to disclose, at or before the sale of municipal securities to a customer, all material facts concerning the transaction, including a complete description of the security. Such requirement encompasses not only material facts known to the municipal securities dealer, but material facts reasonably accessible to the market, for example through official statements, rating agency reports, annual disclosure and material events filings, whether in a primary or secondary market transaction context. The rule distinguishes between inter-dealer transactions and transactions with certain institutional investors by imposing less extensive disclosure obligations on municipal securities dealers engaging in transactions with those entities, but there is no distinction with regard to the prohibition in engaging in deceptive practices.

MSRB rules require that a municipal securities dealer act diligently to assure a customer is purchasing or selling a security at a fair price that reflects the security's market value, in the case of Rule G-18, if the broker is acting as agent, and in the case of Rule G-30, if the dealer is purchasing for or selling from its own account.[14]Additionally, excessive compensation in the form of unreasonable mark-ups in the sale of securities and unreasonable markdowns in the purchase of securities are prohibited under Rule G-30.[15] Rule G-32 requires disclosure of underwriter compensation in a negotiated transaction, enabling the customer to evaluate the reasonableness of the compensation. Rule G-32 also requires disclosure of prices for each maturity, including those that are not being publicly reoffered, which enables a customer to compare the prices he is being offered to prices being offered to others, and the rule requires that customers be provided with official statements, if prepared, for a particular issue. Rule G-13 mandates that a price quotation be based on a municipal securities dealer's best judgment of the fair market value of the municipal securities.

Rule G-19 requires that a municipal securities dealer recommend only securities that are suitable for an investor's particular financial needs. Munic-

---

[14] Fippinger, *The Securities Law of Public Finance* at § 9:3.2 [E].

[15] Id.

ipal securities dealers are required to have an adequate basis for recommending a particular security based on information available from the issuer such as annual disclosure information readily available pursuant to SEC Rule 15(c)2-12. Prior to recommending a municipal securities transaction to a non-institutional investor, a municipal securities dealer is required to obtain information concerning (1) the customer's financial status; (2) the customer's tax status; (3) the customer's investment objectives; and (4) such other information used or considered to be reasonable and necessary by such municipal securities dealer in making recommendations to the customer. In the municipal securities area, a customer's tax status is a key component to making an appropriate recommendation since the benefits to an investor of tax-exempt income can differ substantially depending on the customer's particular tax status and portfolio of investments.[16] The dealer is required to use the information it obtains to make an affirmative determination of suitability with regard to any investment recommendation regardless of whether the recommendation is to an institutional or noninstitutional investor.[17]

Rule G-21 generally prohibits false and misleading advertising by municipal securities dealers of information about their skills and services or about the skills and services of other municipal securities dealers and imposes accuracy requirements with regard to advertisement of new issues (other than preliminary or final official statements). Rule G-24 prohibits municipal securities dealers from using confidential, nonpublic information concerning the ownership of municipal securities obtained while acting in a fiduciary or agency capacity for an issuer or another municipal securities dealer from using such information for the purpose of soliciting purchases, sales, or exchanges of municipal securities or otherwise using such information for financial gain without consent.

MUNICIPAL SECURITIES INFORMATION LIBRARY

Congress included language in the 1975 Amendments prohibiting the MSRB from requiring municipal issuers, directly or indirectly, through municipal securities dealers or otherwise, to furnish the MSRB or prospective investors with any documents, including official statements. The MSRB specifically is permitted, however, to require that official statements or other documents that are available from sources other than the issuer, such as the underwriter, be provided to investors.[18] Following the adoption in 1989 of Rule

---

[16] Id.

[17] Id.

[18] Securities Exchanges, 15 U.S.C. § 780-4 (2001); see also, 53 Fed. Reg. 37778 (1988).

15(c)2-12 by the SEC, underwriters of most municipal offerings greater than $1,000,000 were required to receive an official statement within seven business days after any final agreement to purchase, offer, or sell an issuer's municipal securities. Now that underwriters were required by law to have official statements, the MSRB could, and did, require underwriters to file them with the MSRB. In 1990, the MSRB adopted Rule G-36, requiring each municipal securities dealer acting as an underwriter of municipal securities in a primary offering to file the official statement within one business day of receipt but no later than 10 business days after any final agreement to purchase, offer or sell the municipal securities. In addition, if the underwritten issue advance refunds an outstanding issue of municipal securities, the rule requires delivery of the advance refunding documents as well.[19] The official statements sent to the MSRB under Rule G-36 enter into the Official Statement and Advance Refunding Document-Paper Submission System (OS/ARD), part of the MSRB's Municipal Securities Information Library (MSIL) System. OS/ARD collects official statements and advance refunding documents and makes them available on magnetic tape and paper.[20]

MARKET INTEGRITY

MSRB Rules G-20, G-22 G-23, G-37, and G-38 are designed to require disclosure of or prohibit certain conflicts of interest, limit gifts and gratuities, require disclosure of consultants used to obtain municipal securities business and regulate or prohibit certain political contributions.

Rules G-22 and G-23 require disclosure of certain potential conflicts of interest. Rule G-22 requires municipal securities dealers to disclose control relationships to customers before effecting transactions in such securities, and to memorialize such disclosure in writing. A control relationship with respect to a municipal security is deemed to exist if a municipal securities dealer (or a bank or other person of which municipal securities dealer is a department or division) controls, is controlled by, or is under common control with the issuer of the security or a person other than the issuer who

---

[19] Rule Approval Notice, 55 Fed. Reg. 23333 (June 7, 1990). An advance refunding transaction typically involves the defeasance of an outstanding issue of municipal securities subject to call protection (the "refunded" issue) through the substitution of a pool of escrowed U.S. Treasury securities providing payment of principal and interest to holders of the refunded issue until first call or maturity. The U.S. Treasury securities are purchased by a new issue of municipal securities carrying a lower interest rate (the "refunding" issue). The documents creating the escrow, are the "advance refunding documents."

[20] Proposed Rule Notice, 56 Fed. Reg. 28194 (June 19, 1991); *see also*, Municipal Securities Disclosure, 17 C.F.R. 240 (1994).

is obligated, directly or indirectly, with respect to debt service on the security. Rule G-23 provides procedural, disclosure and consent provisions that apply in the event a financial advisor will also act in the role of underwriter or remarketing agent. The rule also mandates disclosure to customers of the existence of a municipal securities dealer financial advisory relationship with regard to an issue of securities.

Rules G-37 and G-38 relating to political contributions and consultants are intended to curb a practice known as *pay-to-play*, in which contracts for professional services associated with marketing new issues of municipal securities are awarded on the basis of campaign contributions to elected officials responsible for selection.[21] Rule G-37 prohibits municipal securities dealers from engaging in municipal securities business with issuers, including providing financial advisory or consulting services, if such firms or any municipal finance professional associated with the firm or any PAC controlled by the firm or its municipal finance professionals makes certain defined political contributions to officials of such issuers. Notably, municipal securities dealers are not prohibited from making contributions, however they are prohibited from engaging in municipal securities business with an issuer if certain contributions are made.[22] Firms and associated municipal finance professionals, but not PACs, are also prohibited from soliciting contributions for issuers or coordinating contributions made by others. Rule G-37 also prohibits municipal securities dealers and municipal securities professionals from using other persons to avoid the prohibition such as lobbyists or consulting firms, PACS, lawyers spouse, or affiliates. Firms are required to retain records of political contributions and to disclose such records to the MSRB.

Municipal finance professionals include the professionals in the municipal securities department, professionals who solicit municipal securities business, the chain of supervisors of the firm up to the CEO, and anyone who is a member of the executive, or management committee.[23] In general, employees of retail broker firms whose sole responsibility is the sale of securities are not covered by the rule.[24] Contributions include payments "for the purpose of influencing any election for federal, state or local office" as well as other payments generally understood as political contributions.[25] An official of an issuer is a person who, at the time of the contribution, is an incumbent, candidate, or successful candidate for elective office of the issuer where that office can influence hiring of municipal securities dealers and any

---

[21] See "Municipal Machinations," *The Economist* 337, no. 79.39, 4 November 1995, p. 83.

[22] Fippinger, *The Securities Law of Public Finance* at § 9:9.2[C].

[23] Id., § 9:9.2[A].

[24] Id.

[25] Id., § 9:9.2[B].

person holding elective office of the state or another political subdivision if that person has authority to appoint any officials of an issuer who can influence the outcome of the hiring.

Certain exceptions apply regarding the prohibition of engaging in municipal securities business as a result of certain contributions. Municipal finance professionals who are entitled to vote for a particular official may contribute up to $250 to each such official for each election, including a primary, without triggering the prohibitions of the rule, but such professional cannot be reimbursed by the associated firm.[26] Municipal securities dealers are authorized to bid on competitive sales regardless of whether qualifying political contributions were made. No prohibitions apply as a consequence of donating volunteer time to an issuer official.

Municipal securities dealers must have procedures in place to make sure they don't inadvertently violate Rule G-37.[27] Regulatory agencies are required when doing compliance exams to review the information to make sure G-37 is observed. Information about contributions is available in the MSIL. In August 2005, the MSRB abandoned the approach of disclosure of use of consultants and revised the text of Rule G-38 to provide simply that "no broker, dealer or municipal securities dealer may provide or agree to provide, directly or indirectly, payment to any person who is not an affiliated person of the broker, dealer or municipal securities dealer for a solicitation of municipal securities business on behalf of such broker, dealer or municipal securities dealer."

Supplementing the policy of G-37 and G-38, Rule G-20 prohibits municipal securities dealers from directly or indirectly giving any service or anything of value in excess of $100 per year to any person. All gifts are aggregated to compute the $100 limitation and gifts by consultants at a firms' direction are counted toward the limit. There is an exemption for normal business dealings which are defined as occasional gifts of meals or tickets or legitimate business functions that are deductible.

ADDITIONAL INFORMATION REGARDING MSRB

Current MSRB rules, together with proposals to amend existing or adopt new rules, interpretive notices and letters, other guidance, and general information about the MSRB may be found on the MSRB website at www.msrb.org. Releases proposing and adopting MSRB rulemaking proposals may be found on the SEC's website at www.sec.gov/rules/sro/msrb. The releases accompanying rulemaking proposals and Rule adoption available on both web sites provide an informative explanation of the regulatory purpose for each rulemaking.

---

[26] Id., § 9:9.2[C].
[27] Id.

CHAPTER 23

The Role of the Securities and Exchange Commission

Paul S. Maco
Partner
Vinson & Elkins LLP

Cristy C. Edwards
Associate
Vinson & Elkins LLP

P rior to the adoption of the federal securities laws in the early part of the twentieth century, aggrieved investors found whatever recourse the law offered in a combination of common law rights and various state statutes enacted to curb speculation. Codified regulation of securities and securities transactions existed at the state level only, for a few states had specifically enacted "blue sky" statutes regulating the sale of securities within their borders a few decades before adoption of the federal securities laws.

Codified regulation of securities and the securities markets at the national level began in the United States in 1933 and the enactment of the Securities Act of 1933 (the Securities Act) as the first of what have come to be commonly known as the federal securities laws. Together with the Securities Act, the other federal laws commonly considered within the term "federal securities laws" include the Securities Exchange Act of 1934 (the

---

Note: This chapter is intended for educational and informational purposes only and does not constitute legal advice or services. If legal advice is required, the services of a competent professional should be sought. These materials represent the views of and summaries by the author. They do not necessarily reflect the opinions or views of Vinson & Elkins LLP or of any of its other attorneys or clients. They are not guaranteed to be correct, complete, or current, and they are not intended to imply or establish standards of care applicable to any attorney in any particular circumstance.

Exchange Act), the Trust Indenture Act of 1939, the Investment Advisers Act of 1940, and the Securities Investor Protection Act. The Public Utility Holding Company Act, formerly included in this term, was repealed in 2005. The Sarbanes-Oxley Act of 2002, aside from creating the Public Company Accounting Oversight Board, mandating several SEC studies, and amending several of the criminal law provisions of the United States Code, largely consists of amendments to the Securities Act and the Exchange Act. Appropriately, in the minds of many, the term *federal securities laws* has come to also include the Sarbanes-Oxley Act.

Initially, the Securities Act was administered by the Federal Trade Commission. Congress created the Securities and Exchange Commission in 1934 through Section 4 of the Exchange Act, at the conclusion of the Senate Banking and Currency Committee's 1932–1934 investigation of stock exchange practices.[1] The SEC administers the other provisions of federal securities law described above. The SEC also has regulatory and oversight authority over self-regulatory organizations (SROs) such as the Municipal Securities Rulemaking Board (MSRB) and National Association of Securities Dealers (NASD). As succinctly stated on its website, "the mission of the U.S. Securities and Exchange Commission is to protect investors, maintain fair, orderly, and efficient markets, and facilitate capital formation."

In passing the federal securities laws, Congress exercised a lighter regulatory touch on municipal securities. This occurred for a variety of reasons. Direct regulation of the process by which municipal issuers raise funds to finance government activities would have placed the federal government in the position of a gatekeeper to the financial markets for state and local governments.[2] Instead, Congress included exemptions for municipal securities in both the Securities Act and the Exchange Act for reasons that included the local nature of the markets, a perceived absence of abusive practices, the predominantly institutional nature of investors, and federal-state comity.[3] The antifraud provisions served as the sole basis for federal regulation of the municipal market until market abuses prompted the addition of statutory provisions regulating municipal securities dealers in 1975.

Although municipal securities and their issuers are exempt from the great bulk of federal securities laws, the complexity of contemporary securities structures and transactions may bring otherwise exempt securities back

---

[1] Joel Seligman, *The Transformation of Wall Street*, 3d ed. (New York: Aspen Press, 2003), p. 1. Seligman provides a detailed history of the origins and growth of regulation of U.S. financial markets.
[2] Exchange Act Release No. 26100 (September. 22, 1988) (the "88 Release"), 53 FR 37778.
[3] Division of Market Regulation, U.S. Securities. & Exchange Commission, Staff Report on the Municipal Securities Market (September 1993).

within the regulatory web of registration and reporting requirements. Many municipal market participants also look to the reporting requirements of the federal securities laws as a source of guidance in preparing disclosure for municipal securities offerings, even though the offerings are exempt from such provisions. For these reasons, a brief overview of the federal securities laws is offered below, followed by a discussion of those provisions of federal securities laws applicable to municipal securities.

FRAMEWORK OF THE FEDERAL SECURITIES LAWS

Definition of "Security"

Section 2(a)(1) of the Securities Act of 1933, which governs the registration of securities with the U.S. Securities and Exchange Commission (SEC or Commission), broadly defines a *security* as "any note, stock, treasury stock, security future, bond, debenture, evidence of indebtedness, certificate of interest or participation in any profit-sharing agreement, collateral-trust certificate, preorganization certificate or subscription, transferable share, investment contract, voting-trust certificate, certificate of deposit for a security, fractional undivided interest in oil, gas, or other mineral rights, any put, call, straddle, option, or privilege on any security, certificate of deposit, or group or index of securities (including any interest therein or based on the value thereof), or any put, call, straddle, option, or privilege entered into on a national securities exchange relating to foreign currency, or, in general, any interest or instrument commonly known as a 'security,' or any certificate of interest or participation in, temporary or interim certificate for, receipt for, guarantee of, or warrant or right to subscribe to or purchase, any of the foregoing."

The Securities Act of 1933: Registration of Public Offerings, Exempt Securities, and Exempt Transactions

The Securities Act of 1933 (the Securities Act) has two basic objectives: (1) to require that investors receive financing and other information about securities being offered for sale to the public; and (2) to prohibit deceit, misrepresentations, and fraud in the sale of securities offered to the public.[4] To achieve these objectives, the Securities Act requires registration of securities and disclosure of certain financial and other information, in order to permit investors to make informed decisions about whether or not to purchase par-

---

[4] U.S. Securities and Exchange Commission, available at http://www.sec.gov/about/laws.

ticular securities.[5] Although the SEC does not guarantee the accuracy of the information provided by issuers of securities, it provides certain recovery rights to investors who purchase securities and suffer losses if such investors can prove that the information disclosed was inaccurate or incomplete.[6]

The registration forms required under the Securities Act generally require inclusion of the following information: (1) a description of the issuer's properties and business; (2) a description of the security to be offered for sale to the public; (3) information about the management of the issuer; and (4) financial statements of the issuer which have been certified by an independent accountant.[7]

As discussed in Part III, certain securities are exempt from the registration requirements of the Securities Act. Among the exempted securities are most securities issued by municipal, state and federal governments, pursuant to Section 3(a)(2) of the Securities Act. In addition, certain types of transactions are exempted. For example, securities may be exempted under certain conditions if offered to a limited number of qualified persons or institutions or if the par amount of the securities to be offered is relatively small.

The Securities Exchange Act of 1934: Regulation of Securities Markets; Registration and Reporting.

The Securities Exchange Act of 1934 (the Exchange Act) created the Securities and Exchange Commission, and gave it broad authority over all aspects of the securities industry, including the power to register, regulate, and oversee brokerage firms, transfer agents, clearing agencies, and securities self-regulatory organizations (SROs) (including the New York Stock Exchange, American Stock Exchange, and the National Association of Securities Dealers, which operates the NASDAQ exchange).[8] The Exchange Act requires exchanges and broker-dealers to register with the SEC; establishes a system of broker-dealer regulation, and provides for registration and regulation of government securities brokers and dealers, a group over which the SEC, the Federal Reserve Board and the Secretary of the Treasury share regulatory authority.

The Exchange Act also permits the SEC to require annual information filings and other periodic reporting by companies with publicly traded securities.[9]

In addition, the Exchange Act prohibits certain types of conduct in the markets and gives the SEC enforcement power over certain regulated enti-

---

[5] U.S. Securities and Exchange Commission, available at http://www.sec.gov/about/laws.
[6] U.S. Securities and Exchange Commission, available at http://www.sec.gov/about/laws.
[7] U.S. Securities and Exchange Commission, available at http://www.sec.gov/about/laws.
[8] U.S. Securities and Exchange Commission, available at http://www.sec.gov/about/laws.
[9] U.S. Securities and Exchange Commission, available at http://www.sec.gov/about/laws.

ties and persons.[10] Notably, Section 10(b) of the Exchange Act, the antifraud provision, provides that:

> It shall be unlawful for any person, directly or indirectly, by the use of any means or instrumentality of interstate commerce or of the mails, or of any facility of any national securities exchange . . . . (b) To use or employ, in connection with the purchase or sale of any security registered on a national securities exchange or any security not so registered, . . . any manipulative or deceptive device or contrivance in contravention of such rules and regulations as the Commission may prescribe as necessary or appropriate in the public interest or for the protection of investors.

SEC Rule 10b-5, promulgated by the SEC under Section 10(b) of the Exchange Act further provides that:

> It shall be unlawful for any person, directly or indirectly, by the use of any means or instrumentality of interstate commerce, or of the mails or of any facility of any national securities exchange, (a) to employ any device, scheme or artifice to defraud, (b) to make any untrue statement of a material fact or to omit to state a material fact necessary in order to make the statements made, in light of the circumstances under which they were made, not misleading, or (c) to engage in any act, practice or course of business which operates or would operate as a fraud or deceit upon any person, in connection with the purchase or sale of any security.

The Exchange Act exempts issuers of municipal securities from its registration and reporting requirements.[11] Additionally, the Exchange Act contains a section known as the "Tower Amendment," added in 1975, which bars the MSRB from requiring issuer filings, both pre- and postsale, and the SEC from requiring presale filings.[12]

Financing Reporting under Securities Laws

SEC Authority

SEC authority regarding financial reporting is generally based on Section 19 of the Securities Act and Section 13(b) of the Exchange Act. Section 19(a) of

---

[10] U.S. Securities and Exchange Commission, available at http://www.sec.gov/about/laws.
[11] Securities Exchange Act § 3(a)(12), 12(A), 15 U.S.C. § 78c, § 78(i) (2001).
[12] Securities Exchange Act § 15B(d), 15 U.S.C. § 78o-4 (2001).

the Securities Act provides the SEC with authority to "prescribe the form or forms in which required information shall be set forth, the items or details to be shown in the balance sheet and earning statement, and the methods to be followed in the preparation of accounts, in the appraisal or valuation of assets and liabilities, in the determination of depreciation and depletion, in the differentiation of recurring and nonrecurring income, in the differentiation of investment and operating income, and in the preparation . . . of consolidated balance sheets or income accounts of any person directly or indirectly controlling or controlled by the issuer . . . ." Section 13(b) of the Exchange Act provides similar authority to the SEC with regard to financial reports to be made by issuers of securities registered pursuant to the Exchange Act.

Public Company Accounting Oversight Board (PCAOB)[13]

The Public Company Accounting Oversight Board (PCAOB) is a private-sector, nonprofit corporation created by the Sarbanes-Oxley Act of 2002 to oversee the auditors of public companies in order to protect the interests of investors and further the public interest in the preparation of informative, fair, and independent audit reports.

Registration Requirement   Section 102 of the Sarbanes-Oxley Act of 2002 prohibits accounting firms that are not registered with the PCAOB from preparing or issuing audit reports on U.S. public companies and from participating in such audits. Section 106(a) of the Act provides that any non-U.S. public accounting firm that prepares or furnishes an audit report with respect to any U.S. public company is subject to the PCAOB's rules to the same extent as a U.S. public accounting firm. Section 106(a) further authorizes the PCAOB to require that non-U.S. public accounting firms that do not issue such reports, but that play a substantial role in the preparation of the audit reports, register.

Required Inspections   Section 104 of the Sarbanes-Oxley Act of 2002 requires the PCAOB to conduct a continuing program of inspections of registered public accounting firms. In those inspections, the PCAOB assesses compliance with the Act, the rules of the PCAOB, the rules of the SEC, and professional standards, in connection with the firm's performance of audits, issuance of audit reports, and related matters involving issuers. The Act requires the PCAOB to conduct those inspections annually for firms that provide audit reports for more than 100 issuers and at least triennially for firms that provide audit reports for fewer issuers.

---

[13] Information in this section derived from the PCAOB web site, available at http://www.pcaobus.org.

The Act requires the PCAOB to prepare a written report concerning each inspection. Under the Act and the PCAOB's rules, the PCAOB provides a copy of each report, in appropriate detail, to the SEC and to certain state regulatory authorities. The PCAOB also makes portions of those reports available to the public, subject to restrictions in the Act that prohibit, or require a delay in, the public disclosure of certain information.

Establishment of Standards Section 103 of the Sarbanes-Oxley Act of 2002 directs the PCAOB to establish auditing and related attestation, quality control, ethics, and independence standards and rules to be used by registered public accounting firms in the preparation and issuance of audit reports as required by the Act or the rules of the SEC. The PCAOB's Office of the Chief Auditor advises the PCAOB Board on the establishment of such auditing and related professional practice standards. The PCAOB also seeks advice from its Standing Advisory Group and ad hoc task forces and working groups.

Enforcement Section 105 of the Sarbanes-Oxley Act of 2002 grants the PCAOB broad investigative and disciplinary authority over registered public accounting firms and persons associated with such firms. To implement this authority, Section 105(a) directs the PCAOB to establish, by rule, fair procedures for the investigation and discipline of registered public accounting firms and associated persons of such firms. The PCAOB has adopted rules relating to investigations and adjudications, and such rules have been approved by the SEC. These rules permit the PCAOB to conduct investigations concerning any acts or practices, or omissions to act, by registered public accounting firms and persons associated with such firms, or both, that may violate any provision of the Act, the rules of the PCAOB, the provisions of the securities laws relating to the preparation and issuance of audit reports and the obligations and liabilities of accountants with respect thereto, including the rules of the SEC issued under the Act, or professional standards. The PCAOB's rules require registered public accounting firms and their associated persons to cooperate with PCAOB investigations, including producing documents and providing testimony. The rules also permit the PCAOB to seek information from other persons, including clients of registered firms. When violations are detected, the PCAOB will provide an opportunity for a hearing, and in appropriate cases, impose sanctions designed to deter a possible recurrence and to enhance the quality and reliability of future audits. The sanctions may be as severe as revoking a firm's registration or barring a person from participating in audits of public companies. Lesser sanctions include monetary penalties and requirements for remedial measures, such as training, new quality control procedures, and the appointment of an independent monitor.

Regulation of Investment Companies

The Investment Company Act of 1940 is enforced by the SEC and governs companies (including mutual funds) that are engaged primarily in investing, reinvesting, and trading in securities, and whose own securities are offered to the public.[14] The Investment Company Act is aimed at minimizing conflicts of interest and requires certain investment companies to provide public disclosure on a regular basis regarding their financial condition and investment policies.[15]

Regulation of Investment Advisors

The Investment Advisers Act of 1940 governs certain investment advisors and is enforced by the SEC. The Investment Advisers Act generally requires firms or sole practitioners who are compensated for advising clients about securities investment to register with the SEC and conform to certain regulations intended to protect investors.[16] As amended in 1996, application of the Investment Advisers Act is generally limited to advisers with at least $25 million of assets under management or advisers who advise a registered investment company.[17]

The Investment Advisers Act applies to persons who are *investment advisors*, and defines such term to include: "any person who, for compensation, engages in the business of advising others, either directly or through publications or writings, as to the value of securities or as to the advisability of investing in, purchasing, or selling securities, or who, for compensation and as part of a regular business, issues or promulgates analyses or reports concerning securities; but does not include (1) a bank, or any bank holding company as defined in the Bank Holding Company Act of 1956, which is not an investment company; (2) any lawyer, accountant, engineer, or teacher whose performance of such services is solely incidental to the practice of his profession; (3) any broker or dealer whose performance of such services is solely incidental to the conduct of his business as a broker or dealer and who receives no special compensation therefor; (4) the publisher of any bona fide newspaper, news magazine or business or financial publication of general and regular circulation; (5) any person whose advice, analyses, or reports relate to no securities other than securities which are direct obligations of or obligations guaranteed as to principal or interest by the United States, or securities issued or guaranteed by corporations in which

---

[14] U.S. Securities and Exchange Commission, available at http://www.sec.gov/about/laws.
[15] U.S. Securities and Exchange Commission, available at http://www.sec.gov/about/laws.
[16] U.S. Securities and Exchange Commission, available at http://www.sec.gov/about/laws.
[17] U.S. Securities and Exchange Commission, available at http://www.sec.gov/about/laws.

the United States has a direct or indirect interest which shall have been designated by the Secretary of the Treasury, pursuant to section 3(a)(12) of the Securities Exchange Act of 1934, as exempted securities for the purposes of that Act; or (6) such other persons not within the intent of this paragraph, as the Commission may designate by rules and regulations or order."[18]

Under certain circumstances, the Investment Advisers Act may be applied to financial advisors of issuers of municipal securities. The Division of Investment Management of the SEC published a legal bulletin dated September 19, 2000 in order to clarify the circumstances under which the Investment Advisers Act would be applied to financial advisors.[19] Although the bulletin has neither been approved nor disapproved by the SEC and does not constitute a rule, regulation or statement of the SEC, its analysis may be useful to financial advisors.

In general, the Investment Advisers Act is not triggered when a financial advisor merely advises an issuer of municipal securities regarding the advisability of issuing securities and/or the structure, timing, and terms of their financings.[20] However, the Investment Advisers Act may be triggered when the financial advisor advises an issuer of municipal securities concerning the investment of the proceeds of a bond offering or other financing.[21]

There are a number of exclusions from the definition of "investment advisors" in the Investment Advisers Act, as indicated above. If none of those exclusions applies, a person is generally considered to be an investment advisor under the Investment Advisers Act if he or she: (1) provides advice, or issues reports or analyses, regarding securities or as to the advisability of investing in, purchasing, or selling securities; (2) for compensation; and (3) is in the business of providing such services.[22] These three elements have been construed broadly

---

[18] Section 202(a)(11) of the Investment Advisors Act of 1940, 15 U.S.C. § 80b-1 – 80b-21.

[19] U.S. Securities and Exchange Commission, Division of Investment Management: Staff Legal Bulletin No. 11 (September 19, 2000).

[20] Id. (citing Division of Investment Management no-action letter, *The Arkad Company* (available March 19, 1992); Division of Investment Management no-action letter, *Magnuson, McHugh & Co.* (available November 13, 1989); Division of Investment Management no-action letter, *Bruce H. Gemmel* (available July 14, 1976). See also L. Loss & J. Seligman, *Securities Regulation*, at 3345-46 (1991 ed.) ("[T]here is nothing to indicate that Congress intended that the Advisers Act should regulate investment banking functions."))

[21] U.S. Securities and Exchange Commission, Division of Investment Management: Staff Legal Bulletin No. 11 (September 19, 2000).

[22] Id. (citing *Applicability of the Investment Advisers Act to Financial Planners, Pension Consultants, and Other Persons who Provide Investment Advisory Services as a Component of Other Financial Services*, Advisers Act Release No. 1092 (Oct. 8, 1987)).

by the Division.[23] The "in the business" element is met if the person: (1) holds himself or herself out as an investment advisor (whether by advertising, word of mouth, through wording in its contracts with clients, or otherwise); (2) receives compensation for such advice (even if included in an overall compensation amount for a transaction); or (3) provides specific investment advice on anything other than rare, isolated, and nonperiodic instances.[24]

Aside from these elements, the Division takes the position in the Bulletin that advice regarding investments in money market funds provides a special exception to the application of the Investment Advisers Act as well. Because the SEC highly regulates money market funds and requires them to be very liquid and limited to high-quality, short-term investments, the Division asserts that a financial advisor that provides advice to a municipal issuer regarding the structure of its financing may also advise the issuer to invest proceeds of the financing in particular money market funds without meeting the "in the business" element, as long as such advice is incidental to the services provided to the client and the financial advisor does not have discretionary authority over the assets of its client that are invested in the money market funds.[25] However, in order for the money market exception to work to prevent the financial advisor from being considered to be an "investment advisor" under the Investment Advisers Act, the other two elements of the three-prong test must also be met (i.e., the financial advisor receives no compensation for the advice about the money market funds and the financial advisor does not hold itself out as an investment advisor).[26]

Trust Indenture Act

The Trust Indenture Act of 1939 is enforced by the SEC and applies to certain debt securities offered for sale to the public, including certain bonds, debentures, and notes.[27] The Trust Indenture Act requires that, prior to the public offering of such securities, the trust indenture entered into by the issuer of such securities must comply with certain standards and regulations con-

---

[23] U.S. Securities and Exchange Commission, Division of Investment Management: Staff Legal Bulletin No. 11 (September 19, 2000).

[24] U.S. Securities and Exchange Commission, Division of Investment Management: Staff Legal Bulletin No. 11 (September 19, 2000) (citing *Applicability of the Investment Advisers Act to Financial Planners, Pension Consultants, and Other Persons who Provide Investment Advisory Services as a Component of Other Financial Services*, Advisers Act Release No. 1092 (Oct. 8, 1987), at Section IIA.2).

[25] U.S. Securities and Exchange Commission, Division of Investment Management: Staff Legal Bulletin No. 11 (September 19, 2000).

[26] U.S. Securities and Exchange Commission, Division of Investment Management: Staff Legal Bulletin No. 11 (September 19, 2000).

[27] U.S. Securities and Exchange Commission, available at http://www.sec.gov/about/laws.

tained in the Trust Indenture Act.[28] Municipal securities are generally exempt from the requirements of the Trust Indenture Act provided that they qualify as exempt securities under Section 3(a) of the Securities Act of 1933.

APPLICATION TO MUNICIPAL SECURITIES

Exemptions for Municipal Securities

Federal securities laws more loosely regulate governmental than corporate issuers of securities. Congress exempted municipal securities from most provisions of the federal securities law more than 70 years ago because it perceived municipal bonds and other governmental securities to carry less investment risk than the equity and debt of business corporations and because of sensitivity to federal-state comity.[29] This dichotomy was reinforced three years ago by the exemption of municipal issuers from the provisions of the Sarbanes-Oxley Act.[30] As a result, the periodic reporting provisions of the securities laws[31]—which require SEC registrants to file quarterly and annual reports—and the provisions that require SEC registrants to maintain reliable internal controls and accurate books and records[32] do not apply to state or local governmental issuers.[33] The same is true of SEC Regulations S-X and S-K, which provide substantial guidance on the form and content of financial statements and other information filed with the SEC.

In general, when issuing securities, municipal issuers do not need to register the offering with the SEC, comply with the many complex rules relating to the offering process, or subsequently file or furnish periodic reports with the SEC at the times and in accordance with the many detailed rules and regulations governing such reports. Congress likewise chose to exempt

---

[28] U.S. Securities and Exchange Commission, available at http://www.sec.gov/about/laws.

[29] Municipal securities were granted special status in 1933 in the Securities Act and in 1934 in the Exchange Act, due to the financial expertise of institutional investors, the then typical purchasers of municipal securities, and the lack of perceived abuses in the municipal securities markets as compared to the market for corporate securities. Further, Congress was concerned that constitutional issues might arise if it attempted to subject municipal issuers to federal regulation. Division of Market Regulation, U.S. Securities and Exchange Commission, Staff Report on the Municipal Securities Market App. A at 1 (Sept. 1993) (footnotes omitted).

[30] Pub L 107-204, 116 Stat 745 (2002).

[31] Securities Exchange Act of 1934 ("Exchange Act"), § 13(a); Exchange Act Rules 13a-1, 13a-11, 13a-13.

[32] Securities Exchange Act of 1934, §§ 13(b)(2)(A) & (B), 13(b)(5).

[33] *In the Matter of County of Nevada, et al.*, Initial Decision Release No. 153 (October 29, 1999), available at http://www.sec.gov/litigation/aljdec/id153bpm.htm.

issuers of municipal securities from the application of what many consider the most significant expansion of the federal securities laws since the 1930s, the Sarbanes-Oxley Act of 2002. The SEC's authority to establish rules for accounting and financial reporting under Section 19 of the Securities Act and Section 13(b) of the Exchange Act does not extend to issuers of municipal securities. Congress also did not extend to municipal issuers the protections provided to certain forward-looking statements by issuers of securities and others when it amended the Securities Act and the Exchange Act in 1995 to provide such protections to registered issuers and certain others.

While exempt from the application of the great bulk of federal securities law, issuers of municipal securities are subject to the antifraud provisions of Securities Act's Section 17(a) and Exchange Act's Section 10 and Rule 10b-5. In addition, the SEC has fashioned a broker-dealer rule, Exchange Act Rule 15c2-12, that in general limits market access for municipal securities issues to those offerings in which the issuer agrees to file annual financial disclosure as well as reports of certain events, if material, with central repositories designated by the SEC. The SEC considers the antifraud rules to apply to such disclosures, as well as any other statements made to the market.

Securities Act of 1933 Exemptions

Municipal securities are exempted from the registration requirements of the Securities Act under § 3(a)(2), unless the securities are a type of third party conduit financing known as *industrial development bonds* that fail to meet the tax-exempt requirement contained in the exempting section.[34] Many municipal securities today are not simple direct obligations of a municipal issuer, but structured obligations such as certificates of participation. Care must be taken before concluding that a municipal security is exempt under the Securities Act. Although the municipal security is exempt, there may be a "separate security" within the structure of the security offered or sold, which may itself require identification of an exemption from registration, without which the offering will need to be sold in an exempt transaction

---

[34] Securities Act § 3(a)(2), 15 U.S.C. § 77c (2001) (The exemption covers "[a]ny security issued or guaranteed by the United States or any Territory thereof, or by the District of Columbia, or by any State of the United States, or by any political subdivision of a State or Territory or by any public instrumentality of one or more States or Territories, . . . or any security which is an industrial development bond (as defined in section 103(c)(2) of the Internal Revenue Code of 1954) the interest on which is excludable from gross income under section 103(a)(1) of such Code, if by reason of the application of paragraph (4) or (6) of section 103(c) of such Code (determined as if paragraphs (4)(A), (5), and (7) were not included in such section 103(c)), paragraph (1) of such section 103(c) does not apply to such security"), Securities Act § 2(a)(1), 15 U.S.C. § 77b (2001) (definition of "security").

or registered with the SEC.[35] Furthermore, all financing structures require analysis to determine their exempt status under the registration and reporting requirements of the Securities Act and the Exchange Act.

Securities Exchange Act of 1934 Exemptions

Exemption from Registration and Reporting Requirements The Exchange Act exempts municipal securities from its registration and reporting requirements.[36] Additionally, the Exchange Act contains a section known as the Tower Amendment, added in 1975, which bars the Municipal Securities Rulemaking Board from requiring issuer filings, both presale and postsale, and the SEC from requiring pre-sale filings.[37] The Tower Amendment is often confused with the exemptions afforded municipal securities from the registration and reporting requirements of the Securities Act and the Exchange Act, respectively. Such exemptions existed, however, prior to adoption of the Tower Amendment.

Exemption from Tender Offer Rules Except for the antifraud provisions under Section 14(e), the proxy and tender offer provisions of Section 14 of the Exchange Act do not apply to municipal securities, either because of express application to equity securities registered under Section 12 of the Exchange Act or exemptions of application to exempted securities. Section 14(e) provides:

> It shall be unlawful for any person to make any untrue statement of a material fact or omit to state any material fact necessary in order to make the statements made, in the light of the circumstances under which they are made, not misleading, or to engage in any fraudulent, deceptive, or manipulative acts or practices, in connection with any tender offer or request or invitation for tenders, or any solicitation of security holders in opposition to or in favor of any such offer, request, or invitation. The Commission shall, for the purposes of this subsection, by rules and regulations define, and prescribe means reasonably designed to prevent, such acts and practices as are fraudulent, deceptive, or manipulative.

The text of Section 14(e) begins with language similar to that contained in Rule 10b-5 of the Exchange Act; however, while 10b-5 applies "in con-

---

[35] See Securities Act Rule 131. See generally Robert Fippinger, Practicing Law Institute, *The Securities Law of Public Finance*, Chapter 2 (2006).
[36] Securities Exchange Act § 3(a)(29), 12(A), 15 U.S.C. § 78c, § 78(i) (2001).
[37] Securities Exchange Act § 15B(d)(2), 15 U.S.C § 78o-4 (2001).

nection with the purchase or sale of a security," Section 14(e) applies to unconsummated offers, requests, invitations, or solicitations. Congress also delegates rulemaking authority to the SEC under Section 14(e), without excluding application to municipal securities. To date, the SEC has not exercised this authority with respect to municipal securities. As noted in Rule 14d-1: "Regulation 14E shall apply to any tender offer for securities (other than exempted securities) unless otherwise noted therein."

Exemption from Internal Controls Requirements and Sarbanes-Oxley Measures under Sections 10A and 13 The Sarbanes-Oxley requirements affecting audits, financial reporting and internal control significantly increased both the extent of detail and cost of compliance for affected entities. State and local governments issuing municipal securities are exempt from these provisions. Nevertheless, through voluntary implementation of best practices, state legislation seeking to mimic Sarbanes-Oxley reforms at the state and local level, standards imposed by service providers such as independent audit firms, and even SEC enforcement proceedings, state and local government may experience an increase in financial accounting and reporting standards resembling that affecting public companies. In one noteworthy enforcement action, the SEC sanctioned a state sponsor of 529 plans for a failure to disclose known and ongoing weaknesses in internal controls, even though the entity was not within the scope of Exchange Act Section 13b2.[38]

Exemption from Financial Reporting/Accounting Regulation

The SEC's authority to establish rules for accounting and financial reporting under Section 19 of the Securities Act and Section 13(b) of the Exchange Act does not extend to issuers of municipal securities. However, as discussed herein, Exchange Act Rule 15(c)2-12, promulgated by the SEC, generally limits market access for municipal securities issues to those offerings in which the issuer agrees to file annual financial disclosure as well as reports of certain events, if material, with central repositories designated by the SEC. In addition, the antifraud provisions of the Securities Act and the Exchange Act apply to any such disclosures.

Application of Antifraud Provisions

The federal securities laws that do apply to municipal issuers are limited to the antifraud provisions: Section 17(a) of the Securities Act of 1933 ("Secu-

---

[38] *In the Matter of Utah Educational Savings Plan Trust*, Securities Act Release No. 8601, August 4, 2005.

rities Act")[39], Section 10(b) of the Exchange Act,[40] and Exchange Act Rule 10b-5.[41] In a March 1994 Interpretive Release (the "March 1994 Interpretive Release"), the SEC informed the municipal market:

> These antifraud provisions prohibit any person, including municipal issuers and brokers, dealers and municipal securities dealers, from making a false or misleading statement of material fact, or omitting any material facts necessary to make statements made by

---

[39] Section 17(a) of the Securities Act provides:

> It shall be unlawful for any person in the offer or sale of any securities or any security-based swap agreement (as defined in § 206B of the Gramm-Leach-Bliley Act [15 USC § 78c note]) by the use of any means or instruments of transportation or communication in interstate commerce or by use of the mails, directly or indirectly
>
> (1) to employ any device, scheme, or artifice to defraud; or
>
> (2) to obtain money or property by means of any untrue statement of a material fact or any omission to state a material fact necessary in order to make the statements made, in light of the circumstances under which they were made, not misleading; or
>
> (3) to engage in any transaction, practice, or course of business which operates or would operate as a fraud or deceit upon the purchaser.

[40] Section 10(b) of the Exchange Act provides that "[i]t shall be unlawful for any person, directly or indirectly, by the use of any means or instrumentality of interstate commerce or of the mails, or of any facility of any national securities exchange . . .

> b. To use or employ, in connection with the purchase or sale of any security registered on a national securities exchange or any security not so registered, or any securities-based swap agreement (as defined in section 206B of the Gramm-Leach-Bliley Act), any manipulative or deceptive device or contrivance in contravention of such rules and regulations as the Commission may prescribe as necessary or appropriate in the public interest or for the protection of investors."

[41] Exchange Act Rule 10b-5 provides, in part:

> It shall be unlawful for any person, directly or indirectly, by the use of any means or instrumentality of interstate commerce, or of the mails or of any facility of any national securities exchange,
>
> a. To employ any device, scheme, or artifice to defraud,
>
> b. To make any untrue statement of a material fact or to omit to state a material fact necessary in order to make the statements made, in the light of the circumstances under which they were made, not misleading, or
>
> c. To engage in any act, practice, or course of business which operates or would operate as a fraud or deceit upon any person, in connection with the purchase or sale of any security.

that person not misleading, in connection with the offer, purchase or sale of any security.[42]

Following the Orange County, California bankruptcy, the SEC initiated and settled its first comprehensive series of enforcement actions against an issuer of municipal securities, the issuer's governing body, certain officials of the issuer, and certain professionals involved in the offering of Orange County's securities.[43]

The SEC summarized the basics of the antifraud provisions in the settled Administrative Proceeding for Orange County:

> Section 17(a) of the Securities Act and Section 10(b) of the Exchange Act and Rule 10b-5 thereunder make it unlawful for any person, in the offer or sale (Section 17(a)) or in connection with the purchase or sale of any security (Section 10(b) and Rule 10b-5), to employ any device, scheme, or artifice to defraud, to make any untrue statement of a material fact, to omit to state a material fact, or to engage in any act, practice or course of business which operates or would

---

[42] Statement of the Commission Regarding Disclosure Obligations of Municipal Securities Issuers and Others, 59 Fed. Reg. 12,748, 12,749 (March 17, 1994) [hereinafter March 1994 Interpretive Release]. See also *Sonnenfeld v. City and County of Denver*, 100 F.3d 744, 746-47 (10th Cir. 1996) (citing *In re CitiSource Sec. Litig.*, 694 F. Supp. 1069, 1072-75 (S.D. N.Y. 1988)); and *In re Washington Pub. Power Supply Sys. Sec. Litig.*, 623 F. Supp. 1466, 1477-80 (W.D. Wash. 1985), *aff'd on other grounds*, 823 F.2d 1349 (9th Cir. 1987)).

[43] *In re County of Orange, California; Orange County Flood Control District; and County of Orange, California Board of Supervisors*, Securities Act Release No. 7260, Exchange Act Release No. 36730 (January 24, 1996), A.P. File No. 3-8937 ("Administrative Proceeding"); *Report of Investigation in the Matter of County of Orange, California as it Relates to the Conduct of the Members of the Board of Supervisors*, Exchange Act Release No. 36761 (January 24, 1996) ("Report"); *SEC v. Robert L. Citron and Matthew R. Raabe*, SACV 96-74 GLT (CD Cal.), Litigation Release No. 14792 (January 24, 1996) (complaint); *SEC v. Robert L. Citron and Matthew R. Raabe*, Litigation Release No. 14913 (May 17, 1996) (settled final orders); *In re Newport-Mesa Unified School District*, Securities Act Release No. 7589, A.P. File No. 3-9738 (September 29, 1998). *In re CS First Boston Corp., Jerry L. Nowlin and Douglas J. Montague*, Securities Act Release No. 7498, Exchange Act Release No. 39595, A.P. File No. 3-9535 (January 29, 1998); *In re Merrill Lynch, Pierce, Fenner & Smith Inc.*, Securities Act Release No. 7566, Exchange Act Release No. 40352, A.P. File No. 3-9683 (August 24, 1998); *In re RBC Dain Rausche, Inc.*, Securities Act Release No. 8121, Exchange Act Release No. 46346, A.P. File No. 3-10863 (August 13, 2002); *In the Matter of Kenneth D. Ough*, Securities Act Release No. 8141, Exchange Act Release No. 46736, A.P. File No. 10922 (October 29, 2002); *In re Jean Costanza*, Securities Act Release No. 7621, A.P. File No. 3-9799 (January 6, 1999).

operate as a fraud or deceit upon any person through the means or instruments of interstate commerce or the mails. Information is material if there is a substantial likelihood that a reasonable investor would consider it important to an investment decision. See *Basic Inc. v. Levinson*, 485 U.S. 224, 231-32 (1988); *TSC Industries, Inc. v. Northway, Inc.*, 426 U.S. 438, 449 (1976). Furthermore, when the information pertains to a possible future event, materiality will depend upon a balancing of both the indicated probability that the event will occur and the anticipated magnitude of the event in light of the totality of the company activity. "Basic Inc., 485 U.S. at 238 (quoting *SEC v. Texas Gulf Sulphur Co.*, 401 F.2d 833, 849 (2d Cir. 1968) (en banc), cert. denied, 394 U.S. 976 (1969)).

Scienter is required to establish violations of Section 17(a)(1) of the Securities Act and Section 10(b) of the Exchange Act and Rule 10b-5 thereunder. See *Aaron v. SEC*, 446 U.S. 680, 701-02 (1980). Scienter is "a mental state embracing intent to deceive, manipulate or defraud." *Ernst & Ernst v. Hochfelder*, 425 U.S. 185, 193 n. 12 (1976). In the Ninth Circuit, recklessness satisfies the Scienter requirement. *Hollinger v. Titan Capital Corp.*, 914 F.2d 1564 (9th Cir. 1990) (en banc), cert. denied, 499 U.S. 976 (1991). Recklessness is "an extreme departure from the standards of ordinary care, and which presents a danger of misleading [investors] that is either known to the defendant or is so obvious that the actor must have been aware of it." Id., 914 F.2d at 1569.

In settling with one of the underwriters of Orange County securities,[44] the SEC explained that negligence is sufficient for a violation of Securities Act Sections 17(a)(2) and (3):

Sections 17(a)(2) and (3) of the Securities Act make it unlawful for any person, through the means or instruments of interstate commerce or the mails, in the offer or sale of any security: "(2) to obtain money or property by means of any untrue statement of a material fact or any omission to state a material fact necessary in order to make the statements made, in light of the circumstances under which they were made, not misleading; or (3) to engage in any transaction, practice, or course of business which operates or would operate as a fraud or deceit upon the purchaser." Scienter is not required to prove violations of Sections 17(a)(2) or (3) of the Securities Act. *Aaron v. SEC*, 446 U.S. 680, 697 (1980). Violations of these sections may be established by showing negligence. *SEC v.*

---

[44] Securities Act Release No. 7566, supra note 407.

Hughes Capital Corp., 124 F.3d 449, 453-54 (3d Cir. 1997); *SEC v. Steadman*, 967 F.2d 636, 643 n.5 (D.C. Cir. 1992).

Liability for misleading disclosure under the antifraud provisions reaches both "primary violators"[45] and those who "knowingly provide substantial assistance" to the primary violator.[46] In administrative proceedings, moreover, the SEC may seek sanctions against those who "cause" violations of the antifraud provisions.[47]

The sanctions available to the SEC for violations of the antifraud provisions include injunctions and cease-and-desist orders prohibiting future violations of the securities laws, disgorgement of improperly obtained funds, if any, and civil penalties in amounts limited by statute. The government, however, to date has rarely sought civil penalties from governmental units, apparently reflecting the understanding that they are ultimately paid by the public through taxes. No statute of limitations applies to SEC injunctive actions, but the remedy of civil penalties is time-barred after five years from the date of the violation.[48]

Since the Orange County proceedings, the SEC has brought enforcement actions against numerous issuers of municipal securities in a variety of circumstances in which the municipal issuer's disclosure was deemed misleading.[49]

Elements of Cause of Action

Section 17(a)(1) and Rule 10b-5 are substantially similar;[50] indeed Rule 10b-5 was modeled on Section 17(a).[51] As a general matter, these regula-

---

[45] "Any person or entity . . . who employs a manipulative device or makes a material misstatement (or omission) on which a purchaser or seller of securities relies may be liable as a primary violator under 10b-5, assuming all of the requirements for primary liability under Rule 10b-5 are met." *Central Bank of Denver, N.A. v. First Interstate Bank of Denver, N.A.*, 511 U.S. 164, 191 (1994), superseded by statute on other grounds.

[46] See Exchange Act § 20(e). The Ninth Circuit has held that this section was intended by Congress to "preserve the definition of aiding and abetting as it existed pre-*Central Bank*" in SEC actions. *SEC v. Fehn*, 97 F. 3d 1276, 1288 (9th Cir. 1996).

[47] Exchange Act, § 21C(a).

[48] *SEC v. Rind*, 991 F.2d 1486, 1492 (9th Cir 1993); *SEC v. Lorin*, 76 F.3d 458 (2d Cir. 1996) (per curiam).

[49] The SEC posts these cases on its web site at http://www.sec.gov/info/municipal.

[50] The wording of each differs in minor respects: under Securities Act § 17(a)(2) it is unlawful to "obtain money or property through the means of any untrue statement," while under Rule 10b-5 it is simply unlawful "to make any untrue statement:" The activity prohibited under § 17(a)(2) is activity "in the offer or sale of any securities," while in the case of Rule 10b-5 it is "in connection with the purchase or sale of any security."

[51] John C. Coffee, Jr. and Joel Seligman, *Securities Regulation*, 968 (9th ed. 2003) (quoting ABA Sec. Corp., Banking & Bus. Law, *Conference on Codification of the Federal Securities Laws*, 22 Bus. Law. 793, 921–923).

tions provide that it is unlawful for any person, in connection with securities transactions, to make any untrue statement of a material fact or to omit to state a material fact necessary in order to make the statements made, in light of the circumstances under which they were made, not misleading.

The U.S. Court of Appeals for the Ninth Circuit has observed that in order to prove a violation of Section 10(b) and Rule 10b-5, the SEC must prove: (1) a material misrepresentation, (2) in connection with the purchase or sale of a security, and (3) scienter. An additional element of proof is necessary to obtain injunctive relief: a reasonable likelihood of future violations.[52] A lesser standard is applied in administrative proceedings for the imposition of a cease-and-desist order. The SEC explained the application of this standard in the *City of Miami* order.[53]

Scienter

A finding of scienter is necessary to establish a violation of Section 17(a)(1) of the Securities Act and Section 10(b) of the Exchange Act and Rule 10b-5

---

[52] *SEC v. Rana Research, Inc.*, 8 F.3d 1358, 1364 (9th Cir 1993) (citing *SEC v. Hasho*, 784 F. Supp. 1059, 1106, 1110 (S.D.N.Y. 1992) and *SEC v. Tome*, 638 F. Supp. 596, 620 & n. 46 (S.D.N.Y. 1986)).

[53] *In re City of Miami, Florida*, Securities Act of 1933 Release No. 8213 (March 21, 2003), Securities Exchange Act of 1934 Release No. 47552 (March 21, 2003).

In assessing whether a cease-and-desist order is an appropriate sanction, we focus on the risk of future violations.

This inquiry is a flexible one and no one factor is dispositive. This inquiry is undertaken not to determine whether there is a "reasonable likelihood" of future violations but to guide our discretion." In the ordinary case, and absent evidence to the contrary, a finding of past violation raises a risk of future violation sufficient to support our ordering a respondent to cease and desist. "To put it another way, evidence showing that a respondent violated the law once probably also shows a risk of repetition that merits our ordering to cease and desist." We also consider: the seriousness of the violation, the isolated or recurrent nature of the violation, the respondent's state of mind, the sincerity of the respondent's assurances against future violations, the respondent's recognition of the wrongful nature of his or her conduct, and the respondent's opportunity to commit future violations. In addition, we consider whether the violation is recent, the degree of harm to investors or the marketplace resulting from the violation, and the remedial function to be served by the cease-and-desist order in the context of any other sanctions being sought in the same proceeding. We further may consider the function a cease-and-desist order will serve in alerting the public that a respondent has violated the securities laws.

quoting KPMG Peat Marwick LLP, Exchange Act Release No. 43862 (January 19, 2001), 74 SEC Docket 384, 436 *motion for reconsideration denied*, Exchange Act Release No. 44050 (March 9, 2001) 74 SEC Docket 1351, *petition denied*, 289 F.3d 109 (D.C. Cir. 2002) and 74 SEC Docket at 430, 436, and note 148.

thereunder.[54] The Supreme Court has determined, however, that Section 17(a)(2) and (3) of the Securities Act may be violated through merely negligent conduct.[55]

Scienter, as used by the Supreme Court in *Hochfelder*, means "a mental state embracing intent to deceive, manipulate, or defraud."[56] The Court in that case, however, stopped short of considering "whether, in some circumstances, reckless behavior is sufficient for civil liability under § 10(b) and Rule 10b-5."[57] Federal Courts of Appeals since *Hochfelder* have interpreted recklessness to be sufficient to constitute scienter, with slight variations among circuits. In the Ninth Circuit, the standard for reckless conduct sufficient to constitute scienter is interpreted as "highly unreasonable [conduct], involving not merely simple, or even inexcusable negligence, but an extreme departure from the standards of ordinary care, and which presents a danger of misleading buyers or sellers that is either known to the defendant or is so obvious that the actor must have been aware of it."[58]

Negligence

The negligence threshold established for Section 17(a)(2) and (3) of the Securities Act under the Supreme Court's holding in Aaron has been articulated in a recent Ninth Circuit decision involving an underwriter of municipal securities as: one of "reasonable prudence, for which the industry standard is but one factor to consider . . . [E]vidence of compliance with custom or industry practice [is] a relevant, but not a determinative factor, in determining whether the appropriate standard of care [has] been met."[59] In adopting this standard, the Ninth Circuit accepted the definition advanced by the SEC in its brief on appeal. As to what constitutes "the industry standard," when "to the extent there is any industry standard of conduct, . . . the standard is sparse and not particularly helpful," the court ruled that "there are genuine issues of material fact as to what is the appropriate industry standard."[60] In particular, the Ninth Circuit found it difficult to define an "industry standard" for underwriters of municipal securities, a group more

[54] *SEC v. Rana Research, Inc.*, 8 F.3d 1358, 1364 (9th Cir. 1993); *Ernst & Ernst v. Hochfelder*, 425 U.S. 185, 201-02 (1976).

[55] *Aaron v. SEC*, 446 U.S. 680, 695-97 (1980).

[56] *Hochfelder*, 425 U.S. at 193, n. 12.

[57] *Hochfelder*, 425 U.S. at 193, n. 12.

[58] *Hollinger v. Titan Capital Corp.*, 914 F.2d 1564, 1569 (9th Cir. 1990) (en banc) (quoting *Sundstrand Corp. v. Sun Chem. Corp.*, 553 F.2d 1033, 1044-45 (7th Cir 1977)).

[59] *SEC v. Dain Rauscher, Inc.*, 254 F.3d 852, 856-57 (9th Cir. 2001) (*citing Doe v. Cutter Biological, Inc.*, 971 F.2d 375, 383 (9th Cir 1992)).

[60] Id. at 857, 859.

heavily regulated than issuers of municipal securities and their officials.[61] The potential culpability will be considered, based on [Available Evidence,] from the standpoint of whether conduct falls into one of three categories: (1) poor judgment falling short of culpable negligence; (2) conduct sufficiently contrary to the actions expected of a reasonably prudent person under the circumstances to constitute negligent conduct; and (3) conduct sufficiently beyond the conduct expected of a reasonably prudent person to constitute recklessness, as defined in Hollinger. Factors affecting this evaluation include relevant SEC guidance, industry practice, and the expectations of rating agencies.

Available Defenses to Application of Antifraud Provisions

To find that a violation of the anti-fraud provisions has occurred, the finder of fact must determine that each element of those causes of action has been demonstrated by a preponderance of the evidence. The Supreme Court decision in *TSC Industries, Inc. v. Northway, Inc.* highlights the "delicate assessment" of determining violations of the antifraud provisions.[62] Materiality and state of mind are elements as to which evidentiary analyses may be particularly subtle and complex. The presence or absence of many factors, such as recognized standards of industry practice, discussed above, and reliance on advice of counsel or other professionals can be influential in a determination of liability.[63]

Upon proof of a violation, a remedy may not always be available. As noted above, the SEC must demonstrate a reasonable likelihood of future violations. In another SEC Administrative Proceeding, Judge Murray dismissed the proceeding after holding:

> Although it is not necessary to find a likelihood of future violations to impose a cease-and-desist order, where, as here, it is highly unlikely that a respondent will commit future violations and no remedial purpose will be served by issuing a cease and desist order,

---

[61] Id. at 856-59.

[62] 426 U.S. 438, 450 (1976).

[63] Reliance on advice of counsel is not an absolute defense. As noted by the SEC's Chief Administrative Law Judge: "A person asserting reliance on counsel as a defense must show that he/she: (1) made a complete disclosure to counsel; (2) sought and received advice that the proposed conduct was legal; and (3) relied on that advice in good faith." *In re Thorn, Alvis, Welch, Inc.*, 61 SEC Docket 2524 (May 2, 1996), available at http://www.sec.gov/litigation/aljdec/id88bpm.txt, at 26 (citing *Markowski v. SEC*, 34 F.3d 99, 105 (2d Cir 1994); *SEC v. Goldfield Deep Mines of Nevada*, 758 F.2d 459, 467 (9th Cir. 1985); *SEC v. Melchior*, [1992-93 Transfer Binder] Fed Sec. L. Rep. (CCH) ¶ 97,356, at 95,838 (D. Utah January 14, 1993).

such an order need not automatically follow upon finding that respondent has violated the securities laws.[64]

Application of the Antifraud Provisions in the Municipal Market

Despite the restricted application of the federal securities laws to the municipal market, the SEC has been active in policing the accuracy of the securities-related disclosure of municipalities and other government entities.[65] Actions brought by the SEC against municipalities have addressed a variety of disclosure failures, most related to the entity's financial soundness. For example, the SEC opinion *In re Massachusetts Turnpike Authority*[66] addressed a failure to disclose to the public substantial cost overruns from the "big dig" roadway and tunnel project in Boston, Massachusetts, as well as the imposition of liability for statements prepared by one party (the Turnpike) for use in the disclosures of a second party (the Commonwealth of Massachusetts). *In re City of Miami, Florida* addressed a failure to disclose Miami's deteriorating cash position and the possible impact of that trend on its ability to service its debt.[67]

Consequences of Exempt Status

In contrast to a public company, when a municipal government issues its securities, it does not file any documents with the SEC or wait for review, comment and approval of its registration materials before it may sell those securities to investors. While municipal issuers are spared the time and expense associated with completing and filing the detailed forms prescribed by federal securities laws required prior to the sale of most corporate securities, they also do not benefit from the implicit guidance available in SEC forms, rules and regulations surrounding the registration process.

Municipal issuers preparing disclosure also do not benefit from the interaction between their counsel and staff in the Division of Corporation Finance over staff comments to their filings. SEC staff are available and

---

[64] *In re County of Nevada, City of Ione, Wasco Public Financing Authority, Virginia Horler, and William Mckay*, Initial Decision Release No. 153, Administrative Proceeding File No. 3-9524 (October 29, 1999), at 27.

[65] See *Office of Municipal Securities: Cases and Materials*, available at http://www.sec.gov/info/municipal/ mbonds/omstoc.shtml.

[66] Securities Act Release No. 8260 (July 31, 2003), Admin. Proc. File No. 3-11198, available at http://www.sec.gov/litigation/admin/33-8260.htm.

[67] Id. Among other points made by the Commission in its Miami opinion relevant to the present matter is the effect of bond insurance. The SEC stated: "Bond insurance did not give Miami license to misrepresent its financial condition or withhold material information from the marketplace."

often diligent in helping issuers comply with SEC reporting requirements, particularly in unusual situations and times of transition, such as the flood of new rules and regulations following passage of the Sarbanes-Oxley Act.

Municipal issuers have no such guidance available to them and must look elsewhere for guidance in preparing their disclosures, in particular, to the marketplace and best practices. In an Interpretive Release providing guidance on its views of the application of the antifraud provisions to municipal securities, the SEC observed:

> In the absence of a statutory scheme for municipal securities registration and reporting, disclosure by municipal issuers has been governed by the demands of market participants and antifraud strictures. Spurred by the New York City fiscal crisis in 1975 and the Washington Public Power Supply System defaults, participants in the municipal securities market have developed extensive guidance to improve the level and quality of disclosure in primary offerings of municipal securities, and to a more limited extent, continuing disclosure in the secondary market.[68]

As noted above, the SEC's authority to establish rules for accounting and financial reporting under Section 19 of the Securities Act and Section 13(b) of the Exchange Act does not extend to issuers of municipal securities. In the same Interpretive Release, the SEC favorably refers to the best practices promulgated by the Government Finance Officers Association:

> In the primary offering of municipal securities, the extensive voluntary guidelines issued by the Government Finance Officers Association ("GFOA") have received widespread acceptance and, among a number of larger issuers, have been viewed as "in essence obligatory rules."[69]

The SEC continues, observing:

> The GFOA Guidelines call for financial statements that are either prepared in accordance with GAAP or accompanied by a quantified (if practicable) explanation of the differences. To avoid misunder-

---

[68] Securities Act Release No. 33-7049; 34-33741; Statement of the Commission Regarding Disclosure Obligations of Municipal Securities Issuers and Others (March 9, 1994).

[69] Securities Act Release No. 33-7049; 34-33741, referencing *Disclosure Guidelines for State and Local Government Securities*, (January 1991). Unfortunately, these guidelines are out of print.

standing, investors need to be informed of the basis for financial statement presentation. Accordingly, when a municipal issuer neither uses GAAP nor provides a quantified explanation of material deviations from GAAP, investors need a full explanation of the accounting principles followed.[70]

When referring to GAAP, the Interpretive Release points out, it means GAAP "as determined by the Government Accounting Standards Board (GASB)."[71]

When an issuer of municipal securities looks for guidance beyond the general rubric of the antifraud provisions as to disclosure matters, they look to best practices and other available but nonbinding guidance. The federal securities laws applicable to registrants may be a signpost as well. As a joint project of the American Bar Association Committee on Federal Regulation of Securities and the National Association of Bond Lawyers points out: "a comparative review of conduct in registered transactions, however, may be instructive in the formulation of practices for municipal securities transactions."[72]

Inapplicability of Safe Harbors for Forward Looking Statements

Unlike public companies, municipal issuers are not subject to the requirements concerning disclosure of "known trends or uncertainties" found in Item 303 of Commission Regulation S-K. At the same time, municipalities are not protected by the safe harbor for forward looking statements provided public companies under Securities Act Section 27 A or Exchange Act Section 21E. Case law does afford limited protection to issuers using meaningful, specific cautionary language when making projections and other forward looking statements under the "bespeaks caution doctrine."[73]

RULE 15(c)2-12

Prior to the 1975 Amendments, broker-dealer activities in municipal securities were substantially unregulated. Thirteen years after passage of the 1975 Amendments that provided the SEC with new rule-making authority,

---

[70] Securities Act Release No. 33-7049; 34-33741.
[71] Securities Act Release No. 33-7049; 34-33741.
[72] ABA Sec. of Urban, State and Local Government. Law, Disclosure Roles of Counsel In *State and Local Government Securities Offerings*, 2nd ed. 1994, at p. 42.
[73] *Virginia Bankshares v. Sandber*, 501 U.S. 1083 (1991), *In re Donald J. Trump Casino Securities Litigation*, 7 F.3d 357 (3d Cir. 1993).

following its investigation of the Washington Public Power Supply System default, the SEC chose to use the new authority to adopt its first rule for municipal securities, SEC Rule 15(c)2-12.[74] Simultaneously, the SEC issued an interpretation of municipal underwriter responsibilities under the federal securities laws.[75] Rule 15(c)2-12 is a set of mechanical steps required to be taken by underwriters and does not alter the substance of the antifraud provisions. Rule 15(c)2-12 is the principal tool used by the SEC to create the municipal securities market's framework for disclosure.[76] The rule requires underwriters participating in primary offerings of municipal securities of $1,000,000 or more to obtain, review, and distribute to investors copies of the issuer's official statement. Furthermore, it requires underwriters to receive assurances that the issuer will contract to provide annual financial information and operating data and notice of eleven material events to central information repositories. The rule's requirements apply to underwriters;

---

[74] "With the release of the Staff Report, the Commission has determined to close its investigation into transactions in WPPSS securities without initiating any enforcement actions . . . [t]he responsibilities of participants in offerings of municipal securities might be more effectively addressed by regulatory measures that would apply to all participants in the municipal securities markets. . . . " *WPPSS Report*, Transmittal letter of Chairman David Ruder to the Honorable John D. Dingell, Chairman, Subcommittee on Oversight and Investigations House Committee on Energy and Commerce, September 22, 1988.

[75] Municipal Securities Disclosure No. 26100, 53 Fed. Reg. 37778 (September 22, 1988) (codified at 17 C.F.R. 240) (the "88 Release"), (modified following public comment, in 89 Release).

[76] 89 Release; Exchange Act Release No. 34-34961; 59 Fed. Reg. 59590, (codified at 17 CFR Part 240) ("94 Release") (Under the Rule, in a primary offering of municipal securities, the underwriter will be required: (1) to obtain and review a copy of an official statement deemed final by an issuer of the securities, except for the omission of specified information; (2) in noncompetitively bid offerings, to make available, upon request, the most recent preliminary official statement, if any; (3) to contract with an issuer of the securities, or its agents, to receive, within specified time periods, sufficient copies of the issuer's final official statement, both to comply with the Rule and any MSRB miles; and (4) to provide, for a specified period of time, copies of final official statements to any potential customer upon request. The Rule prohibits a broker, dealer or municipal securities dealer ("participating underwriter") from purchasing or selling municipal securities unless the Participating Underwriter has reasonably determined that an issuer of municipal securities or an obligated person has undertaken in a written agreement or contract for the benefit of holders of such securities to provide certain annual financial information and event notices to various information repositories and prohibits a broker, dealer, or municipal securities dealer from recommending the purchase or sale of a municipals security unless it has procedures in place that provide reasonable assurance that it will receive promptly any event notices with respect to that security).

however, underwriters cannot meet them without the agreement of issuers to contract, as detailed in the rule, to provide copies of final official statements to the underwriters and to provide annual disclosure and notice of certain specified events to the information repositories identified in the Rule. An issuer of municipal securities selling directly to investors, absent an underwriter, is not subject to the rule. When an underwriter becomes involved in the process, however, the rule is triggered and the underwriter must meet its requirements.

In some financing structures there may be more than one issuer. Many issues of municipal securities are secured by revenue streams provided by multiple obligors. The question of which issuer or obligors would be required to provide ongoing information is addressed in the rule by use of the term "obligated person," defined as "any person, including an issuer of municipal securities, who is either generally or through an enterprise, fund, or account of such person committed by contract or other arrangement to support payment of all, or part of the obligations on the municipal securities to be sold in the offering (other than providers of municipal bond insurance, letters of credit, or other liquidity facilities)." The primary offering document serves as the template for disclosure. Ongoing information is required for each obligated person for whom financial information or operating data is presented in the final official statement.

The SEC chose private repositories, known as Nationally Recognized Municipal Securities Information Repositories (NRMSIRS) to serve as the central collectors and disseminators of information under the rule. To accommodate the concerns of smaller issuers described below, allowance was made for statewide collection of continuing issuer information at State Information Depositories, or SIDs. Finally, to make use of a centralized information system created by the MSRB in the five years between the original rule creating NRMSIRs and the 1994 amendment, the Rule requires notices of material events be sent to the MSRB's Continuing Disclosure Information (CDI) System. Both SIDs and NRMSIRs are designated through the staff "no action" letter process.[77] The MSRB's CDI System is part of its Municipal Securities Information Library (MSIL) System. The CDI System is a central repository for voluntarily submitted official continuing disclosure documents relating to outstanding municipal securities issues.[78]

Brokers, dealers, and municipal securities dealers are required by federal securities law to have a reasonable basis for recommending a security to

---

[77] See e.g., letter of Brandon Becker, Director, Division of Market Regulation to Monty Humble, Esquire, *Re: SID Status of Municipal Advisory Council of Texas*, August 29, 1995.

[78] Exchange Act Release No. 30556 (April 6, 1992) 57 Fed. Reg. 12534 (April 10, 1992).

a customer. In particular, Rule 15(c)2-12 makes it "unlawful for any broker, dealer, or municipal securities dealer to recommend the purchase or sale of a municipal security unless such broker, dealer, or municipal securities dealer has procedures in place that provide reasonable assurance that it will receive prompt notice of any event disclosed pursuant to" an event notice filed as described in the preceding paragraph. The 94 Release observes that both the SEC's past interpretations of broker-dealer law and MSRB Rules emphasize the type of information produced by the Rule "must be taken into account by dealers to meet the investor protection standards imposed by its investor protection rules."[79]

The net effect of Rule 15(c)2-12 for most offerings over $1,000,000 is to provide copies of the official statement at the time of the offering to underwriters, who can then be required to facilitate its dissemination to central repositories, and to create a stream of annual financial and operating data, as well as material event notices, to central repositories. Dealers can look to this information as a means of forming the required reasonable basis for any recommendation they make to a customer regarding a municipal security. The SEC observed that "[t]he availability of secondary market disclosure to all municipal securities market participants will enable investors to better protect themselves from misrepresentation or other fraudulent activities by brokers, dealers, and municipal securities dealers." The lack of such information "impairs investors' ability to . . . make intelligent, informed investment decisions, and thus, to protect themselves from fraud."[80]

Between adoption of Rule 15(c)2-12 in 1989 and amendment in 1994, the MSRB used its own rulemaking authority to create a repository for primary offering disclosure documents, as described below. With the amendments to Rule 15(c)2-12 in place, primary offering documents for most municipal securities issued since 1990 are now publicly available. Annual financial information and operating data and event notices are publicly available for most municipal securities offerings since July 1995. In addition to the disclosure documents available pursuant to SEC and MSRB rulemaking, MSRB Rule G-14 has made current trade and price information for municipal securities transactions publicly available since January 2005.

---

[79] 59 Fed. Reg. 59590 (1994).

[80] Id.

CHAPTER 24

Sarbanes-Oxley and the Securities and Exchange Commission

Paul S. Maco
Partner
Vinson & Elkins LLP

On July 30, 2002, President Bush signed into law the Sarbanes-Oxley Act of 2002[1] (the Act). The Act creates the Public Company Accounting Oversight Board (the Oversight Board), regulates analyst conflicts, contains provisions affecting corporate governance, disclosure practice, insider transactions and loans to executives, expands the remedies available to the Securities and Exchange Commission (SEC) for violations of the federal securities laws, establishes new types of criminal conduct and increases prior criminal penalties for violation of the law. Many scholars of securities regulation consider the Act the most significant change to the regulatory framework governing U.S. securities markets since enactment in the 1930s of the federal securities laws themselves.[2] Provisions of the Act apply to both domestic and non-U.S. public issuers, but the core provisions of the Act do not apply to issuers of municipal securities. Whether directly applicable or not, the Act may, over time, have a profound effect upon practices in the municipal securities market.

---

[1] Pub L 107-204, 116 Stat 745.
[2] See, Joel Seligman, *The Transformation of Wall Street* 3d. ed. (New York: Aspen, 2003), ix ("the most far reaching federal securities law since the New Deal").

Note: This chapter is intended for educational and informational purposes only and does not constitute legal advice or services. If legal advice is required, the services of a competent professional should be sought. These materials represent the views of and summaries by the author. They do not necessarily reflect the opinions or views of Vinson & Elkins LLP or of any of its other attorneys or clients. They are not guaranteed to be correct, complete, or current, and they are not intended to imply or establish standards of care applicable to any attorney in any particular circumstance.

THE ACT

Who is Covered?

Many provisions of the Act apply exclusively to *issuers*, defined in the Act as any entity that: (1) has securities registered under Section 12 of the Securities Exchange Act of 1934 (the 34 Act); (2) is required to file reports with the SEC under Section 15(d) of the 34 Act; or (3) files or has filed a registration statement that has not yet become effective under the Securities Act of 1933 (the "33 Act") and has not been withdrawn. This definition differs from the definition of issuer provided in Section 3(a)(8) of the 34 Act and Section 2(a)(4) of the 33 Act and, with the exception of certain conduit borrowers, excludes most issuers of municipal securities. For issuers, the Act puts in place new standards of corporate governance, executive responsibility and accountability, limits on executive benefits and new provisions for civil and criminal liability supporting the standards. Later in this section we discuss those provisions of the Act applicable to issuers.

For securities analysts, the Act expands the SEC's authority under the 34 Act, adding Section 15D and directing certain rulemaking activity, much of which was underway at the time of adoption of the Act, as discussed below. In addition, the Act expands SEC remedial authority over broker-dealers and investment advisers. For attorneys providing service to issuers, the Act puts in place new rules regulating conduct for practice before the SEC. However, perhaps the most significant change brought by the Act is for the accounting firms that prepare audit reports for issuers. The Act establishes a board to regulate, inspect, and discipline the accounting and auditing profession, sets standards of audit independence, and under Section 404 requires an extensive, and what has proven to be expensive, annual audit attest function for issuers. The new Section 404 requirement and the other provisions affecting the accounting profession are discussed below. We also discuss those provisions of the Act applicable to any person or entity. Finally, the Act required the conduct and submission to Congress of a variety of studies, as described below.

Audit Committee Requirements

Section 301 of the Act amends Section 10A of the 34 Act by adding a new Subsection (m) setting audit committee standards. New 34 Act Section 10A(m)(1)(A) required the SEC, by April 26, 2003, to direct the national securities exchanges and national securities associations to prohibit the listing of any security of an issuer that failed to comply with certain requirements relating to audit committees and audit committee member independence.

The New York Stock Exchange and the National Association of Securities Dealers (NASD) have since amended their rules to the extent necessary to conform to the Act and the rules promulgated by the SEC.

Under new Section 10A(m)(3), issuers are required to have an audit committee comprised entirely of directors of the issuer that are "independent." To be independent, a member of an audit committee could not, except in his capacity as a member of that committee, the board of directors, or any other board committee, accept any consulting, advisory, or other compensatory fee from the issuer, or be an affiliated person of the issuer or any subsidiary of the issuer. New Section 10A(m)(3)(C) gives the SEC exemptive authority for particular relationships, however, and the SEC has addressed many issues relating to audit committee standards through rulemaking.[3]

Under new Section 10A(m)(2), the audit committee must be directly responsible for the oversight of "any registered public accounting firm" preparing the audit report. Issuers are required to provide the audit committee with the authority to engage independent counsel and other advisers as it deems necessary, as well as appropriate funding, as determined by the audit committee, to pay the accounting firm that issues the audit report and any other advisers retained by the audit committee. Issuers also have to establish procedures for the receipt, retention, and treatment of complaints received by the issuer concerning accounting, internal controls, or auditing issues, and the confidential anonymous submission by employees of concerns regarding questionable accounting or auditing matters.

Certifying Financial Statements

Section 302 of the Act required the SEC to adopt rules (a process that the SEC had previously initiated) requiring each annual or quarterly report filed or submitted by an issuer with the SEC pursuant to Sections 13(a) or 15(d) of the 34 Act to be accompanied by a statement from the chief executive officer (CEO) and chief financial officer (CFO), or their equivalents, certifying that:

- The signing officer has reviewed the report.
- Based on the officer's knowledge, the report does not contain any untrue statement of a material fact or omit to state a material fact necessary in order to make the statements made, in light of the circumstances under which such statements are made, not misleading.
- Based on the officer's knowledge, the financial statements, and other financial information included in the report, fairly present in all mate-

---

[3] *Relating to Listed Company Audit Committees*, Release Nos. 33-8220; 34-47654; IC-26001; File No. S7-02-03 (April 9, 2003).

rial respects the financial condition and results of operations of the issuer as of, and for, the periods presented in the reports.

- The signing officers are responsible for establishing and maintaining internal controls, have designed such controls to ensure that material information relating to the issuer and its consolidated subsidiaries is made known to such officers by others within those entities, particularly during the period in which the report is prepared, have evaluated the effectiveness of such controls as of a date within 90 days prior to the report, and have presented in the report their conclusions about the effectiveness of their internal controls based on their evaluation as of that date.

- The signing officers have disclosed to the issuer's auditors and the audit committee of the board of directors all significant deficiencies in the design or operation of internal controls which could adversely affect the issuer's ability to record, process, summarize, and report financial data and have identified for the issuer's auditors any material weaknesses in internal controls, as well as with any fraud, whether or not material, that involves management or other employees who have a significant role in the issuer's internal controls.

- The signing officers have indicated in the report whether or not there were significant changes in internal controls or other factors that could significantly affect internal controls subsequent to the date of their evaluation, including any corrective actions with regard to significant deficiencies and material weaknesses.

The Act specifically provides that an issuer may not escape responsibility under this Section by reincorporating or otherwise transferring its domicile outside the United States. In addition, Section 906 requires certain certifications and imposes criminal penalties for individuals who certify reports while knowing that they do not comport with the requirements of Section 906.

Section 906 of the Act states that each periodic report containing financial statements filed by an issuer with the SEC pursuant to Section 13(a) or Section 15(d) of the 34 Act must be accompanied by a written statement by the issuer's chief executive officer and chief financial officer (or the equivalent thereof) certifying that such report fully complies with the requirements of Sections 13(a) or 15(d) of the 34 Act and that information contained in the periodic report fairly presents, in all material respects, the financial condition and results of operations of the issuer. Section 906 provides that any officer who makes such a certification knowing that the periodic report accompanying the statement does not comport with the requirements of Section 906 is subject to a fine of up to $1,000,000 and up to 10 years imprisonment. If the officer "willfully" makes such a certification, the officer is subject to a fine of up to $5,000,000 and up to 20 years imprisonment. Section 906 states, in effect, that any periodic report containing financial statements filed with the SEC on or after July 30, 2002, pursuant to Section 13(a) or Section 15(d) of the 34 Act must be accompanied by the required certification.

The SEC adopted rules implementing Section 302 on August 29, 2003.[4] The SEC defined the term "disclosure controls and procedures" to make it explicit that the controls contemplated by Section 302(a)(4) of the Act are intended to embody controls and procedures addressing the quality and timeliness of disclosure. The SEC also included this definition to differentiate this concept of disclosure controls and procedures from the preexisting concept of "internal controls" that pertains to an issuer's financial reporting and control of its assets, as currently embodied in Section 13(b) of the 34 Act. The SEC expects each issuer to develop a process that is consistent with its business and internal management and supervisory practices. The SEC further recommended that issuers create a committee with responsibility for considering the materiality of information and determining disclosure obligations on a timely basis. Officers and employees of an issuer who have an interest in, and the expertise to serve on, the committee could include the principal accounting officer (or the controller), the general counsel or other senior legal official with responsibility for disclosure matters who reports to the general counsel, the principal risk management officer, the chief investor relations officer (or an officer with equivalent responsibilities) and such other officers or employees, including individuals associated with the issuer's business units, as the issuer deems appropriate.

Influence on Auditors Prohibited

Section 303 of the Act prohibits officers or directors of an issuer, or any other person acting under their direction, from taking any action to fraudulently influence, coerce, manipulate, or mislead any independent auditor for the purpose of rendering the issuer's financial statements materially misleading. The SEC adopted rules implementing Section 303 on May 20, 2003.[5]

CEO/CFO Reimbursements of Issuer

Section 304 of the Act provides that if an issuer is required to prepare an accounting restatement due to the material noncompliance of the issuer, as

---

[4] *Certification of Disclosure in Companies' Quarterly and Annual Reports*, Release Nos. 33-8124, 34-46427, IC-25722; File No. S7-21-02.

[5] *Improper Influence on Conduct of Audits*, Release Nos. 34-47890, IC-26050; FR-71; File No. S7-39-02.

a result of misconduct, with any financial reporting requirement under the securities laws, the CEO and the CFO are required to reimburse the issuer for: any bonus or other incentive-based or equity-based compensation received by that person from the issuer during the 12 months following the first public issuance or filing with the SEC (whichever occurs first) of the financial document embodying such financial reporting requirement, and for any profits realized from the sale of securities of the issuer during that 12-month period. The SEC is authorized to exempt any person that it deems necessary and appropriate.

Pension Fund Blackout Periods

Section 306 of the Act makes it unlawful, except to the extent provided by any SEC rule, for any director or executive officer of an issuer of any equity security (other than an exempted security) to purchase, sell, or otherwise acquire or transfer any equity security of that issuer (other than an exempted security) acquired in connection with service or employment as a director or executive officer during any pension fund blackout period. The blackout period would encompass certain periods during which participants in an individual account plan under ERISA are not permitted to acquire or transfer such securities. A cause of action is created under which officers and directors, irrespective of any intention in entering in the transaction, may be forced by the issuer or any owner of any security of the issuer, if the issuer fails to bring such an action within 60 days of request, to disgorge any profits realized in violation of this provision. The issuer is required to notify its directors and officers, and the SEC, of such blackout periods. Section 306 also amends ERISA to require the plan administrator to notify the plan participants and beneficiaries. The SEC adopted Regulation BTR pursuant to Section 306 on January 22, 2003.[6]

Reports Must Reflect Adjustments, Off-Balance Sheet Transactions

Section 401(a) of the Act amends Section 13 of the 34 Act by adding new Subsections (i) and (j). Under new Section 13(i), each financial report that contains financial statements, and that is required to be prepared in accordance with (or reconciled to) *generally accepted accounting principles* (GAAP) and filed with the SEC, must reflect all material correcting adjustments that have been identified by a *registered public accounting firm* in accordance with GAAP and the rules and regulations of the SEC.

---

[6] *Insider Trades During Pension Fund Blackout Periods*, Release No. 34-47225; IC-25909; File No. S7-44-02.

Pursuant to new 34 Act Section 13(j) the SEC issued rules on January 28, 2003 under which annual and quarterly financial reports required to be filed with the SEC must disclose all material off-balance sheet transactions, arrangements, obligations (including contingent obligations), and other relationships of the issuer with unconsolidated entities or other persons, that may have a material current or future effect on the issuer's financial condition, changes in financial condition, results of operations, liquidity, capital expenditures or resources, or significant components of revenues or expenses.[7] Registered investment companies are exempted from this provision.

Pro Forma Information Not Misleading, Reconciled to GAAP

Section 401 also required the SEC to issue rules providing that pro forma financial information included in any periodic or other report filed with the SEC, or in any public disclosure or press or other release, must be presented in a way that does not contain an untrue statement of a material fact or omit to state a material fact necessary to make the pro forma financial information, in light of the circumstances under which it is presented, not misleading and that reconciles it with the issuer's financial condition and results of operations under GAAP. The SEC issued such rules on January 22, 2003.[8]

Loans to Officers and Directors Prohibited

Section 402 amends Section 13 of the 34 Act by adding a new subsection making it unlawful for an issuer, directly or indirectly, including through subsidiaries, to extend or maintain credit, to arrange for the extension of credit, or to renew an extension of credit, in the form of a personal loan to or for any director or executive officer of that issuer. This provision does not apply to existing loans so long as there is no material modification to any terms or any renewal after July 30, 2002. This provision is subject to certain limited exceptions for home improvement and manufactured home loans, consumer credit, open end credit plans, charge cards, and or certain extensions of credit by a broker or dealer registered under Section 15 of the 34 Act to an employee of that broker or dealer. In addition, this prohibition applies only to loans made after the date of enactment, and does not include any loan made or maintained by an insured depository institution if the loan is subject to the insider lending restrictions of Section 22(h) of

---

[7] *Disclosure in Management's Discussion and Analysis about Off-Balance Sheet Arrangements and Aggregate Contractual Obligations*, Release Nos. 33-8182; 34-47264; FR-67 International Series Release No. 1266, File No. S7-42-02.

[8] *Conditions for Use of Non-GAAP Financial Measures*, Release No. 33-8176; 34-47226; FR-65; File No. S7-43-02.

the Federal Reserve Act. Registered investment companies are exempted from this provision.

Transactions by Management and Principal Stockholders

Section 403 amends the list of filings in Section 16(a) of the 34 Act that must be made by officers, directors, and owners of more than 10 percent of any class of equity security (other than an exempted security), which is registered pursuant to Section 12 of that act with the SEC (and, if such security is registered on a national securities exchange, that exchange). As amended, Section 16(a) of the 34 Act requires that (1) at the time of registration of such security on a national securities exchange or by the effective date of a registration statement filed pursuant to Section 12(g) of the 34 Act; and (2) within 10 days after such person becomes a beneficial owner, director, or officer; that such person must file a statement with the SEC (and the national securities exchange, if applicable) indicating the amount of all equity securities of such issuer of which the filing person is the beneficial owner. If there has been a change in such ownership, or if one of the persons listed above shall have purchased or sold a security-based swap agreement involving such equity security, before the end of the second business day following the day on which the subject transaction has been executed, or at such other time as the SEC provides by rule in case the two-day period is not feasible, such person must file with the SEC (and the national securities exchange, if applicable) a statement indicating ownership by the filing person at the date of filing, any such changes in ownership, and such purchases and sales of the security-based swap agreement as have occurred since the most recent such filing. Within one year of the date of enactment, such filings must be made electronically and posted on the SEC's and the issuer's Internet sites. The amendment required by this Section became effective August 29, 2002. All transactions subject to Section 16(a) executed on or after August 29, 2002 are reportable by insiders on Form 4, except when the rules under Section 16(a) provide otherwise. On August 27, 2002, the SEC adopted final rules that:

- Amended the Section 16(a) forms to conform all references to the Form 4 filing deadline to the amended statutory filing deadline and to reflect that Form 4 is no longer a monthly form.
- Amended Rule 16a-6(b), the small acquisitions rule, to conform the description of the Form 4 deadline contained in that rule to the amended statutory filing deadline.
- Amended Rules 16a-3(f) and 16a-6(a) so that transactions between officers or directors and the issuer exempted from Section 16(b) short-

swing profit recovery by Rule 16b-3 previously reportable on an annual basis on Form 5 are required to be reported within two business days on Form 4.

■ Amended Rule 16a-3(g) to calculate the two-business day Form 4 due date differently for the following transactions, for which we have determined that the amended Section 16(a) statutory reporting period is otherwise not feasible:

  • Transactions pursuant to arrangements that satisfy the affirmative defense conditions of Exchange Act Rule 10b5-1(c) where the reporting person does not select the date of execution.
  • Discretionary transactions pursuant to employee benefit plans where the reporting person does not select the date of execution.

Internal Control Report

Section 404 required the SEC to issue rules requiring annual reports made pursuant to Sections 13(a) or 15(d) of the 34 Act to include an internal control report. The internal control report must describe the responsibility of management for establishing and maintaining an adequate internal control structure and procedures for financial reporting, and must contain an assessment, as of the end of the issuer's most recent fiscal year, of the effectiveness of such control structure and procedures. The issuer's auditing firm is required to attest to, and report on, such assessment, in accordance with standards promulgated by the Oversight Board established by the Act. Registered investment companies are exempt from this provision. The SEC adopted rules under Section 404 on June 5, 2003.[9]

Code of Ethics

Section 406 required the SEC to issue final rules requiring issuers to disclose whether or not (and if not, why not) such issuer has adopted a code of ethics for its senior financial officers, applicable to its principal financial officer and its comptroller. The SEC also was directed to revise its regulations concerning matters requiring prompt disclosure on Form 8-K to require the immediate disclosure of any change in or waiver of such code of ethics for senior financial officers. To meet the Act's requirements, a code of ethics must contain such standards as are reasonably necessary to promote: (1) honest and ethical conduct, including the ethical handling of actual or apparent

[9] *Management Report on Internal Control Over Financial Reporting and Certification and Certification of Disclosure in Exchange Act Periodic Reports*, Release Nos. 33-8238; 34-47986; IC-26068; File Nos. S7-40-02; S7-06-03.

conflicts of interest between personal and professional relationships; (2) full, fair, accurate, timely, and understandable disclosure in the issuer's periodic reports; and (3) compliance with applicable rules and regulations. On January 23, 2003, the SEC adopted rules and amendments requiring companies, other than registered investment companies, to include two new types of disclosures in their annual reports filed pursuant to the Securities Exchange Act of 1934. First, the rules require a company to disclose whether it has at least one *audit committee financial expert* serving on its audit committee, and if so, the name of the expert and whether the expert is independent of management. A company that does not have an audit committee financial expert must disclose this fact and explain why it has no such expert. Second, the rules require a company to disclose whether it has adopted a code of ethics that applies to the company's principal executive officer, principal financial officer, principal accounting officer or controller, or persons performing similar functions. A company disclosing that it has not adopted such a code must disclose this fact and explain why it has not done so. A company also will be required to promptly disclose amendments to, and waivers from, the code of ethics relating to any of those officers.[10]

Financial Experts

Section 407 required the SEC to issue final rules requiring each issuer to disclose whether or not (and if not, why not) its audit committee has at least one member who is a *financial expert* as defined by the SEC. In arriving at a definition of financial expert, the SEC was required to consider whether a person has, through education and experience as a public accountant, auditor, principal financial officer, comptroller, or principal accounting officer of an issuer, or from a similar position: (1) an understanding of GAAP and financial statements; (2) experience in preparing or auditing financial statements of comparable issuers and applying such principles in connection with the accounting for estimates, accruals, and reserves; (3) experience with internal accounting controls; and (4) an understanding of audit committee functions. The SEC adopted rules under Section 406 and 407 of the Act on January 23, 2003.[11]

Real-Time Disclosure

Section 409 of the Act amended Section 13 of the 34 Act to require issuers reporting under Section 13(a) or 15(d) of the 34 Act to disclose to the public

---

[10] *Disclosure Required by Sections 406 and 407 of the Sarbanes-Oxley Act of 2002,* Release Nos. 33-8177; 34-47235; File No. S7-40-02.
[11] Id.

on a rapid and current basis such additional information concerning material changes in the financial conditions or operations of the issuer, in plain English, which may include trend and qualitative information and graphic presentations, as the SEC determines, by rule, is necessary or useful for the protection of investors and the public interest. On March 16, 2004, the SEC adopted extensive amendments to Form 8-K.[12]

Enhanced Review of Issuer Disclosures

Section 408 requires the SEC to regularly and systematically review corporate filings by issuers reporting under Section 13(a) of the 34 Act (including reports filed on Form 10-K) and that have a class of securities listed on a national securities exchange or traded on an automated quotation facility of a national securities association. The SEC is required to review each such issuer *at least* once every three years. The review shall include financial statements. In scheduling the reviews, the SEC is required to consider whether an issuer has made material restatements of financial results, has a stock price that has exhibited extreme volatility, has a large market capitalization, is an emerging issuer with a disparity in its price to earnings ratio, significantly affects any material sector of the economy, and any other relevant factors.

In addition to the provisions described above, issuers are also subject to the provisions discussed later.

Securities Analysts

Safeguards for Analyst Objectivity and Disclosure of Potential Conflicts

Section 501 created a new Section 15D of the 34 Act containing provisions relating to securities analysts and research reports. Section requires the SEC, or upon its authorization and direction a registered securities association or national securities exchange, to adopt rules addressing conflicts of interest that can arise when securities analysts recommend equity securities in research reports and public appearances. The rules must be designed to foster greater public confidence in securities research and to protect the objectivity and independence of analysts by (1) restricting prepublication clearance or approval of research reports by persons employed by the broker-dealer and directly responsible for investment banking activities or persons not engaged in investment research (other than legal or compliance staff); (2) limiting the supervision and compensatory evaluation of analysts to officials employed by the broker-dealer who are not engaged in investment banking activities;

---

[12] *Additional Form 8-K Disclosure Requirements and Acceleration of Filing Date,* Release Nos. 33-8400; 34-49424; File No. S7-22-02.

and (3) prohibiting retaliation or threats of retaliation against analysts by broker-dealers or their employees engaged in investment banking activities for reports that adversely affect present or prospective investment banking relationships with the issuer that is the subject of the report (except that the broker-dealer may still discipline analysts for other causes in accordance with the firm's policies). The rules must also define periods during which broker-dealers who have participated, or are to participate, in a public offering of securities as underwriters or dealers should not publish or distribute reports relating to such securities or to the issuer, establish structural safeguards within broker-dealers to ensure that analysts are insulated from review, pressure, or oversight by those whose involvement in investment banking activities might bias the analyst's judgment, and address any other issues the SEC or such association or exchange determines appropriate.

Section 15D of the 34 Act also requires the SEC, or such registered securities association or national securities exchange so authorized and directed by the SEC, to adopt rules requiring analysts to disclose in their public appearances, and broker-dealers to disclose in their research reports, conflicts of interest that are known or should have been known by the analyst or broker-dealer to exist at the time of the appearance or the date of distribution of the report. Such conflicts or potential conflicts include: (1) the extent to which the analyst has any debt or equity investments in the issuer that is the subject of the appearance or report; (2) whether any compensation has been received by the broker-dealer or its affiliates, including the analyst, from that issuer, subject to such exemptions as the SEC determines appropriate and necessary to prevent disclosure of material nonpublic information regarding potential future investment banking transactions of such issuer; (3) whether an issuer whose securities are recommended is or has been, within a one-year period preceding the date of the appearance or the distribution of the report, a client of the broker-dealer, and if so, the services that were provided; (4) whether the analyst received compensation for a research report based on (among other factors) investment banking revenues of the broker-dealer; and (5) any other conflicts of interest that are material to investors, analysts, or the broker-dealer as the SEC or the association or exchange determines appropriate. The SEC may impose civil penalties for violations pursuant to Section 21B(a) of the 34 Act. Note that the definition of "securities analyst" includes any associated person of a broker-dealer that is principally responsible for, and any associated person who reports directly or indirectly to, a securities analyst in connection with the preparation of the substance of a research report, whether or not any such person has the job title of securities analyst and that the definition of "research report" includes all "written or electronic communication that includes an analysis of equity securities of individual companies or industries and that provides information reasonably sufficient upon which to base an investment decision."

The New York Stock Exchange and NASD approved rules regulating analyst conduct shortly before the Act was signed into law, and modified several times since, addressing many of the matters identified in Section 501. On February 20, 2003, the SEC also adopted Regulation AC. Regulation AC requires that brokers, dealers, and certain persons associated with a broker or dealer include in research reports certifications by the research analyst that the views expressed in the report accurately reflect his or her personal views, and disclose whether or not the analyst received compensation or other payments in connection with his or her specific recommendations or views. Broker-dealers are also be required to obtain periodic certifications by research analysts in connection with the analyst's public appearances.[13]

Broker Dealers and Investment Advisers

Enhanced Authority to Limit Broker-Dealers and Investment Advisers

Section 604 amends Section 15(b)(4) of the 34 Act and expands the authority of the SEC to limit the activities of broker-dealers and investment advisers based on final orders of state securities commissions and insurance commissions, and state and Federal banking regulators, that bar such persons from associating with an entity regulated by such body, or from engaging in the business of securities, insurance, banking, savings association activities, or credit union activities, or which constitutes a final order based on violations of any law or regulation prohibiting fraudulent, manipulative, or deceptive conduct.

Attorneys

Authority to Regulate Professional Conduct of Attorneys

Section 307 requires the SEC to issue rules of professional conduct for attorneys appearing and practicing before the SEC in any way in the representation of issuers. The rules must include a rule requiring an attorney to report evidence of a material violation of securities law or a breach of fiduciary duty or similar violation by the company or its agents to the general counsel or CEO of the company, and if the general counsel or CEO does not appropriately respond to the evidence (adopting, as necessary, appropriate remedial measures or sanctions with respect to the violation), requiring the attorney to report the evidence to the audit committee or another committee of the board comprised solely of directors not employed directly or indi-

---

[13] Release Nos. 33-8193; 34-47384; File No. S7-30-02.

rectly by the issuer, or to the board of directors. The SEC issued Rule 205, Standards of Professional Conduct for Attorneys, on January 29, 2003.[14] In certain circumstances, attorneys participating in municipal securities transactions may be subject to Rule 205.[15]

Accountants

Public Company Accounting Oversight Board

Prior to the Act, the SEC deferred the direct exercise of its powers under Section 19(a) of the 33 Act and section 13(b) of the 34 Act to prescribe accounting standards for registration statements to self-regulating private sector bodies, including American Institute of Certified Public Accountants' Auditing Standards Board in setting audit standards and the Financial Accounting Standards Board (FASB) in setting accounting standards. The Act provides for mandatory funding for FASB, which retains its accounting standard setting function[16], but creates the Oversight Board and authorizes the Oversight Board to establish auditing, quality control and ethics standards. The Act also directs the Oversight Board to include in the auditing standards it adopts a requirement that audit reports evaluate the issuer's internal control structure and procedures required under Section 404(b). Foreign public accounting firms that prepare or furnish audit reports with respect to any issuer are made subject to the Act and the rules of the Oversight Board and the SEC issued thereunder. The Act also amends Section 19 of the 33 Act, adding new Section 19(b)(1), which authorizes the SEC to recognize as "generally accepted" any accounting principles established by a standard setting body meeting the criteria stated in the section (effectively, the Oversight Board and FASB) in carrying out its authority under Section a) of the 33 Act and section 13(b) of the 34 Act to prescribe accounting standards for registration statements, prospectuses and filings under the 33 Act and the 34 Act.

Auditor Independence

The Act also adds new sections to Section 10A of the 34 Act establishing boundaries of auditor independence by identifying specific prohibited activities and requiring preapproval of audit and nonaudit services; establishing

---

[14] *Implementation of Standards of Professional Conduct for Attorneys*, Release Nos. 33-8185; 34-47276; IC-25919; File No. S7-45-02; 17 CFR Part 205.
[15] See Paul S. Maco, "Federal Securities Regulation," *The Bond Lawyer* 25, no. 1 (March 1, 2003), p. 42.
[16] See *Commission Policy Statement Reaffirming the Status of the FASB as a Designated Private-Sector Standard Setter*, Release Nos. 33-8221; 34-47743; IC-26028; FR-70.

requirements for preapproval of audit services (including providing comfort letters) and nonaudit services and requiring disclosure of approvals of non-audit functions in periodic reports under 34 Act Section 13(a); requiring audit partner rotation; requiring registered public accounting firms performing audits for issuers to report certain matters to the audit committee; adding to the definitions provided under Section 3 of the 34 Act new definitions for *audit committee* and *registered public accounting firm* and conforming other sections of the 34 Act to the new terminology; amending 34 Act Section 10A(f) by adding a definition of issuer as used in the Section; prohibiting certain conflicts of interest; mandating a study by the Comptroller General of the United States of the effects of mandatory rotation; instructing the SEC to "issue final regulations to carry out" each of the newly added Subsections (g) through (l) by January 26, 2003 (which the SEC has done); making it unlawful for a registered public accounting firm (or associated person) to prepare an audit report for an issuer if it engages in activity prohibited by new 34 Act Sections 10A(g)–(l) or any rule or regulation of the Commission thereunder; and making recommendations for consideration by appropriate state regulatory authorities.

The Audit Committee preapproval requirements of Section 202 of the Act provide that approval by an audit committee of a nonaudit service to be performed by the auditor of the issuer "shall be disclosed to investors in periodic reports required by Section 13(a)" of the 34 Act.

Audit Workpaper Retention

Section 1520 requires any accountant who conducts an audit of an issuer of securities subject to Section 10A(a) of the 34 Act to maintain all audit or review workpapers for a period of five years from the end of the fiscal period in which the audit or review was concluded. Anyone who knowingly and willfully violated this requirement could be fined and/or imprisoned for not more than 10 years. The SEC issued rules relating to the retention of such records on January 24, 2003.[17]

General Applicability

Specific provisions of the Act are applicable to any *person*, a term that encompasses issuers and other corporate entities, including issuers of municipal securities and their officials, as well as other natural persons. A majority of the Act's provisions that apply to *persons* create new penalties for conduct related to violations of the securities laws. These provisions create newly de-

---

[17] *Retention of Records Relevant to Audits and Reviews*, Release Nos. 33-8180; 34-47241; IC-25911; FR-66.

fined crimes, and their enhanced penalties for existing crimes substantially increase the consequences for those who violate the securities laws. At the same time, the SEC and the Department of Justice are given expanded powers to pursue alleged violations of law and the remedies available to the SEC are increased.

Director and Officer Bars and Other Equitable Relief

Section 305 adds to the powers provided to the SEC in Section 21(d) authority to seek, and authorizes federal courts to grant, any equitable relief appropriate or necessary for the benefit of investors. This has potential implications for *any person brought into federal court by the SEC, including any person involved in sales of municipal securities or private sales of securities*. The Act also makes it easier for the SEC to bar persons from serving as officers or directors of public companies, as Section 305 lowers the standard for officer and director bars in Section 21(d)(2) of the 34 Act and Section 20(e) of the 33 Act from "substantial unfitness" to "unfitness." Similarly, Section 1105 of the Act amends Section 21C of the 34 Act to provide that in any cease-and-desist proceeding, the SEC may issue an order to prohibit any person who has violated Section 10(b) of the 34 Act, or the rules or regulations thereunder (which may include violations in connection with private sales of securities), from acting as an officer or director of any issuer with registered securities pursuant to Section 12 of the 34 Act or that files reports pursuant to Section 15(d) of that act if that person's conduct demonstrates unfitness to serve as an officer or director.

Funds for Investors

Section 308 provides that in any judicial or administrative action under the securities laws where the SEC obtains an order against any person requiring disgorgement and civil penalties, the civil penalty shall, on motion or at the direction of the SEC, be added to the disgorgement fund for the benefit of victims of the violation. The SEC is also authorized to accept gifts to such disgorgement funds, and is required to report to Congress by January 26, 2003 the results of a mandated study of disgorgements and civil penalties over the last five years.

Authority to Limit SEC Practice

Section 602 of the Act added new Section 4C to the 34 Act authorizing the SEC to censure any person or bar that person, temporarily or permanently, from appearing or practicing before the SEC if that person is found by the

SEC (after notice and opportunity for hearing): (1) not to possess the requisite qualifications to represent others; (2) to be lacking in character or integrity or to have engaged in unethical or "improper professional conduct"; or (3) to have willfully violated, or willfully aided and abetted the violation of, any provision of the securities laws or regulations. *Improper professional conduct* means, with respect to any registered public accounting firm or associated person: (1) intentional or knowing conduct, including reckless conduct, that results in a violation of the applicable professional standards; and (2) negligent conduct, consisting of a single instance of highly unreasonable conduct that results in a violation of professional standards in circumstances in which the firm or associated person knows or should know that heightened scrutiny is warranted or multiple instances of unreasonable conduct, each resulting in a violation of professional standards, that indicate a lack of competence to practice before the SEC.

Penny Stock Bar

Section 603 amends Section 21 of the 34 Act and Section 20 of the 33 Act to authorize courts to prohibit certain violators of the securities laws from participating in penny stock offerings.

Obstruction of Justice

Section 802 of the Act amends the federal criminal statutes relating to obstruction of justice by adding Section 1519 to Chapter 73 of Title 18 of the United States Code (the Code). The new Section makes it a crime to knowingly alter, destroy, mutilate, conceal, cover up, falsify, or make a false entry in any record, document, or tangible object with the intent to impede, obstruct, or influence the investigation or proper administration of any matter within the jurisdiction of any department or agency of the United States or any case filed under Title 11. Violators may be fined and/or imprisoned for not more than 20 years. These provisions apply to any matter involving any department or agency of the United States.

New Bankruptcy Provisions

Section 803 of the Act amends Section 523(a) of Title 11 of the Code, which contains the exceptions to debts that may be discharged by a *debtor in bankruptcy*. All participants in a bankruptcy proceeding may be potentially affected by this provision. As amended, Section 523(a) limits the discharge of debts that arise under a claim relating to violations of the securities laws or common law fraud, deceit, or manipulation in connection with the sale of any security, and which result from a judgment, order, consent order, or decree in any judicial or administrative proceedings, any settlement agreement, or any court or administrative order for damages, fine, penalty, citation, restitutionary or disgorgement payment, attorney fee, or other cost.

New Statute of Limitations for Securities Fraud

Section 804 amends Section 1658 of Title 28 of the Code, which establishes a four-year statute of limitations for civil actions arising under an act of Congress, to provide that a private right of action that involves a claim of fraud, deceit, manipulation, or contrivance in contravention of the securities laws may be brought not later than the earlier of two years after the discovery of the facts constituting the violation or five years after such violation. The new limits apply only to proceedings commenced on or after the date of enactment. These provisions apply to implied private rights of action under Section 10b-5, which may include lawsuits arising out of private purchases and sales of securities as well as public transactions in securities.

Sentencing Guidelines

Sections 805, 905, and 1104 require the U.S. Sentencing Commission to review and amend the Federal Sentencing Guidelines related to obstruction of justice, fraud (including securities, pension, and accounting fraud), and other criminal misconduct to ensure that they are sufficient to deter and punish violations.[18]

Whistleblower Protection

Section 806 of the Act creates a new Section 1514A in Title 18 of the Code. Section prohibits issuers with a class of securities registered under Section 12 of the 34 Act or required to report under Section 15(d) of the 34 Act, or their officers and employees, contractors and subcontractors, or agents from retaliating against employees who lawfully provide information regarding or assisting in investigations of suspected securities law violations, when the information or assistance is provided to any Federal regulatory or law enforcement agency, any Member of Congress or Congressional committee, or a supervisor of such employee or other person with authority to investigate the matter. It also protects employees who file, testify, participate in, or assist in a proceeding alleging a violation of the securities laws or any fraud against shareholders. In addition, Section 1514A provides for enforcement of those protections and remedies for violations.

---

[18] See *Amendments to the Sentencing Guidelines*, available at http://www.ussc.gov/2003guid/2003cong.pdf.

Fraud

Section 807 adds a new Section 1348 to the criminal statutes relating to mail fraud in Title 18 of the Code. Section makes it a crime, subject to fine and/or imprisonment for 25 years, to knowingly execute, or attempt to execute, a scheme or artifice to defraud any person in connection with any security of an issuer with a class of securities registered under Section 12 of the 34 Act or that is required to file reports under Section 15(d) of the 34 Act, or to obtain, by means of false or fraudulent pretenses, representations, or promises, any money or property in connection with the purchase or sale of any security of such an issuer.

Conspiracy to Commit Fraud

Section 902 amends Chapter 63 of Title 18 of the Code to create a new Section 1349 that subjects anyone who attempts or conspires to commit any offense under that chapter, including securities fraud, to the same penalties as those prescribed for the offense.

Mail and Wire Fraud

Section 903 amends Sections 1341 and 1343 of Title 18 of the Code to increase the possible prison terms for mail and wire fraud from five years to 20 years.

ERISA Fraud

Section 904 amends ERISA to increase the potential monetary penalties and prison terms for violators of that act. For individuals, potential monetary penalties increase from $5,000 to $100,000, and potential prison sentences increase from one year to 10 years. For companies, potential monetary penalties increase from $100,000 to $500,000.

Document Tampering/Impeding Official Proceedings

Section 1102 amends Section 1512 of Title 18 of the Code, which establishes penalties for witness tampering, to make it a crime to corruptly alter, destroy, mutilate, or conceal a record, document, or other object, or attempt to do so, with the intent to impair the object's integrity or availability for use in an official proceeding or otherwise obstruct, influence, or impede any official proceeding or attempt to do so. Violators may be fined and/or imprisoned for up to 20 years. These provisions apply to any matter involving any official proceeding under federal law.

Authority to Request Freeze on Issuer Payments

Section 1103 amends Section 21C of the 34 Act to authorize the SEC, during the course of an investigation of possible securities violations by an issuer or its directors, officers, partners, controlling persons, agents, or employees, to petition a Federal district court for an order to escrow for 45 days (which may be extended to 90 days) any extraordinary payments by an issuer to any of its directors, officers, partners, controlling persons, agents, or employees when it appears likely that such payments will be made. Such an order may be entered only after notice and opportunity for a hearing, unless the court determines that provision of such notice and opportunity for a hearing would be impracticable or contrary to the public interest. If the individual affected by such order is charged with a violation of the Federal securities laws within 45 days of the escrow order, including any applicable extension period, the escrow will continue, subject to approval by the court, until the conclusion of any legal proceedings.

Securities Violations

Section 1106 of the Act increases the penalties for willful violations of the 34 Act. Penalties for individuals are increased from fines of $1,000,000 and/or imprisonment for up to 10 years to fines of $5,000,000 and/or imprisonment for up to 20 years. Fines for persons who are not natural persons are increased from $2,500,000 to $25,000,000. These increased penalties are applicable to violations of the antifraud rules in the context of private purchases and sales of securities as well as public transactions in securities.

Retaliation Against Informants

Section 1107 amends Section 1513 of Title 18 of the Code to make it a crime to knowingly, with the intent to retaliate, take any action harmful to any person, including interference with the employment or livelihood of such person, for providing to a law enforcement officer any truthful information relating to the commission or possible commission of any federal offense. Violators are subject to fine and/or imprisonment of up to 10 years.

Studies

Study of Consolidation of the Accounting Industry

Section 701 requires the Comptroller General to study the consolidation of public accounting firms and the present and future impact of such consolidation on capital formation and on domestic and international securities markets. Findings and recommendations are to be reported to Congress within one year of enactment. The General Accounting Office submitted its report on July 30, 2003.[19]

Study of Credit Rating Agencies

Section 702 requires the SEC to conduct a study of the role and function of credit rating agencies in the securities market. The SEC submitted its report and recommendations to Congress on January 24, 2003.[20] On February 2, 2007, the SEC issued proposed rules regulating certain rating agency activities.[21]

Study of Special Purpose Entities

Section 401 requires the SEC to conduct a study of the use of off-balance sheet transactions within one year of enactment, and to report its findings and recommendations to Congress within six months of the completion of the study. On June 15, 2005, the SEC submitted its report to the President of the United States, the Committee on Banking, Housing, and Urban Affairs of the United States Senate and the Committee on Financial Services of the United States House of Representatives.[22]

Study of Aiding and Abetting by Securities Professionals

Section 703 requires the SEC to conduct a study of the number of securities professionals (including accountants, public accounting firms, investment bankers, investment advisers, broker-dealers, and attorneys) who have aided and abetted securities violations and other associated issues. The SEC submitted its report and recommendations to Congress on January 24, 2003.[23]

---

[19] *Public Accounting Firms: Mandated Study on Consolidation and Competition,* GAO-03-864.

[20] "Report of the Securities and Exchange Commission," *Report on the Role and Function of Credit Rating Agencies in the Operation of the Securities Markets,* available at http://www.sec.gov/news/studies/credratingreport0103.pdf

[21] *Oversight of Credit Rating Agencies Registered as Nationally Recognized Statistical Rating Organizations,* Release No. 34-55231.

[22] *Report and Recommendations Pursuant to Section 401(c) of the Sarbanes-Oxley Act of 2002 on Arrangements with Off-Balance Sheet Implications, Special Purpose Entities, and Transparency of Filings with Issuers,* available at http://www.sec.gov/news/studies/soxoffbalancerpt.pdf.

[23] "Report of the Securities and Exchange Commission: Section 703 of the Sarbanes-Oxley Act of 2002," *Study and Report on Violations by Securities Professionals,* available at http://www.sec.gov/news/studies/sox703report.pdf.

Study of Enforcement Actions

Section 704 requires the SEC to conduct a study of the violations of reporting requirements and restatements of financial statements during the past five years and to identify the areas that are most susceptible to fraud, manipulation, and inappropriate earnings management. The SEC submitted its report and recommendations to Congress on January 24, 2003.[24]

Study of Investment Banks

Section 705 requires the General Accounting Office to study the role investment banks have played in designing transactions. The GAO submitted its report on March 17, 2003.[25]

CONCLUSION

At the time of writing, debate was underway as to whether the Act should be modified, and if so, to what extent.[26] What modifications, if any, will be made to the Act remains to be seen. Likewise, what influence, if any, the provisions of the Act relating to issuers will have on judicial application of the antifraud provisions to other entities such as municipal securities issuers, remains a subject for future evaluation. The new rigors imposed on the auditing profession by the Oversight Board in regulating issuer audits may spread to non-issuer audits as well. One area of relevance to the municipal securities market in which the influence of the Act is already visible is that of best practices.[27]

[24] *Report Pursuant to Section 704 of the Sarbanes-Oxley Act of 2002*, available at: http://www.sec.gov/news/studies/sox704report.pdf.
[25] *Investment Banks, The Role of Firms and Their Analysts with Enron and Global Crossing*, available at http://www.gao.gov/new.items/d03511.pdf.
[26] See *Interim Report of the Committee on Capital Markets Regulation* (November 30, 2006), available at http://www.capmktsreg.org/pdfs/11.30Committee_Interim_ReportREV2.pdf.
[27] See "GFOA Recommended Practice," *Audit Committees* (1997, 2002, and 2006) (CAFR), available at http://www.gfoa.org/services/rp/documents/2006_RP_Audit_Committee_revised.pdf.

CHAPTER 25

Using Auditing Techniques to Develop Investment Adviser Compliance Procedures

Kevin Reilly, CPA
Investments Compliance Specialist
Guardian Life Insurance Company of America

Steal a man's good name, or steal a company's reputation, and you have stolen something priceless. Reputations drive business. It's the basic element of trust. Whether you are buying a television, a life insurance policy, or investment advice, you expect the company on the other side of the transaction to be fair. Damage that expectation, and many reasonable buyers will choose another company. Destroy that expectation, and all reasonable buyers will take there business elsewhere.

In the adviser business, compliance departments help protect their company's reputation. Investment advisers with strong compliance programs have a competitive advantage over those that do not. These programs not only promote compliance with regulations, they protect a company's reputation and foster trust. Therefore, a strong compliance program will actually help the business grow.

The investment adviser industry, as industry in general, has undergone extensive reforms to ensure that the trust between customers and the industry remains strong. In order to "keep the trust," the Securities and Exchange Commission (SEC) adopted a rule which, among other requirements, mandated that investment advisers appoint a chief compliance officer, and that the chief compliance officer adopts written policies and procedures reasonably designed to prevent compliance violations with the Adviser Act by October 2004. Investment companies adopted even more extensive requirements that are not the subject of this chapter. Developing adviser compliance procedures was no easy matter, as many a compliance professional will attest.

Many advisers needed to hire outside consultants to assist the chief compliance officer in this task. Others relied upon external or internal auditors to assist in the development of these procedures.

Auditors have the basic skill set required to understand and document process flows. The word audit itself implies listening, which is critical to this entire process. Others relied on staff with audit backgrounds, or experience in process flow documentation. Regardless, the goal is the same: develop procedures reasonably designed to prevent compliance violations.

This chapter provides detailed instructions on how to use auditing techniques to help investment advisers develop procedures reasonably designed to prevent compliance violations in a bond portfolio. The chapter provides a step-by-step methodology for the development of these procedures. By following these procedures, one can gain a full understanding of any process and then work with legal counsel, if necessary, to revise the process to effectively promote compliance. The method is a four-tiered approach based on auditing techniques: understand the process, document it, review the process, and revise the process documentation.

GETTING STARTED

Before developing these procedures, work with legal counsel to determine the scope of the procedures. In order to determine the scope and sufficiency of any compliance program, compliance professionals need to work closely with legal counsel. Working closely with an attorney, who understands the industry and requirements of the regulations associated with it, will help the compliance officer ensure their procedures are sufficient. Examples of some common procedures in many compliance programs include important functions such as trading, best execution, trade correction, trade allocation, and settlement procedures.

After determining the procedures that need to be developed, follow a four-tiered approach based on auditing techniques: understand the process, document it, review the process, and revise the process documentation.

UNDERSTANDING THE PROCESS

This may sound straightforward, but it's actually quite complicated. Minor differences in procedures can make a huge difference in any process. It is critical that compliance professionals fully understand the processes they are trying to control.

Telephone interviews, relying on the subjects that perform the process to independently provide a process flow, or purchasing "canned" process documentation will not suffice. The use of traditional auditing techniques, a controlled exploratory process with multiple layers, will achieve a full understanding of any process.

Interview the Subject Performing the Process

It is important to remember that the subject performing the process is the expert in your organization on this function. They are the experts in the process. The auditor is the expert in "listening" to the process expert, and in documenting procedures.

The most important factor in getting this step correct is the relationship the auditor develops with the process owner both prior to the initial interview and during the interview process. It is important to remember that the process owner is helping the auditor develop the procedures. The auditor should emphasize the importance in developing these procedures, and thank the process owner for helping them with this function. The relationship must not be adversarial, or the results will not be satisfactory.

The initial and follow-up interviews should be scheduled at a time that is convenient for the process owner. The process owner's main job function is to perform their process, not to answer questions from an auditor. For example, a fixed income trader needs to assess the fixed income market, achieve best execution, and allocate the trades during the trading day. The initial and follow up interviews should be scheduled at the trader's convenience, perhaps at the end of the day after the close of the market.

The initial interview must take nothing for granted. The auditor should never "fill in the gaps" or assume any part of a process. Most process owners, when first describing their process, will initially give a high-level summary of the process. The auditor should not interrupt. Document this high-level process, and then use follow up questions to dig deeper into each step.

For example, when asked to describe the fixed income trading process, a fixed income trader might list the following seven steps in their process flow:

1. Call broker-dealer and negotiate price.
2. Execute trade.
3. Time stamp ticket.
4. Allocate trade.
5. Complete ticket including broker-dealer information and price.
6. Reconcile daily trades to trade blotter
7. Sign or authorize blotter.

The auditor should write each step down on a separate page in their notes, allowing room in the notes for the answers to follow-up questions. These follow-up questions are the key to fully understanding the fixed income trading process.

After obtaining a high-level understanding of the fixed income trading process flow, the auditor should begin digging further. Many of these questions will lead to better fixed income procedures; while other questions will raise red flags to the auditor on other procedures that may be lacking. The auditor then can share this information with their compliance officer. Some typical questions that might be asked follow each of the seven initial steps in the process. The follow-up questions will lead to a better understanding of the process. They may lead to related procedures that may need to be developed.

Call Broker/Dealer and Negotiate Price

Pretrade Compliance?   Before calling the broker-dealer, do you have a pre-trade compliance system to verify that the trade will not violate the investment guidelines for your bond portfolio? Could you show me how the compliance system works? Could I get a printout of a typical compliance system output?

Authorized Brokers-Dealers?   What brokers-dealers do you use? Is there a list of authorized brokers-dealers? How is this list determined? Could I get a copy of the list? Could I interview the individual responsible for maintaining the list of authorized brokers-dealers?

Reasonable Trade Flow and Commissions?   Does anyone review the volume of trades executed by each broker-dealer during the quarter or year?

Gift and Entertainment Policy?   Is there anything you can think of that could lead a trader to give a broker-dealer a price unfavorable to the portfolio? Do you receive any gifts or entertainment from these brokers-dealers? If so, with what regularity does this occur and for what dollar amounts? Are these gifts and entertainment documented? Do you have a gift and entertainment policy? Could I get a copy? Could I interview the individual who wrote the policy? Is there anyone who monitors compliance with this policy?

Other Trading Methods?   Are there other methods of obtaining a price rather than calling a broker-dealer? Do you use any web-based or other system based trading platforms? When negotiating a price, what do you base your initial bid/ask on? Could I get a sample printout of any market information you use to base your initial bid/ask?

Best-Execution? How do you promote best execution? Do you have a best execution policy? Could I get a copy of it? Could I interview the individual responsible for writing and maintaining the policy? Can I see any documentation you maintain on completing bids/offers for trades?

Execute Trade

How are trades executed? What trading platforms are used to execute the trades? Are trades executed over the telephone recorded? How do you confirm that you received the price you negotiated?

Time Stamp Ticket

How many time stamp machines are there? How is the time set and maintained? Is the machine calibrated? Do you always stamp the ticket immediately after the trade is executed?

Allocate Trade

How do you ensure that trades are allocated fairly? What are your allocation procedures? Who wrote them? Can I interview the person who wrote them? Are they monitored?

Complete Ticket Including Broker-Dealer Information and Price

What information is completed uniformly on all trade tickets? Could I have a copy of a trade ticket?

Reconcile Daily Trades to Trade Blotter

Describe your reconciliation procedure? Is it documented? Could I get a copy? Does anyone besides yourself reconcile your trades to the blotter? If so, could I interview that individual? Could I have a copy of yesterday's trade blotter and trade tickets?

Sign or Authorize Blotter

Who signs the blotter? Could I see the signatures on the last 15 trade blotters?

Observe How and Who Performs the Process

It has been my experience that no matter how well intentioned the interviewee (process owner) and the auditor are, the description of the process obtained through the interview almost always varies from the actual process. This may result simply from a lack of communication between the auditor and the process owner. Regardless, small differences in a process can make a big difference in results. The timing of when the trade ticket is stamped is a good example. What if the trader, to save time, stamps several tickets at once prior to executing the trades and then fills in the information on the stamped ticket? It is unlikely, even if the trader perceives the auditor to be "on their side," that any trader would actually say in an interview that sometimes when the desk is hectic they stamp several tickets at once and then execute the trades. So, what is the difference between a couple of minutes? Perhaps in some instances it does not make much of a difference. But what if your bond portfolio is being audited for best execution by a regulatory agency and one of the audit tests reveals multiple groups of tickets consistently stamped at the same time throughout each day tested?

Therefore, it becomes necessary for the auditor to observe the process (perhaps over the course of several days) to ensure that the actual real-life process does not differentiate from the process disclosed in the interview. The auditor should use the opportunity to learn the process from the process owner. Any difference should be thoroughly investigated and resolved. The documented process flow should be updated accordingly.

Using a Sample of Trades: Audit the Process

In order to verify the process owner truly follows the process revealed in the interview, it is important to audit the current process. Using audit sampling techniques and perhaps even audit software that allows auditors to include trades with unusual attributes (such as those with an unusual price) in a sample, the auditor should once again attempt to verify that the process which was developed in the interview and confirmed by observation accurately represents the process. Key points in the process should be part of the audit testing. There is no benefit in documenting incorrect procedures. The only way the auditor will be able to work with counsel to make sure the procedures are reasonably designed to prevent compliance violations, is to fully understand the current procedures and revise them if and when necessary.

Each important step in the trading process should be part of the audit checklist for the sample of trades. For example, in our illustrative example, for a sample of trades, check that the trader:

- Used pretrade compliance system.
- Used authorized brokers-dealers.
- Documented best execution.
- Completed a trade ticket.
- Time stamped the ticket.
- Allocated the trade according to trade-allocation procedures.
- Provided copies of tickets to settlements.
- Reconciled daily trades to trade blotter.
- Signed or authorized the blotter, and had the portfolio manager authorize the blotter.

DOCUMENT THE PROCESS

Documenting the Process via a Process Narrative

After interviewing the process owner, observing the process, and testing the process, the auditor fully understands the process. The auditor is now ready to prepare documentation of the process flow as the process now exists. Each step of the process should be numbered and the corresponding number should appear in the process flowchart for each step of the process. The process narrative should be inclusive and very descriptive. The narrative serves to fully explain the process, whereas the flowchart cannot include the complete descriptions of the process. It provides a simple visual overview of the process.

The process narrative and the flowchart jointly present a simple understanding of the overall process and are "twins" that together help fully document a process flow. Exhibit 25.1 provides an example narrative of fixed income trading procedures. These procedures are for illustrative purposes only and should not serve as standard procedures designed to prevent trading compliance violations in a bond portfolio.

Develop a Corresponding Flowchart to the Narrative

The narrative now needs to be flowcharted. Flowcharting software most often comes installed with standard auditing shapes and arrows that allow the auditor to seamlessly convert a process narrative into a flowchart. Each shape in the flowchart represents part of the process and should be numbered to correspond with the narrative. Key controls within the process, which are descriptively documented in the narrative, should also be readily evident in the flowchart. Exhibit 25.2 is an example flowchart of a fixed income trading procedures. This flowchart is for illustrative purposes only and should not serve as standard procedures designed to prevent compliance violations in a bond portfolio.

EXHIBIT 25.1   Illustrative Fixed Income Trading Procedures Narrative

1. The trader meets with the portfolio manager every morning to discuss the market and the orders to be executed for the day.
2. The trader enters the trade onto the pretrade compliance system, which determines if the trade will violate investment restrictions, or other regulations.
3. If the trade fails any of the compliance tests, the trader calls compliance to discuss the failure.
4. If the trade passes the compliance tests, the trader will begin to assess the market to execute the trade.
5. Trader determines if the issue is widely available and price is relatively consistent.
6. If it is, the trader will execute over a web-based trading platform to execute trades with brokers-dealers that have been preapproved by Legal and Compliance. After entering the trade, it is automatically executed with a preapproved brokers-dealers offering the best price and the information automatically feeds the trade-recording platform.
7. If the issue is not widely available and price not consistent, the trader can also negotiate directly with a broker-dealer on the approved broker-dealer list. Trader enters negotiated trade on trade recording platform.
8. The trader then prints out the execution screen showing the executed price, broker-dealer, amount, CUSIP, description, trade date, and settlement date. Trader completes a trade ticket documenting the broker-dealer, price, buy or sale, quantity, cusip, and description. The ticket is time stamped to document the time of execution. The trader maintains one copy of ticket and one copy is forwarded to the Settlement Department (Operations) to settle the trade.
9. Trader documents at least two competing bids or offers on the *competing bid/offer sheet* to document best execution. The trader also prints out the competing bids/asks at the time of the executed trade to document best execution.
10. After the trade is executed, the trade is allocated to the appropriate portfolios based upon the *allocation procedures* documented and approved by Compliance and Legal.
11. At the end of the day, trader reconciles all trade tickets to the trade blotter and signs the blotter indicating approval of all the information on it. The trader provides the blotter and tickets to the portfolio manager who also reviews it and signs the blotter authorizing the trades. The blotter is then filed by date.

REVIEW THE PROCESS

Review the Documented Process with Subjects

Now the process has been fully documented. It was obtained by interviewing the process owner, observing the process, testing the process, narrating the

EXHIBIT 25.2 Illustrative Fixed Income Trading Procedures Flowchart

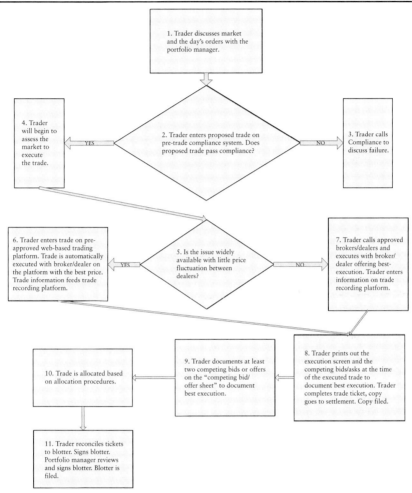

process, and flowcharting the process. It's a critical multitiered, labor intensive method used to understand the process. Have the process owner review, initial, and date the process narrative and flowchart so everyone is completely clear that this is an accurate current representation of the existing process.

Meet with Counsel and Compare the Actual Process to Best Practices

As previously discussed, experienced compliance officers and experienced attorneys need to work together to ensure each procedure is reasonably designed to prevent compliance violations. In addition to their own research and experience, and the knowledge of the process owner, the compliance officers should work with a specialized attorney to ensure their procedures are complete and reasonably designed.

Now that the current process is fully and accurately documented, it is time to schedule a meeting with your in-house counsel or your outside counsel who specializes in your business. Counsel can help you understand the requirements and if your current procedures fall short.

REVISE THE PROCESS DOCUMENTATION

Highlight Revisions

All revisions from the original process narrative and flowchart should be made and highlighted so the process owner can focus on the changes and not the entire process in the final "buy in" meeting.

Meet with Process Owner

This has been a long process. The auditor is now at the "finish" line. A final meeting with the process owner to discuss any deficiencies in the current process and proposed revisions to the process may be necessary. If there were deficiencies and revisions to the process, have the process owner accept the changes by signing and dating the revised narrative and flowchart.

Provide Copies to All Interested Parties

In our illustration, we have now successfully documented one procedure using auditing techniques. It is reasonably designed to prevent compliance violations at our hypothetical bond portfolio. The key was our multitiered approach that leads the auditor to a complete understanding of the current procedures. The auditor then works with counsel to determine deficiencies (if any), and revises the procedures. The final step is to send copies to all interested parties, and then incorporate them with any other completed procedures.

SUMMARY

In 2004, the SEC adopted a rule with a requirement that investment advisers appoint a chief compliance officer and that the officer adopts written policies and procedures reasonably designed to prevent compliance violations with the Advisers Act. This chapter demonstrated how to develop the procedures for a bond portfolio. Developing procedures to prevent compliance violations requires a complete understanding of the processes involved. The use of traditional auditing techniques will achieve a full understanding of any process. It follows a four-tiered exploratory approach after determining the procedures that need to be developed: understand the process, document it, review the process, and revise the process documentation.

CHAPTER 26

Rule 2a-7: Legal and Research Issues for Tax-Exempt Money Market Funds

Stephen A. Keen
Partner
Reed Smith LLP

Leslie K. Ross
Counsel
Reed Smith LLP

Tax-exempt money market funds are unique. No other form of investment provides a combination of tax-exempt interest, stable yield and diversification with the liquidity of wire transfers, check writing and debit cards. Little wonder that the total assets of tax-exempt money market funds were approaching $400 billion at the beginning of 2007.

Tax-exempt money market funds are also unique in their reliance on structured investments. Unlike the taxable money market, with trillions of dollars of Treasury and agency bills, commercial paper, and bank instruments, only a small fraction of tax-exempt securities are issued with original maturities of one year or less. Moreover, the tax-exempt market is not as liquid or transparent as the taxable money market. These circumstances make it practically impossible to manage a tax-exempt money market fund without investing in long-term, adjustable-rate securities with liquidity features.

The unique nature of tax-exempt money market funds demands unique regulations. This has led the Securities and Exchange Commission (SEC) to incorporate special provisions for tax-exempt money market funds into Rule 2a-7,[1] the principal regulation governing money market funds under

---

[1] 17 C.F.R. § 270.2a-7 (2007). Unless otherwise noted, all citations to paragraphs refer to paragraphs of Rule 2a-7.

the Investment Company Act of 1940 (ICA).[2] The fact that the rule includes a definition of a tax-exempt fund exemplifies the extent to which the SEC has crafted Rule 2a-7 to accommodate the practical limits of the tax-exempt money market.

This chapter examines the application of Rule 2a-7 to tax-exempt money market funds and the instruments in which they invest.[3] It begins with the regulatory definition of a tax-exempt money market fund and the general requirements for money market funds. The chapter then summarizes the requirements for eligible securities and for the diversification of tax-exempt money market funds. The chapter also provides an analysis under Rule 2a-7 of various types of instruments commonly held by tax-exempt money market funds. The chapter concludes by reviewing the circumstances under which Rule 2a-7 may require a money market fund to dispose of a portfolio security or cease to maintain a stable value per share.

DEFINITION OF A TAX-EXEMPT MONEY MARKET FUND

Paragraph (a)(24) defines a tax-exempt fund as a "money market fund that holds itself out as distributing income exempt from regular federal income tax." In order to understand the significance of this definition, we must examine what it means to be a money market fund and the implications of a money market fund holding itself out as tax exempt.

Definition of a Money Market Fund

A *money market fund* is a mutual fund[4] that seeks to maintain a *net asset value* (NAV) of $1 per share using either the *Amortized Cost Method* or *Penny Rounding Method*.[5] A money market fund using the Amortized Cost Method determines its NAV based upon the cost (rather than the current market value) of its portfolio (plus any accrued discount and less any amortized premium). Only realized gains and losses can affect the NAV of a fund

---

[2] 14 U.S.C. §§ 80a-1, et. seq. (2007).

[3] This chapter does not address provisions of Rule 2a-7 that generally affect only taxable money market funds. Although the chapter does not purport to be all inclusive even with respect to tax-exempt funds, managers of taxable funds should consult other sources for guidance on Rule 2a-7.

[4] *Mutual fund* refers to an investment company registered with the SEC that is an *open-end company* as defined in ICA § 5(a)(1). Open-end companies are distinguished by having managed portfolios and issuing shares that may be redeemed for their NAV.

[5] *Amortized Cost Method* is defined in ¶ (a)(1) and *Penny Rounding Method* is defined in ¶a)(18).

using the Amortized Cost Method. A money market fund using the Penny Rounding Method determines its NAV based upon the current market value of its portfolio, but rounds its NAV to the nearest cent per share. Both realized and unrealized gains and losses can affect the NAV of a fund using the Penny Rounding Method. We will focus on money market funds using the Amortized Cost Method, because few funds currently use the Penny Rounding Method.

Mutual funds that do not comply with Rule 2a-7 cannot use either the Amortized Cost Method or the Penny Rounding Method to calculate their NAVs. The SEC limits the use of the Amortized Cost Method by other mutual funds to valuing debt securities with remaining maturities of 60 days or less.[6] Moreover, the SEC would require a money market fund that failed to comply with Rule 2a-7 to calculate its NAV "with an accuracy of one-tenth of one percent."[7] Consequently, a mutual fund that attempts to maintain a constant $1 NAV without complying with Rule 2a-7 must use the current market value of all portfolio securities maturing in more than sixty days to calculate its NAV, and then round the calculation to the nearest tenth of a cent.

Even if a mutual fund manages to maintain an NAV within one-tenth of $1, Rule 2a-7(b) would prevent the fund from holding itself as a "money market fund" unless it complied with the rule. This provision also requires any fund that uses *money market*, *cash*, *liquid*, *money*, *ready assets*, or similar terms in its name to comply with Rule 2a-7.

Definition of a Tax-Exempt Fund

Rule 35d-1(a)(4),[8] rather than Rule 2a-7, governs the use of the words "tax exempt" in a fund's name. This rule requires that any fund (including a money market fund) with a "name suggesting that the Fund's distributions are exempt from federal income tax or from both federal and state income tax" adopt a policy:

> (i) To invest, under normal circumstances, at least 80% of the value of its [net assets] in investments the income from which is [tax] exempt, . . . ; or
> (ii) To invest, under normal circumstances, its [net assets] so that at least 80% of the income that it distributes will be [tax] exempt, ...

---

[6] Release No. IC-9786, 42 F.R. 28999 (June 7, 1977).
[7] Id. at 29001.
[8] 17 C.F.R. § 270.35d-1(a)(4) (2007).

To qualify as tax exempt for purposes of this policy, the income from a security must be "exempt from federal income tax under both the regular tax rules and the alternative minimum tax [AMT] rules."[9] The income must also be exempt from state or local income or investment taxes if the fund's name refers to the state or locality. The policy must be "fundamental," in that it may not be amended without approval by a majority of the fund's shareholders.

A money market fund that wishes to retain the right to invest more than 20% of its assets in municipal bonds subject to AMT, or a single state fund that wishes to retain the right to invest more than 20% of its assets in securities not exempt from the state's income tax, will typically use more generic words (such as *municipal*) in its name. There are many money market funds paying dividends exempt from regular federal income tax or partially exempt from state income tax that do not meet the requirements of Rule 35d-1(a)(4).

Therefore, a money market fund that includes "tax exempt" in its name in compliance with Rule 35d-1 should automatically qualify as a tax-exempt fund for purposes of Rule 2a-7. Even if a money market fund's dividends are subject to AMT (so that it cannot refer to "tax exempt" in its name), the fund can still qualify as a "tax-exempt fund" under Rule 2a-7 so long as the dividends are exempt from "regular" income tax. In addition, ¶ (a)(23) defines a "single-state fund [as] a tax-exempt fund that holds itself out as seeking to maximize the amount of its distributed income that is exempt from the income taxes or other taxes on investments of a particular state and, where applicable, subdivisions thereof." We will use these Rule 2a-7 defined terms throughout the balance of this chapter. We will also use the term *national fund* to refer to a tax-exempt fund that is not a single-state fund.

GENERAL REQUIREMENTS OF RULE 2a-7

The essence of Rule 2a-7 can be boiled down to the first three sections of ¶ (c):

First: "The money market fund shall limit its portfolio investments to those United States Dollar-Denominated securities[10] that the . . . board of directors determines present minimal credit risks (which determination must be based on factors per-

[9] Release No. IC-24828, 66 F.R. 8509, 8512 (Feb. 1, 2001).
[10] *United States dollar-denominated* is defined in ¶ (a)(27). This requirement should not raise issues for a tax-exempt fund, as in our experience tax-exempt securities are invariably United States dollar-denominated.

taining to credit quality in addition to any rating assigned to such securities by an NRSRO[11]) . . . ." ¶ (c)(3)(i)

Second: "The money market fund shall maintain a dollar-weighted average portfolio maturity [WAPM] appropriate to its objective of maintaining a stable net asset value per share or price per share." ¶c)(2)

Third: The money market fund shall "continue to use [the Amortized Cost or Penny Rounding] method only so long as the board of directors believes that it fairly reflects the market-based net asset value per share." ¶ (c)(1)

In essence, these provisions require a money market fund's manager to determine the amount of credit and interest rate risk the fund will take, without causing the fund's market-based NAV to deviate too far from $1 per share. Although Rule 2a-7 contains a great many more requirements, they act primarily to limit the scope of these three determinations. In other words, these three provisions of Rule 2a-7 tell a manager what he must do, while the other provisions tell a manager what he cannot do.

Although the SEC expressly charges the money market fund's board of directors ("board") with responsibility for making these determinations, in practice the responsibility for all three determinations falls primarily on the investment adviser. Almost all boards delegate responsibility for determining minimal credit risk and the fund's WAPM to the fund's investment adviser, as permitted by ¶ (e). And, even though Rule 2a-7 does not permit a board to delegate its responsibilities under ¶c)(1), boards typically charge the investment adviser with monitoring the deviation between the market-based NAV and $1. The SEC has provided guidance for boards which should aid investment advisers in performing these delegated responsibilities.

Determination of Minimal Credit Risk

Apart from stating that the determination cannot be based exclusively on an instrument's ratings, the text of Rule 2a-7 provides no guidance as to the meaning of *minimal credit risk* or as to how an instrument's credit risk should be determined. However, the SEC and its staff have provided some general guidance on minimal credit risk in releases and interpretive letters. For example, when the SEC originally adopted Rule 2a-7, it provided the following explanation of why factors other than ratings must be considered in determining credit risk:

---

[11] "NRSRO means any nationally recognized statistical rating organization" that is not an affiliated person of the company being rated. ¶ (a)(17).

However, the mere fact that an instrument has or would receive a high quality rating may not be sufficient to ensure stability. The [SEC] believes that the instrument must be evaluated for the credit risk that it presents to the particular fund at that time in light of the risks attendant to the use of amortized cost valuation or penny-rounding. Moreover, the board may look at some aspects when evaluating the risk of an investment that would not be considered by the rating services.[12]

In other words, a manager must assess credit risk from the perspective of a fund seeking to sell and redeem its shares for a constant $1 NAV, which may differ from the perspective of an NRSRO.

An exchange of letters between the Director of the Division of Investment Management (Division) and the Investment Company Institute (ICI) provides more detailed guidance concerning the credit analysis required by Rule 2a-7. The ICI initiated the exchange in 1989, after certain advisers purchased defaulted commercial paper from their money market funds to avoid "breaking a dollar" (i.e., no longer maintaining a $NAV). In its letter, the ICI urged the SEC to issue an interpretive release that, among other things, "included a list of factors which might be considered in determining whether a particular instrument presents minimal credit risk . . . ."[13] The ICI's letter then provided illustrative factors "that might be considered in assessing credit risk of the issuer or guarantor of money market securities."[14] Exhibit 26.1 sets forth these illustrative factors.

Initially, the Division responded by agreeing that "the board should take into account, as appropriate, the kinds of factors listed in your letter," but declining to issue an interpretive release.[15] However, continued concerns about defaults led the Division to issue a second letter.[16] In this letter, the Division observed that a board must determine credit risk "based upon an analysis of the issuer's capacity to repay its short-term debt," and provided "[e]xamples of elements of such an analysis include[ing]":

(i) a cash flow analysis; (ii) an assessment of the issuer's ability to react to future events, including a review of the issuer's competitive position, cost structure and capital intensiveness; (iii) an assessment of the issuer's liquidity, including bank lines of credit and alterna-

---

[12] Release No. IC-13380, 48 Fed. Reg. 32555, 32560 (July 11, 1983).
[13] *Investment Company Institute, No-Action Letter*, WSB File No. 121889014 at 5-6 (pub. avail. Dec. 6, 1989).
[14] Id. at 6.
[15] Id. at 2-3.
[16] *Letter to Registrants*, WSB File No. 051490039 (pub. avail. May 8, 1990).

EXHIBIT 26.1 Illustrative Factors for Determining Minimal Credit Risk[a]

General factors:	Macroeconomic factors which might affect the issuer's or guarantor's current and future credit quality.
	The strength of the issuer's or guarantor's industry within the economy and relative to economic trends.
Specific factors:	The issuer's or guarantor's market position within its industry.
	Cash flow adequacy.
	The level and nature of earnings.
	Financial leverage.
	Asset protection.
	The quality of the issuer's or guarantor's accounting practices and management.
	The effect of any significant ownership positions.
	The degree of financial flexibility of the issuer or guarantor to cope with unexpected challenges and to take advantage of opportunities, as well as an assessment of the degree and nature of event risks.
	The likelihood of a sudden change of credit quality from external (e.g., hostile takeovers, litigation) and internal (e.g., financial restructuring, acquisitions) sources.
Factors with respect to tax-exempt securities:	Sources of repayment.
	Autonomy in raising taxes and revenue.
	Reliance on outside revenue sources.
	Strength and stability of the supporting economy.

[a] *Investment Company Institute, No-Action Letter*, WSB File No. 121889014 (pub. avail. Dec. 6, 1989).
Source: Reed Smith LLP. Reprinted by permission.

> tive sources of liquidity to support its commercial paper; and (iv) a "worst case scenario" evaluation of the issuer's ability to repay its short-term debt from cash sources or asset liquidations in the event that the issuer's backup credit facilities are unavailable.[17]

The last element may represent a departure from traditional credit analysis, which usually evaluates the probability that an issuer cannot satisfy the conditions for drawing on its credit facilities, rather than presuming that the credit facilities "are unavailable." Failure to address the "worst-case scenario" was a hot topic during SEC examinations of money market funds in the 1990s, and managers are still well advised to address this in their credit procedures.

The Division's letter also noted that the credit analysis "should take into consideration the length to maturity of the security and the percentage of the

---

[17] Id. at 2.

fund's portfolio represented by securities of that issuer."[18] In other words, a manager might determine that an overnight investment of 1% of a fund's portfolio presents minimal credit risk without necessarily reaching the same conclusion with respect to investing 5% of the portfolio in 180-day commercial paper of the same issuer. Finally, the Division warned that minimal credit risk "determinations must be recorded in the books and records of the fund . . . ."[19] Failure to record minimal credit risk determinations remains a frequently cited deficiency in SEC examinations of money market funds.

Determination of Weighted Average Portfolio Maturity

In contrast to the minimal credit risk determination, the SEC and the Division have provided little guidance concerning how a manager should determine an appropriate WAPM. In the release originally adopting Rule 2a-7, the SEC observed that:

> During periods of higher volatility in the market, the [Board] should be aware of the greater difficulty in maintaining a stable price per share and should take steps to ensure that they are providing adequate oversight to the money market fund.[20]

The SEC reiterated this point when it shortened the WAPM requirement from 120 to 90 days.[21]

Cash flow is another important factor for determining WAPM that the SEC has never acknowledged. If cash outflows coincide with increasing interest rates, a money market fund's WAPM can extend rapidly as the fund uses its cash balances and proceeds from maturing investments to pay net redemptions. If this were to push the WAPM beyond 90 days, the SEC has made it clear that "the [board] is obligated to cause the fund to invest its available cash in such a manner as to reduce its [WAPM] . . . as soon as reasonably practicable."[22] This could force the fund to realize losses, creating a deviation between the fund's NAV and $1 that will grow more significant if the net redemptions continue. This risk may explain why taxable money market funds rarely operate near the 90-day limit, particularly when the first year of the yield curve is relatively flat.

---

[18] Id.

[19] Id.

[20] Release No. IC-13380, supra note 12, at 32559.

[21] "[D]uring periods of very high market volatility, a ninety day average maturity may be too long, and the board would be required to take such actions as are necessary to assure that the average maturity is adjusted accordingly." Release No. IC-17589, 55 F.R. 30239, 30246 n. 61 (July 17, 1990).

[22] Release No. IC-13380, supra note 12, at 32559.

The unique nature of the tax-exempt market gives tax-exempt funds less control than taxable funds over their WAPM. Most municipalities issue their short-term notes in conjunction with the beginning of their fiscal year, which is commonly July 1. This creates a large supply of one-year notes during the summer, which rarely become available in the secondary market later in the year. Thus, most tax-exempt funds extend their WAPMs in the summer and then roll down during the course of the year as the notes approach maturity. Still, the WAPMs of most tax-exempt funds rarely approach 90 days.

Determination That Amortized Cost Value Fairly Reflects the Market-Based NAV

Fundamentally, Rule 2a-7 presumes that shareholders of a money market fund are willing to suffer some dilution[23] in their investment in exchange for the predictable liquidity provided by a constant $1 NAV. However, at some point, the dilution may become so great as to become unfair to either shareholders or new investors. In addition, cash flows may cause dilution to systematically disadvantage some shareholders as compared to others. Rule 2a-7 therefore requires the board to determine that the amount of dilution resulting from using the Amortized Cost or Penny Rounding Method remains fair to shareholders.

Paragraph (c)(7)(ii) requires the board to adopt specific procedures to monitor potential dilution through "shadow pricing." Under these procedures, a money market fund must calculate the deviation between the NAV calculated using the Amortized Cost Method and the NAV "calculated using available market quotations".[24] The calculations must occur "at such intervals as the [board] determines appropriate and reasonable in light of current market conditions."[25] The board must periodically review "the amount of the deviation as well as the methods used to calculate the deviation."[26]

---

[23] "If shares are sold based on a net asset value which turns out to be either understated or overstated in comparison to the amount at which portfolio instruments could have been sold, then either the interests of existing shareholders or new investors will have been diluted." Release No. IC-12206, 47 Fed. Reg. 5428, 5430 n. 6 (Feb. 5, 1982).

[24] The procedures may also use "an appropriate substitute [for market quotations] that reflects current market conditions." ¶ (c)(7)(ii)(A)(1). In addition, "all portfolio instruments, regardless of their length of maturity, should be valued based upon market factors and not their amortized cost value." Release No. IC-12206, supra note 23, at 5434. Most money market funds use either a pricing service or a price matrix to calculate their market-based NAV.

[25] Paragraph (c)(7)(ii)(A)(1).

[26] Paragraph (c)(7)(ii)(A)(2).

In the release originally proposing Rule 2a-7, the SEC discussed the relationship between market conditions and the frequency with which the deviation was calculated.

> During periods of high market volatility, this requirement may necessitate that the deviation between such market-based value and price be monitored on a daily basis. During periods of lower volatility, it may be reasonable to monitor such deviation less frequently. The reviews should be frequent enough so that the [Board] may become aware of changes in the market-based per share net asset value before they become material.[27]

Boards typically comply with the need to relate the frequency of the calculation to market conditions by setting a standard frequency for normal market conditions and authorizing the manager to increase the frequency during more volatile conditions. The procedures may also require more frequent calculations if the deviation exceeds a specific threshold (e.g., 25 basis points).

If the deviation exceeds 50 basis points, the board must meet promptly to "consider what action, if any, should be initiated by the [board]." The board must also cause the fund to take action if it "believes the extent of any deviation . . . may result in material dilution or other unfair results to investors or existing shareholders."[28] It is important to keep in mind that a market-based NAV above $1 may be as dilutive during periods of net sales as an NAV below $is during periods of net redemptions.

As we previously noted, Rule 2a-7 does not permit the board to delegate its responsibilities under ¶ (c)(7). However, many boards do require the manager to:

- Review each calculated deviation.
- Report to the board any deviation in excess of a specified threshold or any circumstance the manager "believes may result in material dilution or other unfair results."
- Involve senior management or compliance in addressing deviations in excess of a specified threshold.
- Recommend actions for the board's consideration should the deviation exceed 50 basis points.

As a result, the manager usually bears primary responsibility for managing the deviation, albeit with increasing board oversight as the deviation approaches or exceeds 50 basis points.

---

[27] Release No. IC-12206, supra note 23, at 5434.
[28] Paragraph (c)(7)(ii)(B)-(C).

ELIGIBLE SECURITIES FOR TAX EXEMPT FUNDS

A money market fund may only acquire securities that are eligible securities under ¶ (a)(10).[29] The definition eligible security contains over 400 words and uses a myriad of other defined terms. This section breaks down the elements of the definition that commonly apply to tax-exempt securities. First, it examines the credit quality requirements for rated and unrated securities. Next, it examines the additional requirements for eligible securities subject to guarantees and demand features. Finally, it examines how to calculate the maturity of securities for purposes of the definition.

A money market fund must determine compliance with the eligible security requirement at the time it "acquires" the security. An *acquisition* occurs whenever a money market fund purchases or rolls over a position in a security.[30]

Credit Quality Requirements

Eligible securities must meet an objective standard for credit quality defined by an NRSRO's second highest short-term rating category. Generally, if an obligation has received short-term ratings from an NRSRO, or is comparable in priority and security to other obligations of the issuer that have received short-term ratings from an NRSRO, then Rule 2a-7 treats the obligation as a rated security. A rated eligible security is further categorized as a first-tier security or a second-tier security, depending on whether it has received NRSRO ratings in the first or second highest short-term rating category. Rule 2a-7 has additional rules for obligations that receive different ratings from NRSROs.

If the obligation is not a rated security, then Rule 2a-7 treats it as an unrated security and requires the manager to determine if it is of comparable quality to a rated eligible security. However, the rule limits a manager's ability to make this determination if the unrated security has received long-term credit ratings.

Rated Securities

A money market fund should treat a rated security as having received any short-term rating given by an NRSRO to other obligations of the issuer having comparable priority and security.[31] Long-term ratings have no bearing on whether to treat a security as a rated security. A security that receives

---

[29] Paragraph (c)(3)(i).
[30] Paragraph (a)(1).
[31] Paragraph (a)(19)(i)-(ii).

exclusively long-term ratings from NRSROs is an unrated security for all purposes under Rule 2a-7.

Moreover, a security is not a rated security if the credit support arrangement on which the NRSROs based their ratings has been modified.[32] For example, a money market fund may not treat a security as a rated security if the issuer substitutes financial guarantee insurance from a company without short-term ratings for a letter of credit from a bank with short-term ratings. In such case, the security would remain a rated security only if an NRSRO updates its short-term rating of the security to reflect the modified credit support arrangement. Otherwise, Rule 2a-7 forces analysis of the modification in the same manner as an unrated security.

First- and Second-Tier Securities

To qualify as an eligible security, a rated security must be either a first-tier security or a second-tier security. Generally, a rated security is a first-tier security if it received ratings from NRSROs in the highest short-term rating categories; a rated security is a second-tier security if it received ratings from NRSROs in the second highest short-term rating categories. Rule 2a-7 defines a rating category without regard to subcategories or gradations.[33] Currently, there are five NRSROs: A.M. Best Company (Best), Dominion Bond Rating Service (DBRS), Fitch Ratings (Fitch), Moody's Investors Service, Inc. (Moody's), and Standard & Poor's (S&P). Exhibit 26.2 identifies the two highest short-term rating categories for each NRSRO.

EXHIBIT 26.2 Eligible Security Rating Categories of NRSROs

NRSRO	Best	DBRSa	Fitch	Moody's	S&P
Highest category	AMB-1+ or AMB-1	R-1 (high, middle, or low)	F1+ or F1	Prime-1 or MIG-1	A-1+, A-1, SP-1+ or SP-1
Second highest category	AMB-2	R-2 (high, middle, or low)	F2	Prime-2 or MIG-2	A-2 or SP-2

[a] DBRS defines securities with any level of an R-2 rating as having "adequate" credit quality, while securities with an R-1(low) rating are defined as having "satisfactory" credit quality. In comparison, both S&P and Fitch use "satisfactory" to define their second highest short-term rating categories and "adequate" to define their third highest short-term rating categories. Money market funds should therefore exercise caution in relying on an R-2 rating to classify a security as second-tier or an R-1(low) rating to classify a security as first tier.

Source: Reed Smith LLP. Reprinted by permission.

[32] Paragraph (a)(19)(iii).
[33] Paragraph (a)(12)(i).

If a security has received a short-term rating from only one NRSRO, then that rating determines whether the security is a first- or second-tier security.[34] A rating in the highest category makes the security a first-tier security,[35] a rating in the second highest category makes it a second-tier security.[36] If the security received a short-term rating below the second highest category, then the security is not an eligible security.

If a rated security receives short-term ratings from multiple NRSROs, all in their highest short-term rating category, then it is a first-tier security;[37] if all of the ratings are in the second highest rating category, it is a second-tier security.[38] If a rated security receives multiple ratings in different rating categories, then its status as a first- or second-tier security is determined by the "Requisite NRSROs."[39] The requisite NRSROs are whichever two NRSROs have given a security its highest rating. If both requisite NRSROs rate the security in their highest short-term rating category, then it is a first-tier security. If one requisite NRSRO rates the security in its second highest short-term rating category, then it is a second-tier security, and, if a requisite NRSRO gives the security a lower rating, it is not an eligible security. Exhibit 26.3 illustrates the various permutations of requisite NRSROs.

EXHIBIT 26.3   Ratings by Requisite NRSROs

Two NRSROs:	P-1/A-1	First tier
	P-2/A-1	Second tier
	P-3/A-1	Not eligible
Three NRSROs:	A-1/F-1/P-3	First tier
	A-2/F-1/P-3	Second tier
	A-3/F-1/P-3	Not eligible
Four NRSROs:	F-1/AMB-1/A-3/P-3	First tier
	F-2/AMB-1/A-3/P-3	Second tier
	F-3/AMB-1/A-3/P-3	Not eligible
Five NRSROs:	R-1/AMB-1/A-3/P-3/F-3	First tier
	R-2/AMB-1/A-3/P-3/F-3	Second tier
	R-3/AMB-1/A-3/P-3/F-3	Not eligible

Source: Reed Smith LLP. Reprinted by permission.

---

[34] Paragraph (a)(21)(ii).
[35] Paragraph (a)(12)(i).
[36] Paragraph (a)(22).
[37] Paragraph (a)(21)(i), (a)(12)(i).
[38] Paragraph (a)(21)(i), (a)(22).
[39] Paragraph (a)(21).

Any government security[40] is a first-tier security, regardless of whether an NRSRO has rated the security, or the issuer or guarantor thereof.[41] Shares of another money market fund also are treated as first-tier securities, regardless of whether the other fund holds second-tier securities in its portfolio.[42]

Unrated Securities

Any security that is not a rated security is an unrated security.[43] To be an eligible security, the board must determine that the credit quality of an unrated security is comparable to a rated first-tier or second-tier security.[44] However, the board may only make such a determination if the unrated security satisfies one of the following three conditions:

First: At the time of issuance, the unrated security's maturity did not exceed 397 days.

Second: The unrated security has not received a long-term rating from any NRSRO.

Third: The unrated security has received long-term ratings within the three highest rating categories from the requisite NRSROs.[45]

Generally, the board delegates responsibility for making determinations regarding unrated securities to the fund's investment adviser, as permitted by ¶(e).

---

[40] *Government security* is defined in ICA § 2(a)(16) to include a security that is issued or guaranteed by the United States, or by a person controlled or supervised by and acting as an instrumentality of the United States. Issuers of government securities include the U.S. Treasury, the Federal Farm Credit System, the Federal Home Administration, Federal Home Loan Banks, the Federal Home Loan Mortgage Corporation, the Federal National Mortgage Association, the Government National Mortgage Association, the Department of Housing and Urban Development, the Resolution Funding Corporation, the Small Business Administration and the Student Loan Marketing Association. The World Bank or a similar international organization would not qualify as an instrumentality of the United States, even though the United States participates in this organization, and would therefore not issue a government security.

[41] Paragraph (a)(12)(iv).

[42] Paragraph (a)(iii).

[43] Paragraph (a)(28).

[44] Paragraph (a)(10)(ii).

[45] Paragraph (a)(ii)(A).

Securities Subject to Demand Features and Guarantees

If a security is subject to a demand feature or guarantee, the analysis of whether it is an eligible security is more complex. We will refer to the provider of a demand feature (other than the issuer) or guarantee as an *enhancer*.

A demand feature is the right to tender a security for purchase at a price equal to its amortized cost plus accrued interest as of the date of purchase.[46] A holder may exercise a demand feature at any time or at intervals of not more than 397 days.[47] We will refer to the day on which a security is purchased after exercise of a demand feature as the *tender date*. A demand feature may not require notice of exercise more than 30 days' prior to the tender date.[48] Failure to exercise a demand feature does not constitute an acquisition by a money market fund.

A guarantee is an unconditional obligation of a person other than the issuer of the security to pay the principal amount of the security plus accrued interest when due or upon default.[49] Guarantees include letters of credit and financial guaranty (bond) insurance. A demand feature from an enhancer that may be readily exercised in the event of a default by the issuer, which ¶ (a)(26) defines as an "Unconditional Demand Feature," also qualifies as a guarantee.[50]

A security subject to a guarantee may qualify as an eligible security based on the guarantee's status as a first-tier or second-tier security.[51] The definitions of rated and unrated securities include guarantees, and their tier status is determined in the same manner as other rated or unrated securities. However, to rely upon a guarantee, the security must require notice to the money market fund of any substitution of the demand feature or guarantee.[52] For example, if a security permits the issuer to replace a letter of credit with another credit facility, then the security must provide for notice of any replacement. To protect the money market fund, the security should require sufficient notice to allow the fund to exercise the demand feature before the substitution occurs. A security subject to mandatory tender upon substitution of a demand feature or guarantee, or which does not permit substitution of the demand feature or guarantee, also will satisfy this requirement.

A security that is subject to a guarantee issued by a *noncontrolled person* must either (1) have received a rating based upon the guarantee or (2) be

---

[46] Paragraph (a)(8)(i).
[47] Paragraph (a)(8)(i)(B).
[48] Paragraph (a)(8)(i)(A)-(B).
[49] Paragraph (a)(15).
[50] Id.
[51] Paragraph (c)(3)(iii).
[52] Paragraph (a)(10)(iii)(B).

comparable in priority and security to other rated obligations of the guarantor.[53] A guarantee is issued by a noncontrolled person if the issuer of the guarantee does not control, and is neither controlled by or under common control with, the issuer of the security.[54] Unlike the requirements for a rated security, long-term as well as short-term ratings from an NRSRO will satisfy this requirement. A minimum rating is not required, although the guarantee must qualify as either a first- or second-tier security.

A security that is subject to a *conditional demand feature*[55] must meet additional requirements to qualify as an eligible security.[56] The first two requirements relate to the nature of the conditional demand feature. First, the tender date of the conditional demand feature cannot exceed 397 days.[57] Second, the conditional demand feature must qualify as a first-tier or second-tier security.[58]

The next two requirements relate to the circumstances under which the conditional demand feature terminates, commonly referred to as *tender option termination events* (TOTEs). Specifically, a money market fund must determine that there is minimal risk that any TOTE will occur.[59] Further, TOTEs must be limited to (1) events that can be readily monitored; (2) events for which the security requires sufficient notice to allow the exercise of the conditional demand feature before it terminates; and (3) if the security purports to be tax-exempt, a determination that interest payments are taxable.[60]

The final requirement relates to the creditworthiness of the underlying security.[61] Under this requirement, either the underlying security or a guarantee of the underlying security must satisfy the following quality standards: (1) If the underlying security or guarantee is a rated security, it must have received ratings in one of the two highest long-term or short-term rating categories; or (2) if the underlying security or guarantee is an unrated security, the money market fund must determine that it is of comparable quality to

---

[53] Paragraph (a)(10)(iii)(A).

[54] Paragraph (a)(16). Control means "control" as defined in ICA § 2(a)(19).

[55] *Conditional demand feature* is defined in ¶ (a)(6) to include a demand feature that is not an unconditional demand feature. A conditional demand feature is not a guarantee.

[56] Paragraph (c)(3)(iv).

[57] Paragraph (c)(iv)(A).

[58] Id.

[59] Paragraph (c)(3)(iv)(B).

[60] Paragraph (c)(iv)(B)(1)–(2). Common TOTEs include (1) payment default, (2) events of insolvency, (3) the security being downgraded below investment grade and (4) a final determination of taxability.

[61] *Underlying security* is defined in ¶ (c)(3)(iv) as the security subject to the conditional demand feature.

securities rated by NRSROs in one of their two highest long-term or short-term rating categories.[62]

Ratings for this requirement are determined in the same manner as ratings for first- and second-tier securities (i.e., the rating of the only NRSRO to rate the security, or the two highest ratings if multiple NRSROs rate the security). The rating standard applied should be consistent with the TOTEs. In other words, if a downgrade below a specified long-term rating constitutes a TOTE, then the underlying security or guarantee should be rated or comparable to obligations rated in the two highest long-term rating categories. If a TOTE is defined in terms of short-term ratings, then the underlying security or guarantee should be rated or comparable to obligations rated in the two highest short-term rating categories.

Maturity Limitations

A money market fund may not acquire any instrument having a remaining maturity of greater than 397 days.[63] A security with a longer maturity cannot qualify as an eligible security.[64] For some securities, Rule 2a-7 calculates maturity based on when the final payment is due. For other securities, Rule 2a-7 looks to the availability of a demand feature or a scheduled adjustment to the security's interest rate to determine its maturity.

Stated Maturity

The maturity of a portfolio security generally is equal to the period remaining (calculated from the trade date or other date on which the money market fund's interest in the security is subject to market action) until the date on which, under the terms of the security, the money market fund must unconditionally receive full payment of principal.[65] The maturity of a security that the issuer has called for redemption is the scheduled redemption date. We will refer to this period as the security's *stated maturity*.

The legal obligation to repay the principal must be unconditional insofar as the principal must come due without further action by any person.[66] The money market fund's right to demand payment for a security may create a demand feature, but the money market fund may not use the demand fea-

---

[62] Paragraph (c)(3)(iv)(C).

[63] Paragraph (c)(2)(i).

[64] Paragraph (a)(10)(i).

[65] Paragraph (d).

[66] A standard payment requirement, such as the need to present a security to the paying agent, does not make a payment obligation conditional for purposes of calculating a security's stated maturity.

ture to calculate the security's stated maturity. However, a money market fund can calculate a security's stated maturity based upon a mandatory payment, redemption or tender, even if the money market fund has the option to affirmatively waive its right to payment. In effect, when calculating a security's stated maturity, a money market fund should ignore its option to accelerate or extend principal payments until the money market fund exercises the option.

Exceptions

There are specific exceptions to the general rule that a security's stated maturity determines its maturity for purposes of Rule 2a-7. The exceptions that may apply to tax-exempt securities include exceptions for (1) variable rate securities, (2) floating rate securities, and (3) shares of other money market funds.[67] We refer to this period as the security's *effective maturity*. Exhibit 26.4 summarizes the effective maturity for the foregoing types of securities.

A *variable rate security* is a security whose interest rate adjusts on set dates.[68] We will refer to the date on which a security's interest rate adjusts as the *reset date*. The money market fund must reasonably expect the vari-

EXHIBIT 26.4   Exceptions to Stated Maturity

Type of Security	Stated Maturity	Effective Maturity
Variable rate security	≤ 397 days	Next reset date[a]
Variable rate security subject to a demand feature	≤ 397 days	Earlier of the next reset date and next tender date[b]
Variable rate security subject to a demand feature	> 397 days	Later of next reset date or next tender date
Floating rate security (whether or not subject to a demand feature)	≤ days	Next day
Floating rate security subject to a demand feature	> 397 days	Next tender date
Money market fund securities	Not applicable	Period for redemption (usually seven days)

[a] Date of a scheduled adjustment to the security's interest rate.
[b] Date on which the holder would receive the purchase price for the security following exercise of the demand feature.
Source: Reed Smith LLP. Reprinted by permission.

[67] Paragraph (d)(1)–(8).
[68] Paragraph (a)(29).

able rate security to approximate its amortized cost on each reset date until its stated maturity.[69] A variable rate security with a stated maturity of 397 days or less has an effective maturity equal to the shorter of the period until the next reset date or the next tender date.[70] A variable rate security with a stated maturity of more than days must be subject to a demand feature, and has an effective maturity equal to the longer of the period until reset date or the next tender date.[71]

A floating rate security is a security with reset dates that occur whenever a specified interest rate changes.[72] The money market fund must reasonably expect the floating rate security to approximate its amortized cost continuously until its stated maturity.[73] A floating rate security with a stated maturity of 397 days or less has an effective maturity equal to one day.[74] A floating rate security with a stated maturity of more than days must be subject to a demand feature, and has an effective maturity equal to the period until the next tender date.[75]

Shares of another money market fund mature on the date that the other money market fund is obligated to honor a redemption of the shares.[76] Most money market funds reserve the right to postpone payment of redemption proceeds for up to seven days, making this the effective maturity.[77]

DIVERSIFICATION OF TAX EXEMPT FUNDS UNDER RULE 2a-7

Rule 2a-7 contains two diversification regimes, one of which limits the percentage of total assets[78] that a money market fund may invest in securities of a single issuer (issuer diversification),[79] and the other of which limits the percentage of total assets that a money market fund may invest in securities issued or guaranteed by, or having demand features to, a single entity (enhancer diversification).[80] Rule 2a-7's diversification requirements vary

---

[69] Id.
[70] Paragraph (d)(2).
[71] Paragraph (d)(3).
[72] Paragraph (a)(13).
[73] Id.
[74] Paragraph (d)(4).
[75] Paragraph (d)(5)
[76] Paragraph (d)(8).
[77] Generally, ICA § 22(e) provides that the period between redemption and payment of redemption proceeds cannot exceed seven days.
[78] *Total assets* is defined in ¶ (a)(25) as the total amortized cost value of a money market fund's assets.
[79] Paragraph (c)(4)(i).
[80] Paragraph (c)(4)(iii).

depending on whether the money market fund is a national fund or a single-state fund. Moreover, Rule 2a-7 contains special instructions for diversification of certain securities, including conduit securities and shares of other money market funds.

Issuer Diversification Limitations

Exhibit 26.5 shows the issuer diversification limitations for tax-exempt funds. In order to apply these limitations, a manager must determine whether Rule 2a-7 treats a tax-exempt security as having been issued by its municipal issuer or as a conduit security deemed to be issued by another entity.

Municipal Issuers

Municipal issuers include any state or territory of the United States (including the District of Columbia and Puerto Rico), or any political subdivision or public instrumentality of such a state or territory.[81] This definition corresponds to the entities permitted to issue tax-exempt securities under the Internal Revenue Code. Questions sometimes arise as to whether government agencies or instrumentalities of the same state or locality should be treated as separate issuers. The SEC has stated that: "When the assets and revenues of an agency, authority, instrumentality or other political subdivision are separate from those of the government creating the subdivision and

EXHIBIT 26.5   Issuer Diversification Limits

Type of Security	National Fund	Single-State Fund
Refunded securities	No limit	No limit
Securities subject to guarantees issued by a noncontrolled person	See Exhibit 26.6	See Exhibit 26.6
First-tier securities	5% × 100%	5% × 75%
Second-tier conduit securities[a]	1% × 100%	1% × 100%
Other second-tier securities	5% × 100%	5% × 100%

Note: The first number represents the maximum percentage of total assets that a tax-exempt fund may invest in the specified type of security. The second number represents the minimum percentage of total assets that must comply with the limitation.
[a] A tax-exempt fund may not invest more than 5% of its total assets in second-tier conduit securities in the aggregate.
Source: Reed Smith LLP. Reprinted by permission.

---

[81] Paragraph (a)(7).

the security is backed only by the assets and revenues of the subdivision, such subdivision would be deemed to be the sole issuer for purposes of Section 5(b) (1)."[82] This interpretation has also been understood to apply for purposes of Rule 2a-7.

Conduit Securities

Conduit securities include every security issued by a municipal issuer unless it satisfies one of four criteria:

1. The security is payable from the general revenues of the municipal issuer (e.g., revenues that are not "derived from an agreement or arrangement with a person who is not a municipal issuer that provides for or secures repayment of the security . . .").
2. The municipal issuer fully and unconditionally guarantees the security.
3. The security finances a project owned and operated by a municipal issuer.
4. The security finances "a facility leased to and under the control of an industrial or commercial enterprise that is part of a public project which, as a whole, is owned and under the control of a municipal issuer."[83]

The issuer of a conduit security is the person (other than the municipal issuer) ultimately responsible for payments of interest and principal on the security.[84]

National Funds

A national fund may not invest more than 5% of its total assets in first-tier securities of a single issuer[85]; 1% of its total assets in second-tier conduit securities of a single issuer[86]; or 5% of its total assets in other second-tier securities of a single issuer.[87] In addition, a national fund may not invest more than 5% of its total assets in second-tier conduit securities *in the aggregate.* The diversification requirements apply to 100% of the national fund's total assets.[88]

---

[82] Release No. IC-9785 42 Fed. Reg. 29130, 29130 (May 31, 1977).

[83] Paragraph (a)(7).

[84] Paragraph (c)(4)(ii)(C).

[85] Paragraph (c)(4)(i)(A).

[86] Paragraph (c)(4)(i)(C)(2). A money market fund with less than $100 million in total assets may invest up to $1 million in second-tier conduit securities.

[87] Paragraph (c)(4)(i)(A).

[88] Paragraph (c)(4)(i)(A), (C).

However, national funds have some leeway in complying with the issuer diversification limitations. Specifically, a national fund may invest up to 25% of its total assets in securities of a single issuer subject to three conditions: (1) the securities are first-tier securities; (2) the national fund acquires securities of only one issuer in excess of the 5% limit at any one time; and (3) the national fund exceeds the 5% limit for not more than three business days.[89]

Single-State Funds

A single-state fund may not invest more than 5% of its total assets in first-tier securities of a single issuer[90]; 1% of its total assets in second-tier conduit securities of a single issuer[91]; or 5% of its total assets in other second-tier securities of a single issuer.[92] In addition, a single-state fund may not invest more than 5% of its total assets in second-tier conduit securities *in the aggregate.*

The diversification requirements regarding second-tier conduit securities and other second-tier securities apply to 100% of the single-state fund's total assets.[93] However, the diversification requirement regarding first-tier securities only applies to 75% of the single-state fund's total assets.[94] Accordingly, single-state funds have a permanent 25% basket for first-tier securities that are not subject to the 5% issuer diversification limitation. Moreover, this permanent 25% basket is not subject to any limitations regarding the number of issuers comprising the basket.

Money Market Fund Shares

Tax-exempt funds may invest without limitation in shares of another money market fund.[95] The only requirement is that the board must reasonably be-

---

[89] Paragraph (c)(4)(i)(A). However, the SEC did not intend to permit a national fund to invest continuously up to 25% of its total assets in first-tier securities of a single issuer that roll over every three days. Such a practice would expose a fund "to the risks associated with investing more than 5% of fund assets in a single issuer for an indefinite period of time." Release No. IC-18005, 56 Fed. Reg. 8113, 8117 346–140 (Feb. 20, 1991).

[90] Paragraph (c)(4)(i)(B).

[91] Paragraph (c)(4)(i)(C)(2). A money market fund with less than $100 million in total assets may invest up to $1 million in second-tier conduit securities.

[92] Paragraph (c)(4)(i)(B).

[93] Paragraph (c)(4)(i)(B), (c)(4)(i)(C)(2).

[94] Paragraph (c)(4)(i)(B).

[95] Paragraph (c)(4)(ii)(E). However, ICA § 12(d)(1) generally prohibits a mutual fund from investing more than 5% of its assets in another mutual fund; and limits total investments by a mutual fund in other mutual funds to 10% of assets. But see, 17 C.F.R. § 270.12d1-(2007) (exempting investments of cash balances in money market funds).

lieve that the acquired fund is in compliance with the issuer diversification limitations.[96]

Enhancer Diversification

National funds and single-state funds are treated identically for purposes of enhancer diversification. Specifically, a tax-exempt fund may not invest more than 10% of its total assets in securities issued by or subject to first-tier demand features or guarantees of a single enhancer[97]; or 5% of its total assets in conduit securities issued by or subject to second-tier demand features or guarantees of a single enhancer.[98] Exhibit 26.6 shows the enhancer diversification limitations for tax-exempt funds.

For securities subject to first-tier demand features or guarantees issued by a noncontrolled person, these diversification requirements apply to 75% of the total assets.[99] Accordingly, tax-exempt funds have a permanent 25%

EXHIBIT 26.6   Enhancer Diversification Limits

Type of Security	National Fund	Single-State Fund
Securities not subject to demand features or guarantees	See Exhibit 26.5	See Exhibit 26.5
Securities guaranteed by a government issuer	No limit	No limit
Securities subject to first-tier demand features or guarantees issued by a noncontrolled person	10% × 75%	10% × 75%
Securities subject to other first-tier demand features or guarantees	10% × 100%	10% × 100%
Securities subject to second-tier demand features or guarantees[a]	5% × 100%	5% × 100%

Note: The first number represents the maximum exposure that a tax-exempt fund may have to an entity providing a demand feature or guarantee. The second number represents the minimum percentage of total assets that must comply with this limitation.
[a] A tax-exempt fund may not invest more than 5% of its total assets in second-tier conduit securities in the aggregate.
Source: Reed Smith LLP. Reprinted by permission.

---

[96] Generally, the board delegates responsibility for making such determination to the fund's investment adviser, as permitted by ¶ (e).
[97] Paragraph (c)(4)(iii)(A), (C).
[98] Paragraph (c)(4)(iii)(B).
[99] Paragraph (c)(4)(iii)(A).

basket for issued by or subject to first-tier demand features or guarantees issued by a noncontrolled person that is not subject to the 10% enhancer diversification limitation. Otherwise, the diversification requirements apply to 100% of the total assets.[100] Finally, no more than 5% of the total assets of a tax-exempt fund may, *in the aggregate*, be invested in conduit securities subject to second-tier demand features or guarantees.

Fractional and Layered Demand Features and Guarantees

A fractional demand feature or guarantee is a demand feature or guarantee that applies only to a portion of the principal value of the underlying security. The provider of a fractional demand feature or guarantee is deemed to have issued the demand feature or guarantee only with respect to that portion of the underlying security to which the demand feature or guarantee applies.[101]

Layered demand features or *guarantees* occur where there are multiple demand features or guarantees with respect to the same underlying security, and the obligations of the provider of such demand feature or guarantee are not contractually limited. Each issuer of a layered demand feature or guarantee is deemed to have issued the demand feature or guarantee with respect to the entire principal amount of the security.[102]

APPLICATION OF RULE 2a-7 TO MUNICIPAL SECURITIES

This section applies Rule 2a-7 to common types of tax-exempt money market securities. It also identifies some interpretative issues commonly associated with certain security types. Although nothing can replace an analysis of the specific terms of a security, the generalized examples discussed in this section should give managers an idea of the interplay between such terms and the provisions of Rule 2a-7.

Anticipation Notes

Anticipation notes include tax, revenue, and bond anticipation notes.

Tax and Revenue Anticipation Notes

Unlike most businesses, many municipal issuers do not receive steady streams of revenue. Property taxes, in particular, are typically assessed once

---

[100] Paragraph (c)(4)(iii)(B), (C).
[101] Paragraph (c)(4)(iv)(A).
[102] Paragraph (c)(4)(iv)(B).

a year and collected over a few months. However, expenses need to be paid throughout the year. To fill the gap between revenues and expenses, a municipal issuer may issue *tax and revenue anticipation notes* (TRANs) and use the proceeds to pay its expenses. The municipal issuer then collects taxes or other anticipated revenues to repay the TRANs at the end of its fiscal year. In some cases, a municipal issuer will roll over its debt by issuing new TRANs even as it pays off the old TRANs.

TRANs are relatively simple to analyze under Rule 2a-7. Assuming that they are not credit enhanced, TRANs will be subject only to issuer diversification and the municipal issuer issuing the TRANs will be the "issuer."[103] The manager must conclude that there is a minimal risk that the municipal issuer will fail to repay the TRANs when they come due. If the TRANs are not rated, the manager must determine if the municipal issuer has other short-term ratings or if the TRANs are of comparable quality to other rated eligible securities.

TRANs bearing a fixed rate of interest should be treated as maturing on their stated maturity date. It is important to remember that maturity is calculated from the trade date. A municipal issuer that is rolling notes over may seek binding commitments to purchase new TRANs in advance of their issuance. Rule 2a-7 permits this so long as the stated maturity of the TRAN is not more than 397 days after the date of the commitment. However, the tax-exempt fund will be treated as owning the TRAN once it makes a commitment that is not subject to market action, so the commitment will extend the fund's WAPM immediately. A commitment remains subject to market action if the yield will be established by reference to a benchmark rate, such as a number of basis points over the BMA Municipal Swap Index, as determined on the settlement date.

Although rare, variable rate TRANs are sometimes issued with monthly or quarterly reset dates. So long as the manager reasonably believes that these adjustments will cause the TRANs' market value to approximate their amortized cost value throughout their remaining term, then Rule 2a-7 will treat the TRANs as maturing on the next reset date. However, any cap on the adjusted rate may make it difficult to reach this conclusion, as we discuss in more detail below in the subsection on tender option bonds.

Bond Anticipation Notes

Bond anticipation notes (BANs) are issued to fund initial capital expenditures for a project that a municipal issuer expects to finance eventually

---

[103] Some TRANs are guaranteed by another municipal issuer or supported by a letter of credit or bond insurance. Such TRANs are subject to enhancer diversification, which is discussed at greater length below in the subsection on the diversification of VRDOs and related enhancers.

with long-term bonds. BANs frequently receive long-term ratings due to their dependence on long-term financing for repayment. Rule 2a-7 treats long-term rated BANs as unrated securities unless the issuer has received short-term ratings for obligations of comparable priority and security. Technically, Rule 2a-7 does not require that such BANs receive long-term ratings above any specific category because BANs are issued with stated maturities of 397 days or less. However, a manager may find it difficult to support a determination that, for example, a BBB or Baa rated BAN is comparable in quality to a first-tier rated security if NRSROs uniformly give issuers with such long-term ratings their second highest short-term rating.

Otherwise, Rule 2a-7 generally treats BANs in the same manner as TRANs, except that their minimal credit risk analysis should include consideration of the issuer's ability to access the long-term debt market.

Maturing Bonds

A high-quality municipal bond may become an eligible security once its remaining stated maturity falls to 397 days or less regardless of how long ago the bond was issued. However, such maturing bonds typically have long-term, rather than short-term, ratings. As was just noted, Rule 2a-7 treats long-term rated bonds as unrated securities unless the issuer has received short-term ratings for obligations of comparable priority and security. However, unlike BANs, ¶ (a)(10)(ii)(A) does not permit a manager to determine that an unrated maturing bond that has received long-term ratings is an eligible security unless the requisite NRSROs have rated the bond in one of their three highest rating categories (e.g., single A or higher).[104] For example, a 30-year bond that originally received ratings of A3/BBB+ cannot be treated as an eligible security—even if the rating was issued 29 years ago and the issuer has made every coupon and sinking fund payment on a timely basis.

Apart from this additional eligible security requirement, Rule 2a-7 treats maturing bonds in the same manner as TRANs unless the bonds are conduit securities or refunded securities. We have already discussed conduit securities in the context of issuer diversification.

Refunded Securities

Refunded securities are municipal bonds that are payable from escrowed government securities.[105] The escrow is designed so that proceeds from the

---

[104] As with short-term ratings, gradations and subcategories are ignored for purposes of defining a rating category. Thus, AA+ and AA- are within Standard & Poor's second highest long-term rating category, and Aa1 and Aa3 are within Moody's.

[105] 17 CFR § 270.5b-3(c)(4)(2007) (defining a "refunded security").

maturing government securities will fund all scheduled coupon payments until the bonds may be called, and then will fund the principal repayment and any call premium. Refunded securities result when a municipal issuer refinances an issue of bonds before their first call date, by issuing new bonds at lower interest rates and using the proceeds to purchase the escrowed government securities. An NRSRO that rated the original bonds will normally increase its rating to its highest long-term category following the refunding, provided that the NRSRO receives the escrow documents.

For purposes of issuer diversification, ¶ (c)(4)(ii)(B) treats refunded securities as a direct investment in the escrowed government securities.[106] This means that a tax-exempt fund may invest an unlimited amount of its portfolio in the refunded securities of one municipal issuer. However, to qualify as a refunded security, the bond must satisfy the following requirements of Rule 5b-3(c)(4) under the ICA:

- The municipal issuer must irrevocably place government securities sufficient to pay all remaining principal and interest, and any call premium, on the bonds in escrow with an escrow agent that is not an "affiliated person" (as defined in ICA § 2(a)(3)(C)) of the municipal issuer.
- The escrow agreement must (1) give principal and interest payments priority over any other payments (including expenses of the escrow agent) and (2) prohibit substitution of securities other than other government securities.
- The bonds must have received either (1) a rating from an NRSRO in its highest rating category based on the escrow arrangement or (2) certificate from an independent certified public accountant that the escrowed government securities "will satisfy all scheduled payments of principal, interest and applicable premiums."

Most refunded bonds that receive AAA or Aaa ratings satisfy these requirements.

---

[106] The "look-through" to the underlying government securities is only for purpose of diversification. The government securities do not have to qualify as eligible securities and may have maturities in excess of 397 dates. However, the escrow normally requires that the government securities mature in advance of the maturity of the refunded security. As a result, the escrowed government securities will normally mature within 397 days.

Although Rule 2a-7 does not state this explicitly, treatment of refunded securities as investment in government securities suggests that they should be classified as first-tier securities for purposes of determining their status as eligible securities. See ¶ (a)(12)(iv).

Variable Rate Demand Obligations

Weekly demand "floaters" are the mainstay of *tax-exempt funds*. Until these securities were developed in the 1980s, it would have been impossible to construct a liquid, dieversified tax-exempt portfolio with a WAPM of less than 90 days. Today, *variable rate demand obligations* (VRDOs), including "synthetic" VRDOs known as *tender option bonds*, comprise a majority of most tax-exempt funds' portfolios.

VRDOs are long-term variable rate securities that generally reset on a daily, weekly, monthly or quarterly basis. Daily resets can be tendered for purchase on a same day basis (e.g., if the holder gives notice of tender in the morning, the holder will receive the purchase price by that afternoon). Weekly resets can be tendered at any time with seven-days' notice (e.g., if the holder gives notice of tender on Monday, the holder will receive the purchase price on the following Monday). In contrast, monthly and quarterly resets generally have fixed tender dates (e.g., the holder will receive the purchase price on the last business day of the month or quarter, provided the holder gives notice at least seven days before the tender date). The tender date for monthly and quarterly VRDOs often coincides with the reset date.

Once tendered, a remarketing agent for the VRDO tries to resell the VRDO for settlement on the tender date. Ordinarily, the remarketing agent also sets the interest rate on the VRDO, which enables it to offer a rate that will attract a buyer for the tendered VRDO. If the remarketing is successful, the buyer pays the purchase price for the VRDO on the tender date, and the remarketing agent delivers the purchase price to the holder tendering the VRDO. If the remarketing agent cannot remarket the VRDO, it will normally draw on a letter of credit, standby purchase commitment or other liquidity facility to pay the purchase price to the tendering holder. In most cases, the issuer also is obligated to pay the purchase price if no other source of funds is available.

Maturity of VRDOs

In order to satisfy the maturity requirement for an eligible security, a VRDO must qualify as a variable rate security subject to a demand feature. So long as the remarketing agent fulfills its obligation to set the interest rate at a level that permits the VRDO to be remarketed, a tax-exempt fund manager can justify an expectation that the VRDO will have a market value that approximates its amortized cost on each reset date. Hence, most VRDOs qualify as variable rate securities. The one exception is when the VRDO has a cap above which the remarketing agent cannot set the interest rate. As the interest rate nears the cap, it may become more difficult to expect the market value of the VRDO to return to its amortized cost on the next reset date, in which case the tax-exempt fund would need to exercise the demand feature.

Normally, the right to tender a VRDO will satisfy the requirements for a demand feature. The principal concern here is that the VRDO cannot require a tax-exempt fund to give notice more than 30 days before the tender date. In addition, the purchase price upon tender must include accrued interest. The demand feature also needs to qualify as a guarantee or conditional demand feature, which are considered in more detail below.

If the stated maturity of a variable rate security subject to a demand feature exceeds 397 days, Rule 2a-7 treats the security as maturing on the later of its next reset date or tender date. One consequence of this is that weekly VRDOs maintain a constant maturity of seven days, because the tender date is never less, and the reset date is never more, than seven days away. In contrast, the maturity of monthly and quarterly VRDOs roll down to their tender/reset date, and then reextend to the next tender/reset date.

Diversification of VRDOs and Related Enhancers

Although some VRDOs are general obligations, VRDOs frequently qualify as conduit securities for purposes of issuer diversification. In addition, many VRDOs (particularly conduit VRDOs) are supported by a letter of credit or by bond insurance. VRDO issuers rarely provide liquidity for the demand feature. Instead, most letters of credit also cover payment of the purchase price of VRDOs that are not successfully remarketed. Insured bonds generally have standby purchase agreements to cover such payments.

Letters of credit and bond insurance qualify as guarantees for purpose of Rule 2a-7. A VRDO subject to a guarantee issued by a noncontrolled person is not subject to issuer diversification. Instead, such VRDOs are subject to enhancer diversification with respect to the provider of the guarantee.

In contrast, most stand-by purchase agreements and similar liquidity facilities do not qualify as guarantees, because the obligation to purchase VRDOs is subject to one or more tender option termination events. Such demand features may qualify as conditional demand features for purposes of Rule 2a-7. VRDOs with conditional demand features remain subject to issuer diversification, unless they are also subject to a guarantee from a non-controlled enhancer. This is commonly the case with insured VRDOs, in which case a tax-exempt fund must comply with enhancer diversification with respect to both the bond insurer and the provider of the stand-by purchase agreement rather than complying with issuer diversification.

A few examples will illustrate the interplay between issuer and enhancer diversification of VRDOs. The first example examines securities issued and securities guaranteed by the same enhancer. Assume that State X issues TRANs and also unconditionally guarantees payment of Series 1 VRDOs issued by a school district. Further assume that the TRANs and the Series 1 VRDOs are first-tier securities. Issuer diversification would limit a national fund's investment in the TRANs to 5% of its total assets. However, issuer diversification would not limit investment in the Series 1 VRDOs because they are subject to a guarantee from State X.

On the other hand, enhancer diversification would limit the national fund's investment in the Series 1 VRDOs to 5% of its total assets because the percentage of total assets issued by or subject to a demand feature or guarantee from State X cannot exceed 10%. Alternatively, if 75% of the national fund's Asset were within the 10% limit for enhancer diversification, the national fund could use the 25% basket for nondiversified enhancers to invest up 20% of its total assets in the VRDOs. Note that the TRANs would count towards both the 10% limit and the 25% basket for purposes of enhancer diversification.

The analysis would be different for a single-state fund, because the issuer diversification limits for first-tier securities apply to only 75% of the fund's total assets. This would allow a single-state fund to invest up to 25% of its total assets in State X TRANs. If it did so, however, it could not invest in the Series 1 VRDOs because enhancer diversification applies to securities issued by, as well as those guaranteed by, State X. In other words, a single-state fund could invest up to 25% of its total assets in any combination of TRANs and Series 1 VRDOs subject to two independent limits: first, if the combination exceeds 10% of its total assets, then the TRANs and Series 1 VRDOs will count against the 25% nondiversified basket for enhancer diversification, and second, if the TRANs exceed 5% of its total assets, then the TRANs must count against the 25% nondiversified basket for issuer diversification.

The second example examines the interplay between guarantees and demand features from different enhancers. Assume that Bank Y issues a direct pay letter of credit to secure a series of VRDOs issued by the EDA (Series 2 VRDOs). The Series 2 VRDOs are conduit securities, secured by a loan to Company ABC. Further assume that the EDA issues a separate series of VRDOs (Series 3 VRDOs) insured by a monoline Insurer Z, with a stand-by purchase agreement from Bank Y. The Series 3 VRDOs are also conduit securities, secured by a lease to Company DEF. In order for both series of VRDOs to qualify as eligible securities, we will also assume that (1) both series of VRDOs are rated first-tier securities and are subject to mandatory tender upon any substitution of the letter of credit, bond insurance or stand-by purchase agreement; (2) Insurer Z has received the highest long-term ratings from the requisite NRSROs; and (3) the tender option termination events for the standby purchase agreement are easily monitored and present minimal risks.

Both Series of VRDOs are conduit securities, so Rule 2a-7 will look through to the underlying companies for purposes of issuer diversification, treating Series 2 as issued by Company ABC and Series 3 as issued by Company DEF. However, the Series 2 VRDOs are subject to a guarantee (the letter of credit) from Bank Y and the Series 3 VRDOs are subject to a guarantee (the bond insurance) from Insurer Z. Therefore, issuer diversification will not limit a tax-exempt fund's investment in either Series of VRDOs.

Both series remain subject to enhancer diversification, however, which is uniform for national and single-state funds. Therefore, a tax-exempt fund could invest up to 10% of its total assets in the Series 2 or Series 3 VRDOs, or any combination of the series, and comply with the enhancer diversification limit. This is because the limit applies to securities subject to demand features from Bank Y (the Series 3 VRDOs) as well as those subject to guarantees from Bank Y (the Series 2 VRDOs). Alternatively, if a tax-exempt fund's combined investment in the Series 2 and Series 3 VRDOs exceeds 10%, then the combined investment must be counted against the 25% nondiversified basket permitted by enhancer diversification.

In this second example, Insurer Z is irrelevant to enhancer diversification. The Series 3 VRDOs will either comply with the 10% limit for Bank Y or count towards the 25% nondiversified basket (even if the Series 3 VRDOs do not exceed 10% of total assets by themselves). A tax-exempt fund that invests 15% of its total assets in Series 3 VRDOs and 10% in Series 2 VRDOs will still comply with enhancer diversification so long as the other 75% of its total assets meet the 10% limit on other enhancers. In other words, a tax-exempt fund is not required to double count the Series 3 VRDOs against the 25% nondiversified basket because they have a guarantee from Insurer Z as well as a demand feature from Bank Y, or double count the Series 2 VRDOs because Bank Y provides both a guarantee and a demand feature. The point of the enhancer diversification basket is to limit the portfolio securities issued by or subject to enhancement by nondiversified enhancers to 25% of total assets, regardless of the number of nondiversified enhancers.

The results would be different if a tax-exempt fund owned other securities supported by bond insurance from Insurer Z. Assume that a tax-exempt fund has already invested 5% of its assets in TRANs insured by Insurer Z. The TRANs would not be subject to issuer diversification (due to the guarantee from Insurer Z), but would count towards the 10% enhancer diversification limit for Insurer Z. Thus, if the fund invested more than 5% of its assets in Series 3 VRDOs, both the insured TRANs and Series 3 VRDOs would count against the 25% non-diversified basket. However, the Series 2

VRDOs would not count against the nondiversified basket unless the fund's combined investment in Series 2 and Series 3 VRDOs exceeded 10% of its total assets. Thus, a tax-exempt fund could invest 5% of its total assets in each series of VRDOs (so its exposure to Bank Y would not exceed the 10% limit) and another 20% of its total assets in the insured TRANs (which would use up the 25% basket with nondiversified exposures to Insurer Z). A tax-exempt fund also could invest 8% of its total assets in each Series of VRDOs and in the insured TRANs (which would create a nondiversified exposure to Bank Y and Insurer Z of 24%). However, a tax-exempt fund could not invest 9% of its total assets in each of the securities (because the combined 27% nondiversified exposure would exceed 25%).

Our third example examines *layered guarantees*. Assume that State X's long-term ratings are downgraded, but the Requisite NRSROs continue to rate the TRANs in their highest short-term rating categories. In response, State X obtains a letter of credit from Bank Y to secure the Series 1 VRDOs. However, because its guarantee is irrevocable, State X remains liable for the Series 1 VRDOs.

In this case, the Series 1 VRDOs would have two enhancers providing guarantees: State X and Bank Y. However, a tax-exempt fund may elect not to rely on one of the guarantees, provided that it maintains a record of the election in accordance with procedures adopted by the board. Once a fund makes such an election, it cannot rely on the guarantee for purposes of determining the security's minimal credit risk, status as an eligible security, effective maturity, or liquidity.[107] If a tax-exempt fund does not record such an election, then both guarantees must comply with enhancer diversification.[108]

Therefore, if a national fund or a single-state fund did not record an election not to rely on State X's guarantee of the Series 1 VRDOs, then the fund would remain subject to the issuer diversification and enhancer diversification limits on State X identified in the first example. Moreover, if a tax-exempt fund did not record an election not to rely on Bank Y's guarantee of the Series 1 VRDOs, then the Series 1 VRDOs would be combined with the other two series of VRDOs for purposes of determining the fund's exposure to Bank Y. For example, if a tax-exempt fund had already invested 25% of its total assets in Series 2 and 3 VRDOs, it could not invest in Series 1 VRDOs without violating enhancer diversification.

On the other hand, a national fund that did not own any Series 2 or VRDOs, and that had already invested 5% of its total assets in State X TRANs, could use the entire 25% basket for nondiversified enhancers to invest in Series 1 VRDOs by electing to rely on the Bank Y letter of credit

---

[107] Paragraph (c)(5).
[108] Paragraph (c)(4)(iv)(B).

rather than the State X guarantee. More significantly, a single-state fund making such an election could invest up to 25% of its total assets in the State X TRANs and up to 25% of its total assets in Series 1 VRDOs (assuming that it did not own the other series of VRDOs) because there would not be any overlap between a nondiversified issuer (State X) and a nondiversified enhancer (Bank Y). However, such a single-state fund would have to consider carefully the minimal credit risk implications of the resulting lack of diversification.

Similarly, a tax-exempt fund that had already invested in Series 2 or 3 VRDOs could increase its capacity to invest in Series 1 VRDOs by electing to rely on the State X guarantee to the exclusion of the Bank Y letter of credit. Such an election would permit the fund to invest up to 10% of its total assets in Series 1 VRDOs (assuming that it did not own State X TRANs) while leaving the 25% basket available for any combination of Series 2 and 3 VRDOs. Of course, this assumes that the manager still considers State X a minimal credit risk following the downgrade of its long-term ratings.

Mandatory Tender Obligations

Municipal obligations subject to mandatory tender are the inverse of VR-DOs: instead of opting to tender a VRDO, the holder of the bond must affirmatively opt *out* of remarketing its mandatory tender obligations. Consequently, Rule 2a-7 treats the tender date of a mandatory tender obligation as its stated maturity, because a tax-exempt fund will receive full payment of principal and accrued interest unless it opts to roll over the investment. Rule 2a-7 effectively measures the maturity of mandatory tender obligations in the same manner as commercial paper (i.e., the obligations are treated as maturing on their tender date, and then extended if the tax-exempt fund opts out of the tender). Such obligations are sometimes referred to as tax-exempt commercial paper.

To qualify as an eligible security, the mandatory tender date of the obligation must occur not more than 397 days after the date on which a tax-exempt fund opts out of the mandatory tender. This creates a practical limit on the period of time in which a tax-exempt fund must give notice of its election, even though a mandatory tender is not subject to the 30-day notice limit required for a demand feature. For example, if a bond required the holder to give 90 days notice of its election to opt out of the mandatory tender, then the bond could not qualify as an eligible security unless the next mandatory tender date was not more than 397 days after the fund gave such notice because Rule 2a-7 would treat the notice as a commitment to repurchase the bond. The bond must also satisfy all applicable diversification requirements based on the total assets as of the date of the election to opt out of the tender.

Project finance bonds are frequently subject to mandatory tender during the construction phase of the project. Rather than pay interest during this phase, the project developer may invest the bond proceeds in a *guaranteed investment contract* (GIC) provided by an insurance company, bank or other financial institution. The GIC will provide for periodic payments sufficient to pay interest on the bonds and will mature on the mandatory tender date. Proceeds from the maturing GIC will be used to purchase any bonds that holders did not opt to retain and that could not be remarketed. Otherwise, the proceeds either are reinvested in another GIC maturing on the next mandatory tender date or else used to pay off construction loans (at which point the bonds are no longer subject to mandatory tender).

Normally, the GIC provides the only source of payment for the bonds during the mandatory tender period. Even if the bonds purport to be secured by a loan to the project developer, the developer will not become obligated to repay anything until it draws on the loan. In this situation, Rule 2a-7 treats the bonds as conduit securities and the provider of the GIC as the issuer for purposes of issuer diversification. The bonds would not be subject to enhancer diversification because the GIC provider would be the sole source for payments, not a secondary source enhancing the issuer's payment obligations.

Tender Option Bonds

Tender option bonds (TOBs) represent a growing segment of the tax-exempt money market. These structured products consist of municipal obligations placed in a trust that issues two classes of interest: variable rate interests that may be tendered under a conditional demand feature, which are the tender option bonds, and residual interests, also known as *inverse floaters*. Complex TOBs raise enough issues under Rule 2a-7 to fill a chapter of their own.[109] However, for most purposes under Rule 2a-7, a manager may safely treat a TOB in the same manner as a conduit security subject to a conditional demand feature.[110]

---

[109] See Stephen A. Keen, "Application of Rule 2a-7 Portfolio Quality and Diversification Requirements to Tender Option Bonds," *Investment Lawyer* 14 (June–July 2007).

[110] This was clearly what the SEC intend when it first proposed to deal with TOBs explicitly in Rule 2a-7. Release No. IC-21837, 61 F.R. 13956, 13969 (Mar. 28, 1996). ("In the case of qualifying assets that consist of securities issued by ten or fewer issuers (e.g., most tax exempt tender option bond structures), the issuer of each core security would have been treated as the issuer for issuer diversification purposes.") [Footnote omitted.] Although the SEC ultimately took a different approach, we have not found anything to suggest the SEC intended to reach a different result with respect to TOBs.

This section will limit its analysis to a simple TOB. Assume that a AAA or Aaa rated, fixed coupon, long–term general obligation bond is deposited in a trust that issues TOBs. The TOBs receive a variable portion of the interest paid on the bond so that they qualify as variable rate securities. The TOBs are subject to a seven-day conditional demand feature from Bank Y. The TOTEs of the conditional demand feature are limited to a default, event of insolvency, downgrading or taxability with respect to the bond. The TOBs receive long-term ratings of AAA or Aaa, based on the credit quality of the bond, and short-term ratings of A-1+/VMIG-1, based on the credit quality of Bank Y.

Rule 2a-7 would treat these simple TOBs as rated first-tier securities based on the short-term ratings received from the requisite NRSROs. The conditional demand feature for the TOB appears to meet the requirements of ¶ (c)(3)(iv), insofar as:

- The conditional demand feature is a first-tier rated security with a tender date of seven days.
- The TOTES can be readily monitored and, given the high ratings assigned to the TOBs, the risk of a TOTE occurring should be minimal.
- The underlying securities have received long-term ratings in the highest category.

The seven-day demand feature and weekly reset date should cause the TOBs to have a constant effective maturity of seven days. In short, the TOBs should qualify as eligible securities.

With respect to issuer diversification, it is important to realize that Rule 2a-7 treats TOBs as asset-backed securities.[111] Paragraph (a)(3) defines an *asset-backed security* (ABS) as "a fixed income security (other than a government security) issued by a Special Purpose Entity . . . , substantially all of the assets of which consist of Qualifying Assets . . . ." *Qualifying assets* are defined as "financial assets, either fixed or revolving, that by their terms convert into cash within a finite time period . . . ." A *special purpose entity* is defined as "a trust, corporation, partnership or other entity organized for the sole purpose of issuing securities that entitle their holders to receive payments that depend primarily on the cash flow from Qualifying Assets." In this example, the trust would be the special purpose entity and the bonds would be the qualifying assets.

Paragraph (c)(4)(ii)(D) provides specific rules for calculating diversification with respect to an asset-backed security. The general rule is that:

---

[111] Id. at 13968.

> An Asset Backed Security Acquired by a fund . . . shall be deemed to
> be issued by the Special Purpose Entity that issued the Asset Backed
> Security . . . .[112]

Under the general rule, a tax-exempt fund would treat the trust as the
special purpose entity issuing the TOBs. However, this general rule is subject
to the following proviso:

> Any person whose obligations constitute ten percent or more of
> the principal amount of the Qualifying Assets of the . . . ABS ("Ten
> Percent Obligor") shall be deemed to be an issuer of the portion of
> the . . . ABS such obligations represent . . . .[113]

This proviso applies to the example, because the bond is the sole qualifying asset underlying the TOBs, making the municipal issuer of the bonds a
10% (indeed, a 100%) obligor. Therefore, according to the proviso, a tax-
exempt fund must treat the municipal issuer as the issuer of the TOBs for
purposes of issuer diversification. This means that, assuming that the fund
did not already hold other obligations of the municipal issuer, a national
fund would have to limit any acquisition of the TOBs to 5% of its total assets. A single-state fund, however, could include the TOB in its 25% basket
for nondiversified issuers.

The TOBs also are subject to enhancer diversification. Therefore, a tax-
exempt fund would have to limit any acquisition of the TOBs and other
securities issued by, or subject to demand features or guarantees provided
by, Bank Y to 10% of its total assets, or else include the TOBs in the 25%
basket for nondiversified enhancers. Of course, the VRDOs from our earlier
examples that were subject to letters of credit and standby purchase agreements from Bank Y also would count against the 10% limit or the 25%
basket.

TOBs do not always have demand features (in which case they are not
really tender option bonds, but we will stick with the term). When a state
issues a large amount of TRANs, dealers will sometimes deposit a portion of
the TRANs in a trust and sell variable and inverse classes of interest in the
trust. This can serve to shorten the effective maturity of the variable interest to its reset date, because Rule 2a-7 treats a variable rate security with a
stated maturity of 397 days or less as maturing on its reset date. However,
to qualify as a variable rate security, the manager must expect that the TOB
will have a market value that approximates its amortized cost on every reset
date until its stated maturity. In comparison, a manager only needs to have

---

[112] Paragraph (c)(4)(ii)(D)(1).
[113] Paragraph (c)(4)(ii)(D)(2).

this expectation for a TOB subject to a demand feature for any reset dates occurring prior to the next tender date.

The fixed amount of interest received by the trust from the TRANs necessarily limits the variable rate of interest that it can pay to the TOBs. For example, suppose that a dealer deposits $100 million of TRANs yielding 3% into a trust and issues $60 million of TOBs and $40 million of inverse interests. In this example, the trust will receive $3 million in interest. This means that the highest interest rate that can be paid on the TOBs (assuming all $3 million was paid to the TOBs) would be 5%. If the BMA swap rate is 2.5%, this would not leave much room for changes in the rate paid on the TOBs before they reach the 5% cap.

The Division discussed whether a manager could reasonably expect the market value of a capped adjustable rate security to approximate its amortized cost value in a letter to the ICI.[114] In the letter, the Division reiterated that "interest rate caps on floating or variable rate instruments are inconsistent with the requirement that they can reasonably be expected to return to par upon readjustment." However, the letter continued, "the Division does not object if money market funds purchase variable or floating rate instruments issued by the United States government or agencies thereof the interest rates of which are capped at a rate in excess of 20% to comply with certain state usury laws." The Division noted that money market funds could still invest in capped adjustable rate securities with stated maturities of 397 days or less, but would have to treat them as maturing on their stated maturity date rather than their next reset date for purposes of determining the fund's WAPM. The Division also reiterated that "this position does not affect the ability of money market funds to invest in capped floating or variable rate demand notes or other instruments the maturity of which is determined by reference to a demand feature . . . ." [original emphasis.] The SEC codified the Division's position when it amended the definitions of variable rate and floating rate securities.[115]

The Division's letter only addressed caps on government securities. Given that tax-exempt rates are normally lower than rates for U.S. Treasury Securities, one might suppose that the Division would accept a cap on a adjustable rate TOB without a demand feature below 20%. However, neither the SEC nor the Division have provided any public guidance as to when a cap would prevent an adjustable rate tax-exempt obligation from being treated as a variable rate security. In the absence of such guidance, managers of tax-exempt funds should either (1) treat the obligation as maturing on its stated maturity date or (2) carefully analyze historical market information and document the

---

[114] Investment Company Institute, Interpretive Letter, WSB File No. 072693011 (June 16, 1993).
[115] Release No. IC-19959, 58 F.R. 68585, 68600 at n. 153 (Dec. 17,

minimal likelihood that the interest rate would reach the cap. Obviously, the flatter the yield curve, the more difficult it will be to substantiate an expectation that the cap will not affect the obligation's market value.

POSTACQUISITION CONSTRAINTS IMPOSED BY RULE 2a-7

A money market fund must comply with specific procedures in the event that one of its portfolio securities is downgraded or experiences a default.[116] Moreover, there are specific requirements if the deviation between the market based NAV and amortized cost value exceeds 0.5% of 1%.[117]

Requirements In the Event of a Downgrade

If a downgrade event occurs, the money market fund's board must promptly reassess whether the portfolio security continues to present minimal credit risks.[118] Further, the board must cause the money market fund to take such action as is in the best interests of the money market fund and its shareholders.[119] The board may, and generally does, delegate these responsibilities to the investment adviser. Downgrade events include:

1. A portfolio security ceases to be a first-tier security (either because it is no longer rated in the highest rating category by the Requisite NRSROs or, in the case of an unrated security, because the investment adviser has determined that the portfolio security is no longer comparable to a first-tier security).
2. The investment adviser becomes aware that any unrated security or second-tier security held in the fund's portfolio has been given a rating by any NRSRO below the second highest short-term rating category.[120]

However, if the money market fund disposes of the security (or the security matures) within five business days of the downgrade event, the investment adviser is not required to make such reassessment, provided that the board receives subsequent notification of the disposition.[121]

There is an additional requirement imposed on securities subject to demand features. If a first-tier demand feature is downgraded to second tier,

---

[116] Paragraph (c)(6).
[117] Paragraph (c)(7)(ii)(B).
[118] Paragraph (c)(6)(i)(A).
[119] Id.
[120] Paragraph (c)(6)(i)(A).
[121] Paragraph (c)(6)(i)(B).

and the result is that the money market fund has more than 5% of its total assets invested in second-tier demand features of a single entity, the fund must reduce its investment to 5% or less by exercising the demand features at the next exercise date.[122] However, the money market fund is not required to eliminate its excess positions if the investment adviser determines that disposing of the securities would not be in the best interest of the money market fund.[123]

Requirements in the Event of a Default

If any of the following default events occurs, the money market fund is required to dispose of the security as soon as practicable consistent with achieving an orderly disposition:

1. There is a default with respect to a portfolio security (other than an immaterial default unrelated to the financial condition of the issuer).
2. The portfolio security ceases to be an eligible security.
3. The portfolio security no longer presents minimal credit risks.
4. An event of insolvency[124] occurs with respect to the issuer of the security or the provider of any demand feature or guarantee.[125]

However, the money market fund is not required to dispose of the security if the board determines that such disposition would not be in the best interests of the money market fund.[126] In this regard, the staff of the SEC has said that a board "should consider any and all factors that it believes to be material in assessing whether retention of a security is in the best interests of a money market fund."[127] It has further indicated that the board may "take into account market conditions that could affect the orderly disposition of the portfolio security," noting that such provision was added to Rule 2a-7

---

[122] Paragraph (c)(6)(i)(C).

[123] Id.

[124] *Event of Insolvency* is defined in ¶ (a)(11) to include (1) an admission of insolvency, the application by a person for the appointment of a trustee or similar officer for all or substantially all of its assets, a general assignment for the benefit of creditors, the filing by the person of a voluntary petition in bankruptcy or application for reorganization or any arrangement with creditors; (2) the institution of similar proceedings by another person against the person which are not contested; or (3) the institution of similar proceedings by a government agency responsible for the activities of the person, whether or not contested by the person.

[125] Paragraph (c)(6)(ii).

[126] Id.

[127] *ICI Mutual Insurance Company, No-Action Letter*, WSB File No. 072798007 (pub. avail. July 27, 1998).

because "it may not be in the best interests of a money market fund to dispose of distressed securities in a 'fire sale' environment."[128]

A money market fund is required to give notice to the SEC if any of the default events occur with respect to a portfolio security, and 0.5% or more of the money market fund's total assets is invested in such portfolio security.[129] The notice, which may be made by telephone, facsimile transmission or electronic mail, should specify the event and the action that the money market fund intends to take to address the situation.

Again, there is a special requirement that applies to securities subject to a demand feature or guarantee. A security subject to a demand feature or guarantee is not deemed to be in default if the demand feature has been exercised and the money market fund has received either the principal amount or the amortized cost of the security, with accrued interest; or if the guarantor is, without protest, making payments as due on the security.[130]

Requirements in the Event of a Deviation

If the deviation exceeds 0.5 of 1%, the board is required to consider what action, if any, should be taken to reduce the deviation.[131] Moreover, the board is required to take appropriate action if it believes that the deviation would result in material dilution or other unfair results to investors or existing shareholders, regardless of the extent of the deviation.[132] The board may not delegate the responsibility. However, a board will generally ask the investment adviser for a recommended course of action.

SUMMARY

As we have just seen, the application of Rule 2a-7 to a portfolio containing a wide variety of tax-exempt obligations can become quite complicated. Some of the rule's provisions draw bright lines, particularly relating to eligible securities, maturity and diversification. With regard to these provisions, a manager is principally concerned with properly classifying the obligation and its ratings, issuers and enhancers. Other provisions require the manager to exercise judgment, particularly with regard to the overall credit and interest rate risk taken by the tax-exempt fund. The board plays an important

---

[128] Id.
[129] Paragraph (c)(6)(iii). The percentage of total assets must be determined prior to the default event.
[130] Paragraph (c)(6)(iv).
[131] Paragraph (c)(6)(iii).
[132] Id.

role in overseeing these judgments. Although a manager should take care to comply with the objective requirements of Rule 2a-7, a tax-exempt fund's ability to grow while maintaining a constant $1 NAV will ultimately depend on the manager's judgments.

Fixed Income Analysis of Municipal Products

CHAPTER 27

Evaluation of Municipal Bonds

Gerard Brennan
Senior Municipal Evaluator
Interactive Data Pricing and Reference Data, Inc.

A *municipal bond evaluation* is an independent opinion about the value of a bond. At Interactive Data Pricing and Reference Data, Inc. (Interactive Data), for example, an evaluation represents the firm's good faith opinion as to what a buyer in the marketplace would pay for the security in a current sale. This chapter provides an overview of the factors considered by this pricing service in the evaluation of municipal bonds.

THE NEED FOR EVALUATIONS

Municipal bond evaluations are required by a variety of entities as an important part of the operations and oversight of investment portfolios. Mutual funds use them in their daily calculation of their net asset values. Institutions use them to value holdings, managed portfolios, and other investment products. The availability of third-party bond evaluations helps ensure that portfolios are valued objectively and accurately.

A bond evaluation is not necessary when a bond is first issued. At that point, the underwriters handle the pricing of bonds along a scale.[1] Municipal bonds are typically issued in series, meaning that a set of bonds is issued with different maturity dates. The underwriters price the bonds in the series based on factors such as orders for the securities, levels similar bonds have attained in the secondary market, the current interest rate environment, credit rating, and historical values for comparable issues. Of course, these are also among the factors that bond evaluators will consider once the bonds

---

[1] The Municipal Securities Rulemaking Board defines *scale* as the "prices and/or yields, listed by maturity, at which new issue securities are offered for sale to the public by the underwriter."

enter the secondary market, meaning that they are sold by someone other than the original issuer.

A steady flow of new bonds means a constant flow of new securities into the secondary market. During the first six months of 2006, Muni-View^{SM}, Interactive Data's municipal descriptive database, processed more than 60,000 new municipal securities. New issues join a municipal bond universe of over $1 trillion in outstanding bonds.

The methodology for evaluating municipal bonds has evolved significantly over time. Early evaluations may have been based on a trader giving a conservative opinion of the bid side of a particular bond, sometimes called a *worst case bid*; or were based on simple matrices which compared bonds only on the most basic characteristics, such as ratings, coupon size, and maturity.

Bond evaluation methodologies have become more complex with the rise of fixed income mutual funds and unit investment trusts in the 1960s and 1970s. These products created a demand for more precise, professional, daily evaluations that funds could consider when calculating their *net asset value* (NAV) daily.

As the importance of bond evaluations grew it created the need for full-time bond evaluators familiar with the latest municipal bond trends and products.

TOOLS OF EVALUATION

A typical day for bond evaluators starts before the bond market opens with a review of all block trades[2]—trades that are large enough to assume an informed professional is involved—in the sectors they cover. Throughout the day, evaluators use a variety of tools to help them reach appropriate evaluations.

Internal Yield Curve

At its most basic, bond evaluation consists of placing a value on a bond by comparing it to bonds with similar characteristics for which recent prices are known. Adjustments to the value are made based on how the individual bond differs from the other bonds with which it is compared.

The internal yield curve is a yield curve consisting of all bonds with similar maturities. For example, an evaluator focusing on noncallable general obligation bonds would create a yield curve of bonds to use as a reference.

---

[2] Block trades for municipal bonds are trades with a par value of $1 million or more.

There are also times when a scale needs to be broken down by month or day to assign specific value to a month or even day if the market demands it. This is similar to what underwriters do when they create a new issue scale.

The evaluator then prices a specific bond by comparing it to what the best of the category—the AAA bond—sells for. When a bond is "spread" off another bond, it is positioned a certain number of basis points higher than the base scale. In general, bonds which are perceived by the Street as being less desirable will have higher yields (more basis points in its spread) to attract investors.

The values assigned along this internal yield curve or scale take many factors into account, including recent trades, new issue pricing, quoted two-sided markets (where a dealer or broker is willing to quote both a bid and an ask price), results of brokers' bids wanted, and bids and offers. The bonds are then broken down by particular characteristics, including:

- Issuer
- Coupon
- Maturity
- Type: Revenue or general obligation
- Rating
- Call features
- Purpose
- Use of proceeds
- State
- Bond insurance
- Alternative Minimum Tax status

The evaluator relies mainly on data for block trades, also known as *institutional round lots*. An Interactive Data evaluation typically assumes a minimum par value of $1 million. There are times when smaller amounts are considered. For example, when a bond is rarely traded or was originally issued in a small amount. This occurs most often with high-yield bonds, where the trades are generally smaller due to liquidity problems. Smaller amounts of bonds typically trade cheaper than round lots and might attract less interest from potential buyers.

Municipal Securities Rulemaking Board

The Municipal Securities Rulemaking Board (MSRB) is an important source of data used in municipal bond evaluation since the effective date of amendments to Rule G-12(f) and Rule G-14 in January 2005, which required each dealer to report, within 15 minutes, to the MSRB information about each purchase or sale transaction effected in municipal securities via the Real-time Transaction Reporting System (RTRS). Evaluators look at the MSRB reported trades and the difference between the trade and their evaluation for a particular CUSIP[3] or bond. Using the information in these posted trades, an evaluator makes adjustments either to the internal yield curve or on the particular bond, and potentially other bonds in the series or bonds with similar traits.

Street Contacts

Bond evaluation is an art, and an evaluator must sort through many variables in the process of forming an opinion. That is why information from Wall Street contacts is factored into evaluations. An evaluator starts the day by discussing the market with other evaluators, reading the morning municipal market commentaries in the newspapers and on the Internet, and talking to bond professionals—including traders, underwriters, salespeople, and brokers. These activities help evaluators to form opinions on the current "tone" or possible direction of the market. This activity continues throughout the day as an ongoing dialogue via phone conversations or e-mails with Street professionals.

An evaluator monitors a steady stream of reported trades that the MSRB makes available throughout the day. Once these MSRB trades are matched to the current evaluation of the same security, the evaluator can use tone and movement of the municipal market to make adjustments on an ongoing basis.

As bonds are traded in the secondary market, evaluators use their experience to sift through Street information such as trades on bellwether or benchmark issues,[4] spreads between various bonds, new issue scales, and customer and Street bid wanteds.[5] This information is then utilized for making adjustments in either particular bonds or entire curves or scales.

---

[3] On its web site, the MSRB defines *CUSIP* as follows: "An identification number assigned to each maturity of an issue intended to help facilitate the identification and clearance of securities. In some cases, separate CUSIP numbers may be assigned to different portions of a maturity that bear different interest rates or where differences exist in the terms of the securities of such maturity that may impair the fungibility of the securities within the maturity. For example, if a portion of a maturity has been advance refunded and the remaining portion remains outstanding, each portion will be assigned a separate CUSIP number."

[4] Benchmark issues are bonds that have a large "float" or Street position and are universally recognized by the municipal bond industry as a bond which has many buyers and sellers.

[5] The MSRB web site defines *bid wanted* as the "process by which an investor or broker-dealer actively solicits bids on a position of securities from the marketplace."

EXHIBIT 27.1 Municipal Bonds Group by Credit Quality (as defined by Interactive Data)

Group	Rating Agency	Rating
Investment grade	Moody's Investors Service	Baa3 and higher
	Standard & Poor's	BBB– and higher
	Fitch Ratings	BBB– and higher
	Certain unrated bonds with characteristics of investment grade securities	
High-yield securities	Moody's Investors Service	Ba1 and lower
	Standard & Poor's	BB+ and lower
	Fitch Ratings	BB+ and lower
	Certain unrated bonds with characteristics of high-yield securities	

ADJUSTING FOR DIFFERENT TYPES OF MUNICIPAL BONDS

Municipal bonds are issued by state and local governments or their agencies to raise funds in various amounts and for different reasons. There are two basic types of municipal bond: general obligation or revenue. Bonds may vary based on the type of purpose, such as to build or repair a hospital or highway. In addition, some bonds have more sophisticated characteristics such as active sinking funds or variable rates. An evaluator must take all of these characteristics into account when evaluating a particular bond.

Credit Quality

Credit quality is one of the characteristics that must be taken into account when bonds are evaluated. There are two main groups: investment grade and high yield (see Exhibit 27.1).

Grouping by Purpose, Issuer Type or Other Characteristics

Once bonds are grouped by credit quality, they are subdivided according to other characteristics that affect bond evaluations (see Exhibit 27.2). For example, general obligation bonds are considered more secure than revenue bonds. Evaluators then specialize in one or more of these sectors.

OTHER CONSIDERATIONS

Money Market Bonds

For money market bonds, the scale or internal yield curve is always broken down by month. Money market instruments are bonds or notes with a

EXHIBIT 27.2   Selected Municipal Bond Categories

By type of funding	General Obligations Revenue
Other types	Double-barreled COPS Lease-rent Prerefunded or ETM Tax allocation Tobacco state appropriation Tobacco settlement

By purpose	Airports Bridge and tunnel Charter schools Convention center Gas Highway Hospital Higher education Industrial development Mass transit	Military housing Multi-family housing Pollution control Public power Seaport/marine terminal Single-family housing Solid waste Stadium Veteran housing Water and sewer

Miscellaneous	Active sinking funds Derivatives Distressed and/or defaulted High yield Index floaters Notes (BANs, TANs, RANs, TRANs, etc.) Put bonds Taxable municipals Tax-exempt commercal paper Tender option bonds Variable rates

maturity of 13 months or less. The popularity of money market funds has created a demand for certain notes and bonds which mature in 13 months or less. Demand usually leads to higher prices and lower yields. There are also times in the marketplace when, because of demand or lack of supply, bonds slightly longer than 13 months will trade in line with money market bonds.

Fallen Angels

Bonds whose credit quality is in transition are often called *fallen angels*. Although they were investment grade when initially issued, they have since fallen to high-yield or junk rating levels. At Interactive Data, evaluators decide on a case-by-case basis whether bonds from a particular issue are being treated by the marketplace as high yield or investment grade. Once again, an evaluator will rely on bids, offerings, and markets quoted on the Street and trades reported by the MSRB. In addition, Interactive Data analysts may review the credit.

Natural Disasters

Natural disasters—including floods, blizzards, and hurricanes—can affect the credit worthiness, and evaluation of a particular bond. Evaluators must adjust their evaluations accordingly.

As an example, let us consider how Interactive Data treated an uninsured municipal note issue from New Orleans, LA following Hurricane Katrina in August 2005. Bond Anticipation Notes or BANs 3.00% due July 26, 2006 were issued at par (100) on July 28, 2005. Prior to Katrina, these notes had traded and had been evaluated at or close to par as the market dictated. On August 29, the day the hurricane hit, the notes were evaluated at 100.022. As long as the ratings of the notes were not changed, the evaluation remained at par, which is where they were offered on the Street. However, the evaluator was in constant communication with traders, brokers, and holders of the securities to be aware of any possible bids or offerings posted on these securities.

New Orleans BANs did not trade in the marketplace again until September 21, 2005, when they traded around a dollar price of $94.40. The evaluation was immediately adjusted upon learning of the trades. The next day they traded at $98.00, and again the evaluation was adjusted to reflect this level. The notes then continued to be fairly actively traded or quoted, and the evaluation tracked the different levels. The evaluator had to put extra effort into monitoring a truly unique situation regarding this bond.

High Yield

High-yield, nonrated securities are another challenge. If they have been in the market for at least a year, Interactive Data has an internal team of analysts who can develop credit ratings for internal use only, provided that sufficient financial information is available. We base our credit analysis on offering documents, the most recent available financial statements, material event notices, and credit information obtained from the MuniView database and from trustees, financial advisors, borrowers, Nationally Recognized

Municipal Securities Information Repositories (NRMSIRs)[6] and/or clients. This credit rating plays a key role in assisting the evaluators in determining relationships to similar rated securities, when applicable. As credit situations change, analysts may change our internal ratings.

Individual evaluations on high-yield bonds are based on objectively verifiable information, including credit and market information derived from the market, which the evaluators obtain from the analysts and the evaluators' market contacts.

In addition, there are certain nonperforming high-yield securities which must be approached differently. Distressed municipal securities and defaulted municipal securities are two groups of municipal bonds which are usually inactive, which means that there are few, if any, trades in the secondary market.

Distressed Municipal Bonds

These are bonds that have fallen significantly in price, usually due to diminished financial performance, multiple notch credit rating downgrades (internal or public), and sometimes technical default. Credit surveillance is often tightened on distressed securities because they will tend to trade based on their underlying credit fundamentals. In the absence of current market activity, distressed municipal securities may be evaluated by either referencing corporate bonds in the same sector (e.g., steel, paper, airlines) or based on the liquidation value or restructuring value of the underlying assets. Fallen angels may also be distressed municipal bonds.

Defaulted Municipal Bonds

Defaulted bonds have missed a scheduled debt service payment and are typically traded *flat* (without accrued interest) in the secondary market. Bonds backed by borrowers that have filed for Chapter 11 bankruptcy protection are also considered to be in default. In the absence of current market activity, defaulted securities are often evaluated utilizing liquidation, restructuring or a capitalization-rate[7]/discounted cash flow approach. Analysts seek up-to-date valuations of assets and liabilities by consulting with market experts including real estate brokers. In the case of a bankruptcy filing, the plan

---

[6] The MSRB web site defines *NRMSIR* as an "entity designated by the SEC to receive final official statements, material event notices and annual financial information under Rule 15c2-12." Interactive Data Pricing and Reference Data, Inc. is one of four designated NRMSIRs.

[7] Capitalization rate refers to the net operating income divided by the sales price or value of the assets. It is expressed as a percentage.

of reorganization and disclosure statement are reviewed to help determine potential bondholder recovery.

All defaulted bonds are distressed, but not all distressed bonds are defaulted. Most distressed and defaulted securities do not move with the market. In most cases, these securities are evaluated in an internal "flat" category. Evaluated prices which are disseminated on these types of securities tend to remain constant for relatively long periods.

THE FUTURE OF MUNICIPAL BOND EVALUATION

The evolution of the process of municipal bond evaluations has mirrored the evolution of the municipal bond industry in terms of technology, regulations and other innovations. As computers have become more sophisticated and nimble, so has municipal bond evaluation. When new laws were passed introducing the *alternative minimum tax* (AMT[8]) and bank-qualified[9] issues to the marketplace, evaluations had to adjust to these new dynamics in the bond market.

It is the function of the evaluator to reflect current market values in a timely and professional manner. Evaluators must remain constantly vigilant so that they can adjust to changes in the marketplace and so that evaluations will remain a highly sophisticated tool of the municipal bond industry.

---

[8] The MSRB web site defines the *AMT* as taxation "based on an alternative method of calculating federal income tax intended to ensure that taxpayers are not able to avoid paying any federal income tax. For taxpayers subject to the alternative minimum tax, certain tax preference items, including interest on some private activity bonds, otherwise not subject to taxation are added to the gross income of the taxpayer for purposes of calculating the federal income tax liability."

[9] The MSRB web site defines *bank qualified* as the "designation given to a public purpose bond offering by the issuer if it reasonably expects to issue in the calendar year of such offering no more than $10 million par amount of bonds of the type required to be included in making such calculation under the Internal Revenue Code. When purchased by a commercial bank for its portfolio, the bank may receive an 80% tax deduction for the interest cost of carry for the issue. A bond that is bank qualified is also known as a 'qualified tax-exempt obligation'."

CHAPTER 28

Valuation of Municipal Bonds with Embedded Options

Frank J. Fabozzi, Ph.D., CFA
Professor in the Practice of Finance
School of Management, Yale University

Andrew Kalotay, Ph.D.
President
Andrew Kalotay Associates, Inc.

Michael P. Dorigan, Ph.D.
Senior Quantitative Analyst
Municipal Investment Group
PNC Capital Advisors

Computing formula-based volatility measures for option-free bonds is straightforward. Applying the same calculations to bonds with embedded options (e.g., callable and putable bonds) is inappropriate. This is because the cash flows on these bonds are uncertain. Instead, the analysis of these bonds must take into account the bonds' possible cash flow outcomes.

The valuation method that we describe in this chapter allows the investor to identify if a bond is cheap, rich, or fairly priced. Rather than think in terms of price, investors prefer to look at a bond in terms of *yield spread*. That is, if a valuation model indicates that a municipal bond is cheap by one point, investors seek to translate that amount into a basis point spread relative to the yield of a particular benchmark security. However, as we explain in this chapter, the appropriate benchmark for measuring the yield spread is not a particular point on the municipal yield curve of an issuer, but instead the spread over the theoretical zero-coupon curve of the issuer. This spread, which takes into account the bond's option features, is referred to as the *option-adjusted spread*.

The valuation model presented here is state-of-the-art technology. It is complicated. Our hope here is to provide a general understanding of this methodology, its underlying assumptions, and its applications. In practice, instead of developing their models in-house, institutional investors tend to rely on dealer or vendor models, using their own assumptions.

UNDERLYING PRINCIPLES

The valuation model that we discuss in this chapter requires understanding of two fundamental principles. Accordingly, first, we explain the correct methodology for valuing any bullet municipal bond (i.e., one with no embedded options). Second, we provide a conceptual framework for valuing bonds with embedded options.

OVERVIEW OF BOND VALUATION

The price of a bond is the present value of the expected cash flow. In all of our illustrations until now, we applied a single discount rate to all cash flows, namely the yield to maturity of a corresponding on-the-run issue of the municipal issuer. For example, suppose that a value for a 10-year, option-free, single-A municipal bond is sought. If the yield to maturity of the on-the-run 10-year municipal bond is 5%, then all the cash flows are discounted at 5%. However, this approach is incorrect.

For example, the rate used to discount the cash flows of a 10-year current coupon municipal issue (5% in our example) would be the same as that used to discount the cash flow of a 10-year, zero-coupon municipal issue. But that makes little sense because the cash flow characteristics of the two bonds are different.

Because of this drawback, recognition has been given to the fact that any bond should be thought of as a package of cash flows, with each individual cash flow (such as a coupon payment) viewed as a zero-coupon instrument maturing on the date it is received. As such, each cash flow or zero-coupon instrument should be discounted at the rate that would be offered on a zero-coupon municipal issue with a maturity equal to the maturity of that individual cash flow. Therefore, rather than using one discount rate for bonds with multiple cash flows, multiple discount rates should be used.

Consequently, the first step in valuing a municipal issue is to determine the appropriate zero-coupon rates, or as they are more commonly referred to as, *spot rates*. Since municipal issuers typically do not have zero-coupon bonds with different maturities outstanding, it is necessary to estimate a theoretical spot rate curve. This curve can be estimated from the issuer's on-the-run yield curve by a method called *bootstrapping*.

Exhibit 28.1 shows the first three points on a theoretical on-the-run yield curve for a triple-A rated municipal issuer and the corresponding spot rate curve. For simplicity, we assume that all the issues are annual pay.

If this municipal issuer issued an option-free three-year, 4.5% coupon bond, the theoretical price of this issue would be equal to the present value of each cash flow discounted at the corresponding spot rate. This is illustrated in Exhibit 28.2. The theoretical value for this bond would be $100.

Rather than using the theoretical spot rates, theoretical one-year forward rates can be used. A forward rate is defined as a rate for some specified length of time beginning at some specified time in the future. Forward rates are not the investor's expectations of future interest rates. Instead, they are obtained using arbitrage arguments—the same methodology used for obtaining spot rates. Exhibit 28.1 shows the one-year forward rates for the municipal issuer whose on-the-run yield curve is shown in the exhibit. Letting f_t denote the one-year forward rate t years from now, then the present value of the cash flow for year T is as follows:

$$\frac{\text{Cash flow for year } T}{(1+f_1)(1+f_2)\ldots(1+f_T)}$$

To illustrate, consider the 4.5% coupon bond in Exhibit 28.2. Using the one-year forward rates in Exhibit 28.1, the theoretical value of this bond is

EXHIBIT 28.1 On-the-Run Yield Curve and Theoretical Spot Rate Curve for a AAA Municipal Issuer

Year	Yield to maturity	Price	Spot Rate	Forward Rate
1	3.5%	$100	3.500%	3.500%
2	4.0	100	4.010	4.523
3	4.5	100	4.531	5.580

EXHIBIT 28.2 Theoretical Value of an Option-Free, AAA Municipal Issue with a 4.5% Coupon bond

Year	Coupon per $100 of par	Spot Rate	Present Value
1	4.5	3.500%	$4.348
2	4.5	4.010	4.160
3	104.5	4.531	91.492
		Theoretical value:	$100.00

$$\frac{\$4.5}{(1.035)} + \frac{\$4.5}{(1.035)(1.04523)} + \frac{\$1.045}{(1.035)(1.04523)(1.05580)} = \$100.00$$

Notice that this value agrees with that computed in Exhibit 28.2 using the spot rates.

Conceptual Approach to the Valuation of Bond with Embedded Options

Next let's look at how a bond with an embedded option should be viewed at a conceptual level. An investor in a callable bond holds a long position in the underlying noncallable (or bullet) bond and has sold an option to the issuer to call the bond (i.e., has a short position in a call option on this bond). Therefore a callable bond of the same issuer (or on a bond with the same credit risk) is worth less than a noncallable bond with the same coupon rate. This is because of the risk that the bond will be called when interest rates fall below the coupon rate, forcing the investor to reinvest the proceeds at a lower yield.

In contrast, an investor in a putable bond holds a long position in the underlying bullet bond and has purchased an option to put back the bond to the issuer, and therefore a putable bond is worth more than an otherwise identical optionless bond.

Given the above, conceptually, the price of a callable and putable bond can be expressed as follows:

Callable bond price = Bullet bond price − Value of the call option

Putable bond price = Bullet bond price + Value of the put option

The procedure described below can be used to value bonds in general, both bullet bonds and bonds with embedded options. As a byproduct, it can also provide the theoretical value of the embedded option.

VALUATION MODEL

The value of any municipal bond is determined by the discounting the cash flows from the bond, using rates consistent with the issuer's theoretical spot rate curve. However, the cash flows for a callable or a putable bond are uncertain because they both depend upon future interest rates. All of these factors must be taken into account when valuing bonds with embedded options.

The first step in valuing a bond, with or without embedded options, is to determine the appropriate municipal yield curve.[1] These will be the yields on liquid option-free new issues that are perceived to have the same credit risk as the bond under consideration. We will call this the *benchmark curve*. We then generate the spot and forward rates associated with this curve. The next step is to consider possible paths that interest rates can take over the life of the bond to be analyzed.[2] As will be explained in the illustration that follows, an interest rate tree of forward one-period rates is generated, where each path represents a possible interest rate scenario over the life of the bond and each point (or node) on an interest rate path represents an interest rate at a future point in time. Next, we have to determine the cash flows that would be received from the bond along each interest rate path. Finally, all cash flows must be discounted back to the present time and probability weighted to determine the bond's expected value today.

This is a tedious procedure even for an option-free bond. The bond's cash flow at the final node is discounted by the forward rate set at the beginning of the period (i.e., at the previous node) on the interest rate tree in order to determine the expected value of the bond at that node. The value at each node in that period is then discounted back to the next prior node. This procedure is repeated, where the value and any other cash flows (generally coupon payments) associated with each period are discounted back to the present. The bond's theoretical value is the resulting final price at the beginning of the tree.

For simplicity, we will first discuss the use of this model for valuing a bond with no embedded options. We will then extend the model to analyze bonds with calls, puts, and other embedded options.

Generating the Interest Rate Tree

We must determine the possible interest rate scenarios. To do this we generate an interest rate tree which considers the different paths that interest rates can take over the bond's life, ensuring that this tree is consistent with the on-the-run yield curve, and the assumed distribution and volatility of rates.

An example of an interest rate tree for a three-year bond (assuming, for simplicity annual pay) is shown in Exhibit 28.3. At each node (i.e., each point), the one-year forward rate is shown. Also, the one-year forward rate for the next year is assumed to take on two possible values, each with an equal probability of occurring.

---

[1] The Treasury yield curve should not be used for the valuation of municipal bonds. Although yields of municipal and Treasury securities are generally positively correlated, they are not perfectly correlated. They can even move in opposite directions at times.

[2] A lognormal distribution for rates is assumed and the volatility of interest rates must be estimated and input for the analysis.

EXHIBIT 28.3 Interest Rate for a Three-year, AAA Municipal Issuer Assuming 10% Interest Rate Volatility

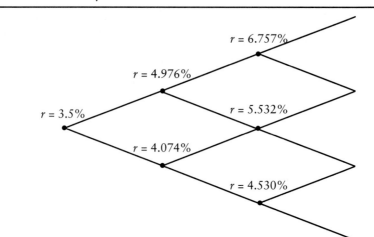

The objective in the valuation process is to obtain an interest rate tree such that when any of the on-the-run issues is valued, it will always correctly value that bond; that is, it will produce the observed market price.

An explanation of the methodology for deriving the interest rate tree is beyond the scope of this chapter.[3] However, it should be noted that it is based on the assumption that the distribution of forward rates follows a lognormal distribution with a 10% volatility.[4]

Valuing a Bond Using the Interest Rate Tree

Let's look at how the interest rate tree in Exhibit 28.3 is used. Exhibit 28.4 shows the cash flow of the bond at each node. These are the coupon interest for years prior to maturity and coupon interest plus par at maturity. The procedure is straightforward. At each node, the value of the bond is found using the following steps:

---

[3] The interested reader is referred to Andrew Kalotay, George Williams, and Frank J. Fabozzi, "A Model for the Valuation of Bonds with Embedded Options," *Financial Analysts Journal* (May–June 1993), pp. 35–46.

[4] In actuality, shorter maturity bonds are included in the benchmark yield curve and shorter time steps (perhaps monthly, or weekly, depending on the maturity of the bond to be analyzed) are used to evaluate the bonds. For brevity, we've chosen to show the analysis for only three time periods, though the actual number of steps often includes 100 or more time steps. A large number of steps and therefore interest rate paths are required for analyzing bonds with embedded options.

EXHIBIT 28.4 Coupon and Par Value at Each Interest Rate Node for a Three-year Municipal Bond

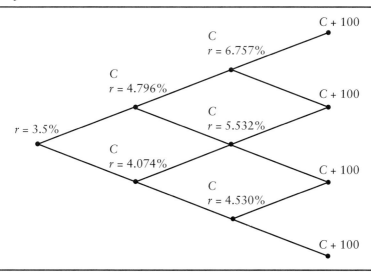

EXHIBIT 28.5 Calculating Value at a Node

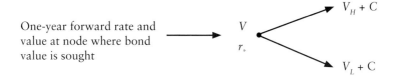

V_H = Bond's value in high-rate state one year forward
V_L = Bond's value in low-rate state one year forward
C = Coupon flow on the bond

Step 1. For a given year, determine the cash flow for the two possible interest rate paths one-year from this node. The cash flow is the value of the bond one-year from this point plus the coupon payment. Hold aside for now how we get these two values because, as we will see, the process involves starting from the last year in the tree and working backwards to get the bond's theoretical value today.

Step 2. Calculate the present value of the cash flows for each of the two possible interest rate paths one-year from now. The discount rate is the one-year forward rate at the node. This is illustrated in Exhibit 28.5

for any node assuming that the one-year forward rate is r_* at the node where the valuation is sought and letting:

V_H = The bond's value for the higher one-year forward rate
V_L = The bond's value for the lower one-year forward rate
C = Coupon payment

Using our notation, the cash flow at a node is either:

$$V_H + C \text{ for the higher one-year forward rate}$$

or

$$V_L + C \text{ for the lower one-year forward rate}$$

The present value of these two cash flows using the one-year forward rate at the node, r_*, is:

$$\frac{V_H + C}{(1 + r_*)} = \text{Present value for the higher one-year forward rate}$$

$$\frac{V_L + C}{(1 + r_*)} = \text{Present value for the lower one-year forward rate}$$

Step 3: Calculate the average of the two values computed in the previous step. Then, the value of the bond at the node is found as follows:

$$\text{Value [at a node]} = \frac{1}{2}\left[\frac{V_H + C}{(1 + r_*)} + \frac{V_L + C}{(1 + r_*)}\right]$$

The same process continues for each node on the interest rate tree. The process begins by starting in the last period and working backwards.[5]

To illustrate these three steps, consider the three-year, 4.5% on-the-run noncallable issue shown in Exhibit 28.1.

Step 2 requires the determination of the cash flow along the interest rate tree. Exhibit 28.6 shows the interest rate tree and the cash flow at each node. The only known cash flows are the coupon payments, and, in year 3, the maturity value ($100) plus the coupon interest of $4.5. To see how to use steps 2 and 3 outlined above to get the value of the bond at for the top node in the second year, we will use Exhibit 28.7, which has four nodes labeled W, X, Y, and Z on the tree. The interest rate tree in Exhibit 28.7 is

---

[5] This process is known as *recursive valuation*, where the value of the bond is determined by taking the final bond value and discounting it and all associated cash flows by the appropriate discount rates back to the current time period.

EXHIBIT 28.6 Cash Flows for a Three-year, 4.5%, AAA Rated Municipal Bond

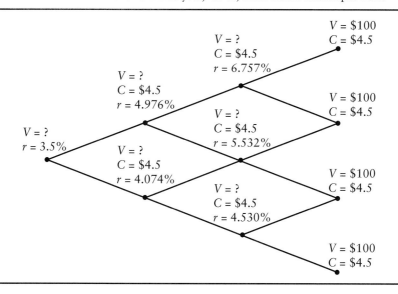

EXHIBIT 28.7 Cash Flows for a Three-year, 4.5%, AAA Rated Municipal Bond with Labels

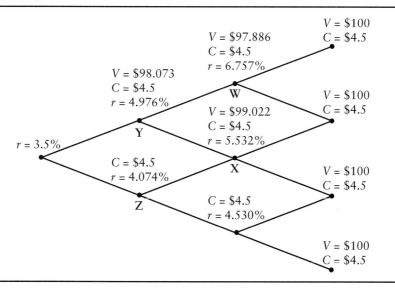

identical to that in Exhibit 28.6, but the labeling of the nodes will make it easier to follow the explanation. In addition, values determined below are also displayed on the nodes in the exhibit.

In terms of Exhibit 28.7, a value for the bond at the end of year two is the node marked with the label W. The value of this bond at node W is the present value of the cash flows for the two nodes to the right of the node (i.e., for the two nodes one year forward that are to the right of node W).

Step 2 indicates how this present value should be calculated at node W to arrive at the bond value at node W. To get the present value, the forward rate at node W, 6.757%, is used. Using the notation V_H for the upper node to the right of node W, then the present value of the cash flow for the upper node is[6]

$$\frac{\$100 + \$4.5}{1.06757} = \$97.886$$

Since the cash flows at the lower node to the right of node W are identical to the upper node, the present value of the cash flow for the lower one-year forward rate is also $97.886.

Step 3 states that the present value for the two cash flows should be averaged (assuming an equal probability of each outcome) to get the value of the bond at node W. Since the two present values are the same, the average value equals $97.886. This is the bond value shown in Exhibit 28.7 at node W.

The value of the bond at node X, and all other nodes in period two, would be determined similarly. At this node, the one-year forward rate that would be used to calculate the present value of the cash flows for the two nodes to the right of node X would be 5.532%. In step 2, since V_H and V_L to the right of node X are both $100 and the coupon is $4.50, the cash flow is identical. The present value of the cash flow at both nodes to the right of node X is then

$$\frac{\$100 + \$4.5}{1.05532} = \$99.022$$

The average of the two present values is then $99.022 and is therefore the value of the bond at node X.

As you can see, getting the bond value for the two nodes for the year just before the maturity date is easy. Now let's look at how to get the value of the bond at node X. At node Y, the two nodes to the right are node W and node X. Now to get the bond value at node X, we need the cash flow at node W and node X. The cash flow is the bond's value at these two nodes plus the

---

[6] Fair value at any node is highly sensitive to the number of decimal places used in each calculation.

coupon rate. The cash flow at nodes W and X will then be discounted at the one-year forward rate at node Y which is 4.976% and then averaged to get the bond's value at node Y. But where do we get the bond's value at nodes W and X? We calculated it above, it is $97.886 and $99.022, respectively. This is why the procedure we are using is called recursive valuation: we work our way backward in the interest rate tree from the maturity date to the root of the tree (today). The bond values at each node are in turn used to get the bond value at an earlier period.

Thus the value of the bond at node Y is determined from the values calculated at nodes W and X. In this case V_H is the value at node W which is $97.886 and V_L is the value at node X which is $99.022. Then:

Present value of cash flow for the higher one-year forward rate

$$= \frac{\$97.886 + \$4.5}{1.04976} = \$97.533$$

Present value of cash flow for the lower one-year forward rate

$$= \frac{\$99.022 + \$4.5}{1.04976} = \$98.615$$

The average present value is then $98.073 [($97.533 + $98.615)/2]. This is the bond's value shown in Exhibit 28.7 at node Y.

EXHIBIT 28.8 Cash Flows of a Three-Year, 4.5%, AAA Rated Municipal Bond

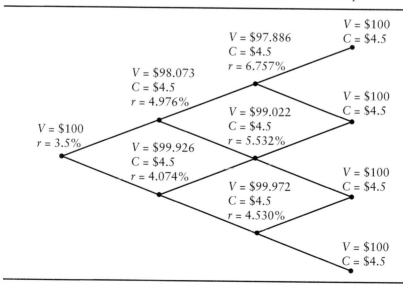

The value of the bond at node Z would be similarly determined. The value of the bond today (node 0) would be determined from the values of the cash flow nodes Y and Z.

Exhibit 28.8 shows the completed interest rate tree with the values shown at each node. Notice that the value at the root (i.e., the value today) is $100, which agrees with the observed market price. Thus, the interest rate tree is consistent with the three-year on-run-issue. If the same procedure is followed for the other two on-the-run issues, the theoretical values would equal the observed market prices. As a result, the resulting interest rate tree is considered to be arbitrage-free.

Valuing a AAA Municipal Bond

In order to evaluate any AAA rated municipal bond, the same interest rate tree shown in Exhibit 28.3 is used. The cash flows of the bond at each node will be discounted by the benchmark forward rate for that period. The steps for determining the theoretical value are the same as the three steps discussed above. If the calculated bond value is greater than its market price, the bond is considered to be cheap. Conversely, if the calculated value from the interest rate tree is less than the market price of the bond, the bond is considered to be rich.

EXHIBIT 28.9   Interest Rate Tree and Values for a AAA Rated 5% Municipal Bond

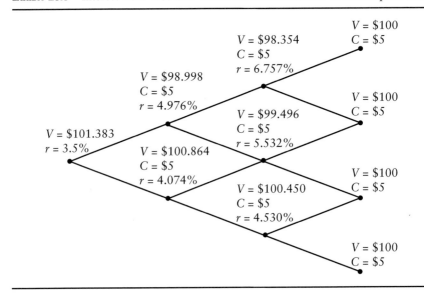

To illustrate this, consider a AAA option-free three-year, 5% coupon bond from the same issuer and thus subject to the same discounting rates (i.e., interest rate tree). Suppose the bond is currently trading at $101.5. Exhibit 28.9 gives the complete interest rate tree with values at each node. The theoretical value of this bond is $101.383. Since the bond's calculated (or theoretical) value is less than its current price, the bond is considered rich and should be avoided. Conversely, if the bond's market price is $101, the bond would be considered cheap, since its theoretical value is above its market price.

Also note that if the same bond were discounted using the spot rates or the forward rates given in Exhibit 28.1, its value would be $101.383. This should not be surprising since if the bond is an option-free, using the spot rates or forward rates will give the same value as the interest rate tree.

Valuing an A Rated Bond

How do we determine the value of an A rated bond? Using the on-the-run, A rated yield curve, an interest rate tree must be generated that can be used for valuing this bond. This can be done directly by generating an interest rate tree using the benchmark A rated yield curve. Alternatively, the zero-coupon credit spreads for A rated bonds over the AAA curve can be added to the yields at each node on the AAA benchmark tree. The resulting interest rate tree will then be consistent with the forward rates implied by the benchmark A rated yield curve determined above.

For example, Exhibit 28.10 shows the interest rate tree for an A rated issuer by adding the following zero-coupon spreads to the AAA interest rate

EXHIBIT 28.10   Interest Rate Tree for an A Rated Issuer

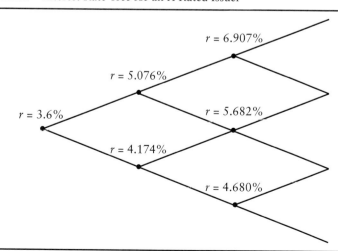

tree in Exhibit 28.3: 1 year, 10 basis points; 2 year, 10 basis points; and 3 year, 15 basis points.

The resulting rates at each node on the interest rate tree are the A rated benchmark one-year forward rates. To determine an A rated bond's value, the bond's cash flows are discounted back to the present using these rates. The result is the value for the bond implied by today's benchmark yield curve for A rated bonds. If the calculated theoretical value is greater than the market price, the bond is considered cheap; if the calculated value is less than the market price, the bond is considered rich.

The same procedure would be used for evaluating bonds of other credit ratings, where the yield curve used in the analysis is the yield curve consistent with the credit of the bonds to be evaluated.

Valuing Callable Bonds

If the bond is callable, the valuation must take into account the possibility that the bond will be called when interest rates decline below the coupon rate.[7] To do this, the cash flow at each node is adjusted to reflect a possible call at the node. Here the bond's price at each node is equal to the lower of the calculated price or the call price plus the coupon payment.

For example, assume a AAA rated, 6% coupon municipal bond with three years to maturity is callable in one year and thereafter at par. The value in each year is the lower of the calculated value and the call price of 100. The value of the bond is then found using the three steps given earlier, using the AAA interest rate tree generated in the previous examples. This is illustrated in Exhibit 28.11.

The value at node M equals the expected value of the bond, $99.291. The value at node N, calculated from the two possible outcomes (i.e., the two nodes to the right of node N), is $100.443. However, since the value exceeds the call price, we assume that the issuer would call the bond at point N, resulting instead in a value of $100, not the $100.44 calculated value.[8] The value at point O is the call price of 100 rather than the calculated value of $101.406, since the issuer would call the bond at this point.

The value at each point of an interest rate tree for a callable bond is the minimum of (1) the calculated value or (2) the call price (plus issuance costs). The same procedure is repeated until we reach the beginning of the interest rate tree, which will be the value of the bond today.

---

[7] Rational exercise of the option by the municipal issuer is assumed.
[8] We assume no issuance costs. In actuality, an issuer will call the bond if the value of the bond is greater than the call price plus issuance costs.

EXHIBIT 28.11   Value of a Three-Year, AAA Rated, 6% Callable Bond, Callable at Par in One Year

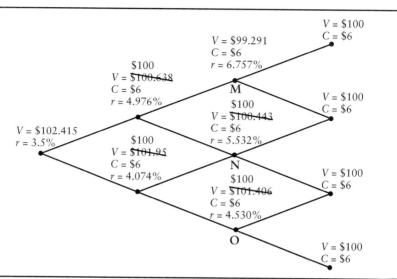

Valuing Putable Bonds

Bonds with embedded put options can be analyzed within the framework outlined above. However, for the interest rate tree, on the upper branches, the maximum of the put price or the calculated bond price will be used. This is because as rates in the market rise above the coupon rate on the putable bond, the investor would prefer to put the bond and reinvest the proceeds in a higher coupon rate bond. If interest rates fall below the coupon rate of the issue, investors will prefer to retain the bond. For example, assume that an AAA rated, 5.5%, bond currently selling at $102 is putable one year forward and each subsequent year at $100. Using our AAA rated benchmark yield curve and valuation, the interest rate tree and bond values are shown in Exhibit 28.12. Therefore, the calculated bond value is $103.051. As can be seen from this example, the bond will be put in the second period, when interest rates rise and the bond begins to sell at a discount.

SPECIFIC ADJUSTMENTS TO THE VALUATION MODEL FOR MUNICIPAL BONDS

The analysis described up to now can also be used to value corporate or callable Treasury bonds, where the benchmark yield curve is a corporate or Treasury yield curve, respectively. However, because of their unique

EXHIBIT 28.12 Value of a Three-year, AAA Rated, 5.5% Putable Bond Putable at Par in Year One

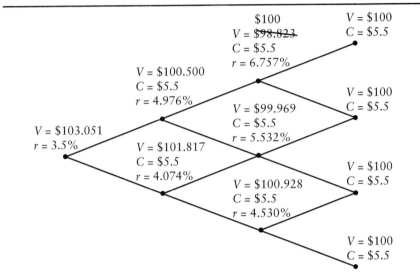

features two adjustments to the model are required to value municipal bonds. The first is a tax adjustment which takes into account that capital gains on municipal bonds are taxable. The second adjustment accounts for the fact that many municipal bonds can be advance refunded. These are described next.

TAX ADJUSTMENTS TO THE MODEL

For the investor's perspective, municipal pricing model must take into account the fact that certain municipal interest is free from federal income taxes (and may be free from state and local taxes). Price increases and decreases on the bond may have tax effects and therefore could affect the cash flow on the bond. The net value of the bond should be compared to the call price of the bond at the appropriate node on the yield curve.

Price changes, especially price appreciation on a tax-exempt bond purchased at a discount, may have tax implications. The tax rules for determining the investor's liability can be very complex, e.g., calculation of accreted original issue discount (OID), calculation of the *de minimus* or market discount cut-off price. For our purposes here, we assume a simple adjustment to the bond cash flows with the understanding that the actual adjustment must be made on a bond-by-bond basis assuming individual investor tax status.

EXHIBIT 28.13 Value of a Three-year AAA Rated, 6% Callable Bond Callable at Par in One Year Adjusted for the Tax Effect (Investor Tax Rate = 36%)

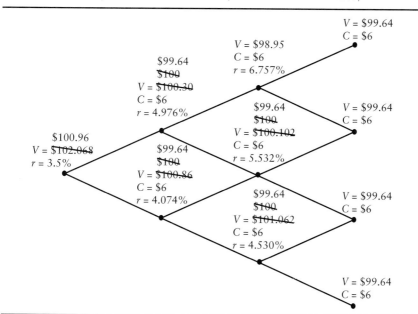

For example, if a bond is purchased at a discount at $99 and is callable at $100, the net cash flow on the call date for the investor would be

$$\$100 - t\,(\$100 - \$99)$$

where t is the marginal tax rate for the investor that applies to the situation. For example, if the situation called for capital gains tax treatment, the marginal tax rate would be the capital gains tax rate. If not, the marginal ordinary tax rate would apply. Since bonds selling at a premium are amortized over time, the difference between the bond's price (or call price) and the adjusted-tax basis (rather than the purchase price) on the bond at that particular point should be used to determine the net cash flow at each node on the interest rate tree. Exhibit 28.13 shows the adjusted values for the callable bond shown in Exhibit 28.11, assuming a purchase price of $99 and a marginal tax rate of 36%.

Similarly, the adjusted-tax basis for an original-issue discount bond is the accreted value of the bond on the call date. The net cash flow on the bond when it is called should be substituted for the call price at the node on which the bond is called. A similar analysis is required for putable bonds.

Adjustments for Advanced Refunding

Callable municipal bonds may be eligible for advanced refunding. Advanced refunding occurs prior to the initial call date. In an advanced refunding transaction the municipal issuer delivers into an irrevocable trust a portfolio of qualified bonds.[9] The cash flows generated by these bonds match those of the outstanding bond until the intital call date, including the call price. The municipality's rationale for advanced refunding is to lock in an interest rate which is below that of the coupon of the outstanding issue, and thereby save interest expense. This eliminates the risk that by the time the bond becomes callable, rates have risen to a level that renders the refunding less attractive.

Once a bond is advanced refunded it becomes default free, if it is collateralized by U.S. Treasury securities, and the issue's rating becomes AAA. Moreover, there is no further uncertainty regarding the call: independent of the subsequent course of interest rates, the bond is certain to be redeemed on the initial call date. Due to these considerations, that is, credit improvement and removal of call risk, advanced refunding increases the bond's value. Specifically, once a bond is advanced refunded, it should be priced by discounting its cash flows to the call date (including the call price) with a negative spread to the AAA municipal curve. These bonds are said to "trade though" the benchmark curve.

When valuing municipal bonds subject to advanced refunding or calling (also referred to as current refunding), investors should take into account various practical considerations that impact upon the issuer's decision. In other words, they should consider the bonds from the perspective of the issuer.

Let's first discuss the effect of insurance. If the bonds are insured, they will be rated AAA and valued using the AAA yield curve.[10] But what if without insurance the issuer's credit rating is BBB? From the perspective of the issuer, the determining factor in the refunding decision is the yield curve corresponding to the uninsured (i.e., BBB) credit. Of course, the issuer can always insure the refunding bonds, but there will be an associated cost. Consequently, the refunding of insured bonds is not going to be based on the AAA yield curve, to the obvious benefit of the investors.

Transaction costs, particularly the cost of underwriting, also affect the refunding decision. These costs, which can be substantial, will impede refund-

---

[9] Typically, U.S. Treasuries are required or a special class of government-issued bonds created to serve as collateral to the trust, called State and Local Government Securities (SLGSs or "slugs"), are used. Certain agency issues are allowed to secure the trust.

[10] Of course, recent events in the monoline insurance industry have put this assertion to the test.

ing. From the perspective of the issuer, the relevant call prices should include transaction costs associated with the issuance of the refunding issue. Transaction costs reduce the value of the call option and increase the cost (i.e., liability) associated with the debt service. Conversely, the call option will not be as onerous to the investor as the simple recursive valuation suggests.

In the case of advanced refunding, the issuer must consider the available return on Treasury bonds. The yield of the escrow is limited to the issuer's current cost of borrowing, but there is no guarantee that this can be actually achieved. If the issuer's borrowing cost exceeds the relevant available Treasury yield, the resulting "negative arbitrage" will be an impediment to advanced refunding. For this reason, advanced refunding is less likely to occur when the applicable Treasury rate is below the issuer's borrowing rate.

The considerations discussed above (i.e. insurance, transaction costs, negative arbitrage) affect the issuer's cash flows. A different dimension of the valuation problem from the perspective of the issuer is the discounting process. The theoretically correct method is to discount the relevant cashflows using the issuer's taxable borrowing rate, because it is unconstrained (not subject to approval). The reason for this is that for the issuer it is irrelevant whether the interest is taxable or tax-exempt. Moreover, that the value of the call option depends on the borrower's tax-exempt borrowing rate adds additional complexity to the valuation process. Finally, corporate issuers of tax-exempt bonds also need to take into account the effect of federal income taxes. From their perspective interest expense is deductible, regardless whether it is associated with taxable or a tax-exempt debt. Furthermore, transactions at a premium or discount to par value may also have tax ramifications.

Occasionally, due to indenture-related considerations rather than interest savings, municipalities advance refund noncallable (or low coupon callable) issues to maturity. As in the case of advanced refunding to the initial call date, such issues benefit from the improved credit, but optionality has no relevance.

The methodology used for dealing with advanced refunding draws on the same principles that are applied in the determination of efficient embedded-option exercise earlier in the chapter. We need a rule to guide us as to when to exercise the option to advance refund. Ideally, this rule should be option-based: act when the resulting savings capture a sufficiently high amount (say 95%) of the forfeited option value, which now includes both the value of the call option and the option to advance refund. A solution, which is beyond the scope of this chapter, is provided by Kalotay and May.[11]

---

[11] Andrew Kalotay and William May in "The Timing of Advanced Refunding of Tax-Exempt Municipal Bonds," *Municipal Finance Journal* (Fall 1998), pp. 1–15.

Obviously, the option to advance refund adds another layer of complexity to the problem. However, the lattice-based valuation methodology is all that is required to assess the value of this new option, while still calculating the value of the bond's embedded call option. What changes is the nature of the decisions at each node on the tree. For example, at nodes prior to the call date, the present value savings of an advance refunding at that node must be calculated via the recursive valuation process, while still accounting for the efficient exercise of the call option later in the tree (i.e., earlier in the recursive process), based on the rules outlined in prior sections of the chapter. Then a decision must be made at the node to advance refund based on the 95% efficiency rule from above.

There are a number of additional considerations that complicate the problem, such as calculating the so-called "true interest cost" from the refunding (i.e., new money) bond in order to satisfy certain tax rules related to arbitrage between the tax-exempt market and the U.S. Treasury market, which usually make up the portfolio in the refunding trust. Again, these issues go beyond our scope in this chapter.

HORIZON PRICE

When the total return is used to assess the potential performance of a bond or a portfolio over some investment horizon, a projection of the price of the bond at the end of the horizon date is required. The price is called the *horizon price*.

Thus far, the model that we have described assumes that the valuation date is the present date. However the analysis can be extended to determine the horizon price or value of the bond. For example, assume a portfolio manager has a four-year investment horizon and is considering the following three AA rated bonds.

Bond	Years to maturity	Today's price	Yield to maturity
A	11 years	$97.5	5.25%
B	5 years	$98.0	4.85%
C	7 years	101.0	5.50%

Since all bonds have a maturity different from the investment horizon, the calculation of total return would require that the portfolio manager calculate the horizon price for each bond. In addition to determining the option-adjusted spread of the bond at today's price and appropriate benchmark yield curve, the portfolio manager must also project how the yield curve evolves from the starting time until the horizon date. The ending yield curve defines an interest rate tree commencing at the horizon date; this tree determines the bond prices on the horizon date. The intermediate yield curves determine the reinvestment rates of any interim interest and principal payments.

OTHER VALUES CALCULATED FROM THE MODEL

There are other byproducts of the valuation model described above. They are described next.

Option Value

The difference between the calculated value of the underlying bullet (option-free) bond and the calculated value of the callable bond is the value of the embedded call option. If the value of a callable bond is $99.5 and the value of the bullet bond is $101, the value of the embedded call option is $1.50. Although this value can be calculated, it is not, by itself, very useful in relative value analysis of bonds with different option types.

Effective Duration and Convexity

Duration is a first approximation of the sensitivity of a bond or a portfolio to changes in interest rates. (More specifically to a parallel shift in the yield curve.) Using modified duration for a callable bond as an interest rate sensitivity measure is incorrect since this measure does not take into consideration that the cash flow can change as yields change. Similarly, the traditional convexity measure does not consider the changes in cash flow. Instead, of modified duration and traditional convexity, effective duration and convexity should be calculated.

Effective duration and convexity are calculated by shifting yield curves up and down by a small number of basis points (usually 30 to 40 basis points) and using the resulting values for the security to determine its sensitivity to changes in interest rates. The new value must reflect the fact that the change in interest rates can change the cash flows.

The effective duration and convexity should be calculated using the valuation model introduced in this chapter. We must shift the entire yield curve, then recalibrate the tree. The value of the bond is recalculated and the resulting price and yield changes are used in the effective duration and convexity calculation.[12] When the valuation model described in this chapter is used to calculate the effective duration and effective convexity, they are also referred to as *option-adjusted duration* and *option-adjusted convexity,* respectively. Lehman Brothers refers to this measure as *modified-adjusted duration.*

RELATIVE VALUE ANALYSIS OF MUNICIPAL BONDS

It is difficult to compare the prices of bonds with different features, such as maturity or coupon, even for option-free bonds. For example, how can one compare the value of a coupon-paying bond with that of a zero-coupon instrument on the basis of price alone? We need a better measure for comparison. Two methods are generally used in the market for relative valuation of bonds with embedded options: option-adjusted spread analysis and implied volatility analysis. Both methods are discussed next.

Option-Adjusted Spread Analysis

In traditional bond analysis of option-free bonds, a spread to the appropriate matched-maturity benchmark yield curve is calculated for each bond. For bonds with embedded options, maturity is made uncertain due to the chance the option is exercised. Hence, instead of a bullet spread, an option-adjusted spread (OAS) is calculated. This is the spread that when added to the benchmark interest rate tree causes the discounted cash flows of the bond to equal today's price. If applied to a bullet bond, the resulting OAS serves as a proxy for the credit component of the bond.

Richness or cheapness is assessed by comparing the OAS of bonds with similar credit rating and effective duration. For example, suppose two bonds, A and B, have embedded options, are of the same credit quality, and have the same effective duration. Suppose further that the OAS of A is 55 basis points while that of B is 65 basis points. On a relative value basis, B would be preferred because it offers a higher OAS.

Although OAS can be calculated based upon the bond's benchmark credit rating curve, they are often calculated as spreads to a widely known or used AAA municipal benchmark curve so that one anchor for comparison on all bonds is used. Then the OAS of bonds with the same credit ratings are compared to determine relative value. If the bond's calculated OAS is greater than that implied by the spread for a comparable bullet bond, the bond is considered cheap and would be a good value if consistent with the

---

[12] For an illustration of how this done, see Chapter 5 in Frank J. Fabozzi, *Duration, Convexity, and Other Bond Risk Measures* (Hoboken, NJ: John Wiley & Sons, 1999).

portfolio manager's investment objectives. If, however, the OAS is less than the spread implied for a fairly priced bullet bond, the bond is considered rich and should be avoided.[13]

Volatility Analysis

Implied volatility is an alternative way to measure the relative attractiveness of bonds. The *implied volatility* for a bond with an embedded option can be calculated given the current price and the OAS. The implied volatility for a bond is that volatility, which when used to generate the interest rate tree, causes the bond's price to equal its calculated value. Given the OAS, the current yield curve, and initial volatility, the interest rate tree is generated and the value of the bond is calculated. Volatility is then shifted and new trees and cash flows are generated until the discounted value of the cash flows equate to today's market price. The volatility which equates the two is the bond's implied volatility.

A high relative volatility (relative to estimated volatility in the marketplace) implies a high price of the embedded call option and, because the investor is short the call, a lower price for the bond. Thus the bond is cheap. For putable bonds, the opposite is true, since the investor is long the put.

SUMMARY

In this chapter we provided an overview of the latest technology for valuing municipal bonds with embedded options. This methodology is far superior to the traditional valuation and yield spread analysis of municipal bonds with embedded options because it takes into consideration the value of the options.

Most municipal bond portfolio managers will not develop their own model or have one developed for them if there is a quantitative group in their firm. Instead, they use the output of models developed by dealer firms or vendors. However, municipal bond portfolio managers should be familiar with the basic procedure, recognize the importance of the critical assumptions in the valuation model, understand how an effective duration and convexity can be calculated, understand how OAS can be incorporated

---

[13] It should be noted here that some OAS solutions use a credit benchmark curve in the analysis that may not represent a parallel shift over the AAA benchmark curve. Here, the OAS calculated is the yield spread to the credit benchmark curve, not to the AAA benchmark curve. Therefore the model will calculate a different OAS to maturity or call or other specified workout date relative to the benchmark AAA curve.

into total return framework analysis, and appreciate how OAS or implied volatility can be used in relative value analysis.

CHAPTER 29

Analyzing and Evaluating Tax-Exempt Indexed Floaters: Investor and Issuer Perspectives

Yingchen Li
Executive Director
JPMorgan Securities

Increasing issuance of indexed bonds is a new trend in the municipal market. All indexed bonds are long-term variable rate bonds that passively reset based on the reference indexes. Common reference indexes include three-month LIBOR, BMA 7-Day Index, and the 5- or 10-year CMS (constant maturity swap rates). The first such bond is the Detroit Sewer Disp Revenue Floater sold on 12/14/2006. The bond pays a quarterly floating coupon of 67% × 3-month LIBOR + 60 basis points and matures on 7/1/2032.

Although relatively new for investors, LIBOR-indexed floaters are equivalent to synthetic floating structures from the issuer's perspective. Suppose an issuer has a fixed coupon bond outstanding and receives 67% of LIBOR swap of the same maturity. The net position for the issuer is a synthetically floating rate position which is equivalent to a LIBOR-indexed floater.

The synthetic floating activities of issuers used to be concentrated within the 10-year maturity and mostly BMA based. From this point of view, LIBOR-indexed floaters represent the issuer's push toward LIBOR-based synthetic floating in the longer part of the curve.

BREAKEVEN EQUATION FOR THE ISSUER

Most of the index bonds sold so far are LIBOR-indexed floaters paying a coupon of the form 67% × 3ML + Fixed spread, where 3ML means 3-month LIBOR. We would like to derive a breakeven equation for the "Fixed Spread" from the issuer's perspective.

EXHIBIT 29.1   The Issuer of a LIBOR-indexed Floater Swaps to Paying Fixed

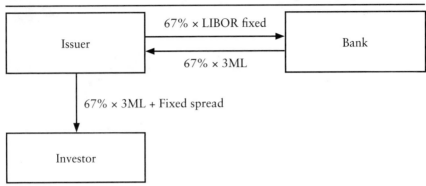

The issuer typically enters a same maturity LIBOR swap to pay fixed on 67% notional amount (see Exhibit 29.1) transforming its floating rate position to a synthetically fixed rate position. Since the issuer can sell fixed coupon bond directly in the market paying AAA yield + Credit spread, no arbitrage argument would force the following equation to hold:

67% × LIBOR fixed + Fixed spread = AAA yield + Credit spread

This equation can be used to compute the fair value of the fixed spread:

Fixed Spread = (AAA/LIBOR ratio – 67%) × LIBOR fixed + Credit spread

Thus a fair-valued LIBOR-indexed floater has a coupon of

67% × 3ML + (AAA/LIBOR ratio – 67%) × LIBOR fixed + Credit spread

RISK ANALYSIS OF LIBOR-INDEXED FLOATERS

Risk characteristics of LIBOR-indexed floaters are unique among municipal bonds. We would like to discuss them in detail in this chapter.

There are three risk components to a LIBOR-indexed floater: interest rate risk, ratio risk, and credit risk. The interest rate risk is small, which can be seen from the coupon structure. The mild interest rate exposures of LIBOR-indexed floaters are reflected in their small durations as well. Exhibit 29.2 shows the modified durations for a typical series of LIBOR-indexed floaters from 10- to 30-years.

EXHIBIT 29.2 Modified Durations and Credit Spread Durations of LIBOR-indexed Floaters with Fair Value Fixed Spreads

Maturity	Modified Duration	Credit Spread Duration
10	0.34	7.80
15	0.51	10.51
20	0.72	12.49
25	0.95	14.00
30	1.11	14.63

EXHIBIT 29.3 Theoretical Price Changes of 10- to 30-year LIBOR-indexed Floaters per 1% Change in AAA Ratios

10	$0.45
15	$0.61
20	$0.73
25	$0.82
30	$0.86

Two main risks of LIBOR-indexed floaters are credit risks and ratio risks. The credit spread duration of a LIBOR-indexed floater is roughly the same as that for a comparable fixed coupon bond (see Exhibit 29.2). As a consequence, any credit spread change should induce price action of similar magnitude for a LIBOR-indexed floater and a comparable fixed coupon bond. For example, should the 10-year credit spread widen by 5 basis points for an issuer, the price of a 10-year LIBOR-indexed floater by the issuer should fall by approximately $5 \times \$0.078 = \$0.39$ per $100 notional.

Ratio changes should have significant price impact on LIBOR-indexed floaters via the fair value calculation of the fixed spread. As an example, suppose the 30-year AAA/LIBOR ratio rises by 1% and the 30-year LIBOR rate is 5.80%. This would result in approximately 5.8 basis points widening in the fixed spread in the primary market, which in turn implies approximately $0.86 decline in price for an existing 30-year LIBOR-indexed floater (see Exhibit 29.3).

OTHER PERCENT LIBOR-INDEXED FLOATERS

The basic design of the 67% LIBOR-indexed floaters can be extended along several directions. In this chapter we would like to introduce the obvious one by replacing 67% with a generic parameter R. Such a more general

LIBOR-indexed floater is paying a coupon of the form $R \times$ 3ML + Fixed spread. Nonarbitrage equation for the issuer would be translated into a formula for the fixed spread:

Fixed spread = (AAA/LIBOR ratio – R) × LIBOR fixed + Credit spread

From the issuer's standpoint, all of the structures with different values of R can be swapped back to the same fixed coupon bond paying AAA + Credit spread, and thus should all be equivalent to each other. For investors, however, different choices of R are not equivalent. In particular, the sensitivity of the bond to interest rates varies as the value of R changes. At one extreme, when $R = 0$, the bond becomes a fixed-coupon bond. At another extreme, when R = Current AAA/LIBOR ratio, the bond is a fully floating-rate bond. The generalization does not end here, however. R does not have to be limited to the range from 0 to Current AAA/LIBOR ratio. If R > Current AAA/LIBOR ratio, the fixed spread would have to be negative, causing the bond to possibly have small negative durations. Also, if $R < 0$, the risk characteristics are not very different than a fixed coupon bond.

PERCENT BMA-INDEXED FLOATERS

The BMA-indexed floating rates bonds are another possibility. Such a bond pays a coupon of the form BMA 7-day index + Fixed spread, or even more generally a coupon of the form $R \times$ BMA 7-day index + Fixed spread, where the percentage parameter R is generally larger than 100%. Again, no arbitrage argument can be employed to derive a formula for the fixed spread:

Fixed spread = AAA – R × BMA fixed + Credit spread

In the case when R = 100%, the above equation reduces to

Fixed spread = Asset swap spread + Credit spread

The asset swap spread in the municipals market is defined as AAA rates less the same maturity BMA swap rates.

For investors, BMA-indexed floaters offer a good alternative to LIBOR-indexed ones. In particular, investors in *tender options bonds* (TOBs) do not need to worry about basis risks as in the case for LIBOR-indexed floaters, nor do they need to worry about the max-rate problem. Such advantages, of course, may sometimes be offset by narrower spreads in the offerings.

CMS AND BMS

All floaters we have discussed so far are based either on 3ML or BMA seven-day index. It is also possible to create floaters based on *constant maturity swap* (CMS) indexes.

A fixed floating CMS is a notional swap contract whose floating leg is based on a spot rate, typically 5 years or 10 years, on the LIBOR swap curve. Constant maturity swaps in the space of BMA swaps would be called *BMS*. A typical example is a $10 million notional 20-year CMS whose fixed leg is paying a semiannual par coupon of 6.19%, while its floating leg is paying a quarterly coupon based on 5-year LIBOR at the time of each reset. The current par coupon for the same maturity plain vanilla LIBOR swap is 5.85%, so there is a spread of 33 basis points (= 6.19% − 5.85%) between the CMS par coupon and the plain vanilla LIBOR swap coupon. The 33 basis point spread is called the CMS spread.

There are well-established valuation models for CMS in the literature such as the so-called SABR model by Hagan, Kumar, Lesniewski, and Woodward.[1] Calculators are also available on Bloomberg (SWPM <GO>). Risk characteristics of CMS and plain vanilla LIBOR swaps, although quite similar, can differ somewhat due to the shape of the LIBOR curve. For example, the CMS mentioned above has a dollar value of an 01 (DV01) of $12,165 per $10 million notional, while the 20-year vanilla LIBOR swap has a DV01 of $11,773 per $10 million notional.

PERCENT CMS-INDEXED STRUCTURES

In a further generalization of LIBOR-indexed floaters, the 3ML Index is replaced by a CMS index such as five-year LIBOR Index to create a percent CMS structure. Likewise, percent BMA-indexed floaters can be extended to percent BMS structures.

For example, an issuer can sell a bond maturing in 20 years, paying a monthly reset coupon of 67% × 5Y LIBOR + Fixed Spread where 5Y means five years. Fair value for the fixed spread can also be computed from the issuer's synthetic fixed trade (see Exhibit 29.4). The issuer selling a percent CMS structure generally swaps back to paying fixed by entering a CMS trade. For example, the issuer selling the 20-year (20Y) bond paying a monthly coupon of 67% × 5Y LIBOR + Fixed spread would enter 67% CMS with an investment bank. The net position for the issuer would be equivalent to a fixed coupon bond paying 67% × (20Y LIBOR + CMS spread) + Fixed spread.

---

[1] S. P. Hagan, D. Kumar, A. S. Lesniewski, and D.E. Woodward, "Managing Smile and Risk," *Wilmott Magazine* (2002), pp. 84–108.

EXHIBIT 29.4   Issuer Swap a 67% CMS to Paying Fixed

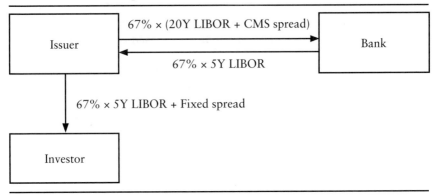

Again, since the issuer can sell fixed coupon bonds directly in the market, no arbitrage argument would force the following equality to hold:

$$67\% \times (20Y\ LIBOR + CMS\ spread) + Fixed\ spread$$
$$= 20Y\ AAA + Credit\ spread$$

Thus,

$$Fixed\ spread = (20Y\ AAA/LIBOR\ ratio - 67\%)$$
$$\times 20Y\ LIBOR - CMS\ spread + Credit\ spread$$

This formula reduces to the fair value formula for a LIBOR-indexed floater when CMS Spread = 0. Higher or lower percent CMS structures are also possible by replacing 67% by a generic parameter R to have a coupon of R × 5Y LIBOR + Fixed spread.

   In a parallel development, % BMS structures can be constructed. For example, percent BMS structures using 5Y BMA swap index would pays a floating rate coupon of the form R × 5Y BMA + Fixed spread. For a 20-year maturity such structure, the formula for the fixed spread is given by

$$Fixed\ spread = 20Y\ AAA - R \times (20Y\ BMA + BMS\ spread) + Credit\ spread$$

RISKS OF PERCENT CMS AND PERCENT BMS

A fair value 20-year percent CMS structure using 5Y LIBOR index has a coupon of

$$67\% \times 5Y \text{ LIBOR index} + (20Y \text{ AAA/LIBOR ratio} - 67\%)$$
$$\times 20Y \text{ LIBOR} - 67\% \text{ CMS spread} + \text{Credit spread}$$

From this equation, one can see that the bond's floating rate exposure is to the 5Y LIBOR index, not the 3M LIBOR. The bond has the same exposure to 20Y LIBOR and 20Y AAA/LIBOR ratio as a 20Y LIBOR-indexed floater. Additionally, the term −67% CMS spread expresses the fact that this structure is exposed positively to the CMS spread widening, which may result from a steepening of the LIBOR curve. As an example, suppose the 5- to 30-year part of the LIBOR curve shifts up by 50 basis points while the 0 to 4.99 sector remains unchanged. Then, the CMS spread would widen by 33 basis points using data on 7/16/2007. This will impact the bond price as follows: 67% × 33 basis points = 22 basis points. This translates into approximately a $2 gains per $100 notional bond.

As another example, suppose the 0- to 5-year sector realizes parallel shift up by 50 basis points while the rest of the curve remains unchanged. In this case, based on data on 7/16/2007 the CMS spread would narrow about 14 basis points which would translate into approximately a $0.85 decline in the bond price per $100 notional.

SUMMARY

Indexed bonds are new to municipal investors. In this chapter, their structures and risk characteristics are described.

Early buyers of LIBOR-indexed floaters included short-intermediate range mutual funds and TOB investors as well as private banks. The buyer's base has expanded significantly since the first deal as the risk/return profiles of the products became more widely understood. Secondary market liquidity and price action should also be more in line with what theory predicts when ratio risks in such products are well understood. However, such risks should not be overly emphasized as ratios are generally much more stable than a decline in interest rates themselves. Moreover, some of the outstanding tax problems normally associated with fixed coupon bonds such as the de minimis rule are less of an issue for these bonds.

CHAPTER 30

Municipal Inverse Floating Rate Securities

Cadmus Hicks, CFA, Ph.D.
Managing Director
Nuveen Investments

Municipal inverse floating rate securities are vehicles are used by institutional investors to increase, through the use of leverage, the tax-exempt income earned on municipal bonds. This chapter describes how inverse floating rate securities are structured and how their market value, duration, coupon, and yield are calculated.

DESCRIPTION

Municipal inverse floating rate securities (*inverse floaters*) are securities that pay a tax-exempt rate of interest that moves inversely with changes in short-term tax-exempt rates. Municipal inverse floating rate securities are created by a sponsor, which establishes a trust into which it deposits tax-exempt bonds. The trust then issues two classes of securities:

- *Floating rate securities* (FRS), which pay money market rates and which can be periodically tendered for redemption at par at the option of the holder (typically every week).
- Inverse floating rate securities that pay to the holder all income from the trust not needed to pay interest on the floating rate securities and expenses of the trust.

The interest rate on the FRS is set by an auction conducted by the remarketing agent. The remarketing agent is usually also responsible for providing liquidity for the FRS by promising to purchase any such securities that are not successfully remarketed.

The market value of the inverse floaters is equal to the market value of the underlying bonds less the par value of the floating rate securities. Because they receive all income not needed to pay interest on the FRS and expenses of the trust, inverse floaters are sometimes referred to as *residuals*. By paying the purchase price of the FRS and instructing the trustee to redeem all outstanding FRS through a mandatory tender event, the holders of inverse floaters have the right to collapse the trust. They can then take possession of the underlying bonds or instruct the trustee to sell the bonds and deliver the proceeds to them.

In addition to the interest paid to the holders of the FRS, the trust has two types of expenses: the fees paid to the trustee and fees paid to the agent for remarketing and providing liquidity for the FRS. The remarketing and liquidity fees are based on the amount of FRS outstanding, while the trustee fees (of about 0.015%) are based on the par value of the entire trust, not just the FRS. Altogether, these fees typically total to about 0.20% to 0.25% of the par value of the FRS.

TAX TREATMENT

The U.S. Tax Code effectively prohibits investors from borrowing for the purpose of investing in securities that pay interest that is exempt from federal income taxes. It does this by disallowing the deduction that one would otherwise take for the interest expense associated with such borrowings. Municipal inverse floaters allow investors to benefit from the leverage through the capital structure of the trusts without engaging in the sort of borrowing that would trigger the loss of the deduction of interest expense.

In order for the trust to make payments to both the holder of the FRS and the holder of the inverse floaters that are exempt from taxation, the holder of the FRS must be deemed to be an owner of securities issued by the trust rather than a lender of funds to the trust. For this reason, the holder of the FRS must share in the risks and benefits of ownership. With respect to risks, the FRS holder loses the right to tender securities if there is an event of default by the issuer of the underlying bonds held in the trust. With respect to the benefits of ownership, the FRS holder shares in any capital gain realized upon the sale of bonds from the trust. Typically, legal opinions regarding the tax-exemption of payments from the trusts stipulate that 5% to 10% of the gains be distributed to the FRS holders. (The distributed gain may be further reduced by the percentage of par value attributable to the holders of the inverse floaters.)

Another requirement under tax law is that the amount of interest paid on FRS may not exceed the amount of tax-exempt interest earned on the underlying bonds.

COMPUTATIONS

When working with inverse floaters, it is necessary to compute values for price, effective coupon rate, and duration that reflect the effect of the leverage inherent in the trust's structure. The following examples assume that a trust is created using a bond with a 6% coupon, priced on 8/1/2006 at $112 to yield 3.75% to an 8/1/2012 call date at par.

Price

Assume that the bonds in a trust have a total par value of $9,000,000, and that the trust has issued $6,000,000 of floating rate securities. The par value attributable to the inverse floaters would then be $3,000,000, and the leverage would be two times. Given a dollar price of $112 and a par value of $9,000,000, the market value of the trust would be $10,080,000 (1.12 × $9,000,000 = $10,080,000). The value of the inverse floaters would be equal to the market value of the trust ($10,080,000) less the par value of the FRS ($6,000,000). In our illustration it is a $4,080,000.

Dividing the market value of the inverse floaters by their par value of $3,000,000, produces a dollar price of $136 ($4,080,000/$3,000,000 = 136%)

Thus, the formula for computing the price of an inverse floater is

$$InvPx = (LinkedPx \times (1 + Lev)) - (Lev \times 100)$$

where

LinkedPx = Price of underlying bond
Lev = Ratio of par value of FRS to par value of inverse floaters
InvPx = Price of inverse floater

Assuming that the underlying bonds have a dollar price of $112 and the leverage factor is 2 times, the price of the inverse floater would be

$$InvPx = (112 \times 3) - 200 = 136$$

Duration

We saw earlier that a dollar price of $112 implies that the value of the bonds in the trust would be $10,080,000, and the market value of the inverse floaters would be $4,080,000. If the market value of the underlying bonds rose by 1%, the dollar value would increase by approximately $100,800. The full amount of that increase in value would be to the benefit of the holders of the inverse floaters. An increase of $100,800 represents an increase in the value of the inverse floaters of 2.47% ($100,800/$4,080,000 = 2.47%). Thus, a 1% increase in the value of the underlying bonds causes a 2.47% increase in the value of the inverse floaters. In other words, the inverse floaters are 2.47 times as volatile as the underlying bonds. Since duration is the standard measure of volatility, this same factor can be applied to the duration of the underlying bonds to compute the duration of the inverse floater. The formula for this adjustment is as follows:

$$InvDur = \left(1 + \frac{Lev \times 100}{InvPx}\right) \times LinkedDur$$

where

LinkedDur = Duration of underlying bond

InvDur = Duration of inverse floater

The bond that we have been considering would have a duration of 5.1 years. Substituting that value in the equation produces the following:

$$InvDur = \left(1 + \frac{2 \times 100}{136}\right) \times 5.1 = 12.6$$

Exhibiti 30.1 illustrates that the price volatility of the inverse floater is 2.47 times as great as that of the underlying bond.

Coupon

If the underlying bond has a coupon of 6%, expenses equal 0.25% of the par of the FRS, and the floating rate is 3.00%, the income available to the holders of the inverse floaters would be as follows:

Income of trust	$9,000,000 × 0.06 =	$540,000
– Expenses	$6,000,000 × 0.0025 =	(15,000)
– Interest cost	$6,000,000 × 0.03 =	(180,000)
		$345,000

EXHIBIT 30.1   Price Changes of Bond and Inverse Floater

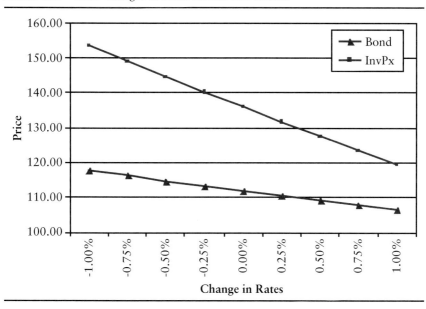

Since the coupon rate of a security is expressed as a percentage of par value, and since the par value of the inverse floaters is $3,000,000, the residual income of $345,000 received from the trust implies an effective coupon rate on the inverse floaters of 11.5% ($345,000/$3,000,000 = 0.115 or 11.5%)

This can be expressed as a formula as well:

Effective coupon = (LinkedCoup × (1 + Lev)) – (Exp × Lev) – (FR × Lev)

where

LinkedCoup = Coupon of the underlying bond
Exp   = Expenses of the trust as percent of the par value of the FRS
FR   = Interest rate paid to holders of FRS

Effective coupon = (6% × (1 + 2)) – (0.25% × 2) – (3.00% × 2) = 11.50%

Given leverage of two times, the change in the value of the effective coupon of the inverse floater will be twice the change in the yield on the FRS, but with an opposite +/– sign.

Yield

While the coupon rate is useful as a measure of the cash flow generated by an inverse floater, it fails to give effect to the amortization of the premium or discount of the underlying bond that will occur as the bond approaches its expected retirement date. To remedy this deficiency and to compare inverse floaters with fixed rate bonds, investors can calculate a measure of the yield of the inverse floater, which is computed in a manner similar to the way yield is calculated on a fixed rate bond, but which assumes that the current floating rate will remain constant over the remaining life of the inverse floater. In our example, a bond with a coupon of 11.5%, a price of $136 and an expected redemption on 8/1/2012 would have a yield of 4.57%, which would be treated as the yield of an inverse floater with those same characteristics. This compares to a yield on the underlying bond of 3.75%.

The following table summarizes the values for the underlying bond and the inverse floater.

	Price	Duration	Coupon	Yield
Underlying bond	$115	5.1	6.00%	3.75%
Inverse floater	$136	12.6	11.50%	4.57%

When computing the yield, one should use the date to which the underlying bond has been priced, not the termination date of the trust, which is typically scheduled to occur before the first optional redemption date.

ACCOUNTING TREATMENT

In December 2006, several major accounting firms changed their interpretation of the rules governing how inverse floaters are treated by mutual funds. Previously, the funds would simply record the market value of the inverse floater as an asset and the interest earned on the inverse floater as income. Under the new interpretation, which applies Statement of Financial Accounting Standards #140 to inverse floaters, if a mutual fund sold the underlying bond to the inverse floater trust, the fund must include the full value of the underlying bonds as an asset of the fund and the par value of the FRS as a liability, and the fund must recognize the full interest earned on the underlying bonds as income and show as expenses of the fund the fees and expenses of the trust and the interest paid to the holders of the FRS. If the mutual fund never owned the underlying bond prior to its deposit into the trust, the fund will follow the former rules and will record as an asset only its residual interest in the trust and will recognize as income only the interest earned on the inverse floater. While this change does not affect the net income reported to shareholders or the net asset value of the fund, it does change the expense ratio.

TENDER OPTION BONDS

In a sense, every inverse floater is a *tender option bond* (TOB) since the holders of the FRS have the option of tendering their securities at par. In general usage, however, participants in the financial services industry generally use *inverse floating rate security* to refer to securities which have leverage of one or two times the par value of the FRS, and use the TOB when referring to securities with significantly greater leverage. When a high level of leverage is employed, the investor will usually enter into a swap to pay fixed and receive floating in order to protect against the heightened price volatility of the TOB. The swap may use a taxable instrument like LIBOR or BMA (an index provided by the Securities Industry and Financial Markets Association, which was formerly known as the Bond Market Association). In the case of LIBOR-based swaps the amount of the hedge needs to be adjusted for the fact that interest rates in taxable markets have historically been more volatile than interest rates on comparable maturities in tax-exempt markets.

SUMMARY

Oscar Wilde spoke of people who know "the price of everything but the value of nothing." A similar distinction exists with reference to inverse floaters. While an increase in the rate paid on the FRS (and a corresponding decrease in the interest rate paid on the inverse floater) might make the inverse floater less valuable to the investor holding it, such a change would not affect the market price of the inverse floater. When the floating rate increases, what becomes less valuable is not the underlying bond, but the utility of employing the trust structure. As long as the price of the underlying bond is unchanged, the price of the inverse floater will be unchanged.

The key to understanding inverse floaters is to remember that the holder of an inverse floater (1) receives all income not needed for paying interest on the FRS and expenses of the trust and (2) bears the full effect of changes in the value of the underlying bond. Thus, if you know the price of the underlying bond and the leverage of the trust, you can compute the price of the inverse floater. And if you know the leverage, you can determine the extent to which the volatility of the price of the inverse floater will exceed the volatility of the price of the underlying bond. Managing that added volatility requires skill and discipline on the part of the portfolio manager.

CHAPTER 31

Analyzing Portfolios Daily

Paul R. Daniels, CFA
Executive Committee Chairman
Investortools, Inc.

As a professional portfolio manager of municipal bonds, it is likely that you represent a financial institution that manages its own assets, or the holdings of a group of publicly available funds or individual investor accounts. You may be responsible for investment decisions at a casualty insurance company, a bank trust department or a specialized money management firm. You could be an employee of a family office or of a very high net worth individual. You may manage a single portfolio—or several.

You probably work with one or more general managers, staff-function colleagues and possibly members of a Board of Directors/Trustees of publicly held funds. Each of your portfolios has investment objectives and restrictions, informal or formal. In the long run, your job performance is connected to your ability to generate acceptable total returns. You expect those returns to be compared with returns of similar portfolios, whether or not you like being graded on a curve. If managing public fund portfolios, you experience performance pressure of peer-group total return comparisons calculated by Lipper and Morningstar. For other portfolios, you deal with the more subtle performance pressure of "risk-adjusted" benchmark comparisons. Even if your mandate is to maximize income, total return almost certainly will be a factor in your long-term success, because of the ultimate importance of principal preservation.

Depending on your organization's style of dividing portfolio management duties, you may operate as a trader, executing transactions directly, in addition to making transaction decisions. You may be your own credit analyst. Alternatively, you may have associates to whom you delegate trading and credit research. The concepts presented in this chapter will apply under any style of dividing duties of asset allocation, trading, research, and managing holdings.

Each asset holding for which you are responsible has income potential and market volatility. There may be constraints on possible transactions because of gain/loss intolerance or transaction turnover restrictions. Subject to such constraints, each day you view every holding as a continual sale candidate. You sell any holding when its proceeds can be reinvested more productively, taking market risks into account. You realize that market risks include the possibility of poor total return performance, reinvestment, issuer redemption, and credit deterioration.

A FOUR-LEVEL FRAMEWORK FOR PORTFOLIO ASSETS

The framework described in this chapter offers four levels or categories for thinking about your municipal bond securities. All securities in a portfolio, and across portfolios, can be assessed at each of the following four levels:

1. *Credits.* A municipal credit is a group of closely related state or local government debt obligations. Each credit is defined by security characteristics of those obligations. For example, if a city has outstanding general obligation bonds, water and sewer revenue bonds, and electric power revenue bonds, that city would have three municipal credits.
2. *Issues.* A credit may have many outstanding issues.
3. *Holdings or CUSIPs.* Each holding is a particular serial or term security, to which a CUSIP number is assigned.
4. *Transactions or tickets.* Tickets express details of buy or sale transactions. The currently held (unsold) portion of any purchase transaction is its tax lot, used in tax accounting.

For an example of the four levels, a portfolio might contain a total of $5,000,000 par Intermountain Power Agency, Utah, Power Supply Revenue Bonds (the credit) from four bond issues, with one or more holdings or CUSIPs of each of those issues. Each CUSIP represents one or several tax lots, each of which provides accounting tracking of the unsold amount of each relevant purchase transaction.

In daily portfolio analysis, the credit and holdings levels deserve primary attention. For example, credit-level reviews will be primarily by sector, via spreadsheets or a specialized credit analysis system. Within a sector, peer group comparisons may include credit rankings, statistical comparisons to medians, distributions of credit indicators and trend analyses. At the holdings level, analysis includes various risk factors including durations, ratings and sectors. Holdings-level calculations can include historical total return analytics, portfolio-index return comparisons, and forward-looking market and/or transactions simulations. Ideally, your credit analysis and portfolio management software systems are integrated so that, for any asset, you can move easily among data representing any of the four levels. In considering the sale of all or part of a CUSIP, an integrated system will allow you to reach up to the credit level to find financial statement data, ratings history, research reports, and the like. With such a system, you can reach down to the tax lot category to calculate effects of tax loss constraints. An integrated credit and portfolio system easily facilitates reporting of which portfolios hold specific credits—useful when there is serious impairment of credits as well as during routine credit surveillance.

CREDIT-LEVEL ANALYSIS

Unless your municipal bond positions are so high grade that there is almost no risk of default or serious credit deterioration, your organization's credit surveillance of existing holdings is a major element of protecting investment values. A well-executed program of monitoring creditworthiness can give timely warnings and reduce losses by prompting early sales of deteriorating positions, preferably well before they are downgraded by rating agencies. Whether credit surveillance is part of your vocation or the responsibility of research specialists, your firm has the difficult task of determining the optimum amount of credit surveillance. Evidently some municipal bond participants have translated the proven creditworthiness of investment-grade (BBB or Baa or higher rating category) bonds into an assumption that these bonds' credit risks will continue to be negligible. With casualness toward credit, their primary portfolio management focus is on bond market (interest rate) risks, as calculated by duration measures and option-adjustment models. Using an analogy from modern portfolio theory, this is something like an equity investor focusing mostly on stock market (systematic) risks and largely ignoring alpha or nonmarket (unsystematic) risks. For any unaware of the perhaps irrelevant 1930s credit experience of municipal bonds, this quotation by a World Bank writer at least provokes reflection:

> Yet absolute default probabilities may not be inferred from the credit rating categories as default occurrences xaaa%, xaa% and xa% are period dependent (with higher concentration of defaults in periods of economic depression). For instance, analyses of corporate debt defaults during the US Great Depression show that, of all corporate issuers rated (by Moody's) as of July 1932, almost one in ten defaulted within one year. Of the US municipal debt issues that

were rated in 1929 and went into default in 1932, 78% had been rated AA or better, and 48% had been rated AAA.[1]

In comparison to "maybe 5,000 to 7,000 stocks that trade on the nation's major markets . . . , there are more than 1 million different municipal bonds issued by more than 50,000 state and local governments."[2] There is no official tracking of numbers of United States municipal credits. Since many states and local government entities have more than one credit outstanding, the total of United States municipal securities credits may be 100,000 or more. Most of these are not regularly followed by any analysts, which largely explains why the municipal bond market is the least efficient of the country's major securities markets. That inefficiency gives opportunity for short-term trading benefits not available in U.S. government, agency, and corporate bond markets. Knowledgeable municipal bond professionals can take advantage of short-term supply/demand imbalances. They can apply publicly available, but unassimilated, information about specific bond holdings. To analyze proposed new positions or to do surveillance on current holdings, you organize financial and other relevant information credit-by-credit, probably grouped by sector, such as general obligation, airport revenue or water/sewer revenue.

Since your review of credits goes beyond considering current ratings, you assess individual credits, especially proposed new exposures, through a gauntlet of standard or customized peer group analysis reports similar to Exhibit 31.1. This example sorts private colleges and universities alphabetically within states. The Exhibit 31.1 report could have been sorted by the last column's Merritt Scores, which are produced by a multivariate-ranking model designed to compare statistics across credit exposures of the same type. With a database of recent financial information (balance sheets, income statements, cash flows reports and derived ratios, and trend statistics), you or your firm can develop similar, proprietary ranking models. By developing multiple such models, results can be compared across models and against ratings in order to validate hypotheses of how best to gauge creditworthiness.

Your organization's credit analysis may compare a credit's key statistics to benchmark tables showing medians for same-sector credits. Benchmark comparisons can be more precise by using medians of rating groups, and for some sectors, other medians (e.g., of urban, suburban and rural hospitals or of small, medium and large hub airports).

---

[1] Samir El Daher, "Credit Ratings—An Introduction (and the Case of Sub-Sovereign Ratings)," *Infrastructure Notes (Transport, Water and Urban Development, Urban No. FM-8c)*, The World Bank (July 1999).

[2] Kathleen Pender, "Pricey Municipal Bonds," *San Francisco Chronicle*, February 12, 2004.

EXHIBIT 31.1   Private Higher Education Peer Group Analysis

Credit Name	City	S&P	Moody	FY Used	Total Unrst Resources	Cur DS Coverage	Profit Margin %	Tuition Revenue %	Unrst Resrc to Debt %	Selectivity Ratio %	Merritt Score
Colorado											
Colorado College	Colorado Springs	AA-	Aa3	2006	380,703	4.81	10.9	37.6	6.8	37.5	78.03
Regis University	Denver	BBB	CE	2006	45,000	4.10	7.4	70.4	1.1	78.1	72.08
University of Denver	Denver	A	A1	2006	205,121	5.50	8.7	61.1	1.3	81.8	92.25
Connecticut											
Connecticut College	New London	CE	A2	2006	61,100	5.66	15.5	53.7	1.3	35.3	21.13
Fairfield University	Fairfield	A-	A3	2006	156,741	9.57	33.1	63.8	0.9		50.21
Loomis Institute	Windsor	CE	A2	2006	100,354	9.88	26.1	39.3	1.9	45.2	72.29
Quinnipiac University & Affiliate	Hamden	A-	A2	2005	188,909	9.43	25.5	66.1	1.6	55.0	76.11
Sacred Heart University Inc	Fairfield	BBB	Baa3	2005	43,369	1.56	7.1	64.5	0.4		44.27
St Joseph College	West Hartford	CE		2006	3,387	3.91	-0.8	51.3	0.3	71.8	14.54
Trinity College	Hartford	A+	A1	2006	170,725	3.44	-6.1	45.5	1.3	39.4	59.98
University of Hartford	West Hartford	BBB-	Baa3	2005	23,161	2.45	4.0	56.6	0.2	60.1	8.81
University of New Haven	West Haven	CE	CE	2006	3,028	3.69	2.4	71.3	0.1		1.17
Wesleyan University	Middletown	AA	Aa3	2006	482,508	8.92	27.8	31.1	2.4	27.6	68.26
Yale University	New Haven	AAA	Aaa	2006	9,255,335	5.88	44.3	8.3	4.7	9.7	98.83
District of Columbia											
American University	Washington	A	A2	2006	367,886	9.31	22.1	58.9	1.7	51.3	41.51
Catholic University of America &	Washington	A	A2	2006	108,178	4.61	6.9	52.2	1.1	81.3	66.99
George Washington University	Washington	A	A2	2006	915,849	3.57	15.8	46.1	1.3	37.0	93.52
Georgetown University	Washington	BBB+	A3	2006	72,015	2.22	4.9	46.9	0.1		27.07
Howard University	Washington	A+	A2	2005	345,686	2.88	2.7	13.5	2.0	46.9	69.75
Florida											
Barry University & Sub	Miami	BBB-		2005	6,241	0.16	-2.5	76.8	0.1	72.5	11.36
Eckerd College Inc & Affiliates	Saint Petersburg	CE		2005	-17,868	3.79	3.9	41.8	-0.6	74.3	18.37

Source: CreditScope Municipal Edition with Merritt Data.

Graph-based techniques of credit analysis, and of portfolio management generally, are particularly efficient. Scatter graphs make outliers obvious, bar graphs intuitively display distribution profiles, and line graphs are well suited for revealing trends. Analysis is further focused if each scatter graph's data point can be identified as a specific credit and each bar of a bar graph can reveal its constituent credits. The following are recommended sector-specific distribution graphs for credit-level analysis of revenue bonds: Various debt service coverage ratios, profit margins, ratings and rating upgrades versus no rating change versus rating downgrades. For selected revenue bond sectors, similar distribution graphs can cover ratios of debt to enplanements for airports, debt to full-time equivalent students for colleges and universities, days cash on hand for hospitals and cash flow to debt. Revenue bond sector-specific line graphs can be developed for displaying historical trends of coverage, leverage, profitability, and working capital ratios.

BASIC HOLDING-LEVEL ANALYSIS

Successful portfolio management is a process of continuously rotating holdings (i.e., reducing or eliminating positions that are expected to underperform) and increasing positions expected to produce superior returns. In the process, you will continuously evaluate expectations for each of your holdings. You may think of yourself as a steward of each dollar of assets, including accrued interest. If an asset's expected contribution to portfolio total return is below average, for its relative characteristics, you usually will consider it to be a sale candidate. You may also think of yourself as a de facto securities dealer and your portfolio assets as inventory. With that kind of trading mindset, you think about portfolio composition by maturity, priced-to-date, duration (modified), effective (option adjusted) duration, rating, insurer, coupon, sector, state and issuer. Distribution or profile graphs by these criteria allow you to visualize relevant asset components and then to drill down to listings of each component's holdings. Exhibit 31.2 is an example of a sector distribution graph for a group of portfolios.

As compositions of your portfolio(s) change, you will continually analyze their current totals and averages (Exhibit 31.3), using these statistics as the framework for thinking about yield potential, appreciation potential, volatility risks, and so on. It also may be instructive periodically to review corresponding historical totals and averages. Your objective is to look for ways to improve overall risk/reward relationships.

The inclusion in Exhibit 31.3 of three option-adjusted statistics and three duration statistics prompts the following comments: First, since effective (option-adjusted) duration, option adjusted yield, and option-adjusted spread are determined by mathematical models, you will want to be familiar with whatever model you are using. Be convinced that the model's variables,

EXHIBIT 31.2   Sector Profile

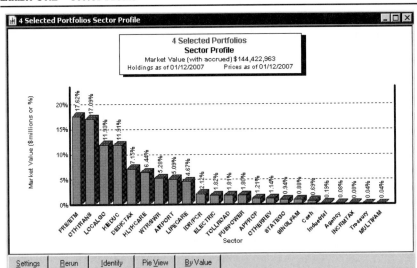

Source: Perform Portfolio Management System.

EXHIBIT 31.3 Totals and Averages

		Priced Securities	All Securities
Total cash	$	1,000,000.00	1,000,000.00
Total par—including cash	$	135,321,000.00	135,321,000.00
Total market value—no accrued interest	$	140,646,574.91	140,646,574.91
Total market value—plus accrued interest	$	142,418,512.42	142,418,512.42
Total annualized coupon income	$	7,400,971.25	7,400,971.25
Annual amotizations (–)	$	–820,848.40	–820,848.40
Annual accretions	$	267,775.29	267,775.29
Net annualized income	$	6,847,898.14	6,847,898.14
Portfolio income[a]		4.87	4.87
Average current return[a]		5.26	5.26
Average market yield[b]		4.231	4.231
Average option adjusted yield[b]		4.076	4.076
Average option adjusted spread[b]		0.186	0.186
Average maturity[b]		08/08/2022	08/06/2022
		(15.55 years)	(15.55 years)
Average priced-to-date[b]		07/02/2011	07/02/2011
		(4.45 years)	(4.45 years)
Average duration—Macaulay[b]		3.760	3.760
Average duration—Modified[b]		3.678	3.678
Average duration—Effective (UA)[b]		4.812	4.812
Average convexity[b]		–0.586	–0.586
Average coupon[c]		5.469	5.469
Average market price[c]		103.936	103.936
Average acquisition yield[c]		4.935	4.935
Average book yield[c]		4.999	4.999
Average book price[c]		99.430	99.430
Gain or loss	$	6,097,381.82	6,097,381.82
Modified duration standard deviation		2.527	2.527
Effective duration standard deviation		3.333	3.333
Futures and swaps market value	$	0.00	0.00
Futures and swaps modified duration impact		0.000	0.000

[a] Based on market value (without accrued interest).
[b] Weighted by total market plus accrued interest).
[c] Weighted by par
Source: Perform Portfolio Management System.

especially its volatility assumptions, are set to be consistent with your market view. Second, there is a common perception that effective (option-adjusted) duration is more sophisticated and therefore a generally more useful analytic tool than modified duration. In this writer's opinion, that perception is an oversimplification. The mathematical model calculating the three option-adjusted statistics in Exhibit 31.3 certainly is more complex than the basic modified duration formula. That probabilistic option-adjustment model uses multiple future interest rate scenarios. However, the simpler modified duration sometimes is more useful than effective (option-adjusted) duration as a volatility proxy for a single callable bond. This is especially the case with short-term and small municipal market moves. The reverse is true where a small market shift could change a callable bond's priced-to-date, a situation that most portfolio managers would intuitively recognize as they review reports of their bonds' coupons, yields, prices, and call features. As a volatility proxy, effective (option- adjusted) duration is of great value with groups of callable bonds (i.e., at the portfolio level). It also is valuable in comparing bonds with dissimilar call features.

With changing market prices, it will be profitable to identify outliers on yield scatter graphs, thinking through the possibilities that these outliers represent threats or opportunities. In order to make it easier to compare callable bonds, similar scatter graphs can be created for option-adjusted spread (Exhibit 31.4) and option-adjusted yield. In all of these cases, you will need to decide the criteria against which you want these yields or spreads to be plotted. They are typically by maturity or by duration, but they could be by priced-to-date, effective (option-adjusted) duration or market value.

Convexity is a crucial risk characteristic of callable bonds, and scatter graphs of convexity are useful. However, that measure is based on a summation of price appreciation and depreciation from hypothetical and symmetrical market movements. Therefore, convexity does not indicate the amount of upside market price potential in terms of downside risk. There is another measure which more directly reflects relative price appreciation/depreciation. That is the ratio of a bull market move to a bear market move. A bull/bear ratio of 1.0 signifies equal size market price moves up and down. Therefore, a bull/bear ratio scatter graph displays data points above and below 1.0. A convexity graph will have its roughly corresponding data points above and below 0.0. Portfolio managers typically create convexity and bull/bear ratio scatter graphs using 100 basis points for the hypothetical market movements up and down. You could use a smaller shift in order to reflect a less volatile market assumption. Because these measures require assumptions about the size of market moves, they cannot be precise predictors.

EXHIBIT 31.4   Option-Adjusted Spread

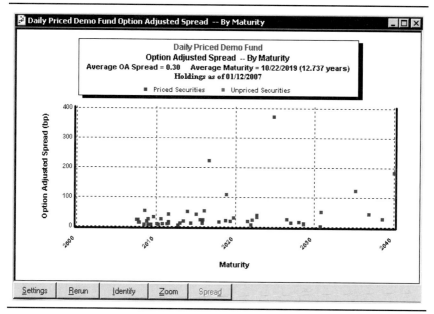

Source: Perform Portfolio Management System.

As you evaluate current holdings as sale candidates, market price volatility of individual bonds can be roughly estimated through duration or effective (option-adjusted) duration. However, volatility of specific bonds does not need to be estimated. It can be calculated exactly and displayed visually in a price curve graph such as Exhibit 31.5. This displays percent price changes caused by upward and downward yield changes, in basis points, for a single bond. In Exhibit 31.5, the Arizona Health Facilities Authority 4.75% bond matures on 10/01/2030 and is priced at 101.35, yielding 4.35. It is priced to the 10/01/2010 to-worst par call, even though it is callable at a premium before that date. It would not take a large bear market move for this long bond to be valued at a discount. Exhibit 31.5 dramatically shows the bond's limited upside potential, because it is priced to a short call, versus its much greater downside risk if it becomes priced to maturity. For comparison, price curves for a small group of bonds can be plotted together. A similar duration curve graph can show percent duration changes associated with yield changes in both directions. These curve graphs can be prepared for any holdings reflected in a portfolio system.

Analyses like those above, as well as the more specialized approaches discussed in the next sections of this chapter, are only some of your most

EXHIBIT 31.5   Perform Price Curve

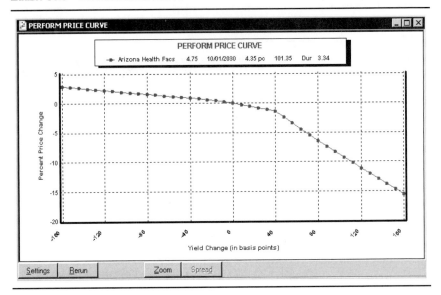

Source: Perform Portfolio Management System.

common analytic endeavors as a municipal bond portfolio manager. You will have occasions to scan your portfolio(s) by CUSIP, maturity, duration, sector, state, subsets and ad hoc criteria. You may study graphs of benchmark yield curves, graphs of spreads to yield curves, various trading reports, cash flow reports and de minimis threshold yield and price reports. Many of these will be standard output of portfolio systems, but some of your portfolio research may be based on your own proprietary ideas translated into custom reports and graphs.

TOTAL RETURN PERFORMANCE

If your portfolios are evaluated (priced) each business day, based on reliable descriptive data, you will be able to calculate total returns for portfolios, portfolio components and individual securities, for any historical period. Less frequent pricing will reduce your historical period options, because accurate performance measurement calculations require market prices at the beginning and at the end of the measurement period. As you plan a framework for performance calculations, an early question will be, "What is the scope of the return analysis? Is it entire portfolio(s) or subsets of portfolios?" Return calculations can be limited to subsets of virtually any bond characteristic, such as bonds of certain rating ranges, callable or noncallable bonds, insured or uninsured bonds, and zero-coupon securities.

Historical total return performance can be analyzed at three levels: portfolio(s), components, and individual securities. Components and their ranges might include years to maturity, years to priced-to-year, (modified) duration, effective (option-adjusted) duration, highest rating, lowest rating, coupon, sector, state and insurer. Components allow comparison, for example, of the performance of a group of bonds with high duration to a group with low duration.

Further framework decisions relate to return methodology frequencies. First, if subperiod returns are to be considered, what will be their compounding frequency? For example, if there is to be reporting of monthly returns within a semiannual performance report, the specified compounding frequency might be monthly. In that case, the six monthly total returns would be geometrically linked to determine the semiannual performance totals. More frequent compounding produces returns that are more isolated from external cash flows; these returns better reflect the value of the portfolio management function, assuming that portfolio management does not cause external cash flows. Daily compounding completely excludes effects of those cash flows.

A similar framework decision is needed to prepare for calculating performance of components: "What will be the regrouping frequency?" In some situations, such as changes in a bond's rating or duration, a bond would properly belong in one component at the beginning of the period and another component at the end of the period. Regrouping frequency determines how often each bond's component classification is determined. Note that regrouping should not be more frequent than compounding. Otherwise, a bond could be assigned to mutually exclusive return components during a single compounding period.

Portfolio performance can be measured against a published index of municipal bonds. Lehman Brothers and Standard and Poor's/Investortools provide detailed municipal bond index reporting. Many index statistics are published, some are customized by a provider, and some are customized by users through specialized software with access to index bonds. Using either published or customized indexes, portfolio and index returns can be compared, as can their percentage weights, yields, and durations. By comparing portfolio returns with corresponding data for indexes, you can determine sources of portfolio outperformance or underperformance.

Return reports may selectively show total return and its two basic elements, market and yield return or, alternatively, coupon and price return. Yield return is the expected return if yield remains constant, whereas market return is the return caused by a change in market yield. Some return reports may include return contributions in basis points, as in Exhibit 31.6.

EXHIBIT 31.6   Total Return by Security

Total Return by Security - By CUSIP (Stacked) - 09/29/2006 through 12/29/2006 - Daily Priced Demo Fund

CUSIP	Par ($000)	Desc	St	Beg Coupon	Beg Mty	S&P Moody	Beginning Ending	Mkt Price	Chg	Yield	BP Chg	Contrib (BP)	Total Return	Yield TR Ann Yld TR	Mkt Return
DEMOFUND - Daily Priced Demo Fund															
013544FA4	1,750	Albuquerque N M	NM	10.125	08/01/2008	AAA	09/29/2006	109.81		4.50				1.13%	-0.20%
						Aaa	12/29/2006	108.32	(1.49)	4.63	13	1.3	0.93%	4.54%	
01752ABK0	1,750	Allen Cnty Ind R	IN	0.000	05/15/2008	NR	09/29/2006	67.00		3.81				0.95%	-0.09%
						NR	12/29/2006	67.57	0.58	3.87	6	0.7	0.86%	3.82%	
040506OX9	1,500	Arizona Health F	AZ	4.750	10/01/2030	AAA	09/29/2006	101.35		4.38				1.08%	0.21%
						Aaa	12/29/2006	101.47	0.12	4.32	(6)	1.4	1.29%	4.31%	
110227CC7	500	Bristol Tenn Hea	TN	6.750	09/01/2010	AAA	09/29/2006	108.64		4.33				1.10%	-0.56%
						Aaa	12/29/2006	107.54	(1.10)	4.50	17	0.2	0.54%	4.40%	
119674YH6	1,380	Buffalo N Y	NY	5.200	02/01/2010	AAA	09/29/2006	102.56		3.43				0.86%	-0.03%
						Aaa	12/29/2006	102.13	(0.43)	3.62	19	0.8	0.84%	3.47%	
127109EQ5	750	Cabrillo Calif Cmu	CA	0.000	08/01/2011	AAA	09/29/2006	83.63		3.73				0.93%	-0.05%
						Aaa	12/29/2006	84.36	0.74	3.74	1	0.4	0.88%	3.73%	
13068HFJ8	2,500	California St Pub	CA	5.400	10/01/2022	A-	09/29/2006	103.13		4.16				1.03%	-0.03%
						A2	12/29/2006	102.82	(0.31)	4.20	4	1.8	1.01%	4.15%	
155048BB6	10,000	Central Puget Sou	WA	4.750	02/01/2028	AAA	09/29/2006	101.07		4.40				1.08%	0.21%
						Aaa	12/29/2006	101.20	0.13	4.33	(7)	9.2	1.29%	4.33%	
167592NZ3	1,425	Chicago Ill O Har	IL	5.500	01/01/2016	AAA	09/29/2006	102.36		3.96				0.98%	0.11%
						Aaa	12/29/2006	102.12	(0.24)	4.05	9	1.1	1.09%	3.94%	
196473V90	3,000	Colorado Health	CO	6.250	05/15/2011	AAA	12/06/2006	110.97		3.56				0.22%	-0.43%
						Aaa	12/29/2006	110.34	(0.62)	3.67	11	-0.5	-0.20%	3.56%	
21969NAS3	7,000	Corona Calif Pub	CA	4.750	09/01/2028	AAA	09/29/2006	101.35		4.37				1.07%	0.35%
						Aaa	12/29/2006	101.61	0.26	4.27	(10)	7.1	1.42%	4.30%	
233433Z87	1,200	Dade Cnty Fla	FL	5.125	10/01/2016	AAA	09/29/2006	102.11		3.76				0.92%	0.33%
						Aaa	12/29/2006	102.11	0.00	3.58	(18)	1.1	1.25%	3.68%	
233455F90	1,845	Dade Cnty Fla A·	FL	5.125	10/01/2022	AAA	09/29/2006	102.24		4.30				1.06%	0.02%
						Aaa	12/29/2006	102.07	(0.17)	4.28	(2)	1.5	1.08%	4.26%	
249481BQ4	3,000	Denver West Me	CO	6.500	12/01/2006	NR	09/29/2006	101.48		3.60				0.62%	0.00%
						NR	12/01/2006	101.00	(0.48)	6.50	290	1.4	0.62%	3.59%	
25457VBE5	1,570	Director St Nev L	NV	7.375	01/01/2040	NR	09/29/2006	104.46		6.36				1.60%	2.21%
						NR	12/29/2006	106.67	2.21	5.56	(81)	4.5	3.81%	6.42%	
25476ABU2	1,000	District Columbia	DC	6.000	06/01/2013	AAA	09/29/2006	113.24		3.74				0.93%	-0.38%
						Aaa	12/29/2006	112.37	(0.87)	3.81	7	0.4	0.55%	3.72%	

Settings | By Subperiod   8 of 6

Source: Perform Portfolio Management System.

Graphs can display performance component total returns, market returns or yield returns, along with beginning market exposures (including accrued interest) for each component. Exhibit 31.7 is an example of beginning exposures and market returns for each of the relevant states. Instead of showing exposures and returns by state, you might find it useful to use a duration grouping, highest/lowest ratings, sectors, and the like.

Scatter graph displays of bonds' total returns by maturity, priced-to date, duration, effective (option-adjusted) duration, and market value can be useful in identifying outlier individual securities that have outperformed or underperformed.

SIMULATIONS

Portfolio management software can be used to specify one or more simulated transactions or one or more hypothetical market scenarios—or both—in order to estimate, in advance, the effects of these "what-ifs." Simulation objectives include estimating market value changes, identifying durations moving outside an acceptable range, estimating future total return performance, and assessing portfolio composition under the specified conditions.

EXHIBIT 31.7   Component Profile—by State—Market Return

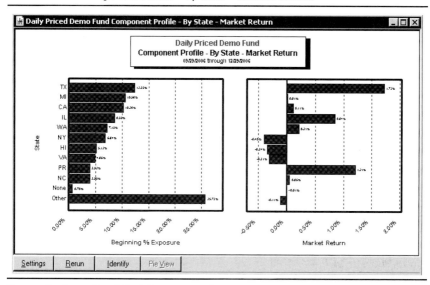

Source: Perform Portfolio Management System.

Simulations can be for entire portfolios, multiple portfolios or defined components of one or more portfolios. Simulations can be targeted to analyze individual securities or groups of securities, including candidates for potential bond swaps.

As a threshold matter for hypothetical market simulations, you may want to consider how they are to be applied. Are the market shifts to be applied directly to bond yields, or are they to be applied to the term structure of an option-adjustment model? If the latter, then should different spreads be applied to different sectors or rating groups? Since bond pricing typically is expressed as yield, the simpler yield-based shifts are intuitive. For example, you might specify a hypothetical parallel market yield shift of up or down 50 basis points. Or you might specify yield increments (up or down) for various non-parallel market yield shifts of steeper or flatter yield curves to be applied to the affected bonds. The alternative approach uses option-adjusted spreads, which can be held constant or can be shifted by sectors, rating groups or other criteria. With this approach, hypothetical market yield shifts are applied to the option-adjustment term structure (theoretically a yield curve for noncallable, triple-A municipals) to create a new option adjustment term structure. The new term structure is used to recalculate simulated bond prices using the original option-adjusted spread

EXHIBIT 31.8   Simulation—Raw Total Return—by Duration

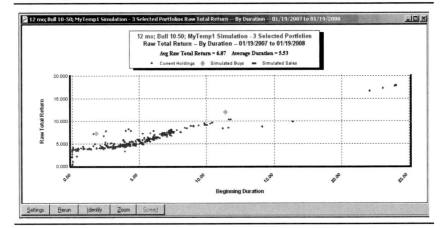

Source: Perform Portfolio Management System.

and applicable spread shifts, if any. With option-adjustment model methodology, the model's variables can significantly affect simulation results.

There are two other simulation choices that can affect the simulated
market values and future total returns: The horizon (the simulations time
period) and, if market shifts are applied directly to bond yields, whether or
not to roll down the yield curve. A simulation which uses a roll-down feature will properly reflect the yield impact of the shortening of bonds which
occurs over the simulation's horizon. A simulation's roll-down feature can
be used to measure the short-term impact of "riding the yield curve." This
is a strategy often used by portfolio managers, that is, systematically selling
bonds well before they mature, so that bonds are held only for selected portions of yield curves. Applied consistently during times of normal, upward-
sloping yield curves, this strategy generally results in yield enhancements
over a buy-and-hold strategy. By running a software simulation with no
transactions, a no-change market scenario, but with roll down, portfolio
managers can isolate estimated market impacts of riding the yield curve over
short-time horizons.

Exhibit 31.8 demonstrates estimated future total returns from a bull
market simulation. There is a data point for each bond, including simulated
buys and sales. Returns are displayed by duration. Also useful can be similar
graphs by maturity, market price or effective (option-adjusted) duration.

PORTFOLIO STRUCTURE: COMPLIANCE AND TARGETS

You may consider some degree of automation of monitoring portfolio compliance. Your portfolio management may be constrained by SEC rules, prospectus requirements, internal policy requirements that are more restrictive than prospectus limitations, and other policy criteria. Some of the "other" criteria may change as market conditions change. Beyond portfolio management software rules to insure compliance with absolute compliance limits, less rigid rules can use targets to help move portfolios closer to cash, duration or other portfolio structure objectives. Reports can show results of portfolio rules tests, whether passing, failing or approaching limits. In order to prevent unacceptable transactions, a portfolio management system can be customized to prevent input of buys or sales that would be inconsistent with specified compliance standards. Rules for municipal bonds may deal with virtually any bond criteria relevant to compliance and portfolio structure targets. Examples are state limitations, block sizes, cash ranges, and duration ranges.

REPORTING

The reports that you use regularly can be batch printed every day, automatically through an overnight process or on demand. Individual favorite reports or groups of them can be set up for frequent printing or on-line archiving. Other reports may be periodically produced for legal compliance or management or marketing, or to give information to a governing board. Making packages of reports and graphs available to high net worth owners of accounts may be helpful in client retention. In the case of nondaily reporting, the as-of date of each report will need to be determined. With frequently changing assets, accurate historical reporting will require either that these reports be saved as of past dates or that you use portfolio software that allows you to reverse transactions back to past dates. If transactions are reversed, relevant bond descriptions need to be historically accurate as of report dates. The more flexible transactions reversal approach will provide far more options for historical reporting.

A SECRET FORMULA?

Of course there are no secret formulas for successful money management. However, the inefficiency of the municipal bond market (the least efficient of the major U.S. securities markets) provides opportunity for aggressive and creative portfolio managers.

Part of the opportunity comes from the dearth of credit information on municipals and the difficulty of obtaining current financial statements associated with many municipal securities. It is vital that aggressive municipal portfolio managers purchasing higher-yielding securities have access to credit analysis (research) based on publicly available credit information. A municipal credit analysis system can make more efficient the obtaining, processing, and comparing of that credit information.

Additional opportunity in municipal bonds comes from that market's fragmentation—and its normal condition of shortages of market supply of desirable types of municipal securities, especially shortages of large blocks of bonds. Whenever you are seeking any specific sector, quality, state or duration range, there normally will be a lack of offerings of large blocks of municipal securities at attractive yields. The problem of availability of municipals typically applies both to primary and to secondary markets. You can turn this problem to competitive advantage and can differentiate yourself from your peers at many other money management organizations, through your roles as both buyer and seller:

- As a securities buyer, you can continually promote your portfolio(s) and investment appetite, with public finance originators, securities sales persons and traders, so that they will contact you early. The ideal is for them to call you first, as they work on new issues or secondary offerings that fit your buying interests. It will help if you give these individuals access to portfolio holdings and sufficient information about your buying objectives. You can encourage them to serve, in effect, as assistant portfolio managers. Periodically providing portfolio holdings to securities sales personnel fits well with the buying objective, for example, of adding small block sizes to existing holdings. By thus aggregating blocks of bonds, the resulting larger blocks become more attractive to subsequent buyers and potentially more valuable.
- As a securities seller, if you are not constrained by tax or accounting loss limitations, you can regularly make selected holdings available to the market—at offering prices determined by you. This can be done through web-based bond market makers, through securities dealers directly or through software available to dealers that allows them to search available holdings.

SUMMARY: 20 INGREDIENTS FOR SUCCESS

This chapter has referred to a number of concepts that can contribute to successful municipal bond portfolio management. These concepts may involve different individuals and/or different departments of a money management firm. As reminders for whoever accomplishes portfolio management tasks, including credit analysis, the following summarizes 20 such concepts into a reference list of ingredients for success:

1. Think of your portfolio securities on four levels: credits, issuers, holdings, and transactions.
2. Use integrated systems covering all four levels.
3. Consciously plan how to take advantage of inefficiencies within the municipal bond market, especially supply/demand imbalances.
4. Decide the appropriate level of credit surveillance.
5. Systematically use graphs for credit analysis.
6. Create and use proprietary ranking models for credits, by sector.
7. Search for holdings whose proceeds can be reinvested more productively.
8. Have a mindset of portfolio holdings as if they were dealer inventories.
9. Review current totals and averages, looking for ways to improve risk/reward relationships.
10. Recognize the circumstances where modified duration is a more useful predictor than effective (option-adjusted) duration, and vice versa.
11. Look for outliers on graphs of yield, option-adjusted yield, and/or option-adjusted spread scatter graphs.
12. Use bull/bear ratios, price curves, and duration curves in considering return potential of individual bonds.
13. Develop your own techniques for measuring total return performance and comparing that with index returns.
14. Develop your own techniques for transactions and market scenario simulations.
15. Plan and implement a strategy for riding selected portions of yield curves.
16. Have a strategy for monitoring compliance and for using targets for portfolio structure objectives.
17. Anticipate needs for historical date reporting.
18. Encourage securities sales persons and dealer traders to function as "assistant portfolio managers."
19. Aggregate bond blocks in order to enhance their market appeal.
20. Make selected holdings available to the market, at offering prices determined by you.

CHAPTER 32

Discovering Relative Value Using Custom Indexes

Daniel J. Garrett, CFA
Vice President
Investortools, Inc.

The scope of this chapter is the database of municipal bonds that comprise the Standard and Poor's/Investortools Municipal Bond Indexes. Competitive advantages can be discovered by comparing various bond groups, individual bonds, or indexes, using price, yield and spread history and comparative value of index constituents. Understanding how these relative values have compared in the past, considering past and current trends, and analyzing how these might reveal future price trends, allow a manager or analyst to improve the quality of decisions and ultimately total return performance. compared to uninformed peers who lack this resource.

INTUITIVE PATTERNS

Most managers of bond portfolios have a feel for pricing patterns among and between groups of alternative bonds. Some of this feel is from empirical evidence of total return comparative breakdowns, but there also is cumulative, intuitive knowledge of historical trading patterns. Spread changes due to credit events are inferred from prices moves. Portfolio managers understand, for example, when an issuer's specific project warrants the spread differences compared to similarly rated or structured deals. Some general conclusions can also be made about certain states' relative value due to supply/demand imbalances or state tax laws. Generalizations become more specific by observing outperforming sectors or credit quality, by noting peers whose funds do better for a period of time and by analyzing competitor holdings and comparing those characteristics to their own fund. From these observations portfolio managers can draw inferences of where the excess returns came from.

EMPIRICAL PATTERNS

Now there are tools and data available to not only validate intuitive presumptions, but discover new ideas and relationships. Previously, data were difficult to obtain or unorganized, but today's analytical tools allow us to arrange data into valuable information where obvious patterns can be transformed into profitable trading ideas.

Standard and Poor's/Investortools indexes are built from a historical record of trades and pricing history reflecting years of market activity. This accumulation of market pricing data can now be organized into comparative groups. This allows differences and similarities to be explored, uncovering relationships between risk characteristics, such as quality, sector or option features and their corresponding price history to see if there are adequate rewards for taking those risks.

The art of portfolio management is enhanced by this new analysis. Conclusions of the new approach are dependent on interpretation of patterns, that is, which inferences are real and which are misleading. Just because there is correlation between events does not imply cause and effect. The practitioner still must know what questions to ask—what should be compared to what? What do the results reveal? And perhaps most important—what is not explained by the patterns?

DISCOVERY

There are over 50,000 bonds, priced historically, in the Standard and Poor's/Investortools Main Municipal Bond index, and thousands of comparisons can be made. Exhibit 32.1 plots yields of five-year insured bonds in the index as of a date in time by modified duration.

Identifying the bond with the highest vertical position and therefore the greatest yield, it is a New York insured bond. Perhaps New York insured bonds are cheap historically. To test this hypothesis, we next plot a history of yield spread differences for New York insured bonds versus the average five-year national municipal bond yield levels. This reveals a pattern of observation points along with a darker line for average and ±1 standard deviation for the years 1999 to 2006 (see Exhibit 32.2).

One inference is that perhaps specialty states like New York and California behave differently than the overall national municipal market. Also, insured may behave differently as well. Exhibit 32.3 shows history of five-year insured bond yield spreads in several specialty states relative to the five-year insured national average.

EXHIBIT 32.1   Scatter of 5-year Insured Yields by Duration—Main Muni Index

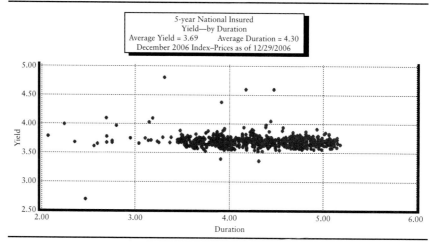

Source: Investortools, Inc. Perform and Custom Index Manager systems & S&P/ Investortools Main Index.

EXHIBIT 32.2   Spread of 5-year Insured New York to 5-year Insured National

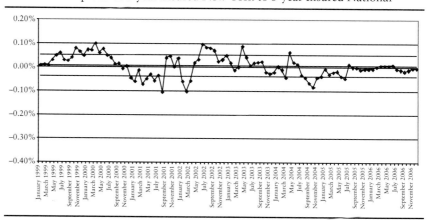

Source: Investortools, Inc. Perform and Custom Index Manager systems & S&P/ Investortools Main Index.

EXHIBIT 32.3   Spread of Specialty State 5-year Insured versus 5-year National Insured

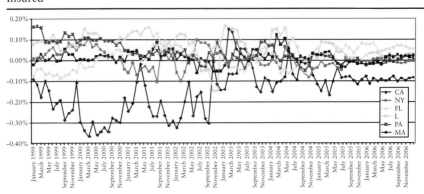

Source: Investortools, Inc. Perform and Custom Index Manager systems & S&P/ Investortools Main Index.

These patterns for comparative groups can be refined to more narrowly compare specific groups, as well as other characteristics like calls or other factors which may explain price differences. Experienced municipal investors know that not all patterns and observations among municipal bonds are easily defined, observed, or explained.

The five-year California insured bonds were high priced throughout the early 2000s, trading 20 to 30 basis points less spread than the average five-year insured bond although only about 10 basis points richer since mid-2005. Based on the graphed relationships, a possible trading strategy would be to sell California and buy five-year insured Florida bonds, which seem to have higher spreads than the national insured average recently because their spread is a little higher than the average (cheaper), all else being equal. Of course, the assumptions include that the Florida spreads won't get wider and the California spreads won't get tighter, relative to national bonds— both of which would be bad for price total return, Florida prices would drop or California prices would go higher, relative to other choices. Also possible, is that Florida bonds may have other risks like more call option risk in bonds which may justify the wider spreads. The point is that there is now a way to identify things to shop for or possibly offer to sell, which can be easily found and then explored deeper. In the above example, it appears that about 15 basis points could be picked up for identical risk—if future price moves are parallel, the total return will be 15 basis points higher solely due to yield advantage, which is a significant number for bond fund total return comparisons.

CAVEATS AND DISCLAIMERS

The aim of this chapter is not to present an exhaustive list of trading ideas nor a complete step-by-step process to capture these pricing differences. There are many logical questions that may explain away any rich or cheap observations that are specific to the issuer, the issue/deal structure, the inability to trade illiquid bonds or perhaps simply pricing flaws not being recognized in the pricing methodologies of some of these seldom-traded municipal bonds.

There are questions to be answered and research to be done to verify and understand this newly revealed information. The goal is to entice the reader to explore and discover value in places heretofore hidden to municipal bond investors.

CONCLUSION

Most people who have been investing in municipal bonds learned early in their experience that the municipal market is filled with inefficiencies, anomalies and quirks unique to this market. However, there is now a rich set of data and tools available for customizable indexes, to dig out valuable patterns of which the majority of investors are unaware. These ideas may lead to profitable discoveries of relative value that could lead to higher total returns.

CHAPTER 33

Municipal Bond Swaps

Evan C. Rourke, CFA
Portfolio Manager
M. D. Sass Tax Advantaged Bond Strategies, LLC

For individual investors, executing bond swaps can be a valuable tool for managing their portfolio. Swaps can be done to reduce an investor's tax liability or to alter the characteristics of the investor's portfolio. Swaps can be used to increase income, to reduce credit risk, to increase liquidity, or to diversify a portfolio. Swaps can be done to restructure a portfolio to meet a revised strategic plan or to adjust to changing circumstances. In this chapter, we describe bond swaps.

DESCRIPTION OF A BOND SWAP

Simply put, a bond swap involves the selling of one bond and the simultaneous purchase of another. The addition of the new bond and subtraction of the old bond should adjust the portfolio to better conform to investment objectives. Swaps are done to adjust coupon, maturity, credit rating, yield, or portfolio diversity.

Investors should remember that transactions have costs and frequent trading can reduce portfolio performance. Investors should include cost considerations before deciding to execute bond swaps. Some broker-dealers charge lower commissions for swaps than for outright purchase and sales. Transaction fees may be lower for municipal bonds held in fee-based accounts.

TAX SWAPPING

The most common form of bond swap involving municipal bond is the tax swap. The objective of tax swapping is to minimize an investor's overall tax liability. Investors should always consult with their tax advisor before entering into tax swaps.

In a tax swap, an investor sells a municipal bond to realize a loss. This is accomplished by selling a bond for less than the adjusted cost basis. At the same time, the investor purchases a similar but not identical bond at approximately the same price. The realized loss can be used to offset capital gains or up to $3,000 of ordinary income per year. Unused losses can be carried forward to reduce tax liability in future years. The tax swap should result in only minor changes in the portfolio's performance characteristics.

The Internal Revenue Service (IRS) will disallow any deduction which is produced from a wash sale. According to the agency, a wash sale occurs when an investor sells and then repurchases the same security or a substantially identical security within 30 days of the sale. Two bonds can be considered substantially different if they differ on at least two of the following three characteristics: issuer, coupon and maturity.

Example of a Tax Swap

Suppose that on 3/11/2004, an investor purchased $1 million par amount of insured Freeport, NY General Obligation 3.50% bonds due 4/01/2017 at the original issue yield of 3.88% and a dollar price of $96.134. For a settlement date of 8/15/2007, the investor sells the bonds at a yield of 3.97% and a dollar price of $96.266. Simultaneous to selling the Freeport General Obligation bonds, the investor purchases $1 million par amount of insured New York State Thruway Revenue 3.75% bonds due 1/01/2017 at a yield of 3.97% and a dollar price of $98.287. Both bonds have Aaa ratings due to bond insurance, both mature in 2017 and both are exempt from New York State taxes. Since the issuer and the coupon are different, the sale creates an acceptable loss. The investor realizes a deductible loss of $7,020 on this position.

Note that according to the IRS code, before calculating a gain or loss, the investors adjusted cost basis must be determined. The adjusted cost basis is determined using the *constant-yield-to-maturity* (CYM) method. In simple terms, the CYM method determines the current dollar price using the effective yield at time of purchase. In this example, it is the dollar price at a 3.88% yield for settlement 8/15/2007, $96.968. Subtracting the cost basis from the sales price, the investor has a loss on the bonds of $7,020.

Example of a Wash Sale

Suppose that on 2/28/2006, an investor bought $2 million par amount of California State General Obligation 4.5% bonds due 12/01/2034 at the original issue yield of 4.54% and a dollar price of $99.366. For a settlement date of 8/15/2007, the investor sells the bonds at a yield of 4.78% and a dollar price of $95.749. The investor realizes a loss of $72,440 on this position.

Simultaneous to selling the bonds, the investor purchases $2 million par amount of California State General Obligation 4.5% bonds due 3/01/2033 at a yield of 4.78% and a dollar price of $95.892. In this case, the investor has bought and sold substantially identical securities. Not enough has changed, this is a wash sale and a tax loss will be disallowed by the IRS.

OTHER TYPES OF MUNICIPAL BOND SWAPS

Other types of municipal swaps are consolidation swaps, quality swaps, and geographical swaps.

Consolidation Swaps

Investors who have accumulated a portfolio over time may have a large number of line items. *Consolidation swaps* can be done to reduce the number of line items and increase their par amount. Larger positions will have greater liquidity and therefore better market value than smaller odd-lot positions. Investors who want to receive tax-exempt income but expect to include their municipal bond portfolio as part of their estate may elect to do consolidation swaps.

Quality Swaps

The purpose of a *quality swap* is to improve the credit quality of a portfolio. In a quality swap, an investor will sell a bond to buy another with a better credit rating. The investor will have improved the credit quality of their portfolio and will reduce the yield on the portfolio—unless they take on a different risk at the same time that they reduce their credit risk. When an investor does a quality swap, they are changing the fundamental character of their portfolio.

There are several reasons why an investor may execute a quality swap. The investor may want to reduce a credit exposure based on the view that credit spreads will widen. This occurs when the yield premium in the market for lower-rated credits widens relative to high-grade credits. The investor may want to realize a profit on a lower-rated credit because credit spreads have tightened. This occurs when strong demand for lower-rated credits has caused the yield premiums to contract.

Geographic Swaps

The purpose of a *geographic swap* is to increase the diversity of the portfolio. Geographic swaps can be done in two ways: interstate and intrastate. An investor might do a geographic swap to insulate their portfolio from the risk of a localized natural disaster or regional economic downturn might.

The most common geographic swaps are interstate swaps. In an *interstate swap*, the investor will sell bonds from one state to purchase bonds from another. Investors may be taking on state tax liability when buying bonds issued outside of their state of residence. As always, they should consult with their tax advisor before executing an interstate swap. When assessing an interstate swap, the investor should consider the after-tax yield of the swapped bonds. An investor should consider an interstate geographic swap when they can increase their portfolio yield, on an after-tax basis, while increasing the diversity of their portfolio. Shifts in the relative value of municipal bonds from different states can create opportunities for investors to reverse geographic swaps and realize gains but investors should be cognizant of the risks of concentrating their portfolios.

For investors from large states or states with distinct regions, the benefits of geographic swaps may be achievable through *intrastate swaps*. For example diversity benefits might be realized by splitting a portfolio between northern and southern California, eastern and western Texas, upstate and downstate New York, or even eastern and western Pennsylvania. Intrastate geographic swaps allow for geographic diversity without creating a potential state tax liability.

SUMMARY

In this chapter, municipal bond swaps are described and the reason for their use are explained. Swaps are used by retail investors in municipal bonds for tax purposes and for such purposes investors must be aware of the wash rule provision in the tax code. Other types of swaps described in this chapter are consolidation swaps, quality swaps, and geographical swaps (interstate swaps and intrastate swaps).

CHAPTER 34

The Tax Treatment of Municipal Bonds

Martin J. Mauro, Ph.D.
Fixed-Income Strategist
Merrill Lynch

Philip Fischer, Ph.D., J.D.
Municipal Strategist
Merrill Lynch

In this chapter, we focus on the tax treatment of municipal bonds. We begin with the federal tax treatment and then move to state and local tax treatment.

FEDERAL TAX TREATMENT OF MUNICIPAL BONDS

Interest received on a bond that is an essential public-purpose or qualified private-purpose obligation of a state or municipality is exempt from federal taxation. *Essential public purpose* means that the proceeds from the bond's sale will be used almost exclusively to benefit the public, and not a private person or corporation. General obligation bonds, water and sewer bonds, municipally owned utility bonds, and highway and public building bonds all fit the definition. Interest income on some other types of bonds is also tax exempt, such as those issued by not-for-profit hospitals, schools, and revenue bonds for airports and convention centers.

Capital gains from municipal bonds are subject to federal taxation.

Alternative Minimum Tax (AMT) and Munis

The federal AMT was designed to prevent individuals or corporations from reducing their tax liability by taking an "excessive" amount of deductions, although its reach has expanded far beyond its original purpose. Individuals must pay the higher of the tax calculated under the regular system and under the individual AMT.

AMT income is broader than ordinary taxable income. It differs from taxable income in its treatment of personal exemptions and itemized deductions and also in its inclusion of income from *preference items*. Preference items for individuals include such things as oil exploration credits, rental depreciation, and most *private-purpose municipal bonds*. Housing and airport bonds are often private-purpose bonds. These are referred to as *AMT bonds*.

Taxpayers must calculate their tax under the regular system and the AMT, and pay the higher amount. The tax rate under the AMT is 26% of AMT income up to $175,000 and 28% of AMT income in excess of $175,000. But in the income range where the AMT exemptions are phased out, the top effective marginal tax rate could be 35%, and the marginal rate on capital gains and dividends could be 22%.

Municipal buyers, who tend to have above-average incomes, will likely be disproportionately subject to the AMT in coming years. The AMT has three consequences for municipal investors:

- Bonds subject to the AMT generally pay a yield spread of 15 to 30 basis points over comparable bonds not subject to the AMT. A few years of being taxed under the AMT could erase the yield advantage from these bonds.
- Many taxpayers who pay the AMT face a 28% marginal rate, compared to the top rate of 35% under the regular system. When comparing munis with taxable instruments, the investor who faces the AMT should consider the AMT tax rate, rather than the higher rate that might apply under the regular system.
- The AMT also disallows the deductibility of state and local taxes. In so doing, the AMT makes out-of-state municipal securities less attractive for most investors who fall under its reach. That is because most states tax the interest income on out-of-state bonds, but not on in-state bonds. Under the regular federal tax structure the deductibility of state taxes reduces the effective tax bite on out-of-state bonds.

Treatment of Par, Premium, and Market Discount Bonds

Federal tax treatment differs according to whether the municipal bond is priced at par, at a premium or at a discount.

A bond purchased at *par* will not have any capital gain or loss at maturity. If the bond is sold prior to maturity, any change in its value is taxable as a capital gain or loss, as with any other investment. If a bond is called, however, the call premium, if any, may be a capital gain.

The amortization of the *premium* on a municipal bond is not considered a capital loss. There would be a capital loss (gain), however, if the bond were sold prior to maturity at a price below (above) its amortized value. The amortized value is the price of the bond at the new issue yield.

For example, consider a bond with 10 years remaining to maturity, a 6% coupon, priced at 107.8 to yield 5%. If the bond is held to maturity, there is neither a capital gain nor a capital loss. If the bond is sold after five years, the capital gain or loss would be the difference between the sales price and the amortized value of 104.4 (using the constant yield method).

A *market discount bond* is one that is selling in the secondary market at a discount for tax purposes A market discount would arise because the yield on the bond has risen since the bond was issued.

- For an original issue discount (OID) bond, the market discount would be the excess of the accreted price over the market price.
- For a non-OID coupon bond, the market discount would be the excess of par over the market price.

For a market discount bond purchased in the secondary market, the investor is taxed on the accrual of the market discount. The accrued market discount is the price change that would occur as the bond approached maturity if the yield stayed the same as when the bond was purchased. For an OID, the accrued market discount is the total accrued discount less the accrued OID. For a bond that is held to maturity, the entire market discount accrues, so the investor is taxed on the full-market discount. The tax on the accrued market discount applies when the bond is disposed of either through a sale, redemption or call, unless the taxpayer has elected to pay tax on the accrual of the market discount on a current basis.

For bonds purchased after April 30, 1993, the accrued market discount is taxable as *ordinary income*, provided the discount exceeds the de minimis criteria: the discount must be at least one quarter point for each full year remaining to maturity on the bond. So, for example, a bond with 10 years remaining to maturity would have to be priced at or below 97.5 (100 minus 10 times 0.25) in order for the de minimis criteria to be exceeded. If the de minimis criteria is not exceeded, or if the bond was purchased before April 30, 1993, the accrued discount is taxed as a capital gain.

If the de minimis criteria is exceeded then:

- If the bond is held to maturity or is called, the entire market discount is taxable as ordinary income at the tax rate that applies at that time.

■ If the bond is sold prior to maturity, the tax liability may involve a combination of ordinary income and capital gain or loss depending upon the proceeds from the sale and how much of the discount was accrued.

Consult your tax advisor for full details concerning market discount and other tax issues.

State and Local Tax Policies

All but eight states impose some form of tax on interest income. Seven of those states have no income tax: Alaska, Florida, Nevada, South Dakota, Texas, Washington, and Wyoming. Indiana has an income tax, but does not tax municipal interest income.

Most of the remaining states tax municipal interest income on equal footing with other forms of income such as wages and salaries. New Hampshire and Tennessee are exceptions. Those states tax the income from interest and dividends only.

Most states follow the basic structure of the federal tax system, but with different tax brackets, different levels for personal exemptions, and sometimes, different allowable deductions. In seven states, federal taxes are at least partially deductible from taxable income. North Dakota allows taxpayers a choice of two methods to compute their taxes, one that allows the deduction of federal taxes and one that does not.

Some *local* governments tax income earned within their boundaries. Localities that tax interest income piggyback their local income tax to the state tax. Examples are: New York City, Philadelphia, certain counties in Maryland, and many school districts in Iowa. Counties in Indiana tax interest income, but not on municipal bonds.

Most states that tax municipal interest income apply the tax only to bonds issued in other states. In other words, most investors who face a state income tax would be subject to tax on the interest income from out-of-state bonds, but not on bonds from their own state. There are exceptions on both sides though:

■ Several states tax the interest income from *some* in-state bonds. Colorado, Illinois, Iowa, Kansas, Oklahoma, and Wisconsin are examples.
■ Indiana does not tax any municipal interest income, and Utah does not tax the interest income from bonds issued in states that do not tax the interest income from Utah bonds. North Dakota does not tax out-of-state municipal interest income for taxpayers who file the ND-1 form, but does tax the income for those who file ND-2 forms. Also, the Dis-

trict of Columbia and Puerto Rico do not tax individuals on interest from municipal bonds.

Most states treat *capital gains* on municipal bonds as ordinary income. But again there are exceptions. About a dozen states tax the capital gains from out-of-state bonds, but not from at least some in-state bonds. Several states give favorable treatment to all capital gains, while Massachusetts imposes an extra tax on short-term capital gains.

Interest on all bonds issued by the Commonwealth of Puerto Rico, its municipalities, agencies and authorities, along with other U.S. territories (i.e., U.S. Virgin Islands, Guam, American Samoa), and the Government of the Northern Mariana Islands is exempt from taxation at any level of government. All bonds issued by the District of Columbia and its agencies are exempt from Federal and District of Columbia taxes. In general, interest income from these bonds is subject to taxation by states.

Kentucky Supreme Court Ruling

In August, 2006, the Kentucky Supreme Court let stand a lower court ruling that the state should apply the same tax treatment to in-state and out-of-state municipal bonds. The state has appealed the decision, and the United States Supreme Court has decided to consider the case in the session that began in October 2007.

If the Kentucky ruling stands, then other states may also be forced to change their tax treatment of municipal bonds in future years. Most likely, the states that now tax the interest income from out-of-state bonds would then no longer do so. A few states might instead opt to tax both in-state and out-of-state bonds at the same rate. It would probably take several years before these legal issues are resolved, so we do not expect major changes in the state tax treatment of municipal bonds soon.

CALCULATING THE EFFECTIVE TAX RATE ON INTEREST INCOME FROM OUT-OF-STATE MUNICIPAL BONDS

What tax rate do you pay on interest income from municipal bonds from other states? The answer begins with your state tax rate, but additional adjustments have to be made for the possible deductibility of state taxes on federal returns, the deductibility of federal taxes on state returns.

Exhibit 34.1 shows the top tax rate on interest income from out-of-state municipal bonds by state. The *effective* marginal tax rate (EMTR) for a given state may be lower than that however, since many taxpayers can

EXHIBIT 34.1   Top Marginal Tax Rates on Interest from Out-of-State Bonds, by State

Alabama[a]	5.00%	Nevada	0.00%
Alaska	0.00%	New Hampshire	5.00%
Arizona	4.54%	New Jersey	8.97%
Arkansas	7.00%	New Mexico	4.90%
California[b]	10.30%	New York	6.85%
Colorado	4.63%	New York City[e]	10.50%
Connecticut	5.00%	North Carolina	7.75%
Delaware	5.95%	North Dakota (ND-1)	0.00%
Dist. of Columbia	0.00%	North Dakota (ND-2)	12.00%
Florida	0.00%	Ohio	6.56%
Georgia	6.00%	Oklahoma	6.25%
Hawaii	8.25%	Oregon	9.00%
Idaho	7.80%	Pennsylvania	3.07%
Illinois	3.00%	Philadelphia[e]	7.33%
Indiana	0.00%	Puerto Rico	0.00%
Iowa	8.98%	Rhode Island[f]	9.90%
Kansas[c]	8.70%	South Carolina	7.00%
Kentucky	6.00%	South Dakota	0.00%
Louisiana[a]	6.00%	Tennessee	6.00%
Maine	8.50%	Texas	0.00%
Maryland[d]	7.25%	Utah[g]	5.00%
Massachusetts	5.30%	Vermont	9.50%
Michigan	4.35%	Virginia	5.75%
Minnesota	7.85%	Washington	0.00%
Mississippi	5.00%	West Virginia	6.50%
Missouri	6.00%	Wisconsin	6.75%
Montana	6.90%	Wyoming	0.00%
Nebraska	6.84%		

Tax rates as of 2007.
[a] State allows deduction of federal taxes.
[b] Rate for California includes the 1% surcharge on incomes over $1 million. Most residents pay a marginal rate of 9.3%.
[c] Kansas rate includes 2.25% intangible personal property tax.
[d] Maryland rate includes 2.5% county tax.
[e] Rates for New York City and Philadelphia include the state taxes.
[f] Rhode Island residents can also use a flat tax option, with an 8.0% rate.
[g] Utah does not tax interest on the bonds of states that do not tax interest on Utah bonds.

deduct state taxes on federal returns. Except for the handful of states that allow deductibility of federal taxes, when the investor deducts state taxes at the federal level, the EMTR calculation is

EMTR = Marginal state tax rate × (1 − Federal marginal tax rate)

For example, in New York Sate, the top marginal tax rate is 6.85%. For somebody in the 35% federal tax bracket, the effective rate applied to out-of-state bonds when state taxes can be deducted at the federal level is:

$$EMTR = 6.85\%(1 - 35\%) = 4.45\%$$

An investor who pays the federal AMT, or who does not itemize deductions at the federal level would not be able to deduct state tax payments. In those cases, the maximum state tax rates on municipal interest income are those shown in Exhibit 34.1.

Evaluating Out-of-State Bonds: Taxable Equivalent Multipliers

Exhibit 34.2 shows the EMTR that applies to out-of-state municipal bonds for some of the higher-tax states with more active municipal markets. The EMTRs are calculated as described above. The exhibit also shows the Taxable Equivalent Multipliers (TEMs) for each of those states. You use the

EXHIBIT 34.2 Taxation on Out-of-State Municipal Interest Income

	Tax Rate	State Taxes Deducted on Federal Return		State Taxes not Deducted on Federal Return	
		Effective Marginal Tax Rate[a]	Taxable Equivalent Multiplier[b]	Marginal Tax Rate	Taxable Equivalent Multiplier
California	9.30%	6.05%	1.064	9.30%	1.103
New York State	6.85%	4.45%	1.047	6.85%	1.074
New Jersey	8.97%	5.83%	1.062	8.97%	1.099
Virginia	5.75%	3.74%	1.039	5.75%	1.061

Calculations use 35% federal bracket.
[a] The effective marginal tax rate adjusts for the deductibility of state taxes on federal returns.
[b] Multiply the yield on an in-state bond by the Taxable Equivalent Multiplier to get the yield needed on an out-of-state bond in order to get the same after-tax yield as on the in-state bond.

TEM to determine how much yield you would need on an out-of-state municipal security in order to match the tax-free yield on an in-state bond. For example, in Virginia the TEM for investors in the top tax bracket who deduct state taxes at the federal level is 1.039. In order to match the yield on in-state bond that yields 4.00%, an out-of-state bond would need to yield 4.16% (4% × 1.039).

Exhibit 34.2 is broken into two sections, one for cases where state taxes are deducted at the federal level, and one for when they are not. With state taxes deducted, both the effective marginal tax rate and the TEM are lower. That is, the deductibility of state taxes on federal returns reduces the sting of state taxation and therefore reduces the extra yield compensation needed on the out-of-state bond.

SUMMARY

A full analysis of the tax advantage of municipal bonds requires a look at both the federal and state and local tax treatment of municipal interest income. Investors who face state income taxation will generally find a tax benefit in owning an in-state bond. Other things being equal, the benefit will vary with the state tax rate. State taxation can be mitigated by the ability to deduct state taxes at the federal level. But the federal Alternative Minimum Tax does not allow the deduction of state taxes, and even under the regular tax system, the deduction does not apply to investors who do not itemized federal deductions. Investors should also be aware of the federal taxation of market discount bonds.

The Buy Side:
Institutional Investors

Managing a National Municipal Bond Fund

Alexander Grant
Managing Director, Investment Department
Guardian Life Insurance Company of America
and
Portfolio Manager
RS Tax-Exempt Fund

This chapter presents the questions that the investor should ask in selecting a total return national municipal bond fund and how a portfolio manager makes trading decisions for such a fund that is primarily high-investment grade in structure and of relatively long duration.

Lipper would categorize a national municipal bond fund under its General Municipal Debt Funds whereas the Morningstar category is Municipal National Long. Funds in these categories generally purchase municipal bonds that are primarily investment grade. Investment grade is any bond that is rated either Baa or better by Moody's or BBB– and better by S&P. Investment-grade issuers can run the gamut from general obligations of a state to investment-grade hospital bonds.

While the skills required in successfully managing such a fund are similar to those required in managing other tax-exempt funds such as specialty state, high-yield, and short-duration funds, long national investment-grade funds have their own unique characteristics and market forces. At a minimum the mantra of all tax-exempt funds is to maximize current income exempt from federal income taxes that is consistent with the preservation of capital.

Although this chapter focuses on portfolio management, it is important to examine other aspects of a national fund. This includes looking at a national fund through the eyes and expectations of the investor and why an investor would choose a national fund over a state-specific fund or a high-yield fund. What tools an investor can use in measuring funds to ascertain the appropriateness of a fund to the investor's objective. This chapter also explores the benefits and advantages of a national tax-exempt fund to the investor and why a national fund can provide not only higher returns but higher credit quality. The chapter also takes the reader through some of the thoughts and observations on how a portfolio manager views the high-grade municipal market. The focus of the chapter will be on a national high-grade tax-exempt municipal bond fund and how a portfolio manager tries to preserve capital and provide current income under the umbrella of high-grade municipal bonds.

State-specific funds, or specialty state funds as they are sometimes called, are funds that invest strictly in bonds issued by municipalities and other tax-exempt issuers in a particular state. This investment restriction, in most cases, insures that coupon income that is generated by the fund is exempt from both federal and state taxation and in some cases city taxation. Whereas, a national tax-exempt bond fund invests in municipalities across the United States. This would include Federal territories such as Puerto Rico, the U.S. Virgin Islands, and Guam. Income generated from a national fund is exempt from federal taxes and national tax-exempt funds also offer geographic diversification.

THE INVESTOR WHO BUYS THE FUND

Whether it is a national municipal fund, state specific municipal fund or high yield municipal fund, the investor is looking for tax-free income and chooses a municipal fund for that reason. If the investor is risk adverse the high-yield fund will lack the credit quality that the investor needs to satisfy that requirement and the choice then becomes either a national fund or state-specific fund. With a state-specific fund the investor will get the added benefit of tax-free income at the state level. Although this added benefit appears to have value that may not always be the case if the investor compares returns to national funds. That is to say, even though you have an in state tax advantage with a state-specific fund the investor may find that the historical return on a national fund may be higher even after the in state tax is paid.

It is sometimes assumed that since a tax-exempt fund is not high yield then it must be high grade. This may not be the case. National and state-specific funds are generally higher quality than high-yield funds but one should not assume that the fund's investments are all investment grade. There can be some overlap in credit quality between a high-yield fund and a high-grade fund. In general, national funds and state-specific funds are higher in credit quality than a high-yield fund. However, this may not always be the case when comparing a national fund to a state specific fund. In either case the potential shareholder should look closely at the holdings of the fund and read the prospectus to determine what are acceptable investments. A few basic questions to ask are:

- Are there limitations on credit quality?
- What percentage of below investment grade is the fund allowed to hold? Is it none, 20% or are there no limitations on credit quality?
- Are derivatives and nonrated bonds acceptable investments for the fund?
- If they are acceptable investments then what are the exposure limitations; if any?
- Does the fund invest in *alternative minimum tax* (AMT) bonds? If so, is there a limit to how much AMT bonds the fund may hold?

Along with fund performance these are a few of the more important questions that an investor should be asking when making decisions on what are appropriate investments to satisfy the investment goal. A national tax-exempt fund has an appeal to a class of investors that are looking for diversified tax-free income with little credit risk. It is important that the fund is positioned to reflect what the investor expects but more importantly it is up to the investor to monitor the investment.

NATIONAL VERSUS STATE-SPECIFIC FUNDS

The benefits for the investor of a national investment-grade long municipal bond fund are twofold. First, the fund provides income that is free from federal income taxes. Some issues may be tax exempt from the state where the investor resides and therefore a portion of the income is also exempt from state income taxes. The second advantage is that with a national investment-grade fund there is diversification of credit risk. Unlike specialty-state funds, regional economic and local budgetary conditions do not dominate the quality of the portfolio.

It is not uncommon for some regions of the country to undergo severe economic stress and for others to enjoy robust economic cycles. Two examples of financial stresses would be the automobile industry and the economic aftermath of Hurricane Katrina. The massive layoffs in the automobile industry had a direct impact on the creditworthiness of various issuers in and including the state of Michigan where many of the automobile plants and suppliers were located. In Louisiana, the economic impact of Hurricane Katrina also was severe. Many state and local credits were downgraded and underwent financial stress. If a fund had a concentration in these regional credits, clearly, the impact on performance would have been extremely negative.

Also, legislative actions within a particular state can negatively impact the performance of a fund that is overly concentrated in credits of that state and also even change a specialty state bond fund into a national one. An example is Florida. As of 2007, Florida no longer had an intangible personal property tax. Prior to 2007, the tax was $0.50 per $1,000 of fair market value of holdings and applied to out-of-state municipal bonds. With the elimination of the tax, the trading appeal of Florida tax-exempt funds and Florida bonds became less so. The funds, in effect, became national funds with a heavy regional concentration.

Since a state-specific fund must have the majority of its assets in a particular state, local economic and legislative tax changes can present problems. If a region in which that state fund invests experiences an economic downturn the state-specific fund may experience multiple downgrades in credits that it holds. This in turn could cause a decrease in market values that would have an impact on the performance of the fund.

A national municipal fund can avoid these regional areas under economic stress and thus avoid the downgrades associated with it. In general, it can be said that a national fund provides greater insulation from a regional economic downcycle, which could significantly hurt the overall performance of the fund. Since investing in a specific state is not a national fund requirement, the portfolio manager can effectively diversity credit risk by selectively buying value across the country. Conversely, value can be found in these previous areas of economic weakness and can become buying opportunities for the national fund manager when economic recoveries and trading anomalies begin to appear.

TOTAL RATE OF RETURN

The specific goals of the portfolio manager are not only to provide tax-exempt income but performance as well. Total rate of return is one measurement of performance. The total rate of return of a fund is used to delineate the rankings of funds within a peer group. Lipper and/or Morningstar are normally used to provide peer group comparisons. They will track the performance of a fund and rank the performance in quartile and percentile expressions. The ranking is determined by performance. The success of a fund is measured in relationship to its benchmarks and how attractive the total rate of return is relative to the other funds in its category with the same objective. Municipal national funds would not be ranked with state-specific funds or high-yield municipal funds. Funds with the same objective would be ranked together. There are different ways to measure performance among funds but the total rate of return metric is the most common.

Total rate of return is measured and reported on a year-to-date, 1 year, 3 year, 5 year, 10 year, and life-of-the-fund basis. Total rate of return is one of the more important tools for the investor to use in measuring the suitability of a fund. It is particularly critical to learn the track record of the portfolio manager who is currently managing the fund and is responsible for its performance.

Two basic questions to ask:

- Are the total rate of return performance data associated with the fund the current portfolio manager's?
- How long has the portfolio manager been managing the fund?

Management and peer group performance should also be key factors in determining the appropriateness of the investment to the potential shareholder.

When comparing various funds on a total rate of return basis it is important to reduce them to a common denominator. If the investor is comparing the performance of a state-specific fund to a national fund, an understanding of the in-state tax code is helpful. It is necessary to adjust the return of the national fund to compensate for the taxes that will be paid. The biggest tax liability is at the federal level while state taxes will vary from state to state. Some cities, such as New York City, have tax liabilities for its residents, which must be taken into consideration when comparing various funds. The whole tax-liability picture must be taken into consideration when trying to compare the return of a national fund to a state-specific fund.

MANAGING A FUND BY RELATIVE VALUE

Portfolio management should be concentrated in the "relative value" aspect of the municipal bond market. *Relative value* is a term that is used to describe historical trading ranges and how the ranges compare to each other. A hypothetical value is assigned to each characteristic of the bond, which is then compared to another bond or a theoretical municipal yield curve. The value assigned to the bond can help the portfolio manager determine whether or not it is a sale candidate, should be purchased or is fair valued. Although the pricing services will try to capture the inefficiencies in the municipal market, this is not always possible given supply and the new issue market. Surges in supply, especially in a particular state or sector, can be disruptive to traditional spreads causing them to widen, which in turn can create opportunities. Conversely, lack of new issuance supply can cause spreads to tighten which also creates opportunity. Being able to recognize opportunities in relative value is a skill a portfolio manager needs to develop.

ISSUES OF COUPON AND STRUCTURE

The high-grade municipal market is sometimes driven by structure and coupon. The coupons can be important when devising a strategy for portfolio management and total return performance. Depending on the interest rate environment, some coupons can be bearish or bullish and have considerable influence on the performance of a portfolio. Historical spreads between coupons are important to monitor as their relationships can vary and can present opportunities for buying or selling.

As an example, in mid-2007 there was a spread relationship between 4.50% and 5.00% coupons that had become very unusual and is an example of the portfolio manager having to be nimble and always be looking for new trading patterns. This was most notable in the trading of uninsured, long California general obligation bonds. The spread between the two coupons over a three-month period had been as wide as 30 basis points (bps) to as tight as 20 bps. What was particularly interesting was that the 4.50% coupon, in a rising interest rate environment that existed toward the end of the second quarter of 2007, was outperforming the 5.00% coupon.

This was occurring despite the fact that the 4.50% coupon was approaching de minimis. *De minimis* is when a municipal bond moves into taxable status based on market discount and is subject to federal capital gains tax. As a tax-exempt bond approaches de minimis status, the spread should be expected to get wider to the 5.00% coupon and underperform. Since this provision of the federal tax code was written in 1993, bonds approaching de minimis status have usually softened in price more than others.

There are two possible reasons for the relatively stronger performance of the 4.50% coupon in mid-2007. First, the 4.50%, on a spread basis, was higher yielding than the 5.00% coupon and that characteristic would have an appeal to an arbitrageur. A relatively new crossover participant in the municipal market who is not driven by income tax considerations, this buyer may not be expected to be concerned about the de minimis issue. Second, because the discount to the coupon is greater for the 4.50% coupon than for the 5.00% there may have been an appeal for the retail investor. Since retail does not typically buy large blocks of bonds, a combination of both arbitrage buyers and some retail buying may have caused the stronger performance of the 4.50% coupon with the arbitrageurs being the dominant players.

TRADITIONAL BUYERS VERSUS THE ARBITRAGEURS

The tax-exempt municipal market has evolved since 2005 into an asset class that is starting to mirror other taxable asset classes. The asset class is attracting not only the traditional buyer, who is seeking tax-exempt income, but a new class of investor that will invest in municipals for other reasons. They find the asset class interesting for various reasons such as percentages to Treasuries or the steepness of the municipal curve, to name just a few. This new class of investor has introduced liquidity to the municipal market and has provided stability but also, at times, can be a volatile participant.

In its simplistic form, the *ratio buyer* or *crossover buyer* (crossover because it is a crossing over into another asset class) will purchase municipals and sell Treasuries, or reverse that based on percentages (municipal yield divided by Treasury yield). The crossover is based on the municipal yield versus the Treasury yield. Typically, it is a 10-year municipal yield versus a 10-year Treasury yield and a 30-year municipal yield versus a 30-year Treasury yield. The higher the ratio the more attractive are municipals relative to Treasuries. Conversely, as the ratio decreases, the relative attractiveness of municipals declines. The ratio can vary based on municipal credit quality but normally the crossover buyer operates in the high-grade market. The high-grade credits for this ratio buyer is usually A or better.

The ratio buyer can have a great deal of influence on high-grade municipals, especially in the 10- and 30-year part of the curve because they are percentage driven rather than spread driven. The ratio buyer will buy and sell municipals based on percentages and does very little differentiation among credit. This in turn can have some credits trading tighter or wider in spread than the historical averages.

The *tender option bond* (TOB) participant looks primarily at the steepness of the synthetic municipal curve and purchases municipal bonds in the long end of the curve. They are then deposited in a tax-exempt trust, which in turn issues tax-exempt variable rate demand notes in the short end of the market. In essence, the TOB investor is taking the spread out between the long end of the curve and the short end of the curve. This structure can be leveraged, allowing the TOB participant to extract the curve in multiples.

The TOB players have, like the ratio buyer, brought liquidity and less volatility to the municipal market. Like the ratio buyer, the TOB buyer is trained to look at credit differently than the traditional municipal buyer.

Participation of the TOB in the long end of the municipal market can have an effect on high-grade municipal spreads. High-grade credits for a TOB program are usually AAA and that would include insured bonds. (Concerning insured bonds, it should also be noted that as of early 2008 as the triple A bond insurers have come under a cloud of financial and rating uncertainities, their use has declined.) The TOB buyer, like the ratio buyer, while bringing new money and liquidity to the municipal bond market, can also disrupt historical spreads.

CONCLUSION

In this chapter, a brief overview of some of the concerns that investors should be aware of in assessing a high-grade, tax-exempt municipal fund as well as the issues that the portfolio manager of such a fund is confronted with on a daily basis while managing such a fund is provided. The interests of the shareholder should be the key concern to the portfolio manager. That is, the portfolio manager should always keep the shareholder in mind when executing a long-term strategy. As noted in the chapter, in managing a fund the long-term strategy can be influenced by other market participants and what their views are of the municipal world on any given day. Over the last few years through early 2008 the municipal market has gone through many changes with new and different participants and untested security structures. The market is constantly evolving. The fund manager has to be aware of these changes with their potential risks and advantages and adapt his strategy accordingly.

CHAPTER 36

Managing a High-Yield Municipal Fund

Wayne Godlin
Managing Director
Morgan Stanley Investment Management

Jim Phillips
Executive Director
Morgan Stanley Investment Management

Bill Black
Executive Director
Morgan Stanley Investment Management

Barnet Sherman
Vice President
Morgan Stanley Investment Management

Mark Paris
Vice President
Morgan Stanley Investment Management

Seth Horwitz
Senior Associate
Morgan Stanley Investment Management

The first high-yield municipal bond funds were offered to investors in the early 1980s. To maximize current yield to shareholders, these funds invested in a new and relatively unknown asset class of bonds that came to market without a rating from Standard and Poor's or Moody's. Lacking a credit or performance history, these bonds were perceived by most investors as having significant risk. But a few portfolio managers and analysts focusing on this promising asset class saw returns that offered value relative to that risk. Nonrated bonds offered borrowers access to capital in sectors previously limited or excluded from the municipal bond market. High-yield investors found additional value in these newly developing sectors or unique bond issuers as well as distressed credits. As this market evolved, new entrants and new borrowers caused anomalies in traditional value relationships to emerge, offering trading opportunities. Moreover, derivatives entered the lexicon of the municipal bond market, offering institutional investors sophisticated new tools to maximize returns. Indexes and benchmarks were developed to measure and compare investment performance. With new sectors and new financial instruments, fund managers found that the internal controls and processes necessary for managing nonrated and high-yield bonds differed from managing a portfolio of general market-rated debt. This chapter covers all these various aspects of the high-yield municipal bond market and how portfolio managers and analysts invest in and manage a high-yield municipal bond fund.

HIGH-YIELD BORROWERS

The vast majority of borrowers in the municipal bond market are states, municipalities, or other public purpose entities with well-established economic credentials. Frequently they achieve the highest investment-grade ratings by Standard & Poor's or Moody's. Correspondingly, they also enjoy the most competitive interest rates.

However, there are other borrowers in this market with significantly smaller capital needs. These generally come to market as one-time project-based financings for charter schools, rural hospitals, nursing homes, retirement centers, or economic development areas that often do not have extensive operating histories, if any. Although these borrowers serve an essential public service, they generally lack the economic track record to achieve an investment-grade rating. Often, they choose to come to the market with no rating at all, accepting a higher rate for access to capital—hence the term "high yield" for this asset class.

Active participants in this market are investors willing to trade off the perceived higher risk, in lower-rated and nonrated bonds, for the higher yields. However, these investors do not go in blindly. Rather, each investment decision requires significant credit analysis to determine the risks—and projected returns—before committing capital.

Consequently, it is often the institutional investor, be it mutual funds or high net worth money managers, with the resources necessary to do that analysis, who are the most active participants in lower-rated and nonrated bonds. While individual bond purchase decisions are complex, managing a portfolio of high-yield bonds adds another dimension to the investment decision-making process. This chapter gives a broad yet concise overview of most of the aspects of managing high-yield municipal portfolios.

HIGH-YIELD MUNICIPAL BOND FUND TRACK RECORD

By taking on additional risk, investors in the high-yield market have been rewarded relative to their peers investing in general market bonds.

Several years ago, many investors fretted about putting lower-rated or nonrated high-yield bonds in their portfolios. Often funding sectors new to the market that, by definition, lacked credit and market performance history, high-yield municipal bonds were purchased almost exclusively by a handful of large institutional investors. Most investors took a wait-and-see attitude. In part because of this and the interest rate environment from 1997 to 2001, high-yield municipal bond funds underperformed general market funds by a cumulative total return of nearly 6%.

However, by 2001, high-yield bonds had an established track record of credit stability. Mutual funds investing in high-yield bonds were increasingly able to distribute a higher dividend to shareholders. To remain competitive, funds that had initially shunned high-yield municipal bonds began to invest in this asset class. As individual investors clamored for above-average tax-exempt income, mutual fund companies began offering, new open and closed-end municipal bond mutual funds to meet investors' demands. Other new entrants to the municipal bond market were hedge funds, who also began participating in the high-yield asset class. Demand for high-yield paper grew proportionately with the inflows from these capital sources and, as demand rose, prices rose too. Consequently, the spread (the difference in basis points) between high-yield bonds and the market benchmark Municipal Market Data AAA (MMD AAA) narrowed. Note on Exhibit 36. 1 that by fall 2003, the HY-AAA Spread was at a high of over 400 basis points. By summer 2006, the spread had tightened to only slightly over 1%. This yield compression largely explains the outperformance of high-yield municipal bond funds relative to the general market funds. As Exhibit 36.2 shows, from 2001 to 2006, on a cumulative total return basis, high-yield bond funds' returns exceeded general market funds by over 11% and insured bond funds by nearly 13%.

EXHIBIT 36.1   High-Yield Compression versus High-Yield Fund Flows

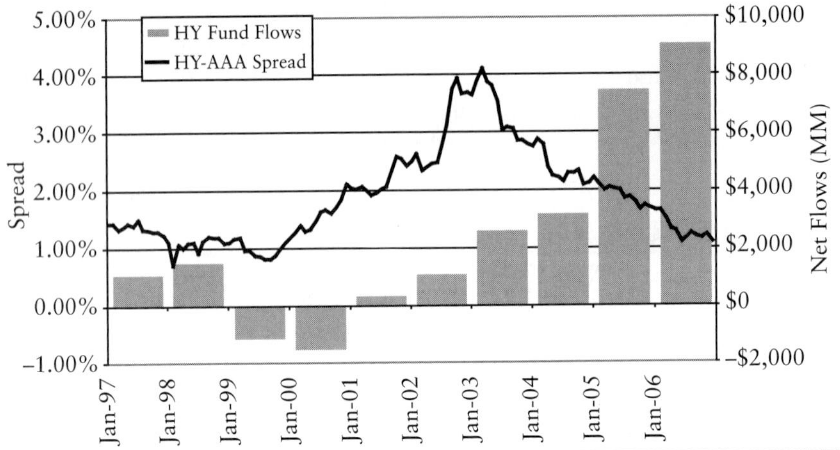

Source: Data obtained from Morningstar and Lipper.

EXHIBIT 36.2   Comparative Municipal Debt Fund Returns

Fund Name	1 Year 01/31/2006 01/31/2007 Cumulative Total Return (%)	3 Years 01/31/2004 01/31/2007 Cumulative Total Return (%)	5 Years 01/31/2002 01/31/2007 Cumulative Total Return (%)	10 Years 01/31/1997 01/31/2007 Cumulative Total Return (%)
High-yield municipal debt funds				
Average/total	6.79	19.75	36.09	67.74
General municipal bond funds				
Average/total	3.98	10.94	24.73	61.21
Insured municipal debt funds				
Average/total	3.48	9.45	23.15	59.06
Intermediate municipal debt funds				
Average/total	2.99	7.33	20.08	55.47

Source: Data obtained from Lipper.

CREDIT ANALYSIS

The challenge for a portfolio manager of a high-yield municipal bond fund is to balance the potential reward of investments that can generate an above average tax-exempt yield against the risk of the loss of capital on each investment.

Without question, the single most important component a portfolio manager can have to accomplish this is an experienced credit research staff. Seasoned high-yield analysts can quickly and effectively analyze the reward/ risk parameters and dynamics in specific credits and across many of the specialized sectors within the high-yield municipal market place. Credit teams are best assembled by areas of sector expertise and geography, working together to collectively and comprehensively analyze a credit's strengths and weaknesses. Careful, methodical, research is of utmost importance. Consistent long-term performance and long-term track records are derived from the collective efforts of an experienced and broad-based high-yield credit research team.

The goal of a high-yield municipal analyst is to make recommendations to the investment management team on which sectors and which specific credits to consider. Many of these sectors include but are not limited to:

1. Healthcare, which involves financing acute care hospitals, not-for-profit nursing homes, stand-alone assisted living projects, community clinics, and continuing care retirement communities.
2. Infrastructure finance, which includes utility district financing (MUD, CDD), *tax increment financings* (TIFs), toll roads, port, and airport facilities.
3. Housing, which includes multifamily and single-family stand-alone financings.
4. Industrial revenue bonds (PCRs, IDBs) used by large taxable corporations that have special tax incentives to borrow in the high-yield municipal market.
5. Education, which includes higher education, charter schools, and private schools.
6. Social service providers that offer education, housing, and healthcare to children and adults with developmental disabilities.

SECTOR ALLOCATION

In early 2007, high-yield municipal bond funds as a group were heavily weighted in the industrial revenue development (including special facility

EXHIBIT 36.3   Standard & Poor's High-Yield Municipal Bond Index Sector Allocations

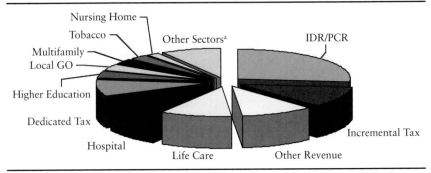

^a "Other Sectors" includes the 12 remaining S&P Sectors, each composing less than 1.50% of the full index.
Source: Standard & Poor's, InvestorTools.

airport revenue bonds) sector and the healthcare sector, (hospitals and life care included), as captured by the Standard and Poor's High Yield Municipal Bond Index, as seen in Exhibit 36.3. An important but smaller sector for the group is bonds secured by payments under the Master Settlement Agreement entered into by many states and the major cigarette manufactures to settle litigation brought by the states against the manufacturers.

One limitation of this index is that it does not list as a sector derivative holdings, such as inverse floating rate securities, that many funds had invested in by 2007 and that can materially contribute to performance. It should be noted that the index only includes funds whose bonds arepriced by Standard and Poor's Evaluations. This is only a minor limitation, however, since Standard and Poor's Evaluations prices the overwhelming number of high-yield municipal bond funds.

TRADING OPPORTUNITIES

While credit remains paramount in high-yield municipal fund management, a portfolio manager would be remiss if he or she did not look to boost returns by looking for trading opportunities in the market. Relative value is the basis for the ultimate decision to buy one bond or sector and sell another. What may cause a security to trade "rich" or "cheap" to another or to its historical spread relationship? Below are a few of the factors that can cause spread relationships to change and thus create trading opportunities.

New Issue Supply

Municipal bonds are issued via underwritings by the dealer community, and are then sold to end users such as mutual funds and individuals. On occasion, a new issue is brought that is larger than the market has demand for at that time. To be able to sell all of this debt, a dealer may have to price the new issue at a higher yield or spread than normal. This anomaly generally corrects itself over time as the market returns to its natural supply/demand equilibrium. A savvy investor can buy these bonds at issuance and hold them until the market reverts as projected.

Dealer Inventory

Broker-dealers in the municipal marketplace buy bonds for their inventory as a matter of course. Reasons for this include proprietary trading, supporting deals underwritten by their investment banking department, and retail distribution needs. From time to time, dealers will find themselves overextended, or maintaining too much inventory, for a number of reasons. As a result, the dealer may feel compelled to sell some securities, causing those bonds to be sold to the market at artificially low prices. This usually creates a widening of the normal spread relationship of the bonds they are selling. Conversely, if dealers feel that they are not holding enough inventory, they may be willing to pay higher prices and tighter spreads than normal.

Supply/Demand Anomalies

Sometimes an institutional investor such as a mutual fund or hedge fund, has a need to purchase a specific issue or sector. If supply of such securities is limited or if holders are unwilling to part with their holdings, the bid side will normally rise. This can create a tightening of the normal spread relationship that could be advantageous to any potential sellers.

Sector versus Sector/State versus State

One reason for tracking the historical yield differences between sectors or states is the fact that these relationships can drift from their historical averages before reverting back. A large seller of one sector, a market overreaction to an event in a particular state, or an institutional account with a large inquiry can skew the relationship of two issuers or sectors. By looking for these anomalies, an investor can take advantage of these changes and reverse the trade when the market normalizes. Of course, this assumes that structural changes in the market have not altered the normal relationship.

Out of Favor Sectors

From time to time, there may be macroevents which cause elevated concern in the market regarding certain borrowers. For example, bonds issued for hospitals and nursing homes came under considerable pressure as the full implications on federal funding of healthcare reimbursement in the Balanced Budget Act of 1998 came to light. While the impact of this legislation affected each healthcare provider differently, many municipal bond market participants viewed the legislation as economically detrimental to the sector as a whole. Speculation of widespread defaults caused alarm. Risk-averse investors had little interest in owning this debt whereas others demanded higher yield premiums for taking on the perceived risk. As a result, prices for hospital bonds declined, causing spreads to widen against other sectors and the market in general. This opinion was so pervasive that even when the market rallied on positive interest rate news, healthcare bonds tended to lag.

However, to the high-yield portfolio manager, this uncertainty meant opportunity. Careful credit research on individual hospitals showed that many continued to perform adequately under the new legislation. Relative to the risk, the depressed prices offered above average yields to investors willing to ignore market consensus. As time passed and fears of massive defaults proved unfounded, the broader market began to reassess its view of risk in this sector. Spreads began to come back to more normative levels and funds that had done quality research were appropriately rewarded.

STORY BONDS

Some credit considerations go beyond fundamental economic analysis. For example, when many of the large tobacco companies agreed to fund a *master settlement agreement* (MSA) as part of resolving a lawsuit brought by the states, many states chose to issue bonds backed by those settlement proceeds. Even so, there were many civil lawsuits still ongoing against the tobacco companies. A successful suit resulting in a large damage award against any one company participating in the settlement agreement could jeopardize that firm's payments to the trust—and by extension, payments to the bondholders. In addition to considering the fundamental economic risk of the tobacco companies, bondholders also had to assess judicial and legislative risk. This initial uncertainty caused investors to demand higher yields from bonds backed by the MSA payments. However, as this market grew and rulings on the civil suits proved favorable to the tobacco companies, investors became increasingly comfortable with the risk. Correspondingly, yield premiums began to decline and investors saw the values of their bonds increase.

OPPORTUNITY BONDS

Broad diversification is the best hedge against credit risk because, in a portfolio of high-yield investments, inevitably there will be some distressed credits. When that happens, it is the role of the portfolio manager to preserve value by both protecting principal as well as maintaining valuable tax-exempt income. Generally, since municipal bonds are for entities that provide an essential public service, there is community and political impetus in finding a way to keep a distressed credit from closing its doors.

Working with managers, and sometimes political leaders, investors can work out the problems afflicting a credit. Depending on the circumstances causing the credit problems, there may be several remedies to preserve value for bondholders and the facility as well. Deferring principal or interest for some time may be all that is needed when an unexpected but short-term problem arises. For example, a sudden drop in occupancy at a retirement center may be a one time, statistically anomalous event. Another option may be a debt restructuring to lessen leverage but ensure long-term credit stability. One security provision in bond documents, often insisted upon by buyers of high-yield debt, is a first mortgage lien. It is a solution of last resort, but bondholders secured by a mortgage have the option of foreclosure and sale of the underlying asset.

From time to time, a distressed credit for one investor may prove an opportunity for another. Some mutual funds invest in high-yield to improve returns but do not have a strong focus on it. When a problem arises in a credit in such a fund, the bond may have to be sold per indenture or simply to avoid reporting underperforming assets to shareholders. However, the high-yield fund manager may see opportunity in a distressed credit. Able to focus on the credit, analyze the risk and values carefully, and purchase the bonds at the right price, the fund manager can achieve substantial returns on principal as well as potentially earn tax-exempt income by putting in the time to do the workout.

CREDIT IMPROVEMENT AND ENHANCEMENT

To get a project financed in the capital markets, a not-for-profit or municipality needs to assemble a team of experienced managers, developers, financial feasibility consultants, architects, and investment bankers. The proceeds of the debt financing fund the construction of the facility. Initially, with nothing built and no established economic track record, the risk seems high. Will the project get built on time and on budget? Will parents send their children to the new charter school? Will seniors move to the new retirement center? Will families buy homes in the community development district? In most cases, after a couple of years, the project is built: the charter school is filled with children, retirement centers with seniors, the district with stores and homes.

The investor takes on the risk of that initial uncertainty, quantified by the yield on the bonds. However, the bonds increase in value as the project turns from a plan on paper to an operating business entity with established financial performance. Correspondingly, the price improves as the credit improves. From time to time, a project supporting a bond issue may perform so well that the fund manager will bring it to the attention of the rating agencies to get it rated. Going from nonrated to investment grade can be quite a boost to the bond's value. Additionally, if the rate environment permits, there may be an opportunity for an advance refunding.

DERIVATIVES

As in virtually every other financial market, the use of derivatives has grown exponentially in recent years within the world of municipals due to their unique ability to cost-effectively monetize the value of certain events . These derivatives have enabled portfolio managers to hedge risks associated with current holdings through credit default swaps (or to offer "insurance" to other investors by taking the other side of such a trade), to make a direct investment on projected changes in the structure of the yield curve using different interest rate swaps, or to leverage their exposure to certain existing holdings through a device called an inverse floater.

While many swaps are still in their infancy in the municipal market, inverse floaters have been an invaluable tool for most managers, and have become even more so for high-yield managers as credit spreads have compressed. Inverse floaters serve a double purpose within the market by allowing a long-term investor to leverage current positions, while simultaneously offering additional liquidity to the short-term tax-free market that is used by institutional money market funds and the like.

An inverse floater is created by selling a long-term, high-grade, fixed-rate bond into a trust that then sells off two certificates, series A (short-term floating rate securities, or floaters) and series B (inverse floaters), to different investors. The trust receives all coupons for the deposited security, and distributes income to series A and series B holders based on a pre-determined formula. The series A certificate, which always has its price maintained at par, has an interest rate equal to the BMA weekly rate (or another floating rate as defined in the trust agreement). The interest rate for the series B, or inverse floater, is equal to the difference between the fixed rate received by the trust on the deposited bond less the adjustable rate paid out on the series A class of bonds. Of major importance, in order to keep the series A bonds priced at par, the series B securities retain all of the price volatility for the whole trust.

As long as the slope of the municipal yield curve is positive, by holding an inverse floater (or series B security), a high-yield manager can "squeeze" extra yield from a security by assuming more risk. To further increase such returns, additional leverage may be placed on the series B securities by selling a greater amount of the series A security. By increasing the leverage ratio, yields on the series B security will rise. (For example, if a bond yielding 5.30% is leveraged 3:1, (A:B) it can yield 9.80% to the inverse floater holder.) As the leverage increases on a trust, the duration of the series B security does as well. This often requires a manager to hedge such floater positions, but, even so, the after-hedge returns of inverse floaters can add significantly to the total return of a high-yield municipal portfolio. Prospectus guidelines for high-yield municipal funds generally limit inverse floaters to 15% to 20% of assets.

Credit Default Swaps

In 2006, *credit default swaps* (CDS) began to be marketed for municipal bonds. In a traditional corporate CDS, one party accepts the risk of a monetary default, bankruptcy or restructuring in exchange for payment of a fee from the other party, typically paid quarterly, but quoted on an annual basis. CDS in the corporate market has become the simplest way to transfer or speculate on risk for a particular credit or basket of credits. The depth of the market has improved to the point that the notional amount of CDS exceeds the amount of outstanding bonds in the corporate market, and bid/ask spreads are often just 1 to 2 basis points.

Because default risk is much lower in the municipal market than in the corporate market, initial interest in municipal CDS has come from parties outside of traditional municipal market participants. Interest in selling municipal CDS (taking a payment in exchange for accepting credit risk) has come from parties that would like exposure to the municipal bond market but do not want the low interest rate from federal tax exemption. To date, sellers of municipal CDS include foreign banks that have become familiar with municipal bonds but cannot use the U.S. federal tax exemption. Buyers of municipal CDS have been newer participants (often international) who find the modest premium for insuring investment-grade municipal bonds worthwhile, often for their own regulatory reasons.

Currently, market activity is inhibited by relatively low CDS premiums and low volatility, compounded by relatively wide bid/ask spreads. As the market grows and should credit risk become more volatile, these issues would decline in importance.

A more fully developed market would allow participants to short the credit risk of a bond, something very difficult to do in the municipal cash market that exists today. Municipal CDS also has the potential to be an alternative to traditional municipal bond insurance, particularly when only short-term protection is desired. For example, an investor may become uncomfortable with a state or territory's credit risk during a particularly contentious budget season; as opposed to bond insurance, a CDS trade can be taken off once that crisis has passed.

THE USE OF BENCHMARKS

The industry standard benchmarks for high-yield municipal portfolios are the Lehman Brothers High Yield Municipal Index and the Standard & Poor's High Yield Municipal Index. There are other well-established indexes that sometimes are used in performance comparisons with the high-yield municipal indexes, such as the Lehman Brothers Municipal Bond Index which includes both high-yield and investment-grade municipal bonds. Additionally, there are proprietary indexes that are developed to specifically try to mimic the assumed holdings of competitors, allowing a manager to make allocation decisions accordingly.

HIGH-YIELD MUNICIPAL FUND INFRASTRUCTURE

To achieve consistent above average results, a high-yield municipal fund must have solid internal processes and procedures. These encompass a wide variety of functions within the investment team. They address how primary and secondary market issues are discussed for purchase, how nonrated issues are assigned internal ratings, how surveillance is conducted on the fund's holdings, how distressed securities are monitored and priced, and how certain holdings may be classified as illiquid. The key to these procedures is that they should be specific enough to address the important topics but also general enough to allow for flexibility and judgment. Adequately documenting how the investment group complies with its own and fund complex procedures is also critical. Finally, the investment team should periodically review its procedures and revise them if they become too cumbersome, onerous or irrelevant due to changes in the market, a shift in investment strategy, or other factors beyond the control of the group.

How surveillance is conducted offers a good example of the importance of procedures and the issues they address. The first question to address is the frequency of team members' formal reviews for a holding. The team must decide how to allocate its resources to analyzing periodic disclosures, researching a sector, or contacting management in connection with existing holdings. The next question to deal with is how to document the surveillance; fund groups typically have a computerized system containing periodic updates that are readily accessible by portfolio managers or analysts to assist in decisions to buy more of a holding or potentially to sell it. Another issue to address is how often the team as a whole will discuss holdings in detail. One approach might be to hold quarterly, all-hands meetings to review in detail holdings that are characterized as developing due to ongoing construction projects or ramp-ups in utilization. These could also include holdings that might need more attention because they are not performing as expected or projected. A semiannual review could then be held to review the more seasoned credits in less detail. By addressing all of the above issues, the investment team fulfills some key objectives. The first is that the team fulfills its pledge to shareholders to adequately monitor fund holdings. The second is that the team identifies in a timely manner specific holdings to add to or to liquidate in an effort to optimize returns—one test of a solid surveillance process is that portfolio mangers can rely on it to quickly give them the latest information on a holding to make an informed investment decision. A related benefit is that the team is able to detect key trends within sectors earlier than competitors without a sound surveillance process, thus enabling portfolio mangers to get a jump on either adding to a particular sector or lightening up in it. The bottom line is that well thought out, systematic, documented surveillance procedures are critical to a high-yield fund fulfilling its investment objectives.

SUMMARY

Investing in high-yield municipal bonds has evolved considerably since the first funds were offered to investors. As new sectors, unique borrowers, distressed debt, and sophisticated financial instruments were introduced into the municipal bond market, fund managers and analysts adapted by creating methodologies to understand and value each new risk and potential reward accordingly. By consistent application of careful investment analysis for each acquisition as well as broad diversification within their portfolios' holdings, institutional investors sought to hedge against the uncertainties of change. It is part of the challenge—and the reward—of investing in high-yield bonds, knowing that more changes and opportunities, both expected and unexpected, are yet to come. Perhaps if all of the lessons of managing a high-yield portfolio over those years were reduced to one, it is that the management of this asset class is the management of change.

CHAPTER 37

Managing Municipal Bonds for Property and Casualty Insurance Companies for Total Return

Karen Szerszen, CFA
Senior Credit Research Analyst
Allstate Investments, LLC

The purpose of this chapter is to discuss some of the strategies and techniques used to manage a property and casualty insurance company's tax-exempt portfolio on a total return basis. The goal of managing a portfolio on a total return basis is to maximize the portfolio's value derived from the combination of interest income, gains or losses on securities sold, plus the change in market value of the portfolio. A property and casualty insurance company's tax-exempt portfolio is managed within the content of maximizing the total return of the company's total investment portfolio, subject to the investment constraints dictated by its management and by statutes unique to insurance companies. We begin with a brief review of the property and casualty insurance industry.

BUSINESS OF PROPERTY AND CASUALTY INSURANCE COMPANIES

Property and casualty insurance companies are primarily in the business of collecting funds in exchange for a promise to payout cash to settle claims. This is known as the *underwriting operations* of an insurance company and, as discussed next, this segment of the company's operations can be profit-

The author thanks Charles Mires, CFA and Robert Zubak of Allstate Investments, LLC for their helpful comments.

able or it can incur losses. Therefore, the investment portfolio of a property and casualty insurance company plays a critical role in the company's operations. The investment portfolio not only helps the company pay claims but can also assist in keeping its premiums competitive.

COMBINED RATIO

The profitability of an insurance company's underwriting operations can be ascertained by computing its *combined ratio*. The calculation for the combined ratio is the sum of claims paid or payable plus underwriting expenses divided by earned premiums([Claims paid + Claims payable + Underwriting expenses]/Earned premiums) for the time period for which the combined ratio is being computed. This ratio is then usually multiplied by 100. A ratio below 100 means an insurance company's underwriting operation is profitable while a ratio above 100 indicates an unprofitable underwriting operation.

In 2005, according to A.M. Best Company,[1] the U. S. property and casualty insurance industry had a combined ratio of 101.2. This means that for every premium dollar earned by the industry in 2005, it incurred over a one cent underwriting loss. In 2004, the industry combined ratio was 98.1, which means, overall, the industry's underwriting operations were profitable. This was the first year since 1978 that the property and casualty insurance industry reported a combined ratio below 100. The preliminary combined ratio for 2006 was 92.4, the lowest combined ratio since 1948. A history of the industry's combined ratio is provided in Exhibit 37.1.

Characteristics and Goals of Property and Casualty Insurance Company's Investment Portfolio

As the history of the combined ratio indicates, as a whole, the underwriting operations of the property and casualty insurance industry are generally not profitable. Therefore, one of the goals of a property and casualty insurance company's investment portfolio is to generate sufficient cash flow to help pay a portion of the company's normal business expenses. For this reason, property and casualty insurance companies' investment portfolios tend to be heavily invested in fixed income securities. These types of securities usually have more reliable cash flows than equities.

---

[1] A.M. Best Company is the source of this information. A.M. Best Company is a privately held company which rates the claims paying ability of individual insurance companies and is a provider of information on the insurance industry.

EXHIBIT 37.1   History of Combined Ratio for U.S. Property and Casualty Industry

Year	Combined Ratio
1970s	100.3
1980s	109.2
1990s	107.8
2000	110.1
2001	115.7
2002	107.2
2003	100.1
2004	98.1
2005	101.2
2006	92.4

Source: A.M. Best.

Besides normal business expenses, the investment portfolio can also assist in paying insurance claims. The potential payout of insurance claims for the common auto accident or house fire can be actuarially calculated. Therefore, these claims can normally be paid from the cash flow generated from the insurance company's underwriting activity or from the cash flow generated from the coupons of its fixed income securities. However, the occurrence of large claims is not predictable. Therefore, the liquidity of the investment portfolio is important and can be a material consideration when constructing and managing fixed income securities for an insurance company. Liquidity, in this case, is the ability to quickly sell needed amounts of the portfolio's securities without materially negatively impacting the prices received for these securities.

Fixed income securities possessing higher credit quality usually have greater liquidity as well as greater reliability of cash flow. Likewise, the securities of frequent issuers—that is, well-known obligors—have greater liquidity. Therefore, property and casualty insurance companies' investment portfolios tend to be heavily invested in the securities of higher rated, larger issuers.

The main characteristics of a property and casualty insurance company's investment portfolio are relatively stable cash flow and good liquidity. Additionally, many property and casualty insurance companies attempt to match assets with their liabilities. This can be accomplished by having the duration of its investment portfolio approximately equal the duration of its estimated liabilities or its projected insurance claims.

TOTAL RETURN VERSUS BENCHMARK

As mentioned earlier, a portfolio's total return, for a specific time period, is the income it generates from the combination of interest income, gains and/ or losses on securities sold, and the change in market value of the portfolio from the start of the measurement period to the last date of the measurement period. The portfolio manager's (or managers') goal is to maximize total return given the constraints provided. The total return results are usually measured against a publicly available benchmark. The measurement result is the difference between the total return of the portfolio versus the benchmark, usually expressed in basis points. The goal is to record a positive spread versus the benchmark—that is, to outperform the benchmark. For example, if the benchmark's total return was 6.4% and the portfolio's return was 6.6%, the portfolio outperformed the benchmark by 20 basis points. Likewise, if the benchmark had a return of –2.2% while the portfolio's return was –2.0%, the portfolio still outperformed the benchmark by 20 basis points. As these examples illustrate, the portfolio's performance is always compared to that of the benchmark as this is the best way to measure how well the portfolio is performing—that is, the absolute total return figure is not a sufficient indicator of how well the portfolio performed. However, while the goal is to outperform the benchmark, negative returns are not viewed favorably, even if the loss is less than the benchmark.

In order to outperform the benchmark, the portfolio manager must know the characteristics of the benchmark to which the portfolio is being compared. By characteristics, we primarily mean the duration of the benchmark portfolio, as well as the credit sectors and/or quality of its securities. The insurance company's portfolio can outperform/underperform the benchmark only if its characteristics are different from the benchmark's— for example, lengthening the portfolio's duration, investing in lower quality credits, or underweighting in a sector. If the insurance company's portfolio has the same characteristics as the benchmark, its performance is expected to be equal to the benchmark.

REGULATORY FACTORS

The portfolio management techniques used to optimize total return, such as managing duration and/or credit quality, are generally the same whether the tax-exempt portfolio is that of a property and casualty insurance company or that of another institutional investor, such as a mutual fund. The main difference is the operating or regulatory environment.

For example, the management of a mutual fund's portfolio is governed by the fund's prospectus. The prospectus usually indicates the interest rate risk of the securities in which the mutual fund's portfolio invests as well as any credit risk requirements. As a tax-exempt mutual fund, the recognition of taxable income is expected to be kept to a minimum.

The management of a property and casualty insurance company's tax-exempt portfolio may allow for more flexibility in changing the portfolio's duration, credit quality of the securities in which it invests, as well as real-izing taxable income. After all, the tax-exempt portfolio is just a portion of the insurance company's total investment portfolio. Most property and casualty insurance companies have sizeable taxable fixed income portfolios. Therefore, the recognition of taxable income may not be an issue. The goal, in a total return world, is to maximize the performance of the insurance company's total investment portfolio.

While a mutual fund is a singular entity with its own financial state-ments, the investment assets and, the investment income these assets gener-ate, are components of the insurance company's financial statements. These financial statements are prepared pursuant to *generally accepted accounting principles* (GAAP) as dictated by the Financial Accounting Standards Board (FASB). Insurance companies can classify its investment assets in one of three categories: (1) hold-to-maturity, (2) available for sales, and (3) trading portfolio.

Securities classified as being held to maturity will be carried at cost on an insurance company's financial statements and their change in market value or unrealized gains or losses will not have any impact on either the company's balance sheet or income statement. However, unrealized gains or losses for securities classified as available for sale will be accounted for in the equity position of an insurance company's balance sheet while unre-alized gains or losses for securities held in the trading portfolio must be accounted for on the insurance company's income statement. Portfolio turn-over is a key factor in determining whether securities should be classified as available for sale or as a trading portfolio. Since stability of earnings is gen-erally important to insurance companies, it is desirable to keep the amount of securities classified as held for trading at a minimum.

The desire for stable earnings, and perhaps more importantly stable cash flow, may also impact the ability of the portfolio manager to actually realize gains or losses. Any limitations on the ability to realize investment gains or losses could impact the portfolio's total return and its performance versus the benchmark.

TAX RISK

All fixed income portfolios possess credit risk (unless they solely invest in U. S. government securities) as well as interest rate risk. Additionally, tax-exempt fixed income portfolios assume tax risk. *Tax risk* is the risk of having the interest earned from tax-exempt securities declared taxable after the debt is initially issued (sold in the primary market). This can occur for a number of reasons. One is changes in the federal tax code. Every investor in tax-exempt securities assumes this risk and there is really no way to alleviate this risk. The risk of having tax code changes, which would negatively impact tax-exempt securities, is greater for longer term maturities as these securities have more time, and more of their cash flows, exposed to legislative changes.

However, federal tax code changes could impact all tax-exempt bonds. For example, the implementation of a flat tax could eliminate the benefits of investing in tax-exempt bonds. In March 1986, the municipal market essentially shutdown for a few days when Senator Bob Packwood of Oregon proposed a 20% alternative minimum tax on all tax-exempt bond income.

There is an effective flat tax rate on all property and casualty insurance companies' tax–exempt interest income as a result of the Tax Reform Act of 1986. The proration rule requires property and casualty insurance companies to reduce their reserves for incurred losses by 15% of their tax exempt interest income when determining their taxable income. This would result in a tax rate of just over 5% on interest income earned from tax-exempt securities for insurance companies in the 35% tax bracket.

While a change in the federal tax code is the greatest source of tax risk for investors in tax-exempt bonds, changes in state and local tax codes can also be a source of tax risk. For example, it is currently common practice for many states to exempt from taxation, interest income earned from tax-exempt bonds issued by the taxing state while taxing tax-exempt income earned from out of state municipal bonds. If this practice of in-state exemption is reduced or eliminated, it will likely negatively impact the value of existing bonds of high-income tax states.

Tax code changes can affect all tax-exempt securities. However, tax risk can also be security specific. This occurs when the Internal Revenue Service (IRS) declares specific bonds as taxable. This can occur for a number of reasons. One such reason is when bond proceeds are used inappropriately, such as for the cost of a portion of a project not eligible for tax-exempt financing. Reliance on the bond opinion of an experienced and known bond counsel can alleviate this risk. Historically this type of tax risk has been minimal and is expected to continue to be minimal, despite the increased enforcement effort by the IRS. Many times, other parties involved in the bond transaction, such as the underwriter or the obligor, will settle with the IRS before a bond issue is declared taxable.

Tax risk associated with tax code changes and IRS enforcement is assumed by all investors in tax-exempt bonds. However, for the property and casualty insurance company industry, there is tax risk associated with the nature of its business—operational tax risk.

Given the history of the industry's combined ratio, one may wonder why a property and casualty insurance company would invest in tax-exempt securities. However, as previously mentioned, the combined ratio only indicates the profitability of a property and casualty insurance company's underwriting activity. Property and casualty insurance companies generate profits from their investment portfolios. The allocation of a company's investment among asset classes is decided by its management and can change from one year to the next as well as within a year's time. The more profitable management expects the company to be, the greater its allocation may be to tax-exempt securities.

The *alternative minimum tax* (AMT) is another operational tax risk for insurance companies. If underwriting income is inadequate, an insurance company may be subject to the AMT. If an insurance company is in an AMT position, all of the interest earned from its tax-exempt securities will be subject to the AMT tax, not just its AMT bonds. To alleviate this operational tax risk, an insurance company's management regularly assesses its tax position. As a result of these periodic assessments, the allocation of the company's investments among asset classes may be changed. For example, if it appears that the insurance company will be in an AMT position, management may direct all future cash flow into taxable assets. Occasionally it may also direct the sale of a portion of its tax-exempt portfolio. The latter strategy is not frequently done as management usually expects the factors causing the AMT situation to be temporary.

CREDIT RISK

As mentioned previously, all fixed-income securities (unless, of course, they are U.S. government securities) possess credit risk. Essentially, credit risk is the risk of default or more broadly, the risk of not receiving the security's principal and interest income on a timely basis. Credit risk can be expanded to include an investment's change in credit quality over time—that is, the likelihood of default or not receiving the timely payment of debt service changes over time. When managing a portfolio on a total return basis, credit risk also includes changes in spread between different rating categories.

Many large insurance companies maintain their own staff of credit analysts. One of the responsibilities of these analysts is to ascertain the credit risk associated with a particular investment security. Like other asset classes, this analysis will include an assessment of the qualitative factors of a credit as well as a financial analysis. An added twist to the analysis of many tax-exempt bonds is a review of the legal provisions of the bond indenture. This can include whether the bonds are secured by a mortgage lien on any real property, and, if there is a lien, whether it is senior or subordinated and, whether there are conditions under which this lien can be released. The flow of funds may be analyzed as well as if there are any financial covenants, what constitutes events of default, and bondholders' remedies if there is an event of default.

There may be a misconception that insurance companies are risk averse. This is not necessarily the case. After all, the nature of an insurance company's business is the assumption of risk. However, historically, some insurance companies were less likely to assume credit risk than others. This appears to be changing as pressure to keep insurance premiums down intensifies. Given the relationship between risk and reward, some insurance companies have moved down the credit spectrum to increase the return generated by their fixed income portfolios. A few insurance companies even dedicate a portion of their investment dollars to the acquisition of below investment-grade securities.

There are a number of ways an insurance company can reduce the amount of credit risk it assumes as it moves down the credit spectrum. One of the most common ways is purchasing bond insurance. This is primarily done when a bond issue is first sold in the market; however, secondary market bond insurance can also be purchased. The impact of purchasing secondary market credit enhancement not only reduces the amount of credit risk assumed, but, may also increase the value of the security, as it will now be rated triple A (assuming insurance from a triple A insurer is purchased). Bond insurance may also increase the liquidity of the security as the market views the bond's credit as that of a well-capitalized, triple-A rated insurer rather than that of the underlying uninsured municipal entity. Penetration of bond insurance has increased significantly over time. According to Thompson Financial, in 1986, only 15.58% of new issue bonds came to market with insurance; by 2005, this percentage had risen to 55.86%. Preliminary figures for 2006 indicate that this percentage fell to around 51%.

Another way an insurance company can alter the risk profile of its fixed income portfolio is by buying or selling credit default swaps. If an insurance company wants to reduce its credit risk, it can buy credit protection via a credit default swap. Likewise, credit risk can be increased by selling credit protection via a credit default swap. The credit exposures involved in credit default swaps are specifically identified, in terms of both the credit involved (e.g., Commonwealth of Puerto Rico) and the dollar amount (e.g., $10 million). By specifically identifying the credit as well as the dollar amount involved, the credit default swap parties know what credit risk they are either mitigating or assuming and to what level.

The key way credit risk can be used to improve a portfolio's total return is by trading credit spreads. Usually credit spreads are associated with the difference in interest rates commanded by different rating categories. However, credit spreads also exist between the different sectors of the municipal market. A single-A general obligation bond will generally command a lower interest rate than a single-A hospital bond, while a double-A general obligation bond will generally command a lower interest rate than a single-A general obligation bond. This statement assumes that the securities all have similar maturity structures, coupons, and call features.

An example of a rating category swap is as follows. Let's say that the normal spread between a general obligation bond issued by triple-A rated State of Virginia and a general obligation bond issued by double-A rated Commonwealth of Pennsylvania is 15 basis points. However, suppose that the current spread is only 5 basis points. The portfolio manager may trade out of the Pennsylvania position and buy State of Virginia bonds. When the spread returns to 15 basis points, the portfolio manager can reverse the trade, if desired.

Sector spread swaps work much the same way. If the spread between a single-A rated Pennsylvania hospital and a single-A rated general obligation debt of a Pennsylvania school district is normally 20 basis points and is now 35 basis points, the portfolio manager may purchase the single-A hospital and sell its school district position. This swap assumes that the hospital's credit quality is stable or improving. Before performing this swap, the portfolio manager should ascertain the credit trend of the hospital securing the bonds. Deteriorating credit quality may be contributing to the widening of the spread between the two bonds.

The above example segues into another way a portfolio manager can use credit to increase the total return of a portfolio—changing credit quality. If the portfolio manager can increase a position in a credit whose credit quality is improving, the value of the credit's bonds should appreciate over time, relative to other bonds, as well as in response to rating upgrades. Likewise, if the credit quality of a position in the portfolio is deteriorating, the portfolio manager will attempt to sell out of the position. The key here is that the trades are done before the securities' market price reflects the change in credit quality.

Remember the portfolio manager's performance is compared to that of a publicly available benchmark. It is important for the portfolio manager to know the composition of this benchmark. One way to outperform the benchmark is to underweight in credits or sectors that are likely to underperform, such as deteriorating ones, and to overweight in credits or sectors expected to outperform, such as improving ones.

INTEREST RATE RISK

Usually the biggest risk associated with a fixed income portfolio is interest rate risk—the impact that changing levels of interest rates has on the value of the securities in the portfolio. The measurement used to indicate a security's or portfolio's sensitivity to changes in interest rates is duration. The higher the duration, the greater the sensitivity to interest rate changes. Interest rate changes have a greater impact on longer-duration securities than shorter-duration ones. Therefore, if a general increase in interest rates is expected, shorter duration bonds should be held in the portfolio and longer-duration securities should be held if interest rates are expected to decline. The coupon rate on a particular bond, relative to current market levels, will also impact its sensitivity to interest changes. Discount bonds, bonds whose coupons are below current interest rates, have longer durations, while premium bonds, bonds whose coupons are higher than current interest rates, have shorter durations.

Managing a portfolio's duration is a common way of managing interest rate risk. If interest rates are expected to rise, duration will be shortened or lowered while, if interest rates are expected to fall, duration will be lengthened or raised. For this discussion, parallel shifts in the yield curve are assumed. Obviously this is not always the case; however, the general techniques are the same, just complicated by the nonparallel shifts.

Changes in a portfolio's duration can be accomplished in the cash market. As mentioned above, this can be done simply by buying longer duration securities and/or selling shorter-duration securities if interest rates are expected to fall and doing the opposite (selling long/buying short) if interest rates are expected to rise. Buying and selling discount or premium bonds can be used to change a portfolio's duration. The most extreme discount bond is a zero-coupon security. By buying these types of securities, the portfolio manager will be lengthening the duration of the portfolio while selling zero-coupon securities will be shortening it. Purchasing premium bonds will have the opposite impact; it will shorten the portfolio's duration while selling premium bonds will lengthen it.

While a portfolio's duration can be modified via the cash market, it may not be the most efficient way of accomplishing such a change. In recent years, the easiest and more efficient way of changing a portfolio's duration is using the derivative market. This market is rapidly evolving, enabling the derivative products to better match interest rate changes in the municipal market. Two derivatives products commonly used to effect a change in a portfolio's duration are interest rate swaps and interest rate futures.

For example, to shorten the duration of a tax-exempt portfolio, the portfolio manager may sell Treasury futures. To shorten duration using interest rate swaps, the portfolio will agree to pay a long fixed rate coupon in exchange for receiving a short floating rate coupon. The interest rate swap may use either LIBOR or the Bond Market Association (BMA) index as the basis for the swap payments. If the portfolio manager believes that municipal bonds are relatively cheap to their historical relationship with taxable rates, he/she may prefer to enter into a swap which utilizes LIBOR rates. Otherwise, the BMA index may be preferred because of its expected higher correlation with holdings of cash municipal securities.

Previously, insurance companies were not allowed to hold long positions in derivative products. Therefore, derivatives could not be used to lengthen the portfolio's duration and the only way to lengthen the portfolio's duration was via the cash market or by offsetting a duration shortening transaction. This began to change a few years ago and now insurance companies can also use derivative products to lengthen its portfolio's duration.

As mentioned with managing credit risk, it is imperative that the portfolio manager know the duration of the benchmark to which performance is being compared. The difference between the duration of the portfolio and the benchmark should be due to the interest rate bets that the portfolio manager consciously wants to take in the portfolio.

CONCLUSION

Optimizing the total return of a property and casualty insurance company's investment portfolio can be a critical component of the company's operations because in more years than not, the company does not realize a profit from its insurance underwriting business.

The risks associated with the company's tax-exempt portfolio are not significantly different from that of any other tax-exempt portfolio. All tax-exempt portfolios assume tax risk, credit risk, and interest rate risk. However, the property and casualty insurance company's portfolio does assume the tax risk associated with the profitability of its insurance operations. Otherwise, the techniques used to manage and/or alleviate these risks are generally the same whether the portfolio is that of a property and casualty insurance company or another institutional tax-exempt portfolio, such as a mutual fund. Therefore, the major difference is in the operating environment.

One's first impression is that the insurance company's operating environment is more restrictive. Due to the nature of insurance claims, the need for liquidity can impact investment policy. However, mutual funds also need liquidity to cover redemptions. Of course, the insurance company's portfolio must be managed such that it helps the company reach other potential objectives, such as stability of earnings. This may restrict the ability to realize investment gains or losses. Insurance companies are also subject to the insurance statutes and oversight body of each state in which it operates as well as the national oversight commission, National Association of Insurance Commissioners (NAIC). Regulations imposed by these commissions may influence investment policy.

Nevertheless, there can be more flexibility in managing a tax-exempt portfolio for a property and casualty insurance company. Given that the tax-exempt portfolio is just a portion of a larger investment portfolio held by a taxable entity, recognizing or receiving taxable income may be acceptable. This is usually highly discouraged for a tax-exempt mutual fund. The ability to receive taxable income can be important if an investment experiences credit problems and is in a workout mode. This also enables the insurance company's portfolio to invest in lower credit quality investments which can increase its total return. A mutual fund's prospectus frequently dictates the fund's duration, whether or not it can use derivative products, as well as the credit quality of its investments. It is possible to modify a fund's prospectus, although this process can be laborious and it is definitely time-consuming. It only takes a discussion with management to make these changes in an insurance company's tax-exempt portfolio. Therefore, quicker response time to changes in the marketplace leads to higher total return.

CHAPTER 38

The Role of Hedge Funds in the Municipal Market

Jonathan A. Fiebach
Cofounder
Duration Capital

The attraction of the municipal bond market for hedge funds can best be defined by the lure of a fundamentally inefficient relationship between supply and demand. Issuers tend to sell long-term debt to finance assets designed for very long-term use such as schools, roads, and utility systems. Investors in municipal bonds prefer to keep the terms of their loans very short, predominately through investments in liquid tax-exempt money market funds. Hedge funds bridge the gap. In this chapter, I explain how arbitrageurs take advantage of this basic supply and demand inefficiency and why it can be a profitable, yet risky, enterprise.

The arbitrage relationship between hedge fund and issuer begins with the relationship of each entity to tax rates. Municipalities are tax exempt; an issuer does not pay taxes so it is indifferent to tax rates. Most issuers have the choice of issuing municipal bonds to finance operations and projects or borrowing money from a bank directly in the form of a mortgage or a loan. Normally, the rate will be lower in the bond market as the interest paid from the issuer to the lender is exempt from federal taxation (tax advantaged). The fair value of a municipal bond for an issuer is

$$\text{Interest rate} < 100\% \text{ of LIBOR swap rates}$$

Interest received by the lender from a municipal bond investment is generally expected to be exempt from federal income taxes. Therefore, fair value for a municipal bond purchaser is

$$\text{Interest rate} > (1 - \text{Tax rate}) \times \text{LIBOR}$$

Hedge funds tend to compare values in the municipal market to values in the corporate bond and agency bond markets, though retail investors are likely to compare tax-advantaged municipal rates to U.S. Treasury note and bond rates. Many hedge funds view LIBOR swaps as a proxy for rates in the taxable market, which can then be compared to municipal bond rates. The vast majority of hedging of tax-advantaged municipal rates is done in the LIBOR swap market, as it is very difficult to borrow and sell short large baskets of corporate bonds or agency debt.

If a 10-year LIBOR swap is 5%, the issuer has an advantage issuing municipal bonds so long as the cost of borrowing, after all fees, is less than 5%. (It is likely that if a municipality went to a bank for a loan, the rate would be the LIBOR swap rate for the term of the loan.) An investor in the 35% tax bracket gains advantage so long as the interest rate on the municipal bond is greater than 3.25%. Top quality municipal bonds with maturity dates of 10 years tend to trade around 75% of a 10-year LIBOR swap. With 5% LIBOR, a 10-year municipal bond would change hands at 3.75%; a win-win situation for both the lender and the borrower. This fundamental arbitrage exists in very few markets around the world and is likely to be around for a long time creating a viable business for hedge funds.

Hedge funds are able to profit from the two specific areas that derive directly from this relationship. First, long-term municipal rates are fairly volatile, and are slightly different for every issuer. Second, due to the demand for tax exempt money market funds, rates for municipal bonds maturing in less than one year tend to average close to 65% of LIBOR and corporate bond rates.

RATIO CURVES

The fact that investors seek short-term investments and issuers need long-dated loans is one contributing factor to the slope of the ratio curve.[1] The *ratio curve* is the guiding light for hedge funds seeking exposure to the municipal bond market; it is the difference in relative value between municipal rates and taxable rates. Historically, demand wanes as the length of the loan increases. The ratio curve expresses the term structure of ratios, much as the yield curve expresses the term structure of interest rates. Therefore, investors have been able to garner higher ratios as time to maturity increases.

---

[1] Municipal bonds are often quoted as a percentage of LIBOR. Industry practice is to refer to the percentage as a ratio. A 10-year municipal bond quoted at a "ratio of 75" would indicate the yield on the municipal bond was equal to 75% of the yield of a LIBOR swap with the same term. The ratio is normally below 100% because the interest rate on the municipal bond is usually exempt from taxation.

A second factor leading to higher ratios in longer maturities is the uncertainty of tax rates. There is a presumption implied by the ratio curve that the value of tax-advantaged income is riskier as the length of the loan extends. Hedge funds have become insurers against this presumption. A hedge fund buys a 10-year municipal bond at 75% of LIBOR, and hedges the interest rate risk in the taxable market; the hedge fund is betting that as the bond rolls down the maturity curve, it will also roll down the ratio curve. That is, the hedge fund is making the bet that 75% compensates them for taking the risk that municipal bonds retain their advantage at an average rate for 10 years of less than 75% of their hedge vehicle, normally a LIBOR swap or a U.S. Treasury bond. If the value of the short-term tax exempt income remains at 65% of LIBOR for the next 10 years the hedge funds wins; if the value of the short-term tax advantaged income rises above 75%, the hedge fund loses. The value of tax-exempt income has many factors. Tax rates are the most popular measure of risk on this trade, but by no means are tax rates the only risk. During 2003 and 2004, short-term municipal rates regularly changed hands at 80% to 100% of LIBOR though the highest U.S. tax rates were 35%.

An easy formula to determine the value of buying long maturity municipal bonds is

$$\text{Muni rate} - \text{LIBOR} \times (1 - \text{Tax rate})] = \text{Arbitrage value}$$

If the 10-year municipal rate is 75% of LIBOR, and 10-year LIBOR swap is 5%, the municipal rate would be 3.75%, then:

$$3.75\% - [5\% \times (1 - 0.35)] = 0.50\%$$

In this example, the edge or theoretical value to the municipal bond is 50 basis points so long as the credit is equivalent to LIBOR. The 50 basis points of arbitrage profit is a direct result of the ratio differential multiplied by the interest rate. Keeping the ratio of the municipal to LIBOR fixed at 75%, but shifting the 10-year LIBOR swap to 2.5% the profit expectation drops substantially:

$$1.625\% - [2.5\% \times (1 - 0.35)] = 0.25\%$$

In this example, the hedge fund is only getting 25 basis points of edge on the same transaction. Therefore, profit from a ratio trade tends to be inversely correlated to interest rates. Consequently, a hedge fund that is invested in ratios is expecting municipals to outperform LIBOR and is going to have higher returns as interest rates rise. An adjustment can be made if the municipal credit is better or worse than LIBOR.

Because there are two points of view on the fair value of a municipal bond the relationship between municipal rates and LIBOR is most influenced by issuer supply and investor demand. If supply increases and overwhelms demand, the ratio will rise toward 100% of LIBOR, which in turn causes issuers to refrain from selling bonds, sending the ratio back down. If supply falls and demand remains constant, the ratio will fall toward 65% until ratios are too low and investors stop buying.

HEDGE FUND ACTIVITY

Hedge funds have found a few ways to gamble on the volatile relationship between tax-free and taxable rates. The most popular method for hedge funds to access the risk between tax-advantaged municipal rates and taxable LIBOR is with the Securities Industry and Financial Markets Swap Index (SIFMA). SIFMA is an index of municipal rates for a one-week term. SIFMA is most often compared to LIBOR because both are short-term rates. LIBOR and SIFMA have an actively traded swap market where investors can exchange fixed and floating cash flows. A SIFMA interest rate swap, like its LIBOR counterpart, is quoted for a fixed term with a fixed rate exchanged for floating rates. A hedge fund may, for example, want to bet that a 10-year SIFMA swap will outperform a 10-year LIBOR swap. To place this bet, it can enter into a trade to receive a fixed rate in SIFMA versus paying the floating rate, and simultaneously pay a fixed rate on a LIBOR swap and receive the LIBOR floating rate. Derivatives traders have found a way to simplify this relationship by creating a product referred to as a *basis swap* or *ratio swap* that combines the cash flows from these two trades into one transaction. In the case of a ratio swap, the hedge fund receives a fixed percentage of LIBOR versus paying the floating SIFMA rate. A hedge fund can receive 71% of 3-month LIBOR every quarter for 10 years and pay out the weekly SIFMA rate, quarterly, for 10 years. So long as the weekly SIFMA rate is below 71% of LIBOR on average for the 10-year period the hedge fund will have a profit. (See Exhibit 38.1.) Because SIFMA is a weekly index it mirrors the rates of liquid money market investments that are so eagerly sought out by risk adverse tax advantaged investors.

EXHIBIT 38.1 Ten-Year Basis (Ratio) Swap

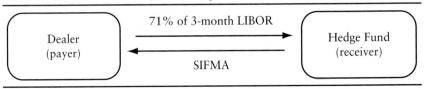

The profit or loss for the hedge fund depends on interest rates. Because the typical transaction is done as a ratio swap, one ratio of profit is equal to the dollar value of 1% of quarterly LIBOR.[2] When the yield curve is inverted, the popularity of ratio trades by hedge funds increases as the profit of a ratio gain is at the point of the yield curve where rates are highest. When the yield curve is steep, or positively sloped the value of a ratio is at the lowest point on the yield curve.

If a hedge fund receives 75% of LIBOR and pays SIFMA, the profit or loss is defined as

$$[75\% - (\text{Average SIFMA rate for 90 days/90-day LIBOR})] \times \text{90-day LIBOR}$$

If LIBOR is 5.25% and SIFMA resets at 67% of LIBOR, the profit for a hedge fund would be

$$[75\% - 67\%] \times 5.25\% = 42 \text{ basis points}$$

Ratio trades can usually be leveraged 20× or more. A hedge fund that enters into the ratio swap in the previous example for $1 million, can get exposure to $20 million of ratio risk. If SIFMA resets at 67% of LIBOR, the profit would be

$$[75\% - 67\%] \times 5.25\% \times \$20,000,000 = \$84,000$$

$$\$84,000/1,000,000 = 8.4\%$$

The hedge fund posts a return of 8.4% plus the 5.25% LIBOR, because the $1 million margin requirement is usually invested at LIBOR. If the term of this trade was 10 years and the 10-year LIBOR swap rate was 5.25%, the hedge find would reap a return of 8.4% over the 10-year swap rate. The major risk a hedge fund takes when entering into a transaction like this is

---

[2] It is important to remember that the profit and loss for a ratio trade changes as short- term interest rates shift. For example, suppose a trader pays 71% of LIBOR for a 10-year term in the morning with one counterparty and receives 72% for a 10 year term in the afternoon from a different counterparty. The profit from the 1 ratio win cannot be determined until both sides of the trade are closed out. The trader's profit is 1% of short-term LIBOR for each quarter for 10 years. If short-term LIBOR was 5%, the profit would be equal to 5 basis points. If short-term LIBOR dropped to 2.5%, the trader's profit would be 2.5 basis points. Investors in ratios have constant P&L risk directly tied to 90-day LIBOR on all of their open positions. If LIBOR were to drop to a very small rate, close to 0%, years and years of P&L may be wiped out for firms with huge books of open positions. After all, 1% of 0 is 0; it does not matter whether it was a profit or loss.

that the value of tax-exempt income dissipates. For example, if the highest marginal income tax rate in the United States were to decline to 15% from 35%, SIFMA would likely reset at 85% of LIBOR, causing a 10 ratio loss in our the previous example. If short-term interest rates were to decline from 5.25% to 2.75%, the return for the hedge fund would also drop. When the yield curve is steep, the expected return could easily fall to levels that may not compensate for the risk. With a 2.75% 90-day LIBOR and 5.25% 10-year LIBOR swap rate, the return profile of the same 10-year ratio swap struck at 75% is

$$(75\% - 67\%) \times 2.75\% \times \$20,000,000 = \$44,000$$

$$\$44,000/\$1,000,000 = 4.4\%$$

As long as the margin relationship remains the same, the hedge fund return drops from 13.65% to 7.15%. If the risks of a tax decrease or some other event that will cause tax-advantaged income to become less valuable arises, the hedge fund is getting a much smaller spread to the risk-free rate on its trades as short interest rates fall. The edge becomes even smaller as the yield curve becomes steeper.

If the term of this example is a 10-year trade, you can see in the first example the hedge fund received a spread of 840 basis points over the 10-year swap rate, yet in the second example the return drops to 215 basis points over the 10-year swap rate.

SIFMA swap popularity among hedge funds accelerated in the early part of 2007 as the combination of a flat LIBOR yield curve and a steep SIFMA ratio curve presented a rare opportunity. With 90-day LIBOR at 5.35%, and a 10-year LIBOR swap at 5%, a hedge fund that received fixed LIBOR for 10 years and paid the floating rate would have negative carry at the start of the trade and hope to get paid off later in the 10-year cycle of the trade. The SIFMA/LIBOR ratio curve, on the other hand, has been fairly steep. The 10-year SIFMA/LIBOR basis has been trading at 72%, while the short-term basis has been averaging 67%.

90-day rate:　　　　$5.35\% \times 67\% = 3.58\%$
10-year swap rate:　$5.00\% \times 72\% = 3.60\%$

A hedge fund could receive 2 basis points of positive carry upon entering a trade to receive the 10-year SIFMA rate and pay the floating rate, while in an identical maturity LIBOR swap the hedge fund would have to pay 35 basis points.

As the yield curve changes, so does this relationship and so will the demand for SIFMA risk by hedge funds. If the 10-year LIBOR swap rate were to rise to 6.5% while the 90-day rate remained at 5.35%, the relationship at the start of the swap transaction would be:

90-day rate: $5.35\% \times 67\% = 3.58\%$

10-year swap rate: $6.50\% \times 72\% = 4.68\%$

In this example the LIBOR yield curve is equal to positive 115 basis points at the start of a trade, while the SIFMA yield curve is equal to 110 basis points. The ratio remained the same in both examples, but as the yield curve shifted and the 10-year rate rose the value of the LIBOR yield curve may become more appealing than the value of the SIFMA yield curve and the risks associated with tax-advantaged yields.

There are many forces acting on the municipal swap rates that can cause changes in the demand for long-dated municipal derivative risk. In this last example, one may walk away feeling that as the yield curve steepens and interest rates increase, the SIFMA/LIBOR swap ratios will also increase. Yet in the previous example we saw how as short-term rates increased, the allure of SIFMA swaps by hedge funds also increased.

As demand will surely ebb and flow with interest rates, ratios and the slope of the yield curves, issuers will continue to focus on selling long-term debt at rates that are most attractive when compared to taxable interest rates.

CONCLUSION

Most hedge funds absorb the excess yield available in long-dated SIFMA swaps and tend to avoid the complexities of the underlying securities markets. The demand for SIFMA swap risk has been accelerating at a very rapid pace in the last decade, opening the door for a second hedge fund trade in the municipal market: single strategy municipal hedge funds that arbitrage the relationship between the municipal securities market and SIFMA swaps. This arbitrage relationship is defined by an asset swap spread. The municipal asset swap hedge fund replaces the basis risk between tax-advantaged and taxable rates with a basis risk between SIFMA and tax advantaged bonds. This single strategy municipal hedge fund would purchase a municipal bond and hedge the interest rate risk with a fixed rate SIFMA swap. Finally, a third strategy that has been gaining popularity, especially with foreign investors, combines the other two strategies. Hedge funds can hedge a long position in municipal bonds with a short position in LIBOR swaps or some other variety of taxable debt. Though this strategy is the riskiest, it attracts a breed of hedge fund investors that do not mind volatility in exchange for potentially high returns. In conclusion, hedge funds enable issuers to meet their needs of selling bonds with long maturities when there is little demand from traditional investors, and they also enable end users to keep their investments in short term money markets. Hedge funds are able to profit from the spread.

CHAPTER 39

Managing Municipal Bond Portfolios for High-Net-Worth Investors

Thomas P. Dalpiaz
First Vice President and Portfolio Manager
Advisor's Asset Management
Fixed Income Securities, L.P.

This chapter will discuss managing municipal bond portfolios for high-net-worth investors. The nature of individual investors and the unique challenges they present to the municipal bond portfolio manager are addressed first. The importance of determining a client's existing situation, uncovering and articulating client objectives, setting portfolio parameters, and explaining performance measurement are then reviewed before various tools designed to add value to clients' portfolios are outlined. A brief discussion of portfolio distributions is followed by a summation recognizing the necessity and effectiveness of municipal bonds as an asset class. Let us first turn to the nature of individual investors and the unique challenges they present.

A LIVING, BREATHING HUMAN BEING

Of course, ultimately a living breathing human being is what exists behind every investment portfolio. And yet, that simple fact is most critical for portfolio managers to recognize when dealing with high-net-worth investors. The central importance of the individual—the presence of the individual—is felt most immediately by high-net-worth individual portfolio managers. In fact, it is the critical difference that separates high-net-worth individual portfolio managers from those who manage portfolios for mutual funds or institutions.

What makes managing municipal bond portfolios for high-net-worth investors different?

EMOTIONAL UPS AND DOWNS

It is a truism on Wall Street that investors allow their investing to be overly influenced by fear and greed, often oscillating between the two. High-net-worth investors are no exception and may be more susceptible to this truism because of their relative lack of investment sophistication. In fact, even quite sophisticated investors can fall prey to the fear/greed trap. The potential for emotional ups and downs and its impact on investor behavior must be kept in mind by bond managers when dealing with high-net-worth investors.

TRANSPARENCY

Recent advances in technology and online reporting have allowed high-net-worth investors with separately managed portfolios of individual bonds to know exactly what is in their portfolio at all times. This real-time transparency adds an element to managing a portfolio that is always present for high-net-worth individual portfolio managers. Since each and every holding is visible and subject to scrutiny, the manager must be aware of the client's potential reaction to each bond placed in the portfolio as well as reactions to possible fluctuations in value for each holding.

EDUCATION

The transparency of separately managed portfolios and the emotional ups and downs that come with high-net-worth investors make it absolutely critical that ongoing education and clear communication are part of the portfolio management process. High-net-worth investors come with various levels of investment knowledge and sophistication. Even though they are not municipal bond professionals, high-net-worth investors can understand and grow comfortable with creative portfolio management strategies through proper education. Portfolio managers that recognize the importance of education and clear communication and base their service on that core conviction can differentiate themselves.

THE STARTING POINT

Always begin by listening. By truly listening to clients, managers can discern where clients presently are and where they need to go. This is critical information to uncover and articulate before any portfolio management can commence. In initial client meetings, many managers make the mistake of routinely jumping directly into a detailed soliloquy about their firms, investment philosophies, portfolio strategies, or investment performance, often giving secondary importance to the task of determining the client's present bond situation and future goals. This approach should be avoided. The prospects for a successful investment relationship improve measurably when, from the very beginning, the client is engaged and a manager's active listening uncovers a client's existing situation and future needs.

THE CLIENT'S EXISTING SITUATION

The manager can uncover the client's existing situation by asking a number of questions:

- *What asset classes make up the client's total investment picture?* This is useful for the bond portfolio manager to know since it can reveal the client's appetite for risk and help articulate goals for the client's bond allocation given what else is in his or her investment picture. For example, a preservation of capital/low volatility objective for bonds becomes clearer when risks taken in the client's other investments are noted.
- *Where has the client placed the funds set aside for bonds? Are they placed in a bond fund, in an existing bond portfolio assembled by a retail broker, in an existing bond portfolio with a money manager on a fee basis, or temporarily in cash?* The answer to this question will give the portfolio manager not only what specifically he or she will be starting with but also an idea of the client's past experience in the bond market. This will help the manager know from what perspective the client is likely to judge the future management of his or her bond assets.
- *What is the client's tax bracket?* Most high-net-worth investors will find themselves in the top federal tax bracket (and top state bracket if there is one) where municipal bonds can often provide a clear yield advantage compared to conservative fixed income alternatives. Since a client's tax bracket may change from year to year though, managers will still want to check with a client's accountant or investment advisor to verify the appropriate tax bracket. The portfolio manager will use that tax bracket when making comparisons of available yields among fixed-income alternatives.
- *In what state does the client officially reside?* This is key information that will help the manager select individual bonds. Clients who reside in states with no income taxes or no taxes on interest and dividends have broad investment flexibility to buy appropriate bonds from all states and territories. For clients who reside in other states, the manager must

compare in-state bond yields with yields on out-of-state bonds after taxes.

UNCOVERING CLIENT OBJECTIVES

The manager who can help clients uncover and articulate their bond objectives will have a strong foundation for a successful investment relationship. The importance of this step in the investment process cannot be overemphasized. Clients and portfolio managers simply must be on the same page when it comes to knowing where the client needs to go in the bond market. While some clients will be better than others at articulating their goals, all clients can benefit from the guidance portfolio managers or investment advisors can provide.

It is the role of the investment professional to help clients define their goals clearly and to cure those goals of any contradictions and unreality. Regarding bond market objectives, it is not unusual for clients to say something such as, "I need you to get me really high levels of income but I want my bonds to be very safe. I need to sleep well at night," or "I want aggressive total returns from my bond portfolio but I don't want to see a lot of volatility." Clients may state specific yield goals of 6%, 7%, 8%, or higher in a 4% municipal-bond-yield world. It is here that education on the municipal bond market, bond yields, and expected volatility can be particularly useful. The goal of this part of the process is to produce clear, realistic objectives that fit the client and can meaningfully guide the portfolio manager.

WHAT IS THE CLIENT REALLY TRYING TO ACHIEVE IN THE BOND MARKET?

Client responses to the above question are likely to include the following statements:

- "I want an attractive level of reliable income."
- "I want attractive total returns."
- "I want to preserve my capital. I don't want to see a lot of volatility."
- "I want my bonds to be safe. I don't want any surprises."
- "I want liquidity. I don't want to be hurt if I need to sell my bonds to raise cash."

Clients may emphasize just one of these statements, mention a few, or insist on all of them! The portfolio manager must determine which of these sentiments is of primary importance to the client. Even when clients insist on income as a primary objective or total return as the main goal, the portfolio manager must be aware that some element of all of the goals listed above will matter to the client regardless. Whether it is income or total return, those overall goals are, in practice, placed in the context of underlying goals such as capital preservation, low volatility, safety, and liquidity. These underlying goals contribute to and are necessary accompaniments to the more clearly stated goals of income or total return. If underlying goals are not given their appropriate recognition up front, they will resurface further along in the investment relationship as concerns regardless of the client's initial protest to the contrary.

ARTICULATING OBJECTIVES AND SETTING PARAMETERS

Managers and clients often talk about "being on the same page." This section refers to the part of the investment process where that "page" is formalized. A broad statement of objectives coupled with a list of parameters that will guide the day-to-day management of the portfolio is the most effective way of articulating where a client wants to go and how the manager will take them there. The objectives and parameters "page" in Exhibit 39.1 is merely a sample and should be modified in its details to fit each particular client. Clients will most likely differ on specific credit quality and maturity/

EXHIBIT 39.1 Sample Objectives and Parameters

- Broadly stated, the objectives for your bond portfolio will be to provide an attractive level of after-tax income within the context of preserving capital, maintaining safety and low volatility, and providing liquidity.

- All holdings will be rated single A or higher by one of the nationally recognized rating agencies (Standard & Poor's, Moody's, or Fitch). The average rating for the portfolio will be AA. Nonrated securities will be used (to a maximum of 20% of the portfolio) only when, in our opinion, the credit quality of the bond under consideration is of equivalent quality to bonds rated single A or higher.

- Your portfolio will have generally scattered bond maturities of 15 years and under with a target portfolio duration of 5.5 years.

- Your portfolio will be managed with diversification and liquidity needs in mind. To ensure adequate diversification, bonds will be purchased in a size so that the market value of each block of bonds will not exceed 7% of the entire portfolio's value. No single credit sector of the municipal bond market (with the exception of bonds backed by U.S. Treasuries) will exceed 25% of the portfolio. No single issuer (with the exception of the bonds backed by U.S. Treasuries) will exceed 12% of the portfolio.

EXHIBIT 39.1 (Continued)

- Since our strategy emphasizes value and security selection, we will exercise patience in creating and managing your portfolio. Our deliberate approach for a portfolio presented as all cash usually results in an initial investment period of about three to six weeks depending on market conditions.

- Once a portfolio is fully invested, cash as a percentage of the total portfolio should not exceed 5% except for extraordinary defensive purposes.

- It is our understanding that you are a New York State resident subject to the top state tax bracket on interest income from non-New York bonds. We will use both New York and (when feasible) non-New York bonds in the portfolio, always basing our decisions on the attractiveness of after-tax yields provided.

- Since you are subject to the highest federal income tax rate, municipal bonds provide the most attractive after-tax yields given the current yield relationships of investment grade taxable and tax-exempt bonds. A tax-effective approach, however, will govern the management of your portfolio. We will monitor the yield relationships of taxable and tax-exempt bonds and, keeping your federal and state tax status in mind as well as liquidity needs and transaction costs, consider shifting to taxable bonds when there is a clear advantage to do so. Such shifts will be implemented only with your consent.

- Until instructed otherwise, all interest income and realized capital gains will be reinvested in your portfolio. Of course, income remittances and other regularly scheduled disbursements will be set up at any time in the future according to your needs.

- The portfolio's investment performance will be compared to the Lehman Brothers seven-year Municipal Bond Index on a quarterly basis.

- These guidelines will direct us in the day-to-day management of your bond portfolio. We will formally review these guidelines with you on an semiannual basis to determine their continued appropriateness for your goals. We will discuss with you any suggestions to change these guidelines as well as suggestions to temporarily go outside of these guidelines. Any changes or portfolio management actions beyond these guidelines will occur only with your consent.

duration parameters as well as whether or not they are reinvesting or taking income. Once clients have read the objectives and parameters "page," they should have a good sense of what will guide a portfolio manager in his or her day-to-day management.

PERFORMANCE MEASUREMENT

The process of uncovering and articulating client objectives illustrates a simple but overlooked reality: clients ask their bond assets to do many things (provide income, total return, low volatility, safety, liquidity). Because of these multiple goals, the task of measuring investment performance (which is really measuring *satisfaction*) must include multiple measures. A hyperfocus on total return investment performance is misguided in that it says nothing about whether or not the portfolio is achieving other goals clients have set. For bond investors in particular, the desire for returns must always include the risk undertaken to achieve those returns.

Listed below are a number of suggestions for making performance measurement in the municipal bond market more meaningful for the high-networth individual investor.

- As much as possible, select a benchmark with a duration that closely matches the duration target of your portfolio. Comparing the investment performance of a portfolio with a benchmark that is perennially longer or shorter in duration provides little meaningful information to clients. The old adage of comparing apples to apples certainly applies here.
- Compare some measure of the return per unit of risk of the benchmark to your portfolio. This measure (Sharpe ratio) will help standardize returns across various risk levels and help investors determine the price (in risk) they pay for various levels of return.
- Compare the results over an entire interest rate cycle. An effective portfolio should produce attractive returns and manage volatility in both up and down bond markets. Having the patience to see how a portfolio performs through an entire interest rate cycle will provide the most complete answer as to whether or not a client's goals are being achieved.
- Know the differences between the attributes of your portfolio and those of the benchmark. Measuring investment performance is more meaningful when there is an understanding of the difference between what an individual is trying to achieve with their bond assets and a benchmark characterizing an entire market. A benchmark may include many bonds that are not appropriate for a particular individual's portfolio (BBB rated bonds, hospital and tobacco bonds, AMT bonds,). Unlike an individual's portfolio of laddered or scattered maturities, a benchmark may be more like a bullet in its maturity structure and have a tight concentration around a particular point on the yield curve. In an individual's portfolio, this maturity structure could result in unwanted reinvestment risk.
- Compare the portfolio turnover of competitors. Higher levels of portfolio turnover can substantially reduce returns on an after-tax basis.
- Compare gross to gross or net to net. Aside from buying Treasury notes and bonds direct from the Federal Reserve, any endeavor into the bond market will cost investors something (i.e., commissions from brokers; expensed and fees from mutual funds and advisors). Of course, a bench-

mark (if you could buy it at all) would cost an investor something to construct as well. Individual portfolio comparisons should be done on a gross basis, or after fees on both the portfolio and the benchmark.

The desire to have a portfolio produce investment performance above a benchmark should not be confused with what clients actually need to achieve in the bond market. It should be noted in the sample objectives and parameters portrayed earlier that a benchmark was included but a specific investment performance goal versus that benchmark was not. Benchmarks are designed to replicate markets or niches in markets. They tell you what markets have done. In the municipal bond market, they are not the passive alternative individual investors can select for simplicity's sake. This contrasts with individual portfolios designed for real-world needs of actual clients, that is, solving actual investment problems for individuals. That difference needs to be explained clearly to clients. Comparing a portfolio to an appropriate benchmark can be a useful exercise when it includes not only the raw numbers but all the understanding outlined above as well.

UNCOVERING VALUE IN THE MUNICIPAL BOND MARKET

Once a portfolio manager has listened carefully to determine a client's existing situation, helped to uncover and articulate client objectives, set portfolio parameters, and explained performance measurement, day-to-day management of the portfolio can begin. Simply put, the overriding quest each day for portfolio managers is to find ways to add value to their clients' portfolios. Value, which by very definition means finding something beyond the ordinary, is uncovered by confronting risks in the marketplace and carefully selecting securities whose returns compensate for those risks. Specific ways to uncover value include confronting interest rate risk, credit risk, call risk, liquidity risk, yield curve analysis, and bond swapping.

CONFRONTING INTEREST RATE RISK

Interest rate risk is the degree to which bonds fluctuate in value due to the general movement of interest rates. A bond's duration is a useful indicator for the approximate fluctuation in principal value investors can expect when interest rates rise or fall. When interest rates rise (fall) 100 basis points, a bond with a duration of five years will tend to experience a 5% decrease (increase) in principal value. Portfolio duration will provide investors with the same information for a portfolio as a whole.

Managers can add value in this area by shifting a portfolio's duration longer in anticipation of a decline in interest rates or shorter in anticipation of a rate increase. These shifts can be large or small, frequent or occasional. The nature of the high-net-worth individual investor and the objectives they bring to the bond market argue for more modest and occasional duration shifts. First, there is the difficulty of being consistently correct for an extended period of time on the direction of interest rates. More importantly, the resulting volatility and possible tax consequences of sharp and frequent adjustments to portfolio duration contradict the objectives individual investors bring to the bond market. It is preferable to add value in this area by acting on the margin. A target duration should be selected for each portfolio and the actual portfolio duration should be kept within a certain band of the target (plus or minus 5% to 10%). Target durations can be lengthened or shortened but only at major cyclical interest rate turning points.

Managers can also add value regarding interest rate risk by changing the mix of interest rate sensitive and defensive paper in a portfolio. All bond prices are influenced by the direction of interest rates. Depending on their structure, however, municipal bonds can react to interest rate movements in varying degrees. When interest rates rise, bonds with higher coupons and call features tend to display a defensive characteristic, that is they decline less in price than similar maturity bonds with lower coupons and noncallable features. The above average coupons in outstanding defensive bonds comprise a greater portion of the bond's yield thus necessitating smaller price movements to produce yields equivalent to newly issued bonds. When interest rates fall, interest rate sensitive bonds, such as those with par type, discount, or zero-coupons. and noncallable features, tend to move in price to a greater degree than defensive bonds. By changing the mix of defensive and interest rate sensitive bonds in a portfolio, managers can add value by emphasizing the type of bond that will perform better in a particular interest rate environment.

A third way to add value in this area is to speed up or slow down the pace at which cash is invested depending on whether interest rates are falling or rising. Managers should be careful to use this tool modestly, focusing on merely speeding up or slowing down the pace. Making all-or-none type decisions on putting cash to work is not recommended, particularly when a portfolio starts as all cash. Adopting an all or none approach to investing cash simply puts too much of the portfolio at risk, making its performance too dependent on a particular interest rate move. In addition, the longer one waits to commit large amounts of cash, the more weight that decision to invest carries and the greater the chance that decision will become infected with unclear thinking. When managers have a strong conviction about the direction of rates over a very short time period (two to five weeks), then varying the pace at which cash is invested can be an effective tool (utilized in small doses).

CONFRONTING CREDIT RISK

For bond investors, credit risk is actually comprised of two components. There is default risk which is the risk that principal or interest is not paid in a timely fashion by the issuer. There is credit deterioration risk which is the risk that an issuer's credit quality and credit rating deteriorate from its current standing. While both of these events can cause bond values to decline, sometimes precipitously, managers can add value to their clients' portfolios by confronting those risks, making judgments about the seriousness of the credit risk actually present, and deciding whether or not their portfolios are being adequately compensated with a bond's yield.

Managers can determine if yield compensation is adequate by tracking the difference between yields of Aaa-insured, single-A and Baa paper historically and comparing the particular yield spread of a bond under consideration to those historical spreads. Even when current spreads are relatively tight compared to average historical spreads, it can be worthwhile to search for the occasional value by confronting credit risk. Many lower rated credits have attractive yields and may be worthwhile additions to a portfolio simply because they have a relatively new security structure, are small entities, are relatively infrequent issuers of debt, or simply misunderstood. Some lower rated credits may not have the large cushions of safety found in higher rated credits but they may provide essential services, be a sole provider, or exhibit relatively stable situations nonetheless.

Confronting credit risk may be a large or small part of how a manager adds value to his or her clients' portfolios. The degree to which managers use this tool depends on current credit spreads, the availability of attractive credit "stories" in the municipal marketplace, and the particular tolerance of each client for any kind of credit risk.

CONFRONTING CALL RISK

Another way for portfolio managers to add value is to confront call risk. The municipal bond market has a wide variety of bond structures available to the investor, many of which have call features or sinking funds. Bond investors often shy away from bonds with call features because of the uncertainty regarding the actual life of their investment. They may also shy away because of the potential shift in duration (and volatility) for callable bonds.

Bonds with above market coupons, premium prices, and large gaps between the first call date and final maturity can experience sharp changes in duration depending on how interest rates move. A premium coupon bond with a 25-year final maturity and a first call in five years may be priced and trade in the market at the yield to first call in one interest rate environment and to the final maturity in another. There is usually some confusion and a dispersion of opinions as to how bonds with these structures should be priced.

To add value with callable bonds, portfolio managers must first be fully aware of all optional and extraordinary call features for each bond they consider for their clients' portfolios. Judgments can then be made about the likelihood of actual calls occurring given the coupon of the bond, the final maturity, the premium call price (if any), the size of the issuer, the size of the issue, and the prospect for changes in the general level of interest rates. When purchasing a callable bond, portfolio managers should price the bond to its various call dates and to maturity to determine its attractiveness under likely interest rate scenarios. An ongoing knowledge of yield spreads between noncallable and callable bonds is essential in selecting attractive callable bonds for clients' portfolios.

CONFRONTING LIQUIDITY RISK

An investment has good liquidity when it can be converted to cash quickly at a price that is reasonably close to its current market value. Liquidity risk is the risk that bonds held in a portfolio may only be sold, with some difficulty, at prices meaningfully lower than current market valuations for reasons unrelated to interest rate movements. Bonds with above average liquidity risk are typically characterized by poor marketability and wide bid/ask spreads. There are many reasons that bonds in the municipal market may carry liquidity risk. They may have poor or declining credit quality, a history of past credit problems, or be part of a municipal bond sector under credit pressures. They may be backed by a relatively new and untested security structure or have complex or out-of-favor bond structures. The bond or the sector of which they are a part may have legal or political issues surfacing in the press, or they might simply be relatively obscure and infrequent issuers.

The tool of confronting liquidity risk has some overlap with the analysis of credit and call features. Whatever the reason for less than stellar liquidity, an examination of these opportunities may garner extra yield for client portfolios. As always, objectives and parameters must be reviewed to determine if the tool of confronting liquidity risk as a way to add value is appropriate for each client. If the portfolio is structured properly to include an amount of highly liquid bonds sufficient for client needs, then most clients can benefit from some portion of their portfolio in bonds with liquidity challenges.

YIELD CURVE ANALYSIS

The portfolio manager tool of yield curve analysis brings into consideration the issue of portfolio maturity structure. A laddered maturity structure (equal amounts maturing each year) is a familiar and frequently suggested approach to constructing a portfolio. A ladder provides the benefit of reinvesting at regular intervals in the interest rate cycle, thus minimizing the difficult endeavor of timing interest rate movements. Bullet structures (emphasizing a particular maturity) and barbell structures (emphasizing very short and long maturities) represent additional approaches to portfolio construction that, unlike ladders, are related to the expectation of particular interest rate moves.

A portfolio maturity structure that includes elements of all these is a scattered approach. With this approach, portfolios are constructed with a portion of the portfolio coming due in each year; however, the mechanical rigidity of a ladder is avoided. Rather, portfolio managers using a scattered approach seek to select attractive bonds maturing each year within the range appropriate for each client and add bonds in those specific years where yield curve analysis highlights particular value. Determining attractive points on the yield curve can be done by assuming a stable interest rate environment and viewing the total return of each maturity over a one-year time frame. Examining the incremental yield provided by moving out each year compared to the incremental duration taken on is another way of determining attractive points on the yield curve. Whatever the method, portfolio managers can make judgments on the particular points of the yield curve that are most attractive and add value to their clients' portfolios.

BOND SWAPPING

Judicious bond swapping is another critical tool for portfolio managers to use in adding value. A bond swap is simply selling one bond and replacing it with a different bond simultaneously to secure some improvement to a portfolio. With markets constantly in flux, some bonds become relatively "rich" in valuation and are candidates to be sold while other bonds become relatively "cheap" and should be purchased. Reasons for a bond to become relatively "rich" include a temporary decrease in the supply of a particular state or sector's issues, an increase in the demand for a particular state, or sector's issues, a refunding event where bonds become secured by U.S. Treasuries in escrow, and a perception of improvement in credit quality. Bonds may become "cheap" for reasons opposite to those just cited.

Swapping from a relatively "rich" bond to a relatively "cheap" bond is called a *yield pick-up swap*. Swapping a short maturity bond with a longer maturity bond is called a *duration extension swap* while selling a long maturity and replacing it with a shorter bond is called a *duration shortening swap*. Other swaps are performed to improve a portfolio's credit quality (*credit improvement swap*) or to diversify a portfolio geographically, by sector, or by bond type (*diversification swap*). In a situation where interest rates have risen meaningfully since a portfolio's original construction, portfolio managers can execute a *tax loss swap* by selling a bond at a loss and replacing it with a different, higher yielding bond. By harvesting a loss, the manager provides the client an opportunity to reduce the client's tax liability by offsetting ordinary income or capital gains and make the portfolio work harder.

USING BALANCE IN PORTFOLIO CONSTRUCTION AND RECONSTRUCTION

Managing municipal bond portfolios is more than simply finding one attractively valued bond after another. Managers also add value in the way they construct and reconstruct portfolios with an eye toward balance and diversity. This portfolio balance helps to avoid the pitfalls and potential volatility that await bond investors who unwittingly concentrate their portfolios. Earlier in this chapter, the variety of objectives that investors bring to the bond market was noted. Even when clients insist on income or total return as their main goal, the portfolio manager must be aware that those overall goals are, in practice, placed in the context of underlying goals such as capital preservation, low volatility, safety, and liquidity. A properly diversified portfolio gives the portfolio manager the best chance to achieve all of their clients' objectives. Some bonds are placed in a portfolio to provide total return. Some may provide an income element while others serve to preserve capital and/or lower portfolio volatility. Portfolios can be diversified by issuer, credit sector, geographic region, bond type (interest rate sensitive, defensive, callable, noncallable), and by maturity. By constructing portfolios in a balanced and diversified way, portfolio managers ensure that all of the varied parts of the portfolio are working to achieve all of the objectives their clients desire to achieve.

PORTFOLIO DISTRIBUTIONS

The question of how much income clients can take from a portfolio is a common one for municipal bond portfolio managers of high-net-worth investors. Many clients focus on the coupon income produced by a portfolio and then withdraw that amount. If a portfolio contains premium coupon bonds and all coupon income is taken, then clients will be "eating into principal" and suffer declines in the value of their portfolio over time regardless of interest rate movements. A preferred method of portfolio distribution is to calculate the yield to maturity for the entire portfolio using original purchase prices (say 4.25%), apply it to the total value of the portfolio ($3,500,000), and derive an amount that can be withdrawn by the client without consuming principal ($148,750). This amount can be simply divided by 12 to derive a monthly distribution figure ($12,395). Even if a client's income needs require that they consume principal to some degree, this process can educate the client so that there is full understanding regarding the extent of principal depletion and expectations of future portfolio values. Deriving an appropriate level of portfolio distribution in the manner described above also provides the benefit of freeing the portfolio manager to pursue value in the marketplace wherever it can be found. A deemphasis on coupon income alone allows the portfolio manager the flexibility to buy par paper, discounts, zeros, premiums—whatever bond structure makes sense to add value to client portfolios.

MUNICIPAL BONDS: A MOST NECESSARY INVESTMENT

Of all the words that could be used to describe municipal bonds as an investment, perhaps the best one would be "necessary." Other investments may garner more attention, have more interesting stories to tell, or generally offer more "punch." But by quietly meeting a number of important needs for high-net-worth investors, municipal bonds can be characterized as a most necessary investment. Municipal bonds can provide safety, liquidity, abundant variety for diversification and customization, attractive after-tax yields among conservative investment choices, and capital preservation characteristics for smoothing the volatility of an investor's total investment picture.

Interest rate and stock market cycles come and go. The lure of attractive yields and returns on a variety of traditional and newfangled investments is constant. Through the ups and downs and the exciting stories promising investment success, municipal bonds continue their quiet, effective work. Through it all—for all that they do for high-net-worth investors—municipal bonds remain a most necessary investment.

CHAPTER 40

Municipal Credit Default Swaps

Frank J. Fabozzi, Ph.D., CFA, CPA
Professor in the Practice of Finance
Yale School of Management

Managers of municipal bond portfolios are experienced in how to control interest rate risk using interest rate derivative instruments. Yet, interest rate risk is only one form of risk faced by investors in the municipal bond market. The other is credit risk.

Credit risk encompasses three types of risk: (1) default risk, (2) credit spread risk, and (3) downgrade risk. Default risk is the risk that the municipal entity that issued the obligation will fail to satisfy the terms of the obligation with respect to the timely payment of interest and repayment of principal. Even in the absence of default, an investor is concerned that the market value of a bond will decline. Credit spread risk is the risk that the debt obligation of a municipal entity will decline due to an increase in the credit spread required by the market. Most investors in the municipal bond market commonly gauge the default risk of a municipal bond issue or municipal bond issuer by looking at the credit rating assigned by the rating agencies—Moody's Investors Service, Standard & Poor's Corporation, and Fitch Ratings. Once a credit rating is assigned to a debt obligation, a rating agency monitors the issuer's credit quality and can reassign a different credit rating. Downgrade risk is the risk that the price of a municipal bond will decline due to a downgrading of the issue or issuer and is closely related to credit spread risk.

To control credit risk, managers in the corporate bond market have employed credit derivatives. These instruments allow a manager to buy or sell credit protection. There are different types of credit derivatives, the most popular being a *credit default swap* (CDS). The growth and liquidity of the CDS market in which the underlying is a corporate credit has been staggering. The market as of the end of 2007 exceeded $17 trillion. The growth in the market is understandable. All the conditions for the development of the market were present. Standardized documentation of CDS trades was created by the International Swap and Derivatives Association (ISDA). The corporate bond market has been characterized by substantial volatility in credit spreads and continued concerns about corporate defaults. Moreover, there were parties ready and willing to take both sides of the trade: buy credit protection and sell credit protection.

The ISDA provided additional provisions when the underlying is a municipal entity. However, unlike the corporate bond market, the municipal bond market until 2006 lacked the other attributes and potential market participants to foster the development of CDS in which the underlying is a municipal entity. Credit spread volatility was low. Defaults were low. Moody's, for example, reports that only 41 municipal deals that it rated from 1970 to 2006 defaulted. Because of this, there were many market participants willing to sell credit protection but few willing to purchase it. However, conditions in the market changed in several ways. First was the introduction of new players into the market: hedge funds, European banks, and life insurance companies. These buy-side players wanted more efficient vehicles for obtaining credit exposure to the market both as buyers and sellers of credit protection. Moreover, they were not concerned with the fact that income generated from a position in a municipal CDS was taxable. Second, credit volatility in the market increased, and there was greater concerns about credit risk resulting from the impact of the meltdown in the subprime mortgage market in the summer of 2007. As a result, the municipal CDS market grew from just a few billion at the end of 2005 to between $40 and $80 billion as of mid-August 2007.[1]

In this chapter, the CDS contract and its potential applications by portfolio managers are described.

SINGLE-NAME MUNICIPAL CDS CONTRACT

The parties to a CDS are the *protection buyer* and the *protection seller*. In a CDS, the protection buyer pays a fee to the protection seller in exchange for the right to receive a payment conditional upon the occurrence of a credit event by the reference entity. Should a credit event occur (1) the payments to the protection seller are made only up to the credit event date and then no further payments are made; and (2) the protection seller must make a payment to the protection buyer.

The elements of a CDS include:

---

[1] I thank Ted Jaeckel of BlackRock for this information which he obtained from an informal poll of major players in the market.

- The reference entity
- The notional amount
- The swap premium payment
- The tenor of the contract
- The payment dates
- Settlement provisions
- The credit events covered by the contract

In a municipal CDS, the *reference entities* are municipal entities, either the issuer of a state or local general obligation bond or the issuer of a revenue bond. When there is only one municipal reference entity, the CDS is referred to as a single-name municipal CDS. As of this writing, this is the most popular type of municipal CDS. The notional amount is the amount that is used to compute the payment made by the protection buyer to the protection seller and should a credit event occur is used to determine the termination value. For municipal CDS, the contract size is typically from $10 million to $25 million. The *swap premium payment* is the payment made by the protection buyer to the protection seller. It is based on the *swap spread* agreed to by the parties in the trade. The swap spread is expressed as a percentage. The product of the swap spread and the notional amount is the dollar amount of the annual premium payment made by the protection buyer to the protection seller. For example, if the swap spread is 20 basis points and the notional amount is $25 million, the annual swap premium payment made by the protection buyer to the protection seller is $50,000 (0.002 × $25 million).

Dealer quotes are two way prices. For example, suppose the quote for a five-year municipal CDS in which the municipal entity is the State of South Carolina is "6/11." This means that the dealer is willing to sell protection for 11 basis points and buy protection for 6 basis points. The rating of South Carolina by both Moody's and Standard & Poor's is triple A as of August 2007. The State of California, in contrast, is A1 (Moody's) and A+ (S&P) and a five-year quote might be "14/19," which is higher than for the State of South Carolina for buying and selling protection due to its lower rating.

The tenor of the contract is the time that the contract is scheduled to terminate if no credit event is realized. The tenor, also referred to as the maturity, can be for the life of a particular issue that the protection buyer seeks protection for or for a shorter period. The typical tenors for a municipal CDS are 5 years and 10 years. The tenor of the municipal CDS affects the swap spread. For example, for the CDS in which the reference entity is the State of South Carolina, a five-year swap spread might be quoted as "6/11," while a 10-year swap spread might be quoted as "9/14." That is, it cost more to buy protection and one receives more for selling protection the longer the tenor.

Periodic payments must be made by the protection buyer to the protection seller. Typically the payment is quarterly and in municipal CDS the payments are typically the 20th of March, June, September, and December. The amount of the swap premium payment is not simply one-quarter of the annual payment but is adjusted for the number of days in the quarter. The day count convention used for CDS is actual/360. A day convention of actual/360 means that to determine the payment in a quarter, the actual number of days in the quarter are used and 360 days are assumed for the year. Consequently, the swap premium payment for a quarter is

Quarterly swap premium payment

$$= \text{Notional amount} \times \frac{\text{Actual no. of days in days in quarter}}{360}$$

To illustrate, assume a hypothetical municipal CDS where the notional amount is $25 million and there are 92 actual days in the quarter and the swap premium is 20 basis points (0.002). The quarterly swap premium payment made by the protection buyer for that quarter would be

$$= \$25,000,000 \times 0.002 \times \frac{92}{360} = \$12,777.78$$

If a credit event occurs, then the protection seller must make an exchange with the protection buyer. For this purpose a *termination value* must be determined for the CDS. The procedure for computing the termination value depends on the settlement terms provided for by the trade. This will be either physical settlement or cash settlement. With *physical settlement* the protection buyer delivers an amount of the face value of the municipal entity to the protection seller equal to the notional amount. The protection seller pays the protection buyer the face value of the bonds. Since all municipal entities that are the subject of a CDS have many issues outstanding, there will be a number of alternative issues of the municipal entity that the protection buyer can deliver to the protection seller. These issues are known as *deliverable obligations*. The trade documentation will set forth the characteristics necessary for an issue to qualify as a deliverable obligation. From the list of deliverable obligations, the protection buyer will select for delivery to the protection seller the cheapest-to-deliver issue.

Cash settlement can be done in one of two ways. The first involves determination of the fair market value of the bonds and then a payment by the protection seller to the protection buyer of cash equal to the difference between the face value and the fair market value. The fair market value is determined in the dealer market. The second way is to stipulate when the trade is executed a fixed recovery value for the reference entity. These trades are referred to as *fixed recovery trades*. The protection seller then delivers to the protection buyer the difference between the notional amount and the fixed recovery value. Market standards for fixed recovery have been 0% (i.e., no recovery) and 50%.

While we have mentioned several times credit events, we have not specifically defined that term thus far. The payout of the protection seller to the protection buyer is contingent upon the occurrence of a credit event. The ISDA provides definitions for various credit events. The *1999 ISDA Credit Derivatives Definitions* publication (referred to as the "1999 Definitions") provides a list of eight credit events: (1) bankruptcy; (2) credit event upon merger; (3) cross acceleration; (4) cross default; (5) downgrade; (6) failure to pay; (7) repudiation/moratorium; and (8) restructuring. For corporate debt obligations, these eight credit events attempt to capture every type of situation that could cause the credit quality of the reference entity to deteriorate. However, they are not all applicable to municipal entities.

The three that are used as credit events in municipal CDSs are bankruptcy, failure to pay, and restructuring. Because credit events may not apply to all types of municipal bonds, the ISDA's standardized confirmation for municipal CDSs requires that the parties to a trade specify the type of municipal bond that is the underlying for a trade. The ISDA confirmation provides the following three choices for the type of municipal bond: (1) those backed by the full faith and credit of the municipal government (full faith and credit obligations); (2) those paid from funds on hand (general fund obligations); and (3) those backed by specific revenue streams (revenue obligations).

Bankruptcy is defined as a variety of acts that are associated with bankruptcy or insolvency laws. *Failure to pay* results when a reference entity fails to make one or more required payments when due. This type of credit event is included for both general obligation bonds and revenue bonds. When a reference entity breaches a covenant, it has defaulted on its obligation. The most controversial credit event is restructuring of an obligation. A *restructuring* occurs when the terms of the obligation are altered so as to make the new terms less attractive to the debt holder than the original terms. In the case of CDSs where the reference entity is a corporate entity, the terms that can be changed would typically include, but are not limited to, one or more of the following: (1) a reduction in the interest rate; (2) a reduction in the principal; (3) a rescheduling of the principal repayment schedule (e.g., lengthening the maturity of the obligation) or postponement of an interest payment; (4) a change in the level of seniority of the obligation in the reference entity's debt structure; and (5) a change in the currency in which payments must be made.

Because of the problems encountered with the definition of restructuring, the *Restructuring Supplement to the 1999 ISDA Credit Derivatives Definitions* (the "Supplement Definition") issued in April 2001 provided a modified definition for restructuring. In January 2003, the ISDA published its revised credit event definitions in the *2003 ISDA Credit Derivative Definitions* (referred to as the "2003 Definitions"). The revised definitions reflected amendments to several of the definitions for credit events set forth in the 1999 Definitions. Specifically, there were amendments for bankruptcy, repudiation, and restructuring. The major change was again to restructuring, whereby the ISDA allows parties to a given trade to select from among the following four definitions: (1) no restructuring; (2) "full" or "old" restructuring, which is based on the 1999 Definitions; (3) "modified restructuring," which is based on the Supplement Definition; and (4) "modified modified restructuring." The ISDA confirmation for municipal CDSs includes modified restructuring for credit events.

USES OF MUNICIPAL CDS BY PORTFOLIO MANAGERS

To appreciate the potential applications of municipal CDS, it is necessary to understand the economic position of the protection buyer and protection seller of a CDS. Let's start with the protection seller. In the absence of a credit event, the protection seller receives the swap premium for the tenor of the CDS. Thus, the protection seller is taking in the equivalent of interest income. If a credit event occurs, the protection seller must do one of the following depending on whether there is physical or cash settlement. With physical settlement, the protection seller buys from the protection buyer bonds of the issuer equal to the notional amount thereby suffering a loss due to the lower value of the bonds in the market. This is the same as if the protection seller had owned the bonds. If there is cash settlement, the protection seller must make a payment equal to the amount of the loss just as if the protection seller had owned the bonds and sold them. Hence, the protection seller is effectively long the credit risk of the reference entity.

The protection buyer, in contrast, is making swap premium payments in the same way that an investor who is short the bond would be making. Also, if there is a credit event resulting in a decline in the value of the bonds of the reference entity, then the protection buyer gains in the same that a shorter seller would gain. Hence, the protection buyer is effectively short the credit risk of the reference entity.

One important distinction between the position of the seller of protection in municipal CDS and owning a municipal bond should be noted. Municipal bond interest received is exempt from federal income taxation.

This is not the case for the swap premium received by the protection seller as of this writing, although the Internal Revenue Service has yet to officially opine on the tax treatment of CDS. This is clearly a disadvantage for portfolio managers who want to consider selling protection as an alternative to owning the bond. Portfolio managers of tax-exempt municipal bond funds, for example, cannot at this time sell protection as an alternative to buying the cash bond.[2] However, there are participants in the market who are not concerned with this difference in the tax treatment. Instead, they have other objectives when using municipal CDS to efficiently take a credit position.

With that background, below we briefly describe four applications of single-name municipal CDSs.

In the corporate sector, the liquidity of the CDS market compared to the corporate bond market makes it more efficient to obtain exposure to a reference entity by taking a position in the CDS market rather than in the cash market. To obtain exposure to a reference entity, a portfolio manager would sell protection and thereby receive the swap premium. The same is occurring for certain municipal credits in the municipal bond market. So a basic application of municipal CDS is to more efficiently take a long credit position in a municipal credit.

Second, conditions in the municipal bond market may be such that it is difficult for a portfolio manager to sell the current holding of a municipal bond of an issuer for which there is a credit concern. Rather than selling the current holding, the portfolio manager can buy protection in the municipal CDS market.

Third, if a portfolio manager expects that a municipal entity issuer will have difficulties in the future and wants to take a position based on that expectation, it will short the bond of that issuer. However, shorting bonds in the municipal bond market is extremely difficult. The equivalent position, as noted earlier, can be obtained by entering into a municipal CDS as the protection buyer where the reference entity is the municipal entity involved.

As a final application, consider a portfolio manager seeking a leveraged position in a municipal bond. Creating such a position may be difficult to do in the municipal cash market. However, this can be done easily in the CDS market. The economic position of a protection buyer is equivalent to

---

[2] In August 2007, Delaware Investors indicated that it would be modifying its prospectus for the open-end and closed-end tax-exempt municipal bond funds for which it is the financial advisor to allow up to 15% of a fund's total net assets to be invested in CDS. In the announcement, it was not clear how the tax issue would be dealt with. It was not clear whether there was an actual plan to use CDS or simply a modification of the prospectus to give the fund managers the opportunity to use CDS should the tax issue be resolved. See Matthew Posner, "Delaware Investments Will Allow Its Funds to Buy, Sell CDS," *The Bond Buyer*, August 28, 2007, p. 4.

a leveraged position in a municipal bond. The use of a CDS does not per se result in leverage, which is a concern to clients. The impact on leverage will depend on how the cash that would have been used to purchase the underlying cash bond is utilized. If all the funds are used to invest in a money market instrument, leverage is not realized. Another way of saying this is that the duration of the portfolio is the same whether municipal bonds are purchased in the cash market or CDS market (by selling protection) if the funds not used to purchase the municipal bonds are invested in a money market instrument.

Furthermore, the selection of a fixed recovery trade rather than a trade requiring physical delivery allows a portfolio manager to lever the swap premium payment. This is because the lower recovery value assumed, the higher the swap spread the protection buyer is willing to pay and therefore the greater the swap spread that the protection seller will receive.

SECOND GENERATION OF CREDIT DEFAULT SWAPS

As in the corporate CDS market, the second generation of municipal CDS is the basket CDS. As the name suggests, a basket CDS or basket default swap has as its underlying more than one reference entity. With a basket default swap, when a payout must be made must be specified in the trade. For example, suppose that a basket default swap has seven municipal reference entities. When does the protection seller have to make a payment if a credit event occurs? Will a credit event for just one of the seven municipal entities trigger a payment by the protection seller? It depends. Basket default swaps can be structured in different ways.

The simplest case is that if there is a credit event for any of the municipal reference entities, there is a payout by the protection seller for that entity and then termination of the swap. This type of swap is referred to as a *first-to-default basket swap*. Similarly, if a payout is triggered only after a credit event for a second municipal reference entity occurs, the swap is referred to as a *second-to-default basket swap*. In general, if it takes k municipal entities to trigger a payout, the swap is referred to as a *k-to-default basket swap*.[3]

The elements of a basket default swap include (1) the municipal reference entities; (2) the notional amount of each municipal reference entity; (3) the tenor of the swap, (4) the type of delivery/termination value; (5) the swap premium; and (6) the type of basket default swap (e.g., first-to-default basket swap).

---

[3] For a further discussion of these types of swaps, see Mark J.P. Anson, Frank J. Fabozzi, Moorad Choudhry, and Ren-Raw Chen, *Credit Derivatives: Instruments, Applications, and Pricing* (Hoboken, NJ: John Wiley & Sons, 2004).

For example, suppose that a basket default swap has seven municipal entities: Arizona, California, Michigan, New York, Ohio, Pennsylvania, and Puerto Rico. The notional amount for each reference entity is $10 million and the tenor of the swap is five years. If a credit event occurs for, say, California in the third year after the trade, then if the trade is a first-to-default basket swap, this triggers a payment by the protection buyer to the protection seller based on the $10 million notional amount. After that payment, the protection seller has no further protection for the other six municipal reference entities because the contract is terminated. Suppose instead that the trade is a second-to-default basket swap. In this case, the occurrence of a credit event by California would not trigger any action by the protection seller. It is not until one of the remaining six municipal reference entities experiences a credit event that the protection seller is required to make a payment on the defaulting entity.

If the municipal market follows the development of the corporate market, basket default swaps will be used by dealers to create synthetic *collateralized debt obligations* (CDOs) in which the underlying is municipal entities.[4]

SUMMARY

Municipal bond portfolio managers face three forms of credit risk: (1) the risk that the issuer will default (default risk); (2) the risk that the credit spread will increase (credit spread risk); and (3) the risk that an issue will be downgraded (downgrade risk). Credit default swaps in which the underlying is one or more municipal entities can be used to buy or sell protection against credit risk. CDS include single-name CDS and basket default swaps. In a CDS, the payment by the protection seller to the protection buyer depends on the occurrence of a credit event. The ISDA defines potential credit events and trade documentation allows the parties to select which are applicable to a particular trade. Municipal CDS can be used to create equivalent credit exposure to a municipal entity that can be obtained in the municipal cash market. The advantage of the municipal CDS market to do so is that for certain credits this market may be more liquid than the cash market and allows the short selling of municipal entities. Moreover, for the new participants in the municipal bond market who seek leverage, the municipal CDS provides an efficient way of obtaining it. The drawback for investors who seek tax-exempt interest is that as of this writing, the swap premium payment is taxable.

---

[4] Municipal cash CDOs are described in Chapter 41. For a discussion of synthetic CDOs, see Douglas J. Lucas, Laurie S. Goodman, and Frank J. Fabozzi, *Collateralized Debt Obligations: Structures and Analysis*, Second Edition (Hoboken, NJ: John Wiley & Sons, 2006).

Municipal Collateralized Debt Obligations

Rebecca Manning
Vice President, Structuring
Harbor Asset Management

Douglas J. Lucas
Executive Director and Head of CDO Research
UBS

Laurie S. Goodman, Ph.D.
Cohead of Global Fixed Income Research and
Manager of U.S. Securitized Products Research
UBS

Frank J. Fabozzi, Ph.D., CFA
Professor in the Practice of Finance
School of Management
Yale University

Given their strong credit profile and historical performance, municipal bonds (*munis*) would seem ideal collateralized debt obligation (CDO) collateral. But munis have only made a couple appearances in CDOs because traditional CDOs cannot pass the tax-exempt interest of munis on to CDO investors. And the cost of a before-tax coupon to CDO debt holders leaves little "arb" for CDO equity investors. However, in September 2006, the first 100% cash muni CDO hit the market: Non-Profit Preferred Trust I (NPPT).

We also thank David Gilliand, CFA and Vaibhav Kumar, of UBS municipal bond trading and CDO structuring, respectively, for providing us with their expertise.

By using a structure that differed slightly from that of a traditional CDO, and focusing on a niche within the muni market, NPPT paved the way for future tax-exempt muni CDOs.

In this chapter, we discuss muni CDOs. Muni CDOs are likely to focus on issues in three sectors: nonprofit corporations, limited recourse housing, and enterprise financing. Nonprofit corporations are tax-exempt entities according to Section 501(c)(3) of the IRS code (why they are often referred to as 501c3s). The subsectors within this sector that are likely to be found in CDOs are healthcare, higher education, charter schools, private primary and secondary schools, and nontraditional, nonprofit corporations that includes community service providers, cultural institutions, charitable organizations, and research institutes. Within the enterprise financing sector, the following are likely to be included in a CDO: airport special facility bonds, tobacco settlement bonds, industrial revenue bonds, and tax increment, special tax, and special assessment bonds.

CDO BASICS

A CDO begins with its assets, which for a muni CDO is a pool of municipal bonds. On the other side of the balance sheet, a CDO's liabilities have a detailed and strict ranking of seniority, going up the CDO's capital structure from equity or preferred shares, to subordinated debt, mezzanine debt, and senior debt tranches. Exhibit 41.1 shows the typical capital structure of a CDO.

Within the stipulation of strict seniority, there is great variety in the features of CDO debt tranches. The driving force for CDO structurers is

EXHIBIT 41.1 Typical CDO Structure

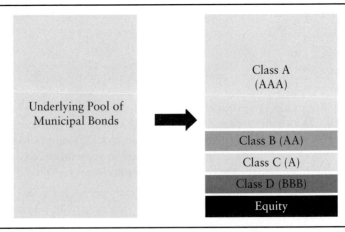

to raise funds at the lowest possible cost. This is done so that the CDO's equity holder, who is at the bottom of the seniority ladder, can get the most residual cash flow.

Purposes

CDOs are created for one of three purposes: balance sheet, arbitrage, or origination. These purposes also dictate how a CDO acquires its assets.

In a *balance sheet* CDO, a holder of CDO-able assets sells the assets to a CDO, thus removing the assets from the holder's balance sheet. This type of CDO is attractive to banks seeking to remove assets from their balance sheet and lower the bank's regulatory capital requirement.

In an *arbitrage* CDO, assets are purchased in the market place from many different sellers and put into the CDO. In this case, the CDO is another means, along with mutual funds and hedge funds, for a money manager to provide his service to investors. The difference is that instead of investors sharing the fund's return in proportion to their investment, investor returns are also determined by the seniority of the CDO tranches they purchase.

The final reason for creating a CDO is *origination*, which, in the case of a muni CDO, allows smaller-size municipalities and special purpose entities to issue bonds directly to the CDO simultaneous with the CDO's issuance of its own liabilities. The muni bonds would not be issued but for the creation of the CDO to purchase them. Non-Profit Preferred Trust I is an origination CDO. The manager has originated loans to 501(c)(3) nonprofits to be placed into the CDO.

These three purposes differentiate CDOs on the basis of how they acquire their assets and focus on the motivations of assets sellers, asset managers, and muni note issuers. But from the point of view of CDO investors, all CDOs have a number of common purposes, which explain why many investors find CDO debt and equity attractive.

One purpose is the division and distribution of the risk of the CDO's assets to parties that have different risk appetites. Thus, a AAA investor can invest in speculative-grade assets on a loss-protected basis and a BB investor can invest in AAA assets on a levered basis.

For CDO equity investors, the CDO structure provides a leveraged return without some of the nasty consequences of borrowing via repo from a bank. CDO equity holders own stock in a company and are not liable for losses of that company. Equity's exposure to a CDO asset portfolio is thus capped at the cost of equity minus previous equity distributions. Instead of short-term bank financing, long-term financing via the CDO is locked in at fixed spreads to LIBOR.

For CDO debt investors, CDOs offer spreads that are usually higher than those of alternative investments, particularly for CDOs rated below AA. And finally, the CDO structure allows investors to purchase an interest in a diversified portfolio of assets. Often these assets are not available to investors except through a CDO.

Cash Flow Waterfalls

The specifics of a CDO's cash flow structure determine the risks taken on by various classes of CDO debt and equity and thus the return profiles of those classes. To understand the cash flow structure of a CDO, one must understand *cash flow waterfalls*. There are two waterfalls in a cash flow CDO: collateral interest and collateral principal. The cash flow waterfalls determine the order in which CDO creditors get paid and thus enforce the seniority of one creditor over another.

Embedded in the waterfalls are *overcollateralization* (OC) *tests*, which can divert cash from subordinated creditors and redirect it to senior CDO creditors. The key to these tests is that defaulted assets are excluded or severely haircut (counted at a fraction of their par amount) in the definition of asset par:

$$\text{Class A OC test} = \text{\textit{Asset par/Class A par}}$$
$$\text{Class B OC test} = \text{\textit{Asset par/(Class A par + Class B par)}}$$
$$\text{Class C OC test} = \text{\textit{Asset par/(Class A par + Class B par + Class C par)}}$$

and so on, for all the debt tranches

To pass these tests, par coverage must be greater than some percentage, perhaps 120% for the Class A OC test, perhaps only 105% for the Class C OC test. The more defaulted assets a CDO has, the more likely it will fail one or more of these tests. Failure of a par coverage test requires that cash be withheld from paying interest on lower-ranking debt tranches. Instead, cash must be used to pay down principal on the CDO's seniormost debt tranche.

Exhibit 41.2 shows simple cash flow waterfalls in which collateral interest and principal is applied to CDO creditors in the order shown.[1]

Diversion of collateral interest can greatly increase protection to senior CDO tranches. Debt tranches can receive all their principal even if collateral losses surpass the amount of subordination below them in the capital structure. The benefit of coverage tests to senior tranches depends on how soon

---

[1] Readers familiar with CDOs will notice that the principal waterfall does not show principal being diverted to pay interest to senior tranches. This is unique to muni CDOs and is discussed further later in this chapter.

EXHIBIT 41.2 Interest and Principal Waterfalls

Interest Waterfall	Principal Waterfall
Trustee Fees & Senior Expenses	Unpaid Senior Fees & Expenses
Senior Management Fee	Class A until paid in full
Class A Interest	Class B until paid in full
Class A OC Test–if failing, amortize Class A until test is met	Class C until paid in full
Class B Interest	Class D until paid in full
Class B OC Test–if failing, amortize Class A and then Class B until test is met	Unpaid Subordinated Fees & Expenses
Class C Interest	Equity Tranche
Class C OC Test–if failing, amortize Class A, then Class B, then Class C until test is met	
Class D Interest	
Class D OC Test–if failing, amortize Class A, then Class B, then Class C, then Class D until test is met	
Subordinated Expenses	
Subordinated Management Fee	
Equity Tranche	

Source: UBS CDO Research.

the tests are breeched. The earlier the diversion begins, the more collateral interest can be diverted over the collateral's remaining life. The amount of cash that can be diverted is smaller if the test fails late in the life of the deal.

CDO Equity in a Portfolio

CDO equity investors should consider the following when analyzing a potential investment:

1. The collateral's promised yield.
2. The CDO's funding cost.

3. The amount of leverage in the CDO structure.
4. The cash flow structure of the CDO.
5. The influence of the CDO manager.
6. The collateral's default and recovery performance.

History makes little difference with respect to most factors impacting CDO equity returns. Only current levels matter. So predicting the performance of a new CDO requires modeling the CDO's collateral spread, funding cost, leverage and structure, and then testing equity returns under different collateral default and recovery assumptions.

This is nothing more than what bankers present in every CDO pitch book. We simply recommend looking at the default and recovery scenarios provided, mindful of the historic default experience of the CDO's assets and current underwriting standards. This, we hope, sounds like a very ordinary, even mundane, suggestion.

MUNI CDOs

As we stated at the outset of this chapter, the first 100% cash tax-exempt muni CDO was issued in September 2006: Non-Profit Preferred Trust I. While NPPT has paved the way for future muni CDOs, not all muni CDOs will look like NPPT. So our discussion on muni CDOs in the remainder of this chapter is based almost entirely on how we believe future muni CDOs will be structured.

A New Dance STEP

The goal of future muni CDOs is for debt tranches to be exempt from federal taxes. Each tranche must be treated as equity for tax purposes, and to do so, muni CDOs must be structured slightly differently from other types of CDOs. Tax exemption is currently achieved by structuring the CDO as a Structured Tax-Exempt Pass-Through or STEP. The main difference is the principal waterfall.

In a typical CDO, collateral principal payments can be diverted from the junior debt tranches to pay unpaid interest on senior debt tranches. But muni CDOs cannot do this. Instead, collateral principal payments may only be used to pay principal payments in order of seniority. As such, the subordination levels of a muni CDO are slightly higher than what they would be if the CDO could divert principal to pay interest. This lowers the CDO's leverage and therefore lowers its equity return. However, preserving the tax benefit of the muni CDO collateral outweighs lower equity leverage on an after-tax basis.

In another difference with most CDOs, muni CDOs are set up as *Delaware partnerships*, rather than as Cayman Island corporations.

Collateral and Capital Structure

Muni CDOs seeking tax-exempt status will be restricted to 100% cash deals. While credit default swaps on munis exist, their premiums are taxable income. Likewise, income earned on interest rate swaps is also taxable, so muni CDOs will not be able to hedge any mismatch in interest rates. Therefore, like most munis, most muni CDO tranches will offer fixed coupons. Muni CDOs will also avoid munis whose distributions are subject to alternate minimum tax.

It is envisioned that every muni CDO tranche will have a CUSIP, pay interest semiannually, and trade and settle like a normal muni bond. Accountants will provide tax reporting on muni CDO tranche distributions quantifying tax-exempt interest, capital gains, and taxable interest (expected to be zero in a muni CDO).

Coupons on muni CDO collateral portfolios will vary greatly. The first muni CDO with nonprofit underlyings had a weighted average coupon on its collateral of MMD + 230–240. Higher-quality muni CDO portfolios will have WACs under MMD + 100 basis points. To provide an idea of how a muni CDO might look, we tranched an example muni CDO with higher-quality assets, as shown in Exhibit 41.3.

SUMMARY

In this chapter, we reviewed the basics of a traditional CDO structure. Finally, we reviewed muni CDOs and their unique attributes.

At this point, muni CDOs are a developing product, with only two deals completed as of May 2007. Rating methodologies and surveillance are still being hashed out, as the rating agencies look to combine the work

EXHIBIT 41.3 Sample Muni CDO Capital Structure

Rating	Size ($ millions)	Subordination
AAA	344	14%
AA	16	10%
A	12	7%
BBB	8	5%
Equity	20	

of their public finance and CDO analysts. While we believe several deals will follow in the pipeline, muni CDOs will be a small niche product in the overall CDO market. Nonetheless, muni CDOs create a unique opportunity for both CDO investors and muni investors to access a new asset class while still enjoying the benefits of tax exemption.

CHAPTER 42

Performance Attribution of Municipal Bonds

Daniel J. Garrett, CFA
Vice President
Investortools, Inc.

Performance is the ultimate measure of success in investing. Investing performance is typically expressed as total return, the measure of income and price change over a period of time for a single investment or group of investments. Performance drives assets accumulated, fees, profits and pay of everyone in an investing institution. As such, the attention paid to total return has become more focused, particularly in relationship to the total return of an index with similar investment objectives and constraints.

One of the most difficult tasks of a portfolio manager, in any asset class, is to tell the story of how day-to-day decisions translate into total return performance. The difficulty is accurately backing claims with facts and figures to illustrate the point. The presentation of these claims in marketing material is of interest to regulators (Securities and Exchange Commission) and those interested in maintaining integrity within the investment profession (CFA Institute, among others). Because total return is a key part of what investors consider in their choice of who will manage their money, nearly everyone from the investment boards who hire portfolio managers to the wealthy individual or young worker choosing their first 401k account have a vested interest in accurate reporting of total return.

However, a single total return number is often not enough to make such manager choices. Beyond just one total return number for a specific time period, an increasing number of more detailed questions about how individual investment decisions impacted each component of return are being asked. Now the focus has become how to isolate and measure each part of a portfolio manager's decision process, from credit, to sector, to maturity length, and the like, and attribute performance to each of those decisions. How did results in each compare to the intended strategy? How can we create a set of measures to clearly tell the story, perhaps even impacting manager pay or their ability to attract and retain clients and ultimately their jobs?

Performance attribution presents a most difficult problem for the municipal bond manager. Measuring the overall total return is fairly easy. There are pricing services that evaluate bond trades and can provide consistent market values on most municipal bonds even if they infrequently trade. The difficulty is determining what factors went into a price change from day to day on particular bonds. Without agreed upon standards of grouping bonds or which factors had what specific impact on price movements, attribution of return becomes subjective and vague.

Therefore, the challenge of any analytical tool is to create a consistent, defensible return method that has several characteristics. It should have standardization and integrity. It should be directly and clearly tied to specific investment decisions. It should have direct connections to price changes. In sum, it should translate into a presentation of sound, understandable, and easy to explain performance attribution.

This chapter describes the methods and reasons that embody a sound, defensible approach to analyzing and attributing performance relative to an index for a portfolio of municipal bonds.

WHICH APPROACH FOR MUNICIPAL BONDS?

Choosing which attribution approach should be used for fixed income, especially municipal bonds, must reflect practical limitations of both the data available and the market characteristics from which comparative yields or prices are available. The two basic attribution approaches are returns-based (top-down) and security-level return breakdowns based on pricing factors (bottom-up).

The *returns-based approach* looks at relative price movements and weights compared to an index and attributes return to similarly matched groupings of characteristics of the target portfolio versus a benchmark group of general market bonds (an index). Both the index and portfolio are hierarchically grouped by duration, quality, sector or other items and compared on over/under weight and return to break out excess return associated with each component. For these purposes, excess return is defined as the portfolio return minus the index return, and is referred to as the *active return*.

The pricing factor-based approach (bottom-up) separates the price change of a bond into component parts. After accounting for the passage of time, each price change can be expressed as a change in yield on the bond relative to the yield of a comparable risk-free bond, the difference in yield being the spread change for that component over that period of time. Usually, because of embedded options in municipal issues (predominately the call option), these yields and spreads are calculated using an option-adjusted pricing model. Each price change can be expressed as a return, by dividing the price at the end of period by price at the beginning of period, and then subtracting one. For each factor (quality, maturity, sector, and so on), a spread change is measured. Each spread change is converted to a corresponding price movement either by estimation using spread change times duration, or by actually computing a price change by adding the factor spread change into a pricing model and discounting the cash flows by a discount rate equaling the risk-free curve point plus spread change. By calculating the return from each spread change, with the ratio of the beginning and ending modeled price for each factor, the return attributable to each factor spread change can be obtained. A similar process is used to explain movements in the risk-free yields over the period, although this aspect of the attribution model will not be covered in detail in this chapter.

The focus for this chapter is the fixed income market in general and the municipal bond market in particular. There are papers written by a variety of practitioners on the subject of attribution, but this chapter will focus on the method used by Investortools in the creation of tools for municipal bond attribution, which follows the principles and mathematical treatment outlined in the model first described by Brinson, Hood, and Beebower[1] and then extended by Brinson and Fachler.[2]

WHAT DOESN'T WORK FOR MUNICIPAL BOND ATTRIBUTION

Perhaps the best place to start is describing what doesn't work in the municipal bond attribution framework and why. Several fixed income attribution methods focus on the price component of total return being a function of price movements which are assumed to be broken into discrete pieces. They are labeled in a variety of ways: factor-based, bottom-up, principal components, pricing factor-based, and so on. In brief, this bottom-up approach does not work well for illiquid markets that have no standard risk-free pricing benchmark curve, and fragmented, infrequent trading on the majority of the securities in the market. The municipal market has all of these limitations and more, so a bottom-up pricing factor approach is inappropriate.

---

[1] Gary P. Brinson, L. Randolph Hood, and Gilbert L. Beebower, "Determinants of Portfolio Performance," *Financial Analysts Journal* (July/August 1986), pp. 39–44.
[2] Gary P. Brinson, and Nimrod Fachler, "Measuring Non-U.S. Equity Portfolio Performance," *Journal of Portfolio Management* (Spring 1985), pp. 73–76.

An Example of What Does Not Work for Municipal Bonds

A simple example is a two-factor model of maturity and rating on a bond with a 10-year maturity, AA credit rating, and a seven-year duration. The approach is to isolate the portion of price movement attributable to spread change in a set of similar-maturity bonds. One way to estimate price changes for small changes in rates is using duration, where price moves opposite of the product of interest rate change times duration.

Assume for a particular period of time that 10-year maturity bonds had, on average, a seven-year duration, and risk-free interest rates moved up 10 basis points. Taking duration of seven times a 0.10 movement in rates gives an estimated price change of a 70 basis point price drop.

Next, we determine that 10-year, AA rated bonds, in general, moved down 5 basis points in spread, all else being equal. The seven-year duration would lead you to attribute 35 basis points of positive price movement due to the rating ($-7 \times -0.05 = 0.35$). The maturity point chosen for AA is arbitrary, but the concept is to isolate the AA spread change. Let's also assume we had 30 basis points of income on the bond. The other piece we were told from our bond system was that the total return for the period on our bond was 20 basis points.

Taking all this into consideration, the total return of 20 basis points can be attributed to these factors: income = +30 basis points, maturity decision= –70 basis points, AA rating = +35 basis points, with the individual bond selection/residual of +25 basis points for the sum total of 20 basis points total return ($30 - 70 + 35 + 25 = 20$). The group of similar bonds for each attribute, be it maturity or rating or some other characteristic, is most often a basket of securities representing the market, that is, an index or benchmark portfolio.

Of course, there are the many other components we could isolate and explain further: the general movement of the risk-free curve, term structure shift changes of parallel moves or slope, and correlations of all the above. The key idea is to isolate spread changes of various baskets of similar securities and set that as the general market movement for that factor and then compare the specific bond to that movement of the general market in isolation, by holding everything else constant and seeing the price change in present value by discounting the cash flows by the spread change of each factor. To keep it simple, duration times spread change to estimate the effect could be a quick alternative to repricing using discounted cash flow modeling, as suggested in the example.

Why Isolating Factor Spreads Does Not Work for Municipal Bonds

However, isolating these characteristics and their spread movements becomes difficult in an illiquid market where there is difficulty finding observations to adequately identify these spread movements. The municipal bond market violates many assumptions that must hold true to make this "pricing decomposition by spread movement" a viable approach. Notice the above phrase "determine that 10-year, AA rated bonds, in general" is not a trivial task. The difficulty of attributing performance to specific spread factors in the municipal bond market is trying to isolate and determine exactly these clearly defined, independent price movements. The main collapse is over the assumption that there is an agreed upon set of general market groups. For starters, there is no agreed upon risk-free yield curve in the municipal market. There are not standardized definitions of sectors. There is no agreement on pricing standards between municipal bond evaluation services for non-traded municipal bonds and even mutual funds using two different evaluation services can have the price on the same CUSIP vary widely between the various services.

Why Isolating Factor Spreads Works Better for Taxable Bonds

The taxable market is more amenable to isolating price movements due to specific factor spreads. For one, there is a Treasury curve that can be the agreed upon starting point for yields to use as discount rates from which spot rates can be derived for use in discounting cash flows. Taking a daily history of Treasury curves and comparing them can lead to a pattern of correlations and pricing models that form a commonly defined starting point. Then spreads for quality, sector, and the like can be added in order to piece together a series of prices for each component that would be comparable for attribution of a single security with like characteristics. The taxable market is more liquid, more trades occur, and pricing and the related spreads/yields associated with market changes can be more readily measured and with more observations adds statistical reliability, clearly delineated sources of the pieces of price movements. The trades are more widely reported and reflected in the form of Treasury curves and spreads by a wide array of securities dealers and information services. Therefore, the averages, standard deviation, and correlation measures based on those price observations are more reliable for drawing some of the broad-market pricing comparisons needed for the bottom-up, pricing component approach. So for taxable bonds as compared to municipal bonds, one has more confidence in conclusions drawn by comparing current prices movements to past patterns because the relationships are more reliable.

As previously noted with municipal bonds, the way to group bonds and even the starting risk-free curve is seldom agreed upon. The reporting of municipal bond trades is sparse and only a small fraction of the municipal market trades relative to the frequency and variety of taxable trades. Even if municipal bond spreads could be discretely known for each factor with proper correlations built-in across factors, there would have to be an agreed upon option pricing model. That option model would need to consistently reflect each price movement for each of those spreads and be consistently applied to each basket of bonds for each factor. As it is, the illiquidity of the municipal market means many prices are actually matrix prices, and detailed return attribution using the pricing factor approach instead provides more information on the matrix pricing process itself rather than market behavior and discovery of excess returns.

Given there are no generally agreed upon risk-free curves or pricing models or even common sets of general market bonds to derive each spread component, the pricing components approach to municipal bond attribution quickly breaks down into a set of violated assumptions, which make the results suspect at best and likely misleading.

Some would argue that the lack of a pricing model or inability to break down price movements into detailed yield curve changes or spread movements (as is done in bottom-up attribution) indicates a less robust result. However, for municipal bonds, as outlined above, stretching assumptions to create relationships based on unclear connections leaves the portfolio manager with explanations based on vague or indefensible reports that can lead to misunderstood or misleading conclusions as to what decisions impacted certain price movements.

THE BETTER APPROACH FOR MUNICIPAL BOND ATTRIBUTION

The better approach for municipal bonds is the returns-based, top-down approach. However, there are some important considerations to employ to ensure this attribution method is reliable, defensible, and explainable to the relevant audience. The key is that the attribution of returns be done in such a way that the portfolio manager can explain how their decisions turned into results. This is sometimes difficult for those close to the portfolio management process, let alone those unfamiliar with the methods and process of how investments in general or bonds in particular are priced and how various decisions impact those prices.

The returns-based approach requires some common ground for comparing groups of bonds, especially important in the world of municipal bonds, where so many additional pricing variables come into play. From call options to how to categorize sectors, the municipal market is full of individualized characterizations of how a bond is described or even traded, which makes the market both full of opportunity for those able to research and identify unique situations as well as full of difficulty for those trying to corral this idiosyncrasy into standard groupings to compare performance.

The Investortools, Inc. solution was to reflect the general market in an index of bonds that represented the majority of traded bonds available to mutual funds. To do this, we partnered with Standard & Poor's which has an evaluation service used by municipal bond fund managers. We take all the bonds of $2 million outstanding that are evaluated by Standard & Poor's, and maintain a portfolio of those bonds internally using our portfolio management tool called *Perform™*. We calculate daily yields, durations, and option-adjusted statistics using full bond descriptions and daily prices from Standard & Poor's. We also received input from the marketplace, through help from a variety of portfolio managers, to arrive at a commonly defined set of sectors and applied those definitions consistently across all the bonds in the index. These various index returns and statistics with bond-level data are made available in various levels of summary in Investortools, Inc. products, Perform and Custom Index Manager. Summary level returns and statistics on indices are available through Standard & Poor's web site, and Bloomberg products, and the *Bond Buyer*.

With the portfolios and index in the same analytical system for municipal bonds, a major hurdle is overcome. Given a common set of data definitions used by both the portfolio and the index for sectors (Perform has a feature for mapping portfolio sectors to index sectors for comparability) and ratings and common calculation methods for duration and option-adjusted calculation assumptions (via Custom Index Manager), we now have a way to group comparable characteristics of both the portfolio and a general market index of municipal bonds. This critical step creates a universe of unmanaged bonds that can be aligned against the portfolio for which price return and yield return can be compared, and characteristics are now consistently defined. Therefore, a manager's active management choices and decisions can be judged against a passively managed index of bonds.

Also critical is a way to customize this general market set of bonds to match portfolio objectives and constraints, a very valuable feature found in Investortools Custom Index Manager product. For instance, if certain sectors or quality levels are not allowed in the portfolio, a portfolio manager can exclude those bonds from the general market index and create a custom index subset of bonds that represent a passively managed index that reflects the portfolio's investment policy (as opposed to day-to-day management decisions). Again, the critical step is be able to show how portfolio decisions, even ones that are taken away from the manager as a result of portfolio guidelines, impact the total return for better or worse. A custom benchmark helps differentiate between performance due to the portfolio policy (represented by the benchmark) and performance due to the active implementation of that policy by a portfolio manager (represented by the excess return), perhaps with some freedom to respond to market conditions. Another benefit is to compare the difference between the custom benchmark and the overall index, to measure the value-added by investment policy (as separate from the performance of the manager).

Another advantage of the top-down method is that it is easy to explain. The explanations tend to involve whether more or less of something is owned relative to the benchmark and whether it did better than the overall average. There are many ways to show the portfolio versus the index and pieces of the index to other parts of the overall index, but the explanation tends to be how much did the portfolio have of something and did it outperform.

The next sections will deal with some of the mathematical equations used in this attribution method, some examples and exhibits to illustrate the mathematical treatment, and finally some client stories and applications.

MATHEMATICS OF RETURNS-BASED ATTRIBUTION

The mathematics for applying the Brinson-Fachler method to a municipal bond attribution approach is the same as the mathematics used for equity attribution. The basic premise is to group the portfolio and index in similar ways, compare the weightings between the portfolio and index groupings (the amount of the decision), and also compare the individual allocation return to overall return to isolate the effect of allocation decisions (was the decision good or bad relative to the overall return).

The following will detail the equations that underlie the specific examples presented in the next section. These will focus on one-level grouping (using duration), and then a two-level grouping scheme, (here duration and rating). For each level of attribution, the portfolio and index bonds are grouped into ranges or bands, for instance the duration example will have four bands groups: 0–2, 2–4, 4–6, and 6+.

One-Level Attribution Mathematics Example

This method (based on the Brinson-Fachler method) rewards allocation decisions based on whether or not the index segment beats the overall index. Each band will have a contribution difference (or *excess contribution*) between the portfolio and index, which is calculated using the following equation:

$$EC_d = W_{dP}R_{dP} - W_{dI}R_{dI}$$

where EC_d is the excess contribution of an individual duration band d, W_{dP} and W_{dI} are the weighting percentages (which sum to 100%) of an individual duration band d for the portfolio P or index I, respectively, and R_{dP} and R_{dI} are the average returns of an individual duration band d for the portfolio P or index I, respectively.

For this example, excess contributions from duration allocation and security selection are calculated using the following equations:

$$ECDuration_d = (W_{dP} - W_{dI})(R_{dI} - R_{TI})$$

$$ECSelection_d = W_{dP}(R_{dP} - R_{dI})$$

where R_{TI} is the *overall* or total index return.

In other words, excess contribution from duration is calculated by multiplying the weighting difference by the amount of that index's duration bands' outperformance relative to the overall index. Excess contribution from selection is calculated by multiplying the portfolio weight by that duration band's excess return.

From here, it can be seen that (assuming the unleveraged case where all portfolio weights are positive), excess contribution from selection is:

- *Positive* when a duration band's excess return is positive.
- *Negative* when a duration band's excess return is negative.

Excess contribution from duration is slightly more complicated, and is:

- *Positive* in the case of overweighting outperforming duration bands or underweighting underperforming duration bands.
- *Negative* in the case of overweighting underperforming duration bands or underweighting outperforming duration bands.

This is summarized in the following sign table:

	Outperforming	Underperforming
Overweighted	+	−
Underweighted	−	+

Excess contribution from duration is summed across all duration bands to provide the overall excess return from duration allocation decisions. Likewise, excess contribution from selection is summed across all duration bands to provide the overall excess return from selection. These two *excess-return-from* terms can be added together to equal the overall excess return.

Two-Level Attribution Mathematics Example

A one-level example will often have a high selection factor because it is often dealing with fairly large bands. Adding another level of breakdown may reduce that selection factor by extracting another allocation factor from it. In addition, portfolio allocation decisions can be made on more than one level, so adding another level may cause the attribution results to better mirror the decision process. This is accomplished by isolating each segment of the first-level breakdown and essentially treating it as a portfolio or index in its own right (and with its own excess return), performing the same kind of attribution analysis on it as is done at the overall level, and then relating the result to the overall excess return.

The following example will involve breaking down both the portfolio and index down by duration bands just as before. However, each duration band will itself be broken into rating bands. Each duration band will have an excess return ERd that is equal to $R_{dP} - R_{dI}$. Within that duration band, each rating band will have a term for *excess contribution from rating* and *excess contribution from selection*. Thus, we can come up with the following equations for a specific *rating-duration band* combination:

$$ECRating_{dr} = (W_{drP} - W_{drI})(R_{dP} - R_{dI})$$

$$ECSelection_{dr} = W_{dP}(R_{dP} - R_{dI})$$

All terms with a dr subscript refer to values for a specific *rating-duration band* combination. Note that for the Market Over/Under-Performance method, an index rating's performance is judged relative to the average return of that duration band (R_{dI}) rather than that of the overall index (R_{TI}). Rating-duration band weightings (W_{drP}, W_{drI}) add up to 100% within each duration band.

When summed over all ratings within a duration band, these numbers produce an *excess return from rating* and *excess return from selection* for each duration band, which themselves sum up to that duration band's excess return. This fact can be used to expand the excess-contribution-from-selection term calculated in the previous one-level example into two new terms:

$$W_{dP}(R_{dP} - R_{dI}) = W_{dP}ER_d = (W_{dP}ERRating^d) + (W_{dP}ERSelection_d)$$

Additionally, the W_{dP} term can be multiplied through to the individual $ECRating_{dr}$ and $ECSelection_{dr}$ terms (since it is constant for all those terms), causing them to relate directly to the overall excess return.[3] Thus, we would have the following modified versions of the equations listed just above that relate to overall excess return instead of the excess return of their duration band:

$$ECRating_{dr} = W_{dP}(W_{drP} - W_{drI})(R_{drI} - R_{dI})$$

$$ECSelection_{dr} = W_{dP}W_{drP}(R_{drP} - R_{drI})$$

This suggests the following master equations for two-level attribution that breaks excess return into terms for duration, rating, and selection:

$$ER = \sum_d \left[(W_{dP} - W_{dI})(R_{dI} - R_{TI}) \right] + \sum_d \sum_r \left[W_{dP}(W_{drP} - W_{drI})(R_{drI} - R_{dI}) \right]$$
$$+ \sum_d \sum_r \left[W_P W_{drP}(R_{drP} - R_{drI}) \right]$$

This master equation produces at the overall level an excess return from duration, excess return from rating, and excess return from selection. It may be evident from this that the excess-return-from-duration result will be the same as that calculated by the previous example; its calculation is not altered by adding another level or levels of breakdown.

It can be demonstrated through equation manipulation that the last two terms (rating and selection) sum together to equal the selection term for one level of duration attribution. This fact provides a fast way for a user to determine what the selection term would have been had the portfolio manager used fewer levels of attribution. If selection increases, you may have increased the noise level or the choice of factors was inappropriate.

Order Dependence of Hierarchy Levels

The preceding explanation may suggest that, due to the hierarchical nature of this analysis, reversing the order of breakdown will produce different results for the allocation factors. This is indeed shown to be the case by the mathematics. For example, breaking the portfolio and index down by duration and then rating will produce different results from breaking them down by rating and then duration. Because of this, it is important to have a rationale for the choice of order in order for the results to be meaningful.

---

[3] Investortools attribution system, Custom Index Manager, displays *all* attribution numbers such that they relate to the overall excess return.

Handling of Empty Groupings

The returns-based attribution method produces the most meaningful results in cases where the portfolio and index are divided into groupings where each band contains securities. For bands in which either the portfolio or the index is missing securities, there can be no meaningful distinction made between allocation and selection effects. The selection term for that factor band becomes zero and the full excess contribution goes to allocation.

If there are many groupings for which this is occurring in a given attribution analysis, it may be an indication that the index being used at that time is not a good match for the portfolio or that the groupings have too many detailed bands. To assist with this problem, the Investortools Custom Index Manager tool provides the ability to create complex custom index definitions in order to provide a benchmark with investment objectives and constraints similar to those of the portfolio and the ranges of the bands are adjustable. For example, for a short portfolio with a limit of less than five-year bonds, the duration factor broken into bands would be empty for longer duration bands, so a properly constructed custom index would avoid empty duration bands beyond five years.

If the portfolio lacks holdings in a grouping for which the index has holdings, then by definition the portfolio weight and return will be zero for that grouping. And, since excess contribution from selection is weighted by the portfolio weight, it will also be zero in this case. The portfolio weight will drop out of the allocation term, leaving only the index weight (for grouping s):

$$ECAlloc_s = -W_{sI}(R_{sI} - R_{TI})$$

The reverse situation of the portfolio containing *out-of-index* holdings is more complicated. If the index weight and return were simply taken to be zero, there would be a reversal of the previous case: all the excess contribution go into selection. However, to achieve results that are more consistent with the previous case, our approach at Investortools is to set the index return equal to the portfolio return, while leaving the index weight at zero. The implication is that bonds do exist for that segment that could have been included in the index but were not, and the portfolio holdings for that segment will be used as a proxy for that universe of index holdings. This has the effect of eliminating the selection term (since the returns of the grouping are now identical between the portfolio and index), and produces the following equations (for grouping s, again assuming that R_{sI} is set equal to R_{sP}):

$$ECAlloc_s = W_{sP}(R_{sI} - R_{TI}) = W_{sP}(R_{sP} - R_{TI})$$

In wrapping up the mathematics discussion, the main point is that decisions and excess contribution to return become very clearly tied under the returns-based approach. Each bond purchase gets grouped in the portfolio with similar bonds and compared against index bonds of exactly the same group. There is clarity about which weightings and returns are being compared. The equations above should help those who want to fully understand the mathematics behind the attribution reports produced by returns-based software packages. However, perhaps examples with actual numbers and labels are more helpful to the reader.

EXAMPLES OF RETURNS-BASED ATTRIBUTION FOR MUNICIPAL BONDS

The following examples use reports created by Investortools' Custom Index Manager product for various scenarios. This is a one-month period where rates were rising. The portfolio is a fund of about 60 securities with an average duration of 3.7 years. The index is a national investment-grade index with an average duration of 5.1 years. The examples will be for a one-level grouping by duration and a two-level grouping by duration rating.

One-Level Attribution Report

The single-factor run of the allocation attribution duration report gives two sets of results, a summary and a detailed breakout of the bands of the duration grouping. Exhibit 42.1 is the summary showing the index had a negative 0.354% total return (–35.4 basis points) and the portfolio had a negative 0.007 (–0.7 basis points) return. So the portfolio outperformed the index by the difference shown in the "Excess Return" column which is 34.7 basis points (bps). The attribution is split between 21.9 bps for duration allocation and 12.8 bps of excess return due to security selection. Any hedging activity using derivatives is also shown at this summary level and excluded from the rest of the analysis, as we wanted to show hedging decisions as being sources of excess return separate from the daily portfolio

EXHIBIT 42.1 Summary of Excess Return from Duration

Portfolio	Total Return	Excess Return (bps)	Attribution of Excess Return (bps)		
			Duration	Selection	Derivatives
Index	–0.354	—	—	—	—
Demo Fund	–0.007	34.7	21.9	12.8	0.0

management buy/sell decisions on long bond positions. In fact, sometimes hedging is done by a separate unit, so including its effect in with the rest of the attribution results would make them less meaningful.

The bulk of the explanation for the returns-based approach can be shown in Exhibit 42.2. Understanding this table and the mathematics of the Excess Contribution columns is the key to understanding the entire methodology, regardless of the number of factor groupings, how many bands they are split into and the order in which the factors are considered. The summary total line of Excess Contribution in Exhibit 42.1 becomes the "Total" line in Exhibit 42.2. The rows are now the groupings or bands referred to in the math equations of the previous section of the chapter.

The two key items that go into the mathematics of Excess Contribution from duration in each row are the "Weighting %" difference column "Diff." and the "Ind. vs. Avg." total return % column. The "Diff." column is simply the portfolio weight minus the index weight and shows the over/under allocation for each band of the factor. For the 0–1.999-year duration band, the overweight is 13.51%.

The second key item is whether that duration band was a "good or bad" allocation decision. The "Ind. vs. Avg." values are calculated by taking the index return for that row of duration and subtracting from it the overall average index return. For the 0–1.999-year duration band in Exhibit 42.2, the index return was 0.234%, while the overall average index return was –0.354%, so this duration band beat the overall average by 0.588% as shown in the "Ind. vs. Avg." column.

The total allocation decision impact on the portfolio is the product of the two key items, weighting and relative return of the grouping. For the 0–1.999 duration band, the result is 7.9 bps which equals 13.51% times 58.8 bps. The excess contribution of return for the 2–3.99 duration band is 3.2 bps which is the product of 9.52% overweight and 33.1 bps market outperformance. The 6+ duration band had a 10.8 bps excess contribution of return for a different reason, in this case an underweight of a "bad" allocation band of –22.5%, avoiding an index band versus the average index disadvantage of –48 bps.

The column of excess contribution from selection explains how much your bond selection within a given grouping did better or worse than the index bonds of the same grouping, as explained in the math equations above. To calculate these numbers, the portfolio weight is multiplied by the return difference of the portfolio band versus the index band for each row which is contained in the column "Diff. (bps)" of the "Total Return %" group in Exhibit 42.2. For example, for the duration band 2.000–3.999, the portfolio weight was 28.46% and the portfolio bonds of 2–4 duration did worse than index bonds of 2–4 duration returns by a "Diff. (bps)" of –4.7,

EXHIBIT 42.2   Attribution of Excess Return from Duration Allocation

Duration	Excess Contribution (in BP)			Weighting %				Total Return %			
	Duration	Selection	Total	Port	Index	Diff. (bps)	Port	Index	Diff. (bps)	Ind. vs. Avg.
0.000–1.999	7.9	0.4	8.4	30.70	17.19	13.51	0.248	0.234	1.4	0.588
2.000–3.999	3.2	–1.3	1.8	28.46	18.94	9.52	–0.070	–0.023	–4.7	0.331
4.000–5.999	0.0	2.5	2.5	26.64	27.18	–0.53	–0.215	–0.309	9.4	0.045
6.000+	10.8	11.2	22.0	14.20	36.70	–22.50	–0.046	–0.834	78.7	–0.480
Total	21.9	12.8	34.7	100.00	100.00		–0.007	–0.354	34.7	0.000

so the impact of –4.7 times 28.46% on the portfolio was –1.3 bps. For the 6+ duration band, the portfolio has 14.2% in 6+ duration bonds with portfolio 6+ bonds only losing 4.6 bps versus the index 6+ bonds losing 83.4 bps, an outperformance of 78.7, which times 14.2% gives a result of 11.2 bps in the selection column.

The total column in Excess Contribution in Exhibit 42.2 adds across each duration band, giving a total excess contribution from duration allocation and bond selection for each duration band. For example, 0–2 duration decisions together were 8.4 bps of excess contribution coming from the allocation decision of 7.9 and the bond selection of 0.4 (the 0.1 discrepancy is due to rounding).

Two-Level Attribution Report

The two-level factor run of the allocation attribution report gives three sets of results. Exhibit 42.3 is the summary, which again shows that the index had a –0.354 bps total return and the portfolio had a negative –0.7 bps return and a +34.7 bps excess return. The excess return is split between 21.9 bps for duration allocation, 1.4 bps for rating allocation and 11.4 bps for security selection. Any hedging activity using derivatives is again shown at this summary level and excluded from the rest of the analysis.

Notice that duration returns in the total on Exhibit 42.3 and on the next level of detail in Exhibit 42.4 are the same as in the one-level example above. We have not changed any duration band weightings or returns so the results are the same. However, we now have split the previous selection result into two parts by adding the factor of rating to the mix. The one-level selection return from Exhibits 42.1 and 42.2 of 12.8 bps is split into a return contribution of 1.4 bps due to allocation amongst various quality ratings within each duration band and the remaining 11.4 bps from security selection.

So the second level of the allocation attribution analysis is shown as Exhibit 42.4, containing another detail column for rating. The column for excess contribution from duration allocation was derived the same as before for each band, with the over/under weight times "Ind. vs. Avg." total return. Also the total and excess return columns are the same as in Exhibit 42.2.

EXHIBIT 42.3   Summary of Excess Return from Duration and Rating

| Portfolio | Total Return | Excess Rtn. (bps) | Attribution of Excess Return (bps) | | | |
			Duration	Rating	Selection	Derivatives
Index	–0.354	—	—	—	—	—
Demo fund	–0.007	34.7	21.9	1.4	11.4	0.0

EXHIBIT 42.4 Attribution of Excess Return by Duration Band

Duration	Excess Contribution (in bps)				Weighting %			Total Return %			
	Duration	Rating	Selection	Total	Port	Index	Diff. (bps)	Port	Index	Diff. (bps)	Ind. vs. Avg.
0.00–1.99	7.9	0.1	0.4	8.4	30.70	17.19	13.51	0.248	0.234	1.4	0.588
2.00–3.99	3.2	0.1	−1.4	1.8	28.46	18.94	9.52	−0.070	−0.023	−4.7	0.331
4.00–5.99	0.0	0.2	2.3	2.5	26.64	27.18	−0.53	−0.215	−0.309	9.4	0.045
6.00+	10.8	1.0	10.2	22.0	14.20	36.70	−22.50	−0.046	−0.834	78.7	−0.480
Total	21.9	1.4	11.4	34.7	100.00	100.00		−0.007	−0.354	34.7	0.000

In order to explain the rating column's excess contribution, another level of detail is needed for each duration band. This example will focus on the 6.00+ duration band which is expanded into rating bands in Exhibit 42.5. From here, we can now do the mathematics for the rating allocation attribution as well as the bond selection, which can only be done at the bottom level of the grouping hierarchy. Only after all the index allocation has been computed is it possible to compare the portfolio bonds and index bonds within this lowest level grouping to find the selection term.

Focusing on the AAA rated securities and again following the mathematics from the equations and our first report example, the AAA band within the 6+ duration band was underweight by −21.12% and 6+ duration bonds were still 14.2% of the portfolio (from Exhibit 42.4). Additionally, the corresponding index band had a return of −87.4 bps versus overall index bond return of −83.4 bps, meaning an underperformance of 4 bps. So the 6+ duration portfolio weight of 14.2% times the −21.1% underweight of AAA in the 6+ duration band avoided an underperformance of 4 bps, resulting in an excess contribution for rating allocation of 0.1 bps for the portfolio (0.142 × 0.211 × 4 bps). Notice the index band's "Ind. vs. Avg." relative performance is compared to the 6+ duration average return of 83.4 not the overall index return from Exhibit 42.3 or Exhibit 42.4. Thus the rating allocation becomes dependent on the duration allocation explained before it, so that all comparisons at this bottom level must be done relative to similar bonds of the next-higher grouping level.

A more significant allocation decision was in the BBB band, which was about 22% overweight for the portfolio within the 6+ duration band (with 6+ duration being 14.2% of the overall portfolio). Here the index bonds did better than 6+ duration index bonds overall by a 30.6 bps advantage (index 6+ duration BBB return was −0.528% compared to overall index 6+ duration of −0.834 %). The mathematics is 0.142 × 0.2196 × 30.6 bps resulting in 0.954 bps which rounds to the 1.0 bp of excess contribution from BBB rating allocation in Exhibit 42.5.

The calculation of excess contribution from selection also becomes a little trickier at the second hierarchy level. In order for this result to relate to portfolio returns, the weights must reflect both how much of the portfolio is in 6+ duration bonds (14.2% from Exhibit 42.4) and the portfolio weighting of each rating band within the 6+ duration band. Again, the selection is based on total return of the portfolio vs. the index at the lowest hierarchical level of the analysis—which is the "Diff. (bps)" column under "Total Return %" in Exhibit 42.5.

For example, in the band of AAA bonds within the 6+ duration band (Exhibit 42.5), the portfolio lost 53.4 bps but the index was worse and lost 87.4 bps, giving the portfolio band an excess return of 34.4 in "Diff. (bps)"

EXHIBIT 42.5 Expanded Rating Bands within the 6+ Duration Band

Rating	Excess Contribution (in bp) from			Weighting %			Total Return %			
	Rating	Selection	Total	Port	Index	Diff.	Port	Index	Diff. (bps)	Ind. vs. Avg.
Aaa/AAA	0.1	2.4	2.5	48.26	69.38	−21.12	−0.530	−0.874	34.4	−0.041
Aa/AA	0.0		0.0		16.87	−16.87		−0.824	82.4	0.010
A2/A	−0.1		−0.1		7.08	−7.08		−0.746	74.6	0.088
Baa2/BBB	1.0	−3.1	−2.1	28.60	6.64	21.96	−1.285	−0.528	−75.7	0.306
Unrated	0.0	10.9	10.9	23.14	0.03	23.11	2.493	−0.824	331.8	0.010
Other						0.00			0.0	0.834
Total	1.0	10.2	11.2	100.00	100.00		−0.046	−0.834	78.7	0.000

column. Relative to the overall portfolio impact, multiply this 34.4 excess return by 48.26% weight of AAA within 6+ duration bonds and 14.2% of 6+ duration relative to overall portfolio weighting. The result is 2.357 bps which rounds to 2.4 bps in the selection column.

By contrast, for BBB selection the portfolio band did terrible relative to the corresponding index band, losing a relative 75.7 bps (–1.285% vs. –0.528% for the index). Multiplying 75.7 bps by the weights of 28.6% of BBB within 6+ duration times 14.2% equals 3.07 bps, which rounds to the –3.1 shown in Exhibit 42.5.

The portfolio's unrated bonds performed very strongly, exceeding the return of similar index bonds by 331.8 bps. The 23.14% unrated bonds portfolio weight times the overall portfolio weight of 14.2% for the 6+ duration band times the band's 331.8 excess return equals the excess contribution from selection of 10.9 bps (331.8 bps × 0.2314 × 142 = 10.902 bps). Note that having no portfolio bonds in AA or A ratings, means there is no selection term for these groupings.

In these examples you can drill down into the higher-level decisions and disaggregate specific explanations for where and by how much various allocations and bond selection choices impacted the overall portfolio results. Showing weightings and returns for each portfolio and index band, as well as totals for each level, help assess the magnitude as well as the offsetting bets of the various decisions. In fact, as a portfolio manager continues to run this analysis over time, there should be certain patterns and observations, if not outright selling points to clients as to what strategies are being employed, whether or not they are working and how well. For example, do over/under performance trends even out due to market swings or are certain decisions consistently good or bad (perhaps some risks will appear as not worth taking). Assumptions in objectives and constraints can be verified. With a custom index software product, an index can be constructed that has the same criteria as the manager's strategy and then the manager can compare the excess returns to the overall index as well as the custom index which represents the strategy. This will show both whether the manager is doing well against the overall market and the strategy selected, but also whether the strategy (as implied in the passive custom index) is a good one compared to the overall market.

CLIENT STORIES: APPLYING MUNICIPAL BOND ATTRIBUTION

This is a practical section from real situations. We have several clients who have used our attribution software in a variety of situations. In this section, we provide a few stories of how our Custom Index Manager and the methodologies described in this chapter have helped with client presentations explaining strategy or decisions made.

Perhaps Duration Wasn't so Neutral

The first story demonstrates the importance of proving a presumption. A manager described their approach as duration neutral to their index with value being added from sector rotation and rich/cheap analysis which helped them excel at bond selection. The analysis was based on option-adjusted duration and overall duration was kept within ±0.5 years of the index as a matter of policy. Indeed the fund did well over a variety of falling and rising rates, but as the yield curve steepened and then flattened, both periods were met with lagging results. In going to the duration, sector two-level attribution reporting it was found that while overall duration was matched, the long and short ends were not matched to the index. Worse, as rates went up on the long end, the manager lengthened which helped when the yield curve flattened, but not enough to keep pace with the index.

The duration bands pointed out the issue quickly. Certain weightings that were assumed to be made were not reflected in the weightings on the report. In fact, the report showed that indeed the individual allocations made were far worse than expected relative to what was going on in the index bonds. Some sector and selection advantages showed up as well, but the description of the approach as being *duration neutral* was just an assumption not reality. The portfolio manager started using the detailed analysis to check adjustments that were made and now the duration-neutral claim can be supported. It can now be demonstrated that hidden duration risk is now not standing in the way of other good decisions. Attribution analysis in most cases shows an excess return from duration of almost zero because the portfolio's duration weights are very close to that of the index. The resulting ability to show true sector and bond selection expertise has increased assets and also led to some better bonuses for the traders who help discover value. They can even isolate results down to the CUSIP level.

Right Can Go Wrong

This is a quick example of why being able to show the details is vital, even if things went right. A manager had done fairly well over the years in a separately managed account by having a decent advantage over the peer group and index by 20 bps to 30 bps and ranking in the upper quartiles consistently. However, one year there was quite an upside surprise with about 150 basis points advantage that might have been due to some "prerefunding events and some good trades." The client wanted more detailed information. Which trades? Some anecdotes followed, but it was all stories and the client suddenly became worried that the opposite might occur, with little understanding as to why on the manager's part. The bottom line was the manager fumbled in getting deeper answers and was fired. Perhaps it was bad reporting or a bad memory when he needed it, but if this manager had been armed with the more detailed reports he probably could have regained some client confidence and perhaps retained the client.

Many Other Stories

I have several other related stories which all have the same message. Communication on how and where results were achieved with details to back it up have led to more clients, retained or saved existing clients and have improved senior managements' understanding of what is going on. Reporting on this detailed level has also revealed poor assumptions or blown theories which were leading to trouble. Detailed analysis can also undercover real strengths which were effective but masked by decisions which were offsetting them, and sometimes even unintended decisions which were revealed by this approach.

Perhaps not all experiences will be as dramatic as winning new clients or avoiding embarrassing meetings that result in lost clients. But having the detailed data and analytical tools to make municipal bond attribution possible to tie performance results back to decision making becomes an attractive solution to consider. It is certainly a problem that many have longed for a way to solve.

SUMMARY

Municipal bond attribution is difficult for a variety of reasons. Nonstandard pricing models leading to discrepancies between evaluation services, option calculation approaches which differ, nonstandard yield curves, and illiquid markets are only a few of the data issues. The data need and analytical tools can be daunting to obtain from scratch. Having a large universe of index bonds with monthly pricing detail is a critical starting point to building a valid benchmark against which to measure the portfolio. Having a flexible way to group factors such as duration, sector and rating and a common analysis engine to compute similar yields, option adjusted durations, and align sector and rating definitions between the portfolio and the benchmark is critical to making valid comparisons to this benchmark. Returns-based attribution is attractive for the above reasons, particularly in a product like Investortools' Custom Index Manager. Returns-based attribution is the same method used in equity portfolios and this has its own advantages. This method can be used for a variety of security types, which brings with it a sense of consistency. High net worth managers as well as mutual fund managers will find that the investment committees or boards are often familiar with this method. Investors with tax-exempt income needs tend to be equity investors as well, so they can benefit from the familiarity and consistency as well. Even for those new to attribution, returns-based attribution is relatively easy to understand and demonstrate mathematically and tie back to the decision making process.

This chapter describes the approaches and choices open to portfolio managers of municipal bonds and encourages the reader to go deeper into understanding and mastering the tools of municipal bond attribution. These are tools that will help to enhance how returns are explained and decisions are made, and they demonstrate the expertise involved in the management of municipal bonds.

Six

Credit Analysis

The Role of the National Federation of Municipal Analysts in Promoting Better Disclosure

Lisa Good
Executive Director
National Federation of Municipal Analysts

Gerry Lian
Executive Director
Morgan Stanley Investment Management

With contributions from

Tom Weyl
Eaton Vance Management

Gregory A. Clark
HVB Group

Gregory Aikman
Mellon Private Wealth Management

The National Federation of Municipal Analysts (NFMA) is a not-for-profit professional association of municipal bond analysts located throughout the United States who specialize in evaluating the creditworthiness of municipal securities issued by state and local governments and underlying political instrumentalities. As set forth in its Constitution, the NFMA's core mission is broad based (1) to promote professionalism in global public finance and credit analysis; (2) to strengthen the skill level of its members through educational programs; (3) to advocate issues of importance to the municipal finance industry; and (4) to facilitate the flow of information between analysts and market participants.

The NFMA was formed in 1983 through the creation of a national federation of municipal analyst groups scattered across the country. This federation included (1) members drawn from four charter organizations: the Boston Municipal Analysts Forum, the Chicago Municipal Analysts Society, the Municipal Analysts Group of New York and the Southern Municipal Finance Society; (2) members associated with the two new constituent societies known as the California Society of Municipal Analysts and the Minnesota Society of Municipal Analysts; and (3) other members composed of an affiliated group of individuals not associated with an established organization. Mirroring the growth of the municipal finance industry as a whole, the NFMA has evolved into a large national professional association composed of over 1,000 municipal analysts.

The purpose of this chapter is to provide a brief history and overview of the role the NFMA has played in the municipal bond market, with an emphasis in depicting the pivotal role this organization has played in developing improved disclosure standards. The discussion will begin with a quick historical summary of key NFMA initiatives, provide a brief timeline of some major initiatives and then turn to a detailed consideration of the NFMA's special role in promoting improved disclosure.

SUMMARY OF NFMA INITIATIVES

For over two decades, the NFMA has assumed an active role in implementing several strategic objectives which aim to advance three core organizational goals: (1) to provide ongoing education and training to its members; (2) to advocate issues of timely importance to its members and the municipal bond industry at large; and (3) to promote better disclosure in the municipal bond market. Set forth below is a chronological summary of several key initiatives undertaken by the NFMA.

- *Education.* The NFMA Education Committee has sponsored Ad-vanced Seminars and Annual Conferences to provide its members with ongoing, in-depth educational programs. These conferences provide a valuable forum for leading analysts and public finance professionals to discuss and evaluate issues and topics of timely interest. An Introduction to Municipal Bond Credit Analysis seminar has been held annually since

1987; it serves to introduce entry-level analysts and other municipal bond market participants—including sales, support staff, public finance and issuers—to the key points of analysis of at least 12 specific sectors in the municipal bond market.

■ *Advocacy.* The NFMA Industry Practices Committee has continuously monitored policy issues and concerns impacting the municipal bond market and has developed an extensive collection of Position Papers pertaining to a wide assortment of topics and concerns.[1]

■ *Disclosure.* Although education and advocacy are important objectives that have been diligently advanced by the NFMA, even greater energy and resources have been channeled toward improving disclosure in the municipal bond market. Exhibit 43.1 provides a timeline of major NFMA Disclosure Initiatives.

THE SPECIAL IMPORTANCE OF DISCLOSURE

Since the inception of the NFMA, the NFMA Disclosure Committee has assumed a leadership position in promoting better disclosure throughout the municipal bond market. The importance of the NFMA contribution toward better disclosure should be viewed in light of three important considerations that typify the municipal bond market:

1. Due to the inapplicability of the registration and reporting requirements of the Securities Act of 1933 and the Securities Exchange Act of 1934 to municipal securities, federal regulation of municipal securities is very

---

[1] Examples of NFMA Position Papers include: NFMA Position Paper on 1994 Amendments to SEC Rule 15(c)2-12 (Spring 1998); NFMA Comments on Yield Burning (Summer 1998); NFMA Letter to GASB Regarding Infrastructure Reporting Issues (May 1999); NFMA Letter to TBMA Regarding Proposed Official Statement Disclaimer Language (December 1999); Letter to NABL Regarding Proposed Form Indenture Project (December 1999); NFMA Comment Letter to SEC Regarding Selective Disclosure and Insider Trading (March 2000); NFMA Comment Letter to SEC Regarding Use of Electronic Media (June 2000); NFMA Letter to MSRB on Improving Disclosure (August 2001); NFMA Position Paper on Recharacterization of Airline Special Facility Leases in Bankruptcy (August 2003); NFMA Position Paper on Tax Opinions Under IRS Circular 230 (March 2004); NFMA Position Paper on NASCT Endorsement of Voluntary Interim Disclosure (October 2004); NFMA Position Paper on Coerced Tenders (June 2005); NFMA Letter to GASB Exposure Draft on Accounting and Financial Reporting for Pollution Remediation Obligations (May 2006); NFMA Position Paper on Recommended Responses by Municipalities to Disasters (March 2007). A complete set of NFMA Position papers is set forth on the NFMA website located at www.nfma.org.

EXHIBIT 43.1 NFMA Disclosure Timeline

1986 NFMA began work on what became the *Disclosure Handbook for Municipal Securities* (NFMA Disclosure Handbook). It took two years and the participation of nearly 100 analysts to compile. There was interaction with other industry groups, including the Municipal Finance Officers association, predecessor to the Government Finance Officer's Association (GFOA), and a lengthy comment period.

1990 The NFMA Disclosure Handbook published.

1992 NFMA Board voted to participate with GFOA on a joint publication regarding exemplary disclosure, the first formal buy-side/sell-side effort in the market's history.

1992 *The Disclosure Handbook for Municipal Securities, 1992 Update*, published, with expanded secondary market sections for each sector.

1992 NFMA surveyed members on adequacy of primary and secondary market disclosure. Nearly 80% of respondents said they would support SEC involvement to force issuers to disclose their intentions regarding periodic reporting. 73% responded that they would not support municipal bond market regulations comparable to those in the corporate market.

1992 NFMA's Certificate of Recognition program established, recognizing issuers who developed policies to provide ongoing secondary market disclosure.

1992 NFMA's Model Language effort results in a *Bond Buyer* advertisement listing names of NFMA members who endorsed continuing disclosure language in offering documents.

1993 NFMA released the first of a series of 16 standardized Secondary Market Disclosure Forms designed for issuers and their trustees.

1994 Amendments to SEC Rule 15(c)2-12 are issued. The purpose of these amendments was to facilitate improved disclosure in the secondary market through ongoing disclosure of financial reports, operating statistics and other material events.

1997 NFMA submits letter to SEC Chairman Arthur Levitt on 15(c)2-12 Amendments.

1998 NFMA issues position paper on 1994 amendments to 15(c)2-12.

2000 NFMA releases the first of 16 Recommended Best Practices in Disclosure and/or White Papers for various sectors of the market.

2000 NFMA releases comment letter on disclosure and insider trading.

2001 NFMA surveyed members on disclosure. Of those surveyed, 64% reported that they use Nationally Recognized Municipal Securities Information Repositories (NRMSIRs) to retrieve official statements. For secondary market information, the percentage using NRMSIRs dropped to 50%. Eighty-seven percent indicated a desire to access documents electronically through a centralized document delivery system.

2004 NFMA published a bound compilation of Recommended Best Practices in Disclosure for dissemination to the municipal bond industry

limited and is almost exclusively grounded in antifraud concepts such as the prohibition against material omissions set forth in SEC Rule 10-b(5), together with a recent amendment that requires municipal underwriters to obtain, review and distribute a disclosure document pursuant to SEC Rule 15(c)2-12.

2. Over the course of time, due to the issuance of a variety of municipal revenue bonds, the volume, risk and complexity of municipal bonds rose dramatically and rendered the federal exemption of municipal bonds from federal securities regulation far less appropriate.

3. To fill this void, since 1986 the NFMA has developed a comprehensive set of recommended disclosure standards that offer practitioners clear and useful guidance on what information investors deem important in making investment decisions.

NFMA efforts to improve disclosure is divisible into three stages: (1) efforts to work cooperatively with other industry groups to develop voluntary disclosure guidelines; (2) development of the NFMA Disclosure Handbook in 1986 that set forth sector specific disclosure guidelines that identified basic informational requirements; and (3) beginning in 2000 and continuing to the present, the NFMA, working in conjunction with industry representatives, has developed Recommended Best Practices to identify on a sector-specific basis all relevant information deemed important in analyzing municipal credit risk.

Early Cooperative Efforts to Improve Disclosure

Early efforts to improve disclosure centered upon an initiative by the NFMA to work cooperatively with other industry groups. One promising avenue related to an attempt by NFMA leaders to work together with the GFOA to supplement their pioneering effort to improve disclosure. To address the growing need for disclosure, in 1976 the Municipal Finance Officers Association, the predecessor to the GFOA, completed a publication entitled Voluntary Disclosure Guidelines (GFOA Voluntary Guidelines). The GFOA Voluntary Guidelines were not intended to be legally binding, but rather to encourage improved disclosure and greater standardization of disclosure practices. The guidelines set forth information that the GFOA believed municipal issuers should disclose to potential investors. In the late 1990's the NFMA offered to formulate a supplement to be appended to the GFOA Voluntary Guidelines but this effort did not reach fruition.

The NFMA Disclosure Handbook

Over time, as the NFMA evolved into a larger professional association, a decision was made that municipal bond analysts, as recognized experts who specialized in evaluating municipal credit risk, ought to develop their own recommendations with respect to municipal disclosure.

First, municipal analysts, as primary users of investment information, had developed specific expertise in municipal finance transactions and were in a unique position to recommend what substantive content ought to be disclosed.

Second, because a large and growing component of municipal analysts represented the buy-side of the market, as investors these analysts had a keen grasp of what specific information was relevant to make informed investment decisions.

Third, over the course of time, as the range of municipal bonds broadened to include a wider spectrum of different revenue pledges, the need arose to develop disclosure guidelines on a sector-specific basis and municipal analysts had the necessary specialized knowledge to develop appropriate guidelines.

Fourth, given the relative absence of meaningful disclosure guidelines, municipal analysts were forced to either assume a proactive approach to spur development of substantive guidelines or face the likelihood that meaningful guidance would not be provided otherwise.

Finally, from a public policy standpoint, analysts felt strongly that in a modern capital securities market the privilege of gaining market access carried with it a corresponding responsibility to provide ongoing material information to investors.

For the foregoing reasons, in 1986 the NFMA Board decided to work together with a group of leading municipal analysts to develop voluntary disclosure guidelines. Over the next two years, a number of analysts developed recommended disclosure guidelines for individual credit sectors that included general obligation bonds, single family housing bonds, multifamily housing bonds, hospital bonds, public power bonds and airport bonds. In 1990, these drafts were distilled into the NFMA Disclosure Handbook. In 1992, to facilitate better disclosure in the secondary market, the NFMA published an update to the Disclosure Handbook that added sector-specific secondary market disclosure guidelines. This led to the creation in 1993 of 16 standardized Secondary Market Disclosure Forms to simplify disclosure reporting for issuers and bond trustees.

NFMA Recommended Best Practices

Commencing in June 2000 and continuing to the present, the NFMA has developed updated disclosure guidelines known as NFMA Recommended Best

Practices (RBP) in disclosure. The RBP disclosure documents are a compilation of 16 sector-specific disclosure guidelines designed to facilitate provision of more accurate, timely and complete investment information. These documents represent an important extension to the NFMA Disclosure Handbook that add significant depth and breadth and also reflect substantive input from the municipal finance industry at large. Whereas the NFMA Disclosure Handbook was the exclusive work product of municipal bond analysts, the RBP represent a collaborative effort undertaken by the NFMA acting in concert with a broad range of municipal professionals that include investment bankers, government issuers, bond counsel and financial advisors.

To date over 200 individuals have been involved in writing, conceptualizing and producing these documents. Diversity of viewpoint is provided by two means (1) analysts are drawn from all segments of the municipal bond industry including the buy side, sell side, rating agencies and bond insurers; and (2) in nearly every instance, each sector committee is also represented by a variety of disciplines including bond attorneys, financial advisors, issuers and trustees. Discussion will now turn toward a detailed consideration of the RBP documents which are also available for download from the NFMA's web site located at www.nfma.org.

A DETAILED LOOK AT THE NFMA'S RECOMMENDED BEST PRACTICES

The NFMA's Recommended Best Practices identify specific information needed by analysts to make an informed investment decision. The process of evaluating credit risk forms the core responsibility of an analyst: to assemble, evaluate and diligently review all material investment information. The NFMA RBPs constitute important tools that summarize key analytical criteria used by municipal analysts in evaluating credit quality on a sector-specific basis.

Development of the RBP documents has been undertaken by scores of municipal analysts drawn from every facet of the market including mutual funds, large corporations, insurance companies, investment banks and rating agencies to improve informational content. To solicit industry support and diversity of viewpoint, each ad hoc committee formed to develop a RBP document included leading investment bankers, bond counsel, governmental issuers and financial advisors. Through thoughtful discussion and constructive dialogue, these committees succeeded in developing an impressive collection of disclosure guidelines that offer invaluable assistance to guide the preparation of Official Statements, Rule 15(c)2-12 annual information reports and other forms of disclosure. At a time when issuers are being actively encouraged to improve municipal disclosure, the NFMA RBP documents have found widespread use and support across the industry.

Three organizing principles of the RBP documents are worth noting: (1) the RBPs represent a collaborative industry effort to develop disclosure guidelines on a voluntary basis; (2) the RPBs duly recognize that the pluralistic nature of municipal finance means "one size does not fit all" and therefore refrain from imposing uniform disclosure standards; and (3) the RBP guidelines strive to elevate increased acceptance of the best or highest disclosure standards, and are not necessarily designed to prescribe minimum disclosure requirements.

Substantive Content of the RBP Documents

The RBPs are divisible into two conceptual areas: (1) disclosure guidelines developed on a sector-specific basis to identify material information used by analysts to evaluate credit risk; and (2) white papers that address discrete transactions, issues and topics in the municipal bond market that impact the credit quality of investments or the ability of analysts to evaluate credit risk. Disclosure guidelines for specific credit sectors generally incorporate a uniform format. Each of these documents begins with an overview and description of a select credit sector, identifies key items of information deemed relevant to credit analysis and often incorporates an operating data segment to facilitate secondary market disclosure. White papers are the preferred format for addressing new emerging industry topics or intricate transactional issues that extend beyond identification of pure analytical credit criteria. To date the NFMA has completed 13 RBP documents for specific credit sectors listed in Exhibit 43.2 and four white papers on specific topics summarized in Exhibit 43.3.

PROCEDURE FOR DEVELOPING RBP DOCUMENTS

Having explained the purpose and rationale behind the development of the NFMA RBPs, it is also important to summarize the painstaking process followed to promulgate these documents. Careful steps have been taken to enlist wide industry participation and discussion every step of the way since inception of the RBP project. Several procedures are followed to solicit broad-based discussion and industry comment.

Collaborative Effort

Great care is taken to involve outside organizations in the formation of each credit committee formed to develop NFMA RBPs. Typically, this includes

EXHIBIT 43.2 Inventory of Completed RBP Disclosure Reports

1. Water & Sewer Transactions	March 2006
2. Toll Roads	August 2005
3. Airports	May 2004
4. Public Power	June 2004
5. Tax Increment Financings	March 2003
6. Variable Rate and Short-Term Securities	February 2003
7. Long-Term Care/Senior Living	October 2002
8. General Obligation and Tax-Supported	December 2001
9. Solid Waste	November 2001
10. Private College and University	May 2001
11. Acute Care Hospitals	August 2000
12. Single & Multifamily Housing	July 2000
13. Land Secured	June 2000

Note: Items 2–12 feature supplemental NFMA Operating Data Guidelines to facilitate secondary market reporting, including downloadable Excel templates.

EXHIBIT 43.3 Inventory of Completed White Papers

Position Paper on Recommended Responses by Municipalities to Disasters (March 2007). Suggests steps that can be taken by local units of government, both before and after a natural or man-made disaster, to maintain effective communication with the financial community following such a disaster.

Project Finance Risk Assessment and Disclosure (August 2006). Covers such topics as construction risk and feasibility studies in more detail than prior NFMA publications.

Recommended Term Sheet and Legal Provisions for Hospital Debt Transactions (December 2005). The lack of standardization in hospital bond legal documents can lead to confusion and potential risk to bondholders, particularly in the "high-grade" market where key transaction participants may not have extensive experience in workouts and bankruptcies. This white paper is to be used as a resource for to assemble recommended provisions that incorporate the lessons learned by its authors in following many deals through the default, workout and bankruptcy cycle.

White Paper on Disclosure for Swaps (February 2004). The size and breadth of the municipal swap market has grown substantially, but disclosure of swap transactions is uneven. This white paper identifies the types of information that analysts need to better evaluate the credit posture of the various swap counterparties.

issuers, investment bankers, financial advisors and bond attorneys in addition to municipal analysts. Thus, the basic structure and composition of each committee is established to capture meaningful input from all corners of the marketplace, including issuers.

Standard of Reasonableness

The NFMA believes that an implicit standard of reasonableness should govern the process by which specific information is requested and solicited in RBP documents. The NFMA systematically includes industry representatives on each Credit Committee to promote healthy discussion and debate. This exchange helps to ensure that information being requested in the RBP document satisfies two criteria: (1) that it is relevant and material to credit analysis; and (2) that is available from issuers within the normal course of business operations.

Generous Public Comment Period

After RBP documents are formulated by a broad-based committee, exposure drafts were provided to the public to solicit further commentary. In many instances, exposure drafts are first introduced at disclosure sessions held at the NFMA Annual Conference. Thereafter, a formal 90-day comment period was announced through a press release in the *Bond Buyer* inviting all interested parties to read, review and comment on an exposure draft. All comments were carefully discussed and considered, and where appropriate, incorporated into the final text of the RBP documents.

Use of Special Forums to Solicit Feedback

In certain instances, exposure drafts of RBP documents are distributed at special forums to solicit industry feedback. Some examples include:

1. The Housing Revenue Bond Committee conferred extensively over a multiyear period with the National Council of State Housing Agencies;
2. The Hospital Debt Committee actively solicited comments from the American Hospital Association, the Healthcare Financial Management Association and the MSRB which established a special task force to spur further critical discussion and commentary.
3. The Long-Term Care Committee presented their exposure draft at a MSRB/AAHSA forum.

4. The GO Bond and the Tax Supported Committee included an officer from the GFOA Debt Committee as a participating representative of that organization

Living Documents Subject to Ongoing Refinement

The RBP documents represent a key strategic investment of the NFMA to which it has allocated and will continue to commit substantial time and resources. RBP documents are considered by the NFMA Board to be "living documents" that require ongoing oversight and modification. As noted in the preface to the RBP documents, all interested parties are encouraged to submit comments at any time for consideration in the development of future versions of NFMA Recommended Best Practices in Disclosure Guidelines.

THE MECHANICAL STEPS USED TO DEVELOP AN RBP DOCUMENT

RBP documents and white papers are produced as part of a process that can take several months to complete. The steps needed to produce one of these documents illustrate the care take to incorporate divergent view points and the highly deliberative nature of this process:

1. *Identification of an analytical issue.* Typically, the idea for a new white paper or RBP begins with one or more NFMA members, who in informal discussions with members of the NFMA Board suggest that NFMA study a particular topic. In addition, board members frequently have their own opinions about what topics should be further analyzed.
2. *Decision by the NFMA Board to authorize a white paper or RBP.* If a board member and/or the chairs of NFMA's Disclosure Committee agree that a topic deserves further study, they will propose at one of NFMA's Board meetings—which are held three times per year—that the topic be covered by a white paper or RBP. If the board as a whole agrees with the member's opinion, the board will authorize the chairs to form a committee that will eventually produce the white paper or RBP.
3. *Formation of a committee.* Chairs of the Disclosure Committee appoint an NFMA member who is an expert on a given issue to form his or her own committee for further study and eventual production of a white paper or RBP. The head of this new committee is asked first to solicit volunteers from the NFMA ranks. Subsequently, non-NFMA members such as local government officials, bond attorneys, financial advisers to issuers, and trustees—are invited to be part of the committee. In short,

the NFMA has always been careful to enlist industry-wide participation and discussion.

4. *Production of a draft report.* As the professionals described above proceed with their work, a draft RBP or white paper is eventually produced. Here the procedures for white papers and RBPs begin to diverge. RBPs are subject to a public comment period—after RBP documents are formulated by their respective committees, exposure drafts are provided to the public to solicit further commentary. Exposure drafts are frequently first introduced at the NFMA Annual Conference, after which time a press release is issued. The press release is typically covered by the *Bond Buyer*, at which time a formal 90-day comment period also begins. During the comment period, interested parties review and comment the exposure draft. All comments are discussed and considered, and where appropriate, incorporated into the final text of the RBP documents.

5. *Release of the final report.* Following the 90-day comment period, the final report is released to the public and made available on NFMA's website.

6. *Release of the final report.* Following the 90-day comment period, the final report is released to the public and made available on NFMA's website.

CURRENT ISSUES AND CHALLENGES FACING THE NFMA

By and large, the NFMA's efforts to improve substantive disclosure, starting with the NFMA Disclosure Handbook and now featuring the NFMA's Recommended Best Practices, provide a reasonable solution to concerns regarding disclosure content. Disclosure content, however, is not the only issue facing the municipal bond market. In addition to concerns regarding the quality of substantive disclosure, better disclosure in the municipal bond market requires that investment information be disseminated to investors in a manner that is at once timely, evenhanded and efficient. These mechanical issues present additional challenges that the NFMA believes also need to be carefully addressed.

Dissemination of Investment Information

A crucial issue facing the municipal bond market centers on the efficient dissemination of investment information to all investors. As capital markets continue to expand and globalize, it becomes increasingly important that access to information on municipal securities be made easily accessible through established distribution channels. These channels should be established for at least two uses: (1) for dissemination of official statements and placement memoranda for new issue offerings; and (2) for dissemination of Rule 15(c)2-12 annual information reports and other interim disclosure reports for secondary market reporting. To date the Central Post Office (CPO) has evolved as a consensus solution developed by the Muni Council, a collaborative effort of a vast body of professional associations and municipal bond industry groups, to facilitate dissemination of secondary market disclosure.

However, challenges remain with respect to dissemination goals that the CPO has not yet fully resolved (1) the CPO has not assumed responsibility in the new-issue market for the collection and redistribution of official statements by electronic means; and (2) secondary market reports filed with the CPO are not made directly available to retail customers or other global investors. The NFMA endorses the creation and fully supports the operation of the CPO but recommends that its function be expanded to serve as a repository for official statements and offering memoranda by devising a workable methodology whereby digital information maintained by the CPO be made available to retail investors free of charge.

Mandatory Filing with the CPO

In order for the CPO to provide full and complete dissemination of investment information, it is appropriate to mandate that all municipal issuers file disclosure documents with this entity and that filings be done through electronic means. If the CPO is judicially invalidated, the MSRB should be delegated this responsibility. Mandatory filing with the CPO, or if necessary, an alternative entity, in this manner confers several advantages:

1. It ensures that the CPO itself contains a complete record of all disclosure documents.
2. It will enable the CPO to provide the market once and for all with a complete and accurate centralized index of disclosure reports, thereby assuring quick and easy access to all information when needed.
3. It will stimulate faster adoption of electronic filing, thereby reducing dissemination costs for issuers, NRMSIRs, investors, and the CPO itself.
4. Establishment of a complete digital library of municipal disclosure will fortify the entire market and render it better able to compete for global investment capital through provision of more complete, timely, and accessible investment information.

Timeliness of Information

If disclosure is going to serve its intended purpose, investment information must be disseminated in a timely manner. In connection with new-issue offerings, disclosure documents must be received by investors far enough in advance of the sale date to permit meaningful and rigorous analysis. The greater the degree of credit risk, the more lead time should be given to promote careful credit review. By allowing the CPO to serve as the designated repository for digital copies of new issue offerings, investors will be afforded quick and ready access to essential documents, thereby eliminating wasteful lag time that inhibits robust analysis and informed investment decision-making. Likewise, for various reasons the dissemination of secondary market reports is frequently subject to substantial delay, often disadvantaging investors with stale information.

Two steps should be taken to promote better timeliness of secondary market reporting: (1) issuers ought to be held to a 120-day filing deadline following the end of a fiscal year for reports mandated pursuant to Rule 15(c)2-12; and (2) these reports should be required to be filed in electronic format, allowing for appropriate phase-in for smaller issuers to ease transition to this new standard.

Dissemination of Information to Municipal Pricing Services

Mutual funds account for substantial ownership of municipal securities. Efficient and timely valuation of securities held by these funds is dependent upon the ability of a small handful of pricing services to accurately evaluate the fair market value of all investments held in these portfolios.

To enable pricing services to properly carry out this responsibility, it is imperative that these firms be provided with a continuing stream of updated financial information pertaining to individual securities. The most effective way to equip pricing services with current information is by providing municipal pricing vendors with immediate and preferential access to digital content maintained by the CPO on the same preferential basis as NRMSIRs.

A fallback solution is to popularize the use of a special dissemination covenant obligating issuers and their agents to send all disclosure reports directly to these pricing services. To avoid the often circuitous and redundant means by which investment information is disseminated to mutual funds, who then reproduce and resend such information to external pricing services, institutional investors are encouraged to incorporate a standardized disclosure covenant in applicable financing documents that require issuers to send all information reports provided under Rule 15(c)2-12 or otherwise to designated pricing services.

The Tower Amendment Revisited

The NFMA has resisted endorsement of full-blown federal regulation of municipal disclosure practices in a manner identical to corporate securities offerings. Due to fundamental differences in risk characteristics, the rationale for the filing and reporting requirements set forth under the Securities Act of 1933 and the Securities Exchange Act of 1934 has limited application to municipal debt offerings.

The NFMA strongly believes that all municipal issuers should properly be required to disclose all material information to investors through official statements prepared for new issue offerings and in Rule 15(c)2-12 annual information reports prepared for secondary market disclosure. Although municipal issuers are generally exempt from providing standardized investment reports resembling either Forms 10-K or 10-Q, they are nevertheless subject to the federal antifraud provisions and are thereby obligated to provide investors with all material information required to facilitate informed decision making.

A recent call has been made by responsible government regulators for reevaluation of the ongoing appropriateness of the so-called Tower Amendment, legislation which prohibits either the SEC or the MSRB, directly or indirectly, from mandating the filing of a written disclosure report prior to the sale of a security. The NFMA believes that this suggestion is worthy of consideration by market participants. At a time when the fate of the CPO is subject to considerable uncertainty due to pending federal litigation, municipal bond market participants must carefully evaluate the full range of options that can and should be taken to ensure that provision of investment information is fully and rigorously maintained. The NFMA plans to work collaboratively with other industry groups to carefully consider the implications posed by the potential dismantlement of the CPO and to develop appropriate alternative solutions, if such action proves necessary.

CHAPTER 44

A History of
Modern Municipal Defaults

James E. Spiotto
Partner
Chapman and Cutler LLP

There is a saying: "While doctors bury their mistakes, in municipal financing, they are refunded." There comes a time, however, when certain financial problems cannot be refunded. Under present economic conditions, the probability has increased that many municipalities will be faced with significant cash flow difficulties and ensuing financial crisis. In such situations, the municipality may consider requesting state support, curtailing spending and services or seeking a debt adjustment to resolve the fiscal emergency. If the municipal crisis is not addressed quickly and effectively, both the state and the municipality could face acrimonious and agitated credit markets. The prolonged crisis could be injurious to the state and municipal credit and harmful to the achievement of an economic solution to the situation.

ANALYSIS OF DEFAULTS OF MUNICIPAL DEBT IN THE UNITED STATES

Causes of Default

In order that the past not be repeated, it is helpful to review the causes and nature of prior defaults. While each default by a local governmental body has unique factors (specific problems of economics, industry or tax revenue

---

Note: A more detailed discussion by the author appears in M. David Gelfand (ed.), *State and Local Goverment Debt Financing,* Cumulative Supplement issued June 2007 (St. Paul, MN: Thomson West).

of the time and place), there are also notable themes that can be guides for the future. The usual causes of defaults by municipalities in the United States are described below.

Economic Conditions

Defaults may be caused by economic conditions such as depressions, recessions, and high interest rates. Such conditions may shake the most stable businesses, and this will, in turn, threaten the tax base for a municipality. Historically, there is a direct link between economic depression in the United States and municipal default. Examples abound. The depression of 1837 led to the default of the city of Mobile in 1839, which was the first recorded municipal default in the United States. The depression of 1857 led to problems in, among other places, the cities of Chicago and Philadelphia. The panic and depression of 1893 brought with it a large number of municipal defaults. Of course, the Great Depression of the 1930s led to the highest municipal default statistics ever recorded in the United States.

Nonessential Services

In the municipal arena, financings developed to pay for services for which there is no long-term need or demand are often the subject of later defaults. Such problems are not exclusively the product of recent times. Railroad stations constructed throughout the southern part of the United States during the 1800s, where railroads were never built, were funded by municipal bonds. Real estate ventures in California in the mid-1800s were ahead of their time and led to troubled financial situations. It is not difficult to think of recent examples of bad ideas such as large housing developments not supported by population or demand and refuse-burning facilities that do not work. These nonessential services are directly related to lack of feasibility issues.

Feasibility of Projects and Industries

As one person remarked, "I never saw a feasibility study which showed the project would not make it." However, there are some industries, businesses, and structures of financing that just are not feasible. When financing is based upon a flawed concept, disaster comes sooner or later. Moreover, there is a life cycle to products and to businesses, and the life cycle of some of these is very short indeed. Ranger, Texas in the early part of the 1900s, grew out of an oil discovery and blossomed to a population of 30,000. Ten years later, Ranger became a town of a few hundred when the oil ran out. The large infrastructure paid for by municipal financing was required to be paid off over decades by a population of less than 1/100 its original size.

Feasibility problems do not always stem from a "crazy idea." Sometimes, for example, the developers of the financing simply misread the future. In the Washington Public Power Supply System (WPPSS) situation, the elasticity of demand for power was not anticipated. Unexpectedly, demand dropped and the projects failed. Small special tax and levy districts have run into difficulties when they are superseded by larger utilities (sometimes private or investor-owner) or become obsolete.

Fraud

When greed exceeds fear, the parties involved with the transaction fail to comply with the terms of the relevant documents and, in essence, convert funds and benefits to the detriment of the creditors. Part of Orange County, California's problem in 1994 was attributable to investment strategies and borrowings to fund derivative investment schemes that were too good to be believed.

Mismanagement

A municipal operation cannot succeed without proper management. It is management's ability to react to the constant changes of economic cycles that can make or break a default situation.

Unwillingness to Pay

Defaults can be caused by an unwillingness to pay which leads to repudiation. Following the Civil War, in the mid 1800s, at least 13 states repudiated their indebtedness. This historical event clarified the difference between default and repudiation. Default occurs when the municipality lacks the ability to pay because of economic problems: The revenues don't come in, there is a general economic depression, or there may be other outside reasons. However, although it may be impacted by economic factors, repudiation is a decision not to pay. Repudiation has always been met with a strong negative response by the municipal bond market.

After the 13 states repudiated their indebtedness, there was a general recognition of the importance of willingness to pay. Eventually, the market demanded numerous protections including rating agencies, clear disclosure of bondholder remedies, and statutory and constitutional provisions with respect to the obligation of municipalities to pay their debts and the use of bond counsel as an independent professional passing on the legal issues. Yet, over a hundred years later, WPPSS and Orange County, California chose not to pay in part due to a breakdown of these necessary protections.

Natural and Man-Made Disasters

Natural disasters can ravage a local government by causing an increase in cost and expense to repair damages that deplete revenues. For example, Galveston, Texas was hit by a hurricane in 1900 which was so devastating that default on the city's bonds was inevitable. Likewise, the terrorist attacks of 9/11 on New York City stressed that city's financings, but federal relief effectively prevented serious consequences to New York City's operations and obligations. Similarly, Hurricane Katrina did not result in any immediate bond defaults.

Frequency of Municipal Defaults in the United States

Since 1839, there have been less than 10,000 municipal (local government) defaults. Almost half of these occurred between 1929 and 1937 in the Great Depression. The number of defaults is quite small given that presently there are over 50,000 municipalities in the United States.

Between 1939 and 1969, there were 6,195 recorded municipal defaults. The defaults between 1839 and 1969 involved 727 counties and parishes, 1,911 incorporated municipalities, 313 unincorporated municipalities, 1,372 school districts, and 1,872 special purpose districts. During the period of time between 1929 and 1937, there were 4,770 defaults by governmental bodies. (See Exhibit 44.1 for further details.)

EXHIBIT 44.1   Defaults by Governmental Bodies During the Period of 1929–1937

Type of Government Unit	Number in Default	Percentage of Total Number in Default	Indebtedness of Defaulting Unit (in $ millions)	Percentage of Debt in Default
Counties	417	13.7	$360	15.1
Incorporated municipalities	1,434	8.3	1,760	19.9
Organized townships	88	0.4	10	2.9
School districts	1,241	0.9	160	7.8
Reclamation, levee irrigation, and drainage districts	944	28.2		
Other special districts	644	12.4	400	25.0
Total	4,770	2.7	$2,690	17.7

Source: "City Financial Emergencies: The Intergovernmental Dimension," Advisory Commission on Intergovernmental Relations, Washington, D.C. July 1973.

During the 1930s, local governmental bodies defaulted on the payment of interest and principal on 17.7% of the principal amount of $15 billion of municipal bonds outstanding. In comparison, between 1945 and 1970, municipal bonds in the principal amount of $450 million went into default, which constituted approximately 0.4% of the principal amount of bonds outstanding in 1970. The pattern, with some notable exceptions, has continued over the years.

Selected Case Studies

The New York and Cleveland Experiences: Problems of Financial Controls and State and Federal Bailouts

In spring 1975, New York City was unable to market its debt because the bond market had discovered that New York had, for more than 10 years, been using questionable accounting and borrowing practices to eliminate its annual budget deficits. The banks refused to renew short-term loans that were maturing or lend additional cash to the city. As a result, only state cash advances were keeping the city afloat. The city's spending for operating purposes had exceeded operating revenues for several years, and the accumulated fund deficit could only be resolved by increasing amounts of short-term borrowing. New York City itself had no funds to meet its short-term obligations. According to several commentators, the causes of this revenue shortfall included changing population and economic characteristics, national economic difficulties, state and federal government action and inaction, and weaknesses in the political system itself. However, New York avoided a default on the payment of its notes in October 1975.

New York City's then-existing financial crises were averted through use of a *deus ex machina* in the form of the State Municipal Assistance Corporation, which issued its own long-term securities to refinance short-term city securities, coupled with a federal loan. One of New York's principal problems then and now is shared by most major metropolitan cities: increasing labor costs in a period of decreasing revenues. It is not unusual for 60% to 75% of municipal budgets to be attributed to labor costs.

In December 1978, Cleveland defaulted on $15.5 million of bond anticipation notes. When a financial emergency was declared by the state auditor in 1980, Cleveland had overdue accounts in excess of $36 million and a large general fund deficit. Again, as in the case of New York, general fund expenditures exceeded revenues. Further, it appeared that restricted funds had been used to meet general obligations. Cleveland was able to solve, at least for a time, its financial problems by borrowing $15 million from the state of Ohio to pay overdue debts and by the issuance and sale of $36.2 million in bonds to Cleveland banks. Although the federal bankruptcy provisions relating to municipal debt adjustment Chapter 9[1] had been amended following the New York City crisis to make this remedy more acceptable to the bond market, a resort to municipal bankruptcy was not seriously considered as an option for Cleveland.

The San Jose School District and Medley, Florida Cases: Excessive Labor Costs or Judgments

The San Jose School District instituted a bankruptcy proceeding on June 30, 1983.[2] Labor problems, coupled with restrictions on real estate taxes, were apparently the primary causes of the municipal insolvency. The vast majority of creditors appeared to be individual teachers. At the time of the filing, the average teacher in the school district made approximately $28,000 a year.[3] The average salary for teachers in the State of California was approximately $24,000.[4]

Bonded debt was not listed by the school district as part of the debt to be reorganized. Prior to 1978, the school district had issued general obligation bonds pursuant to the California Education Code. Section 15250 of the California Education Code[5] provided that it was the duty of the board of supervisors of the county to levy taxes sufficient to pay the principal, interest, and an annual reserve to insure required payments of bonds issued by such school districts.

The San Jose School District made it clear that it did not in any way intend to impair the rights of its bondholders by this bankruptcy. Accordingly, the school district stated that the bonds were secured by a property tax assessed by the county controller's office on property within the school district at rates sufficient to make principal and interest payments. Because the school district had neither the authority to levy taxes nor access to bond reserve funds held by the controller's office, the school district argued that the bondholders were not proper parties to the bankruptcy proceeding. The San Jose School District filed bankruptcy at the same time that an interest payment was due to its bondholders. The school district allowed the tax funds that had been collected to be used to pay the interest payment that was

---

[1] The original provision relating to municipal debt adjustment under the Municipal Bankruptcy Act is Chapter IX. The subsequent treatment of the same topic under the Bankruptcy Code, which became effective in 1979, is termed *Chapter 9*.

[2] *In re San Jose Unified School Dist.*, No. 5-83-02387-A-9 (BC ND Cal. 1983).

[3] Human Resources Development, San Jose School District, March 4, 1993.

[4] United States National Center for Education Statistics, Digest of Educational Statistics 1984.

[5] Cal. Edu. Code § 15250.

due at the time the school district filed its Chapter 9 proceeding. This was a clear recognition by the state and school district of the continuing duty of municipalities to pay the obligations which they had incurred despite a general prohibition for paying interest during a bankruptcy proceeding where a debtor is insolvent. In spring 1984, the school district resolved its differences with its employees. The settlement gave the employees approximately 60% of the increases promised in prior years. Therefore, on June 8, 1984, the Chapter 9 proceeding was dismissed.

The conclusion reached by the San Jose School District is not unprecedented. In 1968, the City of Medley, Florida, a small city of approximately 350 people, instituted a Chapter IX proceeding. The city was then the subject of numerous judgments and writs of mandamus issued in favor of creditors. The city stated that it did not seek in the Chapter IX proceeding to adjust the $850,000 bonded indebtedness but only the $700,000 of nonbonded indebtedness. The city proceeded to propose a plan not altering or impairing bonded indebtedness but merely extending the repayment of its nonbonded indebtedness up to 10 years.

Washington Public Power Supply System: Projects Fail when Expected Demand Evaporates

In 1976, WPPSS entered into agreements with 88 public utilities in the northwest part of the United States under which each participant utility purchased a percentage of the project capability of two nuclear power projects, Projects 4 and 5. Each participant agreed to pay its percentage share of costs incurred by the supply system to finance, construct, and operate those projects. During the next five years, WPPSS issued $2.5 billion in bonds to finance Projects 4 and 5. Because of perceived lack of demand for the power, prior to the completion of Projects 4 and 5, construction of the projects was terminated. The terms of the Participants' Agreements would have obligated the participants to commence payments to WPPSS one year later. Within months of termination of construction, however, various lawsuits were filed by rate payers, certain utilities and the trustee for the bonds. In 1983, the Washington Supreme Court decided that certain of the municipal utilities who were participants had lacked authority under state law to enter into the Participants' Agreements. On remand to the State Superior Court, the Participant Agreements, which had unconditionally obligated the participating utilities to make payments to cover the costs of the projects, whether or not they were completed, operable or operating, were invalidated and rendered unenforceable. A second decision of the Washington Supreme Court released the remaining utilities from the Participants' Agreements. The numerous class action lawsuits that were filed alleged securities law violations in connection with the sale of the bonds. Among the alleged misstatements were the region's need for power, the estimated costs of construction, the dates of operation for the projects, and the participants willingness and authority to pay. It was alleged that the region's need for power did not meet the projected expectations, and the estimated costs of construction and dates of operation were significantly understated.

The Colorado Special Districts: Failed Special Projects

The real estate boom and bust in Colorado that took place during the 1980s had ramifications for municipal finance. The infrastructure for residential real estate development—streets, sewers, utilities, and the like—were financed with bonds issued by special districts created under Title 32 of the Colorado Revised Statutes.

Briefly stated, the Colorado special district bonds are a form of special assessment bond where the land benefited from the capital improvements is charged for the cost of those improvements and their related financing costs through annual real estate taxes. In some incarnations, the bonds outstanding are general obligations of a district payable from unlimited ad valorem taxes on the public property (e.g., Dawson Ridge Metropolitan District). In other incarnations, there is a group of districts that are set up to do staged construction over time, and there is a lead district which issues revenue bonds pursuant to intergovernmental agreements with the underlying districts. They, in turn, promise to make payments to the lead district from taxes levied in and by the underlying districts.

With the bust in the Colorado real estate world, the funded interest was largely paid out to bondholders, and most of the real estate developers were either in some form of bankruptcy themselves, or were otherwise unable to pay the taxes necessary to pay the bonds. Unlike a "real city," these special districts generally were not mature enough to have to tap the municipal credit markets for their day-to-day expenditures, which are generally minimal. Given their circumstances, they also were not likely to be future borrowers in the long-term credit markets. Thus, a liquidation or bankruptcy was the only proper burial for most of these projects.

City of Bridgeport, Connecticut: City Troubled by
Flight of Population and Business and the Use of Intercept

In 1991, the City of Bridgeport, Connecticut created a stir in the municipal finance community by filing a petition under Chapter 9 of the Federal Bankruptcy Code. Bridgeport, the largest city in Connecticut, was the first city of major proportions to so file. Unlike the special purpose district bankruptcies which have become common, Bridgeport is a "real" city with many different creditors who have competing interests. Bridgeport has over $200 million in long-term bondholders. At the same time, some 4,000 people are employed by the city pursuant to union contracts to deliver services to approximately 150,000 citizens.

The financial problems of the city did not arise overnight. Previously, the state of Connecticut had enacted special legislation known as the "Special Act" to recognize the otherwise illegal deficits of the city, to provide a financial oversight review board to supervise and discipline city finances, and to provide certain financial assistance to the city. The Special Act authorized the financing of the deficit and provided certain payments to be made by the state to bondholders of the city in order to enhance the creditworthiness of the troubled city. This intercept mechanism, which functions in connection with the review by the oversight board, is not uncommon but could be subject to challenge in the Chapter 9 proceeding.

After the City of Bridgeport filed for bankruptcy, Connecticut moved to dismiss the bankruptcy petition on a number of grounds. Following an extensive hearing, the court concluded that Bridgeport was not "insolvent" when it filed its petition, and, therefore, the petition should be dismissed. According to the court, financial difficulties short of insolvency are not a basis for Chapter 9 relief. Therefore, the court concluded that Bridgeport was not insolvent when the petition was filed, that the petition must be dismissed, and that Bridgeport must continue with the budget and collective bargaining process.

In summary, while the court agreed with Bridgeport that a city should not have to wait until it runs out of money to qualify for Chapter 9 protection, it ruled that the city must demonstrate as a condition precedent to filing that, in the near future, it will run out of money and be unable to pay its debts as they become due. Because of the election of a new mayor in Bridgeport, the appeal of these rulings was not pursued. Therefore, there was no review of the district court's rulings.

City of Philadelphia: Successful Legislation and State and Local Cooperation Avoid Disaster

In 1991, the city of Philadelphia also encountered a financial crisis which nearly denied it access to the short term municipal bond market. The city was required to have a balanced budget. It had accumulated a long-term operating deficit of approximately $200 million and had another $200 million of short-term tax and revenue anticipation notes maturing that the city expected to "rollover" with a refinancing. Inquiries to the market from the city and its investment bankers indicated that a refinancing would not be possible and default loomed on the horizon.

The Pennsylvania legislature enacted the *Pennsylvania Intergovernmental Cooperation Authority Act for Cities of the First Class*,[6] the effect of which was to avoid default. The Act created an "authority that will enable cities of the first class to access capital markets for deficit elimination and seasonal borrowings to avoid default on existing obligations and chronic cash shortages that will disrupt the delivery of municipal services." A review of the Act's provisions is instructive.

- *Authority created.* The Pennsylvania Intergovernmental Cooperation Authority was created as a public authority and instrumentality of the Commonwealth, exercising public powers of the Commonwealth, as an agency and instrumentality thereof.
- *Governing body.* The Authority's governing body had five members: one appointed by the Governor, one by the President Pro Tempore of the Senate, one by the Minority Leader of the Senate, one by the Speaker of the House, and one by the Minority Leader of the House. The Secretary of the Budget and the Director of Finance of the Commonwealth were *ex officio* members without a vote and not counted for quorum purposes. Actual expenses incurred by the members were reimbursable.
- *Avoidance of particular state constitutional problem.* Because its members were not elected, the Authority had constitutional impediments upon levying any tax under the Pennsylvania Constitution, and care was needed so that the nonelected board was not the entity which caused any taxes to be levied or increased.
- *Use of intergovernmental agreements.* The Authority was given the authorization to enter into intergovernmental cooperation agreements with cities, and such agreements were preconditions to the issuance of any obligations by the Authority.
- *Authority could issue bonds and refund city obligations.* The Authority had the legal ability under the Act to issue bonds and other evidences of obligations for borrowed money, but only at the request of the assisted city. As was true for the New York Municipal Assistance Corporation, the Authority was specifically authorized to issued its bonds to refund the obligations of the city.
- *City and authority develop five-year recovery financial plans.* Assisted cities (Philadelphia) were required to develop, implement, and periodically revise financial plans which projected revenues and expenses over five-year periods. The objectives of the plans were to eliminate deficits, restore special fund account moneys which had been misused, create balanced budgets, provide procedures to avoid future fiscal emergencies, and enhance the ability of the city to regain access to the short-term and

---

[6] 1991 June 5, Pub. L. 9, § 101 et seq. (See 53 P.S. § 12720.101 et seq.).

long-term credit markets. The Act required an ongoing dialogue over the budget, the plan, and actual expenditures to continue between the city and the Authority.

■ *Budget approval.* The Authority was given approval power over the city budget.

■ *Collective bargaining agreements.* Collective bargaining agreements which were in existence were to be honored until they expired by their terms. New collective bargaining agreements were required to comply with the financial plan which itself required the consent of the Authority.

■ *Limited availability of federal bankruptcy.* The act imposed limits or denied the ability of assisted cities to file for protection under the Federal Bankruptcy Code.

■ *New revenue (taxes) created; receipts to state for distribution to authority.* Certain new sales and use taxes, a tax on real estate transfers and a sort of city income tax were created, with the taxes to be initially collected by the Department of Revenue of the Commonwealth of Pennsylvania, paid to the State Treasurer and deposited in the Intergovernmental Cooperation Authority Tax Fund. The taxes were to have a duration so long as bonds of the Authority were outstanding.

■ *Original jurisdiction to State Supreme Court.* The Act gave original jurisdiction to the Supreme Court of the Commonwealth to hear any cases or controversies arising out of the statute and to render declaratory judgment concerning the constitutionality of the Act.

The Pennsylvania structure is one approach to troubled municipal debt. The appendix to this chapter provides a discussion of a general approach to an oversight authority.

Orange County, California: Creative Financing to Solve Tax Revenue Shortfalls

Orange County, California is the fourth largest county by population in the United States with an annual budget of approximately $4 billion. An unwise leveraged investment policy, which in periods of falling interest rates had produced as much as 20% to 30% of the revenues for the county, created a liquidity crisis in the late fall of 1994 as a consequence of rising interest rates during 1994. The county filed a petition for relief under Chapter 9 of the Federal Bankruptcy Code on December 6, 1994. At the heart of the bankruptcy was the Orange County Investment Pool (OCIP), a $20 billion fund that had lost $1.6 billion at the time of bankruptcy.[7] The Orange County debacle was complicated by political fragmentation: over 200 local govern-

---

[7] See Mark Baldassare, *When Government Fails: The Orange County Bankruptcy* (Berkeley: University of California Press, 1998), p. 7.

ment agencies had deposited $7.9 billion in the investment pool, including 29 of the 31 Orange County cities, all of the county's school districts, and most of its transportation, water, and sanitation agencies. These agencies would find their funds frozen by Orange County's Chapter 9 filing.

While the real impact of the Orange County Chapter 9 filing may take decades to determine, a number of observations can be made at this time. The bankruptcy default was shocking in the first instance because of the unwillingness to pay posture originally exhibited by the county. Unlike New York, Philadelphia, and Cleveland, which took extraordinary measures (including raising taxes) to avoid default, the wealthy county of Orange County, California made the surprising and speedy decision to file for bankruptcy after it had suffered a dramatic loss because of investments in derivative securities. A proposal to raise the sales tax by half a cent to help the county out of its financial crisis was defeated in June 1995 during the course of the bankruptcy proceedings. Such action is consistent with the antitax sentiment in California that generated such legislative measures as Proposition 13.

While it is true that Orange County is not the first large municipal user of public debt to experience financial difficulty and default, the demographic and economic setting of the Orange County debacle sets the event apart from the like dramas of Cleveland, New York City, Philadelphia, and Bridgeport, Connecticut. Unlike the situations in those large, established Eastern and Midwestern cities, the Orange County debacle arose without the demographic and economic changes that commentators have attributed to their financial woes: growing social expenditures and declining tax revenues resulting from middle-class flight to the suburbs and general industrial decline. By contrast, Orange County was a growing, suburban county with many high-tech jobs. Thus, the fact that the Orange County crisis occurred in a sprawling suburban region, not a large, urban city, and that the debacle affected many local government entities at once, makes this default situation unique.[8]

The investment losses suffered by Orange County are best attributed to the desperate efforts of a revenue-starved municipality to meet the rising costs of public services under a constitutionally imposed tax cap (Proposition 13). The fiscally conservative Orange County voters may have distrusted their local governments, believing them to be inefficient, and poorly managed. They therefore demanded lower taxes alongside high-quality schools, roads, and law enforcement. Unable to raise revenue through traditional means because of the artificially imposed property tax cap and voters' reluctance to permit sales tax increases, county officials sought to find (and to make) revenue in novel ways.

Approximately $2 billion of Orange County short-term obligations (due in under one year or less) came due in July and August 1995 during the

---

[8] Id. at 35.

pendancy of the bankruptcy. Principal was not paid when due. As part of the Plan of Adjustment, the holders of these obligations voluntarily agreed to have the maturity extended for an additional year (at an increased interest rate). Paying these obligations when they matured depended upon refinancing them in the public markets.

The long-term and short-term debt of Orange County held by the public was paid from the proceeds of two financings: the issuance of tax-exempt certificates of participation and taxable refunding pension obligation bonds. The Orange County securities were sold but at a cost to Orange County. The County paid a penalty of 10 to 23 basis points and, including underwriting fees and costs of bond insurance, Orange County paid approximately $60 million more to borrow because of its status as a bankrupt issuer.

The quick resolution of the Orange County financial crisis sets it apart from the experience of Cleveland or New York. Within 18 months, Orange County was able to access the credit markets. By contrast, over a half-decade would pass before New York and Cleveland were able to independently access the credit markets.[9]

The financial penalty that the marketplace imposed upon Orange County has not been permanent. By January 2007, Standard & Poor's, citing the county's strong economic and financial performance and a paydown of debt in recent years, had upgraded the issuer credit rating of Orange County, California to AA–, Moody's Investors Services had assigned a long-term issuer rating of Aa2, and Fitch Rating had assigned a AA– to Orange County outstanding recovery bonds and pension obligation bonds.[10] Further, the once scorned underwriter that sold the derivative products to the county in the 1990s has rejoined the list of qualified bond underwriters for the county.[11] Of great interest will be whether the fact that Orange County did not attempt to discipline itself, as Philadelphia, Cleveland, and New York had in the face of defaults, will have any further lasting effect on the municipal market and Orange County's treatment in that market.

LESSONS LEARNED FROM TROUBLED MUNICIPAL FINANCING

The Necessity for a Clear and Objective Accounting Standards and Legal Principles

One of the key factors that contributed to problems in the 1800s and early 1900s, and to some extent today, is the lack of coordinated, objective and

---

[9] Id. at 10 citing *California Senate Special Committee on Local Investments*, Hearing, Friday, March 23, 1995 at 43.

[10] *The Bond Buyer*, 17 January 2007, p. 36.

[11] *The Bond Buyer*, 15 December 2006, p. 3.

clearly understood accounting and auditing functions of municipality entities. Without appropriate accounting standards and a background in which to judge the current financial situation of the municipal entity on an objective basis, any form of financing is doomed from the beginning.

The Government Accounting Standard Board (GASB) has published accounting principles applicable to municipalities, including GASB 34, Basic Financial Statements for State and Local Governments. GASB 34 requires government-wide financial statements to be prepared using the accrual basis of accounting and economic resources as a measurement focus. Adopting recognized standards of reporting for municipalities will assist in the proper evaluation of its debt and, if appropriate, acceptance by the investing community.

In addition, as was noted, the expectations of indebtedness of the past support the need for clear statutory provisions outlining the rights, remedies, and redress of the investors if there are defaults. One of the best protections against unnecessary litigation, loss of market creditability or dynamic uncertainty as to the future of a specific credit is defining the rights and remedies of the investors by statute. Clearly defined authorization and limitations for the debt to be incurred by the municipalities (including any support of the national governmental agencies) is required. Any limitations on the indebtedness to be issued or the ability to repay should be fully articulated in the governing law and fully disclosed to the marketplace. A legal and accounting umbrella will protect against future problems and eliminate surprises. If the legal and accounting issues are fully articulated and understood, there should be no shock with respect to the consequences of default.

Creating jobs and encouraging business growth in a locality will require construction of a new public works system or continued maintenance and operation of the present public work system and infrastructure. Significant increases in infrastructure spending at both the national and municipal levels are not only necessary but inevitable. There will be increasing demand on the capital markets to finance these infrastructure improvements over the next 20 years. Obviously, access to the capital markets is enhanced by a workable statutory system of governance supported by objective accounting and auditing standards. This has been a key lesson of defaults in the last two centuries. Transparency and financial literacy should not be goals for municipal finance but a reality.

The Requirement of Clearly Defined and Determined Sources of Repayment

One of the major, contributing factors to the problems that Orange County, California, has suffered and other municipalities in the United States confront, is the growing desire of taxpayers to put constitutional or statutory limits on the ability of governmental bodies to tax. A number of states, including Florida, South Dakota, Oregon, Colorado, Illinois, and others, have some form of tax limitation. Given the aging infrastructure of any established country, a limitation on taxation is bound to cause additional problems. Revenue-starved governmental bodies face shrinking revenues relative to expanding costs, which include providing governmental services and maintaining aging infrastructure. Certain governmental services, including police, fire and education, must be provided and are expected. When revenues are unreasonably restricted, local governments may turn to creative investment vehicles as financings sources such as in Orange County in order to compensate for the other revenues no longer available. Accordingly, it is important that, in undertaking any financing, there is a clearly determined source of repayment for the indebtedness.

It is important, to the extent possible, to make any pledge of revenue or any source of repayment for debt financing immutable until the debt is satisfied. While that clearly is a difficult task to achieve, within reason, certain assurances can be provided to the capital markets to insure an orderly payment when due of principal and interest. Future efforts to curtail, limit or unreasonably restrict those sources of payment will cause governmental bodies to reach for a solution such as in Orange County and to suffer dire consequences.

Recognition of the Continuing Need for Infrastructure Financing and Necessity of Periodic Improvements (The Problem of Delay)

The United States contains one of the most extensive and sophisticated public works systems in the world, including 3,000,866 miles of roads, 565,000 bridges, over 1,000 mass transit systems, 16,000 airports, 25,000 inland and intercoastal waterways, 70,000 dams, 900,000 miles of pipe and water systems, and 15,000 wastewater treatment plants. Local and national welfare and economic growth depend upon the efficient operation of local governmental facilities, most of which are financed by revenue bonds purchased by the municipal bond market.

Our ability to supply jobs and encourage business growth in metropolitan areas will require construction of new public work systems and continued maintenance and operation of present public work systems and infrastructure. Financial markets are not static. They are as dynamic as the forces that will push and shove the growth and development of the country. If there are uncertainties faced by capital market investors in purchasing debt instruments of governmental bodies due to inadequate state statutes or defects in structure and covenants, then the market will begin to question the advisability of such investments. As a result, the market may either demonstrate greater selectivity in the obligations purchased or increase the cost of borrowing, both of which would most dramatically affect those who need financing. Accordingly, it is important that financing is structured to recognize the existence of economic cycles and fluctuation in available revenue sources.

The life cycle for capital improvements in a municipality may be 20, 30 or 40 years depending upon the quality and nature of the improvement. It is clear municipalities need bridge financing to cover those years in which significant cash levies must be made for capital improvements. In addition, municipalities face increased resistance by taxpayers to capital improvements, continuing assessments and taxation. This has caused increased problems for municipalities. Many times, municipalities forego capital expenditures for political expediency and popularity with the electorate only to find the cost of maintenance and repairs has increased, thereby decreasing funds available for other municipal services. In the United States, there could be $1 to $1.3 trillion of infrastructure improvements required over the next 15 to 20 years. Capital improvements are necessary. They are cyclical, and borrowings in the capital markets are necessary to bridge these demands. In addition, financings should be structured so that they take into account the periods in which peak borrowing may occur, and some effort should be made to smooth out those peaks with forward planning. If cycles of financing or the wear and tear of improvements are not taken into consideration, financial problems will result.

Coping with the Effects of Extraordinary Personnel Growth and Future Pension Costs

One of the largest problems that municipalities in the United States face is the ability to deal with the ever-increasing personnel numbers. The increase in related personnel costs, including pensions, salaries, benefits, is caused, in large part, by increases in the marketplace. They generally create a significant problem for municipalities, absent new sources of revenues including taxation. The increasing popularity of tax caps creates a tension with growing pension liabilities. The dynamic is set into motion where there will be less ability to pay the ever-expanding cost of pension obligations. To the extent that pension obligations are not funded, they are a ticking time bomb. Pension problems are of great importance to municipal employees. Accordingly, in reviewing any form of financing and its feasibility and appropriateness, increasing employee costs and labor practices must be analyzed and properly assessed.

Adjusting for Changing Population Centers

In the United States, the dream is frequently the spacious home in the suburbs. Because of this, urban areas that normally house businesses, manufacturing, and major service industries are asked to bear the cost of providing municipal services to those who live elsewhere and use the city only during working hours. The increased tax burden for providing these services is spread upon fewer taxpayers. The City of Bridgeport in the early 1990s is such an example. The institution of head taxes, income taxes, parking taxes, and gasoline taxes are the product of efforts to find some method of bridging the decline of the urban areas and the increase of bedroom communities around them. A recognition that a default by a major municipality will adversely affect the whole metropolitan area will lead to a better understanding of defaults and the interplay of the capital markets. However, such was not always readily apparent during the problems with Orange County. It is important to attempt to bridge these situations and to look at financing from a more metropolitan or regional approach rather than from a specific local government perspective.

Dealing with the Flight from the Rust Belt to the Sun Belt

While there have been certain indications of a decline in the flight from manufacturing centers, it is clear that, at least among the older population groups, the desire for a warmer climate for retirement and vacation has increased. Population demographics indicate an increased aging population with a changing tax base relocating from one area of a country to another. This has lead to a growing tax base together with increasing urban problems and newly required municipal services in the Sun Belt. Likewise, municipalities in colder climates have recognized that departing taxpayers have caused a contraction in the tax base in those areas. The flight has both been of individuals and corporations seeking a perceived better working environment. While there are some trends of a return to colder climates by certain industries, there is no assurance that this pattern will continue. A key part of any long-term governmental financing is the assurance that a sufficient number and diversity of taxpayers will be there when the debt matures. This factor should be taken into consideration.

Providing for the Increasing Costs of Social Services

As the complexity of society increases, the issues of healthcare, childcare, homelessness, public safety, and dependent children loom larger on the horizons of state and local governments. Tax limitations or tax caps do not take into consideration the social problems that are being transferred to local governments to deal with. A legacy of unfunded mandates will be faced by future generations. This does not even touch upon the serious issues of adequate education, healthcare, public safety and the ensuing costs related thereto. Education, healthcare, transportation and public safety are critical factors in business growth and the ability to compete in a global market. The burden of dealing appropriately with these concerns will continue to be a financial challenge to municipalities that could lead to defaults.

The Requirement of Disclosure of Issues Not Only at the Time of Issuance, but Timely Disclosures Thereafter

There is a saying that sunshine is the best disinfectant. Those financings where all known problems are fully disclosed and understood by investors minimize problems later if problems do arise. Further, continuing disclosure of the financial conditions of the relevant governmental bodies responsible for providing revenues to pay for debt is essential. Prompt and timely disclosure of adverse consequences are well received in the market. It may help to bring about a solution. The delay in announcing such problems aggravates the situation. For investors in government debt, market liquidity and volatility are in part a function of timely and full disclosure by the municipal and sovereign.

Protecting Against Lingering Legal Issues and Surprise Court Decisions

Since the mid-1800s, there has been a consistent effort to reduce the problems of unaddressed or undisclosed legal deficiencies. The key experience in the United States was the WPPSS case. As previously noted, WPPSS issued bonds to support up to five power generating facilities in the state of Washington to supply power to the Pacific Northwest. Various local governmental bodies joined together in a joint action structure to provide the support from their local tax base for this financing. Two of the projects, Projects 4 and 5, reportedly suffered from a legal defect in the authorization of the participating municipal bodies to enter into the contracts based on state law. By June 15, 1993, the Supreme Court of the state of Washington decided the participants were not authorized to enter into take-or-pay contracts, which lead to a massive municipal bond default of over $2.25 billion. Also, around that same time, a state court in Oklahoma declared a water resource board financing unconstitutional and a court in Ohio declared unconstitutional the use of general obligation bonds to pay off revenue bonds of the City of Gahanna. Such court decisions are often unpredictable, and therefore can lead to unexpected defaults. However, the key to all these problems and the demand by the market is to make sure that the statutory authority is clear and tested, and, to the degree there is some uncertainty, any legal impediments or problems must be fully disclosed so that the market can appropriately determine the risk.

Beware of Off-Balance Sheet Liability

In the corporate world after Enron and other recent failures of disclosure or accounting in the United States, there is a demand for full understanding of the true assets and true liabilities of any enterprise. It will be true, that investors will want full disclosure of any off-balance sheet liability. Off-balance sheet liabilities can be serious enough to create a risk of default. For example, an undisclosed environmental problem can lead to massive cleanup costs and also the flight of business and population. As discussed above, pension fund liabilities and deferred compensation can be staggering and another source of off-balance sheet liability. Further, unforeseen tragedies, such as in the case of South Tucson, Arizona can arise. A police officer's use of fatal force found to be unwarranted led to a multimillion dollar judgment that forced that municipality into bankruptcy. Other natural or man-made disasters have the same affect with the accompanying crippling costs. These off-balance sheet liabilities may prove to be a cause of future defaults and, to the degree known off-balance sheet liabilities are disclosed, and there is periodic disclosure over the term of the financing, markets will have better clarity and assurance.

The Reality of Transportation and Demographic Issues

The contraction of airlines will become a stress for airports, which rely upon the competition among the airlines for various fees and charges. Also, as set forth above, billions of dollars of highway improvements are necessary. On the other hand, with technical changes pointing to the virtual workplace, dramatic changes may take place. Especially in the era where personal safety is more of a concern, downtown city centers may not be popular in the future. There may not be a rush hour. There may not be the need for superhighways or mass municipal parking structures. Accordingly, if the airline industry continues to contract, the financial health of airports will be impacted. If center cities become a less desirable place to be, tax sources will shift elsewhere. Any form of future financing must attempt to anticipate and bridge these problems by having a source of revenue and taxation that makes rational sense for the future and the dynamics that will be faced.

The Problem of Financing of Nonessentials Services

As was noted in the beginning, there are numerous examples of governmental financing for a perceived need that never materializes. Changes in the way people communicate can also affect the need for recreation, working, and social infrastructures. The need for sports arenas, their location and desirability may change. To the extent governmental bodies finance or attempt to finance something that is not an essential governmental service affecting life, safety, and welfare, such as roads, sanitation, water, health, education and safety, there will be risks that the nonessential nature of the service will impact the anticipated revenues to support the financing.

SUMMARY OF LESSONS LEARNED

Lessons learned that can be used are as follows:

1. *Transparency and financial literacy.* Make sure there is always a back drop of accounting and auditing standards so that the market can clearly know the financial risks involved.
2. *Acceptable legal system.* There should be full disclosure of any and all legal risks or impediments that exist or are threatened to occur in the near future.
3. *Clear and certain investors rights and remedies and political stability.* There should be clearly defined rights and remedies for investors so that both the governmental body and the investor knows the consequences of default and the actions that will be taken. This should include the ability to take action before there is the impairment to any security or pledge of revenues from tax sources. To the extent that any issue is unclear or needs to be determined, the legal system or legislation should be used to clarify the uncertainty in order to protect the rights of the capital markets.
4. *No after-the-fact questioning and a real source of repayment.* The transaction should be structured to comply with the law, the law should specifically permit the type of financing provided and there should be a real and dedicated source of repayment.
5. *Effective covenants and monitoring.* Performance and financial covenants and the use of financial consultants to monitor and detect early problems have been helpful in the past and will be helpful in the future.
6. *Third-party support.* Credit enhancement and insurance provisions can be coordinated to help insure market acceptability and solve questions regarding either tax sources or legal structures.

7. *Sovereign oversight and emergency financial support.* A mechanism or structure should be established whereby the national government can provide oversight to the extent appropriate.
8. *Sensitive to potential problems.* In structuring the financing, the participants should be sensitive to the true necessity of the service funded, changes in revenue or tax source for repayment, uncontrollable risks, demographic changes and economic cycles.

RULES FOR SURVIVAL

Rules for survival in the government finance market in the twenty-first century:

1. Fewer defaults should occur given lessons learned, but you cannot prevent recession, depression, economic downturn and natural disasters. Ill-conceived financings and structures can be and should be avoided. The traditional government financing has been the safest investment this side of national debt obligations in the United States.
2. Municipalities virtually always pay their debts in full for essential service projects and general obligations. This should be true for municipalities assuming appropriate legal structures are instituted. There should be clear and defined rights and remedies for investors.
3. Nonessential financing may be attractive but dangerous. Not every town can provide every service. There are more stadiums than teams. The world is contracting.
4. Artificial caps on tax revenue can be the beginning of the end of sound financing. Sources of repayment should never be curtailed. Expenses may not be capable of being controlled, employee costs may increase, unfunded mandates are more likely and off-balance sheet liabilities can become problems.
5. Infrastructure needs will be funded, but where should the infrastructure be built. Changes in demographics, changes in work habits and location are issues.
6. National governments must work with local governments to solve any financial distress situation. Those who do will be credit-risk winners. If bondholders lose, you do too.
7. Effective regulation prospectively is far better for the market than regulation retroactively. Any change in the legal structure which was the premise for financing should be prohibited to the extent it impairs the ability for repayment on the past debt. Financial standards are required to provide transparency and financial literacy to all.

8. If there are any problems or lingering legal issues, don't buy it, don't sell it, don't issue it. Life is too short. Demand excellence in documents, professionals and disclosure. Full and timely disclosure is the best financial disinfectant.

9. Tax-exempt financings and tax-credits have worked well in the United States but are complicated. Taxable bonds may be the answer when combined with special tax-credits and other devices that may put sizzle in municipal debt financing.

10. Municipal issuers should consider combining to become regional issuers or use pool transactions. Those structures should have less credit risk. Moreover, with fewer issues, there may be lower transaction costs and more bang.

APPENDIX: THE STRUCTURE FOR OVERSIGHT AND EMERGENCY FINANCING

Exhibit 44.2 portrays possible responses to troubled municipal debt. Exhibit 44.3 generally identifies some of the key issues involved in an oversight authority. Municipalities which have encountered financial distress have resorted to financing and oversight authorities (such as New York City and Philadelphia). This approach can involve various degrees of formal oversight and control. In the beginning, it can be as simple and benign as a "commission" that reviews the city budget and makes recommendations based on new revenue sources. The commission can develop into a refinancing authority with full power to refinance existing debt of the municipality and to authorize collection of new revenue sources or withdraw use of new revenue sources if budget recommendations are not followed or met. There are two basic advantages to this approach: (1) The new authority can have financial credibility and, therefore, access to borrowing in the capital marketplace if it has an assured source of revenue to pay debt service that is isolated from the bankruptcy and other legal risks facing creditors of the municipality; and (2) an independent authority can use various tools to enforce fiscal discipline on the municipality because it can be removed from political pressures.

The basic idea is that the authority is given a revenue source. It then borrows and assigns the revenue source to pay debt service on the bonds. The authority makes the bond proceeds available to the municipality to pay its expenses and retire the deficit. A basic legislative choice is whether the municipality levies the new taxes and pledges the proceeds to the authority or the authority is the taxing body authorized to levy taxes. In addition, the municipality's ability to levy new taxes may be conditioned on a balanced budget or approval of the authority.

EXHIBIT 44.2 Responses by the State to a Financially Distressed Municipality

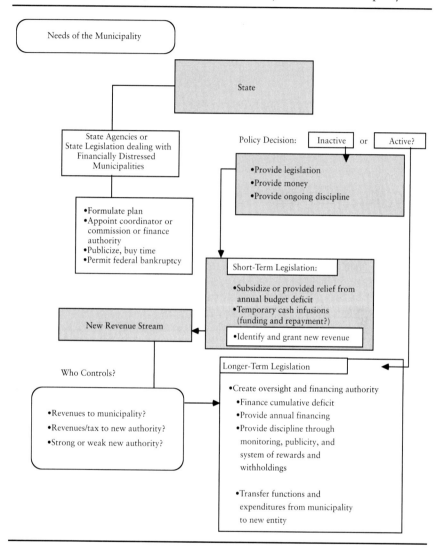

Financing through the authority can be utilized both for a long-term amortization of the cumulative deficit and, if necessary, for an interim period, to accomplish the annual revenue anticipation note borrowings which are necessary for the municipality to operate. Different revenue sources might be utilized for each type of borrowing.

EXHIBIT 44.3   Scenario for Successful Municipal Financial Oversight

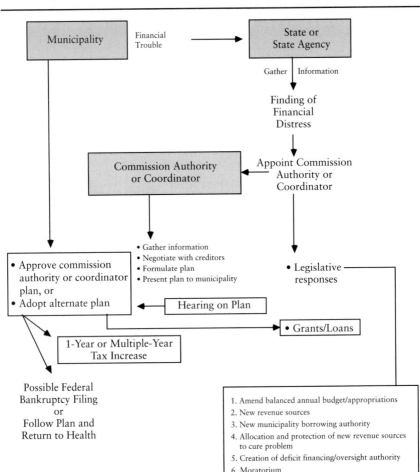

The disciplinary tools are important and a wide range of tools can be constructed including the following:

■ *Grants from the federal, state, or regional governmental bodies.* Obviously, a source of funds has to exist from which to make grants. The grant becomes a tool if the federal, state or regional governmental body imposes performance conditions as a precondition to any grant. The federal, state, or regional governmental body can make the process more politically palatable by freely making a grant to the authority while requiring either in the legislation or in the grant documents that the authority impose performance requirements.

- *Loans from the federal, state, or regional governmental bodies.* Instead of a grant, the federal, state or local governmental body could make loans which require ultimate repayment. The repayment terms can be varied depending upon the municipality's compliance with an approved financial plan and the achievement of goals over time. That is, interest rates could be increased or decreased as needed; in a worst case scenario, principal payment could be accelerated for a default. There can also be in certain states the assumption of the obligations by the state.
- *Intercepts.* Part of the discussion in structuring grants and loans should consider "intercepting" the payments to the municipality. Legislation can be written which permits the state or regional governmental body to withhold these payments if the municipality acts inappropriately or fails to act, or which permits those revenues to be pledged (e.g., paid directly) to lenders or bondholders. In the implementation stage, there is an issue of whether special interest groups, such as unions, local financial institutions, or pension funds might have the ability and willingness to invest in such financing. New York City had support from unions in purchasing significant positions of its refinancing debt.
- *Budget process involvement.* Having a financial plan to work out of the deficit, following that plan, and changing the plan as experience dictates are the keys to a successful workout. The first step is to identify the problems and to stop the financial bleeding to the degree possible.
- *Required financial performance.* The authority can legislatively be given powers to participate in and monitor the municipality's budget process across a broad spectrum. Ultimately, the teeth in the program are that bond proceeds or new tax revenue sources are not made available to the municipality until it complies with the plan, and that continued compliance is required for a continuing revenue flow. The legislation itself can contain the requirements, or it can authorize the authority to develop and establish the requirements.
- *Legislative assistance.* A financially distressed municipality comes as a somewhat recalcitrant beggar to the legislature. An authority that is monitoring (and actively participating in) the municipality's recovery can give it credibility with the legislature, or alternatively, if the municipality fails to make progress, can assist the legislature in developing new criteria and programs.
- *Moral obligations of the state.* Some states may be constitutionally able to assume debt of a municipality. In such states an "extra legal" state guarantee called a "moral obligation" is sometimes used to credit enhance bonds.

- *Appointment of authority members.* The makeup of the governing body of the authority is key to its success. Payment of its staff is important. It is conceivable that some community leaders may be willing to serve without compensation if they believe the authority and its tools are capable of success. Whether or not the municipality is able to appoint or be represented on the authority is a question for the drafters of the legislation.
- *Acceleration of loans.* If the authority makes loans to the municipal, the loan could include in those loans the rights to accelerate the loans if the municipal fails to comply with a financial program.
- *Publicity.* By participating in the municipality recovery process, the authority can become a mechanism for disseminating both good and bad information about the progress of the municipality's recovery efforts. Such information flow and disclosure will be helpful in building credibility with the investment community. The experiences of New York City and Cleveland stress the importance of accurate and clear communication with the financial market.
- *Powers.* The authority can have as many or as few powers as the Legislature may require, including but not limited to:

1. Authorizing filing of a judicial action for municipal debt adjustment by the municipality.
2. Granting, after hearing and notice, a stay against litigation and debt enforcement.
3. Approval or withdrawal of future use of increase tax revenues.
4. Rejecting or approving budget, financial plans and future financing.
5. Determining financial emergency or recovery.
6. Approving, expediting, or withholding state aid and entitlement to taxes distributed to the municipality.
7. Approving or issuing bonds for refinancing or paying municipal deficit or extraordinary operating expenses.
8. Reporting to the state regarding the need for further legislative or disciplinary tools.

Legislation can be written so that some or all of the above-described tools are available to the authority. These tools can be designed and enacted so that they are mandatory or discretionary. The choices and variations can be further delineated.

CHAPTER 45

New Issues in Municipal Accounting

David R. Bean
Director of Research and Technical Activities
Governmental Accounting Standards Board

Dean Michael Mead
Research Manager
Governmental Accounting Standards Board

A key factor in any buy/hold/sell recommendation of a municipal security is the government's ability to repay the debt at issue. A primary source of data that an analyst can use in arriving at that conclusion is the government's financial statements. Whether included in the preliminary offering statement or as a standalone document, a wealth of information is contained in those statements. Knowing what information is included in governmental financial statements and where to quickly find that information is essential to effective analysis.

The Governmental Accounting Standards Board (GASB), which sets *generally accepted accounting principles* (GAAP) for state and local governments, was formed in 1984 to establish and improve standards of state and local governmental accounting and financial reporting that will result in useful information for users of financial reports and guide and educate the public, including issuers, auditors, and users of those financial reports.[1]

Meeting the essential needs of financial statement users is a primary goal of the standard-setting process. In the government environment, the financial community is a primary user of financial statements; however, it is not the only user. The GASB has identified three types of financial statement users

---

[1] GASB mission statement.

The views expressed in this chapter are those of the authors. Official positions of the GASB are determined only after extensive due process and deliberation.

that are considered to be external to the management of the government. Based on Concepts Statement No. 1, *Objectives of Financial Reporting*, the GASB identified external financial statement users to be (1) those to whom government is primarily accountable (the citizenry); (2) those who directly represent the citizens (legislative and oversight bodies); and (3) those who lend or who participate in the lending process (investors and creditors).

This chapter will focus on how the financial community can benefit from financial statements prepared in conformity with GAAP, especially standards that have recently become effective.

STRUCTURE OF GOVERNMENTAL FINANCIAL STATEMENTS

Generally, GAAP financial statements are divided into three communication methods. These distinctions are important because of the differing levels of information that the methods are attempting to convey and the differences in auditor's association with each communication method. That association will be addressed in the following discussion.

The information presented in each one of these communication methods has undergone substantial changes over the past decade. The most significant changes were introduced in the new financial reporting model standards that were issued in 1999 (primarily through Statement No. 34, *Basic Financial Statements—and Management's Discussion and Analysis—for State and Local Governments*). Although some governments implemented those standards before their effective date, most governments have just recently implemented them. The primary financial reporting model standards were followed by standards that changed many of the note disclosure requirements and updated the statistical section. In addition to the core financial reporting model, the GASB also has issued standards that addressed specific types of transactions, including retiree health care benefits, investments, and pollution remediation liabilities.

The basic financial statements are the foundation of every state and local government annual financial report. Those statements not only focus on the government as a whole but also on the major funds of the government. The basic financial statements also include notes that highlight important accounting policies and provide additional detail on the amounts presented in the financial statements. The basic financial statements receive the greatest amount of attention from the auditor's perspective. The auditor expresses an opinion on whether the basic financial statements, including the notes to those statements, are fairly presented in conformity with GAAP in all material respects.

Required supplementary information (RSI) also conveys essential information to the readers of financial statements that places the basic financial statements and notes to basic financial statements in a context. RSI may include explanations of recognized amounts (for example, pension and retiree healthcare costs), analysis of known facts or conditions (for example, Management's Discussion and Analysis [MD&A]), or other information. In certain cases, it also may include budget-to-actual schedules for the major governmental funds that have a legally adopted budget. The auditor does not express an opinion on RSI; however, procedures are performed by the auditor to determine that the information presented does not conflict with the information presented in the basic financial statements and that the information that is actually required by the GASB is or is not presented.

Supplementary information (SI) is used by governments to place the basic financial statements and notes to the basic financial statements in an appropriate operational, economic, or historical context. SI includes items such as combining schedules for nonmajor funds, the tables in the statistical section, and the letter of transmittal. The auditor of a government's financial statements generally has little or no association with this information.

INFORMATION PRESENTED IN BASIC FINANCIAL STATEMENTS AND RSI

To assist an analyst in navigating a government's financial report, the following discussion highlights the key information that can be found in that report.

MD&A

Although the MD&A is classified as RSI, it is often the first item that is prepared by the government that an analyst will encounter in a government's annual financial report. (For governments that prepare a Comprehensive Annual Financial Report (CAFR), the first item presented is a letter that "transmits" the report to the financial statement reader.) The MD&A is a relatively new requirement; however, some MD&As may have already fallen into the boilerplate trap. Despite the potential for some boilerplate language, there is still important information to be found. MD&As will begin with either a summary of major events that occurred during the year or a brief description of the basic financial statements, how the statements relate to each other, and, as previously discussed, the significant differences in the information they provide. (A summary of all the required features of an MD&A is presented in Exhibit 45.1.) The summary can highlight key areas that the analyst may want to focus their attention on. The description of the basic financial statements quickly becomes boilerplate. Once the analyst understands the financial statements for a particular type of government, they can skip over this section and move on to the meatier parts of the MD&A.

EXHIBIT 45.1 Management's Discussion and Analysis Requirements

1. A brief discussion of the basic financial statements, including the relationships of the statements to each other, and the significant differences in the information they provide. This discussion includes analyses that will assist readers in understanding why measurements and results reported in fund financial statements either reinforce information in governmentwide statements or provide additional information.

2. Condensed financial information derived from governmentwide financial statements comparing the current year to the prior year. At a minimum, governments will present the information needed to support their analysis of financial position and results of operations (see below), including these elements:
   a. Total assets, distinguishing between capital and other assets.
   b. Total liabilities, distinguishing between long-term liabilities and other liabilities.
   c. Total net assets, distinguishing among amounts invested in capital assets, net of related debt; restricted amounts; and unrestricted amounts.
   d. Program revenues, by major source.
   e. General revenues, by major source.
   f. Total revenues.
   g. Program expenses, at a minimum by function.
   h. Total expenses.
   i. Excess (deficiency) before contributions to term and permanent endowments or permanent fund principal, special and extraordinary items, and transfers.
   j. Contributions.
   k. Special and extraordinary items.
   l. Transfers.
   m. Change in net assets.
   n. Ending net assets.

3. An analysis of the government's overall financial position and results of operations to assist users in assessing whether financial position has improved or deteriorated as a result of the year's operations. The analysis provides information for both governmental and business-type activities as reported in the governmentwide financial statements and includes reasons for significant changes from the prior year, not simply the amounts or percentages of change. In addition, important economic factors, such as changes in the tax or employment bases, that significantly affected operating results for the year are discussed in this section.

EXHIBIT 45.1 (Continued)

4. An analysis of balances and transactions of individual funds. This analysis presents the reasons for significant changes in fund balances or fund net assets and whether restrictions, commitments, or other limitations significantly affect the availability of fund resources for future use.

5. An analysis of significant variations between original and final budget amounts and between final budget amounts and actual budget results for the general fund (or its equivalent). The analysis includes any currently known reasons for those variations that are expected to have a significant effect on future services or liquidity.

6. A description of significant capital asset and long-term debt activity during the year, including a discussion of commitments made for capital expenditures, changes in credit ratings, and debt limitations that may affect the financing of planned facilities or services.

7. A discussion by governments that use the modified approach (see discussion below) to report some or all of their infrastructure assets including:
   a. Significant changes in the assessed condition of eligible infrastructure assets from previous condition assessments.
   b. How the current assessed condition compares with the condition level the government has established.
   c. Any significant differences from the estimated annual amount to maintain/preserve eligible infrastructure assets compared with the actual amounts spent during the current period.

8. A description of currently known facts, decisions, or conditions that are expected to have a significant effect on financial position (net assets) or results of operations (revenues, expenses, and other changes in net assets).

Extracted from Dean Michael Mead, *An Analyst's Guide to Government Financial Statements* (Norwalk, CT: Governmental Accounting Standards Board, 2001). Reprinted with permission.

All MD&As are required to present condensed financial information derived from governmentwide financial statements comparing the current year to the prior year. These presentations are followed by an analysis prepared by the government that includes the reasons for significant changes from the prior year, not simply the amounts or percentages of change. In addition, important economic factors, such as changes in the tax or employment bases, which significantly affected the economic resource flows for the year, will be discussed in this section of the MD&A.

This section will be followed by an analysis of balances and transactions of individual funds and an analysis of significant variations between original and final budget amounts and between final budget amounts and actual budget results for the general fund (or its equivalent). The fund analysis will note the reasons for significant changes in fund balances or fund net assets and whether restrictions, commitments, or other limitations significantly affect the availability of fund resources for future use.

The budget analysis will present the reasons for significant variations from the original budget to the final budget. In addition, the analysis will include a discussion of the difference between budgeted amounts and actual results using the same basis that was used to adopt the budget (for example, a modified cash—cash plus encumbrances—basis).

The preceding sections, when prepared in accordance the GASB's standards in form and in spirit, will provide information that will either answer questions that an analyst may have had about a government's activities for the year or place the analyst in a position to ask directed questions to the government officials that prepared the MD&A.

The MD&A also will include a description of significant capital asset and long-term debt activity during the year, including a discussion of commitments made for capital expenditures, changes in credit ratings, and debt limitations that may affect the financing of planned facilities or services. Although much of this information will already be known to the analyst, the commitments discussion may prove to be enlightening.

The final section of the MD&A, while not intended to be predictive in nature, has the most forward-looking information provided. This section will present a description of currently known facts, decisions, or conditions that are expected to have a significant effect on financial position or future economic resource flows.

Basic Financial Statements

As previously noted, the basic financial statements contain information from both a governmentwide vantage point and an individual major fund viewpoint. A government can present up to 10 basic financial statements. Although the sheer number may appear to be overkill, each statement plays an important role in assessing a government's financial position and changes in financial position. Those basic statements can include:

- Statement of net assets
- Statement of activities
- Balance sheet—governmental funds
- Statement of revenue, expenditures, and changes in fund balance—governmental funds

- Budget-to-actual comparison—major governmental funds[2]
- Statement of net assets—proprietary funds
- Statement of revenues, expenses, and changes in net fund assets—proprietary funds
- Statement of cash flows—proprietary funds
- Statement of fiduciary net assets—fiduciary funds
- Statement of changes in fiduciary net assets—fiduciary funds

Governmentwide Financial Statements

Governmentwide financial statements include:

- Statement of net assets
- Statement of activities

Statement of Net Assets   Prior to the implementation of the new financial reporting model, an overall presentation of a general purpose government's financial position was not provided in the basic financial statements. The statement of net assets presents all of the government's assets and liabilities. The governmentwide statements focus on the primary government with separate columns for the general government and its business-type activities. The government's discretely presented component units (generally entities for which the primary government is financially accountable) also are presented in a separate column (see Exhibit 45.2). The asset section contains the government's capital assets, including infrastructure assets. Prior to the implementation of the new model, infrastructure assets generally were not included in government reports, and governmental capital assets were not presented net of accumulated depreciation.

   In assessing the government's liabilities it is important to understand the nature of the liabilities reported for government pensions and retiree healthcare benefits. These liabilities are not the unfunded actuarial accrued liability, but they do represent the accumulation of the difference between the annual costs for those benefits and the actual qualifying amounts contributed to the benefit plans since the implementation of the respective GASB standards. Information on the unfunded actuarial accrued liabilities, which are not considered to be accounting liabilities in the state and local government sector, can be found in the notes to the financial statements and in RSI.

   The net asset section is divided into three categories: (1) capital assets net of related debt, (2) restricted net assets, and (3) unrestricted net assets. The capital assets, net of related debt account provides some important

---

[2] This information can be presented as either a statement as part of the basic financial statements or a schedule in RSI.

EXHIBIT 45.2 Illustrative Governmentwide Statement of Net Assets, Local Government

	Primary Government			
Local City—Statement of Net Assets as of December 31, 2002				
	Governmental Activities	Business-type Activities	Total	Component Units
Assets				
Cash and cash equivalents	$13,597,899	$8,785,821	$22,383,720	$303,935
Investments	27,365,221	—	27,365,221	7,428,952
Receivables (net)	12,833,132	3,609,615	16,442,747	4,042,290
Internal balances	175,000	(175,000)	—	—
Inventories	322,149	126,674	448,823	83,697
Restricted cash and cash equivalents	—	1,493,322	1,493,322	—
Capital assets (Note 2):				
Land and nondepreciable infrastructure	88,253,120	6,460,119	94,713,239	—
Depreciable infrastructure, net	30,367,241	30,952,214	61,319,455	751,239
Depreciable buildings, property, and equipment, net	51,402,399	113,976,418	165,378,817	36,993,547
Total assets	224,316,161	165,229,183	389,545,344	49,603,660
Liabilities				
Accounts payable	6,783,310	751,430	7,534,740	1,803,332
Deferred revenue	1,435,599	—	1,435,599	38,911
Long-term obligations (Note 3):				
Due within one year	9,236,000	4,426,286	13,662,286	1,426,639
Due beyond one year	83,302,378	74,482,273	157,784,651	27,106,151
Total liabilities	100,757,287	79,659,989	180,417,276	30,375,033
Net Assets				
Invested in capital assets, net of related debt	103,711,386	73,088,574	176,799,960	15,906,392
Restricted for:				
Capital projects	11,705,864	—	11,705,864	492,445
Debt service	3,020,708	1,451,996	4,472,704	—
Community development projects	4,811,043	—	4,811,043	—
Other purposes	3,214,302	—	3,214,302	—
Unrestricted (deficit)	(2,904,429)	11,028,624	8,124,195	2,829,790
Total net assets	$123,558,874	$85,569,194	$209,128,068	$19,228,627

Extracted from Dean Michael Mead, *An Analyst's Guide to Government Financial Statements*, Governmental Accounting Standards Board. Reprinted with permission.

information. For example, it gives the reader a sense of the extent that the government's capital assets have been leveraged through debt issuance. There are examples in practice in which the amount of related debt actually exceeds the capital assets, which indicates that either a significant portion of the debt is back loaded, the debt maturities exceed the expected useful lives of the related capital assets, or, in some cases, both.

What qualifies as a restricted net asset has been the subject of much debate by the GASB. In addition to addressing the issue in Statement 34, a specific pronouncement was devoted to the topic (Statement No. 46, *Net Assets Restricted by Enabling Legislation*). In an analyst's search for unrestricted resources, it is important to know a government's policy regarding the treatment of restricted assets—what qualifies and when those resources are released. This information can be found in the notes to the financial statements, and the application of those policies will be reflected in the amounts presented in the restricted net asset account.

The unrestricted net asset account is intended to convey to the financial statement reader the amount of net economic resources that a government has as a result of its activities over the years. This is not an amount that is "available for appropriation" because of the presence of long-term assets and liabilities in the calculation. In many cases, when a government chooses to fund the activities (including purchase of capital assets) of another government with the use of long-term debt or chooses not to accumulate resources for the payment of its own long-term liabilities that are not capital related, an unrestricted deficit will be reported. A common case found in practice is where a state or county government will issue debt of the construction of schools that are appropriately reported in a school district's financial statements. The debt is not related to the government's own capital assets, so it is appropriately reflected in the unrestricted net asset account. In these cases, a government often will disclose the amount of the deficit that is related to this type of debt. Some governments also choose not to accumulate resources for the payment of long-term employee benefit liabilities (for example, vacation payment or retiree healthcare benefits). Again, this is a policy decision of the government that is not within purview of standard setters; however, the economic consequence of that policy decision is reflected in this statement.

Statement of Activities   The Statement of Activities title is self-explanatory (see Exhibit 45.3). It reports the results of the government's activities for the year. The statement focuses on the cost of providing government services for that period and also reports what resources were generated to fund those activities. Even though cost of service data generally is of greater interest to other types of financial statement users, this statement still should provide valuable information to the analyst.

EXHIBIT 45.3 Illustrative Governmentwide Statement of Activities, Local Government

Local City—Statement of Activities for the Year Ending December 31, 2002

Functions/Programs	Expenses	Indirect Expenses Allocation	Program Revenues: Charges for Services	Program Revenues: Operating Grants and Contributions	Program Revenues: Capital Grants and Contributions	Net (Expense) Revenue and Changes in Net Assets — Primary Government: Governmental Activities	Net (Expense) Revenue and Changes in Net Assets — Primary Government: Business-type Activities	Net (Expense) Revenue and Changes in Net Assets — Primary Government: Total	Net (Expense) Revenue and Changes in Net Assets — Component Units
Primary Government									
Governmental activities:									
General government	$9,571,410	$(5,580,878)	$3,146,915	$843,617	$ —	$ —	—	$ —	—
Public safety	34,844,749	4,059,873	1,198,855	1,307,693	62,300	(36,335,774)	—	(36,335,774)	—
Public works	10,128,538	3,264,380	850,000	—	2,252,615	(10,290,303)	—	(10,290,303)	—
Engineering services	1,299,645	111,618	704,793	—	—	(706,470)	—	(706,470)	—
Health and sanitation	6,738,672	558,088	5,612,267	575,000	—	(1,109,493)	—	(1,109,493)	—
Cemetery	735,866	55,809	212,496	—	—	(579,179)	—	(579,179)	—
Culture and recreation	11,532,350	1,858,966	3,995,199	2,450,000	—	(6,946,117)	—	(6,946,117)	—
Community development	2,994,389	1,740,265	—	—	2,580,000	(2,154,654)	—	(2,154,654)	—
Education (payment to school district)	21,893,273	—	—	—	—	(21,893,273)	—	(21,893,273)	—
Interest on long-term debt	6,068,121	(6,068,121)	—	—	—	—	—	—	—
Total governmental activities	105,807,013	0	15,720,525	5,176,310	4,894,915	(80,015,263)	—	(80,015,263)	—
Business-type activities:									
Water	3,595,733		4,159,350	—	1,159,909		1,723,526	1,723,526	—
Sewer	4,912,853		7,170,533	—	486,010		2,743,690	2,743,690	—
Parking facilities	2,796,283		1,344,087	—	—		(1,452,196)	(1,452,196)	—
Total business-type activities	11,304,869		12,673,970	—	1,645,919		3,015,020	3,015,020	—
Total primary government	$117,111,882		$28,394,495	$5,176,310	$6,540,834	$(80,015,263)	$3,015,020	$(77,000,243)	—
Component units:									
Landfill	$3,382,157		$3,857,858	—	$11,397				$487,098
Public school system	31,186,498		705,765	3,937,083	—				(26,543,650)
Total component units	$34,568,655		$4,563,623	$3,937,083	$11,397				$(26,056,552)

EXHIBIT 45.3 (Continued)

Local City—Statement of Activities for the Year Ending December 31, 2002

Functions/Programs	Expenses	Indirect Expenses Allocation	Program Revenues — Charges for Services	Program Revenues — Operating Grants and Contributions	Program Revenues — Capital Grants and Contributions	Net (Expense) Revenue and Changes in Net Assets — Primary Government — Governmental Activities	Net (Expense) Revenue and Changes in Net Assets — Primary Government — Business-type Activities	Net (Expense) Revenue and Changes in Net Assets — Total	Net (Expense) Revenue and Changes in Net Assets — Component Units
General Revenues									
Taxes									
Property taxes, levied for general purposes						$51,693,573	$ —	$51,693,573	$ —
Property taxes, levied for debt service						4,726,244	—	4,726,244	—
Franchise taxes						4,055,505	—	4,055,505	—
Public service taxes						8,969,887	—	8,969,887	—
Payment from sample city						—	—	—	21,893,273
Grants and contributions not restricted to specific programs						1,457,820	—	1,457,820	6,461,708
Investment earnings						1,958,144	601,349	2,559,493	881,763
Miscellaneous						884,907	104,925	989,832	22,464
Special item—gain on sale of park land						2,653,488	—	2,653,488	—
Transfers						501,409	(501,409)	—	—
Total general revenues, special items, and transfers						76,900,977	204,865	77,105,842	29,259,208
Change in net assets						(3,114,286)	3,219,885	105,599	3,202,656
Net assets—beginning						126,673,160	82,349,309	209,022,469	16,025,971
Net assets—ending						$123,558,874	$85,569,194	$209,128,068	$19,228,627

The structure of the statement is untraditional in nature when compared to its private-sector counterpart. The format was intended to give the statement reader greater insight into provision of services, the primary goal of governments, and whether those services were funded by program revenues or general revenues of the governments.

Governments do not have a single bottom line. There are bottom lines associated with changes in financial resources and changes in cash. In addition to efficiency measures, there also is interest in how effectively governments have provided services. Even with the diverse set of information that was available to analysts, until the new financial reporting model was put into place, the government was without a single bottom line from an economic resources standpoint. The statement of activities provides that bottom line with the "change in net assets" subtotal.

Fund Financial Statements

The information presentation in what are now the eight fund financial statements (see Exhibits 45.4 through 45.11) remained relatively unchanged from the prior model. The Board was keenly aware that with all the changes introduced in the new financial reporting model, there needed to be some stability. However, there are a number of changes that are noteworthy.

The first noteworthy change was the shift from fund-type reporting (for example, special revenue funds) to major fund reporting. A government identifies major funds based on the following criteria:

1. Total assets, liabilities, revenues, or expenditures/expenses of that individual governmental or enterprise fund are at least 10% of the corresponding element total (assets, liabilities, and so forth) for all funds of that category or type (that is, total governmental or total enterprise funds), and
2. The same element that met the 10% criterion in (1) is at least 5% of the corresponding element total for all governmental and enterprise funds combined.

In addition to funds that meet the major fund criteria, any other governmental or enterprise fund that the government's officials believe is particularly important to financial statement users (for example, because of public interest or consistency) may be reported as a major fund. If an analyst does not find a fund that he or she believes is important, that fact should be communicated to the government. Based on this provision, the government has the ability to react to the analyst's needs.

EXHIBIT 45.4 Illustrative Governmental Funds Balance Sheet, Local Government

Local City—Balance Sheet, Governmental Funds as of December 31, 2002

	General	HUD Programs	Community Redevelopment	Route 7 Construction	Other Governmental Funds	Total Governmental Funds
Assets						
Cash and cash equivalents	$3,418,485	$1,236,523	$ —	$ —	$5,606,792	$10,261,800
Investments	—	—	13,262,695	10,467,037	3,485,252	27,214,984
Receivables, net	3,644,561	2,953,438	353,340	11,000	10,221	6,972,560
Due from other funds	1,370,757	—	—	—	—	1,370,757
Receivables from other governments	—	119,059	—	—	1,596,038	1,715,097
Liens receivable	791,926	3,195,745	—	—	—	3,987,671
Inventories	182,821	—	—	—	—	182,821
Total assets	$9,408,550	$7,504,765	$13,616,035	$10,478,037	$10,698,303	$51,705,690
Liabilities and Fund Balances						
Liabilities:						
Accounts payable	$3,408,680	$129,975	$190,548	$1,104,632	$1,074,831	$5,908,666
Due to other funds	—	25,369	—	—	—	25,369
Payable to other governments	94,074	—	—	—	—	94,074
Deferred revenue	4,250,430	6,273,045	250,000	11,000	—	10,784,475
Total liabilities (Note 2)	7,753,184	6,428,389	440,548	1,115,632	1,074,831	16,812,584

EXHIBIT 45.4 (Continued)

	General	HUD Programs	Community Redevelopment	Route 7 Construction	Other Governmental Funds	Total Governmental Funds
Fund balances:						
Reserved for:						
Inventories	182,821	—	—	—	—	182,821
Liens receivable	791,926	—	—	—	—	791,926
Encumbrances	40,292	41,034	119,314	5,792,587	1,814,122	7,807,349
Debt service	—	—	—	—	3,832,062	3,832,062
Other purposes	—	—	—	—	1,405,300	1,405,300
Unreserved, reported in:						
General fund	640,327	—	—	—	—	640,327
Special revenue funds	—	1,035,342	—	—	1,330,718	2,366,060
Capital projects funds	—	—	13,056,173	3,569,818	1,241,270	17,867,261
Total fund balances	1,655,366	1,076,376	13,175,487	9,362,405	9,623,472	34,893,106
Total liabilities and fund balances	$9,408,550	$7,504,765	$13,616,035	$10,478,037	$10,698,303	

Amounts reported for governmental activities in the statement of net assets are different because:

Capital assets used in governmental activities are not financial resources and therefore are not reported in the funds.	161,082,708
Other long-term assets are not available to pay for current-period expenditures and therefore are deferred in the funds.	9,348,876
Internal service funds are used by management to charge the costs of certain activities, such as insurance and telecommunications, to individual funds. The assets and liabilities of the internal service funds are included in governmental activities in the statement of net assets.	2,994,691
Long-term liabilities, including bonds payable, are not due and payable in the current period and therefore are not reported in the funds	(84,760,507)
Net assets of governmental activities	$123,558,874

With the introduction of the governmentwide statements, reconciliations between the fund financial statements and the new financial statements were added to highlight the key differences between the statements. This reconciliation is illustrated in Exhibit 45.4.

Another change that is worth noting relates to the combined balance sheet. It has been divided into three separate balance sheets. With the introduction of the governmentwide statement of net assets, there was no longer a reason to artificially combine the governmental, proprietary, and fiduciary funds. This gave the GASB greater flexibility in meeting user needs with account classifications and statement formats. The most significant changes included the introduction of a classified statement of net assets for the proprietary funds (for example, enterprise funds) and reformatting the fiduciary net asset statement.

Two significant changes were made in the budgetary reporting arena. First, there is a requirement to present the original budget for the period that was adopted by the government. In some cases, significant changes are made to the budget during the year; however, the financial statement reader may be unaware of those modifications. This addition increases the transparency of this presentation.

The second change reflects the GASB's role in the budgetary process. The GASB cannot require governments to adopt budgets let alone establish specific standards for approaches that should be used in developing a budget. To reflect that role, the GASB proposed that budgetary reporting be reflected in RSI. Based on feedback, primarily from the preparer community, the GASB ultimately decided to allow governments to either present the budgetary comparison as RSI or in the basic financial statements. Therefore the table of contents should be referred to in locating this presentation. It should be noted that the variance columns presented in Exhibit 45.6 are optional. In some cases, one or more of these columns may not be found when reviewing financial reports.

With the complete implementation of the new model in the rear view mirror, the GASB is now redirecting its attention to the governmental funds. The GASB is looking at fund balance classifications. In practice, there are a number of interpretations (including some obvious misinterpretations) of what unreserved, undesignated fund balance is intended to convey. The Board is currently assessing what guidance (tweaking or introducing major changes) is needed to provide greater consistency in financial reporting. In the future, the GASB also will determine what, if any, changes need to be made to the current financial resources model to provide a more consistent basis of what resources are reported in governmental funds (for example, whether certain long-term liabilities of a government that normally are liquidated with available resources should be reported in a governmental fund balance).

EXHIBIT 45.5 Illustrative Governmental Funds Statement of Revenues, Expenditures, and Changes in Fund Balances, Local Government

Local City—Statement of Revenues, Expenditures, and Changes in Fund Balances

	General	HUD Programs	Community Redevelopment	Route 7 Construction	Other Governmental Funds	Total Governmental Funds
Revenues						
Property taxes	$51,173,436	$	$	$	$4,680,192	$55,853,628
Franchise taxes	4,055,505	—	—	—	—	4,055,505
Public service taxes	8,969,887	—	—	—	—	8,969,887
Fees and fines	606,946	—	—	—	—	606,946
Licenses and permits	2,287,794	—	—	—	—	2,287,794
Intergovernmental	6,119,938	2,578,191	—	—	2,830,916	11,529,045
Charges for services	11,374,460	—	—	—	30,708	11,405,168
Investment earnings	552,325	87,106	549,489	270,161	364,330	1,823,411
Miscellaneous	881,874	66,176	—	2,939	94	951,083
Total revenues	86,022,165	2,731,473	549,489	273,100	7,906,240	97,482,467
Expenditures						
Current:						
General government	8,630,835	—	417,814	16,700	121,052	9,186,401
Public safety	33,729,623	—	—	—	—	33,729,623
Public works	4,975,775	—	—	—	3,721,542	8,697,317
Engineering services	1,299,645	—	—	—	—	1,299,645
Health and sanitation	6,070,032	—	—	—	—	6,070,032
Cemetery	706,305	—	—	—	—	706,305
Culture and recreation	11,411,685	—	—	—	—	11,411,685
Community development	—	2,954,389	—	—	—	2,954,389
Education—payment to school district	21,893,273	—	—	—	—	21,893,273

Exhibit 45.5 (Continued)

	General	HUD Programs	Community Redevelopment	Route 7 Construction	Other Governmental Funds	Total Governmental Funds
Debt service:						
Principal	—	—	—	—	3,450,000	3,450,000
Interest and other charges	—	—	—	—	5,215,151	5,215,151
Capital outlay	=	=	2,246,671	11,281,769	3,190,209	16,718,649
Total expenditures	88,717,173	2,954,389	2,664,485	11,298,469	15,697,954	121,332,470
Excess (deficiency) of revenues over expenditures	(2,695,008)	(222,916)	(2,114,996)	(11,025,369)	(7,791,714)	(23,850,003)
Other Financing Sources (uses)						
Refunding bonds	—	—	—	—	38,045,000	38,045,000
Long-term capital-related debt	—	—	17,529,560	—	1,300,000	18,829,560
Payment to bond refunding escrow agent	—	—	—	—	(37,284,144)	(37,284,144)
Transfers in	129,323	—	—	—	5,551,187	5,680,510
Transfers out	(2,163,759)	(348,046)	(2,273,187)	=	(219,076)	(5,004,068)
Total other financing sources (uses)	(2,034,436)	(348,046)	15,256,373	=	7,392,967	20,266,858
Special Item						
Proceeds from sale of park land	3,476,488	—	—	—	—	3,476,488
Total other financing sources (uses) and special items	1,442,052	(348,046)	15,256,373	(11,025,369)	7,392,967	23,743,346
Net change in fund balances	(1,252,956)	(570,962)	13,141,377	(11,025,369)	(398,747)	(106,657)
Fund balances—beginning	2,908,322	1,647,338	34,110	20,387,774	10,022,219	34,999,763
Fund balances—ending	$1,655,366	$1,076,376	$13,175,487	$9,362,405	$9,623,472	$34,893,106

EXHIBIT 45.6 Illustrative Budgetary Comparison Schedule, Local Government

Local City—Budgetary Comparison Schedule for the General Fund
For the Year Ended December 31, 2002

			Actual Amounts, Budgetary Basis	Variances—Positive (Negative)		Budget to GAAP Reconciliation	Actual Amounts GAAP Basis
	Original	Final		Original to Final	Final to Actual		
Revenues							
Property taxes	$52,017,833	$51,853,018	$51,173,436	$(164,815)	$(679,582)	—	$51,173,436
Other taxes—franchise and public service	12,841,209	12,836,024	13,025,392	(5,185)	189,368	—	13,025,392
Fees and fines	718,800	718,800	606,946	—	(111,854)	—	606,946
Licenses and permits	2,126,600	2,126,600	2,287,794	—	161,194	—	2,287,794
Intergovernmental	6,905,898	6,571,360	6,119,938	(334,538)	(451,422)	—	6,119,938
Charges for services	12,392,972	11,202,150	11,374,460	(1,190,822)	172,310	—	11,374,460
Investment earnings	1,015,945	550,000	552,325	(465,945)	2,325	—	552,325
Miscellaneous	3,024,292	1,220,991	881,874	(1,803,301)	(339,117)	=	881,874
Total revenues	91,043,549	87,078,943	86,022,165	(3,964,606)	(1,056,778)	=	86,022,165

EXHIBIT 45.6 (Continued)

	Original	Final	Actual Amounts, Budgetary Basis	Variances—Positive (Negative) Original to Final	Variances—Positive (Negative) Final to Actual	Budget to GAAP Reconciliation	Actual Amounts GAAP Basis
Expenditures							
Current:							
General government	11,837,534	9,468,155	8,621,500	2,369,379	846,655	9,335	8,630,835
Public safety	33,050,966	33,983,706	33,799,709	(932,740)	183,997	(70,086)	33,729,623
Public works	5,215,630	5,025,848	4,993,187	189,782	32,661	(17,412)	4,975,775
Engineering services	1,296,275	1,296,990	1,296,990	(715)	—	2,655	1,299,645
Health and sanitation	5,756,250	6,174,653	6,174,653	(418,403)	—	(104,621)	6,070,032
Cemetery	724,500	724,500	706,305	—	18,195	—	706,305
Culture and recreation	11,059,140	11,368,070	11,289,146	(308,930)	78,924	122,539	11,411,685
Education—payment to school district	22,000,000	22,000,000	21,893,273	—	106,727	—	21,893,273
Total expenditures	90,940,295	90,041,922	88,774,763	898,373	1,267,159	(57,590)	88,717,173
Excess (deficiency) of revenues over expenditures	103,254	(2,962,979)	(2,752,598)	(3,066,233)	210,381	57,590	(2,695,008)
Other Financing Sources (uses)							
Transfers in	939,525	130,000	129,323	(809,525)	(677)	—	129,323
Transfers out	(2,970,256)	(2,163,759)	(2,163,759)	806,497	—	—	(2,163,759)
Total other financing sources (uses)	(2,030,731)	(2,033,759)	(2,034,436)	(3,028)	(677)	—	(2,034,436)

EXHIBIT 45.6 (Continued)

| | Original | Final | Actual Amounts, Budgetary Basis | Variances—Positive (Negative) | | Budget to GAAP Reconciliation | Actual Amounts GAAP Basis |
				Original to Final	Final to Actual		
Special Item							
Proceeds from sale of park land	1,355,250	3,500,000	3,476,488	2,144,750	(23,512)	=	3,476,488
Total other financing sources (uses)							
and special items	(675,481)	1,466,241	1,442,052	2,141,722	24,189	=	1,442,052
Net change in fund balance	(572,227)	(1,496,738)	(1,310,546)	(924,511)	186,192	57,590	(1,252,956)
Fund balances—beginning	3,528,750	2,742,799	2,742,799	(785,951)	=	165,523	2,908,322
Fund balances—ending	$2,956,523	$1,246,061	$1,432,253	$(1,710,462)	$186,192	$223,113	$1,655,366

Explanation of Differences

The city budgets for claims and compensated absences only to the extent expected to be paid, rather than on the modified accrual basis. $(129,100)

Encumbrances for goods and services ordered but not received are reported as expenditures in the year the orders are placed for budgetary purposes, but are reported in the year the goods and services are received for GAAP purposes.   186,690

Net increase in fund balance—budget to GAAP $57,590

The proprietary funds were slightly modified to adopt the net asset presentation of the governmentwide statements, and the clean-surplus approach was introduced in the resource flows statements.

Exhibit 45.7 Illustrative Proprietary Funds Statement of Net Assets, Local Government

	Local City—Statement of Net Assets Proprietary Funds as of December 31, 2002			
	Enterprise Funds			Internal Service Funds
	Water and Sewer	Parking Facilities	Total	
Assets				
Current assets:				
Cash and cash equivalents	$8,416,653	$369,168	$8,785,821	$3,336,099
Investments	—	—	—	150,237
Receivables, net	3,564,586	3,535	3,568,121	157,804
Due from other governments	41,494	—	41,494	—
Inventories	126,674	—	126,674	139,328
Total current assets	12,149,407	372,703	12,522,110	3,783,468
Noncurrent assets				
Restricted cash and cash equivalents	—	1,493,322	1,493,322	—
Capital assets:				
Land	813,513	3,021,637	3,835,150	—
Distribution and collection systems	39,504,183	—	39,504,183	—
Buildings and equipment	106,135,666	23,029,166	129,164,832	14,721,786
Less accumulated depreciation	(15,328,911)	(5,786,503)	(21,115,414)	(5,781,734)
Total noncurrent assets	131,124,451	21,757,622	152,882,073	8,940,052
Total assets	143,273,858	22,130,325	165,404,183	12,723,520
Liabilities				
Current liabilities:				
Accounts payable	447,427	304,003	751,430	780,570
Due to other funds	175,000	—	175,000	1,170,388
Compensated absences	112,850	8,827	121,677	237,690
Claims and judgments	—	—	—	1,687,975
Bonds, notes, and loans payable	3,944,609	360,000	4,304,609	249,306
Total current liabilities	4,679,886	672,830	5,352,716	4,125,929

EXHIBIT 45.7 (Continued)

	Enterprise Funds			Internal Service Funds
	Water and Sewer	Parking Facilities	Total	
Noncurrent liabilities:				
Compensated absences	451,399	35,306	486,705	—
Claims and judgments	—	—	—	5,602,900
Bonds, notes, and loans payable	54,451,549	19,544,019	73,995,568	=
Total noncurrent liabilities	54,902,948	19,579,325	74,482,273	5,602,900
Total liabilities	59,582,834	20,252,155	79,834,989	9,728,829
Net Assets				
Invested in capital assets, net of related debt	72,728,293	360,281	73,088,574	8,690,746
Restricted for debt service	—	1,451,996	1,451,996	—
Unrestricted	10,962,731	65,893	11,028,624	(5,696,055)
Total net assets	$83,691,024	$1,878,170	$85,569,194	$2,994,691

The cash flows statement for the enterprise funds was improved by the requirement that all governments that present this statement should report cash flows from operations using the direct method. Under the direct method, inflows and outflows from operations are separately reported versus being netted for reporting purposes. This allows the readers to more clearly see where the cash is coming from and what it is being used for.

Because of the restrictions associated with fiduciary funds, those funds are not presented in governmentwide financial statements. However, the high level of accountability associated with government was influential in the decision to keep fiduciary fund statements as part of the basic financial statements. As noted earlier, with the disaggregation of the fund statements, it did allow the GASB to introduce a reporting format that is more in line with the fiduciary nature of the activities reported in those funds.

Notes to the Basic Financial Statements The notes to the basic financial statements normally begin with a table of contents. The notes have grown larger over the years in order to provide the context and explanations that are necessary to understand the complex transactions entered into by state and local governments. Therefore, to assist the reader in navigating this material, a table of contents was added with the new reporting model. The following discussion highlights just a portion of the information that is available to the financial statement reader in the notes to the basic financial statements.

EXHIBIT 45.8 Illustrative Proprietary Funds Statement of Revenues, Expenses, and Changes in Fund Net Assets, Local Government

Local City—Statement of Revenues, Expenses, and Changes in Fund Net Assets
Proprietary Funds for the Year Ending December 31, 2002

	Enterprise Funds			Internal Service Funds
	Water and Sewer	Parking Facilities	Totals	
Operating Revenues				
Charges for services	$11,329,883	$1,340,261	$12,670,144	$15,256,164
Miscellaneous	—	3,826	3,826	1,066,761
Total operating revenues	11,329,883	1,344,087	12,673,970	16,322,925
Operating Rxpenses				
Personal services	3,400,559	762,348	4,162,907	4,157,156
Contractual services	344,422	96,032	440,454	584,396
Utilities	754,107	100,726	854,833	214,812
Repairs and maintenance	747,315	64,617	811,932	1,960,490
Other supplies and expenses	498,213	17,119	515,332	234,445
Insurance claims and expenses	—	—	—	8,004,286
Depreciation	1,163,140	542,049	1,705,189	1,707,872
Total operating expenses	6,907,756	1,582,891	8,490,647	16,863,457
Operating income (loss)	4,422,127	(238,804)	4,183,323	(540,532)
Nonoperating Revenues (expenses)				
Interest and investment revenue	454,793	146,556	601,349	134,733
Miscellaneous revenue	—	104,925	104,925	20,855
Interest expense	(1,600,830)	(1,166,546)	(2,767,376)	(41,616)
Miscellaneous expense	—	(46,846)	(46,846)	(176,003)
Total nonoperating revenue (expenses)	(1,146,037)	(961,911)	(2,107,948)	(62,031)
Income (loss) before contributions and transfers	3,276,090	(1,200,715)	2,075,375	(602,563)
Capital contributions	1,645,919	—	1,645,919	18,788
Transfers out	(290,000)	(211,409)	(501,409)	(175,033)
Change in net assets	4,632,009	(1,412,124)	3,219,885	(758,808)
Total net assets—beginning	79,059,015	3,290,294	82,349,309	3,753,499
Total net assets—ending	$83,691,024	$1,878,170	$85,569,194	$2,994,691

EXHIBIT 45.9 Illustrative Proprietary Funds Statement of Cash Flows, Local Government

Local City—Statement of Cash Flows
Proprietary Funds for the Year Ended December 31, 2002

	Enterprise Funds			Internal Service Funds
	Water and Sewer	Parking Facilities	Total	
Cash Flows from Operating Activities				
Receipts from customers	$11,400,200	$1,345,292	$12,745,492	$15,326,343
Payments to suppliers	(2,725,349)	(365,137)	(3,090,486)	(2,812,238)
Payments to employees	(3,360,055)	(750,828)	(4,110,883)	(4,209,688)
Internal activity—payments to other funds	(1,296,768)	—	(1,296,768)	—
Claims paid	—	—	—	(8,482,451)
Other receipts (payments)	(2,325,483)	=	(2,325,483)	1,061,118
Net cash provided by operating activities	1,692,545	229,327	1,921,872	883,084
Cash Flows from Noncapital Financing Activities				
Operating subsidies and transfers to other funds	(290,000)	(211,409)	(501,409)	(175,033)
Cash Flows from Capital and Related Financing Activities				
Proceeds from capital debt	4,041,322	8,660,778	12,702,100	—
Capital contributions	1,645,919	—	1,645,919	—
Purchases of capital assets	(4,194,035)	(144,716)	(4,338,751)	(400,086)
Principal paid on capital debt	(2,178,491)	(8,895,000)	(11,073,491)	(954,137)
Interest paid on capital debt	(1,479,708)	(1,166,546)	(2,646,254)	(41,616)
Other receipts (payments)	=	19,174	19,174	131,416
Net cash (used) by capital and related financing activities	(2,164,993)	(1,526,310)	(3,691,303)	(1,264,423)
Cash Flows from Investing Activities				
Proceeds from sales and maturities of investments	—	—	—	15,684
Interest and dividends	454,793	143,747	598,540	129,550
Net cash provided by investing activities	454,793	143,747	598,540	145,234
Net (decrease) in cash and cash equivalents	(307,655)	(1,364,645)	(1,672,300)	(411,138)
Balances—beginning of the year	8,724,308	3,227,135	11,951,443	3,747,237
Balances—end of the year	$8,416,653	$1,862,490	$10,279,143	$3,336,099

EXHIBIT 45.9 (Continued)

	Enterprise Funds			Internal Service Funds
	Water and Sewer	Parking Facilities	Total	
Reconciliation of operating income (loss) to net cash provided (used) by operating activities:				
Operating income (loss)	$4,422,127	$(238,804)	$4,183,323	$(540,532)
Adjustments to reconcile operating income to net cash provided (used) by operating activities:				
Depreciation expense	1,163,140	542,049	1,705,189	1,707,872
Change in assets and liabilities:				
Receivables, net	653,264	1,205	654,469	31,941
Inventories	2,829	—	2,829	39,790
Accounts and other payables	(297,446)	(86,643)	(384,089)	475,212
Accrued expenses	(4,251,369)	11,520	(4,239,849)	(831,199)
Net cash provided by operating activities	$1,692,545	$229,327	$1,921,872	$883,084

EXHIBIT 45.10 Illustrative Statement of Fiduciary Net Assets, Local Government

Local City—Statement of Fiduciary Net Assets
Fiduciary Funds as of December 31, 2002

	Employee Retirement Plan	Private-Purpose Trust	Agency Fund
Assets			
Cash and cash equivalents	$1,973	$1,250	$44,889
Receivables:			
Interest and dividends	508,475	760	—
Other receivables	6,826	=	183,161
Total receivables	515,301	760	183,161
Investments, at fair value:			
U.S. government obligations	13,056,037	80,000	—
Municipal bonds	6,528,019	—	—
Corporate bonds	16,320,047	—	—
Corporate stocks	26,112,075	—	—
Other investments	3,264,009	=	=
Total investments	65,280,187	80,000	=
Total assets	65,797,461	82,010	$228,050

EXHIBIT 45.10   (Continued)

	Employee Retirement Plan	Private-Purpose Trust	Agency Fund
Liabilities			
Accounts payable	$ —	$1,234	$ —
Refunds payable and others	1,358	=	228,050
Total liabilities	1,358	1,234	$228,050
Net Assets			
Held in trust for pension benefits and other purposes	$65,796,103	$80,776	

EXHIBIT 45.11   Illustrative Statement of Changes in Fiduciary Net Assets, Local Government

Local City—Statement of Changes in Fiduciary Net Assets Fiduciary Funds for the Year Ended December 31, 2002		
	Employee Retirement Plan	Private-Purpose Trust
Additions		
Contributions:		
Employer	$2,721,341	$ —
Plan members	1,421,233	—
Total contributions	4,142,574	—
Investment earnings:		
Net (decrease) in fair value of investments	(272,522)	—
Interest	2,460,871	4,560
Dividends	1,445,273	—
Total investment earnings	3,633,622	4,560
Less investment expense	216,428	—
Net investment earnings	3,417,194	4,560
Total additions	7,559,768	4,560
Deductions		
Benefits	2,453,047	3,800
Refunds of contributions	464,691	—
Administrative costs	87,532	678
Total deductions	3,005,270	4,478
Change in net assets	4,554,498	82
Net assets—beginning of the year	61,241,605	80,694
Net assets—end of the year	$65,796,103	$80,776

The first note encountered is the summary of significant accounting policies. This note contains a treasure trove of information about the government's accounting policies. The following are just some of the policies that might be disclosed in this note:

1. A description of the governmentwide financial statements, noting that neither fiduciary funds nor component units that are fiduciary in nature are included.

2. A brief description of the component units of the financial reporting entity and their relationships to the primary government. This disclosure includes a discussion of the criteria for including component units in the financial reporting entity and how the component units are reported. It also includes information about how the separate financial statements for the individual component units may be obtained.

3. A description of the activities accounted for in each of the following columns—major funds, internal service funds, and fiduciary fund types—presented in the basic financial statements.

4. The measurement focus (economic resources) and basis of accounting (accrual) used in the governmentwide statements.

5. The revenue recognition policies used in fund financial statements, including the length of time used to define "available" for purposes of revenue recognition in the governmental fund financial statements.

6. The policy for eliminating internal activity in the governmentwide statement of activities.

7. The policy for capitalizing assets and for estimating the useful lives of those assets (used to calculate depreciation expense). Governments that choose to use the modified approach for reporting eligible infrastructure assets should describe that approach. (See the discussion in the RSI section.)

8. A description of the types of transactions included in program revenues and the policy for allocating indirect expenses to functions in the statement of activities.

9. The policy for defining operating and nonoperating revenues of proprietary funds.

10. The policy for applying FASB pronouncements issued after November 30, 1989, to business-type activities and to enterprise funds of the primary government.

11. The definition of cash and cash equivalents used in the statement of cash flows for proprietary funds.

12. The government's policy regarding whether to first apply restricted or unrestricted resources when an expense is incurred for purposes for which both restricted and unrestricted net assets are available.

The notes also address specific accounts found in the basic financial statements. These disclosures include information on cash and investments, capital assets, long-term liabilities (for example, debt, leases, liabilities associated with employee benefits), derivatives, and interfund transactions.

Cash and Investments   The cash and investment disclosure focuses on credit and market risks associated with these assets but also provides other important information, including:

1. The methods and significant assumptions used to estimate the fair value of investments, if that fair value is based on other than quoted market prices.
2. The policy for determining which investments, if any, are reported at amortized cost.
3. For any investments in external investment pools that are not SEC-registered, a brief description of any regulatory oversight for the pool and whether the fair value of the position in the pool is the same as the value of the pool shares.
4. Any involuntary participation in an external investment pool.
5. Any income from investments associated with one fund that is assigned to another fund.

The credit risk disclosures include information regarding overall credit risk (for example, the amount of investments are AAA rated), custodial credit risk related to counterparties that are involved in investment transactions, and concentration risk (investments that represent 5% or more of the government's total investments).

The interest risk disclosure is intended to reflect in part how the government identifies and manages that risk. Interest rate risk information is organized by investment type and amount using one of the following methods:

1. Segmented time distribution
2. Specific identification
3. Weighted-average maturity
4. Duration
5. Simulation model (such as shock tests)

Capital Assets and Long-Term Obligations   Major classes of capital assets and long-term liabilities are disclosed in the notes to the financial statements. The liabilities are divided between those associated with governmental activities and those associated with business-type activities. In addition, capital assets that are not being depreciated (for example, land) are disclosed separately from those that are being depreciated. This breakout is provided so that analysts can compare the historical costs to accumulated depreciation to assist in their assessment of potential capital needs. The disclosures also include summary additions and deductions to these accounts during the year.

Because the methods and assumptions used by government have such a significant effect on actuarial accrued liabilities for pensions and other postemployment benefits (for example, retiree healthcare), all of these assumptions will soon be found in notes. These methods and assumptions include:

1. The actuarial cost method (for example, entry age normal).
2. The method(s) used to determine the actuarial value of assets (for example, three-year smooth market value).
3. The assumptions with respect to the inflation rate, investment return (including the method used to determine a blended rate for a partially funded plan, if applicable), postretirement benefit increases if applicable, projected salary increases if relevant to determination of the level of benefits, and, for postemployment healthcare plans, the healthcare cost trend rate.
4. The amortization method (level dollar or level percentage of projected payroll) and the amortization period (equivalent single amortization period, for plans that use multiple periods) for the most recent actuarial valuation and whether the period is closed or open.
5. Employers that use the aggregate actuarial cost method will disclose that because the method does not identify or separately amortize unfunded actuarial liabilities, information about funded status and funding progress has been prepared using the entry age actuarial cost method for that purpose, and that the information presented is intended to be a surrogate for the funding progress of the plan.

In addition, the notes present information on the funding status of pension and *other postemployment benefits* (OPEB), from the most recent actuarial valuation when the employer participates in either a single-employer or an agent multiemployer plan.

Interfund Transactions Analysts have always had an interest in the transactions that occur between funds. To provide financial statement users with better information on these transactions, changes were made to the interfund transaction disclosure requirements with the new model.

The notes to the financial statements provide the following details about interfund balances reported in the fund financial statements to assist financial statement users:

1. Amounts due from other funds by individual major fund, nonmajor governmental funds in the aggregate, nonmajor enterprise funds in the aggregate, internal service funds in the aggregate, and fiduciary fund type.
2. The purpose for interfund balances.
3. Interfund balances that are not expected to be repaid within one year from the date of the financial statements.

The notes to the financial statements provide the following information about interfund transfers reported in the fund financial statements:

1. Amounts transferred from other funds by individual major fund, nonmajor governmental funds in the aggregate, nonmajor enterprise funds in the aggregate, internal service funds in the aggregate, and fiduciary fund type.
2. A general description of the principal purposes of the government's interfund transfers.
3. The intended purpose and the amount of significant transfers that meet either or both of the following criteria:
   a. Do not occur on a routine basis—for example, a transfer to a wastewater enterprise fund for the local match of a federal pollution control grant.
   b. Are inconsistent with the activities of the fund making the transfer—for example, a transfer from a capital projects fund to the general fund.

Other Forms of RSI   Pension and OPEB trend information often dominate the RSI section (other than MD&A) of a state and local government financial report. Like any longitudinal data set, this trend information provides important context to a reader. For example, if a government reports that its pensions are 80% funded in the notes to the financial statements, the RSI will provide information from past valuation so the analyst can quickly assess the direction of the plan's overall funding. For example, a very different conclusion would likely be reached if the prior valuation reported a 70% funded ratio versus a 90% funded ratio.

The RSI for single and agent multiple-employer pension and OPEB plans provide information about the funding progress of the plan, including, for each valuation:

1. Actuarial valuation date.
2. Actuarial value of assets.
3. Actuarial accrued liability.
4. Total unfunded actuarial liability (or funding excess).

5. Actuarial value of assets as a percentage of the actuarial accrued liability (funded ratio).
6. Annual covered payroll.
7. Ratio of the unfunded actuarial liability (or funding excess) to annual covered payroll.

In addition, factors that significantly affect the identification of trends in the amounts reported, including, for example, changes in benefit provisions, the size or composition of the population covered by the plan, or the actuarial methods and assumptions used, are presented.

Some governments, including many state governments, have chosen the option of reporting infrastructure assets (primarily roads and bridges) using what the GASB refers to as the *modified approach*. Under this approach, the government is not required to depreciate these assets. However, all capital replacement costs are expensed instead of being capitalized, and the government is required to perform, at least every three years, asset condition assessment. Information that will be found in RSI for at least the three most recent complete condition assessments include:

1. Dates of the assessments.
2. Assessed condition of the qualifying infrastructure asset (for example, 80 on a scale of 100—see 4. below).
3. Estimated annual amount calculated at the beginning of the fiscal year to maintain and preserve the qualifying infrastructure assets at (or above) the condition level established and disclosed by the government compared with the amounts actually expensed for each of the past five reporting periods.
4. The basis for the condition measurement and the measurement scale used to assess and report condition. For example, a basis for condition measurement could be distresses found in pavement surfaces. A scale used to assess and report condition could range from zero for a failed pavement to 100 for a pavement in perfect condition.
5. The condition level at which the government intends to preserve its eligible infrastructure assets reported using the modified approach.
6. Factors that significantly affect trends in the information reported in the required schedules, including any changes in the measurement scale, the basis for the condition measurement, or the condition assessment methods used during the periods covered by the schedules. If there is a change in the condition level at which the government intends to preserve eligible infrastructure assets, an estimate of the effect of the change on the estimated annual amount to maintain and preserve those assets for the current period also will be disclosed.

Supplementary Information Governments often include information for "nonmajor" funds in combining schedules. Because this information is not required by the GASB, it is presented as SI.

Another major component of SI is the statistical section. Because the statistical section is primarily made up of trend information, it is of particular interest to analysts. Financial trends information is intended to assist users in understanding and assessing how a government's financial position has changed over time. If the summary of significant accounting policies is a treasure trove of information, the statistical section is Davy Jones' locker.

Information that will be found in the statistical section is classified into five distinct categories; however, those categories are not specifically labeled in the presentation. Instead, they are used as organizing themes on which reporting objectives can be applied to a wide range of governmental entities. These categories, including the intent of each category are:

1. Financial trends information is intended to assist users in understanding and assessing how a government's financial position has changed over time.
2. Revenue capacity information is intended to assist users in understanding and assessing the factors affecting a government's ability to generate its own-source revenues.
3. Debt capacity information is intended to assist users in understanding and assessing a government's debt burden and its ability to issue additional debt.
4. Demographic and economic information is intended (a) to assist users in understanding the socioeconomic environment within which a government operates and (b) to provide information that facilitates comparisons of financial statement information over time and among governments.
5. Operating information is intended to provide contextual information about a government's operations and resources to assist readers in using financial statement information to understand and assess a government's economic condition.

A list of statistical tables that is typically presented in a comprehensive annual financial report is presented in Exhibit 45.12.

SUMMARY

No matter what the standards do to improve the transparency of financial reports for state and local governments, if those reports are not produced on

EXHIBIT 45.12 Statistical Section Tables, General Purpose Government with Property Taxes as the Most Significant Revenue Source

Financial Trends
1. Net assets by component, last 10 fiscal years
2. Changes in net assets, last 10 fiscal years
3. Fund balances, governmental funds, last 10 fiscal years
4. Changes in fund balances, governmental funds, last 10 fiscal years

Revenue Capacity
1. Assessed value and actual value of taxable property, last 10 fiscal years.
2. Direct and overlapping property tax rates, last 10 fiscal years.
3. Principal property tax payers, current year and nine years ago.
4. Property tax levies and collections, last 10 fiscal years.

Debt Capacity
1. Ratios of outstanding debt by type, last 10 fiscal years.
2. Ratios of general bonded debt outstanding, last 10 fiscal years.
3. Direct and overlapping governmental activities as of fiscal year end.
4. Legal debt margin information, last 10 fiscal years.
5. Pledged-revenue coverage, last 10 fiscal years.

Demographic and Economic Information
1. Demographic and economic statistics, last 10 calendar years (includes population, total personal income, per capita personal income, and unemployment rate).
2. Principal employers, current year and nine years ago.

Operating Information
1. Full-time equivalent city government employees by function/program, last 10 fiscal years.
2. Operating indicators by function/program, last 10 fiscal years (if information is collected by the government).
3. Capital asset statistics by function/program, last 10 fiscal years.

a timely basis, the effectiveness of those reports are diminished. The GASB cannot wave its magic wand to ensure that all governments issue reports within two or three months of their year end or even six months. To improve timeliness it will take a concerted effort by all parties involved. One way that the analytical community can help is to let the financial statement preparers know that timeliness of financial statements prepared in conformity with GAAP provide valuable information and do make a difference.

Unfortunately, many preparers think that no one cares about their annual financial reports and, therefore, a low priority is placed on those reports. This results in a vicious cycle. The lower the priority often results in financial statements being issued at a later date. When the financial statements are not issued on a timely basis, the information contained in those reports becomes less useful. This cycle needs to be broken.

The GASB will continue to do its part by issuing guidance on important financial reporting topics. Be it retiree healthcare benefits, derivatives, fund balance, public/private partnerships, or pollution remediation obligations, the GASB is taking on the difficult issues. The GASB's efforts result in more complete and consistent information being included in financial reports; however, the Board cannot nor should it issue standards in a vacuum. When proposals are developed and issued for public comment, financial statement preparers and auditors stand ready to provide feedback and the GASB welcomes that input. Preparers and auditors are only two of the three important constituent groups. Financial statement users are the third leg of the stool. Without input from the user community, a vital element is missing. Without that input, the financial statements could be less useful to analysts, and the vicious cycle referred to above gains momentum.

CHAPTER 46

Managing a Buy-Side Municipal Bond Research Department

Richard A. Ciccarone
Managing Director and Chief Research Officer
McDonnell Investment Management LLC
and
President
Merritt Research Services LLC

As an investment asset class, most professional and casual investors often fail to grasp the vast number of issuers, diversity of credit types, unique security structures, and risk parameters that make up the municipal bond market. As such, municipal bond research managers spend a lot of time trying to educate others, especially from outside the municipal market, about the challenges they face.

Municipal bond analysis is rarely taught in the halls of higher education. The relatively low default rate for traditional municipal bonds is probably one of the biggest reasons that business schools and investment courses do not spend a lot of time on municipal security analysis. *Munis* are deemed relatively staid investments that one shouldn't lose too much sleep over. However, municipal bonds can and do experience problems that may result in lowered ratings, lowered prices, and sometimes defaults. When it comes to managing a municipal bond buy-side investment portfolio and the associated research effort in particular, predicting credit outcomes is a critical function but it is not the whole story. Research managers are under pressure to ensure that their analyst teams are identifying bonds that will provide consistently higher yields and total returns than the portfolio next door.

Municipal bond research management demands a generalist's knowledge of a plethora of different types of public finance security structures, geography, governmental functions, state laws, demographics, economic trends, business trends and specialized not-for-profit market sectors to name a few. Orchestrating this knowledge base in conjunction with bond market dynamics are important requirements that determine the team's ability to anticipate credit changes and identify relative value opportunities.

Although credit analysis remains a primary concern, research managers that assume an active role and shared responsibility with portfolio managers in building better bond performance overall are more likely to stand out. Beyond credit, superior research efforts are those that work with portfolio managers to assess bond call risk, bond prepayments, interest rate direction, bond market supply, unique demand elements or tax exemption risks. Successful investment managers are those that have exceeded the expectations of those who have entrusted their money to them.

Centered on the objective of achieving the best results, winning buy-side research efforts are organized around maximizing and harmonizing three key elements: people, technology and process. This chapter is designed to outline the most important goals, obstacles faced, and resources needed to achieve successful municipal research management.

ASSESSMENT OF CHALLENGES

Exceptional research managers are required to be artists who can learn to walk the tight rope which stands between excessive risk and superior performance.

Balancing Capital Preservation versus Total Return

The first responsibility of a buy-side research manager is the ability to assess and promote good bond ideas that delicately balance the twofold objective of capital preservation and producing optimal total portfolio returns. While capital preservation is of utmost importance at all times, the degree to which one is risk-adverse is normally related to the goals and standards of an investor's overall investment strategy and related asset allocation. To the extent that specific investors are looking to achieve their alpha in equities or other markets, bond investment strategies will be more focused on conservative views of fundamental default risk. However, current portfolio management practices commonly expect much more than the return of principal and coupons.

Endeavoring to avoid credit problems remains a basic responsibility for any fixed income research manager. At the same time, most institutional buy-side managers are challenged by the need to identify bonds that will enhance performance relative to industry benchmarks. Striving to achieve alpha, that is the extra kick in performance from well-chosen bonds, echoes from the lips of most bond investment managers these days. Prior to the 1990s, bond managers and research directors stressed almost exclusively the beta risk factor, which focused more on the stability of bond returns. Today, both objectives are critical to the task at hand. This is true not only for bond managers that cater to institutional organizations and mutual funds but also for many of those that cater to high-net-worth individual clients since both groups are held accountable to those that hire them to maintain or exceed peer group measurement standards. Contemporary fixed income investment management standards require securities research analysts to determine whether the risks taken are prudent based on accurate assessments of credit quality and likely outcomes. If the risks appear to be acceptable, then buy-side analysts should become the internal proponents of relevant risk. If they are not, then analysts ought to assume the role of stalwart guardians of capital preservation.

Unique Research Challenges in the Municipal Market

Municipal managers have to understand the unique terrain that can camouflage risks not significant in other securities markets. If it were not for the municipal market's relatively safe track record and the high percentage of insured bonds, the resources relegated to cover the market would seem to be inadequate. Still, the enormous potential list of issuers, the heavy dependence on third-party guarantors, the uneven record of secondary market disclosure information, and the often thin margin for error due to relatively tight quality spreads present a daunting challenge for independent research for both investment-grade and noninvestment-grade municipals.

Multitude of Different Public Finance Credit Sectors and Securities

According to 2002 Census of Governments statistics, there are nearly 90,000 local governments, including 19,429 municipalities, 3,034 counties, 16,504 townships, 13,506 school districts, and 35,052 special governments. This is the first line of potential issuers of municipal bonds. The second line is the hundreds more of bond issuing state and local bond conduit authorities, which each has the power to issue bonds on behalf of thousands of non-profit organizations such as colleges, hospitals, and long-term care facilities as well as quasi-public public entities that build housing projects, power plants, among others. Then, there are still more municipal bonds issued by industrial revenue bond conduits to provide lower cost financing to promote economic development for qualified private borrowers. The plethora of potential borrowers that can tap the municipal bond market poses a potential burden of immense proportions to individual research departments.

Although there is a core of highly visible frequent borrowers that the market sees on a regular basis, which the market is highly familiar, many of the issuers in the market make one-time only or rare appearances in the market.

The uniqueness and enormity of the number of potential credits that may appear is one of the biggest challenges of the municipal market vis-a-vis the corporate bond market. Given the statistics involved here, it is a daunting task for any research department to even attempt to provide intensive coverage of all credits. Yet, historically, municipal bond research department are relatively small compared to their corporate bond and their equity analyst counterparts. While other markets may closely follow 35 to 65 names each year, a municipal analyst may have to review many more, perhaps over 80 to 150 credits dependent on perceived risk level in a single year.

There are two primary mitigating factors that rationalize the high ratio of municipal borrowers to the number of analysts. First, during the 20th Century, the municipal default rate for traditional government entities is relatively low. Most of the governmental municipal bonds that defaulted occurred during the Great Depression of the 1930s. Since then, the overall municipal bond default rate has been relatively low at less than 1% of all bonds outstanding. The default rate is somewhat higher relative to non-governmental tax-exempt borrowers related to land development, health care, and economic development industrial revenue bonds. However, there have been some notable defaults and bankruptcies, such as the debt moratorium on New York City bonds in 1975, the city of Cleveland in 1978, the Washington Public Power Supply (WPPSS) bond default in 1983, the Orange County bankruptcy in 1994, and the Allegheny Health Education and Research Foundation (AHERF) bankruptcy and default in 1998.

Second, bond insurance has become prevalent in the investment-grade municipal market since the 1980s. With many of the governmental and quasi-governmental bonds insured, default risk to individual investors diminishes even more. It is important that bond insurance is not a credit substitute and that investors have a true double-barreled security in which the underlying credit security for an insured municipal bond remains intact for repayment. For that reason, it makes sense for municipal bond investors to be fully aware of the underlying risks and potential for repayment when buying and pricing an insured municipal bond. Theoretically, investors in insured bonds are buying a more valuable bond when the underlying credit quality is strong on its own merits. Research efforts that pay heed to underlying credit quality and do not treat insured municipal bonds as generic could outperform their peers if an underlying credit weakens or if an insurer experiences problems of their own. In the latter case, it is essential that municipal bond researcher be able to assess the credit quality of the bond insurers themselves.

Buy-side research teams tend to be a little larger in the case of research managers who focus on noninvestment grade bonds. This segment of the municipal market has grown substantially since the mid-1980s when the first mutual funds were created to offer diversified portfolios of higher yielding, higher risk municipal bonds. Bonds in these funds are usually concentrated in nonprofit or private-activity issues with an emphasis on health care, housing, economic development, and project financing. The vast majority are uninsured and not rated, unlike junk bonds in the corporate market, making buy-side analysts the only game in town for credit analysis of these financings.

Third-Party Research

Municipal buy-side research departments do not have access to the depth of third-party research coverage available in the corporate bond and equity securities markets either through dealers or independent research services.

Unlike the corporate and equity markets, sell-side research analysts, especially those that follow credit trends and publish their work are few and far between especially since the mid-1990s. The proliferation of bond insurance among investment-grade bonds, lower bond profit spreads to underwriters, relatively low default risk, and the rise in the size and sophistication of many buy-side analytical teams have all combined to diminish the availability of dealer research. There are notable exceptions but sell-side analytical presence is certainly not what it once was. Even in the municipal high-yield market, there are only a scattering of firms that have their own sell-side analysts as underwriters and private placement firms have backed away from giving their own recommendations. In some cases, buy-side firms receive some support from sell-side desk analysts who don't publish but these analysts are probably more helpful to the dealers who rely on them to get advice on quality issues for trading pricing purposes.

The one area of sell-side research that is more widely represented in the municipal bond field is that pertaining to municipal market bond trends and strategies. Their focus on relative value, supply, and general trends in the municipal market provides intelligent commentary to help buy-side analytical teams and portfolio managers as well better understand the patterns that might influence bond performance. Buy-side research managers and teams are still wise to take advantage of the sell-side research analytical opinions and comments in order to check their own impressions of situations or pick up any background nuances that might give them new insights.

Rating agency reports are usually available on investment-grade names from Standard & Poor's, Moody's, and Fitch Ratings for those that subscribe to these services. Rating agencies cover only those bond issuers that request their opinion. That often includes providing an opinion on the underlying quality of bonds insured by one of the financial guaranty firms. Issuers that would likely receive a speculative rating do not usually ask for a rating and are rarely insured. Nonrated issues go straight to the buy-side firms where they are reviewed and monitored internally.

Buy-side research firms may find rating agencies a good credit benchmark to compare against their own opinions; however, few firms rely on them solely. Similar to receiving research from sell-side analysts, it is unwise for sell-side analysts to ignore commentary from the rating agencies just in case insights are offered that might not otherwise have been apparent. There is room to disagree with the final opinion and the direction of where a credit or bond price might be trending. In cases like New York City, Washington Public Power Supply System (WPPSS), Orange County or Allegheny Health, Education, and Research Foundation (AHERF) in which investment-grade credit quality has plummeted rapidly, buy-side analysts have shown that they have a lot to gain and a lot more to lose if they fail to apply their own skills and instincts to investigate further beyond a bond rating.

Secondary Market Disclosure and Information Access

Those not familiar with the municipal bond market are almost always surprised when they discover that municipal bond disclosure and access to periodic information from borrowers are not assured. You would expect that anything to do with a government entity in the United States is certainly bound to be current, available, and transparent. Unfortunately, that's not always the case for many governments but especially related to bonds issued by state- and local-sponsored conduit authorities for quasi-government, non-profits or private parties.

The problem all goes back to the historical roots of munis when local banks, property and insurance companies and a small share of very wealthy individual investors dominated the market. They often bought state and local general obligation and essential service revenue issues that they knew and were comfortable holding. When the New York crisis occurred in 1975, there was an opportunity to upgrade disclosure practices to better reflect standards in the corporate and private markets. However, strong resistance to imposing federal oversight over state and local governments by Congress resulted in the Tower Amendment that prohibited the imposition of securities oversight and regulation directly on municipal bonds, including for disclosure. Not all was lost when the Securities and Exchange Commission (SEC) and the Municipal Securities Rulemaking Board (MSRB) were able to mandate a couple of "end-arounds" the Tower Amendment by tying better disclosure practices to the responsibilities of underwriters. These mandates reduced the problem by requiring underwriters to provide new issue official statements in the late 1970s and later in the 1990s by requiring the promise of some secondary market disclosure when a deal was brought to market.

The relevance of this historical backdrop in the context of managing a buy-side research effort is that credit information may not always be as accessible, complete or standardized in the municipal market as it is in the corporate bond market. With it brings problems that potentially pose timing and content gaps when research departments have the information they need to track the issues they hold for surveillance or buy in the secondary market. In some ways, this gap raises the importance of bond rating agencies since they have the power to request specific information and meetings with borrowers in order to maintain a rating. However, investors then become beholden to rating agency surveillance schedules if they are not able to get adequate information on their own from publicly accessible sources.

Cutting edge research managers who want to stay on top of their holdings have to improvise methods to gather and filter information to smartly make credit decisions. Unlike the SEC sponsored Edgar system to track financial statements on corporate securities, access to vendor databases with specialized software are few and far between in the municipal credit arena. Creditscope with Merritt Research data, DAC, Bloomberg, and Moody's are among the few vendors that offer technology to access a large base of financial statements and updated credit information. At least two of these systems also offer their subscribers the ability to perform complex peer group comparisons as well as customized data sorting and analysis. Whether a research team develops its own in-house database system and software or goes to a third-party provider, technology is a critical part of being able to gauge oncoming trouble spots or identify developing improvements that signal alpha opportunities.

The large number of credits that are often found in institutional municipal portfolios exacerbates the obstacles to casting the net for information and then digesting the data into useful acquisition and surveillance analyses. The key to maintaining appropriate surveillance supervision of a large portfolio or portfolios of municipal bonds necessitates efficient technological monitoring of individual credit names linked to individual bond names or issuers. Unlike stocks which use a simple stock symbol to link to all fundamental and technical factors and information related to the security, municipal bonds are tied to a CUSIP number which may not in itself link to a single obligated party. A case in point relates to a hospital, where the CUSIP is linked to a tax-exempt issuer such as a state health financing authority and not to the individual hospital obligated to secure repayment. In order to tie the issuer to the exact obligated hospital, a manual link or a custom service is needed to identify the proper hospital with the issuer. This linking capability to tie a bond with a specific obligated credit is only in the early years of implementation in the municipal bond market. When issuers and credits are linked, best practice municipal portfolios can be scanned and monitored as financial reports are updated to identify red flag situations in which financial ratio factors and trends signal problems or opportunities. In those cases, managers can better allocate time and priority reviews so that analysts can be assigned to complete the reviews.

Tax Exemption Issues

A distinguishing factor that separates 95% of all municipal bonds from other bonds is the exemption they receive from federal and often state income taxes. While bond counsel provides opinions when a bond is issued that the bonds are not subject to taxation, there are occasions when the bonds can lose their exemption either through actions they take or due to challenges by the Internal Revenue Service (IRS). Analysts as well as portfolio managers should consider this risk assessment when reviewing potential purchases and in the course of surveillance review. Probably 95% of all municipal bonds have little to worry about this risk. Normally, the more plain vanilla the purpose and the structure appears, the lower the risk. To date, this risk has been less apparent for governmental borrowers (except in the case of aggressive advanced refunding situations) than for conduit obligations.

The IRS may investigate and take issue with a bond's tax exemption if it believes that the bonds violate its code in any way. Usually, the threat is related to arbitrage violations related to refundings. Ultimately, a potential violation does not usually result in the loss of tax exemption. The most common resolution of such a situation is a settlement between the IRS and the violating parties that put the issue together. In other cases, the potential for a violation may result in an early call related to taxability. Industrial revenue bonds (IRBs) can risk losing their exemption, for example, if in the case of a merger, the combined entities have IRBs outstanding that exceed the limit of tax-exempt bonds allowed to be outstanding by a single corporation. Even though such an event might trigger a bond call at par, investors might be harmed if the bonds currently are valued at a high premium.

Tax exemption risks can be difficult to detect since bondholders normally rely on bond counsel to make sure that the bond issue is valid in a manner that is consistent with tax laws. Still, buy-side research departments should attempt be cognizant of potential threats to tax exemption if the issue appears to fit a profile that has triggered other investigations. Bond research managers must assume the leadership in their own departments to be on lookout for noncredit related risks such as taxability threats that could adversely affect bond performance.

Knowledge and Skill Sets Needed

Most research managers will probably agree that their best analysts are those with sharp, inquisitive and analytical minds, who can put it all together to come to sound conclusive decisions on not only "what is" but also "what is likely to happen." Research managers, however, are likely to differ on what background, training or certifications, if any, are needed to do the job.

Municipal bond credit analysis, by its very nature, is an eclectic field that requires a wide span of knowledge. It is extremely hard for any one person to adequately cover all the bases, however, striving to be a generalist with specific concentrations of focus is a worthwhile objective.

In equity and corporate bond analyses, an understanding of the business principles of financial analysis and corporate accounting provide an underlying similarity to assess corporate condition across diverse industry groups. Business school and accounting training provide basic preparation for dissecting companies to determine financial condition. In municipal analysis, few schools provide basic principles of analysis for traditional governmental municipal bonds. Even accounting principles and financial analysis may differ more dramatically among municipal credit sectors. *General obligation* (GO) credits are subject to the rules dictated by the Governmental Accounting Standards Board (GASB), while hospital bonds and utilities may be using corporation based accounting rules dictated by the Financial Accounting Standards Board (FASB). Beyond accounting issues, credit assessment techniques for municipal bonds may vary greatly. GO bonds may be analyzed based on more qualitative analysis of what is more likely to influence the soundness of the economic and property tax base while public power analysis may look at similar factors as an investor-owned corporate utility.

In both corporate bonds and municipal bonds, the best analysts are those that can determine what trends are likely to drive the numbers next year or in five years based on the dynamics now and foreseen. The best analytical teams are those that draw upon experience, insight, and skills from diverse work backgrounds, educational experiences, and certifications. Accomplished analysts are those of proven achievement, sometimes those credentials come from MBA, MPA or PhD programs, other times through the Chartered Financial Analyst (CFA) designation or through distinguished backgrounds in areas of expertise related to specializations that are active in the municipal bond market, such as municipal finance or health care. Quantitative analysts are also becoming increasingly more valuable in a research setting to help portfolio management efforts to identify relative value based on statistically significant market trends for the purpose of prognostication.

There is value in mixing the skills and market experience of a fixed income research team. Being able to tap into the experience of a corporate utility analyst to assist or cover public power credits as well as investor-owned utilities has obvious value. It can also be beneficial to share the insights of an airline analyst with an airport analyst or a hospital analyst with a for-profit health care specialist. Many private-activity municipal bonds are more akin to the corporate sector than to governments. Municipal land based nonrated deals can benefit substantially from the expertise of a real estate analyst that may cover the corporate bond market homebuilders or REIT bond sector. Intertwining fixed income research can also have reverse benefits. Taxable municipal bond deals, which may trade at higher spreads than corporate bonds and also have potentially better returns on a risk-adjusted basis, are now included in corporate bond indexes.

Evaluating Analyst Performance

When it comes to assessing individual analytical contributions on a research team, conventional practice has been to evaluate each analyst based on subjective factors such as the upgrade/downgrade calls, defaults experienced, the number of credits reviewed, the quality of interaction with portfolio managers, and professional recognition. While each of these is important, municipal bond performance evaluation based on total returns of bonds covered by an analyst is mostly an elusive goal. Attribution analysis that quantitatively identifies what bond portfolio factors contributed to performance is most relegated to portfolio managers. However, portfolio management teams that are integrated into a collaborative effort with their research team should pay closer attention to attribution contributions to determine total returns related to individual analyst bond recommendations. For example, analysts that recommend overweighted positions in certain credit sectors, states or individual credits should be rewarded or held accountable for returns that exceed or fall below portfolio benchmarks.

Portfolio attribution programs are easier done in equity portfolios where like securities are bought and sold and analyst contributions are not skewed by security variations of the name. In contrast, attribution to evaluate individual credit recommendations are more complicated because a bond's performance may be more influenced by its coupon, maturity, duration, and structure than by credit performance. In order to compare a municipal bond performance based on credit recommendations, one has to isolate a bond of specific structural components with a similar structure benchmark bond or index. In this day and age of increasingly sophisticated bond management assessment, managers are more likely in the future to attempt to assess research contributions based on quantitative methods that are evolving that link the research effort more closely to portfolio results.

SUMMARY

The relative credit safety of most municipal bonds can lead outsiders to underestimate the role, complexity, and importance of municipal bond research and the challenges that must be overcome to manage the process. Factors that are not an issue to analyze corporate bonds such as inadequate disclosure, tax-exemption risk, and local politics can provide a unique challenge to the limited resources often available to cover municipal credits. At the same time, total return performance competition has become increasingly acute to the portfolio management process tempting portfolio managers and analysts to stretch their risk tolerance for just a few more basis points. That is why institutional buy-side research departments remain important to executing successful credit risk management acquisition and surveillance strategies.

CHAPTER 47

The Role of an Activist Bond Analyst

Arthur E. Schloss
Vice President
Morgan Stanley Investment Management

This chapter posits that bond analysts are activists when they properly perform their role. By *activist*, I am referring to an analyst who seeks to improve portfolio performance by being proactive rather than reactive in the face of a deteriorating credit. While activism can present itself in different contexts, it is the assertive analyst who can add value to a stressed credit by following the general guidelines discussed in the following sections.

ACTIVIST BOND ANALYST'S APPROACH TO IMPROVING STRESSED OR DETERIORATING CREDITS

The role of an activist bond analyst is evident in each stage of the credit process. It begins with the initial review of deal-related documents and the framing of credit questions for the site visit. It includes a review of the legal provisions governing the transaction and the request to tighten the terms and conditions for the financing. While each stage of the process contains elements of activism, it is the approach to stressed credits which best illustrates activist bond analysis. An activist analyst will ask probing questions and will ask in-depth follow up questions before suggesting a purchase. Over time the underlying economics of a credit will change and management may also change. An activist analyst will keep up with developments and seek to anticipate where a credit is headed. The acquisition phase for a new credit is a relatively quick process measured in weeks, usually. The holding period may last for many years and it is here where the activist analyst can add enduring value.

There are times when a borrower will delay or stop releasing disclosure materials and where calls to a trustee will not provide much help. In older bond documents, the ability to enforce disclosure may be more limited than in a more recent financing. Lessons to be learned from conducting surveillance and review of borrowers are:

1. Despite the legal requirements of 15(c)2(12), disclosure ultimately depends on a mind set among borrowers—disclosure works optimally when the borrower really understands that they have a stake in keeping the bondholders fully informed.
2. Disclosure must be continuous and where a credit begins to run into trouble, the borrower must document steps being taken or contemplated to resolve issues. Analysts are generally willing to be of help but the borrower must do all in its power to start a remediation. Where a borrower has taken no steps to improve performance, the bond investor cannot be expected to be the entire solution.
3. The amount of time it takes to apply a curative fix to a problem is extensive and the earlier there is a frank recognition of issues facing the borrower, the earlier steps can be taken to resolve them.

After a financing closes, there is a remarkable transformation that occurs. During the period where a bond fund is considering the purchase of a security, the interests of the obligor and the bond fund are diametrically opposite. The bond fund seeks the highest possible return and the strongest bond covenants while the obligor seeks the lowest cost of capital and the most flexible borrowing terms. After the financing, the bond fund buyer, and indeed retail buyers, have the exact same goal as the borrower; a project that works and that improves with the passage of time. For projects that do not come out of the starting gates strongly, any measure of help that can be provided by the bondholder is limited unless that bondholder has all relevant information available.

The most obvious starting point for discussing the role of an activist analyst is disclosure. The bond documents accompanying each new financing detail the frequency and often the content of the disclosure to be provided. The most basic form of disclosure includes information on utilization, occupancy, toll transactions, home sales, enrollment, and the like depending on the credit type. Beyond that, a balance sheet and income statement are normally included. Occasionally, a cash flow statement is also provided which breaks the financials into the following three segments:operating activity, financing activity and borrowing activity. While these are essential, a *management discussion and analysis* has become increasingly recognized as a key component of a full disclosure regimen. Without this, it is easy for the disclosure material to become a book of numbers devoid of any context. At the risk of sounding uncharacteristically erudite, this is akin to the famous cave analogy of Plato, where only the shadows are seen but not the true reality causing the shadows. Unless the factors that are influencing the reported financial measures are discussed, the analyst is at a disadvantage in structuring an appropriate response.

Data on utilization serves as a form of a leading economic indicator. Well before the financial statements indicate either credit stress or improvement, trends in utilization will give a strong clue as to what future financial statements are likely to look like. An activist high-yield analyst will look at current utilization trends and compare them with previous reports to determine seasonality factors, overall trends, and trends in subunits and subcomponents of the credit. These will then be compared with standard benchmarks for that particular high-yield sector. It is also important to understand the context in which a credit exists. Over and above the operational and financial information obtained from the borrower, which can be viewed as a starting point, it is useful to review the economic and demographic environment in which a borrower conducts its business.

The financial statements are the initial point for review—especially a review of the major indicia of leverage, solvency and liquidity. While many of these measures are somewhat standardized, the results must be evaluated based on the specific type of credit being reviewed. As a basic example, all else being equal, a Type A Lifecare credit, where there is a future guarantee of nursing care included in the contract, will have a stronger current financial profile than a Type C facility, where future nursing and other health care costs are provided on a fee for service basis. Similarly, while hospitals are usually thought of as representing a single-credit sector, the reality is that rural hospitals, urban hospitals, hospital systems, and children's hospitals all have very different credit profiles and issues.

Disclosure forms the basis for credit surveillance,the analysis and written follow up to capture not only the credit's current condition but its future prospects. Markets move on expectations, not static credit, so surveillance must be directed to what is and also to what is most likely to be.

Surveillance is critical for several reasons:

1. A robust surveillance regimen enables an activist analyst to keep the portfolio manager up to speed with whether a credit is stable, improving, or declining.
2. This information can serve as an important indicator to the portfolio manager as to whether to hold, sell or buy more of the credit. Of course, credit information and outlooks are only one of many inputs the portfolio manager must take into account.

3. An active surveillance program can pinpoint situations requiring active participation by the analyst in the resolution of credit issues. Further, it can provide important clues as to whether the credit deterioration is a result of poor management or poor markets and this is the first important determinant of the approach to a credit decline.
4. The aggregation of credits, by sector, within a portfolio and their analytical review, can pinpoint issues within that sector and indicate whether an overweight or underweight in that sector makes credit sense.

Surveillance is actually a (bifurcated) form of triage. A percentage of credits in a portfolio will improve over time as demand factors boost utilization and financial indicators. With a well-selected and diversified portfolio of credits, the percentage will be larger. The vast majority of credits will be stable and produce consistent, if unspectacular, financial measures. In the case of both stable and improving credits, there is very little for the activist analyst to do except for recommending whether to add or lighten the weighting in that credit. In both cases, the portfolio manager will need to be informed and kept up to date, but there is no role for remediation as long as performance meets the minimal covenants in the bond documents.

The role of the activist analyst becomes evident where a credit fails to perform. While this often occurs in the early years of a credit, after capitalized interest has been expended, it can occur at any stage. I have seen credits falter almost from the outset and I have also seen credits deteriorate with just a few years left until the final maturity. In new credits, it is construction and fill-up risk that are often the obstacles. In more seasoned projects, it is the accumulated failure to reinvest in the project and large-scale competitive pressure that may be the culprit. In all cases in which an analyst is confronted with a stressed or distressed credit, I have found it absolutely necessary to confer with colleagues. It is often the case that an analyst can become so engrossed in a credit that perspective is lost. Also, other analysts within the group may have extensive experience with similar issues and can be of enormous assistance. While colleagues who have not "lived" with the credit cannot have the same feel for the issues involved, their help can be of enormous benefit in identifying alternate approaches.

WATCHFUL WAITING

In the case of a deteriorating credit, the most basic strategy may prove to be watchful waiting. While this may appear to be the antithesis of activism, it frequently works. Occasionally, a project is financed and the target market for which it is built is not quite ready for it. With the passage of time, market factors sometimes improve and a credit can find its market. For this strategy to be successful, it is a prerequisite that the borrower have access to cash in the form of external financing or strong operating reserves, to ride out the time necessary for the demand factors to become more positive. It is essential, when such an approach is pursued, to monitor liquidity and the "burn rate" of expenditures. This is also a comparatively short-term approach. Typically, a project can find its bearings 12 to 18 months following expected stabilization, but it is rare for a project to function for a much longer period if stabilization has not occurred by that point.

ASSET PRESERVATION

One of the ways that an activist analyst can preserve value and stabilize the performance of a credit during periods of stress, is to focus on the reality that it is the end-user of the services and facilities being financed that is the true security for a financing. Terms such as bankruptcy and default are emotion-laden with the target market and may engender panic. This approach is particularly appropriate with senior housing credits where word of adverse credit issues and financial stringency can spread through an elderly population quickly and can seriously compromise the ability of management to get the facility occupied. Adverse publicity can create a self-fulfilling prophecy, dissuading potential clients from reserving units which, in turn, will worsen financial performance. The activist analyst must consider meeting with both prospective and existing residents to assure them that their interests will not be compromised.

THE CONFERENCE CALL

It has become commonplace for underwriters of financings that begin to underperform to conduct frequent phone calls with the borrower and the bondholders. The purpose of the call is to go beyond the mere numbers and afford analysts the opportunity to ask questions concerning construction issues, marketing, occupancy, and detailed explanations for financial performance. While these are, at least theoretically, a good idea, the unfortunate downside is that long after a credit has improved, many of these calls continue as no one wants to be the party suggesting they be curtailed. As a practical matter, once a credit has been restored to a level of performance in which the covenant package can be met—at the most, a quarterly call probably makes the most sense.

COVENANT WAIVERS/CONSULTANTS

Prior to, or in lieu of, the formal retention of a consultant, it may be necessary for bondholders to waive the formal application of covenants. In projects that do not perform up to covenant levels, it is frequently permissible for bondholders to either retain a consultant or else waive the breach of a covenant. The hiring of a consultant is most likely to bear fruit where bondholders do not have a great deal of confidence in management. There is no really pleasant way to assure management that the retention of a consultant does not, in some measure, reflect lack of confidence in management's capabilities. In virtually all cases where an activist analyst agrees to waive a covenant, it is predicated on the borrower doing something to compensate for this waiver. Most frequently, it is increasing the frequency of disclosure reports and also adding information such as cash flow forecasts, which may not have been provided for in the original bond documents. Covenant waivers are also predicated on the borrower providing a detailed plan of remediation to correct the issues underlying their failure to perform as expected. Waivers are almost always for prior breaches of bond covenants. It is extremely rare to provide waivers on a going forward basis.

If it appears desirable to hire a consultant, the first step is to survey a list of consultants that specialize in that market segment. There are hospital consultants, senior living consultants, housing consultants, and the like. Further, some are more noted for their expertise in marketing and sales issues while others specialize in operational issues. It is rare to get unanimity among a group of high-yield municipal analysts—getting down to a list of three to propose to a borrower is generally the road taken. The borrower then interviews the candidates and selects their choice which begins a process that can take many months. Each month that the process continues until the consultant's report is issued, is foregone revenue. Despite this, there are at least three important reasons for hiring a consultant:

1. The consultant report represents a fresh pair of expert eyes and consultants will often locate corrective actions that will stabilize or improve a credit.
2. The consultant's report will unearth data and information that are helpful in the ultimate restructuring of a credit.
3. The use of a consultant can legitimize the need for a comprehensive restructuring to skeptical colleagues.

Over and above these reasons, the threat of hiring a consultant may force management to take firm action. It is important to emphasize that a consultant cannot reverse basic economics. If the problem is market rather than management, the consultant is less likely to prove helpful.

Before considering the use of more far-reaching rights and remedies, there are several important considerations that must be kept in mind. These include:

1. Is the fund the largest bondholder, the only bondholder, or is it a minority holder?
2. Is there a retail group of holders? How large are they and how can they be identified?
3. At what point will it make sense to contact counsel to advise the bondholder group? Which counsel and firm is most appropriate?
4. Is the largest bondholder's analyst someone I can work with and what experience have I had in prior situations with that person?
5. Are there subordinate holders or other classes of debt and what rights do they have?
6. Do the facts and circumstances presented suggest that a comprehensive restructuring is called for or will modifications lasting no more than two years (the legal limit before a restructuring is classified as a re-issuance) give the credit sufficient time to fiscally stabilize?
7. How fiscally stressed is the credit? How extensive does the corrective action need to be?
8. Will this produce a sustainable recovery?
9. In what specific ways are the interests of different classes of debt holders different?
10. What level of sacrifice can be expected of the vendors and which ones are "mission critical"?

PROJECT SALE TO EXTERNAL BUYER

Occasionally, underperforming projects in the high-yield market are sold to external buyers who may purchase either the underlying asset or just the bonds. This may not be the best approach, however. To begin with, there are a limited number of potential purchasers for projects that are in serious financial distress. Because these buyers are motivated to earn a return, they will likely not offer a level of compensation that makes a sale desirable relative to other options. If a group of holders exists, it may be extremely difficult to establish a price that will appeal to everyone or even a majority of the holders. It is also difficult to establish the value of an asset, particularly in cases where there is no free cash flow that can be discounted. A few projects only cover operations and some do not even cover that in full, although this is rare. In projects that have no discountable cash flow and no benchmark comparable sales, a sale price that can be justified to all stakeholders may prove illusory.

THE DEBT SERVICE RESERVE FUND

Among the most common, if often unpalatable, short term approaches, is to allow a borrower to dip into the *debt service reserve fund* (DSRF). These funds are typically capitalized from bond proceeds and set aside with the trustee. They are generally equal to the maximum amount of debt service in any future year and are designed to be used to cure transitory and relatively minor shortfalls in meeting debt service. They are also designed to be replenished as rapidly as possible. Another way of looking at the DSRF is as a "buyer of time" for the borrower during which more long lasting corrective actions can be taken. An activist analyst will generally not allow for the use of a DSRF unless a more comprehensive strategy is simultaneously used to deal with the underlying problem or unless the problem is clearly short term. One key feature of the DSRF is that, in the event counsel needs to be retained, it may prove to be the only source of funds with which to compensate the attorney and pay associated legal costs.

DELEVERAGING

The next logical step, if all else has failed, is deleveraging, that is reducing the load of debt service to a level that can be supported by the available cash flow. This may involve writing down principal or cutting the coupon, or both. While this may seem straightforward, the initial question is whether to make the deleveraging short term or permanent. Tax law permits a change in coupon for up to two years before considering the transaction a reissuance. Unfortunately, there is no particular science governing the degree of write-down. Even though benchmarks exist for most credit types in terms of what a project is worth and how much debt it can handle, each project is unique and has a different feel to it. One approach that is often used in a debt restructuring is called an A/B structure. In this approach, the A bond is the restructured security and the B bond receives any excess cash flow remaining. It is often the case that by the time there is any excess cash flow, the original financing has improved to the point at which it can be advance refunded. What an activist analyst wants to avoid is developing a short-term solution and then having to revisit it again within a short time period.

Prepackaged bankruptcies, or *prepacks* as they are known, allow both the borrower and creditors to know what the capital structure will look like postbankruptcy and also allow for the discharge or settlement of subordinate debt holders at a fraction of their holdings. They can take several months to accomplish and are often accompanied by exchange bonds—bonds which result in the complete restructuring of the borrower's capital structure.

From the foregoing it should be apparent that the activist analyst has two avenues of attack for credit problems. The first—use of consultants, watchful waiting and intense internal discussion within the community of analysts holding the credit—is oriented to fixing the underlying causes of underperformance or waiting until an issue corrects itself. The second general line of approach—the deleveraging of a project—does not necessarily do anything to resolve the underlying problem, unless it was an overleveraged project to begin with. It is a procrustean solution which fits debt service to the cash flow an impaired credit can sustain.

At the point at which a credit begins the process of being restructured, the activist analyst must, in concert with the portfolio manager and the firm's legal staff, decide when and whether to place the credit on its restricted list. This is crucial because, in the course of a restructuring, the analyst may come into possession of material, nonpublic information which could create a potentially unfair trading advantage based on asymmetrical access to information. The goal of the activist analyst is to make certain, that, to the greatest degree possible, information is made public at the earliest possible time.

While a restructuring is occurring, usually through the exchange of new bonds for the old bonds, the activist analyst should keep his portfolio manager, his legal staff, the pricing services and the Nationally Recognized Municipal Securities Information Repositories (NRMSIRs) informed. The activist analyst should also be in touch with the bond trustee, trustee counsel, and other institutional holders. Any restructuring depends on working cooperatively with the borrower and the achievement of a restructuring represents the culmination of intense negotiations to reconcile competing motivations. Restructurings and bankruptcies are extremely time consuming and often frustrating. Fortunately, they are also relatively rare occurrences when deal selection is done well.

The sine qua non for a restructuring is a highly skilled legal team, which includes both external counsel and in-house counsel. The legal issues surrounding restructurings and prepackaged bankruptcies are discussed in Chapter 9. The selection of counsel is based, not only on the firm's expertise, but on regional factors and compatible personalities.

CONCLUSION

In reality, there is no real breed of analyst one could call an *activist analyst*. To the extent a high-yield municipal analyst is merely doing his or her job, they are by definition an activist analyst.

CHAPTER 48

How to Analyze General Obligation Bonds

Sylvan G. Feldstein, Ph.D.
Director, Investment Department
Guardian Life Insurance Company of America

Terry J. Goode
Head of Tax Exempt Research
Wells Capital Management

In this chapter, the basic analytical issues are discussed in evaluating the credit quality of general obligation municipal bonds that are issued by states and local governments. General obligation bonds are secured by the pledge of the issuer's taxing powers (limited or unlimited). More commonly the general obligation bonds of local governments are paid from ad valorem property taxes and other local general revenues.

It should be noted that there is no universally accepted theory of general obligation bond credit analysis. To a considerable extent it remains more an art than a science. This requires individual judgment and personal interpretation of a range of important factors. The following provides some simple, clear guidelines for the bond analyst to consider when reviewing a *general obligation* (GO) *bond*.

Information relating to the analysis of GO bonds may be grouped into four categories. They are:

Terry Goode has coauthored this chapter for informational purposes only and it is not intended as an offer to sell or a solicitation of an offer to buy any security. The views expressed are based on the judgment and experience of the authors. It should not be assumed that the securities discussed or investments made in the future will be profitable or will equal the performance of those discussed in this commentary.

1. The issuer's debt structure and security for the GO bonds.
2. The issuer's budgetary operations.
3. The issuer's revenue structure.
4. The economy.

These four categories, with slight modifications, may be applied to the GO bonds issued by states, counties, school districts, towns, or cities.

After these four categories are covered, the more important debt ratios that are important in assessing credit risk are discussed. Additionally, it should be noted that at the writing of this chapter in the first half of 2007, the U.S. economy has enjoyed several good years of low interest rates, low unemployment, and high tax revenues on the state and low government levels. In terms of GO defaults of any significant size, there have been none. Consequently, some of the examples presented in this chapter to illustrate analytical principles were drawn from older time periods. Since municipal bonds in many cases have final maturities going out to 40 years from their issuance dates, it is possible that in the future some GO bonds will undergo significant credit stresses again. Therefore, learning the lessons of the past may be helpful in anticipating the credit problems of the future.

THE ISSUER'S DEBT STRUCTURE AND SECURITY FOR GENERAL OBLIGATION BONDS

The first question to ask in assessing the risk of a general obligation bond is: What is the total amount of GO debt outstanding? This figure should include all bonds and notes secured by the general taxing powers, limited and unlimited, of the issuer.

Several issuers have limited-tax GO bonds outstanding. These bonds are secured by the limited power of the issuer to raise taxes. For example, while King County, Washington, issues unlimited-tax GO bonds, it also issues limited-tax bonds. The limited-tax bonds, although they are general obligations, are secured only by the revenues generated by a property tax that cannot exceed $1.80 per $1,000 of assessed value in the county. Nonetheless, when calculating the issuer's true total GO debt, the limited-tax bonds and the unlimited ones, which are secured by the full taxing powers of the issuer, are initially combined. Information is also required on the GO debt trend for the previous five years.

These figures show whether or not the issuer has been using debt to an increasing degree, possibly during periods of local economic adversity and decline when capital improvements are not required. An increase in debt is not automatically negative, however, if one takes into consideration the impact of inflation and the genuine needs of the community. On the one hand, many growing suburban communities have shown rapid increases in debt as they financed the construction of water and sewer systems, new roads, and schools. On the other hand, some declining areas have turned in the past to GO debt as a way of financing budget deficits and priming the local economy. While determining the GO debt trend for five years, the issued GO notes must also be consistently reported. If the record of debt outstanding at the end of the issuer's fiscal year is used, the notes that were issued and redeemed during the course of the year could be overlooked. The analyst must determine the bonds outstanding at the year-end and must also indicate the notes sold during the course of the year.

Security for General Obligation Debt

The security behind the GO bonds sold by states, counties, school districts, and municipalities usually includes a pledge that the issuer will use its full taxing powers to see that the bondholder receives bond principal and interest when due. Under various state and local government constitutions and charters, providing such security usually involves the levy of unlimited taxes on property, a first claim by the bondholder to monies in the issuer's general fund, and the legal duty or pledge of the governing body to pass any legislation needed to increase revenues.

Double-Barreled Bonds

While most GO bonds are secured by only the general taxing powers of the issuer, and by whatever monies are available in the issuer's general fund, some bonds are also secured by earmarked revenues which flow outside the general fund. For example, the state of Illinois issues GO Transportation, Series A bonds. These bonds are general obligations of the state and are secured by the gasoline taxes in the state's road fund. Because, as a matter of actual practice, debt service is paid from monies in the road fund, the bonds are considered to have a double-barreled security. If all other factors are equal, bonds having a double-barreled security should be considered a stronger credit than the issuer's straight GO bonds.

Net General Obligation Debt

In order to determine the debt ratios, it is necessary to determine the amount of the issuer's GO bonds that is not double-barreled, or supported by earmarked revenues, by reviewing the accounting reports of the issuer. While certain funds outside the issuer's general fund may be used to pay debt service, the source of monies in the specific fund determine whether the bonds are operationally double-barreled or just straight GOs. For example, New York State has issued GO bonds for housing that are secured by monies in the state's housing fund. Although the annual debt service on these bonds is, indeed, paid out of the housing fund, the bonds are not genuinely self-supporting (or double-barreled). This peculiarity arises because most of the monies in the fund are appropriated by the state for grants to local governments; these monies are credited to the fund by the state comptroller for payments owed the fund by the local governments.

The net GO figure should include all those bonds that require monies from the general fund to pay debt service. The purpose of the figure is to show the amount of GO debt that the general unrestricted taxing powers of the issuer supports. Some analysts would deduct from this figure the amount of monies at year-end in any sinking funds or debt reserves. Since it is not always certain what these reserves are invested in, we would tend not to deduct these amounts from the debt figures.

Overlapping and Underlying Debt

Still another debt figure necessary for the analyst to determine is the total amount of GO debt for which the issuer's taxpayers are responsible. If the issuer is a municipality, the overlapping debt would include the GO debt of its county, school district(s), and special districts such as water and sewage authorities which have issued GO bonds secured by unlimited property taxes. In determining how much of a county's outstanding GO debt must be included in the municipality's overlapping debt, the analyst must determine the percentage of the full real estate property values of the municipality versus that of the county. That percentage represents the county's overlapping debt that pertains to the municipality's real property taxpayers. Similar approaches are used to determine the overlapping debt of school districts and special districts applicable to the municipality's taxpayers.

When the issuer is a county government, the same procedure is used to determine the applicable GO debt of other jurisdictions. Here, however, the debt is underlying debt and not overlapping debt, though the concept is the same. An analyst must be careful in determining what overlapping or underlying debt the taxpayer is indeed responsible for paying. For example, while Baltimore County, Maryland, physically surrounds the city of Baltimore, its jurisdiction stops at the city's borders. And the city is not legally considered to be within the county's jurisdiction. Therefore, taxpayers in the city of Baltimore are not responsible for the county's GO bonds, and the county taxpayers are not legally responsible for the city's GO bonds.

State Debt

Normally, when determining the overlapping or underlying debt of school districts, counties, or municipalities, the GO debt of their state is not considered. This is because states, unlike local governments, have broader revenue sources and potential powers under their constitutions to pay debt service on their GO bonds without reverting to property taxes, which are the major revenue sources of most local governments. Delaware is the one state that may be an exception. Because of the state's small size and because the state provides many of the services (such as highway and school construction) which in other states are provided by local governments, it may be prudent to use the Delaware state debt in determining the overlapping debt figure for the local units of government.

Special Debt

Besides the net GO debt and the overlapping or underlying GO debt, there are also four other debt obligations that many states, counties, and municipalities incur and which should be considered part of the issuer's debt load. They are outstanding leases, "moral obligation" commitments, unfunded pension liabilities, and postretirement benefits other than pensions.

Lease Debt

Many states and local governments have entered into leases or lease/purchase agreements for the construction of new buildings, highway repairs, and rentals for office space and data processing computers. The rental payments come from various sources, including general fund revenues, earmarked tax revenues, student tuition, patient fees, and amusement park fees. In some instances, such as lease/rentals of computer equipment, the leases are also secured by the equipment itself. Over the last 40-plus years, this borrowing instrument has become increasingly important, and most GO debt issuers have lease/rental debt outstanding. Since this debt usually has a legal claim to the general revenues of the issuer, analysts should include it in their overall debt figures as well.

Moral Obligation Debt

Many states have issued moral obligation municipal bonds. These bonds, structured as revenue bonds with one-year debt reserves, carry a potential state liability for making up deficiencies, should any occur, in their debt reserves. Under most state laws, if a drawdown of the reserve occurs, the bond trustee must report to the governor and state budget director the amount used. The state legislature in turn may appropriate the requested amount, though there is no legally enforceable obligation to do so. Bonds with this makeup provision are the so called *moral obligation bonds*.

Unfunded Pension Liabilities

Still another special debt figure that the analyst must develop is the current unfunded pension liability of the issuer: What is the difference between the expected assets of the public employee pension system at current annual contribution rates and the future benefits to be paid out to the issuer's employees? In assessing this figure, the analyst must determine when the pension system was last audited, who performed the audit, and what the auditor's assumptions were concerning (among other factors) the average age of public employee entry and retirement. The analyst should also determine whether the issuer has a plan in operation to reduce the unfunded liability and, if so, how long it will take (10, 20, or 50 years, for example) to eliminate the liability. Still another question to raise concerning pensions is their legal basis: Can pension benefits unilaterally be reduced by the local governments? Such reduction is allowed in some jurisdictions but not in others. An example of the latter would be New York State, where the state constitution prevents the reduction of pension benefits once they are granted to the public employees. Therefore, the unfunded pension liabilities of local governments in New York must be taken much more seriously than in states where such guarantees do not exist.

Postretirement Benefits Other Than Pensions

Another potential liability for the general obligation bond issuer that came into the forefront of concern in the early years of the twenty-first century involves the actuarially determined costs of providing health care for the governmental retirees. These are postemployment benefits. In many jurisdictions they are not legally mandatory and are paid on a pay-as-you-go basis. There are usually strong political constituencies such as public employee unions and the retirees themselves that support these postemployment health programs. Eliminating or cutting back on them can be politically very difficult. Additionally, they can be quite costly to the general obligation issuer. For most large issuers it is now required by the Governmental Accounting Standards Board (GASB) that after December 15, 2006 they be disclosed to the bondholders.

As an example of the potential size of this liability, in fiscal 2006, ending June 30, 2006, New York City reported its long-term retiree health care liabilities to be $53.5 billion. The city's long-term net general obligation debt outstanding on September 30, 2006 was approximately $35.2 billion.

For purposes of determining the special debt figure—which represents the potential liability in a worst-case environment—the lease obligations, the moral obligations, the unfunded pension liabilities and the retiree health costs could be shown combined and broken out.

Revenue Debt

Besides the general obligation, special lease, moral obligation, and pension liability, many governing bodies have also issued revenue bonds that are secured solely by the monies generated by the revenue-producing enterprises. Municipalities have issued water and sewer revenue bonds, and many states have issued toll road revenue bonds, most of which do not have a legal claim to the general taxing powers of the respective municipality or state. Nonetheless, the analyst should tabulate the issuer's outstanding revenue debt. Though this debt is not factored into the debt ratios, it is important to know the total borrowing activities of the issuer.

Future Bond Sales

While some GO issuers have small amounts of debt outstanding, they may be required to borrow significant amounts of money in the future. In order to factor this possibility into the credit assessment, the analyst must learn what the future financing plans are. As an example, a municipality that will have to issue large amounts of GO bonds to finance the construction of mandatory federal improvements for pollution control is of weaker quality than one that has already met the standards.

However, not all large-scale programs of capital construction are in themselves undesirable. Issuers that are borrowing heavily today to construct their physical infrastructures (such as new roads, schools, and water systems) may be better long-term investments than those issuers who have postponed making improvements and, as a result, have much less GO debt outstanding. The latter may very well face the prospect of extensive capital expenditures somewhere down the road in order to remain attractive for continued economic development and to meet the service demands of the taxpayers.

As an example, in the early 1960s, the GO bonds of Newark, New Jersey, and Parsippany-Troy Hills, New Jersey, were rated by Moody's as A and Baa, respectively. Newark was seen as a mature, developed community with little need for additional borrowing. In contrast, Parsippany Troy Hills, a growing, youthful suburban community, had relatively higher borrowing needs in order to finance new streets and schools. Thus at the time, Moody's considered Parsippany-Troy Hills to be a weaker credit than Newark. Yet as of September 2007, Moody's credit rating for Newark was Baa2 and the credit rating for Parsippany-Troy Hills was Aa3. The credit analyst must make a qualitative judgment on the future of the issuer 10 to 15 years later—no matter how difficult or speculative it is to do so, and regardless of how sizable the financing plans for current or future bonds appear to be.

Debt Limits

For many years, some credit analysts viewed debt limits as major safeguards for the bondholder. Those GO debt limits which are restricted by the need for electoral approvals before bonds can be sold are still meaningful checks on excessive borrowing. However, debt limits that are tied to percentages of the issuer's real estate wealth have become less significant as a result of New York City's experience in 1974–1975. In spite of state constitutional debt limits, the city had sold, over many years, amounts of GO bonds that were beyond its financial means and yet several billion dollars below its debt limits. The city's resulting fiscal crisis revealed the weakness of debt limits as a real safeguard for the bondholder.

THE ISSUER'S BUDGETARY OPERATIONS

The second general category of information required by the analyst is related to the budget. Here, we are concerned about questions of executive powers, budgetary control, public services, accounting history, and the potential impacts of taxpayer revolts.

Powers of the Chief Executives

Learning the form of government of the GO bond issuer is very important to the analyst. Governments that have strong executive systems (i.e., strong governors, strong county executives, or strong mayors) are, in general, preferred to those that do not, because strong, centralized executive systems have the potential to deal quickly and efficiently with unforeseen budgetary and economic problems. Perhaps the importance of this is best seen in the city of Cleveland. In 1978, Cleveland had a weak chief executive with very little power beyond his access to the press. His limitations included the need for electoral approval for increasing property and personal income taxes that were above the state allowed levels; no control over many of the city's essential services; limited appointment and removal powers; and a term of office which at the time was only two years, so that he had to consistently focus on reelection strategies rather than policy directives. As a result of these limitations and the city's overall economic and political problems, the city defaulted in 1978 on its GO notes.

In the 1970s, the cities of Detroit, Baltimore, Newark, and Boston all had similar economic problems. In the cases of Newark and Detroit, the economic problems were far more serious than those of Cleveland. But all of these cities managed to avoid defaults. One possible reason why these cities have managed their problems is that they have strong executive forms of government, whereas Cleveland did not.

There are three basic components of a strong executive, regardless of whether the chief executive is a governor, county executive, or mayor. First, the chief executive must have at least a four-year term of office with the right to seek reelection without limit. Second, the chief executive must control three aspects of the annual budgetary process: (1) the preparation of the budget, which is presented to the legislative body for approval; (2) line-item veto powers over the approved budget; and (3) control over the implementation of the budget, including the power to determine allotment periods, to fill personnel lines, and to award contracts. The third component is the ability to control the bureaucracy through extensive personnel appointment and removal authority.

Services Directly Provided

In order to project future budgetary demands, it is necessary to determine the services that are provided by the issuer. In general, issuers that provide a full range of services have a weaker credit quality than those that provide only basic minimum services. For a municipality, basic services include utilities (such as water and sewage treatment), garbage pickups, street maintenance, police and fire protection, and recreational programs. Large municipalities that provide additional services—including extensive welfare programs, hospital care, housing, mass transportation, and higher education—usually have bureaus and departments that are captives of pressure groups that demand these services without regard to budgetary consequences.

General Budget Appropriations by Function

While many issuers provide the same services, quantitative distinctions should be made in order to determine what the budgetary priorities of the issuer really are. This is best done by determining the general budget appropriations in the current fiscal year by function, amount, and percentage of the total budget appropriation.

Accounting Procedures and Funds

The most desirable accounting system is known as a *modified accrual system.* Generally, in this system, revenues are only considered received when they are physically in the issuer's general fund. At the same time, expenditures are deemed to have occurred when contracts and other legal liabilities are entered into by the issuer, even though warrants for payment of these obligations may not have been made yet. The modified accrual system is the most honest and fiscally conservative accounting system. Many issuers, however, prefer other accounting systems that allow their governing bodies to have greater flexibility in the budgetary process. For example, for issuers who define revenues to include monies that are due but not necessarily received, a budget can quickly be balanced: The governing body levies a new tax or increases projected revenues from existing taxes and then adds the new amount to the revenue side of the budget. On the expenditure side, those issuers that use "cash expenditure accounting" can easily close their fiscal year with a budget surplus by just delaying actual payments until after the new fiscal year has begun.

Audit Procedures

Auditing is yet another important area of concern for the investor and bond analyst. The best auditing procedure is for the issuer to be audited annually by an outside *certified public accountant* (CPA) who applies generally accepted accounting principles, using the modified accrual system of accounting. For sound cost-related reasons, however, many issuers (states, in particular) do not have such audits performed. If no audit by an outside CPA is commissioned, the next best safeguard for the bondholder is to have the issuer's accounts annually audited by a public official who is politically independent of the chief executive. Many states and municipalities have treasurers and comptrollers who are also elected public officials or appointees of the legislative branch. The institutional rivalry and competition between these elected public officials can provide checks and balances in the accounting areas.

Budget Trends

In order to determine the overall budgetary soundness of the issuer, it is necessary for the analyst to determine the revenues and expenditures of the issuer's general fund and all operating funds for at least a three-year period. This examination will show whether the issuer has balanced budgets, budget surpluses, or budget deficits. Clearly, those communities that have yearly budget deficits are serious investment risks, regardless of how positive the other analytical variables may appear to be.

Still another related question to ask is: What was the cash fund balance in the issuer's general fund at the end of the most recent fiscal year? While some issuers may show budget deficits during the previous three-year period, the deficits may be planned in order to reduce a fund balance surplus. Surpluses should accumulate in state governments that have elastic revenue structures made up of income and sales taxes. During expansions in the local economies or during inflationary periods, these revenues will greatly increase. Prudent states should build substantial, though not particularly excessive budget surpluses during such periods. They can then draw upon these surpluses either to meet revenue shortfalls caused by recessions or to meet increased wage and salary demands caused by inflation. Unfortunately, because of tax revolts, many states in the early 1980s—California, Oregon, and Washington, among others have returned their state surpluses to their taxpayers. During recessionary periods these states have experienced severe budgetary stresses.

Short-Term Debt as a Percentage of the General Fund Receipts of the Prior Year

In order to determine how well the issuer matches revenue flows to expenditure flows, it is necessary to determine the percentage of short-term debt in relation to the issuer's general fund revenues of the prior year. The short-term debt does not include the issuer's *bond anticipation notes* (BANs), but does include both *tax anticipation notes* (TANs) and *revenue anticipation notes* (RANs). When committed to policies that require them to borrow large amounts of money to meet expenditure schedules, such issuers are clearly less attractive than issuers that have coordinated expenditure flow with revenue flow so as to minimize the need for issuing annual short-term debt. Of course, it should be noted that some issuers borrow short-term in order to generate additional General Fund revenues through arbitrage. That is, the interest rate on the note proceeds that are invested in U.S. bills is greater than the interest rate that must be paid to the GO note holders.

Budgets and Taxpayer Revolts

In looking at budget trends, the analyst must also assess the potential impacts of newly enacted or anticipated budget and tax limitation measures. Examples of these include (1) the 5% cap laws in New Jersey, which since 1976 have limited the annual budget increases of the local governments to not more than 5%; and (2) Proposition 13 in California, which significantly restricted local property tax revenue growth, the issuance of new GO bonds, and other functions. While each measure must be carefully reviewed, it can be said in general that taxpayer attempts to reduce taxes and government expenditures on the local levels in the long run have positive benefits for GO bonds. At the same time, these measures may have negative consequences for the overlapping GO bonds of the state governments. On the local level, such restrictions on budget expenditures and tax collections can result in reductions in some municipal services; these restrictions can also provide governing bodies and budget directors with the legal weapons and supportive political climates for resisting constituent demands for increased services and for bargaining with their organized local public employees (i.e., with the unions representing firefighters, police, schoolteachers, etc.) In the last 40 years, the militancy of these unions has been very costly. Since approximately two thirds of the annual expenditures by local governments are for salaries, pensions, and related purposes, curbs in these areas can be very beneficial in slowing down the escalating costs of local governments.

While the political activities and effectiveness of public employee unions and other pressure groups have lessened at the local government level, they may be correspondingly increased at the state government level. This pressure results from their attempts to have the states provide increased state aid to local governments or to have the state governments begin to finance and operate public programs that were originally the responsibility of the local governments. An example of this development occurred in California. After the enactment of Proposition 13 in 1978 and as a result of increased political pressures, the funds that the state raised were used to replace the funds that localities were no longer permitted to raise under the Proposition 13 property tax increase restrictions. One result was that the percentage of certain local government budgets financed by local revenues decreased at the expense of the state's own budget. From a long-term point of view a state's GO bonds should have expected to weaken in security as a result of this development, since its budgetary reserves will be expected to decline dramatically. This is what indeed occurred.

In 1978, when Proposition 13 was passed California's GO bond rating was Aaa by Moody's. Over the next 25 years in spite of a growing population and one of the most robust economies in the nation, the rating drifted downward hitting as low as Baa1 by Moody's in 2003 and being by March, 2007 at A1. The decline in the rating from its premier Aaa designation was because of budgetary strains that the state government easily handled prior to 1978.

When looking at both the GO bonds of the local governments and those of the states, credit analysts must determine both the direct and the indirect implications of specific tax and budget restrictions. This is important in order to determine in a budgetary sense who benefits from the specific restrictions, who is not affected, and who is hurt. Obviously, to answer these questions analysts must determine the relationships and interdependencies between pressure groups, such as public employee unions, and political parties and leaders. Credit analysts invite criticism by speculating on the political implications of proposed tax restrictions, particularly if they later are proved to be incorrect. They must nonetheless offer investors their opinions of the direct and indirect political effects of the proposals.

THE ISSUER'S REVENUE STRUCTURE

The third general category of information covers data relating to the nature of the issuer's specific types and the amounts of revenue.

Primary Revenues

The initial question is: What are the issuer's primary revenues? In general, states have the most diversified revenue sources, which can include personal income taxes, a variety of corporation and business taxes, real and personal property taxes, death and gift taxes, sales taxes, motor vehicle taxes, severance taxes, user fees, and federal grants-in-aid. The attractiveness of state bonds over those of counties, municipalities, and school districts is largely a result of the diversity of a state's revenue sources and a state's ability, under its own laws, to make its revenue base even broader.

The local governments, in contrast, rely primarily on property taxes for their revenues. Some counties and municipalities have broadened their revenue bases through sales and income taxes. Such diversification is usually very difficult for a local government unit to initiate, since state legislative approvals are normally required. Nevertheless, many cities in recent years have convinced their respective state legislatures to grant them taxing powers beyond the property tax.

General Fund Revenue Trends

Besides learning what the overall primary revenue sources are, the analyst should determine what the specific revenues have been in the issuer's general fund over a three-year period. This is the governmental fund account in which all unrestricted revenues that can be used for debt service are placed. The reason for going back three years is to identify trends that may be developing in the issuer's revenue flows.

In the case of issuers who pay debt service on their GO bonds from a debt service fund (which, for example, may receive property taxes that do not pass through the general fund), this fund should also be included. The reason for separating general fund revenues from the restricted ones is that many revenues received by issuers, such as certain federal grants, are restricted as to purpose and cannot be used for debt service on GO bonds. Since many local governments, such as school districts and municipalities, include restricted monies in their general fund reporting, the analyst will have to separate the unrestricted portion from the restricted portion.

For urban counties, school districts, and municipalities, real property taxes, state grants, and federal aid monies are the major sources of revenue. In many cities, state and federal monies have displaced the property tax as the major revenue source. In most suburban and rural areas, the property tax is the dominant source of revenue.

THE ECONOMY

The fourth major category of information required by the analyst concerns the overall economic health of the issuer. Indicators of economic activity and well-being include the trends of real estate valuation, population, unemployment, and total personal income.

While separately these economic indicators provide incomplete assessments of the economic vitality of the issuer, taken as a whole they provide clues as to the strengths and weaknesses of each community. Obtaining the data for the informational categories is easy, since data are available from either the local governments themselves or publications of the U.S. Department of Labor, or from business sources.

Real Estate Valuation Trend

A major index of the growth of a community is the yearly change in its real estate value. Here, analysts are not as interested in the assessed real values, which are used for tax purposes, as they are in the full, or market, values of the real estate. This would only include the taxable real property. Tracking these values over a five-year period provides a good measure of the health of the community and can indicate a declining or stagnant community. It is also important to keep in mind that in an inflationary environment, growth in real estate values is not enough to indicate that a community is becoming wealthier; the annual growth must be higher than the annual inflation rate.

Ten Largest Taxable Properties

In looking at counties, municipalities, and school districts, it is useful to identify the 10 largest taxable properties in terms of their full real values and business purposes. In so doing, the analyst can determine how much of the real estate base may be dependent on railroads, utilities, and private corporations. In the Northeast some of the largest real estate holdings belonged to the Penn Central Transportation Company, which for many years paid no real estate taxes on its properties. Additionally, certain communities may be dependent on one major shopping center or a durable goods manufacturing plant for most of their property taxes. The viability of that single property will determine the community's overall economic viability.

Properties: Taxable or Tax-Exempt?

When reviewing counties, municipalities, and school districts, it is necessary to learn what percentages of the total real estate wealth are exempt from local property taxes. Although a municipality can add new office buildings, hospitals, and governmental structures to its inner core, their contributions to the general real estate wealth of the community will be limited if they are tax-abated or tax-exempted. A corollary is to determine the distribution of the community's taxable property by purpose: What percentage is residential, commercial, industrial, held by a utility or railroad? From these figures the analyst can determine accurately which segments of the community's real estate are carrying the burden of the property taxes.

Building Permit Trend

In looking at counties, municipalities, and school districts, another component of economic vitality is the building permit trend. Here the analyst is looking for at least a five-year record of the annual total dollar value of all permits granted by the local governmental bodies for building and construction improvement. These figures are checked to make sure that building permits for tax-exempt properties are not included. One major value of this indicator is its ability to show the degree of business confidence in the future of the local economy.

Five Largest Employers

It is important to learn whom the five largest employers are in each county, municipality, or school district to be analyzed. The analyst should determine the number of workers as well as the nature of the business. In this way the analyst can determine how stable the community is and how dependent the local economy may be on one industry, such as the automobile industry in Michigan, coal mining in West Virginia, and textiles in South Carolina.

Population Trend

Another useful index for investigating states and local governments is the population trend. An increasing population usually means a growing economy, while a declining or stagnant population usually indicates economic weakness. Besides having the raw population figures, it is worthwhile to break down the population by age group and by income level. A community that has a high percentage of senior citizens may have greater political demands for municipal services and reduced property taxes than one that does not. Also, communities with large numbers of unemployed or low income residents usually require costly social services, and these services increase the budgets of the local schools, courts, welfare systems, and police departments.

Job Trend

Employment data are very necessary to the credit analyst. A 10-year comparison of the absolute number of employed people and their percentage of the population provides another clue as to the economic direction of the area. It is also helpful to determine the distribution of the nonfarm employment for at least the most recent year. The employment categories include manufacturing; retail wholesale trade; services; contract construction; and federal, state, and local government employment. This breakdown of employment according to type of job helps indicate, among other things, whether or not the economy is being supported by increased governmental jobs or by a vibrant private sector.

Unemployment Trend

It is helpful to compare local unemployment trends covering at least three years. It is useful to examine both the annual unemployment rate and the average number of workers unemployed during the year. For counties, municipalities, and school districts, the comparisons should focus on the unemployment rates within the boundaries of the local area, the state, and the nation. If the unit of local government is within a metropolitan area, it is also useful to include the unemployment rates of the metropolitan area.

Economic Activity Indicators for States

When reviewing the economies of states, there are five categories of information that are particularly useful:

1. Statewide personal income trend for the past three years.
2. Statewide retail sales trend for the past three years.
3. Statewide motor vehicle registration trend for the past three years.
4. Total number of people within a state who have received welfare for the past three years.
5. Per capita personal income today, compared with the figure five years ago and with the national per capita income figures.

The information gathered for these categories will quickly show, in absolute terms and when compared with other regions of the country, whether a state is becoming wealthier.

Economic Activity Indicators for Counties

When reviewing counties, municipalities, and school districts, the analyst will find that the following seven categories of information are useful:

1. Percentage of the population in the lower-income bracket.
2. Number of residents receiving welfare.
3. Per capita income, compared with the national average.
4. Median family income.
5. Median home value.
6. Percentage of owner-occupied housing.
7. Age distribution of the population.

The Negative Indicators

Perhaps the most critical short-term function of the credit analysis of GO bonds is to identify the negative trends suggesting potential problems in the fiscal stability of states and municipalities. There are four categories of negative trends:

1. Revenue-based indicators:
   a. Decreasing value of taxable property.
   b. Increasing delinquent taxes.
   c. Increasing tax rate.
   d. Decreasing number and value of building permits issued.
   e. Increasing incidence of actual revenues below budgeted amounts.
2. Expenditure-based indicators:
   a. Increasing excesses of expenditures over local revenues.
   b. Increasing expenditures in excess of total revenues.
   c. Increasing expenditures in excess of the inflation rate.

    d. Increasing incidence of actual expenditures in excess of the approved budget.

    e. Continuing increases in the amount of the unfunded portions of the pension programs.

  3. Cash management indicators:

    a. Reducing aggregate short-term investments.

    b. Increasing amounts of unpaid current obligations.

  4. Debt indicators:

    a. Increasing amounts of bonded indebtedness while the property values remain stagnant.

    b. Increasing need to borrow in order to meet debt service requirements.

    c. Use of long-term debt to fund operation expenditures.

    d. Year-to-year increases in the amount of short-term borrowing remaining unpaid at the end of the fiscal year.

These are general signals which indicate the potential decline in the ability of a municipality to perform its functions within fiscally sound parameters.

THE MORE IMPORTANT DEBT RATIOS

In addition to looking for possible early warning signals, the analyst should develop debt-related ratios. The value of the ratios is twofold: (1) The ratios are among the analytical tools for evaluating the credit worthiness of the issuer's GO bonds; and (2) The per capita data allow the analyst to compare bonds of different communities.

Net GO Debt Per Capita

This figure represents the nonself-supporting GO bonds divided by the population. In theory, it represents the amount of debt per person that is supported by the general taxing powers of the issuer in the issuer's general fund. In general, the lower the number, the more attractive the issuer.

Net GO and Overlapping or Underlying Debt per Capita

This ratio applies not to states but to the local units of government. It is a per capita debt figure that includes the issuer's own net GO debt as well as the GO debt of overlapping or underlying jurisdictions.

Net GO Debt as a Percentage of Full Real Estate Valuation

This percentage indicates the debt as compared with the real estate wealth as represented in the most recent real estate evaluation. This statistic is perhaps one of the most important figures for the credit analyst, since it indicates the issuer's ability to pay.

Net GO and Overlapping or Underlying Debt as a Percentage of Full Real Estate Valuation

This figure is also used for counties, municipalities, and school districts. It represents the relationship of the issuer's full real estate value to the sum of the issuer's own GO and overlapping GO debt.

Net GO Debt as a Percentage of Personal Income

For a state this figure is another major indicator of the ability of the taxpayer to support its debt. While this figure is desirable when reviewing all GO bond issuers, such data are often only available concerning states.

GO Debt Payout in 10 Years

This figure shows whether the issuer has a relatively rapid and level debt retirement schedule, which is desirable, or debt service stretched out to, say, 30 or 40 years. In some cases, payment of debt service on bonds may continue beyond the useful life of the capital projects financed by the original bond proceeds. While the debt payout schedule is not a debt ratio, it is necessary for evaluating the actual ratio figures. For example, high debt ratios may be less significant if most of the issuer's debt will be retired within 10 years. But above-average debt ratios combined with a slow debt retirement schedule certainly weakens a security substantially.

CONCLUSION

The analyst can make a generalization about the investment quality of the bond under review (1) after having determined whether the GO bonds are double-barreled or not (and if so, what the quality of the specific revenue stream is); (2) after having gathered the information about the issuer's debt structure, budget, revenue operations, and economic forces; and (3) after having checked for the negative indicators. While all these elements together are important indicators of bond quality, each provides, if taken separately, only a single isolated element not in itself sufficient for full-scale analysis. Therefore, the analyst must carefully review all these indicators so as to arrive at a judicious credit conclusion concerning the degree of risk involved in purchasing an issuer's GO bonds. As noted earlier in this chapter, this evaluation process is more an art than a science. Nonetheless, we have attempted here to identify the basic background information that is required for making an overall credit assessment.

CHAPTER 49

General Analytical Framework for Assessing the Credit Worthiness of Revenue Bonds

Sylvan G. Feldstein, Ph.D.
Director, Investment Department
Guardian Life Insurance Company of America

Revenue bonds are issued for project or enterprise financings that are secured by the revenues generated by the completed projects themselves, or for general public purpose financings in which the issuers pledge to the bondholders tax and revenue resources that were previously part of the general fund. This latter type of revenue bond, sometimes known as a *dedicated tax bond*, is usually created to allow issuers to raise debt outside general obligation debt limits and without voter approvals.

The trust indenture and legal opinion for both types of revenue bonds should provide the investor with legal comfort in six bond security areas:

- The limits of the basic security
- The flow-of-funds structure
- The rate, user charge, or dedicated revenue and tax covenants
- The priority of pledged revenue claims
- The additional bonds test
- Other relevant covenants and issues

This chapter provides the general analytical framework for determining the credit worthiness of revenue bonds by looking at these six areas. The chapters to follow in this book provide the specific characteristics and features of revenue bonds secured by the different economic and dedicated funding sources such as toll road fees, tobacco taxes, airport charges, student loan repayments, mortgage repayments, and the like.

LIMITS OF THE BASIC SECURITY

The legal documents should explain what the pledged revenues for the bonds are and how they may be limited, by federal, state, and local laws. The importance of this is that although most revenue bonds are structured and appear to be supported by identifiable revenue streams, those revenues sometimes can be negatively affected directly by other levels of government. For example, the state of Wyoming in the early 1980s sold a bond issue known as Mineral Royalties Revenue Bonds. On the surface, the bond issue had all the attributes of a revenue bond. The bonds had a first lien on the pledged revenues, and additional bonds could only be issued if a coverage test of 125% was met. Yet the revenues to pay the bondholders were to be received by the state from the federal government as royalty payments for mineral production on federal lands. There was no legal obligation by the U.S. Congress and President to continue this aid program. Therefore, the investor must read carefully the legal opinion as summarized in the official statement to learn if there are shortcomings of the bond security.

FLOW-OF-FUNDS STRUCTURE

The legal documents should explain what the bond issuer has promised to do concerning the pledged revenues received. What is the order of the revenue flows through the various accounting funds of the issuer to pay for the operating expenses of the facility, payments to the bondholders, maintenance and special capital expenditures (known as *cap ex*) and debt-service reserves? This sometimes is referred to as the *waterfall*. Additionally, the legal documents should indicate what happens to excess revenues after they pass through the waterfall. Do they go to the issuer's general fund or do they stay within the indenture to be used to call bonds, or make capital repairs, and the like.

The flow of funds of many revenue bonds is structured as *net revenues* (i.e., debt service is paid immediately after basic operating and maintenance funds, but before paying all other expenses). A *gross revenues* flow-of-funds structure is one where the debt service is paid even before the operating expenses of the enterprise are paid. Examples of gross revenue bonds are those issued by the New York State Metropolitan Transportation Authority. However, although it is true that these bonds legally have a claim to farebox revenues before all other claimants, it is doubtful that the mass transit system could function if the operational expenses, such as wages and electricity bills, were not paid first. Also, many hospital bonds have a *gross revenue pledge* as well. Again, it is difficult to see hospitals closing down vital life and death operations to pay bondholders. The existence of the pledge though does provide the bondholders possibly with some legal leverage in dealing with the hospital in work-out situations.

RATE, USER-CHARGE OR DEDICATED REVENUE AND TAX COVENANTS

The legal documents should indicate what the bond issuer has legally committed itself to do to safeguard the revenues pledged to the bondholders. If user rates are involved, do they only have to be sufficient to meet expenses, including debt service, known as one times debt service coverage. Is the one times coverage test calculated for the *average annual debt service* requirement or for the higher *maximum annual debt service* one? Additionally, is the coverage requirement for higher amounts such as 1.1 times or 1.25 times so as to provide for reserves? The legal documents should indicate whether or not the issuer has the legal power to increase rates or charges of users without having to obtain prior approvals by other governmental units.

THE PRIORITY OF PLEDGED REVENUE CLAIMS

The legal opinion should state whether or not other levels of government or claimants can legally access the revenues of the issuer even before they begin the process through the issuer's flow-of-funds structure. The highway revenue bonds issued by the Puerto Rico Highway Authority are an example. The bond security in part comes from the moneys collected through the Commonwealth of Puerto Rico gasoline tax. Yet, if in a worst case scenario no other funds are available to pay their debt service, under the Commonwealth's constitution the moneys are first to be applied to the Commonwealth's own general obligation bonds.

THE ADDITIONAL BONDS TEST

The legal documents should discuss under what circumstances the issuer can sell more bonds that share equal claims to the issuer's pledged revenues. Usually, the legal requirement is that the maximum annual debt service on the combined new and old bonds be covered at a specified minimum amount by the projected net pledged revenues. This can be as low as one times coverage of annual debt service. Some revenue bonds have stronger additional bonds tests to protect the existing bondholders from credit dilution. Also, how the historical revenues are calculated in making this test is important. Can the issuer select specific prior months to be used such as 12 out of the last 15 months? Who determines the projection numbers for the future revenues. Is it an independent consultant with expertise in the area? How conservative are the projections and how are they certified? Additionally, the definition of revenues is important. Does it include revenues generated by the enterprise or could it also include special supplemental payments. These are all questions that have to be addressed by the analyst in reviewing the additional-bonds test formula.

OTHER RELEVANT COVENANTS AND ISSUES

Lastly, the legal documents should indicate whether there are other relevant covenants for the bondholder's protection. These usually include pledges by the issuer to insure the project (if it is a project financing revenue bond) to have the financial accounts annually audited by an outside certified public accountant and to provide a timely report to investors as well as to employ independent engineers to annually review the capital plant and make mandatory recommendations to keep the facility operating for the life of the bonds.

In addition, two other developments over the past 20 years make it more important than ever to carefully review the legal documents and opinions summarized in the official statements and assess the people who wrote them. The first development involves the mushrooming of new financing approaches that may rest on legally untested security structures and tax opinions.

The second development is the increased use of legal opinions provided by attorneys who may have little prior experience in these areas. Previously, legal opinions were written by a relatively small number of experienced municipal bond attorneys. As a result of the numerous bond defaults and related shoddy legal opinions in the nineteenth century, the investment community, headed by the large commercial banks who bought municipal bonds, demanded that legal documents and opinions be drafted and written by people they recognized as experienced municipal bond attorneys. For 100 years or so a relative handful of municipal bond attorneys provided these opinions. This discipline began to be eroded significantly in the last decade of the twentieth century. By 2008, there were thousands of attorneys located throughout the country who present themselves as being experts in this area of the law and provide various security structure and tax opinions. Sorting out quality distinctions in their work and who is well grounded in public finance law and who is not is difficult.

CHAPTER 50

How to Analyze
Airport Revenue Bonds

William E. Oliver
Senior Vice President
Director, Municipal Research
AllianceBernstein

Daryl Clements
Senior Portfolio Manager
AllianceBernstein

Airport revenue bonds have generally been regarded as one of the more stable and secure revenue bond types, due to the essential role that most major airports play in the nation's air transportation system. Airports are generally operated by municipal governments or public authorities and possess significant flexibility in setting rates and charges at an adequate level to meet all bondholder covenant requirements. They often face limited direct competition within their metropolitan region or have a strong enough economic base to support multiple airports within the same region. In recent years, however, airport operators have faced unprecedented challenges from a variety of sources, including airline bankruptcies, the changing structure of airline routing, the threat of international terrorism, the spreading of contagious diseases around the globe, rising fuel costs and increasing volatility in travel caused by economic fluctuations. While most airport managements have found a way to cope with these difficult challenges, the complacency with which investors once viewed this sector is gone forever.

AIRPORT OWNERSHIP STRUCTURES

Most public airports in the United States and Canada are owned and operated either directly by municipal governments or by local or regional public authorities. This is in contrast to airports in Europe and Australia which are becoming increasingly owned and operated by the private sector. While there has been much discussion of the privatization of airports in the United States, there are significant constraints set forth by the Federal Aviation Administration under current law that limits the operation of airports by private entities. Municipal governments are strongly committed to maintaining control over these facilities and have a strong history of financing these facilities at lower capital costs through the issuance of tax-exempt bonds.

PASSENGER DEMAND CHARACTERISTICS

A key credit factor in analyzing airport revenue bonds is the strength of the service area, particularly for airports that are highly dependent on *origin-destination* (O&D) traffic. Here, the factors used in analyzing general obligation bonds are applicable, focusing on the strength of the regional economy, its diversity of employment, population growth and wealth levels. The broader and wealthier the service area and economic base is, the stronger passenger demand is likely to be over the long-term. Conversely, for economies that are smaller and more dependent on a few dominant employers, passenger demand will be subject to greater volatility. The mix of leisure and business travel is also important, with leisure travel being somewhat more discretionary, making it more susceptible to macroeconomic changes in the economy or changing attitudes toward air travel. Following the terrorist attacks in the United States of September 11, 2001 (9/11), air travel around the world suffered significant declines for a period of up to two years.

The Greater Toronto Airports Authority (GTAA) is a good example of a strong O&D airport that overcame unprecedented challenges over the last decade. GTAA was created as independent authority in 1996 with exclusive jurisdiction over a 75 kilometer service area surrounding Greater Toronto. Its first challenge was to embark upon a C$4.4 billion airport improvement plan, funded primarily in the international bond markets. GTAA was authorized to fully recover all costs, including debt service, from all of its airline operators. From the development of the plan in 1998 to the opening of the first phase of the new terminal in 2004, GTAA was forced to cope with the aftereffects of the 9/11 terrorist attacks in the United States, the SARS epidemic and the bankruptcy of Air Canada, which accounted for roughly two-thirds of passenger traffic. Despite these obstacles, GTAA continued its major construction projects and increased landing fees and charges to the airlines as originally planned. Due to strong management actions, a monopoly position within the region, and the ability to fully recover its costs from the airlines, GTAA was able to successfully meet all of its operational and financial challenges during this period.

The other type of air traffic is connecting traffic through hub airports. Some large airports, such as Chicago and Dallas Ft. Worth, have strong O&D traffic while also serving as primary hubs for east-west traffic across the country. These hubs enjoy an entrenched role in the national transportation system, based on their geographic location. Regional hubs, such as Atlanta and Denver that serve as dominant connecting points for travel in their respective regions are sometimes referred to as *fortress hubs*. There are many other hubs that serve the needs of a dominant carrier in a particular airport and do not enjoy a strategic advantage for serving a region. As long as the dominant carrier is financially sound, passenger demand will be stable at these airports. However, when a dominant airline, such as TWA in St. Louis or USAir in Pittsburgh goes bankrupt, passenger demand can fall precipitously as flights through the airport are greatly curtailed (see the Pittsburgh example below). Airline travel patterns are also shifting with the advent of smaller regional jets and regional carriers that now allow many smaller cities to be served directly from other parts of the country.

Pittsburgh International Airport (PIT) is a good example of an airport that was forced to adapt to the realities of the airline business when its dominant carrier declared bankruptcy in 2003 for the second time in as many years. In 2001, PIT was dominated by USAir, which held an 87% market share of the airport's 9.9 million enplanements. Hub traffic accounted for 59% of enplanements with O&D traffic the remaining 41%. By the time USAir filed for bankruptcy the second time, enplanements at the airport declined 28% to 7.1 million. Despite the steep decline in traffic, debt service coverage was still a respectable 1.4x. This was primarily due to a residual use and lease agreement that allowed the airport to charge the remaining signatory airlines for all amount necessary to cover both operating and debt service costs.

Following the second bankruptcy filing of USAir, the airport needed to increase its competitiveness as it made the transition from a hub to an O&D airport. PIT sought to lower the operating costs for all signatory airlines by appealing to the state for $150 million in funding and to reduce debt service costs by allocating $15 million of *passenger facility charge* (PFC) revenues for that purpose. By 2006, US Airways, the airline formed out of the merger of USAir and AmericaWest, had reduced traffic significantly at PIT, shifting many of its connections to Philadelphia and Charlotte. Enplanements in 2006 fell to 4.9 million, roughly half of the number of enplanements recorded in 2001. US Airways market share had fallen to slightly below 50%, with many of the existing carriers, as well as some new entrants to PIT, making up the remainder. O&D traffic in 2006 accounted for 84% of enplanements, with hub traffic comprising only 16%. The airport's transition plan is now beginning to show signs of success in 2007 as the airport is attracting greater competition which has resulted in significantly lower fares. Due to the use of residual use and lease agreements with the signatory airlines, debt service coverage in 2005 remained virtually unchanged at 1.38×.

COMPETITION

Competition between airports has historically not been a major credit factor due to the dominant role that most airports play within their service areas. Barriers to entry are extremely high and plans to build new airports are increasing subject to a costly and lengthy environmental approval process. Some airports located near major metropolitan areas have been successful in attracting discount carriers that seek to operate more efficiently in less congested airports. These carriers are more attractive to leisure travelers, but have not significantly reduced demand at the major airports for business travelers or those requiring connections to smaller destinations. Even when airports, such as Denver International Airport and Greater Toronto Airport, completed major construction projects, the higher costs for airlines and passengers did not significantly alter passenger demand.

USE AND LEASE AGREEMENTS

The underlying foundation for a general airport revenue bond is the Use and Lease Agreement between the airport and its airline carriers. This agreement establishes the level of revenue that the airport requires to meet its operating and debt service costs. It also sets forth the rate setting formula and procedures through which the revenues are paid by the airlines. Historically, airports felt the need for longer term leases in order to provide stability. In recent years, however, the trend has been toward shorter lease terms, often ranging from 30 days up to five years. This affords both the airport operators and airlines greater flexibility in a highly competitive and rapidly changing business environment. There are two basic rate setting structures underpinning Use and Lease Agreements, although these approaches have become blurred over time. The first is the compensatory approach that charges airlines rent for terminal and airfield usage and a proportionate share of common costs for the airport. Nonairline revenues such as parking, rental car concession fees and retail rents are designed to make up any shortfalls from the airline payments. Under a compensatory approach the airport takes on the risk of running the airport without the backstop of the airlines. The airport generally has a greater amount of control and typically does not share revenues with the airlines. This approach often encourages the airport to become more entrepreneurial in developing its nonairline revenues and can add significantly to the airport's revenues. Credit quality is enhanced by a diversified revenue base that relies on a combination of airline fees and charges, passenger facility charges and concession income from retail, parking, and rental car concessions.

The alternative approach is the residual approach which ensures that the airline will operate on a cost recovery or break-even basis. This is the system used in the previous examples of Greater Toronto and Pittsburgh International Airports. Under this approach, once the airport deducts all non-airline revenues from its operating expenses, the airlines are responsible to pay the residual amount. This amount forms the basis for setting airline rates and charges. The charges are allocated to each airline on a pro rata basis for its share of the operating and capital expenditures made by the airport during the previous year. This approach provides the airport with much greater flexibility in dealing with many of the unforeseen events that affect demand for air travel mentioned above. Under this approach, the airport generally does not feel the direct impact of the bankruptcy of a major airline tenant as all of the costs are reallocated among all of the remaining airlines. It also ensures that adequate funding will be provided over the life of a long-term capital expenditure program, regardless of the fiscal condition of the participating airlines in any given year. Credit quality tends to be stable, offering little upside potential for ratings upgrades.

Mature airports generally have compensatory agreements, while newer airports, which are extremely costly ventures, have residual agreement since the need for airline involvement is greater. Some airports are now utilizing a hybrid approach that will calculate airline rates and charges under a compensatory method while allowing for some form of revenue sharing between the airport and airlines. All approaches have afforded sufficient flexibility for airport operations during the recent period of volatility. The best approach for an individual airport really depends on the ability of the airport to generate nonairline revenue from its concession businesses.

GATE CONTROL

A key operational factor for any airport is the extent to which they have control over the use of the gates at their terminals. There are three different types of structures for airport leases. The most restrictive is *exclusive control*, where airlines are given total control over the use of certain gates at the airport and maintain the ability in bankruptcy to retain control by affirming the lease in bankruptcy court. This approach was generally used to entice a major airline to play a dominant role in an airport's operation. The second approach is *preferential*, under which the airports have the right to require an airline to either share certain gates or give them back to the airport for reassignment if minimum levels of activity are not maintained. The third approach is *common gate control*, whereby the airport controls all of the gates and has the flexibility to moves airlines between gates to meet shifting travel demand and scheduling patterns. With the plethora of airline bankruptcies in recent years, airports are moving more toward the preferential and common gate approaches to increase their flexibility to better serve passenger demand.

AIRPORT MANAGEMENT

The role of management has become more critical in recent years as airport operators face new challenges from airline bankruptcies to terrorism threats. This is evidenced in the measures taken by management in the examples of Pittsburgh and Toronto cited earlier as well as in the case study of Aruba Airport that appears in the Case Studies section of this book. Airport operators have responded in a number of ways: by increasing utilization of their facilities, developing nonairline revenue businesses, reducing costs and deferring less essential capital projects. They have also become more sensitive to the costs incurred by airlines, especially in planning airport expansions. They have become more proactive in increasing security and responding to the threat of infectious diseases. Overall, they have responded well to these challenges and have been able to maintain financial stability in a difficult operating environment.

CONCLUSION

General airport revenue bonds have proven remarkably resilient during the most recent period of high stress. Despite significant declines in passenger traffic related to the post-9/11 trauma, and a large number of major airline bankruptcies, airports were able to survive this period and are now returning to greater financial health as air traffic levels return to pre-2001 levels. Airport managers responded with a variety of approaches that have increased their flexibility in meeting new challenges. The stability provided by their strong competitive positions and the ability, in many cases, to allocate higher costs among their airline tenants, allowed most airports to meet all of their financial requirements. Ratings, for the most part, were not negatively affected by all the turmoil faced by airports during this period. Given the strong credit fundamentals of the sector and the increasing control over airport operations, airport revenue bonds are expected to continue to be stable investments in the future.

CHAPTER 51

Land-Secured Bonds

Ronald L. Mintz, CFA
Principal
The Vanguard Group

L and-secured bonds—sometimes known as *dirt deals*—finance the public infrastructure costs related to new development, including residential, commercial, industrial, and mixed-use projects. The vast majority of land-secured bonds are, at initial issuance, nonrated. They are generally part of the high-yield portion of the tax-exempt bond market and, within that, they are a part of the real estate segment. This segment also includes tax incre-ment bonds, multifamily housing revenue bonds, mobile home park revenue bonds, and other types of transactions. This chapter focuses solely on land-secured bonds and emphasizes an investor's viewpoint of these credits.

ADVANTAGES OF LAND-SECURED BONDS

From the investor's perspective, the advantage of land-secured bonds com-pared with other high-yield issues is that, if the development proceeds as planned, their credit quality tends to improve relatively quickly. Depending on the size of the underlying development project, these bonds can poten-tially move from noninvestment-grade status to a lower investment-grade position when a critical mass of development and a variety of taxpayers are in place. Even if the size or other characteristics of the project are such that

The views expressed herein are those of the author and not necessarily those of The Vanguard Group, Inc. The author gratefully acknowledges the support of the following individuals who responded to questions, provided clarification and data, and helped edit this chapter: Warren Bloom, Ed Delk, Steve Heaney, Michael Hernan, Noah Hugenberger, Mary Lowe Kennedy, Ruth Levine, Dean Lewallen, Peter Raphael, Brett Sealy, Emily Silva, Reid Smith, Craig Stock, and Matthew Walker.

the bonds will not qualify for investment-grade status, there still may be significant credit appreciation as the project reaches build-out. This possibility of appreciation differentiates land-secured bonds from many other high-yield tax-exempt securities. As credit appreciation takes place, depending on the underlying project variables, there is potential for a refunding—as a higher-quality nonrated transaction; as a rated transaction; as an insured transaction; or as a structured senior-subordinate transaction. Such a refunding will, depending on the call features and other variables, provide price appreciation for the investor on the original bond holdings.

As one would expect, land-secured bonds provide the investor with a yield spread to investment-grade bonds. The magnitude of the spread changes with market conditions, but there is compensation—albeit at varying amounts—for the extra risks that these bonds entail and for the credit analysis that they require. Among these risks is the development risk associated with the project; development is, of course, crucial if the credit quality of the bond is to improve. Over time, an investor can build a diversified portfolio of land-secured bonds with different geographic locations, different developers or builders, different development types, and different market focus areas. However, each individual land-secured holding in a portfolio is inherently concentrated.

From the developer's perspective, land-secured bonds are advantageous because the developer either prepays the bond obligation from sales proceeds or passes it through to the next property owners or the end-users. The developer is able to borrow these funds at a tax-exempt rate that should be below the equivalent bank or other taxable rate, even when the costs of issuance and the burden of the debt-service reserve fund are figured in. Another plus: this financing method allows development to "pay its own way," because the direct beneficiaries—developers and future homeowners or end-users—fund the costs of public improvements related to the development. The latter idea tends to have strong political capital.

GENERAL CHARACTERISTICS OF LAND-SECURED BONDS

Purpose of Land-Secured Bonds

The proceeds of land-secured bonds are used to finance the public infrastructure costs associated with new development. Eligible facilities vary from state to state, but can include roads, sidewalks, gutters, landscaping, water facilities, sewer facilities, storm drains, parks, libraries, public safety facilities, schools, and more. Although tax-exempt bonds cannot be used to fund the private costs of development, federal tax law does permit developers and municipalities to take advantage of the relatively lower cost of financing in the municipal markets for these types of public infrastructure facilities.

Development Types

Land-secured bonds can finance residential, commercial, and industrial development. Residential developments tend to be all single-family or a mix of single-family and multifamily, with the latter typically divided among rental and for-sale units. Commercial and industrial developments include retail facilities, office buildings, and industrial uses (mostly light industrial). Many transactions include a mix of development types.

Security

The bonds are secured by revenue from an assessment or tax that the governmental entity levies on properties that benefit from the related improvements. In most cases, the bonds are limited obligations of the governmental entity. The issuing entity's obligation is strictly to pass through the amounts it (or in some cases, a county tax collector) receives and, if there are delinquencies, to commence a foreclosure or tax sale process. In some cases, the bonds are further secured by sources such as incremental property tax revenues brought about by the new development, sales tax revenue generated by the new development, or support from the general fund of the sponsoring governmental entity. This additional support is relatively rare; in most cases, the tax or assessment levy is the primary security for the bonds. In addition, most land-secured transactions have a debt-service reserve fund, typically financed from bond proceeds.

Lien Status

The taxes or assessments constitute a governmental lien. In most cases, that lien is senior to any private lien (including any mortgage loan), regardless of when it was recorded against the property.[1] The provisions for enforcing the governmental lien vary from state to state, but generally entail judicial foreclosure or a tax lien sale of the property if the tax or assessment is not paid. In states where judicial foreclosure is used, the process starts more quickly than the foreclosure provisions for general property tax delinquencies (Vir-

---

[1] In some states, notably California with respect to assessment transactions (but not special tax transactions), there is a "first in time, first in right" provision. In other words, the first assessment liens to be placed on a parcel have a senior status to subsequent liens. However, California special tax liens rise up to senior status. In any case, priority status does not affect payment rights, because property owners have to pay their entire tax bill; still, the seniority status should be a factor in a foreclosure sale.

ginia is an exception). In states that use tax lien sales, the process tends to work more quickly than in states that use judicial foreclosure. When these procedures are necessary, speed is important to investors, because delays increase the minimum bid required to bring the delinquencies current and can reduce the likelihood of a successful foreclosure.

A successful foreclosure or tax lien sale could wipe out any private liens, although the governmental liens—for the assessment or special tax payments, as well as the ongoing lien for general property taxes—stay in place. Accordingly, if the property has positive value (after giving consideration to the governmental liens), then the property owner, a subsequent purchaser, or a mortgage holder should have an incentive—i.e., retaining the land—to bring any delinquencies current; or else the foreclosure or tax lien sale should be successful. If there are sustained delinquencies, if there is no interest in a property sale given the governmental liens, or if the foreclosure or tax lien sale was not successful, then the parcel or parcels in question may in fact be "under water" and the bondholders' security thus impaired. The foreclosure or tax sale provisions are the bondholders' "hammer" to ensure that the taxes or assessments are paid on time.

CREDIT CRITERIA

The critical variable in analyzing land-secured transactions is the likelihood that the development in question will be completed in a reasonable timeframe. To determine this likelihood, an investor should consider the location of the project, the product(s) being offered, competition, developer capitalization, other financing sources, sales to builders or owners, and other variables.

Location

As with all real estate investments, "location, location, location" is the biggest factor to weigh. It is crucial that the "case for development" be solid. In other words, other similar or complementary development should be in place. For example, a commercial-retail development with no surrounding population base or a dense residential development in a remote location would probably be a risky proposition.

Lien Type

There are generally two types of lien: fixed and variable. With a fixed lien, the assessment or tax levy is spread on a proportionate acreage or some other basis, and it never changes over its life. With a variable lien, the amount of the levy can change based on development status. For example, developed parcels (frequently defined as parcels for which a building permit is in place) are taxed at a higher rate than unimproved parcels—although, given the actual value of the parcel once some level of improvement exists, the burden could be a lower percentage of its value. Each type of lien has specific advantages and disadvantages, as shown in Exhibit 51.1.

Fixed liens are usual in an assessment model and are more common nationwide than variable liens. The latter are used primarily in California for transactions that use the Mello-Roos statutes to issue bonds.

Valuation

The valuation of a development relative to the debt outstanding against it is a crucial variable—especially during the development phase. The governmental lien securing the bonds is senior to all private liens, but if the governmental lien is too high, then a property owner could "walk" from the project. This type of valuation is often described as a value-to-lien ratio or

EXHIBIT 51.1   Lien Type Analysis

	Advantages	Disadvantages
Fixed liens	It is easier to determine the burden that the special taxes or assessments place on the land relative to its value.	Unimproved parcels will bear a disproportionate share of the burden relative to their value.
	It is easier to determine the prepayment amount if a property owner wants to prepay the assessment.	Improved parcels will never generate sufficient cash flow to cover debt service on the bonds—until the development is completely built-out.
Variable liens	Improved parcels can carry a proportionately higher share of the burden, but that burden could be a lower percentage of the property value.	The annual levy can be complicated, and property owners can "play with the dates" to pull building permits after the official record date for development status.
	Depending on the formula, it is possible for improved parcels to generate sufficient cash flow to cover debt service on the bonds even before the development is completed.	In a prepayment scenario, the lien calculation is often complex.

a value-to-burden ratio. Valuations are generally derived from appraisals in California[2] and some other Western states; on the other hand, in Florida and the Southeastern states, transactions often come to market without appraisals. In Colorado, some deals have appraisals while others do not, but most transactions have an independent market or absorption study. It is unclear why this divide exists, but there are strong opinions on both sides—and deals do get done without appraisals.

For those projects that have appraisals, it is important to analyze the assumptions the appraiser uses in the sales comparison and discounted cash flow analyses. Sales comparison analyses are standard, but timing differences and property differences can skew the results. A discounted cash flow analysis avoids some of these problems but requires assumptions about absorption pace and prices. The appraiser can develop these assumptions, or an independent third-party market consultant can provide the data. In any case, it is important for the investor to be aware of the assumptions and do sensitivity analyses to determine how much of a sales slowdown or price reduction the project can absorb while retaining a positive net present value. It is also important that all the costs required to bring the property to the assumed condition—whether the goal is finished lots, completed houses or other buildings, or some other state—are incorporated into the appraisal assumptions. Investors should also ascertain if the final value incorporates the effect of the assessment or special tax burden so an investor can properly compare the value-to-lien ratios among different bond issues.

In California, the market standard is a value-to-lien ratio of 3.0× based on convention and, for Mello-Roos transactions, statute. This ratio indicates that the net present value of the project is three times the sum of the governmental liens outstanding against it, meaning that it should withstand a reduction in valuation of 66.6% before a property owner would logically "walk." Note that the ratio should take into account the direct lien and any overlapping liens (including voter-approved general obligation bonds, assessment bonds, and special tax bonds), but should omit the ongoing lien for general property taxes. According to the author's discounted cash flow analyses for several transactions, deals in Florida and other Southeastern states get done at much thinner valuation ratios, but the tax sale process and the paydown nature of some of the bonds mitigate this factor.

---

[2] California regulations require that Mello-Roos transactions have at least a 3.0× value-to-lien ratio in most cases (there are provisions for exceptions). The ratio can be based on assessed valuation or an appraisal, but owing to the effects of Proposition 13, assessed valuation tends to understate the market value. Thus, most transactions come with appraisals. There are standards for appraisals in California land-secured transactions; see the California Debt and Investment Advisory Commission's web site at www.treasurer.ca.gov/cdiac for further details.

Another important valuation variable is the status of the land. For example, if the land is currently vacant, then investors should expect a lower valuation ratio than in a situation where development is already taking place. Note, however, that the overall value-to-lien ratio is based on aggregate valuations for all the assessed or taxed property within a project area; essentially, it is an average. In cases where properties are in different states of development, it is possible for highly valuable parcels to "bring the average up." Investors therefore must be careful to consider the range of property values within a development relative to the liens and burdens outstanding against them.

Coverage

In most cases, and particularly when the lien is fixed, the assessment or special tax revenues are structured to generate no or slight coverage ratios relative to debt service on the bonds. When there is coverage, it tends to range from 1.05× to 1.10×, so it is rather thin. When the lien is variable—California Mello-Roos transactions are an example—there can be higher coverage ratios if the special taxes are levied in full at their maximum rate (although this is not always the case). A higher coverage ratio can be a strong credit advantage because delinquencies with respect to some parcels will not necessarily interrupt debt-service payments on the bonds; in a fixed lien scenario, by contrast, sustained delinquencies that are of any size and not otherwise funded[3] will lead to debt-service interruptions. Variable liens can include an annual escalator as well. If the bonds are structured with level debt service, the presence of an escalator means the coverage ratio will increase over time. Often, though, the bonds are structured with an ascending debt-service schedule that matches the special tax escalator, negating this advantage.

Debt-Service Reserve Funds

Most land-secured transactions have debt-service reserve funds. A reserve fund that is funded to the maximum allowed by federal tax law (i.e., the lesser of (1) maximum annual debt service on the bonds; (2) 10% of the amount of the bonds issued; or (3) 125% of average annual debt service) is ideal, providing some cushion in the event of an interruption of tax or assessment payments. Practices that can be negative to bondholders include these examples:

- In recent years, the sizing of reserve funds in some Florida transactions has fallen below the amount that would be allowed under tax regulations.

---

[3] See the section on the Teeter Plan later in this chapter.

- In some states, notably Colorado and Florida, the reserve fund is sometimes reduced as development takes place and the ratio of debt to assessed valuation is lowered.
- In some cases, the reserve fund is short-funded in the expectation that interest earned will bring the fund to its full amount. Such a practice extends the time needed to reach full funding and, depending on the underlying development variables, could pose a credit risk (although a capitalized interest period can mitigate the risk).

Foreclosure Provisions

Foreclosure provisions are a key credit variable because the right to enforce the governmental lien is the key inducement to payment, particularly when the foreclosure process would wipe out any private liens. In most states, delinquencies accrue interest at a high fixed rate (for example, 18.0% per annum in California) or at an auction rate in the case of tax sales. Delays in foreclosure or tax sales increase the amount that must be bid for a property transfer and reduce the likelihood of success. From a practical perspective, if a property is nearing the foreclosure stage, then there is a strong possibility that the governmental liens are too high relative to the value of the property. Otherwise, the property probably would not be delinquent. If the delinquency were related to the property owner's situation rather than to the underlying economics, the owner would probably sell the property. Still, aggressive foreclosure follow-through can motivate recalcitrant property owners to make their payments. Often, the bond documents provide for a number of permissible delays before the governmental entity is required to pursue foreclosure. Delaying factors may include:

- A minimum aggregate delinquency percentage; 5.0% is typical, but the trigger may be higher.
- A minimum dollar amount (either in aggregate or per property owner); $5,000 is typical, but here too the trigger may be higher.
- Deferral if the reserve fund is fully funded.

The existence of permissible delays to foreclosure, while common, is nevertheless a negative credit element. The provision for using the reserve fund before starting the process is particularly onerous as a credit matter, because a delay reduces the likelihood that the foreclosure will be successful (i.e., that it will result in new ownership and in having the past special tax or assessment payments brought current) and increases the likelihood of missed debt-service payments in the future. In some states, notably Virginia, there is a two-year delay before the foreclosure process even starts. Obviously, such delays are negative for bondholders.

In California Mello-Roos transactions, bond counsel firms are split over who is responsible for foreclosure. In some cases—typically in Northern California—the municipality or school district sponsoring the issue enters into the foreclosure covenant on behalf of the Community Facilities District (CFD). In other cases—mostly in Southern California—the CFD itself enters into the covenant. The latter case is disadvantageous because the CFD generally has no resources except the reserve fund to use in pursuing the action. Drawing on the reserve fund to pursue foreclosure could interrupt debt-service payments earlier than would otherwise have been the case. Also, if the foreclosure process should be delayed for any reason (including a permissible deferral based on full reserve fund) the reserve fund may end up depleted, reducing the resources available to finance the foreclosure action. This divide among bond counsel is not a factor in California assessment district transactions.

If a property owner files for bankruptcy protection, then the foreclosure process is automatically stayed pending resolution of the filing. In most cases, real estate under development—which is the most risky from a credit perspective and therefore the most likely to suffer sustained delinquencies that would trigger foreclosure—is owned by a single-purpose entity created to possess and develop the property. Provisions of the U.S. Bankruptcy Code limit the time during which these entities have an exclusive right to file reorganization plans with the Bankruptcy Court, although extensions are possible.

In a tax lien sale, the delinquency is sold at public auction at a bid price that determines the interest rate and, with the passage of time and other procedural requirements (which vary from jurisdiction to jurisdiction), allows the lien holder to foreclose on the property directly. That process generally works much faster than in states that rely on the judicial foreclosure process. As with all court processes, judicial foreclosure is subject to delays.

Permitting and Environmental Issues

An investor will consider all the permits that are in place allowing the development to proceed. Regulations differ among states, but generally an analyst will want to understand the following elements:

- *Zoning.* Is the property zoned appropriately for the prospective development?
- *Planning.* Is the development consistent with the jurisdiction's planning status?

- *Mapping or platting.* Is the appropriate paperwork in place or easily filed?
- *Building permits.* Are the developers or builders acquiring them, or is doing so a pro forma matter?

The analyst will also want to understand how the development is affected by environmental regulations from local, state, or federal authorities and to know whether relevant studies were completed and all the necessary permits are in place. If the development includes wetlands or waterways, the environmental status is particularly important and could involve the U.S. Army Corps of Engineers. The presence of any endangered wildlife or plants is key information as well.

Obviously, the farther along the project is in the permitting process and the less exposed it is to endangered species, the better from a credit perspective.

Natural Disasters

The potential for natural disasters—including earthquakes, floods, hurricanes, tornadoes, and other calamitous events—is also important to analyze. These events could damage properties and decrease the ability or willingness of the property owners to pay their assessments or special taxes. Because most land-secured transactions cover a small geographic area, the impact of a natural disaster could be greater than for transactions linked to the welfare of, say, an entire city or county.

Site Visits

Many institutional investors will visit the project site and meet with the developer and other consultants before investing in the bonds. Site visits are an integral part of the credit process because they allow an investor to establish a relationship with the developer, verify the location and other attributes of the development, and better understand the surrounding area. Occasionally, investors will visit a project after making an investment for scheduling or other reasons. A prepurchase site visit is generally viewed as the more disciplined approach.

The Teeter Plan in California

California law allows counties to establish a *Teeter Plan*, which is a positive credit factor within limits. Under a Teeter Plan, the county will forward the entire amount of a tax or assessment levy to the cities, school districts, and other agencies in its jurisdiction, regardless of how much money is actually collected. The county uses the fixed penalties and interest that accrue on delinquent tax bills to finance the program. Some counties exclude land-secured transactions from the Teeter Plan, while others include them. When the Teeter Plan applies, bondholders are assured that the next assessment or special tax levy will be received regardless of the actual level of collection. This is a positive credit attribute, of course. However, the county can terminate the Teeter Plan, or remove an assessment district or CFD from the plan, on one fiscal year's notice. Thus, the Teeter Plan is a renewable short-term benefit. If the county experiences sustained delinquencies over time, officials may become motivated to exclude the assessment district or CFD from the plan. Moreover, since the county relies on the accrued penalties and interest on delinquent tax and assessment payments to fund the delinquencies under the Teeter Plan, the county might be less willing to waive them to facilitate a subsequent property transfer following a failed foreclosure sale, bringing the accrued delinquencies current.[4] Thus, the Teeter Plan is an element of additional security when it's not needed, but could complicate matters in a scenario when investors would most like to rely on it.

Colorado Metropolitan Districts

In most states, the special tax or assessment is based on a formula unrelated to the value of the land, but Colorado has a different approach. There, land-secured bonds are issued as limited tax bonds, since the special tax levy is in fact an ad valorem tax, capped typically at no more than 50 mills. Colorado's method for assessing general property taxes is quite complicated. In effect, a cash flow gap is built into each transaction, because there is a two-year lag between the completion of any building and the date when taxes must be paid on it. Underwriters have devised a variety of mechanisms to cover this gap, most commonly funding special reserves with facilities fees paid when building permits are issued or lots are sold to builders. Occasionally, the developer may also be required to post a letter of credit. Nevertheless, development has to take place within a given timeframe and at a certain valuation level for the levy to be sufficient to pay debt service on the bonds. Thus, in addition to the development risk that is present in all land-secured transactions, the Colorado transactions have unique structural and timing risks of which investors should be cognizant. A properly structured deal should include, at a minimum, a market study and/or absorption schedule that demonstrates a stress-case or break-even debt service coverage scenario at a pace of development far slower than that projected by the developer.

---

[4] Such waivers are a frequent tool in workout scenarios.

Illinois Special Service Area Transactions

In Illinois, some land-secured transactions are issued with an assessment structure, while others are issued with a special tax structure. The latter transactions have occasioned some disagreement among counsel. Special taxes are levied on a per-parcel or proportionate benefit basis, not ad valorem. The Illinois Constitution includes a provision that could be interpreted as not allowing special taxes that are levied on any basis other than ad valorem; however, statutory law clearly allows this type of taxation. Illinois bond counsel firms are conflicted on the legality of non-ad valorem special taxes. This is not an issue in assessment transactions.

Control of the District

Matters related to the control of the assessment or special taxing district differ across the country. In some cases, notably in the Western states, the sponsoring governmental entity—for example, a city, county, school district—forms the district and manages it. In other cases, notably in Florida and Colorado, the developer controls the district and appoints its board of directors. Note that there are provisions for the directors to resign if there is a conflict of interest. In cases where the developer is initially in control of the district, the control will shift to individual property owners once a certain number of them are in place.

ROLE OF THE DEVELOPER

Developer Resources and Experience

The relationship between developers and investors in land-secured transactions can be complicated. The debt-service payments on the bonds are not corporate obligations of the developer—and even if they were, in most cases the developer is a special-purpose, thinly capitalized entity created especially to own and develop the property. The security is the governmental lien on the land and the developer's obligation as the property owner to make the special tax or assessment payments. Those funds will be used to pay debt service on the bonds. The ramification for failing to pay is that the developer will face a foreclosure or tax lien sale. Despite this, the ability of the developer to transform the land from an undeveloped state to an improved one is a crucial credit variable. Thus, the financial health of the developer (or at least its access to capital from its parent entity, banks, or other sources) and its ability to carry out the prospective improvements are highly important.

Therefore, the developer's experience, financial resources, and past record are relevant variables to analyze at purchase and during surveillance.

Obtaining the necessary information can present a challenge because developers—especially private entities—are generally reluctant to post their financial and market statistics with the Nationally Recognized Municipal Securities Information Repositories, where competitors could, in theory, gain access to them. On the other hand, private distribution of financial and market statistics can be problematic from a liquidity perspective if the effect is to make bondholders insiders and restrict the securities from trading. Generally, there is some ongoing reporting on the status of the development, but standards are uneven and the reporting may stop well before the development is completed. Thus, although bondholders must depend on the developer to maintain and improve the value of their investment, they rarely have much information about the developer. Even when such information is available, however, investors need to remember that the tax or assessment payments are not personal obligations of the developer. If the development economics turn negative, then a developer—even a financially strong one— could make a rational decision to abandon the property.[5]

Approaches to Development

The various approaches to development are cyclical. At one time, the large public builders wanted to be integrated development companies that improve lots and build houses. This approach enables a builder to purchase land that it can develop and sell to homeowners or other builders (or both), ensuring itself a constant supply of lots when it is ready to build. However, the planning and permitting process is time-consuming and can tie up capital, inflate balance sheets, and reduce performance ratios. Today, many public builders continue to do development and construction, but they often prefer to buy improved or finished lots from a third party or to engage in *land banking*, wherein the builder buys lots from a third party on a predetermined option schedule or as construction appears warranted based on sales activity. In future, the preferences of public builders could change again. For investors, a scenario in which a builder owns the lots directly—and not through a third-party developer pursuant to options or other arrangements—is the cleanest from a credit perspective.

Development Plan

The development plan should make sense on its face. For example, high-priced minimansions in a remote location known for its affordability could

---

[5] See the discussion on disclosure below for more details.

be slow to sell. Similarly, a commercial development without a supporting population base would be problematic. Thus, analysis needs to include local economic indicators—such as historical building-permit patterns, job base and growth, employment statistics, wealth levels, and other demographic data.

Finance Plan

The developer's finance plan also should make ready sense. Variables to consider are whether the developer already controls the land and how that control was financed. Also important is how the developer plans to finance the land development and vertical construction costs (other than the cost of the public improvements that bond proceeds will finance). If the financing is based on bank credit lines, then the bond investor needs assurance that those lines are in place and that the amounts available are adequate (if the lending bank has a mortgage on the property, it is a good idea for the investor to make sure the bank is aware that its lien is subordinated to the governmental lien). If the financing is through internal equity, again the investor will want assurance that the money is definitely available and that it will be sufficient for the project. If the developer plans to sell lots to merchant builders, then an investor will want to know if there will be a single sale or if the transactions will occur via structured takedowns and, in the latter case, what the terms of those options are. From an investor's perspective, the more lots move into in the hands of merchant builders or end-users, the stronger the credit will be in most cases. If bond proceeds will not finance all of the required public infrastructure, then the investor should analyze how the remaining costs will be financed. Generally, investors want to see that a developer has equity in the transaction.

Another variable is whether the financing involves an *acquisition district*. In an acquisition district, the infrastructure is already built and the governmental entity is using bond proceeds to acquire it from the developer. Here, the advantage to investors is that the infrastructure is in place, so the land should be relatively more valuable than would otherwise be the case. Also, there is little (if any) construction risk. The disadvantage is that the reimbursement to the developer reduces its overall equity stake in the project. When there is no acquisition district, the bond proceeds will finance the construction of the public infrastructure, which the governmental entity will acquire at a later date (so it will eventually be an acquisition transaction). This scenario involves construction risk: if the construction costs exceed the amounts available, does the developer have adequate resources to finance the remaining costs?

DISCLOSURE

The primary market disclosure for land-secured transactions is generally good, although there are differences from state to state and among underwriters. But secondary market disclosure varies. As noted earlier, developers (particularly private entities) generally resist providing data about their finances and their sales and construction records. And when they do, the required reporting often terminates well before the development is completed, at a point when investors still want such data to help them monitor the progress of the development and the pace of credit appreciation.

The underlying problem is that investors (particularly institutional investors), engaged in a constant search for yield, have been undisciplined in their disclosure demands. From an underwriter's perspective, since these deals are getting done—and in some cases they are well oversubscribed—there is little incentive to offer better disclosure. This is unfortunate.

In mid-2000, the National Federation of Municipal Analysts (NFMA) issued best-practice guidelines for land-secured transactions. In general, the market has adopted some, but not all, of these guidelines.[6]

THE LAND-SECURED BOND MARKET

Deal Size

Deal sizes in the land-secured sector vary widely. They range from very small—below $1.0 million in some instances—to more than $50.0 million. From January 1, 2000, to June 30, 2006, the average deal size was $17.8 million.[7]

Market

Land-secured bonds are marketed in many states. A search of the Kenny database from January 1, 2000, through June 30, 2006, indicated that 795 nonrated land-secured transactions worth $14.2 billion came to market in that 6.5-year span. These transactions made up 51.3% of all nonrated transactions shown for the period; they also represented approximately 45.3% of the dollar volume of nonrated bonds that came to market. The bulk of the land-secured transactions took place in Florida and California, which combined accounted for approximately 74.5% of the transactions and approximately 70.2% of the total dollar volume over this period. The geographic

---

[6] The original "Recommended Best Practices in Disclosure for Land-Secured Transactions" is available at the NFMA web site at www.nfma.org.

[7] The source is J.J. Kenny, as filtered by the author.

distribution is shown in Exhibits 51.2, 51.3, and 51.4 with percentages based on the number of deals and the dollar amount (in millions) over the period.[8]

Note that the Kenny database does not include every transaction that comes to market. Some other states permit land-secured financing in various forms, but no relevant transactions in these states appeared in the database for the period studied. States not listed in the Exhibit 51.4 that have statutes permitting some kind of land-secured finance include Arkansas, Connecticut, Georgia, Hawaii, Iowa, Idaho, Kansas, Kentucky, Maine, Michigan, Mississippi, Nebraska, North Carolina, North Dakota, Oklahoma, Oregon, South Dakota, Tennessee, Washington State, West Virginia, and Wyoming.[9]

Land-secured bonds are known by a variety of names in different states. Nomenclature includes the following:

- Assessment districts
- Community development authorities

EXHIBIT 51.2   Geographic Distribution of Land-Secured Bond Issuance by Dollar Amount

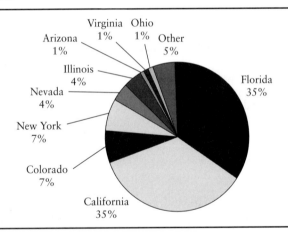

Source: J.J. Kenny and Bloomberg using the author's filters.

---

[8] The sources for the three exhibits are J.J. Kenny and Bloomberg using the author's filters. Note that the list involves some judgment filtering, because land-secured transactions are found in several categories in the Kenny database and not all of the transactions in those categories represent land-secured bonds. Also, for a number of transactions, bond issues that are sold in series could be double-counted; this would affect data about the number of deals but would not affect the dollar volume tables.

[9] The source is Greenberg Traurig, Public Finance Department, Nationwide Selected Statutes Related to the Financing of Development, August 2005. Laws may have been amended post production of document; not a substitute for due diligence.

EXHIBIT 51.3 Geographic Distribution of Land-Secured Bond Issuance by Transactions

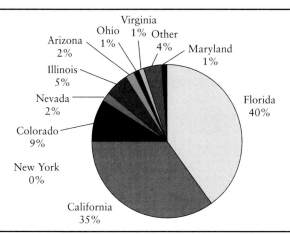

Source: J.J. Kenny and Bloomberg using the author's filters.

- Community development districts
- Community facilities districts
- Economic improvement districts
- Improvement districts
- Local improvement districts
- Mello-roos districts
- Metropolitan districts
- Municipal improvement districts
- Municipal utility districts
- Public improvement districts
- Special development districts
- Special districts
- Special improvement districts
- Special service areas

Bond Types

There are two categories of bonds in the market: long-term and short-term.

Long-Term Bonds

In California and Nevada, issues tend to be structured using serial bonds and term bonds with a set amortization schedule. This practice reflects the retail participation in those markets; historically, retail investors have pre-

EXHIBIT 51.4 Land-Secured Bond Issuance, January 2000–June 2006

State	Deals		Dollars	
	Number	Percentage	Amount	Percentage
Alabama	1	0.1%	$11.9	0.1%
Arizona	12	1.5%	$167.1	1.2%
California	275	34.6%	$4,898.8	34.6%
Colorado	74	9.3%	$986.5	7.0%
Delaware	2	0.3%	$28.4	0.2%
Florida	317	39.9%	$5,021.2	35.4%
Illinois	42	5.3%	$516.7	3.6%
Indiana	1	0.1%	$7.6	0.1%
Louisiana	3	0.4%	$34.0	0.2%
Maryland	10	1.3%	$119.5	0.8%
Minnesota	1	0.1%	$7.3	0.1%
Missouri	3	0.4%	$59.6	0.4%
New Jersey	1	0.1%	$108.9	0.8%
New Mexico	6	0.8%	$90.4	0.6%
Nevada	18	2.3%	$602.2	4.2%
New York	3	0.4%	$980.0	6.9%
Ohio	4	0.5%	$136.3	1.0%
Pennsylvania	4	0.5%	$95.0	0.7%
Rhode Island	1	0.1%	$8.3	0.1%
South Carolina	4	0.5%	$58.6	0.4%
Texas	1	0.1%	$31.5	0.2%
Utah	5	0.6%	$46.2	0.3%
Virginia	7	0.9%	$162.0	1.1%

Source: Greenberg Traurig, Public Finance Department, Nationwide Selected Statutes Related to the Financing of Development, August 2005.

ferred to be shorter on the yield curve. The disadvantage for institutional investors, particularly high-yield investors seeking maximum yields,[10] is that this structure reduces the dollar amount of longer-term maturities. With smaller blocks, the prospect of any liquidity for a particular bond is reduced. Also, in a workout scenario, the presence of retail investors can complicate the decision-making process. The advantage is that the

---

[10] Assumes a positively sloped yield curve.

serial bonds absorb the earlier maturities, so sinking fund payments can start later,[11] creating a possibility of better near-term trading performance. Land-secured transactions in other states include long-term bonds, but rarely with a serial structure.

Short-Term Bonds

In many states, some land-secured bonds have a shorter stated maturity, often 10 years or less. However, these bonds are subject to redemption at par when parcels are sold to homeowners or other end users. Thus, they are frequently called *paydown bonds*. The implication of the early redemption is that the average life is shorter than the stated maturity. Assuming that the bonds are priced to the stated maturity and the short end of the yield curve is fairly steep, early redemption can result in extra yield—meaning that the investor receives more than would have been expected for a stated maturity equal to the average life of the bonds. However, the credit never explicitly improves, because the security is always vacant land. One could argue that with each sale, the case for development becomes stronger and stronger, so the credit does improve; still the land that secures the bonds remains vacant. To examine the question from another angle: All the upside is frontloaded in the yield pickup, but an investor won't know until the final maturity if the investment thesis was correct. Paydown bonds are offered in Alabama, Arkansas, Louisiana, and Utah. In Florida, there are often two tranches of bonds for a particular development, one short that is paid down as improvements take place and one long that is passed through to future property owners. In California, paydown bonds are rare, but a few issuers mandate that an assessment be repaid when a unit is transferred to an end-user.

Call Provisions

In addition to the sinking fund and mandatory redemption provisions discussed above, the long-term bonds are also subject to optional redemption in most cases. Premiums range from zero to 3.0% of par. Based on the coupon and stated maturity date, this factor can produce negative convexity, which is disadvantageous from a trading perspective. Call protection ranges from zero to 10 years.[12]

---

[11] In states such as Arizona, Colorado, Illinois, and Florida that limit retail participation in the land-secured sector, most of the bonds are in longer-term maturities and sinking fund payments start earlier.

[12] California assessment district transactions and transactions in some other states have an *any interest payment date* call provision by statute. Some issuers mandate that assessments be prepaid when properties sell to homeowners.

It is rare for homeowners to choose to prepay their assessments and special taxes, for two reasons: The obligation can be passed through to a subsequent property owner should the homeowner decide to sell, and the interest component of special tax payments or assessments should be deductible from federal income taxes for those who itemize. However, investment bankers sometimes use the prepayment provisions to engineer refunding transactions. Thus, an investor loses a higher-yielding bond when interest rates fall.[13] Also, the negative convexity that exists because of the *any interest payment date* call feature limits the potential price appreciation for that bond during its holding period. Where a call premium exists, investors can count on at least some compensation in the event of a refunding.

Liquidity

Liquidity varies over time for land-secured bonds. Generally, liquidity is strong in the period following issuance, but within a few weeks the bonds tend to be "put away" and trades in specific bonds become rare. Liquidity thereafter is a function of several factors:

- Market demand for high-yield bonds generally and land-secured bonds in particular.
- The coupon and other features of a particular bond issue relative to prevailing market conditions.
- The credit status of the bonds.

Liquidity also depends in part on which firm underwrote the deal. Most dealers tend to support their bonds and, in some cases, other firms' transactions; still, a dealer's capital base, its general interest in market making, and the availability of continuing disclosure are all factors in long-term liquidity for a particular transaction.

Because most land-secured bonds trade infrequently after the initial issuance period, if an investor becomes worried about an issue and chooses to sell it, he or she may not be able to repurchase it later if the credit concerns wane or development variables improve. This reality can present a management challenge, particularly for a high-yield portfolio manager, when such bonds are scarce.

Spread Data

A search of the J.J. Kenny nonrated universe for the period from January 1, 2000, through June 30, 2006, showed that for transactions with a maturity

---

[13] Assumes that the refunding is an economic one.

above 20 years, spreads to the Municipal Market Data (MMD) in the land-secured sector were narrower than for all nonrated transactions. Moreover, the land-secured spreads have narrowed in recent years as can be seen in Exhibit 51.5.

EXHIBIT 51.5   Spread Data, January 2006–June 2006

Year	Spreads for All Nonrated Transactions (bps)	Spreads for Nonrated Land-Secured Transactions (bps)
2000	183	147
2001	202	176
2002	191	165
2003	212	190
2004	154	134
2005	132	111
2006	134	107

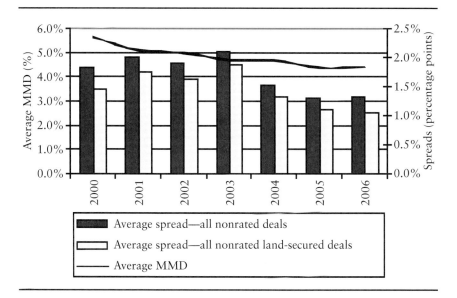

Source: Data obtained from MMD, Bloomberg, J.J. Kenny, author filtering. Based on averages.

BOND STRUCTURES

Maturity Structure

A variety of maturity structures exist in the land-secured market, ranging from short-term bonds usually maturing within 10 years (and often as soon as five years) to long-term bonds with maturities of 30 or more years.

Serials versus Terms

There are examples of shorter serial maturities with a term bond and, sometimes, an intermediate term or terms. Other transactions are structured with just one or more term bonds. The difference seems to be related to retail participation. The states that allow retail investors to buy land-secured bonds—California and Nevada, for example—use the serial structure to take advantage of a positively shaped yield curve and retail investors' traditional preference for bonds with shorter maturities. In the states that generally permit only institutional participation in land-secured transactions (at least at initial issuance)—Arizona, Colorado, Florida, Louisiana, Maryland, South Carolina, and Virginia, for example—the transactions tend to be structured with one or more term maturities based on investor preference. In some cases, these bonds have larger denominations (e.g., $100,000) or require "big boy" letters.

Each structure has advantages and disadvantages. In the case of retail-eligible transactions with serial structures, there is a chance for improved liquidity because the buyer universe is larger. Also, the serial structures take the place of the early sinking fund payments, extending duration and reducing negative convexity for holders of the longer-maturity bonds. The disadvantage of retail participation is that in the event of a workout, it is often difficult to deal with retail investors. Also, when retail investors are absent, more bonds are available for institutions, something that is especially valuable in periods when demand for high-yield bonds is strong. Institutional-only transactions also generally include better disclosure than retail transactions.

Passthrough of the Payment Obligation

For longer-term bonds, the assessments or special taxes "stay with the property." They are passed through to homeowners or end-users. In this case, investors expect the credit quality of the bonds to improve as houses are sold or commercial facilities are built and let. The credit appreciation should lead to price appreciation on the bonds. If the development is large enough, if there is a sufficient level of taxpayer diversity, and if a sufficient level of taxes or assessments is generated from improved parcels, then a rating or bond insurance is possible.

CONCLUSION

Land-secured bonds, which finance the public infrastructure costs related to new development, provide the potential for investing in credits that have tangible security and can improve in quality relatively quickly, yet they offer a spread (of varying magnitudes over time) to rated transactions. They provide developers with access to off-balance sheet finance that can be cost effective because of the tax exemption. Land-secured bonds are issued across the country, although transactions in California and Florida dominate the market segment. Security structures and other credit features differ from state to state based on the laws and practices in those states. In particular, the foreclosure provisions for delinquent assessments and special taxes—which is the crucial security feature—vary in different jurisdictions; delaying mechanisms in the foreclosure provisions, as well as the possibility of a developer bankruptcy filing that could stay the foreclosure process, are credit risks. The value of the land relative to the lien or liens outstanding against it is a key credit variable, but there are no nationwide value-to-lien standards that determine the "proper" amount of leverage. Indeed, while appraisals, a tool for determining the land values, are a requirement in some states for issuing land-secured bonds, they are rare in other states. The developer's role in transforming property from raw land to a substantially improved state is crucial, but in many cases there are limited data about the developer and its financial resources. Also, continuing disclosure standards vary from transaction to transaction. Thus, while land-secured bonds generally provide credit appreciation potential, security selection is important because each transaction is unique.

CHAPTER 52

Hospital Bond Analysis

Lynn Cavallaro
Vice President
Van Kampen Investments

Not-for-profit hospitals account for the greater part of the nearly 5,000 community hospitals located in the United States.[1] A growing number of these tax-exempt hospitals look to the municipal market to access capital. In 2006, Moody's Investors Service reported they maintain ratings for 543 not-for-profit hospitals and health systems. Standard & Poor's rates over 600 hospitals and health systems incorporating well more than 1,000 individual hospitals.[2] In addition, numerous hospitals either unwilling or unable to obtain a credit rating raise capital through the municipal market each year. General acute care hospitals represented 8.5% of all municipal bond issuance during the year 2006, or $30.9 billion in over 500 separate bond issues. Over the near term, hospital bond issuance will be strong as long as hospitals can take advantage of low tax-exempt interest rates. In addition, hospitals will find it necessary to continue to invest in facility and service upgrades simply to stay competitive. Pressure to reduce medical errors is also driving the sector to replace aging facilities with state-of-the-art designs for efficiency and privacy. Recently updated guidelines for hospital design now recommend single-patient rooms for most new hospital construction.

Historically, hospitals have been one of the highest yielding municipal sectors, compensating investors for the risks of owning hospital bonds. Ratings volatility for hospitals is higher than most municipal sectors, also reflecting this risk. Hospitals have suffered a much higher number of rating

---

[1] American Hospital Association, 2005 annual survey. Actual number of U.S. Community Hospitals is 4,936, including 2,958 nongovernmental, non-for-profit hospitals, 1,110 state and local government community hospitals, and 868 investor-owned, for-profit hospitals.

[2] Standard & Poor's, "Why U.S. Not-For-Profit and For-Profit Health Care Credit Quality Differ," 2007.

downgrades compared to upgrades over the past decade. To help distinguish riskier hospitals from stable investments, analysis should go beyond looking solely at the hospital. A top-down approach to hospital analysis is recommended prior to purchasing a hospital bond. This includes analyzing national trends, local market conditions, and a hospital's profile and financial performance. Finally, transaction-specific items, such as security and disclosure, should also be considered.

NATIONAL LEVEL OVERVIEW

With the health care cost trendline continuing to rise and the federally funded programs of Medicare and Medicaid taking up a larger share of spending, pressure to reduce health care costs is great. Those aged above 65 years and those without health care insurance are growing each year. The financial condition of the federal budget, politics, and lobbies, to name a few, continue to have significant influence on health care policy. These issues are pushing the topic of health care reform to the forefront of national debate. Staying in front of national level trends is necessary as each has the potential to impact individual hospitals.

Medicare

In 1965, Congress passed legislation establishing the Medicare and Medicaid programs as Title XVIII and Title XIX of the Social Security Act. During 2006, the Medicare program covered medical care for approximately 43 million beneficiaries. Medicare is the single largest payer of hospital care, and accounts for 17% of national health care spending.[3] On average, Medicare accounts for 43% of a hospital's gross patient revenue.[4]

The Balanced Budget Act of 1997 (BBA '97) created the beginning of one of the toughest periods for the hospital industry. Hospitals entered into a three-year period of seeing little to no increases in Medicare payment rates. Many hospitals suffered downgrades by the rating agencies during the years following the implementation of BBA '97. However, for the years 2001 through 2007, hospitals enjoyed a period of sound Medicare payment rates as Congress restored some of the damage of BBA '97. Many hospitals benefited with improved finances and bond rating upgrades. Recent proposals by the Bush Administration include the possibility of additional Medicare reductions. If passed, hospitals could be in for another rough period of Medicare funding.

---

[3] Centers for Medicare & Medicaid Services.
[4] Moody's Investors Service, Fiscal Year 2005 Not-for-profit Health Care Medians.

Medicaid

Jointly funded by both the federal and state governments, Medicaid provides medical care to low income individuals. The federal government is responsible for at least 50% of the cost of each state's Medicaid program. State Medicaid programs vary considerably since each state establishes its own payment rates, eligibility, and services. States are required to make additional payments to hospitals serving a disproportionate number of Medicaid patients.

The Medicaid program had over 50 million beneficiaries in 2006 and accounted for 17% of the nation's total health spending.[5] Due to its fast growth, health related programs and services now represent one-third of total state spending, and Medicaid represents, on average, 18% of a state's budget.[6] Over the years, states facing deficits continually look to this program for budget relief. With the average hospital's Medicaid burden equal to 10.5% of gross patient revenue.[7] Medicaid policy changes can have a significant impact on a hospital.

Private Payers

Private insurance accounts for 34% of national health care expenditures.[8] Commercial, managed care, and Blue Cross payers, combined, account for 45% of hospital's gross patient revenue.[9] Given the significance of this revenue source, a hospital's ability to obtain rate increases from private payers can be crucial in sustaining a hospital through periods of reduced government reimbursement. Insurance industry consolidation at the national level may increase the local market power of the insurance provider, disadvantaging the hospital in future negotiations. Private insurers experiencing earnings trouble may be reluctant to provide hospitals with historical rate increases. Shifts in the market's balance of power can ultimately lead to a strained negotiating environment and lost revenue for a hospital. Understanding the underwriting cycle, as well as market player clout, will provide key insight into the private payer trends affecting hospitals.

Health Care Cost Trends

Health care expenditures, both public and private, totaled $2.1 trillion in 2006, and accounted for 16% of gross domestic product (GDP).[10] CMS

[5] Centers for Medicare & Medicaid Services.
[6] Moody's Investors Service, "Stable Outlook for State Ratings in 2007 Reflects More Moderate Economic and Revenue Environment."
[7] Moody's Investors Service, Fiscal Year 2005 Not-for-profit Health Care Medians.
[8] Centers for Medicare & Medicaid Services.
[9] Moody's Investors Service, Fiscal Year 2005 Not-for-profit Health Care Medians.
[10] Centers for Medicare & Medicaid Services.

projects national spending on health care will double by the year 2016, rising to over $4 trillion, and representing 19.6% of GDP at that time. Hospital care is the largest portion of health care spending. From 2000 to 2005, total health care spending outpaced the consumer price index, a measure of price inflation. While excellent health care coverage is a hallmark of American Big Business, the rising costs are hitting companies hard. General Motors is a good example of a company suffering from uncontrollable health care costs. According to Fitch, health care costs per GM vehicle doubled over the recent six-year period, and appear insurmountable without labor concessions.[11] Hospitals are also now disclosing other postemployment benefits, comprised primarily of retiree health benefits, with many of these promised benefits sizable. These rising health care spending trends will continue to place pressure on the industry to reduce costs.

Health Care Employment

Some of the country's largest hospital systems are now significant employers, with many employing over 50,000 full-time equivalents. Hospitals are leading employers in markets across the country, providing not only essential services to their communities, but stability to local economies. While health care employment trends are strong, shortages in numerous health care professions, particularly nursing, have hit the industry hard over the past decade.[12] Physician shortages are also increasingly problematic, particularly in markets with poor malpractice environments, driving physicians to more stable locations, or out of the profession entirely.

Legislative/Regulatory/Judicial Environment

The legislative, regulatory, and legal environment for the hospital industry changes frequently and is influenced by federal, state and local matters. Over the years, the hospital industry has faced challenges related to its charity care, community benefit, and bad debt policies. The tax-exempt status of hospitals is in dispute in numerous states, with Congressional level discussion on this topic as well. Federal laws governing hospital/physician relations are increasingly important as hospitals take on strategies such as physician employment. Numerous other laws govern hospital activity, with violation of these laws potentially resulting in the loss of a hospital's tax-exempt status. Regulatory requirements such as Sarbanes-Oxley, while not directly imposed on the not-for-profit sector, are, in many instances, posi-

---

[11] Fitch Ratings.

[12] The American Association of Colleges of Nursing is an excellent source for information on the nursing shortage, both nationally and at the state level.

tively impacting the industry as hospitals adopt stepped-up internal policy, procedures, and disclosure.

National Demand Trends

Over the long term, national demand for medical services is expected to grow stronger. Life expectancy is rising because of the industry's increasing focus on preventative medicine, medical advances, and improved treatment success rates. The nation's population is aging, with those aged 65 years and older projected to increase from approximately 35 million in 2000 to an estimated 71 million in 2030, representing 19.6% of the U.S. population.[13]

Understanding national trends in patient demand offers insight into demand for an individual hospital. There are a couple of ways to follow national industry trends in hospital use. First, the three nationally recognized rating agencies provide annual utilization statistics for the not-for-profit and for-profit hospital sectors.[14] Even tracking the utilization trends of just a few of the nation's largest health care systems can provide a sense of industry demand, as these systems generate thousands of inpatient admissions each year. Second, tracking flu volume can be an indicator of national hospital demand since many flu cases are treated in the emergency rooms of hospitals, and emergency room visits frequently account for 50% or more of a hospital's inpatient admissions.[15]

Other Industry Trends

The dynamic nature of the hospital industry dictates that numerous issues will challenge the sector at any one time. Listed are recent examples:

- Rising drug costs continue to place pressure on hospitals. In recent years, the high costs of pharmaceuticals resulted in numerous states considering overseas purchases of drugs, where costs are considerably lower.
- Industry consolidation/restructurings can change the health care market landscape. New York State is a good example, where a recently released report from the Commission on Health Care Facilities recommended a 7% reduction of hospital beds statewide through closures, mergers, and

---

[13] Centers for Disease Control and Prevention, Public Health and Aging: Trends in Aging—United States and Worldwide.
[14] Moody's Investors Service, Standard & Poor's and Fitch Ratings.
[15] Centers for Disease Control and Prevention, Flu Activity. The CDC publishes national flu activity on its web site.

other downsizing efforts. Other markets will be watching the progress of this market restructuring closely.

- Uncompensated care cost trends are increasingly negative, with many for-profit providers reporting uncompensated care nearing 20% of revenue during 2006.[16] Not-for-profit providers are also reporting rising bad debt and charity care expenses relative to operating revenue.
- Universal coverage is gaining national momentum, with numerous proposals in states such as California and Massachusetts gaining national attention. According to the Census Bureau, 15% of the nation's population is uninsured, or close to 45 million people.[17] Policy debates about universal coverage during the coming years will likely bring systematic change to hospitals in the future.

LOCAL LEVEL REVIEW

Analysis of the local market should include a review of a hospital's state and local jurisdictions, with focus on competition, service area, economy, government influence, and other market-specific factors.

Competition

- A hospital competes not only with other hospitals in its defined service area, but also with nontraditional competitors such as outpatient centers, surgery centers, and physician-run clinics. With physician reimbursement also under pressure at the federal level, physicians are taking profitable services outside of the hospital and into their own setting in order to capture higher reimbursement.
- Understanding the balance of power among all market players is key when identifying competitors. For-profit competitors may have access to deep pockets, possibly providing an edge over its not-for-profit counterpart.
- Competitor hospitals may have exclusive arrangements, partnerships and/or affiliations that may provide them with a competitive edge.
- Barriers to entry are important in competitive local markets. For instance, markets that do not require a certificate of need to construct large projects may become overbedded, such as in the Indianapolis market.

---

[16] For nine months ending 9/30/06, uncompensated care as percentage of revenue: Tenet = 20.3%, Community Health Systems = 19.8%, HCA = 17.8%, Universal Health Services = 17% (Fitch Ratings).

[17] U.S. Census Bureau.

Service Area and Economy

- The service area should be large enough to support the supply of hospital beds within the market.
- Strong demographic trends, stable top employers, and good economic measures in employment and wealth are ideal.
- Payer mix concentration will give the analyst a feel for the characteristics of the economy. For example, a hospital with a 25% Medicaid patient mix may be located in a depressed economy with a high indigent population.

Market Specific Factors

- It is important to understand a state's Medicaid reimbursement history, as well as the outlook for future Medicaid funding.
- States with a hospital provider tax may result in a net benefit or a net payment for the hospital.
- Private insurance companies may engage in exclusive contracting with hospitals and physicians.
- Those states without adequate protection for potential lawsuits are driving malpractice insurance costs higher, forcing physicians to seek more favorable locations to practice medicine.
- Massachusetts and California, as well as other states, are working to implement universal coverage in their respective jurisdictions.

HOSPITAL LEVEL REVIEW

Hospitals of all shapes and sizes raise funds through the municipal capital market, including small, critical access hospitals in remote locations, as well as large, multistate hospital systems serving numerous markets. While risk factors may vary, strong fundamental characteristics and a sound track record in financial performance are key in the hospital level review.

Profile—The Fundamentals

Identifying the distinguishing fundamental characteristics, such as whether a hospital is a standalone provider or a member of a network of hospitals, plays a significant part in analyzing a hospital bond.

- *Market share/service area.* A hospital with a leading market share and limited competition has presumable market influence in pricing its services and negotiating its contracts. Hospitals in highly competitive markets will find it necessary to invest significant capital to keep pace with competitors. Understanding the service area characteristics, competitor affiliations, and reach of patient draw will also offer insight into the market position of each of the market's hospitals.

- *Market niche.* Even hospitals without a leading market share can have a secure place in the market with a well-defined niche. Pediatric hospitals are good examples. Standalone hospitals may be at a disadvantage if competitors are members of larger systems with deep pockets, however many rural hospitals are sole providers, therefore size is not a weakness. Hospitals sponsored by a religious organization may have an advantage in certain markets with a long history of supporting their mission. Other hospitals may benefit from an additional revenue source in a tax pledge or a government subsidy payment. Understanding a hospital's "centers of excellence" may further define their niche. The case mix index measures the level of acuity of services provided by a hospital, with high-end tertiary services typically provided by teaching, urban facilities, and basic primary care services provided by rural and community hospitals.

- *Payer mix.* The revenue mix of a hospital is comprised of governmental payers (Medicare and Medicaid), private payers (Managed Care and Commercial Insurance), and a catchall category that includes self-pay, workers compensation and other smaller revenue sources. Hospital analysis should include identifying any significant concentration or trends in the payer categories. Any shifts in payer trends could mean the loss of a good payer. In markets with high managed care penetration, understand the contract terms. A hospital should have the influence necessary to negotiate adequate rates. The loss of an exclusive contract can negatively affect a hospital. A rise in self-pay patients usually means rising bad debt for the hospital.

- *Medical staff.* A hospital with strong physician relations is critical, as referrals drive a successful hospital business. The quality and age of the active staff, recent turnover, and the concentration of the top admitting doctors on the staff should be scrutinized. A physician shortage may require stepped-up recruitment efforts and the costly use of employment, agency and/or locum tenens. The ultimate test of a hospital staff is physician loyalty, reflected in consistent utilization trends.

- *Management.* Assessing the quality of leadership is not an easy task. A proactive management team with a solid record of financial performance, particularly during periods of slow growth, speaks loudest to the abilities of management. Investors should have the opportunity to assess management's sophistication, depth, and strategic planning efforts. Forward thinking on quality, safety, technology investment, and facility construction is desirable. In addition, management should be willing to fully disclose financial results according to industry standards.

■ *Utilization trends.* Volume trends should be tracked over multiple years in order to detect any changes in admitting patterns, contracts, new competition, physician turnover, and/or new strategies/ventures. Common utilization statistics to analyze should include inpatient admissions, outpatient volume, surgeries, average length of stay, occupancy, and average daily census.

Financial Performance

Hospital analysis includes a comprehensive review of the income statement, balance sheet and cash flow statement, with focus on a number of key financial measures and ratios. A three- to five-year trend should be established, as well as a comparison of actual performance to budgeted ratios and financial projections for out years.

Revenue Trends

■ *Net patient service revenue.* This is equal to gross revenue, net of third party allowances and charity care. Allowances include uncollectible amounts from Medicare, Medicaid and private insurers.
■ *Nonoperating revenue.* Typically includes investment income and contributions from donations, capital fundraising campaigns, and foundations. Take note of unusual periods of strong/weak market returns, and any dependence on these revenue sources.

Expense Trends

■ *Labor.* Salary, wages, and benefits typically account for 50% of a hospital's total expense base. Shortages in nurses, pharmacists, and other technicians are real problems facing the industry. Vacancy and turnover rates, use of agency staffing and *locum tenens*, union activity, and history of work stoppage should all be disclosed by the hospital. Pension expense is also rising for many hospitals.
■ *Bad debt.* This fast growing expense category is under a high level of industry scrutiny. The continuous shift to higher copays and deductibles will cause this expense category to grow further. With nearly 47 million people without health insurance, bad debt will be under pressure for some time to come.
■ *Supply costs.* Supply costs, including drugs, will be a category to watch with federal level focus on reigning in costs to consumers.

- *Pension costs.* Hospitals with underfunded defined benefit pension plans are seeing pension expense increase, with many required to make extremely large payments into their pension plans to stay compliant with required funding levels.

Profitability and Cash Flow Ratios

Monitoring profitability and cash flow can provide early warning signs to a financial downturn. Emphasis should be on ongoing operating profitability; however, nonoperating income can be a significant source of funds as well. Key ratios include:

- *Operating and excess margins.* Operating income as a percentage of total revenue; Excess income as a percentage of total revenue.
- *Cash flow margin.* Cash flow as a percentage of total revenue.
- *Cash flow to debt.* Cash flow from operations to long-term debt.
- *Investment income to total expenses.* Measures a hospital's reliance on investment income.

Capital Spending Ratios

A hospital's spending on capital should be adequate, and should include routine projects as well as future strategies that will grow the business. If pay-for-performance becomes mainstream, then strategic spending for *information technology* (IT) and quality initiatives will likely take up an increasing portion of the capital budget. A hospital should strike a balance between its willingness to invest in capital, and preservation of liquidity. Ratios that evaluate a hospital's capital spending include:

- *Capital spending to EBITDA.* Capital expenditures measured against earnings before interest, taxes, depreciation and amortization (EBITDA).
- *Capital spending to depreciation.* Capital expenditures as a percent of depreciation/amortization expense.
- *Average age of plant.* Depreciation expense relative to accumulated depreciation. Typically, plant above 12-years old is considered an aging facility in need of investment.

Liquidity Ratios

Hospital analysts know the expression, "cash is king," and understand that considerable emphasis is placed on the amount of liquidity reserved for difficult times. Typical liquidity ratios include:

- *Days of cash on hand.* Unrestricted cash and investments relative to daily cash expenditures. Arguably the most important ratio for a not-for-profit hospital.
- *Cash to debt.* Unrestricted cash and investments relative to total long-term debt.
- *Cash to current liabilities.* Measures the amount of unrestricted cash and investments relative to current liabilities.

Leverage Ratios

Leverage measures the amount of debt against a hospital's operations and net worth. The hospital should disclose any plans to issue additional debt. Key ratios include:

- *Debt to capital.* Long-term debt relative to a hospital's net assets.
- *Debt to cash flow.* Long-term debt relative to a hospital's cash flow.
- *Debt to total revenue.* Long-term debt as a percentage of total revenue.

Debt Service Ratios

A hospital's ability to service its debt is measured against cash flow, revenue, and reserves. Important ratios include:

- *Debt service coverage.* Coverage is one of the most important ratios in hospital analysis, that is, EBITDA to peak year debt service (also called *maximum annual debt service*).
- *Debt burden.* Maximum annual debt service as a percentage of total revenue.
- *Cushion ratio.* Unrestricted cash and investments to maximum annual debt service.

Activities Outside of the Obligated Group

Most hospital transactions include an *obligated group*, defined as the core operating entities responsible for paying interest and principal on outstanding debt. Many hospitals are members of a system, and report "up" to a parent along with other *nonobligated* system members. Rating agencies typically incorporate the activities of the entire system when assigning a hospital bond rating, including the non-obligated entities. Therefore, analysis should include not only the obligated group financial results, but also the consolidated financial and operating results of the entire system. Covenants within the legal bond documents should be structured to prevent vital entities from withdrawing from the obligated group and/or system. Covenants should also prevent significant asset transfers that would potentially change the credit quality of the hospital bond.

TRANSACTION-SPECIFIC RISKS

Construction Risk

Hospital bonds issued to finance new construction projects have numerous risks. The analyst should be aware of the potential for construction delays and cost overruns due to rising costs in labor and supplies. Understanding whether the market is able to support the project and whether the hospital can afford the plan is critical. The hospital should provide the investor with a feasibility study conducted by a reputable firm, as well as financial projections that run through the project completion and occupancy dates. A signed guaranteed maximum price contract with experienced and reputable contractors should be in place, with adequate contingencies to absorb unexpected costs.

Security

Having an adequately secured hospital bond is essential in the overall review and analysis of a hospital. Depending on the credit risk and the bond's rating, the security package should provide the investor with a commensurate level of protection in the event the hospital enters into a period of financial difficulty. Riskier hospitals should be required to pledge a higher level of collateral to protect bondholders. Ideally, collateral should include a first lien mortgage on the hospital's core facilities and campus, a gross revenue pledge, and a fully funded debt service reserve fund. Additional protection in bond covenants that test liquidity, additional debt, and debt service coverage should be reasonable, should meet the standards set by the investing community, and should be tested periodically. Be aware of provisions that may strip away pledged security at some future date through carve-out, substitution, release, and springing provisions. An excellent resource for reference is the Recommended Term Sheet and Legal Provisions for Hospital Debt Transactions, published by the National Federation of Municipal Analysts (NFMA). This comprehensive paper is designed to develop standard language and legal provisions for tax-exempt hospital debt transactions.

Disclosure

Reliable, consistent financial disclosure has not always been a strong suit of the municipal industry. Recent efforts over the last decade dramatically improved disclosure for hospitals. Rule 15(c)2-12 by the SEC requires minimum levels of disclosure upon the entire municipal market. Advocates of transparency have pressed the hospital community to improve upon this rule by increasing the frequency and content of disclosure. Efforts by the NFMA have been the most comprehensive. NFMA has published Recommended Best Practices in Disclosure for Hospital Debt Transactions, calling for hospitals to include, at a minimum, annual audited financial statements, quarterly unaudited financial statements, a management discussion and analysis for reporting periods, operating/utilization data, material events, a medical staff discussion, and reporting on any changes to the regulatory environment. This level of disclosure is now expected by institutional hospital investors, creating an industry standard for hospitals issuing debt in the municipal market. However, additional enhancements still need to be made. The best-of-the-best in hospital disclosure provide comprehensive reporting including cash flow statements, multiyear trend comparisons, and detailed management discussion and analysis. Hospital providers also conduct regularly scheduled investor conference calls to give analysts the opportunity to hear management and ask questions. Still, many hospital bond issuers provide only minimal disclosure, excluding relevant information. The hospital investor should pay close attention to a hospital's history of disclosure, as this may be an indication of future actions.[18]

EXAMPLES OF HOSPITAL DOWNGRADES

To illustrate the risks inherent in the hospital sector, it is worthwhile to look at a few examples where seemingly stable hospitals/health systems, some with A category ratings, experienced a series of downgrades over a concise period. All examples reflect Moody's Investors Services ratings.

- *Allegheny Health Education and Research Foundation (AHERF), Pennsylvania.* AHERF was the parent of numerous subsidiary hospitals that held separate bond ratings. Allegheny General, AHERF's flagship hospital, issued over $100 million of debt by 1995, when an A2 rating was assigned—the highest rating of all AHERF affiliates. By 1998, the rating

---

[18] Additional sources for disclosure include rating agency reports, Nationally Recognized Municipal Securities Information Repositories (NRMSIR) filings, and a hospital's own web site. Go to www.sec.gov/info/municipal/nrmsir.htm for a list of NRMSIRs.

was downgraded to Caa1 when a number of AHERF affiliates filed for bankruptcy. Other AHERF affiliate hospitals suffered significant rating downgrades as well. AHERF was the largest default by a not-for-profit hospital system.

- *Detroit Medical Center (DMC), Michigan.* An A3 rating and stable outlook was assigned to DMC's $105 million bond issue in 1998. Over the course of the next five years, DMC was downgraded six notches to Ba3, where the rating remains as of mid 2007.
- *Hillcrest Health System, Oklahoma.* In 1999, Hillcrest issued $225 million bonds with a rating of Baa2 and a positive outlook. A little over a year later, the rating was downgraded to Ba1, and by the end of the year 2000, Hillcrest was downgraded to B3 with a negative outlook. In 2004, the bonds were ultimately refunded after a for-profit health care company purchased Hillcrest.
- *Mount Sinai-NYU Medical Center Health System, NY.* In 2000, $700 million bonds were issued with a Baa1 and stable outlook. By 2003, the rating was downgraded to Ba1. Only after the obligated group was restructured in 2006, did the rating see an upgrade to Baa2.
- *Methodist Hospitals, Inc., Indiana.* $77 million of bonds were issued in 2001, with a rating of A1 and stable outlook. Five years later the rating dropped two notches to A3, and later that same year the rating was downgraded further to Ba1 where it remains today. The outlook remains negative. In total, this was a six-notch decline from the original issue rating.
- *Forum Health, Ohio.* In 2002, Forum Health received an A3 rating and stable outlook on its $60 million bond issue. The following year, a negative outlook was assigned, and over the next three years, Forum was downgraded seven notches to its current rating of B1. A negative outlook remains in place as of mid 2007.

CONCLUSION

Analyzing a hospital bond can be straightforward, especially if a hospital has a high rating and its fundamentals, financial measures, and security are all strong. This is rarely the case; however, as many highly rated providers come to market believing their good standing does not require an adequate collateral pledge. Lower rated hospitals, on the other hand, must compensate investors with a higher level of security to obtain market acceptance.

Uncovering the risks of a hospital can be difficult without careful analysis. For example, a hospital with solid market share, strong demographics, and a favorable patient mix may appear to be on track to perform well.

However, an aggressive or unprepared management team may take this hospital down the wrong path, resulting in declining financial performance and credit deterioration for the hospital bond. Without a high level of diligence on the part of the analyst, these poor management skills may go unnoticed.

While veteran analysts admit that relying on your gut instinct is a small, but necessary part of hospital analysis, the bulk should include a comprehensive review of national, local, and hospital level risk factors. In the end, selecting a solid hospital bond requires spending the time to understand these risks, and obtaining adequate security and disclosure to protect against future credit problems.

CHAPTER 53

Single-Family Housing Bonds

Kurt van Kuller, CFA
Portfolio Manager
1861 Capital Management

Sophisticated investors have long regarded single-family housing bonds as one of the hidden treasures of the municipal bond market. Their inefficient pricing attracts those with the resources to seek excess returns. Research may consistently uncover undervalued opportunities in this sector. Conversely, many traditional bond buyers do not commit the necessary resources to understand this idiosyncratic sector. They are deterred by the volatility of prepayment calls, the opacity of housing bond structures and cash flows, pronounced negative convexity, and uneven disclosure. In this chapter, we explore the attributes that set them apart from other municipal bonds, and allow the reader to determine if these are suitable for their portfolios.

THE APPEAL OF SINGLE-FAMILY BONDS

The investor base for single-family (SF) bonds has waxed and waned over the years, as the sector has cycled in and out of favor. Since 2005, there has been a major influx of new institutional buyers into the sector. There are five reasons for this.

First, SF bonds offer a yield premium over other high-grade municipal bonds of up to 75 (tax-exempt) basis points currently. This is not attributable to credit risk, but call risk. It is analogous to the higher yields that Ginnie Mae passthroughs (GNMAs) carry versus Treasury bonds. The yield premium also compensates for negative convexity and, in most cases, the individual Alternative Minimum Tax (AMT).

This chapter was written when the author was employed as a research analyst at Merrill Lynch.

Second, SF bonds are one of the strongest and most stable credit sectors of the market, with an average rating of AA+ and regular upgrades. Many State Housing Finance Authority (HFA) programs may be seen as very conservatively rated.

Third, SF bonds historically outperform other municipal bonds in periods of flat or moderately rising interest rates. That is because their yield advantage becomes the dominant factor in total return. They also offer important diversification benefits for a municipal bond portfolio.

Significant volume and liquidity are the fourth reason for their popularity. SF bonds are too large a sector for most investors to ignore. Housing bonds account for 7% to 10% of new issues in recent years. Sizable new issue volume and demand has greatly improved secondary market liquidity.

Finally, these bonds are a captive mortgage-backed sector in a bond market. SF term bonds are traditionally sold at 30-year interest rates plus an additional spread for generic redemption risk. Naive buyers traditionally price SF bonds to maturity, although virtually no single-family bond has ever survived its full term. This contradicts a fundamental tenet of securities pricing: valuing a financial asset at the present value of its expected cash flows. Investors may uncover the true value of a single-family bond by pricing it with a spread to its expected average life.

Performance Vehicle

The main reason housing bonds are now in demand is performance. According to the Merrill Lynch Total Return Index, the single-family bond sector outperformed the Master Municipal Index in 2006 by 80 bps and in 2005 by exactly 100 bps as can be seen in Exhibit 53.1. This was no aberration. The SF Bond Index outperformed the Master Municipal Index seven times during the 1990s. Note that these returns reflect the results of a passive index, with no value added from active management. There also was a dismal period in the early part of this decade when the SF Bond Index underperformed by more than 200 bps in four out of five years. This resulted from negative convexity of housing bonds during the major bond rally. Housing bonds had become a specialty niche that mainstream buyers did not participate in.

AMT Penalizes SF Sector

Another factor thinning the market is the AMT. It uniquely penalizes the housing sector which accounts for almost half of all bonds subject to it. It raises yields on interest rate sensitive housing bonds by 20 bps or more. It is a particularly ineffective tax as applied to municipal bonds, as it is easily avoidable

EXHIBIT 53.1 Merrill Lynch Total Return Index

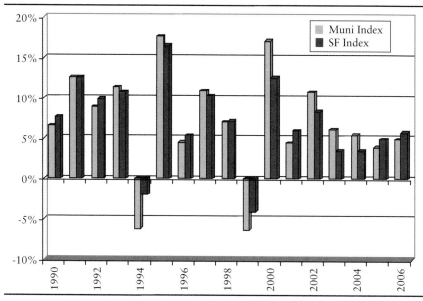

Source: Merrill Lynch.

by purchasing non-AMT bonds. The AMT has the biggest market impact on serial bonds, a province of retail buyers. The AMT mainly causes a shift in the composition of housing bond buyers to institutions not subject to it.

A Segmented Market

Discussions of the thinness of the single-family bond market often ignore its segmented nature. Most buyers favor specific parts of a single-family bond, and rarely change their preference. The dynamics of each segment are strikingly different. The five main segments are:

1. *Serial bonds.* This is traditionally an area for retail buyers.
2. *Planned amortization class (PAC) bonds.* The deepest segment, with demand heavily influenced by tender option bond programs.
3. *Taxable bonds.* Often purchased by Federal Home Loan Banks, at times by other *government-sponsored enterprises* (GSEs).
4. *Variable rate bonds.* Mostly used by issuers for swaps. Bought by money market funds.
5. *Term bonds.* Dominated by Fannie Mae (FNMA), Freddie Mac (FHLMC), and property and casualty (P&C) insurers. Lately this sector has been visited by hedge funds, high-yield funds, and mutual funds.

GSEs Filled a Void

The investor base became very thin at the long end early this decade. Fannie Mae and Freddie Mac came to purchase two-thirds or more of all term bonds. Ironically, this segment had strong new issue pricing due to GSE support. Thus, many would have expected problems in absorption of the record supply in 2006 after Fannie Mae dropped out of the market and Freddie Mac curtailed buying midyear. However, the market easily absorbed this new supply in 2006 with an influx of new buyers. Many investors believe that *single-family mortgage revenue bonds* (SFMRBs) have now entered a sustained period of out-performance. In addition, there are strong prospects for spread tightening due to a combination of less new issue volume and the return of the GSEs in full force. However, this outlook hinges to a large extent on the direction of interest rates. Many new investors that filled the void left by the GSEs may drop out of the sector quickly when the outlook turns.

SF Bond Authorization

For over 30 years, state and local housing finance agencies have sold single SFMRBs to assist low- to middle-income homebuyers purchase first homes. The traditional program offers below market rate mortgage loans funded by tax-exempt bonds. Bond proceeds are utilized to purchase newly originated first mortgages. Upon completion of the mortgage acquisition process, the pool of new mortgages becomes the primary source of repaying the bonds. The program was conceived in a high rate environment as an interest rate subsidy. Tax law permits the weighted average mortgage yields to exceed bond yield by a maximum arbitrage spread of 1.125% over the life of the issue. The largesse of the tax code currently permits HFAs to take this full spread and offer fixed rate, 30-year mortgage loans that are at least 50 bps to 100 bps below market rates. Higher interest rates widen this spread and spur demand for the program. In recent years, down payment assistance (funded by original issue premiums) emerged as a major new product for HFAs. Exhibit 53.2 summarizes the federal legislative history addressing the SFMRB volume.

SF BOND ISSUANCE RECORD IN 2006

Never before in the history of the single-family bonds did issuance approach the heights of 2006 (see Exhibit 53.3). The $24.8 billion sold overtook the previous high of $16.9 billion in 1985 by 47%. As multifamily sales waned, SF bond issuance rose to 80% of the housing sector, tying a previous high.

EXHIBIT 53.2   Federal Legislation Addressing Single-Family Mortgage Revenue Bond Volume

12/5/80	Mortgage Subsidy Bond Tax Act ("Ullman Bill") imposes first time homebuyer requirement, purchase price limits, arbitrage restrictions, and a sunset of 12/31/83.
9/3/82	Tax Equity and Fiscal Responsibility Act loosens many Ullman Bill restrictions.
6/27/84	Deficit Reduction Act reauthorizes MRBs to 12/31/87 and places caps on all IDB issuance. Creates MCCs.
9/27/86	Tax Reform Act imposes income limits, restores Ullman price limits, new arbitrage curbs, and a sunset of 12/31/88. Establishes "private-activity bond" volume caps at $75 per capita or $250 million, decreasing to $50 per capita or $150 million in 1988.
10/21/88	Technical and Miscellaneous Revenue Act imposes recapture on capital gains upon home resale, Ten Year Rule and 42-month Rule for unused proceeds. Extends sunset to 12/31/89.
11/21/89	Omnibus Budget Reconciliation Act reauthorizes MRBs until 9/30/90.
10/27/90	Omnibus Budget Reconciliation Act extends sunset to 12/31/91.
12/11/91	Tax Extension Act moves sunset to 6/30/92.
8/10/93	Omnibus Budget Reconciliation Act makes MRBs permanent.
10/22/98	Omnibus Consolidated and Emergency Supplemental Appropriations Act raises volume cap to $75 per capita or $225 million by 2007, phased-in starting in 2003.
12/16/00	The Consolidated Appropriations Act accelerates the volume cap increase to a two-year period starting in 2001, and indexes it to inflation thereafter.

The single-family boom was driven by a perfect alignment of factors: refinements to HFA underwriting; still heated real estate markets; a modest rise in mortgage rates and decreasing affordability; and a reservoir of private activity bond volume cap carried forward from prior years. (The largest issuers are identified in Exhibit 53.4.) This record may stand for some time. Single-family issuance may decline in coming years—if all market conditions remain identical—because of the exhaustion of volume cap carry-forwards.

Single-family bonds subject to AMT rose the most in 2006 to 70% of the sector. The AMT is a very inefficient tax that mainly causes a shift in the composition of buyers from retail and mutual funds to institutions not subject to it, raising costs without adding revenue to the Treasury. Taxable single-family bond issuance should rise significantly in 2007 and beyond as a means of stretching increasingly scarce volume cap.

EXHIBIT 53.3   SF Housing Bond New Issues by Tax Status, 1980–2006

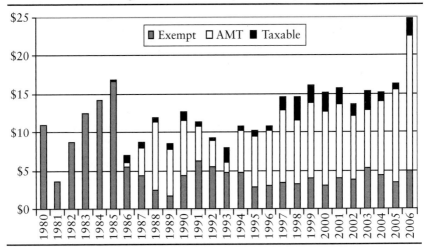

Source: Thomson Financial. Includes private placements and short-term debt.

EXHIBIT 53.4   Leading Issuers of Bonds in 2006

CA HFA	$1,388
OH HFA	$1,300
VA HDA	$890
MD CDA	$770
PA HFA	$768
MN HFA	$695
CT HFA	$676
IN HCDA	$659
WI Hsg & EDA	$628
KY HC	$560

Source: Thomson Financial.

Volume caps are the main reason housing volume appears so stable, as true demand was crimped. Single-family bond issuance often exhibits a countercyclical pattern of rising in tandem with interest rates due to greater borrower demand for the program's below-market rate loans (see Exhibit 53.5). The bulk of annual single-family bond issuance is usually provided through refundings, which do not require volume cap. State HFAs routinely refund prepayments as they accumulate in outstanding bonds, transferring the cash to a new refunding issue and using it to originate new loans. How-

EXHIBIT 53.5   Local HFA versus State HFA Share of SF Bond Market

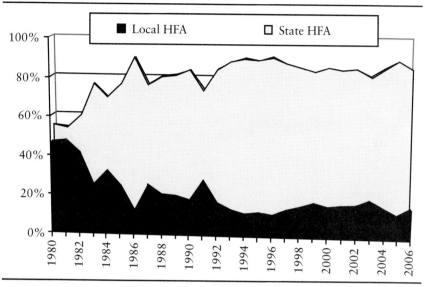

Source: Thomson Financial.

ever, the Ten Year Rule, explained later in this chapter, continues to impair this activity. The outlook for repeal of the Ten Year Rule is much brighter. This could be the main hope for further increases in SF bond issuance in the near future.

CREDIT STRENGTH OF SF BONDS

State HFA SF bonds are one of the strongest credit sectors of the municipal market, rivaling State general obligations. The universe of ratings on these bonds is concentrated between AA to AAA. None have ever defaulted. The ratings are also extraordinarily stable. A trend of upgrades has occurred in this decade, pushing many ratings up a notch. The ratings stability of State HFA SF bonds is by design. These are structured financings—packages of mortgages and redundant credit supports built to withstand Great Depression scenarios for mortgage defaults and extreme prepayment stresses without recourse to the issuer. The multiple layers of security include:

- *First mortgages.* The primary source of repayment for the bonds is a pool of 30-year, fixed-rate first mortgages (see Exhibit 53.6). Servicers are required to foreclose promptly on delinquent loans. Serious delin-

EXHIBIT 53.6   Diagram of Single-Family Bond Financing

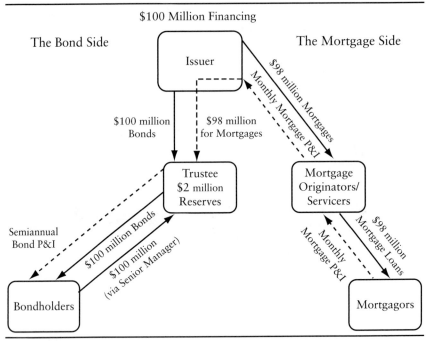

Source: Merrill Lynch.

quencies (60+ days) for seasoned State HFA pools today are generally 0.5% to 3%, much better than averages for Federal Housing Adminis-tration (FHA) loans. State HFAs often combine mortgages from many series into huge pools, so new bonds may be backed by old loans with substantial home equity.

- *Excess collateral.* SF bonds have asset levels equal to 102% to over 110% of outstanding bonds. This is either contributed by the issuer or built up by surplus earnings. A built-in arbitrage is created by the spread of up to 1.125 points between the mortgage coupons and bond rate.
- *Primary mortgage insurance.* All mortgages are credit enhanced if loan-to-value ratios are 80% or above. Many SF bond programs require loans to obtain insurance from the FHA. This federally guaranteed insurance pays 99% of principal following assignment. A minor amount may be insured by the Veterans Administration. Other HFAs utilize private mortgage insurance from companies rated at least AA. A few use state insurance or self-insurance. These policies typically cover 24% to 28% of mortgage principal.

- *Loan loss coverage.* Primary insurance is augmented by additional assets to cover timing and potential gaps in coverage. This may be in the form of pool insurance of 5% to 10% of the loan balances. Alternatively, reserve funds equal to 2% to 10% of the bonds exist.
- *State HFA resources.* Many State HFAs also pledge their general obligation (GO) pledge to their SF bonds. State HFA GO credits are A to AA, although only about half have explicit ratings. Many have hundreds of millions in fund balances, and are vital tools of their state governments. Furthermore, even if a GO pledge is not formally extended, State HFAs provide substantial support through proactive management of their issues. Note that there is no implicit assumption of State GO support factored into these ratings, although that would be a significant probability.

State HFA SF bonds have proven themselves resoundingly by weathering real estate crashes in Texas and other oil-producing states in the 1980s, as well as the Northeast, Southern California, and Hawaii. Only modest downgrades of a rating category occurred to state HFA bonds in Wyoming and Alaska. They were subsequently upgraded. Texas bonds were never downgraded from AA, despite a real estate crash that rivaled the Great Depression in severity.

Facets of Single-Family Bond Credit Analysis

Credit analysis of SF bonds entails a review of the following:

- Mortgage collateral
- Loan loss coverage and liquidity reserves
- Cash flow stress tests
- Legal provisions
- Investments, GICs, other third party supports
- Management
- Local economy

Detailed descriptions on specific criteria for each of these areas are available from rating agencies. In pactice, downgrades have resulted in rare situations for just a few reasons:

- GIC provider downgrades—the main cause of housing bond downgrades (S&P's "Weak Link approach")
- Raids by state general funds—recurs during recessions
- Extreme delinquencies or unused proceeds calls—alters the cash flows
- Negative arbitrage with heavy prepayments

- Mortgage insurer downgrades, disputes, loopholes
- Lack of management
- Call-protected capital appreciation bonds

Causes of Single-Family Bond Credit Stress

The vast majority of downgrades that have occurred among state HFA bonds were caused by downgrades of guaranteed investment agreement providers. These are usually modest in severity. Far fewer have occurred this decade than in the 1980s and 1990s, as providers today are more stable. Most large state HFA programs are highly insulated from exposure to any one *guaranteed investments contracts* (GIC) due to open indentures. Providers may post collateral to reinforce the GIC rating, as could HFAs. Most of the downgrades were by S&P due its weak-link approach to structured financings, which has been modified so as to produce less rating changes. GICs are used for reserves, float, prepayments, and acquisition funds.

Eminently Stable and Often Underrated

A great amount of bonds in the largest indentures have also experienced credit improvement but are not upgrade candidates. Fund balances and profitability have risen. Yet upgrades may not occur for many of the largest, active state HFA indentures because they are programmed for their present A ratings. They are structured to allow new issues, cash withdrawals, GICs from AA entities, cash flow projections set at AA levels, and insurance and reserves set for less than AAA loan loss ratios. A rating of AAA may have always been theoretically available for purchase, but not deemed an inefficient allocation of resources. A number of large HFAs have foregone upgrades because they have not desired to commit to retaining surplus in indentures that permit withdrawals.

Mortgage-Backed Securities versus Whole Loans

In addition to the whole loan credit structure described thus far, about 25% (and rising) of state HFA SF bonds, as well as most local HFA bonds today, are backed by Ginnie Mae, Fannie Mae, and Freddie Mac securities. Trustees exchange the SF bonds mortgages for new *mortgage-backed securities* (MBS) created from the same loans and guaranteed by one of these AAA rated entities. The MBS become the collateral for the bonds, qualifying them for AAA ratings. Alternative structures with reserve fund or collateral guarantees have also been seen. The introduction of MBS into a whole loan indenture often leads to rating upgrades. Most local HFA bonds now use MBS due to a strikingly different credit history.

The Local SF Bond Debacle of the 1990s

By the early 1990s, local single-family, whole loan bonds (not backed by Fannie Mae, Freddie Mac, and Ginnie Mae MBS) became a major municipal junk sector. Harris County, Texas HFC issues ostensibly became the first local single-family bonds to flirt with default in 1987. By the mid-1990s, several dozen had defaulted. The bulk of this local junk was concentrated in four states: California, Colorado, Texas, and Kansas. There were three types of local single-family junk. The first were bonds without ratings due to the failure to submit timely information to the rating agencies. The second had troubled mortgage insurers, most prominently TMIC/Ticor, IMI, and Verex. Some bonds in this category benefited from property appreciation, so that foreclosures were profitable, not requiring insurance.

The third type were those with *asset/liability* (A/L) ratios below 1.00 (parity). Most local single-family bonds started out with slightly less assets than liabilities due to *nonasset bonds* used to cover costs of issuance. They were assigned investment-grade ratings if cash flow projections indicated parity was achieved within five years. A limited number of moderately stressful scenarios were required, such as prepayments at three-year and five-year average lives. A large quantity of local single-family bonds sank further below parity due to extreme unused proceeds and prepayment calls which they were not designed to withstand. The presence of last-to-be-called zero coupons was another structural flaw. Long-term zeros can worsen A/L ratios in the latter stages of an issue's life, accreting liabilities faster than assets earn.

Many also had unprecedented foreclosures. Unforeseen problems arose, such as uninsured losses due to large market value declines, costs of property repairs prior to insurance payouts, challenges by insurance companies, VA no-bids, bankruptcy stays on foreclosure. Administrative errors sometimes exacerbated problems. A major lesson learned from the debacle is the importance of management in a housing issue. This is why state HFA issues largely escaped similar problems.

A UNIQUE BASKET OF CALL OPTIONS

Single-family bonds may be viewed as extremes of the fixed income market because up to six distinct call options may be embedded in any given bond:

1. Prepayments
2. Crosscall

3. Unused proceeds (non-origination) call
4. Optional call
5. Surplus call
6. Cleanup call/sale of mortgages

Many are unique to housing bonds. Most other municipal bonds have just one: the optional call. Taxable MBS have only prepayments plus a cleanup call. SF bonds also differ from MBS due to the behavior of the prepayment calls, and the flexibility reserved by issuers. Housing bond analysts in the municipal market have much more to evaluate.

PREPAYMENTS IN SF BONDS

Mortgage prepayments are a natural occurrence in any pool of mortgages. They arise from mortgage turnover generated by normal economic activity: equity takeout, move-up buying, relocation, partial paydowns, divorces, deaths, mortgage defaults (followed by mortgage insurance payouts), and more. Seasoned mortgage pools prepay in amounts usually ranging from 2% to 15% per annum in the absence of refinancing activity. When rates decline substantially, borrowers with above market rate loans refinance to lower their payments. That may create abnormally high prepayments. Interest rates have an enormous impact on mortgage refinancing activity.

Exhibit 53.7 shows the 30-year fixed mortgage rates versus the Mortgage Bankers Association (MBA) Refinancing Index. The MBA Index gauges refinancing applications at lenders. It sets activity in the week ended 3/16/90 as a benchmark value of 100. It reveals that each succeeding boom has surpassed the prior one in intensity. During 1998, the MBA Index set a new high of 4,389. In 2001, it peaked at 5,535. In 2002, it surged to a high of 6,927. In 2003, the MBA peaked twice, setting a new benchmark of 9,387 in March, and surpassing 9,000 again in June as mortgage rates bottomed out at a 40-year low of 5.21%.

Measures of Prepayments

In the municipal market, there are three ways prepayment speeds are expressed.

PSA (BMA) Index

The Public Securities Association (later named Bond Markets Association and now the Securities Industry and Financial Markets Association) is sim-

EXHIBIT 53.7 MBA Refinancing Index versus Conventional Mortgage Rates, 1/5/90–1/26/07

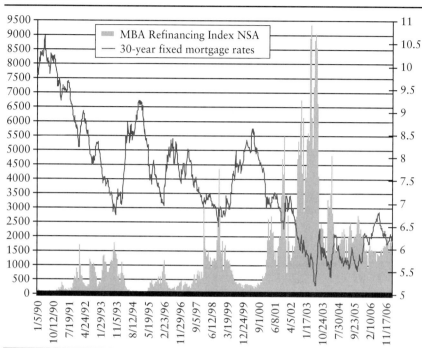

Source: Freddie Mac Primary Mortgage Market Survey for 30-year fixed rate conventional mortgages and the Mortgage Bankers Association Refinancing Index (nonseasonally adjusted).

ply a benchmark, not a predictive model. It assumes a ramp-up of prepayments on newly originated loans by 0.02% per month until the 30th month. Thereafter, the prepayment speed is assumed to remain constant at a 6% CPR. In the absence of refinancing activity, 100% PSA represents a base rate of turnover for market rate loans of 6% for seasoned loans. There is now perceived to be a flaw in the PSA Index. Its seasoning curve has been discredited. The fastest loans in the taxable mortgage markets over the last few years have been those from the last year or two. This ramp-up assumption greatly distorts prepayment speeds.

FHA Index

The FHA Index is based upon the actual terminations experience of FHA loans. Formerly updated annually, it was discontinued by HUD after 1991. Thus, it is woefully out-of-date today. Archaic single-family bond tax code still mandates a 100% FHA assumption for arbitrage calculations. The FHA Index is an anachronism no longer used elsewhere in the mortgage markets. At high speeds, it is faster than the PSA Index.

Conditional Prepayment Rate

A more straightforward measure is a popular standard in the mortgage markets: *conditional prepayment rate* (CPR). This is essentially the compound annualized rate of prepayments as a percent of the pool balance at the beginning of the period. It is interchangeable with PSA speeds. For example, 100% PSA for seasoned loans (i.e., outstanding more than 30 months) equates to a prepayment rate of 6% per year, or a 6% CPR.

MUNICIPAL PREPAYMENT SPEEDS

Single-family bond prepayments are highly sensitive to interest rate movements. Exhibit 53.8 reveals the history of national mean prepayment speeds for SFMRBs mortgages since 1990. The data consist of five active subindices for mortgage coupons of 7%, 6.5% 6% 5.5%, and 5%. Previous subindices for 7.5% to 11% loans were discontinued due to attrition but are shown

EXHIBIT 53.8   SF Bond Prepayment Speed Indexes, 1990–2006

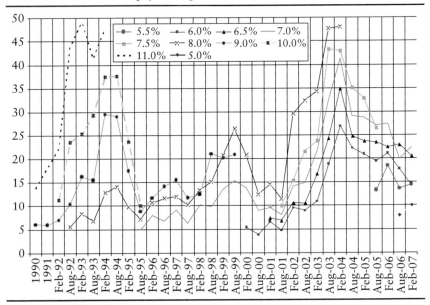

Source: Merrill Lynch.

in grayscale. The index is tabulated semiannually. It is geographically balanced, derived from a database of state HFA single-family bonds from over 20 states totaling over $1 billion outstanding. Only pools with mortgages that uniformly match the subindex rate and which have a "passthrough" approach to prepayments are included. The February 2007 data in Exhibit 53.8 covers current redemptions from October 2006 to March 2007.

The CPR methodology is used for measuring prepayment rates. The value of 20.5 for the 6.5% subindex on February 2007 implies that single-family bonds backed by 6.5% loans would lose 20.5% of outstanding principal to prepayment calls if that rate persisted over an entire year. Most SFMRBs that are backed by pool of loans with 6.5% coupons would have term bonds with coupons in the upper 5%s to 6%. The standard deviations are large, often around 50% of the mean. This attests to a very wide range of speeds among SF bonds with identical mortgage rates.

Volatility is the Norm

The indexes are clearly volatile. Three major prepayment booms are evident: 1993, 1998, and the Great Boom of 2001–2004. However, there is a lag evident in single-family bond calls, due to semiannual redemption cycles and 30-day call notice periods. Peak redemptions for single-family bonds persisted into 1994 and 1999, well after booms subsided in taxable markets. There is a lag of up to eight to nine months before the full impact of interest rate movements are manifest in single-family bond redemptions.

Peak of the Great Prepayment Boom

A main reason that SF bonds were unpopular a few years ago was the torrent of prepayments that peaked in 2003–2004. Semiannual speeds on loans with coupons of 7% and above exceeded 40% calls per annum. This would produce average lives on the entire bond issue of little over 1 year. But fast speeds are not necessarily negative for investors using average life pricing. That's because when the average life of a pool contracts, it is priced using a spread to a shorter benchmark on the yield curve. If the yield curve is rising (the norm for the municipal market), premium loan pools with shorter average lives may offer more spread than premiums with longer average lives.

Bubble in Low-Rate Loans

Although the Great Refinancing Boom of 2003–2004 receded, another type of boom followed due to the "Bubble" in SF home prices. According to the Home Price Index of OFHEO, unprecedented year-over-year nationwide home price increases of 10% to 14% occurred in each of the eight quarters ended December 31, 2006. This has been generating record prepayments in market-rate and below-market rate mortgages. The national mean SF bond prepayment rates in February 2007 of 14% for 5.5% and 6% loans (200% PSA), as well as 10% for 5% loans, evidences still remarkable turnover being generated by surging home values and alternative mortgage products.

Some have postulated that the behavior of prepayments has fundamentally changed. Not long ago, a new pool of market rate 30-year fixed mortgages could reasonably be expected to have an average life of 10 to 11 years at 100% PSA. Now, a new pool of such loans may be expected to have an average life of five to seven years. Nonetheless, SFMRB issuers continue to finance these contracting assets at 30-year bond rates. Investors may take advantage of this increasing mismatch between their assets and liabilities by collecting this extra spread.

Comparisons to Other MBS

MBS whose prepayment speeds most resemble SF Bonds are Ginnie Maes. This is intuitive, as Ginnie Maes consist of FHA/VA loans for borrowers with a profile similar to those of SFMRBs. Federal limitations on SF bonds proscribe maximum purchase prices of 90% of the average for the area, and borrower income limits of 115% of the area median. Moreover, most FHA loans are also made to first time homebuyers. These moderate-income borrowers typically prepay more slowly than higher income conventional loans do, particularly after an interest rate decline. At the height of the Great Boom, SF bond prepayment speeds were the slowest of all MBS by a considerable margin. More affluent Fannie Mae and Freddie Mac mortgagors respond more rapidly to interest rate declines.

However, this correlation is not always consistent for short-term intervals. During periods of rising or higher interest rates, SF bond prepayments may appear relatively vigorous. Periodic inversions of the traditional alignment have been attributed to price appreciation in moderate-income housing, and belated targeting by bankers. Overall, SF bond prepayments appear less volatile.

Geographic Bias in Single-Family Bond Prepayments

Understanding how geographic bias affects SF bond prepayments is a powerful tool for uncovering relative value. All SF bond loans are highly concentrated geographically. This distinguishes them from other residential mortgage-backed securities. Exhibit 53.9 categorizes states by their relative prepayment speeds in the second half of 2006. State prepayment differen-

EXHIBIT 53.9 State Prepayment Ratios for Conventional Loans: Fannie Mae and Freddie Mac Data for Second Half of 2006

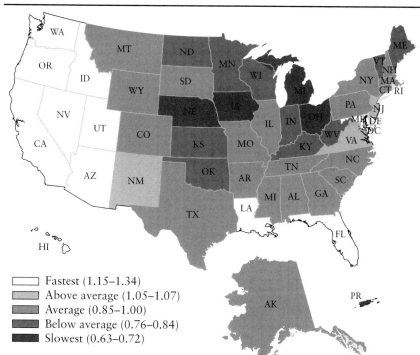

Fastest (1.15–1.34)
Above average (1.05–1.07)
Average (0.85–1.00)
Below average (0.76–0.84)
Slowest (0.63–0.72)

Source: Merrill Lynch.

tials were derived by sorting all conventional and Ginnie Mae loans into cohorts with identical coupons and years of origination, and then ranking the states in each cohort. This neutralizes coupon and seasoning. Within these cohorts, the same states consistently appear at the top or bottom of national averages. A weighted average of all cohorts produces a state factor for modeling.

Many Causes for Prepayment Disparities

Conversely, weak real estate markets inhibit prepayments due to reduced ability refinance, job insecurity or unemployment, and declines in home values. Income levels and loan size are prominent influences on prepayment behavior. Recent declines in the rankings of Midwest states may be partly due to automobile industry weakness. In-migration and population mobility is also associated with higher housing turnover. Marketing efforts by local mortgage originators may be a factor. Moreover, a wide disparity in mortgage recording and transfer taxes may explain the behavior of New York loans. Major prepayment surges in Mississippi and Louisana demonstrate unique prepayment impacts of the Katrina/Rita catastrophes, which generated massive casualty insurance payoffs.

This geographic data appear consistent with current patterns of home price appreciation and developments in mortgage markets (e.g., proliferation of alternative products). This map illustrates the states with fastest prepayments are concentrated in the West. Arizona leads with speeds at 134% of national means. California, Utah, and Nevada are among the fastest. The Pacific Northwest is at recent highs. A highly unusual occurrence was the surge of Louisana in the first half of 2006 to the highest factor ever recorded: 210%. Louisana had been no higher than 70% since 2001. This was due to massive casualty claims from Katrina. Only four times before had a state exceeded 150%. The lowest ratio ever recorded was for Puerto Rico, which registered at 0.30 during the prepayment boom of 2003. Premium bonds from slower states and discounts from fast states may offer greater relative value.

Ranking based upon Ginnie Mae data produces many similar placements. Arizona, is fastest for Ginnie Maes at 170% in the second half of 2006. However, the range of ratios is usually higher for Ginnie Maes for conventional loans.

Flexible Prepayment Structure

Although underlying prepayments may be similar, the manner in which SF bond prepayment redemptions are handled differs greatly from Ginnie Maes or *collateralized mortgage obligations* (CMOs). Many SF bonds have no defined tranche structure for prepayments beyond perhaps a PAC bond. Nonetheless, many tend implement redemptions in a customary pattern. Understanding these patterns is one of the best ways of uncovering undervalued issues. Understanding the issuer's selection method is essential to accurate average life estimates. The two main approaches are to redeem bonds pro rata, or to call the highest coupons first. Exceptions to general patterns can be found within each issuer. Issuers may alter their approach without warning.

Regardless of what the issuer does, the high coupon (usually 30-year maturity) absorbs most of the uncertainty. When opacity is high, the 30-year may appear overvalued. It is merely the uncertainty that detracts from value. One of the most undervalued SF bonds is a 30-year bond of an issuer that consistently calls by high coupons in each series. That is an intermediate average life sold at 30-year bond rates.

OTHER WAYS OF HANDLING PREPAYMENTS

The amount of flexibility retained by many state HFAs is actually far greater than discretion over the order of coupons to call. Indeed, HFAs are often under no indenture requirements to redeem bonds at all. There are six options for handling prepayments at their disposal, enumerated here. Understanding these alternatives is critical to discerning relative value.

1. *Redeem bonds* in the issue.
2. *Recycle into new mortgages.* This may result in no prepayments for some time, but eventually the issuer must stop in order to avoid a cash flow mismatch. (Some bonds have 40 year maturities to accommodate up to ten years of recycling). However, "internal recycling" tends to also increase the volatility of a bond's average life. It extends it when interest rates are high, but fails to prevent calls when rates fall. The efficacy of recycling hinges on the attractiveness of the mortgage rate. Recycling may be done at the same rate as the original loans in the series, at a blended rate for the indenture, or a deep discount has room under the allowable spread.
3. *Reinvest.* Some HFAs reinvest, but earnings are limited under tax code. Some accumulate prepayments in order to do a large current refunding of cash. A lack of prepayment calls is a red flag for investors.
4. *Pay debt service.* Some issues have a front-loaded debt service that is structured assuming some modest level of prepayments. This reduces calls.
5. *Crosscalling* into another series.
6. *Purchase bonds of the issue in the secondary* in lieu of redemptions.

PAC BONDS

One solution for investors seeking investor-friendly, transparent structures is the *planned amortization class* (PAC) bond. PAC bonds are the most successful structural innovation in the history of the SF bond sector. They are a refinement on the former *supersinker* bond. PACs and supersinkers are legally designated as the first-called tranche from prepayments arising from within the series. PACs are only called first up to some readily expected amount, such as 75% to 125% PSA. Unlike supersinkers, PACs become last called for prepayments over this floor. At some high-speed threshold (usually 300% to 500% PSA) they convert to being called pro rata. This call regimen imparts the average life stability within a band of prepayment speeds. This fixed average life within the band distinguishes them from supersinkers, which have a variable average life.

PACs are sold on an average life basis. The vast majority have a target five year average life. If a PAC falls behind or ahead of its schedule of calls, it is busted and may suffer a substantial loss of market value. Note however, that PAC schedules are cumulative, so that a PAC may slip back into its band following some aberrant prepayment activity. Moreover, extension risk may be desirable for a premium PAC. Original issue premium PACs are the most popular type of PAC today by far.

DISCRIMINATING BETWEEN PAC BONDS

Sophisticated PAC buyers look at many other factors besides that PAC pricing speed. Some of these include:

- The broadest band width are 75% to 500% PSA. The lower the floor, the more stable.
- Average life volatility outside of the band.
- The window is the length of time between first and last calls.
- Geographic bias is a crucial determinant of expected speed.
- Ability to be crossed called. PACs may usually not be crosscalled, except if they are behind in their schedules. This is quite important for Premium PACs.
- Unused proceeds call risk. Even if last called from UP, unused proceeds may dramatically extend a PAC. Is the PAC band reduced proportionately? Is a Premium PAC called at the original premium, or some amortized value of that?
- Disclosure, for example, the PAC schedule, speeds of transferred loans, mortgage rates.
- Mortgage collateral, mortgage rates, and loan types.
- Frequency and application of calls. Are semiannual calls mandated? Are pro rata calls required? If not, are projections based on high-to-low calls?
- Lottery calls must be required. This is fundamental to average life pricing. Can the issuer purchase bonds in the secondary market with prepayments in lieu of redemptions?
- Dedication of prepayments to the PAC must not be dependent on perpetuation of the Ten Year Rule (discussed later in this chapter). This is almost always the case.

- Spread to BMA swap curve versus MMD.
- Optional calls of PACs should be at a premium, if the PAC has an average life longer than five years.

The unusually high prepayment speeds now in evidence for low rate loans has created a favorable environment for PACs. The former bane of the PAC market—extension risk—has been banished. Moreover, a moderation in speeds due to a cooling housing market tempers concerns that rapid prepayments will bust bands and impair returns on premium PACs. Investors concerned about contraction risk may generally assign greater relative value to premium PACs from Southern states, the Midwest and Plains, and Puerto Rico.

PASSTHROUGHS

A structure similar to PAC bonds that appears to be proliferating is the *passthrough*. This is also sold on an average life basis in the primary market and meets demands of institutional investors for transparency and a simplified structure that facilitates modeling. However, a passthrough has no band of stability in average life. A passthrough is similar to a supersinker (which is a first-called tranche), but is longer in duration. A passthrough is typically the only maturity in the bond issue and is amortized solely by prepayments and mortgage principal repayments. Thus, its expected average life matches that of the whole underlying pool of loans. There are no other call options (beyond a cleanup call) or interference with the prepayment stream to holders. Crosscalling is prohibited. Spreads may come in as familiarity rises.

LOCKOUT BONDS

For investors at the long end of the market, a structure that greatly mitigates the open-ended optionality of SF bonds is the lockout. This is usually a term bond with no calls allowed for 5 to 10 years. Investors pay for this call protection by sacrificing 10 to 20 basis points of coupon. Some investors are not enticed, suspecting that lockouts are mainly offered on bonds that are not expected to be called anyway. However, these were wonderful investments to own during the Great Prepayment Boom. Lockouts can also add positive convexity. Note that lockouts can usually be called in extreme circumstances to preserve the tax-exempt status. Ten Year Rule restrictions could trigger this.

CROSSCALLING

The option to crosscall between different series distinguishes SF bonds from other MBS. Where practiced, it is often the dominant factor in determining the duration of a SF bond. Analyzing crosscalling is one of the best methods of uncovering undervalued SF bonds. *Crosscalling* is defined as the extraordinary redemption of bonds from redemption funds (e.g., prepayments, surplus, unused proceeds) originating from a different series of bonds. The definition of crosscalling used here refers to transfers of prepayments between series. The term may also be used in conjunction with unused proceeds or surplus revenues. However, prepayments are usually far more significant within an indenture than surpluses. Unused proceeds crosscalls are rarely permitted and seldom encountered.

The Boundaries of Crosscalling

Crosscalling, as defined here, can only occur between series issued under the same general resolution, which share a common, indivisible security. These are parity issues, assigned a common rating. Since all revenues and assets of parity issues are legally commingled, it is efficient debt management to combine prepayments and surpluses derived from individual series and direct them to the highest coupons of all series outstanding. The main benefit to the issuer from crosscalling is rapid retirement of highest cost debt. Crosscalling is also used as a debt management tool, with redemptions sometimes determined by other criteria (e.g., leveling debt service). Crosscalling is overwhelmingly a State HFA phenomenon; only a few local HFAs crosscall.

The legal ability to crosscall is established by the general and/or series resolutions for each issue. Some series within the same indenture may be are crosscallable while others are not. The same applies to individual coupons within a series. Many series are also split into subseries which may be remarketed at different times; therefore it is important to identify which subseries or series are sold on a composite tax plan as a single series. Calls typically occur freely between subseries; however, this does not constitute crosscalling.

Extent of Crosscalling Activity

As of mid-2007, 14 State HFAs (out of 48 that issue SF bonds) crosscall with all eligible prepayments (see Exhibit 53.10). Crosscallers are now clustered in the Northeast and Midwest. There has been little change in the total number or composition of crosscallers over the last three years. However, the number has decreased from 1993, when 20 were active. We have a new

EXHIBIT 53.10 State HFA Crosscalling Status, as of April 2007

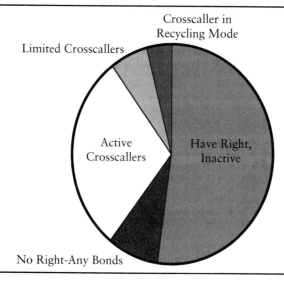

Source: Merrill Lynch.

category this year for crosscallers who have entered the recycling mode (explained below). This includes Connecticut and Virginia. This category is expected to grow. There are 6% of HFAs in the limited crosscalling category. This is a mainly due to a conservative approach to universal cap obstacles. They do not indulge in the reallocation of mortgage assets between series that is characteristic of HFAs that crosscall in the universal cap era.

There are only four state HFAs today that appear to legally prohibit crosscalling in all outstanding series. This category includes Louisana and Mississippi because all their bonds are in closed, standalone indentures. In addition, others have open indentures, but series resolutions are believed to lack explicit authorization for crosscalling.

Most State HFAs Have Latent Crosscall Option

The largest category continues to be state HFAs with the right to crosscall, but who are not presently exercising it. This group now numbers 25 (52%). Many added the ability to crosscall without expecting any offsetting penalization from the market. To be included in this category, it is only necessary to have the crosscall option present in some series (e.g., Arkansas), although others lack it. Some have had the right to crosscall for some time, but never utilized it (e.g., New Hampshire and Montana). Another subgroup is those that may have crosscalled briefly—perhaps once or twice ever—but stopped

(California and Ohio). Others have crosscalled extensively in the past, but have ceased (Vermont and Tennessee), but have ceased. Investors should be cognizant of the potential impacts of changes in crosscalling policies. The majority of state HFAs have materially altered their crosscalling status over the last two decades—although analysts can usually ascertain when a change in policy is forthcoming, due to extensive advance planning and use of specialized financial advisors.

New Era for Crosscalling: Recycling

Crosscalling can be very positive for investors, as it protects many moderate coupons from calls for many years. Throughout most of the history of this sector, progressive declines in interest rates caused new issue coupons to be out-of-the money for crosscalls. Today, we are in a new era for crosscalling. Virtually all are crosscalling in the 5% range. New issue term bond coupons have converged with the targets for crosscalling. Crosscallers find themselves in the awkward situation of attempting to sell new issues that may be near their highest coupons outstanding, and thus may have inordinately short average lives. In reaction to this, many active crosscallers are planning to cease crosscalling in the near future and attempt comprehensive recycling of prepayments. Two have already done so. However, there is no guaranty that issuers will recycle or cease crosscalling if market conditions change again. Connecticut's HFA was in this mode in 2002 before returning to active crosscalling in 2003.

It seems bizarre for an issuer to sell a bond that might be crosscalled in a matter of months at costly 30-year rates. The exhaustion of high coupons may lead to a widespread decline in crosscalling. Crosscalling has already also been increasingly curtailed by two tax laws that Housing bond analysts are very familiar with: the Ten Year Rule and the Universal Cap.

THE TEN YEAR RULE

The *Ten Year Rule* is a major limitation on crosscalling by state HFAs. It was inserted into the Technical and Miscellaneous Revenue Act of 1988. It mandates that, following the tenth anniversary of a SF bond, mortgage repayments and prepayments must be used to redeem bonds no later than the close of the first semiannual period after receipt. The Ten Year Rule preempts crosscalling, recycling, or reinvesting prepayments received after ten years. Specifically, a MRB past the Ten Year Rule limit cannot crosscall out with prepayments, but it could still be crosscalled from prepayments in other series.

It is typical for MRBs to be a combination of new volume cap and current refundings of multiple series. This causes a portion of prepayments to be "restricted" to in-series redemptions, while the "unrestricted" balance may be used for recycling or crosscalling coupons in other series. Restricted prepayments usually exceed unrestricted prepayments within most HFA programs. The percentage that is restricted in a given issue rises over time based upon the dates of the refunded series. Lack of full disclosure of the Ten Year Rule schedule leaves investors unclear as to the extent that the issue may be crosscalled.

Ten Year Rule Constrains Issuance

The Ten Year Rule also limits issuance because it also prevents refundings of prepayments in SF bonds over 10 years old. Most state HFAs routinely refund prepayments accumulated in outstanding series. These current (or "replacement") refundings are not subject to volume cap. The Ten Year Rule costs HFAs many billions of dollars in foregone refundings. The National Council of state HFAs has made repeal of the Ten Year Rule a top priority. Repeal has a significant probability of success in the near term.

Potential Impacts of Repeal of Ten Year Rule

If Repeal is extended to outstanding bonds, then revisions may be necessary to pricing and average life estimates that assumed the Ten Year Rule would last forever. Term bonds of many high coupon callers may face extension risk. Repeal of the Ten Year Rule could lead to increases in crosscalling volume. This would cause faster attrition of highest coupons for active crosscallers. Low coupons would experience average life extension. However, it is likely that Repeal initially may be extended prospectively to new issues. Repeal would eliminate a disclosure matter for investors, and reduce administrative costs for issuers. Investors should consider potential impacts of Repeal in evaluations.

Pre-Ullman Bond Exemption

An exemption from the Ten Year Rule exists for "pre-Ullman" issues. On April 24, 1979, Al Ullman, Chairman of the House Ways and Means Committee, introduced the "Ullman bill." A version was enacted in December 1980 as the Mortgage Subsidy Bond Tax Act of 1980, with some provisions effective as of the date of the bill's introduction. Lenient provisions include: higher 1.5 point spread, absence of income and price limits, non-AMT, and no first time homebuyer requirement. This creates strong incentives for state

HFAs to preserve pre-Ullman money, because of lenient tax provisions and perpetual crosscalling/recycling capability. Calls are avoided through recycling or crosscalling away. Status is usually rolled over through optional refundings.

UNIVERSAL CAP REGULATIONS

If repeal of the Ten Year Rule occurred, the Universal Cap (UCAP) regulation will remain a major deterrent to crosscalling for some HFAs. The UCAP regulations created an accounting mess which has impeded crosscalling between issues sold since July 1993. The trouble is that the UCAP usually forces a matching reallocation of loans from series being crosscalled to the ones that are the source of the prepayments. It requires annual calculations of bond assets to bond par value. Surplus assets over the cap are deallocated—excluded from requirements to rebate arbitrage earnings. A high coupon series receiving prepayments from a low coupon series may be required to deallocate mortgages which will exceed the Universal Cap following the crosscall. Deallocated premium mortgages reallocated to the low coupon series may knock it out of yield compliance.

The main solutions negate financial benefits of crosscalling for the issuer and provide mainly a programmatic benefit for borrowers. These include taking less than full spread, or utilizing 0% participation loans to adjust weighted average mortgage rates. These are very complex and time-consuming transactions which higher legal and advisory fees. Many HFAs abandoned crosscalling which requires a reallocation of loans between series.

THE UNUSED PROCEEDS CALL

This is another major extraordinary call that is unique to SF bonds. It is caused by the failure of the issuer to utilize all the bond proceeds to purchase mortgages. In the 1980s and early 1990s, waves of *unused proceeds* or *non-origination calls* (UP calls) followed major, sustained declines in interest rates. Since the mortgage rate offered by the issuer was derived from the fixed bond rate, a sharp decline in interest rates soon after bond issuance could render the bond money uneconomic. These calls were usually precipitated by a sustained decline of typically at least 50 to 75 basis points, since SF bonds offer below market rate loans initially. Although tax law allows SF bonds 42 months after issuance to utilize their proceeds, most unused proceeds calls happen within one to two years. Note that this is an expiring option not present in seasoned issues. The vast majority of UP calls are pro rata.

Determinants of Unused Proceeds Calls

- *Origination period.* Tax law requires mandatory redemption of SFM-RBs from unused proceeds within 42 months after issuance. However, indentures have origination deadlines of nine months to two years, subject to extension.
- *Prevailing interest rates.* If taxable mortgage rates decline, the below-market rate interest subsidy offered by SFMRBs erodes. Issuer's expectations about rates heavily influences the call decision.
- *Competition.* Points, processing time, and underwriting terms are important factors. HFA loans are not competitive at market rates unless down payment assistance is provided. Additional bonds may undercut it.
- *Negative arbitrage.* Negative spread on mortgage acquisition funds is perhaps the main motivation for UP calls.
- *Guaranteed investment agreement terms.* For the acquisition funds. Investment rate, term, and renewal and rescission provisions are factors. Unused proceeds calls often occur when GICs mature.

UP calls are highly concentrated among inefficient originators. Although interest rate declines are virtually a pre-requisite for these calls, that doesn't entirely explain their causes. Among state HFAs, 10 accounted for 64% of all UP calls in the 1990s, and the top three for 30%.

Improved State HFA Origination Methods Reduce Frequency

Most state HFAs have become so efficient in over the last 10 years that they no longer incur unused proceeds calls, regardless of interest rate movements. The most efficient state HFAs utilize some or all of the origination techniques shown below. These techniques tend to have a similar effect—to shorten the origination period, thereby reducing exposure to interest rate volatility. Some have severed the linkage to bond rates and adjust mortgage rates to market frequently. The cycle of UP calls that used to follow every interest rate downturn has been broken. Following interest rate downturns in 1998 and 2001–2003, no major wave of UP calls materialized. Overall, this is a tremendous achievement for HFAs that have developed techniques to maintain the competitiveness of their product, and a major positive for investors in reducing the risk of UP calls.

Analyzing Unused Proceeds Call Risk

Most state HFAs have had no material UP calls this decade. Thus, research focus has shifted from statistics on actual call volume to a qualitative assessment of the issuer's origination methods. Issuers that engage in these practices attain a marked reduction in UP risk over HFAs using traditional, older origination methods. This is to ensure that the lack of such calls was not merely due to chance. Note that some local HFAs still incur UP calls frequently. The practices of efficient originators include:

- Frequent small issues/short origination pipeline. Efficient originators originate in a few months.
- Regular adjustment of mortgage rates to market.
- First come, first serve single loan reservation system (vs. lender and builder reservations).
- Streamlined, rapid processing of mortgage applications.
- Warehousing of loans /advance commitments.
- Steady pipeline/good lender relations.

OPTIONAL REDEMPTIONS IN SINGLE-FAMILY BONDS

Popular misconceptions exist regarding optional redemption behavior in SF bonds. State HFAs exercise optional call provisions routinely and in a relatively efficient manner. However, their motivations differ from those of other municipal bond issuers. Ostensibly, lowering the cost of debt service does not offer a direct financial benefit to an HFA. Federal tax law proscribes a maximum spread between the mortgage yield and bond yield of 1.125 points; an optional refunding may require rebate of excess earnings to the Treasury. In addition, tax law generally prohibits recovery of call premiums by adjusting the arbitrage spread of a SF refunding bond. Moreover, homeowners are free to prepay their mortgages individually. Heavy prepayment calls may cause such rapid amortization of SFMRBs that optional call provisions may appear superfluous.

Rather, the motivations for HFAs to undertake optional redemptions are mainly program-oriented. Most common are:

1. Blend mortgage yields on transferred premium loans with new super deep discount loans so that the blended rate remains within legal arbitrage limits. Thus, the new issue may be able to originate extremely deep discount mortgages. This is a form of cross-subsidization.
2. Extend the life of pre-Ullman money. State HFAs have strong financial incentives, in the form of liberal arbitrage laws, to preserve "pre-Ullman" series perpetually through optional calls.

A positive spread between the refunded bond coupons and new issue yields is generally, but not always, required. HFAs occasionally have other motivations for optional redemptions besides economic refundings, such as release of overcollateralization in older indentures.

Average life projections should factor in the interactions between multiple call options in a SF bond. Average life projections that extend past "in the money" optional call dates should be viewed with great skepticism. For premium bonds, the optional call should truncate any average life derived from prepayments alone. There have been isolated cases of small local HFAs that sell bonds infrequently, and thus have not taken advantage of optional call opportunities.

Beware of Optional Call Extension

Optional call provisions in SF bonds can be a source of consternation to portfolio managers. Firstly, SFMRBs are not permitted to be advance refunded by a tax-exempt bond. This removes a potential source of capital gains that investors may find in most other municipal bonds. Thus all optional redemptions are current refundings, utilizing active call provisions. Secondly, as interest rates fluctuate, a SF bond may alternate between being a discount and premium bond over its lifetime. Each time it crosses below par, the bond reverts from pricing to optional call date (or average life, if shorter) to maturity. This leverages the extension risk in a SF bond, undercutting performance and raising hedging costs.

PRICING SINGLE-FAMILY BONDS

Many issuers have maximized optionality in SF bonds on the notion that they incur no penalty. Why is this not always perceived to be occur? Is there such a thing as a free lunch? Clearly, there has been a significant influx of major new institutional buyers into the sector that are not selective on structure, since their holding periods are temporary.

However, it may be demonstrated that yields on single family bonds are high. This is not always perceived because the conventional way in which SF bond spreads are measured is off nominal maturity dates. This is "bullet pricing" (by maturity date); it violates the fundamental tenet of securities valuation—which is to value the security at the present value of its expected cash flows. The nominal maturity dates of SF bonds are a fiction. Normal to rapid prepayments cause average lives of many term bonds of different maturity dates to converge. A more meaningful spread is between the average life of the single-family bond to the matching part of the municipal AAA noncallable G.O curve. The basic pricing approaches to SF bonds are:

1. *Bullet pricing.* Pricing to a generic housing spread to the nominal maturity to compensate the investor for the uncertainty of the cash flows. This is what is often quoted as the "Housing bond spread".
2. *Pricing to worst case.* Higher premium issues are often priced to a worst possible case, which may be a current call at par. Pricing to worst is the ultimate in defensive trading.
3. *Simple average life pricing.* This involves calculating the expected average life of the SFMRB, based on the expected scenario for prepayment speed, unused proceeds, and other call options. In its simplest form, the estimated average life is merely substituted for maturity in the bullet pricing approach.
4. *Static cash flow yield analysis.* Yield to maturity (or yield to call) assumes level coupon payments are received until maturity (or to call); it does not recognize prepayments of principal. It is a flawed measure for MBS. Cash flow yield is the internal rate of return on the projected stream of uneven cash flows.
5. *Multiple scenario analysis.* This attempts to price the option or evaluate the effect of the option on prices or yield. This involves expectations analysis. This is an improvement over certainty equivalent cash flows, where the prepay speed is assumed to occur for certain. A better approach is to develop probability weighted yields and returns.
6. *Option-adjusted spread.* The *option-adjusted spread* (OAS) technology in the municipal market evaluates standard municipal bonds with optional call. Different models are widespread in the taxable mortgage markets. The interest rate path dependency of prepayments requires a SFMRB cash flow model and prepayment function coupled with Monte Carlo simulation.

Furthermore, housing bond spreads are often roughly equivalent to those of taxable mortgage market securities in absolute basis points. Adjusted for duration and taxes, single-family yield spreads are greater than spreads of other mortgage backed securities. Thus, the penalty the market imposes on SFMRBs may be viewed as pricing at 30-year interest rates. Housing issuers are financing assets with duration of 6 to 10 years at 30-year rates plus a spread for undefined call risk.

CONCLUDING REMARKS

Pricing inefficiency is sought by sophisticated investors. The single-family sector offers an abundance of opportunities for research to add value. However, there is also a rising tide of interest among investors in SF bonds structured on prepayment assumptions, cleaner structures, and greater disclosure. PAC bonds have been far and away the most successful product for institutional investors in the history of housing bonds. They provide ample evidence of the savings to be derived from tailoring the product to the customers.

CHAPTER 54

Multifamily Bonds

Kurt van Kuller, CFA
Portfolio Manager
1861 Capital Management

The multifamily bond sector is one of the most diverse and innovative in the municipal market in terms of credit types and bond structures. It is an immensely fertile field for sophisticated investors to uncover undervalued bonds with value-added research. For the naive investor, however, caution should be exercised in navigating these waters. In this chapter, we will review the dimensions of this unique market, the characteristics of its main project types and credit structures, and special risks such as extraordinary redemptions.

MULTIFAMILY BOND MARKET PARAMETERS

Housing bond new issuance rose 27% in 2006 to $31.0 billion (including short-term debt of $1.2 billion). This can be see in Exhibit 54.1. This is the second highest annual total ever, exceeded only by $37.9 billion in 1985. However, the boom in 2006 was due entirely to a record amount of single-family mortgage revenue bonds, which surged to a record $24.8 billion sold. This was offset by a 24% decline in multifamily bonds in 2006. Volume of $6.2 billion was only half the total sold in 2003. Multifamily bonds fell to 20% of housing bonds, matching a historic low.

Multifamily bonds have accounted for 34% of the $516 billion housing bonds sold from 1980 to 2006. They peaked in 1985 at 55%, due to a rush to market to beat the effective date of the Tax Reform Act of 1986. That legislation fundamentally altered the landscape for multifamily finance by ending

---

This chapter was written when the author was employed as a research analyst at Merrill Lynch.

EXHIBIT 54.1   Housing Bond New Issues, 1980–2006

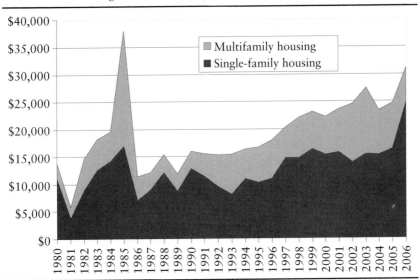

Source: Thomson Financial, Merrill Lynch Research. Includes private placements and short-term notes. Amounts are in $ thousands.

more aggressive forms of syndicated tax shelters and tax deductions. It caused multifamily bond sales to plummet to anemic levels of just over $3 billion between 1987 and 1990. However, the Tax Reform Act contained the seeds of recovery for this sector. It replaced older tax shelters with the Low Income Housing Tax Credit, which, after a slow start, emerged by the late 1990s as the dominant source of equity for for-profit affordable multifamily units.

Multifamily Bond Issuance is Cyclical

Multifamily bond issuance gradually rebounded to a new peak of $12.1 billion by 2003. Volume that year was spurred by a generational low in interest rates. Multifamily volume is highly cyclical. Higher interest rates crimp issuance, as economic refundings of outstanding bonds are curtailed. In addition, many new projects become infeasible at higher interest rates, due to high leverage and modest debt service coverage.

Flipside of the Housing Bubble: Rental Market Weakness

However, the more than 100 basis point rise in mortgage rates after 2003 does not fully explain the sharp decline in multifamily issuance since 2002–

EXHIBIT 54.2 Average Size of Multifamily Bond

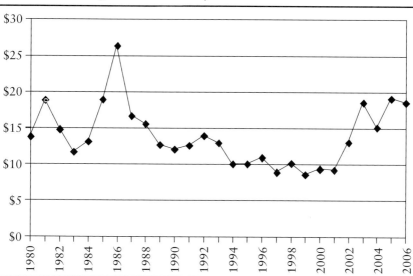

Source: Thomson Financial, Merrill Lynch Research. Includes private placements and short-term notes. Amounts are in $ millions.

2003. The first national downturn in rental markets in 15 years created widespread project financial stress, tighter underwriting guidelines, and reduced investor appetite for high-yield multifamily bonds. The historic boom in single-family home affordability, manifested in the "Housing Bubble" of 2004–2005, sapped demand for apartments. According to Merrill Lynch REIT Research, every 1% increase in home ownership decreases the renter base by roughly 1.1 million households (that equates to over 3% of the estimated multifamily rental housing stock in the United States). An increase in the average size of new multifamily issues (see Exhibit 54.2) somewhat offset the recent decline in dollar volume. The number of deals sold in 2006 (335) is the least since 1991. Moreover, 54% of 2006 MF volume was variable rate.

AMT PENALIZES THE SECTOR

The Tax Reform Act also created a variegated bond market with three types of tax status for Housing bonds: (1) exempt from federal income taxes; (2) taxable; or (3) exempt from the regular income tax but subject to the Alternative Minimum Tax (AMT) on individuals. In general, new multifamily bonds are subject to the AMT if the are owned by a for-profit entity. New multifamily bonds may still be fully tax-exempt if the project is owned by a nonprofit or governmental entity, backed by HUD grants rather than mortgages, or are refundings of original pre-1986 bonds. Taxable bonds are sold for purposes that do not comply with tax code restrictions for tax-exempt multifamily mortgage revenue bonds, such as excess costs of issuance or projects for higher-income tenants.

The AMT is a highly inefficient tax as applied to housing bonds, which are the largest category of municipal bonds subject to it. It raises scant money for the Internal Revenue Service (IRS). However, it has caused retail investors, as well as their intermediaries such as mutual funds, to abandon AMT bonds. It has raised yields on multifamily bonds by typically 15 to 20 basis points. This yield penalty has a negative impact on multifamily production, which is highly sensitive to interest rates. It has left a thinner market dominated by institutional buyers not subject to AMT, including Fannie Mae and Freddie Mac, for whom the AMT penalty is a free lunch.

Over half of multifamily issues sold in 2006 are subject to the AMT. Exhibit 54.3 reveals that the brunt of the decline in multifamily bonds was attributable to a 49% fall in non-AMT sales in 2006. Non-AMT bond sales hit a new low of $1.7 billion (looking back as far as 1980), falling to 28% of MF issuance. This reflects lower refunding volume as well as particular credit weakness among nonprofit 501C(3) developers. Taxable bonds reached a new high of 17%.

EXHIBIT 54.3 Multifamily Bond Issuance by Tax Status, 1980–2006 ($ billions)

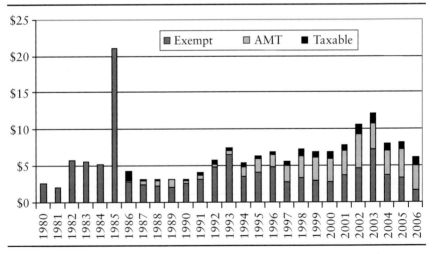

Source: Thomson Financial, Merrill Lynch Research. Includes private placements and short-term notes.

MULTIFAMILY SUPPLY OUTLOOK POSITIVE

Multifamily bond issuance has hit a cyclical low, but will rebound. Robust growth in rents has returned. Weakness in homeownership markets is now boosting demand for rental housing. One mitigating factor that may temper originations is a large inventory of unsold condos in certain local markets, as well as soaring insurance costs. Longer-term, the outlook for steady growth is strong due to several factors:

- Demographic trends—the entry into the rental market of the echo boomers, aging baby boomers, and the steady influx of immigrants should buoy demand for affordable rentals.
- Movements to curb sprawl and revitalize urban cores.
- The housing affordability crisis exacerbated by the long real estate boom.
- Emergence of public housing authorities as a new class of municipal bond issuers.
- Preservation and rehabilitation of existing stock.

VOLUME CAP CONSTRAINS BOND ISSUANCE

The outlook for multifamily bond issuance is constrained by heightened volume cap pressures as a result of burgeoning single-family bond issuance and exhaustion of the stockpile of cap carried forward from recent years. For calendar year 2007, states may allocate the greater of $85 per capita or $256,235,000 in bond cap, and the greater of $1.95 per capita or $2,275,000 for their Low Income Housing Tax Credit cap. Multifamily bonds are a preferred beneficiary for allocations of scarce bond volume cap because they tend to serve a needier population. In addition, affordable housing projects often require a bundling of subsidies from a variety of sources; thus, volume cap leverages resources that might otherwise not be utilized.

GREAT DIVERSITY OF ISSUERS

The largest multifamily bond issuers in 2006 are listed in Exhibit 54.4. The New York City Housing Development Corp. sold $1.7 billion, equivalent to 28% of the sector. New York State Housing Finance Authority (HFA) was second. New York has the highest percentage of households in the nation that rent. However, Local HFAs sold 56% of multifamily bonds in 2006, which is line with historic norms. This contrasts with single-family bonds, 80% of which were issued by state HFAs in 2006.

EXHIBIT 54.4 Largest Multifamily Bond Issuers, 2006 ($ millions)

NYC Housing Dev Corp.	$1,738
NYS Housing Finance Agency	$345
Chicago Public Housing Authority	$284
Colorado Housing & Finance Authority	$256
California Statewide Comm Dev Authority	$205
Washington State Hsg Fin Comm	$171
Michigan State Housing Dev Authority	$155
Illinois Housing Dev Authority	$150
Massachusetts Dev Finance Agency	$140
Virginia Housing Dev Authority	$128

Source: Thomson Financial, Merrill Lynch Research.

EXHIBIT 54.5 New Multifamily Bond Issues by Ratings, 2003–2006

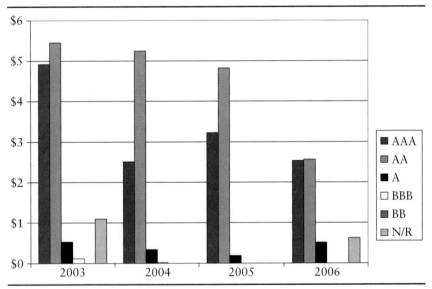

Source: Thomson Financial, Merrill Lynch Research. Includes private placements and short-term notes. Amounts are in $ billions.

Full Spectrum of Credit Ratings

The distribution of ratings on multifamily bonds sold in the last four years is presented in Exhibit 54.5. The great majority of issues are high grade. How-

EXHIBIT 54.6 Percentage of Multifamily New Issues that is High Yield

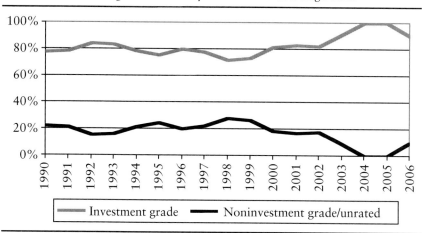

Source: Thomson Financial, Merrill Lynch Research. Includes private placements and short-term notes.

ever, there is also an institutional market for high-yield and unrated multi-family bonds. This area is prone to underreporting due to the prevalence of private placements. These are typically backed solely by the real estate; a lack of credit enhancement often precludes investment grade ratings.

High-Yield Multifamily Bonds

Between 1990 and 2002, unrated and noninvestment grade bonds comprised an average 20.9% of the multifamily issues. (See Exhibit 54.6.) However, no unrated or noninvestment grade multifamily bonds are reported in 2004 or 2005. This may be attributable to higher interest rates and credit stress causing loss of market access. This sector was a rare pocket of credit weakness during a period of very tight credit spreads in the municipal market. In 2006, high-yield multifamily new issuance resurfaced, with $618 million sold, equal to 9.9% of new multifamily deals.

ABUNDANCE OF PROJECT TYPES

An enormous diversity of project types exists in the municipal bond market. The main ones are shown below. They range in tenant profile from market rate developments requiring a minimum "set-aside" of 20% of units for low/moderate income renters ("80/20s"), to Public Housing projects housing the neediest. Thus, generalizations about multifamily projects, even by type, may be perilous.

- *80/20 mixed income market rate developments.* Non-AMT Bonds with pre-1986 tax provisions preserved through refundings. Required to set aside at least 20% of units for tenants with incomes not exceeding 80% of area median. The performance of this type, if unsubsidized, parallels that of market rate apartments.
- *40/60 or 20/50s.* Since 1986, privately owned properties financed by tax-exempt (AMT) bonds must set aside 20% of units for tenants with incomes at 50% or less of median, or 40% for those at 60% of median. This dovetails nicely with LIHTC requirements.
- *Low-income housing tax credit projects ("affordable housing").* Similar 40/60 or 20/50 set aside rule; however, this is usually expanded to 100% of units to maximize amount of credit obtained. Tax credit deals have had an outstanding track record due to low leverage and deep pocket investors that will stand behind these projects.
- *501(c)(3) and governmentally owned projects.* No AMT, volume cap, tenant income, 2% cost of issuance, or advance refunding restrictions. A range of tenant incomes. Many nonprofit have fared poorly during the recent rental market downturn, in part due to lack of resources.
- *Section 8 projects.* Deep federal rent subsidy usually on 100% of units. Income limits revised down numerous times to levels comparable to public housing. Downgrades pervade the non-FHA–insured local HFA sector due to a permanent rent freeze since 1997 for all projects deemed by HUD to have above-market rate rents. According to S&P, their median rating on Section 8 supported projects had slipped to BB in 2006, with average debt service coverage at 1.06×.
- *Section 236 projects.* Federal interest rate subsidy. Incomes allowed up to 80% of median, but often much lower due to the presence of other subsidies. Some "decoupled" project bonds are backed only by the federal subsidy, which continues even if the project defaults.
- *State HFA pools.* Mid to high investment grade due to over-collateralization, HFA oversight and financial resources. A variety of project types, including unsubsidized, exist.
- *Affordable housing projects.* Bonds backed solely by real estate that could initially attain low investment grade ratings under municipal ratings criteria launched in the 1990s. A wave of downgrades to noninvestment grade resulted from their first exposure to a rental market downturn. According to Moody's, 85% of rated projects were initially investment grade. As of May 2006, only 48% were for sophisticated investors only.

■ *High-yield multifamily.* More leveraged, unenhanced bonds backed solely by a mortgage on pledged projects. These usually contain strong legal provisions. Credit distress has pervaded the sector in recent years. Market access has generally closed for subordinate bonds. Many distressed projects are successfully bailed out by sales of underlying real estate, due to strong bids for underlying real estate.

■ *Public housing authority grant bonds.* These bonds are not backed by mortgages at all, but solely by HUD capital grants. These are non-AMT. Generally very stable, with intermediate term credit concerns over cuts in the grant program in recent years.

MULTIFAMILY BONDS: DEFAULT RATES

Concern over the risk in low-income housing projects is warranted. Municipal bond default studies invariably rank the sector as having one of the highest default rates, closer to corporate bonds than essential purpose municipals. For example, a study by Fitch Ratings in 2003 reports that multifamily bonds had a default rate of 4.64% between 1979 and 1997. This was third highest of all sectors, exceeded only by healthcare and industrial development.

Mortgage Default versus Bond Risk

It should be noted, however, that the Fitch study was based largely on a vendor database that counts underlying mortgage defaults as bond defaults— even if no monetary default occurs on the bonds. This neglects the fact that most high-grade MF bonds are structured to withstand mortgage defaults. In an earlier study by S&P/J.J. Kenny, half of the multifamily defaults are attributable to the demise of Executive Life in 1991. These were not true multifamily bonds at all—virtually all were taxable and backed solely by guaranteed investment contracts.

Most Mortgage Defaults Caused Par Calls

Exhibit 54.7 lists the largest mortgage defaults in multifamily bond history (excluding $1.1 billion Executive Life bonds). The only true bond defaults that occurred among them were on a portion of the Mutual Benefit bonds and Ticor bonds, following the demise of those enhancers. All of the others were FHA-insured mortgage defaults that did not cause bond defaults, but a redemption of bonds.

EXHIBIT 54.7   Largest MF Mortgage Defaults in Municipal Market

Mutual Benefit Life Guaranteed Bonds	$650 million
New York State HFA, Co-op City	$390 million
New York State HFA, Starrett City	$363 million
Ticor Mtg Insurance Backed Bonds	$264 million
Battery Park City Authority, 1972 Series	$200 million
Chicago, Presidential Towers	$171 million
NY City HDC, Roosevelt Island Associates	$163 million
Mass HFA, Harbor Point	$154 million
NJ HMFA, Presidential Plaza at Newport	$150 million
NYC HDC Yorkville Plaza/Normandie Court	$133 million
Illinois HDA, Lakeshore Plaza	$63 million

Another shortcoming of multifamily default statistics is that they usually do not account for inequalities in local and proprietary programs. Mortgages of the same type (e.g., 80/20s) vary markedly in experience between *issuers*. In addition, systematic differences between portfolios occur due to diverse underwriting standards, HFA oversight, property management, servicing, and feasibility projections. Some multifamily programs may not be structured to a zero-default tolerance. Industry specialists realize that real estate risk is often a function of leverage, not project fundamentals.

MULTIFAMILY DEFAULT CYCLES

Much of the multifamily bond sector is emerging from the greatest wave of defaults since the savings and loan crisis of early 1990s. This can be measured by FHA default data—the largest national database of multifamily performance. There have been three major waves of defaults since 1971, each about 15 years apart. Exhibit 54.8 reveals the extent of the recent defaults that occurred in the main FHA multifamily program. The surge in claims began in 2003 and peaked in 2004–2005. Latest data indicates a return to moderate levels of defaults in 2006.

Exhibit 54.9 shows cumulative default rates for 221(d)(4) projects by year of initial endorsement. Modern vintages have much lower default rates than pre-1990 ones. However, even modern default rates are well above levels tolerated by bond investors, explaining demand by higher-grade buyers for external credit supports.

EXHIBIT 54.8   Assignments of FHA 221(d)(4) Loans, 1971–2006

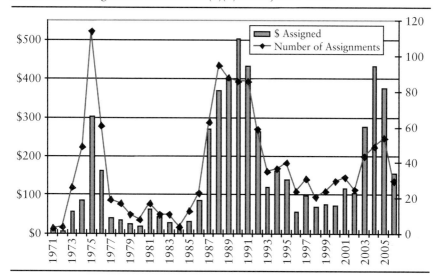

EXHIBIT 54.9   Cumulative 221(d)(4) Assignment Rates by Year of Initial Endorsement, as of 12/31/06

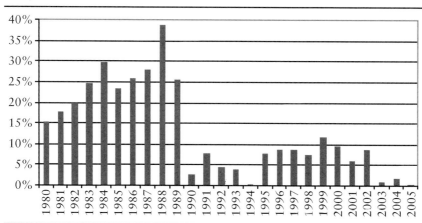

Source: Merrill Lynch analysis of HUD data. Includes only 221(d)(4) loans coded as "OMI" by HUD.

EXHIBIT 54.10 Multifamily Bond Credit Enhancements

- FHA insurance programs (private mortgage insurance is rare).
- GNMA, FNMA, FHLMC collateral.
- Moral obligations of states, cities (legislative appropriation to replenish debt service reserve).
- State mortgage insurance (NY, MD), state rent subsidy (MA), guaranty fund (FL).
- State HFA GO pledge.
- Overcollateralization—seen in state HFA deals. In form of investments or mortgages.
- Senior/subordinate structure—credit tranching.
- Bank letters of credit.
- Federal grants: PHA capital subsidy, HOPE VI, HOME, CDBG.
- Tax increment funds.
- REIT or owner guaranty.
- Multiline casualty insurer guaranty.
- Cross-collateralization and cross-default provisions in pools.

Source: Merrill Lynch.

AN ARRAY OF CREDIT ENHANCEMENTS

No other municipal sector has seen such creativity in credit enhancements (see Exhibit 54.10). A shortage of credit support, rather than fundamental demand for low-income housing, has been the foremost constraint on volume historically. High-grade multifamily bond credit analysis still focuses primarily on the enhancement. The significance of the underlying real estate varies inversely with the strength of the enhancement. Often its primary relevance is to ascertain redemption risk from a mortgage default. In addition to these bond credit enhancements, many of the oldest projects in the municipal market receive federal rent or interest subsidies strong enough to warrant investment grade ratings.

Bondholder Exposure to Real Estate Risks Limited

The vast majority of multifamily bonds are credit enhanced. Indeed, all investment grade rated multifamily bonds required some form of credit enhancement until the advent of S&P's Affordable Housing program in 1993. Previously, unenhanced bonds backed solely by real estate were found only in the unrated market. The next sections will focus on several key credit enhancements and project types.

THE LOW INCOME HOUSING TAX CREDIT

The Section 42 Low Income Housing Tax Credit Program is one of the most successful subsidies for low-income housing production in history. It is involved in over half of all new affordable housing in recent years. The sale of tax credits typically provides cash equity of 25% or more of the total project costs. There are two versions of credit. The more common type provides a tax credit equal to 9% of eligible project costs (excluding land costs). The 9% may not be utilized with tax-exempt bonds. It is a major reason that many developers prefer taxable financing. A special 4% credit is designed for use in tandem with tax-exempt bonds. The 4% credit has no volume cap, since it is constrained by the availability of tax-exempt bonds.

Tax credit projects share certain characteristics. These include a moderate loan-to-value ratio (due to the substantial equity contributed by the credit) and owner/investors highly motivated to maintain the project in order to preserve their credits. Owner support is predicated upon continued economic value of the tax credits. Tax credit deals have had an outstanding track record. An Ernst & Young study reported the cumulative foreclosure rate (or deed-in lieu) since inception at an incredibly low 0.14% through 2000. It is important to note that this does not mean that tax credit projects have not undergone financial stress. In many cases, the owner is motivated to carry them through tough times and avoid recapture of credits through foreclosure. General partners of partnerships need to protect their reputations in order to sell more credits to large corporate investors. The credit requires them to conduct close monitoring of the project, and they can often intervene to remove property management.

However, a potential weakness is their inability to raise rents over 30% of tenant income to offset surges in operating expense (e.g., insurance costs). They have very low-income tenant base (frequently all below 60% of area median income), Another is the likely loss of interest by tax-motivated investors at the end of the 15-year compliance period. Tax credits are earned over the initial 10 years. The earliest tax credit deals face higher credit and prepayment risks. It is conceivable that, in their new postcompliance phase, some may undergo disinvestment, sales to new owners, and management changes. These risks may be compounded in overbuilt areas experiencing increases in vacancies and market rent declines.

FHA INSURANCE

The most common credit enhancement in the multifamily sector is Federal Housing Administration (FHA) insurance. There are several types of FHA multifamily insurance used with bonds (see Exhibit 54.11). The largest is Section 221(d)(4), which historically constitutes over 40% of FHA multi-family initial endorsements. Section 221(d)(4) is designed to for new construction or substantial rehabilitation of projects with for-profit sponsors. The only guideline that restricts the program to the neediest is the loan size limit. However, overlapping requirements for tax-exempt bonds, as well as other subsidies, prevail. A major appeal of the 221(d)(4) program is that it permits construction financing, loan-to-value ratios up to 90% of replacement cost estimates, nonrecourse loans, and debt service coverage ratios of at least 1.10×.

FHA insurance never guaranties a multifamily bond directly. It provides insurance for mortgages that are collateral for bond issues. Rating FHA-insured multifamily mortgage revenue bonds requires thorough review of the complex legal language in the bond indenture that stipulates the actions the servicer and trustee must perform in order to process an insurance claim following a mortgage default in a timely manner. See Exhibit 54.12. A mortgage default should result in the total redemption of the bonds from insurance proceeds. The financial viability of the underlying project is not a fac-

EXHIBIT 54.11 Outstanding FHA-Insured Multifamily Loans, as of 12-31-06

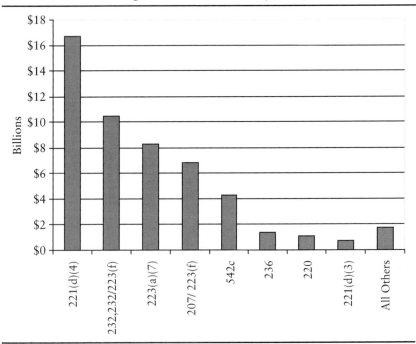

EXHIBIT 54.12   FHA 221(d)3 and 221(d)4 Insurance Payouts

- Two payment options exist: cash or HUD debentures. FHA multifamily bonds must stipulate payment in cash to obtain an investment grade rating. (A rare exception is the debenture lock refunding.) FHA pays 99% (deducting a 1% assignment fee), and also does not cover one month's interest during default. Cash flow projections must also assume 30-day lag.
- Claims are paid in two parts: 90% (or 70% if default is during construction) around 45 days after default, with balance up to 14 months later.

EXHIBIT 54.13   FHA Bond Analysis Focus

- Divergent rating approaches: Moody's caps FHA bond ratings at "Aa" except for Risk Sharing deals. S&P uses complex structured finance approach. State HFA pools usually AA.
- No legal deadline exists for claims payments—timing has shifted in past. Thus, eight months maximum debt service reserve is required.
- Pinhole risks: negative arbitrage between bonds and accrued interest on pending insurance, disallowances from final audit, operating deficit accounts, extensions of filing. Debt service reserve investments may lose market value.
- Bankruptcy courts have stayed claims payments: Trustee and servicer error is possible.
- Weakness in Investment Agreement (GICs) providers are by far the main cause of downgrades, particularly due to S&Ps "weak link theory." This is also true of GNMA and FNMA collateralized ideas.
- Without special reserve funds and required legal language, FHA bonds are non-investment grade.

tor in the ratings process. However, investors often inquire about project finances in order to ascertain the likelihood of a call.

S&P rates many standalone FHA inured mortgage revenue bonds as high as AAA, if the legal structure is deemed to cover all potential timing and payment gaps in the insurance coverage. Moody's generally limiting these ratings to Aa. This is due in large part to the lack of a binding deadline for insurance payments. In particular, 10% of the claims payment may be withheld over a year pending a final audit. In the distant past, longer delays than expected led to an increase in reserve requirements and rating revisions. (See Exhibit 54.13.)

Not an Ironclad Guaranty

A small amount of bond defaults have also occurred as a result of shortfalls in matching the mortgage insurance coverage to bonds. A few bankruptcy courts have also temporarily stayed insurance payments. FHA (d)(4)s serve as an excellent example of the usefulness of ultimate recovery ratings, since the overwhelming majority of bond defaults were tiny (1% to 3%) and/or rapidly cured.

As with state HFA single-family bonds, the main cause of S&P downgrades has been *guaranteed investment agreement downgrades* (GICs). Virtually all FHA bonds have GICs for reserves and float funds over the life of the issue. However, risk of downgrades from GICs is much lower than in the 1980s. Current GIC providers have been less volatile in ratings. New safeguards have been put into GIC contracts to offset ratings risk. Moreover, in 2002, S&P brought its "weak link policy closer to Moody's by allowing the GIC provider to be a full category lower than the bond rating (for AAA rated housing bonds).

RISK SHARING: SUPERIOR FHA PROGRAM

Authorized in 1994, FHA HFA Risk Sharing is a major improvement over other FHA insurance for investors. By holding housing finance agencies liable for a portion of the credit risk, and limiting participation to HFAs with greater resources, underwriting standards are significantly strengthened. State HFAs elect to bear 10% to 90% of default risk. Most take 50%. Bondholders are not exposed to the HFA credit. FHA directly covers mortgage defaults. (See Exhibit 54.14.)

EXHIBIT 54.14   Risk-Sharing: Superior to Traditional FHA Programs

- Begun in 1994, state HFAs elect to bear 10% to 90% of default risk (most take 50%). HUD allows state HFAs with GO ratings above "A" to post no reserves.
- Bondholders are not exposed to HFA's credit. FHA directly covers mortgage defaults. An HFA must notify FHA of a default after 30 days. FHA pays the unpaid principal balance plus interest. The HFA issues a five-year debenture to HUD for amount of the claim. During this term, HFA attempts to workout the project. After five years, HFA and HUD compute their shares in any loss.
- Although bonds may be special obligations, a state HFA's general obligation is pledged to reimburse HUD. This ensures that the underwriting and oversight is high caliber.
- FHA pays 100% of the mortgage note under Risk Sharing rather than 99%. Also, FHA pays claims in one lump sum within six months, rather than withholding final 10% to 30% until final audit.
- This results in a lower debt service requirement (six months maximum). The risk of a shortfall in accrued interest from the default date to the payout date is eliminated by accruing interest at the mortgage note rate, rather than the HUD debenture rate.

FHA pays 100% of the mortgage note under Risk Sharing rather than 99%. Also, FHA pays claims in one lump sum within six months, rather than withholding final 10% to 30% until completion of a final audit. This results in a lower debt service reserve requirement (six months maximum versus eight months). The risk of a shortfall in accrued interest from the default date to the payout date is eliminated by accruing interest at the mortgage note rate, rather than the HUD debenture rate.

The performance of the Section 542c HFA Risk Sharing stands in sharp contrast to the main 221(d)(4) program. As of December 31, 2006, the cumulative default rate remained under 2%, since inception of the program in 1996. These bonds are usually not differentiated from other FHA insured issues in pricing, and may offer more relative value.

Other FHA Programs Used with Bonds

In recent years, project loan refinancings have overtaken new production. The two main refinancing programs, 223(f) and 223(a)(7), together accounted for over 40% of initial endorsements in each of the last three years. Their processes are similar to Section 221(d)(4) and Section 221(d)(3) for nonprofit sponsors.

The 232 program, predominantly for nursing homes, is mired in credit troubles. It does not appear to be rebounding with the market-rate multifamily sector. A major wave of 232 defaults peaked earlier, in 2001, than the one for 221(d)(4)s. See Exhibit 54.15. Claims fell sharply in 2005, raising hopes that a turnaround had commenced. A relapse occurred in 2006. Section 232 loan performance should track the general health of the long-term care industry. The sector faces chronic pressures from Medicaid reimbursement programs. Section 232s have a higher risk of claims than 221(d)(4)s.

GNMA-BACKED MULTIFAMILY BONDS

All GNMAs have FHA insurance underneath the GNMA guaranty. For most of this decade, GNMA has wrapped all new FHA multifamily loans except those in the municipal market still issued as whole loans. The GNMA guaranty is by no means redundant. It facilitates efficient securitization by filling loopholes in FHA insurance coverage. The GNMA blanket guaranty, carrying the full faith and credit of the United States, covers scheduled payments due on the 15th of each month. If the servicer does not receive principal and interest on the first of the month, it must advance the payment. If unable to do so, the servicer notifies GNMA to remit the payment before the due date.

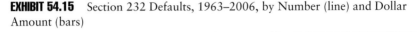

EXHIBIT 54.15 Section 232 Defaults, 1963–2006, by Number (line) and Dollar Amount (bars)

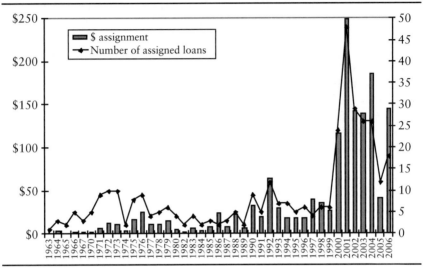

Source: Merrill Lynch analysis of HUD data. Amount shown is original principal balance of terminated mortgages. Data is as of 12/31/06. This includes 232/223(f) purchase/refinancings.

The GNMA guaranty enables efficient securitization of project loans. Without GNMA wrapping or other extraneous enhancements, FHA "whole loans" are typically noninvestment grade, illiquid mortgages. This is notwithstanding the fact that FHA insurance carries the full faith and credit of the United States. It is necessary to fill certain gaps in the insurance coverage in order to attain the maximum security demanded by rating agencies for AAA securities.

Common FHA Insurance Gaps Covered by GNMA

FHA insurance covers only 99% of mortgage principal. This is because FHA deducts a 1% assignment fee from claims payments. In addition, FHA does not reimburse for the 30 days lost interest during a grace period prior to assigning the loan for insurance. Thus, a shortfall of approximately 2% or more of principal is built into most FHA insurance programs. In addition, substantial delays may arise until receipt of insurance proceeds. An initial FHA payment of 90% (70% if default is during construction) is received 10 to 15 days after assignment. However, the balance usually takes up to 6 months to obtain (possibly up to one year). No legal deadline exists as to the timing of the insurance payment. Another common gap arises from differentials between the mortgage rate and the interest rate HUD pays during the period following assignment but prior to final claims payment.

GNMA Promotes Standardization of Project Loans

The GNMA guaranty of payment on the 15th of each month renders the investor indifferent to loopholes in FHA insurance. Mortgage default risk is converted to redemption risk. GNMA requires that FHA insurance be received only in the form of cash. Some FHA programs allow HUD the ability to pay insurance in the form of callable 20-year HUD debentures. This is particularly the case in healthcare projects. This is precluded in GNMA securities.

However, GNMA does not control the timing of the principal returns from FHA claims payments. Defaults are handled by GNMA approved servicers. Following a 30-day grace period, servicers may assign to FHA or foreclose on their own after another 30 to 60 days of delinquency. Most servicers elect to assign after only 30 days to reduce carrying costs. They also have little flexibility to carry defaulted loans past 60 days. GNMA does not permit loan modifications.

FNMA- and FHLMC-Backed Bonds

FNMA-backed bonds come in two main structures: MBS-collateralized and FNMA direct bond guaranty. FNMA also provides liquidity support for variable rate bonds. FHLMC's Forward Commitment program (since 2000) is a direct bond guaranty. Rating agency focus in MBS-collateralized bonds is on legal provisions and cash flows (negative arbitrage; unused proceeds and prepayment scenarios). Credit risk has been downgrade of third-party GIC providers may exist.

PROJECT-BASED SECTION 8

There are several Housing and Urban Development programs under the Section 8 umbrella. The overwhelming majority with above market rents are project-based New Construction or Substantial Rehabilitation, which was utilized for new housing production from 1974 to 1984. Virtually all Section 8 projects encountered in the municipal bond market are older projects from this period. It is a deep subsidy that often pays up to 85% of all project rents, if 100% of the units are subsidized. See Exhibit 54.16. Section 8 also provides portable rent vouchers for low-income tenants; these are not discussed here.

EXHIBIT 54.16   Section 8 Rent Subsidy

- Main federal low-income housing construction program from 1976–84. HUD pays difference between 30% of tenant income and contract rents—a deep subsidy. Usually 100% of units are subsidized.
- Section 8 properties have a wide range of appearances. Elderly projects are reputedly better maintained than family projects. Occupancy commonly near 100%. Defaults modest, but rising.
- Contracts on FHA insured projects generally run 40 years with 20 year renewal option by HUD at midpoint. Uninsured projects usually have 30 year contracts.
- Section 8 acts as a credit enhancement; uninsured ratings largely between BBB to A (A+ for state HFA pools). Coverage usually 1.10× to 1.25×. Subsidy can be reduced for vacancies, revoked for nonhabitability, or terminated for bad owners.

The Housing Assistance Payments (HAP) contract between the mortgagor, HUD and usually the issuer delineates the mortgagor's (owner's) rights to receive monthly housing assistance payments. The owner's rights to HAP payments may be assigned to a mortgagee under loan documents. Original contract terms for new construction projects were for 20, 30, and 40 years. It is important to ascertain that the term of the HAP contract extends as far as the term of the bonds. If it does not, perhaps because a refinancing has extended the bond maturity, the project is subject to contract renewal and appropriation risk.

Permanent Rent Freeze on Section 8s

Meanwhile, all Section 8s with rents above 100% of Fair Market Rents remain subject to a permanent rent freeze since 1997. Owners may furnish a market comparability study if they wish to contest the freeze. However, this is not regularly done due to costs, meager amounts of permissible increases, and challenges in demonstrating rents are low. The freeze has caused progressive credit deterioration for local non-FHA insured Section 8 bonds to high-yield status (median BB), as debt service coverage inexorably declines. Underinvestment is a related problem. State HFA uninsured bonds have remained stable, due to substantial over-collateralization and oversight, and may be additionally secured by an HFA GO or state moral obligation pledge.

Other Section 8 types occasionally seen in the bond market, such as property disposition and preservation, generally have below market rents. This is due to budget-based rents. However, these projects are susceptible to underinvestment.

Credit Crisis for Uninsured Local Section 8s

Fair market rents are formulated annually and used to set maximum rents for Section 8 NC/SR projects. They are fixed at the 40th percentile of renters in standard unsubsidized units for most local markets. Their use in determining project rents has flaws. Perhaps the most glaring shortcoming is their enormous geographic scope, rendering them insensitive to submarket and property distinctions. In addition, comparison of ratios with different denominators creates distortions due to a "scale effect." This may partly explain the systematic presence of high ratios to FMRs in the low rent districts. High-cost areas (e.g., California) have few projects with above-market rents.

HUD and Congress have shown no consistent willingness to intervene in cases where rent freezes may trigger mortgage defaults. HUD's policy is to not grant systematic hardship increases. It is hoped that eventually HUD and Congress will intervene to prevent a defaults and loss of housing stock. It should also be noted that most Section 8s have amortized much of their remaining mortgage debt, and many have experienced significant appreciation.

FHA SECTION 8 MARK-TO-MARKET

The FHA-insured Section 8 projects are in the latter stages of a massive restructuring designed to bring rents down to market. Authorized in 1997, the FHA Section 8 Re-Engineering program (also known as Mark-to-Market or M2M) often entails payment of a partial claim in order to reduce debt to levels sustainable at the lowered rent levels. A complete redemption is required in order to recast the outstanding mortgage. The goal is to bring contract rents down to market levels when FHA Section 8 contracts expire, which is usually after 20 years. Bond-financed projects may be included, as long as their financing agreements are not in conflict. The Mark-to-Market program has just been extended through September 30, 2011 although the bulk of the work is done.

In addition, some prepay ahead of expiration dates due to sales to nonprofits, opt-outs of Section 8, or non-M2M restructurings that may put the project on sounder footing from a preservation standpoint. In addition to the pricing impact of redemption risk, M2M has greatly altered analysis of FHA Section 8s, with potential restructuring becoming the focal point. It has also spawned new breeds of credits, such as transition projects converting from Section 8 to Affordable Housing, and postrestructured Section 8s subject to different rent-setting mechanism, and near-term appropriation risks.

SECTION 236 INTEREST SUBSIDY

The Section 236 program provides an interest rate subsidy that lowers the effective mortgage interest rate to 1% pursuant to 40-year contracts. All bond-financed 236s are in state HFA pools. State HFA projects do not have FHA insurance. All projects are older and generally past lockout expiration. Section 236 was the primary low-income housing program during 1968–1974. Tenants permitted to have incomes up to 80% of median. Payments may be terminated upon foreclosure, but are not if another eligible owner assumes under HFA auspices. These bonds have been exceptionally stable in recent decades. Financing deferred maintenance has been foremost problem.

The HUD Appropriations Act of 2000 and related Notices removed the main constraint on prepayments by permitting continuation of *interest reduction payments* (IRPs) after a refinancing or sale to an eligible owner. The new regulations address both loss of low-income housing stock and the substantial rehabilitation needs in a manner that does not require increased federal funding. Low-income usage is extended another five years. The new rules also permit a new type of financing backed solely by IRP, not total project income. The decoupled IRP may be paid directly to the bond trustee. As before, IRPs can survive foreclosure. With superior oversight, these new structured financings attain very high ratings.

Public Housing Authority Debt

One of the most sweeping pieces of legislation for any subsidized housing was the Quality Housing and Work Responsibility Act of 1998, which created a new class of multifamily bonds for Public Housing Authorities. These are strikingly different from other bonds in the multifamily sector. Most importantly, they are not backed by mortgages at all. They are grant anticipation bonds secured solely by a stream of annual capital grants form HUD. They usually carry rating in the AA category on the basis of debt service coverage of over 2×. The main concern has been appropriation risk. Under the Bush Administration, Congress has enacted cuts of around 2% a year, causing debt service coverages to decline. These bonds have intermediate average terms.

Besides Capital Grant bonds, other bonds have been issued by PHAs. Since 1993, Hope VI grants transform worst PHA projects into privately owned mixed-income developments. Bonds often finance construction, backed by escrowed grant funds. New Housing Authority bonds were guaranteed by the United States—but no new long-term ones have been sold since 1974. In addition, some of the strongest PHAs out of the 3,000 around the nation are accumulating the resources to issue revenue bonds for unsub-

sidized projects. These emerging PHA structures enrich an already variegated multifamily bond landscape.

"AFFORDABLE HOUSING" PROJECTS

As mentioned, unenhanced multifamily bonds—backed by nothing but real
estate—became eligible for investment grade ratings from S&P's municipal
department in 1993. Moody's municipal area began to rate Affordable Housing (AH) bonds in 1998. These programs encountered their first rental market downturn in the last years, and have generally not fared well. S&P's AH
criteria are distinctly different from for-profit, market rate projects (including
tax-exempt 80/20s) rated by its Commercial Mortgage Ratings Dept. (See
Exhibit 54.17.) Most striking are the equity requirements. Established nonprofits are permitted LTVs up to 100% for ratings as high as A. The CMBS
group generally requires around a 60% LTV for a single project financing, as
well as slightly higher coverage ratios. A rationale for this major differential
is that AH deals are at low risk of abandonment, because of their nonprofit
ownership or public purpose. In addition, rent levels are customarily below
market, providing a cushion against downturns, and aiding marketability.
S&P assesses the management and resources of nonprofits.

Affordable Housing is for Sophisticated Only

These bonds are generally appropriate for sophisticated investors only. AH
ratings have proven more volatile than most other investment grade mu-

EXHIBIT 54.17   Key Points on Affordable Housing Projects

- Maximum rating is A+: Most owners have a nonprofit element, or are HFAs. Projects have a public purpose.
- Loan-to-value ratios: How relevant? AHP criteria (up to 100% LTV) contrasts with CMBS group, who require 60% LTV for A rated 80/20.
- "Coverage, coverage, coverage." For best properties, S&P requires 1.25 to 1.50 for an A, 1.15 to 1.40 for BBB. For "good" properties, 1.35 to 1.60 for A, 1.25 to 1.50 for BBB. Moody's requires minimum 1.40 for A3. Tight categories increase volatility.
- Rent levels are usually below market: This is supposed to insulate from eco-nomic cycles. Tax credit deals fit well.
- Construction risk must be covered by rated third party until rent-up.
- Only fully amortizing debt qualifies.
- AHP ratings are more volatile than those of other investment grade municipals. Default rates are already high. Regular monitoring is strongly recommended.

nicipals. According to Moody's, 85% of their rated projects were initially investment grade. As of May 2006, only 48% of their ratings were. Downgrades are caused by a wide range of factors, including changes in physical condition, poor management, weakened local employment or real estate markets, or overly optimistic rent projections. In the last few years, even forecasts of flat rents levels were unrealistic. The volatility of AH ratings is exacerbated by the tightness of the bands of the coverage ratios expected for each rating category. Investors should regularly monitor these projects and ensure that inspections are undertaken, similar to high-yield projects.

TAX OPINION RISKS

The risk of an Internal Revenue Service (IRS) declaration of taxability is remote with standard multifamily bonds. Nonetheless, multifamily bonds do carry much greater ongoing compliance rules than other municipal bonds These involve renter income certification and reporting. Tax risk is greater for obscure local issues with unorthodox or aggressive structures, and using little known tax counsels. Similarly, bond tax exemption may hinge on the nonprofit status of a 501(c)(3)s affiliated with a for-profit developer. Bond accelerations may also be economically impossible for the issue to honor.

The IRS has conducted random audits of multifamily bonds in recent years. No widespread transgressions were uncovered. Projects using the tax credit have fared well in audits of that program. Moreover, if discrepancies are found, the owner has a reasonable period to correct them. Only cases of long-term, intentional breach of covenants are grounds for declarations of taxability.

MULTIFAMILY BOND REDEMPTIONS

High-grade multifamily bonds generally offer the same yield premium over other municipals as do single-family housing bonds. This is not attributable to credit risk, but due to a basket of embedded call options. This is generally reflects inefficient pricing, as the frequency of calls is much lower in most multifamily bonds than in single-family bonds. This creates opportunities for investors to derive relative value from knowledge of multifamily redemption risks.

As can be expected with such an enormous array of multifamily credits and structures, risk of extraordinary call may vary widely between issues. The four most frequently exercised call options are:

Default Redemptions

Par calls from mortgage defaults are associated with invocation of a credit enhancement (e.g., FHA, GNMA, letter of credit). With other enhancements (e.g., state HFA GO pledge, bond insurance), a mortgage default may trigger a par call from a refunding bond pursuant to a workout. Widely divergent experiences occurred due to different underwriting standards, oversight, and local markets. Proactive asset managers intervene to preempt defaults. Virginia Housing Development Authority, for example, has had virtually no default calls in its large multifamily program in over 20 years.

Unused Proceeds Calls

Unused proceeds (UP) calls were a major concern during the 1980s. Many projects fell through during periods of high interest rate volatility. UP calls have become very rare. If firm commitments are in place, UP calls are a function of construction risk and failure to convert to a permanent loan. Multifamily construction is generally not high risk. Unusual small UP calls are possible if a project is completed under budget, or fails to use contingency funds. Multifamily bonds are not subject to the 42-month deadline for expending proceeds that SF bonds are.

Many state HFA multifamily official statements declare the right to substitute projects in event of nonorigination. Although this may seem comforting, substitution is often impractical. Under the Tax Equity and Fiscal Responsibility Act of 1982, projects financed by private activity bonds to be specifically identified in detail in a public hearing (or else by voter referendum). The bonds must be sold within one year of the public approval. Many bond counsels will not permit substitutions unless the alternate project was "TEFRA'd" for the same issue. Moreover, large projects are hard to find replacements for.

Optional Redemption

Like most municipal bonds, multifamily bonds have optional call provisions starting usually 10 years after issuance. However, the manner they are utilized differs in some respects from other municipal bonds. In most state HFA issues, the optional call may be the exclusive right of the issuer. The project owner has a right to prepay under separate provisions.

Furthermore, no financial benefit accrues to the HFA from lowering mortgage rates and widening the spread to the bond rate (to the extent it exceeds the maximum allowed under tax code). Mortgage rates are usually not lowered in state HFA economic refundings, unless the project is in distress or danger of conversion. Instead, the primary technique employed by state HFAs is to do a paired bonding, which transfers the economic benefit of the refunding to other projects in the form of a deeply discounted mortgage rate. The blended mortgage rates are designed to meet allowable spreads.

Tax law also prohibits advance refunding MF private activity bonds with a tax-exempt issue. Forward delivery and forward swaps may achieve similar economic ends. However, advance refundings of 501(c)(3) bonds and governmental bonds are permitted.

PREPAYMENTS IN MULTIFAMILY BONDS

The most important factor in analysis of owner prepayment risk for unsubsidized, market rate properties is the length of the lockout period, or prohibition on voluntary prepayments. A lockout of 10 years is common in the municipal market. Often, optional call provisions cover prepayments. This effectively provides a 10-year lockout. These are the most stringent lockouts in the mortgage markets. This is a major distinction from the single-family bond market, where a 10-year lockout would cost the bond buyer 10 to 15 basis points to obtain.

Hard versus Soft Lockouts

A *hard lockout* is a covenant between the owner and the bondholder that cannot be waived by an issuer. Most state HFA lockouts are soft, meaning they are between the HFA and the borrower. The state HFA can waive the lockout, resulting in an early call. This has happened, but rarely. Other lesser used deterrents are prepayment penalties and yield maintenance premiums.

Recycling prepayment funds into new loans may be feasible with small amounts. It is also be problematical for some tax counsels. Recycling is not common, in part due to a lack of prepayments. It may be difficult to find a qualifying project that the prepayment can be utilized for.

Subsidized Loan Prepayment Behavior

An open prepayment call at par in less than 10 years constitutes a weaker structure. This may be encountered in refundings of older projects whose lockouts have expired. Some state HFAs (New Jersey and California, for example) have continuing restrictions after lockout expiration, such as on project use. Preservation programs may offer alternatives to prepayment, such as soft loans.

Moreover, older subsidized projects exhibit different behavior than market rate properties. Their prepayments are driven by programmatic factors. These owners are not motivated to lower mortgage rates, since the subsidy pays debt service. They usually prepay to extract trapped reserves, convert to market rate, or achieve independence from regulators. Exit taxes on pre-1986 tax shelters constitute a powerful deterrent avoidable only upon death.

Multifamily Prepayment Activity

Market rate properties theoretically exhibit ruthless prepayment behavior, meaning owners prepay efficiently at the first opportunity. That implies that lockout expiration dates should be priced similar to optional call dates are. Evidence suggests that multifamily do not prepay in an efficient manner. Multifamily prepayment models are primitive, due to lack of data and project heterogeneity. No benchmark for municipal multifamily prepayments exists, such as the PSA index for single-family loans. Owner prepayment behavior is governed by complex tax, financial, and personal considerations. Owners are a diverse lot.

However, it is clear that prepayments on unsubsidized multifamily projects evince a pronounced sensitivity to interest rates following lockout expiration. A boom in 221(d)(4) prepayments in 2003–2004 was coincident with one in single-family loans. See Exhibit 54.18.

EXHIBIT 54.18   Prepayments of 221(d)(4) Loans, 1971–2006

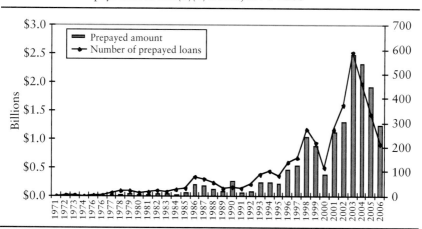

Source: Merrill Lynch analysis of HUD data. Amount shown is original principal balance of terminated mortgages. Data is as of 12/31/06. Loans include those coded as "OMI" in HUD database.

HUD Overrides of FHA Mortgage Lockouts

FHA-insured multifamily bonds are more susceptible to default calls than other multifamily bonds due to the hair trigger mechanism for filing claims after a mortgage default. No workouts or delays are permitted. Another factor that increases call risk for FHA bonds is the right of HUD to override prepayment lockouts or penalties. This emanates from HUD Mortgagee Letter 87-9, published on February 20, 1987. HUD's policy states that an override is only supposed to be exercised in order to facilitate a refinancing or partial prepayment on a defaulted loan, so that HUD can avoid a claims payment. HUD local field offices exercise overrides of lockouts in cases of financial stress.

OTHER CALL OPTIONS IN MULTIFAMILY BONDS

A number of other lesser-utilized extraordinary call options may be present in MF bonds. Exhibit 54.19 lists some common examples. These are infrequently exercised, but could become major concerns in certain situations. Surplus calls may be a significant factor in evaluations of bonds in older indentures. Casualty insurance redemptions are extremely rare. Damaged property can be restored. There have been some in the wake of Katrina catastrophe.

The ability to sell off of performing mortgage collateral in order to collapse a bond issue is a disturbing provision that may be found occasionally. This is a red flag particularly in obscure issues with lesser-known participants. However, if it is contained in optional call or clean-up call provisions pertaining to the tail end of an issuer, it should not be offensive.

EXHIBIT 54.19 MF Redemptions of Concern in Special Situations

- HUD-mandated redemptions: Many Section 8s and other subsidized projects have a separate call option for a HUD requested call.
- Crosscalling with prepayments: Often permitted, virtually never happens due to tax law obstacles, lack of prepayments.
- Sale of mortgages: Some indentures permit sale of mortgage collateral and par calls. NY City HDC action in mid-1980s led to lawsuit by investors.
- Casualty insurance and condemnation proceeds: Terrorism exclusions to be expected now. Battery Park City Authority example.
- Surplus calls: This is important in state HFA open indentures.
- Mandatory tender for failure to renew letter of credit.
- Taxability call: In event of noncompliance with tenant income requirement, or other tax rules. Often handled instead by a gross-up of interest rate.

The right to crosscall with prepayments is often present in state HFA multifamily indentures. However, crosscalling has virtually never been exercised. Many tax counsels are not be comfortable with it. Unlike with single-family bonds, it cannot rest on the defense of being long-standing industry practice.

CONCLUSION

The multifamily bond market is rebounding from the first major rental downturn test since the early 1990s. The impact on the multifamily bonds has been quite even. Most are insulated from direct real estate risk by some form of credit enhancement. High-yield multifamily and unenhanced Affordable Housing have been most susceptible. Uninsured local Section 8s face a chronic rent pressures and appropriation risks. Tax credit projects have been strongly supported by their owners, but may face changing dynamics in coming years. It is therefore important to be highly selective about markets, issuers, and projects.

The rebounding multifamily sector offers an array of credits and structures. A multiplicity of project types renders generalizations perilous. Buyers not in a position to monitor real estate risks should gravitate towards credit enhanced bonds. FHA Risk Sharing has strong advantages over older FHA programs.

However, an ample amount of multifamily bonds offer superior yields, often due to inflated perceptions of call risk. Lockouts typically protect against prepayment risk, while most other call options are infrequently used. Many multifamily bonds offer attractive prospects for outperformance.

Both single-family and multifamily high-grade bonds offer superior credit strength together with extra yield (near that of BBB municipals) due in large part to a basket of embedded call options. However, multifamily bond call options are exercised far less frequently—even though they are typically priced at similar spreads. Thus, they are attractive alternatives to single-family bonds for long-term, yield-oriented buyers.

CHAPTER 55

Tax-Exempt Electric Utility Debt

Gary M. Krellenstein
Managing Director
JPMorgan Securities

Paul R. Bockwoldt
Analyst
JPMorgan Securities

Electric utilities are unique entities with many characteristics that are not shared by other organizations. The electricity that utilities provide is highly essential to consumers and must be manufactured and delivered at the instant of demand. Electric utilities are subject to peculiar economic relationships. This is partly because of the technology involved in providing this type of instantaneous service, the high capital costs of generation and transmission facilities, the unique physical characteristics and essentiality of electricity to a modern society (see Exhibit 55.1 and 55.2).

U.S. utilities are also the largest users of fossil fuels in the nation (mostly coal) as well as the largest producer of CO_2 gas (38%), which appears to be adversely impacting climatic conditions and will likely be subject to regulation in the next few years (see Exhibit 55.3). These organizations are also

EXHIBIT 55.1 Electricity is Fundamentally Different than Any Other Commodity/ Service

- Travels at speed of light—impact of disruptions is immediate.
- Price has weak correlation to value.
- Ethereal—can't be held, difficult to see, not well understood by the public.
- Flawed pricing mechanism.
- Cannot be effectively "routed."
- Cannot be stored—manufactured and delivered on demand.
- Essentiality—blackout: All economic activity stops!

EXHIBIT 55.2   Power's Bizarre Economics

Essentiality, inability to store electricity, and transmission constraints, cause prices to increase exponentially as demand approaches available supply (non-linear step function)

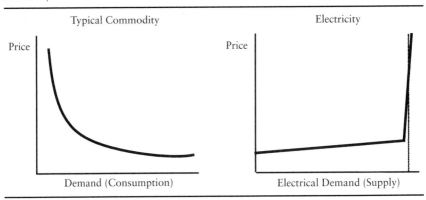

EXHIBIT 55.3   Electric Generation is the Largest Source of CO_2 Emissions in the United States

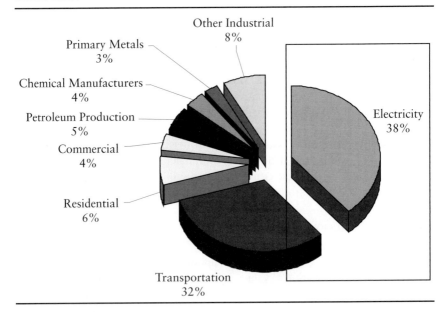

Source: U.S. EIA.

distinct because, until a few years ago, they enjoyed a legally recognized monopoly status. The peculiar nature of electric utilities, the importance of the product they provide, and concerns over pollution, climate change and the geopolitics of energy (particularly, energy independence and national security) make them the subject of numerous public debates questioning their technologies, privileges, and policies. This chapter provides key characteristics of municipal elecric utilities and the major factors needed to understand and evaluate their credit quality.

STRUCTURE OF THE U.S. ELECTRIC INDUSTRY

There are approximately 3,300 electric utilities currently operating in the United States.[1] An electric utility is defined as any corporate or municipal entity that owns and/or operates facilities for the generation, transmission, distribution, or sale of electric energy. In addition to utilities, approximately 32% of the electric energy generating in the United States was produced by *nonutility generators* (NUGs), which sell their power on a wholesale basis or to industrial and large commercial customers. NUGs usually have no defined service area and are often not subject to the same price regulation as utilities, although they are subject to state and federal environmental regulations.

As of January 1, 2006, total installed electric generating capacity in the United States was 1,032 gigawatts (a unit of power equal to 109 watts, or the equivalent of approximately 1,000 large nuclear plants) and total utility electrical production was 3,869 terrawatt-hours (TWH—a unit of energy) including production by nonutility generators of 1,235 TWH.[2]

Although there is some overlap due to traditional utilities that have divested their generation plants, NUGs operate *qualifying facilities* (e.g., independent power producers and cogeneration facilities) under the Public Utility Regulatory Policies Act of 1978 (PURPA) and are not considered to be an electric utility. Each electric service provider in the nation—utilities and NUGs—fall into one of six categories, depending on ownership, regulation, and operating constraints (Exhibits 55.4 and 55.5).

Of the six types of electric service providers shown in Exhibit 55.5 only the first three issue tax-exempt debt on a regular basis. Almost all of the Federal Power Agencies' (FPA) outstanding debt in the public domain (mostly held by the U.S. Treasury) is in the form of taxable long-term bonds. However, tax-exempt bonds issued by several municipal utility systems are directly or indirectly backed by these agencies. For example, the Tennessee

[1] Energy Information Administration Forms EIA-861 and EIA-906/920.
[2] Id.

EXHIBIT 55.4 Structure of U.S. Electric Industry—Total number and percent (in brackets) of Sales to Ultimate Customers

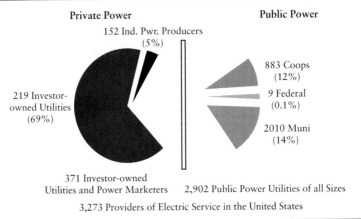

Private Power

152 Ind. Pwr. Producers
(5%)

219 Investor-owned Utilities
(69%)

Public Power

883 Coops
(12%)

9 Federal
(0.1%)

2010 Muni
(14%)

371 Investor-owned
Utilities and Power Marketers

2,902 Public Power Utilities of all Sizes

3,273 Providers of Electric Service in the United States

Source: American Public Power Association (2006–2007 *Annual Directory and Statistical Report*).

EXHIBIT 55.5 U.S. Electric Utility Statistics

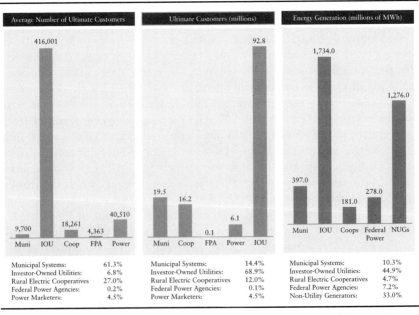

Average Number of Ultimate Customers				
Muni 9,700	IOU 416,001	Coop 18,261	FPA 4,363	Power 40,510

Ultimate Customers (millions)				
Muni 19.5	Coop 16.2	FPA 0.1	Power 6.1	IOU 92.8

Energy Generation (millions of MWh)				
Muni 397.0	IOU 1,734.0	Coops 181.0	Federal Power 278.0	NUGs 1,276.0

Municipal Systems:	61.3%	Municipal Systems:	14.4%	Municipal Systems:	10.3%
Investor-Owned Utilities:	6.8%	Investor-Owned Utilities:	68.9%	Investor-Owned Utilities:	44.9%
Rural Electric Cooperatives	27.0%	Rural Electric Cooperatives	12.0%	Rural Electric Cooperatives	4.7%
Federal Power Agencies:	0.2%	Federal Power Agencies:	0.1%	Federal Power Agencies:	7.2%
Power Marketers:	4.5%	Power Marketers:	4.5%	Non-Utility Generators:	33.0%

Source: American Public Power Association, U.S. Department of Energy/Energy Information Administration.

Valley Authority (TVA) has issued tens of billion of dollars in debt to the public markets; the TVA is indirectly backed the federal government and is rated Aaa/AAA). A brief description of each type of utility will follow below. There is also a breakdown of generating capacity and electric energy production by both fuel and industry segment as well as sector revenues and power sold in Exhibits 55.6, 55.7, and 55.8.

Municipal Utilities

Municipal utilities are electric utilities that are owned and/or operated by municipalities and state agencies to provide service to their constituents. Although municipal systems account for over 60% of the utilities in the

EXHIBIT 55.6   Installed Generating Capacity by Fuel Source Installed Generating Capacity by Fuel Source (in GW)

	U.S. Total	Cooperative	Federal	Investor-Owned	Non-utility	Publicly Owned
Coal	338	24	18	200	66	29
Gas	354	10	4	96	213	29
Nuclear	104	2	7	51	35	8
Oil	66	1	—	28	28	7
Other	19	—	—	0.5	18	0.6
Hydro	96	916	41	24	9	20
Total	979	39	71	400	371	96
% of U.S. Total	100.0%	4.0%	7.2%	40.9%	37.8%	9.8%

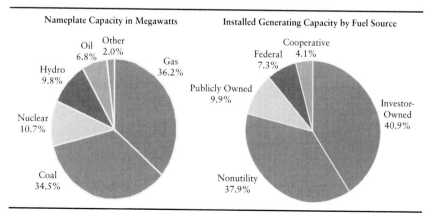

Source: American Public Power Association.

EXHIBIT 55.7   Utility Generating Capacity by Fuel Source (%)

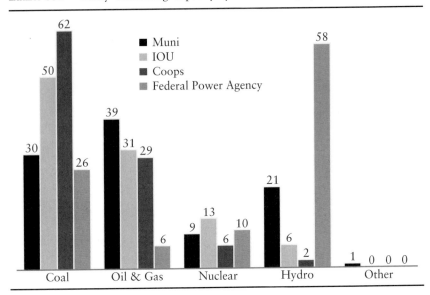

EXHIBIT 55.8   Revenues and Power Sold
Average Revenue Collected Per kWh Sold to Ultimate Customers (cents/kWh)

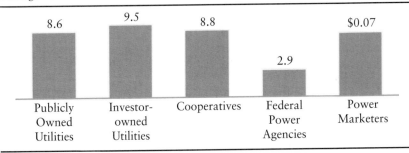

Electric Revenues from Sales to Ultimate Customers ($ billions)

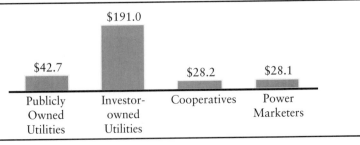

United States, they are generally much smaller than investor-owned utilities and serve only about 15% of the nation's population. The vast majority of municipal electric utilities are individual systems that are state or locally owned (1,962 out of 2,029). The remaining 67 utility systems are *joint-action agencies*, (JAA) comprised of two or more municipal utilities that join together to acquire bulk power supplies. These agencies generate and/or purchase bulk power in order to benefit from economies of scale, and then transmit the power to their members, who distribute it to the ultimate customers.

In general, municipal utility systems are not subject to federal or state rate regulation and their debt is usually exempt from federal taxation. In 2005, municipal systems owned 9.6% (98,686 MW) of the nation's utility-owned generating capacity, had $43.5 billion in total revenues, and sales that accounted for 16.7% (591,062 gigawatt-hours) of the electricity sold to ultimate customers. Exhibit 55.9 shows the ten largest municipal utilities ranked by energy sales, revenues and customers. Exhibit 55.10 shows the geographical location of many of the largest municipal systems.

Investor-Owned Utilities

Investor-owned utilities are utilities organized as tax-paying, profit-oriented businesses that are owned by their shareholders. In general, they have a franchise to serve a specific area and are regulated by state and/or federal regulators. Private power companies are the largest sector of the U.S. electric utility industry. In 2005, they owned 40% (408,699 MW) of the nation's generating capacity, had total combined revenues of $172 billion, and sales that accounted for 63.5% (2,151,720 gigawatt-hours) of the electric energy sold to ultimate customers.

Tax-exempt debt issued by private power companies is almost exclusively in the form of *pollution control revenue* (PCR) bonds or *industrial development authority* (IDA) bonds. Over $70 billion (approximately half) of the total amount of PCR/IDA bonds currently outstanding have been issued on behalf of taxable utilities or their divested generation companies. Under the provisions of the 1986 Tax Reform Act, the ability of investor-owned utilities to use PCR financing was significantly curtailed. Notable exceptions are bonds issued to finance the handling of solid wastes, and a large number of issuers that were specifically grandfathered under the Act's transition rules.

Investor-owned utilities can still utilize tax-exempt IDA financing, although issuance is now limited by numerous restrictions imposed on them by the Tax Reform Act of 1986.

EXHIBIT 55.9 Ten Largest Municipal Utilities

Utility	Ultimate Customers Served
LA Department of Water & Power	1,535,271
Puerto Rico Electric Power Authority	1,410,270
Long Island Power Authority	1,082,903
Salt River Project	802,164
San Antonio City Public Service	601,186
Sacramento Municipal Utility District	547,651
Memphis Light, Gas & Water	404,994
JEA	378,500
Seattle City Light	365,445
Austin Energy	360,873

Utility	MWh Sales
New York Power Authority	47,482,468
Salt River Project	33,084,762
Santee Cooper (SC Public Service Authority)	24,059,568
LA Department of Water & Power	23,916,597
Puerto Rico Electric Power Authority	20,163,433
Long Island Power Authority	19,177,619
San Antonio City Public Service	18,261,632
Nebraska Public Power District	17,571,070
JEA	16,164,540
Seattle City Light	14,564,843

Utility	Electric Revenues (in millions)
Puerto Rico Electric Power Authority	2,581
Long Island Power Authority	2,561
LA Department of Water & Power	2,276
New York Power Authority	2,252
Salt River Project	2,021
San Antonio City Public Service	1,274
Santee Cooper (SC Public Service Authority)	1,033
Sacramento Municipal Utility District	1,014
Austin Energy	844
JEA	832

EXHIBIT 55.10 Location of Major Public Power Utilities

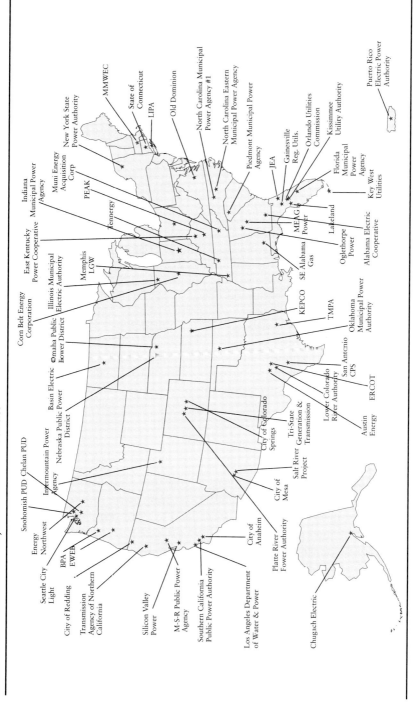

931

Rural Electric Cooperatives

Rural electric cooperatives are nonprofit, customer-owned electric utilities responsible for distributing power in historically rural areas of the nation (although current service territories now include major populations sectors such as the metro area surrounding Atlanta, GA). The existing cooperatives in the United States were developed under the Rural Electrification Act of 1936 (REA Act), which was part of the Roosevelt administration's New Deal. The purpose of the REA Act was to create jobs and bring electricity to small communities. At that time, only about 10% of the farms in the nation had electricity; today over 99% have electricity. The federally subsidized financing offered through the REA Act allowed small communities and farmers to form cooperatives to generate, transmit, and distribute electricity to rural areas. Most of the cooperatives were formed between 1936 and 1960. Today there are 64 power *generation and transmission cooperatives* (G&Ts) supplying electricity to 877 distribution cooperatives. About half of these utilities are subject to state and/or federal rate regulation. Many are also required to adhere to guidelines established by the Rural Utilities Services (RUS), formally called the Rural Electrification Administration or REA.

The majority of the debt issued by cooperative utilities is held by the RUS, although a significant amount of taxable and tax-exempt debt, issued as pollution control/industrial development authority bonds, is also held by the general public. In 2005, cooperatives owned 4.2% (43,225 MW) of the nation's utility-owned generating capacity, had total revenues of $25.5 billion, and sales which accounted for 9.7% (345,157 gigawatt-hours) of the energy sold to ultimate customers.

Federal Power Agencies

Federal Power Agencies (FPAs) are primarily wholesale utilities that sell their power to other utilities (generally cooperatives and municipal utilities) rather than to ultimate customers. They are responsible for operating federally funded and owned power projects such as the Grand Coulee Dam. Most FPA debt is held by the U.S. Treasury, although the TVA has sold several billion dollars of taxable long-term bonds to the public over the past few years. There are nine federal power marketing agencies (TVA, Bonneville Power Authority, Army Corp of Engineers, etc.) and in 2005, they collectively operated 6.9% (71,394 MW) of the installed utility-owned generating capacity in the United States.

Nonutility Generators (NUGs)

NUGs are producers of electricity that are either *independent power producers* (IPPs) (companies like Calpine and Blackrock), GENCOs (the divested generation portion of traditional utilities) or cogeneration plants run by large universities and hospitals, as well as manufacturing and petrochemical entities. In 2005, NUGs accounted for 39.7% of the total installed capacity in the United States (409,689 MW) and delivered 1,235,298 gigawatt-hours of electric energy, a figure that accounts for more than 31% of the total electricity available for distribution in the U.S. NUGs are the fastest growing component of electrical generating capacity and accounted for the majority of new capacity that has came online in the past several years.

Fuel sources used by NUGs in 2005 were as follows: gas (60%), coal (16%), nuclear (9%), oil (7%), hydro (2%), and other including waste, wind, biomass, and so on, representing fewer than 5%. The majority of alternative energy projects planned or under construction is expected to be built by NUGS. To date, only a handful of NUGs projects have utilized tax-exempt financing (e.g., the SMUD's Carson Ice-Gen Project) which produces heat for industrial processes, with the surplus electric or thermal energy sold to utilities or large industrial users.

COST OF ELECTRICITY

Most electric utility costs can be allocated to three functional economic classes:

- Energy or output costs
- Demand or capacity (capital) costs
- Customer costs

Energy or *output costs* are those costs that vary with the total number of kilowatt hours of electricity sold. Fuel cost is usually the largest single component of this category, but wages for production and maintenance personnel are also included. Thus, energy costs vary with the prices that utilities pay for their variable inputs and with the quantity of inputs consumed.

Demand or *capacity costs* are those costs that vary with the maximum demand, or peak load, placed on each utility system. Interest, capital investment, and depreciation expenses are the largest costs in this category but some maintenance, wage, and administrative expenses are included. Variations in these costs rise from the relationship between the peak load and average load on a utility system. The plant capacity maintained to cover the peak load (e.g., a hot summer day in July when air conditioners are on full blast) is not required on most occasions. When the typical load is much lower than the total plant capacity, the capacity costs per unit of electricity sold are high. When the typical load is similar to the peak load, electric utilities benefit from economies of utilization.

The final cost classification, *customer costs*, varies with the number of customers (given the total kilowatt hours sold), and with the maximum rate of consumption per customer. Meter reading, bookkeeping, billing, and some administrative expenses are usually included in this category. While affected by both economies of scale and utilization, customer costs for particular utilities also vary with the distribution of customers among various usage classes (residential, commercial, industrial, and so on as explained below) and with the price of inputs.

CHARGES FOR SERVICE

The relationship between electric utility revenue and cost is complex, largely because of the intricate service rate schedules and accounting procedures of electric utilities. In general, the service charges are a combination of class, block, promotional rates, and fuel cost surcharges.

Electric utility customers are often divided into five classes on the basis of consumption patterns and required services. These are residential customers, commercial customers, industrial customers, customers who purchase or produce electricity for resale, and a small residual class that includes electricity sold for street lighting service. Different rate schedules apply to each class because costs of service differ between classes and must be recouped on a different per-unit basis for each class. Residential rates are typically the highest class, and resale rates are the lowest. Within each class, rates often conform to a declining block pattern.

Block rates are used to reflect capacity and demand costs by relating utilities' cost recovery to consumption per month. Block rates decline as consumption increases because customer and capacity costs are primarily fixed and are recovered in the first blocks for each class. The final block rates only need to cover energy costs and the marginal cost of service to each class. Declining block rates result in a promotional rate schedule, since larger consumers are charged a lower average rate per unit purchased. However, many utilities have moved away from declining block rates because they promote usage and have substituted a variety of complex rate mechanisms that are suppose to promote conservation. Thus, the total revenue of a utility is partially a function of its rate schedule design and distribution of customers among classes.

CREDIT CONSIDERATIONS

In analyzing an electric utility, there are numerous factors that should be evaluated. Unfortunately, due to geographical, political, historical, environmental, economic and regulatory differences between utilities, there is no single formula or cookbook procedure that can consistently be used in determining which attributes are important and which are extraneous. (Identifying the key credit factor is analogous to determining what is the most important organ in the human body; while many might argue that it is the heart or brain, in reality, its which ever one fails to function correctly, leading to the patient's death). Nonetheless, there are several generic factors that should almost always be looked at in attempting to evaluate the credit quality of a given utility, although their relative importance can vary dramatically from one utility to the next. A checklist is provided in Exhibit 55.11, and examples of what to look for are provided below.

- *Regulatory environment.* Does the utility have the ability to set its own rates and issue debt when needed? If not, what is the recent history of obtaining adequate rate relief? Is the regulatory body elected or appointed?

EXHIBIT 55.11   Checklist of Primary Credit Factors
"The most important factor is the one's that's broken."

- Management
- Utility structure—city owned, state agency, JAA, coop, other
- Regulatory environment and rate setting ability
- Legal and security features
- Financial operations
- Capital requirements
- Members' and customer demographics
- Fuel mix and asset concentration
- Contractual obligations
- Counterparty risk
- Ratings and market access
- Liquidity and bank facilities
- Nuclear exposure
- Spot market exposure, long or short power
- Access to transmission
- Completive position
- Ongoing disclosure
- Exposure to pending carbon regulation/state alternative energy mandates

- *Contractual obligations.* Extremely important in evaluating JAAs. Best type of contracts are take-or-pay contracts, which unconditionally obligate members to make payments to the utility. Take-and-pay contracts are conditional on the successful operation of the utility's project(s). Court validation or explicit statutory approval of the contracts is also an important consideration.
- *Competitive position.* How do rates compare with those of other utilities in the area, particularly industrial rates? What are the projections for rate increases of both the utility under evaluation and its competitors? Noncompetitive rates provide strong incentives for customers to find other suppliers, or for members of a JAA to seek legal recourse to get out of undesirable contractual obligations. Transfers of utility revenues to general funds to subsidize property taxes can strain a municipal system's competitive position.
- *Nuclear exposure.* What is the operating history of the utility's nuclear facilities (if any) as measured against other nuclear facilities (capacity factor, fines, etc.). Nuclear exposure does not always constitute a negative credit attribute. A well-run nuclear plant can be an inexpensive source of energy and helps to mitigate fossil fuel volatility as well as the impact of disruptions in oil or coal supplies (e.g., a war in the Middle East, frozen rivers preventing the delivery of coal barges, train line congestion, new air legislation).
- *Capital requirements.* How will future requirements be financed? Is there a large amount of variable rate debt or commercial paper that needs to be refinanced with long term debt? Is the utility about to embark on the construction of any large projects such as a base-load generating station?
- *Fuel mix and asset concentration.* A diverse fuel mix as well as multiple sources of power is almost always preferred.
- *Exposure to pending carbon regulation and/or mandated "alternative energy portfolios."* As a result of the growing concerns over global warming and electric generation of the primary source of CO_2 gases emitted in the United States, investors need to be cautious about a utility's financial and credit exposure to potential regulations that will require reductions in greenhouse gas emissions and/or mandate alternative energy portfolios (see Exhibit 55.12).
- *Excess capacity margin.* If the utility has excess capacity, does it have the ability to make profitable off-system sales? Due to low growth rates and increased competition, excess capacity can represent a major credit problem for some utilities.
- *Financial operations.* Debt service coverage, inclusive of power purchase obligations and other off-balance-sheet debt, is the single-most

EXHIBIT 55.12 States' with "Renewable Energy Mandates"

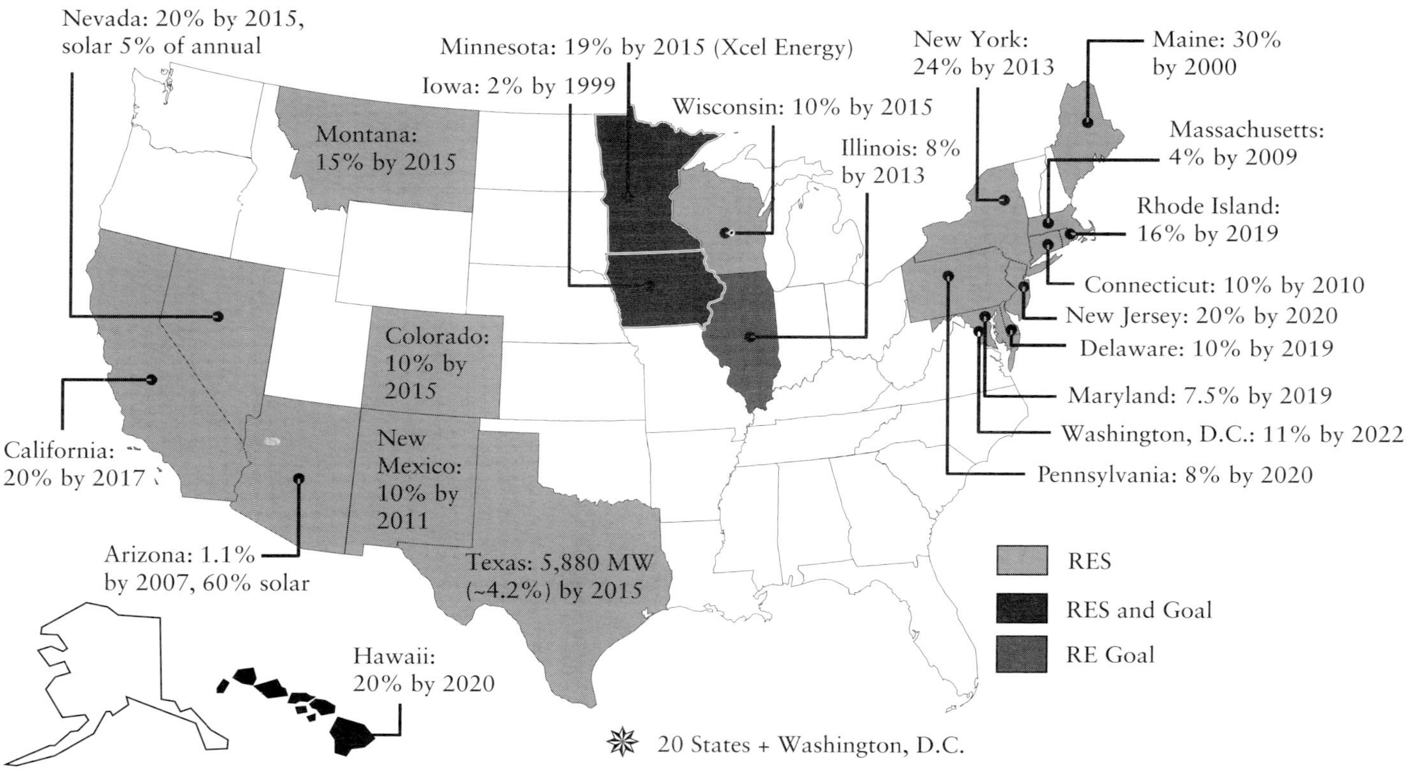

Nevada: 20% by 2015, solar 5% of annual

Montana: 15% by 2015

California: 20% by 2017

Arizona: 1.1% by 2007, 60% solar

Colorado: 10% by 2015

New Mexico: 10% by 2011

Texas: 5,880 MW (~4.2%) by 2015

Minnesota: 19% by 2015 (Xcel Energy)

Iowa: 2% by 1999

Wisconsin: 10% by 2015

Illinois: 8% by 2013

New York: 24% by 2013

Maine: 30% by 2000

Massachusetts: 4% by 2009

Rhode Island: 16% by 2019

Connecticut: 10% by 2010

New Jersey: 20% by 2020

Delaware: 10% by 2019

Maryland: 7.5% by 2019

Washington, D.C.: 11% by 2022

Pennsylvania: 8% by 2020

Hawaii: 20% by 2020

RES

RES and Goal

RE Goal

20 States + Washington, D.C.

937

common measure of financial performance. However, coverage ratios are less important for muni systems and coops than they are for investor-owned utilities since their goals do not include maximizing profits.

- Typical values for municipal electric utilities serving more than 50,000 customers range from 1.3x to 1.8x. Joint-action agencies usually have lower coverage ratios (1.0x to 1 .3x) due to the structure of the contractual obligation between the agency and the participating members.
- For IOUs, the value most commonly looked at is the pretax interest coverage, excluding Allowance for Funds Used During Construction (AFUDC)—a noncash revenue item. The industry median in 2005 for pretax interest coverage was approximately 2.9x.[3]
- For Coops, the value most commonly calculated is the *times-interest-earned ratio* (TIER), as defined by the REA. Typical values for *generation and transmission* (G&T) cooperatives are 1.1x to 1.4x.

■ *Economics and demographics of the service territory.* In general, utilities do best in service areas with modest growth rates. Very high growth rates can be even more of a problem than an economically declining service area. This is because the construction of new generating capacity needed to meet rapid growth is very expensive and entails significant project and forecasting risks.

■ *Access to transmission.* As competition becomes an increasingly important credit factor in evaluating utilities, access to and ownership of transmission facilities will become more critical, since transmission access allows utilities to shop around for the most attractive power sources and/or effectively market their own surplus capacity. Ability to enter into regional transmission compacts with other utilities should be viewed as a positive credit factor.

■ *Customer mix.* In general, a high percentage of residential customers (as measured by energy sales) and a low percentage of industrial customers are preferable. Residential customers change their consumption patterns slowly. Industrial customers, particularly large manufacturing and petrochemical companies, can opt to generate their own electricity or enter into a wholesale power purchase agreement with another utility. Consequently, the presence of a large industrial load subjects a utility to greater competitive risks and makes long-range planning more difficult.

■ *Management style.* Difficult to evaluate, but rapidly management style is becoming one of the most important credit considerations. Look for

---

[3] *Moody's Sourcebook: Power and Energy Companies.*

management that takes an active role in cost cutting, establishes conservation and integrated resource programs, and develops marketing plans to sell and/or purchase power from outside the utility's traditional boundaries.

SUMMARY

Although not meant to be all inclusive, this chapter attempts to provide an overview of the U.S. electric utility industry, including credit factors that investors should review and comparative statistics between the different types of electric service providers. Electric demand growth in the United States is projected to increase 40% by 2025 at a cost of over $500 billion. This growth will lead to public utilities growing need to access the capital markets, and seems to indicate public power will be one of the key growth industries in the municipal sector.

CHAPTER 56

How to Analyze Startup Continuing Care Retirement Community Bonds

Edward C. Merrigan
Director of Research
B.C. Zeigler & Company

In the municipal bond arena, a *continuing care retirement community* (CCRC) is a nonprofit corporation providing or arranging for housing and designated health-related services to an elderly person pursuant to a residency agreement or agreements effective for the rest of the person's life or for a specified period exceeding one year. To provide such designated health-related services, the CCRC (1) accepts an advance fee deposit or other type of entry fee and (2) charges a full or discounted periodic monthly fee. This discussion does not delve into rental communities.

The collection of advance fee deposits sets a CCRC apart from other housing bonds or, from a consumer's point of view, from other senior living options. An analyst's understanding of the accounting and cash flow aspects of advance fee deposits, as well as their timing and refund attributes, is critical to making an informed investment decision about a startup CCRC. Furthermore, practically all startup CCRC bond issues are floated with feasibility studies. These studies provide the core raw information that must be analyzed to discern good projects from potentially bad ones.

The purpose of this chapter is to help analysts understand the subtleties of this high-yield investment category.

ACCOMMODATION AND SERVICE OPTIONS

Accommodations at a CCRC generally include independent living units, assisted living units, and nursing care beds. The terms *unit* and *bed* identify the place within the CCRC and the level of services a resident will receive.

941

The range of accommodations and square footage of an independent living unit go from small studios, to grand three-bedroom deluxe suites. The size is dictated by the CCRC's economics and by local market demand. The typical overall accommodation mix in a startup, single-site CCRC is about 65% independent living, 20% assisted living, and 15% nursing.

Today's typical startup CCRC bond issue is highly complex and highly structured. While still a revenue bond, a CCRC has a special debt structure that mixes accounting revenues with substantial cash flows in the early years of a community's life. Because of the significant cash flow associated with advance fee deposits, typical plans of finance involve so-called temporary and permanent debt structures. The temporary debt is letter-of-credit-enhanced, *variable rate demand bonds* (VRDBs). The sizing of the VRDB temporary debt is based of a percentage of the expected pool of total advance fee deposits, and usually is sized at about 85% of such pool. The VRDBs are called "temporary" because they are expected to be retired and redeemed via optional call within a few years of the CCRC coming online. The source of the VRDB principal repayment is advance fee deposits. The permanent debt consists of fixed rate serial and term bonds with a final maturity of 30 to 32 years. The fixed rate portion generally is structured with a level debt service schedule.

Variations on the typical plan of finance abound, with underwriting firms introducing unenhanced variable rate bonds with soft put features. Also, either the fixed or variable rate demand debt will be swapped. The swap counterparty's security (which sometimes is on parity) is of a concern to some who fear early swap termination ramifications or collateral postings, but most swaps are carried to term.

Startup CCRC bond issues are brought to market unrated. The industry has seen its fair share of historical defaults and is considered high risk and high yield by most institutional investors. However, defaults have been waning compared to say 15 years ago. If a default occurs, it is usually after the CCRC is built, not necessarily during construction. While there are significant construction risks in a CCRC, mitigating the risks can be achieved if reasonable answers to the following questions are evident:

- What is the general contractor's experience?
- Is there an executed guaranteed maximum-price contract?
- Have the costs been reasonable researched, with identified and reasonable construction contingencies and allowances?
- Has all of this been based on design documents in the advanced stage?

Less than solid good answers to these questions should raise a red flag for an investor.

Typical defaults have occurred because the time it took to fill the units spanned a much longer period than originally forecasted. Reaching stable, full occupancy in a startup situation consumes time and capital. Achieving full and stabilized occupancy as quickly as possible is critical. When absorption of newly constructed units takes too long, funds are exhausted and bond default occurs.

Loan-to-value ratios may be calculated for startup CCRCs if the fear of default is real. Certain value investors (versus tax-exempt income investors) think calculating the scrap value upon foreclosure and sale of the property, plant, and equipment is important. However, this author feels that such a calculation is a distant consideration for the typical tax-exempt bond issue underwritten by an investment bank.

A CCRC's debt issue is primarily a revenue bond, not an asset-backed or overcollateralized or traunched transaction. Timely payment of debt service from free cash flow is more important than realizing any residual value from a foreclosure and asset sale in bankruptcy.

In order for a startup CCRC bond issue to be floated, there must have been seed money provided earlier in its life cycle. The taxable seed capital investors are taken out at the time of closing the tax-exempt debt issue. Seed money pays for architectural plans, land acquisition, and most important, presale marketing cost. For the issue to come to market, presales of a sufficient magnitude need to occur. Presales need to occur so that there is enough critical mass demonstrated to both letter of credit banks and long-term, fixed rate investors that there is adequate demand for the CCRC's contemplated independent living units. A bond issue will usually not be brought to market if the presale level is not high enough (see the discussion of presales later in this chapter).

RESIDENCY CONTRACTS

CCRC residents sign a contract that remains in effect for the rest of the resident's life or, in some contracts, only while the resident occupies the *independent-living unit* (ILU). This legal document spells out the obligations of the resident and the CCRC. In states with regulations regarding CCRCs, the form of the contract may be subject to governmental approval. In addition to the financial obligation of both parties, the contract outlines the supportive services and amenities available related to: the property (e.g., gardening and maintenance); hospitality (dining, housekeeping, and laundry); and care (assisted living, nursing, and medical checkups). Residency contract agreements exist in three types: extensive, modified, and fee-for-service. Each contract presents a significantly different risk profile.

Extensive Agreement (Type A)

Extensive agreement or Type A contract includes an unlimited amount of long-term nursing care. The resident pays the same rate for care while occupying a nursing unit in the health center as they would in a residential unit. Management may increase monthly fees for normal operating costs and inflation adjustments. In a Type A arrangement, the resident's advance fee deposit funds the insurance obligation of the CCRC to provide the nursing bed, if needed, at a discounted rate. The discount comes about because the posted monthly charge for an independent living unit is substantially lower than the nursing care bed's posted charges for the same period. When transferred to a nursing care bed, the resident pays the independent living unit rate; thus, the discount.

Modified Agreement (Type B)

The key difference between a modified agreement and a Type A, is the limitation of nursing care bed days. For example, only 60 days per year will be covered. After the covered period expires, the transferred nursing care bed resident pays the higher daily fee set at the posted or prevailing charge rate.

Fee-for-Service Agreement (Type C)

Often called a straight rental, a fee-for service agreement (or Type C contract) includes housing, residential services, and amenities. Residents usually have guaranteed access to the CCRC's nursing beds, but pay the accommodation's prevailing rates when transferred. Essentially, residents pay only for services used.

Advance Fee Deposits

The CCRC industry offers a wide variety of contract options. Each contract specifies its own payment plan and varies according to the amount of health care service obligation assumed by the CCRC. The contracts require a resident to make a lump-sum payment before or upon admission; hence, the term *advance fee deposit*. Key bond analytical considerations include the accounting treatment of advance fee deposits, the credit and financial ratio implications surrounding their cash flow, the hidden actuarial obligation to provide future services, and the contingent refund liability. As previously mentioned, an analyst looking a CCRC bond issue must understand special concepts relating to advance fee deposits.

The word *deposit* is more frequently being appended to the term *advance fee*, so that many in the industry now use the term *advance fee deposit*. In some 100% refundable situations, the word *fee* is being completely dropped and only the word *deposit* is being used.

Advance fee deposits usually are incrementally paid. Each incremental payment demonstrates a prospective resident's interest in moving into the CCRC. The incremental payments count toward the ultimate full price of the advance fee deposit. In the early seed money stages of a CCRC's development, several years before a bond issue is floated, a small refundable deposit will be collected from seriously interested prospective residents. This *priority deposit* represents a down payment of only a very small fraction of the advance fee deposit; usually $1,000 or less. These deposits indicate interest in perhaps committing to bigger payment of about 10% of the advance fee deposit. Analysis of priority deposits come into play with seed capital analysis, which is not the main subject of this writing.

After a priority deposit is received, the next phase of development is to move to a *presale*. A presale has traditionally been thought of as a remittance by the perspective resident of 10% of the full advance fee deposit; with the balance due upon occupancy. Conceivably, the move-in may not happen for another two or three years. Bond issues are not floated until at least 65% to 70% of the independent living units expected to be built have been presold with 10% deposits.

The presale level is one of the most important factors in analyzing startup CCRCs. The 10% dollar amount is paid to reserve a unit; hence the historical connotation of "presale," with the balance due upon occupancy. Analysts should review the presale statistics and see what procedures the feasibility consultant has undertaken to ensure their validity. Between 65% and 70% presale level is the norm before a startup CCRC bond issue comes to market to finance construction.

Review of the presale velocity and the attrition rates also can be telling indicators of demand. Velocity is the rate at which new units have been reserved, beginning with the first month of acceptance of 10% deposits and ending with the most recent statistics available as show in the Preliminary Official Statement's Feasibility Study. A presale period longer than two years indicates demand may be less than compelling.

Each of the reserved independent living unit type categories should be fairly represented with presales. For example, if there is a disproportionate amount of presales for the smaller units compared to the larger, this is cause for concern. The same holds true if the unit count demand is reversed.

Advance fee deposit refunds, if offered, are paid either directly to the resident or, if the resident is deceased, to the estate. Refundable advance fee deposits (in varying proportion depending on the percentage of the advance fee deposit subject to refund) primarily affect the sensitivity analysis performed on the debt service coverage ratio because advance fee deposit refunds somewhat offset fee receipts. With fully refundable advance fee deposits, the CCRC's net cash inflow from this source is reduced substantially after initial fill-up with stabilized occupancy. Refunds of advance fee deposits tend to eliminate or reduce revenue production from this source; the revenue production coming through the amortization process. Thus, net assets (fund balance or equity) accumulation through retained earnings must come from other sources.

Another aspect of creditworthiness affected by the presence of partial or full refunds of advance fee deposits involves the timing of any refund payable. The best credit outcome is when the refundable portion of any advance fee deposit is paid only when the vacated unit is resold and the CCRC has received a new advance fee deposit. This stipulation mitigates credit concerns regarding sudden and material draws on cash reserves when demand for vacated units does not materialize as a fast as needed.

While traditional, self-amortizing, earnable nonrefundable advance fees are still in place in many CCRCs, the increasing prevalence and trend of residents wanting a partial or full refund cannot be ignored.

OWNERSHIP, GOVERNANCE, AND MANAGEMENT

A basic concept analysts must understand in the world of not-for-profit corporations is how they are owned. Nonprofits are not owned by stockholders but rather "members." In many nonsectarian instances, the members/owners also serve on the board of trustees. Typical startup CCRC boards usually do not have the expertise to successfully bring a large project to completion. While board members may have a good mix of professional and business backgrounds, the complex nature of a CCRC usually compels a board to contract hire the talent to get the CCRC marketed, built, and managed. In general, development of a startup CCRC demands highly qualified outside consultants for construction, marketing, and operational management. A contract firm's prior experience in these areas is a must. There are only a handful of firms with the experience and depth of capability to bring a startup CCRC from concept to successful stabilized occupancy.

Exceptions to the mandatory hiring of outside consultants are usual in seasoned multisite operators who are in the business of expansion and have tract records to prove their abilities to add communities. These multisite communities can be unincorporated operating divisions. If they are operated as separately incorporated entities, then a question arises as to if they are part of an obligated group under a master trust indenture arrangement.

DEMAND ANALYSIS OF INDEPENDENT LIVING UNITS

The market segment that can afford to choose a CCRC has a variety of living accommodation options available to it. Generally, the vast majority elderly couples or individuals will most likely choose to simply stay in their own home. Movement into a CCRC, or any other type of congregate setting for that matter is not desired or affordable for these individuals. As such, demand for a CCRC's independent living accommodation, and the related services that go along with living in such a unit, is extremely discretionary. Regardless of such inertia, CCRCs do attract seniors, and demand for the community can be analyzed.

Defining the Primary Market Area

Two interconnected principles define a CCRC's primary market area: (1) specific geographic boundaries; and (2) the count of age and income qualified persons (or households) living within the primary market's boundaries. The existing pool of soon-to-be residents who have paid their 10% advance fee deposit helps draw the startup CCRC's geographic market boundary because their home addresses serve as the best indicator of potential residents' origins. Most CCRC geographic primary market areas do not exceed a 15-mile radius from the central location of the community. If a CCRC's primary market area extends farther, its ability to capture residents living in the outer portions of the boundary becomes questionable. The mileage number is a rule of thumb and each market's population density will affect it.

After establishing its geographic boundaries, a CCRC's consultant can then focus on researching demographics and can quantify the potential size of the market in terms of number of eligible people or households.

Age Eligibility Factor

Most seniors, if they do move into a CCRC, will not make the move until they are at least 75 years of age, with recent trends pushing that number towards 80, although admission of younger residents occurs. Thus, feasibility consultants usually stratify the market area's population or households in five-year intervals starting with age 65 seniors. By identifying area residents in the age brackets of 65–69 and 70–74 years, potential long-term future residents can be identified.

Income Eligibility Factor

Income qualification identifies a prospective resident's ability to meet the monthly fee. Generally, a retiree's main sources of annual recurring income include social security, pension payments, investment income, and return of capital. Living in a CCRC requires an annual income of about 150% to 175% of the annualized weighted average monthly service charge. If a person makes less than this, they are usually counted as ineligible.

Home Sales Analysis

A CCRC must quickly fill newly constructed units. How quickly and for what price a prospective resident can sell a home before entering a CCRC becomes a credit concern when researching demand. Since the local real estate market and, to some extent, the local economy influence home prices, feasibility studies will convey the following statistical information:

- The average length of time homes remain on the market
- The median price of a home
- Number of home sales
- Change in home prices
- Quantity of housing stock

While some prospective residents may have sufficient cash and investments on hand to pay the full advance fee deposit without selling their home, the desire to sell the house before entering the CCRC usually supersedes their financial wherewithal. Concern has been expressed that if the general housing market sees a period of extended weakness, this will translate into lower or delayed CCRC independent living unit presales, slower move-ins, or outright presale cancellations. As mentioned previously, a longer absorption period than that forecasted in the feasibility study could be fatal to a bond issue.

House sale concerns have their premise from the common notion that the full advance fee deposit primarily comes from the sale proceeds of a house. Conventional thinking is that a CCRC's primary service area's average or median home sale price should be at or above the average advance fee deposit of the CCRC. A slowdown in home sales, set off by buyer lack of demand, will cause a CCRC's unit demand to suffer. The scenario continues that seniors would be slow or unwilling to commit to moving into a CCRC because of a lower than originally anticipated house price. Such experience would delay the senior from moving in. Seniors would also be cognizant that a lower than expected house sale price would translate into lower investable funds and lower than expected reinvestment earnings over their remaining lifetime. Some argue that the senior faced with a lower market sale house price will choose to delay the move into the CCRC. At worst, they would cancel their movement plans.

This author posits that the ups and downs of housing market cycles do not necessarily come into play as a major risk for a startup CCRC because of several reasons. Most senior sellers have so much equity in their home that a fluctuation or diminished sale price is not an overriding concern, and not a concern that would, on the whole, result in a material reversal or material delay of a decision to move into a CCRC. Anecdotal information says that most seniors have house prices well above the median sale price of a service area. Furthermore, the choice of living in a CCRC, with all the attendant lifestyle benefits, is the main determinant of a move, all else being equal. A lower sale price for a hose, assumed with a substantial capital gain, can overcome so-called lost profit negatives had the housing market been more robust. Finally, the difference between the sale price and the advance fee deposit (assuming there is a positive difference) certainly will be invested by the senior in securities, but the exact earnings or investment rate would be variable and not tied to the real estate market.

Penetration Rate

A useful ratio tool in measuring demand is a calculation called the *penetration rate*. It is determined by dividing the CCRC's independent living units by the number of eligible people in the primary market. The eligible market size equals the number of households with people over the age of 75 who meet the minimum income criteria. The startup CCRC will target the potential residents in this pool. Calculating a CCRC's penetration rate helps measure the degree to which the primary market is underserved or saturated. The higher the penetration rate, the harder filling units becomes.

Despite the calculation's simplicity, multiple variations and methodologies exist to determine the numerator and denominator. In its simplest form, the penetration rate's numerator includes the subject CCRC's number of independent living units expected to be occupied by residents originating from the defined primary service area. The denominator (the age- and income-eligible households in the market area) will be a large number.

The numerator can then go through several iterations to account for area competitor's vacancies and planned additional units at all competitors. The result of these iterations will increase the small numerator number, thus having an adverse effect on the penetration rate. Whereas minor changes to the large denominator number do not affect the rate. Generally, penetration rates range from below 5%, which is very good, to over 15%, which is cause for concern.

THE ANALYSIS OF ADVANCE FEE DEPOSITS AND MONTHLY SERVICE FEE PRICES

A CCRC tries to cater to a certain market economic segment it aims to capture via the fees it charges. Fees directly affect demand. Advance fee deposits are sized based on cost to build the community, what competitors are charging, stated mission, home values, operating service level, and to a large extent, if the advance fee deposit is refundable. With the exception of the home value and the refundablility aspect, monthly service fees are similarly sized.

Information about deemed competitor's prices are usually summarized in the feasibility study. The information includes the number, types, and square footage (and number of bedrooms) of units, the service program and services included in monthly fees. The level or degree of competition is somewhat proportional to the distance between the CCRC and its identified competitor. The closer a competitor's location to the CCRC, the more it influences demand.

Identified and unidentified new CCRC entrants into the market area pose a major competitive threat. CCRCs that have experienced problems filling newly constructed units can usually attribute their problems to another CCRC coming into the market and flooding the services area with empty units needing to be filled. Potential residents who would have otherwise moved into the subject CCRC instead move into the competitor. This threat ceases to be a major factor once the units are filled, but while absorption is occurring, slow fill problems can arise.

ASSISTED LIVING UNIT AND NURSING CARE BED DEMAND ANALYSIS

An existing CCRC can point to its experience in terms of movement of residents through the continuum of care. However, a startup CCRC's assisted living and nursing care beds must be filled from the outside, not necessarily in the early years with continuum transfers from independent living units. Measuring demand for outside direct admissions to an assisted living unit is subject to many unknown variables because the need is urgent and a move decision must be concluded within a short time span. This is unlike an independent living unit decision which can take years. The defined service area is usually the same geographic boundary as that for the independent living units. Gauging the functional dependency of the frail elderly usually comes from surrogate Census Bureau studies which measure activities of daily living. Despite these unknowns, revenue from assisted living units is not the prime determinate of a CCRCs overall success, so analysis is cursory.

The demand for inpatient nursing services is regarded as purely need driven and not subject to long deliberations. The catchment area's borders are the same as independent and assisted living. The focus of analysis shifts toward payer mix of the beds. Mostly all the beds will be filled with outside admits; very few internal transfers will come in the early years of a CCRC's life. As such, private pay residents will dominate the payer mix. Issues surrounding Medicaid are less of a concern. Some mention of seeking Medicare certification should be present in the offering materials because, at least as of this writing, Medicare is a good payer.

UTILIZATION AND FILL-UP EXPECTATIONS

The early years of a startup CCRC do not show significant unit turnover in the independent living units. Key to success is filling the newly constructed units as fast as possible to reach stabilized occupancy. Generally, the fill rate as shown in the feasibility study spans a two-year period. Feasibility schedules will show move-ins are elevated at the beginning, then trail off towards the end as the CCRC approaches 95% expected stabilized occupancy in the independent living units. The actual fill-up speed is expected to exceed this rate, with almost 50% occupancy sometimes coming in the first six months. The fill-up assumptions have a direct effect on the anticipated receipt of advance fee deposits, Therefore, a sensitivity analysis is performed using a longer absorption period than expected.

FINANCIAL STATEMENT ANALYSIS

The feasibility consultant-prepared forecasted financial statements typically presented in a bond offing extend two years past the date of expected stabilized occupancy.

The cash flow statement is the most important of the three main financial statements to analyze because it provides critical data needed to evaluate the CCRC. Receipt of advance fee deposits for first-time-occupied units are booked as a financing activity, not an operating activity. It is also important to note that the receipt of cash from advance fee deposits does not involve the recognition of revenue; it is only a cash flow item. The corresponding credit entries to the debit of cash are spread between two balance sheet liability accounts. The proportion of the advance fee deposit that is refundable is booked into an account called *refundable advance fee deposits*; the proportion that is earnable is booked as *deferred revenue*. Again, all of these accounts appear on the balance sheet, hence there is no recognition of revenue.

In situations where 90% of the advance fee deposit is refundable, then 10% is earnable. The amortization of earnable advance fee revenue is all noncash. This accounting concept involves the earning over time of the portion of the lump sum cash payment for the advance fee. Since it is not a cash flow number, less emphasis is needed to analyze this number when examining a CCRC bond issue.

In terms of the income statement operating revenue, the majority of a CCRC's revenue comes from three sources: resident services (monthly maintenance fees or rent); amortization of deferred advance fee deposits (a noncash revenue source); and health center revenue (which generally includes patient nursing services). Less proportional revenues are investment income and donor contributions.

Unlike seasoned CCRCs, analysts do not need to devote a disproportionate amount of time analyzing the startup CCRCs revenue mix. Independent and assisted living services are effectively all private pay. Nursing care revenues, in the early years of a CCRC, are also significantly private pay, with state Medicaid or federal Medicare reimbursement providing a small portion of the mix. The private pay portion of the skilled nursing services can be a mixture of full and discounted (transferees) receipts. However, transfers from independent living units to skilled nursing beds are not that significant in the early years of a startup CCRC; the beds are filled with outside admits.

Noteworthy evolving changes in skilled nursing payor mix category involve Medicare Managed Care insurance payments. This is the result of beneficiaries signing up for the new prescription drug benefit and, in turn, relinquishing their indemnity Medicare coverage for managed care benefits. As such, relationships with managed care organizations—ones that enroll Medicare-eligible plan members—are becoming more important to the overall analysis of health insurance sources of revenue for a CCRC. Without a contract, a CCRC may find it difficult to receive payment for its covered resident.

Contributions and returns on investments (or investment income) is usually presented in the "operations" section of the income statement. This is not universal as some consider these line items as "nonoperating" in nature. Unless an adjustment is made by analysts to reclassify these amounts, the line classification will affect how certain financial ratios are computed. Regardless of line placement classification, for a startup CCRC, contributions are not a significant source of revenue.

RATIO ANALYSIS

Industrywide financial ratios were first introduced and published in the early 1990s. Due to the standardization of financial statement presentation brought about by the constantly updated publication of the AICPA's *Health-Care Audit Guide*, widely accepted financial ratios based on consistently presented financial statements are now an industry norm. Standard & Poor's and FitchRatings annually publish financial ratio medians for the universe of bonds for which they have issued bond ratings; Moody's as of this writing is not active in rating CCRC bonds. The Commission on Accreditation of Rehabilitation Facilities—Continuing Care Accreditation Commission (CARF-CCAC) annually publishes guidelines called *Financial Ratios and Trend Analysis*. As such, general but not universal agreement exists about methods and formulas for computing ratios.

Generally, only about two financial ratios will make it to a typical preliminarily official statement: the debt service coverage ratio and the debt-to-cash ratio. Generally, for a startup CCRC's bond to be seriously marketable, the debt service coverage ratio needs to be at 1.3x and the debt-to-cash ratio needs to be at least 30%. Ratios below this threshold indicate heightened vulnerably to default.

LEGAL SECURITY FEATURES AND COVENANT CONSIDERATIONS

As is the case with most health-care-related municipal bonds, debt of a CCRC is secured at the highest level. In other words, substantial subordinate debt structures are very rare. CCRC debt offerings are secured by a first mortgage or deed of trust lien on real property and a perfected security interest in personal properly, including a gross revenue pledge. The CCRC is expected to make monthly underlying loan or master trust indenture note payments to the bond trustee. A debt service reserve fund, sized at maximum annual for the fixed rate piece of debt, is also the norm. Provisions permitting the substitution of the master note, while prevalent in hospital bonds, are limited (but not completely removed) in CCRC debt issuances.

Because of the ubiquitous presence of bank letters of credit enhancing the temporary debt as represented by VRDBs, there is concern about the rights and prepayment provisions of the VRDBs. The bank's experience and commitment to the CCRC industry should be assessed. Bank reimbursement agreements for letters of credit are generally secured by a parity master trust indenture note. These reimbursement agreements contain significant business covenants that are at times the same, and at other times more restrictive than covenants in a typical master trust indenture. The banks will sometimes set the thresholds of covenants at a higher level of performance than that of the fixed rate master trust indenture covenants. In some instances, this disparity of covenants is a point of concern among fixed rate bondholders. In a worst case scenario, a covenant violation of a reimbursement agreement may invoke a draconian remedy by an inexperienced bank; the remedy being acceleration of the VRDBs through the termination of the letter of credit. If such a scenario were to arise, the CCRC would be forced to pay principal associated with VRDBs in a much more accelerated time frame than the nominal original redemption schedule of the VRDBs. In some instances such a scenario can cause a master trust indenture event of default. Not all bond issues come with an intercreditor agreement that spells out the rights and remedies of the two parties and what happens to the shared collateral upon default. However, analysts should make sure collateral is shared pari passu.

Besides the extra and elevated covenants associated with bank reimbursement agreements, startup CCRCs have a host of unique nonfinancial business and operating provisions. These covenants are not universally worded and no two investment banks have the same underwriting standards. Nonetheless, the DSCR covenant is worth discussing in greater detail.

Rate covenants in CCRCs can be and usually are worded such that an event of default cannot immediately be declared if the ratio falls below 1× in any one year. The event of default can only be declared if multiple years of being below 1× are experienced. The reasoning behind this is the uncertain nature of net cash receipts from net advance fee deposits in a stabilized CCRC. In many instances, if turnover is not experienced, coverage will be below one times because of the lack of net advance fee deposits. Yet debt service is being paid on time and without a problem from cash on hand.

Presale minimums during and after construction, as well as absolute occupancy minimums are also the subject of fine-tuned covenants. An event of default should not be triggered by failure to achieve a certain presale level once the CCRC is open and has far exceeded its minimum occupancy covenants.

CONTINUING DISCLOSURE

Compared to a dozen or so years ago, significant improvement in this area has occurred over and above the minimums set by the SEC's Rule 15(c)2-12. Unrated CCRC debt is somewhat illiquid for trading purposes but would be even more illiquid if important and strong continuing disclosure provisions were not forced onto the CCRC by institutional investors. In some instances, the frequency of interim reporting may be monthly. This is especially so during the construction phase, as the bonds must be monitored for significant change orders and any delays. The fill-up stage, after the certificate of occupancy is received, must go according to plan. Sustained marketing efforts cannot be underemphasized. The fill-up of independent living units, and attendant pay down of the temporary VRDBs, is vital to the long-term success of the CCRC. Monitoring of all these factors cannot happen unless extensive secondary market reporting is promised and delivered by the CCRC. Furthermore, and to prevent selective disclosure, all information promised to bondholders should also be sent to the NRMSIRS.

SUMMARY

Successful investing in a nonrated, high-yield, startup CCRC can be summarized as follows: (1) buying a CCRC bond that came to market with an appropriately wide spread to the AAA scale; (2) watching the project finish its construction phase on time and within budget; (3) seeing the CCRC fill up at a rate faster than what was forecasted in the feasibility study; and (4) upon reaching stabilized occupancy, being advance refunded out of the bond at time when there is about five years left to the first premium call date and at a time when current interest rates and spreads are lower than what the original deal came at. That is success.

CHAPTER 57

How to Analyze Tobacco Bonds

Gerry Lian
Executive Director
Morgan Stanley Investment Management

O n November 23, 1998 a total of 46 U.S. states, the District of Columbia, the Commonwealth of Puerto Rico, and four U.S. territories entered into the Master Settlement Agreement (MSA) with four major U.S. tobacco companies: Philip Morris Inc., R.J. Reynolds Tobacco Co., Lorillard Tobacco Co., and Brown & Williamson Tobacco Corp. This agreement represents the largest civil settlement in U.S. history. Following its execution and approval by these participants, the "settling states," have issued over $36.5 billion of tax-exempt revenue bonds secured by a pledge of tobacco settlement revenues provided under the MSA.

The purpose of this chapter is to set forth an analytical framework to evaluate the credit risk of bonds secured by tobacco settlement revenues ("Tobacco Settlement Revenue bonds" or "TSR bonds"). Due to an unusual bundle of risks, TSR bonds) constitute a highly unique and challenging type of municipal bond that is subject to a wide risk spectrum. This spectrum includes structural risk, corporate credit risk, cash flow risk, and litigation risk. The following discussion shall proceed to define and evaluate the specific elements comprising each risk category.

BACKGROUND

Before proceeding to the analysis, it is important to provide an overview and summary of the MSA and to illuminate the structural characteristics of TSR bonds.

The Master Settlement Agreement

The MSA is a complex legal agreement negotiated between two classes of litigants: (1) state governmental entities, comprised of 46 U.S. states, the District of Columbia, Puerto Rico, the Virgin Islands, the Northern Mariana Islands, America Samoa, and Guam (collectively, the "settling states"); and (2) four U.S. tobacco companies, noted above, known collectively as the Original Participating Manufacturers (OPMs). Four U.S. States (Florida, Texas, Mississippi and Minnesota), known as "nonsettling states," entered into separate agreements with the tobacco firms and are not parties to the MSA.

The purpose of the MSA is to resolve on a consensual basis numerous legal and equitable claims filed by the settling states against the OPMs to recover monetary damages for health care costs that have resulted from cigarette consumption. As in any negotiated contract, the parties reached agreement by making certain concessions in return for valuable benefits. The settling states agreed to release the OPMs from all past, present, and future liabilities in connection with state monetary damage claims and to permit subsequent tobacco firms to enter the MSA. In exchange, the OPMs agreed to three key provisions: (1) to make specified tobacco settlement payments, in perpetuity, pursuant to detailed formulas described below; (2) to abide by a series of new regulations restricting the marketing, advertising, sponsorship, and sale of cigarettes to the public, particularly young consumers; and (3) to fund a national foundation that would better educate the public about the dangers of tobacco use.

Classification of Tobacco Firms Under the MSA

The MSA divides tobacco firms into three classifications: OPMs, Subsequent Participating Manufacturers (SPMs), and Non-Participating Manufacturers (NPMs). Since OPMs and SPMs are signatories to the MSA, both classes collectively are deemed to constitute Participating Manufacturers (PMs) to the MSA. Conversely, since NPMs are not parties to the MSA, all escrow payments tendered to the settling states pursuant to the Model Statute are not part of Tobacco Settlement revenues pledged under the MSA. According to the National Association of Attorneys General, as of January 3, 2006 a total of 47 tobacco firms have signed the MSA consisting of three OPMs and 44 SPMs. In order to fully understand cash flow dynamics under the MSA it is necessary to consider differences in payment obligations between OPMs and NPMs.

Original Participating Manufacturers

OPMs are comprised of the largest tobacco firms that originally signed the MSA on November 23, 1998. These firms are comprised of:

1. Philip Morris USA, owned by Altria Group.
2. R.J. Reynolds, owned by Reynolds American Inc.
3. Brown & Williamson, formerly owned by British American Tobacco but subsequently acquired by Reynolds Tobacco Holdings pursuant to a merger agreement that was consummated in July 2004 that led to the creation of Reynolds American Inc.
4. Lorillard, owned by Loews Corporation since 1968.

Whereas, in 1997, the OPMs accounted for 97.1% of total U.S. tobacco shipments, due to increased competition from SPMs and NPMs who have enjoyed a pricing advantage under the MSA, OPMs have experienced an erosion of market share to approximately 85% as of 2006. Despite this erosion in market share, the financial position and operating performance of OPMs has remained robust due to stronger margins. OPMs carry the greatest payment obligation under the MSA and are responsible for contributing *initial payments, annual payments*, and *strategic contribution fund payments*, calculated in accordance with each OPM's relative market share. A detailed explanation and description of each of these payments is set forth below.

Subsequent Participating Manufacturers

SPMs are comprised of all tobacco firms that entered into the MSA following its execution on November 23, 1998 and presently include 44 entities. Under the MSA, SPMs are divided into two subcategories: (1) exempt SPMs, comprised of 14 firms that signed the MSA within 60 days of its original execution; and (2) nonexempt SPMs who signed the MSA on or after February 24, 1999. Exempt SPMs are not obligated to make payments of any kind under the MSA. Nonexempt SPMs, on the other hand, are obligated to make annual payments and Strategic Contribution payments if, and only if, their individual market share exceeds a base market share equal to the greater of (1) their 1998 market share or (2) 125% of their 1997 market share.

Nonparticipating Manufacturers

Due to enactment of a model statute by each settling state, all tobacco firms who have not signed the MSA are obligated to tender annual escrow payments within each jurisdiction in which they operate in amounts intended to be the economic equivalent of MSA payments by SPMs. As originally enacted, however, the Model Statute did not, in fact, create pricing parity with PMs. The original formula for assessing escrow payments required each NPM to make escrow deposits in an amount that the NPM would have had to pay had it been a PM, but only with respect to jurisdictions in which it was doing business. As a result, NPMs that restricted operations to a limited number of states were accorded a pro rata release on excess escrow payments, thereby enabling these regional firms to underprice PMs. However, recent enactment of an amendment to the Model Statute by at least 44 settling states, known as the Allocable Share Release Amendment, has effectively eliminated this loophole in most jurisdictions.

Tobacco Settlement Revenues Under the MSA

In general, the dollar amount of tobacco settlement payments amounts to an estimated $206 billion over the first 25 years, although actual payments will depend upon overall consumption trends, market share levels of the OPMs, as well as other variables. The dollar amount of annual Tobacco Settlement Revenues (TSR) payments are set forth under Article IX to the MSA and includes three payments: (1) initial payments; (2) annual payments; and (3) strategic contribution payments. These payments are subject to a number of adjustments and offsets, as hereafter described. Here is a brief description of each of the foregoing payments:

Initial Payments

Initial payments consist of payments tendered by OPMs from 1998 through 2002 based upon their original market capitalization percentage. The initial payment amounts payable each year run for the first five years are pre-scribed under Article IX (b) of the MSA. Scheduled payments are summarized in Exhibit 57.1. Scheduled payments are subject to modification based upon the volume adjustment, the nonsettling states reduction and for dis-

EXHIBIT 57.1   Initial Payments

Date	Base Amount	Amount Paid
Dec-98	$2.400 billion	$2.40 billion
Dec-99	$2.472 billion	$2.43 billion
Dec-00	$2.546 billion	$2.04 billion
Dec-01	$2.622 billion	$1.89 billion
Dec-02	$2.701 billion	$2.14 billion

puted payments. The actual amounts paid during this time frame are also presented in Exhibit 57.1.

Annual Payments

Article IX (c) provides that beginning April 15, 2000 and continuing April 15 of each year thereafter in perpetuity, OPMs and applicable SPMs shall individually pay their relative market share of the base amounts set forth in Exhibit 57.2, subject to the adjustments discussed below. Due to the application of several adjustments, actual payments tendered are running below base amounts. Applicable adjustments include the *inflation adjustment*, the *volume adjustment*, the *previously settled states reduction*, the *nonsettled states reduction*, the *NPM adjustment*, an offset for miscalculated or disputed payments, the *federal tobacco legislation offset*, the *litigating parties releasing offset*, and offsets for claims described in subsections XII(a)(4)(8) of the MSA.

Strategic Contribution Payments

Article IX (c) of the MSA provides that beginning April 15, 2008 through 2017 OPMs and applicable SPMs shall pay their relative market share of an additional annual payment of $861 million, subject to adjustments discussed below. Applicable adjustments include the inflation adjustment, the volume adjustment, the NPM adjustment, an offset for miscalculated or disputed payments, the federal tobacco legislation offset, the litigating parties releasing offset, and offsets for claims described in subsections XII(a)(4)(8) of the MSA. The scheduled amount of strategic contribution payments before adjustments is set forth in Exhibit 57.3.

EXHIBIT 57.2 Annual Payments

Year	Base Amount	Actual Amount	Difference	% Change
2000	4,500,000,000	3,500,000,000	1,000,000,000	–22.20%
2001	5,000,000,000	4,100,000,000	900,000,000	–18.00%
2002	6,500,000,000	5,200,000,000	1,300,000,000	–20.00%
2003	6,500,000,000	5,100,000,000	1,400,000,000	–21.50%
2004	8,000,000,000	6,200,000,000	1,800,000,000	–21.30%
2005	8,000,000,000	6,300,000,000	1,700,000,000	–21.30%
2006-17	8,139,000,000			
thereafter	9,000,000,000			

EXHIBIT 57.3   Strategic Contribution Payments

Date	Scheduled Amount
15-Apr-08	$861,000,000
15-Apr-09	$861,000,000
15-Apr-10	$861,000,000
15-Apr-11	$861,000,000
15-Apr-12	$861,000,000
15-Apr-13	$861,000,000
15-Apr-14	$861,000,000
15-Apr-15	$861,000,000
15-Apr-16	$861,000,000
15-Apr-17	$861,000,000

Measuring Adjustments

The key to deriving an accurate and reliable projection of pledged TSRs lies in formulating realistic adjustments to the scheduled stream of payments. Therefore, careful consideration must be paid to understanding each of the seven adjustments to revenue prescribed under the MSA. These include: (1) volume adjustment; (2) inflation adjustment; (3) previously settled states reduction; (4) offset for miscalculated or disputed payments; (5) nonparticipating manufacturer adjustment (NPM adjustment); (6) litigation releasing parties offset; and (7) an offset for claims over. Each of these adjustments are summarized below.

Volume Adjustment   All MSA payments are increased or decreased each year by an adjustment which reflects the fluctuation in the total number of cigarettes shipped by the OPMs within the U.S. relative to a base year volume. The base year volume is 1997 in which total cigarette shipments by the OPMs within the United States was 475,656,000,0000 (the "base volume"). If the annual volume shipped by OPMs exceeds the base volume, payments increase by an identical percent. Conversely, if actual volume falls below this amount, payments are reduced by a factor equal to 98% of the rate of decrease. However, in the event that the OPMs' aggregated actual operating income exceeds $7,195,340,000 after adjusting for inflation, all or a portion of the volume reduction is eliminated pursuant to a formula set forth in Exhibit E to the MSA.

Inflation Adjustment   The base amounts of both annual payments and strategic contribution fund payments are increased annually to account for inflation. The increase each year will be equal to either a minimum rate of 3% or any greater percentage increase reflected in the Consumer Price Index. The inflation adjustment percentages are compounded annually on a cumulative basis beginning in 1999 and then first applied in 2000.

Previously Settled States Reduction   The base amount of the annual payments and strategic contribution fund payments are subject to a reduction reflecting payments made to the four states that had previously reached a settlement with the OPMs: Florida, Texas, Mississippi and Minnesota. The exact percentage reduction prescribed by the MSA is as follows: (1) 12.45% for each year prior to 2007; (2) 12.2373756% for each year between 2008 and 2017; and (3) 11.0666667% each year thereafter. In the event that the MSA terminates as to any settling state, the remaining annual payments and strategic contribution fund payments shall be reduced to account for the absence of such state.

Nonparticipating Manufacturers Adjustment   The NPM Adjustment is based upon the market share increases of tobacco firms that refuse to sign the MSA and is designed to reduce OPM payments for losses arising from lost market share resulting from the MSA. Three conditions must be satisfied in order to trigger an NPM adjustment: (1) the aggregate market share of the PMs in any year must fall more than 2% below the aggregate market share held by all PMs in 1997; (2) a qualified independent third-party consultant must determine that the MSA was a significant factor contributing to the PM's lost market share; and (3) the settling state(s) in question must be shown not to have diligently enforced their model statute(s). The NPM adjustment will reduce the amount owed by subtracting from the MSA payment due the product of the amount due multiplied by a factor equal to three times the PM's lost market share, provided that the market share loss is less than 16.67%. If market share loss exceeds 16.67%, the NPM adjustment is 50% plus an additional setoff prescribed by formula under Section IX(d) of the MSA.

Offset for Miscalculated or Disputed Payments   If the MSA auditor receives notice of a miscalculation of an initial payment made by an OPM, or an annual payment made by a PM within the last four years or a strategic contribution fund payment made by a PM within the last four years, then the MSA Auditor will recalculate the payment and make provision to correct any error. Although there are no time limits specified for recalculations, the MSA auditor is required to determine such amounts promptly.

Litigation Releasing Parties Offset If any releasing party initiates litigation against a PM for any of the claims released under the MSA, the PM may be entitled to an offset against such PM's payment obligation under the MSA. A defendant PM may offset dollar-for-dollar any amount paid in settlement, stipulated judgment or litigated judgment against the amount to be collected by the applicable settling state under the MSA only if the PM has fully taken all appropriate measures to defend that action, provided that any settlement or stipulated judgment was consented to by the state attorney general. Any reduction in MSA payments as a result of the litigating releasing parties offset would apply only to the settling state of the releasing party.

Offset for Claims Over If a releasing party pursues and collects on a released claim against an NPM or a retailer, supplier or distributor arising from the sale or distribution of the tobacco products of any NPM or the supply of component parts of tobacco products to any NPM, and the nonreleased party, in turn, successfully pursues a claim for contribution or indemnification against a released party, the releasing party must: (1) reduce or credit against any judgment or settlement such releasing party obtains against the nonreleased party the full amount of any judgment or settlement against the released party; and (2) obtain from such nonreleased party for the benefit of such released party a satisfaction in full of such nonreleased party's judgment or settlement against the released party.

ANALYSIS OF STRUCTURAL RISK

Due to the complex nature of the MSA, TSR bonds are subject to a wide risk spectrum which includes structural risk, corporate credit risk, cash flow risk, and litigation risk. The following sections shall proceed to define and evaluate each specific risk element. We begin in this section with structural risk.

Securitization of tobacco settlement receivables is based upon an irrevocable transfer by each state or its political instrumentalities of its allocated share of MSA revenues to a special purpose legal entity. This special purpose entity, in turn, then sells asset-backed bonds to investors in exchange for a right to receive an assignment of pledged Tobacco Settlement Revenues. An initial risk with TSR bonds centers upon the certainty and irrevocability of this transfer and whether the special purpose legal entity is insulated from bankruptcy risk of the governmental entity.

The rating agencies undertake an exhaustive structural analysis which considers several issues. The first prong of this analysis centers upon determining if the transfer of MSA revenues to a special purpose entity is irrevocable. This is accomplished through the legislative creation of a public corporation that is an instrumentality of a state or through creation of a not-for-profit entity, thereby avoiding involuntary filings. While states and their instrumentalities are not eligible to invoke bankruptcy protection, cities and counties may be eligible to do so. Although state law may permit cities and counties to file bankruptcy petitions, use of a not-for-profit organization in connection with the issuance of TSR Bonds limits bankruptcy risk for this type of special purpose entity to voluntary petitions.

ANALYSIS OF CORPORATE CREDIT RISK

Since a very large percentage of MSA payments are made by OPMs which account for 85% or more of pledged revenue, a key factor bearing upon the credit quality of TSR bonds is the underlying credit strength of the OPMs themselves. Although there were four OPMs in existence at the time the MSA was executed, due to the subsequent merger of R.J. Reynolds Tobacco Co. (RJRTC) and Brown & Williamson in 2004, there now exists three remaining OPMs: (1) Altria Group Inc., the parent of Philip Morris USA; (2) Reynolds American Inc. (RAI), the parent of RJRTC; and (3) Loew's Corporation, the parent of Lorillard. The ratings of the three largest tobacco firms, who are the OPMs to the MSA, reflect each company's exposure to declining domestic cigarette consumption, fierce competition from smaller discount manufacturers typically operating as NPMs and continued financial uncertainty arising from litigation risk. Set forth below is a concise overview of the U.S. tobacco industry, followed by a credit profile of each OPM.

Overview of U.S. Tobacco Industry

The U.S. tobacco industry is composed of OPMs, SPMs and NPMs and is highly competitive. From 1996 to 2006, cigarette consumption within the U.S. has declined at an average compound rate of 2.4% per year. According to Global Insights, an econometric firm that serves as special consultant to issuers of Tobacco Settlement bonds, under base case assumptions the average rate of cigarette consumption decline is projected to run approximately 1.8% per year going forward. As discussed below, although the financial position of each OPM is very strong, the key driver impacting credit ratings centers upon litigation risk, which is hereafter evaluated in greater detail.

In general, OPMs manufacture, distribute and sell better advertised, higher-priced products known as premium cigarettes. NPMs, on the other hand, compete against OPMs by marketing lesser known, lower-priced cigarettes that are sold at a substantial discount. Following enactment of the MSA in 1998, the ability of OPMs to maintain market share has been challenged by NPMs who succeeded in increasing retail sales by underpricing premium products. By 2005 the estimated market share of OPMs declined to 85% while the market share of NPMs rose to approximately 6.00%.

Although conventional wisdom holds that cigarette consumption is subject to demand inelasticity because it is highly addictive, the rise of NPM market share contradicts this precept because NPM market share growth is attributable to discount pricing. Until recently, NPMs have succeeded in underpricing OPMs by limiting business operations to a regional scope. Under the original terms of the MSA, NPMs that restricted operations to a limited number of states were accorded a pro rata release on excess escrow payments, thereby enabling regional NPM firms to underprice PMs. However, recent enactment of the Allocable Share Release Amendment by 44 settling states has effectively eliminated this loophole in most jurisdictions. As noted below, it remains to be seen whether repeal of the Allocable Share Release provision will withstand legal challenges predicated upon the U.S. Commerce Clause and federal antitrust law.

Altria Group, Inc.

Altria Group Inc.'s (Altria) investment-grade rating (Baa1/Stable, BBB+/Positive as of April 1, 2007) reflect the strength of its domestic tobacco company, Philip Morris USA (PM USA), which ranks as the clear market leader in the domestic tobacco industry. These ratings are also supported by Altria's ownership of Philip Morris International and Kraft Foods, a packaged food manufacturer. Altria's net sales through September 30, 2006 were $70 billion which included sales from its domestic tobacco, international tobacco and food packaging segments. However, Altria's ratings are negatively impacted by tobacco litigation risk. PM USA contributed 21% of net sales and 25% of operating income in fiscal year 2005. PM USA ranks as the leading domestic cigarette manufacturer with a 48.7% retail market share. PM's core brands include Marlboro, Virginia Slims, Parliament, Benson & Hedges, and Merit. As of December 31, 2005, Altria had $6.3 billion of cash and equivalent resources.

PM USA's debt ranks senior to Altria's debt but debt used to finance the acquisition is expected to be repaid rapidly. Kraft Foods Inc. had $700 million of short-term debt outstanding and $3.8 billion of credit lines available. Altria does not guarantee the debt of either Kraft or PMI.

Altria's Board recently announced that it was considering unbundling the company into separate entities. The timing and mechanics of the breakup are uncertain and it is not expected to occur unless PM USA achieves favorable financial results. If divestiture is allowed and separation occurs, Kraft would benefit from a stronger credit profile as a standalone packaged food company while the ultimate credit ratings of Altria's domestic and international tobacco businesses would depend upon how the separation is executed and the new capital structure. Altria's financial ratios are very strong: (1) sales revenue has been trending higher from $63.9 billion in 2004 to $68.9 billion in 2005; (2) net income has also surged higher, increasing 10.8% in 2005; (3) EBITDA to interest expense coverage is ample at 12.2 times; (4) margins are all strong, with gross margins at 46.7%, operating margins at 25.1% and profit margins at 15.1%; and (5) leverage is modest with long-term debt to total capital at 27.9%.

Reynolds American Inc.

Reynolds American Inc.'s (RAI) ratings (Ba2/Positive, BB+/Stable as of April 1, 2007) are based upon management's conservative financial policies and substantial cash resources which mitigate tobacco litigation risk. R.J. Reynolds Tobacco Co. (RJRTC), its indirect subsidiary, ranks as the second-largest cigarette manufacturer in the United States with a 30% share of the U.S. cigarette market. These ratings also reflect RAI's substantially lower leverage compared to that of RJRTC prior to the Brown & Williamson combination. As a result of the merger, RAI has started to realize certain synergies. Reynolds has improved profitability considerably through larger scale efficiencies. However, it remains uncertain whether RAI can achieve market share growth longer term due to its reliance on only two flagship brands: Kool and Camel cigarettes.

RAI has begun to diversify its revenue base. Through its recent $3.5 billion acquisition of Conwood Companies, RAI owns the second-largest smokeless tobacco firm. This has enabled RAI to benefit from higher margin sales and offers valuable growth potential. RAI also intends to achieve greater growth in its flagship brands to counteract potential share declines in other brands.

RAI's financial measures are favorable: (1) sales revenue and cash flow for 2005 and through nine months ended September 30, 2006 are strong, as are profit metrics, with RA achieving a gross margin of 40.4%, operating margin of 20.9% and a profit margin of 12.6% in fiscal year 2005; (2) RAI's return on equity and return on assets were strong at 16.4% and 7.2%, respectively; and (3) coverage and leverage ratios are also favorable, with the ratio of EBITDA to interest expense at 17.0 times and total debt to total capital at a very modest level of 21.1%.

Loews Corporation

Loews Corporation's ratings (A3/Stable, A/Stable as of April 1, 2007) are supported by the operating performance of Lorillard and CNA Financial Corporation (CNA), combined with Loews' substantial portfolio of cash and short-term investments. Loew's ratings reflect its diverse business portfolio, strong liquidity, and ample cash flow. Loew's owns the third largest domestic tobacco firm, Lorillard, which holds a 9.2% share of the retail market. In addition to tobacco, Loew's revenue mix includes commercial insurance, offshore gas and oil exploration, gas pipelines, and hotel ownership. Unlike Philip Morris USA and RJRTC, Lorillard does not sell cigarettes in foreign markets to offset declining U.S. consumption. Moreover, over 90% of Lorillard's cigarette revenue derives from one brand, Newport, which exposes it to significant concentration risk.

Loews showed its commitment to CNA with significant financial support. In March 2005 Fitch affirmed CNA's senior debt rating at BBB– and revised the rating outlook to stable from negative. The change in Rating Outlook reflected CNA's improved balance sheet and sound operating results. Loew's financial ratios are very favorable: (1) robust growth in sales revenue from $690.9 million in the first quarter of 2006 to $800.2 million in the third quarter of 2006, combined with a jump in net income from $150.1 million to $202.9 million; (2) unusually strong profitability, evidenced by a 65.5% return on equity and 30.9% return on assets; and (3) an extremely strong balance sheet marked by the absence of long-term debt.

ANALYSIS OF CASH FLOW RISK

A key factor used to evaluate TSR bonds centers upon careful analysis of the sufficiency of pledged tobacco settlement revenues to support related debt service. In essence, this analysis entails thoughtful consideration about critical assumptions that determine the level of MSA payments. The volume of annual payments and strategic contribution fund payments by all PMs under the MSA is tied to a handful of critical variables that drive cash flow: (1) the market share of OPMs and SPMs that are making MSA payments; (2) the income elasticity of demand for cigarettes in relation to spiraling cigarette prices; (3) trends with respect to the price of domestic cigarettes; and (4) changes in volume of domestic cigarette consumption. To properly evaluate cash flow risk of TSR bonds, development of a *cash flow model* (CFM) is extremely useful.

A carefully constructed CFM facilitates analysis of the adequacy of pledged cash flow to pay debt service on all related debt and also provides important guidance in depicting weighted average life forecasts of different bond maturities. The CFM has three key credit applications: (1) to depict total expected revenue pledged under the Master Settlement Agreement; (2) to calculate debt service on *senior current interest bonds* and any *capital appreciation bonds* (CABs); and (3) to measure the sufficiency and timeliness of pledged cash flow to pay debt service under a broad range of assumptions.

In evaluating cash flow adequacy, it is also extremely useful to employ sensitivity analysis to evaluate cash flow under different scenarios that test differences in elasticity of cigarette demand, rates of cigarette consumption decline and OPM market share levels and other key variables. Using sensitivity analysis to evaluate cash flow characteristics yields several important findings. Here is a summary of some general observations.

Consumption Trends

A pivotal variable that determines the ultimate performance of TSR bonds is the annual rate of change in the volume of cigarette consumption. Revenue estimates and coverage levels are very closely tied to the level of consumption decline. Cash flow analysis generally indicates that if the rate of annual consumption decline remains at or below 3%, pledged MSA payments will be sufficient to pay debt service on the senior bonds as well as any subordinate CABs. On the other hand, if the annual rate of consumption decline should increase substantially higher than 4%, both Senior Bonds and CABs may experience cash flow shortage leading to payment shortfalls.

Extension Risk

If the annual rate of consumption decline substantially exceeds 4.00%, declines in cash flow also mean that pledged tobacco settlement revenues are apt to prove inadequate to meet base case turbo redemptions, leading to deferred payments under the sinking fund schedule for many *turbo term bonds*.

NPM Adjustment and Liquidity Analysis

Because the Brattle Group has made a formal determination in a report released March 27, 2006, which concluded that the MSA was a significant contributing factor leading to tobacco market share loss of PMs, the risk of an NPM adjustment now turns upon consideration and analysis of MSA enforcement practices within each settling state. Therefore, in considering cash flow characteristics of TSR bonds, a timely concern relates to the adequacy of cash resources to cover the risk of an NPM adjustment. Whether a given state is subject to an NPM adjustment depends upon determining if it has satisfied an as yet undefined standard of due diligence in the enforcement of the Model Statute, a law designed to create economic pricing parity between tobacco firms that joined the MSA and NPMs that did not. If an NPM adjustment is invoked against a particular state, this could exhaust available liquidity, particularly if (1) the loss of more than 2% market share of OPMs continues for more than one year; and (2) the lapse in diligent enforcement is also found to span more than one calendar year.

Diligent Enforcement

Closely tied to the issue of NPM Adjustment is the question whether settling states have been diligently enforcing their respective Model Statutes. If so, settling states are not subject to an NPM adjustment. Although no state or forum has yet made a substantive determination about diligent enforcement practice, quite a bit of evidence was compiled by the Brattle Group about state enforcement efforts with respect to the MSA Model Statute. This evidence consists of enactment dates of model statutes, complementary legislation and repeal of the Allocable Share Release Provision (ASRP) within the MSA. Although not necessarily indicative that a State is diligently enforcing its model statute, this type of data is at least probative of the speed and responsiveness of a specific jurisdiction in complying with the MSA.

To uncover additional information about diligent enforcement practice, it is advisable to submit detailed questions to law enforcement agencies of the settling states. Criteria to be considered are (1) the number of NPMs doing business within the jurisdiction in question; (2) a record of escrow payments collected by the settling state from each NPM; (3) a description of enforcement actions initiated against all NPMs who failed to make escrow payments; (4) a profile of the size of the administrative staff charged with overseeing and enforcing the model statute; and (5) other information that provide evidence that facilitates analysis of whether the issuer has been exercising due diligence in collecting escrow payments and otherwise enforcing the terms of the model statute.

Impact of PM Market Share Loss

Another factor to be analyzed in a CFM is the impact of further erosion in market share by the PMs to the NPMs. From 1997 to 2006, the market share of PMs declined from 97.5% to roughly 85.1%. As market share declines, total MSA revenues will diminish unless NPMs opt to join the MSA rather than tender escrow payments under the MSA. Although NPM payments may succeed in creating cigarette pricing parity between PMs and NPMs, since NPM escrow payments are not pledged to secure tobacco bonds, any growth in NPM sales will reduce the total volume of MSA payments. The only way tobacco bonds benefit if escrow payments are levied on NPMs is if these payments induce smaller tobacco firms to join the Master Settlement Agreement. To date, even with enactment of ASRP amendments to the model statutes, only a handful of NPMs have elected to become SPMs.

Future Trends in PM Market Share

The probability whether PMs will experience further market share loss is difficult to assess. On the one hand, if recent enactment of the ASRP proves successful, many NPMs may be induced to opt in to the MSA rather than pay dramatically higher escrow payments. But, it is still unclear if PMs will preserve existing market share for two reasons: (1) the future effectiveness of NPM escrow payment collections hinges upon the legal validity of the repeal of the ASRP to the Model Statute, and this amendment has been temporarily enjoined in New York and could be enjoined elsewhere; and (2) even if a preliminary injunction against the ASRP is not granted by a majority of states, it is hard to predict whether NPMs will decide to opt in to the MSA rather than trying to exhaust legal challenges through a full and complete trial.

ANALYSIS OF LITIGATION RISK

Litigation risk comprises a crucial and extremely challenging analytical component integral to an understanding of TSR bonds. Just as a golfer is admonished never to take his eye off the ball, a tobacco bond analyst should never lose sight of the risk of mutlifaceted legal challenges. Litigation risk is pervasive and encompasses all uncertainty relating to the sufficiency and timeliness of debt service payment due to the potential risk of interruption, delay or dilution of the payment of Tobacco Settlement Revenues caused by potential unfavorable legal rulings. Adverse decisions can undermine the financial position of tobacco firms, impair enforceability of the MSA and trigger NPM adjustments if diligent enforcement practices of the settling states are found to be substandard. The settlement reached as a result of the MSA is comprehensive but nonetheless provides tobacco firms with an incomplete release from all legal liability. Although the settling states themselves are barred from recovering damages for past, present, and future claims against PMs, the scope of the settlement offers no protection against individual or class action lawsuits. Moreover, the MSA itself is the object of numerous lawsuits challenging its constitutionality and enforceability under the commerce clause to the U.S. Constitution and the Sherman Antitrust Act.

Legal Background

The last several years have witnessed substantial price volatility with respect to TSR bonds, much of which is attributable to changing perceptions regarding legal risk. In 2003, tobacco firms were adversely impacted by numerous unfavorable rulings which included the *Price Lights* decision in Illinois, the *Engels* decision in Florida and a Department of Justice claim predicated upon violations of the federal RICO statute for damages estimated as high as $289 billion (the "DOJ claim"). These cases, particularly the *Price Lights* judgment which exceeded $10 billion, posed a serious challenge to the financial position of large tobacco firms and resulted in successive rating downgrades by all three rating agencies. As a result, market prices of tobacco bonds plunged, causing quality spreads to widen by as much as 300 basis points over the benchmark MMD scale.

Improving Litigation Climate

By 2004, however, the litigation climate for tobacco firms began to improve. The U.S. Supreme Court ruled in the *State Farm* decision that punitive damages could not exceed a limited multiple of actual economic damages. Thereafter, this ruling was augmented by three landmark decisions that greatly benefited tobacco firms. The Illinois Supreme Court overturned the *Price Lights* decision, thereby releasing Philip Morris from a potentially ruinous $10 billion judgment. The U.S. Supreme Court upheld a decision by the District of Columbia Circuit Court that held that the federal RICO statute did not provide the Department of Justice with a remedy of disgorgement, effectively eliminating the federal government's claim for $289 billion in damages. The Florida Supreme Court in *Engles* upheld a lower court decision that disallowed the use of a class action lawsuit to recover $140 billion in damages against tobacco firms. Taken together, this improving litigation climate triggered a dramatic reversal in the financial outlook for large tobacco firms. As a direct consequence, between 2004 and 2005 prices on TSR bonds rose sharply, reducing yields on long-term maturities on average from roughly 6.25% to 5.00%. The spread on TSR Bonds to MMD also tightened dramatically, falling from 175 basis points to 80 basis points.

Lingering Uncertainty

In 2006, the litigation climate for tobacco firms continued to stabilize, although, more recently, three notable lawsuits have received significant attention and pose renewed risk for tobacco bonds. These include: (1) *Grand River v. William Pryor*; (2) *Freedom Holdings v. Spitzer*; and (3) *Schwab v.*

Philip Morris. Although no significant risk is thought to exist regarding the *Schwab* class action lawsuit, over the next 3 to 12 months, mixed results may be reached with respect to *Grand River* and *Freedom Holdings*. That could create both short-term volatility and trading opportunities. In both cases, it is likely that favorable rulings will be rendered by the lower district courts, followed by the potential for unfavorable decisions by the Second Circuit Court of Appeals. Any unfavorable decisions reached by the Second Circuit Court of Appeals, however, are eventually subject to possible reversal by the U.S. Supreme Court. A digest of the procedural history and status of each decision is summarized below.

Second Circuit Cases Await Final Rulings

To evaluate the risk of adverse decisions by the Second Circuit Court of Appeals on the value of tobacco securitization bonds, the following discussion provides an approximate timetable when upcoming decisions will be rendered with respect to these cases and the potential substantive outcomes once decisions are rendered.

Grand River v. William Pryor   This case involves a commerce clause challenge to the MSA that implicates New York State as well as 30 other state attorney generals (AGs) and has attracted greater attention after the U.S. Supreme Court decided not to grant a writ of certiorari to release these state AGs from this action. The underlying lawsuit was brought by NPMs tobacco firms who challenged the legal validity of the 1998 MSA on two grounds. First, plaintiffs allege that the MSA constituted an output cartel in violation of Section 1 of the Sherman Antitrust Act. Second, the plaintiffs also allege that the MSA and related legislation enacted by the Settling States amounted to extraterritorial control in violation of the Commerce Clause to the U.S. Constitution.

On September 29, 2003 the U.S. District Court for the Southern District of New York found against the plaintiffs and ruled: (1) procedurally, that the District Court itself lacked jurisdiction over the 30 non-New York defendant State Attorney Generals; and (2) substantively, that the plaintiff NPMs failed to state a valid cause of action with respect to claims under the Constitution and the Sherman Antitrust Act. Thereafter, plaintiffs appealed the lower court decision to the Second Circuit Court of Appeals.

Second Circuit Holding

On September 28, 2005, the Second Circuit reversed the lower court on two grounds. First, the Court ruled that since the MSA was negotiated and executed by all state AGs within the State of New York, the defendant attorney generals were subject to personal jurisdiction under New York law. According to Leonard Violi, Esq., the plaintiff's litigation attorney who represents Grand River, this finding is extremely well supported by established precedent. Second, the Court ruled that the District Court erred in dismissing a Commerce Clause claim against the MSA. The Court specifically found that the issue whether the MSA was invalid under what is known as the "extraterritorial control" aspect of the U.S. Commerce Clause was a potentially valid legal claim that is entitled to adjudication and should not have been dismissed. The state AGs next proceeded to seek a writ of certiorari from the U.S. Supreme Court to challenge the Second Circuit's ruling that they were subject to New York jurisdiction.

U.S. Supreme Court Holding

On October 8, 2006 the U.S. Supreme Court voted to deny the request for certiorari filed by the defendant non-New York state AGs in Grand River challenging the jurisdictional ruling by the Second Circuit. As is customary in ruling on writs of certiorari, no written opinion, vote or explanation accompanied the Supreme Court's decision. Nevertheless, since the U.S. Supreme Court has refrained from intervening, the state AGs are now subject to the jurisdiction of the courts below in this proceeding which has been remanded to the lower district court for a trial on the merits.

Appeal to Second Circuit on Preliminary Injunction

Although the Second Circuit remanded the Grand River case back to Judge Keenan of the District Court, the case has temporarily shifted back to the Second Circuit. Subsequent to the Second Circuit's remand in 2005, Grand River moved for the District Court to grant a preliminary injunction barring the defendant states from enforcing their allocable share statutes, including most importantly the repeal of the ASRP. In May 2006, the District Court denied Grand River's requests for a preliminary injunction. Grand River then appealed the District Court's denial of the injunction barring enforcement of the amendment to the ASRP. Note that the preliminary injunction granted in *Freedom Holdings* enjoining repeal of the ASRP in New York alone was issued by Judge Hellerstein of the District Court but was never passed upon by the Second Circuit. *Grand River* is thus shaping up as a critical litmus test of the Second Circuit's underlying position not only on the legality of the preliminary injunction but also as to the validity of the underlying challenges to the MSA.

On March 6, 2007, the Second Circuit Court of Appeals affirmed a ruling by the U.S. District Court for the Southern District of New York that denied Grand River's motion for a preliminary injunction to prevent repeal of the ASRP. In upholding the lower court, however, the Second Circuit based its decision on the failure of the plaintiff, Grand River, to prove that it would incur irreparable harm, without addressing the larger and more important issue of whether Grand River was likely to prevail on the merits. Although this ruling removes the imminent risk that the ASRP will be invalidated, the final outcome on the merits of Grand River's constitutional challenge to the repeal of the ASRP hinges on the Second Circuit's ultimate ruling on the merits of these claims once this case reaches a full trial. In the meantime, the plaintiff Grand River has petitioned the Second Circuit to reconsider its ruling on the preliminary injunction and this motion also awaits a final ruling.

Potential Investment Impact is Substantial

The potential significance of this case increased considerably after the U.S. Supreme Court declined to issue a writ of certiorari requested by the 31 state AGs. Since 31 states are now subject to the jurisdiction of the U.S. District Court and the Second Circuit Court of Appeals, in the months ahead this lawsuit bears careful and continuous monitoring. The substance of the antitrust challenge is identical to *Freedom Holdings* discussed below. The Commerce Clause issue before the Court is whether the aggregate effect of the states' Escrow and Contraband Statutes, enacted by all 46 states in accordance with the MSA, creates a uniform system of regulation that results in higher prices nationwide.

If so found, these provisions may potentailly be declared unconstitutional because they effectively vest these states with the right to regulate interstate commerce, a power that the U.S. Constitution exclusively reserves for Congress. It is, of course, exceedingly difficult to predict how the U.S. District Court and Second Circuit Court of Appeals are likely to rule on this question. In my opinion, however, the risk that these interrelated state regulatory enactments would be found to usurp Congressional regulatory power is significant, given the manner in which the Second Circuit has framed this issue and the operative facts at hand. However, in the event of an unfavorable ruling, an appeal is certain to be taken to the U.S. Supreme Court which would be more apt to construe constitutional remedies more narrowly given its new, more conservative membership, so that the ultimate risk of MSA invalidation is substantially reduced.

Freedom Holdings v. Spitzer This is another landmark case that is also under review by both the U.S. District Court (Southern District of New York) and the Second Circuit Court of Appeals. This suit was originally based upon an antitrust challenge to the MSA and corresponding New York State enforcement statutes known as the Escrow Statute, the Contraband Statute, and Allocable Share Release Provision (collectively, the "Enforcement Statutes") of the MSA. In this case, tobacco firms who were not signatories to the MSA brought suit challenging the validity of the Enforcement Statutes arguing that these provisions were preempted by Section 1 of the Sherman Act as per se illegal because the Enforcement Statutes created an "output cartel."

Although the District Court granted summary dismissal of the antitrust claim, the Second Circuit reversed, holding that plaintiffs had stated a potentially valid legal claim and remanded the case back to the lower district court for a full trial on the merits. Plaintiffs have also amended the complaint to add a Commerce Clause claim similar to that set forth in *Grand River v. Pryor.*

With respect to the antitrust claims, the key issues in *Freedom Holdings* turn upon whether the Enforcement Statutes and the MSA create an unlawful output cartel against NPMs in violation of the Sherman Antitrust Act. The revised complaint of the NPMs is now based upon two distinct challenges which allege: (1) that the MSA violates Section 1 of the Sherman Antitrust Act; and (2) that the MSA violates the commerce clause of the U.S. Constitution. Thus far, plaintiffs have succeeded in procuring a preliminary injunction from the lower federal district court that enjoins the State of New York from implementing the ASRP. However, until this case is fully adjudicated, it is far from clear whether the ASRP will be permanently enjoined.

Previous Ruling by the Second Circuit

In its 2005 ruling, the Second Circuit noted that market share stratification created under the MSA between OPMs, SPMs, and NPMs was anticompetitive on a number of grounds: (1) it creates incentives that preserve the market share of the OPMs; (2) it links PM's MSA payments to unit sales rather than dollar revenue; (3) it grants one class of SPMs preferential standing over subsequent SPMs and NPMs; (4) it imposes fees on NPMs, which force them either to raise prices and forfeit competitive advantage or reduce sales altogether; and (5) it deprives NPMs of tax deductions for fees that are otherwise available to OPMs and SPMs.

Rehearing in District Court

According to Walter Loures, Esq., litigation counsel to the Freedom Holdings plaintiffs, the case has been remanded to U.S. District Court and assigned to Judge Hellerstein. In oral arguments held September 26, 2006, both sides submitted the following motions to the Court: (1) a request for summary judgment to rule on the ultimate disposition of each claim; and (2) submission to a Rule 51 process whereby litigants agree to be bound by submitted written evidence without the need for additional further fact finding.

Potential Investment Impact

Even though the Freedom Holdings action is limited to a challenge of the New York enforcement statutes and does not directly implicate other state AGs, any decision reached by the Second Circuit has potential spillover application in other jurisdictions because of the close similarity of statutory enforcement provisions in all 46 jurisdictions. The essential Commerce Clause issue before the Court is identical to *Grand River* and therefore has a similar likelihood of success. The novel question here is whether the antitrust claim will carry and this presents more complicated public policy questions. Counterbalancing the federal interest in promoting competition are other important policy objectives. The State of New York will continue to argue that the MSA confers other "redeeming social benefits" that should override federal interest in antitrust policy. These include: (1) a reduction in the overall incidence of cigarette smoking; (2) shifting the costs of health care arising from tobacco related illnesses from States to tobacco manufacturers; (3) implementing antismoking programs prescribed by the MSA such as advertising and marketing restrictions; and (4) funding antismoking educational programs and clinics directed at youth. Although it is difficult to predict the outcome, should the Second Circuit rule against New York State, an appeal is again likely to be taken to the U.S. Supreme Court.

Schwab v. Philip Morris

Judge Weinstein's decision on September 25, 2006 to certify a national class action lawsuit against tobacco firms in *Schwab v. Philips Morris* is likely to be overturned by the Second Circuit Court of Appeals. The cause of action centers upon allegations that plaintiff smokers who purchased cigarettes that were falsely called "lights" wound up smoking cigarettes that were not less harmful and were therefore deprived of the benefit of the bargain.

Legal experts contend that Judge Weinstein, in certifying a national "lights" class action suit, has "pushed the limits of legal formality" on three key issues: (1) as to calculation of damages, under RICO, the statutory basis for the cause of action, the measure of damages is not measured by "out-of-pocket loss" but a failure of consideration yet it is far from clear whether the proper measure of damages should be calculated by the full price paid for lights cigarettes or by some lesser amount; (2) assuming damages can be properly measured, how are damages to be allocated to members of the class in the absence of evidence as to who among the class members bought how many cigarettes, and at what price; and (3) under RICO, the requisite showing of detrimental reliance may ultimately be impossible to substantiate in a large class action suit of this scope.

Since Judge Weinstein's certification of the *Schwab* class action lawsuit is simply not supported by legal precedent, the Second Circuit is expected to decertify the class and overturn the lower court decision.

Potential Investment Impact Minimal

The risk of class certification in *Schwab* thus appears small. The defendant tobacco firms have already announced plans to challenge this decision. Equity analysts expect the industry to file an interlocutory appeal of Judge Weinstein's ruling to the Second Circuit Court of Appeals shortly. The Second Circuit has previously invalidated a class action certified by Judge Weinstein, and legal experts expect the same result here due to two substantial problems: (1) the sheer breadth and size of the class of potential plaintiffs, which would include anyone who smoked light cigarettes as far back as the 1970's; and (2) the inherent difficulty in measuring economic damages sustained by these same individuals from smoking "lights" versus "regular" cigarettes.

CONCLUSION

Analysis of the credit risk posed by Tobacco Settlement bonds poses a unique challenge for the municipal analyst. Evaluation of risk entails consideration of at least four major issues: (1) structural risk; (2) corporate credit risk; (3) cash flow risk; and (4) litigation risk. Each risk category poses a special set of problems that demand careful consideration and analysis. Because the volume of pledged Tobacco Settlement Revenue under the MSA is intricately linked to the overall level of domestic cigarette consumption, this sector is exposed to a host of exogenous factors that shape individual smoker habits. These factors include national and global economic variables impacting overall employment and per capita income, health issues and government initiatives that affect public awareness of the dangers of cigarette smoking and new scientific developments that could lead to breakthroughs in anti-smoking cessation products. At the same time, Tobacco Settlement bonds face ongoing litigation risk arising from several sources including class action and individual lawsuits filed against tobacco firms, litigation challenging the enforceability of the MSA, the model statutes and applicable complementary legislation and proceedings instituted by tobacco firms themselves challenging the due diligent enforcement practices of the 46 settling states.

Nevertheless, despite these challenges, the Tobacco Settlement bond sector has proven to offer investors attractive yield and has recently achieved the highest total returns for all investment grade municipal bonds for the past two years, producing total returns of roughly 16.5% in 2005 and 11.7% in 2006, thereby outperforming both the Lehman Brothers and S&P indices by substantial margins. As of April 1, 2007, of the 46 settling states and six jurisdictions with potential bonding capacity, Tobacco Settlement bonds have been issued by only 15 states and 4 other jurisdictions. Therefore, barring an unfavorable legal ruling with respect to the MSA, since most states have thus far refrained from issuing Tobacco Settlement Revenue bonds, total volume can be expected to grow appreciably. For these reasons, analysts who can effectively evaluate the wide risk spectrum presented by this sector will enable fund managers to add impressive potential incremental returns to enhance portfolio performance.

CHAPTER 58

Toll Road Analysis

Robert H. Muller
Managing Director
JPMorgan Securities

T his chapter describes the methodology and approaches needed to analyze toll road revenue bonds. Distinctions between the analysis required to study an already established entity and that needed to determine the risks entailed in a new project for a "greenfield" road will be explored as well. Because defaults have occurred on startup toll road projects, the analyst faces a potentially greater burden in evaluating these kinds of bonds than what is the norm for a typical government-created entity.

HISTORY

We begin the chapter with a look at the short history of toll road financing in the United States.

1792–1940

Toll roads have been part of the United States transportation system since the time of George Washington. "Pennsylvania chartered the first, connecting Philadelphia and Lancaster, in 1792 and it opened in 1794."[1] The road was heavily used by Conestoga wagons heading westward. Its success "led other states to adopt the new plan. By 1800, 69 companies had been char-

---

[1] Daniel B. Klein and Gordon J. Fielding, "Private Toll Roads: Learning from the 19th Century," *Transportation Quarterly* (July 1992), pp. 321–341.

I would like to thank Elizabeth Hillenbrand and Benjamin Djiounas, Associates at JPMorgan Securities, for reviewing this chapter.

tered."[2] Many of these turnpikes were privately run, but some were publicly built or subsidized. This wave began to peter out as canals and railroads displaced the toll roads and many eventually failed. Beginning in the 1920s, toll revenues were used to secure the construction and financing of the Holland Tunnel between New York and New Jersey and the Benjamin Franklin Bridge in Philadelphia. The Golden Gate Bridge in San Francisco followed in the 1930s. The use of tolls became an accepted, if not always popular mechanism, to meet the burgeoning demand resulting from the rise of the automobile.

1940–1970s

The first modern intercity toll road, the Pennsylvania Turnpike, opened in 1940. The road faced financing challenges. "Since bankers were skeptical of supporting the unproven nature of a toll superhighway, the project wound up being financed by a loan from the New Deal's Reconstruction Finance Corporation for almost $41 million at 3.75 percent."[3] Bankers' fears proved groundless as traffic levels surged in the initial years. Following World War II, many states such as New Jersey, New York, Ohio, Massachusetts and others followed Pennsylvania's example and built their own super highways. These projects were financed primarily through the issuance of various forms of revenue bond debt principally secured by toll revenues, but often with some added support from the state. Some of these projects struggled in their initial years, but most of them have succeeded financially and operationally. Many of the bond sales used to finance construction represented some of the largest issues of that era.

As with most good infrastructure financing ideas, success is not universal. Less well conceived projects were developed that ran into financial difficulties. The West Virginia Turnpike, the Chicago Calumet Skyway, and the Chesapeake Bay Bridge and Tunnel defaulted on at least some of their bonds. In each case, forecasts of usage were significantly overestimated. These defaults were not remedied quickly and some continued well into the 1990s. Investor reaction to the defaults, which were highly unusual during that period, was quite negative. The response helped curtail the use of revenue bonds and tolls to build new highways.

The passage of the Interstate Highway Act in 1956, during the administration of Dwight Eisenhower, represented another challenge. Eisenhower secured its passage in Congress under the guise of creating a national limited access highway system for defense purposes. This huge program was

---

[2] Klein and Fielding, "Private Toll Roads: Learning from the 19th Century."

[3] Official site of the Pennsylvania Turnpike, Turnpike History www.paturnpike.com/geninfo/history/history.aspx

financed with funds from the federal gasoline tax combined with state transportation taxes. With "free" expressways being built, states no longer felt the need or desire to finance the construction of additional toll roads.

Throughout the 1960s and early 1970s, established toll road agencies continued to issue bonds primarily to add lanes to already established roads or, in some cases, to expand those systems. As a means of meeting the nation's ground transportation needs, however, new highways were rarely financed using toll revenues. The first hint of change began to emerge in the mid-1960s. Several governments in growing urban centers in the Sunbelt found that federal moneys were insufficient to meet their needs. The energy price explosion during the next decade, which curtailed the growth rate of federal gasoline tax receipts, exacerbated the insufficiency. Exhibit 58.1 highlights the weakness in tax receipts during this period. Several Sunbelt cities embarked on the construction of new toll roads backed principally by the toll revenues expected to be generated when the roads opened. These new toll roads tended to differ substantially in several ways from the earlier period. They were largely urban highways, shorter in length than the older toll roads and designed to provide added mobility within metropolitan areas rather than between cities or regions.

This trend has accelerated steadily since the 1970s, and both federal and state gasoline taxes continue to prove inadequate as mileage per gallon has improved. Furthermore, tax rates have not been increased since the early 1990s as opposition to gasoline tax increases has stiffened and ris-

EXHIBIT 58.1   Federal Tax Collections, 1965–2005

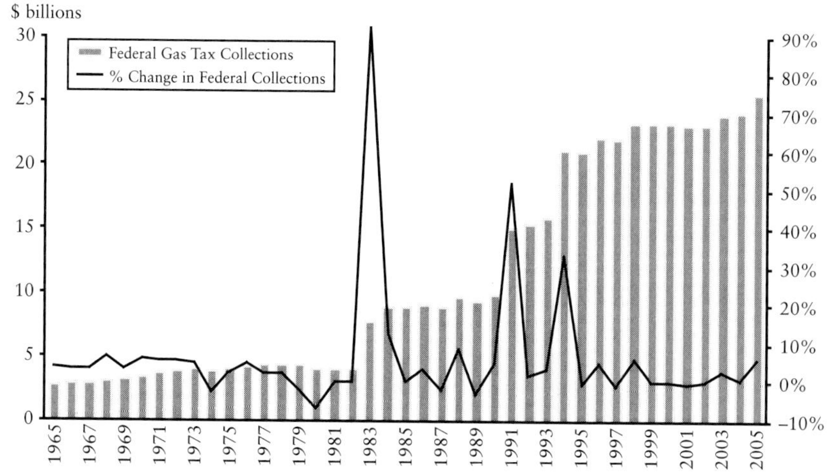

Source: Bureau of Economic Analysis.

ing maintenance expenses on the existing interstate system have consumed funds to the detriment of new construction. At the same time, measures of urban mobility have shown steady deterioration, with particularly sharp declines shown in rapidly growing areas of the Sunbelt.

1980s to the Present

More than 20 authorities and agencies have been created to finance new urban toll roads and bridges. These authorities are scattered throughout the country in locations as diverse as Southern California, Atlanta, Houston, South Carolina, Miami, and Denver. Innovative financing techniques, such as capital appreciation bonds, which produce ascending debt service structures and a need for periodic toll increases have been frequently used in debt structures. As with the earlier period of intercity toll road financing, fiscal problems have surfaced with some of these projects and a few monetary defaults have occurred.

KEY ANALYTICAL FACTORS

In this section we will describe the key factors in the analysis of toll roads.

Importance of Traffic and Revenue Models

The basic approach used by an analyst reviewing an established toll road or bridge and a startup project is similar. The key credit factors and variables, the measuring tools and data sources are interchangeable. What is different is that historical traffic and operating data are available for an established toll road, while for a planned new road, they are not. For new projects, analysts must review the output of sophisticated traffic and revenue models that incorporate regional travel patterns and economic numbers and attempt to simulate the existence of the new toll road. For most established roads, the need to scrutinize many of the key variables is greatly lessened and the reliance on traffic and revenue models is greatly reduced. Nevertheless, many established toll road agencies maintain a close relationship with forecasting firms and will rely upon models particularly when considering the impact of new projects or substantial toll increases on traffic levels. The exception to this rule relates to recent efforts to privatize established toll roads during which time reliance on models is substantial. For most startups, the inter-relationship among key factors is more complex and requires more detailed knowledge and attention to key inputs. Moreover, startup projects have risks associated with construction and ramp up that are not a consideration for established entities.

Importance of Traffic

No matter which type of project is being analyzed, the level of traffic, the number of passenger cars, trucks, and other vehicles paying tolls is the single most important factor needed to determine viability. Traffic usage can be expressed in numerous ways from the actual number of toll transactions incurred to measures such as the *average annual daily traffic* (AADT) or *vehicles per day* (VPD). These two measures will differ depending upon whether tolls are collected at regular, frequent intervals—often called a *barrier system*—or only at entrances and exits from the highway. Barrier systems may show far more toll transactions than the alternative because of the frequency of toll payments, but have a lower AADT. For an established road, the overall pattern of usage, annual changes in traffic levels, and how they respond to economic and other factors generally provide an important component of the analytical information needed to develop a credit opinion. Usage patterns, once established, tend to be highly predictable and growth rates usually can be extrapolated into the future by applying historical trends.

Traffic demand is a result of many consumer choices including the primary motivation of drivers who utilize the road (i.e., trips to work, leisure travel), the type and number of alternative or competing highways, levels of economic growth and personal income, the time savings obtained from using the road, toll rates, the development of electronic toll collection systems, and even signage and marketing.

Most of the nation's toll facilities were constructed to facilitate the movement of goods and people between disparate urban centers. These intercity roadways generally carry a greater percentage of long distance trucks making regular trips, whereas auto trips may be less frequent. In contrast, roads serving daily commuters, many of whom are going to jobs, schools, or other regularly attended activity centers predominate in urban areas. Commuters may make up anywhere from 50% to 70% of all trips taken. These trips are generally short in distance but high in frequency. Determinations of trip purpose are often gleaned by doing travel surveys of roadway users (in the case of a startup, potential users). These surveys provide detailed information on travel patterns, including the origin and destination of their trips. In recent years with the growth of urban centers, many of the turnpikes that were built primarily to accommodate intercity traffic have become more commuter-dependent, which makes the motivating factors and modeling of their traffic patterns more complex. In some cases, the roads traverse several important urban concentrations each with their own economic drivers.

Daily traffic counts and transactions are generally much higher on urban highways because of the frequency of use and overall traffic levels within an urbanized area. A few examples might illustrate the different categories of roads. Predominantly intercity turnpikes include such turnpikes as those in Kansas and Ohio. They generally traverse relatively open space or touch the fringes of urban areas. In contrast, the New Jersey, Florida, and Pennsylvania Turnpikes have become hybrids combining intercity and even out of state users with large commuter populations along their now urbanized sections. Finally, we have numerous local and regional authorities that serve only urbanized areas such as Harris County Toll Road Authority, the North Texas Tollway Authority, and the Orlando-Orange County Expressway Authority. These three roads have expanded rapidly during recent years with growth of their urban areas.

Value of Time

The level of competition from adjacent free expressways and arterial highways is a key determinant of traffic volumes. Drivers choosing a toll alternative go through a series of decisions reflecting a trade-off between paying tolls, the time savings, and the ease of travel provided by a toll road. One of the equations or variables that traffic consultants and economists use to translate these concepts into their models is known as the *value of time*. The value of time incorporates both quantitative and qualitative inputs. It varies substantially among each individual user based on income levels, the purpose of the trip, and the value of truck cargoes. Essentially the higher an individual's income or the more expensive and perishable a truck cargo, the higher the assumed value of time for that trip and the higher the toll rate that can be charged. Trips with a high degree of time urgency have a higher value of time associated with them. In general, these individual differences are homogenized into a numerical input in a model, often expressed as cents per minute or dollars per hour.

The development of new toll collection technologies has become another factor influencing the willingness of drivers to choose toll roads. Beginning in the 1990s, *electronic toll collection* (ETC) emerged as an effective and efficient way to collect tolls. ETC replaces coin or token collection with a noncash system. The technology greatly reduces delays at toll collection points reducing travel times, but the prime benefit is a reduction in the awareness of the cost of a toll trip since no immediate cash is exchanged. Consultants have also identified other factors that can be indirectly linked to the assumed value of time such as the relative amount of comfort, predictability, and ease a toll facility may provide relative to more congested free alternatives. Frequent rest stops on turnpikes, for example, provide such relative advantage. Also, in some studies, women have shown a greater willingness to use toll roads because of a desire or need to get home to their families. These qualitative factors have been called the toll road bonus.

By itself, value of time provides little guidance on this choice between a free or toll road but is an essential building block in the model. Two other key pieces of information are needed by the analyst or traffic consultant. First for urban roads, a keen knowledge of the entire regional traffic system is required. *Metropolitan planning organizations* (MPOs) created under federal requirements track regional traffic movements. These entities have developed models of traffic movements within an entire metropolitan region. They have been developed from an array of information such as actual traffic counts on roadways, the travel surveys discussed above, and the development of so-called trip tables that attempt to measure all movements within a region. They incorporate and aggregate data from small areas, called *traffic analysis zones* (TAZs, for short) that permit all of the above data to be gathered and entered in substantial detail, creating greater reliability. These network models form the basis for forecasting congestion levels and defining alternative routes that can be compared for time savings.

Consultants or analysts also simply compare actual time traveled on different competing routes. This procedure involves a lot of common sense but also requires thinking like a potential driver. These readings are usually obtained through actual trips taken at select times (rush hour, nonrush hour, weekends or in different months) to account for different levels of usage and congestion. On the intercity portions of most turnpikes, these times generally vary little, but in congested urban areas, travel times vary considerably even over the course of the peak rush. The competing roads for an intercity turnpike might be arterial roads with numerous lights and intersections with generally lower travel speeds. Time savings are generally very high on these roads. Yet, even some intercity roads have considerable variation since vacation and weekend travel is important to usage on some of these roads. Travel times may actually be the worst on weekends and before holidays.

For urban roads, numerous alternatives including both free and tolled expressways as well as arterials exist and each major alternative generally needs to be driven. Meanwhile, toll bridges are generally less subject to competition than land-based toll roads and in many cases represent near monopolies providing the only travel route across a water crossing. Time savings are generally expressed in minutes saved between using alternative routes.

The assumed likelihood of a toll road user choosing a toll road results from a comparison of the value of time against the time saved. Since existing toll roads are already in the model, the consultant's forecasting task is greatly simplified. Modeling a new road is more difficult since the existing network must be adjusted to simulate traffic movements after incorporating the new toll road. Those simulations, in turn, are derived from the complex interplay of the value of time, regional traffic movements, and time savings. In general, toll roads must offer a reasonable time savings versus free alternatives.

Traffic Diversion Models

Toll rates are the last element of this analytical equation. In the end, a driver decides to use a toll road because paying a toll remains attractive when measured against time savings and the value of time. A model translates this implicit response into specific numbers that permit toll rates to be compared against the other model inputs. The trade-off between toll rates and the other inputs produces what are known as *diversion curves*. These curves attempt to reflect the interplay between toll rates and the willingness of drivers to select the free alternatives over the toll alternative. Higher toll rates tend to divert traffic but also increase revenues and the curves attempt to reflect this trade-off. For established toll roads, diversion curves can be readily developed from actual results. In terms of startup toll roads, these curves are one of the most important model outputs and remain the center of an ongoing debate among traffic consultants and economists. If the revenues resulting from traffic diversion to the toll alternative are insufficient, debt cannot be paid. All of the above inputs are critical to the determination of the financial feasibility of a new project.

Toll Setting

Toll setting regimes and policies have begun to change in recent years. For many years, the majority of toll road agencies only increased their toll rates in response to substantial increases in borrowing to finance capital improvements. As a result, toll rates for many U.S. toll roads tend to be well under their foreign counterparts, generally averaging less than 12 cents per mile and in some cases below five cents per mile for passenger vehicles. During the past 15 years, however, many startup toll roads have been financed with debt structures that require periodic toll increases to achieve their forecasts. Initial toll rates also have been quite high, often exceeding 20 cents per mile. With the emergence of privatization, various formulas permitting annual periodic toll increases have been applied to already established toll roads. The impact of frequent toll increases and ascending toll rates on future traffic patterns remains uncertain.

As toll regimes change, new attention is being paid to maximizing toll revenues. The theoretical peak of revenues occurs where further toll increases will divert more traffic than is generated through charging higher tolls. Governments, in general, do not set toll rates at this level. They do not operate toll roads as profit-making enterprises. Rather, government-owned toll roads are interested in having sufficient revenue to pay for expenses, debt service, capital improvements, and meeting covenant requirements. In addition, revenue maximization may interfere with other policy goals such as improving regional mobility. Conversely, a private toll road operator is very interested in revenue maximization as bottom line earnings and *earnings before interest, taxes, depreciation, and amortization* (EBITDA) are the principal business drivers. For a startup project, determining the shape of these curves is critical in properly setting initial toll rates to ensure that the mix of forecasted traffic and tolls will be sufficient to pay debt service.

Importance of Economic Growth

Economic growth is the last important determinant of traffic levels, particularly in the future. Population and employment growth correlate strongly with the rate of increase in traffic. Increases in population and income lead to the purchase of more automobiles. Employment growth is highly correlated with rush hour traffic levels in urban areas and, in the past few decades, the increase in two wage earning households has also stimulated work-related travel. Higher incomes also lead to more leisure-related travel and increase the value of time. Income levels are perhaps the key component in the value of time calculation. Growth in each of these variables varies greatly among different metropolitan areas and states.

Economic growth rates are very important for even established roads since they are so highly correlated with past patterns of traffic growth. Changes in economic variables can accelerate or reduce future growth rates. For startup projects, determining the existing level of economic activity and more importantly, ascertaining where growth is likely to occur over the succeeding decade or more is critical to the success of the forecast. Because many startups are constructed in rapidly growing areas on the fringes of metropolitan areas, growth rates can vary dramatically.

To ensure more reliability, forecasts of future economic activity used in traffic forecasts have been developed in recent years by experienced regional economic forecasting firms. Although forecasts of future economic activity can prove incorrect, a rigorous approach is favored over past practices when unnecessary reliance was placed upon plans and forecasts made by developers. Many startup toll roads have been conceived to support development plans that proved overly optimistic. Developer input is necessary but needs to be balanced by a greater knowledge of regional and national economic outlooks. Also, many economic projections fail to provide for recessions, which can result in the overstatement of traffic and revenue when economic downturns actually occur.

Toll Road Elasticity

With so many variables potentially affecting traffic and toll revenues, the analysis of a toll road can be a complex undertaking. As noted, for most established toll roads and bridges, forecasts of future usage are surprisingly straightforward and predictable. Once established, traffic patterns do not change materially unless new highways are constructed. Recessions temporarily slow traffic growth, and in the case of truck traffic often cause outright decline. However, in the recovery, patterns return to the previous trend. The same is true with gasoline prices. One study examined traffic trends on several established toll roads during the period following the Arab oil embargo in 1973 and found that growth slowed on many toll roads but, in general, the impacts were modest.[4]

A substantial increase in toll rates is generally the most important factor that can alter traffic on established toll roads. Traffic consultants often are utilized by established roads when contemplating a large toll rate change. Drawing on their models, these consultants effectively try to determine the potential economic elasticity of a specific toll change. For example, a doubling in tolls might produce a 10% traffic decline on one road, expressed as –0.1 elasticity, while another road loses 20% of traffic, expressed as –0.2. The differences reflect the sensitivity of users to the change in tolls and their perceived value of time. Most well-established roads tend to be more inelastic. In other words, tolls can be increased and revenues will rise nearly as much as the percentage increases in toll rates. Conversely, newer roads can be very different in their response to toll increases and may be more elastic.

Private companies and governments have looked at the privatization of toll roads because of this accepted inelasticity. Revenue streams are deemed fairly predictable in the future based upon certain defined toll regimes. The reliability of revenues also makes tolls an attractive alternative to finance other governmental activities. Bridges operated by the Triborough Bridge and Tunnel Authority and the Port Authority in New York that subsidize mass transit operations serve as a principal example of this phenomena.

Traffic and Revenue Model Concerns

While the performance of established roads is generally highly predictable, the analyst can be challenged by the complexity and uncertain risks of startup

[4] Peter C. Stettler, "Toll Roads 1972–1994: Traffic Growth Overcomes a Few Bumps in the Road," *Journal of Public Finance* (Spring 1997), pp. 18–39.

toll roads sometimes known as *greenfields*. Potential traffic and revenue levels are almost entirely based on the inputs into customized models created by the traffic consultants. This leaves the analyst often trying to draw conclusions from the output of "black boxes." Moreover those models are based on the other models developed by the MPOs and by projections obtained from economic forecasting models.

The forecasts derived from these models have often been overly optimistic. In two studies published in 1996 and 2002 by JPMorgan, analysts compared actual performance in the initial years of operation for newly constructed urban toll roads to the forecasts provided at the time of the initial bond financing.[5] Actual revenue during the first three years of operation was, on average, 40% below the projected level. Numerous factors appeared to contribute to the shortfalls including: overly optimistic forecasts of economic growth or recessions, overstating the amount of traffic congestion on competing roads, miscalculating time savings and the value of time, poor connections to the existing traffic networks, bad signage, and excessive toll charges. Forecasting error increased as the amount of existing development decreased. The best forecasts were for roads built through more congested, higher-income suburban areas where time savings were substantial, whereas the worst performing roads were on the fringe of metropolitan areas and often dependent on the input of optimistic developers.

Analysts of startup toll roads must pay close attention to each assumption in the traffic and revenue models. They also must understand the way variables interrelate. The analyst needs to visit the location of a prospective project, drive on competing highways, exercise best judgment about whether a traffic and revenue forecast seems to recreate real traffic movements, and equate it with driver perception of value. That is a substantial undertaking and burden.

Bond Analysis

Revenues are, in general, a derivative of traffic levels and the toll regime. For established toll roads, a long history may exist of actual revenue collections, the impact of prior toll increases, and operating expenses. Analysts can easily develop calculations for debt service coverage using standard methodologies applied to all types of revenue bonds. For a new project, all of these numbers are projections. Debt service coverage levels range between 1.2× to better than 2×, depending upon the toll road. Because of the inelasticity of

---

[5] Robert H. Muller, "Examining Toll Road Feasibility Studies," *Journal of Public Finance* (Spring 1997), pp. 39–49, and Robert H. Muller and Kristin L. Buono, "Start-Up Toll Roads: Separating Winners from Losers," *JPMorgan Municipal Credit Monitor* (May 10, 2002).

traffic on many established toll roads, high levels of coverage are generally unnecessary for favorable ratings.

Single-purpose entities operate most toll roads and bridges in the United States. The revenue generated from tolls can be used only for the toll road and bondholders have a lien on such revenues. The legal documents supporting these roads provide for a closed flow of funds structure. Revenues are generally placed in a revenue fund and then allocated to pay for operating and maintenance expenses as well as debt service and is used to create various reserves for capital replacement and major renovation, including for purposes such as road resurfacing or bridge repair. In most legal documents, after providing for these purposes, revenues are transferred to a surplus account that can be used for any purpose supporting the toll road including debt repayment. Many toll roads also maintain a debt service reserve fund, however in recent years, some well established roads have dropped this requirement.

Although the flow of funds discussed above is the most common, bonds of some recently constructed toll roads are secured in a fashion more akin to a gross revenue pledge. Revenues are first set aside to pay debt service. In these cases, the expenses for operation and maintenance are often paid by some other governmental entity. This absorption of expenses represents a form of subsidy for these projects and allows for more revenues to be available to pay bonded debt service, permitting large bond financings and more debt service coverage.

Although most toll roads do not allow the transfer of excess revenues, a few governments have realized that established toll roads generate a substantial level of excess and predictable revenues that can be used to finance other transportation needs, particularly mass transit. The bond documents for these agencies allow for the transfer of excess revenues once expenses for debt service, operation and maintenance, and reserves have been met. In general, debt service coverage for the bonds of these agencies is higher.

Most toll road revenue bonds also have other legal safeguards built into their legal documents that are quite similar to those found in other types of municipal revenue bonds. Most important is the rate covenant. It stipulates that the toll agency is required in each year to set toll rates such that after paying for operation and maintenance expenses, remaining net revenues will provide debt service coverage at levels ranging from 1x to 1.5x or more. Restrictions also exist on the issuance of additional parity bonds generally requiring the achievement of a specific coverage level on an historical and pro forma basis after accounting for debt service on any debt proposed.

CONCLUSION

With highway congestion growing steadily, states have finally embraced toll roads as a principal source of funding new highways. New toll collection technologies have made it easier for the public to accept paying tolls. Numerous states from North Carolina to Oregon to Alaska have passed legislation authorizing the financing of toll roads and bridges within their boundaries for the first time. Several states have permitted toll roads to be built and operated by private owners. New groups of investors, not just those who purchase tax-exempt debt must learn how to analyze toll supported projects. Analysts at the forefront of the discussions in the years ahead need to understand more fully the risk factors for startup toll roads. Traffic and revenue models will need to be more transparent. Finally, the impact of the interrelationship of new toll setting regimes, economic growth, and the value of time requires more historical data.

CHAPTER 59

Water and Sewer Bond Analysis

Brian Winters
Vice President
Van Kampen Investments

Water has played a central role in all civilizations from earliest of times to the most contemporary of advanced cities. Societies settled near rivers, lakes and seas for the benefits of protection, transportation, commerce, and irrigation. Across the span of history, water and its employment have had a profound impact on the growth and development of mankind as witnessed in the accounts of the Noahic flood, the ancient Sumerian canals, dikes and reservoirs, the Hanging Gardens of Babylon, the Egyptian's controlled irrigation of the fertile Nile River Valley, the extensive Phoenician maritime trading of the Mediterranean, the engineering marvel of the Roman aqueducts, the breadth of overseas Spanish exploration and the British Empire, and the widespread achievement of municipal water and sewer utilities in the United States.

The quest for potable water is ever more urgent with growth in global population and the increasing size of large urban centers. Also, safe and efficient sewerage is just as necessary to keep the local environment clean in order to prevent and reduce the spread of disease. Fresh water accounts for only 2.5% of all the water in the world, and of that two-thirds is frozen in glaciers and polar ice caps.

The procurement and distribution of clean drinking water and the safe disposal and treatment of wastewater has been successfully accomplished by local municipalities for many decades in the United States.

In this chapter on water and sewer bond analysis, we will consider the structure and management of water and sewer utilities, as well as the underlying economic base supporting the service area, important bond security provisions, established financial ratios, and lastly the growing responsibility of environmental issues.

STRUCTURE

Water and sewer services began in villages, towns, and cities as local projects to provide the populous with potable water and safe and reliable sewerage. These municipalities obtained rights to sources of water and built distribution systems to deliver the water to residential, commercial, and industrial customers. Management of the utilities was at the discretion of city councils and utility boards. Often general obligation water bonds were issued to fund the utility capital projects. Over time, water revenue bonds were issued secured by revenues of the water and sewer utility. Revenues were derived from various rates and fees, most often on usage and connections. This model is still the predominant means by which water and sewer services are provided today. Cities and towns procure water, deliver the water through a city-owned distribution system, and bill and collect payments from customers. Due to water shortages, population growth, more restrictive environmental regulation and a host of other reasons, the procurement of water has changed the most for water and sewer utilities.

Where water sources have been inadequate to meet increased demand, local communities have turned to the formation of water districts and wholesalers. Joining with other towns with similar resource needs to secure a common source of water tends to be more economical and efficient versus going it alone. Besides the primary benefit of obtaining sources of water, shared responsibility for financing, management and operation of projects is a major advantage for small to medium-sized utilities and communities. Water districts are generally governed by a board of directors composed of representatives from communities that belong to the district. Often larger state districts make provision for the governor to appoint a certain number of the district board. Revenues of most water districts are derived primarily from rates and charges on usage and in some cases from assessments. Larger or regional water districts are often comprised of smaller local water districts and stand-alone cities and towns. Two examples of large water districts include (1) the Massachusetts Water Resources Authority that provides wholesale water and sewer service to 2.5 million people and 5,500 large industrial users in 61 metropolitan Boston communities; and (2) the Metropolitan Water District of Southern California serving 18 million people in 26 cities and local water districts. The economies of scale obtained by these water districts results in lower water rates and a constant flow of clean water for customers.

Another water utility structure used in less-populated rural and agricultural areas mostly in the West, is the irrigation or improvement district. To create and maintain viable agricultural business ample water supplies are obtained and delivered via an irrigation system. Many of these irrigation districts supply other utility services such as electricity. The largest irrigation district in the country is the Imperial Irrigation District in California. The district has over 3,000 miles of canals and drains providing 3.1 million acre-feet of water per year to over one-half million irrigated acres.

MANAGEMENT

Management of water and sewer systems is an often overlooked aspect of credit analysis in this sector. The relatively basic nature of pumping water through pipelines and collecting wastewater for treatment lacks the dynamic changes and pressing issues associated with many industries. As a result, management of municipal water and sewer systems is not the first thought of aspiring new graduates of management degree programs. Yet, management of these systems is important to the safe and efficient operation of a basic necessity. Management of water and sewer systems incorporates several aspects of varying nature including the degree of decision making, rate setting authority, staff experience and labor issues to name a few.

The degree of authority in decision making depends on the structure of the system. Whether management responsibility resides with a city council, in an elected or appointed board, a stand alone enterprise fund, or a regional organization will affect the types of decisions made by management. The more political the process, the longer it may take to implement changes and initiatives. Also, the greater the commitment to regional organizations and associations, the less independence management has in enacting certain programs.

Investors look closely at management's rate setting authority. The ability of management to set water and sewer rates and fees autonomously is viewed favorably by investors. With the flexibility to adjust rates on a timely basis, the financial position of the water and sewer entity tends to be more stable and not subject to the often politicized atmosphere of management having to obtain city council approval for changes in rates.

ECONOMIC BASE

The economic stability and vitality of an issuer's service area is of utmost importance in assessing the soundness of a water and sewer credit. An established local economy can support rates for service that allow for routine and necessary maintenance and improvements of the system. An unhealthy local economy will have a more difficult time sustaining rates and sound financial position. Several parameters are helpful in assessing the health of a local economy including population trends, assessed valuation growth, employment rates and industry sector diversification, top 10 employers in the area, and wealth and income measures. Each of these parameters will give an indication of the number of customer connections and the ability of the system to maintain appropriate water and sewer rates for financial strength. In faster-growing service areas, with above-average population gains and new commercial and industrial development, prudent management is needed to provide the required capacity at reasonable rates. In older and slower growing service areas, the ability to maintain quality service is paramount in the face of aging infrastructure.

FINANCIAL RATIOS

Water and sewer systems tend to be some of the safest investments amongst the various municipal bond sectors mainly due to their necessity in any well-developed society. Other services be they education, healthcare, electricity or transportation are all important elements of daily life, but basic water and sewer service ranks above these even with our high-tech dependence. The use of financial ratios is one of the primary tools in ascertaining the creditworthiness and viability of a water and sewer entity. While a plethora of margins and ratios can be derived from the financial statements of a credit, we will focus on the standard and straightforward numbers most often used by investors. These financial ratios will be presented in broader categories to obtain the full scope of financial health.

Operating Performance

Reviewing the operations of a water and sewer entity is the most basic of analysis and yields valuable information of its creditworthiness. Generally, a five-year financial history gives enough information for a dependable trend line. Operating revenues consist of the total water and sewer sales and the rates charged. A pattern in operating revenues should be dissected for the cause, whether it is due to an increase or decrease in sales or the result of changes in rates charged. A trend of increasing operating revenues is a good sign but could be misleading if increased rate charges mask declines in total sales. Operating expenses should also be judged for their reasonableness in relation to other similar entities. The most widely used financial measures of operating performance and profitability is the operating margin and profit margin. Operating margin gives the investor an idea of how well operating revenues cover the variable costs of the entity. Profit margin includes nonoperating revenues and expenses and gets to the bottom line, or overall profitability. With nonoperating revenues and expenses, the investor would want to look for unexpected gains or losses that need to be investigated further. Another indicator to use would be cash flow margin which accounts for noncash items such as depreciation and amortization. A water and sewer issuer with sound operations and profitability is usually a healthy credit.

Leverage

The use of debt to fund capital projects allows water and sewer issuers to build assets and pay for them over the life of the asset instead of using cash and current investments. While debt issuance can be beneficial, too much debt can overburden the issuer and cause weak financial performance. The primary gauge of appropriate leverage is long-term debt to total capitalization. The investor may want to add other noncurrent liabilities such as capital leases or notes payable to long-term debt to get a truer indication of overall leverage and the utilities ability to meet its long-term obligations. Higher debt to capitalization ratios are common with older systems upgrading aging assets or complying with environmental regulations, and with newer systems expanding capacity to meet increasing population demands.

Liquidity

The ability of a water and sewer utility to meet its short-term obligations and day-to-day operations is of highest priority. Sufficient cash and short-term investments provide the means whereby the utility pays for its current liabilities. A review of unrestricted cash and its trend over a number of years is helpful. The best measures of available liquidity are: current ratio, days cash on hand, and unrestricted cash to long-term debt. The current ratio simply divides current assets by current liabilities. Days cash on hand quantifies in number of days how much unrestricted cash and investments is available to cover operating expenses. Lastly, the percentage of unrestricted cash to long-term debt gives a relative measure of how liquid a utility is to its longer-term fixed costs.

Coverage

Chief among financial ratios for bond investors is annual debt service coverage. Ultimately, covering annual requirements for repayment of principal and interest must be at least 1.0 times, yet most bond indentures include covenants requiring annual debt service coverage some percentage above 1.0 times. Other measures of coverage include maximum annual debt service coverage and cash flow to total debt. Failure to satisfy covenanted debt service coverage requirements each year usually triggers a default and thus this ratio is the main hurdle utility management strives to clear after expenditures for operations and maintenance.

These are but a few of the widely used financial ratios and margins used in assessing credit quality of water and sewer utilities. To gain additional insight, these calculations should be compared with other water and sewer utilities of similar size and characteristics.

BOND SECURITY

The security underlying a water and sewer bond issuance has evolved over the years as the sector has matured and individual issuers have proven stability in operations and debt repayment. Historically, water and sewer capital projects were funded through the local municipality and the use of their general obligation bond security. As capital projects increased in size and scope due to population growth, additional environmental mandates and aging infrastructure, and municipal debt levels rose, funding for water and sewer capital requirements shifted from bonds backed by the municipalities general obligation pledge to the revenues derived from water and sewer operations. System revenue could be generated from several sources including rates on volume use, tap fees, connection fees or system development fees, and generally was pledged as either gross or net of operations and maintenance for bond repayment. Additionally, the pledge of revenues of the system would be a senior-lien or a junior-lien. The security as well as other legal provisions protecting investors is defined in the bond indenture. The stricture of many of these provisions has weakened over the years, due to a well-established trend of stable financial performance and thus a perception that such protective provisions are unnecessary, to provide less security for bond investors.

Rate Covenant

The rate covenant is designed to provide protection for the investor that the water and sewer issuer will fix, establish, maintain and collect rates, charges and fees for water and sewer services each year sufficient to cover operation and maintenance expenses, and debt service requirements by net revenues by a determined percentage. In other words, the issuer is covenanting to set rates such that net revenues will exceed annual debt service payments by a minimum level. Typically, the rate covenant for water and sewer bond issues is between 1.00× to 1.20×.

Debt Service Reserve Fund

Another bondholder protection is the debt service reserve fund. This reserve fund provides temporary support for the water and sewer entity to make debt service payments at times of unforeseen net revenue shortfalls. The common funding requirement for the debt service reserve fund is an amount equal to the lesser of 10% of the principal amount of the bonds, 125% of the average annual debt service on the bonds, or the maximum annual debt service on the bonds. If the debt service reserve is tapped to meet current principal repayment and interest expense, the amount of withdrawal is usually required to be restored over a defined course of time, typically one year. So as not to tie up potentially needed funds, some issuers are allowed to substitute a letter of credit, surety bond or other credit enhancement for funds on deposit in the reserve fund. Another wrinkle used by stronger credits that likely will not need the extra financial cushion provided by a debt service reserve fund is to provide investors with a "springing" reserve fund in the event certain specified parameters are not met.

Additional Bonds Tests

To prevent a water and sewer issuer from using too much leverage, and weakening their ability to meet debt service coverage levels, a bond covenant is placed in the indenture limiting additional parity debt. A standard additional bonds test requires that the annual net revenues of a water and sewer system for the most recent fiscal year be at least 125% of the maximum annual debt service requirement including the additional bonds proposed to be issued. An alternative test is commonly included and is more prospective requiring an independent consultant to project annual net revenues and whether they will be equal to at least 125% of maximum annual debt service including the additional bonds to be issued.

Flow of Funds

The bond indenture will also outline the application of revenues earned by the water and sewer system prioritizing them in a flow of funds. Generally, a revenue fund is created to accept all revenues derived and collected from the operation of the system, and is held separate from all other funds. On a timely basis, moneys flow out of the revenue fund to other funds as specified in the indenture. Typically, the flow of funds goes from revenue fund to an operation and maintenance fund to a bond fund to a debt service reserve eventually ending in surplus fund. The investor should analyze the sequence of the flow of funds and the various funding requirements for each of those funds. Of special note in reviewing the flow of funds requirements, is the ability of the water and sewer issuer to transfer out surplus funds to a municipality's general fund. It is important that if transfer of surplus funds is allowed that the timing and amount be clearly specified. The concern for the investor is the excessive transfers from the utility to the municipality could harm the credit quality of the utility.

ENVIRONMENTAL ISSUES

Water and wastewater public utilities are mandated to comply with both the Safe Drinking Water Act of 1974 and amended in 1996, and the Clean Water Act of 1972. These two federal laws provide standards on drinking water and wastewater that apply to all utility systems in the country. In addition to the federal laws and regulations, each state has its own set of regulations and requirements. The costs of meeting the regulatory mandates are significant as most often new capital projects must be built in order for utility systems to be in compliance. Also, as regulations change and amendments to previous provisions are made, the water and sewer utility must have the financial and operational flexibility for implementation.

OTHER CONSIDERATIONS

Increases in global population, technological advancements, and the threat of terrorism warrant other considerations in the analysis of water and sewer systems. With growing demand for fresh water, and the fact that a small percentage of the total global water supply is fresh water, societies are turning to the vast oceans of salt water. Developments in technology allow for the desalinization of salt water. At this time, desalinization is still cost-prohibitive, but as populations grow and supplies of fresh water are used, greater use of desalinization is likely. Another consideration for water and sewer systems is the threat of terrorism. With the pervasive and ever-present threat of terrorist acts, utilities must secure sources of water supplies and protect distribution channels from contamination and interruption of service. The additional costs of securing these assets is significant and will result in increased user fees as surveillance and monitoring devices, as well as other security measures, are installed.

CONCLUSION

Within the universe of investment choices, municipal water and sewer bonds represent a relatively safe option based upon their low rate of default itself a function of the essential nature of the service provided. The inelasticity of demand for water and sewer services is nearly unmatched in the municipal revenue bond sector, and when coupled with sound security provisions makes a wise investment for the prudent investor. The quantity of municipal water and sewer bond issuance is likely to be sustained at current levels or higher in future years as aging infrastructure is renovated and replaced, and tighter environmental requirements demand new facilities.

Special Security Structures and Their Analysis

Evaluating Tax-Exempt Commercial Paper

Maria C. Sazon
Vice President and Senior Research Analyst
AllianceBernstein

T he purpose of this chapter is to set forth an analytical framework to ana- lyze the credit risk of tax-exempt commercial paper. The discussion begins with the definition and purpose of commercial paper notes, identifies differ- ent forms of repayment methods, and proceeds to list various types of pay- ment enhancement otherwise known as *credit backstops*. The chapter con- cludes with criteria to consider in analyzing unenhanced commercial paper.

OVERVIEW OF COMMERCIAL PAPER

Commercial paper (CP) is a short-term promissory note of an issuer (a mu- nicipal issuer or corporation) of high-credit standing, which is bought and sold in the open market. It is issued to provide working capital or interim financing. CP has a term of 30 to 120 days, or any maturity in between. The maximum term that CP can be issued is 270 days. CP programs are typically open-ended with maturities being rolled over on a regular basis. If used as an interim or bridge financing, the CP program is retired when the long-term financing has taken place, generally upon issuance of long-term bonds.

Extendible CP is similar to traditional CP with one major difference: the issuer has the option to extend the stated maturity in the event of a failed rollover or remarketing. As such, extendible CP has a maturity that could stretch beyond 270 days. An extension is not considered a default. An issuer would choose to issue extendible CP because it provides flexibility in managing its liabilities and precludes the need to provide liquidity. The discussion in this chapter covers only traditional CP.

The high credit quality of CP makes it easily transferable from one investor to another, hence the high liquidity. Issuers of CP, including commercial banks that provide credit enhancement to these instruments, are generally highly rated issuers. Because of the relatively short maturity and high credit quality, CP notes are held primarily by money market funds. If so, it is likely that issuers are in the AAA-, AA-, and A-rating categories since those would qualify for tier-one ratings under Rule 2a-7, the SEC guidelines for money market funds (see Exhibit 60.1). Other investors in CP are banks, insurance companies, endowments, municipalities, and investors or institutions that prefer or require safety and liquidity.

REPAYMENT OF COMMERCIAL PAPER NOTES

Similar to floating rate and variable rate demand notes, CP notes are repaid by means of rollover, remarketing or payment made at maturity. The high credit quality of these notes makes it attractive to money market funds rendering it a highly liquid security. When a CP note matures, it is reset and upon its sale, the proceeds of the sale will be used to repay the prior holder.

EXHIBIT 60.1 Relationship between Long-Term Credit Ratings and Commercial Paper Ratings

Moody's		S&P		Fitch	
Aaa		AAA		AAA	
Aa1		AA+		AA+	
Aa2		AA	A-1+	AA	F1+
Aa3	P-1	AA−		AA−	
A1		A+		A+	
A2		A	A-1	A	F1
A3		A−		A−	
	P-2		A-2		
Baa1		BBB+		BBB+	F2
Baa2	P-3	BBB	A-3	BBB	F3
Baa3		BBB−		BBB−	

Note: P-1, P-2, P-3 stand for Prime-1, Prime-2, Prime-3.

There are only a handful of circumstances that can cause CP investors to avoid a credit and therefore result in a failed remarketing. If this occurs, it is likely due to a rating downgrade or any situation that can adversely affect the rating such as a major lawsuit, management changes or a scandal. In the rare case that it is not related to credit, it could be due to a market condition like a steep yield curve where there is a significant difference between short- and long-term tax-exempt interest rates and demand for all short-term instruments, including CP notes, is low. This situation is only temporary because the market will reestablish equilibrium by repricing the notes to a level that renders it attractive and thereby increase demand.

ANALYZING VARIOUS SOURCES OF REPAYMENT FOR COMMERCIAL PAPER

CP with payments or credit backstop come in various forms: CP with credit enhancement, CP with partial enhancement, and CP with a revolving credit agreement. These are discussed in detail in the following subsections.

CP with Credit Enhancement

The most widely used credit enhancement for CP notes is the irrevocable *direct-pay letter of credit* (LOC). LOCs are issued by highly rated commercial banks. The LOC is issued by the bank on behalf of its client, the municipal issuer. The LOC is addressed to the trustee, who has the legal right to draw from the LOC to pay the principal and interest when due, absent a successful rollover. The LOC is sized so that it covers principal and interest at maturity. Any draws to the LOC becomes a loan from the bank whereby it is repaid or reimbursed by the issuer at a loan rate that is defined in the reimbursement agreement. In some instances, a bank may issue a standby LOC instead of a direct-pay LOC because the issuer has the means to provide liquidity on its own but there is a chance that a timing delay could occur.

By issuing a LOC, the bank is unconditionally obligated to advance funds whenever necessary to meet debt service payments. Because of this legal commitment, full credit substitution is applied and the bank's short-term rating is substituted for the issuer's rating. CPs backed by LOCs are typically rated by at least one of the Nationally Recognized Statistical Rating Organization (NRSRO).

Because the investor's risks now lie entirely with the credit quality of the bank, the most important consideration centers upon the investor's comfort level and assessment of the bank. In addition to the high credit ratings of the bank, the analyst must also be confident that the risk of a downgrade is minimal. (In money market terms, under SEC Rule 2-a7, the bank is then referred to as an approved name.) Once an LOC is issued, bankruptcy and/ or insolvency of the bank are probably the only circumstances when an LOC cannot be drawn upon. This will rarely occur because the issuer has the right to replace or substitute the bank once a rating downgrade is triggered. In the event of a bank substitution, either due to replacement or non-renewal, the existing LOC should cover the repayment of all outstanding CP prior to the substitution. To avoid administrative problems, CPs are typically reset at the same time that the new LOC becomes effective.

Another important detail to check is the maturity date of the LOC. The expiry date of the LOC should extend beyond the maturity of the CP. Outstanding CP should always be covered under the LOC prior to its expiration date.

CP with Partial Enhancement

CP programs with partial enhancement are those where the credit facility is provided to pay principal only. In other words, the issuer is responsible for the interest portion that is due and the bank is responsible for the principal portion only. The analyst's job in this case is to ascertain whether the issuer has enough liquid resources to pay interest when due.

CP with Revolving Credit Agreement

For CP backed by a revolving credit agreement, the issuer makes an arrangement with a financial institution to provide an alternate source of liquidity other than its own. In this arrangement, a bank commits to provide a revolving line of credit for the purpose of making advances on behalf of the issuer for the payment of maturing notes. The interest portion may or may not be included. A revolving credit agreement is different from a LOC in that the former is a backup facility and has conditions attached to it prior to making an advance or draw. In a revolving credit agreement, the bank has a set of conditions that the issuer covenants to meet prior to any advances. Breach of, or violations against, these covenants could trigger an event of default that renders the credit agreement legally unavailable to be drawn upon. Certain events of default give the bank the right to deliver a *no issuance notice*, which would suspend continued issuance of the notes. The bank will issue such notice to limit its exposure under this scenario. Generally, CP notes issued prior to this notice (outstanding notes) are covered and therefore will be repaid under the credit agreement. On the other hand, there will be defined *events of default*, also known as *material adverse change clauses*, that would permit the bank to terminate its commitment immediately and hence, would no longer be obligated to fund loans to repay outstanding notes. The key here is to identify which events of default are credit related because those can be monitored. Covenant- or performance-related defaults are difficult, if not impossible, to monitor and therefore, should not be included as events of default triggering immediate termination.

In reviewing the events of default, the analyst must pay attention to the rights and remedies of the bank. The analyst should have a clear understanding under what circumstances draws are allowed pursuant to the credit agreement.

Other important terms of the agreement are the expiration date, when the bank can be substituted, when the bank can transfer its rights and obligations, and the means by which note holders are to be notified of the aforementioned changes.

ANALYZING COMMERCIAL PAPER WITHOUT ENHANCEMENT

CP notes without enhancement are obligations where repayment solely rests on the creditworthiness of the issuer and analysis is focused on the issuer's ability to access the market and its resources to provide liquidity, both internal and external. Note that successful rollover of the CP or issuance of long-term take out bonds are directly related to the credit quality of the security.

Evaluating unenhanced CP entails a two-step analytical process. First, the credit quality of the issuer must be assessed. Second, the issuer's liquidity strength must also be considered. Analyzing CP credit quality is identical to analyzing the credit quality of any long-term bond. High credit quality confers access to the capital markets and facilitates successful rollover of the CP. Similarly, if the CP is expected to ultimately be taken out by long-term bonds, the long-term rating of the bonds and the expectation that it will remain high quality makes the CP highly liquid. Hence, the short-term rating is directly related to the issuer's overall long-term credit rating (see Exhibit 60.1).

To determine credit quality, it is necessary to analyze the creditworthiness of the issuer including the strength of the pledged revenue. CPs can be general obligations of the issuer or backed by a specific revenue stream such as water and sewer fees, sales taxes, general student fees, and other sources, depending on the type of municipal issuer. When CP notes are backed by specific pledged revenues, they are typically subordinate to the long-term bonds. If so, it is important to check if there is a cap or limit to the issuance of senior bonds or an additional bonds test for senior bonds so that the security pledged on the CP notes is not weakened or diluted. Also, when subordinate to the long-term bonds, a covenant is typically made for the issuance of long-term senior bonds to retire the CP.

In terms of liquidity strength, municipal issuers, particularly state governments, retain a sufficient amount of cash and short-term investments to fund daily operational expenses. Although amounts may vary and at times can be substantial, it is likely that those are not at a level that will be sufficient to pay all outstanding CP in case of a failed rollover. One of the ways to address this risk is through the establishment of a liquidity covenant. For example, the issuer is obligated to keep a sufficient amount of high quality investments equal to the amount of CP outstanding, which can be liquidated if necessary. A good rule of thumb is to maintain high quality securities in an amount equal to 100% to 110% of the outstanding CP. While it would be a hard sell to convince an issuer to pledge these investments to the repayment of the notes, what is important is that these securities be unencumbered and remain free from any prior claims and therefore available for CP note repayment, if necessary. In addition, there should be a written liquidation plan in place. The plan should include the timing of funding requests, procedures for liquidation, and individuals responsible for these steps. Another way to assess liquidity is through the availability of a bank line of credit, also known as working capital facility. The line of credit is often made available for general operating purposes which include CP funding. Although highly conditional, the line can either supplement the issuer's own liquidity or can be an alternate source of liquidity. Usually, only the size and expiration date of the line of credit is disclosed in the CP offering memorandum. Hence, it is up to the analyst to ask questions and if necessary, review the underlying line of credit agreement. The analyst must also examine the issuer's cash needs and practices. What are its seasonal cash flow needs and at its low point, does it draw on the line? How often does the issuer borrow from the line of credit? What are the amounts of the draws and when are they repaid? By answering these questions, the analyst will be able to evaluate whether or not the issuer has the financial flexibility and capacity to pay the CP when it matures.

SUMMARY

CP is an alternative for issuers who seek to lower their borrowing costs by taking advantage of short-term interest rates. Issuers have the option to have their notes guaranteed, partially enhanced, or use their own resources to provide liquidity support for their notes. An issuer may also choose to use its own financial assets in combination with bank facilities to provide support to its notes. Not all CP notes are the same despite the high ratings assigned to it. In this chapter, we identified the various forms of credit backstops that analysts can rely on for repayment, and how to assess risks in cases where liquidity facilities are not as strong. We also discussed how to evaluate an issuer's creditworthiness and its correlation to the continued rollover of the CP and an issuer's ability to provide self-liquidity. In conclusion, CP is a widely used and effective tool for any investor who desires stability, quality and liquidity. Analysts who exercise due diligence and proper analysis can be assured that their investment capital is preserved.

CHAPTER 61

The Use of Letters of Credit in Connection with Municipal Securities

Todd P. Zerega, ESQ.
Reed Smith LLP

etters of credit (LOCs) are frequently used by issuers[1] of municipal securities to enhance the creditworthiness, and thus marketability, of municipal debt securities. LOCs are issued by banks or other financial institutions and typically evidence an obligation by the bank or financial institution to pay the principal and interest on a municipal security to the beneficiary of the LOC.[2] By using a LOC in connection with the issuance of their municipal securities, issuers seek to reduce their borrowing costs by increasing the creditworthiness and liquidity of their securities. Similarly, purchasers of municipal securities backed by a LOC are attracted to the increased creditworthiness of the security and the increased liquidity the LOC may provide in case of an event of default, exercise of a tender option or maturity of the security. This chapter will outline the basic mechanics of a LOC-backed municipal security (LOC-backed security) and review some of the considerations that an analyst for a potential investor should consider before investing in such a security.

---

[1] For purposes of this chapter, the term *issuers* of municipal securities will refer to both municipalities that issue the securities directly, as well as the underlying obligor on a municipal security where such security is issued by a conduit municipal entity.
[2] The beneficiary of a LOC is normally the trustee appointed under the trust indenture pursuant to which the securities are issued. The trustee will draw on the LOC for the benefit of the holders of the securities.

Note: This chapter is presented for informational purposes only and is not intended to constitute legal advice.

OVERVIEW OF LOCS

LOCs issued in the United States are generally governed by Article 5 of the Uniform Commercial Code (UCC) as it has been enacted in the various states. The UCC is a collection of model laws jointly published by the American Law Institute and the National Conference of Commissioners on Uniform State Laws.[3] Additionally, a LOC may be subject to the Uniform Customs and Practice for Documentary Credits (UCP). The UCP, which is published by the International Chamber of Commerce, is a set of rules "that apply to any documentary credit ("credit") (including, to the extent to which they may be applicable, any standby letter of credit) when the text of the credit expressly indicates that it is subject to these rules."[4] Therefore, an LOC whose terms incorporate the UCP will be subject to its rules. The official comment to section 5-116 of the UCC states that "letters of credit that incorporate the UCP or similar practice will still be subject to Article 5 in certain respects."[5] The official comment then continues by noting that: (1) the UCP would not override the nonvariable terms of Article 5; (2) both the UCC and UCP would apply if there was no conflict between the UCP provision and the UCC provision; and (3) the UCP provision would not be effective if it provides a term that excuses liability or limits remedies for failure to perform obligations within the meaning of U.C.C. 5-103(c).[6]

Parties to LOCs

There are generally three parties to a LOC. First, there is the issuer of the LOC (the "LOC Issuer"). A LOC issuer is typically a state or national bank. However, a nonbank may also issue a LOC.[7] Second, there is the issuer of the municipal security (the "Municipal Issuer"),[8] who requests the LOC Issuer to issue a LOC in connection with the issuance of its securities. The Municipal Issuer will be obligated to reimburse the LOC Issuer for any payment draws honored under the LOC. The reimbursement obligation is usually

---

[3] For more information, see www.nccusl.org.

[4] Article 1 of International Chamber of Commerce, Publication Number 600 (2007 Revision).

[5] Official Comment 3 to U.C.C. § 5-116. This Comment notes that New York takes a different position from the model Article 5 and provides that a letter of credit that incorporates the UCP is not governed in any respect by Article 5.

[6] Id.

[7] U.C.C. § 5-102(a)(9) defines an *issuer* as "a bank or other person that issues a letter of credit, but does not include an individual who makes an engagement for personal, family or household purposes."

[8] U.C.C. § 5-102(a)(2) refers to the person requesting the LOC Issuer to issue the LOC as the "applicant."

contained in an agreement, appropriately referred to as the reimbursement agreement, entered into between the Municipal Issuer and the LOC Issuer. The third party to the LOC is the beneficiary (the "LOC Beneficiary").[9] The LOC Issuer issues a LOC in favor of the LOC Beneficiary who is typically the trustee under the trust indenture (the "Indenture Trustee") pursuant to which the LOC-Backed Securities are being issued.

The Independence Principal

One of the key features of a LOC is that the rights and obligations under the LOC are generally considered to be completely independent from the rights and obligations contained in other contractual agreements among the parties that arise out of or underlie the LOC.[10] This is generally referred to as the "independence principal." The independence principal was codified in the 1995 revisions to Article 5 of the UCC.[11] The prefatory note to the 1995 revisions to Article 5 of the UCC states:

> Revised Article 5 clearly and forcefully states the independence of the letter of credit obligations from the underlying transactions that was unexpressed in, but was a fundamental predicate for, the original Article 5 (sections 5-103(d) and 5-108(f)). Certainty of payment, independent of other claims, setoffs or other causes of action, is a core element of the commercial utility of letters of credit.[12]

Application of this principal to LOC-Backed Securities results in the rights and obligations under the LOC generally being considered separate from the rights and obligations of the reimbursement agreement between the LOC Issuer and the Municipal Issuer. Therefore, any dispute that the LOC Issuer might have with the Municipal Issuer under the reimbursement agreement should not affect the rights of the LOC Beneficiary under the

---

[9] U.C.C. § 5-102(a)(3).

[10] For an informative discussion of the scope of the independence principal, see Gerald T. McLaughlin, "Exploring Boundries: A Legal and Structural Analysis of the Independence Principal of Letter of Credit Law," *Banking Law Journal* (June 2002), pp. 501–553.

[11] See, U.C.C. § 5-103(d) which provides that the "[r]ights and obligations of an issuer to a beneficiary or a nominated person under a letter of credit are independent of the existence, performance, or nonperformance of a contract or arrangement out of which the letter of credit arises or which underlies it, including contracts or arrangements between the issuer and the applicant and between the applicant and the beneficiary."

[12] Prefatory Note to 1995 revisions to Article 5 of the UCC as published by the National Conference of Commissioners on Uniform State Laws.

LOC. It should be noted, however, that the independence principal does not preclude the LOC Issuer from dishonoring a draw on a LOC due to fraud or forgery.[13]

The independence principal is important in analyzing the status of the LOC in a bankruptcy proceeding involving the Municipal Issuer. Generally, bankruptcy courts have respected the independence principal and have held that proceeds of a LOC are not property of the bankrupt's estate.[14] In *Zenith Laboratories v. Securities Pacific National Trust Co.*, an action involving a LOC supporting certain industrial revenue bonds, the bankruptcy court in dismissing a complaint filed by the debtor held that the "letter of credit and the proceeds therefrom are not property of the debtors' estate."[15] The court in *Zenith* cited the general law as to the nature of a LOC by citing a Fifth Circuit decision which stated that "[i]t is well established that a letter of credit and the proceeds therefrom are not property of the debtor's estate under 11 U.S.C. § 541."[16] However, there have been instances in which courts have declined to follow the independence principal or have found distinguishing factual circumstances.[17] Therefore, an analyst should be cognizant of, and may wish to consult with counsel on, the extent to which courts are honoring the independence principal and holding that the proceeds of a draw on a LOC are not part of the debtor's estate in the case of the bankruptcy of the Municipal Issuer.[18]

---

[13] U.C.C. § 5-109 and § 5-108(d).

[14] For an informative discussion on the general rule and court decisions that follow the general rule see, Brooke Wunnicke, Diane B. Wunnicke, and Paul S. Turner, "Insolvency," Chapter 9 in *Standby and Commercial Letters of Credit* (New York: Aspen, 2007).

[15] 104 B.R. 667, at 671 (D.N.J. 1989).

[16] Id. at 671, citing *Matter of Compton Corp.*, 831 F.2d 586 at 589 (5th Cir. 1988).

[17] See, *Wysko Investment Co. v. Great American Bank*, 131 B.R. 146 (D. Ariz. 1991) (court permitted the Bankruptcy Court to enjoin payment on letter of credit due to "unusual circumstances"); *In re Prime Motor Inns, Inc. v. First Fidelity Bank N.A. New Jersey*, 123 B.R. 104 (S.D. Fla. 1990) (court issued an order which restrained and enjoined the trustee from disbursing funds it received pursuant to a draw on a LOC).

[18] To the extent they are provided, preference opinions issued by legal counsel in connection with a LOC-Backed Security may also give the analyst guidance. Typically, they will opine that receipt of a draw under the LOC will not be a preference under 11 U.S.C. §§ 547 and 549 of the United States Bankruptcy Code in the event that a voluntary or involuntary petition is subsequently filed by or against the Municipal Issuer.

Types of LOCs

For purposes of reviewing LOCs in connection with the issuance of municipal securities, there are normally three types of LOCs with which a potential investor should be familiar. *Direct-Pay LOCs* typically give LOC Beneficiaries the most comfort from a credit prospective. A Direct-Pay LOC permits the LOC Beneficiary to draw upon the LOC for the payment of principal and interest on the LOC-Backed Securities upon the occurrence of certain events, such as the occurrence of an event of default, a tender draw, interest payment or upon the maturity of the securities. Under a Direct-Pay LOC, the beneficiary does not receive payment directly from the Municipal Issuer and there is no obligation on the part of the Indenture Trustee to first request payment from the Municipal Issuer. In contrast to a Direct-Pay LOC, a *Standby LOC* usually only enables the LOC Beneficiary to draw upon the LOC after the Municipal Issuer fails to pay principal and/or interest when due under the municipal securities. Therefore, under a Standby LOC, the Indenture Trustee will first seek payment from the Municipal Issuer and only if the Municipal Issuer is unable to pay does the Indenture Trustee draw upon the Standby LOC. The last type of LOC is generally referred to as a *Confirming LOC*. A Confirming LOC is a second LOC that is only drawn upon if a primary LOC Issuer fails to pay a draw request. Confirming LOCs may be issued by large national banks to "confirm" LOCs issued by smaller local banks.

CONSIDERATIONS IN REVIEWING A LOC-BACKED SECURITY[19]

When reviewing LOC-Backed Securities, analysts for potential purchasers need to carefully review and consider the LOC in connection with the trust indenture and other applicable offering documents. In reviewing the documentation, the analyst should ensure that the documents are consistent, work well operationally, and provide the Indenture Trustee with clear instructions on when to draw on the LOC and when to pay the proceeds to the holder of the securities. The following is a discussion of some additional points that an analyst should consider in reviewing a LOC-Backed Security.

An analyst should determine the type of LOC that is supporting the LOC-Backed Security. If the analyst wishes to rely on the creditworthiness

---

[19] The considerations are drawn from the author's experience in reviewing LOC-Backed Securities which have a variable interest rate, are subject to an optional tender provision in favor of the holder of the security and are supported by a Direct-Pay LOC. Other types of LOC-Backed Securities may involve additional or different considerations.

of the LOC Issuer to the maximum extent possible, then the analyst should ensure that the LOC is a Direct-Pay LOC. Conversely, if the analyst is comfortable with the creditworthiness of the Municipal Issuer or is merely seeking some additional credit support, then a Standby LOC may suffice. Lastly, if the security is backed by a LOC from a bank with which the analyst is not familiar, the analyst may want to request that the Municipal Issuer add a Confirming LOC from a larger national bank.

An analyst will be able to identify the type of LOC by the language in the trust indenture and the LOC. With regard to a Direct-Pay LOC, the trust indenture will direct the Indenture Trustee to draw upon the LOC for the payment of principal and interest, with the LOC Issuer's own funds, upon the occurrence of certain events such as monthly interest payments, the acceleration of the securities due to an event of default, or upon the tender, redemption or maturity of the securities. With regard to a Standby LOC, the Indenture Trustee will first be required to request payment from the Municipal Issuer. Lastly, it should be evident whether a security has a Confirming LOC because there will be two LOCs provided for review and described in the offering documentation.

An analyst should review the mechanics of when and how the Indenture Trustee is instructed to draw upon the LOC under both the indenture and the LOC. The LOC should clearly state the circumstances in which the Indenture Trustee can draw upon the LOC and will normally have attached different forms of draw requests to be presented by the Indenture Trustee to the LOC Issuer when making a draw request. For example, there may be different forms of draw certificates for a principal drawing due to the redemption, acceleration or maturity of the securities, a drawing for the purchase of the securities upon the tender of such securities, and a draw request for interest payments. The trust indenture will also detail when the Indenture Trustee should make a draw upon the LOC. An analyst that is reviewing a Direct-Pay LOC should ensure that the Indenture Trustee is both instructed and able to draw on the LOC whenever there is an event that triggers the payment of principal and/or interest under the indenture.

The analyst also needs to review the size of the LOC. The LOC will clearly state the maximum total amount that is permitted to be drawn upon under the LOC and will usually allocate the total amount among a portion that can be drawn upon for principal payments and a portion that can be drawn upon for interest payments. The portion allocated for interest payments will usually be stated both as a numerical amount and as the number of days of interest which the amount represents.[20] The analyst will then

---

[20] With regard to LOC-Backed Securities with a variable interest rate, the maximum amount of interest permitted under the offering documents is usually used to calculate the number of days' interest represented by the interest portion of the LOC.

need to work through a calculation to ensure that the size of the LOC is sufficient to cover the payment of principal and interest when required to be paid under the indenture.[21] Determining whether or not the LOC contains the proper amount of principal coverage should be relatively straightforward. The analyst should compare the principal amount of the securities to be issued under the indenture and compare that with the amount that is allocated to pay the principal of the securities under the LOC. The amounts should match.[22]

When determining whether or not the interest portion of the LOC is sufficient, the analyst should calculate the following: (1) the number of days between interest payments; (2) the number of days until the interest portion of the LOC is automatically reinstated;[23] and (3) the number of days that it would take to get paid under the LOC, pursuant to the acceleration of the securities (or pursuant to a mandatory tender or redemption), if a notice of nonreinstatement of the interest portion of the LOC were delivered by the LOC Issuer on the last day permitted under the LOC.[24]

By way of illustration, assume that the securities pay interest on a monthly basis, and the monthly interest is paid on the first business day of the following month. In this case, the analyst should assume the worst case scenario of a 31-day month with a three-day holiday weekend to start the following month. Therefore, the analyst should calculate 34 days of interest for the first prong of the calculation. Next, assume that under the LOC the LOC Issuer is entitled to give notice of nonreinstatement of the interest portion of the LOC for five days following an interest draw on the LOC. The

---

[21] If the security permits the payment of a premium in the event of the redemption of the security then the LOC should cover the amount of the premium in addition to the principal and interest coverage.

[22] However, if the indenture permits the issuance of additional principal amount of securities, then a provision would have to be made to increase the size of the LOC accordingly if such option were ever exercised.

[23] LOC Issuers typically have a period under the LOC in which they can deliver a notice of nonreinstatement of the interest portion of the LOC to the LOC Beneficiary following an interest draw on the LOC. An LOC Issuer would typically deliver such a notice if it was not getting reimbursed for the interest payment by the Municipal Issuer under the reimbursement agreement. If no notice is given by the LOC Issuer, then the interest portion of the LOC will usually be automatically reinstated at the end of the expiration of the notice period.

[24] For the specific methodology used by rating agencies to size the interest portion of a LOC, see, "Moody's Rating Methodology," *Moody's Rating Methodology for Letter of Credit Supported Transactions* (August 2005) p. 4; "Standard & Poor's Criteria & Methodologies," *Public Finance Criteria: LOC-Backed Municipal Debt* (October 2006); and Fitch Ratings, *Guidelines for Rating Direct-Pay LOC-Supported Debt* (February 2005) p. 2.

amount calculated under the second prong of the calculation would therefore be five days. Lastly, assume the following: (1) a nonreinstatement notice was delivered by the LOC Issuer on the last day permitted; (2) the delivery of the notice triggered an event of default under the indenture resulting in an immediate acceleration of the notes; (3) interest continues to accrue after an acceleration; and (4) the payment of the securities pursuant to a draw on the LOC must occur within three days following the acceleration of the securities. Under these assumptions, an additional three days of interest coverage should be required. Adding the three prongs of our example together, an analyst should consider requiring 42 days of interest coverage under the LOC.

Lastly, the analyst should consider the situations in which the LOC will expire and the consequences of such expiration. As a general matter, a LOC is irrevocable unless the LOC states that it is revocable.[25] However, situations under which the LOC may expire or terminate include the following: (1) the stated expiration date of the LOC[26]; (2) substitution of the LOC, if permitted under the indenture; and/or (3) acceleration of the securities due to an event of default, mandatory tender, or redemption due to the failure of the LOC Issuer to reinstate the interest portion of the LOC, due to the conversion of the securities to a interest rate mode which is not supported by the LOC, or due to a default under the reimbursement agreement due to the failure of the Municipal Issuer to reimburse the LOC Issuer for draws made under the LOC. Generally, the LOC will have a stated expiration date that may be well before the maturity of the securities. The LOC may also provide for one or more extensions of the expiration date, usually for a minimum of one year, upon notice to the LOC Beneficiary. The analyst should ensure that the indenture contains a mechanism, usually a mandatory tender or redemption, which will pay the LOC Beneficiary the necessary principal and interest pursuant to a draw on the LOC prior to the expiration of the LOC. Similarly, if the indenture permits the substitution of the LOC with another LOC, the analyst should ensure that the holders of the LOC-Backed Securities will receive sufficient advance notice of the substitution of the LOC so that the analyst is able to evaluate the issuer and terms of the new LOC.[27] If the analyst does not wish to have to monitor notices of substitute LOCs, then the analyst may insist that the delivery of an alternate LOC trigger a mandatory tender under the indenture and require that the existing LOC be drawn upon to fund the mandatory tender. Lastly, if an event of default,

---

[25] U.C.C. § 5-106(a).

[26] If the LOC has no stated expiration date, U.C.C. § 5-106(c) provides that the expiration date will be one year from the date of issuance.

[27] If the analyst is not satisfied with the new LOC issuer, then they may wish to exercise their optional tender rights, if applicable, and tender the securities prior to the effective date of the substitution.

mandatory tender, or mandatory redemption occurs under the indenture, either because the LOC Issuer has failed to reinstate the interest portion of the LOC, because the securities are converting to an interest rate mode that is not supported by the LOC, or because there is an event of default under the reimbursement agreement, the analyst should ensure that there is a provision for the Indenture Trustee to draw upon the LOC to pay the principal and interest in such a circumstance.

CONCLUSION

A Municipal Issuer may use a LOC in connection with the issuance of securities in order to enhance the creditworthiness, and thus marketability, of the securities. A potential purchaser of the LOC-Backed Security may be attracted to the enhanced creditworthiness and liquidity provided by the LOC. However, prior to purchasing a LOC-Backed Security, an analyst should consider the type of LOC (i.e., Direct Pay, Standby) that is supporting the security. Once the analyst determines the type of LOC, the analyst should consider whether or not the size of the LOC is sufficient, consider the circumstances under which the Indenture Trustee is instructed to draw on the LOC, and consider the circumstances under which the LOC may terminate and the consequences of such termination.

CHAPTER 62

How to Analyze Tax, Bond, and Grant Anticipation Notes

Sylvan G. Feldstein, Ph.D.
Director, Investment Department
Guardian Life Insurance Company of America

Frank J. Fabozzi, Ph.D., CFA, CPA
Professor in the Practice of Finance
School of Management
Yale University

Notes are temporary borrowings by states, local governments, and special jurisdictions to finance a variety of activities. Usually, notes are issued for a period of 12 months, though it is not uncommon for them to be issued for periods of as short as three months and for as long as three years. In this chapter the structure and credit risk factors of notes are discussed.

TWO MAJOR PURPOSES OF NOTES

There are two general purposes for which notes are issued. One is to even out cash flows. The second is to temporarily finance capital improvements. Each is explained in this section.

Evening Out Cash Flows

Many states, cities, towns, counties, and school districts, as well as special jurisdictions sometimes borrow temporarily in anticipation of the collection of taxes or other expected revenues. Their need to borrow occurs because, while payrolls, bills, and other commitments have to be paid starting at the beginning of the fiscal year, property taxes and other revenues such as intergovernmental grants are due and payable after the beginning of the fiscal year. These notes—identified either as *tax anticipation notes* (TANs), *revenue anticipation notes* (RANs), or *grant anticipation notes* (GANs)—are used to even out the cash flows which are necessitated by the irregular flows of income into the treasuries of the states and local units of government. In some instances, combination *tax and revenue anticipation notes* (TRANs) are issued, which usually are payable from two sources.

Temporarily Financing Capital Improvements

The second general purpose for which notes are issued is in anticipation of the sale of long-term bonds. Such notes are known as *bond anticipation notes* (BANs). There are three major reasons why capital improvements are initially financed with BANs.

First, because the initial cost estimates for a large construction project can vary from the construction bids actually submitted, and since better terms are sometimes obtained on a major construction project if the state or local government pays the various contractors as soon as the work begins, BANs are often used as the initial financing instrument. Once the capital improvement is completed, the bills paid, and the total costs determined, the BANs can be retired with the proceeds of a final bond sale.

Second, states and cities that have large, diverse, and ongoing capital construction programs will initially issue BANs, and later retire them with the proceeds of a single, long-term bond sale. In this instance, the use of BANs allows the issuer to consolidate various, unrelated financing needs into one bond sale.

The third reason why BANs are sometimes issued is related to market conditions. By temporarily financing capital improvements with BANs, the issuer has greater flexibility in determining the timing of its long-term bond sale and possibly avoiding unfavorable market conditions.

SECURITY BEHIND TAX AND REVENUE ANTICIPATION NOTES

Tax anticipation notes are generally secured by the taxes for which they were issued. For counties, cities, towns, and school districts, TANs are usually issued for expected property taxes. Some governmental units go so far as to establish escrow accounts for receiving the taxes and use the escrowed monies to pay note holders.

RANs and GANs are also usually, but not always, secured by the revenues for which they were issued. These revenues can include intergovernmental grants and aid as well as local taxes other than property taxes. In one extreme case, and as the result of the New York City financial crisis in 1975, RANs were issued by New York City for expected educational aid from the state of New York that provided for the note holder to go directly to the state comptroller and get the state aid monies before they were sent to the city's treasury, if that was necessary to remedy a default. Most RANs just require the issuer itself to use the expected monies to pay the note holders once they are in hand. Additionally, it must be noted that most TANs, RANs, and GANs issued by states, counties, cities, towns, and school districts are also secured by the general obligation pledge.

INFORMATION NEEDED BEFORE BUYING
TAX OR REVENUE ANTICIPATION NOTES

Before purchasing a TAN, RAN, or GAN, the analyst should obtain information in five areas in addition to what is required if long-term bonds are being considered for purchase. The five areas are:

1. Determining the reliability of the expected taxes and revenues.
2. The dependency of the note issuers on the expected monies.
3. The soundness of the issuers' budgetary operations.
4. The problems of "rollovers."
5. The historic and projected cash flows by month.

Each area is discussed next.

Determining the Reliability of the Expected Taxes and Revenues

If a TAN is issued in anticipation of property taxes, a question to ask is: What were the tax collection rates over the previous five years? Tax collection rates below 90% usually indicate serious tax collection problems. Additionally, if the issuer is budgeting 100% of the tax levy while collecting substantially less, serious problems can be expected.

If a RAN or GAN is issued in anticipation of state or federal grant monies, the first question to ask is if the grant has been legislatively authorized and committed by the state or federal government. Some RAN issuers, which included New York City prior to its RAN problems in 1975, would issue RANs without having all the anticipated grants committed by the higher levels of government. This practice may still be used by other local governments that are hard pressed to balance their budgets and obtain quick cash through the sale of RANs. A safeguard against this is to see if the issuer has in its possession a fully signed grant agreement prior to the RAN or GAN sale.

The Dependency of the Note Issuers on the Expected Monies

One measure of the credit worthiness of the TAN or RAN issuer is the degree of dependency of the issuer on the temporarily borrowed monies. As examples, some jurisdictions limit the amount of TANs that can be issued in anticipation of property taxes to a percentage of the prior year's levy that was actually collected. The state of New Jersey, which has one of the most fiscally conservative local government regulatory codes in the country, limits the annual sale of TANs and RANs by local governments to no more than 30% of the property taxes and various other revenues actually collected in the previous year. Many other states are more permissive and allow local governments to issue TANs and RANs as high as 75% to 100% of the monies previously collected or even expected to be received in the current fiscal year.

The Soundness of the Issuers' Budgetary Operations

Another critical element of the TAN or RAN issuer's credit worthiness concerns determining whether or not the issuer has an overall history of prudent and disciplined financial management. One way to do this is to determine how well the issuer, over the previous five fiscal years, has maintained end-of-year fund balances in the major operating funds.

The Problems of "Rollovers"

Key indications of fiscal problems are revealed when issuers either retire their TANs and RANs with the proceeds of new issues or issue TANs and RANs to be retired in a fiscal year following the one in which they were originally issued. Such practices, known as *rollovers*, are sometimes used by hard-pressed issuers to disguise chronic operating budget deficits. To leave no doubt as to the soundness of their budgetary operations, many states, local governments, and special jurisdictions have established, either by statute or by administrative policy, that all TANs and RANs issued in one fiscal year must be retired before the end of that fiscal year. While such a policy reduces the flexibility of the issuer to deal with unexpected emergencies that may occur, it does help provide protection to the note holders against TANs and RANs ever being used for hidden deficit financing.

It must be noted that in some circumstances RANs and GANs can be properly issued for periods greater than 12 months. RANs have been issued in anticipation of receiving the federal share of the costs of certain interstate highway construction projects. In this instance, the Federal Highway Administration had established a 36-month reimbursement schedule. Therefore, the RANs could be outstanding for a period greater than 12 months to match this federal payment schedule.

The Historic and Projected Cash Flows by Month

The last area for investigation by the analyst is the TAN or RAN issuer's cash flow history and projections. Initially, what is required here is a monthly accounting, going back over the previous fiscal year, which shows the beginning fund balances, revenues, expenditures, and end-of-month fund balances. In the analysis of this actual cash flow, the investor should determine how well the issuer has met its fiscal goals by maintaining at least a balanced budget and meeting all liabilities, including debt service payments.

Exhibit 62.1 is an actual monthly cash flow summary for the previous twelve months prior to the sale of $82 million in TANs by the Municipality of Anchorage in 2006.

The second cash flow table to review is the one on the projected monthly cash flows for the fiscal year in which the TANs or RANs were to be issued. Here, the investor should look to see if the issuer has included in the projections sufficient revenues to retire the TANs or RANs, and if the estimated revenue and expenditure amounts are realistic in light of the prior fiscal year's experience.

Table 62.2 is a projected monthly cash flow summary for the same TANs that were issued by the city of Anchorage, Alaska.

It should be noted that this approach toward rollovers is not universally shared. Some may think that the ability to refinance (rollover or renew) a maturing note has been regarded as a valuable backstop to notes of the revenue-anticipation type and that the evaluation of a note must therefore consider the availability of refinancing through market rollover. However, the New York City general obligation note crisis of 1975—which occurred largely because the use of the rollover mechanism had allowed the city to avoid retiring its notes and, instead, to annually increase its short-term debt until it had become unmanageable, has raised questions about this approach.

SUMMARY

While the credit analysis of notes has certain similarities to the analysis of long-term bonds, note analysis presents some additional challenges for the analyst. In the above discussion, the more important areas of concern are identified. They should be explored in detail for determining the degree of insulation from adversity of any particular note.

EXHIBIT 62.1 Municipality of Anchorage Actual General Funds (101–191) Cash Flow, 12 Months Ended 12/31/2005 (dollars in thousands)

	Jan-05	Feb-05	Mar-05	Apr-05	May-05	Jun-05	Jul-05	Aug-05	Sep-05	Oct-05	Nov-05	Dec-05	Year to Date
Beginning balance	$88,659	$50,665	$36,024	$0	$0	$0	$29,237	$23,029	$157,336	$140,996	$136,826	$138,101	
Receipts													
Property taxes	1,764	791	1,248	1,092	15,072	159,322	8,826	149,872	6,185	11,451	4,488	1,749	361,859
MUSA	0	0	0	0	309	12,559	0	0	426	0	0	11	13,305
H/M, rental vehicle, and tobacco taxes	2,172	-1,398	997	1,345	2,416	2,018	2,746	4,138	4,997	2,209	3,572	6,320	31,531
Building permit fees	377	513	549	667	541	717	371	494	365	344	362	512	5,813
State revenue share and safe cities	0	0	0	0	0	0	0	1,009	1,333	0	0	0	2,342
Other revenue	1,792	1,825	2,869	4,235	2,398	5,292	3,972	3,986	4,545	3,668	5,556	74,587	114,725
Contribution from MOA trust	0	0	0	0	0	0	0	0	0	0	4,000	2,600	6,600
IGCs to other funds	157	9,746	9,823	8,588	6,549	4,417	6,984	6,302	9,061	7,619	7,595	11,639	88,481
Receivables decrease (increase)	1,324	4,784	236	30	41	-50	-208	-13	223	20	115	-4,900	1,602
TAN proceeds	0	0	0	0	0	0	0	0	0	0	0	0	0
Borrowing from other funds	0	0	13,445	54,183	29,043	0	0	0	0	0	0	0	96,671
Total receipts	7,585	16,262	29,167	70,140	56,369	184,275	22,691	165,789	27,136	25,311	25,687	92,517	722,930

EXHIBIT 62.1   (Continued)

	Jan-05	Feb-05	Mar-05	Apr-05	May-05	Jun-05	Jul-05	Aug-05	Sep-05	Oct-05	Nov-05	Dec-05	Year to Date
Disbursements													
Salaries and benefits	10,392	13,179	13,120	19,611	13,096	13,304	13,504	13,459	20,783	13,378	15,216	10,975	170,017
Services and supplies	4,227	4,529	7,050	5,586	5,627	6,143	5,874	6,925	5,575	5,967	5,404	11,315	72,440
Transfers to ASD	27,334	0	27,334	27,334	27,334	27,334	0	0	0	0	0	27,526	166,196
Contributions to others	11	0	3,333	651	2,551	339	1,241	238	69	-396	36	1,287	9,359
Debt service	103	2,144	2,136	4,927	43	9,666	371	4,335	7,165	3,410	12	73,767	108,080
Payables (decrease) increase	2,049	349	-172	737	-37	1,379	363	-161	-202	-651	-4,143	-3,605	-4,095
TAN payment	0	0	0	0	0	0	0	0	0	0	0	0	0
IGCs from other funds	1,639	11,145	12,155	11,292	8,245	505	7,462	7,629	9,699	7,457	7,993	11,523	96,745
Repayments to other funds	0	0	0	0	0	96,671	0	0	0	0	0	0	96,671
Other	-176	-444	235	4	-489	-304	84	-942	387	316	-106	-911	-2,344
Total disbursements	45,579	30,903	65,191	70,140	56,369	155,038	28,899	31,483	43,476	29,481	24,412	133,879	714,849
Ending balance	50,665	36,024	0	0	0	29,237	23,029	157,336	140,996	136,826	138,101	96,739	

Source: Official Statement, Municipality of Anchorage, Alaska $82,000,000 2006 General Obligation Tax Anticipation Notes (February 15, 2006), p. 17.

EXHIBIT 62.2 Municipality of Anchorage Projected General Funds (101–191) Estimated Cash Flow, 12 Months Ended 12/31/2006 (dollars in thousands)

	Jan-06	Feb-06	Mar-06	Apr-06	May-06	Jun-06	Jul-06	Aug-06	Sep-06	Oct-06	Nov-06	Dec-06	Year to Date
Beginning balance	96,739	59,111	121,962	71,223	17,356	0	130,692	127,921	267,367	253,701	249,622	245,971	
Receipts													
Property taxes	1,769	791	1,254	1,091	30,061	159,511	12,236	149,853	6,236	11,606	4,473	1,757	380,639
MUSA	0	0	0	0	331	13,442	0	0	456	0	0	12	14,241
H/M, rental vehicle, and tobacco taxes	491	491	1,206	1,622	2,902	2,437	3,287	4,988	6,104	2,650	4,084	7,579	37,840
Building permit fees	405	541	579	712	584	762	409	533	400	376	386	565	6,253
State rev. Share and safe cities	2,496	0	0	0	0	0	0	0	0	0	0	0	2,496
Other revenue	4,581	1,611	4,154	5,866	2,956	5,950	4,055	10,035	6,383	3,942	6,859	2,743	59,134
Contribution from MOA trust	0	0	0	0	0	0	0	0	0	0	3,818	2,482	6,300
IGC's to other funds	170	10,539	10,622	9,287	7,082	4,776	7,553	6,815	9,798	8,239	8,213	12,585	95,678
Receivables decrease (increase)	0	0	0	0	0	0	0	0	0	0	0	0	0
TAN proceeds	0	81,422	0	0	0	0	0	0	0	0	0	0	81,422
Borrowing from other funds	0	0	0	0	0	0	0	0	0	0	0	0	0
Total receipts	9,911	95,395	17,815	18,577	43,916	186,879	27,539	172,223	29,377	26,812	27,833	27,724	684,003

EXHIBIT 62.2 (Continued)

	Jan-06	Feb-06	Mar-06	Apr-06	May-06	Jun-06	Jul-06	Aug-06	Sep-06	Oct-06	Nov-06	Dec-06	Year to Date
Disbursements													
Salaries and benefits	11,828	14,999	14,932	22,319	14,905	15,142	15,369	15,318	23,654	15,226	17,318	12,491	193,501
Services and supplies	4,381	4,694	7,306	5,789	5,831	6,366	6,087	7,177	5,777	6,184	5,600	11,727	76,919
Transfers to ASD	29,526	0	29,526	29,526	29,526	29,526	0	0	0	0	0	29,526	177,157
Contributions to others	9	0	2,864	559	2,192	292	726	204	60	0	31	1,106	8,044
Debt service	46	958	955	2,203	19	4,321	166	1,938	3,203	1,525	5	32,979	48,318
Payables (decrease) increase	0	0	0	0	0	0	0	0	0	0	0	0	0
TAN payment	0	0	0	0	0	0	0	0	0	0	0	81,422	81,422
IGC's from other funds	1,748	11,893	12,970	12,049	8,798	539	7,962	8,140	10,350	7,957	8,529	12,296	103,232
Repayments to other funds	0	0	0	0	0	0	0	0	0	0	0	0	0
Other	0	0	0	0	0	0	0	0	0	0	0	0	0
Total disbursements	47,539	32,544	68,554	72,445	61,272	56,187	30,310	32,778	43,043	30,891	31,484	181,547	688,594
Ending balance	59,111	121,962	71,223	17,356	0	130,692	12,7921	267,367	253,701	249,622	245,971	92,148	

Source: Official Statement, Municipality of Anchorage, Alaska $82,000,000 2006 General Obligation Tax Anticipation Notes (February 15, 2006), p. 19.

CHAPTER 63

How to Analyze Refunded Municipal Bonds

Sylvan G. Feldstein, Ph.D.
Director, Investment Department
Guardian Life Insurance Company of America

While originally issued as either general obligation or revenue bonds, municipals are sometimes refunded. A *refunding* usually occurs when the original bonds are escrowed or collateralized by either direct or indirect obligations or by those guaranteed by the U.S. government. Sometimes the escrows for the refunded bonds are allowed to hold lesser credit worthy investments.

The maturity schedules of the securities in the escrow fund are such so as to pay when due bond, coupon, and premium payments (if any) on the refunded bonds. Once this cash flow match is in place, the refunded bonds are no longer secured as either general obligation or revenue bonds. They now have a new security: the escrow fund and the securities that it contains. Such bonds, if escrowed with U.S. government securities, have little if any credit risk. They are the safest municipal bond investments available.

This chapter provides the analytical framework for determining the structure and credit quality of municipal bonds that have been refunded. Refunded bonds are discussed in terms of (1) the general structure of an escrow fund; (2) the reasons why bond issuers refund their bonds; (3) the two major types of refunded bonds; and (4) how the analyst or investor should determine the degree of insulation from adversity of an escrow fund and, thereby, the creditworthiness of the refunded bonds.

PURE VERSUS MIXED ESCROW FUNDS

An escrow fund is an irrevocable trust established by the original bond issuer usually with a commercial bank. Government securities are deposited in an escrow fund that will be used to pay debt service on the refunded bonds. A pure escrow fund is one in which the deposited securities are solely direct or guaranteed obligations of the U.S. government whereas a mixed escrow fund is one in which the deposited securities are not 100% direct or guaranteed U.S. government securities. Other securities that could be placed in mixed escrow funds include federal agency bonds, certificates of deposit from banks, other municipal bonds, and even annuity policies from insurance companies.

WHAT ARE THE REASONS FOR REFUNDINGS?

There are three reasons for refunding a bond issue. We discuss each in the following subsections.

Removing Restrictive Bond Covenants

Many refunded municipal bonds were originally issued as revenue bonds. Revenue bonds are usually secured by the fees and charges generated by the completed projects, such as toll roads, water and sewer systems, hospitals, airports, and power generating plants. The specific security provisions are promised by the bond issuer in the bond trust indenture before the bonds are sold. The trust indenture describes the flow-of-funds structure, the rate or user charge covenant, the additional-bonds test requirements, and other covenants. Many refundings occur because an issuer wants to eliminate restrictive bond covenants such as rate charge covenants, additional bonds tests, or mandatory program expenditures. A refunding eliminates, or defeases, the earlier covenants since the bonds are deemed to have been paid once they are refunded and cease to exist on the books of the issuing jurisdiction.

Changing the Debt Maturity Schedule

Some bonds are refunded in order to change the issuer's debt maturity schedule—either to make the yearly debt service payments more level or to stretch out the maturity schedule. By stretching out the maturity schedule the result can provide budgetary relief for the original issuer or to allow for additional borrowing. In any event it does not effect the credit quality of the properly escrowed refunded bonds.

Saving Money for the Bond Issuer

Still another reason for issuers to refund municipal bonds is to reduce their interest payment expenses. Typically, substantial interest cost savings can occur when interest rates decline approximately 200 to 300 basis points from the levels when the bonds were originally issued. By refunding the outstanding bonds with a new issue, the bond issuer in effect is refinancing the loan at a lower interest rate.

TWO TYPES OF REFUNDED BONDS

The escrow fund for a refunded municipal bond can be structured so that refunded bonds are to be called at the first possible date established in the original bond indenture. The call price usually includes a premium of from 1% to 3% above par. This type of structuring usually is used for those refundings that either reduce the issuer's interest payment expenses or change the debt maturity schedule.

While many refunded bonds are to be retired at the first callable date, some escrow funds are structured differently. In these refundings, the maturity schedules of the escrowed funds match the regular debt-service requirements on the refunded bonds as originally stated in the bond indenture. This type of structure usually is used when the objective is to defease any restrictive bond covenants. Thus bonds are known as being *escrowed to maturity* or EMTs.

It should be noted by the investor that refunded bonds can be called by the trustee before the first call date and prior to the stated maturity of the bond if there is a mandatory sinking fund provision in the original bond indenture. One example of this occurred in 1977. The state of Massachusetts refunded an issue of 9% general obligation bonds that had been issued in 1976 and were to mature on June 1, 2001. Under the 1977 refunding, the bonds—now fully secured with an escrow of U.S. government securities—were to be called on June 1, 1987 at 104%. However, under the original sinking fund provisions, each June 1 from 1978 to 1987 a preset portion of the still outstanding 9% bonds were to be called to fulfill the sinking fund requirement.

While this occurred a quarter century ago, a more recent related example occurred in January of 2007. The state of New Jersey refunded, with a new $3. 6 billion bond issue, tobacco settlement bonds that had been originally issued in 2003. The 2024 maturity of the refunded bonds that had a 6 1/8% coupon and known in the industry as *turbos*, are now to be called at par on June 1, 2012. The original 2003 bonds had certain assumptions about the flow of tobacco settlement revenues collected that could call the bonds prior to the stated maturity. In structuring the refunding, these assumptions were made a certainty. While the refunded bonds had a call at par on June 1, 2012, there were also now these earlier calls that worked somewhat like a mandatory sinking fund. The schedule is:

June 1, 2008	$7,400,000
June 1, 2009	$43,355,000
June 1, 2010	$47,540,000
June 1, 2011	$50,975,000
June 1, 2012	$6,000,000

Because of these earlier calls, the average life of the refunded bonds was reduced. While the credit quality of the bonds dramatically improved for the investor, going from a Moody's Baa3 (barely investment grade) to its premier #*Aaa* rating as a refunded bond, the value of the refunded bonds went down in the secondary market. The #Aaa is known as *Moody's hatch mark triple A*, its highest rating, because the bonds are secured by escrowed funds made up of direct U.S. government obligations unconditionally guaranteed by the U.S. government or the Resolution Funding Corporation. On January 29, 2007, a day before the refunding and with only the Baa3 rating the bonds were yielding approximately 4.552% and had a dollar price of 108.564. The next day after they were refunded and rerated #Aaa, the same bonds were priced to the worst, that is, to the average life of June 1, 2010 to yield 4.849% and had a lower dollar price of 106.875. So, as the result of this refunding, the value of the bonds went down.

DETERMINING THE SAFETY OF THE REFUNDED BONDS

Refunded municipal bonds, from a credit perspective, are generally the safest investments because they are the most insulated from adversity, provided that the escrow funds have only direct noncallable U.S. government securities, or those unconditionally guaranteed by the U.S. government (i.e., that they are pure escrows).

Specific questions for the investor to ask are:

1. Have sufficient monies been deposited in an irrevocable escrow fund at a commercial bank or state treasurer's office to pay the bondholder?
2. Has the bond issuer signed an escrow agreement naming the bank or state treasurer as the irrevocable trustee for the escrow fund?

3. Have certified public accountants reviewed the contents of the escrow fund to determine if it consists of noncallable either direct U.S. government obligations (U.S. Treasury notes, state and local government series, known as *slugs*) or obligations unconditionally guaranteed by the U.S. government? Examples of the latter would include: obligations of the Government National Mortgage Association (Ginnie Mae), obligations that have a Ginnie Mae guarantee, Farmers Home Administration (FmHA) Insured Notes, and Export-Import Bank obligations, among others.

4. Have the certified public accountants also certified that the cash flow from the escrow fund will provide sufficient revenue to pay the debt service as required in the refunding?

5. Has a qualified, nationally recognized attorney reviewed the complete transaction and given an opinion that no federal, state, or local laws have been violated, including arbitrage limitations in Section 103 of the Internal Revenue Code of 1954, as amended?

6. What size commercial bank is involved? Preferably a large bank that is well capitalized should be used so as to minimize the impact if an embezzlement of funds or other irregularity should ever occur.

7. Have all the sinking fund or unusual call features been defeased or are they still operating?

CHAPTER 64

Pollution Control Revenue, Industrial Development Revenue, and Conduit Financing Bonds

Gary M. Krellenstein
Managing Director
JPMorgan Securities

Pollution control revenue (PCR) bonds and industrial development revenue (IDR) bonds are the generic names for tax-exempt debt issued by municipal authorities to finance projects or facilities used by private corporations (e.g., investor-owned utilities, airlines, petrochemical companies). Between 1996 and 2006, over $90 billion in PCR/IDR bonds were sold. Of that amount, roughly half was issued on behalf of private utility companies. At the end of 2006, total PCR/IDR debt outstanding was estimated to be approximately $150 billion. Exhibit 64.1 shows the issuance by year and type from 1996 to 2006.

Although the distinction between PCR and IDR bonds has blurred in recent years, they were originally two distinct types of securities. PCR bonds were issued primarily on behalf of electric utilities and manufacturers to finance the construction and acquisition of pollution-control equipment. IDRs were usually issued as inducements for private companies to locate, utilize, and/or construct certain facilities that were expected to enhance local economic activity. Today, the terms are commonly used interchangeably[1] and the classification of a specific bond issue as a PCR or an IDR often depends on arbitrary distinctions such as the name of the issuing authority rather than the use of the bond's proceeds.

---

[1] PCR and IDR bonds are also referred to as industrial development authority (IDA) bonds, industrial development bonds (IDBs), and environmental facility control (EFC) bonds.

EXHIBIT 64.1   PCR/IDR Bond Issuance: Total Volume, 1996–2006

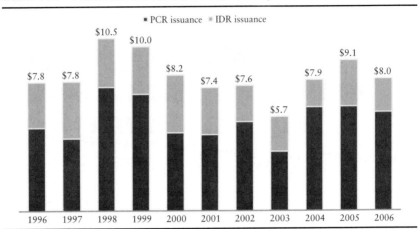

Source: Created from data from Thomson Financial.

PCR/IDR bonds can offer some of the best values in the tax-exempt market. As a result of their complex call features and hybrid nature (municipal bonds backed by a corporate credit), many investors in the tax-exempt market have undervalued these bonds. This is particularly true for small PCR/IDR issues that are secured by corporate entities that are not widely known by municipal market participants. These bonds typically yield more than comparable plain vanilla municipal bonds of similar credit quality and maturity, although they are also somewhat less liquid.

SECURITY

Security for PCR/IDR bonds is derived from the credit of the taxable entity on whose behalf they are issued, rather than the actual municipal issuer, which functions solely as a conduit to allow tax-exempt financing (the bonds do not constitute a lien on the municipal issuer.) Usually, the private entity pledges to make payments to the municipal issuing authority in amounts sufficient to meet all debt service obligations. The pledge is often structured as a note, lease or loan repayment agreement. (See Exhibit 64.2.)

Project Dependence

Most PCR/IDR issues are not directly secured by the operations of the specific project(s) being financed by their sale. Instead, the bonds represent an obligation of the entire corporation on whose behalf they are issued. The

EXHIBIT 64.2   Security Structure

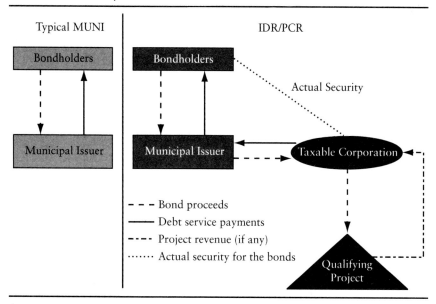

project name, which is often included in the bond's title, identifies the project being financed, and should not be confused with the source of security. Only in instances where the project being financed represents a significant portion of the underlying credit's assets and revenue sources is there a strong correlation between project operations and security on the bonds. For example, the Farmington, NM, Pollution Control Bonds, Series 1993—Four Corners Project, issued on behalf of Southern California Edison, are secured by a pledge of the utility to make payments sufficient to meet debt service on the bonds. Because of Southern California Edison's large size and asset base, the (potential) failure of the Four Corners coal-fired plant to operate successfully for a prolonged period would not materially impact the Company's ability to make debt payments on the bonds.

Collateralized versus Unsecured

Taxable corporations that have PCR/IDR debt issued on their behalf often issue both collateralized and unsecured bonds. Collateralized (secured) bonds have a mortgage lien against the underlying credit's properties and assets in addition to the company's legally binding pledge to make payments to the issuing authority sufficient to meet debt service requirements. Unsecured bonds (debentures) do not have a specific lien on the underlying company's properties and assets and are generally rated one notch lower than the collateralized bonds by Moody's and S&P (e.g., secured Al/A+ and unsecured A2/A).

Collateralized bonds' significant advantage over unsecured PCR/IDR debt is often inadequately reflected in the relative price and yields of secured and unsecured bonds. Under the Bankruptcy Code, holders of secured debt are supposed to be paid off in full before the next class of creditors (the debenture holders) receives any funds. In practice this is rarely the case due to "cramdowns" and other actions initiated by stockholders and unsecured creditors. Nonetheless, the collateralized bondholders are almost always accorded better treatment in bankruptcy reorganizations. This is particularly true for electric utilities, as was demonstrated in the bankruptcy case of PS New Hampshire.

RESTRICTIONS ON ISSUANCE AND REFUNDING OF PCR/IDR DEBT

New Money

The tax exemption for "new money" PCR bonds was essentially eliminated by the Tax Reform Act of 1986, although transition rules allowed several corporations, mostly electric utilities, to issue new money PCR bonds for projects that were already under construction. Issuance of IDR bonds was also significantly curtailed by the 1986 Act. Under the Act's Private-Activities provisions, tax-exempt IDR bonds may be issued on behalf of private companies (subject to the alternative minimum tax) only for a small number of specific activities, such as:

- Local furnishing of gas and electric service ("two county restriction")
- Water distribution systems
- Wastewater systems
- Small issue IDA bonds (less than $10 million)
- Airports, docks, and wharves[2]
- Solid waste[3]

The issuance of IDR bonds is also limited by a state volume cap (as seen in Exhibit 64.3). The Tax Reform Act of 1986 restricts the amount

---

[2] Under certain conditions, bonds issued for these purposes are not counted as part of the state volume cap.

[3] Several electric utilities have been able to finance a portion of their pollution-control equipment through the sale of new money IDR bonds. About 25% to 50% of the pollution-control equipment at coal-fired plants is used to handle solid wastes. This equipment qualifies for IDR financing under the solid waste private-activity provision.

of private-activity bonds that can be issued within any state based on population—$75 per person per state per year, with each state allocated an annual minimum of $263 million regardless of population. Since the cap also applies to non-IDR private activity issuers (i.e., certain types of housing and hospital bonds), only a portion of each state's volume cap is available for new money IDR bonds.

EXHIBIT 64.3 State Allocation of Private-Activity Bonds ($ millions)

State	2007 Cap	State	2007 Cap
Alabama	$391	Montana	$256
Alaska	$256	Nebraska	$256
Arizona	$524	Nevada	$256
Arkansas	$256	New Hampshire	$256
California	$3,099	New Jersey	$742
Colorado	$404	New Mexico	$256
Connecticut	$298	New York	$1,641
Delaware	$256	North Carolina	$753
District of Columbia	$256	North Dakota	$256
Florida	$1,538	Ohio	$976
Georgia	$796	Oklahoma	$304
Hawaii	$256	Oregon	$315
Idaho	$256	Pennsylvania	$1,057
Illinois	$1,091	Rhode Island	$256
Indiana	$537	South Carolina	$367
Iowa	$256	South Dakota	$256
Kansas	$256	Tennessee	$513
Kentucky	$358	Texas	$1,998
Louisiana	$364	Utah	$256
Maine	$256	Vermont	$256
Maryland	$477	Virginia	$650
Massachusetts	$547	Washington	$544
Michigan	$858	West Virginia	$256
Minnesota	$439	Wisconsin	$472
Mississippi	$256	Wyoming	$256
Missouri	$497	Montana	$256
		Total	$28,186

EXHIBIT 64.3   (Continued)

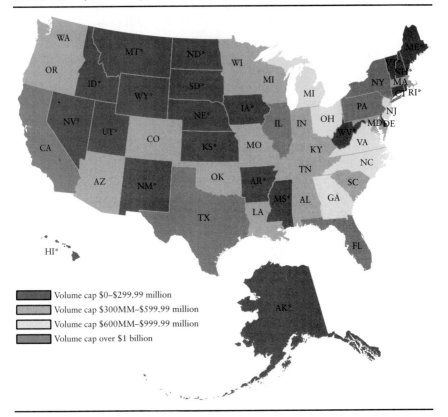

* Represents over a 3.1% change.

Refunding

The ability to advance refund PCR/IDR bonds was abolished in the early 1980s, although current refundings (the sale of a refunding bond issue within 90 days of the first call) remain a viable option. The majority of fixed rate PCR/IDR debt sold in 1993 consisted of current refundings issued to replace outstanding high-coupon bonds and the "remarketing" of variable rate bonds sold in previous years (current refundings and remarketings are not counted under the state volume cap allocations). Most of the current refunding and remarketing issues sold in recent years were not subject to the *alternative minimum tax* (AMT), with the determining factor being the original issuance date of the refunded or remarketed bonds. The refunding restrictions are summarized in the following table:

Advanced refundings	No longer allowed for PCR/IDB Bonds
Current refundings (refundings issue sold within 90 days of call)	Unrestricted except that bond maturity cannot exceed 120 percent of project life. Does not count as issuance under volume caps. Bonds sold to refund PCR/IDR bonds originally issued prior to the 1986 Tax Reform Act are not subject to the AMT provisions of the tax code

Several corporate obligors of PCR/IDR bonds, particularly large electric utilities, have used modified *optional dutch auction tenders* to retire high-coupon bonds prior to their first call date. The obligor notifies bondholders of its offer to purchase, at a premium price, outstanding bonds in the secondary market. Bondholders who accept the offered price tender (sell) their bonds to the obligor, allowing the bonds to be "retired." Concurrent with the tender, the obligor issues a new series of tax-exempt refunding bonds at current rates. However, because of the hefty premiums that often must be paid before bondholders are willing to accept the tender, this refunding technique has met with mixed results.

CALL FEATURES

Standard Calls

Fixed rate PCR/IDR debt is usually issued with 10-year call protection. It is also common for the bonds to have a mandatory sinking fund requirement, particularly on small nonutility-backed deals.

Extraordinary Calls

Virtually all PCR/IDR issues have an extraordinary call feature referred to as an "act of God" or "calamity" calls. This call provision allows the bonds to be redeemed at par on any date should the project(s) financed by the PCR/IDRs (1) be destroyed; (2) be confiscated by eminent domain; or (3) incur a loss of economic viability. Although the third provision—loss of economic viability—sounds like it would allow almost any PCR/IDR-financed project incurring difficulties to exercise an extraordinary par call, the legal requirements of that call feature are extremely difficult to meet. To date, Lehman Brothers' Municipal Research Department has been able to document only a small handful of PCR/IDR issues that were called via the "loss of economic viability" provisions.[4] Other extraordinary call features found on many PCR/IDR issues include loss of tax-exemption, transfer of project ownership, merger or sale of the corporate obligor, and calls from excess bond proceeds.

SUMMARY

PCR/IDR bonds offer private corporations an opportunity to issue tax-exempt debt on projects designed to benefit the communities they are located in. These bonds offer investors additional opportunities in the tax-exempt market and are some of the best values, due to many investors poor understanding of them. The most important point to keep in mind when evaluating PCR/IDR bonds is that you should not be focusing on the issuing authority, but on the credit of the corporation backing the deal. Additional factors to consider include call provisions, securitization, and tax implications (AMT versus non-AMT).

---

[4] For example, the Midland, Michigan, Series 1983 PCR bond issued on behalf of Dow Chemical. Called due to "loss of economic viability" when the equipment financed by the bonds-pollution-control equipment at a (no longer operating) Dow-owned power station was taken out of service, fully depreciated and demolished by the company.

CHAPTER 65

How to Analyze FHA-Insured Mortgage Hospital Bonds

Sylvan G. Feldstein, Ph.D.
Director, Investment Department
Guardian Life Insurance Company of America

Administered jointly with its partner, the Department of Health and Human Services, the Department of Housing and Urban Development's Federal Housing Administration (FHA) hospital mortgage insurance program was enacted in 1968 under Section 242 of the National Housing Act and permits FHA to insure (FHA insurance) mortgages used to finance the construction, rehabilitation or replacement of hospitals. As of May 2007, the Section 242 program has allowed FHA to insure more than 350 mortgages, many of which were funded from the proceeds of tax-exempt revenue bonds (Bonds). As a result of the FHA mortgage loan insurance, Bond financings of this type have received the benefits of AA/AAA investment ratings. The New York Presbyterian Hospital, Montefiore Medical Center, the University of New Mexico, and the Medical University Hospital Authority of the Medical University of South Carolina are examples.

The Section 242 insurance program has experienced only a modest number of defaults and insurance claims since 1968, and as of May 2007, only two in the past 12 years. This chapter describes the security features provided by this program and outlines the questions the analyst should consider when determining the creditworthiness of tax-exempt revenue bonds when collateralized by FHA-insured mortgages. It should be noted that these security structures themselves are complex, and this short chapter covers only the general areas that should be addressed by the credit analyst. The

The author wishes to thank Michael E. Mazer and Roderick D. Owens, partners at the law firm Krooth & Altman LLP of Washington, D.C. and Joseph Spiak for their assistance.

analyst should carefully review the indenture and any offering statements and discuss each aspect of the transaction with the underwriter.

FHA HOSPITAL MORTGAGE INSURANCE

FHA insurance under the Section 242 Program does not insure the bonds or timely payment on the bonds. It insures the mortgage loan only. However, the FHA-insured mortgage bond structure is designed to demonstrate that either debt service on the mortgage, or the proceeds of the FHA insurance in the event of a mortgage default, together with other funds held under the bond trust indenture (the "indenture"), will be sufficient to assure that the principal and interest due on the bonds will be timely paid.

FHA insurance contains both a principal component and an interest component. With regard to the principal component, FHA insurance is paid in the amount of 99% of the unpaid principal balance of the mortgage at the time of default. Additionally, FHA insurance includes accrued mortgage interest from the date of default through the date that the assignment of the mortgage loan and all related loan/assignment documents are required to be submitted to FHA. Because FHA determines the date of default as the date of the first missed mortgage payment, interest for the month preceding the date of default is not included in the FHA insurance settlement. As a result, a loss of one month's interest can be expected in the case of an insurance settlement, as well as 1% of mortgage principal (together, the "Assignment Fee"). Further, the interest component of the FHA insurance benefits is calculated at the applicable FHA debenture rate (as opposed to the interest rate in effect in the note) in effect on the date that the mortgage is insured by FHA and may be higher or lower than the rate on the Bonds.

FHA-insured hospital mortgage revenue bonds are *structured financings*, and as noted above, are designed to assure that if timely payments are made on the FHA-insured mortgage, those payments, together with other funds held under the Indenture, will be sufficient to pay bond debt service. If there is a mortgage loan default, these financings are structured so that FHA insurance, together with other funds held under the Indenture, will be sufficient pay bond debt service (in the case of a debenture payout) or redeem bonds (in the case of a cash payout). Other indentured funds may include cash, letters of credit or other collateral with ratings comparable to those on the bonds necessary to cover the assignment fee, and other possible payment shortfalls demonstrated by the related bond cash flow schedules.

Once a hospital fails to pay the mortgage debt service, the indenture should require the bond trustee, in its capacity as FHA lender, to file a claim for FHA insurance benefits. (The trustee for the bonds in Section 242 transactions is, with few exceptions, the FHA lender of record. In some cases, the bond issuer has served as the FHA lender, as in the case of the Dormitory Authority of the State of New York.) In turn, federal regulations provide that FHA has the option to pay benefits in federal debentures, in cash, or in a combination of cash and debentures. Debentures are 20-year interest-only federal obligations maturing 20 years from the issuance with interest paid semiannually. They are also redeemable at par plus interest by the U.S. Treasury on any January 1 and July 1 payment date.

Because the timing of the payment of an FHA insurance claim cannot be predicted with accuracy, FHA has advised the national rating agencies that in the case of bond financed transactions it would use every effort to pay a claim within six months of a completed filing. To assure that there will be sufficient funds to make bond payments until an insurance settlement, the rating agencies require that the Bonds include a fully funded 12-month debt service reserve fund in order to provide comfort that bond interest and maturing principal will be paid while the insurance claim is being processed. Funds remaining in the debt service reserve fund after settlement will be used to redeem additional bonds.

Recently, FHA has agreed prior to the closing of a Section 242 Mortgage loan to pay an insurance claim in cash and not in debentures. This "cash lock" arrangement permits shorter maturity term bonds and the issuance of more serial bonds than would otherwise be possible if an insurance claim were paid in debentures. In any event, the FHA mortgage interest rate will be set at a level to assure that mortgage payments will be sufficient to assure the payment of bond interest and maturing principal. It is typical in the current market to find a triple-A rated monoline insurer "wrapping" these forms of FHA-insured mortgage collateralized revenue bonds, adds an additional layer of protection to the bondholder and eliminates the risk of a delay or unanticipated shortfall in the FHA insurance settlement.

CREDIT RISK

Several features of the FHA hospital mortgage insurance program could, if not properly collateralized, present impediments to the timely payment of Bond debt service if there is a mortgage payment default. These potential problems result because of the following factors:

1. FHA insurance covers only 99% of the outstanding principal balance of the mortgage, rather than the bonds, when the mortgage payment default occurs and will not include the 30 days' interest accruing on the FHA mortgage prior to the date of default (i.e., the assignment fee).

2. At FHA's option, the claim may be paid in 20-year, interest bearing debentures, not cash, unless FHA has agreed otherwise at the time of the loan closing.
3. Unless agreed to prior to the mortgage closing, FHA is not required to pay an insurance claim, whether cash or debentures, within a specific time period, and debt service on the bonds could become due before an insurance settlement is finalized. As noted above, a debt service reserve fund is required by the rating agencies to offset this potential risk.
4. Should the bond trustee, as FHA lender, fail to properly process the FHA insurance claim or otherwise fail to comply with governing FHA regulations, the insurance settlement may be insufficient to fully redeem the bonds. The quality and experience of the bond trustee should be evaluated.
5. When transactions of this type are wrapped by a monoline insurance company, the potential concerns expressed above are significantly mitigated.
6. Risks to bondholders that are unrelated to the structured nature of Section 242 collateralized bond financings are typically disclosed in the related official statements and should be carefully reviewed by the credit analyst as well.

Of course, the security features described above are in addition to the traditional security features of the conventional hospital revenue bond, including prepayment restrictions. Notwithstanding the foregoing, a credit analyst may consider the possibility of bonds being redeemed as a result of an unanticipated mortgage default, and as such may consider determining the range and quality of health care provided, (i.e., primary, secondary, and tertiary), whether the hospital is a startup or ongoing facility, the historical and projected annual hospital occupancy rates, the degree of dependency of patient day revenues derived from Medicare and Medicaid, and the hospital's operating ratio among other ratios and financial health indicators.

It should be noted that hospitals participating in the Section 242 program may be of lower credit quality than monoline insured or other hospital projects. In some instances, the size of the new debt financings have caused rating agencies to downgrade facilities. As a result the FHA 242 program is viewed as a means of accessing competitive financing rates. It should be noted that many hospitals, especially ones constructing major replacement projects or projects whose feasibility is dependent on future operating results, often finance out of the Section 242 program once they have gained their operating footing. Even so, the analyst should still determine if the hospital is of at least barebones investment quality (i.e., it has the basic financial viability and cash flow to pay debt service).

THE "PRUDENT MAN" EVALUATION APPROACH

While FHA mortgage insurance does not, by itself, provide complete back-up security to bondholders, it does (when properly supplemented by special debt and reserve fund structures) provide a high degree of safety, particularly when wrapped by national bond insurance companies. For any particular hospital revenue bond that has FHA mortgage insurance, the analyst should be concerned about the following:

1. To collateralize the assignment fee (i.e., 1% principal and one-month's loss of interest) the bond structure should have a reserve fund (often referred to as a *collateral account* or *mortgage reserve account*), that contains cash, letters of credit, or surety bonds at least equal to the amount by which the outstanding bonds exceeds the sum of all amounts on deposit in the various bond funds plus 1% of the principal balance of the FHA-insured note and one month's interest.

2. The debt service reserve fund should contain an amount at least equal to maximum annual debt service on the bonds. If repurchase agreements (repos) are used, they must be overcollateralized with direct or indirect U.S. government guaranteed securities; evaluated periodically with prompt makeup provisions and remedies given to the trustee; and provided by well-capitalized credit worthy financial institutions.

3. The structure of the bond issue is especially important if FHA retains the option to pay insurance claim in debentures, which as noted above mature 20 years after the date of issuance. Should a mortgage default occur when less than 20 years of bond maturity remain, or any intermediate maturity is due, the debenture interest received should be shown to be sufficient to provide for all scheduled bond principal and interest payments. On the other hand, should a mortgage default occur when more than 20 years remain for ultimate bond maturity, the semiannual debenture interest and maturing principal (due 20 years after the date of the default) should be able to provide for bond principal and interest requirements. This is usually accomplished by setting the mortgage interest rate sufficiently above the rate on the bonds so that the bonds are amortized faster than the mortgage loan because of the fact that cash flow from note payments will provide for sinking fund redemptions of bonds. This structure reduces the risk that the FHA insurance benefits, which are based on the outstanding balance of the note, will be insufficient to redeem the bonds outstanding because asset parity between the FHA insurance and the Bonds will be assured. This structure, along with the debt service reserve fund (which also contains the collateral account), should provide strong assurance of timely bond

repayments. The cash flow schedules reviewed by the rating agencies and others including municipal bond insurers in connection with the bonds should provide comfort on the quality of the cash flow proofs.

4. Since HUD could redeem debentures for cash prior to their stated 20-year maturities, the projected cash flows must demonstrate the ability to retire the outstanding bonds in case of early debenture redemptions.

5. Because of the possible need to be utilized to assure bond debt service, the investments in the collateral account and debt service reserve funds must be of high quality and be liquid. Additionally, the investments must be controlled by the trustee.

SUMMARY

Conceptually, the FHA-insured mortgage hospital bonds program can provide a high degree of security to the bond investor. It is a little more complicated than most other revenue bonds with federal and cash flow timing considerations involved. Learning the actual detailed structure of the deal is critical. The answers to the issues discussed in this chapter will aid the credit analyst in assessing the creditworthiness of an FHA-insured mortgage hospital bond.

CHAPTER 66

How to Analyze Higher Education Bonds

Bradley D. Mincke
Vice President–Senior Fixed Income Analyst
Van Kampen Investments

Higher education bonds are issued by public and private colleges and universities for the construction or renovation of academic buildings, student housing, recreational facilities, libraries, student unions, administrative buildings, and to purchase land. The bonds can be secured by a general obligation of the institution, specific student fees, or the revenues of a particular project. The schools range in size from less than 1,000 students to several hundred thousand students for a state university system. Credit ratings vary in quality from nonrated to triple A. Degrees and programs offered differ from a single focus mission to comprehensive academic programs. Providing access to quality education with pressure to limit tuition increases and produce favorable financial performance is the challenge of every college and university, regardless of size, reputation or credit rating.

In evaluating the credit quality of higher education institutions and their ability to repay debt, it is necessary to understand the school's mission, governance, degrees and programs offered, student demand, enrollment, revenue sources, fundraising abilities, and debt management. It is important to use a broad spectrum of financial and demand ratios. Ratio analysis provides a means of determining how well an institution is performing relative to itself over time and in comparison to other institutions that are similar in nature. How a college or university compares with sector medians provides a framework for credit analysis but institutional trends play an essential role as well.

The following discussion will present the key elements to analyze the credit quality, long-term viability, and vulnerability of higher education institutions.

THE INSTITUTION

With over 4,200 colleges and universities in the United States, students have many options and it is important to understand the institution and the environment in which it operates. Therefore, knowing the history and mission of the institution, its market niche, competition, as well as the location and size of the campus, the physical plant, and unique challenges, are critical in assessing the creditworthiness of a given institution.

The history of an institution can play a vital role in its long-term viability. An institution with a long history means that not only has it stood the test of time but also that it has built a sizeable alumni base from which it can draw upon for fundraising. For public universities with a long history, some comfort can be drawn from the annual state funding support. A review of funding fluctuations during economic down cycles will indicate the state's commitment to its higher education program. For private colleges and universities, a history of sufficient student demand and student-generated revenues to cover rising expenses can add to an institution's likelihood of survival going forward. An institution with a relatively short history, on the other hand, faces more challenges and uncertainty of survival concerning student demand and its ability to weather the down years with a weaker balance sheet.

In general, colleges that successfully define a distinct market niche that is attractive to students are most likely to achieve prolonged financial health. It is particularly critical for small, private colleges to focus on a specific area or areas in order to set the institution apart from other schools. Colleges and universities with religious affiliations tend to create their own market niche with the students from the religious organization. This can be either a positive or negative factor in determining student demand and will be influenced by the size of the religious organization, the trend in membership, and how pronounced the affiliation is with the school. An extremely strong affiliation could keep some students from applying.

Knowing an institution's competition will help in determining the school's creditworthiness as it relates to enrollment and financial flexibility. Key competitors are generally selected based on acceptance criteria, data regarding cross applications, location, and/or availability of majors. Knowing the tuition, room and board, and student fees of the competing institutions will indicate the level of flexibility a school has to increase its own student charges. The amount of financial flexibility of an institution is particularly important when a school has the need to increase its debt burden but is already at its optimal student body size or cannot increase its enrollment given land constraints. The location of the competing schools will also indicate the geographic draw of the schools. Schools in close proximity to one another will likely indicate a regional draw for enrollment while diverse national locations could likely mean a more favorable national draw. Schools with regional geographic draws are considered more vulnerable because they are susceptible to changes in demographic and economic changes for a smaller, less diverse area.

The size of the campus and available property to expand can influence the school's ability to grow enrollment in the future. Multiple campuses can also add to the success of an institution if these sites are located in higher population growth areas or are more convenient for nontraditional students taking evening or graduate courses. The condition of the physical plant could have a direct impact on future debt needs if there are deferred maintenance issues, particularly if it is unable to raise sufficient funds through a capital campaign drive. An institution with an above average age of plant will eventually need to either raise the cash or issue debt. Whether or not the school has the financial flexibility to handle the additional debt could be critical to its long-term viability.

What to Look For

An analyst should concentrate on determining what sets an institution apart from other schools. A market niche that is of interest to students will likely result in favorable student demand. Next, knowing how the institution compares with competing schools regarding cost, degrees offered, and amenities, will be factors in assessing revenue flexibility and ability to attract students.

USE OF BOND PROCEEDS

Identifying the purpose of a bond issue is important in understanding the priorities of the administration in carrying out its mission. Whether the bond proceeds will be additional debt of the institution or used to refund outstanding bonds will have an impact on many financial ratios. If the purpose of the bonds is to replace or enhance the capital base, student demand could be positively impacted. Replacing or renovating outdated student housing, or constructing educational facilities to allow for the expansion or addition of degrees or programs offered, could also lead to increased student demand.

Construction Risk

If the bond proceeds will be used to build new facilities, construction risk factors must be assessed. These include the experience of the architect, contractor, and construction manager. How much experience does each of the players have and has the institution used this team before and what were the results? Does this project involve any unusual or complicated design factors or materials that could delay the completion date? How tight is the construction schedule? How close does the projected completion date come to the beginning of classes in the fall? If construction is not completed for the start of classes, what contingency plans are in place? A guaranteed maximum price contract from the contractor will protect the college or university from cost overruns and is highly desired.

Bond proceeds that are used to construct projects that are self-supporting, such as student housing that is expected to pay debt service from room and board charges along with the general obligation pledge of the college or university, will have less of an impact on the school's debt burden. This debt, however, should be included in the debt burden analysis given the institution's GO pledge.

SECURITY

Source of Payment for the Bonds

Most higher education bonds issued for the construction and/or renovation of educational buildings, faculty offices, student centers, student housing, athletic facilities, libraries, and infrastructure are a general obligation of the institution, secured by a revenue pledge. In general, the pledged revenues consist of student charges (tuition, room and board, and student fees), grants and contracts, as well as any state support. Some bonds that are issued for specific facilities, such as student housing, are secured solely by that facility's revenue stream. In the case of student housing, the pledged revenues would be room and board charges. Assessing the creditworthiness of student housing bonds involves many of the same criteria as bonds with a broader revenue pledge but will focus more on the type of housing (dormitory, suite or apartment style) and the acceptance by students. Other factors include the age of the student housing stock, housing options (both off campus and on-campus if only select student housing revenues are pledged), historical occupancy levels, breakeven occupancy, room and board rates compared to the off-campus options, and whether the institution implements any policy requiring freshmen to live on-campus. Another example of a narrower revenue pledge is student activity fees for athletic facilities or student unions.

Mortgage Pledge

The assignment of any interests in real mortgaged property may be pledged as additional security. The entire university campus, including property and buildings, can be pledged or just specific properties. A mortgage lien pledge is particularly important in lower rated credits.

Rate Covenant

Colleges and universities generally covenant to maintain tuition, fees, rentals, and other charges, together with the general funds or other legally available moneys, at a level sufficient to pay all obligations when they become due. The debt service coverage ratio for a given period of time, usually the fiscal year-end, is typically used as the rate covenant test. A common rate covenant would be defined as pledged revenues sufficient to pay all operating expenses of the college and cover annual debt service of all parity bonds by 110%.

Additional Bonds Test

The additional bonds test is a financial test that must be satisfied before more bonds secured by the same assets can be issued. A typical additional bonds test would require that net income available for debt service for the fiscal year immediately preceding the incurrence of additional bonds must be sufficient to pay an amount not less than 120% of the combined maximum annual debt service for the currently outstanding long-term bonds and the debt to be incurred. The test is usually historical or historical and projected, but can be based solely on projections, which is the weakest test.

Debt Service Reserve Fund

The debt service reserve fund is available to pay principal and interest on the bonds if revenues are insufficient. The debt service reserve fund constitutes a margin of safety and as a protection against default. The debt service reserve fund requirement is typically the lesser of (1) 10% of the principal amount of bonds; (2) 100% of maximum annual debt service of the bonds; or (3) 125% of the average annual debt service on the bonds. It is highly preferred to have the debt service reserve fund fully funded at the time of bond issuance rather than when the rate covenant falls below a specified level.

What to Look For

An analyst should concentrate on ensuring the security pledge is appropriate for the level of risk. A small, private college with weak student demand, slim liquidity, and/or above average debt burden, is likely to require a general obligation of the college, gross revenue pledge, mortgage lien on all real property, a fully funded debt service reserve, an above average rate covenant, and a more restrictive additional bonds test. A large, state flagship university, however, may be able to issue debt with fewer security pledges and less restrictive covenants.

DEGREES AND PROGRAMS

An institution's academic programs play an important role in student demand. Small colleges with a narrow market niche could be negatively impacted if that degree falls out of favor with students or employers. Senior management and the board of trustees for public and private institutions of all sizes must be flexible and willing to adapt its academic programs to the changing demands of applicants and the marketplace. A study of the history of degrees and programs offered will provide some insight into the school's governance.

STUDENT DEMAND

Student demand is a critical factor in assessing the creditworthiness of an institution. The main factors of demand for higher education are demographic growth of high school graduates, the college participation rate, the economic benefit of obtaining a college degree, and the cost comparison of the various colleges and universities. Application and enrollment trends should be assessed according to state and national averages. Depending on the school's geographic draw, future demographic trends and the projected growth in the number of high school graduates will directly impact future demand. According to a study conducted by the Western Interstate Commission on Higher Education, the projected number of students graduating from high school will peak at 3.2 million in the 2008–2009 school year, then remain relatively stable until 2017–2018. The study shows, however, that growth will vary by region with the South and the West projected to experience the greatest growth with the Northeast and the Midwest regions projected to decline. The states with the highest increase in high school graduates will be Arizona, California, Colorado, Florida, Georgia, New Jersey, Nevada, North Carolina, Texas, and Utah. The states with the greatest decline in high school graduates will be Iowa, Louisiana, Maine, Minnesota, North Dakota, South Dakota, Vermont, West Virginia, Wisconsin, and Wyoming. In all, the number of high school graduates are projected to increase in about 20 states and decline in 30 states.

Applications

Applications have been trending upward at many institutions due to favorable demographics but also partially due to the ease of online application at a moderate cost. Students are applying to more institutions than ever before. Despite this fact, the number of freshmen applications still indicates the demand for an institution.

Selectivity Ratio

The selectivity ratio, or acceptance rate, is the percentage of applications that are accepted by an institution. The desired trend of this ratio is downward. The lower the selectivity ratio, the more selective an institution is in accepting students for admittance and the more flexibility a school has to increase enrollment in the future, if and when applications decline. Conversely, the higher the selectivity ratio, the lower the student demand, the less the enrollment flexibility and the greater the pressure is on a school to maintain or increase applications in order to keep enrollment stable.

Matriculation Ratio

The matriculation ratio is the percentage of accepted students that actually enroll. The desired trend of this ratio is upward. A higher matriculation ratio indicates a school of first choice among its applicants.

Student Quality

The initial quality of entering freshmen, typically stated in terms of an average SAT or ACT score, primarily reflects the quality of the students attracted to an institution of higher education. Its attractiveness to high school graduates is also impacted by the college-age population in the state, region, or nation given the school's geographic draw. The trend in student quality combined with the trend in selectivity is a strong indicator of student demand for an institution.

Another measure of student quality is the position of entering freshmen in their high school class. Grade point averages or the percentage of freshmen that rank in the top quartile of their high school graduating class are indications of student quality. A school's student quality should be compared with mean scores for freshmen nationwide, its competition, and itself.

Enrollment

Enrollment is the one factor that drives revenues and expenditures. The ability to attract sufficient qualified applicants to achieve enrollment goals and have adequate cushion to weather declines in applications is critical to an institution's survival. Enrollment trends fluctuate over time for the various segments: undergraduate, graduate, and professional levels. These changes can be caused by many factors including demographic shifts, economic swings, and changes in college enrollment rates.

According to the National Center for Education Statistics, overall college enrollment is expected to increase by 15% to 20% from 2002 to 2014. Undergraduate enrollment is projected to go up 16%; graduate enrollment by 22%, and professional degrees by 32%. The Center expects private college enrollment to increase 17% and public colleges by 19%. Full-time student enrollment is projected to increase by 20% and part-time by 14%.

Headcount and Full-Time Equivalency

There are several ways to count enrollment. Headcount enrollment is the measure of how many individual students are actually enrolled and attending classes. Headcount enrollment is usually stated in fall enrollment to allow for national comparisons with other colleges and universities. Each student is counted equally regardless of the number of courses taken. *Full-time equivalent* (FTE) enrollment is based on the number of full-time students and a full-time equivalency of the part-time students. The methodology involves taking the total number of credit hours divided by the number of credits hours considered to be full-time. A college will typically have an undergraduate FTE and a graduate FTE due to different credit hours for a full-time student. State legislatures typically use FTE enrollment for state funding of public universities.

Factors Affecting Enrollment

Both headcount and full-time equivalent enrollment are directly impacted by other factors. Actual enrollment can vary from planned enrollment due to a matriculation that is higher or lower than projected. If a college projects that 40% of those students admitted will actually enroll, but 55% decide to enroll, then the college could be faced with housing and classroom capacity issues and it may not receive state funding for the additional students. Retention rate, which is the percentage of students who reenroll the following term, is another factor impacting enrollment. As retention rates increase, enrollments will increase with more students taking classes and more credit hours of instructional effort.

Changes in the economy can also impact enrollment levels. A decline in the economy can reduce state funding for public colleges and universities, shift some students from attending private colleges to public colleges and universities due to cost, make college attendance unobtainable for some, or influence students to stay in school to obtain another degree due to a poor job market.

Demographics play a critical role in college enrollment. Between academic years 2002–2003 and 2015–2016, the National Center for Education Statistics projects the number of high school graduates will increase 5.5% nationally. The increases are expected to impact both public and private higher education institutions but will vary by region. The West and South regions are projected to see increases of 13.8% and 9.6%, respectively. The Midwest and Northeast regions, on the other hand, are expected to see decreases of 3.5% and 1.1%, respectively. Individual states within the Midwest and Northeast regions, however, are expected to see strong increases just as some states within the West and South regions will likely experience declines in high school graduates. Therefore, a college's student demand going forward will be influenced by its geographic draw.

Student Profile

The mix of undergraduate, graduate and graduate-professional students at a school plays a role in an institution's dynamics. Graduate programs are generally more profitable than undergraduate programs because there is far less tuition discounting. Many employers will pay an employee's tuition for graduate studies, which decreases the need to reduce tuition costs to students. For this reason, a college with solid and reputable graduate programs, is typically more stable than a school that provides only undergraduate degrees and programs.

Enrollment versus Capacity

A comparison of current enrollment and current capacity will indicate the amount of flexibility a school has to increase enrollment and revenues without incurring significant debt for plant expansion. A school that is at or near capacity has fewer options to increase its revenues than a school with cushion to increase enrollment.

Key Data and Ratios

The key data ratios to be analyzed are:

- Headcount enrollment
- Full-time equivalent enrollment
- Applications

- Acceptances
- Selectivity ratio
- Matriculation ratio
- Average SAT score
- Undergraduate percentage
- Net tuition per student
- Retention rate
- Total tuition discount

What to Look For

An analyst should concentrate on how selective an institution is and the trend over time, while studying enrollment levels. A rising selectivity ratio, weakening student quality of incoming freshmen, and an increasing tuition discount rate are all warning signs, particularly if these actions only result in flat enrollment levels.

MANAGEMENT AND GOVERNANCE

The strength and experience of a college's senior management and its board of directors are a critical credit factor. Decisions involving the mission of the school, the degrees and programs offered, debt, tuition and fees, plant, institutional financial aid, expenses, and faculty salaries and benefits, each play an important role in an institution's success. As a result, it is important to analyze senior management and the board of trustees and understand their level of experience and roles. The number of years that senior management has with the school and a review of financial performance during their tenure will reveal their ability to produce positive results and respond to challenges. The level of experience of the board of trustees and their length of service at the college or university will indicate the ability of the institution to attract and retain quality governance. Several new key members on the senior management team could indicate that change was needed to improve performance or a new direction for the school is desired, which could take several years before their abilities are proven or the turnaround occurs.

The questions to ask regarding management are:

- Is senior management and the board of trustees long-tenured?
- Is there a well-defined strategic plan?
- Does it have disciplined budgeting practices?
- Does it have a solid track record of break even or positive operating performance?

■ Does management understand its competition; that is, does it track where the students that are accepted but do not matriculate, end up enrolling?

FACULTY AND STAFF

Labor Relations

Faculty and staff at colleges and universities are provided with an extensive range of employee benefits, including health care insurance, dental plans, long-term disability coverage, group life insurance, and retirement plans. The fair and equitable treatment of faculty members is important to an institution's success. The faculty turnover rate indicates an institution's ability to retain experienced faculty members.

Faculty

The faculty profile will indicate an institution's ability or choice to attract experienced professionals, the makeup of the faculty (full-time versus part-time; tenured versus nontenured), and the ability to retain faculty. An above average percentage of part-time and nontenured track faculty is viewed by students and parents as weaker quality, but to investors and governance it is viewed as allowing more financial flexibility if expenses ever need to be reduced.

Key Data and Ratios

The key data and ratios to be analyzed are:

■ Number of full-time tenure track faculty
■ Number of part-time faculty
■ Percent of tenure-track faculty that are tenured
■ Percent of faculty with a Ph.D. or other terminal degree
■ Faculty turnover rate

Pension Plans

Colleges and universities provide retirement benefits for its academic, administrative, and support staff. An understanding of the employee pension benefits, including the type of plan, the benefit obligation, fair value of plan assets, assumptions used (discount rate, expected rate of return), and asset allocation, is necessary in order to assess total long-term liabilities.

TUITION AND FINANCIAL AID

Tuition and Fees

Reviewing a school's tuition and fees over a period of time will reveal its ability and willingness to raise rates and the impact of those increases on student demand when other factors are included in the analysis, such as the number of applications, selectivity and student quality. A comparison of an institution's tuition and fees structure with colleges and universities considered to be competitors will indicate the amount of financial flexibility of an institution. A college or university whose tuition and fees are already at the upper end of the competitive group will have limited flexibility to increase its student charges in order to increase revenue. Conversely, an institution with tuition and fees that are below or near the median for the competitive group, will have more flexibility to increase its rates in the future.

The impact of the economy on tuition can be significant. A downturn in the economy, however, typically affects pubic and private schools differently. Private colleges find it more difficult to implement tuition increases because of actual or perceived declines in wealth levels and the fact that private colleges are already more expensive than public institutions. Public colleges and universities, on the other hand, are often forced to raise tuition to compensate for stagnant or reduced state funding during weak economic cycles.

Financial Aid

Students may be awarded financial aid based on merit, need or a combination of both. Funds for student financial aid come from governmental programs, foundations, individuals, and the college or university itself. Aid is awarded in two forms: (1) grants and scholarships that do not need to be repaid and (2) self-help aid that usually consists of student loans and campus employment. College funded financial aid awards are generally the largest source of financial aid for college students. Institutionally funded financial aid provides access to higher education for many needy students and encourages some students who are unable or unwilling to pay the generally higher cost of private colleges and universities. Tuition discounting allows some students to pay less than the full tuition. The amount of an institution's tuition discount is the difference between gross tuition revenue and net tuition revenue. The tuition discount rate is this difference divided by gross tuition revenue. When an institution's tuition discount rate increases to the point that net tuition revenue is declining year over year, this is a warning sign that the school is having difficulty maintaining student demand and enrollment.

Loan programs supported by the federal government are also a significant source of student financial aid funds. Under current federal guidelines for the Stafford Loan program all U.S. citizens or eligible noncitizens who are identified as dependent may borrow up to $23,000 in pursuit of an undergraduate degree. Independent students may borrow up to $46,000. These loans may be subsidized or unsubsidized depending on the financial need of the student. Additionally, parents of undergraduate students may borrow up to the full cost of education (less any financial aid) under the Parent Loan for Undergraduate Students (PLUS) program. Loans under these programs do not appear on the college's financial statements.

FINANCIAL STATEMENTS

There are three basic statements contained in the financial statement section of the *comprehensive annual financial report* (CAFR) for an institution of higher education: balance sheet, income statement, and cash flow statement. The financial statements allow analysts to assess the college's ability to repay indebtedness in a timely manner. In addition to reviewing each of these statements, you should always read the entire footnotes section. There is sometimes very important and revealing information reported.

Balance Sheet

The balance sheet highlights the financial condition of an institution at a single point in time. It tells you whether the college or university has enough money to fund its own growth or if it is going to need to issue additional debt in order to continue operations. While cash flow and income statements record performance over a period of time, the balance sheet is a snapshot at that particular point in time. The balance sheet describes what is owned and what is owed by an institution on a given date. The balance sheet lists all of the assets in addition to the portion of these assets that are financed by debt. Net assets are broken down into unrestricted, temporarily restricted, and permanently restricted.

During periods of strong demographics, with increasing high school graduates and rising college participation rates, it is sometimes necessary to expand and/or improve facilities in order to accommodate student demand. These facilities can be funded with internal funds or through the issuance of debt. It is important, however, for an institution to issue only the debt that it can handle when this cycle ends and enrollment returns to more normal levels. A capital improvement plan is a long-range plan of approximately five years that details a college's capital projects, the timetable of the projects, and its financing options. If this information is not provided in the official statement, it should be obtained from management.

Off-Balance Sheet Financing

Student demand for quality housing has increased along with the trend of apartment-style living. Privatized student housing has grown since the mid-1990s as many schools have chosen to finance these facilities off-balance sheet without exhausting the debt capacity of the school. This allows institutions to focus their efforts on using debt for educational facilities. Although this debt is off-balance sheet, if there is a strong link between a housing project and its sponsoring institution, it should be included as a direct or indirect obligation of the institution. Criteria that would warrant including off-balance sheet debt in an institution's total leverage would include debt that carries the full or contingent guaranty of the school; the school has granted an occupancy guaranty; the school has contracted to pay operating expenses; the school manages the project as one of its own on-campus student housing facilities; and if the project is essential to the institution.

Key Balance Sheet Ratios

The key balance sheet ratios are:

- Debt burden ratio: debt service divided by total expenditures
- Leverage ratio: unrestricted and temporarily restricted net assets divided by debt outstanding
- Liquidity ratio: cash and investments to operating expenses
- Expendable financial resources to debt
- Expendable financial resources to operating expenses
- Endowment to debt

What to Look For

An analyst should first concentrate on the current assets, such as cash and cash equivalents, accounts receivable, and short-term investments, because it is from current assets that ongoing, day-to-day operations are paid. Long-term investments will indicate an institution's ability to raise funds through capital campaigns and investment income.

The next thing you should look at is the amount of current liabilities. Colleges usually convert some of its current assets into cash to pay off its current liabilities. Compare the amount of current assets to current liabilities.

Next, review the debt burden. The overall long term debt of an institution commonly includes debt that is on its balance sheet as well as off-balance sheet debt that is issued by another entity for a facility that is important to the mission of the school. Debt burden, also known as debt burden ratio, is calculated by dividing the maximum annual debt service of the total outstanding debt by total expenditures. The debt burden of an institution should be compared relative to itself over time and to the median for similar colleges and universities.

Income Statement

The income statement details income that was generated or received, and all expenses that were incurred during the fiscal year. The difference between revenue received and expenses incurred is the net income or net loss of the institution. For colleges and universities, the income statement reveals the institution's reliance on state funding, student charges, research grants, or private gifts. Some of these revenue sources are under the control of the institution while others are in the hands of other governments, institutions or individuals.

Revenue Sources

Most private colleges and universities obtain a majority of their revenues from three sources: student charges (tuition, fees, and auxiliary enterprises, including room and board and parking), private gifts and grants, and investment income. Student charges are generated by the institution's ability to attract and retain students who are able to pay the tuition rate. Private gifts come from the college's ability to complete successful fundraising campaigns. Grant revenue comes from research monies from the federal government, foundations or institutions. Investment income is derived from the university's accumulated financial resources, primarily endowments.

Most public colleges and universities are dependent on state support through annual appropriations of the state legislature for operating and capital needs. This support is vulnerable to changes in the state's funding priorities and the general economy. Rebounds in state support typically lag the economy by a year. Public colleges are less dependent on private gifts, investment income, and student charges than private institutions. Student charges are still a critical revenue source, however, as tuition rates are typically increased when the state support does not keep up with the increase in expenditures.

Externally generated research dollars can be a sizeable portion of overall revenues for some institutions. The stability of these revenues can vary greatly and should be evaluated. Patient care revenue from a university hospital can be significant for many universities. Health care revenues are vulnerable to changes in reimbursement rates and can dramatically impact a higher education institution's financial performance and ultimately credit rating.

Other revenue sources include auxiliary enterprises, which are usually comprised of room-and-board charges for university-owned student housing; and net assets released from restrictions. These are typically endowment funds that were temporarily restricted by donors that have met their requirements and are being used for operations or financial aid.

Expenditures

The income statement also provides insight into how effectively management is able to control expenses. A comparison of the year-over-year percentage change in total operating expenses versus the year-over-year percentage change in total operating revenue is a good starting point. Salaries and benefits are the largest expense items for most colleges and universities. The faculty profile, as discussed earlier, will affect an institution's ability to reduce their salary expense when a school needs to cut expenditures. Similar to revenue sources, auxiliary enterprise expenses relate to operating student housing and hospital operation expenses relate to a university hospital.

Factors Affecting Financial Performance

Economic downturns can challenge both private and public institutions. Private colleges are impacted in the areas of tuition revenue, investment performance and private gifts. Declines in wealth and income levels may impact tuition revenue with students needing to shift from attending private colleges to public institutions due to cost as well as impact fundraising with declines in private giving. Public institutions are affected by strained state budgets, which can lead to cutbacks in state operating and capital funding. Tuition increases are generally necessary to compensate for declines in state support. Investment performance will likely decrease during times of weak financial markets for both private and public institutions.

Key Ratios

The key ratios to analyze are summarized in the following subsections.

Debt Service Coverage Ratio   The debt service coverage ratio is a widely used benchmark that measures a college's ability to pay its debt. The debt service coverage ratio is the amount of cash flow available to meet annual principal and interest payments. A debt service coverage ratio of less than one would mean negative cash flow. A debt service coverage ratio of 0.9 times would mean that net operating income was only sufficient to cover 90% of annual debt service payments. Nonrecurring or extraordinary revenues or expenses are excluded from the calculation of net operating income. A more conservative test of this ratio uses maximum annual debt service in place of the current year's debt service to calculate coverage.

Tuition and Auxiliary Dependency   Tuition and auxiliary dependency measures the reliance on student charges (tuition, fees, and student housing revenue) as a percent of total revenue.

Operating Margin   The operating margin tells you the profitability of the college or university as well as the success of the school's pricing strategy and operating efficiency. Operating margin is calculated by dividing net operating income by total operating revenue. Nonrecurring cash flows are excluded from the calculation.

Net Tuition per FTE Student   Indicates the tuition pricing power of a college, after deducting institutional financial aid, on a per pupil basis for easy comparison to national medians for similar schools, competing colleges and universities and itself.

What to Look For

An analyst should concentrate on trends over time when looking at the income statement. Focus on the various revenue sources and assess their vulnerability historically and their stability during swings in the economy. Next, assess management's ability to control expenditures compared to the growth in revenues.

Cash Flow Statement

The cash flow statement shows how cash made its way from the income statement to the balance sheet. This statement is similar to the income statement in that it records a school's performance over a specified period of time. The difference between the two is that the income statement also takes into account some noncash accounting items such as depreciation. The cash flow statement strips away all of this and tells how much actual money the school generated. It also shows how management has performed in managing inflows and outflows of cash and provides a sharper picture of a school's ability to pay its bills and to finance growth.

What to Look For

Although the cash flow statement is comprised of operating activities, investing activities, and financing activities, an analyst should concentrate on operating activities because it follows the cash from the college's operations. The bottom line is the net cash provided by operating activities, or the true cash profit or loss.

ENDOWMENT FUNDS

Endowment funds are derived primarily from fundraising and investment performance. Fundraising programs seek gifts from donors, including individuals, foundations, and corporations. A strong endowment can provide long-term financial strength and allows a college to attract and support top students, retain the best faculty, and support academic programs. A school with a long history and large alumni base has a distinct advantage in raising funds. Fundraising campaigns are undertaken to meet various capital needs, provide additional endowment funds, and funds for operational support. Donors can specify gifts as permanently restricted, temporarily restricted or unrestricted. Endowment investments that are permanently restricted by its donors require that the principal be invested in perpetuity and only the interest income be utilized. Temporarily restricted gifts require the principal to be held until certain conditions are met, such as a specified period of time has expired or the total endowment has reached a set amount. Unrestricted gifts are available for use by the college or university as it determines.

Colleges and universities spend a percentage of its endowment each year, known as the *endowment spending rate*. Institutions should have an endowment spending policy. The rating agencies set an endowment spending limit that, when exceeded, results in downward adjustments to the income statement and its financial ratios. The opposite is also true. When schools spend less than the spending rate, upward adjustments are made to the income statement. For example, if the rating agency endowment spending limit is 5% of a five-year rolling average of the endowment's market value, but an institution spent 7% of its endowment in order to attract students and pay operating expenses, then the amount of revenue from institutional financial aid on the income statement would be reduced to the 5% limit.

Private college and universities are more dependent on gifts and investment income to support operations than public institutions. As a result, the financial markets directly impact the market values of endowment funds. Additionally, fundraising is more difficult during periods of declines in the stock market and economy as people feel less wealthy due to decreased net worth.

One liquidity test for colleges compares the market value of a school's endowment with its outstanding debt.

What to Look For

An analyst should first concentrate on the ability of the school to increase its endowment. Look at the trend in endowment funds over time. Next, compare the endowment to other schools. Endowment per student is commonly used to compare schools of different sizes. An analyst also needs to determine if the endowment funds are managed internally or by outside fund managers as well as the asset allocation model being used. This details how the endowment is invested as a percentage of equity investments, fixed income investments, and alternative assets (hedge funds, real assets, private equity). The overall risk for a given level of expected return should be assessed. If the investments include participation in some of the more complex derivative products, senior management should understand the specifics of the investments and be able to explain them to investors. If it cannot, it probably should not be involved in the investment.

PLANT AND FACILITIES

Facilities wear out over time and require improvements to satisfy student and faculty needs. It is important to measure the financial resources a school has devoted to maintaining its physical plant and the outstanding deferred maintenance that will likely be a future liability.

The *age of plant ratio* is commonly used to determine the amount of deferred maintenance. The calculation is accumulated depreciation divided by depreciation expense. Accumulated depreciation is found on the balance sheet and depreciation expense is found on the statement of cash flows. This ratio is useful in comparison to sector medians for similar institutions and the institution's trend.

The capacity of the current plant, stated as the number of students the existing were designed to handle, when compared to current enrollment will indicate revenue flexibility, assuming favorable student demand ratios.

What to Look For

An analyst should concentrate on the condition and capacity of the plant. An age of plant over 10 years is an indication of deferred maintenance, which could mean additional long-term debt in the future. Next, you need to determine how much additional debt the college can handle before a rating downgrade could occur.

FUNDRAISING ABILITIES

Gift revenue from fundraising campaigns can be an important revenue source for private colleges and universities. Fundraising proceeds can be used to construct or renovate facilities or added to an endowment fund, a portion of which can be used annually to fund institutional financial aid to students. A comparison of a school's three-year average gift revenue to similarly rated schools will indicate an institution's ability to raise support and reduce its dependence on debt. Fundraising can be influenced by many factors including the economy, the purpose of the campaign, the size of alumni, and the frequency of the campaigns. Changes in the economy can impact fundraising when a campaign is underway. The actual amount of money collected can be significantly less than was originally committed when a downturn in the economy occurs during a fundraising campaign. Additionally, when affected by economic down cycles, fundraising performance typically trails the financial markets by one or two years.

DEFINITIONS OF CERTAIN TERMS

Each official statement will have a definition of certain terms section. It is recommended to review the list of words and read the definitions. Many times, commonly used words in the industry that appear on this list have different meanings than the industry standard.

CONTINUING DISCLOSURE

Disclosure of material information by the higher education institution to investors is necessary and needs to be included in the documents and enforced. This reporting primarily falls into the two categories of annual reporting and material events. In the case of higher-risk, lower-rated credits, semiannual or quarterly reporting may be warranted.

Annual Reporting

- Audited annual financial statements contain the balance sheet, income statement and statement of cash flows.

- Student enrollment data details the number of undergraduate and graduate students by headcount and full-time equivalent enrollment.
- Applications, acceptances and enrollment of first-year students allows the calculation of selectivity and matriculation ratio, which help in assessing student demand.
- Academic profile of new first-year students indicates student quality of the entering freshmen class by SAT/ACT scores and high school class ranking.
- Geographic distribution of entering first-year students will indicate whether the school has a regional or national draw.
- Student retention rate tells the percentage of freshmen that enroll for their sophomore year.
- Tuition and fees will show the annual percentage increases and the ability to compare rates with its competition.
- Endowment funds indicate the school's ability to raise funds through capital campaigns and investing.
- Fund drives detail any current capital campaigns underway with the goals, status, and how the school plans to use the proceeds detailed.

Material Events

- Principal and interest payment delinquencies must be disclosed to investors immediately in order to bring about a solution.
- Nonpayment related defaults include the violation of the rate covenant, which typically triggers bringing in a consultant to resolve the problem.
- Unscheduled draws on debt service reserves, which would indicate financial difficulties.
- Unscheduled draws on credit enhancements reflecting financial difficulties.
- The substitution of credit or liquidity providers, or their failure to perform as this impacts the security of the bonds.
- Adverse tax opinions or events affecting the tax-exempt status of the bonds impact liquidity of the bonds and pricing evaluations.
- Release, substitution, or sale of property securing repayment of the bonds directly impacts the security and value of the bonds.
- Rating changes by the rating agencies impact pricing evaluations and liquidity and must be disclosed.

CONCLUSION

The wide range in credit quality of the higher education sector creates the need to analyze, compare, and understand the institution before investing.

Of all the factors to consider, student demand and tuition pricing power are the most important as they will strongly influence financial performance. Senior management's strength and experience is critical as well as it will impact managing the operating, investing, and financing activities. Historically, the higher education sector has been relatively stable which creates opportunity but analysts need to understand the risks and challenges that affect student demand, financial performance, credit ratings, and price evaluations.

CHAPTER 67

Analyzing Human Service Provider Bonds

Ruben Selles
Director, Head of Municipal Risk
CIFG

Over the last several decades many of the social and human services that had been the responsibility of state and local governments have been assumed by private providers. A movement toward deinstitutionalization has resulted in a shift in the care for people with mental or developmental disabilities. Many large, governmentally run institutions have been closed down and replaced with small community-based providers that provide educational, vocational, and residential services. As this trend continues the capital needs of these private providers will be met in large part by the public capital markets and for the not-for-profit operators this means the tax-exempt bond market.

The definition of *human service providers* (HSPs) has been expanded so that it now includes private providers of care and services to people with mental or developmental disabilities, those with drug and alcohol dependencies, and those in prison. The broadest definition includes providers of services to the unemployed, day care for children and the elderly, and a wide range of family services.[1] Although there are some similarities among these providers, there are significant differences that make a common analytical approach to evaluate the creditworthiness of these providers difficult to develop.

The focus of this chapter will be on those providers that specialize on people with mental and developmental disabilities. This segment of the human service provider sector is one of the most evolved in terms of gov-

---

[1] Kirsten A. Grønbjerg, "The U.S. Nonprofit Human Service Sector: A Creeping Revolution," *Nonprofit and Voluntary Sector Quarterly* (June 2001), pp. 276–297.

ernmental support and acceptance by the capital markets. The State of New York is also an area of focus because it has developed strong legal, regulatory, and funding support for this sector. Investors in the human service provider sector should look for similar legal and regulatory backing as those provided in New York.

MILESTONES IN THE DEVELOPMENT OF HUMAN SERVICE PROVIDERS

Community Mental Health Act of 1963

In 1963, President John F. Kennedy signed the Community Mental Health Act, which had the goal of creating a network of community mental health centers in which services would be provided outside of an institutional setting.[2] The programs created by the act were severally underfunded and had little impact on significant portions of the disabled. Although the act was not completely successful, it did clearly establish deinstitutionalization as the preferred approach to providing care and services to the targeted population.

Willowbrook

Built in the 1930s, the Willowbrook State School was located in Staten Island, New York to provide services to and house the developmentally disabled and mentally retarded.[3] By the mid-1960s, the school, which was built to hold 4,000 people, contained over 6,000 patients. In November 1971, the local newspaper, *Staten Island Advance*, began reporting on the appalling conditions at the school. In early 1972, Geraldo Rivera, then a reporter for the local ABC television affiliate, exposed the conditions at the school to the wider New York and national audience. The parents of some of the children began legal action against the State. The plaintiffs were eventually deemed a class. In 1975, the State of New York entered into a consent degree in which it agreed that among other things that the developmentally disabled would be provided services in the least restrictive environment. The State also agreed that it would provide full education services to those less than 21 years of age. For those over 21, the state would provide six hours of daily training.

[2] Steven Sharfstein, "Whatever Happened to Community Mental Health?" *Psychiatric Services* (May 2000), pp. 616–620

[3] James Kaser (ed.), *A Guide to Willowbrook State School*, CSI Library (last updated in February 2006).

New York State Office of Mental Retardation and Developmental Disabilities Program

In order to fully comply with the Willowbrook Consent Degree, the State of New York restructured the Department of Mental Hygiene and created the New York State Office of Mental Retardation and Developmental Disabilities Program (OMRDD). The stated mission of the OMRDD is as follows:

- To develop a comprehensive, integrated system of services which has as its primary purpose the promotion and attainment of independence, inclusion, individuality and productivity for persons with mental retardation and developmental disabilities;
- To serve the full range of needs of person with mental retardation and developmental disabilities by expanding the number and types of community based services and developing new methods of service delivery; and
- To improve the equity, effectiveness and efficiency of services for persons with mental retardation and developmental disabilities by serving persons in the community as well as those in developmental centers, and by establishing accountability for carrying out the policies of the state with regard to such persons; and
- To develop programs to further the prevention and early detection of mental retardation and developmental disabilities.[4]

In order to meet its statutory mandate, the OMRDD contracts with not-for-profit human service providers. Since 1980 the number of community beds has increased from 9,000 to approximately 36,000 in 2005. The OMRDD has a 2007–2008 operating budget of over $3.5 billion.

Developments in Other States

Minnesota

At the same time that New York was addressing the issues that were raised by Willowbrook, other states were experiencing similar controversies. In 1972, six Minnesota institutions that housed the mentally retarded were sued because of the conditions at the institutions.[5] As in New York, the case was turned into a class action suit with the plaintiff asking that the residents

---

[4] New York Office of Mental Retardation and Development Disabilities Mission, http://www.omr.state.ny.us/document/hp.c1.mission.jsp (14 March 2007).
[5] Luther A. Granguist, "A Brief History of the Welch Case," presentation to AAMD, Boston in 1982.

be treated in the least restrictive environment. After many years of litigation and legislative inaction, the state entered a consent degree in 1980. The consent decree required that discharged residents "shall be placed in community programs which appropriately meet their individual needs."

Alabama

In 1970, the state of Alabama was sued because of the conditions at Bryce State Hospital in Tuscaloosa. At that time, Alabama was ranked 50th among all U.S. states in mental health spending. The poor conditions at the hospital were exacerbated by a cut in cigarette tax revenues that were earmarked for mental services. In the case of *Wyatt v. Stickney*, the judge hearing the case determined that patients "unquestionably have a constitutional right to receive such individual treatment as will give each of them a realistic opportunity to be cured or to improve his or her mental condition."[6] The judge also found that the state's hospitals failed to provide the necessary level of care. As a result of this case, the population of the state's psychiatric hospitals was reduced by two thirds by 1975 and funding was increased by over 300%.

National Initiatives

Civil Rights of Institutionalized Person Act of 1980

In response to the developments at the state level, Congress passed the Civil Rights of Institutionalized Person Act of 1980 (CRIPA). CRIPA authorized the U.S. Attorney General to conduct investigations and litigation relating to conditions of confinement in state or locally operated institutions.[7] The Act does not cover private facilities, which may be a factor in the growth of private providers. Among the people covered by the Act are prison inmates, juvenile inmates, residents in state mental health or mental retardation facilities. The act also provides for protection for residents of public nursing home. Since its creation, CRIPA has lead to the investigation of 430 facilities in 39 states.

Olmstead v. L.C.

In 1999, the U.S. Supreme Court determined that under the Americans with Disabilities Act of 1990, states were discriminating against some people

---

[6] Lauren Wilson, "Wyatt v. Stickney: A Landmark Decision," *Alabama Disabilities Advocacy Program Newsletter* (July 2004), pp. 1–3.

[7] *Civil Rights of Institutionalized Persons.* Jan 4, 2007. U.S. Department of Justice, Civil Rights Division (March 13, 2007).

with mental disabilities by not giving them the opportunity to be placed in community based programs.[8] States are now under continued judicial pressure to address the needs of people with disabilities within their borders.

RISK FACTORS ASSOCIATED WITH HUMAN SERVICE PROVIDERS

There are significant risks in investing debt issued by HSPs, among the most critical are:

- *Operational risks.* Many HSPs are relatively small businesses with limited streams and weak balance sheets.
- *Competitive risks.* Given the small business nature of this sector, there are limited barriers to entry and in some areas insufficient demand for services.
- *Limited funding sources.* HSPs are highly dependent on a small number of governmental programs, which are themselves are subject to budgetary constraints.

Risk Mitigants: Security Factors

Regulatory Framework

A critical credit factor in analyzing the risks of investing in debt secured by the revenues of a human service provider is the comfort provided by the strong regulatory oversight provided by state and local agencies. In the case of New York, strong legal protections are supported by a network of governmental agencies that provide funding and oversight. In addition to OMRDD, New York providers may receive funding from the New York State Department of Education, the Department of Health, the New York State Office of Mental Health, and other municipal agencies.

The State of New York has a Certificate of Need (CON) process that providers must undergo before they can receive funding. In the CON, the provider describes the type of individuals it plans to serve and the kind of services that are to be provided.

A critical aspect of New York's CON process is the development of a Prior Property Approval (PPA). Through the PPA, the State establishes the reimbursements levels that the providers will receive for capital projects.

---

[8] *Olmstead v. L.C..* 98-536 Supreme Court (June 22, 1999).

The CON process provides some assurance that there will be sufficient cash flow to repay debt incurred by the provider.

Another significant factor in the regulatory environment in New York is the operating certificate provided by the State Mental Health Commissioner. Under the operating certificate, the Commissioner has the ability to ask a court to appoint a receiver to take over a failing provider. The receiver is required under state law to honor all existing mortgages, leases and chattel mortgages.

Investors in debt secured by human service providers outside of the State of New York should look for similar evidence of governmental support and involvement. The existence of judicial involvement in the form of consent decrees or other judicial mandates provides another level of comfort that governments are motivated to support the development of HSPs.

Mortgages

The most important security factor in debt issued by human service providers is the presence of a mortgage. Unlike healthcare providers where mortgage can have little or no value, the properties securing HSP debt can be residential in nature and their value can be readily assessed at the time the debt is incurred.

In the case of New York, the mortgage assures the debt holder that their interests will be protected in the event the State Mental Health Commissioner requests a court appointed receiver.

Pledge

As is traditional with health care providers, the debt of HSPs should be additionally supported with a pledge of revenues. The revenue pledge also creates the flow of funds that assures that debt repayment is at the top of the providers' obligations. The revenue pledge can also restrain the HSP's ability to issue additional debt.

Risk Mitigants: Credit Factors

Financial Performance

As has been noted, HSPs can be small companies with revenues of less than $5 million and limited liquidity. In reviewing the financial performance of HSPs an investor should expect a history of profitability and timely payment of debt service. Providers can sometimes receive quarterly or semiannual payments under some of their contracts; this can create cash flow difficulties. To mitigate these strains, the provider should have adequate balance sheet liquidity. It is not unusual for providers to obtain letters or lines of credit to provide for additional liquidity.

Competitive Environment

HSPs operate in a competitive environment with low barriers to entry. In reviewing a provider, an investor should examine the competitive landscape and determine the provider's position in the market. A key consideration in evaluating the demand for the provider's service is the existence of a waiting list of potential clients. This assures that providers will not be fighting for the same limited pool of clients and that there is a source from which to draw if a client is lost.

Management

As with all companies, the key to a successful human service provider is good management. The operators are providing a necessary service to a highly vulnerable clientele and are subject to a high level of governmental scrutiny. The management of an HSP must thrive in this highly constrained environment. It should demonstrate that it can successfully navigate the regulatory waters and can maximize its revenue sources. A demonstrated ability to contain operating costs is necessary for success. An investor in this sector should look for a history of positive financial results over a long period of time.

The provider's performance is subject to periodic governmental review and inadequate performance can be subject to the loss of a franchise. It is important to know that an operator has successfully passed all required reviews. Accreditation by the Commission on Accreditation of Rehabilitation Facilities or other national group is another positive factor.

The quality of the board of trustees should be examined to determine the breadth of community and political support. The board should contain family representatives of those being treated by the provider.

SUMMARY

Investors in debt issued by human service providers should understand the risks associated with these credits. They are small businesses with limited financial flexibility. They are subject to significant competitive risks and have limited sources of funding. However, the essential nature of the services they provide combined with strong governmental mandates give comfort that if the HSP is providing quality services within its constrained revenue stream it will attract clients and the governmental support it needs to assure its survival.

CHAPTER 68

How to Analyze the Municipal Bond Insurers and the Bonds They Insure

Donald King Cirillo
Principal
Municipal Disclosure Advisors, Inc.

T he role of municipal bond insurance in the marketplace has grown greatly since it was first introduced in 1971. Today, almost $600 billion worth of outstanding municipal bonds carry some form of enhancement and up until 2008 approximately 50% of all new issues coming to the primary market annually had been insured by one of the guarantors providing this service.

This chapter explains what municipal bond insurance is, how it works, the different types available, and how and why an issuer would go about choosing this option. Also addressed will be why a potential buyer of the bonds would be interested in this service and, additionally, what operational highlights an analyst needs to look at in terms of comparing the various municipal bond insurers. Finally, this chapter comments on some of the most important financial points for evaluation and comparison purposes and what major points an analyst needs to know in order to arrive at a proper credit decision concerning the choice of one insurer over another.

WHAT IS MUNICIPAL BOND INSURANCE?

To better understand how municipal bond insurance works and its effect on the trading market, an analyst must be fully aware of both the public ratings system and the relative value and creditworthiness of one credit versus another.

What is important to remember about municipal bond insurance, in a general way, is that it works much like any other type of insurance in that an outside third-party, in a simple buy/sell transaction, acts as a protector against loss to the buyer. In the specific case of municipals (whether they are direct governments or agencies acting on their behalf), the bondholders will be insured against any type of default by the bond issuer and the potential loss of both *principal and interest* (P&I) to the bondholders that would be caused by such default.

At no time does the municipal bond insurer act in any capacity as the issuer other than guaranteeing the payment of that issuer's specifically insured debt. The actual insurance policy does not cover any other losses that may result from the issuer not performing its other functions and at no time are the insurance proceeds made available directly to the issuer, even in a bankruptcy scenario.

The only entity eligible to receive the benefits of the municipal bond insurance policy, or any and all monetary remuneration under the conditions and terms of that policy, is the actual debt holder. The debt holder may be from the original placement (sale) of the bonds or they may have obtained these rights because they bought the bonds in the secondary market like any other debt instrument. No matter, the municipal bond insurance stays attached to the bond until it has matured.

In order to avoid default, the issuer may, of course, refinance the insured bonds and then call these bonds at par or with a premium (if such action is permitted under the original indenture), in which case the insured bonds will cease to exist and the insurance will no longer apply.

The municipal bond insurance also ceases on any bonds that may be redeemed at par by the issuer under a sinking fund payment or extraordinary call scenario. Other than that, the insurance always follows the municipal bonds no matter who owns them and for however long they are outstanding. Furthermore, the municipal bond insurance policy is nontransferable to any other type of the issuer's debt. Each bond issue must carry its own separate policy. Many issuers do choose to follow this option of insuring only one of their issues, even when more than one series of bonds is being issued simultaneously.

The analyst must never assume all bonds in a certain series are insured without checking first. Also, the analyst can not assume that any other parity debt issued under an open indenture is also insured simply because some of the bonds do have such coverage. The official statement must clearly show on its cover which series is insured and the name of the bond insurer (or insurers, if there is more than one which is not uncommon) must be prominently displayed. Also, if there is a mix of insured and uninsured bonds within the same issue, either by individual series or by maturity, then that fact needs to be prominently noted on the official statement as well. If there is ever any doubt, the analyst should assume there is no insurance until proven otherwise. Note that, if not mentioned on the official statement's title page, the bonds are clearly not insured as a primary issue.

Basically, for the primary market or first day of issue bonds, the municipal bond issuer buys an insurance policy on the debt instrument before it is placed with the bondholders and those unknown bondholders (represented by a trustee) are then named as sole and ultimate beneficiaries of the insurance policy and its payout.

This municipal bond insurance policy is unconditional, irrevocable by either party, and must pay out all P&I to the bondholders in a predetermined and proscribed manner should the issuer be incapable of doing so at any time and/or for any reason.

The analyst needs to know that the municipal bond insurance policy cannot be canceled by the issuer, the bondholder, the trustee, the underwriter, a bankruptcy judge or even the insurance provider itself. However, it should be remembered that in the case of all legal contracts, fraud or misrepresentation of material facts can be grounds for the cancellation of an insurance policy. Although this appears to have happened in the case of corporate-collateralized or asset-backed debt, the likelihood of it happening in the municipal field is highly unlikely as such insurance policies are not based on mathematical calculations, computer models and the like. It is the straight forward nature of the municipal bond market that does not lend itself to fraud or deliberate miscalculations, so a cancellation of an insurance policy because of those events has never happened and remains extremely unlikely.

For all legal purposes the bond insurance company (or other type of entity underwriting the policy) acts as the true obligor of the debt and so the credit rating already assigned to that corporate entity goes on the new municipal bonds permanently. Should the insurer be downgraded, or upgraded for those below triple A (AAA or Aaa), so would the insured bonds. Thus, the municipal bond issuer's original public rating on its own debt, if it ever had one, is now superseded and replaced by the insurer's own public rating, whatever that rating level may be.

MUNICIPAL BOND INSURANCE BENEFITS

Under normal circumstances, municipal bonds, be they rated or unrated, are issued and sold either publicly or privately. It is the perceived ability of the issuer to pay back its debt that determines the cost of the borrowing, that is, the interest rate paid back to the money lender or bondholder. The higher the creditworthiness of the issuer, normally noted as such by a high investment grade rating issued by a rating agency, the less the cost of the interest on the borrowed money. This happens mainly because of the typical economic reality of risk and reward factors being applied to the situation. One indicator of strong credit quality is a low borrowing cost and, of course, the reverse on both counts also holds true—poor underlying credits pay more to borrow money.

A history of unsteady past performance, or weak underlying fundamentals, or even a nonexistent track record can all lead to a less than desirable rating for the municipal entity, which translates into a higher cost of borrowing for that issuer. This is where municipal bond insurance comes into play.

The investment banker representing the issuer is interested in assisting his or her client in saving money by cutting the costs of issuance and is usually the one who will often recommend that the client apply for a municipal bond insurance policy. It should be noted that the company providing this insurance policy must have an outstanding public rating itself that equals or exceeds the issuer's own underlying rating or buying the insurance policy would not make much sense.

By getting such a bond insurance policy, the issuer will save interest costs over the life of the bonds but it must be enough of a savings to justify the cost of the total premium. The bond insurance premium expense is almost always paid upfront, although annual payments can also be arranged.

Oftentimes a municipal bond issuer that is rated single A will buy an insurance policy against potential default that comes from a policy provider that is rated, let us say, triple A instead. Various circumstances such as the underlying stability of the issuer, whether it is a state, county or city government with a tax base versus a project financing based on anticipated revenues, volatility of the marketplace, a rising interest rate environment, and the like, will all determine the cost of the initial borrowing. Moving up, though, from merely a single-A rating to a high investment-grade rating of triple-A may save the issuer a borrowing cost of as much as two full percentage points (2% or 200 basis points) on the long end of the 30-year maturity scale. Over the life of all of the bonds, depending on the maturity schedule, the net interest cost savings to the issuer might be as much as 160 basis points per year for all outstanding debt.

Let us assume an issuer has only a $20 million series of municipal bonds that it wants to issue with an average life of 20 years. Now assume an interest cost saving to that issuer because it obtains an insurance policy on the bonds, however, that comes to just 80 basis points a year. Over the life of the bonds, that basis point differential alone equals a $3.2 million savings on the total cost of the borrowing for the municipal entity issuing the debt. Clearly this simple mathematical equation shows the high inherent value in obtaining a municipal bond insurance policy if the total premiums paid out to get the insurance were to equal only half that number. For a small town, college or hospital issuing the debt, that is a real dollar cost savings.

In addition to an interest cost savings and the improvement in the overall bond series rating, there are some other reasons for an issuer to obtain municipal bond insurance.

ADDITIONAL BENEFITS OF BOND INSURANCE

Outlined thus far are the economic benefits to an issuer that a municipal bond insurance policy can provide. Specifically, interest cost savings. Although the financial aspects are often the driving force behind an issuer taking out such a policy, other benefits can accrue as well.

The issuer improves access to the market by trading off of the known name of the insurance provider and its higher rating. Where a potential bond buyer may not have heard of the issuer, due to its limited past access to the market or because of just plain obscurity, the municipal bond insurers are all well-known entities to the marketplace, in some cases for over 30 years. However, even the newer municipal bond insurance entities often underwrite policies on a weekly or daily basis and, as such, they too are well known and closely watched by traders, sales personnel, analysts and the like even though they may not be well known to the general public.

Another potential benefit to the bondholders of having their municipal debt insured is that the issue will often trade straight off the insurance and its rating, thus providing a type of homogeneity for similar paper that would not be achieved otherwise and a level of market stability as well, especially in the case of smaller issuers.

The larger and more established municipal bond insurance providers have all experienced P&I claims due to defaults by issuers and the payouts on the insurance policies have all been timely and have worked according to the original policies. This strong performance has built up confidence in the idea of municipal bond insurance as a whole while providing a proven track record that enhances the reputation of not just the original insurance company itself, but also the overall concept of placing a municipal bond insurance policy on an issue.

As of this writing, no municipal bond insurer has failed to make any P&I payments on any municipal bond that it had insured and which later went into default.

Both the bond issuers and the bondholders can benefit greatly from municipal bond insurance. The former saves interest rate costs and the latter gets a strong, highly rated and easily traded debt instrument.

TYPES OF MUNICIPAL BOND INSURANCE

So far only direct municipal bond insurance has been discussed in this chapter. However, these insurance companies also provide other types of insurance that benefit bondholders more than issuers. The idea is the same but the method of delivery varies slightly.

In some cases, a municipal bond that is trading in the secondary market can be insured by itself. This means that the individual bond lot, usually at least $100,000 in value but often worth several million dollars, can get its own personalized insurance policy attached to it for a negotiated premium. This is done to add an extra layer of protection, get a higher rating and to make the bond lot in question easier to sell. If such a policy is attached to that bond lot, both the CUSIP number and the rating on the insured lot only are permanently changed to reflect that fact.

The analyst should remember that it is possible to have two lots of bonds from the same series issued by the same municipal entity with the same coupon and maturity date but where one lot has secondary-market insurance and the other does not!

To be sure, a secondary-market insurance policy exists on the bonds being traded, the analyst should always check with the insurance provider. All municipal bond insurers maintain a *secondary-market desk* for just such a purpose. A quick telephone call during business hours and providing a CUSIP number are usually all it takes to prove to the analyst that the secondary-market insurance policy is registered and in full force.

Another form of municipal bond insurance is called a "wrap" policy. This is where closed-end funds or a *unit investment trust* (UIT) will purchase a group of bonds and form a special *insured portfolio*. While the bonds remain in the fund, they are insured by a special municipal bond insurance policy that wraps around the UIT. However, should the bonds ever be sold out of the fund due to a redemption by a fund participant, the municipal bond insurance policy will no longer apply and the policy will not follow the bonds to the new purchaser. The next buyer does not get the insurance policy unless it makes arrangements to continue it.

Should the issuer default on its P&I while the fund or UIT holds the bonds, the insurance will apply and the policy would pay off. Basically, this is a temporary and conditional municipal bond insurance policy that is in force for only the benefit of the UIT or closed-end fund participants.

Of course it is also possible for a small UIT to provide, all by itself, each individual bond inside the trust with its own insurance policy by way of secondary-market insurance, in which case the insurance policy would indeed then follow the bonds until maturity, even after they are sold out of the UIT. However, that should not be confused with a wrap policy.

MUNICIPAL BOND INSURANCE PROVIDERS

As mentioned at the outset of this chapter, the concept of municipal bond insurance dates back to 1971 when the AMBAC Indemnity Corporation (now known as Ambac Assurance Corp. or AMBAC) issued its first policy. Since then, AMBAC has been joined in this business line by a few other insurers that also make this service available to issuers and bondholders and who are still in competition with them for market share.

What the analyst needs to remember is that not all such municipal bond insurers are rated triple A and, of those that are, not all are rated by the three major rating agencies—Moody's Investor Services, Standard & Poor's, and Fitch). This point may or may not be important to some analysts as it can be argued that obtaining the triple-A rating from one agency is sufficient for marketing and trading purposes.

The analyst is urged to keep checking the public record as new municipal bond insurers are appearing on the scene all the time and many of these new entities are still pursuing their multiple ratings and often are not licensed to do business in every state.

For the purposes of this chapter, it should be noted that as of this writing, the following municipal bond insurance providers are all rated triple A (AAA or Aaa) by at least one of the major rating agencies. These are:

- Ambac Assurance Corp. (AMBAC or Ambac)
- Assured Guaranty Corp.
- CIFG Financial Guaranty
- Financial Guaranty Insurance Corp. (FGIC)
- Financial Security Assurance Inc. (FSA)
- MBIA Insurance Corp. (MBIA)
- XL Capital Assurance, Inc. (XL)

The analyst should also be aware, just for the historical record, that several other municipal bond insurance companies used to be in the market place but either no longer write policies or they were taken over by one of the larger firms mentioned above. To cite a few well-known examples: Connie Lee (1988–1997) was assumed by AMBAC while Bond Investors Guaranty (BIG, 1985–1989) and Capital Markets Assurance Corp. (CapMAC, 1985–1998) were both taken over by MBIA.

OTHER MUNICIPAL BOND INSURANCE PROVIDERS

Previously in this chapter, it was eluded to that municipal bond insurance policies can also be written by guarantors that are rated below triple A. There are many reasons why an issuer would choose to go this route but the main reason is that the issuer usually does not qualify under all of the criteria that the triple-A provider needs in order to feel secure in underwriting the policy. Basically, the issuer's own creditworthiness may be too weak to justify moving it up to the highest investment-grade rating that the policy would provide. Some of the triple-A rated insurers insist that the issuer have at least an A rating in its own right. In other instances, the triple-A rated providers may simply have too much exposure to that type of credit on their books already or it is a sector that they do not underwrite, like, for example, multifamily housing or nursing homes.

In other cases, the issuer may not have been in existence for enough years, such as a new Municipal Utility District (MUD) or the triple-A rated provider has too much saturation in that geographic area. As insurance companies like to underwrite to a zero-loss expectation, an issuer just may not measure up against all standards and is viewed as being too risky.

Whatever the reason for not having triple-A rated insurance, the issuer can seek the alternative option of being insured by a double-A rated municipal insurer such as Radian Asset Assurance, Inc. (formerly Asset Guaranty) or they may choose to go with a single-A rated insurance provider, such as ACA Financial Guaranty (formerly American Capital Access).

One could argue that the payments of P&I to the bondholder are just as safe and secure under these policies as they are from the triple-A rated providers due to the fact that the issued policies are all "money good" because of capitalization requirements and cash reserves being set aside at the time of underwriting the policy. However, the cache of the highest rating is clearly missing and these lower-rated municipal bond insurance policies are definitely viewed differently by the marketplace and, as a consequence, they trade accordingly off of the top investment-grade, triple-A scale.

It should also be noted by the analyst that the underlying credit is clearly of a somewhat weaker nature by definition and will often be viewed, rightly or wrongly, as more speculative. The risk tolerance for single-A- or double-A rated insured municipal paper must obviously be higher than for the triple A.

The analyst must also remember that even though the insurance policies for the nontriple-A rated underwriters are also unconditional and irrevocable the statutory capitalization requirements and cash reserves will be lower. If these insurers suffer stress scenarios, which has happened in the recent past, the public rating of the insurance itself may go down or be placed on credit watch by a rating agency. Such negative actions will thus affect all bonds with outstanding insurance policies from these bond insurers.

REINSURANCE

The analyst needs to be aware of the expanding role that is being played by the reinsurance companies in the municipal bond insurance industry. *Reinsurance*, as it is called, takes place when a primary bond insurer assigns over to another party (usually also a municipal bond insurer but not always) some or all of the risk from a particular bond issue that the primary had originally agreed to insure. The reinsurer, in turn, indemnifies the primary. For all intents and purposes, however, the primary insurer is still liable for the proper performance of its original insurance policy vis-à-vis the bondholder. In fact, the primary insurer often enters into this reinsurance agreement unbeknownst to the bondholders.

The analyst needs to remember that the primary insurer is not relieved of its direct responsibilities to the bondholders in the event of a missed P&I payment just because it has obtained reinsurance. However, it now has access to another source of outside revenue to make those payments, which is definitely a credit positive.

Another benefit of reinsurance is that it allows the primary municipal bond insurer to increase its own overall capacity for insurance policies written because these reinsured bonds are now technically listed as being "off the books." This is because, the direct liability for the missed payments of the issuer's P&I is assumed by another party with funds from a different and outside source. This action also allows the primary insurer to manage its risk to a given credit, or even an entire portfolio, while also satisfying the rating agencies and/or regulatory authorities' standards of compliance.

The analyst also needs to be aware that the same rating values and regulatory rules apply to the reinsurers but usually at a reduced level.

As of this writing, this niche market has seven reinsurers and is dominated, at least in terms of total claims' paying resources available, by Radian Asset and XFLA (XL Financial Assurance, Ltd.), which together account for more than half of all reinsurance.

It should be noted that Radian (as mentioned earlier) also provides direct primary and secondary municipal bond insurance. However, it used to reinsure bonds under the company name of Enhance Reinsurance, which is now doing business as Radian. On the other hand, XLFA is a Bermuda-based reinsurer owned by XL Insurance (Bermuda) and FSA Holdings.

The additional reinsurers doing business are all fairly well balanced in terms of available funds.

In alphabetical order, these other five reinsurers are (1) ACA Financial Guaranty Corp.; (2) AGRe (Assured Guaranty Re, Ltd.); (3) BluePoint Re Limited; (4) Channel Reinsurance Ltd.; and (5) RAM Reinsurance Co., Ltd.

Most of these reinsurers are wholly owned subsidiaries of the primary monoline insurers, but they operate "offshore" and have access to other sorts of capital that the primary insurer itself usually cannot have access to due to regulatory restrictions and the analyst would do well to keep this in mind.

The analyst also should be aware that municipal bond reinsurance can be provided in two distinct ways: (1) either by what is called *treaty* or (2) through a facultative process. Under a treaty, the reinsurer must take all of the bonds falling under a specific class of risk that is underwritten by the primary according to the percentage and other conditions outlined in the reinsurance agreement. In the case of a facultative agreement, the reinsurer always takes the previously agreed upon percentage of the deal but reserves the right to reject a credit commitment and can negotiate terms and price.

As a final point, the analyst should look at a reinsurer's statutory capital versus insurance-in-force and also note that the reinsurer must have a financial enhancement rating of its own that is investment grade.

TELLING THE DIFFERENCE

At first glance, the analyst might be tempted to assume that all of the municipal bond insurers in the same rating category are all the same, especially if all of the insurers under review are rated triple A. This would not necessarily be an error as the rating agencies keep a very close watch on these players and the rating must be affirmed at least once a year. However, this would not be the best judgment the analyst can make without additional research and information. The analyst must bear in mind that the marketplace does not treat all of the municipal bond insurers equally. Often bond traders will place basis point differentials into the effective annual yields of similar bonds that are covered by different insurers, even though the issuers and the maturities may be the same.

A good analyst will look first at the underlying credit of the issuer before making an assessment on the overlapping insurer. What is important to look at here is the ability of the issuer to survive on its own should some catastrophe render the bond insurance provider incapable of paying a P&I claim on its policy. Equally important for the analyst to look at is the likelihood of default on the underlying credit as this could lead to the insurer paying off the bonds sooner than the original maturity date, as that may be an option available to them. This type of call risk should not be overlooked, especially if a premium for the bonds is being paid.

Another point worth checking on by the analyst should be to see if the bond insurer in question has expertise in this area of issuance. Is the bond insurer known for insuring these types of bonds or are they breaking into a new field? On the other hand, is the insurer's overall insured portfolio top heavy in this type of credit, either geographically speaking or industry wise? Is the insurer's overall portfolio balanced with quality credits in various sectors and are these spread out throughout the country? What if a natural disaster, for example, the Katrina Hurricane of 2005, hits an area where 15% of the insurer's premiums come from and/or 80% of its claims in one year might be filed from there? The analyst would do well to remember that even if everything works well on the insurance policy, an event of default will weaken the trading value of those specific bonds and, in a general way, will have a negative ripple effect on all bonds insured by that particular insurer. A major catastrophe will also weaken the trading value of all insured bonds, despite strong solvency by the insurance issuers.

The analyst also needs to pay attention to the track record of the municipal bond insurer and see if it has been in existence for a few years or if it is a new entry into the market. Furthermore, is the insurer licensed to do business in only a few states or regions or is it licensed nationwide?

What kind of a management team does the insurer have is also an important question. Established corporate enterprises will have a working and profitable business model backed up by many years of proven expertise on the behalf of the managers. A startup company or a new entrant to the business of municipal bond insurance may be more aggressive in its underwriting criteria and thus a bit less demanding on underlying creditworthiness and with higher risk tolerance levels than longer established parties in the business.

The analyst must try to be fair and objective when comparing and weighing all of the positives and negatives before making a recommendation. On a case-by-case basis, the analyst's final decision on which insurer is preferred over another should be backed up by a trading price reflective of these pros and cons.

If the insurer has already had claims made against its policies, the analyst should ascertain how these payments were handled. Was the transition of the actual payout of the P&I, from issuer to insurer, smooth and uneventful? Did the trustee bank, acting on behalf of the bondholders, need to sue the insurer in order to receive P&I or was a simple notification of a claim sufficient? Did the insurer threaten not to pay the P&I for any reason or were they hesitant to pay due to legal technicalities or tax questions?

What is the overall reputation of the bond insurer in the marketplace in terms of professionalism, accountability, responsiveness to professional inquiries and the like? Does the insurer make its own financial information available in an easily accessible and transparent manner? Are the insurers in good standing with the rating agencies and are their own internal analysts made available for questions? In answering questions, are they forthcoming?

In addition to annual reports, are quarterly updates readily open to the analyst? Transparency on many levels is important in maintaining a solid reputation of integrity.

The analyst also needs to look closely at the historical record of the municipal bond insurer not just in terms of past performance but also how it has been viewed by the public rating agencies, different municipal bond trading desks and even the front line brokers and sales personnel. A poor reputation for the municipal bond insurer will translate into poor trading value even when there is no real justification for such treatment.

The analyst will also need to note if the insurer has ever had its public rating downgraded. Additionally, has it ever been on credit watch by a rating agency or similar type of watch list portending a rating downgrade, even once? Did the insurer ever have a problem raising capital when required to meet regulatory standards? Have the municipal bonds, insured by the particular insurance provider in question, ever traded off of the usual, comparable trading scale? If so, why did they do so and did they quickly recover or get worse over time?

As a final general point, the analyst needs to pay attention to his or her client's view of the insurer. Does the client have a preference for one municipal bond insurer over the other, even though no substantive reasons are provided? The analyst cannot ignore these attitudes. Knowing the ultimate customer and what the customer wants is always important to an analyst.

FINANCIAL FACTORS

Analysts should also be aware that municipal bond insurers are usually owned by a conglomeration of large institutional investors and/or public holders by way of stocks. While several municipal bond insurance providers are privately held, still others have their stock listed on an exchange and are openly traded with the usual fluctuations in price.

Typically all insurers operate at a statutory risk-to-capital leverage ratio that lies somewhere between 100 and 200-to-1. The actual dollar value of this statutory capital can go from a low of just a few hundred million dollars up to several billion dollars. Although this aspect of the analysis is important, it needs to be taken in conjunction with the value of the *unearned premium reserve* and the *present value of annual premiums*. Taken together these points will give the analyst a better view of all money available to the insurer which is otherwise known as *contingent capital*.

Analysts also need to pay attention to what is often referred to as third-party capital support. These dollar amounts represent any firmly established lines of credit or direct pay letters-of-credit available to the municipal bond insurer as backup revenue. Perhaps these capital commitments are not yet fulfilled by the insurer but they should be readily available to be drawn on in an emergency. These soft capital contingency reserves are worth looking at for comparison purposes before the analyst decides the total claims paying ability of the insurer.

OTHER FINANCIAL FACTORS

The analyst should remember that like any other insurance company, municipal bond insurers must be licensed in any state they do business or write policies in. To that end, there are all sorts of statutory financial requirements that need to be met in order to maintain that business. For the analyst's purposes, the most important criteria are those that help the insurer retain its rating and not just its solvency.

The analyst should look at all of the financial data that is important to the rating agencies and pay particular attention to any actions or trends (either by the individual bond insurer or industry wide) that would cause them concern and thus lead to a downgrade.

The rating agencies all use a total loss or some multiple of the 1930s Great Depression stress test scenario to measure and test the survival of the municipal bond insurer. The analyst needs to be familiar with this type of stress model in order to understand the projection of the likelihood of a municipal bond insurer missing a payout or being viewed as weak by a rating agency.

Weighted averages of the insured portfolio risk are another favorite statistic that is compared industry wide. Basically what is done here is the analyst looks at the average annual debt service commitment as a percentage of the public finance capital charge but also must take into consideration other asset backed (nonmunicipal) par exposures, if there are any.

Previously mentioned in this chapter was statutory capital requirements for the insurers and their claims paying ability based on resources available but the analyst may want to look further at specific ratios that give a quick overview of the situation.

Testing coverage levels of net exposure to capital and/or funds available is always good to look at and so is the same check being performed on net insured annual debt service versus the same criteria.

A review of the average life of the entire insured portfolio and the classic calculation of total annual expenses divided by total available revenues is a ratio of coverage that is always good to know.

Other important ratios for the analyst to get a handle on are the paid loss ratio (net losses paid/net premiums), total assets divided by net exposure and net underwriting over net premiums (the expense ratio).

It is also useful for the analyst to know how the insurer handles its own investment portfolio in terms of distribution of available assets.

Finally, the analyst should look for trends within the issuer's past financial history. Such things as the unearned premium reserve, loss reserves, net premiums written and/or earned as well as "total assets" are all figures that should show positive growth and be trending up over time while "loss and loss expenses incurred" are preferably stable or going down.

Additionally, "net annual income" should always be growing over several fiscal years.

OTHER BUSINESSES

Like all insurance companies, municipal bond insurers are always looking for ways to diversify their product line while enhancing their bottom line. This is why in recent years many municipal bond insurers have expanded their service into other areas, such as asset backed securities, derivative products, and even going overseas for project financings. While these new and expanded service areas can increase income, they also carry a higher risk level as they often involve corporate financings that have historically carried a higher default rate than the safer and more secure arena of municipal debt.

The analyst would be wise to ascertain exactly how much of this new risk is part of the municipal bond insurer's overall underwriting portfolio. Special attention should be paid to determining how much of the claim losses suffered by the insurer are linked to this product line as it may ultimately jeopardize the claims' paying ability of the insurer on the municipal side as well.

On more than one occasion municipal bond insurers have been burned with defaults linked specifically to asset-backed securities that were not in the municipal marketplace and thus were not well known to the players normally associated with following the credit of the insurer. A quick check by the analyst of the balance sheet of the municipal bond insurer will reveal the existence of this type of exposure and the dollar level of the risk.

Lastly, the analyst should also take a moment to note if the parent company of the municipal bond insurer (assuming there is one) has a corporate rating and how has that rating fared over time? An indication of a downward rating trend on the part of the parent will no doubt ultimately impact the subsidiary (the municipal bond insurer) sooner or later and the analyst should not take that issue lightly.

CONCLUSION

The municipal bond insurance provider industry is far reaching in its impact on the market and it has transformed the way business is done. Issuers now have available to them a finance option that allows them greater access to the marketplace at a lower cost. For the most part, this type of flexibility did not exist 35 years ago and was not widely available until the middle 1980s.

All well-rounded analysts need to know something about this group and must be able to speak authoritatively about the players because their presence can not be ignored. Not a day goes by on the average municipal bond trading desk where insured municipal bonds are not presented for buying or selling. In fact, it would not be wrong to say that any one of the major insurers have more debt outstanding and actively trading than any single issuer and, taken collectively, no state in the nation (including all authorities and agencies acting on its behalf) even comes close to the total amount of municipal debt outstanding as that which has been insured.

Furthermore, of all the players in the municipal marketplace, not one of them is as dependent upon its public rating (whatever level it might be) as a municipal bond insurer. A city, county or even a state that suffers a rating downgrade only has its own bonds affected. The negative implications can be contained and in the instance of an infrequent issuer, the problems are not actually highlighted until the issuer attempts to reenter the marketplace of municipal debt.

However, the municipal bond insurers play a huge role in providing liquidity to the market and any type of problem with a rating will play havoc with many different municipal bonds spread across every type of sector in the industry and will also hurt the ability of small towns and cities across the nation to borrow needed funds.

No other player in the municipal bond market is as dependent upon its public rating as a municipal bond insurer. Without a rating, these municipal bond insurance providers are out of business for a simple and basic reason: what they are selling is their rating. Even a severe downgrade or a mild credit warning on claims paying ability of an insurer will damage the insurer's ability to enter the market and/or make a profit.

The analyst would do well to remember that the biggest risk to the municipal bond insurer is a problem with its rating, which will probably come about long before it has a problem with its claims paying ability. If no issuer defaults or if there are no large demands for payouts of P&I, in theory one may never know there was a problem with an insurer as no claims were made or turned away. This is why checking on the fundamentals becomes most important. Municipal bond insurers can run into trouble long before it is commonly known. Also, the analyst must remember that rating downgrades are often lagging indicators of a problem as these actions will usually only come about after an annual review.

The analyst needs to be diligent in following the ratings of the municipal bond insurers but also must do his or her own research on total risk. It must never be assumed that the municipal bond insurers are too big to fail. History has shown that a changing environment can weaken even the strongest of players.

The keyword for any analyst monitoring the municipal bond insurance industry is "diligence" and the operative word is *verification*. Good analysts must always do their own fact checking and not count on others to do it for them.

CHAPTER 69

Student Loan Financing: Risk Evaluation Tax-Exempt and Taxable Markets Converge

Diane R. Maurice
Vice President
Morgan Stanley–Investment Management

Ankur Goyal
Associate
Morgan Stanley–Risk Department

Student loan finance and the assessment of related risk evolved dramatically since the 1980s. One significant trend is the convergence between tax-exempt and taxable strategies to finance student loans. Historically, student loan financing relied to a greater extent on tax-exempt public financing sources. Today, tax-exempt issuers are just as likely to access taxable markets as they are tax-exempt funding sources as the demand for financing has grown over time and tax-exempt cap allocation has not increased to meet the need for all issuers. Often the same issuer will tap both markets in the same transaction. Whether, taxable or tax-exempt, the risk profile is essentially the same for Family Federal Education Loan Program (FFELP) backed student loan financings. Issuers consistently utilize the same securitization financing techniques, or repackaging of student loans, as a dominant financing vehicle.

To better frame the risk profile, this chapter begins by evaluating systemic shifts in the student loan industry. The ownership of long-standing

The authors thank Karen Rockoff in Morgan Stanley Risk Department for her assistance. Dana Ricciardi assisted in the chapter's organization.

issuers has changed hands. The sale of Sallie Mae, for example, as well as not-for-profit student loan entities represent one ongoing trend. Increasingly, the formation of strategic public/private partnerships and a reduced government role has blurred the lines between public and private financing initiatives. Robust growth and a continued move away from fully guaranteed loans and public sector subsidies are expected to define both student loan financing and its sponsoring organizations over the next quarter century. The profile of risk has shifted solidly away from public sector subsidies to private sector initiatives.

Public financing, specifically the U.S. Department of Education guaranteed FFELP program are increasingly inadequate to fuel the 12% compounded annual growth rate in student loan volume experienced over the past decade as noted in Exhibit 69.1. As one of the fastest growing consumer lending sectors the focus on funding secondary educational needs is expected to continue. Exhibit 69.2 provides the breakdown of financial aid for academic year 2005–2006. Rising secondary school attendance, moderate personal income growth and increases in educational expenses all weigh in on the dynamics of change as noted in Exhibits 69.3 and 69.4. Solid growth is expected to continue spurred by predictable tuition increases and the increase in post-secondary enrollment, which is projected to reach 19.5 million by 2014.

EXHIBIT 69.1   Federal Student Loan Origination Volumes

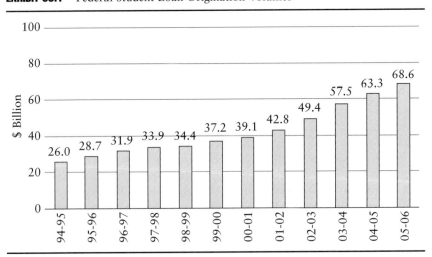

EXHIBIT 69.1 (Continued)
Private Student Loan Origination Volume

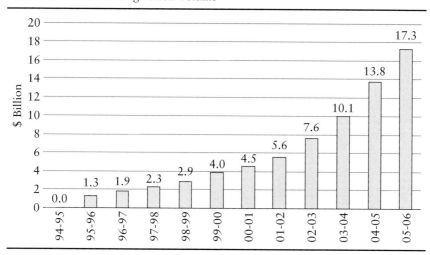

EXHIBIT 69.2 Total College Financial Aid, $152 Billion, Academic Year 2005–2006

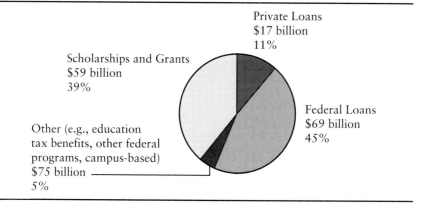

TAX-EXEMPT ISSUERS AND PRIVATIZATION TRENDS

New opportunities anticipated by continuing sector growth has brought new market entrants. There is a relatively low barrier to entry for new market participants, especially in the direct to consumer channel, where long standing relationships with schools and a large sales force to call on financial aid officers are not needed. New and often unexpected alliances have emerged in an effort to keep pace with increased competition. EduCap, for example,

EXHIBIT 69.3   Rising Cost of Attendance, Dollar Amount ($000) and Cumulative Growth (%), Academic Year 1992–2006

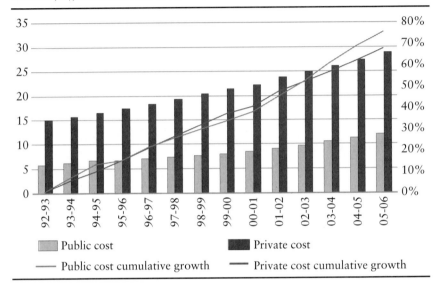

EXHIBIT 69.4   Growing Undergraduate Enrollment, Number of Students in Degree Institutions

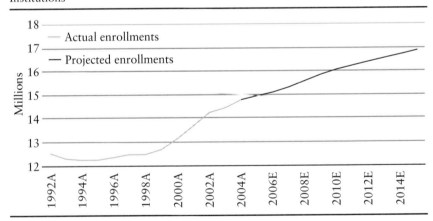

formed a partnership with Lending Tree, to provide "direct to consumer" for both private and FFELP student loans.

Private equity continues to target tax-exempt and traditional student loan issuers. On April 16, 2007, Sallie Mae manager of over $150 billion in educational loans serving nearly 10 million customers announced plans to privatize.[1] Hybrid institutions, pairing not-for-profit issuers with for-profit institutions has evolved in response to a more competitive environment. The Education Resources Institute, Inc. (TERI) alliance with First Marblehead Corporation best epitomizes this. TERI, organized as a not-for-profit organization, was set up to increase financing options for higher education by offering private guarantees. Revenues include the fee paid for the guarantee, which replace the FFELP guarantee as well as fees for delinquent loans. Unlike traditional student loan programs, TERI also extends guarantees in the U.S. and Canada for traditional postsecondary schools, international schools and elementary education (K–12).[2] First Marblehead Corporation, a for-profit institution, provides a consumer marketing channel for originating private, nongovernment guaranteed loans guaranteed by TERI.

In addition to the growing competition from new market participants, FFELP faces dramatic cuts from current legislative proposals (see the appendix to this chapter) which aim to reduce lenders' yields. Many of the smaller not-for-profit entities will face extreme financial pressure as they do not have the economies of scales that larger lenders and bank lenders have to sustain some of the yield reductions, although current proposals may allow for not-for-profit entities to have a lower reduction. As a result, not-for-profit student loan entities may continue to privatize, form strategic alliances and outsource key business functions such as servicing, guarantee services and portfolio retention services which may be less costly if performed by a third-party entity. Some not-for-profit entities have even had to sell all or a portion of their businesses to raise the necessary funds for their respective states' grant and scholarship programs.

Tax-exempt issuers move to embrace a wider array of product offerings to meet growing demand. Consumers are offered payment deferrals, consolidation loans and often terms of up to 20 years (see the appendix to this chapter). Consumers are increasingly faced with a potentially increased debt burden extending well into middle age. For the risk manager, this changing consumer profile coupled with systemic changes in student loan origination and servicing, presents new dynamics in assessing the risk of loss. Both individual's ability to repay and the institutional commitment to support underperforming loan portfolios impose complexities in evaluating this sector.

---

[1] PR Newswire Association LLC, http://www.newscom.com/cgi-bin/prnh/20030617/ SLMLOGO-a (17 May 2007).
[2] *DBRS US Structured Finance Newsletter*, May 3, 2007.

Tax-exempt issuers faced with both a new lending dynamic and increased competition from a number of sources have also embraced more efficient funding techniques. Securitization has become the single most common form of financing for both tax-exempt and taxable issuers. Student-loan-backed securitizations surpassed credit card issuances in terms of asset-backed securitization in 2006 according to industry reports.[3] Near term, Moody's expects the 2007 issuance of U.S. student loan asset-backed securities to stabilize in market contrast to the dynamic growth experienced since 2001. The 2007 issuance is expected to be either comparable to 2006's $82.4 billion or slightly lower. Growth will continue along with securitization techniques designed to tap additional tax-exempt and taxable investors.

New investors for securitizations backed by student loans may ultimately mean a lower the cost of funds. More efficient funding sources often come as the result of structural complexity with uncertain implications for risk. Two recent innovative offerings backed by student loans designed to access new types of investors in the capital markets. Short-term commercial paper and both senior and subordinated term investors participated.

Student Loans Funded in the Short-Term Asset Backed Commercial Paper Market

In August 2006, Moody's assigned a Prime-1 rating to a new asset-backed commercial paper (ABCP) program sponsored by Nelnet, Inc. (Nelnet). Nelnet Student Asset Funding Extendable CP, LLC (Nelnet SAFE CP) will be purchasing eligible FFELP loans originated by Nelnet with proceeds from the issuance of up to $5 billion of extendable commercial paper notes. While student loans have long been funded in the ABCP market, this transaction is the first single-seller program backed exclusively by student loans originated by one sponsor. The program relies on the inherent liquidity of the student loans for both the timely and ultimate repayment of the issued ABCP. Nelnet SAFE CP issues extendible ABCP with an initial maturity of up to 307 days. If, at any time, commercial paper cannot be issued to repay maturing ABCP, the maturing ABCP may be extended for an additional ninety days. During that time, Nelnet will be required to either sell the underlying pool of student loans or securitize it in the term ABS market, and use the proceeds to redeem the ABCP by their final maturity date.

Student Loans Financed By Senior and Subordinated Term Debt

DBRS rated a unique student loan transaction that offered investors the opportunity to buy a "senior tranche" receiving first cash flow, and a junior class or second cash flow from the student loans portfolio. The GCO Series

---

[3] "Hot Topics In Student Loan Securitization," Standard and Poor's, November 1, 2006.

2007-1 transaction included a $55 million junior subordinate class of notes. Certain characteristic of consolidation FFELP-backed SLABs like strong collateral quality, stable excess spread and associated structural elements facilitate inclusion of additional subordinate classes in the SLABs structure. These structural features provide adequate support to more senior notes and include a note trigger that redirects junior subordinate note interest to pay principal on senior notes. The note trigger is tied to collateral defaults. In the absence of a trigger event, the junior subordinate notes receive interest sequentially and their interest is paid before principal payments are made to any class of notes. In addition, junior subordinate note principal is paid only after required payments are made to senior and senior subordinate notes and targeted overcollateralization levels are met.[4] DBRS concludes by noting the inclusion of additional classes of subordinate notes facilitate better execution for the student loan issuers while adding investment opportunities for investors with higher risk tolerance levels.

SYSTEMIC SHIFT-RISK TRANSFERENCE

Risk managers challenged by the changing financial profile must not only consider how evolving financing structures contribute or detract from risk, but more fundamentally, how loans are repaid with full or partial government support. As federal guarantees are replaced with private or nonguaranteed loans, three distinct risks emerge. The first centers on the quality of the underlying borrower. Understanding the consumer's willingness and ability to repay is a key parameter often highlighted by the student loan originators' underwriting standards. Evaluating FICO and other income scoring mechanisms employed by the originator provides risk managers one metric to partially evaluate repayment potential. Secondly, given industrywide change, credit evaluation must consider how servicer/originator maintains consistent student loan portfolio performance. How does the transition from tax-exempt status for an issuer alter underwriting parameters? Can the student loan servicer collect payments on a timely basis? When are calls made to determine which payments will be made or if forbearance is necessary? Lastly, to insure bonds backed by student loans are repaid in full and on time, the risk analysis also considers structural components of the financing. How does the structure compensate for payment delays or defaults by from the underlying consumer or borrowers? Is cash advanced by the student loan companies to cover temporary shortfalls? Are there reserves or other forms of reliable support in place to cover potential deficits? Alternatively, are highly rated third parties required to provide this support to protect investors over time?

---

[4] *DBRS US Structured Finance Newsletter*, March 5, 2007.

New financing strategies in the securitization market may focus on structural mechanisms to protect bondholders and ensure repayment. Securitizations or repackaging of student loans comes in various forms. Credit enhancement to cover losses or ultimate defaults on the underlying loan is perhaps the easiest to conceptualize. If the student fails to make a payment, who makes up the difference? It may be the government under a FFELP transaction for example. Overcollateralization (in excess of parity) or extra reserves may be part of the structure to compensate for shortfalls not covered by government guarantees.

In tax-exempt and taxable securitizations, cash flow captured in the student loan transactions builds up to cover losses often through excess spread. This is typically defined as additional interest, which may not be needed to repay bondholders. Excess spread levels are driven by two key factors: (1) the low level of collateral losses (FFELP loans are guaranteed to at least 97% of principal and interest); and (2) the slower and stable level of prepayments (only for consolidation loans, Stafford/Plus have very high levels of prepayments), which vary depending on the type of student loans. Consolidation loans, for example, where the student has consolidated several loans for under graduate and graduate programs can only be refinanced under very limited circumstances. Therefore, excess spread levels may be relatively stable and enable FFELP transactions to close with total assets match total liabilities (i.e. parity levels reach 100%). Parity levels may increase over two to four years, through the retention of excess spread; ideally, investors are protected as the value of the collateral rises to 101% to 105%. Other programs actually cover interest shortfalls that are temporary in nature.

Government guaranteed programs may be replaced totally with other forms of support. Parental cosigners or other types of support as highlighted in the appendix to this chapter can change the dynamics of risk. Counterparty support from highly rated third parties is also a consideration in increasing numbers of student loan transactions where financial guarantors "wrap" entire loan portfolios (AMBAC/MBIA/FGIC/FSA). In some tax-exempt structures, a highly rated bank provides liquidity for transactions accessing the auction rate market If market access stalls, liquidity banks may also provide temporary support and in some structures results in full risk transference. Counterparty quality, rating, and market access adds other important risk elements for consideration.

GUARANTEED VERSUS PRIVATE LOANS

Risk managers and investors in student-loan-backed products are increasingly asked to accommodate the blurring of lines between public and private sector subsidies. As tax-exempt issuers privatize increased participation in private student loans is a likely next step. As noted below, the menu of student loan options continues to expand along with new market entrants. Repayment to investors more often centers on who qualified lenders are and their ability to collect repayment on a timely basis.

Student loan financing techniques have expanded along with the universe of providers. Assessing the risk of the originator is increasingly complex given the wider variety of providers (see Exhibit 69.5).

RISK PROFILE EVOLVES

Issuers financing in the tax-exempt market may pass on a lower interest rate to borrowers but share the same credit concerns as their taxable counterparts. A declining government role has shifted the emphasis to underwriting and borrower quality. Analyses of securitized pools of student loans require additional levels of analysis. Sophisticated cash flow models allow various stress factors, including probability of default and speed of student loan prepayments, to be captured. Whether evaluating tax-exempt or taxable issuances backed by student loans, investors and risk managers increasingly use these quantitative techniques to complement the analytical checklist and qualitative techniques highlighted in Exhibit 69.6.

SUMMARY

Three major characteristics that influence whether the student loan investor is repaid include (see Exhibit 69.7):

- Student loan or borrower quality takes a front role in the analysis especially as government guarantees become less of a factor.
- Servicer and originator financial strength and operational history are key drivers especially in light of private equity involvement and organizational shifts created as a result.
- Structural complexity is an increasing concern. How the underlying servicer and loan performance contributes to overall performance may be enhanced by various structural features. For example, programs structured with extendable liabilities as seen with recent asset backed commercial paper programs may be the perfect way to accommodate student loan forbearance or deferrals in the context of a wider structure.

The analyst's job in the 1980s focused on the role of government . Today, structural complexity and shift to the private sector guides the analysis.

EXHIBIT 69.5 Major Loan Programs

U.S. Government Guaranteed Student Loans		Private Loans
Federal Family Education Loan Program (FFELP) (Established by the Higher Education Act of 1965)	**Federal Direct Loan Program (FDLP)**	
Qualified Lenders:	**Qualified Lenders:**	**Qualified Lenders:**
• Banks (national and state-chartered, mutual and stock savings) • Credit unions and pension funds • Insurance and trust companies • State agencies • Other entities authorized by HEA of 1965	• Department of Education	• Student loan companies • Finance companies • Not-for-profit entities • Banks
Loan Types:	**Loan Types:**	**Loan Types:**

• Subsidized Stafford
  – Needs-based loans made to postsecondary students for which the federal government pays interest on behalf of the student during school, grace and deferment (subject to limits and 10-year term 1)
• Unsubsidized Stafford
  – Loans made to postsecondary students with needs in excess of Subsidized Stafford loan (subject to limits and 10-year term 1)
• PLUS
  – Loans made to parents of eligible dependent students (subject to total cost of education and 10-year term 1)
  – Graduate PLUS became effective July 1, 2006 as a result of the Deficit Reduction Act of 2005. This new loan type allows graduate students to borrower under the FFEL program up to the total cost of education
• Consolidation
  – Loans comprised of multiple FFELP loans consolidated into a single loan with one payment schedule (up to 30-year term 2)
	• Subsidized Stafford
	• Unsubsidized Stafford
	• PLUS
	• Consolidation
		• Various
		  – Private loan programs are not administered by the federal government. In turn, terms, conditions and options under these programs vary according to the lender
		  – Loans are credit based (vs. needs based) and are originated pursuant to underwriting criteria
		  – Limited to total cost of education with terms of 15 to 30 years

1110

EXHIBIT 69.6 Risk Profile—Analytical Check List

Risk Consideration	Issue
Asset quality	FFELP Guaranty or private loans Percent loans in repayment Lending against delinquent borrower Undergraduate/graduate Professional schools FICO scores
Structural enhancements	Overcollateralization Interest rate reserves—losses and capitalized interest Excess spread—minimum requirements Performance-based triggers
Management/servicer expertise	Track record; management continuity; alliance with third-party servicing platform
Insolvency remoteness of servicer to insure borrowers have unfettered rights to the student loan collateral	Nonprofit Section 501(c)3 or special purpose vehicle UCC filings on collateral Limits on comingling of cash
Hedging	Interest rate mismatches—student loans and bonds Special Allowance Payment (SAP).1
Mark to market	Price volatility—is collateral marked to market with requirements to add more collateral?
Refinancing risk/extended payout	Repayment terms/refinancing risk

APPENDIX: RECENT INVESTIGATORY AND LEGISLATIVE DEVELOPMENTS

Brief History of the Guaranteed Student Loan Program

Federal student aid comes in the form of loans, grants; work-study programs and educations tax benefits. Currently there are two programs sponsored by the federal government that are governed by the Higher Education Act (HEA) of 1965 and administered by the U.S. Department of Education (ED). The HEA is administered by ED and is scheduled for reauthorization by Congress every five years. HEA is subject to frequent amendments, including several amendments that impact the terms and eligibility requirements under these programs.

EXHIBIT 69.7 Shifting Risk Profile

Emphasis Twenty-Five Years Ago: Government Role	Today's Emphasis: Structural Complexity
Key focus: Quality of the Federal Guarantee Management of loan agency	Key focus: Risk sharing: Servicer/originator Underwriting performance: Financial strength Student loan borrower quality
Recourse for improperly originated loans	
Is servicing of the loans by the loan agency done directly or by an independent servicer? What is the servicer's record and experience?	Servicer risk Performance: Percent claims rejected by the Department of Education
What type of automation has the loan agency implemented?	Management consistency
Ability to meet operating expense requirements	
Will adequate loan servicing revenue be available when loans go into repayment?	Underwriting/collection systems: Servicing platform
What portion of the portfolio is presently in repayment?	
What percent of the issue is nonasset? What provisions exist for recovering nonasset bonds?	Exceptional servicer designation status from the Department of Education
Is there protection against parity bonds increasing nonasset bonds as a percentage of outstanding bonds?	Borrower risk
Is any "nonbond" funding of reserves or payment of bond issuance expenses required?	Funded/unfunded loans
Reinvestment risk: Are bonds being issued to provide money to make new loans, or to finance existing loans?	Revolving aggregation
What call provisions exist if cash flow from loans is more rapid than projected?	

EXHIBIT 69.7 (Continued)

Emphasis Twenty-Five Years Ago: Government Role	Today's Empahsis: Structural Complexity
What maturities are allowed for investment of the debt service reserve fund?	Private loans:
Risk of fluctuating special allowance? Is the issue being sold at a rate exceeding 7 percent? If being sold as additional parity bonds, what is the weighted average rate of all bonds outstanding, and what are the maturities of prior issue.	Underwriting
	(See structural considerations listed above)
	FICO scores and income requirements
If secured by a Sallie Mae or bank-forward commitment, can the commitment be exercised in the event of negative arbitrage?	Structural considerations:
Cash flow risk: What are the assumptions regarding loan repayment? Default? Can the debt service reserve be used to smooth out cash flow without creating a default?	Liquidity
	Yield supplement
	Loss coverage
	Reserves
	Excess spread
Will the issuance of additional parity bonds and the making of additional loans be necessary to create a loan portfolio of sufficient size to cover operating expenses? Is this likely?	Parity clauses (100% collateral: under/overcollateralization)
	Performance triggers
	Refinancing: Takeout/rollover risk
Takeout risks	Structural complexities: ABCP and covered bonds

The Federal Family Education Loan Program (FFELP), also known as the Guaranteed Student Loan Program was created by Title IV of the Higher Education Act of 1965 and allows students to borrow federal funds from banks and other financial institutions. Under this program, state agencies or private nonprofit corporations administering student loan insurance programs are reimbursed for portions of losses sustained in connection with FFELP Loans and holders of certain loans are paid subsidies for owning such loans. In its initial form, student loans were available through private lenders at a fixed rate of 6% and were backed by a federal or state guarantee for 80% of the loan amount. The interest rate charged was increased in the late 1960's to 7% spurred by increase in market rates. In 1972, Congress enacted a change to make student loans more competitive by allowing lenders to receive a special allowance[5] from the federal government above the 7% fixed rate. Thereafter, Education Amendments of 1976 eliminated the uncertainty inherent in determination of special allowance rates if special allowance is calculated as bond equivalent average, less 3.5%, of the 91-day Treasury bills auctioned during the quarter. The federal government reimbursement to loan servicers for defaulted claims is 99% for Exceptional Performers (EP)[6] and 97% for the rest on all loans originated after July 1, 2006.

The William D. Ford Direct Loan Student Loan Program (FDLP) was established by the Omnibus Budget Reconciliation Act of 1993. The FDLP allows students to borrow directly from ED. The motivation for launching this program was to make student loan lending more cost efficient buy direct involvement of the federal government. To date FDSLP has originated less loan volume; furthermore, the majority of schools that have participated in the FDSLP are trade/proprietary schools whole graduates historically have higher default rates of all school types.[7]

In addition to the FFELP and FDSLP education loan, Private Student Loans or Alternative Loans are provided by private institutions with no federal government involvement. Such loans have more conservative underwriting criteria and have historically performed better than unsecured consumer loan products.

---

[5] Special Allowance Payment (SAP)–FFELP loans originated prior to July 1, 2006 generally earn interest at the greater of the borrower rate or a floating rate determined by reference to the average of the applicable floating rates (91-day Treasury bill rate or commercial paper) in a calendar quarter, plus a fixed spread that is dependent upon when the loan was originated and the loan's repayment status. If the floating rate exceeds the borrower rate, the ED pays the difference directly to the FFELP lender.

[6] Exceptional Performer Designation is determined by the Department of Education in recognition of a servicer meeting certain performance standards set by the ED in servicing FFELP loans.

[7] "Student Loan Criteria," *Standard & Poor's Structured Finance*, p. 5.

Types of Loans

Various loan products mentioned below are available to students under the FFELP and FDLP programs.

Subsidized Stafford Loans

Subsidized Stafford loans are made to undergraduate and graduate students who meet a financial needs test. The ED makes quarterly interest subsidy payments on behalf of borrowers while the borrowers are in in-school, grace, and deferment periods. As a result, interest is not capitalized during those periods.

Unsubsidized Stafford Loans

Unsubsidized Stafford loans are made to undergraduate and graduate students who do not qualify for subsidized Stafford loans or have financial needs beyond the subsidized Stafford loan limits. The ED does not make any interest subsidy payments on unsubsidized Stafford loans, as the borrower has the option to begin paying interest 60 days after disbursement or capitalize the interest during periods of in school, grace, or deferment. The repayment terms are the same as those for subsidized Stafford loans.

PLUS and GradPLUS Loans

PLUS loans are made to parents of eligible dependent students who have financial needs beyond the Stafford loan limits. In addition to the student meeting the same requirements for the Stafford loan, the parent or graduate student borrower must not have adverse credit history as determined by the ED. Since repayment begins 60 days after disbursement, the ED does not make any interest subsidy payments on PLUS loans. PLUS loans have 10-year repayment terms.

Effective July 1, 2006, graduate and professional students are eligible to borrow PLUS loans up to the cost of attendance.

Consolidation Loans

A borrower can combine multiple FFELP and FDLP (Stafford and/or PLUS) loans into one consolidation loan, to more effectively manage repayment. The repayment term is determined by the loan balance and can range from 10 to 30 years.

Private Education Loans

Private loans are originated outside federal programs, primarily by financial institutions, and as such, are not guaranteed by the ED against default. Still, originators may obtain third-party insurance to protect against default, and, similar to Stafford and PLUS loans, private education loans originated for borrowers attending schools eligible to participate in federal student loan programs are generally nondischargeable in bankruptcy.

Legislative Overview

Student loan legislation is a politically charged process and there is always a power struggle over educational funding reform. A review of the major relevant changes and proposals is as follows:

On March 30, 2006, the U.S. House of Representatives passed H.R. 609 College Access and opportunity Act of 2006 (CAOA), which extended the Higher Education Act of 1965 for six years and reauthorized certain provisions that were not part of the Higher Education Reconciliation Act of 2005 (HERA). CAOA repealed the single-holder rule for consolidation loans received on or after July 1, 2006 where HERA maintains the single-holder rule. This CAOA provision will likely be addressed by the Senate; the remaining provisions are not expected to influence the analysis of student loan revenue bonds issues.

The President's 2008 budget proposal reduced SAP by 50 basis points and raised the consolidation loan fee by 50 basis points. It reduced the EP insurance from 99 to 97 percent and the non-EP insurance from 97% to 95%. It also proposed to reduce guaranty agency collection payment and account maintenance fees. These budget proposals are offset to an extent by the College Student Relief Act that was approved in the House by a vote of 356-71 on January 17, 2007 and proposes an interest rate reduction from 6.8% to 3.4% for all new subsidized Stafford loans for undergraduates. The rate reduction reverts on January 1, 2012.

The Student Aid Reward Act (STAR Act) is aimed at encouraging participation in direct lending by providing reward payments to the participants. Savings generated through direct lending to the Federal government will be distributed to the participating school in form of reward payments in an amount not less than 50% of generated savings, these reward payment must be used to provide grants to students by the school.

The Student Loan Sunshine Act proposes to protect students and parents from exploitation of private lenders. It seeks to ensure that student loan borrowers make an informed choice of the loan product especially since private loans offer less protection that federal student loans and may include stiff penalties and exorbitant interest rates. Increased used of direct-to-consumer marketing allows students to take out loans before getting crucial advice from financial aid administrators. The Student Loan Sunshine Act requires lenders to provide an annual report in addition to disclosures requirements under federal law and also amends the Truth in Lending Act to require disclosures related to private educational loans. It forbids institutions to brand private education loans with school name, emblem, mascot, or logo and requires maintenance of a preferred lender list as part of their program participation agreement. It bans lenders from offering gifts worth $10 and imposes a fee on both lenders and institutions of no less than $25,000 for any violations.

The Student Borrower Bill of Rights Act is another proposal to provide student borrowers with basic rights regarding timely information about their loans and make reasonable and fair loan repayments.

Impact

The proposed legislation is not expected to be retroactive but does pose a threat to the federal student loan program by reducing FFELP margins, altering relations of lenders with schools and borrowers and encouraging direct lending. These changes could fundamentally alter the FFELP program. Subsidy cuts of this magnitude would almost certainly cause a significant reduction in the number of participants, limiting options for students.[8] Consolidation of loans lead by removal of the single-holder rule will result in business moving away from smaller state agencies. As lenders reengineer their business in anticipation of further legislative changes and the growth surge in private loans continues, strong underwriting discipline and good infrastructure will become paramount for success for players in the student loan market. The recent dislocation in the mortgage market has made cash-flow management at the borrower level an equally important factor for performance of student loans in the primary and the secondary markets.

Scrutiny Into Student Lenders Practices

In March 2007, an investigation was launched by New York Attorney General Andrew Cuomo into the practices of education lenders. Cuomo's probe centers on allegations that a group of lenders, including Sallie Mae, CIT Group, EduCap, and Nelnet, are paying kickbacks to colleges in the state in exchange for loan-writing assignments. He also claims the companies set up improper lines of credit for schools and paid for financial aid officers' vaca-

---

[8] *Education Finance Council Statement on FY 2008 Budget*, February 5, 2007.

tions.[9] While there is likely to be no impact on the performance of student-loan bonds, the investigation could lead to a minor reduction in the lenders' origination volumes thereby resulting in a slight cutback in securitization volumes.

---

[9] "Student Lenders Meets Minor Obstacle," *ABS Alert,* March 23, 2007.

CHAPTER 70

Analysis of Tribal Casino Bonds

Megan Neuburger
Director
Fitch Ratings

Michael Paladino, CFA
Director
Fitch Ratings

Jessalynn Moro
Senior Director
Fitch Ratings

David Litvack
Managing Director
Fitch Ratings

In recent years, Native American governments have increasingly sought and gained access to the larger capital markets. Fitch expects this trend to continue as the financial resources and capital needs of Native American governments grow. Notably, there are stark differences that exist in the size and scope of current day Native American gaming operations. A small group of tribes with significant financial resources has had the ability to greatly expand their operations. Noteworthy recent developments include the Seminole Tribe of Florida's acquisition of Hard Rock from Rank Group Plc; the partnership of the Mashantucket Pequot Tribal Nation, owner of the Foxwoods casino, with MGM Mirage; and the Mohegan Tribal Gaming Authority, owner of Mohegan Sun, being awarded a gaming license to operate slot machines at the Pennsylvania Downs race track.

However, many of the Native American gaming issuers now entering the debt markets own and operate much smaller gaming enterprises, and many are issuing debt to construct their first gaming facility. Most of these Native American gaming issuers operate single-site gaming enterprises with limited diversity in the revenue stream. The gaming operations often function with minimal liquidity levels due to the desire of tribal management to maximize distributions to the tribal government. Other credit concerns may include short operating histories and limited experience in project development. There is also some concern that enforcing bondholder rights in a workout situation may be problematic, given that a tribe is defined under federal law as a sovereign nation

While sovereignty raises questions on recovery, it also provides unique credit strengths, including a more protected regulatory and competitive environment and stronger financial metrics than those of most corporate casinos. Stronger financial metrics are mainly due to revenue sharing arrangements with states that can result in lower required payments compared to taxes paid by corporate casinos. Fitch notes that lower financial risk through strong credit metrics helps to mitigate concerns regarding the higher business and legal risks inherent to Native American gaming issuers relative to corporate gaming issuers.

Debt issued by Native American tribes is typically issued either by the tribal entity itself or by a corporation, which is wholly owned by the tribal government. The bond indenture typically assigns the cash flow of a tribal casino operation to a trustee, for the benefit of bondholders, creating a security interest in the cash flow stream. In addition to creating a security interest in the cash flow stream, the bond indenture governing Native American transactions sometimes provides additional protections for bondholders including cash trapping by the trustee at certain debt service coverage ratio triggers and the establishment of debt service reserve funds. There is typically little or no hard asset collateral.

The most creditworthy Native American gaming issuers operate their casino enterprises within a favorable competitive environment with strong market demographics and an expectation of a sustainable competitive advantage. Other important credit strengths may include a history of stable operations, experience with project development, some diversity in the revenue stream, and a stable governance and enterprise management structure.

In this chapter we discuss the key credit factors to consider in analyzing the debt of tribal casino bonds.

ISSUER CREDIT FACTORS

The following factors affect the financial viability of the gaming operation, and ultimately determine the issuer's capacity to pay debt service:

- Tribal governance
- Business profile
- Financial performance
- Management practices

Tribal Government Analysis

A thorough understanding of the operation of the tribal government and its approach to the management of the gaming enterprise is critical to the credit rating process. The gaming operation is often viewed as the tribe's most important economic driver, with contributions from gaming revenues for governmental services and member distributions dwarfing the amounts generated by other tribal enterprise operations. Because management of the tribal government will seek to maximize distributions from the gaming operation, it is important for Fitch to gain an understanding of the governmental operation and the political climate of the tribe. Key credit considerations include the governance model and the financial health of the governmental operation.

Governance Model

Fitch considers the overall philosophy of tribal leadership as it pertains to meeting the demands of the tribal members, and what role tribal leadership feels the gaming enterprise plays in meeting those demands. This entails a review of management policies and procedures. For example, if per capita distributions of gaming revenues are made to tribal members, what is the procedure for setting the amount of the distribution, how often is the policy reviewed, and what kind of approval is required for a change in the policy? Ideally, management policies have been codified, providing some level of comfort that policies and procedures will weather a change in political leadership.

Native American gaming transactions often include a limited waiver of sovereign immunity, whereby the tribe waives its rights of sovereign immunity as it pertains to covenants and performance under the bond documents. Additionally, the tribe submits to the jurisdiction of federal or state courts in the event of a dispute related to the bond documents. In the event the applicable courts deny jurisdiction, the tribe agrees to submit to arbitration to resolve the dispute. A limited waiver of sovereign immunity has never, to Fitch's knowledge, been tested as it relates to a bond agreement, resulting in a level of risk that bondholders would not be able to enforce their rights under the bond documents should it prove to be ineffective.

An additional risk unique to Native American gaming issuers stems from questions related to the status of Native American governments under the U.S. Bankruptcy Code. As currently written, a Native American government does not fit the description of any entity permitted to file for bankruptcy under the code. In the event a tribe is permitted to file a bankruptcy petition, there is the additional question of whether the U.S. bankruptcy courts would accept jurisdiction in a case involving a sovereign entity.

Financial Operations

Another key rating factor is an assessment of the financial operations of the tribal government. An important consideration is the diversity of the revenue stream supporting operations. If a tribal government is heavily dependent upon distributions from the gaming operation, analysts will seek to determine whether the tribal government has sufficient reserves on hand to withstand a drop in the distribution level in the event of financial stress at the gaming operation. Fitch views favorably the contribution of governmental assets to the gaming operation for capital expenditures or other purposes, as this demonstrates commitment of the tribal government to the health of the gaming operation, which will ultimately benefit bondholders. Fitch will also review outstanding debt obligations of the tribe not secured by gaming revenues and the past payment history of those obligations.

Business Profile of Gaming Operation

The following four issues are key to assessing the business profile of a Native American gaming operation:

- The regional gaming market
- Relationship with state government
- Competitive environment
- Project development fundamentals, if applicable

The Regional Gaming Market

An analysis of the gaming market includes a review of the relative saturation of the market, using metrics such as *win per gaming unit* to determine the depth of the market relative to other gaming markets nationwide. In addition, Fitch will evaluate the demographics of the local market area, past cyclicality or volatility in the local gaming market, the impact any volatility has had on the enterprise's revenue stream, and future threats to the viability of the market (e.g., the potential for a material increase in gaming supply). An integral part of the credit review will include a visit by Fitch analysts to the casino or project site as well as nearby competitor facilities to assess the market area.

Relationship with State Government

If a gaming compact with the state is in place, analysts will review the revenue sharing structure and any limitations placed on the number or type of devices or number of gaming facilities a tribe can operate. A key consideration is exclusivity provisions included in state compact agreements for Native American gaming issuers. Exclusivity provisions limit the number and type of competitors that can enter the marketplace, reducing the volatility of the competitive environment. The number of tribes allowed to open gaming facilities is limited by the fact that tribes must first obtain federal recognition as well as land in trust, which is often a lengthy and difficult process. Tribes and bondholders gain comfort that states will honor the compacts to avoid interruption of the revenue sharing cash flow. To avoid renewal risk related to a state compact, debt secured by gaming revenues can be structured to mature before the expiration of the compact.

Competitive Environment

Fitch considers the current competition in the market and potential threats related to new entrants or substitute products to the market. Issuers with the strongest credit characteristics are able to demonstrate a sustainable competitive advantage. One risk factor typical of Native American gaming issuers is that they often operate single-site facilities, since they must be located on reservation land. The limited market area exacerbates business risks, in addition to event risks due to severe weather, earthquakes, and other incidents that would cause business interruption. Three Fitch-rated issuers, the Seminole Tribe of Florida, the Agua Caliente Band of Cahuilla Indians, and the Laguna Development Corp. have the advantage of operating multiple sites. The Seminoles operate seven gaming facilities throughout the state of Florida, providing for good diversification across gaming markets. A unique checkerboard reservation allows the Agua Caliente Tribe to operate two facilities in the same market area, targeting different clientele at each. Laguna's two properties offer a lower level of diversification, as both properties are fueled largely by the same highway traffic.

Project Development Fundamentals

For construction of a new facility or expansion of an existing facility, analysts will review details of the development project including:

- The project budget, including the scope of the project, adequacy of contingency funds, and the equity contribution from the tribe.

- The construction process, including related contracts, required approvals and permits.
- A consideration of whether the economic fundamentals of the service area, including customer demographics, can support the new or expanded facility.
- An analysis of the management and operational oversight that will be utilized during the construction process.
- Any protections for bondholders built into the indenture should the project not reach completion by a certain date.
- Capacity of the existing operations to meet debt service payments without incremental revenues from the project?

Financial Profile of Gaming Operation

Fitch notes that Native American gaming enterprises often produce stronger financial results than corporate gaming companies, mainly as a result of a more favorable regulatory environment. However, due to the other risk factors unique to the typical Native American gaming business model, which include single-site risk and a lack of diversity in the pledged cash flow stream, a Native American gaming issuer needs to realize stronger financial results to offset the higher level of business risk.

Financial metrics considered by Fitch when rating the debt of any gaming issuer fall into the following two main categories:

- *Debt profile.* An analysis of an issuer's debt profile uses key credit metrics including debt service coverage ratios—earnings before interest, taxes, depreciation, and amortization (EBITDA) to principal and interest, and leverage ratios (total debt to EBITDA).
- *Liquidity profile.* Native American gaming issuers often have very limited levels of liquidity at the enterprise due to the practice of transferring income remaining after debt service to the governmental operation. In addition, unlike their corporate counterparts, few Native American gaming issuers utilize external sources of liquidity. As a result, Native American gaming issuers may be less able to handle financial stress. This risk may be addressed through provisions included in the bond indenture, such as debt service reserve funds and liquidity tests.

To assess the liquidity position of a Native American gaming issuer, Fitch considers:

- *Distribution ratio.* Percent of net operating cash flow of the gaming operation that is transferred to the governmental operation.

- *Retained cash flow.* Cash flow of the gaming operation remaining at the enterprise following distribution to the governmental operation, as measured by EBITDA minus distributions.

In general, a Native American gaming issuer with a lower distribution ratio and higher level of retained cash flow will be able to achieve a higher credit rating.

Fitch views favorably adherence to a policy to limit distributions to the governmental operation to a set percent of the cash flow of the gaming enterprise, thereby allowing cash to build up at the enterprise that may be used for capital investments or emergency working capital. Other liquidity sources that can provide comfort to bondholders include access to outside sources of capital or debt service reserve funds.

Historical financial operations are reviewed at the time a rating is assigned initially, and on an ongoing basis while the rating is outstanding. In addition, Fitch requests that issuers provide pro forma financials regarding developments that may impact the financial profile of the operation, such as changes in the marketplace or regulatory environment as well as future expansion plans. Financial stress tests are also developed by Fitch to determine the level of financial stress the enterprise could withstand while maintaining coverage on its operations and debt service.

Of key concern when considering pro forma financial operations is a review of plans for additional debt issuance secured by gaming revenues. Ideally, additional leverage will be incurred only for projects that will enhance the pledged revenue stream. Fitch will also consider the possibility of changes in the gaming market or regulatory environment that may lead to additional leverage, such as an amendment to a state gaming compact agreement that will allow for expansion of gaming facilities.

Management Practices of Gaming Operation

During its credit review Fitch analysts will seek to understand the relationship between the tribal government and the enterprise management and assess the quality of management in operating the enterprise.

Relationship with Tribal Government

An initial consideration is the legal structure that has been put it place by the tribe to act as the owner and operator of the gaming enterprise and issuer of the enterprise related debt. Native American gaming issuers commonly use two types of governance structures:

- The tribe is the issuer/obligor and directly manages the enterprise operation.

■ A federally chartered corporation is created and acts as the issuer/obligor and management for the enterprise operation. This corporation is wholly owned by the tribe.

Fitch notes that there are some advantages to the establishment of a separate corporation that may result in limitations on the influence that can be exerted by tribal membership over the operations of the enterprise. However, in most instances the board of the corporation is appointed by and can be removed by the tribe, at will. Fitch evaluates the enterprise governance structure on a case-by-case basis to determine the impact on the credit profile of the issuer.

Other issues when assessing the relationship of enterprise management with the tribal government include:

■ Does the enterprise management report directly to the tribal government, or to the board of a separate corporation?
■ The frequency of formal reports to the tribal government.
■ In the case of a separate corporation, the composition of the board and the background and professional expertise of the board members.
■ Whether outside consultants are utilized by the tribe to assist the enterprise management team.

Quality of Management

Another important credit factor is an analysis of the management directly responsible for the operations of the casino enterprise, including the depth and stability of key management functions, and the experience of individuals in these positions. For tribes operating a single-site casino, management depth is often limited.

An assessment of the operations of the enterprise will take place during a visit by analysts to the facilities. This assessment will involve discussion with management regarding all major functions of the facility such as operation of the gaming floor, marketing, food and beverage and, if applicable, related hotel operations.

BOND STRUCTURE AND SECURITY FEATURES

Fitch also considers in its rating analysis the security structure of the debt. The most important structure and security provisions are the collateral provided by pledged revenues, debt service reserves funds, and the trustee security structure that provides for trapping of pledged revenues at certain debt service coverage ratio triggers.

Collateral Package

As mentioned previously, the collateral package associated with debt issued by Native American entities typically includes little or no hard asset value, which may limit the prospects for bondholders in a recovery situation. Debt is usually secured only by an interest in the cash flows of the gaming operation, which are unlikely to be available in a severe financial stress scenario. Bond indenture provisions such as cash traps and debt service reserves funds will not have the impact of increasing the likelihood of recovery in a default scenario. However, these provisions can reduce the probability of default by elevating the bondholder's interest in the cash flow stream as the credit approaches distress.

Debt Service Reserve Funds

Fitch considers the funding of debt service reserves to be among the most important bond security provisions. The funding of a reserve somewhat mitigates the lack of liquidity often seen at Native American gaming enterprises. It is recognized that a debt service reserve fund cannot be liquidated to provide working capital, and can only be utilized to cure a deficiency in required debt service payments. However, the availability of these monies can free up more of the cash flows of the operation to be used for working capital in a time of distress. Fitch views most favorably bond indentures that require both a fully funded debt service reserve at closing, and an additional springing reserve funded through the flow of funds at certain minimum debt service coverage ratio triggers.

Cash Trapping by the Trustee

Security provisions that provide for the trapping of the pledged cash flow by the trustee at certain debt service coverage ratio triggers serve to elevate the interest of bondholders in the pledged cash flow to a position above that of the tribe, which typically controls the cash flow in the absence of debt service coverage falling below a trigger point. Although the typical Native American gaming revenue bond indenture creates a security interest for bondholders senior to the claim of the tribal government, there can be concern related to the tribe's potential actions to divert the cash flows for other purposes in a financial distress scenario. The assurance that the cash will be trapped by the trustee mitigates this risk.

Fitch also considers in its rating analysis structural features such as additional bonds tests, liquidity tests, any hard asset security, and requirements to fund additional reserves, such as a renewal and replacement reserve, through the flow of funds.

SUMMARY

In this chapter, we discussed the key credit factors to consider in analyzing tribal casino bonds. Issuer credit factors to consider are tribal government analysis, business profile of gaming operation, financial profile of gaming operation, and management practices of gaming operation. The most important bond structure and security features to consider are the collateral package, debt service reserves, and cash trapping by the trustee.

CHAPTER 71

Understanding Variable Rate Demand Obligations

Mitchell Savader
Chief Executive Officer
The Savader Group LLC
and
Managing Director
Civitas Funding Group LLC

This chapter focuses on *variable-rate demand obligations* (VRDOs) including important considerations when issuing or investing in municipal bonds that use this structure. VDROs have played an increasingly important role in the public finance market in recent years as they provide an attractive investment alternative for investors seeking highly liquid short-term, tax-exempt investments. They are typically purchased by money market funds due to the need to maintain a stable share price. As for obligors, VRDOs provide an efficient and effective tool for managing interest expenses by allowing for the issuance of long-term obligations using short-term interest rates. These instruments are popular with a wide variety of obligors, including state and local governments, regional, and municipally owned utilities and various not-for-profit entities such as hospitals and institutions of higher learning. The availability of municipal interest rate swaps has also contributed to the increased use of VRDOs in recent years by providing a mechanism to eliminate a major risk associated with VRDOs: exposure to increasing interest expenses over time.

HOW VRDOs WORK

Generally speaking, VRDOs are financial instruments whose yield is reset on a regular basis, such as daily, weekly, monthly, or even semiannually. As rates in the overall market move up or down, the VRDO's yield is adjusted in order to bring it in line with the broader interest rate market. The rate reset is typically based on yield data published on a pool of high-quality, short-term, tax-exempt investments.

VRDOs also come with a put feature that allows the investor to return the obligation to the obligor or its agent. Upon each interest rate reset, the investor has the right to put the instrument back to the obligor and be paid face value plus any accrued interest. The ability to return the security provides the investor with the ability to walk away from the investment in the event the newly reset rate is deemed inadequate. Despite most VRDOs being issued with final maturities in line with more traditional fixed-rate instruments (typically 20 to 30 years), the flexibility provided by the interest rate reset and put features virtually eliminates interest rate risk typically present with long-term obligations.

THE NEED FOR CASH

When an investor decides to exercise a put option, the issuer is required to pay the investor from available cash. If the bond can be remarketed quickly, the necessary liquidity will be readily available. However, in the event a remarketing cannot be accomplished, additional liquidity may be required to pay the investor.

Some obligors, such as large not-for-profit universities, maintain substantial levels of readily available liquidity and therefore can provide their own liquidity to meet any potential puts. This liquidity usually takes the form of cash or highly liquid assets such as securities backed by the U.S. government or its agencies or triple-A rated money market funds. The goal is to always have sufficient liquidity to meet any potential demand for payment, even on a single-day's notice. In addition, the assets should be above and beyond what is needed to meet the obligor's normal operating liquidity requirements. For those obligors maintaining large investment portfolios to accomplish various goals, such as meeting future capital needs or funding unforeseen budget gaps, the ability to forego external sources of liquidity—along with their related costs—for VRDOs can present an added financial benefit.

However, as most public-purpose entities lack substantial cash reserves, they must look to third-party liquidity providers to provide the necessary cash to cover the repurchase of put bonds. Many VRDOs are supported by a *letter of credit* (LOC) or *standby bond purchase agreement* (SBPA) from a highly rated financial institution. Furthermore, even if a public entity maintains substantial reserves and liquidity, it may want the flexibility to invest these assets in ways that tie them up for a period of time, thereby reducing or eliminating their availability in the event of a put. For these obligors, an external source of liquidity may also be desirable.

With an LOC, the financial institution is the primary source of liquidity. When VRDOs are put back to the obligor, the financial institution becomes the primary provider of liquidity. With a SBPA, the financial institution agrees to serve as liquidity provider of last resort by purchasing the VRDO in the event the instrument cannot be remarketed. Regardless of which structure is used, the liquidity provider is the ultimate source of liquidity and therefore the VRDO instrument carries its short-term rating.

Ideally, the term of the agreement between the issuer and liquidity provider should cover the life of the debt. To the extent that the liquidity arrangement terminates prior to the obligation's final maturity, there may not be sufficient liquidity to pay the investor in the event of a put after the agreement terminates. To avoid such an occurrence, the obligor must either secure a replacement facility or refinance and convert the bonds into a fixed-rate instrument.

THE ROLE OF BOND INSURANCE

VRDOs are also typically sold with credit enhancement that protects the investor and liquidity provider from long-term credit risk. This credit enhancement typically takes the form of a municipal bond insurance policy provided by one of the primary triple-A rated monoline bond insurers.

Municipal bond insurance provides the investor with the absolute and unconditional guarantee of the insurer to pay all scheduled debt service requirements for the life of the bond. As a result, the obligation carries the bond rating assigned to the claims-paying ability of the insurer, typically triple A. If an issuer cannot make a debt service payment on a particular bond, the bond trustee notifies the insurer of the default and that it will be making a claim on the insurance policy. The insurer typically has one business day to make the payment to the trustee, who then distributes the payment to the bondholders. Furthermore, there are no exceptions to the insurance guarantee, including war, terrorism, act of God or environmental disaster. According to the Association of Financial Guaranty Insurers, the industry trade association, no member insurance firm has ever failed to promptly fulfill a payment obligation.

In addition, insured bonds are highly liquid instruments with prices tied primarily to the insurance commitment of the insurer. Every day, large numbers of insured bonds are traded in the secondary market. Given their broad acceptance, insured bonds can usually be sold with relative ease. In the event a liquidity provider becomes the owner of an insured bond, the credit enhancement provided by bond insurance should help with the remarketing of the bond.

CHAPTER 72

State Credit Enhancement Programs for School Districts and Municipalities

Harold B. Burger
Assistant Vice President and Research Analyst
AllianceBernstein

State credit enhancement programs are designed to assist local governments with obtaining improved credit ratings where, all things equal, the natural underlying credit rating of a local government would be weaker. Although credit enhancement programs are typically structured and sponsored by state governments for their underlying governmental units, often local school districts and their GO debt, other types of enhancement programs, such as a public pension fund guarantee of another entity's debt, exist. However, this chapter exclusively focuses on state credit enhancement programs designed for local school districts and municipalities. This chapter will provide an overview of the differences between enhancement program types; the rating agencies' approach to assessing enhancement programs; and the advantages and disadvantages of such programs.

State credit enhancement programs exist to provide a credit substitute to an otherwise weaker underlying governmental unit when there is a need for the local unit to access the capital markets. In many cases, the enhancement program is either directly or indirectly tied to the state government's credit quality. There are generally four types of credit enhancement programs identified by the rating agencies: state intercepts, state GO guarantees, non-GO state support, and state permanent funds. We discuss each of these in this chapter as well as how to assess them.

TYPES OF STATE CREDIT ENHANCEMENT PROGRAMS

Although there are some variants, state intercepts are generally structured so that the state sponsor is able to divert a local government's aid revenue directly to a trustee or paying agent in the event of an anticipated or actual payment default. Intercept programs can be broken into pre- and postdefault types that are defined by underlying state laws. In the case of a predefault intercept program, the underlying governmental unit must typically deposit sufficient funds to a trustee or paying agent prior to the principal or interest payment date. In the event the local government deposits insufficient funds, there should be adequate time to notify the state sponsor so that revenues required to make up any deficiency can be provided to a paying agent or trustee. An example of a predefault state intercept program is Ohio's Intercept Program under Section 3317.18 of the Ohio Revised Code. Conversely, postdefault enhancement programs are where the state is notified of a payment default subsequent to the principal or interest date. While postdefault programs may not ensure the timely repayment of a debt obligation, they can provide investors with the security of principal and interest recovery. Examples of postdefault intercept programs include New York State's Section 99-b program and Pennsylvania's Section 633 program.

Some credit enhancement programs are backed by a GO pledge of the state sponsor; therefore, they receive a credit rating on par with such state and their assessments move in tandem with the state. This form of credit enhancement is straightforward: The state sponsor supplies its guarantee, in the form of a GO pledge, as a back up in the event there is a default at the local level. Examples of credit enhancements that are GO pledges of the state sponsor include the Michigan School Bond Loan Fund and the Oregon School Bond Guaranty Act.

A third category includes those programs that supply a pledge that is not a GO of the state sponsor. Essentially, a non-GO state credit enhancement program is a "commitment to paying defaulting debt service from all or part of their (the state sponsors) general funds or another funding source."[1] This form of credit enhancement is more closely related to an appropriation-type of obligation by a state. For instance, Standard & Poor's differentiates this type of enhancement program by "standing or annual appropriation,"[2] with both types maintaining a relationship to the overall credit quality of the

---

[1] David T. Litvack, "The ABCs of State School Credit Enhancement Programs," *Fitch Ratings, Tax Supported Special Report* (April 1999), p. 5.

[2] John Sugden-Castillo, "Public Finance Criteria: State Credit Enhancement Programs," Standard & Poor's, *Public Finance Criteria* (October 2006), p. 2.

state. Examples of non-GO enhancements include the programs available in South Carolina and West Virginia.[3]

The credit enhancement program with little direct or indirect relationship to a state sponsor are permanent funds, which are segregated funds whose assets are leveraged to support the debt service of an underlying government. Permanent funds are somewhat similar to pension funds in that they are separate and distinct trusts where the fund's assets are pledged for specific purposes. Some permanent funds were created through the sales of natural resources, such as land and minerals. States with permanent fund enhancement programs include Nevada and Texas. These funds function in the same manner as a monoline bond insurance company, although the ability to leverage their asset base is significantly lower.

ASSESSING STATE CREDIT ENHANCEMENT PROGRAMS

The rating agencies have published extensive guidelines identifying their analytical approaches to assessing state credit enhancement programs. Although there are numerous state credit enhancement programs assessed and followed by the agencies, there are shared factors that the agencies focus on when conducting their analysis. For the most part, these factors include the enhancement program's structure, oversight, and pledged revenues, as well as the general credit quality of the state sponsor.

A primary area of analysis pertains to the structure of the credit enhancement program. A structural analysis includes understanding the legal basis for the program, which could be based on a constitutional provision or legislative action. One should determine whether there is a separate trustee or paying agent involved with making debt service payments. Additionally, timing features are an essential factor in determining the effectiveness and credit quality of an enhancement program: Does an enhancement program assure full and timely payment before or after payment default has occurred? Are there reimbursement requirements for the local government if enhancement program assets are deployed? What are the various reporting and notification responsibilities and who are the participants at the state level? Furthermore, enhancement programs have eligibility requirements that must be fully understood in order to determine if the program has the appropriate authority and capability of backing third-party debt obligations.

Oversight at the state and local government level is a key area of focus when analyzing any state credit enhancement program. Oversight is important in order to ensure that in the event of an anticipated debt service payment disruption, the enhancement program operates effectively so that bondhold-

---

[3] Sugden-Castillo, "Public Finance Criteria: State Credit Enhancement Programs."

ers are paid. One would hope that oversight takes place at the local government level so that any anticipated fiscal distress can be identified in a timely manner. Yet, the nature and purpose of a credit enhancement program implies that if ever needed to assist a local government, there would likely already be some level of distress, potentially relating to insufficient local oversight. In other words, oversight at the local governmental level should be desired, but not assumed. Hence, the most important area of program oversight lies with the state sponsor: Aside from the monitoring of the enhancement program's mechanics, it is important that the state maintain some level of supervision over local governments, particularly after fiscal distress is realized and/or the enhancement program has been invoked. Separately, internal oversight of a state's revenue profile and cash flow requirements is imperative in order to ensure sufficient resources for potential debt service make up payments are available. School districts participating in such programs should schedule their debt service payments so that there is sufficient time remaining in the state fiscal year to tap into state appropriations still to be paid to the district.

It is important to understand what resources are pledged under an enhancement program. In the case of a state intercept for school districts, pledged revenues may include state education aid. A debt service coverage test that is tied to pledged revenues and local government debt service can be performed in order to gauge credit enhancement program flexibility—rating agencies frequently require and perform such coverage tests. For other types of enhancement programs, such as a permanent fund pledge, legally permitted guarantee capacity levels should be analyzed, along with the fund's management, and investment guidelines and performance.

Other than permanent funds, the underlying GO credit quality of the state sponsor will play either a direct or indirect role in the continuing assessment of a corresponding credit enhancement program. Additionally, the spread between a state's GO credit rating and the enhancement program assessment will tie to whether there is an outright GO pledge, a state appropriation, or a pre- or postdefault intercept. Postdefault intercept enhancement programs could be assessed at a level several notches from the state credit rating.[4]

CREDIT ENHANCEMENT PROGRAM ADVANTAGES AND DISADVANTAGES

The primary advantage of state credit enhancement programs is to provide bondholders with additional security, so that in the event of fiscal dis-

---

[4] Linda Hird Lipnick, "Moody's Approach to Rating School District Enhancement Programs: Quality of Credit Enhancement Varies," *Moody's Investors Service Global Credit Research, Rating Methodology* (June 2003), p. 3.

tress at the local government level, there is a mechanism in place to ensure continued payment and/or recovery of principal and interest. From a local government's perspective enhancement programs represent a means to more easily and affordably access the debt markets.

From a bondholder's perspective, there are some disadvantages to holding paper backed by a state credit enhancement program. One such disadvantage, as in the case of other municipal securities, is the potential for an event to occur that would result in the lowering of the enhancement program's credit rating. An adverse credit event is a factor that has the potential to negatively affect a bonds' price. In the case of a bond that exclusively maintains an enhanced rating, credit events are completely out of the control of the local government obligor. Events that can affect the credit quality of an enhancement program include a change in the state sponsor's GO rating or change in legal structure or climate. For instance, on July 11, 2005, Standard & Poor's lowered South Carolina's GO rating to AA+ from AAA.[5] Consequently, South Carolina's school credit enhancement program, which is rated one-notch below the state's GO rating, was lowered to AA from AA+.[6] South Carolina's credit enhancement program rating is considered a non-GO state obligation, whereby debt service payments are made up from state school aid on behalf of a local school district upon notification, prior to actual principal and interest payment dates.[7]

A second example pertains to a change in a state law relating to an enhancement program. On May 15, 2007, Moody's Investors Service put its credit rating on the New Mexico School District enhancement program on its "watch list" for a possible downgrade due to "changes in New Mexico law that affect the amount of eligible state resources that can be advanced for debt service."[8] Although it is unclear if and how the law change will affect the New Mexico enhancement program's rating, it is clear that with enhancement programs, bondholders are exposed to distinct factors that do not pertain to the actual local government obligor.

A separate potential disadvantage pertains to the assumption that local school district finances will be monitored and state sponsors will be notified in the event of a payment delinquency. A recent example is the Roosevelt Union Free School District in Long Island, New York. As a school district

---

[5] Eden Perry, "South Carolina Rating Lowered to 'AA+'; Off Watch; Outlook Stable," *Standard & Poor's RatingsDirect* (July 2005), p. 1.

[6] Eden Perry, "South Carolina State Aid Intercept Program Tax Secured, School State Program," *Standard & Poor's RatingsDirect* (July 2005), p. 1–5.

[7] Sugden-Castillo, "Public Finance Criteria: State Credit Enhancement Programs."

[8] Mireya Loewe, "Moody's Places Aa2 Rating of NM School Enhancement Program on Watchlist for Possible Downgrade," *Moody's Investors Service, Rating Update: New Mexico Sch. Dist. Enhancement Program* (May 2007), p. 1.

that had been experiencing significant financial difficulties, the district had already come under much closer scrutiny by New York State. It was recently discovered that Roosevelt had not fully made its interest payments to the Depository Trust Company (DTC) on its series 2003 GO bonds on December 15, 2005 and December 15, 2006. According to the filed material event disclosure, the December 15, 2006 delinquent interest payment amount was $19,125.[9] The event disclosure further states that the missed payments to the DTC were attributable to "inadequate administrative oversight"[10] at the school district. Interestingly, actual payment to bondholders was not disrupted due to the DTC making up the interest delinquencies. Furthermore, "following notification by the DTC of the interest payment delinquency, the school district wired $19,125 to the DTC on January 25, 2007,"[11] a full month after the delinquency occurred. Under section 99-b of the New York State Finance Law:

> In the event a holder or owner of any such bond or note shall file with the state comptroller a verified statement describing such bond or note and alleging default in the payment thereof or the interest thereon or both such principal and interest, it shall be the duty of the state comptroller to immediately investigate the circumstances of the alleged default and prepare and file in his office a certificate setting forth his determinations with respect thereto and to serve a copy thereof by registered mail upon the chief fiscal officer, as such term is defined in the local finance law, of the city, city school district, or school district which issued such bond or note . . . . Upon the filing of such a certificate in the office of the state comptroller, the state comptroller shall thereafter deduct and withhold from the next succeeding allotment, apportionment or payment of such state aid or assistance due such city, city school district, or school district . . . such amount thereof as may be required to pay the principal of and interest on such bonds and notes . . . then in default.[12]

In the case of Roosevelt, the section 99-b state intercept program did not activate because there was no formal notification to the state comptroller because payment to bondholders had not been interrupted. The DTC bridged the payment gap and then notified the school district itself about the revenue deficiencies. Although the delinquent interest payment was eventually made

[9] Notice of Material Event Information Cover Sheet (February 2007), p. 3.
[10] Id.
[11] Id.
[12] Laws of New York, Consolidated Law, New York State Finance Law § 99-B, "Withholding of State Aid for School Purposes Upon," p. 1.

public, this example illustrates a potential disadvantage of credit enhancement programs: There is a fundamental assumption that there is some basic level of oversight and notification at both the local and state levels.

A similar concern pertains to the lack of testing of credit enhancement programs. Defaults at the local level on GO debt are very rare, and even though credit enhancement program legal provisions are well established, there is an absence of a thorough track record. As Fitch puts it, "because triggering the intercept would necessarily divert funds away from school operations, political and legal pressures to keep aid targeted to the classroom could be intense . . . . Nonpayment by a school district, particularly a sustained period of nonpayment creates the risk, albeit remote, that the intercept protection will not be implemented as set forth by law."[13] Also, because enhancement programs are seldom activated, there is the risk that the various actors involved may not know what procedures should be followed.

SUMMARY

State credit enhancement programs are an important tool used by local governments to more easily and affordably access the capital markets. The various types of enhancement programs have generally received solid credit assessments from the rating agencies, and security provisions provide bondholders with comfort of timely debt service and recovery of principal and interest. Many of the bonds in these programs are additionally insured with a triple-A rating provided by a monoline bond insurance company. Although state credit enhancement programs possess relative disadvantages, the low risk nature of local GO debt may make enhancement program paper desirable to the conservative investor.

---

[13] Litvack, "The ABCs of State School Credit Enhancement Programs."

CHAPTER 73

The ABCs of Charter Schools

Mitchell Savader
Chief Executive Officer
The Savader Group LLC
and
Managing Director
Civitas Funding Group LLC

Although still in its infancy, the charter school movement has expanded rapidly over the last decade and a half, growing from a single school in 1992 to several thousand schools today. This growth has fueled the need for numerous school buildings and the related capital necessary to fund construction of new facilities or the purchase and upgrading of existing facilities. Though still a relatively small proportion of the overall public finance market, the issuance of charter school backed debt has created growing investment opportunities, with further growth expected to reflect the ongoing expansion of this relatively young sector. However, investors should be aware of the unique attributes associated with this sector as well as their implications for credit quality. This chapter focuses on some of these unique credit attributes and what analysts should know about them in order to make well-informed investment decisions.

UNDERSTANDING CHARTER SCHOOLS

Charter schools are publicly funded schools typically created to achieve two results: to provide students with educational opportunities not otherwise available and to hold schools accountable for the results they produce. In addition, charter schools can often operate with significant autonomy and flexibility as they are not normally held to many of the same legal and regulatory requirements imposed by each state on its local public school systems.

The creation and ongoing existence of a charter school is based on the terms of the school's *charter*. Each charter is granted, for a fixed period of time, to an organization or group of individuals, by a state authorized entity. The charter serves as a contract between those supporting the creation of the school and the entity granting the charter. The charter spells out many aspects of the school's character including how it will operate, what the educational focus will be and the various methods for measuring success.

The majority of a charter school's funding is typically provided by the state in which it is located and is based on the school's student enrollment. This characteristic serves as a major distinction between charter schools and traditional public schools. Charter schools lack the ability to impose and collect local property taxes to fund operating and debt service costs; a fundamental attribute of most public school systems. As a result, charter schools must operate as quasi-businesses, while traditional public schools function as governmental entities not subject to the same operational pressures. In fact, if not managed properly, charter schools can and have gone "out of business."

The concept of charter schools first began in Philadelphia in the late 1980s. As the local school system sought to increase the educational alternatives available to its students, it created a number of new charter schools within several of its existing school buildings. By the beginning of the next decade, the charter school movement took a giant step forward as Minnesota passed the first state-wide law providing for the creation of charter schools. Over the following 15 years, the sector realized tremendous growth as parents and other supporters sought alternatives to what many perceived as the substandard traditional public school system.

In 1995, some 100 charter schools were operating throughout the nation. By 1999, the number had grown to almost 1,500 schools in 37 states and the District of Columbia. Currently, almost 4,000 charter schools are operating in 40 states as well as Washington D.C. and Puerto Rico. Charter school enrollments are reportedly approaching 1.2 million students nationwide.

THE CHARTER

The very existence of a charter school is dependent upon the granting of a charter by an entity authorized to do so by the state in which the school will be located. The nature of the granting entity and its relationship with the charter school is critical to the school's creation and ongoing management. In fact, some granting authorities are more closely linked to the schools they have created than are other types of authorizing entities.

As of 2005, there were reportedly some 600 charter school authorizers operating throughout the nation including local school districts, regional agencies, state education agencies, independent chartering boards, colleges and universities, certain municipalities and various not-for-profit organizations. The need to operate as a quasi-business concern makes a strong supportive relationship between authorizing entity and charter school very important. A charter school created by a local school district is far more likely to benefit from its relationship with that district whereas a charter school formed by a statewide agency may function as competition for a local school district. This can prove a problem given a charter school's need to successfully overcome competitive pressures.

Keep in mind that state aid typically follows a student. Therefore, state aid for a student moving from a traditional public school to a newly formed charter school moves with the student, subject to certain adjustments. Therefore, if a public school experiences the loss of a student to a charter school, it will also lose most, if not all, of the state revenue associated with that student. The need for revenue may cause traditional public schools to compete aggressively with local charter schools for area students

A school district that grants a charter for a new charter school is likely to have a more cooperative arrangement with the school and see it as an extension of its own operating structure. Furthermore, the charter school will not be competing with the school district for state aid as the district presumably created the charter school with the expectation that some state aid will shift to the new school.

However, regardless of the type of entity providing the charter, the credit analyst should still examine the nature of the relationship between the granting authority and the charter school as well as understand the motivations of the grantor. Even a charter school formed by a local school district may one day find its existence inconsistent with the district's evolving interests. For example, some public school districts may create a charter school to expand their capacity to accommodate increasing student enrollments. However, if over time the pattern reverses itself, the local school district may find itself competing with area charter schools for a shrinking pool of students. Analyzing the relationship between a charter school and the charter provider should closely examine the authorizer's motivations and how they may change over time.

As charters are authorized for a fixed term—usually five to seven years— charter schools must constantly strive to meet the terms and requirements of their charters to ensure continued renewal by the authorizing entity. Without this renewal, the charter school will lose its legal right to exist when the charter expires. By contrast, traditional public schools are creatures of the state, operate pursuant to state law and are not required to actively maintain their legal existence. A charter school that has successfully won renewal of its charter has demonstrated an ability to meet the requirements of the authorizing entity as well as the state in which it operates. Charter schools that have yet to secure a renewal provide less comfort regarding their ability to satisfy its charter requirements over time, leaving an open variable in the analysis.

Offsetting this concern is the practice of many charter authorizers to regularly provide feedback to a charter school on those issues that could preclude the school's charter from being renewed. In this way, the charter school is made aware of, and therefore can address, the issues prior to the formal charter renewal process. In addition, by learning about necessary adjustments prior to the formal process, the charter school will have additional time to develop the financial resources that may be required to fund any related operating or capital expenses.

THE RELATIONSHIP BETWEEN DEMAND AND FINANCIAL SUCCESS

Traditional public schools are typically funded from a combination of locally generated property taxes and financial support provided by the state in which they exist. However, charter schools do not have the right to impose taxes and, being a public school, cannot collect tuition from students wishing to attend. Instead, charter schools rely almost exclusively on state support which is based on enrollment. Generally speaking, the more students a charter school attracts, the more funding it receives. A failure to attract students will limit funding, possibly below the minimum amount necessary to maintain ongoing operations and pay debt service on outstanding bonds.

Charter schools are typically dependent upon the generation of net revenues—those revenues available after the prior payment of operating and maintenance expenses—to pay debt service requirements. Therefore, reviewing the credit quality of these bonds rests on three analytically important considerations: (1) revenues; (2) operating and maintenance expenses; and (3) debt service requirements. The relationship between these three attributes determines whether or not the charter school will have the funds necessary to meet it operating needs and its financial obligations.

As previously mentioned, state payments comprise the dominant component of a charter school's financial resources. Broadly speaking, these payments are dependent upon an equation that multiplies state aid per student by the number of students attending the school. With regard to the first variable, severe financial stress can cause state aid per student to decline year-over-year. However, most years typically see at least a modest increase in state financial support for education. To better understand the stability, or vulnerability of this revenue stream, the analyst should consider the state's financial profile, including the economic sensitivity of its revenue base, and the importance the state places on its financial support for public education.

Understanding the school's operating expenses can draw an analyst's focus to another interesting feature of charter schools. Many charter schools are managed by former public school officials who have tired of a system that in their opinion was unnecessarily burdened by various legal and bureaucratic constraints. The opportunity to take the initiative by creating a new school and operating it in the best interests of the students they serve can be very attractive. However, it must be remembered that charter schools differ from traditional public schools in ways that force them to behave as quasi-businesses. While a charter school's management team may be great at developing and implementing a school's curriculum and building a first-rate educational program, they may not necessarily be focused on running the school as a business. The desire to fund what may be a costly educational initiative must be balanced with the dispassionate need to maintain a structurally balanced financial profile

The analyst should consider all available sources of financial information when developing an understanding of a management team's financial competency. Often, the most crucial of all available documents are the charter school's audited financial statements. The analyst should focus on several key items including the school's annual operating results, budget versus actual performance, management's discussion of financial highlights, and the maintenance of satisfactory reserves and liquidity. Of these, the comparison of budget to actual performance may shed the most light on a management team's financial philosophy. Given that the charter school movement is still in its infancy, and most charter schools have not been in existence for more than just a few years, management teams are largely untested and therefore somewhat unproven. As a result, a conservatively managed charter school could be perceived as being better positioned to deal with unbudgeted expenses or revenues below expectation.

Also important is management's foresight and ability to develop contingency reserves. Charter schools may require such reserves to offset instances where state payments are reduced or delayed without much warning. The appropriate level of reserves should reflect several variables including the historical level and timing of state aid and the charter school's flexibility to quickly reduce expenses in times of financial stress.

Another important feature of charter schools is their need to maintain or grow enrollments. Given the method by which charter schools are funded, a school's ability to recruit and retain its enrollment is critically important to its ability to maintain a structurally balanced financial profile. Those schools demonstrating a favorable enrollment trend over several years, especially when measured against original expectations of initial demand, provide a measure of comfort that future expectations will be realized. In addition, those schools that have historically maintained enrollments in excess of what is required to generate sufficient financial resources are less likely to face the pressures associated with the need to increase future enrollments.

By providing opportunity, charter schools give students a choice of where to attend school. But students are not necessarily compelled to take advantage of the opportunity represented by a charter school. Students can decide to stay right where they are, within the local public school system or area charter school, or may even decide to attend a different charter school.

This part of the analysis is generally limited for a newly created charter school given the lack of historical enrollment demand. A charter school may have indications of interest from numerous prospective students, but history has shown that many students exhibiting interest do not necessarily translate that interest into action. Improvements at existing traditional public or charter schools, as well as the opening of new charter schools, will increase a student's options and may cut into a charter school's enrollment.

To gauge a charter school's competitive profile, the analyst should consider several variables, including (1) the school's reputation; (2) the nature of the curriculum and its role in the larger marketplace for educational services; (3) the historical enrollment pattern; (4) offerings by other traditional public, charter or private schools; (5) the size and currency of the school's waiting list; (6) the school's ability to translate waiting list students to enrolled students; (7) class sizes; and finally (8) neighborhood demographics.

A review of a charter school's ability to attract students would not be complete without an understanding of the potential universe of students that could enroll at the school. A growing population of school age area residents can mitigate some competitive pressures, while a declining school age population will only increase these pressures. Also, the location and accessibility of an existing or proposed school facility can affect enrollment if the facility is difficult or expensive to reach.

SUMMARY

The discussion in this chapter is based on an understanding of the charter school sector as it has rapidly evolved since the late 1980s. However, the sector remains relatively young and unseasoned and there is no reason to doubt that further change will occur. As a result, some analytically important variables may wane while others come more clearly into focus. Therefore, analysts should be flexible in their approach and be prepared to make adjustments based on the attributes of the specific credit under review.

Case Studies of Innovative and Other Security Structures

New York City Uses Taxable Municipals After 9/11 for Budget Relief and Affordable Housing

Emily A. Youssouf
Managing Director
JP Morgan Public Finance

New York City faced a time of fiscal distress in the aftermath of the terrorist attacks of September 11, 2001, which resulted in the deaths of more than 2,800 people, the destruction of more than 11 million square feet of office space and 650,000 square feet of retail space and the loss of more than 100,000 jobs. Early in 2002, the city government faced a budget deficit of $4.8 billion[1] created by a down turn in the economy that reduced property, sales and income taxes.

As the city struggled to close that gap, it sought and found innovative solutions. The issuance of these bonds by a public benefit corporation affiliated with the city government generated $308 million for the city while maintaining steady services to city residents.

FILLING A BUDGET GAP

The New York City Housing Development Corporation (HDC), a New York State-chartered public benefit corporation that works with the New York City government to finance the construction and preservation of affordable housing, issued $285 million in federally taxable, variable rate bonds (the 2002 Series D Bonds). Using proceeds from the sale of these

---

[1] Office of Management and Budget, City of New York, *Financial Plan: The City of New York Fiscal Years 2002–2006: Summary Book*, February 13, 2002. Available at http://www.nyc.gov/html/omb/pdf/sum1_02.pdf.

bonds, HDC paid the city $223 million to purchase a 100% interest in the cash flows generated by approximately 380 city-originated and city-owned mortgage loans, and a mortgage-backed security evidencing the city's interest in 90 other mortgages first sold by the city in 1995 (this pool is known as the "Sheridan Trust"). Because HDC purchased only the mortgages' cash flow, and not the underlying mortgages, the city retained its rights to the cash flows generated by the mortgages after HDC's bonds are retired.

In addition, to protect itself from the risks associated with variable-rate bonds, HDC purchased an interest rate cap for $22.2 million from the city's Transitional Finance Authority (TFA). This cap ensured that if the interest rate on the 2002 Series D Bonds ever rose above 7.5%, the TFA would pay the difference. Between the $223 million HDC paid the City of New York to buy the mortgage cash flows and the $22 million paid to the city's TFA, HDC's bond sale provided more than $245 million to the city as an upfront cash infusion, which helped close a yawning city budget gap. The loan servicing operations moved from a city agency to HDC resulted with no noticeable change to the residents in the buildings covered by them. HDC would use the revenues generated by the mortgage cash flows to repay the bonds, and anything left over was placed in a pool of money HDC uses to provide low-interest second mortgages to further finance the creation of affordable housing.

The transaction was so successful that a year later, a second similar one was pursued. This time, HDC issued $64.1 million in federally taxable, variable-rate bonds (the 2003 Series D Bonds) to generate $63 million for the city. These bonds financed the purchase of the cash flows generated by approximately 314 mortgage loans to affordable apartment buildings in New York City, and the cash flows from 24 additional mortgages within the Sheridan Trust. Between the 2002 Series D bonds and the 2003 Series D Bonds, the Housing Development Corporation had generated more than $308 million for the City of New York, and now held rights to the cash flows generated by approximately 694 mortgage loans and 114 mortgage loans in the Sheridan Trust, for a total of 809 mortgage loans.

Both series of bonds were directly placed with the Federal Home Loan Bank of New York. The bonds were issued under HDC's "Open Resolution," a nearly $2 billion, overcollateralized parity debt pool created in 1993. Using the Open Resolution gave these bonds a AA rating from Standard & Poor's without the need to use a credit enhancement instrument. HDC charges 1.25% interest fee for the credit enhancement that comes with using the Open Resolution. As of December 2006, 82 bond series had been issued under the Open Resolution, collateralized by 895 mortgage loans worth $1.97 billion.[2] Bonds issued under the resolution are secured on a parity basis with all previous bond series.

GENERATING MONEY FOR AFFORDABLE HOUSING

Between 2003 and 2006, the composition of the mortgage loans held in these loan pools changed. Evolving economic conditions encouraged many of the borrowers to pay off their mortgages ahead of schedule while the value of the remaining properties increased substantially. HDC realized these conditions created a pool of wealth that could be borrowed against for public benefit.

Seeking to generate money for its housing programs and to reduce its risk, HDC refunded the 2002 and the 2003 bonds in 2006 in a transaction that generated $107 million for affordable housing in New York City while reducing the use of variable rate debt in conjunction with this loan portfolio. At the same time, the TFA sought to be released from its obligation to tie up capital needed to provide the interest rate cap.

Both series were refunded in April 2006 by a third bond issue, known as 2006 Series A, which consisted of $306.1 million in federally taxable, fixed and auction rate bonds underwritten by Bear, Stearns & Co. and Goldman, Sachs & Co. Of this total, HDC issued $256 million in 20-year bonds bearing a fixed interest rate of 6.42%. The remainder, $50.1 million, was issued as auction rate bonds with rates set each business day by Goldman, Sachs. No longer needing the TFA's interest rate cap, HDC sold it back to the TFA.

By this point, 205 of the original 809 mortgage borrowers had prepaid their mortgages, leaving a portfolio of 604 mortgage loans on buildings that contained 48,528 affordable apartments. The cash flow from the underlying mortgages had been stronger than had been anticipated in 2002 and 2003 and the properties that remained in the portfolio were strong enough to generate a surplus of $106.9 million for HDC after refunding the holders of the 2002 and 2003 bonds. HDC dedicated this money to an ongoing program to issue second-position mortgages at 1% interest to developers of low- and middle-income housing.

SOURCES

Official Statement. New York City Housing Development Corporation, Multi-Family Housing Revenue Bonds, 2002 Series A, B, C and D, June 14, 2002.

---

[2] New York City Housing Development Corporation, Official Statement, Multi-Family Housing Revenue Bonds, 2006 Series H-1, H-2, I, J-1, and J-2, December 14, 2006, p. II-16.

Official Statement, New York City Housing Development Corporation, Multi-Family Housing Revenue Bonds, 2003 Series B-1, B-2, C and D, June 26, 2003.

Official Statement, New York City Housing Development Corporation, Multi-Family Housing Revenue Bonds, 2006 Series A, April 25, 2006.

City of New York Office of Management and Budget, *Financial Plan: The City of New York Fiscal Years 2002-2006: Summary Book*, February 13, 2002, Available at http://www.nyc.gov/html/omb/pdf/sum1_02.pdf.

Official Statement, New York City Housing Development Corporation, Multi-Family Housing Revenue Bonds, 2006 Series H-1, H-2, I, J-1 and J-2, December 14, 2006.

9/11, Subprime Loans, and the Magnolia Park Apartments Bond Default

Michael J. Ross, CFA
Senior-Vice President
Morgan Keegan & Company, Inc.

This is a case study of a multifamily mortgage revenue bond issue of the Housing Authority of Clayton County, Georgia. The bonds were issued in 1999 for the Magnolia Park Apartments and secured by payments from the apartment project. They were issued in June 1999 as the Series 1999 bonds and consisted of:

1. $10,310,000 Series A (tax-exempt)
2. $300,000 Series B (taxable)
3. $2,300,000 Subordinate Series C (tax-exempt)

OVERVIEW OF THE PROJECT AND THE OWNER

The bond proceeds were used for the acquisition and rehabilitation of the 328-rental unit, Magnolia Park Apartments, located in Jonesboro, Georgia, This is outside the city of Atlanta within proximity of the Hartsfield International Airport. The project was constructed in the 1970s and situated on a rectangular shape tract of approximately 28.6 acres.

The owner of the complex was an RHA/Housing, Inc., a Georgia not-for-profit corporation that was established on August 19, 1994. RHA received its 501 (c)-3 determination from the Internal Review Service on March 15, 1995. Prior to the acquisition of Magnolia Park in 1999, RHA had acquired a 768-unit complex in Orlando and another 151-unit low-income housing project also located in Orlando, Florida. In addition to these two complexes, RHA had acted as codeveloper of a new construction 230-unit low-income housing project in Jonesboro, Georgia. All of the units owned by RHA were financed through tax-exempt bonds issues.

During the late 1990s, it was commonplace for many not-for-profits that included affordable housing in their mission statements to seek ownership of apartment complexes. Also, other not-for-profits that did not have defined housing components in their mission statements, but had tangentially related services also sought entry into the affordable housing sector. Under the tax laws, 501(c)-3 corporations have the ability to issue tax-exempt bonds to finance affordable housing bonds, under the stipulation that a specified number of units are made available to qualifying tenants. RHA-affiliated group operations prior to the acquisition of the various housing projects were directed toward the operation of three types of long-term health care facilities.

PITFALLS AND RISKS TO INVESTORS

The various housing complexes owned by RHA were standalone facilities. There was not a formal guarantee or cross-supports among any of the housing complexes, therefore investors made decisions to purchase Magnolia Park on the basis of its individual ability to service the debt. Qualitative factors such as the depth and experience of the owner were one of the many factors that may have weighed in the investment decision process. In this case, this assumption was flawed because the owner created Magnolia Park as a standalone entity. The problem with this structure is that it provided upside potential to the owner and minimal incentive for the not-for-profit owner to support the project if cash flows fell short or the project needed a capital infusion. For example, if the project were able to generate sufficient revenues to meet operating expenses, debt service requirements, and fund the various reserve requirements, then any surplus revenues would be for the benefit of the owner. These surplus revenues would flow to the owner, who could use the proceeds to support other missions or finance the costs of other acquisitions. This was the lure for many not-for profits. In their view, they would be able to acquire large rental apartment facilities with residual income potential with little capital requirements and without putting their other operations at risk. Magnolia Park was acquired in this manner.

The downside risk of the project was borne by bond investors. If the project failed to meet debt service requirements, then bondholders would have the ability to foreclose on the project. While this provided security for bondholders there was no assurance that the project would be able to receive a sufficient amount from the sale to satisfy the various classes of bondholders. Bondholders in the Subordinated Series C were the most vulnerable in this bond issue. This tiered-structure that was used had little history, hence there was not any data to suggest valuation history. However, bond investors relied on appraisals to assess their degree of asset protection.

DETERMINANTS OF VALUE AND ASSET PROTECTION

CB Richard Ellis, Inc. of Atlanta, Georgia, was retained to prepare an appraisal of the market value of the project. The appraisal was made available to investors during the initial offering period upon request to the underwriter of the bonds. In the opinion of the appraiser, as of March 1999, in its "as is" condition, Magnolia Park's value was $11,700,000. The prospective value of the project after completion and stabilization as of March 2000 was $12,350,000. The project had $12.9 million of debt at issuance and only $12.3 million of value. The Senior Series A and B bonds totaled $10.610 million, which produced a debt-to-value ratio of 86% for the Senior Series, which appeared to provide some downside protection. In addition to the security provided by the physical asset, bondholders were secured by their respective fully funded debt service reserves. Appraised value at issuance is less meaningful if an asset's condition trends toward the distressed spectrum. This is something that we review again later in this case study.

PROBLEMS WITH THE SENIOR/SUBORDINATE BOND STRUCTURE

This senior/subordinate structure was a not an entirely new concept to the municipal bond market. Yet, in some respect, at the time, it was innovative and on the surface appeared to meet the security requirements of municipal investors. Municipal investors were accustomed to holding bonds whose debt service requirements were met after payments were made to the senior/first priority of cash flows were made. This waterfall concept was something that was quite commonplace for many revenue-backed bonds where indenture covenants would limit the amount of parity bonds that could be issued. In order to meet the funding requirements subordinated bonds could be issued by the respective municipal governmental agency and debt service requirements would be paid after the debt service and various reserve-funding requirements were achieved on the senior series. Moody's initially rated the Senior Series A and B bonds Baa1.

The subordinate bonds were secondary in terms of receipt of debt service payments and were also behind the senior bonds for asset collateralization. If we assume that the debt-to-value ratio (86%) for the senior bonds is correct, then the Series C Subordinate bonds would be secured by the remaining 14% of appraised value, plus the Series C's own fully funded debt service reserve of $195,875. In exchange for this subordinated position, the investors were paid an incrementally higher yield, but would not have the ability to accelerate or have any remedies if the borrower was unable to make full and/or timely debt service payments. Both the Senior A and Subordinate C bonds had maturities in 2030. The A bonds were priced to yield a 6.324%, while the C bonds were 7.5% priced at par.

Therefore, in actuality the subordinate bonds would be the first line in the capitalization structure to absorb any potential losses, making it quasi-equity in many respects without the ability to participate in the upside. As we mentioned earlier the downside risk in the project would be borne by bondholders and the upside and any related surpluses in cash flow would accrue to the owner who had little in any meaningful equity invested in the project.

ANALYSIS OF THE REAL ESTATE

In real estate, location is the key. While the property was located off Tara Boulevard, a major thoroughfare in Jonesboro, it was not located directly on Tara Boulevard, but behind this major street. Also, it was not directly visible from Tara Boulevard. There were only signs pointing to its location. In a highly competitive market, visibility is a key factor.

The *official statement* (OS) did not include a feasibility study and the appraisal had to be requested. In retrospect, these reports should have been included with the preliminary official statement and certainly in the OS. During the peak issuance cycle from 1996 to 2001 of multifamily housing bonds, most of the cash flow and valuation were based on 5% vacancy rates and annual rental increases of 3% to 5% upon stabilization. Based on history, these standards appeared quite reasonable for this project.

The appraisals were based on the three common valuation approaches: (1) a stabilized net operating income (NOI); (2) recent comparable sales in the market; and (3) replacement costs methods. For the most part, the *discount cash flow* method was given the most credence. If the value is based on the assumptions that new management can improve the operations, rental increases are sustainable, the market's demand for affordable housing remains strong, and that compliance with affordable income requirement for the tenant profile can be achieved, then it would appear that the valuation could be overstated. Magnolia Park was beset from all sides by events that materially impacted its value.

CHALLENGES FACED BY MAGNOLIA PARK

As noted, location is such a vital intangible and Magnolia suffered not only from its lack of direct visual sight from Tara Boulevard. Its proximity to Hartsfield International Airport was also an important negative factor. After September 11, 2001, the economy around the airport was hurt by the sharp labor reductions that occurred when the airlines started layoffs and most carriers sought to deal with their financial woes by reducing costs. These layoffs had rippling effects on the local economies and nearby rental markets. Those with the least amount of financial cushion were on the lower end of the income spectrum, which happened to be the targeted market. Additionally, Monsanto announced a plant closure in the area and that too may have impacted demand in the sub-market.

The home ownership housing boom in the Atlanta marketplace impacted rental demand as well. In Georgia, there was a proliferation of "no doc loans." When you add in the growth of the subprime market, it was not surprising that many potential renters, who would have been good Magnolia Park renters, were removed from the market, creating a demand imbalance in the submarket. This shift meant that either 5% vacancy rates were not attainable, or it could only be accomplished through rental discounts and concessions, which directly impacted operating cash flows and the ability of Magnolia Park apartments to pay its expenses.

Magnolia Park started off producing good cash flow in the early years of operations. One of the key features that may have been an important marketing factor was the operations of a daycare center on campus and a computer room made accessible to tenants. These were features that were unique to the market place at that time. Also, the recent face-lift fueled demand.

However, post September 11 vacancy rates began to edge higher. And, when combined with a vibrant homeownership market (supported in part as noted above by loan applications that did not require income verifications and subprime lending standards), a softening in the rental submarket occurred.

To counter the weakening market, Brencor, the management company for Magnolia Park apartments, replaced the site manager and implemented various concession strategies to maintain occupancy. Rent concessions were implemented that lowered rents, but the benefits to tenants were mitigated. This was because management shifted the basic utility services from being inclusive in the rents to an expense borne by tenants. While this may have been a commonplace feature in the submarket, the tenant profile served by Magnolia Park did not possess the flexibility to pay.

Lower occupancy and lower margins caused the management company to make decisions that in hindsight were highly detrimental. Cash flow became thin and the ability of management to turn units diminished. Units could not be rented because there were not sufficient proceeds to prepare the unit for rental. Consequently, the number of available rental units began to shrink. Therefore, the appraised value of the project based on a 5% vacancy became immediately questionable. To complicate matters, a decision was made to increase the insurance deductible as a way to counter rising insurance costs. Nationally, insurance premiums showed significant increases in underwriting of casualty insurance post 9/11. After the decision was made to increase the deductible to $100,000, there was a fire in one of the buildings. These fired-damaged units were taken offline and, when combined with the units that could not be prepared for rental, caused vacancy rates to rise precipitously at the project. Even if all of the available units were rented the occupancy rate would have been in the mid-80% range.

In March 2002, Moody's downgraded the senior bonds to Baa2, in what was going to be a downward rating spiral. Debt service coverage slid to 1.21× in 2001 versus 1.26×. In December 2001, physical occupancy fell to 82%. With occupancy dipping to such levels, it was apparent that the subordinate bonds were underwater as it related to asset collateralization. This erosion in perceived value was based on the fact that the appraised value was largely dependent on stabilization at 95% occupancy and that the stress test was set at a 10% vacancy. At these levels, pro forma coverage would have been 1.35× and 1.11×, respectively for the senior and subordinate bonds. With physical occupancy significantly below the project levels and rising operating expenses, it would be only a matter of time before RHA would look to the debt service reserve funds as a source of infusion. Use of the debt service reserve funds would further impair bondholder security. The shortfalls in the valuation assumptions were apparent because vacancy rates alone do not drive the value. It must viewed in the context of the realization of monthly rentals. When lower rental and vacancy rates are combined, the net operating income levels are much lower: hence appraised values have little choice than to fall. NOI would fall and if a buyer were to express an interest in the property a higher capitalization rate would be inevitable. Under this scenario, it was clear that the senior series bonds would also have less asset protection.

RECALCULATION OF THE CAPITALIZATION RATE FOR DISTRESS CREDITS

The argument can be made that the confluence of events caused the demise of the credit and resulted in eroded asset value. These unforeseen events are part of the risk profile. The lower income levels from lower occupancy and market rents eroded any potential security protection that could have been accorded the subordinate bond investors.

The cap rate applied to discount NOI is very important and something that should be given even greater consideration by the analyst when determining value and asset protection. The reason is quite apparent: the lower the capitalization rate, the higher the value of the asset. Conversely, the higher the cap rate, the lower the value of the asset when the NOI is held constant.

The appropriate capitalization rate has to be more than an arbitrary number. Its basis for use must be clear and market relevant. There is often a great deal of discussion about the right cap rate. In many cases, lenders claim the cap rate is too low, while borrowers complain that it is too high. One of the factors that can put multifamily housing bonds in such a precarious position is that the cap rate is often associated with the cost of capital. When tax-exempt bonds are used, the interest rates are always lower than the taxable rates that would otherwise apply. The tax-exempt rate accorded borrowers in the municipal market can result in higher values for municipally financed projects. As long as occupancy and rental projections are achieved, the proper cap rate is less of a concern. But when properties become distressed they will often change hands at a time when occupancy is not ideal or stabilized; hence capitalization rates are higher. The use of the proper capitalization rate (usually higher) is designed to offset some of the uncertainty about the potential variability of cash flows.

When these bonds were issued the valuation benefited from the low tax-free rate. This created a value that was probably more than what the project would have been given through conventional financing. One would argue that the value was overstated and that it should have been based on prevailing market rates and not related to tax-free rates.

RECOVERY RATES FOR THE SENIOR SECURED BONDS

In May 2004, the trustee reported that the property was foreclosed and sold for a cash purchase price of $6.725 million. This effectively made the Subordinate Series C bonds worthless. By 2004, the Series B bonds had fully amortized. The not-for-profit owner of the project did not provide any meaningful support to the property. The risks were clearly borne by bondholders. The Series C bonds became equity and absorbed the first loss and the senior bondholder was the next group to absorb the loss. The owner did not have a duty to provide any meaningful financial support. When this deal was finally sold to an investor each senior holder received $3,224.56 per $5,000 in principal. Accrued interest amount ranged from $88.66 to $100.77 per $5,000 of bond interest. We think a key reason why bondholders realized recovery rates that were substantially less was because the buyer's lender used a higher cap rate to value the cash flows of the project.

The higher cap rate was required because the project had experienced lower occupancy, deferred maintenance, lower cash flows, and an unstable rental market. A new purchaser required a higher return because of perceived risk factors. The purchaser of Magnolia Park was not another 501 (c)-3 not for profit; therefore, the borrowing costs (and the cap rate) were based on higher levels than what the municipal market had provided at the time of RHA's acquisition of the property.

SUMMARY

There were many problems encountered by the Magnolia Park Apartments during its brief operating history. Some of these events were internal and were also accompanied by a myriad of external factors that were not foreseen, but these were risks inherent in any multifamily housing bond issue. The key mistake made by investors was probably the assumption there would be sufficient asset protection to cover the bonds. When a project is foreclosed and sold, unless another 501(c)-3 is able to purchase the asset and use tax-free bonds, a higher cap rate is almost certainly assured. If this cap rate is higher, then value will be lower and there will likely be a loss of principal incurred by investors who purchased the higher secured bonds. There are exceptions to this, but that would be a function of location, location, location. In the absence of a premium location, the buyer would have no incentive to pay above market for the property, or assume a lower capitalization rate. If a higher cap rate had been initially used, the project would have been appraised for $12.3 million.

Newport News Issues an Energy Savings COP

A. Theodore Palatucci
J.P. McGowan & Company

For more than 15 years, the Federal government has encouraged its departments and agencies to install massive upgrades to their energy utilization infrastructure in an attempt to contain costs and expenditures for electricity and natural gas. Through various Executive Orders and Congressional legislative initiatives, a multitude of energy projects were developed and installed at governmental installations around the world. As might be expected, the Department of Defense has been among the largest implementing agencies. Projects for upgrades of energy infrastructure have taken place at major U.S. Air Force facilities both in the contiguous lower 48 states and in Alaska. The Army, Navy and the United States Marine Corps have all installed new lighting; heating, ventilation, and air conditioning (HVAC); fiber optics; heat pumps; swamp coolers; and other energy saving projects at shipyards, ammunition depots, and other bases throughout the country and at offshore facilities as well.

An interesting aspect of all this activity was the requirement for all of this new equipment installation to occur without the expenditure of capital on the part of government. The various service agencies were expected to effect the installation of massive amounts of new boilers, air conditioners, wiring, lighting, controllers and associated wiring, and so on, within the confines of their then-current budgets.

The solution to this apparent enigma was found in the expedient of "Energy Savings" finance. The installed equipment would be leased by the vendors to the governmental agency and would be paid for out of the savings generated by the efficiencies inherent in the new equipment. *Energy services companies* (ESCOs), appeared out of the ether to offer their expertise to admirals, generals, assistant secretaries, and their staffs. As might be expected, virtually every major utility company in the country had an ESCO subsidiary trying to share a piece of the pie. Over the course of time, many of these operations have disappeared and today only a handful of ESCO's are actively pursuing the business opportunities that still exist.

As the projects took shape the ESCO's were faced with the problem of acting as lease finance providers to their customers when what they preferred being was equipment sellers and installers. The solution was found in securitizing the payment streams from the governmental agencies and offering the securities to appropriate institutional investors. Although there were some impediments to this solution as a result of quirks in Federal regulations, the government, over time, has worked hard to accommodate itself to the needs of its vendors and their investment banking partners, adapting much of the regulatory environment to the realities of the capital markets.

State and local governments have also been faced with the problems of dealing with outdated and poorly maintained physical infrastructure, particularly in periods of economic weakness and the concomitant pressures on treasury receipts. The growth and expansion of *certificates of participation* (COPs) and other lease financing vehicles at the local level is evidence enough of the adaptability of governmental agencies that are less monolithic than their Federal counterparts.

In 2002, the school board of the city of Newport News, Virginia, issued a *request for proposals* (RFP) for an energy services provider. In October of that year they named Ameresco, Inc. as the winner. Ameresco would be required to provide performance-based services for the design, execution and financing of a cost reduction plan for the school board to achieve energy cost saving, and other ancillary cost savings. In early 2003, the client and vendor executed an energy services agreement, which served as the basis for Ameresco's work on the school board's behalf. As a direct result of the agreement and on audits of energy needs, the school board implemented and financed more than 10 major conservation measures in its first phase of work.

The financing of these projects required a three-party agreement. The school board entered into an agreement with a third party lender and a trustee for the lease payments and with the ESCO for the performance based contractual obligations. While the requirement for the ESCO to provide performance remained, the payment stream for the COP was based solely on the school board's annual appropriations under the lease.

In early May 2003, Dolphin & Bradbury, Inc. was retained to arrange the placement of $12,480,000 COP issued on behalf of the school board of the city of Newport News. The issuer had not heretofore been a presence in the municipal bond market, relying instead on the City of Newport News for its capital needs. The issuer would be an unrated entity but its real value would approach that of a AA borrower, based on the credit quality of Newport News.

The underlying energy conservation measures had an estimated lease life of 12 years and the COP would mirror that requirement. The deal structure unfolded as follows:

$12,480,000 Certificates of Participation
(Energy Management System Project) Series 2003
Evidencing Ownership Interests in Lease Payments Payable, Subject to Annual
Appropriation by the School Board of the City of Newport News, Virginia
(Newport News School Board)
Pursuant to a Master Municipal Lease Agreement

Dated: Date of Delivery			Due: November 1, as Shown Below
Maturity	Amount	Rate	Reoffering[a] Yield
2004	710,000	2.50%	1.70%
2005	750,000	2.50%	2.10%
2006	790,000	2.50%	2.40%
2007	835,000	3.00%	2.80%
2008	885,000	3.20%	3.10%
2009	940,000	3.20%	3.40%
2010	995,000	3.30%	3.70%
2011	1,055,000	3.50%	3.90%
2012	1,125,000	3.65%	4.05%
2013	1,195,000	3.75%	4.15%
2014	1,270,000	4.00%	4.25%
2015	1,930,000	4.10%	4.35%

[a] Originally shown as *Not Reoffered.*

The securities were offered only to several sophisticated bond funds and were easily placed. The investors were, in fact, familiar with the concepts introduced in the transaction, primarily as a result of previous exposure to federal contract finance transactions.

Tax-Exempt Airport Finance: Tales from the Friendly Skies

James E. Spiotto
Partner
Chapman and Cutler LLP

According to the Federal Aviation Administration (FAA), as of 2006, there are a total of 19,847 airports in the United States (up from 6,881 in 1960), of which 26% are publicly owned. Traditionally, the municipal- or government-owned airports have financed improvements through reliance upon forms of municipal finance.

The United Airlines bankruptcy resulted in several decisions by the Seventh Circuit Court of Appeals of particular interest to municipal bond professionals and investors. These decisions illuminate potential issues arising from popular methods of airport finance and provide important lessons for structuring future deals. Originally, general obligation bonds, backed by the taxing authority of the municipal issuer, were widely used for airport development. As efforts were made to streamline the municipal balance sheet, airport capital funding was modified to transfer the obligation for airport finance from the municipality itself. While traditional airport revenue bonds, whereby the airport's revenue stream is pledged to repay bondholders, have been an important financing mechanism for capital improvements, the United Airlines decisions deal with the treatment of special facility revenue bonds, which are revenue bonds that are usually secured by the credit of the airport tenant. In contrast to the older, general obligation bond types of financing, municipal operators of airports are not liable under such special facility revenue bonds. Although the municipal issuer has an interest in insuring this type of financing will continue to be available as a way of financing airport

Note: This is a summary prepared for discussion purposes and is not intended and should not be construed as a statement of substantive law.

improvements, because such structures typically are based on the ultimate credit of the airline user, the bankruptcy of the airline presents holders of bonds with unchartered territory. In the United Airlines case, the airline, by asserting that the structures were disguised financings, rather than true leases, attempted to treat such bonds as prepetition claims as opposed to lease financings which are required to be cured if assumed under the Bankruptcy Code. Key controversies in the United Airlines bankruptcy were the obligation of the airline under financings for the airports in San Francisco, New York, Los Angeles, and Denver. This case study will analyze the crucial factors that influenced the ultimate judicial resolution of the disputes.

BACKGROUND

United Airlines leased several airport facilities financed, in whole or in part, by tax-exempt special facilities revenue bonds issued on behalf of United. As of December 31, 2004, approximately $1.7 billion in municipal bonds of United were outstanding. A list of the municipal bond financings of United as of the date of the bankruptcy filing is provided in Appendix A of this case. Pursuant to the municipal bond financing agreements, United had to fund amounts sufficient to cover semiannual interest payments, premium (if any), and principal payable at maturity, on the municipal bonds. After it filed for Chapter 11, United asserted that none of its municipal bond obligations were lease obligations; rather they constitute prepetition, general unsecured claims (or possibly in some cases partially secured claims). Therefore, pursuant to the Bankruptcy Code, United stated it could not and was not obligated under the Bankruptcy Code to pay such claims during the Chapter 11 cases absent specific authority from the Bankruptcy Court. However, a number of indenture trustees for certain municipal bonds disagreed with United's conclusions as to certain of the issuances, viewing United's obligations as rent under various so-called "leases," payable during the Chapter 11 Cases under Section 365 of the Bankruptcy Code. United refused to make any postpetition payments under the municipal bond arrangements that the indenture trustees alleged were "rent" payable under Section 365.

The "True Lease" Controversy

Litigation between United Airlines and the trustees for the holders of special facility bonds at San Francisco International Airport (SFO), John F. Kennedy International Airport (JFK), Los Angeles International Airport (LAX), and Denver International Airport (DEN) has concluded. In each case, United brought an adversary proceeding seeking a declaratory judgment that certain of its payment obligations related to airport improvements were not obligations under leases pursuant to Section 365 of the U.S. Bankruptcy Code. All four adversary proceedings stemmed from a similar situation: tax-exempt bonds were issued to finance the construction of airport improvements for the benefit of United with the debt service on the bonds to be paid with funds received from United. Each of the transactions included an agreement denoted as a "lease." The question at issue was whether these agreements were true "leases" or disguised financing transactions. United requested that all four transactions be treated as financing arrangements, not as leases.

In three of the four adversary proceedings, the Seventh Circuit Court of Appeals ultimately ruled that the "leasehold-assignment-and-leaseback" arrangement at issue was not a "true lease" but a disguised financing.[1] In reaching its conclusion with respect to the financing arrangements at airports in San Francisco and Los Angeles, the Seventh Circuit reversed the decisions of District Court Judge John W. Darrah finding the transactions to be leases, and affirmed the initial findings of the Bankruptcy Court. With respect to the New York transaction, the Seventh Circuit affirmed the District Court's holding with an unpublished court order.

Finally, with respect to the Denver transaction, the Seventh Circuit ruled that United's Special Facilities and Ground Lease is a single, inseverable whole, and that as such, must be treated as a true lease for the purposes of Section 365.[2] In so ruling, the Seventh Circuit affirmed the decisions of both the Bankruptcy Court and District Court Judge John Darrah; both had characterized the Denver transaction as a true lease. The outcome of the Denver decision—which required that United Airlines pay $260 million of outstanding special facilities revenue bonds—contrasts with the outcomes with respect to the San Francisco, New York, and Los Angeles transactions. The critical distinction between what the court deemed in Denver to be a true lease and in San Francisco and Los Angeles to be a disguised financing is the fact that United and Denver cemented both the ground lease and facilities improvement arrangement in a single document. By contrast, in the San Francisco and Los Angeles cases, the underlying ground leases were provided in separate documents. In reaching its decision, the Seventh Circuit relied heavily on Colorado state contract law, which "places a heavy burden on the party seeking to sever a contract."[3] Having concluded that the facili-

---

[1] See *United Airlines, Inc. v. HSBC Bank USA, N.A.*, 416 F.3d 609 (7th Cir. 2005), *cert. denied*, ___ U.S. ___, 126 S.Ct. 1465 (2006) (San Francisco); *United Airlines, Inc. v. Bank of New York*, (7th Cir. 2005) (unpublished order) *cert. denied* ___ U.S. ___, 126 S.Ct. 508 (2006) (New York); and *United Airlines, Inc. v. U.S. Bank National Assoc., Inc.*, 447 F.3d 504 (7th Cir. 2006) (Los Angeles).

[2] *United Airlines, Inc. v. HSBC Bank USA, N.A.*, 453 F.3rd 463 (7th Cir. 2006).

[3] Id. p. 9.

ties improvement financing could not be treated separately, the court ruled that the agreement must be treated as a true lease.[4]

The pertinent facts of each of the airport transactions are summarized in Appendix B to this case. As indicated in the Appendix B, the SFO, JFK, and LAX transactions were lease/leasebacks and have a common feature: a bond-issuing agency received an interest in a leasehold held by United and leased that interest back to United in exchange for rent equaling the debt service and administrative costs associated with bonds issued by the agency, with a lease term ending with final payment of the bonds. The Denver transaction, however, did not include any leaseback feature, and the Bankruptcy Court determined that the arrangement was a true lease (and therefore subject to Section 365 of the Bankruptcy Code to be assumed or rejected based on whether the airline needed the leased property to reorganize). By contrast, the Bankruptcy Court determined that the SFO, JFK, and LAX transactions were financing transactions, and the Seventh Circuit Court of Appeals has agreed.

THE DIFFERENCE IN TREATMENT OF A LEASE AND A MORTGAGE UNDER THE BANKRUPTCY CODE: WHY DOES IT MATTER?

As transactions involving assets have become more complicated because parties are attempting to take advantage of tax, accounting, and other considerations, the difference between true leases and financing arrangements has become more and more difficult to ascertain. The two most common financial arrangements in which one party occupies real property while making payments to another party which has an interest in the property are mortgages and leases. In both, the party occupying the property, the mortgagor or lessee, has an obligation to make periodic payments to the other party, the mortgagee or the lessor. And in both, the consequence of a default in the required payments is a loss of occupancy rights, either through foreclosure or eviction. Under the Bankruptcy Code, the two situations are treated quite differently.

Mortgage

If a Chapter 11 debtor occupies nonresidential real property as owner under a mortgage, the debtor may retain the property without paying the full amount of the debt but only the current value of the property, with any additional amounts owing on the mortgage (in excess of the current value of the facility) treated as an unsecured claim. Bankruptcy Code Section 506(a).

---

[4] Id., p. 15.

Lease

If the debtor holds the property as tenant under a lease, the situation is governed by Section 365 of the Bankruptcy Code, under which the debtor may retain its occupancy and other rights only by "assuming" the lease. Lease assumption requires that the debtor cure any defaults that occurred before the bankruptcy, maintain payment obligations during the bankruptcy, and give assurance that there will be no defaults in future payment obligations. If the debtor surrenders the property and rejects the lease, the landlord is entitled to an unsecured claim as limited by Section 502(b)(6) of the Bankruptcy Code, which may be less than the balance due under the lease (namely, a limitation on claims from the termination of leases of real property to "rent reserved by the lease without acceleration, for the greater of one year, or 15 per cent, not to exceed three years, of the remaining term of such lease").

The Bankruptcy Code gives greater protection to the occupancy rights of the owner of leased property than to the occupancy rights of a lender on mortgaged property, but it gives less protection to the owner's total claim. The owner of leased property is denied repossession only if the debtor makes full payment under the lease, but the owner may receive a claim for less than the full amount due under the lease if the debtor surrenders the property. The lender on mortgaged property will be denied repossession if the debtor merely pays the lender's claim up to the value of the property, but the lender receives an unsecured claim in the full amount of any deficiency. While a possible interpretation of the United decisions is that a true lease more attractive to bondholders, such assumption ignores the limitation on liability in the event of a rejection of a true lease pursuant to Section 502(b)(6) of the Bankruptcy Code. As noted, the rejection damages are capped at the rent reserved by such lease without acceleration for the greater of one year or 15%, not to exceed three years of the remaining term of such lease. Accordingly, unless it can be concluded with certainty that the facility will be deemed necessary by the user for the entire life of the bond issue, the true lease structure presents its own risks.

FACTORS COURTS TYPICALLY CONSIDER TO DETERMINE IF A LEASE IS A TRUE LEASE OR A FINANCING ARRANGEMENT

As noted, the term *lease* is not defined in the Bankruptcy Code. However, the court decisions construing Section 365 of the Bankruptcy Code uniformly hold that the simple employment of the word *lease* does not bring every agreement calling itself a lease within that section. Whether a *lease* is a true or bona fide lease or, in the alternative, a financing "lease" or a lease intended as security, depends upon the circumstances of each case. The chief requirement is that the lessor retain significant risk and benefits as to the value of the real estate at termination of the lease. Beyond the risk issue courts have considered a variety of factors in determining the status of a lease for purposes of Section 365 of the Bankruptcy Code. Those factors are:

1. whether the "rental" payments were calculated to compensate the lessor for the use of the land, or rather were structured for some other purpose, such as to ensure a particular return on an investment.
2. whether the [lessor's] purchase price was related to the fair market value of the land, or whether it was calculated as the amount necessary to finance the transaction.
3. whether the property was purchased by the lessor specifically for the lessee's use.
4. whether the transaction was structured as a lease to secure certain tax advantages.
5. whether the lessee assumed many of the obligations normally associated with outright ownership, including the responsibility for paying property taxes and insurance.

THE BANKRUPTCY COURT'S ANALYSIS OF THE SFO, JFK, AND LAX TRANSACTIONS AS FINANCING ARRANGEMENTS

Looking to the economic substance of each transaction, the Bankruptcy Court recharacterized the SFO, JFK, and LAX transactions as financing arrangements and held that the leaseback transactions at issue are the economic equivalent of leasehold mortgages, a recognized real estate financing mechanism. The court did not determine whether they were *enforceable* leasehold mortgages.

The Bankruptcy Court found that first and most importantly, the status of the three leasebacks is governed by the principle that there cannot be a true lease where the lessor has no ownership interest at the end of the lease term.

Unlike a true lease, where the leased property reverts to the lessor at the end of the lease term with substantial value remaining, as to which the lessor takes the ownership risk, the leasebacks terminate with no property interest reverting to the bond-issuing agencies. Since the leasehold that is the subject of each leaseback expires during the term of the leaseback, its entire economic value is exhausted during the leaseback, and nothing reverts to the agencies.

Secondly, the Bankruptcy Court found that the factors confirm this determination:

1. The rental payments from United under the leasebacks were not calculated to compensate the agencies for the use of the transferred leasehold, but were defined by the amounts needed to pay the bonds.
2. The agencies did not acquire the interests that they leased back to United for market value. Rather, they paid nominal (if any) consideration to United, and the real consideration for the leaseholds transferred by United was the promise by the agencies to issue bonds on United's behalf.
3. The property interest involved in the leasebacks (the leasehold interest under the ground leases) was acquired by the agencies specifically for United's use.
4. The leases were part of an arrangement structured to obtain tax advantages (although tax exempt bonds might have been issued without leasebacks, as was done in the Denver transaction).
5. The lessee (United) had all of the ordinary obligations associated with ownership, including the need to maintain insurance and pay property taxes.

The Bankruptcy Court rejected the argument that the LAX Leaseback and the LAX Ground Lease should be integrated and treated as a single instrument for purposes of a Section 365 determination. The court found that (1) the purposes of the agreements were different; (2) the consideration for the two agreements was separate; and (3) the obligations of the parties were distinct under each agreement. The court also refused to adopt a quasi-estoppel argument that because United treated the leasebacks as leases for accounting purposes and for obtaining financing and tax benefits, United should not be allowed to deny that the leasebacks are true leases under Section 365 of the Bankruptcy Code.

THE BANKRUPTCY COURT'S ANALYSIS OF THE DENVER TRANSACTION AS A TRUE LEASE

The Bankruptcy Court found the Denver Lease to be substantially different from the leasebacks. The Court determined that unlike the bond-issuing agencies who were the nominal lessors in the leasebacks, the City of Denver unquestionably occupies a traditional lessor's position under the Denver Lease. The Bankruptcy Court found that (1) the City owns the leased property, and at the conclusion of the lease term it will receive the return of the property, with a substantial part of its economic life remaining; and (2) the City bears a genuine risk of changes in the property value at the end of the lease term.

THE DISTRICT COURT'S REVIEW OF THE DENVER, SFO, JFK, AND LAX TRANSACTIONS

On appeal, the District Court reviewed the Bankruptcy Court's holding with respect to the above transactions with varied results.

Denver

The District Court held that the Bankruptcy Court properly found the lease was a true lease for Section 365 purposes. The District Court found that while the Bankruptcy Court incorrectly applied the "economic reality substance test," a federal law application, such did not alter the correctness of the ruling of the Bankruptcy Court that the lease was a true lease. The District Court held that state not federal law should apply in this determination. Under Colorado law whether a lease agreement is a true lease is determined by the intent of the parties. According to the District Court, the most important factor in distinguishing a lease from a secured transaction is whether the lessee retains any equity in the leased property. Here, the lessor retained an economically significant interest in the property leased to United, and United retained no interest in the property. The lessee does not have an option to purchase at the end of the lease. Therefore, the District Court held the transaction was not a disguised financing.

San Francisco

The District Court disagreed with the Bankruptcy Court's recharacterization of the lease. The District Court reversed the lower court, holding that the Bankruptcy Court erred in applying the federal rule of law known as the economic realities test to the question. The District Court ruled that, under California law, the lease was presumed to be a true lease which assumption could be rebutted by clear and convincing evidence that the parties intended the lease to disguise the substantive transfer of ownership or an encumbrance of the facility. The District Court held that, under California law, factors to be considered included (1) whether the transaction actually transfers the normal risks and responsibilities of the landlord to the lessor; (2) whether the payments under the lease are reasonably designed to compensate the lessor for the use of the property or simply reflect the payment of the lessor's acquisition cost plus interest; and (3) whether the lessor retains an economically significant interest in the property. Applying these facts, the District Court found that the lease was a true lease. Accordingly, the District Court reversed the Bankruptcy Court decision that found that United Airlines was not obligated to repay the $155,000,000 special facilities bond issue as a condition of its lease. The District Court found that the SFO/United lease met various standards under California law in that it designated the parties to the agreement, included a definite description of the property, provided for periodic payment of rent over the lease term and provided United with rights to occupy the facilities. The District Court found the lease to be a true one as United's payments did not transfer risks associated with ownership of the property and, at the end of the lease term, the airline retained no interest. The District Court rejected United's position that its rental payments were tied solely to repayment of the bonds because the amount also represented reasonable compensation of its use of the facilities. The District Court also rejected a key argument cited in the Bankruptcy Court's decision that the lease was not a true one because at the end of the rental term the conduit issuer did not retain ownership. It reverted back to the managing authority of the airport. The District Court found this to have no bearing on its decision.

Los Angeles

The District Court has reversed the Bankruptcy Court and found the lease to be a true lease. The District Court found the court erred using Federal law in applying various economic tests in determining whether the facility's lease was a so-called true lease. Instead, as in the SFO ruling, the District Court said applicable state law should be used. Under state law, an agreement is assumed to be a lease of real property if it includes a designation of the parties a description of the leased property and provides for periodic payment of rent for the lease term and exclusive occupation rights. In an analysis similar to the San Francisco ruling, the decision of the lower court recharacterizing the lease was reversed.

New York

The District Court affirmed the Bankruptcy Court, holding that the Bankruptcy Court's application of Federal law in this instance was harmless error since the proper application of New York State Law would have lead to the same result. The lease was a financing lease. The application of the *Hotel Syracuse* factors indicated that the lease was not a true lease. The development agency does not possess an economically significant interest in the property. If United defaults on the sublease, the development agency retains no right to the property and may not relet the property. The nominal purchase price paid by the development agency was not related to the fair market value of the land, and United's payments under the sublease are not tied to the fair market value of the property. United must make the lease payments even if part of the property is condemned. Moreover, United must pay the Port Authority regardless of whether United is occupying the property.

THE SEVENTH CIRCUIT'S REVIEW OF THE SFO, JFK, LAX, AND DEN TRANSACTIONS

On appeal, the Seventh Circuit reviewed the District Court's holdings with respect to the San Francisco, New York, Los Angeles and Denver transactions.

San Francisco

In a lengthy opinion written by Judge Frank Easterbrook, the Seventh Circuit Court of Appeals reversed the District Court's reversal of the Bankruptcy Court's recharacterization of the transaction as a disguised financing and not a true lease. In reaching the conclusion that the transaction was not a true lease within the meaning of the Bankruptcy Code, the court noted that substance rather than form ought to control. While noting that "a state law that identified a 'lease' in formal rather than a functional manner would conflict with the Code," the Court nonetheless consulted California law to determine which economic features of a transaction have what consequences because "a state approach that gives a little more or a little less weight to one of several 'factors' does not conflict with any federal rule, because there is none with which it *could* conflict." Furthermore, the Circuit Court rejected the District Court's contention that California allows form to control. Finally, in its determination that the financing was a secured loan and not a lease, the court cited five elements of the transaction: (1) the fact that United's "rental" payments were tied to the amount borrowed; (2) the presence of a balloon payment; (3) the presence of a "hell or high water" clause; (4) the fact that prepayment would terminate the arrangement; and (5) the fact that the "lesssor" would not have a remaining interest in the property at the end of transaction. The Supreme Court has denied certiorari.

New York

In an unpublished order, the Seventh Circuit affirmed the District Court's holding that the transaction was not a true lease and noted that, "in New York, as in California, a transaction with the form of a lease but the function of secured credit is not treated as a true lease." The Supreme Court has denied certiorari.

Los Angeles

In a lengthy opinion relying heavily upon the Seventh Circuit's earlier decision with respect to the San Francisco airport financing, Judge Manion held that the leasehold-assignment-and-leaseback arrangement with respect to LAX was not a true lease, but a disguised "security agreement." In reaching his conclusion, Judge Manion cited the same five factors deployed by Judge Easterbrook with respect to the San Francisco transaction. Noting the similarity between the two transactions, the Court determined that because (1) United's "rent" was based not upon the market value but upon the amount borrowed; (2) the arrangement called for a balloon payment when the bonds mature; (3) the agreement included a "hell or high water" clause; (4) prepayment would terminate the arrangement; and (5) the "lesssor" would not have a remaining interest in the property at the end of transaction, the leasehold-assignment-and-leaseback arrangement was not a true lease.

Denver

In an opinion relying heavily on Colorado state contract law, the Seventh Circuit, per Judge Manion, affirmed both the District Court and the Bankruptcy Court's determination that the Denver agreement must be treated as a true lease for the purposes of Section 365 of the Bankruptcy Code. The Seventh Circuit first determined that the interdependent ground and facilities provisions of Denver and United's Special Facilities and Ground Lease constitute an inseverable whole, and then ruled that the agreement as a whole must therefore be treated as a true lease. In light of the severability determination, the court found the question of whether the agreement's facilities provisions are a stealth financing moot.

United O'Hare Bond Litigation

The dispute among United, the trustees for the bond issue, and the City of Chicago involved the right of the trustees to enforce provisions of United Airlines' special facility agreements that required repayment of the bonds. United instigated the litigation by filing an action for declaratory judgment against Chicago to declare unenforceable the provision in the airport use agreement that obligates United to repay the debt. United argued that the cross default provisions could not be enforced for several reasons including the fact that it would, in effect, elevate what United contends is unsecured debt to a level above other unsecured creditors. Chicago requested the Bankruptcy judge to rule that the provision is a condition of the lease and not simply a cross default. The dispute between United and the trustees was settled. The complex settlement forgave $450,000,000 of the bond debt. Under a plan of reorganization United issued $150,000,000 of new taxable convertible securities for distribution to the bondholders who selected that option. Under the settlement, most bondholders had the option to take a distribution of cash being held by the trustees in capitalized interest and unspent construction funds and the payment United made to its unsecured creditors. While the settlement resolved all issues between the airline and the bondholders, the city retained the right to seek a court ruling on whether the cross default mechanism was enforceable. The settlement with bondholders was incorporated into United's plan of reorganization. Following confirmation of the plan, the bankruptcy court ruled that the cross-default provision in the airport use agreement was unenforceable in conjunction with the assumption of the agreement by United because payment of the bonds was unrelated to the city's interests under the airport use agreement.

CONCLUSION

What is the important lesson to be taken from the decisions in United Airlines? In earlier times, the airport authority typically was the lessor and the bondholders could look to the credit of the authority which normally had ownership or the ground lease on the facility. The key relationship was between the issuing authority and the bondholders. If there was a problem with the airline, the issuing authority would work to pay off the bonds either through that airline or another carrier. In recent years, the pass-through financing, made attractive by off-balance sheet benefits and other considerations, has led to a form of financing in which the credit of the airline is key. Under the more recent forms of sale leaseback, the fate of the airline is a determining factor in whether or not bonds will be paid. This is a far cry from the old revenue and general obligation bond financing for airports. Now either the financing enjoys a mortgage on the basic ground lease or facility that is collateral from the authority or an obligation of the airline to pay the bonds as part of its lease obligation. It is likely that the cost of such financing will significantly increase. It may be that, when the dust settles, the market will consider returning to a structure premised on the credit of the authority and a security interest in the authority's ownership or ground lease rather than a relationship with a specific airline credit. This is particularly true given the often precarious state of the airline industry and the limitation on the claim for rejected real estate leases under the Bankruptcy Code.

APPENDIX A

United Municipal Bonds

Eighteen series of special revenue bonds due through 2035 were been issued to finance the acquisition and construction of certain facilities in Los Angeles, San Francisco, New York, Denver and certain other locations:

Series	Issue Date	Maturity	Original Principal Amount ($ in millions)
California Statewide Communities Development Authority Special Facility Revenue Bonds, Series 1997 (United Airlines, Inc.–Los Angeles International Airport Projects)	November 1, 1997	October 1, 2034	$190.2
California Statewide Communities Development Authority Special Facility Revenue Bonds, Series 2001 (United Airlines, Inc.–Los Angeles International Airport Cargo Projects)	April 1, 2001	October 1, 2035	$34.6
California Statewide Communities Development Authority Special Facility Lease Revenue Bonds, 1997 Series A (United Airlines, Inc.–San Francisco International Airport Projects)	August 1, 1997	October 1, 2033	$154.8
California Statewide Communities Development Authority Special Facility Lease Revenue Bonds, 2000 Series A (United Airlines, Inc.–San Francisco International Airport Terminal Projects)	November 1, 2000	October 1, 2034	$33.2
City of Chicago, Chicago O'Hare International Airport, Special Facilities Revenue Refunding Bonds (United Airl ines, Inc. Project) Series 1999A	February 1, 1999	September 1, 2016	$121.4
City of Chicago, Chicago O'Hare International Airport, Special Facilities Revenue Refunding Bonds (United Airlines, Inc. Project) Series 1999B	February 1, 1999	April 1, 2011	$40.3
City of Chicago, Chicago O'Hare International Airport, Special Facilities Revenue Refunding Bonds (United Airlines, Inc. Project) Series 2000A	June 1, 2000	November 1, 2011	$38.4
City of Chicago, Chicago O'Hare International Airport, Special Facilities Revenue Bonds (United Airlines, Inc. Project) Series 2001A-1	February 1, 2001	November 1, 2035	$102.6
City of Chicago, Chicago O'Hare International Airport, Special Facilities Revenue Bonds (United Airlines, Inc. Project) Series 2001A-2	February 1, 2001	November 1, 2035	$100.0
City of Chicago, Chicago O'Hare International Airport, Special Facilities Revenue Refunding Bonds (United Airlines, Inc. Project) Series 2001B	February 1, 2001	November 1, 2035	$49.3
City of Chicago, Chicago O'Hare International Airport, Special Facilities Revenue Refunding Bonds (United Airlines, Inc. Project) Series 2001C	February 1, 2001	May 1, 2016	$149.4

Series	Issue Date	Maturity	Original Principal Amount ($ in millions)
City and County of Denver, Colorado, Special Facility Airport Revenue Bonds (United Airlines, Inc. Project) Series 1992A	October 1, 1995	October 1, 2032	$261.4
Indianapolis Airport Authority 6.50% Special Facility Revenue Bonds, Series 1995A (United Airlines, Inc., Indianapolis Maintenance Center Project)	June 1, 1995	November 15, 2031	$220.7
Massachusetts Port Authority Special Facility Bonds (United Airlines, Inc.) Series 1999A	December 1, 1999	October 1, 2029	$80.5
Miami-Dade County Industrial Development Authority Special Facilities Revenue Bond (United Airlines, Inc. Project) Series 2000	March 1, 2000	March 1, 2035	$32.4
New York City Industrial Development Agency Special Facility Revenue Bonds, Series 1997 (1997 United Airlines, Inc. Project)	July 1, 1997	July 1, 2032	$34.2
Regional Airports Improvement Corporation Adjustable-Rate Facilities Lease Refunding Revenue Bonds, Issue of 1984, United Airlines, Inc. (Los Angeles International Airport)	October 1, 1984	November 15, 2001	$25.0
RAIC Facilities Lease Refunding Revenue Bonds, Issue of 1992, United Airlines, Inc. (Los Angeles International Airport)	October 1, 1992	November 15, 2012	$34.4
		Total	$1,702.8

As of December 31, 2004, there were approximately $1.7 billion principal amount of municipal bonds outstanding and, as of the petition date, there was an aggregate of $16.0 million of accrued and unpaid interest on the municipal bonds. UAL, the parent corporation, guaranteed United's obligations under the (1) RAIC Adjustable-Rate Facilities Lease Refunding Revenue Bonds, Issue of 1984, United Airlines, Inc. (Los Angeles International Airport); and (2) RAIC Facilities Lease Refunding Bonds, Issue of 1992, United Airlines, Inc. (Los Angeles International Airport).

APPENDIX B

Transaction Summaries (Per Summary In the Bankruptcy Court's Memorandum of Decision)

	San Francisco International Airport (SFO)	JFK International Airport (JFK)	Los Angeles International Airport (LAX)	Denver International Airport (DEN)
Summary	At the San Francisco International Airport, United entered into a Ground Lease with the City and County of San Francisco, administered by their Airports Commission, on June 18, 1973 (the "SFO Ground Lease"). United was to use the leased land for "construction and operation of aircraft maintenance hangar, test and storage facilities" and for administrative and supervisory operations, rather than for loading and unloading commercial passengers and cargo. The lease had an initial term of 20 years and was subject to two ten-year extensions at the option of United. Thus, the lease would expire no later than 2113 [sic 2013].	At JFK International Airport in New York, United leases land from the Port Authority of New York and New Jersey (the "Port Authority") under an Agreement of Lease (the "JFK Ground Lease") dated August 1, 1995. The Port Authority's rights in the property derive from an "Agreement with respect to Municipal Air Terminals" between the Port Authority and the City of New York, dated April 17, 1947. The JFK Ground Lease involves premises consisting of two adjacent areas. United was required to surrender one of the areas (Area 2) no later than July 31, 1999. The lease on the other area (Area 1) has an initial term expiring on December 30, 2015, subject to extension to July 31, 2024 if the Port Authority procures an extension of its lease with the City of New York.	United conducts terminal operations at Los Angeles International Airport (LAX) on property rented from the City of Los Angeles pursuant to a Terminal Facilities Lease (the "LAX Ground Lease") dated June 4, 1981. This lease anticipated that United would construct expanded terminal facilities with financing possibly provided by or through the Regional Airports Improvement Corporation (RAIC), a governmental agency authorized to issue bonds. The term of the lease, as amended, was to commence November 15, 1981 (or later, in the event of delayed City Council approval) and was to extend for 40 years, subject to earlier termination at the time of the expiration of any long-term, tax-exempt bond financing.	At the Denver International Airport, United entered into an agreement entitled the "Special Facilities and Ground Lease" with the City and County of Denver (collectively, "Denver"). Through this agreement, United leased ground space and also certain to be built facilities at the Airport. Denver agreed to have United build the facilities that United would be using. To fund the construction by United, Denver issued tax-exempt municipal bonds in the principal amount of $261,415,000 for this project. The term of the lease was for 31 years with an operational nine year extension to October 1, 2032.

1179

Transaction Summaries (Continued)

	San Francisco International Airport (SFO)	JFK International Airport (JFK)	Los Angeles International Airport (LAX)	Denver International Airport (DEN)
Background on the Financing Relationship	Some 24 years after the Ground Lease was executed, United, the California Statewide Communities Development Authority (CSCDA, a governmental agency authorized to issue bonds), and an indenture trustee (now HSC Bank USA, the "SFO trustee") entered into four interrelated agreements, all dated August 1, 1997, in order to finance a number of improvements in United's facilities at the airport. The agreements included (1) a site sublease (the SFO sublease); (2) a facilities lease (the SFO leaseback); (3) an indenture of mortgage and deed of trust (the SFO indenture); and (4) a guaranty agreement.	Within two years of the execution of the JFK Ground Lease, United, the Port Authority, the New York City Industrial Development Authority (NCIDA, a governmental agency authorized to issue bonds), and an indenture trustee (now the Bank of New York, Inc., the "JFK trustee") entered into a series of agreements to finance construction of a United cargo handling and warehousing facility and a ground service equipment facility at the airport. These agreements-all but the first of which are dated July 1, 1997-include (1) a company sublease agreement, dated January 1, 1997 (the "JFK Sublease"); (2) a lease agreement (the "JFK Leaseback"); (3) a consent to subleases agreement (the "consent agreement"); (4) an indenture of trust (the "JFK indenture"); (5) a first supplemental indenture of trust (the "JFK supplemental indenture"); and (6) a guaranty agreement.	On November 15, 1982, United, the City of Los Angeles, the RAIC, and an indenture trustee entered into a series of agreements to effectuate the anticipated financing, including: (1) a partial assignment of terminal facilities lease (the "LAX assignment"); (2) a facilities sublease (the "LAX lease-back"); (3) a contingent lease agreement; (4) an indenture of mortgage and deed of trust (the "LAX indenture"); (5) a first supplemental indenture of mortgage and deed of trust (the "LAX supplemental indenture"); and (6) a guaranty agreement.	At the Denver International Airport, the financing of improvements for United was accomplished by three documents: (a) a "special facilities and ground lease" (the "Denver lease"), dated October 1, 1992; (b) an ordinance of the City of Denver, Ordinance No. 712, approved on October 14, 1992 (the "ordinance"); and (c) a guaranty of United, dated October 1, 1992.

Transaction Summaries (Continued)

	San Francisco International Airport (SFO)	JFK International Airport (JFK)	Los Angeles International Airport (LAX)	Denver International Airport (DEN)
Underlying Financing Structures	The SFO Sublease. Pursuant to the SFO sublease, United leased to the CSCDA a portion of the property covered by the SFO ground lease. The term of the SFO Sublease is defined as the period from September 1, 1997 to October 5, 2033, unless a shorter or longer period (ending no later than October 5, 2038) is required to retire bonds to be issued by the CSCDA (with the parties expressly	The JFK sublease. Pursuant to the JFK sublease, United leased to the NYCIDA the "facility realty," consisting of Area 1 of the JFK Ground Lease. The term of the sublease has several variables, but will extend no longer than the maturity date of the bonds to be issued under the JFK indenture (October 1, 2032). The sublease also terminates with the expiration or earlier termination of the JFK leaseback or the JFK ground lease. The rental to be paid by the NYCIDA to United for the entire term of the sublease is $10, and there is no provision for remedies on the part of United for any default by the NYCIDA.	The LAX assignment. In the LAX assignment, United assigned to the RAIC all of United's right and interest in the LAX ground lease "as it relates and applies to the RAIC Facilities," the facilities that would be constructed with the financing to be obtained through the RAIC. The only consideration stated for this assignment is "the agreements and undertakings by the parties hereto." The LAX assignment terminates upon termination of the LAX leaseback.	The Denver lease. The Denver lease conveys rights to United in two distinct sets of property: (1) about 45 acres of real property (described in Exhibit B to the Denver lease); and (2) a number of "facilities," including buildings, fixtures, and personal property (set out in Exhibit A), whose purchase and construction were to be financed through bonds issued by the City of Denver. United's obligations to pay rent under the lease have two components: (1) "ground rentals," payable monthly, based on a rate per square foot plus costs for common use services; and (2) "facilities rentals," payable at the times and in the amounts necessary for debt service on the bonds through which the facilities are financed. Failure by United to make payment of either type of rent is an event of default, which may result in termination of the lease and removal of United from possession.

Transaction Summaries (Continued)

	San Francisco International Airport (SFO)	JFK International Airport (JFK)	Los Angeles International Airport (LAX)	Denver International Airport (DEN)
The Leaseback Relationship	The SFO leaseback. Under the SFO leaseback, the CSCDA leased back to United the identical property leased to it in the SFO sublease. The term of the SFO leaseback is also identical to the term of the SFO sublease. However, the rent United agreed to pay for leasing back the property that it subleased to the CSCDA is defined by the amounts necessary to make payments on the bonds to be issued under the SFO Indenture, together with the costs of administering the financing. The SFO Leaseback provides a full set of default provisions and remedies, including the CSCDA's right to take possession of the leased facilities and relet them if United fails to make the required payments.	The JFK leaseback. Under the JFK leaseback, the NYCIDA leased back to United the identical property leased to it in the JFK sublease. The term of the JFK leaseback is also substantially identical to the term of the JFK sublease. However, the rent United pays for leasing back the property that it subleased to the NYCIDA is defined by the amounts necessary to make payments on the bonds to be issued under the JFK indenture. The JFK leaseback provides a set of default provisions and remedies, including the right on behalf of the NYCIDA (with the consent of the JFK trustee) to terminate United's interests in the subleased property if United fails to make the required payments, but not including a right to take possession of the leased facilities and relet them. The consent agreement. In the consent agreement, the Port Authority consented to the JFK sublease and leaseback, with the proviso that "the subleases and the financing transaction of which the Subleases are a part . . . are expressly and in all respects subject and subordinate to . . . all of the terms . . . of the [JFK ground lease]."	The LAX Leaseback. In the LAX leaseback, the RAIC leased back to United the right and interest in the RAIC facilities that the RAIC received through the LAX assignment. The term of the LAX leaseback commenced on November 15, 1982 and extends "until payment or redemption of the Bonds" to be issued under the LAX indenture and supplemental indenture. The rent to be paid by United for leasing back the right and interest that it assigned to the RAIC is defined as the amounts necessary to make payments on the bonds to be issued under the LAX indenture together with RAIC's expenses of administering the financing project. The LAX leaseback contains a full set of default and remedy provisions, including an authorization for the RAIC to remove United from the RAIC facilities in the event of default and to "make efforts to relet the RAIC facilities." The contingent lease agreement. The contingent lease agreement effectuated the RAIC's rights in the event of a default by United under the LAX leaseback. The agreement provides that, in the event that United's rights under the LAX leaseback are terminated because of United's default, the City of Los Angeles will grant the RAIC a 90-day option to enter into a new ground lease, on the same terms offered to United, for the balance of the remaining term of the ground lease.	

Transaction Summaries (Continued)

	San Francisco International Airport (SFO)	JFK International Airport (JFK)	Los Angeles International Airport (LAX)	Denver International Airport (DEN)
Indenture Provisions	The SFO Indenture. The SFO Indenture generally provides (a) for the issuance of tax-exempt bonds by the CSCDA; (b) for the SFO trustee to receive the proceeds of the sale of the bonds for purposes of funding construction of defined improvements benefiting United; and (c) for the SFO trustee to receive the rental payments from United under the SFO leaseback for the purpose of paying the debt service on the bonds and ultimately retiring them. The SFO indenture makes clear that the bonds are "limited obligations" of the CSCDA, payable only from revenue received from United and earnings on this revenue.	The JFK indenture and supplemental indenture. The JFK indenture and supplemental indenture generally provide (a) for the issuance of tax-exempt bonds by the NYCIDA; (b) for the JFK trustee to receive the proceeds of the sale of the bonds for purposes of funding construction of defined improvements benefiting United; and (c) for the JFK trustee to receive the rental payments from United under the JFK leaseback for the purpose of paying the debt service on the bonds and ultimately redeeming them. The indenture makes clear that the bonds are "limited obligations" of the NYCIDA, payable only from revenue received from United and earnings on this revenue.	The LAX indenture and supplemental indenture. The LAX indenture and supplemental indenture generally provide (a) for the issuance of tax-exempt bonds by the RAIC; (b) for the LAX trustee to receive the proceeds of the sale of the bonds for purposes of funding construction of the RAIC facilities; and (c) for the LAX trustee to receive the rental payments from United under the LAX leaseback (either directly from United or from RAIC within one day of RAIC's receipt of the payment from United) for the purpose of paying the debt service on the bonds and ultimately redeeming them. The bonds issued under the indentures are to be "payable both as to principal and interest, and premium, if any, from the Revenues to be derived by the [RAIC] from the lease[back] of the RAIC facilities to [United] . . . and from amounts received by the [Indenture] Trustee from UAL, Inc. . . . pursuant to [the] Guaranty Agreement."	The ordinance. The ordinance provides (a) for the issuance and sale of tax exempt bonds by the City; (b) for a "paying agent" (now HSC Bank USA) to receive the proceeds of the sale of the bonds for purposes of funding construction of the facilities; and (c) for the paying agent to receive the facilities rentals from United under the Denver lease for the purpose of debt service on the bonds and their ultimate redemption The bonds issued under the ordinance are "payable solely from the Facilities Rentals payable under the Lease and amounts payable under the Guaranty."

Transaction Summaries (Continued)

	San Francisco International Airport (SFO)	JFK International Airport (JFK)	Los Angeles International Airport (LAX)	Denver International Airport (DEN)
The Airline Guaranty	Guaranty agreement. The guaranty agreement sets out a guaranty from United to the SFO trustee of all payments due under the bonds.	The Guaranty Agreement. The guaranty agreement sets out a guaranty from United to the JFK trustee of all payments due under the bonds.	The Guaranty Agreement. The LAX guaranty agreement sets out a guaranty agreement sets out a guaranty from UAL, Inc., the parent of United (and a debtor in one of the related bankruptcy cases) to the indenture trustee of all payments due under the bonds issued pursuant to the LAX indenture. The guaranty does not address United's obligations under the LAX leaseback.	The Guaranty. The guaranty sets out a guaranty from United to the paying agent of all payments due under the bonds issued pursuant to the ordinance.

Toronto's Highway 407

William E. Oliver
Senior Vice President
Director, Municipal Research
AllianceBernstein

Highway 407 in Toronto, Ontario is one of the earliest and most significant infrastructure projects in North America to be developed under a *public-private partnership* (PPP). The project began as a design build contract in 1993 and ultimately was turned into a long-term concession agreement in 1998 when the province decided to lease the road to a private operator for 99 years. The first bonds were issued in 1999 and helped create an infrastructure sector for the Canadian corporate bond market. All of the bonds have been issued in Canadian dollars and are in strong demand by North American pension funds and insurance companies seeking stable long-term assets with a built in inflation hedge to match their long-term liabilities.

Highway 407 was planned as part of the Greater Toronto Area highway network from the late 1950s to relieve congestion on two of the province's most congested routes, Highway 401 and the Queen Elizabeth Highway. The province had been improving the highway network in small increments; due to funding constraints, however, it is estimated that the highway would not have been completed for another 15 years without utilization of a PPP. The province chose to build the highway as a barrier-free, all-electronic toll road that would be the first in the world. This innovation was dictated by land constraints, operational difficulties of collecting tolls linking to existing highways as well as the desire to maximize traffic flows. The PPP was a true risk-sharing effort, with the province laying off risks best borne by the private sector, including the construction risk of the road and the development and implementation of a new tolling system. The Province of Ontario retained the risk of financing the road and retained ownership, so that it would have flexibility to remove tolls if they failed to generate sufficient revenues to repay the debt.

The provincial government, acting through the Ontario Transportation Capital Corporation (OTCC), solicited bids from private firms in 1993 to design, build, operate, and finance a 69-kilometer, barrier-free toll road under a 30-year concession. The province awarded a C$923 million design build contract for the highway construction and a C$102 million contract for the development and installation of an electronic tolling system. When the bidders became reliant on provincial guarantees to finance the project, the province chose to eliminate the operating concession and issue the bonds itself through the Ontario Finance Authority, backed by its own credit. Bond proceeds were then on lent to the OTCC and were expected to be repaid by tolls from 407. Independent traffic studies confirmed that the project would be self-supporting and the province was allowed to carry this debt as a fully supporting off-balance sheet obligation. There was no equity sponsorship in the project. Construction began in 1994 and the central section's 69 kilometers of highway was completed in June 1997, on time and within budget. The PPP was able to benefit from the private sector's expertise in designing and building the project in a much more cost effective manner, adhering to a tight schedule and employing innovative systems and technology in the process.

By the time that the first phase of the highway had been completed, the Provincial government had undergone a change of leadership. The NDP government, which initiated the project, had been voted out of office in 1995 and was replaced by the Progressive Conservative Party, led by Mike Harris. The new government held a strong ideological view that Highway 407 could be operated more efficiently by the private sector. In February 1998, a plan was announced to sell a long-term concession for the operation and expansion of Highway 407 from 69 kilometers to 108 kilometers. The proceeds of the sale would ultimately be programmed as part of a budget balancing action for the fiscal 1999–2000 budget.

The 407 Act was passed later in 1998, authorizing the province to proceed with the privatization of the highway under a long-term concession agreement. The province issued a request for proposals to operate the Highway 407 concession and ultimately selected the winner from the two finalists, who were asked to re-bid the project after their initial bids were within 5% of each other. The government awarded the concession for C$3.1 billion to a consortium led by Cintra Concessiones de Infrastructuras de Transporte (Cintra), a Spanish toll road operator, SNC-Lavalin, Inc., a Canadian engineering firm, and Capital D'Amerique CDPQ, Inc. a wholly owned subsidiary of the provincially owned Caisse de Depot et Placement du Quebec. Proceeds were used to retire the C$1.5 billion in debt used to build the project, with the remaining C$1.6 billion in excess revenue accruing to the provincial treasury.

The concession agreement constituted two different levels of risk. The first was a contract to design, build, and operate two extensions totaling 41 kilometers, with financing provided by the concessionaire. A design-build agreement for a fixed price contract of C$422.3 million was signed with two of the consortium's partners, Ferrovial (a major investor in Cintra) and SNC-Lavalin. The concessionaire was charged with constructing a 24 kilometer extension westward to Oakville, a 15 kilometer eastern extension toward Markham, and seven new interchanges. All of the work was scheduled for completion by December 31, 2001 with penalties for missing the deadlines. The project was completed on time, although only the most essential interchanges were completed according to this timetable. The second element was to operate the 108 kilometer highway in an efficient and profitable manner over the 99-year life of the concession. At the outset, this involved taking ramp-up risk for a new highway as well as overcoming concerns that the toll road might not gain public acceptance in a country with very little tradition of utilizing them.

The project, subsequent to the issuance of all of its long-term debt, had a capital structure of C$775 million in equity and C$3.55 billion in debt. The debt to capital ratio of 82% was fairly typical for a project of this magnitude. Additional debt was issued to finance highway expansion, bringing the total debt to roughly $4.3 billion by June 30, 2006. Over time, the equity ownership also changed, with Cintra owning 53%, Macquarie Infrastructure Group 30% and SNC-Lavalin 17%.

A key part of the partnership was the Tolling, Congestion Relief, and Expansion Agreement. This agreement sets forth future toll regimes, but also traffic growth targets that must be maintained for the operator to avoid paying financial penalties to the province. The primary goal was to mitigate congestion by requiring traffic lanes to be expanded within the large right-of-way provided by the province. This had the twin effects of relieving congestion as well as allowing the operator to maximize revenues. The agreement contained limits on toll rate increases during the construction period, but were not limited thereafter, as long as traffic growth thresholds were met. The goal was to provide an incentive to the operator to continually make roadway improvements that would maximize traffic flows in peak periods, while allowing toll rates to be set at a level that did not divert traffic to the free alternative highways. The lack of any limitation on toll increases would become the most contentious part of the PPP during the subsequent Provincial election.

Upon opening the road without tolls in June 1997, average daily weekday traffic reached 250,000 vehicles. Traffic fell to 100,000 trips with the advent of tolling in October 1997 and slowly climbed back to the 250,000 within two years. However, the early toll road operations were characterized by a myriad of problems related to the functioning of the transponders and cameras that read and recorded all transactions. This produced massive billing problems, creating a customer service nightmare. The bills became so unreliable that the operator voluntarily asked the province in February 2000 to suspend the License plate denial program until more accurate billing procedures could be put into effect; unbillable trips peaked at 10% of total revenues in the fourth quarter of 2000. These difficulties drove up expenses significantly in the early years, primarily for bad debt write-offs and higher staffing levels. These problems were ultimately addressed through a concerted customer service program and improved technology.

By 2003, traffic began to level off for the first time, largely due to the SARS epidemic and the blackout that affected Ontario and the northeastern United States average daily traffic continued to average over 300,000 trips and demand had become relatively inelastic, even after four prior toll increases. Despite the relative popularity of the road with motorists, toll rates on Highway 407 became an issue in the 2003 election. Dalton McGuinty, the liberal leader, had campaigned to roll back toll increases if his party was elected. Upon assuming office in fall 2003, the new government turned its sights on Highway 407.

In January 2004, the Ontario government initiated the dispute resolution process under the concession agreement to challenge the right of 407 to raise tolls again in February 2004 without approval of the province. After failing to reach an agreement, 407 raised its tolls on February 1 and the next day the province filed a notice of default. This began a long dispute that carried on for more than two years, with the province refusing to reinstate the license tag denial program and making other claims that would have negatively affected the highway's revenues. 407 ultimately prevailed on all of the key legal challenges in a settlement agreement signed with the province on March 31, 2006. Under the agreement, the province agreed to drop all legal challenges while 407 agreed to establish a discount program for frequent users, set up an ombudsman to represent 407 users and to construct an additional 100 kilometers of lane miles by 2007, accelerating the original schedule by several years. Having prevailed in their fight to raise tolls without limitation, peak tolls were increased again in February 2007 by 8.3%.

The sale of a long-term concession to a private operator has not been without its critics. When the concession was sold, there were many uncertainties concerning future traffic, the acceptance of tolls, the functioning of new technology and the construction risk borne by the private sector. The price paid for the concession at that time reflected these risks, and exceeded the expectations of the province. In less than seven years, Highway 407 has reached a fairly robust level of traffic stabilization, improved operational efficiencies, achieved high levels of transponder usage and has seen key elements of the concession agreement validated in the courts. By June 30, 2006, Macquarie valued the equity in project at June 30, 2006 at roughly C$8.8 billion, 11 times higher than the initial $775 million equity contribution.

An area where the province is more frequently subject to second guessing is the lack of any limitations on toll increases following the completion of the initial construction program. However, the main focus of the Tolling Agreement was the alleviation of traffic congestion. This part of the agreement has worked well. As long as traffic continues to grow and required highway improvements are made, the province really places no limitations on toll increases. Taking advantage of the inelasticity demand, the operator has been able to raise tolls annually over the past five years by a cumulative total of 53%. This will have a significant impact on revenues over the life of the concession.

The second area is the length of concession. Although longer concessions are clearly preferred by the operators, the present value of cash flows out beyond 50 years is negligible. As a result, the government actually gets very little cash for the extension, but cedes control was nearly twice as long. While some in the Harris government may have preferred to have sold the road outright, it finally granted a 99-year concession.

Highway 407 was a significant breakthrough for PPPs in North America and has become the catalyst for the development of such partnerships in Canada and the United States. The lessons learned from this experience are very instructive. The PPP itself was a great success, allowing the province to accelerate the construction of the highway by many years. The road was built in a very efficient and timely manner and incorporated state-of-the-art toll road technology. Despite early operational problems, the road continues to experience steady growth in traffic, exceeding all traffic demand forecasts. The province's experience with 407 continues to provide a cautionary tale, however, for the development of PPP projects. Some new concession agreements in the United States and Canada have addressed some of the concerns raised by 407 and are incorporating formula-based toll regimes, shorter concession periods and, in some cases, revenue sharing with the concessionaire.

Disney's California Adventure and Tax-Exempt Bonds

Hilary E. Feldstein
Consultant

The City of Anaheim in 1997, through the Anaheim Public Financing Authority, issued $510,427,465.45 in municipal lease revenue bonds. This is a joint-powers authority between the city and the Anaheim Redevelopment Authority. The authority was established as a vehicle to reduce local borrowing costs and facilitate existing and innovative financial instruments and structures. The governing body is the Anaheim City Council, whose members serve in separate session as the members of the financing authority. Anaheim has a council-manager form of government.

Anaheim covers 50 square miles and is located in northwestern Orange County, approximately 28 miles southeast of downtown Los Angeles and 90 miles north of San Diego. Its population is over 300,000.

The proceeds of the bond issue were used to fund the expansion of the city's convention center and public improvements such as a parking structure with parking for approximately 7,500 vehicles to support the expansion of the Disneyland new theme park, Disney's California Adventure. This second theme park opened in early 2001 and is adjacent to Disneyland Park that opened in 1955. The bond issue was an innovative private-public venture involving the Disney Corporation. The Disneyland Resort by 2006 had approximately 21,950 employees and was the largest employer in Anaheim with 13% of the workforce. It was situated on approximately 292 acres and after the expansion would occupy 454 acres with the new theme park and its hotel, The Grand Californian, with 750 rooms occupying approximately 60 acres. Before the completion of the California Adventure theme park in 2001, its major facilities were Disneyland Park, the Disneyland Hotel, and Disneyland Pacific Hotel. Total hotel rooms on the Disney property were 1,638. Overall, there were 17,200 parking spaces at Disneyland.

The bond issue was unique and received *The Bond Buyer's* "Deal of the Year" award in 1997 for primarily three reasons. First, it had a unique dedicated revenue structure tied to Disneyland visits to provide lease payments to the city. Second, Disney financially guaranteed that the projects would be completed on time, meaning no later than June 30, 2001. And third, it was a closed revenue stream, where excess collected revenues stayed within the indenture and could be used to call bonds.

Of the $510 million, $239,215,000 are tax-exempt Senior Lease Revenue Bonds, Series A, $221,627,465.45 are tax-exempt Subordinate Lease Revenue Bonds, Series C, and $49,585.00 are taxable Senior Lease Revenue Bonds, Series B. The subordinate bonds were Capital Appreciation Bonds and the other two issues are made-up of term bonds and serials. The bonds were issued under the State of California's Marks-Roos Local Bond Pooling Act of 1985.

HOW THE SECURITY STRUCTURE WORKS

The bonds are insured by FSA, a commercial municipal bond insurer. The debt service is paid under a lease from the City of Anaheim's general fund. The revenues available for the lease payments are specific dedicated revenue streams tied to tourism and therefore will vary from year to year. They include a portion of the local hotel tax and certain sales and property taxes collected from Disney at the new theme park. These revenues are specifically defined as (1) 3% of the 15% *transient occupancy tax* (TOT), that is 20% of TOT collected on all hotel properties in Anaheim, excluding the Disney hotels; and (2) 100% of the incremental TOT, sales, and property tax revenues from all Disney properties over the 1995 base. This base is adjusted each year by the CPI change, with a minimum 2% annual increase. These earmarked revenues are referred to as *lease payment measurement revenues* (LPMR's). Anaheim is not required to pay any additional moneys if the LPMR dedicated revenues fall short of the debt service payment amount.

Also, in order to obtain municipal bond insurance to provide the bonds Aaa ratings from Moody's and S&P, the Walt Disney Company provided a guarantee.

THE FLOW OF FUNDS

The LPMR began on January 1, 2001, with the first payment made to the trustee on July 7, 2001. Since then the LPMR is collected monthly and remitted to the trustee.

BOND RATINGS

The bonds were insured by the municipal bond insurer, FSA, and consequently carried the triple-A rating by Moody's and S&P's. At the time of sale, Moody's rated the senior lien Series A and B bonds Conditional Baa2. They did not rate the subordinate lien Series C bonds. At the writing of this case study in January 2008, Moody's maintained a stable rating of A3 on the Series A and B bonds.

CONCLUSION

Because of the 9/11 terrorist attacks and the sharp decline of tourism to Disneyland after 2001, the revenue projections in the original 1997 bond issue were not met. As an example, in September 2001 the hotel portion of the LPMR declined 57% from August 2001. In fiscal 2002, ending June 30, 2002, the TOT revenues had been budgeted at $70.7 million, but because of the ripple effect of 9/11, TOT revenues were only $57.8 million. Nonetheless, collected revenues were adequate to pay debt service and, in the years since 9/11, revenues have improved. Between fiscal 2004 and 2006, the TOT revenues progressively increased going from $63,268,000 in 2004 to $75,979,000 in fiscal 2006.

As of the writing of this case study in early 2008, some of the bonds are still outstanding though the Series A and B bonds have been subject to a premium call beginning on September 1, 2007.

SOURCES

Official Statement, $510,427,465.45 Anaheim Public Financing Authority Lease Revenue Bonds, February 4, 1997.

Moody's New Issue Credit Report, Anaheim Public Finance Authority, California, January 31, 1997.

Moody's Rating Update, City of Anaheim, California, November 26, 2001.

City of Anaheim Comprehensive Annual Financial Report for Year Ended June 30, 2006, December 8, 2006.

City of Anaheim Comprehensive Annual Financial Report for Year Ended June 30, 2002, October 4, 2002.

Super Bowl XXXII Helps Resolve Bond Default

Bill Huck
Managing Director
Stone & Youngberg LLC

Before John Elway and the Denver Broncos could take the field in Super Bowl XXXII, the City of San Diego needed to get its house in order. In this case, the "house" was the 69,000 seat Qualcomm Stadium located about eight miles northeast of downtown.

Among the conditions for granting the 1998 Super Bowl to America's Finest City, was the NFL's requirement for San Diego to extend its light rail line to Qualcomm Stadium. With the development of the Metropolitan Transit System's Green Line, fans could take bright red trolleys from downtown to the big game. The extension included building about six miles of rail line east from the existing Old Town station to a new station to be built in the parking lot at Qualcomm.

The proposed alignment for the Green Line ran along the banks of the San Diego River in Mission Valley. Between miles four and five on the proposed route was located the First San Diego River Improvement Project or FSDRIP ("Fizz-Drip"). That was a problem, because in 1995—two and half years before the kickoff for Super Bowl XXXII—$24 million of FSDRIP bonds defaulted because the largest land owner within a special assessment district was deeply delinquent in its property taxes and assessments.

How could San Diego keep its commitment to the NFL if the Transit Development Board was unable to lay track across tax-delinquent property tied up in bankruptcy and foreclosure? How could Denver snap its four game losing streak in the game with Roman numerals if the Bronco's orange-clad fans couldn't take a trolley to Qualcomm?

FIRST SAN DIEGO RIVER IMPROVEMENT PROJECT

FSDRIP was formed in 1987 by the City of San Diego as a means to finance $24 million in flood control work by dredging the Tijuana River channel, building three river crossings and eight small islands, restoring vegetation, and creating pedestrian and bicycle paths a mile west of Qualcomm. FSD-RIP was a special district formed using California's well-seasoned assessment district laws (adopted in 1913 and 1915) to issue bonds secured by assessments levied on property that derived special benefit from the public improvements being financed. (Today, most California communities use the Mello-Roos Community Facilities District Act of 1982 to finance similar infrastructure.) FSDRIP included about 225 acres of property owned by four different real estate developers.

A 32-acre parcel principally owned by a local developer was assessed $18 million of the total $24 million in FSDRIP. The proposed Park in the Valley project received two-thirds of the total assessment because it received the greatest benefit from the project: the parcel was literally created from the former flood plain. The official statement for the 1987 bonds stated that the Park in the Valley development "cannot be begun until the proposed relocation of the floodway channel has been assured and any proposed building site has been raised above flood level. It is estimated that phased construction will commence in 1987 and that the first phase will be completed in 1992."

It was the middle of 1993 when I received a call from the City Manager advising me that the still-undeveloped Park in the Valley property had not paid its assessments since 1990. As a result, the $24 million issue was headed toward becoming San Diego's first bond default in memory.

COULD WE KEEP THE BONDS CURRENT?

These days, the FSDRIP property is clogged with traffic and developed with hundreds of apartments, condos, restaurants, shops, and offices. However, during the depths of the real estate recession that gripped California during the early 1990s, many real estate projects, including the proposed Park in the Valley, were put on hold or simply failed. Since Stone & Youngberg had purchased the FSDRIP bonds at a competitive sale in July 1987, the City Manager's office was both affording me the courtesy of making our firm aware of the impending default and asking for our advice on what to do next.

In truth, I had no idea what steps might be useful in heading off a bond default. During my 12 years in the municipal bond business, the only bond default I could even remember reading about was the colossal $2.25 billion debacle of the Washington Public Power Supply System in the early 1980s. But WPPSS was just a series of headlines for me. This was personal: it was my city, my bond firm, and our investors that were involved.

At my first of what would become at least two dozen finance team meetings on FSDRIP, I learned that the delinquencies on the Park in the Valley property then totaled about $4.5 million. From reading the bond law, I knew that the statutorily imposed 10% delinquency penalty and 1.5% per month redemption penalties would have grown to almost $2 million. I also knew that the FSDRIP bond documents required the City of San Diego to commence foreclosure proceedings after a 150 day grace period. And, I had read the warning in the official statement that the city's foreclosure process could be stayed in the event a delinquent land owner filed for federal bankruptcy protection. Of course, that is exactly what the Park in the Valley ownership entities had done a year earlier.

At our first workout team meeting, we also learned that the debt service reserve originally funded at $2.4 million had been virtually depleted. There would be sufficient cash to make the March interest payment—if other land owners in the FSDRIP district continued to pay their assessments—but unless the Park in the Valley delinquency could be resolved soon, the city would have an actual bond default on its hands in September.

THE LAW WORKS (SLOWLY)

It's important to note that under California law, the City of San Diego and other issuers of assessment (or now Mello-Roos bonds) have absolutely no obligation to advance city funds to make payments to bond owners. Rather, the bond issuing agency is required to levy amounts due, receive from the San Diego County Tax Collector the assessments that are actually paid by property owners and pass these payments through to bond holders. The issuer is also required to ensure that bond funds are properly spent, keep appropriate records and attempt to foreclose on any delinquent land. The City of San Diego did all these things and much more—including advancing $2 million of city funds—in order to protect its bond holders.

California law also provides that foreclosure on delinquent assessments is a judicial, rather than an administrative, process. Because of the Chapter 11 filing by the landowner entities, the city's lawyers could not push forward with the state court litigation until the federal bankruptcy court gave its approval. As the fall of 1993 ground into the winter and spring of 1994, the workout team listened as the city's bankruptcy counsel explained the challenges they had to overcome to obtain relief from the stay that precluded foreclosure. Finally, the federal judge appointed a receiver for the Park in the Valley ownership entities, the stay was lifted and the city's foreclosure attorneys were given the green light to proceed in the summer of 1994.

Old-timers in the California muni bond business had always referred to the remedy protecting assessment bond holders as "fast foreclosure". I can only conclude that these old hands had never actually been through a foreclosure process themselves. The legal proceedings may only be described as s-l-o-w. Land owners who are delinquent on their assessments and taxes are given more due process and protections that those hosting the Boston Tea Party could have ever imagined. The city's bond counsel firm had two crackerjack attorneys working on the case. We believe they set a world record in moving the foreclosure case to a judgment and sale—but it still took 13 months.

WHAT DO YOU MEAN "THE NUMBERS DON'T WORK"?

While a room full of attorneys became excited about finally getting the delinquent land to the foreclosure auction block, we bean counters were growing concerned. State law requires that property with delinquent assessments must be offered at auction with a minimum bid equal to the delinquent assessment installments plus a 10% delinquency penalty plus a 1.5% per month (that's 18% per annum!) redemption penalty plus the legal/other costs of bringing the property to sale. And the buyer must also assume that the obligation to pay the outstanding balance of the assessment lien and any regular San Diego County taxes, penalties, and interest that were due. The legal process had dragged on for three years, during which time the delinquencies and penalties grew rapidly. By the time the Park in the Valley land would reach the auction block, we projected that the aggregate tax and assessment liens would exceed $26 million.

Our concern was this: The real estate experts said that the land's value had declined during the recession to about $19 million. State law required the city to set a minimum cash bid of $10 million *plus* the buyer must accept an additional $16 million in assessment and tax liens. Who was going to buy land worth $19 million for a total cost of $26 million? "San Diego, we have a problem."

The assessment bond law does provide that the minimum foreclosure bid may be reduced upon two-thirds consent of the bondholders. Stone & Youngberg had sold about 70% of the bonds to a single institutional account, with the remaining 30% sold to high net worth retail buyers. Upon initial contact with our institutional account to advise them of the pending default and request their consent to reduce the minimum bid, their attorneys acted like—well—like attorneys for a large institution: cautious. They suggested that the city first try to auction the $19 million piece of property for the required $26 million. Maybe, we'd get lucky. That did not seem likely.

On a bright sunny day in San Diego, a dozen of us stood on the courthouse steps as the sheriff's deputy asked for a $10 million cash bid for the 32 acres of heavily delinquent property. After 90 seconds of complete silence, the sale was declared a failure and the workout team returned to the conference room to discuss Plan B.

CITY OF SAN DIEGO—AND SUPER BOWL XXXII— TO THE RESCUE

The City of San Diego's workout team did *not* expect the foreclosure sale to succeed. We understood the numbers, but we first needed to pursue the judicial foreclosure remedy to satisfy our institutional investor and before city staff felt it appropriate to ask the Mayor and Council to try a more creative approach. With the September payment date on the bonds looming, we felt as though we were watching a train wreck unfold in slow motion. We knew Plan B would take time. We knew there wasn't enough money left in the Reserve Fund to pay debt service. The city's team had given it our best shot and we couldn't yet reload. All we could do was watch as the FSDRIP bonds defaulted on September 2, 1995.

However, because the city workout team did, in fact, know the numbers, we had already prepared a Plan B that was destined to succeed. Our approach recognized two facts: (1) the City of San Diego and the Metropolitan Transit Development Board had already agreed on the alignment of the Green Line extension to Qualcomm Stadium—which ran across the Park in the Valley land; and (2) the FSDRIP bond holders and county tax collector were not the only creditors on the Park in the Valley property. There was also a $12 million note secured by a deed of trust. Of course, the land owners were also delinquent on their payments to the note holder. The bean counters and legal minds all agreed on an approach that made both economic and legal sense:

1. The note was subordinate to the $26 million in assessment and tax liens. The failed foreclosure sale convinced the note holder that its $12 million note was, in fact, worthless. However, the note holder did see value in helping the city of San Diego solve a problem and sold its delinquent note to the city for a modest amount.
2. The city then acquired fee title to the Park in the Valley property by using the deed of trust securing the delinquent bank loan. Having obtained

ownership of the land, the City Council was then willing to advance nearly $2 million to bring the bonds back out of default.

3. The legal team discovered a little-used section of the Taxation Code that enabled the city to request cancellation of the delinquent county taxes and penalties. Infused with its own Super Bowl spirit, the County Board of Supervisors cooperated by eliminating about $3 million in County tax liens.

4. As the property's new owner, the City of San Diego next subdivided the land into two pieces. The city first sold a strip of land along the River to the Metropolitan Transit Development Board for extension of the Green Line to Qualcomm, thereby keeping San Diego's promise to the National Football League. To recover the city's $2 million advance to FSDRIP and move the property toward construction, the city then sold the remaining land to a new developer who was able to create a vibrant retail center still called Park in the Valley.

5. With the formerly delinquent land in the hands of a capable new developer and the economy emerging from the depths of the recession, the city team then structured a refunding bond issue underwritten by Stone & Youngberg to redeem the once-defaulted FSDRIP bonds at their full par amount plus all accrued interest.

Perhaps no one boarding the Green Line after Denver's 31–24 upset of Green Bay knew how Super Bowl XXXII and the new light rail line had contributed to resolving San Diego's only bond default. But a handful of us on the city's bond workout team felt like we were part of the Bronco's offensive line: We helped John Elway get into the Qualcomm end zone that day.

A Tax-Exempt Prepay Natural Gas Purchase Bond

Sandra McDonald
Principal
McDonald Partners, Inc.

The City of Roseville, California owns and operates a municipal electric system, Roseville Electric, that provides electric service to 48,500 retail customers. To serve the city's growing load, the city commenced construction of a 160 MW natural gas fired generating plant in 2005. Once operations commenced in mid-2007, the plant would require a reliable supply of natural-gas. To this end, the city utilized a tax-exempt prepaid structure for a portion of its fuel requirements. The $209,350,000 of Roseville Natural Gas Financing Authority Revenue Bonds, Series 2007 were issued in early February 2007.

In a prepaid natural gas transaction, the net proceeds of municipal debt are used to prepay a natural gas supplier for a fixed volume of gas. The prepaid price is based on the forward price of the future gas deliveries at the time the transaction is executed. The supplier discounts the contract cash flows using a discount rate that makes the supplier indifferent to whether he receives a lump sum up-front or is paid monthly as gas is delivered over time. The amount of the prepayment, credit enhancement costs and other costs of issuance determine the amount of municipal bonds that must be sold. If the transaction is structured efficiently, the semiannual debt service can be substantially less than the natural gas payments the municipality would otherwise pay on a monthly basis. The basic prepayment structure is illustrated in Exhibit 8.1.

ROSEVILLE TRANSACTION STRUCTURE

The city developed a transaction structure that addressed several concerns. First, the transaction had to satisfy current requirements for tax exemption.

EXHIBIT 8.1   Natural Gas Prepayment Transaction

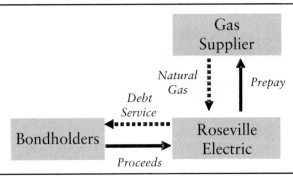

Second, the city needed to have flexibility to resell any prepaid natural gas whenever market prices make it uneconomic to dispatch the electric generator. Third, the city did not want to take the risk that it might execute a long term, fixed price, prepaid contract at a time when natural gas prices were high. Finally, the city did not want to put pressure on its financial ratios or jeopardize its existing bond ratings (A1/A+).

Tax Analysis

The city retained a nationally recognized bond counsel who determined that the city could execute a tax-exempt prepay under U.S. Treasury Regulations in existence at the time of issuance. The tax analysis requires that at least 90% of the prepaid gas be used by a municipal entity. The transaction documents require the city to track how much of the prepaid gas is actually used by the city or sold to other governmental entities. Numerous provisions of the transaction were designed to minimize the risk that that nonqualified use approaches the limitations in the regulations.

Remarketing and Long-Term Price Risk

The city's concern about remarketing and long-term price risk was addressed by including a natural gas price swap in the prepay transaction. The commodity swap enables the city to exchange the fixed gas price that is the basis for the prepayment for a floating price obligation. The floating price is a monthly natural gas index that closely approximates the spot price of natural gas in Northern California. With the commodity swap included in the prepay transaction, the city can resell surplus prepaid gas with very low risk of a significant gain or loss. In addition, converting the fixed price prepayment to a market-based index transaction enables the city to manage gas price volatility on the prepaid volumes with short-term financial products in a manner that is consistent with the city's existing risk management policies.

Conduit Borrower

At the time of the gas prepayment, the city had several series of certificates of participation secured by net revenues of Roseville Electric outstanding. Like many electric system revenue bonds, the installment sale agreement that is the basis for the certificates includes both rate covenants and additional bonds tests. Direct issuance of additional bonds to finance a tax-exempt prepayment would have the unintended consequence of lowering the city's electric system coverage ratios. The city avoided any balance sheet implications and shifted credit risk by forming the Roseville Natural Gas Financing Authority (the Authority), a joint-action agency whose members include the city and the City of Roseville Redevelopment Agency, to issue the debt and make the prepayment. The City Council serves as the Board of Directors of the Authority. Roseville Electric purchases the prepaid gas from the Authority under a standard pay as you go gas contract. Payments to the Authority are considered operating expenses of Roseville Electric.

Credit Profile

An important element of the prepayment transaction is the allocation of credit risk. Tax-exempt, prepay transactions are highly structured borrowings that require the performance of numerous parties. The rating on the Authority's bonds is based on a weak link theory. The city selected Merrill Lynch Commodities Inc. (MLCI) to serve as their gas supplier. Once the prepayment is made to MLCI, it is imperative that MLCI provide natural gas for the Authority to resell. Without the proceeds from the sale of gas, the Authority will have insufficient funds to make timely debt service payments. For this reason, MLCI's obligations are guaranteed by its parent, Merrill Lynch & Co (Aa3/AA–/AA–).

The performance of the city is equally important. If the city fails to pay for gas received, the Authority will have insufficient revenues to pay debt service. In order to achieve the highest possible rating, the city purchased an insurance policy from Financial Security Assurance (FSA) to provide a limited guarantee of Roseville Electric's payment obligations. The FSA policy covers the city's gas payments for a period of approximately two months in a very high gas price environment. The gas purchase contract between the Authority and the city requires the Authority to terminate the contract and suspend all further deliveries to the city upon a payment default by the city. The FSA policy covers only receivables due from the city and is not a guarantee of full principal and interest on the bonds.

The third party that plays a critical role in receiving and maintaining a high credit rating is the commodity swap counterparty. Since the city's payment to the Authority for gas received is based on a monthly index, the Authority will require payments from the swap counterparty when gas prices are low to make timely debt service payments. For this reason, the bond indenture requires that the swap counterparty be rated at least Aa3/AA–/AA– and that the swap be collateralized or replaced if the counterparty's rating falls below that level.

The Authority and the trustee—MLCI—executed a forward supply agreement for the investment of the monthly debt service deposits. Since timely payment of the investment earnings are necessary for the Authority to pay debt service when due, the investment provider is also required to be rated Aa3/AA–/AA– or better. With strong legal requirements and highly rated initial counterparties in place, the transaction received structured finance ratings of Aa3/AA–/AA–. The Roseville Natural Gas Financing Authority transaction structure is illustrated in Exhibit 8.2.

Flow of Funds

All of the Authority's revenues are required to be paid directly to the trustee. The Bond Indenture requires the trustee to make monthly deposits to

EXHIBIT 8.2   Roseville Natural Gas Financing Authority Prepaid Gas Transaction Structure

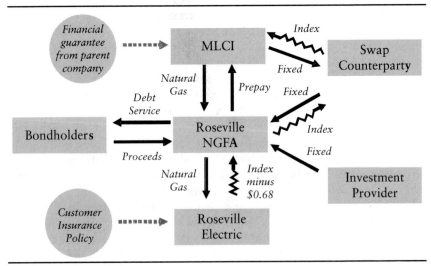

the debt service fund. After debt service deposits are made, the trustee is to make any monthly payments due to the swap provider. Excess cash is released on a monthly basis to the Authority. There is no debt service reserve or operating reserve account. While the transaction is structured to avoid a shortfall, if one should exist, a funding agreement with MLCI, and guaranteed by Merrill Lynch and Co., is available to cover certain deficiencies.

Transaction Size

With the tax requirement that the city use 90% of the prepaid gas in its electric operations or resell the gas to another municipal utility, the city determined that it would prepay approximately 50% of its current projections for natural gas use. The seasonal utilization of gas-fired generation in California resulted in a gas purchase profile that includes more gas, with a higher certainty of use, in the summer months. On average, the city prepaid approximately 6,500 million-Btu/day of natural gas. The annual volumes remain constant over the contract term.

Transaction Term and Bond Structure

The bonds were structured with approximately level debt service for a term of 20 years. The 20-year bond term matches the term of the prepaid Gas Purchase Agreement between the Authority and MLCI and the pay-as-go gas supply agreement between the Authority and the city. All of the bonds bear a fixed rate of interest. The bonds include an extraordinary call provision that will enable the issuer to unwind the transaction at par in the event the gas purchase agreement with MLCI is terminated for any reason. The gas purchase agreement requires MLCI to make a termination payment that is sufficient, together with other available funds, to redeem the bonds in full. The bonds are also callable in the event the city is required to take remedial action to preserve the tax exemption of the bonds. The city's decision to prepay only 50% of its projected gas supply was intended to minimize this extraordinary redemption risk for bondholders. The bonds also include a make-whole optional redemption provision.

BENEFITS TO THE CITY

The transaction, which was well received by bond investors, resulted in savings of $0.68 milion-Btu for the City of Roseville, relative to a typical gas purchase agreement. The city has locked in this benefit for the 20-year term of the bonds so long as all of the transaction participants honor their obligations. On a cash flow basis, the savings represent approximately $1.6 million in reduced operating expenses for each fiscal year. By forming a new joint action agency to issue the bonds, the city successfully shifted performance risk to bondholders. However, by developing a highly structured financing with strong credit requirements and solid termination provisions, the city and the Authority provided strong protection for bondholders.

Universal Studios Road Financing: First with Special Assessment Bonds and Second with Tax Increment Financing Bonds

Hilary E. Feldstein
Consultant

In 1996, a bond was issued by the City of Orlando to address transportation blight. Proceeds were used to construct a series of roadway access ramps and overpasses to facilitate the projected increased traffic along Interstate 4 at one particular interchange, identified as the Republic Drive Interchange. This interchange is adjacent to the main entrance to the Universal Studios entertainment and film production complex in Florida. The highway construction to accommodate increased vehicular traffic was substantially completed on time and on budget by September 30, 1998. The interchange was renamed the Universal Boulevard.

The roadway improvements were necessitated by the estimated $3 billion expansion by Universal Studios on its adjacent site. This included a second daytime theme park, a multitheme nighttime facility, five hotels with 5,000 rooms, and two 9,500 automobile parking garages. This was in addition to the existing theme park and production facilities for film and TV already located there.

The $47,400,000 bond issue to finance the highway access infrastructure improvements was the City of Orlando, Florida Special Assessment Revenue Bonds (Republic Drive Interchange Project), Series 1997A. The maturities went from 1999 out to 2017 and the coupons went from 6% in 1999 out to 6.75% in 2017. Through an interest rate hedge swap mechanism, the issue was a variable rate with weekly resets backed by a direct-pay letter of credit.

HOW THE SECURITY STRUCTURE WORKED
IN THE FIRST BOND ISSUE

Special assessments to pay for the bonds were levied on those who benefited from the road improvements. These were the property owners within the special assessment district. The largest taxpayer in the district of 945 acres owned 98.6662% of the assessment property. This was the Universal City Development Partners, a part of Universal Studios. The special assessments were to be levied beginning October 1, 1996 and continue for a period of 25 years or until the bonds were no longer outstanding, whichever was sooner. The City of Orlando was also expected to collect certain transportation fees from Universal Studios in connection with the issuance of building permits for the Universal Studio property improvements.

BOND RATINGS

The bond issue was rated Aa1/VMIG1 by Moody's. This was based on a direct-pay letter of credit provided by Morgan Guaranty Trust Company of New York which was sized for the full bond principal plus 54 days of interest at the maximum rate of interest on the bonds.

THE SECOND BOND ISSUE

The Universal Studios interchange experienced continued growth, largely due to the development of the Universal Studios entertainment and film production facilities after 1998. By 2002, the assessed taxable improvements were $757.8 million. The base original land value was $248.3 million and the total assessed property valuation for tax purposes was now $1,006,100. The improvements included $192.7 million at the Universal Studios Theme Park; $177.4 million for parking garages and a "people mover," and $17.9 million dollars in the Universal Studios film and TV studios and production lots, among other capital improvements.

In 2002, the City of Orlando, as contemplated in the cooperative agreement with Universal Studios in 1996, issued a refunding issue: City of Orlando, Florida $45,620,000. Republic Drive (Universal Boulevard) Tax Increment Revenue Refunding Bonds, Series 2002. The security for these tax increment financing bonds, known as TIFs, came from the increased property taxes levied by the city and Orange County on the property owners in the special district. This was done by a formula that taps the increase in taxable assessed values above the base year before the Universal Studios capital improvements were made. This was a tax increment financing for an assessment district that encompasses 945 acres.

This second bond issue refunded the first bond issue. It has level debt service with a final maturity of 2025. The coupon rates go from 2% in fiscal 2004 out to 4.875% in 2025, almost 200 basis points less than the coupon rates in the first bond issue. The 2002 bonds are insured by AMBAC and consequently at the time were triple-A rated by Moody's, Standard & Poor's, and Fitch.

This bond issue occurred approximately two years ahead of the original 1997 forecast and was initiated to take advantage of the lower interest rate environment. While Universal Studios had met each of its progress benchmarks, it was still two or more years away from the targeted completion benchmark. The key to refunding the earlier letter of credit-backed issues was that the refunding issue was insured by a AAA insurer. Critical to this was the fact that there was a two-year record of having 2× debt service coverage and an additional secondary debt reserve funded by Universal Studios. By doing this second bond issue, the fixed rate debt coupon was reduced and thereby increased the excess tax increment revenues available to the city of Orlando. In fiscal 2005, debt service coverage was 2.1×.

CONCLUSION

The first bond issue was sold in 1996 to finance the construction improvements to the Interstate 4 exit. They were secured by a special assessment on the nearby property owners who directly benefited from the improvements. Universal Studios was the dominant taxpayer and beneficiary. Over the following years, Universal Studios made capital improvements on its own property as planned in 1996, focusing on its theme park and film production lots. Because of these improvements, the property assessments for tax purposes was dramatically increased. The increased valuations were then tapped in the second bond issue to secure the TIF bonds.

SOURCES

Official Statement for $47,400,000.00 City of Orlando, Florida Special Assessment Revenue Bonds (Republic Drive Interchange Project), Series 1997A, August 26, 1997.

Official Statement for $45,620,000.00 City of Orlando, Florida Community Redevelopment Agency Tax Increment Revenue Refunding Bonds (Republic Drive [Universal Boulevard] I-4 Interchange Project) Series 2002, August 1, 2002.

Moody's Credit Report: City of Orlando, Florida, August 25, 1997.

Comprehensive Annual Financial Report for the City of Orlando, Florida for the Year Ended September 30, 1998.

Comprehensive Annual Financial Report for the City of Orlando, Florida for the Year Ended September 30, 2003.

Comprehensive Annual Financial Report for the City of Orlando, Florida for the Year Ended September 30, 2002.

California's Workers' Compensation Insurance Crisis and the Financing of the California Insurance Guarantee Association

Anthony H. Fisher
Managing Director
UBS Investment Bank

The California Insurance Guarantee Association (CIGA) was created by the California Legislature in 1969 to pay claims of insolvent insurance carriers, including workers' compensation insurers, that are licensed to do business in the state (the "member insurers"). Like its guaranty fund counterparts organized in most other states, CIGA serves as California's "safety net" for insured claimants whose insurance companies have become insolvent. CIGA operates three separate business lines: (1) workers' compensation; (2) homeowners and automobile; and (3) all other insurance provided by Member Insurers (e.g., product liability and commercial property).

CIGA's operations are subject to the regulation of California's Insurance Commissioner. A 13-member board of governors (the "CIGA board") oversees the operations of CIGA. Nine of the CIGA board members are appointed by the Insurance Commissioner and are required to be representative, as nearly as possible, of all the classes of insurance provided by the member insurers. Additionally, there are four public members, two of whom are appointed by the Insurance Commissioner and two who are appointed by the state's legislative leadership.

Since its creation in 1969, CIGA has successfully taken over the claims-paying responsibilities of over 100 insolvent workers' compensation member insurers. Between the years 1969 and 2000, CIGA's payments for workers' compensation claims averaged $14.6 million per year. By 2001, a wave of member insurer insolvencies—triggered by deregulation and subsequent rate competition, as well as rapid claims cost inflation—greatly increased CIGA's claims payments, to $405 million per year. For its fiscal year 2003, CIGA paid $787 million in workers' compensation claims. By 2003, it became evident that CIGA's premium assessments (which are limited by State law) and other capital and assets available to pay workers' compensation related claims would be insufficient to pay the level of claims expenditures anticipated in the future.

In addition, as insolvencies of workers' compensation insurance companies grew, the State Fund, a public enterprise fund intended to serve as a workers' compensation insurer of last resort for California employers, and the largest workers' compensation insurer in the United States and CIGA's largest member, assumed an even larger percentage of the workers' compensation market. Its market share grew from 20% to 53% of the California workers' compensation market.

In response to the expected insufficiency of CIGA's assets in its workers' compensation fund, the state legislature enacted the Financing Act in 2003. The Financing Act authorized the California Infrastructure and Economic Development Bank (CIEDB), a state financing agency, to issue up to $1.5 billion of bonds at the request of CIGA and to loan the bonds proceeds to CIGA. The Financing Act further authorized CIGA to charge workers' compensation member insurers a *special bond assessment* (SBA) to be used exclusively to pay debt service on bonds.

PLAN OF FINANCE

The cash flow modeling required to develop CIGA's plan of finance was challenging, as CIGA could have faced a very wide range of cash flow outcomes. Ironically, if workers' compensation reforms were effective in reducing premiums, CIGA would require much more financing, and its assessments would potentially need to be higher. Conversely, if recoveries from insolvent insurers' estates were significant, CIGA would need to accelerate the retirement of its debt from these recoveries. In order to accommodate this wide range of outcomes, the initial borrowing was structured with $400 million of fixed rate bonds maturing through 11 years and $350 million of auction rate bonds maturing thereafter. This structure was designed to minimize CIGA's borrowing costs as well as meet its need for "optionality," that is, to be able to call bonds annually from estate recoveries and from excess assessment revenues.

SECURITY FOR THE BONDS

The bonds were secured by CIGA's covenant and statutory authority to set the SBA on its workers compensation member insurers at levels adequate to meet its rate covenant. CIGA's rate covenant requires CIGA to set its SBA to collect 110% of projected annual debt service, counting variable rate debt at 150% of recent variable rates. CIGA agrees to test its revenue sufficiency quarterly. It must impose a supplemental SBA to prevent any projected debt service payment deficiency. The SBA is not subject to approval by the Insurance Commissioner and is unlimited in amount. The bonds were also secured by a debt service reserve fund. Considerable care was taken to insure that CIGA had adequate time to bill its members, receive their payments, impose a supplemental SBA if needed, and collect such revenues, prior to the beginning of a bond year so that any insurer delinquencies could be remedied.

BOND RATINGS AND CREDIT ENHANCEMENT

CIGA's bonds received ratings of Aa3 from Moody's and AA– from Fitch. The ratings reflected the many strengths of the credit:

- Workers compensation insurance is mandated by the California Constitution.
- All workers compensation insurers, including the State Fund, are mandated to be CIGA members and to pay its assessments, or risk forfeiture of their license.
- CIGA's financing solution represented the workers' compensation industry's desired approach to solving CIGA's need for recapitalization.
- CIGA's assessments were both nonbypassable and affordable—they were projected to not exceed 2% of total insurance premiums.
- Self-insurance, while permitted, was shown not to be a viable option for a large majority of employers in California, and hence not a source of material reduction in the percentage of the market paying CIGA's assessments.
- CIGA's assessment and collection methods assured a high level of cash flow security.

Perhaps the biggest credit concern during the rating process centered upon the role of the State Fund. With 52% market share, the State Fund would initially pay a majority of CIGA's debt service. The State Fund's only credit rating had been dropped below investment grade, and then suspended. The adequacy of the State Fund's loss reserves were under dispute by the state's Insurance Commissioner, and one scenario was that the State Fund might become subject to control by the Department of Insurance. Ultimately however, analysts became comfortable that (1) the State Fund's finances were sound; (2) as an essential agency in the state's workers compensation system, it could never be permitted to fail; and (3) the State Fund would always be obligated to pay CIGA's assessments.

Bond insurance bids were received from five insurers following a lengthy solicitation process, necessitated by the novel nature of the credit, and the many concerns surrounding the state of the workers compensation industry in California, the state of workers' compensation reform legislation, and the financial health of the State Fund, among others. AMBAC assurance was selected to insure the entire transaction as it offered CIGA the most favorable cost and terms.

SUBSEQUENT EVENTS

CIGA's claims payouts peaked in fiscal year 2004 at $887 million, but have declined for 2007 to an estimated $375 to 400 million. However, its assessment revenues have also declined, as statewide workers compensation premiums, which hit a high of $16 billion in 2004, are expected to be in the range of $11.5 billion in 2006. While CIGA's 2004 base-case projections showed that an additional $260 million of bond proceeds would be required in 2006, CIGA has received significant estate recoveries in subsequent quarters and presently estimates no new financing will be required until 2009 at the earliest. Its underlying bond ratings are unchanged and stable.

Dreamworks Tries to Issue Tax-Exempt Bonds

Rich Saskal
Far West Bureau Chief
The Bond Buyer

Tax-exempt bonds were part of Los Angeles officials' dreams to have movie studio DreamWorks SKG build a studio as part of the Playa Vista development. The proposal became public in 1995. At the time, city officials said they planned to issue $280 million in so-called "Mello-Roos bonds" to support the entire Playa Vista project, a massive residential and commercial real estate development plan near Marina del Ray on the city's west side.

Mello-Roos bonds, named after the California lawmakers who sponsored the legislation to create them, are land-secured financings that are repaid by special taxes levied on landowners within a special district created for the purpose.

They require voter approval, which is typically secured before development begins when the land in the proposed community facility district is under the control of a single landowner or a handful of landowners. They were devised as a way to finance the infrastructure required for new development without tapping existing taxpayers. Mello-Roos bonds typically finance streets, storm drains, sewers, gas and electrical lines, and utilities beneath the streets—the public infrastructure needed to make development possible. In the Playa Vista DreamWorks bond issue, the bonds were also planned to finance the creation of marshlands as part of the environmental remediation required for the project.

Director Steven Spielberg and entertainment executives Jeffrey Katzenberg and David Geffen founded DreamWorks in 1994. They set out to create a new major Hollywood film studio, complete with its own lot to be built on a 47-acre Playa Vista property. It would have been the first large-scale film studio complex to be built in Southern California for decades.

The project was to incorporate the former Hughes Aircraft Company hangar, where the famous "Spruce Goose" flying boat was built in the 1940s. DreamWorks said its studio plans would bring more than 8,000 jobs to Playa Vista. The entire Playa Vista project was originally planned to include 13,000 residential units, more than 4.25 million additional square feet of office space, 750 hotel rooms, and 600,000 square feet of retail.

It quickly became a lightning rod for environmental activists opposed to the development and its impact on adjoining wetlands. According to public accounts in *The Bond Buyer* at the time, their lawsuits in 1997 forestalled plans to issue the first tranche of the municipal bonds.

The ensuing complications led city officials to split the original community facilities district planned at Playa Vista into three districts, including one focused on the DreamWorks "entertainment campus."

The city still moved forward with the split in late 1998 and early 1999 after obtaining a commitment from DreamWorks that it would purchase the required land. The DreamWorks district was expected to require about $50 million in Mello-Roos bonds to be issued and to be used for infrastructure improvements.

DreamWorks announced that it had closed escrow on the property but shortly afterward, in July 1999, the studio changed course, announcing it was backing out of the project, citing an inability to put together satisfactory financing terms.

The 47-acre parcel was transferred back to the Playa Vista developers and the entire Playa Vista project remained bogged down in environmental litigation. Eventually, the Playa Vista project was scaled back to less than 3,300 residential units and 400,000 square feet of combined commercial and retail space. It was not until 2003 that the first Playa Vista bonds were issued; $135 million to finance infrastructure in City of Los Angeles Community Facilities District No.4, a largely residential component of the project.

As of early 2007, the original DreamWorks site still remained undeveloped. A community facilities district does remains in place to finance the infrastructure when it is developed, said Natalie Brill, chief of debt management for Los Angeles.

Where the DreamWorks studio had been planned, developers are expected to build office space. Ironically, some films are made at Playa Vista—in the former Hughes Aircraft hangars, which are protected as historic structures. They are rented out as film soundstages.

As for DreamWorks' plans to create a new major film studio, they have gone by the wayside. In 2004, the studio spun off its animation arm, DreamWorks Animation SKG, in an initial public offering, and in 2005, the remaining live-action side of the business was sold to Viacom's Paramount, which operates DreamWorks Pictures as a subsidiary.

Financings of the Medical University Hospital Authority of South Carolina

Joseph A. Spiak
Managing Director
UBS Securities LLC

The Medical University of South Carolina (MUSC) has served the citizens of South Carolina since 1824. MUSC has expanded from a small private medical college to a state university with an adult and children's medical center and six colleges: Medicine, Pharmacy, Nursing, Graduate Studies, Dental, and Health Professions. For the past 183 years, MUSC has served as the principal teaching and research hospital for the people of South Carolina and has the distinction of being the oldest medical school in the South.

Over the years, since its founding, a number of institutions have served as the teaching hospital of MUSC. For a long period, Roper Hospital, a local not-for-profit hospital, served as the clinic teaching facility of the University. In 1955, through funding by the legislature of South Carolina and the Hill-Burton Program, The Medical University Hospital was built and serves in part today as the clinical teaching facility of MUSC. Operations of the hospital proceeded fairly well until the 1990s, when the pressure of reduced Medicare payments, growing Medicaid caseloads and increased indigent care brought about an economic concern at the hospital. Operating losses mounted and the future viability of the hospital was in question.

A debate began within the South Carolina Legislature, the hospital, MUSC, and the medical community on how to fix the economic problems of what had now become known as MUSC Medical Center and to assure future access to new facilities, equipment, and medical procedures. Several avenues were explored, including leasing the MUSC assets to a for-profit health care management company, thereby tapping into the business expertise that had been developed by the for-profit business sector.

REORGANIZATION FOR THE FUTURE

An alternative approach was investigated that relied on the establishment of a separate government public benefit agency to own and operate the hospital and clinical assets of MUSC, but operate those assets outside the framework of government as a not-for-profit enterprise. This option was selected by the Legislature and Governor of South Carolina and led to the establishment of the Medical University Hospital Authority (MUHA).

MUHA was established on June 9, 1999 to own and operate the hospitals and clinics of MUSC. The board of trustees of MUSC serves as the trustees of MUHA, when functioning as the governing body of the hospitals and clinics. Acting as the trustees of MUHA, the members of the MUSC board act in the best interest of MUHA and promote cooperation with MUSC in furthering the education, research, and clinical care mission of MUSC.

MUHA inherited a severe financial and operating situation when it took over the operation of the adult hospital at MUSC Medical Center, the MUSC Children's Hospital and the Institute of Psychiatry. Cash was in short supply, personnel discipline was lacking, cost controls were wanting, and third party payments were limited. Taking aggressive charge, a team lead by President Ray Greenberg and hospital chief executive officer Stuart Smith, developed and implemented a turnaround plan. Special retirement benefits were offered to employees who chose not to continue with the new organization. Other employees were offered the opportunity to remain and choose either the new MUHA retirement and benefits program or remain as State employees.

Financial performance by the new organization was off to a shaky start. Operation began on June 16, 2000 under the new governance structure. First year operations resulted in a significant operating loss. MUHA had assumed along with the assets and clinical facilities of MUSC, certain long-term debt that had been incurred by the Medical University to construct and equip the Medical Center and Children's hospitals. Total debt outstanding was approximately $75,000,000. *Days-of-operating-expense-on-hand*, also known as *cash-on-hand*, was very limited for an organization of the size and complexity of MUHA.

MUHA obtained a Baa2/BBB rating on its existing debt and proceeded in 2001 to issue $102,835,000 in refunding and new money bonds. The refunding was fortuitous in that because MUHA had previously made monthly payments of debt service to the State Treasurer and its trustee; those funds not yet paid to bondholders could be returned to it and made available for desperately needed cash.

STRATEGIC PLANNING

In 1998 a long over due strategic development planning process was begun by MUHA. For several years, South Carolina, and especially the Atlantic coastal region, which MUHA and MUSC served had grown rapidly with new residents retiring from the Northeast into the coastal region of South Carolina. The new residents were more selective in their choice of health care providers and were expecting and demanding academic based medical care. MUHA needed to replace its cardiovascular and digestive medicine facilities to remain competitive and to meet the needs of its growing community.

PHASE I

In December 2001, MUHA engaged architects as well as health care strategy and planning consultants to develop a comprehensive hospital replacement plan. That plan was submitted to the MUHA Board in October 2002 authorizing management to move forward with a financial feasibility study and the related programming and design for a Phase I hospital replacement project.

Phase I was a consolidation of MUHA and Charleston Memorial Hospital, a former County medical facility, purchased by MUHA. To be constructed was a four-story diagnostic and treatment facility, a seven-story hospital bed tower and a garden atrium uniting the two buildings. These three structures encompass 541,000 square feet. A primary construction focus is the Heart Center, which will provide state-of-the-art emergency, diagnostic, interventional, and therapeutic cardiology services. In addition, digestive disease procedure suite, clinic, and educational center will be provided.

A dedicated Central Energy Plant will also be constructed on the campus of MUHA to supply high-pressure steam and chilled water for this project and future phases of the hospital replacement.

STRUCTURE OF THE FINANCING: FHA SECTION 242 HOSPITAL MORTGAGE INSURANCE

Although encouraged by the South Carolina Legislature to pursue a replacement facilities program, MUHA was advised that neither the state nor the university was prepared to guarantee or assist directly the proposed financing. Furthermore, the addition of $400,000,000 of new long-term debt threatened the end of the MUHA investment grade rating.

MUHA chose to seek FHA Section 242 Mortgage Insurance because that Federal Housing Administration (FHA) program was designed for and focuses on the "needed and necessary" community providers, which have limited access to traditional tax-exempt and monoline insured transactions. After some 20 months of feasibility studies, planning, and negotiation, FHA committed to insure a mortgage of $401,000,000, funded by a taxable and tax-exempt bond issue of $422,060,000. The mortgage insurance proceeds together with other assets provided for under the bond indenture are pledged to the bond trust to secure payment on the bonds. MBIA Insurance Corporation further provided a municipal bond insurance policy that guarantees the scheduled payment of principal and interest when due.

The bonds were rated triple A and sold in two series: Series A, $158,970,000 of tax-exempt bonds in serials from 2020 to 2028, and two term bonds due in 2031 and 2034. All bonds were premium bonds with serial coupons at 5.25% and term bonds at 5.00% and 5.25%. Because the prior bonds were refunding bonds, and therefore not eligible for tax-exempt funding, Series B of $118,095,000 was sold as taxable municipal bonds as all serials due from 2009 to 2020. Serial coupons ranged from 3.921% to 5.38%.

CREATION OF THE ENHANCED TOTAL RETURN CONTRACT

It was anticipated that MUHA would not be able to invest unspent bond proceeds at a rate equal to or above the coupon rate on its bonds and thereby incurring a "negative carrying cost, or negative arbitrage" between the investment rate on the unspent proceeds and the bond interest rate. To assist MUHA with this issue, the *enhanced total return contract* (ETRC) was created. The ETRC was entered into with a commercial bank for the notional amount of $127,650,000. The tax-exempt bonds covered by the ETRC were those serial bonds maturing between 2027 and 2028 and the term bonds maturing in 2034. The ETRC essentially converted MUHA's borrowing cost from fixed to variable during the construction period. A fixed cap of 4.93% was provided as part of the transaction. The termination date of the ETRC is December 1, 2009. MUHA further invested its unspent bond proceeds in a variable rate investment contract, thereby anticipating a rise in investment returns parallel to the rise in variable rate costs under the ETRC subject to the 4.93% cap. The potential benefits to MUHA were estimated as between $10,137,185 and $12,715,467. Any savings generated by the ETRC will be used to reduce the principal outstanding on the mortgage through a subsequent extraordinary mandatory redemption of bonds at par.

THE CENTRAL ENERGY PLANT

To accommodate the request of FHA, MUHA, in cooperation with MUSC and the MUSC affiliate, Medical University Facilities Corporation (MUFC) a limited liability subsidiary of MUFC was created to be the owner of the Central Energy Plant. The owner, Medical University Facilities Corporation Central Energy Plant (CEP) leased land from MUSC, entered into a construction agreement with MUHA, and an operating agreement. MUHA entered into an energy services agreement under which MUHA is obligated to purchase all of the output of the CEP and pay the additional operating and maintenance expenses, if any, as long as the bonds are outstanding. A consortium of banks, domestic and foreign, provided a direct pay letter of credit to guarantee the bonds. The central energy plant was funded by a $61,000,000 South Carolina Jobs-Economic Development Authority tax-exempt bond issue.

EQUIPMENT LEASE/PURCHASE PROGRAM

The South Carolina Office of State Treasurer maintains a tax-exempt funded equipment-leasing program for agencies and municipalities in South Carolina. In anticipation of some $58,800,000 of new equipment purchases for Phase I, it was determined that short-term, five to seven year, financing was more appropriate than 25 year funding of the new equipment needs. MUHA will pay a variable or fixed tax-exempt interest rate on the leased equipment to a vendor selected by the Office of State Treasurer.

SUMMARY

MUHA achieved a cost-effective financing plan for a deemed "needed and necessary" teaching and research institution located in one of the fastest growing regions of the country. By the cooperation and willingness of the FHA, the South Carolina Office of State Treasurer, the South Carolina Jobs-Economic Development Authority, and several domestic and foreign commercial banks, MUHA will be assured of its Phase I project. The estimated fixed mortgage rate to be paid by MUHA is 4.88%.

Niagara Falls Memorial Medical Center

Herman R. Charbonneau
Senior Vice President & Manager
Public Finance Department
Roosevelt & Cross, Inc.

This case study discusses a creative financing plan that was developed by a regional banking firm for a client that presented a challenging financial profile.

The Niagara Falls Memorial Medical Center is a 107-year-old facility with 195 certified beds located in the city of Niagara Falls, New York. It is the largest health care provider in Niagara County, with 7,500 admissions annually, 80,000 outpatient visits, and 25,000 emergency room visits. The hospital's child advocacy center has cared for nearly 1,300 physically and sexually abused children since 1995. The hospital, which employs a staff of 1,200, has had an affiliation with the Buffalo School of Medicine for over 25 years, and provides onsite training for 12 family practice residents. The hospital is a vital part of its community, and provides a disproportionate share of care for indigent, elderly, and otherwise medically underserved constituencies.

The New York State Department of Health granted the hospital approval in 2004 for a $13 million capital project to correct code deficiencies and improve operating efficiencies in its emergency department and noninvasive cardiac services units. My firm undertook the task of financing this improvement. This represented a significant challenge for the firm, as the hospital was viewed by investors as a below-investment-grade credit with substantial financial problems.

Paul T. Lamas, Senior Vice President and Manager of Project Finance at Roosevelt & Cross, Inc., acted as the senior banker for this assignment. He first explored the availability of credit enhancement, either in the form of bond insurance or a ratable commercial bank letter of credit. Both of these options proved to be unavailable, due to questions regarding the hospital's credit quality and financial operations.

The banker then refocused his efforts on effecting a traditional private placement with a major institutional investor, but the anticipated rate of 7.5% to 8.0% demanded by the buyer presented the hospital with a very heavy financial burden.

As an alternative, we also began to explore the use of a credit backup from a private pension fund. This effort proved to be successful. It was a device to obtain financing at a lower overall cost, and at the same time increase the hospital's future financial flexibility. The hospital's financial advisor, Health Care Network Associates, LLP, participated fully in this effort.

The final structure the banker used in this transaction encompassed the following key points.

- The bonds were issued by the Niagara County Industrial Development Agency on behalf of the hospital.
- The bonds were purchased as tax-exempt securities by a major mutual fund. However, there were two significant intermediate steps in accomplishing the sale. First, the bonds were purchased by an agent for the pension fund (an independent pension fund advisor), as evidence of a loan to the hospital by that fund. Second, the bonds were then resold to the mutual fund by that same agent.
- The bonds had a fixed interest rate of 5.5% on a term bond maturing in November 2035, with a sinking fund commencing in 2005.
- The bonds were subject to mandatory tender three years after their date of issuance.
- The bonds are, in the first instance, secured by the corporate guaranty of the Niagara Falls Memorial Medical Center.
- Additional security is available to the bondholder during the first three years in the form of a junior loan agreement between the pension fund and the hospital, under which the pension fund agrees to pay certain costs of issuance on the bonds, to make debt service payments on the bonds if necessary (or provide the hospital with other working capital), and to purchase the bonds subject to mandatory tender under the bond indenture.
- The pension fund also agreed to collateralize its obligations under the junior loan agreement (for the benefit of the bondholder) by the deposit of securities to a custodian bank escrow account in an amount equal to the principal and accrued interest on the bonds; this collateral is marked to market monthly.

- The pension fund charges a fee of 1.5% of the principal amount per annum for its credit enhancement during the three-year initial term.
- At the end of the three-year term, there are a number of possible outcomes, including: (1) extension of the pension fund arrangement; (2) location of a new substitute credit facility; (3) remarketing the bonds without credit enhancement if the hospital's financial condition so permits.
- If none of the above options proves available, the bonds will be acquired by the pension fund.

The hospital found this financial structure attractive because (1) it obtained a fixed rate financing at a moderate cost of 5.5%; and (2) the initial credit enhancement, with its cost of 1.5%, has a duration of three years, permitting the hospital to explore other options at the end of that term. The hospital is confident that its financial prospects are improving, and believes there is a reasonable prospect of either obtaining lower-cost enhancement in the future, or sustaining the 5.5% with no enhancement at all.

This transaction closed in December 2004. The Niagara Falls Memorial Medical Center achieved its financial objectives by utilizing the structure recommended by my firm. While the ultimate outcome for the hospital depends on a number of variables, including its own financial performance, possible consolidations with other regional institutions, and the state of the market for health care-related credit enhancements, this structure financed the near-term needs of the hospital and created a number of future options for the institution.

Roosevelt & Cross created this structure, which was successful in mobilizing a previously untapped credit enhancement source, and thus provided capital to an institution that would not otherwise have had access to the markets.

Aruba Airport Authority Airport Revenue Bonds

William E. Oliver
Senior Vice President
Director, Municipal Research
AllianceBernstein

The Aruba Airport Authority (the Authority) was one of the earliest examples of a foreign infrastructure project being financed in the U.S. taxable bond market. The bonds were structured along the lines of a traditional general airport revenue bond, relying heavily on legal provisions to enforce fixed price construction contracts and bondholder covenants. However, the Authority has faced significant challenges in implementing its airport expansion program from the start and has been constantly struggling with a wide range of issues, some unique to the Authority and other more symptomatic of airport operations globally. Difficulties began with the design and construction of the airport expansion program, and continued with the implementation of key bondholder covenants, political interference from the Government of Aruba, post-9/11 airline bankruptcy and rate covenant violations. Through it all, the Authority board and management responded well to the challenges, often helped by the active role played by investors and the bondholder's trustee. This case study will examine many of the things that can go wrong with airport revenue bonds and how management and bondholders respond to these challenges.

Aruba is a tiny island nation covering 73 square miles in the southern Caribbean, located 19 miles north of Venezuela. Historically, Aruba was part of the Netherlands Antilles until 1986, when it became an autonomous state of the Kingdom of the Netherlands with its own constitution based on western democratic principles. The kingdom now consists of three constituents: Holland, the Netherlands Antilles (five islands), and Aruba. While the

Queen of the Netherlands appoints a governor, the legislative, executive and judicial powers in Aruba are vested in the parliament that is elected by universal suffrage. The majority party in the parliament forms the executive branch and is headed by a prime minister. Jurisdiction in Aruba lies with a common court of Justice of Aruba and the Netherlands Antilles and a Supreme Court of Justice in the Netherlands.

With a population of less than 88,000 people and an economy almost totally dependent on tourism, one of the first orders of business for the new government was to upgrade the island tourist facilities. The existing airport opened in 1934 and the passenger terminal that was built in 1974 was badly outdated. In order to compete effectively with neighboring tourist destinations in the Caribbean, a decision was made to build a new airport terminal with a new preclearance facility for U.S. Customs.

Aruba faced a dilemma over the best way to finance the new airport, eventually deciding that it wanted to privatize the airport. However, it did not want to sell or lease the facility to a private entity, ceding control over a facility that was closely intertwined with the island's economy. It chose to create a public authority that would operate independently, but whose equity would be 100% owned by the government. The separation from the government would allow the authority to operate as a distinct legal entity, improving its access to the capital markets.

The Authority commissioned a long-term capital plan that recommended the construction of a new terminal that would triple existing capacity from slightly over 800,000 passengers per year to 2.6 million. The construction of a new preclearance facility for U.S. Customs was another key improvement, reinforcing Aruba's competitive advantage over other Caribbean airports that did not offer this service. The new terminal was to contain eight loading bridges serving 17 aircraft that could now all be serviced directly from the terminal, instead of requiring passenger to brave the elements when they got on and off the aircraft.

In spring 1997, the Authority issued $61.6 million in airport revenue bonds to finance a portion of the $88 million total funds required for the construction of the new terminal and the funding of capitalized interest and reserve accounts. The issue was structured as a traditional general airport revenue bond pledging all net revenues of the airport as bond security. However, the airport was dedicating the revenue from a $20 *passenger facility charge* (PFC) to directly finance the improvements. This fee was to be collected by the airlines as part of the ticket price and remitted to a paying agent for the bondholders on a monthly basis. To further improve bondholder security, all international airlines were required to make their payments directly to a U.S.-based trustee in U.S. dollars in order to mitigate local currency fluctuations and potential foreign currency controls.

There were also concerns related to sovereign risk and the insulation of the Authority from political interference. These issues were addressed by pledging the stock in the Authority owned by the Aruban government to bondholders and restricting dividends paid to the government until certain debt service coverage levels had been attained. The bonds were given low investment grade ratings by two rating agencies and the majority of the bonds were insured by a monoline bond insurance company and therefore rated AAA. The one-third that was not insured was rated BBB by Fitch and Baa2 by Moody's.

Once the construction program started, the reality proved quite different than what had been envisioned by the Authority. The initial designs were revised to fit an overall cost structure that was affordable, so that sufficient debt service coverage was generated to satisfy the rating agencies and bond insurers. However, once construction commenced, it was clear that some of the deleted items were essential to airport operations and were reinserted into the construction program. Within two months of beginning the project, the original architect was terminated and replaced by another firm to complete the designs and administer the construction process. Airport management also underwent a change with a member of the Board's finance committee taking over as General Manager to increase financial oversight of the Authority. Many items were more expensive than originally projected and change orders required by airlines, tenants and the U.S. Customs Service increased costs further. Delays from faulty engineering also increased costs, as the relocation of an electrical ductbank was required before some of the foundation work could begin. All of these difficulties resulted in suits by the contractor that were eventually resolved in a settlement agreement in March 1999.

Once the revised costs had been established by an outside consultant, the final cost of the airport construction had increased by roughly 40%. The completion of Phase One was delayed by 10 months and Phase Two by 12 months. In order to finance the remainder of the construction program, the Authority had to issue $18.4 million in completion bonds on parity with the first issue. The second bond issue was considerably more difficult to sell, given the poor record of the Authority in managing its construction program, the small size of the issue and the lack of bond insurance. A private placement was done with an institutional investor and at a cost that was significantly higher than the first bond issue. Once financing was in place, construction proceeded relatively smoothly and the airport was able to achieve its new projected opening date of September 1, 2000 within the revised budget.

While the airport was experiencing construction difficulties, bondholders were feeling no ill effects as interest was still capitalized through May 1,

2000. However, once capitalized interest ran out, it was apparent that the international airlines had deliberately ignored the requirement in the bond indenture that all PFC revenues be remitted directly to the offshore bond trustee located in the United States. According to the airlines, this arrangement created a higher level of tax liability, so they ignored the instructions and remitted payment in local currency. Once the trustee discovered that the indenture was not being adhered to, its staff informed bondholders and the bond insurer and a committee was formed with the trustee, airport management, bondholders and insurers. The process was eventually straightened out after the Aruban legislature passed a bill eliminating the taxation provision that adversely affected the airlines. This is indicative of the risks faced with investing in international public finance issues where there is insufficient knowledge or experience to carry out very detailed and often complex requirements set forth in the bond indenture.

The Aruba Airport Authority has faced a wide variety of challenges since the opening of the new terminal, the most significant resulting from the aftermath of the terrorist attacks in the United States on September 11, 2001. International air travel declined significantly, especially for tourist-oriented destinations. This put significant pressure on the tourist industry in Aruba and led to the bankruptcy of Air Aruba, the airport's largest carrier. The financial distress of Air Aruba and other smaller carriers exacerbated the financial pressures already being felt by the Authority from diminished levels of traffic. These carriers were not only reducing levels of service at the airport, but also withholding revenue from passenger facility charges that belonged to the Authority. The Authority ultimately required weaker airlines to establish collateralized bank accounts to cover a few months of revenue collections and actually prevented an Air Aruba plane from landing until the carrier agreed to address its accounts receivable problem with the Authority. Ultimately, the system was changed and passengers were charged directly at the terminal before being allowed to proceed through customs.

While the airport was beginning to experience weakening financial performance, political interference from the Aruban government began to increase. In October 2001, there was a change of political control in the Aruban parliament. Less than one month after the election, there was an attempt by a political appointment of the previous administration to assume the role of General Manager of the Authority and also bring in a highly paid assistant. This was vigorously contested by bondholders and the bond insurer who felt that the current management had done a good job putting the airport back on course. The bondholders prevailed, but the problems were just beginning. In late 2002, the new administration began trying to play a stronger direct role in the Authority's affairs than appeared to be permitted by the bond documents. The first move was to attempt to shift some costs from the Aruban government onto the Authority. Next, there was another demand to replace the current General Manager with yet another political operative. Bondholders and the bond insurer were also becoming increasingly concerned that attempts to collect an unrelated $20 million legal judgment against the government could disrupt the flow of pledged airport revenues. A delegation representing bondholders, bond insurers, and the bond trustee met with representatives of the new board of directors and the government to assert the independence of the Authority and the legal rights established for bondholders in the trust indentures for the bonds. The meetings resulted in a better understanding of appropriate roles for the government, the airport authority and the investors. For example, the government recognized the need for greater airport authority by agreeing to a change in the charter requiring staggered terms for board members, ensuring greater continuity of authority leadership during periods of political transition. Ultimately, the existing general manager was replaced by an experienced management team from Schiphol International B.V., a subsidiary of the operator of the airport in Amsterdam. The bondholders and bond insurers played an advisory role on such issues as the content of the operating agreement and the development of a new retail plan.

In 2002, the airport faced bigger problems as air traffic continued to decline as a result of public resistance to flying in the aftermath of September 11, 2001. Weak demand led to the financial deterioration of many airlines, which subsequently reduced service to the island. Enplanements fell nearly 10% in 2002, producing insufficient revenues to meet its rate covenant of 1.35×. This triggered the hiring of an independent consultant to assess the best course of action in the short run. Recommendations focused on maintaining existing airport fees and charges in a difficult operating environment while reducing spending in both the operating and capital budgets. Other recommendations for long-term operating and capital budget planning were ultimately implemented and would lead to the restoration of financial stability. Traffic remained weak, falling another 3% in 2003 before leveling off in 2004.

Financial performance gradually improved as the world economy began to expand again and the long-term recommendations to grow revenues and constrain spending began to take effect. For the year ending December 31, 2006, debt service coverage was 1.93×. The credit quality of the Authority has now stabilized and investment-grade ratings have been restored.

In conclusion, the Aruba Airport Authority overcame a myriad of problems following the issuance of its first international bond issue in 1997. There are three main factors that contributed to this success. The first was the establishment of the Authority as an independent political body with the ability to enter into binding contract and legal agreements. The second was the strong role played by management at both the operating and board level to preserve their independence and to make the tough decisions that were required. Finally, the investors and their trustee played an active role to assert bondholder rights and ensure that the bond indenture was adhered to. These three factors allowed the Authority to overcome the significant number of challenges that they faced in their first decade of existence.

Yankees versus Mets:
A Subway Series

Mitchell Savader
Chief Executive Officer
The Savader Group LLC
and
Managing Director
Civitas Funding Group LLC

T he movement to replace aging sports venues with more modern facilities has affected a number of communities throughout the nation. Spectators demanding better views and state-of-the-art amenities, as well as owners seeking greater revenue, have pushed the movement forward and driven the construction or planning of all types of new sports facilities.

Baseball has been a major beneficiary of this movement, and no city has produced grander plans than New York City. As home to two major league baseball teams—the Mets and the Yankees—and two major league baseball stadiums—Shea Stadium and Yankee Stadium—New York City had long been considered a likely candidate for the construction of new facilities.

After much planning and negotiation, the city took a major step forward in August 2006 to fund the construction of two new baseball stadiums. The New York City Industrial Development Agency (NYCIDA)— acting on behalf of the City of New York—sold two separate tax-exempt bond issues totaling approximately $1.6 billion to fund the construction of the new ballparks: one in the Bronx for the New York Yankees and the other in Queens for the New York Mets. Both of the new facilities are to be constructed alongside each team's existing stadium.

When completed, the new Yankee Stadium is expected to have more than 50,000 seats, 60 luxury boxes, and room for about 2,000 standees. The stadium will also have a 30,000 square foot plaza as well as restaurants, media facilities, concourses, player's space and other related amenities. The overall project will also provide for the development of four new parking garages containing a total of approximately 4,735 spaces. The overall project cost is estimated at approximately $966 million.

Citi Field Stadium, along with several parking facilities, will be constructed on a 51-acre site adjacent to Shea Stadium. When completed, the new ballpark will accommodate approximately 45,000 spectators, including 49 luxury boxes and five party suites with a combined total of approximately 965 seats and 3,125 club seats. The stadium will also have retail space, corporate business space, function space, and facilities for the media as well as other functions. The overall cost of the project, better known as the Queens Baseball Stadium Project, is projected at approximately $815 million.

Both ballparks are expected to be completed in time for the start of the 2009 season.

Although the construction of each ballpark is funded from a combination of resources, each of the large bond issues sold in August 2006 comprise the single largest component of each respective program. With regard to construction of a new stadium for the New York Mets, the NYCIDA issued $547.355 million of Pilot Bonds (Queens Baseball Stadium Project) Series 2006. The bonds carry triple-A ratings from both Moody's Investors Service and Standard & Poor's reflecting bond insurance provided by AMBAC Assurance Corporation. Construction of the new Yankee Stadium is being funded with proceeds of the NYCIDA's $942,555,000 Pilot Revenue Bonds, Series 2006 (Yankee Stadium Project). These bonds are rated triple A, reflecting insurance policies issued by Financial Guaranty Insurance Co. and MBIA Insurance Corp. Also, the two transactions were assigned underlying ratings of BBB– by Standard & Poor's based on the credit quality of each security absent the benefit of bond insurance. Citigroup Global Markets, Inc. served as underwriter for the Mets bond deal, while Goldman Sachs & Co., played a similar role in the Yankee Stadium transaction.

The two bond issues share a number of characteristics that reflect then current market conditions as both series of bonds were originally sold within a day of one another. However, other elements of the two financings are different and reflect the evolving state-of-the-art within the public finance sector and choices made by the players involved in each transaction.

First, both transactions encompass a complex series of leases, subleases, and related agreements that reflect the complicated ownership, responsibility, and power arrangements either preexisting or newly created between the City of New York, the ball clubs (and their agents), and several other involved parties. For example, the land underlying both facilities is owned by the city. However, the responsibility for building the two facilities falls to the ball clubs acting through their authorized agents: Yankee Stadium LLC and Queens Ballpark Company LLC.

Second, the security pledge backing both series of bonds issued consists primarily of payments-in-lieu-of taxes (PILOTs) to be paid by each ball club's respective agent under agreements between the issuer and the agents who are responsible for the construction and management of each respective stadium. The use of PILOTs accomplishes several goals. Simply put, the use of PILOTs places the responsibility of repaying the debt (indirectly) on those parties benefiting from each project: the ball clubs. Both the Yankees and Mets, acting through their agents, are responsible for repaying the debt financing the construction of each respective project.

For both financings, PILOTs are expected to be paid each year in an amount sufficient to pay the total amount of debt service as well as certain related expenses due in that year. The PILOT payments are expected to be derived from various revenues generated from the ongoing operation of each respective stadium, including revenues related to attendee admissions.

Although the city and the state were intimately involved with the negotiations and under certain circumstances retain certain responsibilities going forward, neither entity is obligated in any way to pay debt service on the bonds. Furthermore, the NYCIDA is only required to pay debt service on the bonds to the extent that PILOT revenues are available and sufficient. The NYCIDA is not obligated to pay investors from any other funds, and the agency does not possess the right to levy property taxes. In addition, neither the Mets nor the Yankees is directly obligated to the payment of debt service on the respective bonds financing the two ballparks. The PILOT payments are made by each ball club's agent.

Both of the elements just mentioned are reflective of the long-term sensitivities as well as powers, responsibilities, and goals of the various parties involved in the two projects. All want to accomplish the same thing, the economical construction of a new baseball stadium, while making sure those entities responsible for successfully completing certain aspects of the project have the rights and powers necessary to meet those responsibilities. Furthermore, the costs of each project should be borne by those who will benefit from the development of the projects.

While several aspects of the two transactions appear virtually identical to one another, other aspects of the transactions appear quite different from one another. First and perhaps most meaningful, while both transactions were issued using 40-year debt structures, the two transactions were sold using interest rate formats that reflect the growing choices available to issuers of long-term municipal debt. Approximately $198 million of the bonds issued for the new Yankee stadium (maturing between 2016 and 2027) are scheduled to pay variable rates of interest; while in contrast, all the bonds issued for the new Mets stadium were issued using fixed rates of interest.

Furthermore, in order to mitigate the uncertainty that follows from the payment of debt based on variable rates of interest, the Yankee Stadium transaction makes use of an interest rate swap known as a *fixed annuity basis swap*. The swap provides for the payment of floating rates of interest pegged to the BMA index—which is based on one-week-tax-exempt note yields—while receive a floating rate that is formulated using 68% of LIBOR—which is based on rates of interest paid by the world's largest banks for deposits from one another.

The swaps provide the Yankees with several benefits. First, the Yankee structure reportedly generates annual savings of approximately ten basis-points, the equivalent of between $5 million and $10 million a year in present-value savings. Second, based on current market conditions, the Yankees stand to receive an annual cash payment of about $4 million.

Although these benefits appear compelling, the structure is not without its risks. Perhaps the most significant of these risks is tax risk: the risk that tax rates can change, thereby significantly affecting the relationship between taxable and tax-exempt rates of interest. If this were to occur, the relative values of the two cash-flows will change, possibly in a way that would generate a loss to be realized at some future date by the Yankees.

In the end, both bond issues were received very favorably by investors. The Yankee transaction reportedly had about $3.5 billion of orders and produced an estimated yield of 4.51%. The bond issue for the new Queens stadium received about $3.2 billion of orders and produced a yield of 4.57%.

SOURCES

Official Statement, $942,555,000 New York City Industrial Development Agency Pilot Revenue Bonds, Series 2006 (Yankee Stadium Project), August 16, 2006.
Official Statement, $547,355,000 New York City Industrial Development Agency Pilot Bonds (Queens Baseball Stadium Project), Series 2006, August 15, 2006.

Good Swap, Bad Swap

Peter Shapiro
Managing Director
Swap Financial Group

The vast majority of interest rate swaps entered into by state and local governments are done for good reasons, most frequently to reduce the cost of debt service. The most commonly used swap structure is what is known as a *synthetic fixed rate financing*. This structure consists of the issuance of floating rate bonds, generally tax-exempt variable rate demand bonds or auction rate bonds, which are accompanied by a swap where the issuer pays a fixed rate and receives a floating rate designed to offset the floating rate paid on the bonds. The net result is a fixed rate equal to the fixed rate on the swap, assuming the two floating rates match. To the extent that the two floating rates differ, the all-in fixed rate may be slightly more or less than the fixed swap rate.

GOOD SWAPS

In our experience, one of the best and most successful examples of the use of synthetic fixed rate financing is the program of the California Housing Finance Agency. CalHFA, as the agency is known, has entered into more than 100 such financings since 1999. The benefits for the agency and the public it serves have been manifold. As a result of the use of swaps and the lower fixed rates that swaps have made possible, according to the CalHFA, the agency has been able to expand its single-family lending programs to reach more than 50% more first-time homebuyers than it could have without the use of swaps, and it has been able to reduce its mortgage rates for affordable apartment developments by as much as one third.

These savings have not been without risk, but the risks are the ones the agency has analyzed closely and mitigated carefully. To lessen counterparty risk, the agency has diversified its swaps among nearly a dozen counterparties, and required a minimum credit rating of double A from at least one rating agency. It requires all counterparties to post collateral if there credit rating drops below the double-A category. And it includes a provision in its swap documents allowing the agency to terminate a swap early, at no out of pocket cost, if the counterparty falls below a single-A rating.

There are two special risks the agency takes on to help produce lower rates. First, it takes on *basis risk*—the risk that the floating rate on the swap will fail to offset the floating rate on its bonds. The floating swap rate for most of the agency's swaps is indexed to a percentage of one-month LIBOR, a taxable rate. Historically, the percentage of LIBOR employed by CalHFA has closely matched the rate on its tax-exempt bonds, but there is a risk, called *tax risk*, that a major change in future tax laws could affect the relationship negatively. The agency has carefully measured this risk and determined that the benefits it is accruing more than offset the risk. The other special risk the agency has taken on is *amortization risk*. When it enters into swaps, CalHFA take special steps to match the scheduled amortization of its swaps with the expected amortization of its bonds. Because the bonds are backed by mortgages, there is an inherent unpredictability of mortgage prepayment that results in bond amortization. To protect against this unpredictability, CalHFA has taken a variety of special steps, including the purchase of early termination options, to give it the flexibility it needs to avoid a mismatch between its swaps and its bonds.

CalHFA's program was the first major swap program of any state housing finance agency. A sign of its success is that by today it has been widely replicated by most other state HFA's, and has helped produce an expansion of public benefit in the form of more affordable housing across the nation.

BAD SWAPS

There are many examples of bad swaps that we have come across in our practice advising issuers. Here is one of a small number of swap transactions that have produced trouble for an issuer.

West Basin Municipal Water District, a medium-sized water utility in the Los Angeles–metropolitan area, entered into what is known as a *basis swap* in 2001 in order to generate an expected financial benefit. The swap structure itself was fundamentally sound, although not without real risks. The problem was in the pricing, and even more significantly, in the events surrounding the district's decision to enter into the swap.

The district serves a portion of Los Angeles County with a large minority population. Its board of directors is elected by the people it serves, but as with many such agencies, the voters historically paid little attention to it. In the period leading up to the swap, things changed. Several minority representatives were elected to the board, and among their priorities was making sure that minority firms were included in the district's procurement process. Included in this policy was a desire to see minority firms represented among the district's banking relationships. In 2001, both Citibank and a minority firm, presented basis swap ideas to the district. Citibank was the district's incumbent investment bank, and the district's staff (who had been hired prior to the arrival of the new board members) supported Citibank's proposal. The board, however, favored the other firm's proposal, and it was chosen to handle the swap.

The swap was a slightly leveraged basis swap. Under its terms, the district agreed to pay the tax-exempt benchmark BMA index (today known as the *SIFMA index*), multiplied by a factor of roughly 1.66, in order to receive one-month LIBOR plus a fixed spread equal to 105 basis points. This firm's analysis was that 1.66 times BMA had roughly equaled one-month LIBOR historically, and they were successful in persuading the district that this relationship would likely hold in the future. Thus, if the future looked like the past, the district would gain a financial benefit equal to 105 basis points per year times the notional amount of the swap of $141,780,000.

The fundamental structure of the swap was sound, and, in fact, dozens of similar tax-exempt issuers have entered into such swaps, although mostly without leverage. The problem was in the pricing. The pricing of the swap determined the amount of the fixed spread—105 basis points, as it was negotiated between the district and the firm.

Because of board-staff tensions, the board wanted to be directly involved in the pricing, and specifically asked that the swap be priced during a board meeting. While this is an unusual request, it is not unheard of. The problem was that the board met at night, in Pacific Time, when all markets were closed. The firm agreed to price the swap under these conditions, and the pricing of the swap most certainly included an added cushion that any dealer would demand for taking overnight risk, when they would be unable to hedge until markets opened the next morning. Compounding the problem was the fact that the night that was chosen for pricing was not just any ordinary night. The pricing was done in the immediate aftermath of the terrorist attacks of September 11, 2001. Market uncertainty was significantly higher than normal, and overnight risk was thus greater. The district did not have a swap advisor (although it did have a general financial advisor).

Roughly a year after the pricing, a federal investigation resulted in the indictment and conviction of a member of the board on charges related to the swap. As alleged in the indictment, the minority firm had entered into a joint-marketing arrangement with another broker-dealer, who had in turn hired a consultant to assist in gaining the business. This consultant was offered a $50,000 success fee. In order to secure the district's business, he allegedly entered into an agreement with the board member to split the fee if the swap was awarded to the firm. The firm denied any knowledge of the corrupt arrangement, and was not charged.

When the scandal broke, the district hired three outside firms (including that of the author) to investigate whether the pricing of the swap had been fair. All firms concluded that the pricing was off-market by a significant amount. Over the next several years, with changes on the district's board, the district took legal action against all of the participants in the swap, including the minority firm and its financial advisor, to have the swap nullified. In 2007, the firm and the district entered into a settlement.

Westminster-Canterbury of the Blue Ridge Continuing Care Retirement Community

Marie S. Pisecki
Managing Director
BB&T Capital Markets

T his case study assesses the strengths and weaknesses of the Westminster-Canterbury of the Blue Ridge *continuing care retirement community* (CCRC) project that were apparent at the time the bonds were sold, as well as the lessons learned through the benefit of hindsight. We also discuss how an investor might weight the risks against the rewards of 6.375% tax-exempt yield in deciding whether to invest in this project.

OVERVIEW

CCRC bonds are typically sold on an unrated basis, often at aggressive spreads compared to other unrated bonds. One reason for the favorable pricing is the liquidity provided by strong retail appetite for this paper, particularly in Virginia. Issue details are provided in Exhibit 17.1. The $79.8 million in Series 2001 bond proceeds were used to finance a major expansion to this life care retirement community in Charlottesville, Virginia, consisting of 122 new *independent living unit* (ILU) apartments and a new kitchen, dining area, and community center. The apartments and common areas were to be completed in November 2003 and achieve 95% occupancy by June 2005. Separately, management planned to cash-fund 10 new cottages after the apartments were completed. The cottages would become available for occupancy in November 2004. Prior to the expansion, the unit mix at Westminster-Canterbury of the Blue Ridge consisted of 136 ILUs, 57

EXHIBIT 17.1   Issue Details

Issuer	Albemarle County Industrial Development Authority, Virginia
Issue	Residential Care Facility Mortgage Revenue Bonds (Westminster-Canterbury of the Blue Ridge), Series 2001A and Series 2001B adjustable rate bonds
Par Amount	$79,815,000
Dated Date	9/1/01
Final Maturity	1/1/31
Coupon/Yield	6.2%/6.375%
Spread to AAA[a]	130 bps
Ratings	Not rated
Underwriters	UBS PaineWebber, Inc., Tucker Anthony, Legg Mason Wood Walker, Inc., BB&T Capital Markets

[a] Spread to yield on September 24, 2001, on AAA general obligation bond due in 2031, Municipal Market Data (MMD) scale.

Source: Official Statement, Residential Care Facility Mortgage Revenue Bonds (Westminster-Canterbury of the Blue Ridge), Series 2001A and Series 2001B adjustable rate bonds.

EXHIBIT 17.2   Project Details

Facility Type	Continuing Care Retirement Community (CCRC)
Contract Type	Lifecare
Location	Charlottesville, VA
Date Opened	1990

Unit Mix (Preproject)	Preproject	Postproject
Independent living units (ILUs)	136	268
Assisted living units (ALUs)	57	57
Nursing beds	54	54
Total	247	379

Source: Official Statement, Residential Care Facility Mortgage Revenue Bonds (Westminster-Canterbury of the Blue Ridge), Series 2001A and Series 2001B adjustable rate bonds.

assisted living units (ALUs), and 54 nursing beds. Postproject, including the cash-funded cottages, the number of ILUs was forecast to increase by 95%. (The project details are summarized in Exhibit 17.2.)

STRENGTHS

The strengths of this issue are:

- Even though each of the six Westminster-Canterbury projects in Virginia are separately managed and financed, the Westminster-Canterbury name has strong brand-name recognition in the Virginia and greater mid-Atlantic markets that is synonymous with quality.
- The Blue Ridge facility serves a high-end client base. At the time the bonds were sold, weighted average entrance fees were $287,000 on existing units and $320,200 on the new units under the 50% refund plan. This represents a 12% pricing differential. In 2006, the weighted average entrance fee for all units had increased to $440,707. High-end facilities generally have wider profit margins and more financial flexibility than more modestly priced projects.
- Demand for both existing and new ILUs appeared satisfactory, but not strong. Because the majority of residents and depositors come from outside the *primary market area* (PMA), we classify Blue Ridge as a *destination facility*. Destination facilities can be more difficult to market. Historical occupancy had been in excess of 93% for the five years prior to financing (1997–2001). ILU occupancy below 90% constitutes a red flag, while occupancy of 95% or higher is the typical goal, so Blue Ridge landed in a solid middle ground area. CCRC projects generally come to market only after 70% of units have been presold with 10% refundable deposits. If it takes too long to reach this threshold, then the list becomes stale and attrition increases. We look for a velocity of three to six units per month. At Blue Ridge, the velocity of presales on the new units was average at 4.1 sales per month.

WEAKNESSES/RISKS

The weaknesses/risks of this issue are:

- In order to be repaid—as with all expansions—the project must be successfully completed on time and on budget (construction risk), followed by the depositors moving in on schedule (fill-up risk).
- The expansion resulted in a 265% increase in debt, from $30,070,000 to $109,885,000. Despite this increase, most leverage ratios were forecast to be well within the normal range for a CCRC. Since funds were spent on bricks and mortar, the increased value of the building offset the increase in debt in ratios, such as debt to capitalization. Fees from initial

move-ins, known as first generation entrance fees, would pay down $32 million in intermediate term bonds due Jan. 1, 2007. Nevertheless, debt per bed would still be high at $205,501.

- Like many life care CCRCs, this facility was dependent on entrance fees for debt service coverage. Although overall debt service coverage was a healthy 1.95x in fiscal 2001 (June 30 fiscal year), coverage without entrance fees was negative 0.77x. This means investors would be exposed to potentially large swings in coverage, depending on unit turnover in any given year. KPMG forecast coverage without entrance fees to improve to a more comfortable 0.60x at stabilization in fiscal 2006.

- Liquidity of 274 *days-cash-on-hand* (DCOH) and 35.6% cash to debt were acceptable, but not ideal for a life care project. KPMG forecast these ratios to improve to 402 DCOH and 40.7% cash to debt by stabilization in fiscal 2006, but included board restricted funds in their calculation. Unrestricted cash, consistent with our analytic calculation in fiscal 2001, was forecast to grow to 340 DCOH and 36.3% cash to debt.

- Assisted living and nursing occupancy was 63% and 78%, respectively, in fiscal 2001. As with many CCRCs, direct admits from the community were not permitted for nursing beds. Low occupancy in health care units (assisted living and nursing) is not necessarily a problem as long as lower levels are anticipated and beds are staffed appropriately. In this case, however, the forecast had occupancy climbing to 91.2% and 92.6% in ALUs and nursing respectively by fiscal 2003.

STATUS UPDATES

Status updates for 2003, 2004, and 2006 are summarized below.

Status Update in 2003

- Construction proceeded on time and on budget, with the expansion opening in October 2003, one month earlier than the initial expectation of November. Common areas opened in the spring, which turned out to have a negative impact on cash flows as this early opening increased staffing expense without any corresponding increase in revenue.

- Although presales for the new units had dropped from 93% in June 2002 to 80% in February 2003, attrition of this magnitude is not unusual as a project gets closer to opening and was not considered a problem, in our view.

EXHIBIT 17.3   Recommended Rate Increases

	2005	2006	2007
Entrance fees	15%	10%	8%
Monthly fees	10%	8%	7%

Source: Larson Allen report, April 20, 2004.

- In fiscal 2003, average annual occupancy was 96.3%, 87.0%, and 83.0% in ILUs, ALUs, and nursing, respectively. While ILUs were fine, occupancy in both ALUs and nursing lagged the KPMG forecast.
- The most serious problem was that liquidity had fallen to 79 days cash on hand (based on BB&T Capital Markets' calculation) compared to a KPMG forecast of 269 days (adjusted to exclude board restricted funds for an apples to apples comparison). Management cited underperforming investments, expense pressures, and lower ALU and nursing occupancy as the primary causes. About 67% of investments were held in equities at the time. Expenses were 10% higher than the fiscal 2003 forecast, and as discussed health care occupancy was underperforming the forecast.
- In addition, the debt service coverage ratio for fiscal 2003 fell to 0.41x. This covenant miss required the hiring of a consultant, who recommended a combination of significant revenue increases and expense cuts. (The recommended rate increases are summarized in Exhibit 17.3.)

Status Update in 2004

- Occupancy of existing ILUs, which had been healthy prior to the project opening, plummeted after the opening, exacerbating the other preexisting problems. By April 30, 2004, occupancy in the existing apartments had fallen to 84% and the older cottages to 76%. The transfer of 15 residents from old ILUs to the new ILUs, the virtual doubling of ILU product in one year, and the contrast between the old and new product all contributed to the problem.
- The new ILUs reached 93.4% by April 2004, a full year ahead of schedule. Occupancy in ALUs and nursing continued to underperform at 84.2% and 79.6%, respectively.[1]
- Entrance fee cash flow from resales of existing units evaporated as those new units were not marketable. Entrance fees from new units were dedicated to repayment of the intermediate term bond debt.

---

[1] Westminster-Canterbury of the Blue Ridge Financial Performance Review for the period ending April 30, 2004.

Status Update in 2006

- The marketing campaign for ILUs was successful. By fiscal year end, the old apartments were 95% occupied. In addition, 100% of the new units and 100% of available cottages were occupied. Nine of the less marketable cottages were taken out of service, leaving 259 rather than 268 total ILUs available.
- ALU occupancy averaged 86.0% and nursing averaged 79.6% for fiscal 2006. This was in line with the more realistic revised forecast undertaken by Larson Allen in 2005 that called for 88.6% and 64.8% occupancy in assisted living and nursing for fiscal 2006. (Series 2005 Official Statement, June 29, 2005.)
- Debt service coverage improved to 1.84× in 2006, up from 1.31× in 2005. Coverage without entrance fees improved from negative 0.06× in 2005 to 0.43× in 2006.
- Days cash on hand remains slim, but improving, at 94 and 174 in fiscal 2005 and 2006, respectively, inching up to 183 days by year-end.

LEARNED IN HINDSIGHT

In hindsight, the following was learned from this project:

- The pricing differential between old and new units was not substantial enough, creating a preference in the market for the newer units. One early indication of this may be a desire for existing residents to transfer to the new units.
- Occupancy in existing units routinely suffer during the construction and fill-up of a major expansion because residents resist moving into a construction site and often prefer new to existing product. Feasibility studies seldom assume that this will occur, usually holding existing units at preproject occupancy levels throughout the forecast period.
- Because a major improvement in occupancy relative to historical experience was forecast for ALUs and nursing, a sensitivity analysis should have been run at existing occupancy levels to test how significantly the cash flows would be impacted by underperformance in this area.
- During an expansion, management can lose sight of monitoring existing operations in the excitement of a major construction project. Expense creep is common and is best kept under control with operating ratio covenants that serve as an early warning signal when the relationship between monthly fees and operating expenses go awry.

WEIGHING THE RISKS

The greatest risk in any CCRC project, in our view, is accurately assessing demand. While volumes have been written on how to do this, occupancy in existing units and velocity of pre-sales are two of the best indicators, in our opinion. One of the strengths of CCRCs is the high levels of liquidity found in most CCRCs, relative to other health care projects such as hospitals and nursing homes. Even if the pace of fill-up has been misjudged, the influx of entrance fees during the fill-up period makes a project particularly flush with cash during the fill-up process. This provides time to implement longer-term solutions, such as changes in the pricing strategy or expense cuts. In some cases a refinancing may be necessary to extend the life of intermediate-term bond debt intended to be paid with first generation entrance fees, but market access for these refinancings has historically been available. As a result, a serious meltdown is unlikely to occur unless demand was completely miscalculated and cannot be resuscitated even with the help of industry consultants.

SUMMARY

Although we questioned the forecast for occupancy in the health care units from inception, the other assumptions appeared reasonable. Operating expense overruns and occupancy problems in existing units should have been addressed sooner, but were ultimately dealt with successfully, in part by a change in the chief executive officer. Despite a somewhat challenging market, the new units sold and filled quickly. The dependency on entrance fees did lead to volatility of debt service coverage, including a missed rate covenant, but this was not a long-term credit problem. The more lasting effect for this credit has been diminished liquidity. It will take a number of years of careful management controls to rebuild the lost cash.

Preserving Housing Affordability with Taxable Municipals

Emily A. Youssouf
Managing Director
JPMorgan Public Finance

Bond financing can be used to preserve the affordability of housing developments built with government assistance that face expiring affordability requirements, averting political turmoil that can result when previously below-market residents are displaced by wealthier households. Through innovative bond financing, the New York City Housing Development Corporation was able to preserve the affordability and physical structure of more than 14,500 apartments where continued affordability for the current residents was threatened.

In 1955, the New York State legislature passed the Limited Profit Housing Companies Law, legislation aimed at creating affordable rental and cooperative housing by providing developers with tax abatements, land, and low-interest mortgages. In exchange, the law required limitation on profits, income limits on tenants, and supervision by New York State. The law, sponsored by State Senator MacNeil Mitchell of Manhattan and Assemblyman Alfred Lama of Brooklyn, has been known ever since simply as *Mitchell-Lama*.

Most developments built under the Mitchell-Lama program were eligible to "buy out" of the program after 20 years by prepaying their government-sponsored mortgage debt. There were originally 105,000 apartments in 269 developments built under the Mitchell-Lama program,[1] and the mortgages were held by city and state agencies. There were 28,800 units

---

[1] New York State Division of Housing and Community Renewal, "Mitchell-Lama Housing Program," http://www.dhcr.state.ny.us/ohm/progs/mitchlam/ohmprgmi.htm (16 March 2007).

that were covered by mortgages held by the New York City Housing Development Corporation, a public benefit corporation aligned with the New York City government.

Between 1989 and February 2004, nearly 15,800 apartments left the Mitchell-Lama program.[2] Between February 2004 and May 2006, the pace at which the units left the program accelerated as an additional 12,603 Mitchell-Lama units left the program, and nearly 13,000 had begun the process of withdrawing.[3] The threatening loss of the affordability of Mitchell-Lama apartments spurred community activism to try to save the buildings as politicians spoke of the need to preserve the affordability in a city where housing costs were skyrocketing. Seeking to find a solution that would preserve the affordability of apartments while repairing the buildings, HDC created two Mitchell-Lama preservation programs: the Mitchell-Lama Repair Loan Program and the Mitchell-Lama Mortgage Restructuring Program. Working in tandem, these programs provided building owners (housing cooperatives in most cases) with below-market mortgage refinancing, brought a fresh infusion of capital to finance building repairs, and ensured that residents would be able to remain in place.

Both programs involved the issuance of taxable bonds. Under the Mitchell-Lama Mortgage Restructuring Program, bond proceeds were used to offer attractive refinancing that encouraged building owners to remain in the program. Through the Mitchell-Lama Repair Loan Program, HDC issued taxable bonds to create low-cost access to capital for building repairs on these aging properties. In some cases, below-market repair loans were made with money from HDC's corporate reserves, which were then reimbursed through the sale of bonds backed by those loans. HDC also used its corporate reserves to pay costs of issuance associated with these bonds.

Between December 2004, when the program launched, and the writing of this case study in March 2007, HDC issued more than $400 million in federally taxable, fixed and auction rate bonds in connection with Mitchell-Lama preservation. The majority of these bonds were issued under HDC's "Open Resolution," an overcollateralized parity debt pool created in 1993 and valued at nearly $2 billion as of 2007. Unlike standalone bond issues, in which the repayment of the bonds is directly linked to the mortgage payments on one building or a small collection of buildings, bonds issued under the Open Resolution are secured on a parity basis with all previous bond series under the resolution, or nearly 900 mortgage loans as of 2007. This allowed the bonds to be given a AA rating from S&P without the need to use a credit enhancement instrument.

As a result of these bond issues, HDC was able to preserve the affordability and physical structure of 14,598 apartments at 33 complexes, more than half of HDC's original portfolio of Mitchell-Lama apartments. The programs remain active and more buildings are expected to participate.

SOURCES

City of New York, Office of the Comptroller, "Affordable No More: New York City's Looming Crisis in Mitchell-Lama and Limited Dividend Housing," February 14, 2004.

Official Statement, New York City Housing Development Corporation, Multi-Family Housing Revenue Bonds, 2004 Series F, G, H, I-1, I-2 and J, December 17, 2004.

Official Statement, New York City Housing Development Corporation, Multi-Family Housing Revenue Bonds, 2004 Series D, E-1 and E-2, December 23, 2004.

Official Statement, New York City Housing Development Corporation, Multi-Family Housing Revenue Bonds, 2005 Series A-1, A-2 and B, May 20, 2005.

Official Statement, New York City Housing Development Corporation, Multi-Family Housing Revenue Bonds, 2005 Series E, F-1 and F-2, September 19, 2005.

Official Statement, New York City Housing Development Corporation. Multi-Family Housing Revenue Bonds, 2005 Series G, H, I, J-1, J-2, K and L, December 21, 2005.

City of New York, Office of the Comptroller, "Affordable No More: An Update: New York City's Mitchell-Lama and Limited Dividend Housing Crisis Is Accelerating," May 25, 2006.

Official Statement, New York City Housing Development Corporation, Multi-Family Housing Revenue Bonds, 2006 Series C, D-1, D-2, E and F, June 23, 2006.

Official Statement, New York City Housing Development Corporation, Multi-Family Rental Housing Revenue Bonds (Seaview Towers), 2006 Series A, December 14, 2006.

New York State Division of Housing and Community Renewal, "Mitchell-Lama Housing Program," http://www.dhcr.state.ny.us/ohm/progs/mitchlam/ohmprgmi.htm (16 March 2007).

Massachusetts Sells LIBOR Index General Obligation Bonds with an Interest Rate Swap

Sylvan G. Feldstein, Ph.D.
Director, Investment Department
Guardian Life Insurance Company of America

Patrick Landers
Assistant Treasurer
Commonwealth of Massachusetts

This case study describes a new type of long-term bond issue that came into vogue in the early part of 2007 in the tax-exempt municipal bond market. It is a form of a structured note called *LIBOR index bonds*. What is unique about it is that the coupon payment to investors is reset every quarter and established in a formula based on LIBOR, the London Interbank Offered Rates for U.S. dollar deposits. Prior to this new structure, tax-exempt floating rates were determined by a remarketing or auction process. This structure already exists in the corporate markets and is known as a *floating-rate note* (FRN).

In May 2007, the Commonwealth of Massachusetts sold $1,046,710,000 of general obligation bonds. What was innovative about this issue was that approximately two-thirds came as LIBOR index bonds with term bonds of (1) $65,750,000 due on November 1, 2018; (2) $31,665,000 due on November 1, 2020; (3) $348,380,000 due on November 1, 2025; and (4) $400,000,000 due on May 1, 2037. The rest of the bond issue came as

---

The authors were assisted by Johan Rosenberg of Sound Capital Management, swap advisor on the transaction.

fixed rate serial bonds. Half of the bond proceeds were used for refunding outstanding issues and half of the bond proceeds were for new money. The bonds have call features and sinking funds.

As general obligations of Massachusetts, the underlying ratings on the bonds were Aa2 by Moody's, AA by Standard & Poor's, and AA by Fitch. A portion, $400,000,000 of term bonds due May 1, 2037, were rated AAA because they were insured by CIFG ($100,000,000) and FGIC ($300,000,000).

The LIBOR index bond term issues were priced as:

1. The $400,000,000 bonds due May 1, 2037 insured by CIFG and FGIC, in two separate tranches, in each case the coupon is determined as 67% of three-month LIBOR plus 57 basis points.
2. The $65,750,000 bonds due November 1, 2018 were sold as 67% of three-month LIBOR plus 46 basis points.
3. The $31,665,000 bonds due November 1, 2020 were sold as 67% of three-month LIBOR plus 46 basis points.
4. The $348,380,000 bonds due November 1, 2025 were sold as 67% of three-month LIBOR plus 55 basis points.

The LIBOR index bonds are subject to an optional call in whole or in part by the Commonwealth. If called prior to the call date in 2017, the redemption price will be equal to 100% of the principal amount plus the fixed spread for LIBOR bonds of that maturity plus accrued interest to the date of redemption. On or after the call date in 2017 the redemption price is par, without premium, plus accrued interest.

As is typical with synthetic fixed rate structures, a fixed payer swap is entered into that pays to the LIBOR index bond issuer the required quarterly amounts due and payable to LIBOR index bondholders.

The overall benefits to the issuer in this transaction are threefold. First, the Commonwealth diversified its issuance to reestablish investor capacity for fixed rate Commonwealth debt and to meet new areas of demand, that is, the hedge fund and nontraditional municipal bond buyer. Second, the refunding portion of the bond issue generated approximately $27.5 million in net present value savings, or 5% of the existing bond amount. Third, it was estimated that by using the fixed payer swap to offset the LIBOR-indexed coupon payments, the Commonwealth obtained a lower cost of funds than it would have on a full fixed long-term coupon.

As compared to a fixed long-term coupon, the following equality should hold from an arbitrage viewpoint:

AA Yield + Credit spread = 67% of LIBOR swap rate + Fixed spread

From an issuer's perspective, as long as the fixed spread is less than AAA yield plus the credit spread minus 67% of the LIBOR swap rate, the issuer would be better off selling FRNs. Likewise, a hedge fund arbitrageur could garner profits by being long or short on either side of that equation.

While obtaining a lower cost of funding than issuing a fixed long-term coupon bond, the FRN synthetic structure also provides additional benefits over the more traditional synthetic structure of variable rate demand obligations (VRDOs) coupled with a percent of LIBOR swap. These benefits include:

1. No liquidity risk; FRNs do not require a liquidity facility or letter of credit.
2. No remarketing fees; FRNs have passive resets.
3. No basis risk; as a "cost of funds swap," the floating leg of the swap exactly offsets the floating payment on the FRNs.
4. No put risk; FRNs are a long-term committed financing.
5. "Super Integration" for calculating the bond yield which has the effect of lessening the administrative burden of related escrow investments.[1]

One advantage for the investor is that the LIBOR index bond is paying a fixed 67% of LIBOR plus the spread thus if the highest federal tax rate ever increases above the level it was at the time the bonds were priced and sold, the percentage of LIBOR on new issues should decrease, thus making the outstanding bonds more attractive to investors.

This financing also removed $1.5 billion of the Commonwealth's long-term fixed rate municipal bonds from the market. As a result, buyers of the Commonwealth's long-term bonds have less inventory to buy or to work with, which should improve the Commonwealth's future financings. As noted above, half of the LIBOR index bonds refunded $500,000,000 of outstanding Massachusetts general obligation bonds. In addition, the two term bond issues came to the market as three-month LIBOR resets not as full long-term, fixed rate coupons.

The profile of a tax-exempt bond investor has changed significantly since 2002 with the decline of the traditional bond fund and insurance company investors and the emergence of the hedge fund and international investors. The rise of hedge fund participation in the tax-exempt market has been supported by dealers willing to carry higher bond portfolio balances and thereby support liquidity of all types of bonds. Similarly, the investor of the LIBOR index bonds to date have been predominantly hedge funds. It will be

---

[1] The LIBOR synthetic fixed rate VRDOs structure does not qualify for super integration. By using the superintegration method, certain IRS tax yield calculations are simplified.

interesting to see if the dealer community supports and develops liquidity in this case, or if the investors ultimately must assume the risk of illiquidity.

SOURCES

Preliminary Official Statement for the Commonwealth of Massachusetts $500,000,000 General Obligation Bonds Consolidated Loan of 2007 Series A and $500,000,000 General Obligation Refunding bonds 2007 Series A, May 3, 2007.

Developing Hudson Yards with a $2 Billion Bond Issue

James McSpiritt
General Counsel
Phipps Houses

This case study describes the $2 billion Hudson Yards Infrastructure Corporation's bond issue that was sold at the end of 2006. It was a complicated and unique financing that provided funds for the economic development of an underdeveloped section of New York City.

The area of New York City, renamed Hudson Yards, is on the West Side of Manhattan and bounded generally by 42nd Street on the north, 11th Avenue on the west, 31st Street on the south and 8th Avenue on the east. As of mid-2007, it consisted primarily of railyards, older industrial buildings and parking lots. In the early years of the twenty-first century and under Mayor Michael Bloomberg, the city rezoned the area and through the bond issue funded the extension of subway service from Times Square to 11th Avenue and 34th Street. It is hoped that this will result not only in the westward expansion of Manhattan's midtown office district but also in the creation of a new mixed use community that will include significant residential development, as well as a new park and boulevard.

This case study focuses on the innovative financing of the infrastructure improvements and the planning steps that were taken which will make possible the realization of the city's vision for the Hudson Yards: the westward extension of the No. 7 subway line, the new park and the creation of a new midblock boulevard between 10th and 11th Avenues.

City Hall assembled an interdisciplinary team from around city government with representation from the Law Department, the Department of

---

James McSpiritt worked on this financing while Deputy Chief of the Municipal Finance Division at the New York City Law Department.

City Planning, the Office of Management and Budget, and the New York City Economic Development Corporation, as well as outside bond counsel and investment bankers. In the course of the effort, the City created a new local development corporation, the Hudson Yards Development Corporation (HYDC), whose sole purpose would be to realize the project. A second local development corporation, the Hudson Yards Infrastructure Corporation (HYIC), was created to issue bonds the proceeds of which will fund the infrastructure improvements.

The challenge the team faced was to create a mechanism pursuant to which revenue streams attributable to the anticipated new development in the Hudson Yards area could be trapped, deployed and directed in support of the HYIC bonds issued to fund the subway extension and other public improvements. Law Department attorneys achieved this desired objective by creatively recombining a set of previously employed devices to fashion a new apparatus for the issuance of bonds.

SOURCES OF FINANCIAL SUPPORT

The Hudson Yards zoning text approved by the city council contains two of the financial supports for the Hudson Yards bonds: a district improvement fund and a provision allowing the sale of transferable development rights. The *district improvement fund* (DIF) is a refinement of zoning bonuses otherwise available pursuant to the city's zoning resolution. For example, pursuant to other well-established zoning text provisions, a developer may be permitted to construct a larger building than otherwise allowed "as-of-right" if the developer also constructs a related improvement to adjacent transit infrastructure. The assumptions underlying such bonuses, and the Hudson Yards, increased floor area bonus as well, is that the infrastructure improvements—which the DIF payments will finance—support the increased density contemplated by the new zoning. No single developer, however, could be expected to fund the entire No. 7 subway line extension and other infrastructure necessitated by the development of the Hudson Yards. Also, such infrastructure will be built in stages as the infrastructure supports and makes possible the development which, in circular and symbiotic sequence, generates the revenue to pay for the infrastructure. The public sector will therefore undertake these infrastructure projects immediately, relying, inter alia, on anticipated revenues from the district improvement fund.

A second source of financial support for the Hudson Yards bonds is the sale of transferable development rights available from a publicly owned real property parcel within the Hudson Yards Special District. Using transferred development rights, real estate developers may seek to build above the new "as-of-right" density otherwise applicable to the Hudson Yards Special District. Generally, density is the product of the floor-area-ratio methodology, established by the Zoning Resolution, that determines the number of square feet of floor area to which a building may be built. Ordinarily, such development rights can be transferred among contiguous parcels within a city block. In the case of the Hudson Yards Special District, the zoning text promulgates a large-scale plan in which development rights may be transferred throughout the large-scale plan area, generally the new commercial district between 10th and 11th Avenues, from 30th Street to 36th Street east of the new park and boulevard and from 30th Street to 41st Street west of the new park and boulevard. The source of the development rights available for transfer and sale in the Hudson Yards area from publicly owned land is the real property known as the Eastern Rail Yards—the superblock between 10th Avenue and 11th Avenue and 33rd Street and 30th Street controlled by the Metropolitan Transportation Authority (MTA). The placement of a park on the site reduces development below the total floor area otherwise achievable under the rezoning on the superblock. The development rights available for transfer may, consistent with the overall zoning constraints of the district, be transferred to other sites in the commercial corridor in exchange for payments by the developers of those sites into a fund. The MTA has agreed to make the proceeds of any such payments available to the HYIC, up to a certain limit, to be used to pay debt service on the HYIC bonds issued to finance the subway extension and other infrastructure costs of the Hudson Yards project.

In addition to the zoning-based revenues, the largest revenue source for the funding of infrastructure improvements in the Hudson Yards area is expected to be real property taxes on new development—or their equivalent. The Hudson Yards financing will capture real property tax-equivalent-related revenues through PILOTs, an acronym for *payments in lieu of taxes.* PILOTs represent a form of development incentive. They consist of payments under essentially synthetic leases from the New York City Industrial Development Agency (IDA) to developers which payments substitute and are a surrogate for real property taxes. They are, in form, "additional rent" payments pursuant to the IDA-to-developers leases. They are generally fixed in amount for a prescribed period of time. The "incentive," if payment is not appreciably lower than what taxes would otherwise be, lies in the certainty of what the owner can expect to pay as "taxes" for the prescribed period. PILOTs are most commonly part of commercial development deals structured by the IDA. Pursuant to its statutory authority, the IDA may enter into an agreement with a commercial developer which renders a site tax exempt in exchange for payment by the developer of a PILOT that is fixed but somewhat lower than the otherwise applicable real property tax for the site. In August 2006, the IDA adopted an amendment specifically for the Hudson Yards area to its Uniform Tax Exemption Policy, which sets forth the standards for its imposition of PILOTs in Hudson Yards deals. Pursuant to this amendment, deeper reductions are offered the sooner and the further west in the Hudson Yards area the development occurs. So, depending on timing and location, developers may be entitled to the benefit of substantially reduced taxes. The countervailing benefit to the public of the deeper "tax abatements" would be that revenues to pay infrastructure bond debt service would be generated sooner, thereby not exposing the city's general fund to the same extent as discussed in the next section.

In the usual case, PILOTs collected by the IDA are required to be paid to the affected tax jurisdiction—in this case, the city. In the "unusual" case of Hudson Yards where the PILOT revenue stream is to be directed, the city must assign these payments to the HYIC to support the repayment of its infrastructure bonds. An agreement between the city council and the mayor that was concluded in 2005 provides that PILOTs generated in the Hudson Yards area be assigned to the HYIC to pay the debt service on the Hudson Yards infrastructure bonds, with any excess flowing back to the city.

OVERCOMING DELAY IN REALIZING REVENUES

Although studies showed that revenues to be generated from new development in the Hudson Yards area would eventually be sufficient to cover the HYIC bonds, a substantial delay inevitably will occur between the issuance date of the bonds and the projected receipt of sufficient revenues. Proceeds from PILOTs and from the transfer of development rights will become available when development of the Hudson Yards occurs. The subway extension and other infrastructure improvements, however, which are predicates of much of the expected development, must be funded now, before the development takes place or contemporaneously with it. This problem was addressed by the city council's passage of a financing resolution in connection with the Hudson Yards rezoning approval. In the financing resolution, the council approved a support agreement between the city and the HYIC that permits the city to make payments, subject to appropriation, of interest on HYIC bonds if the revenues of the HYIC are insufficient for debt service in any year.

In addition, the support agreement permits the city to pay annually to the HYIC, subject to appropriation, an amount equal to the property tax revenue from new development in the area to the extent not covered by PILOT arrangements. In this manner, taxes on new development not captured as PILOTs are available for debt service on the HYIC bonds.

In order to complete the credit structure for the bond transaction, final arrangements had to be made with regard to development of the Eastern Rail Yards, owned by the Triborough Bridge and Tunnel Authority (TBTA) a constituent authority of the MTA. In connection with the development of property that it owns, the MTA has authority to enter into an agreement with a developer obligating the developer to pay a PILOT to the TBTA or MTA. In September 2006, the MTA undertook to assign all PILOTs from development of the Eastern Rail Yards to the HYIC in support of its bonds. It also undertook to impose on developers PILOTs in amounts consistent with the IDA's amended Uniform Tax Exemption Policy for the Hudson Yards area. In addition, HYIC acquired from the MTA, in exchange for a payment of $200 million, a 50% interest in prospective MTA proceeds from the transfer of development rights off of sites within the Eastern Rail Yards to other Hudson Yards sites. An important feature of this development rights transaction is that MTA has conferred on HYDC concomitant authority, in consideration of the $200 million payment, to market the available development rights to potential Hudson Yards real estate developers. To the extent HYDC successfully arranges transactions for transfer of development rights, the MTA will be obligated to seek to effect the transactions. Proceeds from these transfers will be available for HYIC debt service. The proceeds of such development rights transfers will first be paid to the HYIC in support of its bonds and then to the MTA after the HYIC's interest has been exhausted.

The MTA has also agreed to plan with the city for development of the Western Rail Yards (owned by the MTA/TBTA and located between 11th Avenue and West Streets and 30th Street and 33rd Street), an area that has not been rezoned. The MTA has committed that any developer of or within the Western Rail Yards will be required to pay a PILOT consistent with the IDA's Uniform Tax Exemption Policy for the Hudson Yards, and any such PILOT will be assigned by the MTA to the HYIC.

The final piece of the project structuring was the arrangement for the expenditure of the bond proceeds. A further arrangement negotiated with the MTA in September 2006, and embodied in a memorandum of understanding among the MTA, the city, HYIC and HYDC, provides for MTA Capital Construction to undertake and contract for the westward extension of the No. 7 subway. The city, through proceeds from the sale of HYIC bonds, will make available a capital commitment of $2 billion, with a $100 million contingency. The city has agreed to deliver the real property and easements necessary for the extension through the exercise of the city's power of eminent domain.

THE BOND SALE

The planning and the structure of the Hudson Yards program met with success in the bond market. In September 2006, with the necessary agreements in place for securing the revenues and for the expenditure of the proceeds, HYIC, with its advisers and bond counsel, brought the deal to the ratings agencies so that the bonds could be marketed. Two billion dollars in Hudson Yards Senior Revenue Bonds were sold in December 2006 at a true interest cost (which calculates the actual yield on the bonds, accounting for costs and proceeds) of 4.71%. The bonds are an appropriation obligation of the city for the net interest due on the bonds only.

$800,000,000.00 came as 5 percents due February 15, 2047 at a yield of 4.28%. Moody's rated these appropriation bonds A3. Moody's rating the city's general obligation bonds is A1. The rating on the Hudson Yard bonds was A by Standard & Poor's and A– by Fitch. $700,000,000.00 came as 5 percents due February 15, 2047 and a yield of 4.10%. These bonds were insured by FGIC and thereby rated triple A. $500,000,000.00 came as 4.5 percents due February 15, 2047 with a yield of 4.40%. Being insured by MBIA, they were rated triple A.

With the bond proceeds in hand, the Hudson Yards project turned to implementation. As of the writing of this case study in mid-2007, Law Department attorneys and outside counsel are working to complete the necessary property acquisitions. The MTA is preparing the request for proposals for the first construction contract for the No. 7 subway line extension, and anticipates awarding the contract this summer. The city is working with the MTA on the planning principles for the Western Rail Yards and to prepare a request for proposals for development of that site. Change in the Hudson Yards is underway.

Seminole Tribe Bets on Taxability

Joseph Krist
Senior Municipal Analyst
Lord Abbett & Co. LLC

In the late 1990s, the Indian gaming industry began to undergo a huge expansion across the country. This industry was expanding after the passage of the Indian Gaming Regulatory Act (IGRA) in 1988. The legislation provided a framework for federal regulation of the industry and established a basis for negotiations between tribes and the states. By 2001, there had been several tax-exempt bonds issued to finance projects where the source of revenue for repayment derived from tribally owned gaming facilities. These included large hotel and gaming complexes at sites in the northeast—Mohegan Sun and Foxwoods.

The Seminole Tribe of Florida had historically been one of the more successful tribes in terms of commercial business operations. Among these were significant, but limited bingo-based facilities that the tribe had operated for many years at sites in Tampa and Hollywood, Florida. The development nationwide of the Indian gaming industry and the successful partnerships achieved between other tribes and private gaming operators encouraged the Seminole's to take advantage of legislative changes in Florida that permitted the expansion of the Seminole's gaming activities.

In April of 2002, the Capital Trust Agency issued $290,000,000 of municipal bonds, the proceeds of which were distributed to the Seminole Tribe of Florida. The tribe planned to apply the proceeds to the cost of development and construction of resort facilities which would include hotel and gaming facilities which would be owned and operated by the tribe but operated privately by the Hard Rock Café hotel chain. Specifically, the use of funds included in the official statement included resort facilities, repayment of a bridge loan, capitalization of interest, funding of a debt service reserve fund, and costs of issuance. These facilities would replace the existing gaming facilities at both existing sites.

Issuance of municipal bonds by and on behalf of Native American tribes has always presented a number of unique legal challenges. Federally recognized Indian tribes are independent nations with sovereign powers except as they have been limited by treaty or by the U.S. Congress. Indian tribes maintain their own governmental systems and, in many cases, their own judicial systems. Congress may regulate Indian tribes. States do not generally have the authority to regulate Indian tribes. In the case of tribal gaming, the National Indian Gaming Commission exercises primary federal regulatory control over Indian gaming. Contracts are governed by tribal law. Indian tribes enjoy sovereign immunity from unconsented suit.

The Seminole bonds were secured pursuant to a master indenture that granted a security interest to the master trustee for the bonds in pledged revenues. These revenues would consist of all of the revenues from the ownership or operation of then-existing gaming facilities and subsequently the resort and gaming facilities to be operated under agreements entered into between the tribe and the Hard Rock Hotel chain to manage the facilities to be financed by the bonds. The projects were successfully completed and went into operation. They consisted of the hotel portions of the expanded resort facilities at Tampa and Hollywood and infrastructure to support the operation of the resort facilities.

The bonds were issued with opinions from special tax counsel that the interest on the bonds was excludable from gross income for federal tax purposes under Section 103 of the Internal Revenue Code (IRC) of 1986 and was exempt from all present intangibles personal property taxes imposed by the State of Florida pursuant to Chapter 199, Florida Statutes. The tax opinion relied on the opinion of bond counsel that the bonds had been validly issued under state law. Section 103 establishes that gross income does not include interest on any state or local bond. Section 7871 of the IRC defines the status of the tribes for purposes of applying Section 103 to tax-exempt obligations issued by or on behalf of the tribes and establishes that Indian tribal governments are to be treated as states for purposes of Section 103.

At the time of issuance, the use of proceeds did cause enough concern among potential investors that they sought protection in the event of a finding of taxability. Other substantial outstanding issues secured by tribal gaming revenues had presented uses of funds that included a wide range of typically tax-exempt facilities even a museum. The final terms of the issue provided for the eventuality that the interest on the bonds could be declared taxable at some later point by the Internal Revenue Service (IRS). The bonds would be subject to mandatory redemption prior to maturity at a date to be selected by the issuer at the direction of the tribe within one year of any determination of taxability. The bonds would be redeemed in that event at a price of 108% of principal. The bonds were not required to be called if a settlement agreement with the IRS resulted in the interest on the bonds remaining tax exempt.

The IRS often enters into so-called "settlement agreements" with issuers that allow issuers to be punished for misuse of municipal bond proceeds under the IRC without penalizing individual holders of bonds who relied in good faith upon the representations and opinions of the professionals associated with individual bond issues. This process often results in a payment by the issuer or other parties to the deal to the IRS that allows for the continued existence of the issue and continuing tax-exemption for the interest on the bonds and/or early redemption of the bonds often at a premium to the investor.

In the loan agreement securing the tribe's payments to the Capital Trust Agency, the tribe agreed that it would at all times do and perform all acts and things permitted by law which are necessary to assure that the interest paid on the bonds would be excluded from gross income for federal tax purposes. The tribe also agreed that it would contest any challenge by the IRS or any other agency to the exclusion of interest on the bonds.

In April 2004, the tribe received a notice from the IRS that the tax-exempt debt issued for the project was to be the subject of an examination to determine compliance with federal tax requirements. The notice indicated that the IRS had selected the issues for examination through the receipt of information from both external sources and internally that caused a concern that the debt issuance might have failed one or more provisions of Sections 103, and 141 through 150 of the IRC.

The IRS took the position that the Seminole Tribe issued an obligation to the Capital Trust Agency (a loan agreement) substantially all the proceeds of which were not to be used in the exercise of an essential governmental function of the tribe. The primary question centered on whether or not convention, restaurant, and hotel facilities including all related support and ancillary facilities represent an essential governmental function of the tribe. Section 141 of the code limits the use of proceeds used by a person other than a state or local governmental unit and reinforces the requirement that the transaction involve an essential governmental function.

Over the ensuing months, the IRS contacted a variety of parties to the transaction including counsel, underwriters, financial advisers, and other participants in the bond issue. In December 2004, the IRS issued to the Capital Trust Agency as issuer of the bonds, a preliminary adverse determination letter stating that the bonds had not been validly issued under state law and the interest was therefore not excluded from gross income. The notice also indicated that the questions as to whether the tribe should be treated as a state for purposes of Sections 103 and 141 through 150, whether the use of proceeds was an essential governmental function of the tribe, and whether the use of proceeds satisfied private activity bond tests had arisen in the course of the examination of the issue. These matters would be addressed at a future date.

In May 2005, the Capital Trust Agency received a second preliminary adverse determination letter. The letter cited five reasons for determining that the bonds bore interest that was not excludable from gross income. The IRS opined that the bonds were not validly issued because the Capital Trust Agency had no statutory authority, the Capital Trust Agency did not issue the bonds on behalf of a State or political subdivision or on behalf of the tribe itself, the facilities had not been represented as essential governmental facilities, that the facilities were not used in the exercise of an essential governmental function and thus the bonds were private activity bonds, and that the bonds were private activity bonds because of agreements between the facilities and a private operating entity.

The Capital Trust Agency and the tribe contested the findings included in both preliminary notices of adverse determination as they had covenanted to do in the underlying bond documents. The issuer, the Capital Trust Agency, took the position that the tribe's role was more that of a conduit issuer. The tribe took a position that it was not the ultimate obligor (a corporation owned by the tribe was the obligor under the loan agreement) and it was contended that this allowed the use of proceeds to satisfy the private activity tests. The tribe also cited the use of tax exempt bonds by state and local governments to finance 15 large urban hotels over a period beginning in 1995. The tribe's position was that the resort and gaming facilities financed by the proceeds of the bonds were no different than facilities such as hotels in state parks. These facilities, the tribe argued, were within the realm of economic activities that have been considered essential governmental functions.

The ongoing examination was taking its toll on investors in the bonds. The looming taxability finding limited trading in the bonds and complicated the evaluation of a fair market price. Over the same period of time, interest rates were trending lower and credit spreads were narrowing. The construction and startup risk associated with the credit at the time of issuance of the bonds was no longer an issue. The project was a commercially successful entity. This combined to create a strong environment to refinance the issue on a taxable basis.

It was under those circumstances that the tribe exercised its right to redeem the bonds prior to redemption within one year of a finding of taxability. The redemption occurred on October 24, 2005, some three and one-half years after issuance. The bonds were redeemed at a price of 108% plus accrued interest pursuant to the bond document requirements. No investor was required to make any payment to the IRS. This ended the saga on a practical basis for investors. For the tribe, however, the story was not yet over. It still had outstanding issues pertaining to the IRS findings in its second preliminary adverse determination letter.

In December 2006, the Capital Trust Agency was informed that the IRS had concluded that the tribe might be treated as a governmental unit for purposes of Section 103 of the IRC only if the proceeds are used in the exercise of an essential governmental function. The IRS determined that the construction and operation of the project financed with the proceeds of the bonds was not an exercise of an essential governmental function under Section 7871 of the Code. The IRS asserted that the Capital Trust Agency not the tribe was the issuer of the bonds and that this meant that the tribe was not functioning as a governmental unit in connection with the issuance of the bonds. The decision reflected both the language of the statutes in question as well as their legislative history.

The use of tax-exempt bonds by Indian tribes was the subject of evolving law through the 1980s. Various regulatory and legislative actions by Congress established limits on the scope and nature of the facilities which could be financed by Indian tribes with such bonds. These culminated in the enactment of Section 7871 in 1987. The legislation appears to limit the tax exemption on bonds issued by tribes only to those where the proceeds are to be used in the exercise of an "essential government function." In the case of those issues, tribes were to be treated as states for purposes of the IRC.

The IRS determined that the tribe had failed to establish that the ownership and operation of facilities comparable to the project was sufficiently prevalent or long-standing to establish such ownership as an essential governmental function. The IRS went further and found the facilities to be commercial facilities not considered within the scope of the government function exception. The project was found to have the characteristics of a commercial activity because it competed directly with commercial businesses in the local area and it operated in a manner consistent with that of commercial enterprises. It was adjudged to have a profit-making objective and not to provide a direct pubic benefit to local citizens. The Capital Trust Agency and the tribe had also asked that any finding taxability be prospective from the time of determination. This was not granted by the IRS.

This case is an example of the ongoing process of evolution in the regulation of the municipal bond market. Issuers and their clients and representatives will always seek to test and expand the boundaries of the regulatory system while regulators (in this case the IRS) seek opportunities to establish clearer standards for compliance within an innovative and evolving market. In this situation the right mix of client, issuer, project, counsel, and regulator combined to create an opportunity for the IRS to significantly clarify its position. It is now clear what sort of projects must be financed with municipal bonds secured from tribal gaming facilities. This results in clear guidance to the marketplace and reduces the potential for investor risk resulting from unintended taxability issues arising in connection with future issues.

Subsequent issues of bonds secured by revenues derived from tribal gaming facilities have continued. Investors have been reminded of the importance of the tax opinion and the value of protection of a taxability call. The issuers have been more explicit about the governmental nature of the facilities to which proceeds of those issues are applied.

A Pictorial History of Municipal Bonds

Sylvan G. Feldstein, Ph.D.
Director, Investment Department
Guardian Life Insurance Company of America

Peter O'Brien
Manager, Investment Reporting
Guardian Life Insurance Company of America

In Chapter 44 municipal bankruptcies and bond defaults were discussed. In this appendix, we highlight with pictures some of the more colorful and interesting bond defaults as well as representative municipal bonds that have been issued over the years, going all the way back to Colonial times. These bonds are known as *bearer bonds*; since the early 1980s bearer bonds cannot be issued.

Because the defaulted municipal bonds, becoming worthless, were not physically cancelled or destroyed some of them have survived. Over time,

---

Bonds and coupons shown in this appendix are from the personal collections of the authors. Historical sources for this appendix include: A. M. Hillhouse, *Municipal Bonds* (New York: Prentice Hall, 1936); George H. Hempel, *The Postwar Quality of State and Local Debt* (New York: National Bureau of Economic Research, 1971); William A. Scott, *The Repudiation of State Debts* (New York: Thomas Y. Crowell and Co., 1893); selected back issues of *The Bond Buyer* and *Banknote Reporter*; Francis Butler Simkins and Robert Hilliard Woody, *South Carolina During Reconstruction* (Chapel Hill: University of North Carolina Press, 1932); *The Clinton Collection* (New York: NASCA, 1985); "City Wins In Fight On Old Bond Issue," *New York Times*, June 5, 1919; and an Official Statement for a sale of State of Louisiana General Obligation Bonds, dated June 13, 1978. Informant interviews were also held between 1984 and 1985 with Clarence Rareside and Douglas B. Ball, numismatic collectors and dealers specializing in old municipal bonds.

the original owners gradually parted with them and they were bought and sold by coin and "paper money" dealers. The value was usually determined by the detail and beauty of the vignettes. Their scarcity and level of engraving were also critical factors in determining value. In this market, the fact that they were municipal bonds was largely ignored.

Most of the municipal bonds that did not default and were redeemed by the issuer on schedule and at face value were usually physically destroyed by the state or local government involved. In some instances, they were kept, but physically cancelled, and eventually entered the paper money market as collector's items. Some of them are shown here as well.

THE COLONIAL PERIOD

Municipal bonds were even issued in Colonial times. Exhibit A.1 is a non-interest bearing note issued by the "Province of North Carolina." It appears to be dated December 1751 and has four authorizing signatures. It is for two shillings and six pence and payable at the public treasury.

Exhibit A.2 is another noninterest bearing North Carolina note. It was for ten shillings and was issued approximately 20 years later. It is payable upon demand at the public treasury at any time after June 10, 1772. This note is in greater detail than the earlier one and carries warnings printed on both the left and right margins that state "Death to counterfeit."

EXHIBIT A.1   1751, Province of North Carolina Two Shillings and Six Pence Noninterest Bearing Note

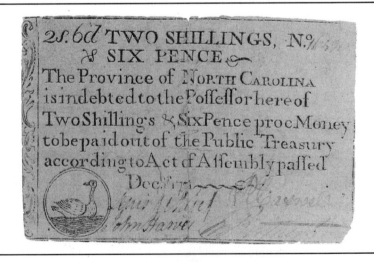

EXHIBIT A.2 1768 Province of North Carolina Ten Shilling Noninterest Bearing Note Number 2628

Lower Manhattan in what is now the City of New York, with its numerous printers, engravers, bankers, salesmen, and lawyers, was from Colonial times up until the almost the end of the twentieth century the center of the municipal bond industry. It was also where possibly the first municipal bond was issued for an identifiable public works project. This was a municipal bond financing that we would describe today as a general obligation debt. In 1774, the governing body of New York, at that time known as the Common Council, began a major construction project and sold bonds to finance it. The bond proceeds were used to pay for the land and construction of the city's first water system for Lower Manhattan, then the sole center of New York City's commercial and residential life. As shown in the illustration of note number 2077 in Exhibit A.3, the two-shilling note was for the New York Water Works.

The construction project was designed by an English civil engineer, Christopher Colles. The note proceeds were used to build a reservoir near a water collection pond. The basin was filled with water pumped from wells. Hollow log pipes were then laid for local distribution. The project was abandoned at the outbreak of the Revolutionary War, soon after it had been put into service, and the Common Council, the obligor for the bonds did not survive.

In Exhibit A.3 are shown the front and back of one of the water works notes. The back of the note depicts the type of water pump that was used.

EXHIBIT A.3   1776 New York Water Works Note Number 2077

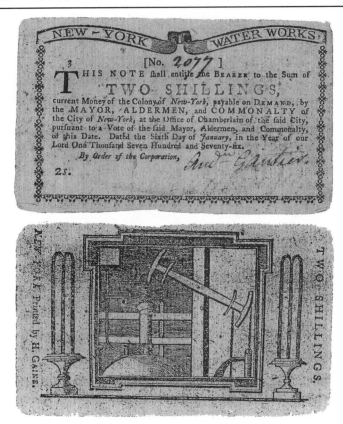

In Exhibit A.4 is a bond issued by the state of Massachusetts in 1780 and due at the end of 1786. It had an annual interest rate of 5%. The front of the certificate is stamped in red ink showing interest had been paid for one year. The back of the bond has detailed engraving and is signed so as to make it more difficult to be counterfeited. It also shows that the US government, by a resolution of Congress, "ensure" payment.

The municipal note in Exhibit A.5 was issued by the state of Connecticut in 1789 and has an annual interest rate of 6% in either "Spanish milled dollars" at the rate of six shillings or gold or silver coins at the interest rate of 6%. The back appears to indicate that interest payments were made for three years through 1792. This municipal note is also of interest as it is signed by Peter Colt, the State Treasurer. It is believed he was related to Samuel Colt, the inventor of the Colt 45 handgun.

EXHIBIT A.4   1780 State of Massachusetts 5% Bond Number 19,369

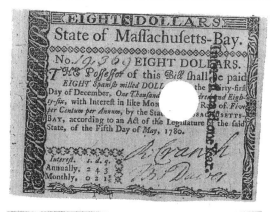

In Exhibit A.6 is a $100.00 note issued on March 17, 1840 by the Fund Commissioner of the State of Illinois and is for public works. Interest is at the rate of 6% per year and is to start on April 20, 1840.

In Exhibit A.7 is a $100.00 note issued on May 9, 1843 by "Municipality Number Two" in New Orleans. It is to pay interest at an annual rate of 6%. The back of the note shows that interest of $25.08 was paid on July 14, 1847.

CIVIL WAR RELATED DEFAULTS

In February 1861, at a convention in Montgomery, Alabama, seven states seceded from the union and created the Confederate Constitution. In April, four more southern states joined them. While the Confederate government issued bonds, many of the states and some cities in the South issued municipal bonds as well.

Ironically, during the Civil War, investors throughout the South and in Europe preferred to buy state and local municipal bonds instead of Confederate bonds. Their thinking was that even if the South lost the war, the state and local governments would still pay their debts. Unfortunately, this belief proved to be incorrect. Section 4 of the14th Amendment to the United States

EXHIBIT A.5   1789 State of Connecticut 6% Note Number 2424

EXHIBIT A.6   1840 State of Illinois 6% Note Number 637

EXHIBIT A.7   1843 New Orleans "Municipality No. Two" 6% Note Number 190

Constitution specifically stated that "neither the United States, nor any state shall assume or pay any debts or obligations incurred in aid of insurrection or rebellion against the United States, or any claim for the loss or emancipation of any slave; but all such debts or obligations shall be held illegal and void."

In Exhibit A.8 is a $5 dollar bearer Arkansas Treasury Warrant issued by the state of Arkansas on March 28, 1862. Interest was to be payable at the rate of 8% per year and the securities were to be "paid in the order of their number." Because of the scarcity of paper in the South, the local printer in Little Rock printed the certificate on the back of a sheet of paper that originally had been printed for another purpose.

In Exhibit A.9 is a more elaborate municipal bond with coupons issued by the state of Georgia on December 16, 1861 and was due in 1881. It is a $1,000 bond and has semiannual interest at an annual rate of 7%. This bond is identified as number 40 and it has been reported that only 1,000 bonds were printed. The bond indicates that it is issued in the Confederate States of America. Like many municipal bonds issued today, it has a call fea-

EXHIBIT A.8   1862 8% Arkansas Treasury Warrant Numbers 61623/339

EXHIBIT A.9 December 16, 1861 State of Georgia 7% Bond Number 40

ture. The bonds are redeemable at the state's opinion at any time after five years from date of issue. Several coupons were paid until November 1863.

After the Civil War, several Southern states and local governments issued municipal bonds that involved fraud and defaults.

South Carolina is also worthy of special mention. As reported in the press at the time, the governor of the state in the early 1870s, Robert K. Scott, had a strong desire for women and drink. Every night he would go to a local house of ill repute and the "employees" there would assist him in signing state general obligation bonds. On at least one occasion, the star of the local burlesque stage was given a percentage commission to induce the drunken governor to sign the bonds. An investigation was eventually undertaken and it was discovered that while the state was supposed to issue only $1.2 million in the bonds, the governor instead had issued over $22 million. Some of these bonds were refunded at 50% of face value and the others repudiated. These bonds are now known among municipal bond history buffs as the "whorehouse" bonds. Exhibit A.10 is of one of these bonds.

Louisiana is also interesting for its history of defaults during Reconstruction—or the "Carpetbagger Era" as it was called in the south. Immediately following the Civil War, Louisiana was governed by a federally appointed governor and legislature who sold $100 million in state bonds, the proceeds of which were misappropriated by them. After Reconstruction, the bonds were repudiated on the basis that since proceeds had been stolen by these officials; the state had received no benefit from the bonds and therefore had no obligation to pay them. The state did authorize and sell some $2 million worth of bonds in $5 denominations to refund by exchange the bonds sold in the Reconstruction era, with the exchange being only for pennies on the dollar of par value of the bonds surrendered.

The $2 million of bonds issued subsequent to Reconstruction, having a picture of a small girl on the front, were called Baby Bonds. The plates used for the original Baby Bond issue were held in the custody of the state treasurer. While he was vacationing in Europe during the 1880s, it was discovered that the plates had been used to reprint the bonds with identical numbers at least three times. The treasurer had allegedly taken $420,000 of the Baby Bonds with him, and another $300,000 was purportedly found in his safety deposit box. He had also taken cash from the state treasury, for which it was said he had substituted additional Baby Bonds to keep all funds and accounts in proper balance. Since the treasurer extended his vacation permanently, he was not available to make full disclosure concerning his transactions. The state subsequently used surplus revenues in the general fund to buy up some of the irregularly issued Baby Bonds, the purchase price being 50 cents for each of the bonds. In Exhibit A.11 are two of these bonds.

EXHIBIT A.10 $1,000.00 State of Carolina Bond Number 2898, Dated January 1, 1869

EXHIBIT A.11   1873 $5.00 State of Louisiana Bond Numbers 45563 and 45562

OTHER INTERESTING BONDS

At a time when bedlam was taking place for bondholders of Southern municipal bonds, others quietly clipped their coupons and went about their businesses. In Exhibit A.12 is a cancelled $1,000 bond issued by the City of Philadelphia in January of 1872. The interest rate is 6% and the principal was due July 1, 1900. The bond was paid on schedule. On the face of the bond it clearly states in red ink that it is "free from all taxes."

But the North was not without its defaults. One occurred in what is now New York City. In 1880, Long Island City was a standalone unit of local government unaffiliated with the City of New York. Under an 1874 State law, it was authorized to issued $1,000,000 in special assessment

EXHIBIT A.12   January 8, 1872, City of Philadelphia Bond Number 43449

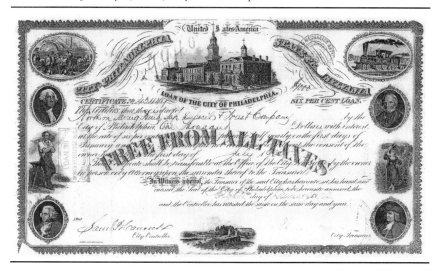

bonds. Proceeds were used for improvements in a section of Long Island City identified as the "First Ward." At the time of the sale, the bonds were to pay an annual interest rate of 7% to the bondholders. The security was from assessments on property in the First Ward. If property were sold for nonpayment, they could not be for less than the property assessments, and these proceeds had to be used to redeem the bonds.

Subsequently, the security provisions were amended to allow the properties to be sold by the Long Island City treasurer for less. The outstanding bonds became worthless. After Long Island City was incorporated into New York City in 1898, the bondholders sued in state court to try to force New York City to pay off the bonds, as it was the legal successor to the Long Island City government. In 1919, the court held that the City of New York was not responsible for this defaulted debt.

In Exhibit A.13 is a $100 bond issued on February 24, 1880.

Below are municipal bonds issued later that show the detail of the engraving and beauty of the bond certificate.

In Exhibit A.14 is a $ 1,000 cancelled general obligation bond number 111 issued by the City of Philadelphia in 1895. It had an interest rate of 3.5% and was retired at the end of 1914.

In Exhibit A.15 is a cancelled City of Providence, Rhode Island general obligation bond number 226.

In Exhibit A.16 is a $1,000 general obligation bond of San Francisco number 11 issued on July 1, 1904 with a 3.5% interest rate and retired on

EXHIBIT A.13   1880 Long Island City, New York 7% Bond Number 2696

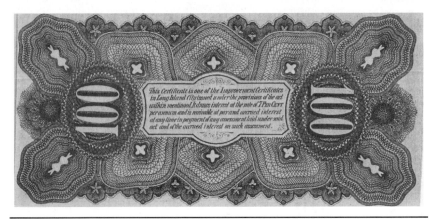

December 31, 1905, a little over three months before the San Francisco Earth-quake. On the upper left side margin is what appears to be a burn mark.

In Exhibit A.17 is a $1,000 4.5% coupon general obligation bond issued by the City of Los Angeles in 1907 for water system improvements. The certificate has a detailed engraving of Mount Whitney, the highest peak in the lower 48 states. High up in the Sierra Nevada mountains, it is a major source of water for Los Angeles. The bond was redeemed in 1923.

In Exhibit A.18 is a $1,000 2.90% coupon, Korean Combat Veterans' Bonus bond issued by the State of Louisiana in 1957. It was retired in 1961. Proceeds were used to pay bonus to service men and women who served in the military between June 27, 1950 and July 26, 1953. It was secured by a portion of the state's beer tax.

EXHIBIT A.14 1895 $1,000.00 City of Philadelphia Bond Number 111

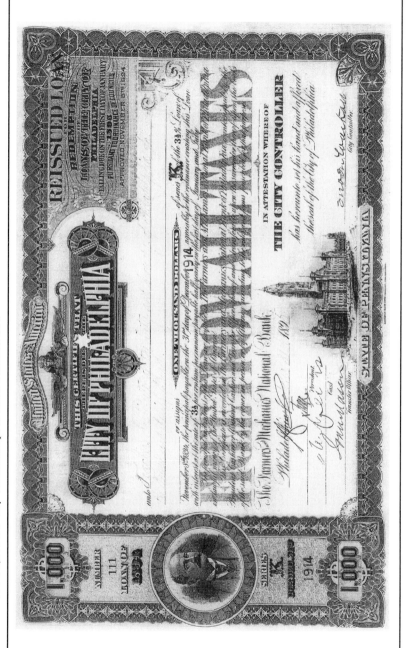

EXHIBIT A.15 1897 $1,000.00 4% City of Providence, Rhode Island Bond, Number 226

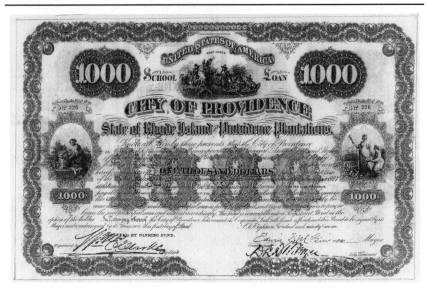

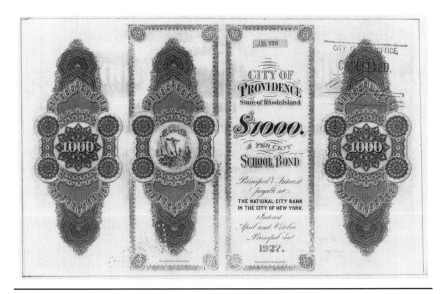

EXHIBIT A.16 1904 City and County of San Francisco Library Bond Number 11

EXHIBIT A.17   1907 City of Los Angeles Water Works Bond Number 20487

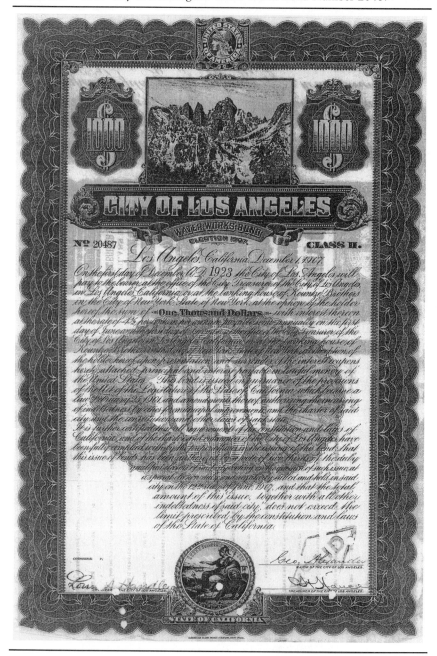

EXHIBIT A.18 1957 State of Louisiana Korean Combat Veterans' Bonus Bond Number 42

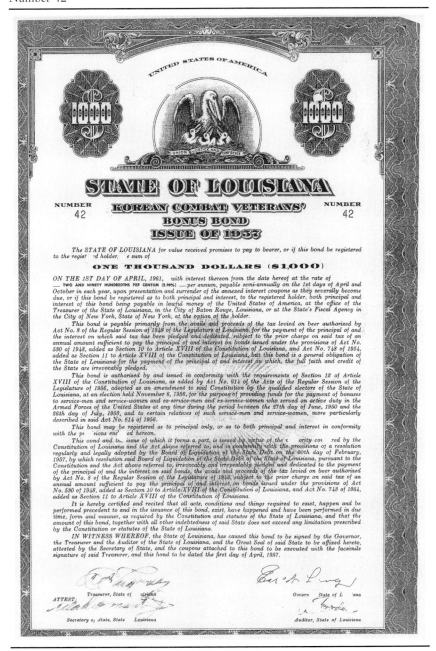

MUNICIPAL BOND COUPONS

Exhibits A.19 to A.22 are some representative nineteenth century municipal bond payment coupons. Such coupons were usually *clipped*, that is, cut from the bond certificate and presented to the issuer for payment every six months until the maturity of the bond. The last two coupons were for bonds issued when Idaho was still a territory; one immediately after the Civil War and the other nine years later.

EXHIBIT A.19   1871 State of Tennessee $30.00 Coupon Number C456

EXHIBIT A.20   1859 Commonwealth of Pennsylvania $25.00 Coupon Number 13

EXHIBIT A.21   1866 Territory of Idaho $8.56 Coupon Number 10

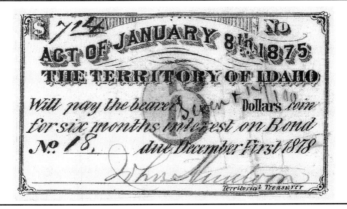

EXHIBIT A.22   1878 Territory of Idaho $7.14 Coupon number 18

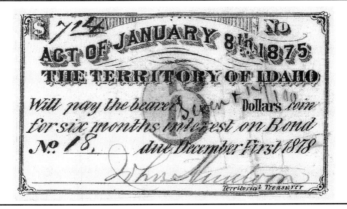

Glossary of Terms

Mitchell Savader
Chief Executive Officer
The Savader Group LLC
and
Managing Director
Civitas Funding Group LLC

Accrued interest   Interest costs that have been incurred, but not yet paid to the bondholder.

Additional bonds test   A legally binding covenant that requires the obligor to meet predetermined requirements before additional, identically secured bonds can be issued.

Ad valorem tax   A tax levied on the value of property owned by the taxpayer. Commonly refered to as *property taxes*.

Advanced refunding   A refunding of a bond that uses money from a new bond that is issued in advance of the date that the original bond can be paid off. The moncy from the new bond is usually invested in an irrevocable escrow account until the date when it is used to pay off the original bond.

Amortization   The gradual repayment of a bond according to a specific time schedule.

Appropriation   An authorization by a government's legislative body to make an expenditure or expenditures for a specific purpose.

Assessed valuation   The value of property for purposes of levying ad valorem— property taxes.

Audit   The examination of an entity's (such as a city, county or state) financial data, systems, and procedures to assess their accuracy and compliance with legal requirements.

Balloon payment   A principal payment that is far larger than prior or future individual principal requirements.

Basis point   A basis point is equal to 1/100th of 1% (i.e., a one basis point increase in an interest rate of 4.25% would raise it to 4.26%).

Bond   A financial obligation whereby an obligor makes a legal binding pledge to repay a specific amount of money with interest at a specific point, or points, in time.

Bond anticipation note   A short-term debt typically issued to fund initial project costs in advance of the issuance of long-term financing.

Bond counsel   A lawyer or law firm acting on behalf of the issuer by providing an opinion as to the legality and tax implications of the proposed bond.

Bond counsel opinion   An opinion given by a qualified attorney or law firm on the legality and tax status of a bond.

Bond covenant   A legally binding promise by an issuer or obligor to take, or refrain from taking, a specific action.

Bond election   The process by which a municipality's voters are given the opportunity to approve a proposed issue of bonds by that municipality.

Bond insurance   A noncancelable insurance policy that guarantees the insurer will pay all insured debt service requirements on time and in full.

Bond proceeds   The funds generated from the sale of a bond.

Bondholder   The owner of a bond to whom principal and interest payments are made.

Call premium   A payment made above a bond's face value to compensate the bondholder for the bond's redemption prior to its stated maturity.

Callable bond   A bond that can be repaid at the option of the issuer prior to the bond's stated maturity.

Competitive sale   A bond sold by means of sealed bids submitted by prospective purchasers of the bond. See also *Negotiated sale.*

Conduit financing   A financing undertaken by an issuer on behalf of an obligor such as a not-for-profit hospital. This is typically done to allow the entity to take advantage of tax-exempt interest rates. See also *Issuer* and *Obligor.*

Coupon rate   The annual rate of interest to be paid on a bond.

Covenant   See *Bond covenant.*

Coverage   See *Debt service coverage.*

Credit enhancement   A formal and legally binding pledge of financial support (i.e. bond insurance), that is provided by a source other than the issuer or obligor, thereby improving the creditworthiness of the bond.

CUSIP   A nine-character alphanumeric identifier used to identify specific securities, CUSIP is the acronym for Committee on Uniform Security Identification Procedures.

Dated date   The date usually used as the starting point for computing a bond's interest requirements.

Debt limit   A legally binding limit on the amount of debt a municipality can incur.

Debt service   The amount of principal and interest required to be paid on a bond during a specified period of time.

Debt service coverage   The relationship between revenues available to pay debt service requirements and the amount of debt service due. Usually expressed as a ratio, with available revenues divided by debt service requirements.

Debt service reserve requirement   A legally binding covenant of an obligor to maintain a specific available liquid reserve to meet debt service requirements in the event pledged revenues are insufficient.

Default   The failure of an issuer or obligor to satisfy a legally binding agreement, including but not limited to a failure to pay debt service on time and in full. See also *Technical default.*

Defeasance   The termination of an issuer's obligation and bondholder's rights upon satisfaction of certain predetermined requirements. usually the provision for payment of all future debt service requirements.

Discount   The dollar amount by which the sale price of a bond is less than the par amount of that bond. See also *Premium.*

Double-barreled bond   A bond backed by a legally binding pledge to pay debt service from at least one of two separate sources of funds.

Escrowed to maturity   See *Advanced refunding.*

Extraordinary mandatory redemption   A mandatory redemption of a bond by the issuer due to the occurrence of an extraordinary event (i.e., the loss of the bond's tax exemption).

Extraordinary optional redemption   The right of an issuer to redeem a bond due to the occurrence of an extraordinary event (i.e., the destruction of the facility financed through the issuance of the debt).

501(c)3   See *Section 501(c)3 organizations.*

Fiscal year   The 12-month period used to account for an organization's financial affairs. *Fiscal year* and *calendar year* are not necessarily the same.

Flow of funds   The legally required sequence that determines how pledged revenues are deposited and used to pay expenses, including those related to oustanding financial obligations.

Full faith and credit bond   A bond backed by the obligor's legally binding pledge to repay the debt from any revenues not otherwise restricted as use, including the obligor's general taxing powers.

General fund   The primary operating fund for most general purpose municipalities. This fund is used to account for revenues and expenditures not accounted for elsewhere.

General obligation bond   See *Full faith and credit bond.*

Gross revenue pledge   A security pledge requiring that all revenues are pledged to the payment of debt service prior to their use for any other purpose.

Housing revenue bonds   A bond secured by revenues generated from mortgage payments paid on single or multifamily housing.

Indenture   See *Trust indenture.*

Industrial development/revenue bond (IDS or IRS)   A bond issued by a municipality on behalf of a commercial entity.

Interest   Compensation paid for the use of borrowed money.

Investment grade   A designation used to refer to a credit rating that symbolizes a high probability of repayment. See also *Noninvestment grade.*

Issuer   A legal entity that borrows money through the creation and sale of debt. The issuer of a debt instrument is not necessarily the obligor that pledges to provide the revenues to repay the debt. See also *Obligor* and *Conduit financing.*

Joint and several obligation   A legally binding obligation that can be enforced against any and all obligors for the full amount of the obligation.

Junk bonds   See *Noninvestment grade bonds.*

Junior lien See *Subordinate lien.*

Lease rental bond A bond secured by revenues derived from the leasing of a facility or other asset.

Limited tax pledge A pledge to repay a bond from proceeds of a tax that is limited as to the tax rate or dollar amount.

Liquidity The cash value of assets. Usually refers to assets that are maintained as cash, or that can be converted into cash quickly and easily.

Mandatory redemption Refers to the requirement—triggered by certain predetermined circumstances—that an issuer redeem its bonds prior to the bond's stated maturity.

Maturity The date on which a bond is scheduled to be repaid.

Maximum annual debt service The greatest amount of annual principal and interest requirements due on a bond over the life of the bond.

Mill rate/millage The tax rate that is applied to each $1,000 of a property's assessed value.

Moral obligation bond A bond that, along with the legally binding pledge of its obligor to repay the debt, also carries the pledge of another entity to consider paying debt service in the event the obligor is unable, or unwilling to do so.

Municipal bond A broad term generally used to identify a debt issued by a state or local municipality.

Municipality A governmental unit such as a county, city, town, village, school, or special district.

Negotiated sale The sale of a debt based on terms negotiated between issuer and underwriter purchasing the debt. See also *Competitive sale.*

Net revenues Gross revenues minus normal operating and maintenance expenditures.

Nonappropriation The failure of a municipality to authorize the payment of a specific expense.

Noncallable bond A bond that cannot be repaid in advance of its stated maturity.

Noninvestment grade A designation used to refer to a credit rating that symbolizes a probability of repayment below that of investment grade. Noninvestment grade bonds are also known as *junk bonds.* See also *Investment grade.*

Note A short-term debt typically issed to meet short-term cash requirements. See also *Bond anticipation note.*

Obligor The entity that pledges to provide the revenues necessary to repay a bond. The obligor is not necessarily the issuer of the debt. See *Issuer* and *Conduit financing.*

Official statement (OS) A document prepared by, or on behalf of, a municipal issuer that provides information to investors about a specific bond being offered. See also *Preliminary official statement.*

Optional redemption The right of an issuer to redeem a bond in advance of its stated maturity.

Original issue discount (OID) The difference between the offering price of a newly issued bond and the par amount of that bond when the price is less than the par amount.

Parity debt   Two or more issues of debt that are identically secured in terms of the revenues pledged for repayment.

Par value   The amount of principal that must be repaid at maturity.

Paying agent   A financial institution that pays debt service to bondholders on behalf of issuer/obligor.

Payment default   An obligor's failure to pay debt service on time and in full.

Pledged revenues   Revenues legally pledged to the repayment of a bond.

Preliminary official statement (POS)   A preliminary version of the official statement. See also *Official statement*.

Premium   The dollar amount by which the sale price of a bond exceeds the par amount of that bond. See also *Discount*.

Prerefunded   See *Advanced refunding*.

Principal   The face amount of a debt obligation; also referred to as *par*. See also *Par value*.

Private activity bond   A bond issued to provide financing for a commercial purpose such as a factory, store, or hotel.

Put bond   A bond that the bondholder can require be repurchased by the issuer according to predetermined terms.

Rate covenant   A legally binding requirement that the obligor maintain rates and charges at a particular level. The covenant is usually expressed as a ratio of available pledged revenues to debt service requirements.

Rating agencies   Companies that assess the relative creditworthiness (payment in time and in full) of specific bonds.

Refunded bond   A bond that is to be repaid in advance of its stated maturity using the proceeds of another bond.

Refunding bond   A bond that is issued to provide those funds necessary to repay a previously issued bond in advance of the original bond's stated maturity.

Revenue bond   A bond secured by revenues generated from a specific enterprise (i.e., a sewer revenue bond secured by revenues generated from the operation of a municipality's sewer system).

Section 501(c)3 organizations   Public purpose, not-for-profit entities as defined under Section 501(C) 3 of the IRS code.

Security   A legally binding pledge of specific revenue sources or assets that back the repayment of a bond. It can also refer to bond covenants that protect bondholder interests.

Self-supporting bond   A bond whose debt service is paid from a source other than tax revenues and typically tied to the project orginally funded from proceeds of the bonds.

Senior lien   A revenue bond that has a legally valid first claim on revenues also pledged to repay other classes of debt. See also *Subordinate lien*.

Serial bond   A bond that is scheduled to be repaid using pre-determined periodic installments.

Subordinate lien   A revenue bond backed by a pledge of revenues first pledged to the repayment of other obligations. See also *Senior lien*.

Tax increment bond   A bond secured by a pledge of tax revenues generated from the incremental growth of a specific area's tax base over a defined period of time.

Tax limit   A legally binding limit—either either in terms of tax rate or dollars—on the amount of taxes that a municipality can impose on its taxpayers.

Technical default   The failure by an issuer to meet all bond covenants, excluding the failure to pay debt service on time and in full. See also *Default*.

Tender bond   See *Put bond*.

Term bond   A bond that is scheduled to be repaid on a single or very limited number of maturity dates.

Tobacco bond   A bond backed by revenues to be received by certain states and other U.S. territories under the Master Settlement Agreement reached between the states and territories and several U.S. tobacco companies.

Trustee   A bank or other financial institution acting on behalf of bondholders by tracking and enforcing the legal agreements securing the bond.

Trust indenture   A contract between the issuer of a bond and the trustee that establishes such things as the rights and responsibilities of the issuer, and trustee, the source of the pledged revenues backing the bond and the remedies available to bondholders in the event of a default.

Underwriter   A securities dealer that purchases a new issuance of a bond for purposes of reselling the bond.

Unlimited tax bond   A bond secured by the pledge of the municipality's taxing power unlimited as to tax rate or dollar amount.

Variable rate bond   A bond with an interest rate that can change over time.

Yield to call   The rate of return on a bond redeemed before its stated maturity. This calculation takes into consideration any call premium.

Yield to maturity   The rate of return on an obligation taking into consideration the interest rate, length of time to maturity, and price paid. This calculation assumes that interest received on the bond is reinvested at the same rate as the bond.

Zero-coupon bond   A deeply discounted municipal bond on which no interest is paid. Instead, interest is reinvested and paid out at bond maturity.

Index